Keep this book. You will need it and use it throughout your career.

About the American Hotel & Motel Association (AH&MA)

Founded in 1910, AH&MA is the trade association representing the $85.6 billion lodging industry in the United States. AH&MA is a federation of state lodging associations throughout the United States with 11,000 lodging properties worldwide as members. The association offers its members assistance with governmental affairs representation, communications, marketing, hospitality operations, training and education, technology issues, industry research, and more. Members have the opportunity to network and share knowledge with other hospitality industry professionals through the association's many committees and through national conventions and leadership forums.

About the Educational Institute of AH&MA (EI)

An affiliate of AH&MA, the Educational Institute is the world's largest source of quality training and educational materials for the lodging industry. EI develops textbooks and courses that are used in more than 1,200 colleges and universities worldwide, and also offers courses to individuals through its Distance Learning program. Leading hotel chains, management companies, and independent properties rely on EI for training resources that focus on every aspect of lodging operations. Industry-tested videos, CD-ROMs, seminars, and skills guides prepare employees at every skill level to succeed in hospitality. EI also offers professional certification for the industry's top performers.

About the American Hotel Foundation (AHF)

An affiliate of AH&MA, the American Hotel Foundation provides financial support that enhances the stability, prosperity, and growth of the lodging industry through educational and research programs. The foundation has awarded hundreds of thousands of dollars in scholarship funds for students pursuing higher education in hospitality management. AHF has also funded research projects on topics of importance to the industry, including occupational safety and health, environmental action, turnover and diversity, and best practices in the U.S. lodging industry.

HOSPITALITY INDUSTRY FINANCIAL ACCOUNTING

Educational Institute Courses

Introductory

INTRODUCTION TO THE HOSPITALITY INDUSTRY
Fourth Edition
Gerald W. Lattin

AN INTRODUCTION TO HOSPITALITY TODAY
Third Edition
Rocco M. Angelo, Andrew N. Vladimir

TOURISM AND THE HOSPITALITY INDUSTRY
Joseph D. Fridgen

Rooms Division

FRONT OFFICE PROCEDURES
Fifth Edition
Michael L. Kasavana, Richard M. Brooks

HOUSEKEEPING MANAGEMENT
Second Edition
Margaret M. Kappa, Aleta Nitschke, Patricia B. Schappert

Human Resources

HOSPITALITY SUPERVISION
Second Edition
Raphael R. Kavanaugh, Jack D. Ninemeier

HOSPITALITY INDUSTRY TRAINING
Second Edition
Lewis C. Forrest, Jr.

HUMAN RESOURCES MANAGEMENT
Second Edition
Robert H. Woods

Marketing and Sales

MARKETING OF HOSPITALITY SERVICES
William Lazer, Roger Layton

HOSPITALITY SALES AND MARKETING
Third Edition
James R. Abbey

CONVENTION MANAGEMENT AND SERVICE
Fifth Edition
Milton T. Astroff, James R. Abbey

MARKETING IN THE HOSPITALITY INDUSTRY
Third Edition
Ronald A. Nykiel

Accounting

UNDERSTANDING HOSPITALITY ACCOUNTING I
Fourth Edition
Raymond Cote

UNDERSTANDING HOSPITALITY ACCOUNTING II
Third Edition
Raymond Cote

BASIC FINANCIAL ACCOUNTING FOR THE HOSPITALITY INDUSTRY
Second Edition
Raymond S. Schmidgall, James W. Damitio

MANAGERIAL ACCOUNTING FOR THE HOSPITALITY INDUSTRY
Fourth Edition
Raymond S. Schmidgall

Food and Beverage

FOOD AND BEVERAGE MANAGEMENT
Third Edition
Jack D. Ninemeier

QUALITY SANITATION MANAGEMENT
Ronald F. Cichy

FOOD PRODUCTION PRINCIPLES
Jerald W. Chesser

FOOD AND BEVERAGE SERVICE
Second Edition
Ronald F. Cichy, Paul E. Wise

HOSPITALITY PURCHASING MANAGEMENT
William P. Virts

BAR AND BEVERAGE MANAGEMENT
Lendal H. Kotschevar, Mary L. Tanke

FOOD AND BEVERAGE CONTROLS
Fourth Edition
Jack D. Ninemeier

General Hospitality Management

HOTEL/MOTEL SECURITY MANAGEMENT
Second Edition
Raymond C. Ellis, Jr., David M. Stipanuk

HOSPITALITY LAW
Third Edition
Jack P. Jefferies

RESORT MANAGEMENT
Second Edition
Chuck Y. Gee

INTERNATIONAL HOTEL MANAGEMENT
Chuck Y. Gee

HOSPITALITY INDUSTRY COMPUTER SYSTEMS
Third Edition
Michael L. Kasavana, John J. Cahill

MANAGING FOR QUALITY IN THE HOSPITALITY INDUSTRY
Robert H. Woods, Judy Z. King

CONTEMPORARY CLUB MANAGEMENT
Edited by Joe Perdue for the Club Managers Association of America

Engineering and Facilities Management

FACILITIES MANAGEMENT
David M. Stipanuk, Harold Roffman

HOSPITALITY INDUSTRY ENGINEERING SYSTEMS
Michael H. Redlin, David M. Stipanuk

HOSPITALITY ENERGY AND WATER MANAGEMENT
Second Edition
Robert E. Aulbach

HOSPITALITY INDUSTRY FINANCIAL ACCOUNTING

Second Edition

Raymond S. Schmidgall, Ph.D., CPA
James W. Damitio, Ph.D., CMA

EDUCATIONAL INSTITUTE
American Hotel & Motel Association

Disclaimer

...ccurate and authoritative information in regard to the subject matter covered. It is sold with the understanding that the publisher is not engaged in rendering legal, accounting, or other professional service. If legal advice or other expert assistance is required, the services of a competent professional person should be sought.

> —From the Declaration of Principles jointly adopted by the American Bar Association and a Committee of Publishers and Associations

The authors, Raymond S. Schmidgall and James W. Damitio, are solely responsible for the contents of this publication. All views expressed herein are solely those of the authors and do not necessarily reflect the views of the Educational Institute of the American Hotel & Motel Association (the Institute) or the American Hotel & Motel Association (AH&MA).

Nothing contained in this publication shall constitute a standard, an endorsement, or a recommendation of the Institute or AH&MA. The Institute and AH&MA disclaim any liability with respect to the use of any information, procedure, or product, or reliance thereon by any member of the hospitality industry.

Library of Congress Cataloging-in-Publication Data
Schmidgall, Raymond S., 1945–
    Hospitality industry financial accounting/Raymond S. Schmidgall,
  James W. Damitio. — 2nd ed.
      p. cm.
    Includes bibliographical references and index.
    ISBN 0-86612-189-7 (pbk.)
    1. Hospitality industry—Accounting. 2. Accounting   I. Damitio
  James W. II. Title.
  HF5686.H75S338 1999
  657'.837—dc21   98–51690
                                                           CIP

Editor: Thaddeus Balivet

Contents

Congratulations. . .

You have a running start on a fast-track career!

Developed through the input of industry and academic experts, this course gives you the know-how hospitality employers demand. Upon course completion, you will earn the respected American Hotel & Motel Association certificate that ensures instant recognition worldwide. It is your link with the global hospitality industry.

You can use your AH&MA certificate to show that your learning experiences have bridged the gap between industry and academia. You will have proof that you have industry-driven competencies and that you know how to apply your knowledge to actual hospitality work situations.

By earning your course certificate, you also take a step toward completing the highly respected learning programs—Certificates of Specialization, the Hospitality Operations Certificate, and the Hospitality Management Diploma—that raise your professional development to a higher level. Certificates from these programs greatly enhance your credentials, and a permanent record of your course and program completion is maintained by the Educational Institute.

We commend you for taking this important step. Turn to the Educational Institute for additional resources that will help you stay ahead of your competition.

Preface

Hospitality Industry Financial Accounting, Second Edition, is designed for individuals wishing to learn the fundamentals of financial accounting through hospitality industry examples. The illustrations and examples in this text cover all areas of the hospitality industry including hotels, restaurants, and clubs.

All 18 chapters in this book include review questions and problems that reinforce the key points in the respective chapters. Several new problems have been added to each chapter for this edition. Chapter 1 provides an introduction and overview of financial accounting. The organizations that affect accounting are discussed in this chapter along with the basic accounting principles.

Chapter 2 explains accounting for basic business transactions. The five basic groups of accounts are introduced along with numerous transactions that involve many specific accounts in these groups. Chapter 3 illustrates the basic accounting adjustments that are necessary at the end of accounting periods.

Chapter 4 covers the procedures for the closing of the books and summarizes the entire accounting cycle. The chapter introduces the concept of the worksheet and demonstrates the preparation of the balance sheet and the income statement.

Chapters 5 and 6 cover in detail the most common financial statements: the income statement and the balance sheet. These financial statements are discussed in the context of the *Uniform System of Accounts for the Lodging Industry,* the *Uniform System of Financial Reporting for Clubs,* and the *Uniform System of Accounts for Restaurants.*

Chapter 7 focuses on the special journals and related subsidiary ledgers typically used in the hospitality industry. Chapter 8 begins a section of the book that covers in detail the accounting for specific items on the balance sheet. The chapter explains the specific accounting procedures for cash, including petty cash funds and bank reconciliations.

Chapter 9 covers both receivables and payables, while Chapter 10 describes inventory procedures. Property, equipment, intangibles, and other assets are discussed in Chapter 11, and Chapter 12 covers current liabilities and payroll.

Chapter 13 covers the major aspects of partnership accounting, including formation of a partnership, procedures for profit sharing, and dissolution of a partnership entity.

Chapter 14 introduces accounting procedures used in the most complex form of business, the corporation. Chapter 15 focuses on the issuance of bonds and accounting for leases and long-term mortgages.

Investments in corporate securities are discussed in Chapter 16. The cost and equity methods are discussed, and consolidated financial statements are introduced. The statement of cash flows, now mandated by the Financial Accounting Standards Board, is explained in Chapter 17. The text concludes with Chapter 18, which offers a detailed discussion of the analysis and interpretation of financial statements.

About the Authors

Raymond S. Schmidgall   James W. Damitio

Raymond S. Schmidgall is a professor in the School of Hospitality Business at Michigan State University. He holds a B.B.A. in accounting from Evangel College and an M.B.A. and a Ph.D. in accounting from Michigan State University. He is also a Certified Public Accountant. He has published articles in *Lodging, Club Management, The Bottom Line, The Consultant, Restaurant Business,* and the *Cornell Hotel and Restaurant Administration Quarterly.* Dr. Schmidgall has also written or co-written five accounting textbooks oriented to the hospitality industry, including basic texts on financial management, financial accounting, and managerial accounting. He conducts workshops and seminars for the Club Managers Association of America, American Hotel & Motel Association, National Restaurant Association, Hospitality Financial and Technology Professionals, Golf Course Superintendents Association of America, and Meeting Planners International. Dr. Schmidgall is Secretary of the Association of Hospitality Financial Management Educators, a member of the AH&MA's financial management committee, a member of International CHRIE's finance committee, a member of HFTP's communications and CHAE committees, serves on the editorial board of CHRIE's *Journal of Hospitality and Tourism Research,* and is a member of several professional accounting associations.

James W. Damitio is a professor in both the Department of Accounting and the Department of Marketing and Hospitality Services Administration at Central Michigan University, where he is also Director of the Perry Schools of Banking and Director of the Entreprenership Program. He received a B.S. in accounting from Central Michigan University and an M.B.A. in finance and a Ph.D. in curriculum and instruction for business from Michigan State University. He is a Certified Management Accountant and a member of the editorial review board of the Association of Hospitality Financial Management Educators. He is also a member of Hospitality Financial and Technology Professionals and the Institute of Management Accountants. He is a contributing author of a financial management text and has published numerous articles in the area of hospitality accounting in *Internal Auditing, Lodging, The Bottom Line,* the *Journal of Hospitality and Tourism Research,* the *Cornell Hotel and Restaurant Administration Quarterly, Florida International Review,* and the *Journal of Hospitality Management.* Dr. Damitio worked for Ernst & Young CPAs and was self-employed in retailing for 14 years.

Study Tips for Users of Educational Institute Courses

Learning is a skill, like many other activities. Although you may be familiar with many of the following study tips, we want to reinforce their usefulness.

Your Attitude Makes a Difference

If you want to learn, you will: it's as simple as that. Your attitude will go a long way in determining whether or not you do well in this course. We want to help you succeed.

Plan and Organize to Learn

- Set up a regular time and place for study. Make sure you won't be disturbed or distracted.

- Decide ahead of time how much you want to accomplish during each study session. Remember to keep your study sessions brief; don't try to do too much at one time.

Read the Course Text to Learn

- *Before* you read each chapter, read the chapter outline and the competencies. If there is a summary at the end of the chapter, you should read it to get a feel for what the chapter is about.

- Then, go back to the beginning of the chapter and *carefully* read, focusing on the material included in the competencies and asking yourself such questions as:

    —Do I understand the material?

    —How can I use this information now or in the future?

- Make notes in margins and highlight or underline important sections to help you as you study. Read a section first, then go back over it to mark important points.

- Keep a dictionary handy. If you come across an unfamiliar word that is not included in the chapter's key terms, look it up in the dictionary.

- Read as much as you can. The more you read, the better you read.

Testing Your Knowledge

- Test questions developed by the Educational Institute for this course are designed to measure your knowledge of the material.

- End-of-the-chapter Review Quizzes help you find out how well you have studied the material. They indicate where additional study may be needed. Review Quizzes are also helpful in studying for other tests.

- Prepare for tests by reviewing:

  —competencies

  —notes

  —outlines

  —questions at the end of each assignment

- As you begin to take any test, read the test instructions *carefully* and look over the questions.

We hope your experiences in this course will prompt you to undertake other training and educational activities in a planned, career-long program of professional growth and development.

Chapter 1 Outline

Accounting Defined
    Bookkeeping Versus Accounting
Branches of Accounting
Organizations Influencing Accounting
Forms of Business Organization
    Sole Proprietorships
    Partnerships
    Limited Partnerships
    Limited Liability Companies
    Corporations
    S Corporations
The Accounting Function in the Hospitality
    Industry
Principles of Accounting
    Cost
    Business Entity
    Continuity of the Business Unit (Going
        Concern)
    Unit of Measurement
    Objective Evidence
    Full Disclosure
    Consistency
    Matching
    Conservatism
    Materiality
Overview of Financial Statements
    Balance Sheet
    Income Statement
    Statement of Cash Flows
Cash Versus Accrual Accounting
The Fundamental Accounting Equation
    Effects of Transactions on the
        Accounting Equation

Competencies

1. Define *accounting* and distinguish it from bookkeeping.

2. Describe the six branches of accounting.

3. Identify and describe organizations that have influenced hospitality accounting practices.

4. Describe basic forms of business organization and their advantages and disadvantages.

5. Describe the responsibilities of a hospitality firm's accounting department.

6. Apply generally accepted accounting principles to hospitality situations.

7. Describe the major types of financial statements: balance sheets, income statements, and statements of cash flows.

8. Describe the fundamental accounting equation and apply it to accounting situations.

1

Introduction to Accounting

ACCOUNTING is simply a means to an end. Businesses, governments, and other entities use it as a means to account for their activities. Generally, this is accomplished through the use of numbers; thus, many people associate accounting with mathematics. However, accounting is much more than numbers.

Accounting assists in providing answers to many questions that hospitality managers raise, such as the following:

- How much cash is available to pay bills?
- What was the total payroll last pay period?
- What amount of property taxes did we pay this year?
- What amount of interest did we pay on long-term debt last year, and how much must be paid during the current year?
- How much does a current guest owe the hotel?
- What were the total food sales for the dinner period last night?
- What amount of food inventory was on hand at the beginning of the month?
- When did we purchase the kitchen range, and how much did it cost?
- How much do we owe the bank on the mortgage?
- What are payroll costs as a percentage of room sales?
- What amount of dividends did we pay to stockholders this past year?
- What is the ratio of food and beverage sales to room sales this past month?
- How much do we owe the meat purveyor?
- When is the utility bill, received yesterday, due?
- How was this hotel corporation financed?

The list of such questions is endless. Hospitality operations, whether hotel, motel, resort, club, restaurant, airline, or hospital, perform a multitude of activities each day. They sell assorted products as well as provide a variety of services. The need to keep track of these many activities has produced modern accounting systems.

Accounting Defined

The American Accounting Association defines **accounting** as "the process of identifying, measuring, and communicating economic information to permit informed judgments and decisions by users of the information."[1] The economic information is generally financial and is stated in monetary terms. For example, room sales for the period were $1,500,000 and net income was $150,000. The accounting process includes observing events in order to identify the events that are of a financial nature. These events must be measured in monetary terms; that is, a monetary value is placed on the observed activity. For example, a meal is sold to a guest. This activity is of a financial nature and is measured by the sales price of the meal. Next, accounting requires recording, classifying, and summarizing the economic events, such as food sales. In the case of the above example, the sale is recorded on a sales slip. This sale is then classified as a food sale as opposed to other types of sales and, at the end of the accounting period, will be summarized in a financial statement along with other economic events. The accounting process continues as financial statements and other reports are provided to users.

A key element of accounting is communication. In other words, not only must information be accumulated and properly summarized, it must be communicated in a way that users understand. The statement of cash flows (SCF) is an example of a report that communicates accounting information. For many years, cash flow information was communicated indirectly at best. Now the SCF provides details of cash inflows and outflows. This information is considerably more useful than what has been communicated in the past.

Bookkeeping versus Accounting

There is a difference between bookkeeping and accounting, though many think they are the same thing. **Bookkeeping** is only a part of accounting—that of recording and classifying transactions. Accounting also includes summarizing and interpreting, which is beyond the scope of bookkeeping.

A bookkeeper records and classifies transactions, usually a routine, clerical task, whereas an accountant supervises the work of the bookkeeper, summarizes the accounting information, and interprets the financial statements. The accountant must also be able to survey a business's transactions, determine how its accounting data are to be used, and so on, and then be able to design an accounting system to fit the business. After the designed system is installed, the accountant must be able to supervise the bookkeeper's work, review it for accuracy, and report to management and others, in quantitative terms, the firm's activity for the period and its financial position at a given time. Thus, the demands on an accountant are much greater than those on the bookkeeper, and the required training is more extensive.

Branches of Accounting

Accountants classify accounting activities in various ways. However, most accountants agree that there are distinct but overlapping branches of accounting. These include financial accounting, cost accounting, managerial accounting, tax accounting, auditing, and accounting systems.

Financial accounting refers to accounting for revenues, expenses, assets, and liabilities. It involves the basic accounting processes of recording, classifying, and summarizing transactions. This area is often limited to the accounting necessary to prepare and distribute financial reports. Financial accounting is historical in nature; that is, it deals with past events. Managerial accounting, on the other hand, deals with proposed events.

Cost accounting is the branch of accounting dealing with the recording, classification, allocation, and reporting of current and prospective costs. Cost accountants determine costs by departments, functions, responsibilities, and products and services. The chief purpose of cost accounting is to help operations personnel control operations.

Managerial accounting is the branch of accounting designed to provide information to various management levels in the hospitality operation for the purpose of enhancing controls. Management accountants prepare performance reports, including comparisons to the budget. One major purpose of these reports is to provide in-depth information as a basis for management decisions. Although managerial accounting may vary among segments of the hospitality industry and certainly among different establishments, many management accountants use various management science techniques and tools. Algebra and forecasting are examples of these techniques.

Tax accounting is the branch of accounting relating to the preparation and filing of tax forms with government agencies. Tax planning to minimize tax payments is a significant part of the tax accountant's work. Tax accounting usually focuses on income tax at the federal, state, and local levels, but may also include sales, excise, payroll, and property taxes. Many hospitality operations employ tax accountants, while some operations contract the services of tax accountants employed by certified accounting firms.

Auditing is the branch of accounting involved in reviewing and evaluating documents, records, and control systems. Auditing may be either external or internal. It is most often associated with the independent, external audit called a **financial audit.** The external auditor reviews the financial statements of the hospitality operation, its underlying internal control system, and its accounting records (journals, vouchers, invoices, checks, bank statements, and so forth) in order to render an opinion of the financial statements. Financial audits may be conducted only by certified public accounting firms who generally also provide recommendations for strengthening the operation's internal controls.

Over the past several years, hospitality operations have increasingly employed internal auditors, whose primary purpose is to review and evaluate internal control systems. Many large hospitality firms have a full staff of internal auditors who conduct audits at individual properties to help management maintain the internal control system.

The final branch of accounting is **accounting systems.** Accounting systems personnel review the information systems of hospitality organizations. Information systems include not only the accounting system but other elements such as reservations. Because many hospitality operations are now computerized, many accounting systems experts are electronic-data-processing specialists, such as programmers and systems analysts. The trend toward larger accounting systems staffs in hospitality organizations continues as the information revolution continues into the twenty-first century.

Organizations Influencing Accounting

Several organizations have influenced the accounting practices used in the hospitality industry. Most have affected accounting in general, while Hospitality Financial and Technology Professionals is hospitality specific. Each organization has contributed in a different way.

The *American Institute of Certified Public Accountants (AICPA)* consists *only* of certified public accountants (CPAs). It was the dominant organization in the development of accounting standards in the United States through 1973. Its Committee of Accounting Procedure issued 51 *Accounting Research Bulletins* recommending generally accepted accounting principles (often referred to by the acronym *GAAP*). The Committee of Accounting Procedure's successor, the Accounting Principles Board (APB), issued 31 Opinions from 1959 to 1973 that established GAAP. In addition, the AICPA influences accounting development through its research division and other committees.

The *Financial Accounting Standards Board (FASB)* replaced the APB in 1973 as an independent, seven-member, full-time board to issue statements on financial accounting standards (principles). The FASB is the major influence in the private sector in the development of these standards, and it was this board that required the recently mandated statement of cash flows.

The *Securities and Exchange Commission (SEC)* was created by Congress when it passed the *Securities and Exchange Act of 1934*. It administers laws dealing with the interstate sale of stocks and bonds. The SEC has been empowered by Congress to prescribe accounting principles for U.S. companies whose capital stock or bonds are sold publicly. For all practical purposes, this involves most major hospitality lodging and food service companies. Even though the SEC has the authority to develop accounting standards for publicly listed companies, it works closely with the FASB, generally adopting the FASB standards as appropriate to companies under its jurisdiction.

The *Internal Revenue Service (IRS)* is the federal government agency charged with enforcing federal tax laws. Many *smaller* companies generally keep their records on an accounting basis that facilitates the preparation of their tax returns. Therefore, the IRS has indirectly influenced their accounting practices. Larger companies in essence keep two sets of books: one that follows GAAP and another that follows the Internal Revenue code.

Hospitality Financial and Technology Professionals (HFTP), formerly known as the *International Association of Hospitality Accountants (IAHA)*, consists primarily of financial executives of hospitality companies. Its major purpose is to enhance financial management and technology in the hospitality industry. HFTP's professional certifications are the Certified Hotel Account Executive (CHAE) and the

Certified Hotel Technology Professional (CHTP).[2] HFTP is responsible for developing and upgrading the *Uniform System of Accounts for the Lodging Industry,* which is published by the Educational Institute of the American Hotel & Motel Association in conjunction with the Hotel Association of New York City.

Forms of Business Organization

A business organization, generally referred to as a *business entity,* is any business existing separately from its owners. A diner, a motel, and a travel agency may be small businesses, but they are separate businesses and must be accounted for separately from the records of their owners. For example, assume the fictitious Barbara Collins owns a 30-unit lodging property. She may drive her car to and from her motel; however, her car is her personal asset. Assume her motel has a van to provide transportation service for its guests. The van is equipment belonging to the motel and should be properly accounted for by the business, not by the owner of the business.

There are four basic forms of business organization: sole proprietorships, partnerships, limited liability companies, and corporations, and some hybrid forms such as limited partnerships and S corporations. Each is discussed briefly in the following sections.

Sole Proprietorships

In terms of sheer numbers, the **sole proprietorship** form of business organization is the most frequently encountered in the hospitality industry. However, revenues from corporate lodging businesses total nearly two-thirds of the lodging revenue across the United States.[3]

As the name implies, a sole proprietorship is a business owned by a single individual who generally (but not necessarily) manages the business. Its popularity stems from the ease with which it is formed. Establishing a sole proprietorship may simply require filing an assumed business name statement with the proper authorities, such as the county government.

From a legal viewpoint, the owner of a sole proprietorship is not separable from the business and is held legally responsible for all debts of the business. For accounting purposes, the business is a separate business entity.

The owner of a sole proprietorship is not paid a salary or wage by the business, but simply withdraws cash from it. These withdrawals are not considered an expense of the business, nor are they deductible for tax purposes. The business does not pay income taxes, but the income or loss from the business is reported on the owner's personal income tax return.

Furthermore, medical insurance and other fringe benefits are deductible for tax purposes only if they benefit employees. Since the owner is not an employee, any payments made by the business to benefit the owner are accounted for as withdrawals by the owner.

In addition to the nondeductibility of benefits, disadvantages include unlimited liability of the owner for the debts of the business, and the difficulty the owner may have in raising large amounts of cash for use by the business.

The sole proprietorship may be an ideal form of organization if the anticipated risk is minimal and is covered by insurance, if the owner is either unable or unwilling to maintain the necessary organizational documents and tax returns of more complicated business entities, and if the business does not require extensive borrowing.

Partnerships

A **partnership** is a business owned by two or more people joined together in a non-corporate manner for the purpose of operating a business. Partnerships are created by either oral or written agreement. The written agreement is better because it provides a permanent record of the terms of the partnership. The written agreement should include the duties and initial investment of each partner, and the sharing of profits and losses. Each partner is responsible for the debts of the partnership and the actions of other partners acting within the scope of the business.

The advantages of a partnership are as follows:

1. Greater financial strength is provided since there is more than one owner. The added capital can provide greater resources for expansion of the business.

2. Businesses organized as partnerships do not pay any income taxes. Income or losses from the business are distributed to the partners according to the partnership agreement. The owners then include the income or losses on their own personal tax returns.

Major disadvantages of the partnership form of operation are as follows:

1. Partners are taxed on their share of the profits regardless of whether cash is distributed to them.

2. Partners may become frustrated in sharing the decision-making process, which can prove cumbersome. Partners may hold different opinions, and, theoretically, each has an equal right to manage the business.

3. Partners generally have unlimited legal liability for obligations of the business. This can be a significant factor where uninsurable business risks exist. This disadvantage may be partially overcome within the partnership form by the use of a limited-partnership form of organization.

Limited Partnerships

A **limited partnership** is a form of partnership that offers the protection of limited liability to its **limited partners.** In order to have limited liability, limited partners may not actively participate in managing the business. In addition to at least one limited partner, a limited partnership must have at least one **general partner** who is responsible for the debts of the partnership—that is, the general partner has unlimited liability. Unlike a general partnership agreement, which can be oral, the limited partnership must be in writing, and the certificate of limited partnership must be filed with the proper government authorities. Most states regulate the public sale of limited partnership interests. Furthermore, public offerings must be filed with the Securities and Exchange Commission; thus, sizable legal fees may be incurred. Smaller private issues generally seek an exemption from registration.

The major unique feature of limited partnerships is the limited liability afforded to limited partners. The extent of limited partners' liability is limited to their investments. However, to ensure limited liability, limited partners cannot actively participate in controlling or managing the hospitality business.

In recent years, the limited partnership has become an attractive financing vehicle for the expansion of hospitality operations. Limited partnerships have been formed for specific projects, with the hospitality establishment acting as the general partner and investors as the limited partners. Thus, the use of the limited partnership enables the hospitality establishment to obtain needed capital and still maintain control over operations.

The basic tax advantages available to general partners are also available to limited partners. Nontax advantages include limited liability and the fact that, within certain limits, the limited partners' interests may be transferred to others without prior approval of the general partners. The latter option is available only to limited partners, not to general partners.

Limited Liability Companies

A **limited liability company (LLC)** is a relatively new form of business organization. The LLC has been gaining in popularity because it combines the corporate feature of limited liability with the favorable tax treatment of partnerships and sole proprietorships. The LLC, unlike the S corporation, may have an unlimited number of owners (who are referred to as *members*) and is not restricted to one class of stock. Unlike a partnership, the LLC may have a single owner.

Corporations

A **corporation** is a legal entity created by a state or another political authority. The corporation receives a charter or articles of incorporation and has the following general characteristics:

1. An exclusive name

2. Continued existence independent of its stockholders

3. Paid-in capital represented by transferable shares of capital stock

4. Limited liability for its owners

5. Overall control vested in its directors

While hospitality businesses organized as sole proprietorships account for the largest number of businesses, hospitality corporations account for the greatest volume in terms of sales, assets, profits, and employees. Several hospitality corporations, such as Holiday Corporation, Marriott Corporation, and McDonald's Corporation, have annual sales in excess of $2 billion.

The major advantages of the corporate form over other forms of business organization include the following:

1. Its shareholders' liability is normally limited to their investment.

2. Owners are taxed only on distributed profits.

3. Employees can be motivated by equity participation, such as stock bonus plans and stock options, and by certain tax-favored fringe benefits.

4. Equity capital can be raised by selling capital stock to the public.

5. Tax rates are generally lower for small corporations than they are for individuals.

6. The corporation's life continues irrespective of the owners' lives.

As with other forms of business organization, there are disadvantages of the corporate form. The major disadvantage is **double taxation,** which means that corporate profits are taxed twice. First, they are taxed on the corporation's own income. Then, any profits paid out as dividends are considered taxable income to the individual stockholders.

In addition, with many corporations, stock is sold to new but unknown stockholders. If these stockholders are able to buy a sufficient quantity of stock, the original owners may lose control of their business. Of course, this can be precluded by maintaining more than 50 percent ownership of the corporation's stock.

S Corporations

Double taxation, a major drawback of the corporate form of operation, can be overcome if the corporation files as an **S corporation** for tax purposes. In essence, this allows the corporation to be taxed like a partnership.

The philosophy behind the S corporation provisions of the Internal Revenue Code is that a firm should be able to select its form of organization free of tax considerations. The S corporation is a hybrid form allowing limited liability for owners but avoiding the corporate "curse" of double taxation.

To qualify as an S corporation, the corporation must meet several tests, including, but not limited to (1) having 75 or fewer stockholders and (2) having only one class of stock.

This form of organization can be very useful when corporate losses are anticipated and owners have taxable income that can absorb the losses. It can also be very useful when corporations are profitable without having uses for extra capital that may be taxed on accumulated earnings. Since profits are passed through to stockholders, they are not taxed as accumulated earnings.

The Accounting Function in the Hospitality Industry ──────

The accounting function in hospitality industry properties is provided by a group of specialists ranging from bookkeepers to executives with such titles as Executive Vice President and Controller (or Comptroller). Chief accounting executives are responsible for typical accounting functions such as receivables, payables, payroll, and, in some cases, storage and security. Exhibit 1 summarizes a survey of 319

Exhibit 1   Responsibilities of Hotel Controllers

Area	Percentage Reporting Responsibility
Accounts Receivable	100%
Accounts Payable	99
Payroll	95
Night Auditors	94
Cash Management	86
Food Controls	78
Cashiers	77
Computer System—Accounting	77
Purchasing	77
Receiving	66
Storage	66
Computer System—Front Office/Reservations	65
Tax Returns	61
Internal Auditors	46
Investments	40
Risk Management	37
Security	25

Source: A. Neal Geller, Charles Ilvento, and Raymond S. Schmidgall, "The Hotel Controller: Revisited," *The Cornell Hotel and Restaurant Administration Quarterly,* November 1990, p. 94.

hotel *property* (as opposed to *corporate*) controllers and shows a wide range of reported responsibilities.

The sizes of accounting staffs may vary widely, from one part-time bookkeeper in a small ten-room motel to several hundred people in a large hotel or restaurant chain. For example, the accounting staff at a certain major worldwide hotel firm totals approximately 190, while the corporate accounting staff (accounts payable, payroll, internal audit, tax, etc.) at Pizza Hut, Inc., headquarters totals 138. A large hotel corporation's accounting staff covers many areas, as reflected by the sample organization chart in Exhibit 2.

The size of the accounting staff at an individual property depends on the size and diversity of the hotel's operations. The accounting staff at hotels with more than 1,000 rooms ranges from 30 to 50 people, consisting of personnel ranging from receiving clerks to the hotel controller. Exhibit 3 is a sample organization chart for the accounting function at a large hotel.

The accounting function within a lodging property is information oriented; that is, its major role is providing information to users. For external users such as financial institutions, accounting usually communicates through financial statements. Internally, accounting provides a wide variety of financial reports, including operating statements. Exhibit 4 lists various management reports generally prepared by accounting department personnel. The operating statements are

Exhibit 2   Sample Organization Chart for Large Corporate Accounting Staff

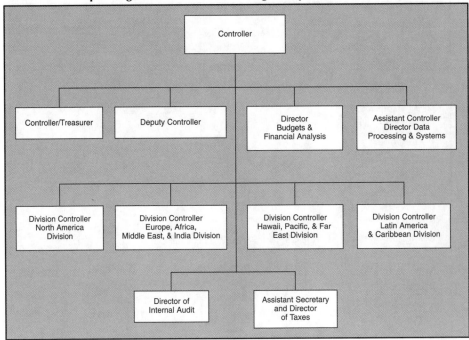

formatted to reflect revenues and related expenses according to areas of responsibility. In addition to reports on the income of the property as a whole, statements are prepared for each department that generates revenues and incurs expenses, such as rooms, food and beverage, and telecommunications. The accounting department also prepares separate statements for service centers such as marketing and property operation and maintenance.

Regardless of the size of an operation's accounting department, the diversity of its responsibilities, or the number and types of reports produced, the accounting staff is responsible for providing *service*. The accounting staff must work closely with operating management and other service departments if the hospitality property is to meet its objectives.

Principles of Accounting

In order to understand accounting methods, you must understand basic accounting principles. These generally accepted accounting principles provide a uniform basis for preparing financial statements. Although not "etched in stone" by boards of accountants, accounting principles have become accepted over time through common usage and also through the work of such major accounting bodies as the American Institute of Certified Public Accountants, the American Accounting Association, and the Financial Accounting Standards Board (FASB).

Exhibit 3   Controller's Department Organization Chart

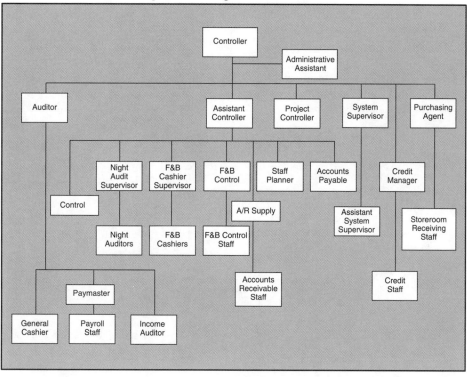

Students of hospitality accounting may wonder why an accounting transaction is recorded in a particular way at a particular time or why some asset value is not changed at some point. Generally, the reasons relate to accounting principles. For example, a fixed asset may have cost $10,000 but may have a suggested value per the manufacturer's catalog of $12,000. The **cost principle** dictates that the fixed asset be recorded on the books at its cost of $10,000 rather than at the suggested value of $12,000. A second example is the accrual of payroll at the end of the month. Assume that employees have worked the last few days of the month and that the next pay date falls in the following month. The matching principle dictates that the unpaid payroll for the period be recognized both as an expense during the current accounting period and as a liability.

The following sections briefly discuss several generally accepted accounting principles.

Cost

The cost principle states that when a transaction is recorded, it is the transaction price (cost) that establishes the accounting value for the product or service purchased. For example, if a restaurateur buys a dishwasher, the agreed-upon price between the restaurant and the supplier determines the amount to be recorded. If

Exhibit 4   Management Reports

Report	Frequency	Content	Comparisons	Who Gets It	Purpose
Daily Reports of Operations	Daily, on a cumulative basis for the month, the year to date.	Occupancy, average rate, revenue by outlet, and pertinent statistics.	To operating plan for current period and to prior year results.	Top management and supervisors responsible for day-today operation.	Basis for evaluating the current health of the enterprise.
Weekly Forecasts	Weekly.	Volume in covers, occupancy.	Previous periods.	Top management and supervisory personnel.	Staffing and scheduling; promotion.
Summary Report-Flash	Monthly at end of month (prior to monthly financial statement).	Known elements of revenue and direct costs; estimated departmental indirect costs.	To operating plan; to prior year results.	Top management and supervisory personnel responsible for function reported.	Provides immediate information on financial results for rooms, food and beverages, and other.
Cash Flow Analysis	Monthly (and on a revolving 12-month basis).	Receipts and disbursements by time periods.	With cash flow plan for month and for year to date.	Top management.	Predicts availability of cash for operating needs. Provides information on interim financing requirements.
Labor Productivity Analysis	Daily, weekly, monthly.	Dollar cost; manpower hours expended; hours as related to sales and services (covers, rooms occupied, etc.).	To committed hours in the operating plan (standards for amount of work); and to prior year statistics.	Top management and supervisory personnel.	Labor cost control through informed staffing and scheduling. Helps refine forecasting.
Departmental Analysis	Monthly (early in following month).	Details on main categories of income; same on expense.	To operating plan (month and year to date) and to prior year.	Top management and supervisors by function (e.g., rooms, each food and beverage outlet, laundry, telephone, other profit centers).	Knowing where business stands, and immediate corrective actions.
Room Rate Analysis	Daily, monthly, year to date.	Actual rates compared to rack rates by rate category or type of room.	To operating plan and to prior year results.	Top management and supervisors of sales and front office operations.	If goal is not being achieved, analysis of strengths and weaknesses is prompted.
Return on Investment	Actual computation, at least twice a year. Computation based on forecast, immediately prior to plan for year ahead.	Earnings as a percentage rate of return on average investment or equity committed.	To plan for operation and to prior periods.	Top management.	If goal is not being achieved, prompt assessment of strengths and weaknesses.
Long-Range Planning	Annually.	5-year projections of revenue and expenses. Operating plan expressed in financial terms.	Prior years.	Top management.	Involves staff in success or failure of enterprise. Injects more realism into plans for property and service modifications.
Exception Reporting	Concurrent with monthly reports and financial statements.	Summary listing of line item variances from predetermined norm.	With operating budgets.	Top management and supervisors responsible for function reported.	Immediate focusing on problem before more detailed statement analysis can be made.
Guest History Analysis	At least semi-annually; quarterly or monthly is recommended.	Historical records of corporate business, travel agencies, group bookings.	With previous reports.	Top management and sales.	Gives direction to marketing efforts.
Future Bookings Report	Monthly.	Analysis of reservations and bookings.	With several prior years.	Top management, sales and marketing, department management.	Provides information on changing guest profile. Exposes strong and weak points of facility. Guides (1) sales planning and (2) expansion plans.

Source: *Lodging,* July 1979, pp. 40–41.

the agreed-upon price is $5,000, the dishwasher is initially valued at $5,000 in the restaurant's accounting records. The supplier may have acquired the dishwasher from the manufacturer for $4,000 and the restaurant may receive an offer of $5,500 for it the day it is purchased; however, it is the cost that establishes the amount to be recorded. If amounts other than cost (such as estimates or appraisals) were used to record transactions, accounting records would lose their usefulness. When cost is the basis for recording a transaction, the buyer and seller determine the amount to be recorded. This amount is generally an objective and fair measure of the value of the goods or services purchased.

When the value of a *current* asset is clearly less than the cost recorded on the books, it is acceptable to recognize this decline in value. Thus, the *conservatism principle* (to be discussed later in this chapter) overrides the cost principle. For example, many properties carry inventory at the *lower* of cost or current market value. On the other hand, property and equipment (also frequently called *fixed assets*) normally are carried at cost less the depreciated amounts and are not reduced to market value as long as management plans to retain them for their useful lives. This treatment of property and equipment is based on the *going-concern principle* (also discussed later in this chapter).

Business Entity

Accounting and financial statements are based on the concepts that (1) each business is a **business entity** that maintains its own set of accounts, and (2) these accounts are separate from the other financial interests of the owners. For example, if a hotel owner decides to take some food home from the hotel for personal use, it should be properly charged to the owner's account. Recording a business activity separately from the owner's personal affairs allows a reasonable determination of the property's profitability. Not only does separate recording provide excellent information for managing the business, it is also necessary for properly filing tax returns. Whether the hospitality business is organized as a sole proprietorship, partnership, or corporation, separate tax forms or portions of forms must be filed for the business.

Continuity of the Business Unit (Going Concern)

According to the **continuity of the business unit principle**, in preparing the accounting records and reports, it is assumed that the business will continue indefinitely and that liquidation is not a prospect—in other words, that the business is a **going concern**. This assumption is based on the concept that the real value of the hotel or motel is its ability to earn a profit, rather than the value its assets would bring in liquidation. According to this concept, the market value of the property and equipment need not appear on the financial statements, and prepaid expenses are considered assets. If there is a reasonable chance the hospitality property may be unable to continue operations in the near future, allowance for this future event should be reflected in the financial statements. This may be best accomplished by reducing asset values to their market values.

Unit of Measurement

The financial statements are based on transactions expressed in monetary terms. Thus, in the United States, the **unit of measurement** is the U.S. dollar. The monetary unit is assumed to represent a stable unit of value so that transactions from past periods and the current period can be included on the same statement. However, there have been significant changes in price levels in the United States in recent years, and the dollar is not as stable as it has been in the past.

In the late 1970s and early 1980s, inflation, as measured by the Consumer Price Index, exceeded 10 percent. The FASB responded by requiring large hospitality firms to show current replacement costs of their property and equipment in footnotes to their financial statements. For some lodging properties, the current values of property and equipment exceeded twice the amount of the fixed assets carried on the books. Since inflation has been relatively low for the past few years, the FASB has rescinded this reporting requirement.

Objective Evidence

Accounting transactions and the resulting accounting records should be based as much as possible on **objective evidence.** Generally this evidence is an invoice or a canceled check. However, estimates must be assumed in the absence of such objective evidence. For example, suppose that the owner of a restaurant contributes equipment, purchased several years ago for personal use, to a restaurant corporation in exchange for 100 shares of stock. Further assume that there is no known market value for the restaurant corporation's stock. The owner may believe the equipment is worth $1,000, while the original catalog shows the cost several years ago of $1,400, and an appraiser appraises the equipment at $850. In this example, the most objective estimate of its value today would be the appraiser's estimate of $850.

Full Disclosure

The financial statements must provide information on all the facts pertinent to the interpretation of the financial statements. This **full disclosure** is accomplished either by reporting the information in the body of the financial statements or in the footnotes to the financial statements. Footnote disclosures might include the accounting methods used, changes in the accounting methods, contingent liabilities, events occurring after the financial statement date, and unusual and nonrecurring items. An example of each type of disclosure is presented in Exhibit 5.

Consistency

Several accounting methods are often available for reporting a specific kind of activity. Management selects the method most appropriate under the circumstances. For example, there are several ways to determine inventory values, and there are several methods of depreciating fixed assets. The **consistency principle** requires that once an accounting method has been adopted, it should be followed from period to period unless a change is warranted and disclosed. The consistency principle

Exhibit 5   Types of Disclosure and Examples

Type of Disclosure	Example
Accounting methods used	Straight-line method of depreciation
Change in the accounting methods	A change from depreciating a fixed asset using the straight-line method to using the double declining balance method
Contingent liability	A lawsuit against the company for alleged failure to provide adequate security for a guest who suffered personal injury
Events occurring after the financial statement date	A fire destroys significant uninsured assets of the hotel company one week after the end of the year
Unusual and nonrecurring items	A hotel firm in Michigan suffers significant losses due to an earthquake

allows a user of financial information to make reasonable comparisons between periods. Without consistent accounting, trends indicated by supposedly comparable financial statements might be misleading. When it becomes necessary to change to another method, the change must be disclosed and the dollar effect on earnings or on the balance sheet must be reported.

The consistency principle does *not* dictate that a hospitality operation must or even should use the same accounting methods for preparing tax returns that it uses for preparing financial statements for external users. The principle does not even require that a method selected for one element of a company be used for all similar elements. For example, the straight-line method of depreciation may be used to depreciate one hotel, and an accelerated method of depreciation may be used to depreciate another hotel owned by the same company.

Matching

The **matching principle** refers to relating expenses to revenues. For example, suppose that a hotel purchases a computerized reservations system that will benefit the hotel for several years. The cost is therefore recorded as a fixed asset and the cost of the system is written off over the system's life. The result is a partial write-off of the cost of the fixed asset each year against the revenues generated in part by using the system. This process is referred to as *matching* and is the basis for adjusting entries at the end of each accounting period. The matching principle is used when transactions are recorded on an accrual basis rather than a cash basis. The accrual basis and cash basis of accounting are discussed later in this chapter.

Conservatism

The **conservatism principle** calls for recognizing expenses as soon as possible, but delaying the recognition of revenues until they are ensured. The practical result is to be conservative (low) in recognizing net income in the current year. It is not proper to deliberately understate net income; however, many accountants wish to be cautious in recognizing revenues and "generous" in recognizing expenses.

A good example of this is the accounting treatment of lawsuits. If a hotel is a plaintiff in a lawsuit and its legal counsel indicates the case will be won and estimates the amount of settlement, the amount is not recorded as revenue until a judgment is rendered. On the other hand, if the same hotel is a defendant in a lawsuit and its legal counsel indicates the hotel will lose the lawsuit and most likely will pay a stated amount, the "expense" should be recognized immediately.

Conservatism is apparent in the valuation of inventory at the lower of cost or current market value and the recognition of nonrefundable deposits for future banquets as a liability until the banquet is catered.

Materiality

According to the **materiality principle**, events or information must be accounted for if they "make a difference" to the user of the financial information. An item is material in comparison to a standard. Some accountants have attempted to establish materiality by rules of thumb; for example, an item must be recognized if it exceeds a certain percentage of total assets or total income. However, this approach fails to address an item's relative importance over time. In addition, several immaterial items may be material when viewed collectively.

The materiality principle is often applied to fixed assets. Tangible items with useful lives beyond one year are commonly recorded as fixed assets. However, when such items cost less than a certain amount (specified by the board of directors of the purchasing organization), they are expensed because the cost is considered immaterial. An example would be a wastebasket. A $39 wastebasket might have a useful life of ten years, but since it costs less than the (for example) $100 limit for recording expenditures as fixed assets, it is expensed. In this case, the expenditure was immaterial to record as a fixed asset.

When a hospitality property provides footnotes to supplement the body of its financial statement, only material or potentially material items are presented.

Overview of Financial Statements

Hospitality enterprises often have several objectives, such as being profitable, being a leader in the marketplace, and growing in size, as in adding more restaurants or lodging operations. However, three basic objectives of every hospitality business are solvency, profitability, and having a positive cash flow. *Solvency* is the ability to pay debts on time, which is reflected in part by the enterprise's balance sheet. *Profitability* is the ability to generate net income, which is shown on a firm's income statement. *Cash* is used to pay the firm's bills as they come due. The cash flow of the hospitality enterprise is shown on the statement of cash flows.

Exhibit 6   Sample Simplified Balance Sheet

Kathy's Catering Service	
Balance Sheet	
December 31, 20X1	
ASSETS	
Cash	$ 1,000
Accounts receivable	2,000
Van	15,000
Equipment	500
Total Assets	**$18,500**
LIABILITIES AND OWNER'S EQUITY	
Liabilities:	
Accounts payable	$ 2,000
Notes payable	12,000
Total Liabilities	**14,000**
Owner's Equity	
Kathy Spring, Capital	4,500
Total Liabilities and Owner's Equity	**$18,500**

Balance Sheet

The **balance sheet** is also called the *statement of financial position*, because it reflects the financial position at a point in time. The balance sheet consists of things the business owns, called **assets,** and claims to those assets, called *liabilities* and *equities.* Assets include cash and equipment used in the business. The claims to assets by parties external to the business are called **liabilities,** while claims by owners are referred to in general terms as **owners' equity.**

To illustrate the relationships among assets, liabilities, and owners' equity, consider Kathy's Catering Service. Kathy Spring purchased a van for the business, paying $3,000 cash and financing the remaining amount of $12,000 with a loan from the bank. Further, she purchased service equipment for the company for $500. The balance sheet for Kathy's Catering Service would show assets of $15,500 (van, $15,000; equipment, $500), liabilities for $12,000 (the amount the business owes the bank), and owner's equity of $3,500 (the amount Kathy has invested in her business).

All financial statements have headings that include (1) the name of the hospitality business, (2) the title of the financial statement, and (3) the date of, or period covered by, the financial statement. Exhibit 6 is a simplified balance sheet for Kathy's Catering Service at the end of its first year of operation. Assets consist of cash of $1,000, accounts receivable (amounts due from customers for services provided) of $2,000, the van at its cost of $15,000, and service equipment that cost $500. Liabilities consist of accounts payable (amounts due to suppliers of food and operating supplies) of $2,000, and the notes payable due the bank of $12,000. Owner's equity consists of $4,500. This is calculated by subtracting total liabilities of $14,000 from the total assets of $18,500 to equal $4,500.

The balance sheet of Kathy's Catering Service reflects the financial position on December 31, 20X1. However, the balance sheet does not reflect the enterprise's profitability or its cash flow for 20X1. These will be shown on the income statement and the statement of cash flows, respectively.

Income Statement

The **income statement** shows the results of operations (that is, revenues and expenses) for a period of time. The period of time covered by the income statement usually ends at the date of the balance sheet. The income statement is generally prepared monthly for management's purposes and generally less frequently for outside users. For example, the information in the income statement is provided annually to the Internal Revenue Service. The income statement has various other names, such as the *earnings statement, profit and loss statement (P&L)*, and *statement of income and expenses.*

The income statement shows both revenues and expenses of the hospitality enterprise for a period of time. **Revenue** is an inflow of assets (such as cash) resulting from the sale of goods or services to customers, while an **expense** is the use of assets to produce revenues. When revenues exceed expenses for a period of time, the hospitality enterprise earns a profit commonly referred to as *net income.* If expenses exceed revenues, a net loss is incurred.

Exhibit 7 shows the income statement for Kathy's Catering Service for the year ended December 31, 20X1. The income reflects catering revenue of $120,000 and expenses of $119,000, resulting in net income of $1,000.

The net income of $1,000 is added to the amount of Kathy's original investment of $3,500 to equal owner's equity of $4,500, as shown on the balance sheet. This process is called the *closing process.*

The income statement reflects the profitability of a hospitality business. However, the cash flows of Kathy's Catering Service are not shown on either the balance sheet or the income statement, so we proceed to the statement of cash flows.

Statement of Cash Flows

The **statement of cash flows (SCF)** reflects the cash inflows and outflows for a period of time. Cash inflows come from a number of sources, such as cash sales, collection of accounts receivable, infusions of cash from owners, and bank loans. Cash outflows result from the purchase of equipment, the payment of wages, the purchase of food, and so on. When cash inflows exceed cash outflows for the period, the result is an increase in cash flow. When cash outflows exceed cash inflows for the period, there is a decrease in cash flow.

Exhibit 7 Sample Simplified Income Statement

Kathy's Catering Service
Income Statement
For the year ended December 31, 20X1

Revenues:

Catering services	$120,000

Expenses:

Cost of food	$36,000	
Wages	75,000	
Other operating expenses	8,000	
Total expenses		119,000
Net Income		$ 1,000

Note: This is a simplified income statement, since neither depreciation expense nor interest on the notes payable with the bank is shown.

Exhibit 8 Sample Statement of Cash Flows

Kathy's Catering Service
Statement of Cash Flows
For the year ended December 31, 20X1

Cash inflows:

Invested by owner		$ 3,500
Proceeds from bank loan		12,000
Cash sales		118,000
Total cash inflows		133,500

Cash outflows:

Purchase of van	$15,000	
Purchase of service equipment	500	
Payment for food	34,000	
Payment of wages	75,000	
Payment of operating expenses	8,000	
Total cash outflows		132,500
Increase in cash		$ 1,000

Exhibit 8 shows a simplified statement of cash flows for Kathy's Catering Service. Cash inflows of $133,500 come from Kathy's investment of $3,500, proceeds from the bank loan of $12,000, and cash sales of $118,000. (The cash sales from customers is the net result of $120,000 of sales and accounts receivable of $2,000.)

Cash outflows of $132,500 include the purchase of the van for $15,000 (cash of $3,000 and the notes payable of $12,000), purchase of service equipment of $500, the payment of food for $34,000 (which is the cost of food sold of $36,000 less the $2,000 owed suppliers and shown on the balance sheet as accounts payable), payment of wages of $75,000, and payment of other operating expenses of $8,000.

The SCF shows the cash flow for the period. Remember, bills are paid with cash, not with profits. Hospitality enterprises often have cash flows that are different from their net incomes as shown on their income statements.

The balance sheet, the income statement, and the SCF are the three major financial statements prepared periodically by hospitality enterprises. A key to excellent communication is to provide this information in sufficient detail to be useful to the reader of the financial statements.

Cash versus Accrual Accounting

The cash and accrual bases of accounting are two methods of determining when to record a transaction.

Cash basis accounting recognizes an accounting transaction at the point of cash inflow or outflow. For example, cash received in 20X2 for rooms sold in 20X1 would be treated as 20X2 revenues. Likewise, expenses incurred in 20X1 for which cash was disbursed in 20X2 would be treated as 20X2 expenses. Because of these improper assignments of revenues and expenses, cash basis accounting is generally not a fair reflection of business operations. Cash basis accounting usually violates the generally accepted accounting principles discussed earlier. However, using this method is acceptable if the results do not differ materially from those that accrual basis accounting would produce. Although cash basis accounting is the simpler of the two methods, its use is generally limited to very small hospitality operations where the owner is also the manager.

The more commonly used **accrual basis accounting** recognizes all revenues according to the accounting period in which they were earned, and, similarly, records all expenses incurred to earn the revenues in that same period. Since revenues earned, whether or not they have been received, and expenses incurred, whether or not they have been paid for, are all recognized within the accounting period, expenses are matched with revenues. At the close of any accounting period, accrual basis accounting allows a more meaningful evaluation of the business's operation because it matches expenses with revenue.

Under accrual basis accounting, procedures must be set up to record all transactions relating to a particular time period during that same period. For instance, a telephone bill for June may arrive late in July, yet the expense must be recognized in June, when it actually occurred. Another problem is that some expenses, such as payroll, do not exactly match the accounting period. Payrolls are paid periodically on a certain day of the week. Only occasionally would that date correspond to the end of the accounting period. It is necessary, therefore, to adjust payroll costs to the accounting period.

Other kinds of transactions receive special treatment under accrual basis accounting. Purchases of furniture and equipment are not considered expenses only of the period in which they were purchased. Instead, a pro rata share of the cost in the form of depreciation expense is charged to each accounting period during the useful life of long-lived purchases. Inventory purchase transactions are another example. Only when the inventory is sold does it become a cost in determining operating performance. Calculation of the cost of goods sold involves beginning and ending inventories plus purchases. For example, $2,000 of beginning food inventory plus $10,000 of food purchases during the accounting period less $2,500 of ending food inventory equals cost of food sold of $9,500.

Accrual basis accounting requires a number of **adjusting entries** at the end of each accounting period. Once the adjusting entries have been recorded, the income and expense for the period will provide a reasonable basis for measuring the business's financial and operating progress.

The Fundamental Accounting Equation

In accounting, a business's properties are called its *assets*, and ownership rights to these assets are called *equities*. Therefore, assets must equal equities. For example, if Kathy Spring establishes a catering business separate from her personal effects and invests $3,500 in it, the business, Kathy's Catering Service, will show assets of $3,500 and equities of $3,500. In this case, the assets of $3,500 are cash, and the equities of $3,500 are the ownership rights to assets. The accounting value of the ownership rights of the proprietor in the assets of the business enterprise is commonly shown under the name of the proprietor followed by the word *Capital*, as shown below.

ASSETS	=	EQUITIES
Cash, $3,500	=	Kathy Spring, Capital, $3,500

As Kathy Spring acquires assets such as a van and equipment for the business, she may find that she is unable to finance all the assets acquired with her personal resources. She will finance these additional assets by borrowing money from others and then purchasing the assets, or by buying the assets on account, that is, buying with a promise to pay at a later date. The businesspeople from whom Kathy Spring buys assets on account are known as *creditors*. The creditors of a business also have a claim to the assets of the business.

Assume that Kathy's Catering Service purchases a van for $15,000 for its catering business by paying $3,000 down and obtaining financing from First Bank for $12,000. Kathy signs a promissory note that indicates, among other things, the amount, the due date, and the interest rate. The accounting equation is now expanded.

ASSETS		=	LIABILITIES		+	OWNER'S EQUITY	
Cash	$ 500			$ —			
Van	15,000		Loan	12,000		Kathy Spring, Capital	$3,500
	$15,500	=		$12,000	+		$3,500

The accounting equation now shows that there are two types of claims on assets: the claims of the owner, Kathy Spring, and the claims of the creditor, First Bank. If Kathy Spring does not pay First Bank the amount due when required per the loan agreement, First Bank has the right to force sale of the van to secure its money.

The equation Assets = Liabilities + Owners' Equity is the **fundamental accounting equation** upon which all double-entry bookkeeping is based. The equation may be rearranged as:

Assets − Liabilities = Owners' Equity

Assets − Owners' Equity = Liabilities

The balance sheet, a basic financial statement that expresses the business's financial position at a point in time, is an expression of the basic accounting equation: Assets = Liabilities + Owners' Equity. The balance sheet for Kathy's Catering Service after the first two transactions would be:

Kathy's Catering Service
Balance Sheet

Assets		Liabilities & Owner's Equity	
Cash	$ 500	Notes payable	$12,000
Van	15,000	Kathy Spring, Capital	3,500
Total Assets	$15,500	Total Liabilities and	
		Owner's Equity	$15,500

Before introducing more transactions and their effects on the accounting equation, let us define what we have so far. *Assets,* simply stated, are anything of value owned by a business. They include cash, investments, accounts receivable, food inventory, beverage inventory, buildings, equipment, prepaid insurance, and so forth.

Liabilities are obligations to pay money or other assets, or to render services, to an outside party (a person or a business enterprise) either now or in the future. Liabilities represent claims that nonowners have on the firm's assets. Liabilities include accounts payable, loans payable, wages payable, rent payable, unearned revenue, bonds payable, notes payable, and so on.

Owners' equity is the excess of assets over liabilities. The claims of the firm's owners to the firm's assets are represented by owners' equity. Owners' equity is also called *net worth* at times.

Equities, then, are all claims to assets. This term includes both liabilities (the claims of creditors), and owners' equity (the claims of the owner).

Effects of Transactions on the Accounting Equation

The previous discussion of the accounting equation included two transactions:

1. Kathy Spring, owner, invested $3,500 in the business.

2. She purchased a van for the business for $15,000 by paying $3,000 from the business and borrowing $12,000 from the First Bank.

Each transaction affects the elements of the accounting equation. As previously shown, assets were increased from $-0- to $3,500 when the proprietor invested in the business. Further, assets were increased when the van was purchased. The effects of these two transactions on the accounting equationare shown again below. Note that the equation remains in balance after each transaction.

ASSETS			LIABILITIES		OWNER'S EQUITY
Cash	+ Van	=	Notes payable (First Bank)	+	Kathy Spring, Capital
(1) $ 3,500	$ —		$ —		$3,500
(2) − 3,000	15,000		12,000		—
$ 500	+ $ 15,000	=	$ 12,000	+	$3,500

Then four more transactions followed:

3. The business purchased service equipment for $500 cash.

4. Kathy invested $2,000 more in the business.

5. The business purchased on account $200 worth of operating supplies from Gordon Food Supply.

6. The business paid one month's rent of $1,000 on its office building.

The effects of these transactions are shown in Table I.

Table I

	Assets					=	Liabilities		+	Owner's Equity
Cash	+ Operating Supplies +	Prepaid Rent +	Equip-ment +	Van	=	Accounts Payable (Gordon Food Service) +	Notes Payable (First Bank)	+	Kathy Spring, Capital
(1) $3,500	$—	$—	$—	$—		$—	$—		$3,500
(2) − 3,000	—	—	—	15,000		—	12,000		—
500				15,000			12,000		3,500
(3) − 500	—	—	500			—			
0			500	15,000			12,000		3,500
(4) 2,000	—	—				—			2,000
2,000			500	15,000			12,000		5,500
(5) —	200	—				200			
2,000	200		500	15,000		200	12,000		5,500
(6) − 1,000	—	1,000				—			
$1,000 +	$ 200 +	$1,000 +	$ 500 +	$15,000	=	$ 200 +	$12,000	+	$5,500

Transaction 3 results in the exchange of one asset, Cash, for another asset, Equipment. Liabilities and owner's equity remain the same.

Transaction 4 increases an asset, Cash, and owner's equity.

Transaction 5 results in the increase of an asset, Operating Supplies, and the increase of a liability account, Accounts Payable.

Transaction 6 results in the increase of an asset, Prepaid Rent, and the decrease of an asset, Cash.

Kathy Spring's primary objective in investing her resources in the catering business is to increase her owner's equity by earning profits. She will accomplish this objective by selling food to customers. Profits will be earned only if the revenue from selling food is greater than the expenses incurred. To illustrate the effect of revenues and expenses on owner's equity, consider three additional transactions:

7. Kathy's Catering Service catered a dinner party for Walter Adams and received $800.

8. The business paid employees $300 to work on the dinner party.

9. The cost of food purchased for cash and used totaled $300.

The effects of these transactions on the accounting equation are found in Table II.

Table II

	Assets					=	Liabilities		+	Owner's Equity
Cash +	Operating Supplies +	Prepaid Rent +	Equip-ment +	Van	=	Accounts Payable (Gordon Food Service) +	Notes Payable (First Bank) +			Kathy Spring, Capital
(1) $3,500	$—	$—	$—	$—		$—	$—			$3,500
(2) − 3,000	—	—		15,000		—	12,000			—
500				15,000			12,000			3,500
(3) − 500	—		500							
0			500	15,000			12,000			3,500
(4) 2,000	—	—								2,000
2,000			500	15,000			12,000			5,500
(5)	200	—				200				
2,000	200		500	15,000		200	12,000			5,500
(6) − 1,000	200	1,000	500	15,000		200	12,000			5,500
1,000	200	1,000	500	15,000		200	12,000			5,500
(7) 800										800
1,800	200	1,000	500	15,000		200	12,000			6,300
(8) − 300										− 300
1,500	200	1,000	500	15,000		200	12,000			6,000
(9) − 300										− 300
$1,200 +	$200 +	$1,000 +	$500 +	$15,000	=	$200 +	$12,000 +			$5,700

$17,900

$17,900

Transaction 7 results in an increase in cash, an asset, of $800, and an increase in owner's equity of $800. The claim to the $800 received is by Kathy Spring, proprietor, since the $800 was paid for services rendered to the customer, Walter Adams. The $800 collected from the customer is known as a *revenue*. In this illustration, a **revenue** is an inflow of cash, accounts receivable, or other asset in exchange for food and services.

Transaction 8 is an example of an expense. This transaction results in an equal decrease of assets and owner's equity by $300. The $300 paid to employees for their services reduces cash and owner's equity by the same amount.

Transaction 9 is another example of an expense. In this illustration, $300 was paid for food used to cater the dinner party for Walter Adams. The result is a decrease in cash and a similar decrease in owner's equity. All expenses decrease owner's equity and either decrease assets or increase liabilities.

After Transaction 9, the assets of $17,900 equal the liabilities of $12,200 plus the owner's equity of $5,700. Thus, the accounting equation remains in balance after the nine transactions.

Summary

All types of business entities use accounting to "account" for their business activities. Accounting is the process of identifying, measuring, and communicating economic information to permit users of the information to make informed judgments and decisions. Accounting differs from bookkeeping in that accounting includes summarizing and interpreting information, while bookkeeping simply involves recording and classifying transactions.

There are several distinct yet overlapping branches of accounting. They are financial accounting, cost accounting, managerial accounting, tax accounting, auditing, and accounting systems.

Accounting is regulated and influenced by several different organizations. The Financial Accounting Standards Board (FASB) issues statements regarding generally accepted accounting procedures and financial statements. The Securities and Exchange Commission (SEC) and the Internal Revenue Service (IRS) administer various laws dealing with stock sales and income taxes, respectively. Hospitality Financial and Technology Professionals (HFTP) enhances accounting in the hospitality industry, and several of its members were members of the AH&MA's Finanacial Management Committee, which periodically updates the *Uniform System of Accounts for the Lodging Industry*.

Businesses can be organized in several different ways. The four major types are sole proprietorships, partnerships, limited liability companies, and corporations. There are also hybrid forms, such as S corporations and limited partnerships. Two major concerns when choosing a business form are the legal responsibility for the debts of the business and the method of taxation used.

In a hospitality firm, the accounting function is performed by several specialists who oversee many activities such as receivables, payables, and payroll. Sizes of accounting departments can vary considerably, depending on the sizes and degrees of complexity of their host organizations.

Generally accepted accounting principles are guidelines that help to keep all businesses' accounting records consistent. These are not laws but the basis for accounting methods. The principles include the cost principle, the matching principle, the business entity principle, the going concern principle, the unit of measurement principle, the objective evidence principle, the full disclosure principle, the consistency principle, the matching principle, the conservatism principle, and the materiality principle.

Three major financial statements required for most businesses are the balance sheet, the income statement, and the statement of cash flows. The balance sheet is a statement of financial position on a certain date. The balance sheet shows the relationship of the fundamental accounting equation. The fundamental accounting equation is the basis of all double-entry accounting. It states the relationship between assets of the business and the claims to those assets, namely liabilities and owners' equity. The equation is Assets = Liabilities + Owners' Equity.

The income statement is a statement of the revenues and expenses of a business over a certain period of time. The income statement is a statement of profitability, since the difference between revenues and expenses is net income or profit.

The statement of cash flows shows a business's cash inflows and outflows over a certain period of time. This statement differs from the income statement when accrual basis accounting is used rather than cash basis accounting. In accrual basis accounting, the revenues and expenses of a business are recognized when they are actually earned or incurred, rather than when actual cash inflow or outflow occurs. The statement of cash flows enables its users to know the various types of cash flows and related amounts.

Endnotes

1. *A Statement of Basic Accounting Theory* (Evanston, Ill.: American Accounting Association, 1966), p. 1.

2. The Educational Institute of the American Hotel & Motel Association has developed a study guide used by candidates who are preparing to take the CHAE examination.

3. Albert Gomes, *Hospitality in Transition* (Houston, Texas: Pannell Kerr Forster, 1985), p. 92.

 ## Key Terms

accounting—The process of identifying, measuring, and communicating economic information to permit users to make informed judgments and decisions.

accounting systems—The branch of accounting that covers the review of a firm's entire information system, not just the accounting system.

accrual basis accounting—System of reporting revenues and expenses in the period in which they are considered to have been earned or incurred, regardless of the actual time of collection or payment.

adjusting entries—Entries required at the end of an accounting period to record internal adjustments of various accounts due to the matching principle of accounting.

assets—Resources available for use by the business—that is, anything owned by the business that has monetary value.

auditing—The branch of accounting that examines a firm's financial statements and internal controls for the purpose of expressing opinions regarding the financial statements.

balance sheet—Statement of the financial position of the hospitality establishment on a given date, giving the account balances for assets, liabilities, and ownership equity.

bookkeeping—The recording and classification of transactions.

business entity principle—An accounting principle that requires that a business maintain its own set of records and accounts that are separate from other financial interests of its owners.

cash basis accounting—System of reporting revenues and expenses at the time they are collected or paid, respectively.

conservatism principle—An accounting principle that requires accounting procedures that recognize expenses as soon as possible, but delay the recognition of revenues until they are ensured. For example, nonrefundable deposits for future services should be recognized as liabilities until the service is actually performed.

consistency principle—An accounting principle that requires that once an accounting method has been adopted, it should be followed from period to period in the future unless a change in accounting methods is warranted and disclosed.

continuity of the business unit principle—The assumption in preparing the accounting records and reports that the business will continue indefinitely and that liquidation is not a prospect—in other words, that the business is a going concern.

corporation—A form of business organization that provides a separate legal entity apart from its owner or owners.

cost accounting—The branch of accounting dealing with the recording, classification, allocation, and reporting of current and prospective costs in order to aid operations personnel in controlling operations.

cost principle—An accounting principle that requires recording the value of transactions for accounting purposes at the actual transaction price (cost).

double taxation—This occurs when both corporate profits and dividends paid to stockholders are taxed.

expenses—Costs incurred in providing the goods and services offered.

financial accounting—A branch of accounting dealing with recording, classifying, and summarizing transactions involving revenues, expenses, assets, and liabilities.

financial audit—An independent, external audit.

full disclosure principle—An accounting principle that requires that a business's financial statements provide information on all the significant facts that have a bearing on their interpretation. Types of disclosures include the accounting methods used, changes in the accounting methods, contingent liabilities, events occurring subsequent to the financial statement date, and unusual and nonrecurring items.

fundamental accounting equation—The equation upon which all double-entry bookkeeping is based: Assets equal liabilities plus owners' equity. This equation is a balance to be tested and proven, not a formula to be calculated.

general partner—The member(s) of a limited partnership who has (have) unlimited liability for the debts of the partnership.

going concern principle—An accounting principle that requires the preparation of accounting records and reports under the assumption that the business will continue indefinitely and that liquidation is not a prospect; also referred to as *continuity of the business unit principle.*

income statement—A report on the profitability of operations, including revenues earned and expenses incurred in generating the revenues for the period of time covered by the statement.

liabilities—Claims to a business's assets by parties external to the business.

limited liability company—An unincorporated business entity that is not restricted to one class of stock and may have any number of owners. It combines the corporate feature of limited liability with the favorable tax treatment of partnerships and sole proprietorships.

limited partner—The member(s) of a limited partnership who has (have) limited liability. Limited partners may not actively participate in managing the business.

limited partnership—A partnership in which one or more of the partners have limited liability; that is, their liability is limited to the amount of their investment in the partnership and their personal assets are not vulnerable to their business's creditors. Every partnership must have at least one general partner, and there are several criteria that must be met in the case of a limited partnership.

managerial accounting—The branch of accounting that provides information to various management levels for the enhancement of controls, usually in the form of budgets.

matching principle—An accounting principle that requires that expenses and revenues be matched to the period in which they were incurred or earned regardless of when they are actually realized.

materiality principle—An accounting principle that states that only items that are "material" or that "make a difference" should be presented in financial statements. For example, materiality may be established by a rule of thumb that states that an item is recognized if it exceeds a certain percentage of total assets or income.

objective evidence principle—An accounting principle that states that all accounting transactions and the resulting accounting records should be based on objectively determined evidence to the greatest extent possible.

owners' equity—Financial interest of the owners of a business in that business— equal to assets minus liabilities.

partnership—An unincorporated business owned by two or more individuals. The partners co-own all the assets and liabilities of the business and share in some manner in its profits or losses.

revenues—Inflows of assets resulting from sales of goods or services to customers.

S corporation—A type of corporation in which profits are taxed in the same manner as those of a partnership; S corporations thus avoid double taxation.

sole proprietorship—An unincorporated business entity that is owned by a single individual.

statement of cash flows—A statement that reflects the cash inflows and outflows of a business for a period of time. It explains the change in cash by showing the effects on cash of a business's operating, investing, and financing activities for the accounting period.

tax accounting—The branch of accounting dealing with the preparation and filing of tax forms with the various governmental agencies.

unit of measurement principle—The accounting principle that requires financial data to be recorded with a common unit of measure. In the United States that common unit is the dollar.

 # Review Questions

1. How are bookkeeping and accounting different?
2. What are the various fields of accounting and how do they differ?
3. What are the major advantages and disadvantages of the corporate form of organization?
4. If a firm did not use the continuity of the business unit principle, what effect would this have on its financial statements?
5. How does cash basis accounting differ from accrual basis accounting?
6. Why are footnote disclosures in financial statements necessary, and what forms do they take?
7. Why should accountants adhere to the conservatism principle?
8. What are the differences among the three major financial statements?
9. How would *liabilities* be defined in terms of the basic accounting equation?
10. How do room sales transactions on account affect elements of the accounting equation?

 # Problems

Problem 1

Fill in the following blanks with the accounting principle that best applies.

a. Cost
b. Business Entity
c. Going Concern
d. Unity of Measurement
e. Objective Evidence

f. Full Disclosure
g. Consistency
h. Matching
i. Conservatism
j. Materiality

1. A fire occurred in your hotel during the previous year. The estimated loss due to a pending lawsuit is recorded because of the _____ principle.

2. You purchased a new dishwasher from Mike's Machines for $1,250, and, because of the _____ principle, it is recorded at $1,250, even though you could now sell it for $1,500.

3. Although the last biweekly pay period ended December 26, your employees have worked through the end of December. The unpaid salaries and wages are accrued as of December 31 because of the _____ principle.

4. Your firm is the defendant in a major lawsuit. Your attorney believes you may lose. Although the attorney is unable to estimate the potential loss, the lawsuit is briefly mentioned in a footnote to the financial statements because of the _____ principle.

5. In the past, you have depreciated furniture in your hospitality firm using the straight-line method. You are going to change to an accelerated method, even for the furniture you previously depreciated using the straight-line method. Changing depreciation methods violates the _____ principle.

Problem 2

Indicate which branch of accounting would likely be most involved with each activity listed below. Consider the branches of financial accounting, cost accounting, managerial accounting, tax accounting, auditing, and accounting systems.

1. Prepares the firm's federal income tax return.
2. Reviews procedures for purchasing, receiving, and issuing food stocks.
3. Processes the payroll for the biweekly pay period.
4. Evaluates the need for upgrading the point-of-sale system in the restaurant.
5. Works closely with the hotel's general manager and department heads in preparing the five-year budget for the hotel.
6. Records food service charge sales in the restaurant and posts the charges to the guests' accounts.

Problem 3

The following are balance sheet accounts for Blair's Catering:

Accounts payable	$ 5,000
Accounts receivable	4,000
Blair Douglas, Capital	15,000
Cash	1,000
Equipment	10,000
Food supplies	2,000
Prepaid rent	3,000

Required:

Prepare a simplified balance sheet. Consider following the example of Kathy's Catering Service shown in the chapter.

Problem 4

You have been hired as a bookkeeper by Henry Holiday, owner of Henry's Inn. During your first week on the job, the following transactions occur:

1. New furniture costing $10,000 was purchased with a loan from the bank.
2. Mr. Holiday contributed $5,000 to the business as new capital.
3. Cash of $1,000 is paid on the $10,000 loan.
4. Office supplies of $50 are bought on account from Stu's House of Office Supplies.
5. A new computer costing $1,500 is paid for with cash.

Required:

Show and describe how the transactions affect the fundamental accounting equation, Assets = Liabilities + Owner's Equity.

Problem 5

Dwayne Kent on January 1, 20X1, opened the Double K Inn, a ten-room lodging facility. During the first three days the following transactions were completed.

a. He invested $50,000 of his personal cash in a bank account opened in the name of Double K Inn.

b. He paid $2,000 for the month of January to lease a building containing the ten guest-rooms.

c. He rented rooms for the three days and collected an average of $50 per room for the 15 rooms that were "sold." Treat this activity as a single transaction to keep things simple.

d. He purchased guest supplies on account from Hotel Suppliers, Inc., for $300.

e. He paid an advertising bill of $500.

Required:

1. Arrange the following asset, liability, and proprietorship titles in an expanded accounting equation like that shown in the chapter: Cash, Guest Supplies, Prepaid Rent, Accounts Payable, and Dwayne Kent, Capital.

2. Show by additions and subtractions the effects of each transaction on the assets, liabilities, and proprietorship of the Double K Inn. Show net totals for all items after each transaction.

Problem 6

Melvin Dwight owns a small catering business called M.D.'s Catering. At the beginning of the current month, the business had the following assets: cash, $2,500; food inventory, $500; beverage inventory, $2,500; office supplies, $200; and delivery truck, $2,000. M.D.'s owed $500 to

Lawrence Supply Co., and $1,500 on a note to First Auto Bank. On the first day of the month, M.D.'s Catering completed the following transactions:

a. Melvin invested $500 more in M.D.'s Catering.

b. Food costing $250 was purchased on account from Lawrence Supply Co.

c. Twenty dinners were served to L&M Trucking Co. Board of Directors, and L&M was charged $5.50 for each dinner. Cash was received from L&M. The costs of food and beverages served were $40 and $15, respectively.

d. Melvin paid $20 for repair work to the delivery truck. (Note: This expenditure should be considered an expense.)

e. Melvin paid J.D. Hill $15 for labor services received.

f. Melvin paid First Auto Bank $450 on account.

g. Melvin withdrew $300 from the firm for personal use.

Required:

1. Arrange the asset, liability, and proprietorship titles in an expanded accounting equation like that shown in Table II in this chapter.

2. Enter the assets and liability of M.D.'s under the titles of the equation. Determine Melvin Dwight's equity and enter it under the title of Melvin Dwight, Capital.

3. Show by additions and subtractions the effects of each transaction on the elements of the equation. Show new totals after each transaction.

Problem 7

Using the account names and account balances from Problem 6, create a balance sheet (dated December 31, 20X2) for M.D.'s Catering. Follow the example given in Exhibit 6.

Problem 8

Charlie Reps owns the Spring Valley Motel. It is the end of the year 20X5 and he has asked you to help him prepare his balance sheet. His account balances are as follows:

Accounts receivable	$ 300
Inventory	50
Notes payable	2,500
Cash	250
Prepaid insurance	50
Accounts payable	200
Building	5,000
Wages payable	150
Owner's equity	?????

Required:

1. Find the missing account balance, using the fundamental accounting equation.

2. Prepare Charlie's balance sheet for 20X5, using the form shown in Exhibit 6.

Problem 9

Melanie Anastor is the owner and manager of Mel's Diner, a popular eatery and gathering place. She believes things are going very well, but she needs to have an income statement prepared for the IRS for 20X7. She has hired your consulting firm to prepare one.

Melanie's sales from food and beverages for the year were $575,000. Labor costs for her cooks, servers, and buspeople were $190,000. Cost of food used was $165,000. General maintenance and upkeep costs for the year were $20,000. Other operating costs (including your consulting fee of $10,000) came to $90,000.

Required:

Prepare an income statement for 20X7 for Mel's Diner according to Exhibit 7.

Problem 10

Juan and Wendy Carlos own a small roadside motel called the Carlos Inn. They prepare their own financial statements and are learning about the importance of the statement of cash flows. They desire your assistance in preparing a statement of cash flows for the Carlos Inn.

The following series of transactions occurred at the Carlos Inn during 20X3:

- It paid cash for wages to employees of $60,000.
- It acquired loan from Lone Star Bank for $25,000. Used loan to buy new shuttle van for $30,000.
- It paid cash for cleaning supply purchases of $2,000.
- It had sales (no credit sales are made at the Carlos Inn) of $155,000.
- It paid operating expenses with cash of $45,000.
- It paid fees for a reservation system of $5,000.
- The owners withdrew cash of $10,000.

Required:
1. Prepare a statement of cash flows for the Carlos Inn for 20X3.
2. Assuming there is a surplus in cash, suggest some ways in which it could be used.

REVIEW QUIZ

When you feel you have covered all of the material in this chapter, answer these questions. Choose the *best* answer.

1. Bookkeeping and accounting differ in that:

   a. bookkeeping includes accounting.
   b. accounting includes bookkeeping.
   c. bookkeeping requires more training than accounting.
   d. bookkeeping has more to do with computers than accounting.

2. Which of the following branches of accounting is often limited to preparing and distributing financial reports?

   a. financial accounting
   b. cost accounting
   c. managerial accounting
   d. auditing

3. Which of the following is a disadvantage of the sole proprietorship form of business organization?

   a. unlimited liability
   b. double taxation
   c. complicated rules for formation
   d. unfavorable tax treatment

4. Which of the following statements about the role of the accounting department of a hotel is *true?*

   a. Accounting staff only provide reports to the front desk staff and top managers.
   b. Accountants' most crucial role in a business is their preparation of tax forms.
   c. Hospitality accounting firms usually communicate financial information to external users such as banks through financial statements.
   d. It is common for headquarters of large hospitality chains to have less than 10 accounting staff members, because so much work is done with computers.

5. The generally accepted accounting principles number whose application requires that significant amounts of inventory be carried at the lower of cost or market value is the:

   a. cost principle.
   b. conservatism principle.
   c. disclosure principle.
   d. materiality principle.

REVIEW QUIZ *(continued)*

6. Percy wants to examine the most recent expense reports for his hotel. Revenues and expenses are shown on:

    a. the balance sheet.
    b. the income statement.
    c. the statement of cash flows.
    d. any of the above.

7. What happens to the fundamental accounting equation when the purchase of an asset is financed entirely with debt?

    a. Assets increase, liabilities increase, and owners' equity decreases.
    b. Assets remain the same, liabilities increase, and owners' equity decreases.
    c. Assets remain the same, liabilities increase, and owners' equity increases.
    d. Assets increase, liabilities increase, and owners' equity remains the same.

Answer Key: 1-b-C1, 2-a-C2, 3-a-C4, 4-c-C5, 5-b-C6, 6-b-C7, 7-d-C8

Each question is linked to a competency. Competencies are listed on the first page of the chapter. An answer reading 3-b-C4 translates to:

    3: the question number
    b: the correct answer
    C4: the competency number

Chapter 2 Outline

Accounts
    Asset Accounts
    Liability Accounts
    Owners' Equity Accounts
Debit and Credit
    Mechanics of Double-Entry
        Accounting
    Recording Changes in Assets,
        Liabilities, and Owners' Equity
    Recording Changes in Revenues and
        Expenses
    Recording Owner's Withdrawals
    Determining Account Balances
    Normal Balances
General Ledger
Journalizing
    Standard Account Forms
    Posting
    The Trial Balance
    Compound Journal Entries
Comprehensive Illustration—Journalizing,
    Posting, and Preparing a Trial Balance

Competencies

1. Explain the functions of accounts and T-accounts, and classify accounts into the major account categories.

2. Define the terms *debit* and *credit*, explain the basis of the double-entry accounting system, and identify the normal balances of commonly used accounts.

3. Define *general ledger*, distinguish between balance sheet and nominal accounts, and describe the relationship between general ledger accounts and the chart of accounts.

4. Demonstrate how to journalize and post accounting entries, and prepare a trial balance for accounts.

2

Accounting for Business Transactions

IN THIS CHAPTER, we introduce the T-account, the concepts of debits and credits, the journal, the recording process of journalizing, the ledger, the process of posting, and the trial balance. These tools are all basic to a double-entry accounting system.

Business transactions are the raw data of accounting. First, business events are observed and those of an economic nature are identified. For example, suppose a customer purchases a meal for $8.00. From the seller's viewpoint, the purchase of the meal is a business event of an economic nature. The seller exchanges food and service for $8.00. An example of an event that is not of an economic nature is "a potential guest has entered our hotel." No goods or services have been provided yet; thus, the event is insignificant from an accounting viewpoint.

In the first example, the sale of food and accompanying services for $8.00, an economic event, has occurred. The measure of this transaction is the sales price of $8.00, which must be recorded as a sale and as a receipt of cash. At the same time, the provision of food and use of labor have occurred. These activities must also be recorded, but the detail of this recording will be provided later.

Accounts

Economic events, such as those in the preceding illustration, are reflected in accounts. An **account** is the basic element used in an accounting system to classify and summarize business transactions. Think of the account as a basic storage unit for data. Thus, accounts must be established for each separate classification. For example, each business will have a cash account, as well as accounts to record different types of sales and expenses.

To illustrate accounts, we start with a **T-account** that has three basic parts: the title, the left side, and the right side. The T-account's name is derived from its appearance. A T-account looks like the letter *T*, as shown below:

(Name of Account)	
(left side)	(right side)

Increases in accounts are recorded on one side of the account, and decreases are recorded on the other side. Which side (left or right) is used for increases and which is used for decreases depends on the type of account. For example, let us consider Cash, an asset account. Assume $100 is received and $50 is disbursed in two separate transactions. This cash activity would be shown as follows:

Cash			
Received	100	Disbursed	50

Notice that the increase in cash is shown on the left side, while the decrease in cash is shown on the right side. This is generally true for all asset accounts.

The decreases are subtracted from the increases in our Cash account to yield the account balance. In this example, the Cash account has a $50 balance:

Cash			
Received	100	Disbursed	50
Balance	50		

Future cash activities would be recorded in the Cash account in a similar fashion, except the balance would reflect both increases and decreases.

Hospitality businesses have many accounts. The general classifications include assets, liabilities, and owners' equity. Under the owners' equity classification, there are capital, revenue, and expense accounts.

A few of the more common accounts are described in the next sections.

Asset Accounts

Cash. Cash includes cash on hand in the custody of cashiers and other employees, plus the cash on deposit with banks. Accountants generally maintain a separate cash account for each cash fund and for each account with the bank.

Notes Receivable. A formal written promise to pay a sum of money at a fixed future date is called a *promissory note.* Businesses refer to these notes as *notes receivable* when they receive them from debtors. Generally, the Notes Receivable account contains only notes receivable from debtors who maintain open accounts with the enterprise. Notes receivable from officers, employees, and affiliated companies are shown in separate accounts.

Accounts Receivable. Goods or services are often sold to guests on the basis of the guests' oral or implied promises to pay in the future. Such sales are known as *sales on account*, and the promises to pay are known as *accounts receivable.* Accounts receivable are segregated by type of debtor. Accounts receivable from guests would be shown in one account, while amounts due from officers, employees, and companies affiliated or associated with the business would be shown in separate accounts.

Accrued Interest Receivable. This account consists of interest earned on interest-bearing assets that the business has not yet received at the date of the balance sheet.

Marketable Securities. Securities (stocks and bonds) that are purchased as short-term investments and are thus readily convertible to cash are classified as marketable securities.

Inventories of Merchandise. Several accounts will be maintained for the inventory of goods for sale, including but not limited to Beverage Inventory, Food Inventory, and Gift Merchandise Inventory.

Office Supplies. Postage stamps, stationery, paper, pencils, and similar items are known as *office supplies.* They are assets when purchased. As they are used in the business, they become expenses.

Other Prepaid Expenses. Prepaid expenses are items that are assets when purchased but become expenses as they are used. Prepaid items include prepaid rent, unexpired insurance, and prepaid taxes. Each type of prepaid expense is accounted for in a separate account.

Investments. Investments in securities of affiliated or associated companies and other securities purchased as nontemporary investments are included in an investment account.

Property and Equipment. This class of assets includes land, buildings, furniture, carpets, linen, china, glassware, and uniforms. A separate account is maintained for each type of property and equipment.

Liability Accounts

Notes Payable. This account includes promissory notes given to creditors. Promissory notes given to banks may be shown separately from notes to other creditors.

Accounts Payable. An account payable is an amount the business owes to a creditor, resulting from an oral or implied promise to pay at some future date.

Taxes Charged to Guests and Withheld from Employees. All taxes collected from guests or withheld from employees are generally recorded in separate accounts, such as Sales Taxes Payable, FICA Payable, Federal Income Taxes Withheld, State Income Taxes Withheld, and City Income Taxes Withheld.

Income Taxes Payable. The firm will record the amount of federal, state, and city income taxes due for prior fiscal years in separate accounts. The estimated liability for income taxes on the current year's net income to date will also be recorded in these accounts.

Accrued Expenses. Expenses for a period not yet paid at the end of the accounting period (such as wages, salaries, interest, and utilities) are recorded as well as the liability. A separate account is maintained for each item.

Unearned Income. This is the unearned portion of revenue resulting from cash received from a guest for a period following the end of the accounting period. Deposits on banquets and room reservations may also be shown as unearned income.

Mortgage Payable. A mortgage payable is a long-term debt for which the creditor has a secured prior claim against one or more of the hospitality firm's assets.

Owners' Equity Accounts

Many transactions affect the owners' equity of a business enterprise, including the investment of a proprietor, withdrawal of assets by a proprietor, and revenues earned and expenses incurred by the organization. So that an accountant can readily obtain information on the various kinds of increases and decreases in owners' equity, a different account is used for each type of increase or decrease.

Capital Account. When an individual invests in a business organized as a sole proprietorship, the investment is recorded in an account bearing the investor's name. All other capital accounts will be "closed" into this account periodically. If the firm is incorporated, the Capital account is replaced by two types of accounts: (1) Capital Stock, in which different accounts are maintained for different types of stock; and (2) Retained Earnings, in which net income or loss, the results of operations less dividends declared, is recorded.

Revenue and Expense Accounts. Revenues increase owners' equity, whereas expenses decrease it. The prime objective of a business enterprise is to earn a profit. If the enterprise is to succeed, detailed information regarding the kinds of revenues and expenses must be supplied to management on a timely basis. This information is maintained in a separate account for each revenue and expense item. Common revenue and expense accounts include the following:

Revenues	Expenses
Room Sales	Beverage Expense
Food Sales	Food Expense
Beverage Sales	Wages Expense
Gift Shop Sales	Payroll Taxes
Green Fees	Office Supplies
Pro Shop Sales	Rent
Banquet Sales	Cleaning Supplies
Interest Income	Electricity
Dividend Income	Fuel
	Insurance
	Interest
	Advertising Expense
	Travel Expenses
	Property Taxes
	Depreciation Expense
	Income Taxes

The kind of revenue or expense recorded in each of these accounts is reasonably evident from its title, as is true of most revenue and expense accounts.

Debit and Credit

The left side of any account is always called the **debit** side and the right side is always called the **credit** side, as arbitrarily established by accountants. Debit and credit are abbreviated "dr" and "cr," respectively. To *debit* an account is simply to record an amount on the *left* side of the account; to *credit* an account is to record an amount on the *right* side. The difference between the total debits and credits of an account is called the *balance*. Thus, an account may have either a **debit balance** or a **credit balance.** Accounting personnel will often use the term *charge* in place of *debit*.

When Michael Miller invests $10,000 in his lodging business, cash is increased (debited) for $10,000, and the $10,000 is recorded on the left side of the Cash T-account. The account Michael Miller, Capital is also increased (credited in this account) for the $10,000. This is recorded on the right side of the account, as shown:

Cash		Michael Miller, Capital	
10,000			10,000

When Michael Miller invested $10,000 in his business, both cash and Michael Miller's proprietorship increased. Observe, however, that the cash increase is recorded on the left side of the Cash account, while the owners' equity increase is recorded on the right side of the Michael Miller, Capital account. This results from the mechanics of double-entry accounting.

Mechanics of Double-Entry Accounting

In **double-entry accounting,** every transaction affects and is recorded in at least two accounts, and the debits of the entry must equal the credits of the entry. Since every transaction is recorded with equal debits and credits, the sum of the debits recorded must equal the sum of the credits recorded. When the accounts are balanced, each account has either a debit or credit balance. The equality of debit and credit accounts is tested by preparing a trial balance, discussed in detail later in this chapter. The equality of these two groups of accounts provides some assurance that the arithmetic of the transaction recording process has been properly completed.

Equal debits and credits in recording transactions result under a double-entry system because the system is based on the fundamental accounting equation, Assets = Liabilities + Owners' Equity. Increases in assets are recorded with debits, and decreases in assets are recorded with credits. Increases in liabilities and owners' equity are recorded with credits, while decreases are recorded with debits. These rules are shown below:

Assets		=	Liabilities		+	Owners' Equity	
+	−		−	+		−	+
dr	cr		dr	cr		dr	cr

The rules can be restated in this way:

1. Asset accounts are increased by debits and decreased by credits.

2. Liabilities and owners' equity accounts are increased by credits and decreased by debits.

Applying these two rules keeps the accounting equation in balance; that is, assets equal liabilities plus owners' equity.

Recording Changes in Assets, Liabilities, and Owners' Equity

The following three transactions from the hypothetical Mable Motel will illustrate these concepts.

For Transaction 1, assume that Molly Mable invests $100,000 in her lodging enterprise, the Mable Motel. The Mable Motel records the $100,000 that Molly invests as follows:

Cash		Molly Mable, Capital	
(1) 100,000			(1) 100,000

This transaction increases cash of the Mable Motel and also increases Molly Mable's equity in her business. Since Cash is an asset account, it is debited for the $100,000 received. Molly Mable, Capital is an owner's equity account, so it is increased by a credit entry of $100,000. Recording this transaction as shown results in debits equaling credits and assets equaling owner's equity. At this point there are no liabilities.

For Transaction 2, assume that Molly Mable borrows $50,000 from First Bank. She signs a note, which in this case is a written promise to pay the bank the $50,000 in three years. The transaction is recorded as follows:

Cash		Notes Payable—First Bank	
(2) 50,000			(2) 50,000

The asset account Cash is increased with a debit for the $50,000 cash received. The liability account, Notes Payable—First Bank, is increased with a credit for the $50,000 of cash borrowed. First Bank has claims to the Mable Motel's assets of $50,000. The above recording results in debits equaling credits, and assets (cash) of $150,000 equaling liabilities of $50,000 and owner's equity of $100,000.

Transaction 3 for this lodging enterprise is the purchase of $80,000 worth of furniture by the Mable Motel. The transaction is recorded as follows:

Furniture		Cash	
(3) 80,000			(3) 80,000

The asset account Furniture is increased (debited) for $80,000, while another asset account, Cash, is decreased (credited) for $80,000. This transaction is recorded, as all transactions must be, with debits equaling credits. Further, the accounting equation of $A = L + E$ is in balance, as follows:

Assets	
Cash	$ 70,000
Furniture	80,000
Total	$ 150,000
Liabilities and Owner's Equity	
Notes Payable—First Bank	$ 50,000
Molly Mable, Capital	100,000
Total	$ 150,000

Recording Changes in Revenues and Expenses

In theory, revenues and expenses can be recorded directly in the Owners' Equity account. However, in the real world, revenues and expenses are recorded in separate accounts to facilitate the communication of this information in the income statement. Revenues increase owners' equity, so increases in revenues are recorded with credits. Expenses decrease owners' equity, so increases in expenses are recorded with debit entries. The expanded accounting equation, including the debit and credit rules for each account classification, is as follows:

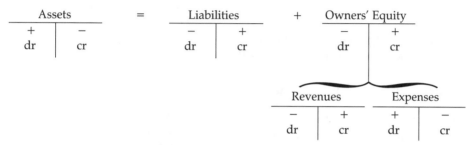

Note: At the end of the accounting period, revenue and expense accounts are closed to the Owners' Equity account.

Two transactions (Transactions 4 and 5) of the Mable Motel will illustrate the rules of debit and credit for revenue and expense accounts. Transaction 4 is the receipt of $50 for a room rented to Susan Smith, a guest. The transaction is recorded as follows:

Cash			Room Revenues	
(4)	50			(4)	50

Cash and Room Revenues are increased by the rental of a room for one night and Susan Smith's payment of $50. The Cash account is debited for $50 to reflect the increase, while the revenue account, Room Revenues, is increased (credited) for $50.

Transaction 5 is a $30 cash payment to Jason Jones for work performed for the motel. The transaction is recorded as follows:

Wages Expense			Cash	
(5)	30			(5)	30

Wages Expense is increased with a debit of $30, while Cash is decreased with a credit entry of $30.

Recording Owner's Withdrawals

The owner of an unincorporated business such as the Mable Motel may decide to withdraw cash from his or her business. Withdrawals reduce the owner's equity in the business and have the same effect as an expense on the owner's equity. The

drawing account is not an expense account, however. Owners' withdrawals are recorded in a drawing account that is a subclassification of the owners' equity account, similar to revenue and expense accounts. Since withdrawals reduce owners'
equity, the drawing account is increased with debits and decreased with credits in
the same way expense accounts are increased and decreased.

Transaction 6 for the Mable Motel illustrates the withdrawal of $100 by Molly
Mable from her business. The transaction is recorded as follows:

Molly Mable, Drawing		Cash	
(6)	100	(6)	100

The drawing account is increased with a debit entry of $100, while the cash
account is decreased with a credit of $100.

Determining Account Balances

The difference between the sum of the debits and the sum of the credits of each
account results in the account balance. When the debit total exceeds the credit total,
the account has a debit balance. When the credit total exceeds the debit total, the
account has a credit balance. For example, the Cash account for the Mable Motel
has a debit balance of $69,920, since the sum of the debit entries of $150,050 exceeds
the sum of the credit entries of $80,130, by $69,920:

Cash			
(1)	100,000	(3)	80,000
(2)	50,000	(5)	30
(4)	50	(6)	100
	150,050		80,130
Debit Balance	69,920		

The balance of the Molly Mable, Capital account is a credit balance, since the
credit entry of $100,000 exceeds debits which, in this case, are zero:

Molly Mable, Capital		
	(1)	100,000
	Credit Balance	100,000

Normal Balances

The **normal balance** of an account is the kind of balance, either debit or credit, that
an account generally shows. This balance results from increases in the account, and
only on occasion does the balance of an account result from an excess of decreases
over increases. The major classes of accounts have the following normal balances:

Type of Account	Normal Balance
Asset	Debit
Liability	Credit
Owners' Equity:	
Capital	Credit
Revenue	Credit
Expense	Debit
Drawing	Debit

Accountants know the normal balance of every account of the accounting system of their lodging business and are skeptical of an account with a balance opposite from normal. Investigating accounts with suspicious balances will usually show either an error or an unusual transaction. For example, if the Furniture account has a credit balance, an error has most certainly been made. On the other hand, a credit balance in a guest's account would probably not attract attention, because such credits occur whenever the guest makes a deposit with his or her reservation.

General Ledger

A group of accounts is defined as a *ledger*. The **general ledger** is the group of general accounts that includes accounts for assets, liabilities, owners' equity, revenues, expenses, and owner's drawing. The **balance sheet accounts,** also called *real accounts* since they are permanent accounts and are never closed, include the asset, liability, and owners' equity accounts. The remaining accounts are temporary accounts and are often called **nominal accounts.** These accounts include revenue, expense, and drawing accounts, which are closed at the end of each year into the Owners' Equity account. The general ledger may be a binder housing all accounts, or, if the general ledger is computerized, all accounts may be printed on a continuous form.

Each hospitality business should have a complete listing of all accounts. This is called a **chart of accounts.** The chart of accounts lists all account numbers and account titles. The major purpose of the chart of accounts is to guide accountants as they record business transactions.[1] Rather than invent new accounts, accountants generally record all transactions in accounts that are listed in the chart.

Accounts are numbered according to their classification. For example, a chart of accounts for a lodging firm might look like this:

Classification	Account Numbers	Examples of Accounts	
Assets	100–199	Cash on Hand	100
		Petty Cash	101
		.	
		.	
		.	
		Furniture	151
		.	
		.	
		Building	171

Liabilities	200–299	Accounts Payable	200
		Notes Payable	201
		·	
		·	
		·	
		Mortgage Payable	249
Owner's Equity and Drawing	300–399	Owner's Name, Capital	300
		Owner's Name, Drawing	301
Revenues	400–499	Rooms Revenue	400
		Food Revenue	401
Expenses	500–599	Wages Expense	500
		Supplies Expense	501
		·	
		·	
		·	
		Depreciation	550

Exhibit 1 is the Assets section from the sample chart of accounts from the *Uniform System of Accounts for the Lodging Industry.* The suggested three-digit account numbers for each classification are listed here:

Assets	100–199
Liabilities	200–280
Equity	281–299
Revenue	300–399
Cost of Sales	400–499
Payroll and Related Expenses	500–599
Other Expenses	600–699
Fixed Charges	700–799

Thus, this system has four separate classifications of expenses from "cost of sales" through "fixed charges." Many lodging operations use a very extensive chart of accounts like this to classify and summarize business activity and facilitate financial reporting.

Journalizing

Thus far, we have recorded transactions directly in the T-accounts. Each account reflects only the activity affecting that account. For example, the Mable Motel's Cash account reflects only the cash portion of the cash transactions. The Cash account shows only the changes in cash and does not reveal the sources of cash receipts or the uses of cash disbursements.

In actual practice, transactions are seldom recorded directly in ledger accounts for three reasons:

1. There is not room for much detailed information in a ledger account. Accounts are mainly for classifying and summarizing financial information. If an

Exhibit 1   Assets Section from a Sample Chart of Accounts

ASSETS

100 Cash
 101 House Funds
 103 Checking Account
 105 Payroll Account
 107 Savings Account
 109 Petty Cash
110 Short-Term Investments
120 Accounts Receivable
 121 Guest Ledger
 122 Credit Card Accounts
 123 Direct Bill
 124 Notes Receivable (Current)
 125 Due from Employees
 126 Receivable from Owner
 127 Other Accounts Receivable
 128 Intercompany Receivables
 129 Allowance for Doubtful Accounts
130 Inventory
 131 Food
 132 Liquor
 133 Wine
 135 Operating Supplies
 136 Paper Supplies
 137 Cleaning Supplies
 138 China, Glassware, Silver, Linen, and Uniforms (Unopened Stock)
 139 Other
140 Prepaids
 141 Prepaid Insurance
 142 Prepaid Taxes
 143 Prepaid Workers' Compensation
 144 Prepaid Supplies
 145 Prepaid Contracts
 146 Current Deferred Tax Asset
 147 Barter Contracts Asset
 149 Other Prepaids
150 Noncurrent Receivables
155 Investments (not short-term)
160 Property and Equipment
 161 Land
 162 Buildings
 163 Accumulated Depreciation—Buildings
 164 Leaseholds and Leasehold Improvements
 165 Accumulated Depreciation—Leaseholds
 166 Furniture and Fixtures
 167 Accumulated Depreciation—Furniture and Fixtures
 168 Machinery and Equipment

(continued)

Exhibit 1   *(continued)*

ASSETS
169 Accumulated Depreciation—Machinery and Equipment
170 Information Systems Equipment
171 Accumulated Depreciation—Information Systems Equipment
172 Automobiles and Trucks
173 Accumulated Depreciation—Automobiles and Trucks
174 Construction in Progress
175 China
176 Glassware
177 Silver
178 Linen
179 Uniforms
180 Accumulated Depreciation—China, Glassware, Silver, Linen, and Uniforms
190 Other Assets
191 Security Deposits
192 Deferred Charges
193 Long-Term Deferred Tax Asset
196 Cash Surrender Value—Life Insurance
197 Goodwill
199 Miscellaneous

Source: *Uniform System of Accounts for the Lodging Industry,* 9th rev. ed. (East Lansing, Mich.: Educational Institute of the American Hotel & Motel Association, 1996), pp. 191–192. ©Hotel Association of New York City.

account includes all the details, it does not serve well as a device for classifying and summarizing.

2. Account entries fail to record a complete record of each transaction in any one place, since a ledger has many accounts, each located on a separate page. As noted, each transaction affects at least two accounts.

3. If transactions are recorded directly in the accounts, errors are easily made and are difficult to locate.

Therefore, rather than recording directly in the accounts, the accountant records the transaction first in a journal. This process is called **journalizing.** The information recorded in the journal is then "transferred" to the ledger accounts.

A journal is commonly called a *book of original entry,* since the transaction is first recorded there, while the ledger is referred to as a *book of final entry.*

Firms in the hospitality industry maintain several kinds of journals. However, the simplest and most flexible is the general journal. A general journal provides for recording:

1. Date of the transaction (in the date column)

2. Titles of the accounts used (in the account titles and explanation column)

3. Explanation of the transaction (in the account titles and explanation column)

Exhibit 2   Transactions 1 and 2 for the Mable Motel

Date		Accounts/Explanation	Post. Ref.	Debit	Credit
		General Journal			Page 1
20X1					
Jan.	*1*	Cash		1 0 0 0 0 0	
		Molly Mable, Capital			1 0 0 0 0 0
		To record investment by Molly			
		Mable in the Mable Motel.			
Jan.	*1*	Cash		5 0 0 0 0	
		Notes Payable—First Bank			5 0 0 0 0
		To record amount borrowed from			
		First Bank.			

4. Page numbers of ledger accounts to which the debit and credit amounts of the transaction are "transferred" (in the Post. Ref. [posting reference] column)

5. Debit and credit effects of the transaction on the accounts listed (in the debit and credit columns)

Exhibit 2 shows how Transactions 1 and 2 for the Mable Motel are recorded in the general journal. The date of the transactions, January 1, 20X1, is recorded for each. Then the account titles and amounts and an explanation for each transaction are recorded. Note that the account title for the credit entry of each transaction is indented. The account numbers in the posting reference column are recorded when the amounts are transferred from the journal to general ledger accounts. Generally, dollar signs, commas, and decimal points are not used in lined journals or ledgers. Also, when amounts are in even dollars, the accountant may leave the cents column blank or simply draw a dash across the column.

Standard Account Forms

T-accounts are commonly used in teaching, since details are eliminated and the student can concentrate on ideas. Hospitality businesses, however, do not use T-accounts to record transactions. Exhibit 3 illustrates the account form that businesses with manual accounting systems most often use.

Exhibit 3   Account Form Used with Manual Accounting Systems

Account Title	Cash				Account No.			

Date		Accounts/Explanation	Post. Ref.	Debit	Credit	Balance
Jan.	1	Initial investment		1 0 0 0 0 0		1 0 0 0 0 0
	1	Loan from bank		5 0 0 0 0		1 5 0 0 0 0

In Exhibit 3, the Cash account is not divided into two sides as is the T-account. Instead, it has debit and credit columns next to each other. Further, this account has a balance column so the balance of the account can be maintained at all times. After the two transactions mentioned before are recorded in the Cash account, the balance is $150,000.

The balance column in Exhibit 3 does not indicate whether the Cash account has a debit or credit balance, since the balance of an account is always assumed to be the normal type unless otherwise indicated. Therefore, the Cash account will have a debit balance. If a transaction causes an opposite balance, such as a credit balance in the Cash account, the accountant indicates it by entering the balance in red, by circling the balance, or by enclosing the balance in brackets or parentheses.

Posting

The process of transferring amounts recorded in the general journal to ledger accounts is called **posting.** Posting is done periodically, sometimes daily, but always by the end of an accounting period. When the accountant posts the amount to the ledger account, he or she completes the posting reference column in the general journal by indicating the account number to which the amount is posted. In the posting reference column of the corresponding ledger account, the accountant lists the general journal page where the posted amount was journalized. Journal debits are posted as ledger account debits and journal credits as ledger account credits.

Exhibit 4 shows Transactions 1 and 2 recorded in the Mable Motel's general journal on January 1, 20X1, and the posting of these amounts in the general ledger accounts. The relationships are shown with arrows for the first transaction, as follows:

1. The date of the journal entry in the general journal (January 1, 20X1) is shown on both the Cash account and the Molly Mable, Capital account.

2. The cash received of $100,000 and recorded in the general journal is posted to the Cash account.

3. In the posting reference of the general journal, the Cash account number 100 is written to indicate the completion of the posting.

Exhibit 4 Illustration of Relation of Journal and Ledger Accounts

			General Journal			Page 1	
Date		**Accounts/Explanation**	**Post. Ref.**	**Debit**		**Credit**	
20X1							
Jan. ①	1	Cash	100	1 0 0 0 0 0			
		Molly Mable, Capital	300			1 0 0 0 0 0	
		To record investment by Molly					
		Mable in the Mable Motel.					
Jan.	1	Cash	100	5 0 0 0 0			
		Notes Payable—First Bank	220			5 0 0 0 0	
		To record amount borrowed from First Bank.					

General Ledger Accounts

	Account Title *Cash*				Account No. *100*			
Date		**Accounts/Explanation**	**Post. Ref.**	**Debit**		**Credit**	**Balance**	
Jan.	1	Initial investment	GJ 1	1 0 0 0 0 0			1 0 0 0 0 0	
	1	Loan from bank	GJ 1	5 0 0 0 0			5 0 0 0 0	

	Account Title *Molly Mable, Capital*				Account No. *300*			
Date		**Accounts/Explanation**	**Post. Ref.**	**Debit**		**Credit**	**Balance**	
Jan.	1	Initial investment	GJ 1			1 0 0 0 0 0	1 0 0 0 0 0	

	Account Title *Notes Payable—First Bank*				Account No. *220*			
Date		**Accounts/Explanation**	**Post. Ref.**	**Debit**		**Credit**	**Balance**	
Jan.	1	Loan from bank	GJ 1			5 0 0 0 0	5 0 0 0 0	

4. In the posting reference column of the general ledger Cash account, the source and page (*GJ 1* for *general journal,* page *1*) are recorded.

5. The posting of $100,000 to the Molly Mable, Capital account is shown, including the posting reference of the account number 300 for Molly Mable, Capital in the general journal and GJ 1 as the posting reference in the Molly Mable, Capital account.

The recording of account numbers in the general journal and page numbers from the general journal in the general ledger accounts at the time of posting is called *cross-indexing*. It allows accountants to check and trace the origins of the transactions.

The Trial Balance

The trial balance of accounts, generally shortened to just **trial balance**, is a listing of the accounts and their debit and credit balances. The trial balance is prepared to test the equality of debits and credits. Accountants prepare the trial balance using the following procedure:

1. Determine the balance of each account in the ledger.

2. List the accounts and show debit balances in one column on the left and credit balances in a separate column to its right.

3. Add the debit balances.

4. Add the credit balances.

5. Compare the totals of the debit and credit balances.

When the total of the debit balance accounts equals the total of the credit balance accounts, the trial balance is in balance. If the trial balance does not balance, someone erred in recording the transactions, in determining the balances of each account, or in preparing the trial balance. However, a balanced trial balance is not proof that all transactions have been recorded properly. For example, an accounting employee may mistakenly record the payment of advertising expense by debiting Wages rather than Advertising. The trial balance would still be in balance, yet the amount of wages and advertising will have been incorrectly recorded. The trial balance, if correct, indicates only that debits equal credits.

Exhibit 5 shows the balance of each account of the Mable Motel after Transactions 1 through 6 were recorded. The exhibit also shows the Mable Motel's trial balance. Since the total of debit balance accounts of $150,050 equals the total of credit balance accounts of $150,050, the trial balance is in balance.

Compound Journal Entries

Up to this point, all transactions used in illustrations have affected only two accounts. Business transactions will often involve three or more accounts. Journal entries recording these transactions are called **compound journal entries.** As with all journal entries, debits must equal credits.

Exhibit 5 Mable Motel Accounts and Trial Balance

ASSETS	=	LIABILITIES	+	OWNER'S EQUITY

ASSETS

Cash

(1) 100,000	(3) 80,000
(2) 50,000	
(4) 50	(5) 30
	(6) 100
150,050	80,130
69,920	

Furniture

(3) 80,000	
80,000	

LIABILITIES

Notes Payable—
First Bank

	(2) 50,000
	50,000

OWNER'S EQUITY

Molly Mable,
Capital

	(1) 100,000
	100,000

Molly Mable,
Drawing

(6) 100	
100	

Room Revenues

	(4) 50
	50

Wages Expense

(5) 30	
30	

Mable Motel
Trial Balance

	Debit	Credit
Cash	$ 69,920	
Furniture	80,000	
Notes Payable—First Bank		$ 50,000
Molly Mable, Capital		100,000
Molly Mable, Drawing	100	
Room Revenues		50
Wages Expense	30	
Total	$150,050	$150,050

To illustrate a compound journal entry, consider the Mable Motel's purchase of office supplies from Kay's Business Supplies. The motel paid $50 and charged $50 for the purchase of $100 of office supplies. The transaction would be recorded as follows:

		Dr	Cr
20X1			
Jan. 1	Office Supplies	100	
	Cash		50
	Accounts Payable—Kay's Business Supplies		50
	To record the purchase of office supplies.		

This journal entry shows $100 debited to office supplies and $50 credited to two accounts: Cash and Accounts Payable—Kay's Business Supplies.

Comprehensive Illustration—Journalizing, Posting, and Preparing a Trial Balance

This last major section of the chapter contains a comprehensive illustration of the accounting process from journalizing through the preparation of a trial balance. The hypothetical hospitality enterprise is Carson Catering, owned by Don Carson. Since the business is new, only a few transactions are incurred during the first month of operations. Each will be fully analyzed, explained, and journalized in the general journal.

The chart of accounts and a description of each account for Carson Catering is as follows:

Account No.	Account Title	Description
100	Cash	Cash in the bank and on hand
105	Accounts Receivable	Amounts due the company from customers
110	Operating Supplies	Supplies to be used in catering parties for customers
120	Van	Vehicle used in catering business
200	Accounts Payable	Amounts owed suppliers for items purchased on account
210	Notes Payable—Big Motors Acceptance Corporation (BMAC)	Amount due BMAC from loan for van
300	Don Carson, Capital	Owner's equity in the business
301	Don Carson, Drawing	Amount of withdrawals by owner
400	Catering Revenue	Amounts earned from catering parties
500	Wages Expense	Wages paid to employees of the business
501	Advertising Expense	Cost of advertising purchased
502	Food Expense	Cost of food catered to customers
503	Gas Expense	Cost of gas, oil, and so on, used in van

Each business transaction incurred during December 20X1 will be provided and analyzed using T-accounts, and a brief explanation will be given.

Transaction 1: Don Carson forms Carson Catering on December 1, 20X1, and invests $5,000 of his personal funds in the business. The accounts affected are as follows:

Cash		Don Carson, Capital	
(1) 5,000			(1) 5,000

Cash is increased with a debit entry, and Don Carson, Capital is increased with a credit entry.

Transaction 2:   On December 5, Carson Catering pays $500 for advertising in the local paper. The accounts affected are as follows:

Advertising Expense		Cash	
(2) 500			(2) 500

Advertising Expense is increased with a debit entry, while Cash is decreased with a credit entry.

Transaction 3:   In anticipation of catering events, Carson Catering purchases a van on December 8, 20X1, costing $15,000. A down payment of $3,000 is made, and the remainder ($12,000) is financed through Big Motors Acceptance Corporation (BMAC). The transaction is analyzed as follows:

Van		Cash		Notes Payable—BMAC	
(3) 15,000		(3) 3,000			(3) 12,000

With the purchase of the van, the Van account is increased with a debit for its cost of $15,000. Cash is reduced by $3,000, which is the amount of the down payment, so Cash is credited. The difference between the cost of $15,000 and the down payment of $3,000 is financed by BMAC. Don Carson signs a note that requires 12 quarterly payments starting April 1, 20X2. The note for $12,000 is recorded with a credit to the Notes Payable—BMAC account.

Transaction 4:   On December 12, 20X1, Carson Catering purchases food costing $200 to be served at a party for M.J. Jolly.

Food Expense		Cash	
(4) 200			(4) 200

Food Expense is increased by $200 with a debit entry, while Cash is decreased with a credit entry of $200. In many hospitality food service businesses, the purchase of food is recorded in an asset account, Food Inventory, and, as the food is used, the Food Expense account is charged and Food Inventory is credited. However, since Carson Catering is purchasing only the food necessary for a particular catered event, Food Expense is charged directly.

Transaction 5:   On December 13, 20X1, Carson Catering purchases $300 of operating supplies on account from Supplies, Inc. These supplies will be used for several catered events over the next few months. The transaction will affect the accounts as follows:

Operating Supplies		Accounts Payable (Supplies, Inc.)	
(5)	300	(5)	300

An asset account, Operating Supplies, is increased with a debit entry for $300, and Accounts Payable is increased with a credit by $300. The debit is made to an asset account rather than an expense account, since the operating supplies purchased will be used during catered events beyond the current period. If the operating supplies purchased were expected to be used in their entirety in December, an Operating Supplies expense account would have been charged. The terms of sale require Carson Catering to pay the amount due Supplies, Inc., on December 28.

Transaction 6:   On December 13, Carson Catering caters the party for M.J. Jolly and receives payment of $800. The transaction is analyzed as follows:

Cash		Catering Revenue	
(6)	800	(6)	800

Cash is debited by the increase in cash of $800, and Catering Revenue is increased with a credit to the account for $800.

Transaction 7:   On December 19, 20X1, Carson Catering purchases food for a party to be catered for Mary Chris Smith. The accounts affected are as follows:

Food Expense		Cash	
(7)	300	(7)	300

This transaction is the same as Transaction 4. Food Expense is increased by (debited for) $300, and Cash is decreased by (credited for) $300.

Transaction 8:   On December 20, 20X1, Carson Catering caters the party for Mary Smith for $1,000. She pays $300, and Carson agrees to allow Mary two weeks to pay the remainder due of $700. Thus, three accounts are affected as follows:

Cash		Accounts Receivable (Mary Smith)		Catering Revenue	
(8)	300	(8)	700	(8)	1,000

Cash is debited for the $300 increase, while Accounts Receivable is increased with a debit for $700. Catering Revenue is increased with a credit for the total cost to the customer of $1,000.

Transaction 9:   On December 22, 20X1, Carson Catering purchases $25 of gasoline for its van. The transaction is analyzed as follows:

Gas Expense		Cash	
(9)	25	(9)	25

Gas Expense is increased by (debited for) $25, and Cash is decreased by (credited for) $25. Quite possibly, Carson Catering will not use the entire amount of gasoline purchased during the rest of the month. However, it is impractical to account for gasoline put into the van as an asset and account for it on a usage basis. Further, the $25 is also an immaterial amount, so the expedient way to account for this expenditure is to expense it.

Transaction 10:   On December 28, 20X1, Carson Catering pays $400 to part-time employees who assisted with the two catered events. The accounts affected are as follows:

Wages Expense		Cash	
(10)	400	(10)	400

Wages Expense is increased by (debited for) $400, and Cash is decreased by (credited for) $400.

Transaction 11:   On December 28, 20X1, Carson Catering pays Supplies, Inc., the $300 due. Two accounts are affected as follows:

Accounts Payable (Supplies, Inc.)		Cash	
(11)	300	(11)	300

The payment to Supplies, Inc., of $300 decreases the Accounts Payable account so that account is debited, and Cash is decreased with a credit for the $300.

Transaction 12:   On December 28, 20X1, Don Carson withdraws $200 from Carson Catering for his personal use. The Cash and Drawing accounts are affected as follows:

Don Carson, Drawing		Cash	
(12)	200	(12)	200

The withdrawal by the owner of Carson Catering is accounted for by increasing (debiting) Don Carson, Drawing for $200. The Cash account is credited for $200, since cash is reduced by the amount of the owner's withdrawal.

The T-accounts used in the preceding 12 transactions are shown only for analysis purposes. In the real world, the transactions are recorded first in a journal. For illustrative purposes, Exhibit 6 contains the general journal that shows how each of the 12 transactions are journalized.

Exhibit 7 contains the general ledger of accounts for Carson Catering. The 12 transactions recorded in the journal (Exhibit 6) have been posted to the appropriate ledger accounts. The posting reference column indicates the source of the amount, which is either page 1 or 2 from Carson Catering's general journal.

Exhibit 8 shows the trial balance of Carson Catering at the end of the month. The balance of each general ledger account has been placed in the appropriate debit and credit columns, and the columns each add up to $18,800. Therefore, the trial balance at December 31, 20X1, for Carson Catering is in balance.

Exhibit 6   General Journal, Carson Catering

Date			Accounts/Explanation	Post. Ref.	Debit	Credit
			General Journal Carson Catering			Page 1
20X1						
Dec.	1		Cash	100	5 0 0 0	
			Don Carson, Capital	300		5 0 0 0
			To record Don Carson's investment in			
			Carson Catering.			
	5		Advertising Expense	501	5 0 0	
			Cash	100		5 0 0
			To record advertising expense.			
	8		Van	120	1 5 0 0 0	
			Cash	100		3 0 0 0
			Notes Payable—BMAC	210		1 2 0 0 0
			To record purchase of van.			
	12		Food Expense	502	2 0 0	
			Cash	100		2 0 0
			To record food expense.			
	13		Operating Supplies	110	3 0 0	
			Accounts Payable (Supplies, Inc.)	200		3 0 0
			To record the purchase of operating			
			supplies on account.			
	13		Cash	100	8 0 0	
			Catering Revenue	400		8 0 0
			To record catering revenue.			
	19		Food Expense	502	3 0 0	
			Cash	100		3 0 0
			To record food expense.			
	20		Cash	100	3 0 0	
			Accounts Receivable (Mary Smith)	105	7 0 0	
			Catering Revenue	400		1 0 0 0
			To record catering revenue.			
	22		Gas Expense	503	2 5	
			Cash	100		2 5
			To record gas expense.			

Exhibit 6 *(continued)*

Date		Accounts/Explanation	Post. Ref.	Debit	Credit
		General Journal **Carson Catering**			Page 2
20X1					
Dec.	28	Wages Expense	500	4 0 0	
		Cash	100		4 0 0
		To record wages expense.			
	28	Accounts Payable (Supplies, Inc.)	200	3 0 0	
		Cash	100		3 0 0
		To record payment on account.			
	28	Don Carson, Drawing	301	2 0 0	
		Cash	100		2 0 0
		To record cash withdrawal by Don Carson.			

Summary

Accounting is based on transactions that occur in the business world. Many transactions occur every day in a major organization. Double-entry accounting is designed to classify and summarize these transactions.

An account is the basic unit of accounting. It is represented in this chapter by a T-account, which is a simple tool used to teach accounting.

Accounts have two sides. Increases in the accounts are recorded on one side, while decreases are recorded on the opposite side. There are several different classifications of accounts such as asset, liability, and owners' equity. Owners' equity accounts are subclassified as capital accounts, revenue accounts, and expense accounts.

The left side of an account is defined as a *debit,* and the right side is defined as a *credit.* The account balance is the difference between the sum of the debits and the sum of the credits. When total debits exceed total credits, the account has a debit balance. When credits exceed debits, the account has a credit balance. In general, different account classifications have different balances, which are called *normal balances.* For example, an asset account under normal circumstances will have a debit balance, and a liability will have a credit balance.

In double-entry accounting, every transaction affects and is recorded in at least two accounts, and the debit entry must equal the credit entry. This is tested with the preparation of a trial balance. If each transaction has been recorded with equal debits and credits, the account balances should equal. This does not ensure, however, that all transactions have been recorded correctly; it simply shows that the transactions have been recorded with balanced debits and credits.

Exhibit 7 General Ledger, Carson Catering

Account Title _Cash_ **Account No.** _100_

Date		Accounts/Explanation	Post. Ref.	Debit	Credit	Balance
20X1						
Dec.	1	Investment in Carson Catering	GJ 1	5 0 0 0		5 0 0 0
	5	Payment, advertising expense	GJ 1		5 0 0	4 5 0 0
	8	Partial payment on van	GJ 1		3 0 0 0	1 5 0 0
	12	Payment of food expense	GJ 1		2 0 0	1 3 0 0
	13	Catering revenue	GJ 1	8 0 0		2 1 0 0
	19	Payment of food expense	GJ 1		3 0 0	1 8 0 0
	20	Receipt of cash—catering revenue	GJ 1	3 0 0		2 1 0 0
	22	Payment of gas expense	GJ 1		2 5	2 0 7 5
	28	Payment of wages	GJ 2		4 0 0	1 6 7 5
	28	Payment on account	GJ 2		3 0 0	1 3 7 5
	28	Withdrawal by D. Carson	GJ 2		2 0 0	1 1 7 5

Account Title _Accounts Receivable (Mary Smith)_ **Account No.** _105_

Date		Accounts/Explanation	Post. Ref.	Debit	Credit	Balance
20X1						
Dec.	20	Partial charge sale	GJ 1	7 0 0		7 0 0

Account Title _Operating Supplies_ **Account No.** _110_

Date		Accounts/Explanation	Post. Ref.	Debit	Credit	Balance
20X1						
Dec.	13	Purchase of operating supplies	GJ 1	3 0 0		3 0 0

Account Title _Van_ **Account No.** _120_

Date		Accounts/Explanation	Post. Ref.	Debit	Credit	Balance
20X1						
Dec.	8	Purchase of van	GJ 1	1 5 0 0 0		1 5 0 0 0

Exhibit 7 *(continued)*

Account Title _Accounts Payable (Supplies, Inc.)_ **Account No.** _200_

Date		Accounts/Explanation	Post. Ref.	Debit	Credit	Balance
20X1						
Dec.	13	Purchase of operating				
		supplies on account	GJ 1		3 0 0	3 0 0
	28	Payment on account	GJ 2	3 0 0		- 0 -

Account Title _Notes Payable—BMAC_ **Account No.** _210_

Date		Accounts/Explanation	Post. Ref.	Debit	Credit	Balance
20X1						
Dec.	8	Loan for van	GJ 1		1 2 0 0 0	1 2 0 0 0

Account Title _Don Carson, Capital_ **Account No.** _300_

Date		Accounts/Explanation	Post. Ref.	Debit	Credit	Balance
20X1						
Dec.	1	Investment in Carson Catering	GJ 1		5 0 0 0	5 0 0 0

Account Title _Don Carson, Drawing_ **Account No.** _301_

Date		Accounts/Explanation	Post. Ref.	Debit	Credit	Balance
20X1						
Dec.	28	Withdrawal of cash	GJ 2	2 0 0		2 0 0

Account Title _Catering Revenue_ **Account No.** _400_

Date		Accounts/Explanation	Post. Ref.	Debit	Credit	Balance
20X1						
Dec.	13	Receipt of cash for catering				
		revenue	GJ 1		8 0 0	8 0 0
	20	Record catering revenue—				
		M. Smith	GJ 1		1 0 0 0	1 8 0 0

Account Title _Wages Expense_ **Account No.** _500_

Date		Accounts/Explanation	Post. Ref.	Debit	Credit	Balance
20X1						
Dec.	28	Payment of wages	GJ 2	4 0 0		4 0 0

(continued)

Exhibit 7 *(continued)*

Account Title	Advertising Expense		Account No.	501		
Date		**Accounts/Explanation**	**Post. Ref.**	**Debit**	**Credit**	**Balance**
20X1						
Dec.	5	Payment of advertising expense	GJ 1	5 0 0		5 0 0

Account Title	Food Expense		Account No.	502		
Date		**Accounts/Explanation**	**Post. Ref.**	**Debit**	**Credit**	**Balance**
20X1						
Dec.	12	Payment of food expense	GJ 1	2 0 0		2 0 0
Dec.	19	Payment of food expense	GJ 1	3 0 0		5 0 0

Account Title	Gas Expense		Account No.	503		
Date		**Accounts/Explanation**	**Post. Ref.**	**Debit**	**Credit**	**Balance**
20X1						
Dec.	22	Payment of gas expense	GJ 1	2 5		2 5

Exhibit 8 Trial Balance of Carson Catering

Carson Catering
Trial Balance
December 31, 20X1

Account Numbers		Debits	Credits
100	Cash	$ 1,175	
105	Accounts Receivable	700	
110	Operating Supplies	300	
120	Van	15,000	
200	Accounts Payable		$ –0–
210	Notes Payable—BMAC		12,000
300	Don Carson, Capital		5,000
301	Don Carson, Drawing	200	
400	Catering Revenue		1,800
500	Wages Expense	400	
501	Advertising Expense	500	
502	Food Expense	500	
503	Gas Expense	25	
	Totals	$ 18,800	$ 18,800

A group of accounts is defined as a *ledger.* The most common ledger is the general ledger, which includes the general accounts such as cash, accounts receivable, and accounts payable. All transactions are eventually recorded in these accounts; however, each account shows only one part of the transaction. For this reason, accountants record the entire transaction in a journal. This keeps track of all transactions and preserves the details of them. It also makes finding mistakes much easier. After transactions are recorded in the journal, they are posted to the proper accounts. After all transactions are posted, the trial balance is prepared.

It is also possible for a transaction to affect more than two accounts. This results in a compound journal entry. For example, cash sales may be paid partially in cash and partially on account. In this case, the debits would be to the Cash account and the Accounts Receivable, and the credit would be to Sales.

Endnotes

1. Generally, bookkeepers record and classify transactions, while accountants supervise the bookkeepers' work, summarize accounting information, and interpret financial statements.

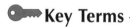

Key Terms

account—The basic element in an accounting system used for classifying and summarizing business transactions.

account balance—The difference between the sum of the debits and the sum of the credits in an account.

balance sheet accounts—Accounts that are never closed, such as asset, liability, and owners' equity accounts.

chart of accounts—A listing of the titles (names) of all the accounts used by a particular business's accounting system. A chart of accounts should be sufficiently flexible to allow individual owners or managers to add or delete accounts to meet the specific needs of their properties. A company's chart of accounts defines the amount of detail that may be shown on its financial statements.

compound journal entries—Entries in the general journal that involve more than two accounts.

credit—Decrease in an asset or increase in a liability or capital—entered on the right side of an account; such amounts are said to be *credited* to the account.

credit balance—A balance in which the sum of the credits is greater than the sum of the debits.

debit—Increase in an asset or decrease in a liability or capital—entered on the left side of an account; such amounts are said to be *debited* or *charged* to the account.

debit balance—A balance in which the sum of the debits is greater than the sum of the credits.

double-entry accounting—A system of accounting in which every transaction affects and is recorded in at least two accounts, and the debits of the entry must equal the credits of the entry.

general ledger—The principal ledger, containing all of the balance sheet and income statement accounts (including assets, liabilities, owner's equity, revenues, expenses, and owner's drawing).

journalizing—The recording of transactions in a journal before they are entered in a ledger; the journal keeps a record of details of the transactions.

nominal accounts—Temporary accounts that are closed after each accounting cycle, such as revenue and expense accounts.

normal balance—The kind of balance, either debit or credit, that an account usually has.

posting—The process of transferring amounts recorded in the journal to the appropriate ledger accounts.

T-account—A representation of an actual account; it consists of a title, a right side, and a left side.

trial balance—A listing of the general ledger accounts and their debit and credit balances in order to test the equality of the balances.

 Review Questions ———————————————————————

1. What is the difference between the terms *debit* and *credit?*
2. What is the normal balance of each major class of accounts?
3. What is the purpose of preparing a trial balance?
4. What are three reasons for journalizing?
5. What is the difference between a journal and a ledger?
6. What is the posting process?
7. Does an "in-balance" trial balance ensure that the bookkeeper has performed flawlessly? Why or why not?
8. What is the difference between balance sheet accounts and nominal accounts? What are some examples of each?
9. How do revenues and expenses affect the owners' equity account?
10. Why are revenues and expenses recorded separately from the owners' equity accounts?

 Problems ———————————————————————————————————

Problem 1

D&G Inn has experienced several transactions on April 1 as follows:

a. Cash received from cash sales totaled $1,750.20.

b. Cash paid to the IRS for payroll taxes equaled $2,430.00.

c. Check #8752 was written to Statewide Electric for $2,419.22.

d. Sales on account for the day equaled $3,690.00.

e. An insurance refund of $180.26 was received.

f. Checks received in the mail and deposited in the firm's checking account totaled $5,100.00.

g. Food supplies totaling $942.15 were purchased on account.

Required:

Determine the balance of the cash account at the end of April 1. Assume a cash balance of $6,700.00 on March 31.

Problem 2

The following transactions have occurred at the Litchfield Inn:

a. A new computer was purchased by paying 30 percent down and signing a bank note for the remainder.

b. Salaries for the month were paid from cash.

c. Kati Litchfield, the owner, withdrew cash for her personal use.

d. Office supplies were purchased on account. The supplies will be expensed.

e. Sales to guests were made on account.

f. Excess cash was invested in temporary investments.

g. A supplier was paid on account for supplies purchased 20 days ago.

h. Rent for the following month was paid out of cash.

Required:

For each of the transactions, state which accounts are affected, state the normal balance for each account, and indicate whether the transaction is a debit or credit to that account. Set up your answers in columns, as indicated below:

Accounts Affected	Normal Balance	Debit or Credit

Problem 3

In order to better analyze revenue and expenses, accountants classify all revenues and expenses in separate accounts. Below is a list of revenue and expense account balances.

Wages Expense	$ 2,000
Food Sales	5,500
Rent Expense	700
Beverage Sales	400
Cost of Food Sales (Expense)	1,700
Cost of Beverage Sales (Expense)	100

Required:

1. Create T-accounts for the revenue and expense accounts.
2. Enter the account balances in the T-accounts (be sure to enter them on the correct side of the account).

Problem 4

You are a temporary bookkeeper hired by the Three-Ring Circus Company for the busy season. Your job is to journalize transactions that occur. The food service operation is run by Barney Bailey. He has given you the following transactions:

a. Purchase of food (hot dogs and popcorn) with cash, $75. All of this food will be sold this month.

b. Purchase of equipment on account from Circus Supply for $150.

c. Cash food sales of $300.

d. Payment of wages in cash, $110.

e. Beverage sales of $100.

f. Purchase of beverages, $12. These beverages will be sold this month.

g. Payment on account to Circus Supply for $10.

Required:

Prepare the necessary journal entries showing the debit and credit entries. In addition, provide a brief explanation of each entry.

Use the following account names: Cash; Equipment; Accounts Payable (Circus Supply Co.); Food Sales; Beverage Sales; Wage Expense; Food Expense; Beverage Expense.

Problem 5

The Turner Café has a general ledger with only twelve accounts. It is the end of the month and Josie Turner (owner) needs a trial balance in order to prepare the month's financial statement. The following are the general ledger accounts:

Cash	$ 3,500
J. Turner, Capital	10,500
Food Inventory	4,500
Prepaid Expenses	700
Accounts Payable	2,100
Equipment	15,400
Notes Payable	7,400
Sales	42,000
Cost of Food Sold	14,000
Rent Expense	2,000
Wages Expense	16,000
Other Expenses	6,900

Required:
Prepare a trial balance for the Turner Café.

Problem 6

The following alphabetically arranged accounts and their balances were taken from the ledger of Chuck's Supply Company on December 31 of the current year:

Accounts Payable	$ 2,400	Office Equipment	1,600
Accounts Receivable	4,500	Office Supplies	85
Building	25,500	Prepaid Insurance	160
Cash	2,000	Prepaid Interest	15
Chuck Franko, Capital	18,300	Revenue	35,950
Delivery Equipment	2,500	Store Equipment	5,450
Interest Expense	200	Store Supplies	155
Interest Payable	150		
Land	8,200	Taxes Payable	250
Merchandise Inventory	9,500	Telepcommunications Expense	110
Mortgage Payable	6,500	Truck Repairs	130
Notes Payable	1,200	Wages Expense	4,420
Notes Receivable	300	Wages Payable	75

Required:

Without changing the alphabetical arrangement of the accounts, prepare a trial balance for the company. That is, leave the account names in the same order, and arrange debits and credits in their proper columns. Then prepare the trial balance.

Problem 7

The following is an excerpt from the general journal of Mary's Motel:

		Dr	Cr
20X1			
Oct. 2	Cash	12,000	
	Equipment	10,000	
	Mary Ramaker, Capital		22,000
Oct. 3	Prepaid Rent	1,000	
	Cash		1,000
Oct. 3	Food Expense	2,000	
	Beverage Expense	500	
	Accounts Payable (Bixbie Food)		2,500

Oct. 4	Cash		500	
	Accounts Receivable		200	
	Food Sales			600
	Beverage Sales			100
Oct. 4	Wages Expense		195	
	Wages Payable			195
Oct. 6	Cash		100	
	Accounts Receivable			100

Required:

1. Write a general journal explanation for each of the foregoing entries.
2. Open the following T-accounts: Cash; Equipment; Mary Ramaker, Capital; Prepaid Rent; Accounts Payable (Bixbie Food); Accounts Receivable; Food Sales; Beverage Sales; Food Expense; Beverage Expense; Wages Expense; Wages Payable.
3. Post the journal entries to the proper accounts.

Problem 8

The trial balance of Stephanie's Steakhouse at the beginning of the day, July 1, 20X1, was:

Cash	$ 1,500	
Marketable Securities	5,000	
Accounts Receivable (Erica Lee)	20	
Accounts Receivable (Monica Ray)	15	
Office Supplies	2,250	
Cleaning Supplies	500	
Furniture	1,000	
Equipment	2,000	
Accounts Payable (Stacie Supply, Inc.)		$ 400
Notes Payable (Mineral State Bank)		1,500
Stephanie Smith, Capital		2,085
Food Sales		25,000
Beverage Sales		7,000
Food Expense	10,000	
Beverage Expense	2,000	
Wages Expense	8,000	
Utilities Expense	1,000	
Rent Expense	2,000	
Insurance Expense	500	
Office Supplies Expense	100	
Advertising Expense	100	
	$ 35,985	$ 35,985

Transactions for July 1, 20X1, were as follows:

    a. Received cash on account from Erica Lee, $10.

    b. Paid rent for the month of June, $200.

    c. Purchased food (to be expensed) on account from Stacie Supply, Inc., $250.

    d. Paid utilities bill for June, $100.

    e. Paid advertising bill for newspaper advertisement for July 1, $5.

    f. Paid temporary help for their labor for the day, $20.

    g. Sales on account to Monica Ray, $5 ($4 for food and $1 for beverages).

    h. Cash food sales for the day and beverage sales for the day, $250 and $60 respectively.

Required:

1. Set up T-accounts for each account listed in the trial balance of Stephanie's Steakhouse. Record the balance in each T-account per the trial balance. (Be sure to record the amounts on the proper side of the account.)
2. Record the transactions for July 1, 20X1. Identify each amount by its transaction letter.
3. Prepare a trial balance for July 1, 20X1 (end of day).

Problem 9

Paul Olivia opened a pizza business under the name of Olivia's Pizza Parlor, and during the first week completed the following transactions:

    a. Invested cash of $2,000 and the following assets at their fair market values: furniture, $2,000; equipment, $3,000; and building, $8,000.

    b. Purchased food and beverages on account, costing $500 and $100, respectively, from Edgar's Food Supply.

    c. Purchased a typewriter with cash, $200.

    d. Paid for newspaper advertising, $30.

    e. Paid utility bills, $50.

    f. Paid wages for the week, $250.

    g. Paid for cooking supplies used during the week, $10.

    h. Paid $100 on account to Edgar's Food Supply.

    i. Received $900 from customers for pizza and beverages sold. Pizza sales amounted to $750, the remainder was beverage sales.

Required:

1. Set up the following T-accounts: Cash; Furniture; Equipment; Building; Accounts Payable (Edgar's Food Supply); Paul Olivia, Capital; Food Sales; Beverage Sales; Advertising Expense; Utilities Expense; Wages Expense; Cooking Supplies Expense; Food Expense; Beverage Expense.
2. Record the transactions in the accounts with each amount identified by its transaction letter.
3. Prepare a trial balance.

Challenge Problem

Problem 10

Jack Wicks is the owner and manager of the Rodeside Motel, which caters to family travelers. He has hired you to do his bookkeeping. The following transactions occurred in August:

  a. Cash of $1,000 was paid on August 15 for September's rent.
  b. Cash room sales of $15,000.
  c. Room sales on account, $250.
  d. Purchase of cleaning supplies for cash, $290.
  e. Purchase of office supplies on account from Bing's Office Supply Hut, $150.
  f. New investment by owner of $1,000.
  g. Payment on account (Bing's), $50.
  h. Rental income from vending machines, $75.
  i. Payment of wages with cash, $5,700.

Further, he has account balances for the beginning of August as follows:

Cash	$ 3,120
Accounts Receivable	200
Cleaning Supplies	30
Office Supplies	100
Accounts Payable, Bing's Office Supply Hut	50
Notes Payable	400
Jack Wicks, Capital	3,000

Required:

  1. Enter the transactions into the general journal, showing debits and credits, and an explanation for each.
  2. Open T-accounts for each balance sheet account as well as for the revenue and expense accounts. Enter the beginning balances.
  3. Post the August transactions to the T-accounts. Determine the ending balance for each account.
  4. Prepare a trial balance for August 31, 20X3.

REVIEW QUIZ

When you feel you have covered all of the material in this chapter, answer these questions. Choose the *best* answer.

1. All of the following are asset accounts *except:*

    a. Notes Receivable.
    b. Marketable Securities.
    c. Unearned Income.
    d. Office Supplies.

2. Which of the following accounts normally has a credit balance?

    a. Cash
    b. Accounts Payable
    c. Inventory
    d. Marketing Expense

3. Which of the following financial statements reflects the fundamental accounting equation?

    a. income statement
    b. balance sheet
    c. statement of cash flows
    d. aging of accounts receivable report

4. Which of the following types of accounts typically carry a debit balance?

    a. liability accounts
    b. expense accounts
    c. capital accounts
    d. revenue accounts

5. Ali is trying to locate the ledger for Accounts Receivable for a certain guest. Which of the following documents would most help Ali locate this ledger?

    a. a balance sheet
    b. an income statement
    c. a classification of accounts
    d. a chart of accounts

6. Accountants or bookkeepers record transactions first in the _____, then in the _____.

    a. journal; ledger
    b. ledger; journal
    c. balance sheet; income statement
    d. income statement; balance sheet

REVIEW QUIZ *(continued)*

7. Cathy just purchased a shuttle bus for her upscale resort. This transaction would appear in which of the following ways in the general journal?

   a. as a credit
   b. as a debit
   c. as a credit to one account and a debit to one or more others
   d. as a balance for one account and a posting reference for another

Answer Key: 1-c-C1, 2-b-C2, 3-b-C2, 4-b-C2, 5-d-C3, 6-a-C4, 7-c-C4

Each question is linked to a competency. Competencies are listed on the first page of the chapter. An answer reading 3-b-C4 translates to:

   3: the question number
   b: the correct answer
   C4: the competency number

Chapter 3 Outline

The Need for Adjustments
Cash versus Accrual Accounting
Classification of Adjusting Entries
Deferral Adjustments Illustrated
    Prepaid Insurance/Insurance Expense
    Depreciation Expense
    Unearned Revenues
Accrual Adjustments Illustrated
    Accrued Wages Payable
    Accrued Utilities
    Accrued Assets
Failure to Prepare Adjustments
Comprehensive Illustration—Adjustments

Competencies

1. Explain the need for and timing of accounting adjustments, and distinguish between cash basis accounting and accrual basis accounting.

2. Describe the major classes of accounting adjustments and use them to classify adjustments.

3. Demonstrate how to enter deferral adjustments, and use straight-line depreciation for adjusting depreciation expense.

4. Demonstrate how to enter accrual adjustments.

5. Explain how a failure to make accounting adjustments affects financial statements.

3

Accounting Adjustments

AT THE END of an accounting period, a trial balance of the general ledger accounts is taken. However, during the accounting period, certain assets are partially consumed but not recorded as expenses, and some liabilities are incurred but not recorded as expenses. Such "activities," along with others to be described in this chapter, must be recorded with journal entries called *adjustments* or **adjusting entries.**

The Need for Adjustments

The time period principle of accounting states that the life of an enterprise is divided into segments of time generally as short as a month, and the operations for the period and the financial position at the end of the period are reported in the financial statements. The income statement, which shows revenues and expenses, reports operations of the business enterprise, while the balance sheet reports the financial position at the end of the accounting period. Even though all transactions have been properly recorded and posted, several accounts must be adjusted to reflect the proper balances and to ensure that the financial statements prepared therefrom are reasonably accurate. Think of the adjusting process as a "fine-tuning" of the books. With the adjusting process, accountants attempt to make financial statements more accurate. Notice two things that are common to every adjusting entry: (1) Each entry involves a balance sheet account and an income statement account; and (2) no adjusting entry involves cash.

The matching principle is the major reason for adjustments. Expenses incurred must be *matched* with revenues generated. Two examples illustrate this requirement:

1. A vehicle is purchased at a cost of $10,800 and recorded in the Equipment account (a fixed asset). Assume the vehicle has a three-year life, after which it will be useless and worth $–0–. The expense related to this equipment is depreciation; therefore, each month the accountant records $\frac{1}{36}$ of the vehicle cost as depreciation expense. In this case, then, depreciation expense of $300 is recorded monthly via an adjusting entry. Not only are expenses increased monthly by $300, but fixed assets are reduced monthly by $300 to reflect the reduction in the value of the vehicle.

2. Assume a lodging firm pays $24,000 on January 1, 20X1, for fire insurance protection for the year. Since the firm benefits beyond one month from this expenditure, the entire amount is recorded as Prepaid Insurance (an asset) for

$24,000. However, at the end of January 20X1, the firm must recognize the expense for the month and reduce the value of the asset (Prepaid Insurance). This is accomplished with an adjusting entry of $2,000. Insurance Expense is debited and Prepaid Insurance is credited for the $2,000. The continuous using up of insurance coverage is referred to as a *continuous event*, and the expense relating to this item could be recognized continuously as time passes. However, accountants customarily record the adjusting entries to recognize insurance expense just before preparing the financial statements. Therefore, if the financial statements are prepared monthly, a monthly adjustment is made; if the firm issues statements quarterly instead of monthly, a quarterly adjustment is made.

When making adjustments, accountants must also consider how material or significant an item is. For example, a large firm may store great amounts of office supplies in inventory to ensure that the supplies are on hand when someone needs them. This way, the firm would not have to order an item each time someone needs to use it. Theoretically, office supplies should be recorded as assets and expensed as they are used. However, the accountant might not record office supplies expense every time an item is removed from inventory for usage. Instead, he or she might wait until the end of the accounting period to make a single entry to recognize the entire office supplies expense for the period. The cost of making an entry each time an item is removed from inventory is greater than the benefit realized from any accuracy achieved. In addition, perhaps the office supplies expense in total is quite immaterial in relation to the firm's activities. When the expense is insignificant, the item (office supplies in this case) may simply be expensed when purchased, with no asset recognized.

Cash versus Accrual Accounting

Cash basis accounting recognizes an accounting transaction at the point of cash inflow or outflow. This method of accounting does not require the adjustments discussed in the previous example of the vehicle. Instead of accounting for depreciation expense, this method of accounting would expense the vehicle one time only: when it was purchased. Similarly, the fire insurance coverage would be expensed only once in cash basis accounting: when the invoice was paid. Although cash basis accounting is simpler than accrual basis accounting, its use is generally limited to the smallest of hospitality firms.

Accrual basis accounting recognizes expenses when they are incurred regardless of when payment is made, and recognizes revenue when it is earned regardless of when cash is received. At the end of an accounting period, accrual basis accounting allows a more meaningful evaluation of the business's operation because it more accurately matches expenses with revenue.

Under accrual basis accounting, procedures must be set up to record all transactions relating to a particular time period during that period. That is, costs must be recorded when they are actually incurred and revenues recorded when they are actually earned, regardless of when cash actually changes hands. For instance, the electric bill for April may arrive late in May, yet the expense must be recognized in

April when it actually occurred. In addition, some expenses, such as payroll, do not exactly match the accounting period. Payrolls are paid periodically on a certain day of the week. Only occasionally would that date correspond to the end of the accounting period. Therefore, it is necessary to adjust payroll costs to the accounting period.

Other kinds of transactions receive special treatment under accrual basis accounting. For example, purchases of buildings are not considered expenses only of the period in which they are purchased. Instead, a pro rata share of the cost in the form of depreciation expense is charged to each accounting period during the useful lives of long-lived purchases. Inventory purchase transactions present another example. Only when the inventory is sold does it become a cost in determining operating performance. Calculation of the cost of goods sold involves beginning and ending inventories plus purchases.

Classification of Adjusting Entries

Adjusting entries consist of two major classifications: deferrals and accruals. **Deferrals** include adjustments for amounts previously recorded in accounts, while **accruals** include adjustments for which no data have been previously recorded in the accounts.

Deferred items include the following two types of adjustments:

Type of Adjustment	Example
Previously recorded assets become expense	Prepaid insurance (an asset) becomes insurance expense as time elapses
Previously recorded liabilities become revenue	Deferred service revenue (a liability) becomes revenue as services are provided

Accrued items include the following two types of adjustments:

Type of Adjustment	Example
Assets and revenues not previously provided	Recording a service provided but not previously recorded as a receivable (an asset) and a revenue
Liabilities and expenses not previously recorded	Recording the amount due the utility company (liability) and the corresponding expense

First, we will illustrate adjustments for deferral items. The asset/expense adjustments will include insurance and depreciation, while the liabilities/revenue adjustment will include the recognition of services provided.

Then, we will illustrate the adjustments for accrual items with liability/expense adjustments for accruing payroll and accruing utility expenses. We will illustrate the second type of accrual adjustment, the asset/revenue adjustment, with accrual of assets.

We will use the hypothetical rooms-only Michaels Motel to illustrate adjusting entries. The Michaels Motel records monthly adjustments and has a fiscal year-end of December 31.

Deferral Adjustments Illustrated

Prepaid Insurance/Insurance Expense

Assume the Michaels Motel paid a one-year fire insurance premium of $12,000 on January 1, 20X2. The payment was initially recorded in the Prepaid Insurance account (an asset account) since the benefit from the insurance payment lies in the future. Cash (another asset) was reduced by the amount of payment. At the end of January 20X2, an adjusting entry must be prepared to recognize the expiration of the asset (Prepaid Insurance) and to recognize Insurance Expense. The journal entry on January 31, 20X2, is recorded as follows:

Insurance Expense	$1,000	
Prepaid Insurance		$1,000
To record insurance expense for January.		

The T-accounts for Prepaid Insurance and Insurance Expense for the January 1 payment and the end of the month adjustment would appear as follows:

Prepaid Insurance

Jan. 1 (payment)	12,000	Jan. 31 (adjustment)	1,000
Jan. 31 (balance)	11,000		

Insurance Expense

Jan. 31 (adjustment)	1,000	

The Prepaid Insurance account now reflects the amount of unexpired insurance of $11,000, which is 11 months of insurance at $1,000 per month, or the amount for 12 months of $12,000 less the expired insurance cost of $1,000. The Insurance Expense account reflects the amount of insurance expense for January, which is $\frac{1}{12}$ of the annual insurance premium of $12,000.

Remember, the major reason for making this adjustment is so that the financial statements will properly reflect results of operations for the month and the financial position at the end of the month. Therefore, the income statement for the month would show $1,000 of insurance expense, and the balance sheet would include prepaid insurance of $11,000 as an asset.

Depreciation Expense

Just as prepaid insurance indicates a gradual continuous use of an asset, so depreciation is the expense of a depreciable asset. There are major differences between the two. First, prepaid insurance is written off over its relatively short life (generally one year), while the costs of property and equipment are expensed over long useful lives (often ranging up to 40 years). Second, the cost of property and equipment is generally relatively large compared to the cost of insurance. Still, the adjustment process involves an asset being expensed in both cases.

Depreciable assets are property and equipment such as buildings, furniture, vehicles, and equipment that have lives in excess of one year and are used in the business to generate revenues. The reduction in the value of depreciable assets is simply called *depreciation.* There are several different methods of accounting for depreciation; this chapter will present only the simplest, the straight-line method. The following three elements are involved in computing depreciation expense using the straight-line method:

1. **Cost of the asset.** This is the amount the enterprise pays to purchase the depreciable asset. In our illustration, the Michaels Motel was purchased on January 1, 20X2, at a cost of $3,500,000.

2. **Estimated useful life.** This is the estimated useful life of a depreciable asset. Unfortunately, since we are dealing with the future, we cannot be completely sure of the life of any depreciable asset. In our illustration, we will assume the building (the motel) has a useful life of 25 years.

3. **Estimated salvage value** (sometimes called *residual value*). This is the estimated market value of the depreciable asset at the end of its useful life. In our illustration, we estimate the motel will be worth $500,000 at the end of 25 years.

The equation for determining the depreciation expense for the accounting period is as follows:

$$\text{Depreciation Expense} \ = \ \frac{C - SV}{n}$$

$$
\begin{aligned}
\text{where } C \ &= \ \text{Depreciable asset cost} \\
SV \ &= \ \text{Estimated salvage value} \\
n \ &= \ \text{Number of periods of useful life}
\end{aligned}
$$

Therefore, the monthly depreciation expense of the building for January 20X2 is $10,000, determined as follows:

$$
\begin{aligned}
\text{Monthly Depreciation Expense} \ &= \ \frac{\$3,500,000 - \$500,000}{300 \text{ months}} \\
&= \ \underline{\underline{\$10,000}}
\end{aligned}
$$

The depreciation expense for January 20X2 is recorded with an adjusting entry:

Depreciation Expense	$10,000	
Accumulated Depreciation, Building		$10,000
To record depreciation expense of the building		
for January.		

The T-accounts after the recording and posting of this adjusting entry would appear as follows:

Depreciation Expense

Jan. 31 (adjustment)	10,000		

Accumulated Depreciation, Building

		Jan. 31 (adjustment)	10,000

Depreciation Expense will be reported on the income statement while the Accumulated Depreciation, Building, will be shown on the balance sheet as a deduction from the Building account.

The Accumulated Depreciation account is a contra-asset account that contains the total depreciation recorded on the building through the balance sheet date. This account normally carries a credit balance. The balance of this account is subtracted from the Building account to report the *net* book value (or *carrying value*) of the building on the balance sheet. Thus, the Michaels Motel would show the net book value of $3,490,000, determined as follows:

Cost of building	$3,500,000
Less: Accumulated depreciation	10,000
Net book value	$3,490,000

Unearned Revenues

A liability/revenue adjustment involving **unearned revenues** generally covers instances in which a guest pays cash for future services. In a lodging enterprise, a customer may pay for banquet space in advance. This payment would be recorded as a liability until the hotel rendered the service, thereby earning the revenue. To illustrate this type of adjustment, assume James Bell, a guest of the Michaels Motel, checks into a room on January 17 for 30 days. The Michaels Motel records the $600 it receives from Bell on January 16 as unearned room revenues. Since Bell will not be charging any amounts to his account, his record is not kept at the front desk. Instead, it is placed in monthly rentals, which Michaels Motel's accountants adjust at the end of the month or at check-out, whichever comes first. James Bell stays at the Michaels Motel through the rest of January, which is 15 days. Therefore, of the

$600 deposit, $300 should be recognized as revenue at the end of the month, since $\frac{15}{30}$ times $600 equals $300.

At the end of January, the adjustment to record the revenue and reduce the liability account would be recorded in this way:

Unearned Room Revenues	$300	
Room Revenues		$300
To record reduction in unearned room		
revenue account of James Bell.		

The T-accounts after the entry is recorded and posted would appear as follows:

Unearned Room Revenues

		Jan. 17 (cash received)	600
Jan. 31 (adjustment)	300		
		Jan. 31 (balance)	300

Room Revenues

	Jan. 31 (balance before adjustment)	65,000
	Jan. 31 (adjustment)	300
	Jan. 31 (balance)	65,300

The Unearned Room Revenues account is shown as a liability on the balance sheet dated January 31, 20X2. The room revenue of $65,300 earned in January will be reported on the firm's income statement.

All deferral adjustments are made to financial data already recorded in an enterprise's asset and liability accounts.

Accrual Adjustments Illustrated

Accrual adjustments are made for business data that have not yet been recorded on the firm's accounting records. Accrual adjustments include two types: liability/expense adjustments and asset/revenue adjustments. The liability/expense adjustments to be illustrated with the hypothetical Michaels Motel include the accrual of wages payable and the accrual of utilities expense. The asset/revenue adjustment includes the accrual of interest income on investments owned by the motel.

Accrued Wages Payable

Wages are paid periodically to employees, generally weekly, biweekly, or monthly; however, the pay period seldom ends—and employees are seldom paid—on the last day of the month, unless employees are paid on a monthly basis. Therefore, to record all wages for the month, wages must be accrued using an adjusting entry. The accrual recognizes both Wages Expense and the liability Accrued Wages Payable.

Assume the Michaels Motel pays its employees every two weeks, and the last payday in January is January 24. Therefore, wages for the period of January 25–31 must be accrued. For simplicity's sake, let us assume that all employees' wages total $10,000 every 14 days. Since the January 25–31 period covers seven days, the accrual should be $5,000, according to this calculation:

$$\$10,000 \quad \times \quad \frac{7}{14} \quad = \quad \underline{\underline{\$5,000}}$$

The adjustment would be recorded as follows:

Wages Expense	$5,000	
Accrued Wages Payable		$5,000
To record accrued wages at the end of January.		

The T-accounts after posting from the journal would appear as follows:

Wages Expense

Jan. 24 (balance)	17,143	
Jan. 31 (adjustment)	5,000	
Jan. 31 (balance)	22,143	

Accrued Wages Payable

	Jan. 31 (adjustment)	5,000

The income statement would reflect the Wages Expense of $22,143 for January, while the balance sheet would include the liability of $5,000 for Accrued Wages Payable.

Accrued Utilities

The Michaels Motel must record additional liability/expense adjustments at the end of the month, since the motel has not yet received invoices for utility services it has used, such as telephone, electricity, and water. To illustrate this type of adjustment, we will show how the Michaels Motel would accrue the electricity expense.

Assume the Michaels Motel is billed on the fifth day of the month for service it received the previous month; that is, on February 5, the motel receives the January electric bill. However, this hospitality enterprise wishes to record all of its adjustments on January 31 and prepare its financial statements as soon as possible.

Therefore, the Michaels Motel must estimate its January electric bill. There are several ways to do this; however, the Michaels Motel's accountant simply reads the electric meter and multiplies the kilowatt hours (kwh) of electricity used by the electric rate. For the month of January, assume the Michaels Motel used 71,050 kwh. The electricity expense for January based on the kwh use and the assumed electric rate of $.06 per kwh is calculated as follows:

$$71,050 \quad \times \quad .06 \quad = \quad \underline{\underline{\$4,263}}$$

The adjustment to accrue electricity expense is recorded in this way:

Electricity Expense	$4,263	
Accrued Expenses Payable		$4,263
To accrue electricity for January.		

The T-accounts after the accrual is posted would appear as follows:

Electricity Expense		
Jan. 31 (adjustment)	4,263	

Accrued Expenses Payable		
	Jan. 31 (adjustment)	4,263

Thus, the electricity expense for the period is recorded in keeping with the matching principle. In addition, the corresponding liability, the amount the Michaels Motel will owe the electric company, is recorded.

The income statement would reflect the Electricity Expense of $4,263, while the balance sheet would show the Accrued Expenses Payable of $4,263 as a liability.

Accrued Assets

Accrued assets are assets that exist at the end of the accounting period but have not yet been recognized. These assets reflect the right to receive future cash payments, and the corresponding revenue recognizes earnings. Examples of accrued assets include unbilled services and accrued interest receivable. The following example will illustrate the recording of accrued interest receivable for the Michaels Motel.

Assume the Michaels Motel invests $50,000 in a certificate of deposit on January 16, 20X2. The six-month certificate will generate $2,000 in interest at an annual interest rate of 8 percent. The Michaels Motel will receive the investment of $50,000 plus the interest of $2,000 on July 15, 20X2. Even though the Michaels Motel received no interest at the end of January 20X2, it has earned interest and records it with an adjusting entry.

The amount of interest earned is determined using the following equation:

$$\text{Interest} = P \times R \times T$$
$$\text{where } P = \text{Principal (the amount invested)}$$
$$R = \text{Annual interest rate}$$
$$T = \text{Portion of year covered by time of investment}$$

Therefore, the Michaels Motel should record $164.38 interest which is calculated in this way:

$$\text{Interest} = \$50,000 \times .08 \times \frac{15}{365}$$
$$= \underline{\$164.38}$$

The T element of the equation includes the number of days in January during which the $50,000 was invested, divided by the number of days in the year. Incidentally, the day the investment was made, January 16, is not included in the count of 15 days, so we assume the certificate was purchased at the end of the business day.

The adjusting entry would record the interest income in the following way:

Accrued Interest Receivable	$164.38
Interest Income	$164.38
To record interest earned for January.	

An asset account, Accrued Interest Receivable, reflects the amount due the Michaels Motel at the end of January, while the revenue account, Interest Income, reflects the interest earned for January.

The T-accounts after the accrual was posted would be as follows:

Accrued Interest Receivable

Jan. 31 (adjustment) 164.38	

Interest Income

	Jan. 31 (adjustment) 164.38

The Accrued Interest Receivable is reported on the balance sheet as an asset, while Interest Income is shown on the income statement as revenue.

Failure to Prepare Adjustments

The failure to prepare and record adjusting entries will affect both the balance sheet and the income statement. Exhibit 1 shows the impact this failure would have on each statement. As Exhibit 1 shows, each type of adjusting entry not recorded has a different impact on the balance sheet and the income statement. In addition to the adjustments discussed in this chapter, many more adjustments are possible. The adjustments presented in this chapter serve simply as examples.

Exhibit 1   Impact on Financial Statements of Failure to Prepare Adjustments

Type of Adjustment	Example	Impact on Balance Sheet			Impact on Income Statement		
		Assets	Liabilities	Owners' Equity	Revenue	Expenses	Net Income
Deferral—Asset/Expense	Depreciation	over	none	over	none	under	over
Deferral—Liability/Revenue	Unearned Income	none	over	under	under	none	under
Accrual—Liability/Expense	Wages Accrual	none	under	over	none	under	over
Accrual—Asset/Revenue	Accrued Interest Receivable	under	none	under	under	none	under

Note: "Over" indicates *overstated*, "under" indicates *understated*, "none" indicates *no change*.

Comprehensive Illustration—Adjustments

We will use Carson Catering to provide a comprehensive illustration of adjustments. Assume that Carson Catering had just been formed and had a few transactions during its first month, December 20X1. Now we find Carson Catering on November 30, 20X2, at the end of its first fiscal year of operations. The chart of accounts includes the following:

Account Number	Account Title	Description
100	Cash	Cash in the bank and on hand
101	Certificate of Deposit	Investments in certificates of deposit with First Bank
105	Accounts Receivable	Amounts due the company from customers
107	Accrued Interest Receivable	Account for recording interest accrued but not received
110	Operating Supplies	Supplies to be used in catering parties for customers
115	Prepaid Rent	Account for recording rent paid in advance
120	Van	Vehicle used in catering business

121	Accumulated Depreciation, Van	Account for accumulating depreciation on van
125	Equipment	Account for recording equipment purchases
126	Accumulated Depreciation, Equipment	Account for accumulating depreciation on equipment
200	Accounts Payable	Amounts owed suppliers for items purchased on account
201	Accrued Wages Payable	Account for accruing unpaid wages
202	Accrued Interest Payable	Account for accruing unpaid interest
210	Notes Payable— Big Motors Acceptance Corporation (BMAC)	Amount due BMAC from loan for van
300	Don Carson, Capital	Owner's equity in the business
301	Don Carson, Drawing	Amount of withdrawals by owner
400	Catering Revenue	Amounts earned from catering parties
410	Interest Income	Account for recording interest earned
500	Wages Expense	Wages paid to employees of the business
501	Advertising Expense	Cost of advertising purchased
502	Food Expense	Cost of food catered to customers
503	Gas Expense	Cost of gas, oil, and so on, used in van
504	Rent Expense	Account to charge for rent expense
505	Supplies Expense	Account to charge for supplies expense
506	Interest Expense	Account for recording interest expense
507	Utility Expense	Account for recording utility expense
508	Depreciation Expense	Account for recording depreciation expense

Carson Catering's trial balance, which was figured at the end of its last business day and doesn't yet include any adjustments, is shown in Exhibit 2.

The following adjustments for Carson Catering at the end of November 30, 20X2, are required:

Adjustment	Explanation
1. Accrued Interest Receivable/Interest Income	No interest income has been accrued on the certificate of deposit that was purchased on July 1. The annual interest rate is 8 percent.
2. Prepaid Rent/Rent Expense	On July 1, 20X2, an office was leased for 12 months for $12,000. The rent for the 12 months was paid on July 1, 20X2. Prepaid Rent and Rent Expense have been adjusted for July through October, but not for November.

Exhibit 2   Trial Balance before Adjustments

Carson Catering
Trial Balance (Before Adjustments)
November 30, 20X2

Account Number	Title	Debits	Credits
100	Cash	$ 3,000	
101	Certificate of Deposit	10,000	
105	Accounts Receivable	6,200	
110	Operating Supplies	500	
115	Prepaid Rent	8,000	
120	Van	15,000	
125	Equipment	10,000	
200	Accounts Payable		$ 5,500
210	Notes Payable—BMAC		9,385
300	Don Carson, Capital		25,000
301	Don Carson, Drawing	8,000	
400	Catering Revenue		137,418
410	Interest Income		500
500	Wages Expense	37,000	
501	Advertising Expense	10,000	
502	Food Expense	60,000	
503	Gas Expense	2,200	
504	Rent Expense	4,000	
505	Supplies Expense	2,100	
506	Interest Expense	1,003	
507	Utilities Expense	800	
	Total	$177,803	$177,803

3. Operating Supplies/
   Supplies Expense

A physical inventory of operating supplies on November 30, 20X2, reflects $250 in operating supplies on hand at the end of the fiscal year. This amount differs from the Operating Supplies balance of $500.

4. Depreciation of Equipment
   and Van

Depreciation expense has not been calculated on either the van or the equipment. The straight-line method will be used. The van was purchased for $15,000 on December 8, 20X1, so it will be depreciated for one full year. Its expected useful life is 4 years, and the estimated salvage value is $1,000.

The catering equipment was purchased on January 1, 20X2, and it will have a useful life of 5 years. Further, it will have a zero salvage value. The equipment will be depreciated for 11 months.

5. Accrued Wages Expense/   Wages expense of $2,500 related to November
    Accrued Wages Payable   20X2 were not paid by the end of November
                                    20X2.

6. Accrued Interest Payable/   The last payment to BMAC was on October 1,
    Interest Expense   20X2. Two months of interest will be accrued. The
                                    annual interest rate is 12 percent, and the amount
                                    owed BMAC after the last payment is $9,385.

7. Utilities Expense/Accrued   Carson Catering has not received the electricity
    Expenses   bill for the month of November. A reading of the
                                    electric meter reveals 2,000 kwh were used, and
                                    the electric rate is $.08 per kwh.

Exhibit 3 shows (1) the calculation of the amount to be recorded with an adjusting entry, and (2) the journal entry. All adjusting entries are rounded to the nearest dollar to reduce the detail in this illustration.

Adjustment 1 records interest earned on the $10,000 certificate of deposit purchased July 1. No interest earned had previously been recorded. The interest is calculated for the five-month period of July through November 20X2. The effect on the financial statements is to increase Interest Income shown on the income statement and to increase Accrued Interest Receivable included on the balance sheet.

Adjustment 2 records rent expense for the month of November 20X2. Each month since July, this adjustment has been prepared to recognize the monthly rent expense of $1,000. So Rent Expense to be shown on the income statement is increased by $1,000, and the asset, Prepaid Rent, shown on the balance sheet, is reduced by $1,000.

Adjustment 3 records the difference in the operating supplies per the accounting records and the physical inventory of operating supplies at the end of November 20X2. Carson Catering's accounting procedure for operating supplies is to record purchases in the asset account Operating Supplies, and to determine the usage (expense) for the month by subtracting the dollar amount of the physical inventory of operating supplies from the amount shown in the asset account. The amount shown on the trial balance for Operating Supplies is $500. Since the physical inventory reveals only $250, Operating Supplies must be reduced by $250 and Supplies Expense increased by $250. The impact of this adjustment on the financial statements is an increase in the income statement's Supplies Expense of $250 and a reduction of the balance sheet's asset Operating Supplies by $250.

Adjustment 4 records depreciation expense on the van and the equipment for the year. Like many small businesses, Carson Catering waits until the end of the year to record its depreciation expense. The compound journal entry shows depreciation expense of $5,333 and increases in the two contra-asset accounts by a total of $5,333. Even though the van was not purchased on December 1, depreciation expense is calculated for the entire year. The difference between December 1, 20X1 (the first day of the fiscal year), and the purchase date of December 8, 20X1, is deemed to be insignificant. On the other hand, depreciation expense on the equipment is calculated for 11 months, since the equipment was purchased one month into the fiscal year.

Exhibit 3 Adjusting Entries

Carson Catering
Adjusting Entries
November 30, 20X2

Adjustment No.	Type of Adjustment	Calculation				Journal Entry		
1	Accrued interest	Interest	=	Principal × 10,000 ×	Rate × .08 ×	Time 5/12	Accrued Interest Receivable	333	
			=	$333			Interest Income		333
							To record interest income earned through November, 20X2.		
2	Rent expense	Monthly Rent	=	Annual Rent × 12,000 ×	1/12 1/12		Rent Expense	1,000	
			=	$1,000			Prepaid Rent		1,000
							To record rent expense for November 20X2.		
3	Operating supplies	Operating supplies per books Physical count of operating supplies Reduction in operating supplies		$500 250 $250			Operating Supplies Expense	250	
							Operating Supplies		250
							To record the reduction in operating supplies on hand.		
4	Depreciation expense	Depreciation of Van Depreciation	=	(C – SV)/n			Depreciation Expense	5,333	
			=	(15,000 – 1,000)/4			Accumulated Depreciation, Van		3,500
			=	$3,500			Accumulated Depreciation, Equipment		1,833
		Depreciation of Equipment Annual depreciation	=	$10,000/5 2,000			To record depreciation expense for the year.		
		Depreciation for 11 months	=	2,000 (11/12) $1,833					
5	Accrued wages	Simply $2,500					Wages Expense	2,500	
							Accrued Wages Payable		2,500
							To record accrued wages at November 30, 20X2.		
6	Accrued interest expense	Interest	=	Principal × 9,385 ×	Rate × .12 ×	Time 2/12	Interest Expense	188	
			=	$188			Accrued Interest Payable		188
							To record interest expense since last debt payment.		
7	Utilities expense	Expense	=	kwh × 2,000 ×	Cost/kwh .08		Utilities Expense	160	
			=	$160			Accrued Expense Payable		160
							To accrue utilities expense (electricity) for November 20X2.		

The impact of this adjustment is that depreciation expense of $5,333 is shown on the income statement, and the same amount is shown as a reduction of the two depreciable assets on the balance sheet.

Adjustment 5 records unpaid wages at the end of November 20X2. Employees worked during November; however, the pay period during which the $2,500 in unpaid wages were earned ends during December 20X2 and will be paid then. Still, because of the matching principle, the expense is recognized with this adjustment as well as the liability Accrued Wages Payable. This adjustment results in an increase in Wages Expense to be shown on the income statement and an increase in Accrued Wages Payable, a liability account, which is shown on the balance sheet.

Adjustment 6 is prepared to record interest expense on the unpaid balance owed to BMAC. When the van was purchased, $12,000 of its cost was financed with a loan from BMAC. Since the last payment was made on October 1, 20X2, interest expense must be accrued for the two months of October and November 20X2. The interest expense is determined based on the balance due BMAC after the last payment. This adjustment results in an increase in the Interest Expense account of $188 to be reflected on the income statement. Accrued Interest Payable is a liability account that will be included on the balance sheet.

Adjustment 7 is recorded to recognize the electricity used during November 20X2. Utilities Expense is shown on the income statement, while the Accrued Expenses account is a liability that will be reflected on the balance sheet.

Exhibit 4 lists Carson Catering's revenue and expense accounts. The pre-adjustment balances of revenue accounts total $137,918, while pre-adjustment balances of expense accounts total $117,103. The difference of $20,815 is Carson Catering's preliminary net profit for the fiscal year ended November 30, 20X2. However, seven adjusting entries were required to reflect the proper amounts in revenue and expense accounts. Each of the adjustments affects one revenue or expense account. The net impact of the seven adjustments is the reduction of net profits by $9,098 to $11,717 for the year. Thus, the failure to record these adjustments would have shown an overstatement in net profits of $9,098, which is 77.6 percent of the net profit for the year.

Summary

In an accrual basis accounting system, the goal is to produce an accurate picture of revenue, expenses, and therefore net income. Revenues are recorded when earned, and expenses are recorded when incurred. However, because the financial statements of a business are produced at the end of arbitrary time periods (months, for example), certain adjustments must be made to accounts to ensure that account balances are accurate for each time period. For example, certain assets may have been used and should be expensed although the entry has not been made, or a liability may have been incurred but not recorded. These entries are called *adjusting entries*. Adjusting entries always involve an income statement account and a balance sheet account. Adjusting entries never involve cash.

There are two types of adjusting entries: deferrals and accruals. Deferrals are adjustments for amounts previously recorded in accounts, while accruals are

Exhibit 4   Impact of Adjustments on Carson Catering's Net Profits

Revenue/ Expense Accounts	Pre-Adjustment Balances Debits	Credits	Adjustments Debits	Credits	Adjusted Balances Debits	Credits
Revenue:						
Catering Revenue		$137,418				$137,418
Interest Income		500		(1) $333		833
Expenses:						
Wages Exp.	$ 37,000		(5) $2,500		$ 39,500	
Adv. Exp.	10,000				10,000	
Food Exp.	60,000				60,000	
Gas Exp.	2,200				2,200	
Rent Exp.	4,000		(2) 1,000		5,000	
Supplies Expense	2,100		(3) 250		2,350	
Interest Expense	1,003		(6) 188		1,191	
Utilities Expense	800		(7) 160		960	
Depreciation Expense	-0-		(4) 5,333		5,333	
Totals	$117,103	$137,918	$9,431	$333	$126,534	$138,251

Pre-Adjustment Total Revenues	$ 137,918	Total Adjustments to Revenue	$ 333	Adjusted Total Revenue	$ 138,251
Pre-Adjustment Total Expenses	117,103	Total Adjustments to Expenses	9,431	Adjusted Total Expenses	126,534
Pre-Adjustment Net Profit	$ 20,815	Total Adjustment to Net Profit	$ 9,098	Adjusted Net Profit	$ 11,717

adjustments for which no data have been previously entered. Depreciation is a special adjustment designed to match expense to revenue from the use of property and equipment.

Unearned revenues occur when a guest pays for services before they are actually rendered. Such unearned revenues are actually liabilities of the business until the revenues are earned.

If adjusting entries are not prepared, the revenue and expenses will not be accurate. Therefore, net income will not be accurate. In addition, some balance sheet accounts will be overstated or understated. Adjusting entries must be recorded if businesses are to achieve reasonably accurate financial statements.

Key Terms

accrual basis accounting—System of reporting revenues and expenses in the period in which they are considered to have been earned or incurred, regardless of the actual time of collection or payment.

accruals—Adjusting entries made for business data that have not yet been entered into accounts.

adjusting entries—Entries required at the end of an accounting period to record internal adjustments of various accounts due to the matching principle.

cash basis accounting—Reporting of revenues and expenses at the time they are collected or paid, respectively.

cost of asset—Amount paid by a business to purchase an asset.

deferrals—Adjusting entries made for business data that have already been recorded in other accounts.

depreciable assets—Property and equipment owned by a business that last more than one year and are used to generate revenue.

estimated salvage value—The estimated market value of a depreciable asset at the end of its useful life.

estimated useful life—The estimated length of time that a depreciable asset will be used to help generate revenue.

unearned revenues—The offset for cash received for services before they are rendered.

Review Questions

1. What is the purpose of adjusting entries?

2. Are adjusting entries used in an accrual basis accounting system or in a cash basis accounting system? Why?

3. What are two examples of an accrual adjusting entry?

4. What are two examples of a deferral adjusting entry?

5. Why do adjusting entries never involve cash?

6. Why does each adjusting entry involve both a balance sheet account and an income statement account?

7. What is the relation between the matching principle and adjusting entries?

8. What is unearned revenue? When does it occur? How is the unearned revenue account classified?

9. In what situation would it be necessary to record accrued wages?

10. What method is used to adjust prepaid expenses to account for partial use?

 **Problems** ——————————————————————————

Problem 1

Kathy's Kitchen bought a van to deliver Kathy's famous pies. The van cost $20,000. Kathy estimates that, with the hard use the van will get, it will be of use for 4 years. At the end of the four years, it will be sold for parts for $2,000.

Required:

1. Determine the monthly depreciation expense using the straight-line method.
2. Make the journal entry to record depreciation expense for January.

Problem 2

Dave Townsend paid the fire insurance premium of $1,200 for the Townsend Café on April 24. The insurance coverage is from May 1 through October 31. Monthly financial statements are prepared for the Townsend Café.

Required:

1. Record the payment of April 24 for $1,200.
2. Based on the information above, what is the amount of insurance expense for April?
3. What is the monthly insurance expense for each month over the insurance coverage period?
4. What is the balance of the Prepaid Insurance account at the end of June?

Problem 3

The Valley Catering Company has been contracted by a wedding planner to cater wedding and rehearsal dinners. Valley Catering requires an advance deposit of $200 for all engagements. On June 15, the wedding planner sends a check to Valley Catering for $400 ($200 for the wedding and $200 for the rehearsal dinner). The rehearsal dinner is on July 2, and the wedding is on July 3. The total cost for the rehearsal dinner is $300 and for the wedding, $800.

Required:

1. Make the journal entry to record the receipt of the deposit check on June 15.
2. Make the adjusting entries for July 2 and 3 to record the actual revenue earned and to adjust the unearned revenue account.

Problem 4

The Hilltop Inn pays its employees on a biweekly basis. The last day of the pay period for January is the 25th. The biweekly gross pay for Hilltop's employees has averaged $4,200. Assume a biweekly pay period covers 14 workdays.

Required:

1. Estimate the amount of wages payable at the end of January.
2. Record the adjusting entry for January.

Problem 5

The following are examples of adjusting entries in the general journal of Diane's Diner. Identify the accounts that are affected by each entry, and state whether it is a deferral or accrual entry.

1. Adjusting entry for wages that have been earned by workers but not yet paid or recorded
2. Adjusting entry for revenue that has now been earned, but was paid for previously
3. Adjusting entry to record periodic depreciation expense
4. Adjusting entry to record the use of one month's worth of prepaid rent
5. Adjusting entry to record interest earned on an investment but not yet received
6. Adjusting entry to record the cost related to electricity expense used, but not yet paid for

Problem 6

Diane Ososki owns O's Place. On March 1, O's Place borrowed $5,000 from the Poulan Bank. The annual interest rate is 8 percent. At the end of each quarter, O's Place must pay $500 on the debt plus the interest on the loan for the quarter. Assume interest is due only on the unpaid amount of the loan.

Required:

1. Determine the interest accrual for March 31.
2. Make the adjusting entry to record the interest accrued on March 31.
3. Make the adjusting entry to record the interest accrual as of April 30.
4. Record the payment due May 31.

Problem 7

Required:

State (1) whether the following failures to record adjusting entries will understate or overstate net income, and (2) what the effect on the balance sheet accounts will be.

1. Not recording depreciation expense
2. Not adjusting unearned revenue when revenue is earned
3. Not adjusting prepaid rent when rent is used
4. Not recording accrued interest on investments
5. Not recording accrued interest on loans
6. Not recording services rendered, but not yet billed
7. Not recording accrued wages
8. Not recording the electric expense used but not yet paid for

Challenge Problems

Problem 8

Don Donuts, owned by Donald Weeks, has annual accounting periods ending each December 31. On December 31, 20X3, after all transactions were recorded, the bookkeeper prepared the trial balance of accounts:

Don Donuts
Trial Balance
December 31, 20X3

Cash	$ 2,500	
Supplies	1,250	
Prepaid Insurance	1,000	
Food and Beverage Inventory	2,000	
Equipment	10,000	
Accumulated Depreciation, Equipment		$ 4,000
Building	40,000	
Accumulated Depreciation, Building		6,000
Land	3,000	
Accounts Payable		600
Mortgage Payable		20,000
Donald Weeks, Capital		12,750
Donald Weeks, Drawing	4,000	
Food and Beverage Sales		85,000
Cost of Food and Beverage Sales	26,600	
Salaries Expense	30,000	
Advertising Expense	1,000	
Utilities Expense	3,000	
Supplies Expense	2,000	
Interest Expense	2,000	
	$128,350	$128,350

Required:

1. Open the following T-accounts: Supplies; Prepaid Insurance; Food and Beverage Inventory; Accumulated Depreciation, Equipment; Accumulated Depreciation, Building; Salaries Payable; Cost of Food and Beverage Sales; Salaries Expense; Depreciation Expense, Equipment; Depreciation Expense, Building; Supplies Expense; Insurance Expense.

2. Prepare and post adjusting journal entries based on the following information.

   a. The physical count of the food and beverage inventory at December 31, 20X3, is $1,650.

   b. Insurance expired during the year, $500.

c. Estimated depreciation of equipment for the year, $1,500.

d. Estimated depreciation of the building for the year, $2,500.

e. Salaries earned by workers between December 28 (payday) and December 31, $200.

f. Physical count of supplies at December 31, 20X3, $1,100.

Problem 9

The following is the December 31, 20X3, trial balance for Norm's Diner.

Norm's Diner
Trial Balance
December 31, 20X3

Cash	$ 6,750	
Accounts Receivable	1,400	
Food and Beverage Inventory	3,400	
Office Supplies	900	
Prepaid Rent	800	
Furniture	26,000	
Accumulated Depreciation, Furniture		$ 3,000
Equipment	60,000	
Accumulated Depreciation, Equipment		8,000
Accounts Payable		4,300
Unearned Revenue		300
Notes Payable		32,700
Norm Kamp, Capital		48,500
Food and Beverage Revenue		87,000
Cost of Food and Beverage Sold	35,880	
Wages and Benefits	29,000	
Rent Expense	8,800	
Office Supplies Expense	1,000	
Repairs and Maintenance	7,000	
Interest Expense	1,500	
Advertising Expense	1,370	
	$183,800	$183,800

Required:

Using the information in the trial balance, make the journal entries for the following transactions. You will need to use these additional accounts: Accrued Wages, Interest Payable, and Depreciation Expense.

1. Food and Beverage inventory was taken on December 31 after closing. The physical inventory was $2,650. (Hint: use Cost of Food and Beverage Sold as the expense account.)

2. A physical inventory of office supplies shows $810.

3. The furniture was bought last year. At that time, it had a useful life of six years and a salvage value of $8,000. Determine this year's depreciation using the straight-line depreciation method.

4. The equipment was bought two years ago. At that time, it had a useful life of 12 years and a salvage value of $12,000. Determine this year's depreciation using the straight-line depreciation method.

5. Norm paid his entire rent for the year on January 1. He has used the expense for 11 months in equal amounts. Determine the rent expense for December.

6. The last payday of the year falls on December 24. Determine the accrued wages for the staff. Average daily wages are $150.

7. Norm has a note payable with the Wooden Nickel Savings and Loan for part of his equipment. The payment is made every six months and is due on January 1 and July 1. The annual interest rate is 8.5 percent. Determine the amount of interest payable to WNSL (round to the nearest dollar).

8. Norm hires an independent firm to tend to the repairs and maintenance. However, the bill for December has not yet arrived. Norm's accountant expects repairs and maintenance to be about 6 percent higher than November due to the extensive holiday decorations Norm likes. November's expense was $600.

9. Norm catered a dinner on New Year's Eve for which he had received an advance deposit of $300. The dinner was paid for at the end of the night for a total of $525. The $225 in cash received has already been recorded as cash receipts. Record the advance deposit as earned revenue.

Problem 10

The following is the trial balance for the Mason Motel as of December 31, 20X2.

Mason Motel
Trial Balance
December 31, 20X2

Cash	$ 5,650	
Marketable Securities	10,000	
Accounts Receivable	8,000	
Cleaning Supplies	2,500	
Prepaid Insurance	4,500	
Interest Receivable	300	
Furniture	40,000	
Accumulated Depreciation, Furniture		$ 20,000
Equipment	10,000	
Accumulated Depreciation, Equipment		5,000
Building	300,000	
Accumulated Depreciation, Building		100,000
Land	20,000	
Accounts Payable		5,000
Unearned Revenue		650

Notes Payable		5,000
Mortgage Payable		54,000
Melvin Mason, Capital		103,000
Room Revenue		146,800
Manager's Salary	15,000	
Housekeeper's Wages	15,000	
Cleaning Supplies Expense	2,000	
Office Supplies Expense	1,000	
Utilities Expense	5,000	
Advertising Expense	500	
	$439,450	$439,450

Required:

Using the information in the trial balance, make the journal entries for the following transactions. You will need to use these additional accounts: Accrued Wages, Insurance Expense, Interest Income, and Depreciation Expense.

1. Mason Motel bought a three-year insurance policy on July 1, 20X2, for the period of July 1, 20X2, through June 30, 20X5. Determine the insurance expense for 20X2.

2. A physical inventory shows $1,000 of cleaning supplies. Determine cleaning supplies expense for the year.

3. The furniture was bought two years ago. At that time, it had a useful life of four years and no salvage value. Determine this year's depreciation using the straight-line method.

4. The equipment was bought five years ago, and, at that time, had a useful life of ten years and no salvage value. Determine this year's depreciation using the straight-line method.

5. The building was bought five years ago, and the estimated useful life was 10 years. The salvage value is expected to be $100,000. Determine this year's depreciation using the straight-line method.

6. The last payday of the year falls on December 27. Determine the accrued wages for the housekeeper. There is one housekeeper on the staff who works eight hours a day. The housekeeper's hourly wage is $6.25.

7. Mason has owned the marketable debt securities since October 1, 20X2. The annual interest rate is 7 percent. Determine the amount of interest receivable on this investment.

8. Mason's utilities bill has not yet arrived. Mason's accountant estimates the utilities expense to be $500.

9. Mason owes $240 to an advertising firm. However, the advertising firm has not sent the bill yet.

10. Mason had guests whose rooms were paid for with an advance deposit of $650. The guests are now gone, and the entire deposit was earned.

11. Mason has guests who are staying at the hotel and will not leave until after December 31. They have three rooms, each costing $20. The guests have been at Mason's since December 27. Mason has not yet billed these guests. Calculate the amount of unbilled revenue to December 31.

REVIEW QUIZ

When you feel you have covered all of the material in this chapter, answer these questions. Choose the *best* answer.

1. The generally accepted accounting principle most closely associated with accrual accounting is the:

    a. cost principle.
    b. matching principle.
    c. disclosure principle.
    d. materiality principle.

2. Which of the following is an example of an accounting adjustment that records assets or revenues that were not previously recorded?

    a. Prepaid Insurance decreases and Insurance Expense increases.
    b. Utilities Payable decreases and Utilities Expense increases.
    c. Unearned Room Revenue decreases and Room Revenue decreases.
    d. Accrued Interest Receivable increases and Interest Income increases.

3. Which of the following adjustments is an example of a deferral adjustment?

    a. a liability/expense adjustment involving unpaid wages
    b. an asset/expense adjustment involving insurance
    c. an asset/revenue adjustment involving accrued interest income
    d. a liability/expense adjustment involving utility expenses

4. A depreciable asset that cost $20,000 is expected to have a salvage value of $5,000 after a useful life of ten accounting periods. What is the depreciation expense per period, using the straight-line method?

    a. $2,000
    b. $1,500
    c. $1,000
    d. $500

5. A certain hotel building depreciates by $8,000 each accounting period. To record this figure at the end of an accounting period, accountants should:

    a. debit Depreciation Income and credit Depreciation Expense.
    b. debit Cash and credit Depreciation Expense.
    c. debit Accumulated Depreciation, Building and credit Depreciation Expense.
    d. credit Accumulated Depreciation, Building and debit Depreciation Expense.

REVIEW QUIZ *(continued)*

6. Sandy's Resort used 200,000 kilowatt hours of electricity in August. The resort pays $.07 per kilowatt hour. The resort paid for 120,000 of August's usage in the last payment. To ensure the accuracy of August's month-end accounting reports, accountants at the resort should adjust:

    a. Cash with a credit of $5,600 and Electricity Expense with a debit of $5,600.
    b. Electricity Expense with a credit of $14,000 and Cash with a debit of $14,000.
    c. Accrued Expenses Payable with a credit of $14,000 and Electricity Expense with a debit of $14,000.
    d. Accrued Expenses Payable with a credit of $5,600 and Electricity Expense with a debit of $5,600.

7. Jeremy failed to make adjusting entries to account for depreciation of the assets of his hotel. This mistake affects which of the following financial statements?

    a. the balance sheet
    b. the income statement
    c. the statement of cash flows
    d. a and b

Answer Key: 1-b-C1, 2-d-C2, 3-b-C2, 4-b-C3, 5-d-C3, 6-d-C4, 7-d-C5

Each question is linked to a competency. Competencies are listed on the first page of the chapter. An answer reading 3-b-C4 translates to:

    3: the question number
    b: the correct answer
    C4: the competency number

Chapter 4 Outline

The Accounting Cycle
    Adjusted Trial Balance
    Preparation of Financial Statements
    Closing Entries
    Post-Closing Trial Balance
The Worksheet
Reversing Entries
Comprehensive Illustration—Completing
    the Accounting Cycle

Competencies

1. Explain the steps in the accounting cycle.

2. Explain the purpose of the adjusted trial balance and the relationships between the adjusted trial balance, the balance sheet, the income statement, and the statement of owner's equity.

3. Describe the closing process, and explain the function of the post-closing trial balance.

4. Describe the worksheet and explain its function.

5. Explain the purpose of reversing entries and identify the circumstances under which they can be used.

4

Completing the Accounting Cycle

In THIS CHAPTER, we discuss the accounting cycle, focusing on the last five steps of the cycle as follows:

- Journalizing and posting adjusting entries
- Preparing an adjusted trial balance
- Preparing the income statement and the balance sheet
- Journalizing and posting closing entries
- Preparing a post-closing trial balance

In addition, this chapter will present a worksheet approach for adjusting entries and preparing the income statement and the balance sheet. Finally, the chapter will discuss reversing entries.

The Accounting Cycle

The **accounting cycle** consists of the many steps the accounting staff follows, beginning with analyzing transactions and ending with preparing a post-closing trial balance.

Exhibit 1 lists the ten steps in the accounting cycle. The length of the cycle depends on how often the business prepares financial statements. Most businesses prepare monthly financial statements. For these businesses, the cycle is one month long. However, for smaller businesses that prepare only annual financial statements, the accounting cycles last one year. Regardless of its length, the cycle starts when the accountant analyzes source documents to determine how to record the business transaction. Thus, the basic input of the accounting cycle consists of the various source documents, including sales invoices, purchase invoices, and time cards for hourly employees. The output from the accounting cycle consists of the financial statements.

Only the three basic financial statements (the income statement, the balance sheet, and the statement of owners' equity) are discussed in this chapter. In addition to the basic statements, accountants must prepare explanations called *notes to the financial statements* to accompany the financial statements.

The remaining steps in the accounting cycle involve the processing of accounting data that will generate the information included in the financial statements.

Exhibit 1   Steps in the Accounting Cycle

Step	Explanation
1. Analyzing transactions	Examining source documents such as sales invoices
2. Journalizing transactions	Recording transactions in a journal
3. Posting	Transferring the debits and credits from journals to the ledger accounts
4. Preparing a trial balance	Summarizing the ledger accounts to prove the equality of debits and credits
5. Preparing adjusting entries	Determining the adjustments and recording them in the general journal
6. Posting adjusting entries	Transferring the adjusting entries from the journal to the ledger accounts
7. Preparing an adjusted trial balance	Summarizing the ledger accounts to prove the equality of debits and credits after the posting of the adjusting entries
8. Preparing the financial statements	Rearranging the adjusted trial balance into an income statement and a balance sheet
9. Recording and posting closing entries	Journalizing and posting entries that close the revenue and expense accounts for the period to the capital account
10. Preparing a post-closing trial balance	Summarizing the asset, liability, and owners' equity accounts to prove the equality of debits and credits

Only journalizing and posting take place day after day during the accounting cycle. In theory, accountants prepare the various trial balances and prepare, record, and post adjusting and closing entries on the last day of the accounting cycle. In practice, accountants make adjusting entries and close accounts a few days into the following month or cycle, but record them as of the last day of the previous accounting period.

Adjusted Trial Balance

Adjustments are recorded in the general journal at the end of each accounting period, generally as of the last date of the month. The recorded amounts are then posted to the general ledger accounts as of the last day of the accounting period.

Accountants record and post adjustments in the same way that they record and post business transactions. The difference is only one of timing: business transactions occur every business day, but adjusting entries are recorded and posted on the last day of the accounting period. After posting the adjustments, the accountant prepares an **adjusted trial balance** to prove the equality of debits and credits.

Exhibit 2   Adjusted Trial Balance

Mason Motel
Adjusted Trial Balance
December 31, 20X1

	Debits	Credits
Cash	$ 5,000	
Marketable Securities	10,000	
Accounts Receivable	8,000	
Cleaning Supplies	1,800	
Prepaid Insurance	3,000	
Furniture	40,000	
Accumulated Depreciation, Furniture		$ 24,000
Equipment	10,000	
Accumulated Depreciation, Equipment		6,000
Building	300,000	
Accumulated Depreciation, Building		110,000
Land	20,000	
Accounts Payable		5,000
Notes Payable		5,000
Accrued Wages		150
Mortgage Payable		100,000
Melvin Mason, Capital		113,000
Melvin Mason, Drawing	10,000	
Room Revenue		150,000
Manager's Salary	15,000	
Assistant Manager's Salary	7,500	
Room Attendants' Wages	15,150	
Payroll Taxes	3,000	
Cleaning Supplies Expense	2,700	
Office Supplies	1,000	
Utilities	5,000	
Advertising	500	
Repairs and Maintenance	9,000	
Insurance Expense	1,500	
Depreciation Expense, Furniture	4,000	
Depreciation Expense, Equipment	1,000	
Depreciation Expense, Building	10,000	
Property Taxes	22,000	
Interest Expense	8,000	
Total	$ 513,150	$ 513,150

Remember that, before the accountant records adjusting entries, he or she will have prepared a trial balance; the only difference between that trial balance and the adjusted trial balance is the adjustments.

Exhibit 2 shows the adjusted trial balance for the Mason Motel, prepared at the end of the accounting period, which, for this illustration, is December 31, 20X1. Notice that the sums of the debit and credit columns are equal: both total $513,150.

Preparation of Financial Statements

The adjusted trial balance is used to prepare the income statement and the balance sheet. The revenue accounts make up the revenue (or sales) of the hospitality enterprise, while the expense accounts make up the expenses of the business. The difference between the revenues and expenses is either net income or net loss. Net income results when revenues exceed expenses, while a net loss results when expenses exceed revenues. The relationship between the adjusted trial balance for the Mason Motel and its income statement is shown in Exhibit 3. The net income for the year for the Mason Motel is $44,650, since revenues of $150,000 exceed expenses of $105,350.

A **statement of owners' equity** is a financial statement that summarizes transactions affecting the owners' capital account. The accountant prepares this schedule using information—the balances of the owners' capital and drawing accounts—from the trial balance. The accountant also takes the net income (or net loss) for the period from the income statement. The statement of owners' equity shows the following:

Owners' Equity—beginning of period	$ XXX
Plus: Net income for the period	XX
Less: Owner withdrawals for the period	(XX)
Owners' Equity—end of period	$ XXX

If a net loss is incurred for the period, the net loss would be subtracted in preparing the statement of owners' equity.

Exhibit 4 shows the statement of owner's equity for the Mason Motel for 20X1. During 20X1, Melvin Mason's capital account increased from $113,000 to $147,650 as the net result of net income for the Mason Motel of $44,650 and his withdrawals of $10,000.

The statement of owners' equity serves as a link between the income statement and the balance sheet, since the net income for the period, in essence, is transferred from the income statement to the balance sheet via this statement.

Exhibit 5 shows the Mason Motel's balance sheet dated December 31, 20X1. As expected, assets of $257,800 equal the sum of owner's equity (proprietorship) and liabilities, $257,800. (The balance sheet is the embodiment of the fundamental accounting equation.) Rather than tracing the Melvin Mason, Capital and Drawing accounts from the adjusted balance, the accountant simply takes the balance for the Melvin Mason, Capital account from the statement of owner's equity shown in Exhibit 4.

Closing Entries

Revenue and expense accounts are nominal accounts, since they are subclassifications of owners' equity. Accountants separate revenue and expense accounts to get more detailed information for use in preparing the financial statements. Once the financial statements are prepared, the accountant closes the revenue and expense accounts, clearing the accounts to zero by transferring the balances to the

Exhibit 3 Adjusted Trial Balance and the Income Statement

Mason Motel
Adjusted Trial Balance
December 31, 20X1

	Debits	Credits
Cash	$ 5,000	
Marketable Securities	10,000	
Accounts Receivable	8,000	
Cleaning Supplies	1,800	
Prepaid Insurance	3,000	
Furniture	40,000	
Accumulated Depreciation, Furniture		$ 24,000
Equipment	10,000	
Accumulated Depreciation, Equipment		6,000
Building	300,000	
Accumulated Depreciation, Building		110,000
Land	20,000	
Accounts Payable		5,000
Notes Payable		5,000
Accrued Wages		150
Mortgage Payable		100,000
Melvin Mason, Capital		113,000
Melvin Mason, Drawing	10,000	
Room Revenue		150,000
Manager's Salary	15,000	
Assistant Manager's Salary	7,500	
Room Attendants' Wages	15,150	
Payroll Taxes	3,000	
Cleaning Supplies Expense	2,700	
Office Supplies	1,000	
Utilities	5,000	
Advertising	500	
Repairs and Maintenance	9,000	
Insurance Expense	1,500	
Depreciation Expense, Furniture	4,000	
Depreciation Expense, Equipment	1,000	
Depreciation Expense, Building	10,000	
Property Taxes	22,000	
Interest Expense	8,000	
Total	$513,150	$513,150

Mason Motel
Income Statement
For the Year Ended December 31, 20X1

Room Revenue		$150,000
Manager's Salary	$15,000	
Assistant Manager's Salary	7,500	
Room Attendants' Wages	15,150	
Payroll Taxes	3,000	
Cleaning Supplies Expense	2,700	
Office Supplies	1,000	
Utilities	5,000	
Advertising	500	
Repairs and Maintenance	9,000	
Insurance Expense	1,500	
Depreciation Expense, Furniture	4,000	
Depreciation Expense, Equipment	1,000	
Depreciation Expense, Building	10,000	
Property Taxes	22,000	
Interest Expense	8,000	105,350
Net Income		$ 44,650

Exhibit 4 Statement of Owner's Equity

Mason Motel	
Statement of Owner's Equity	
For the year ended December 31, 20X1	
Melvin Mason, Capital, January 1, 20X1	$113,000
Plus: Net Income for 20X1	44,650
Less: Melvin Mason, Withdrawals	10,000
Melvin Mason, Capital, December 31, 20X1	$147,650

owners' equity capital account. The accountant closes these accounts with **closing entries** that must be recorded in the general journal and then posted to the general ledger accounts.

The revenue and expense accounts are often closed to the capital account through a **clearing account** called Income Summary. Thus, the balance of the Income Summary account after the closing of all revenue and expense accounts is the net income or net loss for the period. This balance is then closed to the owners' Capital account, resulting in a zero balance in the Income Summary account. The closing process transfers revenues and expenses to the Owners' Equity account, and also reduces the revenue and expense accounts to zero to prepare them for receiving data during the following accounting period.

The owners' Drawing account is also closed at the end of the accounting period, but not to the Income Summary account. Instead, it is closed directly to the Owners' Equity account.

The three basic steps of the closing process are as follows:

1. Close the revenue and expense accounts to the Income Summary account.

2. Close the Income Summary account to the Owners' Equity account.

3. Close the owners' drawing accounts to the Owners' Equity account.

Exhibit 6 shows the flow of the amounts from the revenue and expense accounts through the Income Summary to the Capital account. This exhibit also shows the closing of the Drawing account to the Capital account.

In closing entry 1 (CE#1), the amounts from the expense accounts (A and B) are transferred to the Income Summary account. Each expense is credited for the amount of its previous debit balance, and the total of $220 is debited to the Income Summary account.

CE#2 effectively closes the revenue account (R) to the Income Summary account by debiting Revenue R by $250 and crediting the Income Summary account by $250.

CE#3 transfers the balance of the Income Summary account of $30 to the Capital account by debiting the Income Summary account and crediting the Capital account.

Exhibit 5 Adjusted Trial Balance and the Balance Sheet

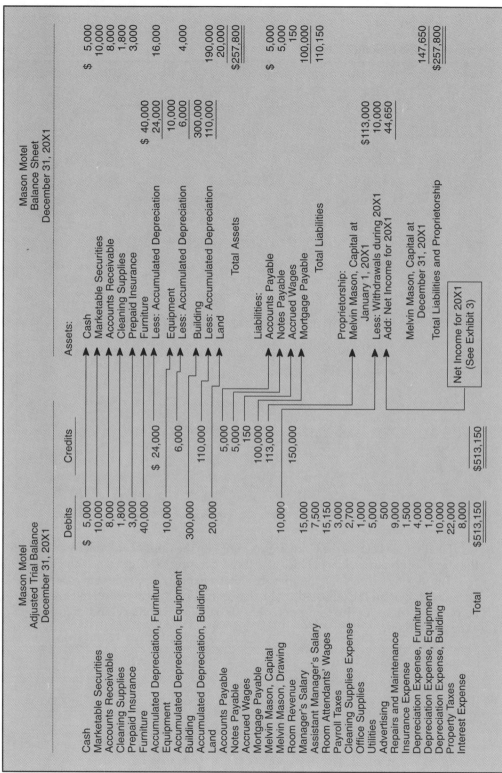

Mason Motel
Adjusted Trial Balance
December 31, 20X1

	Debits	Credits
Cash	$ 5,000	
Marketable Securities	10,000	
Accounts Receivable	8,000	
Cleaning Supplies	1,800	
Prepaid Insurance	3,000	
Furniture	40,000	
Accumulated Depreciation, Furniture		$ 24,000
Equipment	10,000	
Accumulated Depreciation, Equipment		6,000
Building	300,000	
Accumulated Depreciation, Building		110,000
Land	20,000	
Accounts Payable		5,000
Notes Payable		5,000
Accrued Wages		150
Mortgage Payable		100,000
Melvin Mason, Capital		113,000
Melvin Mason, Drawing	10,000	
Room Revenue		150,000
Manager's Salary	15,000	
Assistant Manager's Salary	7,500	
Room Attendants' Wages	15,150	
Payroll Taxes	3,000	
Cleaning Supplies Expense	2,700	
Office Supplies	1,000	
Utilities	5,000	
Advertising	500	
Repairs and Maintenance	9,000	
Insurance Expense	1,500	
Depreciation Expense, Furniture	4,000	
Depreciation Expense, Equipment	1,000	
Depreciation Expense, Building	10,000	
Property Taxes	22,000	
Interest Expense	8,000	
Total	$513,150	$513,150

Mason Motel
Balance Sheet
December 31, 20X1

Assets:		
Cash		$ 5,000
Marketable Securities		10,000
Accounts Receivable		8,000
Cleaning Supplies		1,800
Prepaid Insurance		3,000
Furniture	$ 40,000	
Less: Accumulated Depreciation	24,000	16,000
Equipment	10,000	
Less: Accumulated Depreciation	6,000	4,000
Building	300,000	
Less: Accumulated Depreciation	110,000	190,000
Land		20,000
Total Assets		$257,800
Liabilities:		
Accounts Payable		$ 5,000
Notes Payable		5,000
Accrued Wages		150
Mortgage Payable		100,000
Total Liabilities		110,150
Proprietorship:		
Melvin Mason, Capital at January 1, 20X1	$113,000	
Less: Withdrawals during 20X1	10,000	
Add: Net Income for 20X1	44,650	
Melvin Mason, Capital at December 31, 20X1		147,650
Total Liabilities and Proprietorship		$257,800

Net Income for 20X1
(See Exhibit 3)

Exhibit 6   The Closing Process

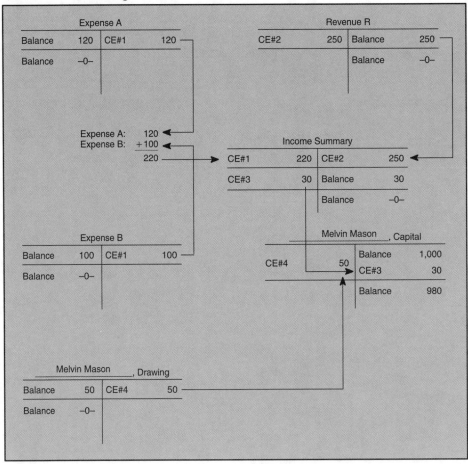

Finally, CE#4 closes the Drawing account into the Capital account by crediting the Drawing account by its balance of $50 and debiting the Capital account for $50.

The closing entries for the Mason Motel's expense accounts have debit balances as shown on the adjusted trial balance (Exhibit 2). Therefore, to close these accounts, a compound closing entry debits Income Summary and credits each expense account.

Dec. 31	Income Summary	$105,350	
	Manager's Salary		$15,000
	Assistant Manager's Salary		7,500
	Room Attendants' Wages		15,150

(continued)

Payroll Taxes	3,000
Cleaning Supplies Expense	2,700
Office Supplies	1,000
Utilities	5,000
Advertising	500
Repairs & Maintenance	9,000
Insurance Expense	1,500
Depreciation Expense, Furniture	4,000
Depreciation Expense, Equipment	1,000
Depreciation Expense, Building	10,000
Property Taxes	22,000
Interest Expense	8,000
To close the expense accounts at year-end.	

The Room Revenue account, as shown in Exhibit 2, has a credit balance. Therefore, to close and clear this revenue account, the account must be debited for the balance and the Income Summary account must be credited for the same.

Dec. 31	Room Revenue	$150,000	
	Income Summary		$150,000
	To close the Room Revenue account at year-end.		

When a firm's revenue and expense accounts are closed into the Income Summary account, the balance reflects the result of the year's operations as either net income or net loss. After the two previous closing entries, the Mason Motel's Income Summary T-account has a credit balance of $44,650, the amount of net income earned for 20X1.

Income Summary

CE#1	105,350	CE#2	150,000
		Balance	44,650

To close and clear the Income Summary account for the Mason Motel, the account is debited for $44,650 and Melvin Mason, Capital is credited for $44,650. The journal entry is recorded as follows:

Dec. 31	Income Summary	$44,650	
	Melvin Mason, Capital		$44,650
	To close the Income Summary account		
	at year-end.		

Finally, the Drawing account is closed to the Capital account. Since the Melvin Mason, Drawing account has a $10,000 debit balance, it is credited by $10,000 and the Capital account is debited for $10,000 as follows:

Dec. 31	Melvin Mason, Capital	$10,000	
	Melvin Mason, Drawing		$10,000
	To close the Drawing account at year-end.		

After the closing entries have been posted, the revenue and expense accounts, the Drawing account, and the Income Summary account have zero balances. The Melvin Mason, Capital account has been increased from $113,000 to $147,650, as shown in the statement of owner's equity (Exhibit 4).

Post-Closing Trial Balance

After the accountant records and posts the closing entries, the only accounts with balances that remain in the general ledger are the balance sheet accounts. These accounts must be in balance; that is, the total of debit balance accounts must equal the total of credit balance accounts. To test this equality and to check the accuracy of the closing process, the accountant prepares a **post-closing trial balance**. As with the trial balance prepared before the closing process, account balances are listed in debit and credit columns and totaled to ensure that debits equal credits.

Exhibit 7 shows the post-closing trial balance of the Mason Motel as of December 31, 20X1. The account balances have been taken from the ledger accounts for inclusion on this trial balance. Note that no revenue, expense, or drawing accounts are included, because they have been closed for the accounting period to the Melvin Mason, Capital account through the closing entries.

The Worksheet

The accountant may use a **worksheet** in the adjusting process and in completing the accounting cycle. A worksheet is a columnar sheet of paper on which accountants list the general ledger accounts before making adjustments and preparing the income statement and balance sheet. It is only a tool and is not part of the formal accounting records. Accountants generally use it to reduce the chance of errors in adjusting accounts and producing the financial statements. The worksheet helps the accountant accomplish the following:

1. Prepare the trial balance.

Exhibit 7   Post-Closing Trial Balance

Mason Motel
Post-Closing Trial Balance
December 31, 20X1

	Debits	Credits
Cash	$ 5,000	
Marketable Securities	10,000	
Accounts Receivable	8,000	
Cleaning Supplies	1,800	
Prepaid Insurance	3,000	
Furniture	40,000	
Accumulated Depreciation, Furniture		$ 24,000
Equipment	10,000	
Accumulated Depreciation, Equipment		6,000
Building	300,000	
Accumulated Depreciation, Building		110,000
Land	20,000	
Accounts Payable		5,000
Notes Payable		5,000
Accrued Wages		150
Mortgage Payable		100,000
Melvin Mason, Capital		147,650
Total	**$ 397,800**	**$ 397,800**

2. Adjust the accounts without immediately having to post adjustments to the ledger accounts. Instead, the adjusting entries can be journalized and posted after the worksheet is completed.

3. Prepare the adjusted trial balance.

4. Segregate the adjusted account balances into columns for preparing the income statement and the balance sheet.

5. Determine the net income or loss for the accounting period.

To reiterate, the worksheet is merely an accountant's tool; it is neither published nor given to management to use. Each individual accountant decides whether or not to use a worksheet. He or she must weigh the advantage of reducing the chance of errors and the time required to prepare the financial statements (since recording and posting of the adjustments can be done later) against the disadvantage of the additional time required to prepare the worksheet.

The worksheet for the Mason Motel for the end of 20X1 is shown in Exhibit 8. Observe the following concerning this worksheet:

1. Column 1 lists the Mason Motel's accounts. These were taken from general ledger accounts, except for the five located at the bottom of the list. They result from adjustments.

Exhibit 8 Worksheet

Mason Motel
Worksheet
For the year ended December 31, 20X1

(1) Account Title	(2) Trial Balance Debit	(3) Trial Balance Credit	(4) Adjustments Debit	(5) Adjustments Credit	(6) Adjusted Trial Balance Debit	(7) Adjusted Trial Balance Credit	(8) Income Statement Debit	(9) Income Statement Credit	(10) Balance Sheet Debit	(11) Balance Sheet Credit
Cash	5,000				5,000				5,000	
Marketable Securities	10,000				10,000				10,000	
Accounts Receivable	8,000				8,000				8,000	
Cleaning Supplies	2,500			(b) 700	1,800				1,800	
Prepaid Insurance	4,500			(a) 1,500	3,000				3,000	
Furniture	40,000				40,000				40,000	
Accumulated Depreciation, Furniture		20,000		(c) 4,000		24,000				24,000
Equipment	10,000				10,000				10,000	
Accumulated Depreciation, Equipment		5,000		(d) 1,000		6,000				6,000
Building	300,000				300,000				300,000	
Accumulated Depreciation, Building		100,000		(e) 10,000		110,000				110,000
Land	20,000				20,000				20,000	
Accounts Payable		5,000				5,000				5,000
Notes Payable		5,000				5,000				5,000
Mortgage Payable		100,000				100,000				100,000
Melvin Mason, Capital		113,000				113,000				113,000
Melvin Mason, Drawing	10,000				10,000				10,000	
Room Revenue		150,000				150,000		150,000		
Manager's Salary	15,000				15,000		15,000			
Assistant Manager's Salary	7,500				7,500		7,500			
Room Attendants' Wages	15,000		(f) 150		15,150		15,150			
Payroll Taxes	3,000				3,000		3,000			
Cleaning Supplies Expense	2,000		(b) 700		2,700		2,700			
Office Supplies	1,000				1,000		1,000			
Utilities	5,000				5,000		5,000			
Advertising	500				500		500			
Repairs and Maintenance	9,000				9,000		9,000			
Property Taxes	22,000				22,000		22,000			
Interest Expense	8,000				8,000		8,000			
	498,000	498,000								
Insurance Expense			(a) 1,500		1,500		1,500			
Depreciation Expense, Furniture			(c) 4,000		4,000		4,000			
Depreciation Expense, Equipment			(d) 1,000		1,000		1,000			
Depreciation Expense, Building			(e) 10,000		10,000		10,000			
Accrued Wages				(f) 150		150				150
			17,350	17,350	513,150	513,150	105,350	150,000	407,800	363,150
							44,650			44,650
							150,000	150,000	407,800	407,800

2. Columns 2 and 3 show the trial balance that the accountant prepared before making any adjustments. The total of the debit column (column 2) of $498,000 equals the total of the credit column (column 3) of $498,000. If the Mason Motel accountant had not used a worksheet, he or she would have prepared a separate trial balance.

3. Columns 4 and 5 list six adjustments, as follows:

Adjustment	Amount	Purpose
a	$ 1,500	To record insurance expense for 20X1.
b	700	To record additional cleaning supplies used as expense for the year.
c	4,000	To record depreciation expense of furniture for the year.
d	1,000	To record depreciation expense of equipment for the year.
e	10,000	To record depreciation expense of the building for the year.
f	150	To accrue unpaid wages at the end of 20X1.

Notice that each adjusting entry has a debit and a credit. The total of the debits of $17,350 equals the total of the credits of $17,350. When the accountant completes the worksheet and prepares the financial statements, he or she records the adjusting entries in the general journal and then posts them to the ledger accounts.

4. Columns 6 and 7 show the adjusted trial balance. As discussed previously in this chapter, the adjusted trial balance is simply the trial balance of ledger accounts after adjustments have been prepared. As with all trial balances, the total of the debit column should equal the total of the credit column. Further, the totals of columns 6 and 7 equal the totals of the Mason Motel's adjusted trial balance that is shown in Exhibit 2. This adjusted trial balance is simply a duplicate of that shown in Exhibit 2. However, remember that if the Mason Motel accountant had decided to use a worksheet in completing the accounting cycle, the trial balance on the worksheet would have sufficed, and he or she would not have prepared a separate adjusted trial balance.

5. Columns 8 and 9 include only the revenue and expense accounts, since these are the only accounts for which amounts are shown on an income statement. The amounts in columns 8 and 9 are those shown on the income statement as provided in Exhibit 3. In actual practice, a more detailed income statement is generally prepared for management's internal use, and a less detailed income statement is prepared for external uses. Room revenue of $150,000 is the only revenue account and, since it has a credit balance, it is shown in the credit column. All the amounts from the expense accounts in column 6 are written in column 8, since they represent debit balances. The difference between the totals of columns 8 and 9 (that is, expenses and revenue) equals the net income for the accounting period. The Mason Motel's net income for 20X1 is $44,650.

6. Columns 10 and 11 include the remaining accounts, those that are shown on the balance sheet. The total of the debit column (column 10) exceeds the total of the credit column (column 11) by $44,650, which is the same amount as the net income earned in 20X1 by the Mason Motel. The net income figure thus serves as a "balancing amount" for the balance sheet columns of the worksheet.

After the worksheet is completed, the accountant would prepare the formal income statement and balance sheet as shown in Exhibits 3 and 5, respectively, for the Mason Motel. If the accountant used a worksheet, he or she would complete the accounting cycle in the following way:

- Record and post adjusting entries.

- Record and post closing entries.

- Prepare a post-closing trial balance.

Reversing Entries

Reversing entries are journal entries made the first day of an accounting period to reverse the effects of adjusting entries made on the last day of the previous accounting period. The sole purpose of reversing entries is to simplify the first journal entries related to the same items during the next accounting period.

For example, on December 31, 20X1, the Mason Motel recorded accrued wages payable of $150 as adjusting entry (f). If the Mason Motel's accountant uses reversing entries, this adjustment is reversed on January 1, 20X2, with the following entry:

Accrued Wages	$150	
Room Attendants' Wages		$150
To reverse the accrual of Room Attendants' Wages.		

After this reversing entry is recorded, the expense account (Room Attendants' Wages) has a credit balance of $150. This credit will be more than offset when the Mason Motel records the first payroll in January 20X2. Assume the first payroll is paid on January 12, 20X2, and the total room attendants' wages are $1,350. Of the $1,350, $150 relates to the employees' work performed during 20X1 and $1,200 is for work performed in 20X2. The matching principle requires that expenses for each period be *recorded* in that period, though not necessarily paid in the separate periods. The $150 for 20X1 was recorded in 20X1 using an adjusting entry. The Mason Motel would record the payroll in January as follows:

Room Attendants' Wages	$1,350	
Cash		$1,350
To record the payroll for Room Attendants' Wages.		

It appears that the entire $1,350 is expensed in January 20X2. However, because of the reversing entry, the net effect is that only the $1,200 of expense pertaining to 20X2 is reflected as the balance. At this point, the Room Attendants' Wages T-account would look like this:

Room Attendants' Wages

Jan. 12 Pay period	1,350	Jan. 1 Reversing	150
Balance	1,200		

If the Mason Motel had not used reversing entries, the accountant would still have recorded the proper amount in the Room Attendants' Wages expense account by using the following compound entry when the first payroll in January was paid:

Room Attendants' Wages	$1,200	
Accrued Wages	150	
Cash		$1,350
To record the payroll for Room Attendants' Wages.		

Generally only those adjusting entries that are accruals of assets and liabilities may be reversed. For example, the accrual of interest income and the related interest receivable, as well as the accrual of interest payable and the related interest expense, may be reversed. On the other hand, certain adjustments, such as the adjustment of prepaid insurance to recognize insurance expense at the end of the accounting period, may *not* be reversed. In this case, there is no transaction in the following period to offset a reversing entry as there is for the accrual of assets and liabilities. Thus, the end result in the ledger accounts is the same, regardless of whether or not reversing entries are used. It is up to the accountant to decide which approach is easier to use, since the use of reversing entries has no effect on the financial statements.

Comprehensive Illustration—Completing the Accounting Cycle

After adjusting entries are recorded and posted, an adjusted trial balance is prepared. Exhibit 9 shows the adjusted trial balance for Carson Catering on November 30, 20X2. The total debits of $186,317 equal the total credits of $186,317, so the accounts are in balance. The next step is preparing the income statement, the statement of owner's equity, and the balance sheet for Carson Catering. Exhibits 10 through 12 show these financial statements.

The income statement (Exhibit 10) covers the entire fiscal year for Carson Catering of December 1, 20X1, through November 30, 20X2. Revenues total $138,251, while expenses total $126,534, giving a net income of $11,717. (This particular income statement is very simplistic.)

Exhibit 9 Carson Catering Adjusted Trial Balance

Carson Catering
Adjusted Trial Balance
November 30, 20X2

Account Number	Account	Debits	Credits
100	Cash	$ 3,000	
101	Certificate of Deposit	10,000	
105	Accounts Receivable	6,200	
107	Accrued Interest Receivable	333	
110	Operating Supplies	250	
115	Prepaid Rent	7,000	
120	Van	15,000	
121	Accumulated Depreciation, Van		$ 3,500
125	Equipment	10,000	
126	Accumulated Depreciation, Equipment		1,833
200	Accounts Payable		5,500
201	Accrued Wages Payable		2,500
202	Accrued Interest Payable		188
203	Accrued Expenses Payable		160
210	Notes Payable—BMAC		9,385
300	Don Carson, Capital		25,000
301	Don Carson, Drawing	8,000	
400	Catering Revenue		137,418
410	Interest Income		833
500	Wages Expense	39,500	
501	Advertising Expense	10,000	
502	Food Expense	60,000	
503	Gas Expense	2,200	
504	Rent Expense	5,000	
505	Supplies Expense	2,350	
506	Interest Expense	1,191	
507	Utilities Expense	960	
508	Depreciation Expense	5,333	
	Total	$186,317	$186,317

The statement of owner's equity (Exhibit 11) reflects Don Carson's initial capital investment of $5,000 in Carson Catering on December 1, 20X1, and also his additional investment of $20,000 during the fiscal year ended November 30, 20X2. This statement also reflects the net income for the year as well as Don Carson's withdrawals of $8,000 during the year. The final balance of $28,717 will be carried over to the balance sheet and shown as Don Carson, Capital as of November 30, 20X2.

The balance sheet (Exhibit 12) reflects the financial position of Carson Catering as of the last day of the accounting period, November 30, 20X2. Assets total $46,450, while liabilities and owner's equity total $46,450. This statement reflects

Exhibit 10   Carson Catering Income Statement

Carson Catering
Income Statement
For the year ended November 30, 20X2

Revenue:

Catering Revenue		$ 137,418
Interest Income		833
Total		138,251

Expenses:

Wages	$ 39,500	
Advertising	10,000	
Food	60,000	
Gas	2,200	
Rent	5,000	
Supplies	2,350	
Interest	1,191	
Utilities	960	
Depreciation	5,333	126,534
Net Income		$ 11,717

Exhibit 11   Carson Catering Statement of Owner's Equity

Carson Catering
Statement of Owner's Equity
For the year ended November 30, 20X2

Don Carson, Capital, December 1, 20X1	$ 5,000
Plus: Capital investment during the year	20,000
Plus: Net income for the year	11,717
Less: Don Carson, Withdrawals	$ 8,000
Don Carson, Capital, November 30, 20X2	$ 28,717

the fundamental accounting equation: assets equal liabilities plus owner's equity. Notice that Don Carson, Capital reflects the $28,717 from the statement of owner's equity rather than the $25,000 as shown on the adjusted trial balance (Exhibit 9) for Don Carson, Capital. This particular form of the balance sheet is very simplistic. Discussion of the proper balance sheet form is beyond the scope of this chapter.

Now Carson Catering's accountant begins closing the nominal accounts (the revenue, expense, and drawing accounts). The revenue and expense accounts will be cleared and closed through the Income Summary account. The closing entries for Carson Catering are as follows:

Exhibit 12 Carson Catering Balance Sheet

Carson Catering
Balance Sheet
November 30, 20X2

Assets

Cash	$ 3,000
Certificate of Deposit	10,000
Accounts Receivable	6,200
Accrued Interest Receivable	333
Operating Supplies	250
Prepaid Rent	7,000
Van	15,000
Less: Accumulated Depreciation, Van	(3,500)
Equipment	10,000
Less: Accumulated Depreciation, Equipment	(1,833)
Total Assets	**$ 46,450**

Liabilities and Owner's Equity

Accounts Payable	$ 5,500
Accrued Wages Payable	2,500
Accrued Interest Payable	188
Accrued Expenses Payable	160
Notes Payable—BMAC	9,385
Don Carson, Capital	28,717
Total Liabilities and Owner's Equity	**$ 46,450**

1. Closing Entry #1: Revenue Accounts

Catering Revenue	$137,418	
Interest Income	833	
Income Summary		$138,251
To close the revenue accounts.		

2. Closing Entry #2: Expense Accounts

Income Summary	$126,534	
Wages Expense		$39,500
Advertising Expense		10,000
Food Expense		60,000

(continued)

Gas Expense	2,200
Rent Expense	5,000
Supplies Expense	2,350
Interest Expense	1,191
Utilities Expense	960
Depreciation Expense	5,333
To close the expense accounts.	

3. Closing Entry #3: Income Summary

Income Summary	$11,717	
Don Carson, Capital		$11,717
To close the Income Summary account.		

4. Closing Entry #4: Drawing Account

Don Carson, Capital	$8,000	
Don Carson, Drawing		$8,000
To close the Drawing account.		

After the closing entries are posted from the general journal to the general ledger accounts, all the nominal accounts have zero balances and are ready for posting of activity for the following accounting period.

The last step in the accounting cycle is preparing the post-closing trial balance. Exhibit 13 shows Carson Catering's post-closing trial balance for November 30, 20X2. The total debits of $51,783 equal the total credits of $51,783, thus proving the equality of debits and credits.

Summary

The accounting cycle consists of a set sequence of steps the accounting staff performs during each fiscal period. The accounting cycle begins when the accountant analyzes transactions and ends when he or she prepares a post-closing trial balance.

At the end of the accounting period, after making, journalizing, and posting adjusting entries, the accountant prepares an adjusted trial balance to prove the equality of debits and credits. Because the accountant prepared a trial balance before making adjustments, the only differences between that trial balance and the adjusted trial balance should be the adjustments themselves. The accountant uses the adjusted trial balance in preparing the income statement and balance sheet, taking account balances directly from the adjusted trial balance.

Exhibit 13   Carson Catering Post-Closing Trial Balance

Carson Catering
Post-Closing Trial Balance
November 30, 20X2

Account Number	Account	Debits	Credits
100	Cash	$ 3,000	
101	Certificate of Deposit	10,000	
105	Accounts Receivable	6,200	
107	Accrued Interest Receivable	333	
110	Operating Supplies	250	
115	Prepaid Rent	7,000	
120	Van	15,000	
121	Accumulated Depreciation, Van		$ 3,500
125	Equipment	10,000	
126	Accumulated Depreciation, Equipment		1,833
200	Accounts Payable		5,500
201	Accrued Wages Payable		2,500
202	Accrued Interest Payable		188
203	Accrued Expenses Payable		160
210	Notes Payable—BMAC		9,385
300	Don Carson, Capital		28,717
	Totals	**$ 51,783**	**$ 51,783**

The statement of owners' equity is prepared using information from the income statement and the trial balance. The statement of owners' equity is a summary of the transactions affecting the owners' equity account. Net income is added to owners' equity from the beginning of the period, and then owners' drawing accounts are subtracted, resulting in owners' equity at the end of the period. The statement of owners' equity is a link between the income statement and the balance sheet, since net income is essentially transferred from the income statement to the balance sheet through this statement.

After the accountant prepares financial statements, he or she closes revenue and expense accounts. The accountant closes these accounts with closing entries that he or she records in the general journal and then posts to the general ledger accounts. In a very simple accounting system, revenues and expenses may be reflected directly in the owners' equity account. However, to more clearly see the amounts that lead to net income, the accountant records revenue and expenses in separate temporary equity accounts. These accounts are closed at the end of a fiscal period and the balances are brought to zero. The accountant often does this by transferring the balances to a clearing account called Income Summary. Once all revenue and expense accounts are closed to Income Summary, the balance in the Income Summary account should be net income. This balance is then closed out to the Owners' Equity account. After all closing entries are journalized and posted, only balance sheet accounts are left with balances. At this time, the accountant prepares a post-closing trial balance to prove the equality of debits and credits of the permanent accounts, and the accounts are ready for the start of a new fiscal period.

The worksheet is a tool that an accountant may use in the adjustment process and in completing the accounting cycle. A worksheet is used to list general ledger accounts in columns by debit and credit.

Reversing entries are journal entries made at the beginning of an accounting period to reverse the effects of adjusting entries made in the previous period. This is done to simplify the first journal entry related to that same item during the new period. Reversing entries can usually be made only on accruals of assets or liabilities. Reversing entries are not mandatory, so each firm must weigh the benefits and costs in deciding whether to prepare them.

Key Terms

accounting cycle—The sequence of principal accounting procedures of a fiscal period: transaction analysis, journal entry, posting to ledger accounts, trial balance, adjustments, adjusted trial balance, preparation of periodic financial statements, account closing, and post-closing trial balance.

adjusted trial balance—The trial balance prepared to prove the equality of debits and credits after adjusting entries have been posted to accounts.

clearing account—An account used to temporarily store information as part of an accounting procedure.

closing entries—Journal entries prepared at the end of the period (normally yearly) to close the temporary proprietorship accounts into permanent proprietorship accounts.

post-closing trial balance—The trial balance prepared after closing entries have been posted to accounts to prove the equality of debits and credits in the permanent accounts.

reversing entries—Journal entries made on the first day of an accounting period to reverse the effects of adjusting entries made on the last day of the previous accounting period.

statement of owners' equity—A financial statement that summarizes transactions affecting the owners' capital account(s).

worksheet—A working paper used as a preliminary to the preparation of financial statements.

Review Questions

1. What are the differences between a trial balance, an adjusted trial balance, and a post-closing trial balance?

2. What is the purpose of a worksheet?

3. What are closing entries? When are they prepared?

4. What is the Income Summary account? When is it used?

5. What are the ten steps in the accounting cycle?

6. What is a reversing entry?

7. Why would an accountant prepare reversing entries?

8. How is the owner's drawing account closed?

9. What are the three main steps in the closing process? What are the features of each?

10. Why do only balance sheet accounts have balances in the post-closing trial balance?

 **Problems** ────────────────────────────

Problem 1

The following is a list of some accounts used by a food service business:

a. Food Inventory	i. Equipment
b. Prepaid Insurance	j. Notes Payable
c. Food Sales	k. A.M. Smith, Drawing
d. Utility Expenses	l. Income Summary
e. Cash	m. Wages Expense
f. Accounts Receivable	n. Operating Expenses
g. Accounts Payable	o. Depreciation Expense
h. A.M. Smith, Capital	p. Accumulated Depreciation

Required:

For each account:

1. State what type of account it is (permanent, temporary, clearing).
2. State whether it is closed during closing entries. (yes/no)
3. If it is closed during closing entries, state to which account it is closed.

Problem 2

The Roadhouse Inn's activities for 20X1 and 20X2 that affect the Emily Road, Capital account are as follows:

	20X1	20X2
Net income for the year	$55,000	$58,500
Withdrawals by Emily Road	$20,000	$25,000
Investment by Emily Road	–$0–	$10,000

In addition, the balance of the Emily Road, Capital account on January 1, 20X1 was $52,500.

Required:

1. Prepare a statement of owner's equity for the Roadhouse Inn for 20X1.
2. Determine the balance of the Emily Road, Capital account as of the end of 20X2.

Problem 3

The following is an income statement for Chuck's Steakhouse:

Chuck's Steakhouse
Income Statement

Food and Beverage Revenue		$ 474,500
Expenses:		
Wages	$ 142,350	
Cost of Food Sold	156,585	
Advertising Expense	9,490	
Repairs and Maintenance	40,333	
Rent Expense	33,215	
Depreciation Expense	15,000	
Utilities Expense	18,980	415,953
Net Income		$ 58,547

The balance of the Owner's Equity account is $96,000 at the beginning of the period. During the year, the owner has drawn out 5 percent of his equity (use beginning Owner's Equity to calculate this).

Required:

Prepare a statement of owner's equity for Chuck's Steakhouse.

Problem 4

The following is a trial balance for the Albatross Motel:

Albatross Motel
Trial Balance
December 31, 20X2

Cash	$ 6,100	
Marketable Securities	15,000	
Accounts Receivable	2,900	
Prepaid Insurance	2,250	
Equipment	10,000	
Accumulated Depreciation, Equipment		5,000
Building	275,000	
Accumulated Depreciation, Building		100,000
Land	130,000	
Accounts Payable		5,000
Unearned Revenue		200
Notes Payable		7,000
Mortgage Payable		49,000
Melvin Mason, Capital		217,050
Room Revenue		98,500

Manager's Salary	19,000
Housekeepers' Wages	15,000
Office Supplies Expense	1,000
Utilities Expense	5,000
Advertising Expense	500

$481,750	$481,750

Required:

1. Post the following adjusting entries to the proper T-accounts.

Adjusting Entries

a.	Dec. 31	Insurance Expense	$ 325	
		Prepaid Insurance		$ 325
b.	Dec. 31	Depreciation Expense	$ 1,000	
		Accumulated Depreciation, Equipment		$ 1,000
c.	Dec. 31	Depreciation Expense	$20,000	
		Accumulated Depreciation, Building		$20,000
d.	Dec. 31	Housekeepers' Wages	$ 130	
		Accrued Wages, Housekeepers		$ 130
e.	Dec. 31	Utilities Expense	$ 500	
		Accounts Payable		$ 500
f.	Dec. 31	Unearned Revenue	$ 200	
		Room Revenue		$ 200

2. Prepare an adjusted trial balance.

Problem 5

The following is an adjusted trial balance for Tinker's Motel:

Tinker's Motel
Adjusted Trial Balance
December 31, 20X1

Cash	$ 15,900	
Supplies	3,400	
Accounts Receivable	8,000	
Furniture	100,000	
Accumulated Depreciation, Furniture		$ 20,000
Building	250,000	
Accumulated Depreciation, Building		140,000
Accounts Payable		6,090
Mortgage Payable		57,900
Tinker Bell, Capital		81,000
Room Revenue		219,000

Wages	43,800	
Utilities Expense	19,710	
Insurance Expense	15,330	
Supplies Expense	32,850	
Depreciation Expense	35,000	
	$523,990	$523,990

Required:

1. Prepare the journal entries to close the revenue and expense accounts to the Income Summary account.
2. Prepare the journal entry to close the Income Summary account to the Owner's Equity account.

Challenge Problems

Problem 6

The following is an adjusted trial balance for Steven's Motel for the month of November. Steven's accountant has prepared the trial balance and adjusting entries. Now the financial statements must be prepared from the adjusted trial balance.

Steven's Motel
Adjusted Trial Balance
November 30, 20X1

Cash	$ 2,300	
Accounts Receivable	200	
Equipment	35,000	
Accumulated Depreciation, Equipment		$ 5,000
Building	77,000	
Accumulated Depreciation, Building		19,000
Accounts Payable		2,000
Note Payable		4,500
Mortgage Payable		10,000
Steven Schultz, Capital		72,598
Steven Schultz, Drawing	1,450	
Room Revenue		6,045
Wages	1,028	
Payroll Taxes	242	
Repairs and Maintenance	302	
Utilities Expense	121	
Depreciation Expense	1,500	
	$119,143	$119,143

Required:

From this adjusted trial balance, prepare (1) the income statement, (2) the balance sheet, and (3) the statement of owner's equity.

Problem 7

The following is an adjusted trial balance for Mary's Miracle Pastries, a successful coffee shop. Mary's accountant has prepared the trial balance and adjusting entries. Now the financial statements must be prepared from the adjusted trial balance.

Mary's Miracle Pastries
Adjusted Trial Balance
December 31, 20X3

Cash	$ 32,522	
Marketable Securities	12,000	
Accounts Receivable	17,000	
Food and Beverage Inventory	9,200	
Equipment	35,000	
Accumulated Depreciation, Equipment		$ 5,000
Building	167,000	
Accumulated Depreciation, Building		40,000
Accounts Payable		7,000
Accrued Wages		600
Note Payable		15,000
Mortgage Payable		79,000
Mary Ramaker, Capital		58,999
Mary Ramaker, Drawing	4,600	
Pastry Revenue		361,350
Cost of Food Sold	126,473	
Wages	108,405	
Advertising Expense	14,454	
Repairs and Maintenance	18,068	
Insurance Expense	7,227	
Depreciation Expense	15,000	
	$566,949	$566,949

Required:

From this adjusted trial balance, prepare (1) the income statement, (2) the balance sheet, and (3) the statement of owner's equity.

Problem 8

The trial balance and adjusted trial balance for Twyla's Diner are as follows:

Twyla's Diner
Trial Balance and Adjusted Trial Balance
December 31, 20X3

	Trial Balance	Adjusted Trial Balance
Cash	$ 7,750	$ 7,750
Accounts Receivable	1,400	1,400
Food Inventory	3,400	2,800

	Trial Balance		Adjusted Trial Balance	
Office Supplies	900		800	
Prepaid Rent	800		-0-	
Equipment	75,000		75,000	
Accumulated Depreciation, Equipment		$ 8,000		$ 12,000
Accounts Payable		4,230		4,230
Notes Payable		28,200		28,200
Accrued Wages		-0-		1,000
Twyla Kamp, Capital		48,500		48,500
Food Revenue		80,500		80,500
Cost of Food Sold	35,880		36,480	
Wages and Benefits	31,000		32,000	
Rent Expense	8,800		9,600	
Office Supplies Expense	1,000		1,100	
Interest Expense	3,500		3,500	
Depreciation Expense	-0-		4,000	
	$169,430	$169,430	$174,430	$174,430

Required:

By analyzing the differences between the figures in the trial balance and the adjusted trial balance, determine the adjusting entries that recorded (1) adjustment of food inventory, (2) office supplies, (3) depreciation expense, (4) adjustment of prepaid insurance, and (5) accrued unpaid wages.

Problem 9

1. Using the adjusted trial balance from the solution of Problem 8, prepare the proper closing entries for Twyla's Diner. Close all revenue and expense accounts to Income Summary.
2. Close Income Summary to the Owner's Equity account.
3. Prepare a post-closing trial balance for Twyla's Diner.

Problem 10

The following is an adjusted trial balance for Fleischer's Motel as of December 31, 20X2. The accountant for Fleischer's needs to close out the temporary revenue and expense accounts to Income Summary, and then to the Owner's Equity account.

Fleischer's Motel
Trial Balance
December 31, 20X2

Cash	$7,100
Accounts Receivable	700

Supplies	1,300	
Prepaid Insurance	4,500	
Investments	15,000	
Accounts Payable		$ 200
Note Payable		3,000
Mark Fleischer, Capital		13,000
Room Revenue		47,900
Rental Revenue		670
Wages	13,740	
Supplies Expense	2,000	
Utilities Expense	5,960	
Rent Expense	9,760	
Insurance Expense	4,500	
Interest Expense	210	
	$64,770	$64,770

Required:

1. Open the T-accounts for the revenues and expenses as well as the Income Summary and Owner's Equity accounts.

2. Prepare the journal entries necessary to close out the temporary accounts to Income Summary, and post the entries to the proper T-accounts.

3. Close the Income Summary out to Owner's Equity and post the entry to the proper T-account.

4. Prepare a post-closing trial balance.

REVIEW QUIZ

When you feel you have covered all of the material in this chapter, answer these questions. Choose the *best* answer.

1. Transferring amounts from journals to ledger accounts is called:

    a. adjusting entries.
    b. posting.
    c. debiting.
    d. crediting.

2. The statement of owner's equity serves as a link between which of the following?

    a. the statement of cash flows and the income statement
    b. the income statement and the general ledger
    c. the income statement and the balance sheet
    d. the balance sheet and the statement of cash flows

3. Which of the following best describes the difference between the adjusted trial balance and the trial balance?

    a. The trial balance does not include adjusting entries; the adjusted trial balance does.
    b. The adjusted trial balance is usually higher than the trial balance.
    c. The adjusted trial balance includes post-closing entries.
    d. The trial balance serves as a link between the income statement and the balance sheet.

4. Closing the Wages Expense account usually involves:

    a. crediting it for the amount of its balance.
    b. debiting it for the amount of its balance.
    c. deleting it from the general ledger.
    d. none of the above.

5. The main function of compiling the post-closing trial balance is to:

    a. make adjusting entries.
    b. prove that adjusting entries have been properly entered.
    c. test the equality of credits and debits and ensure the accuracy of the closing process.
    d. test the equality of revenues and expenses and ensure the accuracy of the closing process.

6. Accountants sometimes use worksheets when preparing financial statements. A worksheet lists:

    a. balance sheet accounts.
    b. the general ledger accounts.
    c. revenue and expense accounts.
    d. clearing accounts.

REVIEW QUIZ *(continued)*

7. A reversing entry of an accrual of interest expense results in a(n) _____ to the _____ account.

    a. increase; Interest Expense
    b. debit; Interest Expense
    c. credit; Interest Expense
    d. credit; Accrued Interest

Answer Key: 1-b-C1, 2-c-C2, 3-a-C2, 4-a-C3, 5-c-C3, 6-b-C4, 7-c-C5

Each question is linked to a competency. Competencies are listed on the first page of the chapter. An answer reading 3-b-C4 translates to:

    3: the question number
    b: the correct answer
    C4: the competency number

Chapter 5 Outline

Major Elements of the Income Statement
Relationship with the Balance Sheet
Sales
Cost of Goods Sold
Expenses
Gains and Losses
Income Taxes
Extraordinary Items
Earnings per Share
Income Statements for Internal and
    External Users
Uniform System of Accounts
Internal Income Statements—A
    Contribution Approach
Contents of the Income Statement
Departmental Statements
Uniform System of Accounts for
    Restaurants
Statement of Retained Earnings

Competencies

1. Identify the purpose of the income statement, its major elements, and its relationship to the balance sheet.

2. Identify when a sale is recorded, describe how to account for allowances and returns, and describe how to account for the cost of goods sold.

3. Identify some common operational expenses and explain how they are recorded, and describe how to calculate and account for gains and losses.

4. Explain how earnings per share is calculated and reported, and describe how income statements for internal and external users differ.

5. Explain the purposes of uniform systems of accounts and identify those systems that are relevant to the hospitality industry.

6. Outline the contents of the income statement and identify the purpose of departmental statements.

7. Describe the purpose of and information reported on the statement of retained earnings.

5

Income Statement

FINANCIAL STATEMENTS are the major result of the accounting cycle. Data is accumulated, analyzed, summarized, and reported in meaningful formats to users of financial statements. The financial statement used to convey operating performance is the **income statement**. Also called the *statement of operations,* the *profit and loss statement,* and various other titles, the income statement reports sales and expenses that ideally result in net income but sometimes in a net loss for an accounting period. This information is provided in fairly abbreviated statements to outsiders such as bankers and suppliers and in considerable detail to internal users such as the property's general manager and various department heads.

In this chapter, we will focus on the income statement and discuss its major users and its major elements. We will also discuss earnings per share, external versus internal statements, and the various uniform systems of accounts.

Owners and potential owners, creditors such as suppliers and financial institutions, and managers are all users of financial information. In general, users are divided into two groups: internal and external users. **Internal users** are the managers of the business. **External users** include potential investors, creditors, and owners not active in managing the hospitality enterprise. The information needs of the two groups are generally quite different.

External users are given a statement that reflects only the basics, that is, sales and a few categories of expenses. More detailed information, such as breakdowns by department and comparisons to the operating budgets, is best kept within the particular operation lest it fall into the hands of competitors. This information is often provided in accordance with the uniform system of accounts for the appropriate segment of the hospitality industry.

Each user of financial information seeks operations information for his or her own reasons. Owners and potential owners are interested in profitability as an indicator of potential cash dividends and increases in market prices of publicly traded stocks. Creditors are interested in profitability as an indicator of the firm's ability to pay its bills, perhaps thinking, "Today's profits lead to tomorrow's cash for paying bills." Management wants the operating results to indicate the degree of its success in managing operations. In addition, management expects the operating results to reveal problem areas so it can ensure that the firm generates profits in accordance with the operating plans.

Major Elements of the Income Statement

With an accrual basis accounting system, revenues are recorded when they are earned. When a hotel guest is served a meal, the food sales have been earned.

How to find a Company's Annual Report Online

Many companies have created online *Investor Relations* pages which contain a version of their Annual Report(s) as well as copies of quarterly 10-K and other information for current and potential investors. Company websites can be usually located quickly by searching Yahoo! or one of the Useful Investor Relations Sites listed by National Investor Relations Institute. The Investor relations page is usually linked from the company's home page.

An alternative is to use Yahoo! Finance to find a company's finance page.

alternatives

| | Get Quotes | Basic ▼ | symbol lookup |

Hint: Select "Profile" under **More Info**

Another option is Hoover's Company Capsules. These contain information on more than 10,000 of the largest public and private companies in the United States and around the world. Each capsule includes a description of the company, address, officers, sales and employment figures, and hyperlinks to more information, like financial reports, stock quotes, S.E.C. filings, and news searches. Check: Global Symbol Database

By Company Name: [   ] find

By Ticker Symbol: [   ] find

Other useful places to look ...
- Silicon Investor - top 300 Technology Stocks!
- InvestorsEdge.com - a list of the 100 largest companies in Northern California
- Business Connections - from the *NY Times*
- Finance Site List - from Journal of Finance
- ACGNJ Investing SIG Links Page
- Annual Report Gallery A-Z

The Annual Report Library's Internet site (at http://www.zpub.com/sf/arl/arl-how.html) gives users ways to look up companies' annual reports. (Courtesy of the Annual Reports Library)

When funds are invested in a certificate of deposit, revenue in the form of interest is earned over time. So, generally, with sales and interest, revenue is recorded before cash is received. When future lodging guests pay cash as a room deposit, the amount is initially recorded as a liability, then recognized later as revenue when services are provided to the guest. The revenues shown on an income statement generally are net revenues—that is, the amounts charged (gross sales) less any allowances granted after the sale.

Expenses recorded include outflows related to the accounting period *and* expenses that have been matched to revenues. Expenses related to the period are expenses incurred, even though revenues may not have been earned. For example, insurance on a building provides coverage regardless of the hospitality firm's level of sales. The prepaid insurance is reduced periodically to reflect the insurance expense based on time, not revenue. Many expenses, however, are incurred in direct relation to revenue, and adjusting entries at the end of the accounting period are recorded to match expense to revenue.

Relationship with the Balance Sheet

The income statement covers a period of time, while the balance sheet is prepared as of the last day of the accounting period. Thus, the income statement reflects operations of the hospitality property for the period between balance sheet dates, as shown below:

The result of operations, net income (net loss), for the period is added to (subtracted from) the proper owners' equity account and shown on the balance sheet at the end of the accounting period.

Sales

The sale of goods or services occurs between the seller (the lodging property) and the buyer (the lodging guest). The goods or services are provided by the seller in exchange for the guest's cash or promise to pay at a later date.

Services are recorded as sales as the services are provided. For example, when a lodging guest occupies a guestroom, a sale is recorded. Likewise, food or other merchandise sales are recorded at the time of the sale. The server's check is the source document for the sale of goods such as food and beverages. The revenue from the sale is recorded at the time of the sale for the following reasons:

1. Legal title to the goods (food and beverages) has passed from the seller to the buyer.

2. The selling price has been established.

3. The seller's obligation has been completed.

4. The goods have been exchanged for another asset, such as cash or accounts receivable.

Each time sales are made, the appropriate sales accounts are credited and Cash or Receivables is debited. Sales are recorded at the agreed-upon price. When the lodging guest is dissatisfied with the goods or services, an allowance may be made; that is, the guest may be given partial credit. For example, assume a guest is displeased with his or her room. Management may decide to give a $10 allowance. In this case, the account Room Sales Allowances is debited and the guest's Accounts Receivable is credited for the $10. In effect, room revenue is reduced by $10, since room sales allowances are offset against room revenue in determining net room revenue to be shown on the firm's income statements.

When a hospitality firm sells items not consumed on the premises, such as gift shop merchandise, there may be some returns. For example, the merchandise may have been damaged at the time of the sale. If the guest had charged the purchase from the gift shop to his or her room, the sales returned would be recorded as follows:

Gift Shop Sales Returns	$XXX	
Accounts Receivable		$XXX
To record a sales return by a hotel guest.		

If the hotel guest had paid cash for the merchandise, cash generally would be disbursed from the cash register, and the Cash account would be credited instead of Accounts Receivable.

Allowances and returns are recorded in contra-sales accounts to track the amount of such activities. Many firms use one account for both returns and allowances for a given department, such as Gift Shop Sales Returns and Allowances.

Cost of Goods Sold

The sales of food, beverages, and other merchandise require that the cost of the goods sold also be recorded. Generally, when goods are purchased for resale, they are recorded as inventory. When they are sold, the costs are transferred to a **cost of goods sold** account. The costs may be transferred at the time of sale, or they may be recorded at the end of the accounting period. At this point, for the sake of simplicity, we will assume that food, beverage, and other merchandise purchased are recorded in separate purchases accounts. For example, $100 of food purchased is recorded as follows:

Food Purchases	$100	
Cash		$100
To record food purchases.		

At the end of the accounting period, a physical inventory of food is taken and the cost of the food inventory is determined. Cost of food sold for the period is determined as follows:

Food inventory, beginning of period	$ XX
Plus: food purchases	XXX
Food available for sale	XXX
Less: food inventory, end of period	XX
Cost of food sold	$ XXX

This assumes that no food was used for other purposes during the period. If food was used for other purposes, additional adjustments are required. Other uses could include employee meals provided free of charge, transfers to the beverage department, and food used for promotional purposes. If food is used for these purposes, the line "Cost of food sold" is changed to "Cost of food used," and adjustments are made as follows:

Cost of food used	$ XXX
Less: Cost of employee meals	XX
Less: Promotional meals	XX
Less: Transfers to beverage department	XX
Cost of food sold	$ XXX

For example, assume a hotel's food service department provides the following information at the end of its accounting period, December 31, 20X1:

Food inventory, beginning of month	$ 5,000
Food purchases (during December)	20,000
Food inventory, end of month	6,000
Cost of employee meals	300
Cost of promotional meals	200
Food transfers to beverage department	50

The cost of food sold to be reported on the income statement would be determined as follows:

Food inventory, December 1, 20X1	$ 5,000
Food purchases	20,000
Food available	25,000
Less: food inventory, December 31, 20X1	(6,000)
Cost of food *used*	19,000
Less: cost of employee meals	(300)
Less: cost of promotional meals	(200)
Less: transfers to beverage department	(50)
Cost of food sold	$18,450

The journal entry to record the cost of food sales and the ending inventory would be as follows:

Cost of Food Sold	$19,000	
Food Inventory	1,000	
Food Purchases		$20,000
To record cost of food sales and to adjust food inventory to its ending inventory.		

The debit to food inventory of $1,000 effectively increases the food inventory account to the physical inventory of $6,000, since $1,000 plus the food inventory account balance of $5,000 as of December 1, 20X1, equals $6,000. The $19,000 debit to Cost of Food Sold and the $1,000 debit to Food Inventory are offset by the $20,000 credit to Food Purchases. Remember, debits must equal credits. The credit of $20,000 reduces the Food Purchases account to a zero balance.

The journal entry to record the cost of employee meals, promotional meals, and transfers to the beverage department would be as follows:

Employee Meals (food department)	$300	
Promotional Meals (marketing department)	200	
Transfers to Beverage Department	50	
Cost of Food Sold		$550
To record food used in operations.		

This entry records the expense of using food in operations (employee meals and promotional meals) and transfers to the beverage department. In addition, the Cost of Food Sold account is credited to reflect the cost of food sold for the month as previously calculated, since $19,000 less $550 equals $18,450. This entry assumes all employee meals are consumed by food department employees. The Employee Meals (food department) account is an expense account in the food department. The Transfers to the Beverage Department account and the Beverage Purchases account are treated similarly when determining the cost of beverages sold for the period. The Promotional Meals account is an expense account of the marketing department.

Expenses

Expenses other than cost of goods sold include day-to-day operational expenses such as supplies and labor as well as depreciation, interest expense, and income taxes.

Expenses are generally recorded for each department. Labor costs related to the rooms department are recorded as expenses of that department, while labor costs of the food and marketing departments are recorded in their respective departments. Labor costs include the three major areas of (1) salaries and wages, (2) fringe benefits, and (3) payroll taxes.

Assume a hotel's payroll for the month included the following wages:

Rooms department employees		$10,000
Food department employees		5,000
General manager		2,000
	Total	$17,000

Further, assume the related payroll taxes were as follows:

Rooms department employees		$1,000
Food department employees		500
General manager		200
	Total	$1,700

Finally, assume the only fringe benefit is health insurance, which is assigned to departments based on coverage of their respective employees:

Rooms department employees		$2,500
Food department employees		1,400
General manager		300
	Total	$4,200

The total labor costs by department would be as follows:

	Rooms Dept.	Food Dept.	General Manager
Salaries/wages	$10,000	$5,000	$2,000
Payroll taxes	1,000	500	200
Fringe benefits	2,500	1,400	300
Totals	$13,500	$6,900	$2,500

A hospitality business normally has separate accounts for each major category by department.

Hospitality businesses record other expenses in selected accounts for each department. Departments that sell goods or services to guests, such as the rooms department, food department, and gift shop, are commonly called **profit centers**. Departments that provide services to profit centers, such as accounting and human resources (personnel), are called **service centers**. Each department has several accounts for recording their various other expenses. These classifications are typically based on the uniform system of accounts (discussed later in this chapter) and facilitate the preparation of the income statement. Several expenses are not directly related to any department and are simply recorded in separate (nondepartmental) accounts. These expenses usually relate to the operation as a whole rather than to individual parts, and include depreciation, interest, insurance, rent, and property taxes.

Gains and Losses

Gains are defined as increases in assets, reductions in liabilities, or a combination of both. Gains result from a hospitality operation's incidental transactions and from all other transactions and events affecting the operation during the period, except those that count as revenue or investments by owners. For example, there may be a gain on the sale of equipment. The business uses equipment to provide goods and services and, when that equipment is sold, only the excess proceeds over its net book value (purchase price less accumulated depreciation) is recognized as gain.

For example, assume a lodging business sold a van that it had used to transport guests to and from the airport for $6,000. Further, assume the van cost $15,000 when purchased and had accumulated depreciation of $10,000. Its net book value would be determined as follows:

Cost	$ 15,000
Accumulated depreciation	− 10,000
Net book value	$ 5,000

The gain on the sale is the result of the selling price exceeding the net book value as follows:

Selling price	$6,000
Net book value	− 5,000
Gain on sale	$1,000

Finally, **losses** are defined as decreases in assets, increases in liabilities, or a combination of both resulting from a hospitality operation's incidental transactions and from other transactions and events affecting the operation during a period, except those that count as expenses or distributions to owners. In the earlier equipment example, if the proceeds were less than the net book value, a loss would occur and would be recorded as "loss on sale of equipment." Another example would be a loss from an "act of nature," such as a tornado or hurricane. The loss reported is the reduction of assets less any insurance proceeds received.

In income statements for hospitality operations, revenues and gains are reported separately, and expenses are distinguished from losses. These distinctions are important in determining management's success in operating the hospitality property. Management is held accountable primarily for operations (revenues and expenses) and only secondarily (if at all) for gains and losses.

Income Taxes

The order of elements of the income statement presented is shown as follows:

    Revenue (sales)
    −   Cost of goods sold
    −   Labor expenses
    −   Other expenses
    =   Operating income
    +   Gains
    −   Losses
    =   Income before taxes

Income tax expense shown on the income statement is based on relevant revenues and expenses on the income statement. Textbooks are written on the topic of income taxes; however, for our purposes it is sufficient to say that the income taxes shown on the income statement are seldom the same taxes shown on the firm's income tax return. The major reason for this is the difference between the accounting method used for financial statement purposes and that for income tax purposes.

For example, consider a hypothetical restaurant company that has $100,000 of pre-depreciation income. Assume that the only additional expense to be considered before the calculation of income taxes is depreciation. However, many companies use accelerated methods of calculating depreciation for tax purposes and the straight-line method for book purposes. Assume that this restaurant firm has $40,000 of depreciation for book purposes based on the straight-line method and $60,000 of depreciation for tax purposes. Then the income tax expense for books and taxes, assuming a tax rate of 25 percent, would be as follows:

	Books	Taxes
Pre-depreciation income	$100,000	$100,000
Depreciation expense	40,000	60,000
Taxable income	60,000	40,000
Tax rate	× .25	× .25
Taxes	$ 15,000	$ 10,000

This restaurant would show $15,000 as income taxes on its income statement and $10,000 due on its tax return. The journal entry to record income taxes would be as follows:

Income Tax Expense	$15,000	
Income Tax Payable		$10,000
Deferred Income Taxes		5,000
To record income taxes for the year.		

The Deferred Income Taxes account is a liability account and will be included on the firm's balance sheet.

Extraordinary Items

In addition to the preceding elements of an income statement, a hospitality firm may very infrequently report an **extraordinary item** on its income statement. Extraordinary items are reported at the bottom of the income statement after income taxes and just above the bottom line of net income.

To show an item as extraordinary, the hospitality firm must meet two major criteria:

1. Unusual nature—the underlying event should possess a high degree of abnormality and be clearly unrelated to the ordinary and typical activities of the hospitality enterprise.

2. Infrequency of occurrence—the underlying event should not reasonably be expected to recur in the foreseeable future.

If an event does not meet both criteria, it is not reported as an extraordinary item. Of course, what is extraordinary for one firm may not be for another. A hotel in California suffering loss from an earthquake may not consider that loss extraordinary, while a Michigan hotel may have a casualty loss from an earthquake that would probably be considered extraordinary.

Extraordinary items are reported net of tax. That is, if an extraordinary loss results in taxes saved, the tax savings are offset against the loss in reporting the loss. For example, consider a hotel that has an extraordinary loss of $40,000 and a tax rate of 25 percent. Because of the $40,000 loss, $10,000 of taxes are saved. The extraordinary loss is shown on the income statement as $30,000.

Earnings per Share

Owners and potential investors of a hospitality enterprise are most interested in the bottom line of the income statement, that is, in net income. However, the net income amount by itself often lacks meaning. To provide a more meaningful number, accountants include **earnings per share**. Earnings per share (EPS) in its simplest form is determined with this equation:

$$\text{EPS} = \frac{\text{Net Income}}{\text{Common Shares Outstanding}}$$

EPS is calculated only for hospitality businesses organized as corporations or limited liability companies, since proprietorships and partnerships do not issue shares of stock. If a firm has types of stock other than common outstanding stock, net income is reduced by the amount of income that "belongs" to non-common stockholders. Further, EPS must be shown on the income statement before extraordinary items and net income.

Income Statements for Internal and External Users

Hospitality properties prepare income statements for both internal users and external users. These statements differ substantially. The income statements provided to external users are relatively brief, providing only summary detail about the results of operations. Exhibit 1 is the income statement presentation of Marriott International, Inc., from its Annual Report for 1997. Marriott's income statement shows the following:

- Sales by segment

- Operating expenses by segment

- Operating profit by segment (sales less operating expenses)

- Corporate expenses

- Interest expense

- Interest income

- Income before income taxes

- Provision for income taxes

- Net income

- Earnings per share

Footnotes, which generally appear after the financial statements in the financial report (but are not included in Exhibit 1), are critical to interpreting the numbers reported on the income statement.

Although the amount of operating information shown in the income statement and accompanying footnotes may be adequate for external users, management requires considerably more information, on a more frequent basis, than outsiders do. In general, the more frequent the need to make decisions, the more frequent the need for financial information. Management's information needs are met, in part, by detailed monthly operating statements that reflect budget numbers and report performance for the most recent period, the same period a year ago, and year-to-date numbers for both the current and the past year.

Many firms in the hospitality industry revise their budgets and show the latest forecast of results if they expect a major difference between the year-to-date numbers and the originally budgeted numbers. Management can then compare actual

Exhibit 1   Income Statement—Marriott International, Inc.

MARRIOTT INTERNATIONAL, INC.   *1997 Annual Report*

Home   Highlights   Letter   Brands   Businesses   Financials   Directors   Awards   Sitemap

COMBINED STATEMENT OF INCOME

Fiscal Years Ended January 2, 1998, January 3, 1997 and December 29, 1995	1997	1996	1995
($ in millions, except per share amounts)	*(52 weeks)*	*(53 weeks)*	*(52 weeks)*
SALES			
Lodging			
Rooms	$4,288	$3,619	$3,273
Food and beverage	1,577	1,361	1,289
Other	1,143	874	765
	7,008	5,854	5,327
Contract Services	2,038	1,413	928
	9,046	7,267	6,255
OPERATING COSTS AND EXPENSES			
Lodging			
Departmental direct costs			
Rooms	964	843	772
Food and beverage	1,195	1,038	973
Remittances to hotel owners (including $541, $438 and $300, respectively, to related parties)	1,493	1,256	1,120
Other operating expenses	2,787	2,265	2,102
	6,439	5,402	4,967
Contract Services	1,998	1,357	898
	8,437	6,759	5,865
OPERATING PROFIT			
Lodging	569	452	360
Contract Services	40	56	30
OPERATING PROFIT BEFORE CORPORATE EXPENSES AND INTEREST	609	508	390
Corporate expenses	(88)	(73)	(59)
Interest expense	(22)	(37)	(9)
Interest income	32	37	39
OPERATING PROFIT BEFORE CORPORATE EXPENSES AND INTEREST	609	508	390
Corporate expenses	(88)	(73)	(59)
Interest expense	(22)	(37)	(9)
Interest income	32	37	39
INCOME BEFORE INCOME TAXES	531	435	361
Provision for income taxes	207	165	142
NET INCOME	$ 324	$ 270	$ 219
EARNINGS PER SHARE			
Pro Forma Basic Earnings Per Share (unaudited)	$ 1.27	$ 1.06	$ .88
Pro Forma Diluted Earnings Per Share (unaudited)	$ 1.19	$ .99	$ .83

Source: http://www.marriott.com

results against the most recent forecasts. In addition to the monthly operating statement, a major report prepared more often for management is the daily report of operations.

Accountants may meet management's need for financial information on a monthly basis, to a large degree, by using an income statement and accompanying departmental income statements as discussed in the various uniform systems of accounts.

Uniform System of Accounts

The **uniform systems of accounts** are standardized accounting systems prepared for various segments of the hospitality industry.[1] A uniform system of accounts provides a turnkey system for new entrants into the hospitality industry by offering detailed information about accounts, classifications, formats, and the different kinds, contents, and uses of financial statements and reports. For example, the *Uniform System of Accounts for the Lodging Industry (USALI)* contains not only the basic financial statements, but also over 25 supplementary departmental operating statements and sections covering budgeting and forecasting, a discussion of compiling revenue by market source, forms of statements, breakeven analysis, and a uniform account numbering system.

The uniform system of accounts also allows for a more reasonable comparison of the operational results of similar hospitality properties. As similar establishments follow a uniform system of accounts, the differences in accounting among these hospitality properties are minimized, thus ensuring comparability.

A uniform system of accounts is a time-tested system. The *Uniform System of Accounts for Hotels (USAH)* was first produced in 1925–26 by a designated group of accountants for the Hotel Association of New York City. Since then, the *USAH* has been revised many times by committees, in the beginning by New York City accountants and, most recently, by accountants from across the United States. The ninth revised edition of the *USALI* was prepared by a select subcommittee of the Financial Management Committee of the American Hotel & Motel Association. During the work on the ninth revision, consultations on changes were made with various other accounting groups including the British Association of Hospitality Accountants.

Finally, the uniform system of accounts can be adapted for use by large and small hospitality operations. The ninth revised edition of the *USALI* illustrated in this chapter contains many more accounts and classifications than a single hotel or motel will generally use. Therefore, each facility simply selects the schedules and accounts that it requires and ignores the others.

The *USALI* is designed to be used at the property level rather than at the corporate level of a hotel. The format of the income statement is based on **responsibility accounting;** that is, the presentation is organized to focus attention on departmental results such as the rooms and food and beverage departments. The income statements prepared at the corporate level, where more than one lodging property is owned by the lodging corporation, would most likely be considerably different. They would likely include sale of properties, corporate overhead expenses, and other items that would not necessarily appear on an individual lodging property's income statement.

Internal Income Statements—A Contribution Approach

The income statement format in the *USALI* approach consists of the following:

	Revenue
Less:	Direct operating expenses
Equals:	Departmental operating income
Less:	Overhead expenses
Equals:	Net income

Revenue less direct operating expenses equals departmental operating income. (**Departmental operating income** is the *contribution* by profit centers to both overhead expenses and net income.) Departmental operating income less overhead expenses equals net income. **Direct operating expenses** include not only the cost of goods sold, but also the direct labor expense and other direct expenses of the profit centers. Direct labor expense is the expense of personnel working in the profit centers, such as the rooms, food, and beverage departments. Other direct expenses include supplies used by these revenue-producing departments.

The income statements based on the *USALI* provide separate line reporting by profit center. Sales and direct expenses are shown separately for the rooms, food, beverage, and telecommunications departments, among others. In addition, the overhead expenses are divided among **undistributed operating expenses** and the group of management fees and **fixed charges**. The undistributed operating expenses are further detailed on the income statement by major service centers such as marketing and information systems. The detail provided by both profit centers and service centers reflects reporting by areas of responsibility and is commonly referred to as *responsibility accounting*.

Thus, the *USALI* income statement is useful to managers in the hospitality industry because it is designed to provide the information necessary to evaluate the performance of managers of the lodging facility by area of responsibility.

Contents of the Income Statement

The income statement per the *USALI* (illustrated in Exhibit 2) is divided into three major sections: Operated Departments, Undistributed Operating Expenses, and a final part that includes management fees, fixed charges, gain or loss on sale of property, and income tax.

The first section, Operated Departments, reports net revenue by department for every major revenue-producing department. Net Revenue results when allowances are subtracted from related revenues. Allowances include refunds and overcharges at the time of sale that are subsequently adjusted. For example, hotel guests may have been charged $100 (rack rate) for their rooms when they should have been charged the group rate of $80. The subsequent adjustment of $20 the following day is treated as an allowance. Revenues earned from activities such as

Exhibit 2   Income Statement per *USALI*

SUMMARY STATEMENT OF INCOME

	SCHEDULE	NET REVENUES	COST OF SALES	PAYROLL AND RELATED EXPENSES	OTHER EXPENSES	INCOME (LOSS)
OPERATED DEPARTMENTS		$	$	$	$	$
Rooms	1					
Food	2					
Beverage	3					
Telecommunications	4					
Garage and Parking	5					
Golf Course	6					
Golf Pro Shop	7					
Guest Laundry	8					
Health Center	9					
Swimming Pool	10					
Tennis	11					
Tennis Pro Shop	12					
Other Operated Departments	13					
Rentals and Other Income	14					
Total Operated Departments						
UNDISTRIBUTED OPERATING EXPENSES[1]						
Administrative and General	15					
Human Resources	16					
Information Systems	17					
Security	18					
Marketing	19					
Franchise Fees	19a					
Transportation	20					
Property Operation and Maintenance	21					
Utility Costs	22					
Total Undistributed Operating Expenses						
TOTALS		$	$	$	$	
INCOME AFTER UNDISTRIBUTED OPERATING EXPENSES						
Management Fees	23					
Rent, Property Taxes, and Insurance	24					
INCOME BEFORE INTEREST, DEPRECIATION AND AMORTIZATION, AND INCOME TAXES[2]						
Interest Expense	25					
INCOME BEFORE DEPRECIATION, AMORTIZATION AND INCOME TAXES						
Depreciation and Amortization	26					
Gain or Loss on Sale of Property						
INCOME BEFORE INCOME TAXES						
Income Taxes	27					
NET INCOME						$

[1] A separate line for preopening expenses can be included if such costs are captured separately.
[2] Also referred to as EBITDA—Earnings before Interest, Taxes, Depreciation and Amortization

Source: *Uniform System of Accounts for the Lodging Industry*, 9th rev. ed. (East Lansing, Mich.: Educational Institute of the American Hotel & Motel Association, 1996), p. 33. ©Hotel Association of New York City.

investments are shown with rentals. If these amounts are significant, they should be reported separately.

Direct expenses are reported for each department generating revenue. These expenses relate directly to the department incurring them and consist of three major categories: Cost of Sales, Payroll and Related Expenses, and Other Expenses. Cost of sales is normally determined as follows:

	Beginning inventory
Plus:	Inventory purchases
Equals:	Goods available for sale
Less:	Ending inventory
Equals:	Cost of goods consumed
Less:	Goods used internally
Equals:	Cost of goods sold

The second major direct expense category of operated departments is Payroll and Related Expenses. This category includes the salaries and wages of employees working in the designated operated departments, such as servers in the food department. Salaries, wages, and related expenses of departments that do not generate revenue but provide service, such as marketing, are recorded by service departments. The "Related Expenses" of "Payroll and Related Expenses" includes all payroll taxes and fringe benefits relating to employees of each operated department. For example, in the rooms department, the front office manager's salary and related payroll taxes and fringe benefits would be included in the Payroll and Related Expenses of the rooms department.

The final major expense category for the operated departments is Other Expenses. This category includes only other direct expenses. For example, the 14 major other expense categories for the rooms department (per the *USALI*) are Cable/Satellite Television, Commissions, Complimentary Guest Services, Contract Services, Guest Relocation, Guest Transportation, Laundry and Dry Cleaning, Linen, Operating Supplies, Reservations, Telecommunications, Training, Uniforms, and Other. Expenses such as Marketing, Administration, and Transportation are recorded as expenses of service departments. They benefit the rooms department and other profit centers but only on an indirect basis.

Net revenue less the sum of cost of sales, payroll and related expenses, and other expenses results in departmental Income or Loss. The departmental income or loss is shown on the income statement (Exhibit 2) for each operated department.

The second major section of the income statement is Undistributed Operating Expenses. This section includes the nine general categories of Administrative and General Expenses, Human Resources, Information Systems, Security, Marketing, Franchise Fees, Transportation, Property Operation and Maintenance, and Utility Costs. These expense categories are related to the various service departments. In the income statement, two of the expense elements—Payroll and Related Expenses, and Other Expenses—are shown for each category. The Administrative and General expense category includes service departments such as the general manager's office and the accounting office. In addition to salaries, wages, and related expenses of service department personnel covered by Administrative and General, other expenses include, but are not limited to, credit card commissions, professional fees, and provision for doubtful accounts. The appendix at the end of this chapter includes *USALI*'s recommended schedule for administrative and general expenses, which details the several expense categories for administrative and general expenses, as well as a complete set of recommended schedules.

The *USALI* recommends a separate departmental accounting of information systems expenses for those lodging operations with significant investments in information systems. As with most other service centers, the two major sections of expense are Payroll and Related Expenses, and Other Expenses. If information systems expenses are not considered significant, the *USALI* recommends that they be included as part of administrative and general expenses.

Another service center for which the *USALI* recommends separate departmental accounting is the human resources department. This schedule includes the labor cost of departmental personnel and other expenses such as employee housing, recruiting expenses, the cost of relocating employees, and training costs.

The fourth service department is security. The purpose of this service department is to provide security services for the lodging facility and the guests. The expenses to be included on the security department schedule include payroll and related expenses and other expenses such as armored car service, operating supplies, safety and lock boxes, and training. If security expenses are not considered significant, then the *USALI* recommends security expenses be included as part of the administrative and general expenses.

Marketing expenses include costs relating to personnel working in marketing areas of sales, advertising, and merchandising. In addition, marketing expenses include advertising and merchandising expenses such as direct mail, in-house graphics, point-of-sale materials, and print, radio, and television advertising. Agency fees and other fees and commissions are also included as marketing expenses. Franchise fees, when applicable and significant, should be listed as a separate line item on the summary statement of income. If the franchise fees are insignificant, they would be included as part of the marketing expenses.

The transportation service department provides transportation services for lodging guests, such as transportation to and from the airport. The expenses to be included on the transportation department schedule include payroll and related expenses, and other expenses such as fuel, operating supplies, and repairs and maintenance. If guest transportation expenses are not considered significant, then the *USALI* recommends transportation expenses be included as part of the rooms department expenses.

The eighth major category of undistributed operating expenses is Property Operation and Maintenance. Included in Property Operation and Maintenance are salaries and related payroll costs of the personnel responsible for property operation and maintenance, and the various supplies used to maintain the buildings, grounds, furniture, fixtures, and equipment.

The final category of undistributed operating expenses is Utility Costs. The recommended schedule includes separate listings of the various utilities, such as electricity and water. Sales by the hotel to tenants and charges to other departments are subtracted in determining net utility costs.

Subtracting the total undistributed operating expenses from the total operated departments income results in Income after Undistributed Operating Expenses.

Many industry personnel continue to refer to this difference between operating revenue and expense as *gross operating profit,* or simply *GOP,* but this is terminology from an earlier edition of *USALI*'s format for the income statement.

Operating management is considered fully responsible for all revenues and expenses reported to this point on the income statement, as they generally have the authority to exercise their judgment to affect all these items. However, the management fees and the fixed charges that follow in the next major section of the income statement are the responsibility primarily of the hospitality property's board of directors. The expenses listed on this part of the statement generally relate directly to decisions by the board, rather than to management decisions.

Management fees are the cost of using an independent management company to operate the hotel or motel. The fixed expenses are also called *capacity costs,* since they relate to the physical plant or the capacity to provide goods and services to guests.

The fixed charges include rent, property taxes, insurance, interest, and depreciation and amortization. Rent includes the cost of renting real estate, computer equipment, and other major items that, had they been purchased instead, would have been recorded as fixed assets. Rental of miscellaneous equipment for specific functions such as banquets is shown as a direct expense of the food and beverage department.

Property taxes include real estate taxes, personal property taxes, business and transient occupation taxes, taxes assessed by utilities, and other taxes (but not income taxes and payroll taxes) that cannot be charged to guests.

Insurance includes the cost of insuring the building and its contents against damage from fire, weather, and similar agents. In addition, the general insurance costs for liability, fidelity, and theft are included in this category.

Interest expense is the cost of borrowing money and is based on the amounts borrowed, the interest rate, and the length of time for which the funds are borrowed. Generally, loans are approved by the operation's board of directors, since most relate to the physical plant. Thus, interest expense is considered a fixed charge.

Depreciation of fixed assets and amortization of other assets are shown on the income statement as fixed charges. The depreciation methods and useful lives of fixed assets are normally disclosed in footnotes.

The income statement per the *USALI* shows gains or losses on the sale of property and equipment. A gain or loss on the sale of property results from a difference between the proceeds from the sale and the carrying value (net book value) of a fixed asset. This item (gain or loss) is included on the *USALI*'s income statement just before income taxes. Gains are added while losses are subtracted in determining Income before Income Taxes.

Finally, Income Taxes are subtracted from Income before Income Taxes to determine Net Income.

Departmental Statements

Departmental statements, which supplement the income statement and are called *schedules,* provide management with detailed information by operated department

Exhibit 3   Rooms Department Schedule—Honeymoon Inn

Honeymoon Inn Rooms For the year ended December 31, 20X1	Schedule 1
Revenue	
Transient—Regular	$ 543,900
Transient—Group	450,000
Permanent	48,000
Other	2,000
Allowances	(2,700)
Net Revenue	1,041,200
Expenses	
Salaries and Wages	159,304
Employee Benefits	26,030
Total Payroll and Related Expenses	185,334
Other Expenses	
Cable/Satellite Television	4,900
Commissions	5,124
Contract Cleaning	3,200
Contract Services	3,100
Laundry and Dry Cleaning	12,706
Linen	9,494
Operating Supplies	12,742
Reservations	9,288
Telecommunications	4,685
Training	4,315
Uniforms	1,400
Other	8,126
Total Other Expenses	79,080
Total Expenses	264,414
Departmental Income	$ 776,786

and service center. The classifications listed in the income statement suggest up to 30 schedules. Each of these schedules is included in the appendix at the end of this chapter.

Exhibit 3 illustrates an operated department schedule using the rooms department of the Honeymoon Inn. The operated department schedule reflects both revenue and direct expenses. Totals from the operated department schedules are reflected on the income statement. In the rooms department illustration, the following totals are carried from the department statement to the property's income statement:

- Net Revenue $1,041,200
- Payroll and Related Expenses $185,334
- Other Expenses $79,080
- Departmental Income $776,786

Exhibit 4   Summary Income Statement—Honeymoon Inn

Honeymoon Inn
Summary Income Statement
For the year ended December 31, 20X1

	Schedule	Net Revenue	Cost of Sales	Payroll and Related Expenses	Other Expense	Income (Loss)
Operated Departments						
Rooms	1	$1,041,200	$ 0	$ 185,334	$ 79,080	$ 776,786
Food	2	420,100	160,048	160,500	44,013	55,539
Beverage	3	206,065	48,400	58,032	22,500	77,133
Telecommunications	4	52,028	46,505	14,317	6,816	(15,610)
Total Operated Departments		1,719,393	254,953	418,183	152,409	893,848
Undistributed Operating Expenses						
Administrative and General	5			47,787	24,934	72,721
Human Resources	6			22,625	4,193	26,818
Information Systems	7			20,421	11,622	32,043
Marketing	8			33,231	33,585	66,816
Transportation	9			13,411	7,460	20,871
Property Operation and Maintenance	10			31,652	49,312	80,964
Utility Costs	11			0	88,752	88,752
Total Undistributed Operating Expenses				169,127	219,858	388,985
Income after Undistributed Operating Expenses		$1,719,393	$254,953	$ 587,310	$372,267	504,863
Rent, Property Taxes, and Insurance	12					200,861
Interest	13					52,148
Depreciation and Amortization	14					115,860
Income before Income Taxes						135,994
Income Tax	15					48,707
Net Income						$ 87,287

Exhibit 4 is the Honeymoon Inn's income statement. The figures from the rooms department schedule are reflected in the top row of figures on the income statement.

In contrast to the profit center schedules prepared by the revenue-producing operated departments of a hospitality operation, a service center schedule reports only expenses by area of responsibility. Although these activity areas do not generate revenue, they do provide service to the operated departments and, in some cases, to other service centers. Exhibit 5 illustrates a service center departmental schedule by using the property operation and maintenance schedule of the Honeymoon Inn. The three numbers that are carried over to the Honeymoon Inn's income statement (Exhibit 4) for this department are total payroll and related expenses of $31,652, other expenses of $49,312, and total expenses of $80,964.

The number and nature of the supporting schedules reported in a lodging facility depends on the size and organization of the establishment.

Uniform System of Accounts for Restaurants

Operations of a commercial food service operation differ from operations of a lodging business or a club and, therefore, the financial information as presented in

Exhibit 5   Property Operation and Maintenance Schedule—Honeymoon Inn

Honeymoon Inn Schedule 10	
Property Operation and Maintenance	
For the year ended December 31, 20X1	
Salaries and Wages	$ 27,790
Employee Benefits	3,862
Total Payroll and Related Expenses	31,652
Other Expenses	
Building Supplies	8,900
Electrical and Mechanical Equipment	8,761
Engineering Supplies	1,981
Furniture, Fixtures, Equipment, and Decor	14,322
Grounds and Landscaping	6,241
Operating Supplies	2,651
Removal of Waste Matter	2,499
Swimming Pool	2,624
Uniforms	652
Other	681
Total	49,312
Total Property Operation and Maintenance	**$ 80,964**

financial statements also differs. The income statement recommended for commercial food service operations is prescribed in the *Uniform System of Accounts for Restaurants (USAR)* published by the National Restaurant Association.

The benefits of the *USAR* are similar to those of the *USALI*. The *USAR*:

- Provides uniform classification and presentation of operating results.

- Allows easier comparisons to food service industry statistics.

- Provides a turnkey accounting system.

- Is a time-tested system prepared by some of the food service industry's best accounting minds.

Exhibit 6 is the statement of income for the hypothetical Steak-Plus Restaurant. As with the *USALI*'s income statement, there are several recommended subsidiary schedules to this statement of income. Although they are not shown here, they provide supplementary information, as do the subsidiary schedules for the *USALI*'s income statement.

The basic similarities and differences between the *USAR*'s and *USALI*'s income statement formats are as follows:

	USALI	*USAR*
Sales segmented	yes	yes
Cost of sales segmented	yes	yes
Payroll and related costs segmented	yes	no

Exhibit 6   *USAR* Summary Statement of Income

Summary Statement of Income
Steak-Plus Restaurant
For the year ended December 31, 20X1

	Exhibit	Amounts	Percentages
Sales:			
Food	D	$1,045,800	75.8%
Beverage	E	333,000	24.2
Total Sales		1,378,800	100.0
Cost of Sales:			
Food		448,000	32.5
Beverage		85,200	6.2
Total Cost of Sales		533,200	38.7
Gross Profit		845,600	61.3
Operating Expenses:			
Salaries and Wages	F	332,200	24.1
Employee Benefits	G	57,440	4.2
Direct Operating Expenses	H	88,400	6.4
Music and Entertainment	I	14,200	1.0
Marketing	J	30,000	2.2
Utility Services	K	37,560	2.7
General and Administrative Expenses	L	56,400	4.1
Repairs and Maintenance	M	28,600	2.1
Occupancy Costs	N	82,200	6.0
Depreciation	N	31,200	2.3
Other Income	O	(5,400)	(0.4)
Total Operating Expenses		752,800	54.6
Operating Income		92,800	6.7
Interest	P	21,600	1.6
Income before Income Taxes		71,200	5.2
Income Taxes		22,000	1.6
Net Income		$ 49,200	3.6%

Other direct costs segmented	yes	no
Controllable expenses separated from fixed charges	yes	yes
Fixed charges segmented	yes	yes

Statement of Retained Earnings

Most businesses include four financial statements in their annual reports: a balance sheet, an income statement, a statement of cash flows, and a statement of retained earnings.

Incorporated businesses typically provide a **statement of retained earnings**, while unincorporated businesses provide a statement of owners' equity.

Exhibit 7   Statement of Retained Earnings—Honeymoon Inn

> **Honeymoon Inn**
> **Statement of Retained Earnings**
> **For the year ended December 31, 20X1**
>
> | | |
> |---|---|
> | January 1, 20X1 balance | $285,000 |
> | Add: Net income for 20X1 | 87,287 |
> | Less: Dividends | 25,000 |
> | Less: Adjustment for failure to record depreciation in prior year | 2,000 |
> | December 31, 20X1 balance | $345,287 |

The statement of retained earnings is a formal statement showing changes in retained earnings during the accounting period. Exhibit 7 shows the statement of retained earnings for the Honeymoon Inn.

Since the statement covers the accounting period of one year in this illustration, the retained earnings balance at the beginning of the period is the first line of the statement. Net income for the period is added; a net loss would be subtracted. Dividends declared during the year, regardless of when they are paid, are subtracted. Dividends become a legal liability of a corporation when they are declared by the corporation's board of directors. At that point, Retained Earnings is reduced (debited) and Dividends Payable is increased (credited). Later, when the dividends are paid, Cash is credited and Dividends Payable is debited.

The next item on the statement of retained earnings is called a **prior period adjustment**. The correction of an error in a financial statement of a prior period is shown on the statement of retained earnings rather than as part of operations for the current year. In our illustration, the Honeymoon Inn failed to record depreciation in the prior period for a piece of equipment it had purchased. The depreciation expense which should have been recorded was $2,000. Therefore, rather than reduce net income for 20X1 when the depreciation relates to the prior year, Retained Earnings is simply reduced. The journal entry to record this prior period adjustment would be as follows:

Retained Earnings	$2,000	
Accumulated Depreciation, Equipment		$2,000
To record depreciation on equipment for the prior year.		

Some corporations provide a statement of stockholders' equity that explains changes in retained earnings and the contributed capital accounts such as Capital Stock, Paid-In Capital in Excess of Par, and Treasury Stock. Exhibit 8 is a statement of stockholders' equity from Marriott Corporation.

Exhibit 8   Statement of Stockholders' Equity—Marriott International, Inc.

MARRIOTT INTERNATIONAL, INC. AND SUBSIDIARIES

Fiscal years ended January 3, 1997, December 29, 1995 and December 30, 1994 (dollars in millions, except per share amounts)

Common shares outstanding *(millions)*		Common stock	Additional paid-in capital	Retained earnings	Treasury stock, at cost
125.7	Balance, December 31, 1993	$126	$ 552	$ 18	$ —
—	Net income	—	—	200	—
3.1	Employee stock plan issuance and other	2	55	—	22
—	Dividends ($.28 per share)	—	—	(35)	—
.7	Conversion of debt	1	16	—	—
(7.0)	Purchases of treasury stock	—	—	—	(190)
122.5	Balance, December 30, 1994	129	623	183	(168)
—	Net income	—	—	247	—
3.4	Employee stock plan issuance and other	—	(6)	—	97
—	Dividends ($.28 per share)	—	—	(35)	—
(.4)	Purchases of treasury stock	—	—	—	(16)
125.5	Balance, December 29, 1995	129	617	395	(87)
—	Net income	—	—	306	—
3.4	Employee stock plan issuance and other	—	36	(32)	100
—	Dividends ($.32 per share)	—	—	(41)	—
(3.0)	Purchases of treasury stock	—	—	—	(163)
125.9	Balance, January 3, 1997	$129	$ 653	$628	$ (150)

See notes to consolidated financial statements.

Courtesy of Marriott International, Inc.

Summary

The income statement, complete with all departmental statements, is considered the most useful financial statement for management. It reports sales and expenses that ideally result in net income, but sometimes in a net loss, for the period. The income statement has different uses for different groups of people. External users such as creditors and potential investors need general information about profitability, sales, and some expenses. Internal users such as managers need detailed information so they can manage operations.

The income statement shows four major elements: revenues, expenses, gains, and losses. Revenues (increases in assets or decreases in liability accounts) and expenses (decreases in assets or increases in liability accounts) are directly related to operations while gains and losses result from transactions incidental to the property's major operations.

The original *Uniform System of Accounts for Hotels* was written in 1925–26 to standardize income statements within the hospitality industry. Changes and revisions have been made since then, the most recent being the ninth revised edition of the *Uniform System of Accounts for the Lodging Industry (USALI)*, published in 1996. A uniform system of accounts provides a turnkey accounting system for a complete and systematic accounting for the hotel's operations. The various uniform systems also facilitate comparison among large and small hospitality operations.

To enhance the usefulness of the income statement, the format set up by the *USALI* includes statements of departmental income showing the revenues produced by each profit center (operated department) and subtracting from each the corresponding direct operating expenses. Included in the direct operating expenses are the cost of goods sold, the direct payroll, and other direct expenses. Next, undistributed operating expenses, which consist of nine major service center categories—Administrative and General Expenses, Human Resources, Information Systems, Security, Marketing, Franchise Fees, Transportation, Property Operation and Maintenance, and Utility Costs—must be subtracted to determine Income after Undistributed Operating Expenses. This is followed by management fees and fixed charges (rent, property taxes, insurance, interest, and depreciation and amortization). Next, gains (losses) on the sale of property and equipment are added (subtracted) to determine Income before Income Taxes. Finally, income taxes are subtracted, resulting in Net Income.

Departmental income statements supplement the income statement and are called *schedules*. They provide management with detailed information by operated department and service center. The number and nature of the supporting schedules that a firm uses depend on the size and organization of the firm.

The statement of retained earnings is a formal statement that shows the changes in owners' equity during the accounting period. It is through the retained earnings account that the impact of the income statement is shown on the balance sheet. This statement is prepared for companies that are incorporated, as opposed to proprietorships, which prepare a statement of owners' equity.

Endnotes

1. Uniform systems of accounts are available as follows:

     Uniform System of Accounts for the Lodging Industry, 9th rev. ed. (East Lansing, Mich.: Educational Institute of the American Hotel & Motel Association, 1996). © Hotel Association of New York City, Inc.

     Uniform System of Financial Reporting for Clubs (Washington, D.C.: Club Managers Association of America, 1996).

     Uniform System of Accounts for Restaurants, 7th rev. ed. (Washington, D.C.: National Restaurant Association, 1996).

 # Key Terms

cost of goods sold—The cost of the products that are sold in the operation of the business.

departmental operating income—The difference between an operating department's revenue and direct expenses.

departmental statements—Supplements to the income statement that provide management with detailed financial information by operating department and service center; also referred to as *schedules*.

direct operating expenses—Expenses related directly to the department incurring them and consisting of cost of sales, payroll and related expenses, and other expenses.

earnings per share (EPS)—A ratio providing a general indicator of the profitability of a hospitality operation by comparing net income to the average common shares outstanding. If preferred stock has been issued, preferred dividends are subtracted from net income before calculating EPS.

external users of financial statements—Creditors, potential investors, and passive owners of a business who need general information regarding sales, expenses, assets, and liabilities.

extraordinary item—An item (usually a loss) reported at the end of the income statement that is both highly unusual and also highly infrequent in occurrence.

fixed charges—A category of expenses reported on the income statement that relates to decisions outside the area of control of operating management and consisting of rent, property taxes, insurance, interest, and depreciation and amortization.

gains—Increases in assets, reductions in liabilities, or a combination of both, resulting from a hospitality operation's incidental transactions and from all other transactions and events affecting the operation during the period, except those that count as revenues or investments by owners.

income statement—A report on the profitability of operations, including revenues earned and expenses incurred in generating the revenues for the period of time covered by the statement.

internal users of financial statements—The managers of the hospitality firm who need detailed information to most effectively run daily operations.

losses—Decreases in assets, increases in liabilities, or a combination of both, resulting from a hospitality operation's incidental transactions and from the other transactions and events affecting the operation during a period, except those that count as expenses or distributions to owners.

management fees—The cost of using an independent management company to manage the hospitality operation.

prior period adjustment—The correction of an error in a financial statement from a prior period, shown on the statement of retained earnings.

profit center—An operating department within a hospitality operation that generates revenues and incurs expenses.

responsibility accounting—The organization of accounting information (as on an income statement) that focuses attention on departmental results such as the rooms, food, and beverage departments.

service center—A department within a hospitality operation that is not directly involved in generating revenue but that provides supporting services to revenue-generating departments within the operation.

statement of retained earnings—A formal statement that is prepared for an incorporated business and that shows changes in retained earnings during the accounting period.

undistributed operating expenses—Expenses not directly related to income-generating departments and consisting of Administrative and General Expenses, Human Resources, Information Systems, Security, Marketing, Franchise Fees, Transportation, Property Operation and Maintenance, and Utility Costs.

uniform system of accounts—Standardized accounting systems prepared by various segments of the hospitality industry offering detailed information about accounts, classifications, formats, the different kinds, contents, and uses of financial statements and reports, and other useful information.

 Review Questions ———————————————————

1. Why are internal and external users interested in the income statement?

2. What is the relationship between the income statement and the balance sheet?

3. How do accountants treat employee meals, transfers, and promotional meals when determining cost of food sold?

4. What are three examples of departmental operating expenses for the rooms department?

5. Why are certain kinds of expenses classified as fixed?

6. What are the characteristics of direct expenses and undistributed operating expenses?

7. What are the advantages of a uniform system of accounts?

8. What is the purpose of separate departmental schedules or statements?

9. What is the difference between a profit center and a service center?

10. What are the rules for declaring an extraordinary item? How might the guidelines change for different hotels in different locations?

 Problems ———————————————————————————

Problem 1

The following is information for the Texas Two-Step Bar and Grill.

Purchases	$57,900
Food Inventory Beginning of Year—20X3	1,160
Food Inventory End of Year—20X3	1,450
Transfers from the Bar to Kitchen	95
Employee Meals	732
Transfers from Kitchen to Bar	50
Promotional Meals	432

Required:

Using the information provided, calculate the cost of food sold for 20X3.

Problem 2

The New York Strip Steak House is undergoing renovation. A consulting firm has recommended that the NYS Steak House replace its old ovens and grills with new ones that will make the kitchen more efficient.

The old equipment was purchased 10 years ago for $35,000. The annual depreciation was $2,500.

The consulting firm has found a buyer who is interested in the ovens and grills and who will pay $13,000 cash for them.

The new equipment will cost $75,000.

Required:

Using the information provided, determine the amount of gain or loss on the sale that will be incurred if the NYS Steak House takes the consulting firm's advice and replaces the ovens and grills.

Problem 3

The Southwest Hotel issues a full set of financial statements annually to its stockholders. Buzz Barr, the chief accountant, has provided you with the following information:

Retained earnings account balances:

December 31, 20X1	$150,000
December 31, 20X2	$200,000

Sale of capital stock:

20X2	$10,000
20X3	$15,000

Dividends *declared*:

20X2	$20,000
20X3	$30,000

Dividends *paid*:

20X2	$15,000
20X3	$25,000

Operating results:

20X2 net income	$70,000
20X3 net loss	$10,000

Required:

Using the information provided, prepare statements of retained earnings for 20X2 and 20X3.

Problem 4

The Upper Room Inn (URI), an incorporated lodging operation, prepares its income tax return using the same information as it shows on its annual report to its owners with the exception of depreciation. The pre-depreciation income of the URI for 20X2 is $200,000. Assume that depreciation expenses for book and tax purposes are $50,000 and $100,000, respectively. Further assume the relevant tax rate is 25 percent.

Required:

Determine the amount of taxes (1) to be shown in its annual report, (2) to be shown on its tax return, and (3) to be recorded as deferred taxes.

Problem 5

Lisa Brandt is the owner of Brandt's Bed and Breakfast. Even though she runs a small operation, Lisa still likes to use the *USALI*. The following are some accounts pertaining to the rooms division of her business.

Salaries and Wages	$16,560
Operating Supplies	2,484
Linen	500
Sales	82,800
Laundry	5,500
Commissions	700
Dry Cleaning	120
Uniforms	200

In addition, Lisa's fringe benefits and payroll taxes are 30 percent of Salaries and Wages. She incurs other expenses of 2 percent of sales.

Required:

Prepare a rooms department schedule for Brandt's Bed and Breakfast according to the *USALI*.

Problem 6

The following are several accounts and balances from the general ledger of the Hilltop Motel.

Allowances—Rooms	$ 500
Commissions	1,000
Contract Cleaning	1,800
Dry Cleaning	1,200
Fringe Benefits	3,000
Laundry	3,000
Linen Expense	1,000
Operating Supplies	1,500
Other Expenses	1,800
Payroll Taxes	2,000
Salaries	10,000

Sales—Transient—Group	50,000
Sales—Transient—Regular	100,000
Uniforms	500
Wages	15,000

Required:

Prepare a rooms department schedule following the *USALI*.

Problem 7

The following are several accounts and balances from the general ledger of the Shifting Sands Casino and Hotel that pertain to property operation and maintenance.

Building Supplies	$ 1,125
Operating Supplies	11,250
Furniture	5,250
Uniforms	300
Employee Benefits	18,750
Grounds and Landscaping	6,750
Other	750
Engineering Supplies	4,050
Swimming Pool	4,725
Removal of Waste Matter	3,720
Salaries and Wages	75,000
Electrical and Mechanical Equipment	12,000

Required:

Prepare a property operation and maintenance schedule following the *USALI* for the month ended July 31, 20X4.

Challenge Problems

Problem 8

Goran Blomberg is interested in investing in a new rooms-only lodging property. He needs some financial projections for a single year for the proposed operations. He provides the following:

1. Room sales:
   a. Average room rate—$50
   b. Average daily occupancy—65%
   c. Available rooms per day—50

2. A&G fixed labor—$12,000/month

3. Variable expenses (as a % of total room sales):
   a. Rooms labor—20%
   b. Rooms other expense—10%

    c. A&G other—3%
    d. Marketing—5%
    e. Maintenance—5%

4. Other fixed expenses:
    a. Depreciation—$5,000/month
    b. Utilities—$3,000/month
    c. Insurance—$1,000/month
    d. Property taxes—$2,000 for the year
    e. Maintenance—$500/month

5. Income tax rate—20 percent (as a percentage of income before taxes).

6. Assume the property will be open 365 days of the year.

Required:

Prepare an income statement in accordance with the *USALI*.

Problem 9

The general ledger of Ramsey's, a 100-seat restaurant, as of December 31, 20X3, includes revenue and expense accounts as follows:

Salaries	$ 150,000
Wages	280,000
Payroll Taxes	30,000
Fringe Benefits (excludes employee meals)	50,000
Employee Meals	5,000
Food Sales	1,200,000
Beverage Sales	500,000
Food Purchases	460,000
Beverage Purchases	130,000
Other Sales	20,000
Direct Operating Expenses	100,000
Music	20,000
Marketing	30,000
Heat, Light, and Power	35,000
Rent	152,000
Interest Expense	20,000
Depreciation	50,000
Repairs	30,000
Administrative & General	92,000

Other information is as follows: Income tax rate—30 percent on pretax income

Inventories	1/1/X3	12/31/X3
Food	$20,000	$22,000
Beverage	15,000	17,000

Required:

Prepare Ramsey's income statement for 20X3 in accordance with the *USAR*.

Problem 10

The Wilson Motel has two major operated departments: Rooms and Food. The following information is supplied as of December 31, 20X6:

Account	Account Balance
Insurance (Fire)	$ 5,000
Rooms Department—Salaries and Wages	80,000
Food Department—Salaries and Wages	60,000
Other Expenses—Food Department	20,000
Food Purchases	55,000
Rooms Sales	380,000
Interest Income	1,000
Interest Expense	?
Cost of Food Sold	?
Food Sales	180,000
Administrative & General—Wages	50,000
Advertising	10,000
Maintenance—Expenses	30,000
Depreciation	50,000
Heat	15,000
Power and Lights	12,000
Amortization of Franchise Fee	2,000
Supplies and Other—Rooms Department	30,000
Property Taxes	12,000
Administrative & General—Other Expense	10,000

Other information is as follows:

1. The Wilson Motel borrowed $50,000 on January 1, 20X6 at 10 percent, and no payments were made during 20X6.
2. The beginning and ending inventories of food were $2,000 and $3,000, respectively. Food consumed by the Food and Rooms department employees during the year (free of charge) totaled $500 and $300, respectively.
3. Fringe benefits and payroll taxes for all employees, excluding free food, are 20 percent of gross salaries and wages.
4. The Wilson Motel's average income tax rate is 25 percent of pretax income.
5. The management fee to be paid to the management company is 3 percent of room sales and 10 percent of total income before management fees and fixed charges.

Required:

Prepare an income statement in accordance with the *USALI*.

Chapter Appendix:
Departmental Schedules from the
Uniform System of Accounts for the Lodging Industry

ROOMS

Rooms—Schedule 1

	Current Period
REVENUE	$
ALLOWANCES	————
NET REVENUE	
EXPENSES	
Salaries and Wages	
Employee Benefits	————
Total Payroll and Related Expenses	————
Other Expenses	
Cable/Satellite Television	
Commissions	
Complimentary Guest Services	
Contract Services	
Guest Relocation	
Guest Transportation	
Laundry and Dry Cleaning	
Linen	
Operating Supplies	
Reservations	
Telecommunications	
Training	
Uniforms	
Other	
Total Other Expenses	————
TOTAL EXPENSES	————
DEPARTMENTAL INCOME (LOSS)	$ ————

FOOD

Food—Schedule 2

	Current Period
TOTAL REVENUE	$ _____
REVENUE	$
ALLOWANCES	_____
NET REVENUE	
COST OF SALES	
Cost of Food	
Less Cost of Employee Meals	
Less Food Transfers to Beverage	
Plus Beverage Transfers to Food	
Net Cost of Food	_____
Other Cost of Sales	_____
Total Cost of Sales	_____
GROSS PROFIT (LOSS) ON FOOD SALES	
OTHER INCOME	
Meeting Room Rentals	
Miscellaneous Banquet Income	
Service Charges	_____
Total Other Income	_____
GROSS PROFIT (LOSS) AND OTHER INCOME	
EXPENSES	
Salaries and Wages	
Employee Benefits	_____
Total Payroll and Related Expenses	_____
Other Expenses	
China, Glassware, Silver, and Linen	
Contract Services	
Laundry and Dry Cleaning	
Licenses	
Miscellaneous Banquet Expense	
Music and Entertainment	
Operating Supplies	
Telecommunications	
Training	
Uniforms	
Other	_____
Total Other Expenses	_____
TOTAL EXPENSES	_____
DEPARTMENTAL INCOME (LOSS)	$ _____

BEVERAGE

Beverage—Schedule 3	Current Period
TOTAL REVENUE	$ _____
REVENUE	$
ALLOWANCES	_____
NET REVENUE	
COST OF SALES	
Cost of Beverage	
Less Beverage Transfers to Food	
Plus Food Transfers to Beverage	
Net Cost of Beverage	_____
Other Cost of Sales	_____
Total Cost of Sales	_____
GROSS PROFIT (LOSS) ON BEVERAGE SALES	
OTHER INCOME	
Cover Charges	
Service Charges	
Total Other Income	_____
	_____
GROSS PROFIT (LOSS) AND OTHER INCOME	
EXPENSES	
Salaries and Wages	
Employee Benefits	
Total Payroll and Related Expenses	_____
Other Expenses	
China, Glassware, Silver, and Linen	
Contract Services	
Gratis Food	
Laundry and Dry Cleaning	
Licenses	
Music and Entertainment	
Operating Supplies	
Telecommunications	
Training	
Uniforms	
Other	_____
Total Other Expenses	_____
TOTAL EXPENSES	_____
DEPARTMENTAL INCOME (LOSS)	$ _____

TELECOMMUNICATIONS

Telecommunications—Schedule 4

	Current Period
REVENUE	$
ALLOWANCES	————
NET REVENUE	
COST OF CALLS	
Long-Distance	
Local	
Utility Tax	
Other	————
Total Cost of Calls	
GROSS PROFIT (LOSS)	
EXPENSES	
Salaries and Wages	
Employee Benefits	————
Total Payroll and Related Expenses	————
Other Expenses	
Contract Services	
Printing and Stationery	
Telecommunications	
Training	
Other	————
Total Other Expenses	————
TOTAL EXPENSES	————
DEPARTMENTAL INCOME (LOSS)	$ ════

GARAGE AND PARKING

Garage and Parking—Schedule 5

	Current Period
REVENUE	$
ALLOWANCES	_____
NET REVENUE	
COST OF MERCHANDISE SOLD	_____
GROSS PROFIT (LOSS)	
EXPENSES	
Salaries and Wages	
Employee Benefits	_____
Total Payroll and Related Expenses	_____
Other Expenses	
Contract Services	
Licenses	
Management Fee	
Operating Supplies	
Telecommunications	
Training	
Uniforms	
Other	_____
Total Other Expenses	_____
TOTAL EXPENSES	_____
DEPARTMENTAL INCOME (LOSS)	$ _____

GOLF COURSE

Golf Course—Schedule 6

	Current Period
REVENUE	$
ALLOWANCES	_____
NET REVENUE	
EXPENSES, EXCLUDING COURSE MAINTENANCE	
Salaries and Wages	
Employee Benefits	_____
Total Payroll and Related Expenses	_____
Other Expenses	
Contract Services	
Gasoline and Lubricants	
Golf Car Batteries/Electricity	
Golf Car Repairs and Maintenance	
Laundry and Dry Cleaning	
Operating Supplies	
Professional Services	
Telecommunications	
Tournament Expenses	
Training	
Other	_____
Total Other Expenses	_____
TOTAL EXPENSES EXCLUDING COURSE MAINTENANCE	_____
COURSE MAINTENANCE EXPENSES	
Salaries and Wages	
Employee Benefits	_____
Total Payroll and Related Expenses	_____
Other Expenses	
Contract Services	
Fertilizers, Insecticides, and Topsoil	
Gasoline and Lubricants	
Repairs and Maintenance	
General	
Irrigation	
Machinery and Equipment	
Refuse Removal	
Sand and Top Dressing	
Seeds, Flowers, and Shrubs	
Telecommunications	
Training	
Uniforms	
Water	
Other	_____
Total Other Expenses	_____
TOTAL COURSE MAINTENANCE EXPENSES	_____
TOTAL GOLF COURSE EXPENSES	_____
DEPARTMENTAL INCOME (LOSS)	$ _____

GOLF PRO SHOP

Golf Pro Shop—Schedule 7

	Current Period
TOTAL REVENUE	$ _____
REVENUE	$ _____
ALLOWANCES	
NET REVENUE	
COST OF MERCHANDISE SOLD	_____
GROSS PROFIT (LOSS)	
OTHER INCOME	
GROSS PROFIT (LOSS) AND OTHER INCOME	
EXPENSES	
Salaries and Wages	
Employee Benefits	_____
Total Payroll and Related Expenses	_____
Other Expenses	
Contract Services	
Operating Supplies	
Telecommunications	
Training	
Other	_____
Total Other Expenses	_____
TOTAL EXPENSES	_____
DEPARTMENTAL INCOME (LOSS)	$ _____

GUEST LAUNDRY

Guest Laundry—Schedule 8a

	Current Period
REVENUE	$
ALLOWANCES	_____
NET REVENUE	
EXPENSES	
Salaries and Wages	
Employee Benefits	
Total Payroll and Related Expenses	_____
Other Expenses	_____
Contract Services	
Laundry Supplies	
Operating Supplies	
Telecommunications	
Training	
Uniforms	
Other	
Total Other Expenses	_____
TOTAL EXPENSES	_____
DEPARTMENTAL INCOME (LOSS)	$ _____

Guest Laundry—Schedule 8b
(where only one laundry is operated)

REVENUE	$
ALLOWANCES	_____
NET REVENUE	
COST OF LAUNDERING	_____
DEPARTMENTAL INCOME (LOSS)	$ _____

HEALTH CENTER

Health Center—Schedule 9

	Current Period
REVENUE	$
ALLOWANCES	————
NET REVENUE	
COST OF MERCHANDISE SOLD	————
GROSS PROFIT (LOSS)	
EXPENSES	
Salaries and Wages	
Employee Benefits	————
Total Payroll and Related Expenses	————
Other Expenses	
Contract Services	
Laundry and Dry Cleaning	
Licenses	
Linen	
Maintenance	
Operating Supplies	
Professional Services	
Telecommunications	
Training	
Uniforms	
Other	————
Total Other Expenses	————
TOTAL EXPENSES	————
DEPARTMENTAL INCOME (LOSS)	$ ════

SWIMMING POOL

Swimming Pool—Schedule 10

	Current Period
REVENUE	$
ALLOWANCES	_____
NET REVENUE	
EXPENSES	
Salaries and Wages	
Employee Benefits	_____
Total Payroll and Related Expenses	_____
Other Expenses	
Chemicals	
Contract Services	
Laundry and Dry Cleaning	
Linen	
Operating Supplies	
Professional Services	
Telecommunications	
Training	
Uniforms	
Other	_____
Total Other Expenses	_____
TOTAL EXPENSES	_____
DEPARTMENTAL INCOME (LOSS)	$ _____

TENNIS

Tennis—Schedule 11	
	Current Period
REVENUE	$
ALLOWANCES	————
NET REVENUE	
EXPENSES	
Salaries and Wages	
Employee Benefits	————
Total Payroll and Related Expenses	————
Other Expenses	
Contract Services	
Court Maintenance	
Nets and Tapes	
Operating Supplies	
Professional Services	
Telecommunications	
Tournament Expense	
Training	
Other	————
Total Other Expenses	————
TOTAL EXPENSES	————
DEPARTMENTAL INCOME (LOSS)	$ ════

TENNIS PRO SHOP

Tennis Pro Shop—Schedule 12

	Current Period
REVENUE	$
ALLOWANCES	_____
NET REVENUE	
COST OF MERCHANDISE SOLD	_____
GROSS PROFIT (LOSS)	
OTHER INCOME	
GROSS PROFIT (LOSS) AND OTHER INCOME	
EXPENSES	
Salaries and Wages	
Employee Benefits	_____
Total Payroll and Related Expenses	_____
Other Expenses	
Contract Services	
Operating Supplies	
Telecommunications	
Training	
Other	_____
Total Other Expenses	_____
TOTAL EXPENSES	_____
DEPARTMENTAL INCOME (LOSS)	$ _____

OTHER OPERATED DEPARTMENTS

Other Operated Departments—Schedule 13

	Current Period
REVENUE	$
ALLOWANCES	_____
NET REVENUE	
COST OF MERCHANDISE SOLD	_____
GROSS PROFIT (LOSS)	
PAYROLL AND RELATED EXPENSES	
Salaries and Wages	
Employee Benefits	_____
Total Payroll and Related Expenses	_____
Other Expenses	
China and Glassware	
Contract Services	
Laundry	
Linen	
Operating Supplies	
Telecommunications	
Training	
Uniforms	
Other	_____
Total Other Expenses	_____
TOTAL EXPENSES	_____
DEPARTMENTAL INCOME (LOSS)	$ _____

RENTALS AND OTHER INCOME

Rentals and Other Income—Schedule 14

	Current Period
Space Rentals and Concessions	$ _____
Commissions	
Cash Discounts Earned	
Cancellation Penalty	
Foreign Currency Transactions Gains (Losses)	
Interest Income	
Other	_____
TOTAL RENTALS AND OTHER INCOME	$ _____

ADMINISTRATIVE AND GENERAL

Administrative and General—Schedule 15

	Current Period
PAYROLL AND RELATED EXPENSES	
Salaries and Wages	$
Employee Benefits	_____
Total Payroll and Related Expenses	_____
OTHER EXPENSES	
Bank Charges	
Cash Overages and Shortages	
Communication Systems	
Contract Services	
Credit and Collection	
Credit Card Commissions	
Donations	
Dues and Subscriptions	
Head Office	
Human Resources	
Information Systems	
Internal Audit	
Internal Communications	
Loss and Damage	
Meals and Entertainment	
Operating Supplies and Equipment	
Postage	
Printing and Stationery	
Professional Fees	
Provision for Doubtful Accounts	
Security	
Telecommunications	
Training	
Transportation	
Travel	
Other	_____
Total Other Expenses	_____
TOTAL ADMINISTRATIVE AND GENERAL EXPENSES	$ _____

HUMAN RESOURCES

Human Resources—Schedule 16

	Current Period
PAYROLL AND RELATED EXPENSES	
Salaries and Wages	$ _____
Employee Benefits	_____
Total Payroll and Related Expenses	_____
OTHER EXPENSES	
Contract Services	
Dues and Subscriptions	
Employee Housing	
Employee Relations	
Medical Expenses	
Operating Supplies and Equipment	
Printing and Stationery	
Recruitment	
Relocation	
Telecommunications	
Training	
Transportation	
Other	_____
Total Other Expenses	_____
TOTAL HUMAN RESOURCES EXPENSES	$ _____

INFORMATION SYSTEMS

Information Systems—Schedule 17

	Current Period
PAYROLL AND RELATED EXPENSES	
Salaries and Wages	$ _____
Employee Benefits	_____
Total Payroll and Related Expenses	_____
OTHER EXPENSES	
Contract Services	
Equipment Maintenance	
Operating Supplies	
Printing and Stationery	
Software—Commercial Applications	
Telecommunications	
Training	
Other	_____
Total Other Expenses	_____
TOTAL INFORMATION SYSTEM EXPENSES	$ _____

SECURITY

Security—Schedule 18

	Current Period
PAYROLL AND RELATED EXPENSES	$
Salaries and Wages	
Employee Benefits	_____
Total Payroll and Related Expenses	_____
OTHER EXPENSES	
Armored Car Service	
Contract Services	
Operating Supplies	
Safety and Lock Boxes	
Telecommunications	
Training	
Uniforms	
Other	_____
Total Other Expenses	_____
TOTAL SECURITY EXPENSES	$ _____

MARKETING AND FRANCHISE FEES

Marketing—Schedule 19

	Current Period
SELLING	
PAYROLL AND RELATED EXPENSES	
Salaries and Wages	$
Employee Benefits	
Total Payroll and Related Expenses	
OTHER EXPENSES	
Complimentary Guests	
Contract Services	
Dues and Subscriptions	
Meals and Entertainment	
Printing and Stationery	
Postage	
Trade Shows	
Telecommunications	
Training	
Travel	
Other	
Total Other Expenses	
TOTAL SELLING EXPENSES	
ADVERTISING AND MERCHANDISING	
PAYROLL AND RELATED EXPENSES	
Salaries and Wages	
Employee Benefits	
Total Payroll and Related Expenses	
OTHER EXPENSES	
Collateral Material	
Contract Services	
Direct Mail	
Frequent Stay Programs	
In-House Graphics	
Media	
Outdoor	
Point-of-Sale Material	
Special Promotional Vouchers	
Telecommunications	
Other	
Total Other Expenses	
TOTAL ADVERTISING AND MERCHANDISING EXPENSES	
FEES AND COMMISSIONS	
Agency Fees	
Other	
Total Fees and Commissions	
OTHER MARKETING EXPENSES	
TOTAL MARKETING EXPENSES	$

Franchise Fees—Schedule 19a

	Current Period
FRANCHISE FEES	$ _____

TRANSPORTATION

Transportation—Schedule 20

	Current Period
PAYROLL AND RELATED EXPENSES	
Salaries and Wages	$
Employee Benefits	_____
Total Payroll and Related Expenses	_____
OTHER EXPENSES	
Contract Services	
Fuel and Oil	
Insurance	
Operating Supplies	
Repairs and Maintenance	
Telecommunications	
Training	
Uniforms	
Other	_____
Total Other Expenses	_____
TOTAL TRANSPORTATION EXPENSES	$ _____

PROPERTY OPERATION AND MAINTENANCE

Property Operation and Maintenance—Schedule 21

	Current Period
PAYROLL AND RELATED EXPENSES	
Salaries and Wages	$
Employee Benefits	_____
Total Payroll and Related Expenses	_____
OTHER EXPENSES	
Building Supplies	
Contract Services	
Curtains and Draperies	
Electrical and Mechanical Equipment	
Elevators	
Engineering Supplies	
Floor Covering	
Furniture	
Grounds and Landscaping	
Heating, Ventilating, and Air Conditioning Equipment	
Kitchen Equipment	
Laundry Equipment	
Life/Safety	
Light Bulbs	
Locks and Keys	
Operating Supplies	
Painting and Decorating	
Removal of Waste Matter	
Swimming Pool	
Telecommunications	
Training	
Uniforms	
Vehicle Maintenance	
Other	_____
Total Other Expenses	_____
TOTAL PROPERTY OPERATION AND MAINTENANCE EXPENSES	$ _____

UTILITY COSTS

Utility Costs—Schedule 22

	Current Period
UTILITY COSTS	
Electricity	$
Gas	
Oil	
Steam	
Water	
Other Fuels	_____
Total Utility Costs	
RECOVERIES	
Recoveries from other entities	
Charges to other departments	_____
Total Recoveries	_____
NET UTILITY COSTS	$ ========

MANAGEMENT FEES

Management Fees—Schedule 23

	Current Period
BASE FEES	$ _____
INCENTIVE FEES	_____
TOTAL MANAGEMENT FEES	$ ========

RENT, PROPERTY TAXES, AND INSURANCE

Rent, Property Taxes, and Insurance—Schedule 24	
	Current Period
RENT	
Land and Buildings	$
Information Systems Equipment	
Telecommunications Equipment	
Other Property and Equipment	
Total Rent Expense	————
PROPERTY TAXES	
Real Estate Taxes	
Personal Property Taxes	
Business and Transient Occupation Taxes	
Utility Taxes	
Other	————
Total Property Tax Expense	
INSURANCE	
Building and Contents	
Liability	————
Total Insurance	————
TOTAL RENT, PROPERTY TAXES, AND INSURANCE	$ ————

INTEREST EXPENSE

Interest Expense—Schedule 25	
	Current Period
Amortization of Deferred Financing Costs	$
Mortgages	
Notes Payable	
Obligation Under Capital Leases	
Other Long-term Debt	
Other	————
TOTAL INTEREST EXPENSE	$ ————

DEPRECIATION AND AMORTIZATION

Depreciation and Amortization—Schedule 26

	Current Period
Assets Held Under Capital Leases	$
Buildings	
Furnishings and Equipment	
Leaseholds and Leasehold Improvements	
Intangibles	
Other	_____
TOTAL DEPRECIATION AND AMORTIZATION	$ =========

INCOME TAXES

Federal and State Income Taxes—Schedule 27

	Current Period
FEDERAL	
Current	
Deferred	$ _____
Total Federal	_____
STATE	
Current	_____
Deferred	_____
Total State	
TOTAL FEDERAL AND STATE INCOME TAXES	$ =========

HOUSE LAUNDRY

House Laundry—Schedule 28

		Current Period
PAYROLL AND RELATED EXPENSES		
Salaries and Wages		$ _____
Employee Benefits		_____
Total Payroll and Related Expenses		_____
OTHER EXPENSES		
Cleaning Supplies		
Contract Services		
Laundry Supplies		
Printing and Stationery		
Telecommunications		
Training		
Uniforms		
Other		_____
Total Other Expenses		_____
TOTAL EXPENSES		
CREDITS		
Cost of Guest and Outside Laundry		
Concessionaires' Laundry		
Total Credits		_____
COST OF HOUSE LAUNDRY		_____
CHARGED TO:		
Rooms	Schedule 1	
Food	Schedule 2	
Beverage	Schedule 3	
Golf Course	Schedule 6	
Health Center	Schedule 9	
Swimming Pool	Schedule 10	
Other Operated Departments	Schedule 13	_____
Total		$ _____

SALARIES AND WAGES

Salaries and Wages—Schedule 29

	Number of Employees or Full-Time Equivalents	Current Period
ROOMS		
Management		$
Front Office		
House Attendants		
Housekeeper and Assistants		
Linen Control		
Reservations		
Service		
Total Rooms (Schedule 1)		
FOOD		
Management		
Food Preparation		
Food Service		
Restaurants		
Banquets		
Room Service		
Food General		
Total Food (Schedule 2)		
BEVERAGE		
Management		
Beverage Service		
Lounges		
Banquets		
Mini-Bars		
Total Beverage (Schedule 3)		
TELECOMMUNICATIONS (Schedule 4)		
GARAGE AND PARKING (Schedule 5)		
GOLF COURSE (Schedule 6)		
GOLF PRO SHOP (Schedule 7)		
GUEST LAUNDRY (Schedule 8)		
HEALTH CENTER (Schedule 9)		
SWIMMING POOL (Schedule 10)		
TENNIS (Schedule 11)		
TENNIS PRO SHOP (Schedule 12)		
OTHER OPERATED DEPARTMENTS (Schedule 13)		
ADMINISTRATIVE AND GENERAL		
Manager's Office		
Finance		
Accounting Department		
Guest Accounting		
Credit Department		
Revenue Night Auditors		
Food and Beverage Control		
Storeroom and Receiving		

Salaries and Wages—Schedule 29 *(continued)*

	Number of Employees or Full-Time Equivalents	Current Period
ADMINISTRATIVE AND GENERAL *(continued)*		
Purchasing		$
Total Administrative and General (Schedule 15)		
HUMAN RESOURCES (Schedule 16)		
INFORMATION SYSTEMS (Schedule 17)		
SECURITY (Schedule 18)		
MARKETING (Schedule 19)		
TRANSPORTATION (Schedule 20)		
PROPERTY OPERATION AND MAINTENANCE		
Carpenters and Furniture Repairers		
Carpet Repairers		
Chief Engineer and Assistants		
Electricians		
General Mechanical		
Grounds and Landscaping		
Kitchen Mechanics		
Masons		
Office, Storeroom, and Other		
Painters and Paperhangers		
Plumbers and Steam Fitters		
Plant Operators		
Radio and Television		
Refrigeration		
Upholstery and Drapery Repairers		
Total Property Operation and Maintenance (Schedule 21)		
HOUSE LAUNDRY		
Finishing		
Manager and Assistants		
Washing		
Other		
Total House Laundry (Schedule 28)		
TOTAL SALARIES AND WAGES		$ _____

PAYROLL TAXES AND EMPLOYEE BENEFITS

Payroll Taxes and Employee Benefits—Schedule 30

	Current Period
PAYROLL TAXES	
Federal Retirement (FICA)	$
Federal Unemployment (FUTA)	
Medicare (FICA)	
State Disability	
State Unemployment (SUTA)	————
Total Payroll Taxes	
EMPLOYEE BENEFITS	
Auto Allowance	
Child Care	
Contributory Savings Plan (401K)	
Dental Insurance	
Disability Pay	
Group Life Insurance	
Health Insurance	
Meals	
Nonunion Insurance	
Nonunion Pension	
Profit Sharing	
Stock Benefits	
Union Insurance	
Union Pension	
Workers' Compensation Insurance	
Other	————
Total Employee Benefits	————
TOTAL PAYROLL TAXES AND EMPLOYEE BENEFITS	$ ═══
Charged to	
Rooms	
Food	
Beverage	
Telecommunications	
Garage and Parking	
Golf Course	
Golf Pro Shop	
Guest Laundry	
Health Center	
Swimming Pool	
Tennis	
Tennis Pro Shop	
Other Operated Departments	
Administrative and General	
Human Resources	
Information Systems	
Security	
Marketing	
Transportation	
Property Operation and Maintenance	
House Laundry	
Total	$

REVIEW QUIZ

When you feel you have covered all of the material in this chapter, answer these questions. Choose the *best* answer.

1. Which of the following statements best summarizes the relationship between the income statement and the balance sheet?

    a. The income statement represents the operations of the hospitality firm between balance sheet dates.
    b. The income statement contains all of the balance sheet's information and more.
    c. The balance sheet contains all of the income statement's information and more.
    d. The income statement is the version of the balance sheet that is compiled for external users.

2. A journal entry to record the cost of employee meals would:

    a. credit Food Sales.
    b. debit Cost of Food Sold.
    c. debit Cash.
    d. debit Employee Meals.

3. A van that cost $10,000 was sold for $3,000. The accumulated depreciation on the van at the date of sale was $8,000. The _____ on the sale equaled _____.

    a. gain; $3,000
    b. loss; $5,000
    c. gain; $1,000
    d. loss; $1,000

4. Which of the following best describes how to calculate earnings per share?

    a. Determine the product of gains and losses.
    b. Divide the number of non-common stockholders by the amount of retained earnings.
    c. Add gross income to the number of common shares outstanding.
    d. Divide net income by the number of common shares outstanding.

5. The *Uniform System of Accounts for the Lodging Industry,* ninth revised edition, has all of the following features *except:*

    a. the set of accounts and account numbers that all properties must use.
    b. formats for departmental operating statements.
    c. a uniform account numbering system.
    d. formats for basic financial statements.

REVIEW QUIZ *(continued)*

6. In an income statement, the overhead expenses for hospitality firms are represented:

   a. in the revenue section.
   b. as undistributed operating expenses, management fees, or fixed charges.
   c. as departmental expenses, according to the costs each department incurred.
   d. as direct operating expenses.

7. The Panda Hotel's retained earnings at the beginning of the year was $100,000. Earnings for the year totaled $150,000, while dividends paid during the year equaled $80,000. Dividends declared during the year totaled $90,000. Based on this information, the ending balance of retained earnings is:

   a. $100,000.
   b. $160,000.
   c. $170,000.
   d. $250,000.

Answer Key: 1-a-C1, 2-d-C2, 3-c-C3, 4-d-C4, 5-a-C5, 6-b-C6, 7-b-C7

Each question is linked to a competency. Competencies are listed on the first page of the chapter. An answer reading 3-b-C4 translates to:

   3: the question number
   b: the correct answer
   C4: the competency number

Chapter 6 Outline

Purposes of the Balance Sheet
Limitations of the Balance Sheet
Balance Sheet Formats
Content of the Balance Sheet
    Current Accounts
    Noncurrent Receivables
    Investments
    Property and Equipment
    Other Assets
    Long-Term Liabilities
    Owners' Equity
    Footnotes
    Consolidated Financial Statements

Competencies

1. Explain the purposes of the balance sheet.

2. Identify the limitations of the balance sheet.

3. Define the various elements of assets, liabilities, and owners' equity as presented on the balance sheet.

4. Explain the use of footnotes in balance sheets, and describe the use of consolidated financial statements.

6

Balance Sheet

THE BALANCE SHEET is a major financial statement prepared at the end of each accounting period. It reflects a balance between an organization's assets and the claims to its assets called *liabilities and owners' equity.* This statement is also called the *statement of financial position.*

The balance sheet answers many questions that managers, owners (investors), and creditors may ask, such as:

1. How much cash was on hand at the end of the period?

2. What was the total debt of the hospitality operation?

3. What was the mix of internal and external financing at the end of the period?

4. How much did guests owe to the hotel?

5. What amount of taxes did the operation owe to the various governmental tax agencies?

6. What is the operation's ability to pay its current debt?

7. What is the financial strength of the operation?

8. How much interest do stockholders have in the operation's assets?

In this chapter, we will address the purposes and limitations of the balance sheet. We will also consider the formats and contents of balance sheets, paying special attention to the suggested balance sheet from the *Uniform System of Accounts for the Lodging Industry (USALI).* In addition, we will discuss the kinds and purposes of footnotes attached to financial statements. The appendix to this chapter includes the financial statements and the accompanying footnotes from the 1998 annual report of the Hilton Hotels Corporation.

Purposes of the Balance Sheet

Other major financial statements—the income statement, the statement of retained earnings, and the statement of cash flows—pertain to a period of time. The balance sheet reflects the financial position of the hospitality operation—its assets, liabilities, and owners' equity—at a given date.

The balance sheet was considered the major financial statement issued to investors in the early 1900s, since many firms did not issue income statements.

Management believed the income statement contained confidential information that, if issued to external users, would end up in the hands of competitors. After the stock market crash of 1929 and subsequent governmental regulation, the Securities and Exchange Commission required businesses under its regulation to issue income statements. In the past, so much emphasis was placed on earnings that investors largely ignored the balance sheet. However, in recent years, investors have shown much more interest in the balance sheet.

Management, although generally more interested in the income statement and related department operations statements, will find balance sheets useful for conveying financial information to creditors and investors. In addition, management must determine if the balance sheet accurately reflects the financial position of the hospitality operation. For example, many long-term loans specify a required **current ratio** (current assets divided by current liabilities). An operation's failure to meet this ratio requirement may result in all its long-term debt being reclassified as current and thus due immediately. If the firm were unable to raise large sums of cash quickly, it might go bankrupt. Therefore, management must carefully review the balance sheet to ensure that the operation is in compliance with its current ratio requirement. For example, assume that at December 31, 20X1 (year-end), a hotel has $500,000 of current assets and $260,000 of current liabilities. Further assume that the current ratio requirement in a bank's loan agreement with the hotel is 2 to 1. Based on these numbers, the hypothetical hotel's current ratio is less than 2 to 1. The required current ratio can be attained simply by taking the appropriate action. In this case, the payment of $20,000 of current liabilities with cash of $20,000 results in current assets of $480,000 and current liabilities of $240,000, resulting in a current ratio of 2 to 1.

Creditors are interested in the hospitality operation's ability to pay its current and future obligations. The operation's ability to pay its current obligations is shown, in part, by a comparison of current assets and current liabilities. The ability to pay future obligations depends, in part, on the relative amounts of long-term financing by owners and creditors. Everything else being the same, the greater the financing from investors, the higher the probability that long-term creditors will be paid and the lower the risk that these creditors take in "investing" in the enterprise.

Investors are most often interested in earnings that lead to dividends. To maximize earnings, an organization should have financial flexibility, which is the operation's ability to change its cash flows to meet unexpected needs and take advantage of opportunities. Everything else being the same, the greater the financial flexibility of the hospitality operation, the greater its opportunities to take advantage of new profitable investments, thus increasing net income and, ultimately, cash dividends for investors.

In addition, the balance sheet reveals the liquidity of the hospitality operation. **Liquidity** measures the operation's ability to convert assets to cash. Even though a property's past earnings may have been substantial, this does not in itself guarantee that the operation can meet its obligations as they become due. The hospitality operation should have sufficient liquidity not only to pay its bills, but also to provide its owners with adequate dividends.

Text only | Search non-EDGAR documents | Search EDGAR Archives
SEC & Year 2000 | Site Map

U.S. SECURITIES AND EXCHANGE COMMISSION

"We are the investor's advocate."
William O. Douglas
SEC Chairman, 1937-1939

About the SEC

Investor Assistance & Complaints

EDGAR Database

SEC Digest & Statements

Current SEC Rulemaking

Enforcement Division

Small Business Information

Other Sites to Visit

Current News:

Paul F. Roye Named Director of the Division of Investment Management

SEC Names David Becker and Meyer Eisenberg Deputy General Counsels

SEC Charges 44 Stock Promoters in First Internet Securities Fraud Sweep

SEC Issues "Plain English" Handbook and Staff Legal Bulletin

New Information Technology Employment Opportunities Available at the SEC

ITTOC RFP Available

About this site

Privacy Act Notice

More information about the U.S. Securities and Exchange Commission is available on its Internet site (at http://www.sec.gov). Information about such commissions in other countries is available through the site of the International Organization of Securities Commissions (at http://www.iosco.org).

Analysis of balance sheets for several periods will yield trend information that is more valuable than single period figures. In addition, comparison of balance sheet information with projected balance sheet numbers (when available) will reveal management's ability to meet various financial goals.

Limitations of the Balance Sheet

As useful as the balance sheet is, it is generally considered less useful than the income statement to investors, long-term creditors, and especially to management. Since the balance sheet is based on the cost principle, it often does not reflect current values of some assets, such as property and equipment. For hospitality operations whose assets are appreciating rather than depreciating, the difference between an asset's book value (shown on the balance sheet) and its current value can be significant. Hilton Hotels Corporation presents a good example of what this limitation of the balance sheet might lead to. In one annual report, the corporation revealed the current value of its assets (footnote disclosure only) to be $4,027,000,000, while its balance sheet showed the book value of its assets to be $1,892,500,000. The difference between current value and book value was $2,134,500,000. The assets reflected in the balance sheet for Hilton were only 47 percent of their current value.[1] This "understatement," if unknown to or ignored by management, investors, and creditors, could lead to less than optimal use of Hilton's assets and less borrowing potential.

Another limitation of balance sheets is that they fail to reflect many elements of value to hospitality operations. Most important to hotels, motels, restaurants, clubs, and other sectors of the hospitality industry are people. Nowhere in the balance sheet is there a reflection of the human resource investment. The major hospitality firms spend millions of dollars in recruiting and training to achieve an efficient and highly motivated work force, yet this essential ingredient for successful hospitality operations is not shown as an asset. Other valuable elements not directly shown on the balance sheet include such intangibles as goodwill, superiority of location, customer loyalty, and so on.[2] Understandably, it is difficult to assign a dollar value to these elements. Nevertheless, they are not only of significant value to an operation, but also essential to its success.

Balance sheets are limited by their static nature; that is, they reflect an operation's financial position only at a particular moment. Thereafter, they are less useful because they become outdated very quickly. Thus, the user of the balance sheet must be aware that the financial position reflected at year-end may be quite different one month later. For example, a hospitality operation with $1,000,000 in cash may appear financially strong at year-end. However, if it invests most of this cash in fixed assets two weeks later, its financial flexibility and liquidity are greatly reduced. The user of financial documents would generally know about this situation only if another balance sheet or other financial statements were available for a date after this investment had occurred.

Finally, the balance sheet, like much of accounting, is based on judgment; that is, it is *not* exact. Certainly, assets equal liabilities plus owners' equity. However, several balance sheet items are based on estimates. The amounts shown as

Exhibit 1   Balance Sheet Account Format

Morrison Motel				
Balance Sheet				
December 31, 19X1				

ASSETS			LIABILITIES AND OWNERS' EQUITY	
Current Assets:			Current Liabilities:	
Cash	$ 2,500		Notes Payable	$ 23,700
Accounts Receivable	5,000		Accounts Payable	8,000
Cleaning Supplies	2,500		Wages Payable	300
Total	10,000		Total	32,000
Property & Equipment:			Long-Term Liabilities:	
Land	20,000		Mortgage Payable	120,000
Building	300,000		Total Liabilities	152,000
Furnishings and Equipment	50,000		Marvin Morrison, Capital at	
	370,000		January 1, 20X1	64,500
Less Accumulated			Net Income for 20X1	38,500
Depreciation	125,000		Marvin Morrison, Capital at	
Net Property &			December 31, 20X1	103,000
Equipment	245,000		**Total Liabilities**	
Total Assets	**$ 255,000**		**and Owners' Equity**	**$ 255,000**

accounts receivable (net) reflect the estimated amounts to be collected. The amounts shown as inventory reflect the *lower of cost or market* (that is, the lower of its original cost and its current replacement cost) of the items expected to be sold. The amount shown as property and equipment reflects the cost less estimated depreciation. In each case, accountants use estimates to arrive at "values." To the degree these estimates are in error, the balance sheet items will be wrong.

Balance Sheet Formats

The balance sheet can be arranged in either the account format or the report format. The **account format** lists asset accounts on the left side of the page and liability and owners' equity accounts on the right side. Exhibit 1 illustrates this arrangement.

The **report format** shows assets first, followed by liabilities and owners' equity. The group totals on the report form can show either that assets equal liabilities and owners' equity or that assets minus liabilities equal owners' equity. Exhibit 2 illustrates the report format.

Content of the Balance Sheet

The balance sheet consists of assets, liabilities, and owners' equity. Simply stated, assets are things owned by the firm, liabilities are claims of outsiders to assets, and

Exhibit 2   Balance Sheet Report Format

Morrison Motel
Balance Sheet
December 31, 20X1

ASSETS

Current Assets:

Cash		$ 2,500
Accounts Receivable		5,000
Cleaning Supplies		2,500
Total Current Assets		10,000

Property and Equipment:

Land	$ 20,000	
Building	300,000	
Equipment	10,000	
Furnishings	40,000	
Less Accumulated Depreciation	125,000	
Net Property and Equipment		245,000
Total Assets		**$255,000**

LIABILITIES AND OWNER'S EQUITY

Current Liabilities:

Notes Payable	$ 23,700	
Accounts Payable	8,000	
Wages Payable	300	$ 32,000
Long-Term Liabilities:		
Mortgage Payable		120,000
Total Liabilities		152,000

Owner's Equity:

Marvin Morrison, Capital		103,000
Total Liabilities and Owner's Equity		**$255,000**

owners' equity is claims of owners to assets. Think of the asset portion of the balance sheet as a "pool of valuable things" owned by the firm. The liability and equity portion is a pool of rights or claims to those valuable things. The two "pools" must be equal; assets must equal (balance) liabilities and owners' equity. Assets include accounts such as Cash, Inventory for Resale, Buildings, and Accounts Receivable. Liabilities include accounts such as Accounts Payable, Wages Payable, and Mortgage Payable. Owners' equity includes Capital Stock and Retained

Exhibit 3   Order of Balance Sheet Elements

Assets	**Liabilities and Owners' Equity**
Current Assets	Current Liabilities
Noncurrent Assets:	Long-Term Liabilities
Noncurrent Receivables	Owners' Equity
Investments	
Property and Equipment	
Other Assets	

Exhibit 4   Normal Operating Cycle

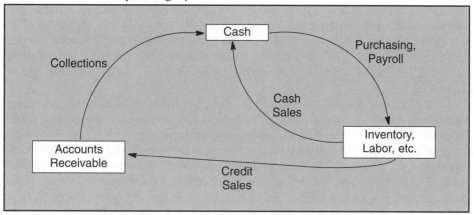

Earnings. These major elements are generally divided into various classes as shown in Exhibit 3. While balance sheets may be organized in different ways, most hospitality operations follow the order shown in Exhibit 3.

Current Accounts

The Assets section and the Liabilities section each include a current-accounts classification. **Current assets** normally refer to items that are to be converted to cash or used in operations within one year or within a normal operating cycle. **Current liabilities** are obligations that are expected to be satisfied either by using current assets or by creating other current liabilities within one year or a normal operating cycle.

Exhibit 4 reflects a normal operating cycle that includes (1) the purchase of inventory for resale and labor to produce goods and services, (2) the sale of goods and services, and (3) the collection of accounts receivable from the sale of goods and services.

A normal operating cycle may be as short as a few days, as is typical for many quick-service restaurants, or it may extend over several months for some hospitality operations. It is common in the hospitality industry to classify assets as current or noncurrent on the basis of one year rather than on the basis of the normal operating cycle.

Current Assets. Current assets, listed in the order of decreasing liquidity, generally consist of cash, marketable securities, receivables, inventories, and prepaid expenses. Cash consists of cash in house banks, cash in checking and savings accounts, and certificates of deposit. The exception is cash that is restricted for retiring long-term debt, which should be shown under Other Assets. Cash is shown on the balance sheet at its face value.

Marketable securities include investments in stocks and bonds of other entities. For example, a hotel company may own 100 shares of stock in General Motors Corporation. Marketable securities are shown as current assets when they are immediately salable at a quoted market price and expected to be converted to cash within a year of the balance sheet date. Marketable securities that are not available for conversion to cash are considered noncurrent investments. Generally, the critical factor in deciding whether an asset is current or noncurrent is management's intent. Marketable securities are usually shown on the balance sheet at their market value.

The Current Assets category of receivables consists of Accounts Receivable—Trade and Notes Receivable. Accounts Receivable—Trade includes open accounts carried by a hotel or motel on the guest, city, or rent ledgers. Notes receivable due within one year are also listed, except for notes from affiliated companies, which should be shown under Noncurrent Receivables. A note receivable is a promissory note held by the payee that states the amount due and the maturity date, and often states an interest rate, since interest is generally paid on notes receivable. Both accounts receivable and notes receivable should be stated at the amount estimated to be collectible. An allowance for doubtful accounts, the amount of receivables estimated to be uncollectible, should be subtracted from receivables to provide a net receivables amount.

Inventories of a hospitality operation consist of merchandise held for resale and the usual stock of china, glassware, silver, linen, uniforms, and other items such as guestroom supplies. Inventories are generally an insignificant percentage of the total assets of a hospitality operation and may be valued at cost. If the amount of inventory is material and the difference between cost and market is significant, the inventory should be stated at the lower of cost or market.

Prepaid expenses represent purchased goods and services to be used by the hospitality operation within one year. For example, assume that a fire insurance premium of $6,000 affords insurance protection for one year after the transaction. At the date of the expenditure, the $6,000 is classified as prepaid insurance or unexpired insurance and, thereafter, is amortized by a monthly reduction of $500 ($\frac{1}{12}$ of $6,000), which is shown on the operating statement as insurance expense. Other prepaid expenses include prepaid rent, prepaid property taxes, prepaid interest, and prepaid maintenance and service contracts.

Prepaid expenses that will benefit the operation beyond one year from the balance sheet date should be classified as Other Assets. For example, assume a three-year fire insurance policy costs $18,000. The entry to record the cash disbursement would be to debit Prepaid Insurance for $6,000 (the cost of coverage for the next 12 months) and to debit Deferred Charges—Insurance for $12,000 (the cost of insurance coverage paid that benefits the operation for periods beyond 12 months from the balance sheet date). The entry would credit Cash for $18,000.

Current assets, according to the *USALI,* may also include deferred income taxes. Deferred Income Taxes—Current is a line that represents the tax effects of temporary differences between the bases of current assets and current liabilities for financial and income tax reporting purposes. For example, if the allowance for doubtful accounts is not deductible for tax purposes until such time as the debt is written off, the allowance for doubtful accounts will result in a current deferred tax asset. Current deferred income taxes are presented as net current assets or net current liabilities as circumstances dictate.

Other current assets include items not shown elsewhere that are reasonably expected to be realized in cash or otherwise used in the business within the next 12 months. The category Other under Current Assets is normally used to capture minor items that are not separately disclosed.

Current Liabilities. In order for an obligation to be classified as a current liability, the obligation must be due within one year and management must intend to use existing current assets or create other current liabilities to satisfy the debt. For example, the debt related to the purchase of food and beverages would be classified as a current liability since the amount due is expected to be paid in the near future. On the other hand, if a debt payment due in one month is to be paid with restricted cash funds (a noncurrent asset that will be discussed later), this obligation would be classified as a noncurrent liability.

Current liabilities generally consist of one of the four following types:

1. Payables resulting from the purchase of goods, services, labor, and the applicable payroll taxes

2. Amounts received in advance of the delivery of goods and services, such as advance deposits on rooms and banquet deposits

3. Obligations to be paid in the current period relating to fixed-asset purchases or to reclassification of long-term debt as current

4. Dividends payable and income taxes payable

The major classifications of current liabilities according to the *USALI* are Accounts Payable, Notes Payable, Current Maturities of Long-Term Debt, Income Taxes, Deferred Income Taxes, Accrued Expenses, and Advance Deposits. Notes payable include short-term notes that are due within 12 months. Current maturities of long-term debt include the principal payments of long-term debt such as notes and similar liabilities, sinking fund obligations, and the principal portions of capitalized leases due within 12 months. Accounts payable include amounts due to creditors for merchandise, services, equipment, or other purchases. Deferred

Income Taxes—Current includes amounts that represent the tax effects of timing differences attributable to current assets and current liabilities being accounted for differently for financial and income tax reporting purposes. (The concept of deferred income taxes is discussed in greater detail in the Long-Term Liabilities section of this chapter.) Accrued expenses, such as accrued payroll, are expenses incurred before but not due until after the balance sheet date. Advance deposits include amounts received for services that have not been provided as of the balance sheet date.

Obligations to be paid with **restricted cash** (that is, cash that has been deposited in separate accounts, often for the purpose of retiring long-term debt) should be classified not as current, but rather as long-term.

Current liabilities are often compared with current assets in two ways. Current assets minus current liabilities is commonly called **net working capital**. Current assets divided by current liabilities is called the *current ratio*. Many hospitality properties operate successfully with a current ratio approximating 1 to 1, compared with a reasonable current ratio for many other industries of 2 to 1. The major reason for this difference lies in the relatively low amount of inventories required and relatively high turnover of receivables by hospitality operations as compared with many other industries.

Noncurrent Receivables

Noncurrent receivables include both accounts receivable and notes receivable that are not expected to be collected within one year of the balance sheet date. If a hospitality organization is uncertain of its ability to collect noncurrent receivables, an allowance for doubtful noncurrent receivables should be used (similar to the allowance account for current receivables) and subtracted from total noncurrent receivables to provide net noncurrent receivables.

In the balance sheet based on the *USALI*, noncurrent receivables are divided between noncurrent receivables from "owners, officers, employees, and affiliated entities" and "others."

Investments

Investments consist of long-term investments that are to be held for more than one year. Included as investments are investments in securities (capital stock and debt instruments), cash advances to affiliated companies, and investments in property not currently used in operations. For example, a hotel company may have invested in center city land with the expectation of constructing a hotel in the future. The land purchase should be shown as an investment and not listed under Property and Equipment on the balance sheet. Certain investments are generally stated on the balance sheet at cost, while others are stated at their market values.

For example, suppose a hotel corporation invests $10,000 in 100 shares of a large firm ($100 per share), intending to hold the shares for several years. At the balance sheet date, the market value per share is $85. The market value for the stock is $8,500, which should be reflected on the balance sheet.

Property and Equipment

Property and equipment consists of fixed assets including land, buildings, furnishings and equipment, construction in progress, leasehold improvements, and china, glassware, silver, linens, and uniforms. Property and equipment under capital leases should also be shown in this section of the balance sheet. With the exception of land, the cost of all property and equipment is written off to expense over time due to the matching principle. Depreciation methods used should be disclosed in a footnote to the balance sheet. The depreciation method used for financial reporting to outsiders and that used for tax purposes may differ, resulting in deferred income taxes. Deferred income taxes are generally a liability and will be discussed later in the chapter. On the balance sheet, fixed assets are shown at cost and are reduced by the related accumulated depreciation.

Other Assets

Other Assets consists of all assets not included in the aforementioned categories. The *USALI* identifies examples of Other Assets as follows:

1. Goodwill represents the excess of the purchase price over the fair value of net assets acquired in the purchase of a business. Goodwill should be amortized over the period during which it is expected to benefit the business, but the amortization period should *not* exceed 40 years.

2. The cash surrender value of life insurance is the amount of cash the lodging company would receive if it surrendered the life insurance policy it had on the lives of key individuals.

3. Deferred charges are charges for services received that should benefit future periods, such as advertising and maintenance. Deferred expenses also include financing costs related to long-term debt.

4. Deferred Income Taxes—Noncurrent represents the tax effects of temporary differences between the bases of noncurrent assets and noncurrent liabilities for financial and income tax reporting purposes. For example, if a liability is accrued that will not be paid for an extended period of time and the expense is deductible only when paid for tax purposes, the accrual will result in a noncurrent deferred income tax asset.

Other assets also include the costs to organize the hospitality operation (organization costs), security deposits, and unamortized franchise costs. Organization costs consist of any cost of establishing a business, including incorporation costs, legal and accounting fees, promotional costs incidental to the sale of stock, printing of stock certificates, and so forth. Theoretically, organization costs benefit the business over its entire life; however, this asset is generally written off over a five-year period. Thus, the amount shown on a balance sheet for organization costs is the unamortized amount. Security deposits include funds deposited with public utility companies and similar types of deposits. The initial franchise fee paid by the franchisee should be recorded under Other Assets and amortized against revenue over the life of the franchise agreement.

Long-Term Liabilities

Long-term liabilities are obligations at the balance sheet date that are expected to be paid beyond the next 12 months or, if paid in the current year, will be paid from restricted funds. Common long-term liabilities consist of notes payable, mortgages payable, bonds payable, capitalized lease obligations, and deferred income taxes. Any long-term debt to be paid with current assets within the next year is reclassified as a current liability.

A long-term *note payable* is a formal promise to pay an amount at a date more than 12 months beyond the balance sheet date. A promissory note is signed and, generally, interest is paid on the note at the interest rate stated on the note. To the payee, the note is a note receivable, as discussed previously. Unpaid interest on notes payable at the balance sheet date should be accrued as Accrued Interest, a liability. If the accrued interest is to be paid within a 12-month period from the balance sheet date, it should be reported as a current liability; otherwise, as a long-term liability.

A *mortgage payable* is a debt that is secured by using real property, such as a building, as collateral. The amount due within 12 months or less of the balance sheet date is classified as a current liability.

Bonds payable are certificates of indebtedness that take on many forms. Bonds due within 12 months of the balance sheet date are reclassified as current, while other bonds are classified as long-term.

Lease obligations reported as long-term liabilities generally cover several years, while short-term leases are usually expensed when paid. *Deferred income taxes* result from timing differences in reporting for financial and income tax purposes—that is, the accounting treatment of an item for financial reporting purposes results in a different amount of expense (or revenue) from that taken for tax purposes. Generally, the most significant timing difference for hotels and motels relates to depreciation, since many operations use the straight-line method for financial reporting purposes and an accelerated method for income tax purposes.

For example, suppose a hotel decides to depreciate a fixed asset on a straight-line basis at $15,000 a year for reporting purposes, and depreciates the same asset $25,000 for the year using an accelerated method for tax purposes. If the firm's marginal tax rate is 30 percent, the difference in depreciation expense of $10,000 ($25,000 − $15,000) times 30 percent results in $3,000 cash saved and reported as a noncurrent liability. The book entry to record this savings is as follows:

Income Tax Expense	$3,000	
Deferred Income Taxes		$3,000

Owners' Equity

The Owners' Equity section of the balance sheet reflects the owners' interest in the operation's assets. The detail of the Owners' Equity section is a function of the organization of the business. The four major types of business organization are corporations, sole proprietorships, partnerships, and limited liability companies

(LLCs). The Owners' Equity section of a corporation includes capital stock, additional paid-in capital, retained earnings, and treasury stock. Capital stock for most hospitality operations is common stock; however, a few operations have also issued preferred stock. When more than one type of stock has been issued, each type should be reported separately. **Capital stock** is the product of the number of shares outstanding and the par value of the shares.

The **Additional Paid-In Capital** category consists of payments for capital stock in excess of the stated or par value of the capital stock. For example, cash of $50 received from the sale of common stock with a par value of $10 would be recorded as $10 to the common stock account and the remainder ($40) as Paid-In Capital in Excess of Par.

Retained earnings reflect earnings generated but not distributed as dividends. Changes in this account during the year are commonly shown on a statement of retained earnings.

Treasury stock represents the property's own capital stock which it has repurchased but not retired. The cost of the treasury shares is shown as a reduction of owners' equity.

Exhibits 5 and 6 are the prescribed formats of the Assets section and the Liabilities and Owners' Equity section of the balance sheet from the *USALI*. Note that the Owners' Equity section of the balance sheet pertains to a lodging operation organized as a corporation.

When a lodging operation is organized as a sole proprietorship, all the owners' equity is reflected in one account as illustrated in Exhibit 2, Marvin Morrison, Capital. Marvin Morrison's $103,000 of capital would have been spread across at least two accounts, Capital Stock and Retained Earnings, if the Morrison Motel had been incorporated.

Many lodging businesses are organized as partnerships. The Owners' Equity section of a partnership should reflect each partner's equity. The balance sheet for a partnership with many partners simply refers to a supplementary schedule showing each partner's share. The Owners' Equity section of a business organized as a partnership by its three owners is illustrated as follows:

M. Kass, Capital	$ 50,000
J. Ninety, Capital	25,000
R. Chicklets, Capital	25,000
Total Owners' Equity	$100,000

Finally, when a lodging operation is organized as a limited liability company, the owners are called *members* and the Owners' Equity section is similar to that of a partnership.

Footnotes

The balance sheets of hospitality operations, although filled with considerable financial information, are not complete without the other financial statements and footnotes. The full disclosure principle requires that businesses supply sufficient financial information to inform the users—creditors, owners, and others. This can

Exhibit 5   Assets Section of the *USALI* Balance Sheet

BALANCE SHEET

Assets

	Current Year	Prior Year
CURRENT ASSETS		
Cash		
House Banks	$	$
Demand Deposits		
Temporary Cash Investments	_____	_____
Total Cash		
Short-Term Investments		
Receivables		
Accounts Receivable		
Notes Receivable		
Current Maturities of Noncurrent Receivables		
Other	_____	_____
Total Receivables		
Less Allowance for Doubtful Accounts	_____	_____
Net Receivables		
Inventories		
Prepaid Expenses		
Deferred Income Taxes, Current		
Other	_____	_____
Total Current Assets		
NONCURRENT RECEIVABLES, Net of Current Maturities		
INVESTMENTS		
PROPERTY AND EQUIPMENT		
Land		
Leaseholds and Leasehold Improvements		
Furnishings and Equipment		
Buildings		
Construction in Progress		
China, Glassware, Silver, Linen, and Uniforms	_____	_____
Less Accumulated Depreciation and Amortization		
Net Property and Equipment	_____	_____
OTHER ASSETS		
Goodwill		
Cash Surrender Value of Life Insurance		
Deferred Charges		
Deferred Income Taxes—Noncurrent		
Other	_____	_____
Total Other Assets	_____	_____
TOTAL ASSETS	$ _____	$ _____

Source: *Uniform System of Accounts for the Lodging Industry*, Ninth Revised Edition (East Lansing, Mich.: Educational Institute of the American Hotel & Motel Association, 1996), p. 4. ©Hotel Association of New York City.

Exhibit 6   Liabilities and Owners' Equity Section of the *USALI* Balance Sheet

BALANCE SHEET
Liabilities and Owners' Equity

	Current Year	Prior Year
CURRENT LIABILITIES		
Notes Payable		
Banks	$	$
Others		
Total Notes Payable	————	————
Accounts Payable		
Accrued Expenses		
Advance Deposits		
Income Taxes Payable		
Deferred Income Taxes—Current		
Current Maturities of Long-Term Debt		
Others		
Total Current Liabilities	————	————
LONG-TERM DEBT, Net of Current Maturities		
Mortgage Notes, other notes, and similar liabilities		
Obligations under Capital Leases		
Total Long-Term Debt	————	————
OTHER LONG-TERM LIABILITIES		
DEFERRED INCOME TAXES—Noncurrent		
COMMITMENTS AND CONTINGENCIES		
OWNERS' EQUITY		
———% Cumulative Preferred Stock, $——— par value, authorized ——— shares; issued and outstanding ——— shares		
Common Stock, $ ——— par value, authorized ——— shares; issued and outstanding ——— shares		
Additional Paid-In Capital		
Retained Earnings		
Less: Treasury Stock, ——— shares of Common Stock, at cost	————	————
Total Owners' Equity	————	————
TOTAL LIABILITIES AND OWNERS' EQUITY	$ ————	$ ————

Source: *Uniform System of Accounts for the Lodging Industry,* Ninth Revised Edition (East Lansing, Mich.: Educational Institute of the American Hotel & Motel Association, 1996), p. 5. ©Hotel Association of New York City.

be accomplished only by providing footnote disclosure in addition to the financial statements. Thus, **footnotes** are an integral part of the financial statements of a hospitality operation. They contain additional information not presented in the body of the financial statements. They should not contradict or soften the disclosure of the financial statements, but should provide additional explanations. The financial statements of publicly held companies generally include the following footnotes:

1. Summary of Significant Accounting Policies

2. Accounts and Notes Receivable

3. Inventories

4. Investments

5. Property and Equipment

6. Current Liabilities

7. Long-Term Debt

8. Income Taxes

9. Capital Stock

10. Employee Benefit Plans

11. Segments of Business

12. Leases

13. Commitments and Contingent Liabilities

14. Supplementary Financial Information

Consolidated Financial Statements

Many major hospitality companies consist of several corporations. For example, the hypothetical XYZ Hotel Company consists of a parent corporation, XYZ Hotel Company, and three separately incorporated hotels—Hotel X, Hotel Y, and Hotel Z. The XYZ Hotel Company owns 100 percent of the capital stock of each of the three hotels. Each hotel has its own set of financial statements, but for purposes of financial reporting, they are combined with the parent's financial statements. The combined statements are referred to as **consolidated financial statements**. The first footnote usually includes a brief description of the principles of consolidation used to combine the statements of a parent corporation and its subsidiary corporations.

Hilton Hotels Corporation's financial statements in the appendix to this chapter are consolidated financial statements. The "Notes to Consolidated Financial Statements" cover the basis of presentation and principles of consolidation for the reports.

In effect, consolidated financial statements reflect a single economic unit rather than the legal separate entities resulting from separate corporations. Generally, more than 50 percent of the voting stock of a subsidiary should be owned by the holding company or by the same interests if the associated companies' financial statements are to be combined. Complex procedures involving consolidation are covered in advanced accounting textbooks.

Summary

Although the balance sheet may not play the vital role in management decision-making that other financial statements play, it is still an important tool. By examining it, managers, investors, and creditors may determine the financial position of the hospitality operation at a given point in time. It is used to help determine an operation's ability to pay its debts and purchase fixed assets.

The balance sheet is divided into three major categories: Assets, Liabilities, and Owners' Equity. Assets are the items owned by the operation, while liabilities and owners' equity represent claims to the operation's assets. Liabilities are amounts owed to creditors. Owners' equity represents the residual interest in assets for investors. Both assets and liabilities are divided into current and noncurrent sections. Current assets are cash and other assets that will be converted to cash or used on the property's operations within the next year. Current liabilities represent present obligations that will be paid within one year. The major categories of noncurrent assets include Noncurrent Receivables, Investments, Property and Equipment, and Other Assets. Long-term liabilities are present obligations expected to be paid beyond the next 12 months from the date of the balance sheet.

Owners' equity generally includes common stock, paid-in capital in excess of par, and retained earnings. Common stock is the product of the number of shares outstanding and the par value of the shares. Paid-in capital in excess of par is the amount over the par value paid by investors when they purchased the stock from the hospitality corporation. Retained earnings are the past earnings generated by the operation but not distributed to the stockholders in the form of dividends.

Since assets are the items owned by the property, and liabilities and owners' equity are claims to the assets, the relationship involving the three is stated as follows: Assets = Liabilities + Owners' Equity. The balance sheet is prepared either with assets on one side of the page and liabilities and owners' equity on the other (account format) or with the three sections in one column (report format).

Endnotes

1. *Hilton Hotels Corporation 1988 Annual Report* (Beverly Hills, Calif.: Hilton Hotels Corp., 1989), pp. 32–44.

2. The exception is that **purchased goodwill** is shown on the balance sheet. This goodwill results when a purchaser of a hospitality operation is unable to assign the entire purchase price to the operation's individual assets. The excess of the purchase price over the dollars assigned to the individual assets is labeled *goodwill*. Self-generated goodwill, which for many hospitality operations is significant, is not shown on the balance sheet.

Key Terms

account format—An arrangement of a balance sheet that lists the asset accounts on the left side of the page and the liability and owners' equity accounts on the right side. Compare *report format*.

additional paid-in capital—Payments for capital stock in excess of the stated or par value of the capital stock.

capital stock—Shares of ownership of a corporation.

consolidated financial statements—The combined financial statements of a parent corporation and its subsidiary corporations.

current assets—Resources of cash and items that will be converted to cash or used in generating income within one year or a normal operating cycle.

current liabilities—Obligations at the balance sheet date that are expected to be satisfied either by using current assets or by creating other current liabilities within one year or a normal operating cycle.

current ratio—Ratio of total current assets to total current liabilities expressed as a coverage of so many times; calculated by dividing Current Assets by Current Liabilities.

footnotes—Disclosures in the financial statements that contain additional information that is not presented in the body of the financial statements.

liquidity—The ability of a hospitality operation to meet its short-term (current) obligations by maintaining sufficient cash or short-term investments that are easily convertible to cash.

long-term liabilities—Obligations at the balance sheet date that are expected to be paid beyond the next 12 months or, if paid in the current year, they will be paid from restricted funds; also called *noncurrent liabilities*.

net working capital—Current Assets minus Current Liabilities.

noncurrent receivables—Accounts and notes receivable that are not expected to be collected within one year of the balance sheet date.

other assets—A category of the balance sheet that includes purchased goodwill, cash surrender value of life insurance policies, deferred charges, noncurrent deferred income taxes, security deposits, organization costs, and unamortized franchise costs.

property and equipment—A category of the balance sheet in which accountants record the values of fixed assets such as land, buildings, furniture, equipment, construction in progress, leasehold improvements, and property such as china, glassware, silver, linens, uniforms, and so on.

purchased goodwill—The excess of a hospitality operation's purchase price over the dollars assigned to its individual assets.

report format—An arrangement of a balance sheet that lists the assets first, followed by liabilities and owners' equity. Compare *account format*.

restricted cash—Cash that has been deposited in separate accounts, often for the purpose of retiring long-term debt.

retained earnings—An account for recording undistributed earnings of a corporation.

treasury stock—A corporation's own capital stock that the corporation has repurchased but not retired or reissued.

Review Questions

1. What is the importance of the balance sheet to management, investors, and creditors?

2. How do the three major parts of the balance sheet (Assets, Liabilities, and Owners' Equity) relate to each other?

3. Why is liquidity important to a hospitality firm?

4. What are some limitations of the balance sheet?

5. What is the difference between current and noncurrent assets?

6. Why are marketable securities shown before accounts receivable on the balance sheet?

7. What does the phrase *lower of cost or market* mean?

8. What is the difference between short-term and long-term debt?

9. When would a corporation have an Additional Paid-In Capital account?

10. What is the purpose of footnotes?

 # Problems

Problem 1

The following are accounts from the balance sheet of the Stewartville Hotel.

Building	Note Payable (2 Year)
Prepaid Insurance	Investment in GM Stock (100 shares)
House Banks	Organization Expenses
Obligations under Capital Leases	Construction in Progress
Common Stock, Par Value $150,000	Accounts Payable
Petty Cash	Additional Paid-In Capital
Accrued Payroll	Deferred Income Taxes (Long-Term)*
Retained Earnings	Treasury Stock
Supplies Inventory	Notes Payable (6 Months)
Advance Deposits	Security Deposits

* Relates to how businesses depreciate property and equipment.

Required:

Classify these accounts using the major classifications from the *USALI* balance sheet (see Exhibits 5 and 6).

Problem 2

The TexMex Café has recently purchased new office equipment. The owner, José Tex, wonders how the cost will be shown on the balance sheet and where the cost will be expressed.

Assume the equipment cost $20,000 and has a useful life of six years. Further, assume the estimated value of this equipment at the end of the six years is $2,000.

Required:

1. Using the straight-line method of depreciation, determine the amount of depreciation expense for years 1 through 6.

2. What net book value (cost-accumulated depreciation) will be shown on the balance sheet for the office equipment at the end of each year from years 1 through 6?

Problem 3

The Bravo has the following current balance sheet accounts:

Cash	$ 10,000
Accounts Receivable	200,000
Accounts Payable	50,000
Inventory	20,000
Income Taxes Payable	30,000
Prepaid Expenses	10,000
Accrued Expenses	40,000
Current Portion—Long-Term Debt	100,000
Wages Payable	30,000
Marketable Securities	25,000
Allowance for Doubtful Debts	5,000

Required:

1. Determine the Bravo's total current assets.
2. Determine the Bravo's total current liabilities.
3. Determine the Bravo's net working capital.
4. Determine the Bravo's current ratio.

Problem 4

The following are account balances from the trial balance of the Village Inn at October 31, 20X1 (the end of the Inn's fiscal year), arranged in alphabetical order.

	Debits	Credits
Accounts Payable		$ 77,000
Accounts Receivable	$ 96,900	
Accrued Liabilities		91,000
Accumulated Depreciation		338,400
Additional Paid-In Capital		25,000
Building	1,786,400	
Cash	47,800	
Common Stock		300,000
Current Portion—Long-Term Debt		14,000
Furniture and Fixtures	275,400	
Inventories	19,900	
Land	115,500	
Long-Term Debt		1,527,000
Other Assets	172,200	
Other Current Liabilities		40,800
Prepaid Expenses	2,400	
Retained Earnings		103,300

Required:

Prepare the balance sheet for the Village Inn according to the *USALI.*

Problem 5

Listed below are asset, liability, and owners' equity accounts for Sue & Jerry's Sleepy Hollow as of December 31, 20X7.

Common Stock	$144,600
Inventories	23,241
Treasury Stock	7,278
Land	111,158
House Banks	11,738
Deferred Income Taxes (Noncurrent/Credit Balance)	190,038
Paid-In Capital in Excess of Par	115,501
Notes Payable	42,611
Retained Earnings	327,137
Demand Deposits	8,803
Other Current Liabilities	21,246
Accounts Receivable	128,179
Accrued Salaries	78,293
Certificates of Deposit	2,934
Prepaid Expenses	13,499
Notes Receivable	22,420

Building	682,093
Marketable Securities	134,634
Long-Term Debt	262,930
Investments	30,049
Accounts Payable	58,690
Allowance for Doubtful Accounts	16,316
Deferred Charges	12,794
Advance Deposits—Banquets	14,203
Equipment	250,424
Current Maturities of Long-Term Debt	25,824
Security Deposits	8,569
Accumulated Depreciation, Equipment	150,424

Required:

Prepare the Assets section of the balance sheet for Sue & Jerry's Sleepy Hollow according to the *USALI.*

Problem 6

Using the account balances given in Problem 5, prepare the Liabilities and Owners' Equity sections of the balance sheet for Sue & Jerry's Sleepy Hollow according to the *USALI.*

Problem 7

Noreen Bayley, the owner/manager of Winkie's Motel, has come to you with some accounting questions. As a result of a fire at the motel, many of the records as of December 31, 20X2, were either burned or soaked by the sprinkler system.

Required:

You are to help Ms. Bayley determine the following balances:

1. In one report, the current ratio for the motel is 1.2 to 1. In addition, you have determined the amount of current liabilities (including $14,736 of current portion of long-term debt) to be $105,380 and long-term debt to be $60,000. What is the amount of current assets for Winkie's Motel?

2. Ms. Bayley has her December 31, 20X2, bank statement, which says she has $49,765 in her savings account and $36,072 in her checking account. She has a copy of the inventory sheet, which states total inventory on December 31, 20X2, of $15,491. Assuming that the only current assets are cash, inventory, and accounts receivable, what is the total accounts receivable owed to Ms. Bayley?

3. Ms. Bayley has a copy of the balance sheet from November 30, 20X2, which states that Current Assets was 30 percent of Total Assets. Assuming this relationship is the same at December 31, 20X2, what is the amount of total assets as of December 31, 20X2?

4. Based on the information in parts 1 through 3, what is the Owner's Equity as of December 31, 20X2?

Challenge Problems

Problem 8

The Spartan Inn, a sole proprietorship, has several accounts as follows:

Room Sales	$1,000,000
Land	80,000
Cash	5,000
Accounts Payable	20,000
Inventories	15,000
Accounts Receivable	80,000
Bonds Payable (Long-Term)	300,000
Jerry Spartan, Capital (1/1/20X3)	300,000
Accrued Expenses	10,000
Prepaid Expenses	8,000
Temporary Investments	25,000
Building	500,000
Equipment and Furnishings	200,000
Franchise Fees (Deferred)	15,000
Accumulated Depreciation	150,000
Income Tax Payable	10,000
Deferred Income Taxes (Long-Term Liability)	20,000

Other information is as follows:

The Spartan Inn's net income for 20X3 was $145,000, and Jerry Spartan withdrew $27,000 for personal use during 20X3.

Required:

Prepare a balance sheet for the Spartan Inn as of December 31, 20X3, in accordance with the *USALI*.

Problem 9

Julie Wayne is the new owner of the Moby Hotel in Washington, D.C. However, she has no experience in the hospitality industry and has hired you to help the newest employee, Carol Niks, computerize the back office operations. The first job you must tackle is teaching Carol about the balance sheet. The following is (1) a list of selected account balances in the general ledger on December 31, 20X1, and (2) some additional information.

Bank Balance	$ 141,022
Marketable Securities	550,000
Accounts Payable	1,530,761
Land	3,861,725
Retained Earnings	462,476
Current Portion—Long-Term Debt	392,000

Building	4,768,333
Accounts Receivable	1,843,999
Furniture & Equipment	2,000,741
Paid-In Capital in Excess of Par	1,795,463
Prepaid Insurance	??
Accumulated Depreciation	847,937
Long-Term Debt	??
Capital Stock	??

Additional information:

1. The market value of the marketable securities as of December 31, 20X1, is $532,000.

2. On January 1, 20X1, the previous owner purchased a two-year insurance policy for $40,000 to cover years 20X1 through 20X2.

3. On December 31, 20X1, there were 50,000 shares of stock issued and outstanding with a par value of $10 per share. The 50,000 shares were sold for $2,295,463.

4. Long-term debt can be calculated by subtracting owners' equity and all liabilities other than long-term debt from total assets.

Required:

Prepare the balance sheet in accordance with the *USALI.*

Problem 10

The trial balance of balance sheet accounts of Lancer's, a popular casual dining spot, as of December 31, 20X3, is as follows:

	Debits	Credits
Cash	$ 5,000	
Marketable Securities	10,000	
Accounts Receivable	100,000	
Allowance for Doubtful Accounts		$ 5,000
Food Inventory	15,000	
Prepaid Rent	5,000	
Prepaid Insurance	8,000	
Investments	50,000	
Land	80,000	
Building	420,000	
Equipment	100,000	
Accumulated Depreciation		100,000
Accounts Payable		15,000
Income Taxes Payable		–0–
Accrued Expenses		25,000
Dividends Payable		–0–
Long-Term Debt		300,000
Capital Stock		89,000

Paid-In Capital in Excess of Par	68,000
Retained Earnings (1/1/X3)	61,000

Additional information:

1. Dividends declared during 20X3 totaled $30,000. Only $20,000 of the dividends declared in 20X3 have been paid as of December 31, 20X3. The unpaid dividends have not been recorded.

2. Operations generated $800,000 of revenue for 20X3. Expenses recorded totaled $650,000. Additional adjustments required are as follows:

    a. The allowance for doubtful accounts should be adjusted to 10 percent of accounts receivable.

    b. Prepaid insurance of $8,000 is the premium paid for insurance coverage for July 1, 20X3, through June 30, 20X4.

    c. Unrecorded depreciation expense for 20X3 totals $41,000.

    d. Income taxes have not been recorded. Lancer's average rate is 20 percent.

3. The Long-Term Debt account includes $50,000, which must be paid on June 30, 20X4.

Required:

Prepare a balance sheet according to the *USALI*.

Appendix

Consolidated Statements of Income

(in millions, except per share amounts)	Year Ended December 31, 1998	1997	1996
Revenue			
Rooms	$ 952	779	441
Food and beverage	414	326	188
Management and franchise fees	104	115	105
Other revenue	299	255	213
	1,769	1,475	947
Expenses			
Rooms	237	205	127
Food and beverage	315	254	147
Other expenses	686	556	393
Corporate expense, net	67	65	43
	1,305	1,080	710
Operating Income	464	395	237
Interest and dividend income	13	17	26
Interest expense	(137)	(90)	(52)
Interest expense, net, from unconsolidated affiliates	(4)	(8)	(7)
Income Before Income Taxes and Minority Interest	336	314	204
Provision for income taxes	136	124	79
Minority interest, net	12	7	5
Income from Continuing Operations	188	183	120
Income (loss) from discontinued gaming operations, net of tax provision (benefit) of $111, $63 and $(25)	109	67	(38)
Net Income	$ 297	250	82
Change in unrealized gains and losses, net of tax	(19)	7	11
Comprehensive income	$ 278	257	93
Basic Earnings Per Share			
Income from continuing operations	$ .71	.68	.61
Discontinued gaming operations	.44	27	(.20)
Net income per share	$ 1.15	.95	.41
Diluted Earnings Per Share			
Income from continuing operations	$ .71	.68	.61
Discontinued gaming operations	.41	.26	(.20)
Net income per share	$ 1.12	.94	.41

See notes to consolidated financial statements

Courtesy of Hilton Hotels Corporation.

Consolidated Balance Sheets

(in millions)	December 31, 1998	1997
ASSETS		
Current Assets		
Cash and equivalents	$ 47	5
Accounts receivable, net of allowance of $12 and $6, respectively	204	155
Receivable from discontinued gaming operations	73	—
Inventories	54	39
Deferred income taxes	48	31
Other current assets	43	32
Total current assets	469	262
Investments, Property and Other Assets		
Investments	262	233
Long-term receivable	625	—
Property and equipment, net	2,483	1,373
Net assets of discontinued gaming operations	—	3,381
Other assets	105	29
Total investments, property and other assets	3,475	5,016
Total Assets	$ 3,944	5,278
LIABILITIES AND STOCKHOLDERS' EQUITY		
Current Liabilities		
Accounts payable and accrued expenses	$ 410	268
Current maturities of long-term debt	62	31
Income taxes payable	34	9
Total current liabilities	506	308
Long-term debt	3,037	1,437
Deferred income taxes	65	36
Insurance reserves and other	149	114
Total liabilities	3,757	1,895
Commitments and Contingencies		
Stockholders' Equity		
8% PRIDES convertible preferred stock	—	15
Common stock, 261 and 249 shares outstanding, respectively	663	628
Additional paid-in capital	—	1,759
Retained (deficit) earnings	(347)	1,040
Other	—	11
	316	3,453
Less treasury stock, at cost	129	70
Total stockholders' equity	187	3,383
Total Liabilities and Stockholders' Equity	$ 3,944	5,278

See notes to consolidated financial statements

Consolidated Statements of Cash Flow

(in millions Year Ended December 31, 1998	1997	1996
Operating Activities		
Net income $ 297	250	82
Adjustments to reconcile net income to net cash provided by operating activities:		
(Income) loss from discontinued gaming operations (109)	(67)	38
Depreciation and amortization 125	93	67
Non-cash items —	(2)	22
Amortization of loan costs 2	1	1
Change in working capital components:		
Inventories (15)	10	(42)
Accounts receivable (42)	5	(44)
Other current assets (17)	(5)	(8)
Accounts payable and accrued expenses 124	4	135
Income taxes payable 25	4	(8)
Change in deferred income taxes 9	(63)	(11)
Change in other liabilities 5	(46)	(10)
Unconsolidated affiliates' distributions (less than) in excess of earnings (17)	6	37
Other 3	39	26
Net cash provided by operating activities 390	229	285
Investing Activities		
Capital expenditures (171)	(93)	(49)
Additional investments (98)	(97)	(53)
Change in temporary investments —	25	53
Proceeds from asset sales —	123	—
Payments on notes and other 49	49	1
Acquisitions, net of cash acquired (842)	(67)	(432)
Net cash used in investing activities (1,062)	(60)	(480)
Financing Activities		
Change in commercial paper borrowings and revolving loans 355	(1,218)	1,041
Long-term borrowings 400	1,393	492
Reduction of long-term debt (247)	(95)	(1,457)
Issuance of common stock 25	38	31
Purchase of common stock (81)	(40)	—
Cash dividends (90)	(93)	(60)
Net cash provided by (used in) financing activities 362	(15)	47
Net transfers from (to) discontinued gaming operations 352	(191)	(110)
Increase (Decrease) in Cash and Equivalents 42	(37)	(258)
Cash and Equivalents at Beginning of Year 5	42	300
Cash and Equivalents at End of Year $ 47	5	42

See notes to consolidated financial statements

Consolidated Statements of Stockholders' Equity

(in millions, except per share amounts)	8% PRIDES Convertible Preferred Stock	Common Stock	Additional Paid-In Capital	Retained (Deficit) Earnings	Other	Treasury Stock
Balance, December 31, 1995	$ —	494	—	909	(7)	(142)
Exercise of stock options	—	—	—	—	—	31
Bally acquisition	15	133	1,735	—	—	—
Cumulative translation adjustment, net of deferred tax	—	—	—	—	6	—
Change in unrealized gain/loss on marketable securities, net of deferred tax	—	—	—	—	5	—
Deferred compensation	—	—	10	—	—	—
Net income	—	—	—	82	—	—
Dividends ($.305 per share)	—	—	—	(60)	—	—
Balance, December 31, 1996	15	627	1,745	931	4	(111)
Issuance of common stock	—	1	4	—	—	5
Exercise of stock options	—	—	—	(48)	—	76
Treasury stock acquired	—	—	—	—	—	(40)
Cumulative translation adjustment, net of deferred tax	—	—	—	—	(4)	—
Change in unrealized gain/loss on marketable securities, net of deferred tax	—	—	—	—	11	—
Deferred compensation	—	—	10	—	—	—
Net income	—	—	—	250	—	—
Dividends						
PRIDES ($.89 per share)	—	—	—	(13)	—	—
Common ($.32 per share)	—	—	—	(80)	—	—
Balance, December 31, 1997	15	628	1,759	1,040	11	(70)
Issuance of common stock	—	1	10	—	—	—
Exercise of stock options	—	—	—	—	—	22
Treasury stock acquired	—	—	—	—	—	(81)
Conversion of PRIDES	(15)	34	(19)	—	—	—
Cumulative translation adjustment, net of deferred tax	—	—	—	—	(9)	—
Change in unrealized gain/loss on marketable securities, net of deferred tax	—	—	—	—	(10)	—
Deferred compensation	—	—	10	—	—	—
Net income	—	—	—	297	—	—
Dividends						
PRIDES ($.67 per share)	—	—	—	(10)	—	—
Common ($.32 per share)	—	—	—	(80)	—	—
Spin-off of Park Place Entertainment Corporation	—	—	(1,760)	(1,586)	8	—
Balance, December 31, 1998	$ —	663	—	(347)	—	(129)

See notes to consolidated financial statements

Notes

NOTES TO CONSOLIDATED FINANCIAL STATEMENTS

December 31, 1998

BASIS OF PRESENTATION AND ORGANIZATION

On December 31, 1998, Hilton Hotels Corporation ("Hilton" or the "Company") completed a spin-off that split the Company's operations into two independent public corporations per an agreement dated June 30, 1998, one for conducting its hotel business and one for conducting its gaming business. Hilton retained owner-ship of the hotel business. Hilton transferred the gaming business to a new corpo-ration named Park Place Entertainment Corporation ("Park Place") and distributed the stock of Park Place tax-free to Hilton stockholders on a one-for-one basis. As a result of the spin-off, Hilton's financial statements reflect the gaming business as discontinued operations. Also on December 31, 1998, immediately fol-lowing the spin-off, Park Place acquired, by means of a merger, the Mississippi Gaming Business of Grand Casinos, Inc. ("Grand").

Hilton is primarily engaged in the ownership, management and development of hotels, resorts and vacation ownership properties and the franchising of lodging properties. Hilton operates in select markets throughout the world, predominately in the United States.

SPIN-OFF OF GAMING OPERATIONS

As discussed above, on December 31, 1998, the Company completed a spin-off of its gaming operations. Accordingly, results of operations and cash flows of Park Place have been reported as discontinued operations for all periods presented in the consolidated financial statements of Hilton. The consolidated balance sheet as of December 31, 1997 also reflects the Company's gaming business as discontinued operations. Summarized financial information of the discontinued operations is presented in the following tables:

Net assets of discontinued gaming operations:

(in millions)	1997
Current assets	$ 450
Current liabilities	334
Net current assets	116
Property and equipment, net	3,621
Other assets	1,559
Long-term debt, including allocated debt	1,272
Other liabilities and deferred taxes	643
Net assets of discontinued gaming operations	$3,381

Income (loss) from discontinued gaming operations:

(in millions)	1998	1997	1996
Revenues	$2,295	2,145	958
Costs and expenses	1,993	1,944	866
Operating income	302	201	92
Net interest expense	79	67	29
Income before income taxes and minority interest	223	134	63
Provision for income taxes	111	63	27
Minority interest, net	3	4	—
Income before extraordinary item	109	67	36
Extraordinary loss on extinguishment of debt, net of tax benefit of $52	—	—	(74)
Income (loss) from discontinued gaming operations	$ 109	67	(38)

SUMMARY OF SIGNIFICANT ACCOUNTING POLICIES

Principles of Consolidation

The consolidated financial statements include the accounts of Hilton Hotels Corporation and its majority owned and controlled subsidiaries. The Company adopted EITF 97-2 "Application of FASB Statement No. 94 and APB Opinion No. 16 to Physician Practice Management Entities and Certain Other Entities with Contractual Management Arrangements" in the fourth quarter of 1998, and, as a result, no longer consolidates the operating results and working capital of affiliates operated under long-term management agreements. Application of EITF 97-2 reduced each of revenues and operating expenses by $1.3 billion and $1.6 billion for the years ended December 31, 1997 and 1996, respectively. Application of the standard reduced each of current assets and current liabilities by $240 million at December 31, 1997. Application of EITF 97-2 had no impact on reported operating income, net income, earnings per share or stockholders' equity.

All material intercompany transactions are eliminated and net earnings are reduced by the portion of the earnings of affiliates applicable to other ownership interests. There are no significant restrictions on the transfer of funds from the Company's wholly owned subsidiaries to Hilton Hotels Corporation.

Cash and Equivalents

Cash and equivalents include investments with initial maturities of three months or less.

Currency Translation

Assets and liabilities denominated in most foreign currencies are translated into U.S. dollars at year-end exchange rates and related gains and losses, net of applicable deferred income taxes, are reflected in stockholders' equity. Gains and losses from foreign currency transactions are included in earnings.

Property and Equipment

Property and equipment are stated at cost. Interest incurred during construction of facilities is capitalized and amortized over the life of the asset. Costs of improvements are capitalized. Costs of normal repairs and maintenance are charged to expense as incurred. Upon the sale or retirement of property and equipment, the cost and related accumulated depreciation are removed from the respective accounts, and the resulting gain or loss, if any, is included in income.

Depreciation is provided on a straight-line basis over the estimated useful life of the assets. Leasehold improvements are amortized over the shorter of the asset life or lease term. The service lives of assets are generally 40 years for buildings and eight years for building improvements and furniture and equipment.

The carrying value of the Company's assets are reviewed when events or changes in circumstances indicate that the carrying amount of an asset may not be recoverable. If it is determined that an impairment loss has occurred based on exected future cash flows, then a loss is recognized in the income statement using a fair value based model.

Pre-Opening Costs

Costs associated with the opening of new properties or major additions to properties are deferred and amortized over the shorter of the period benefited or one year. In April 1998, the AICPA issued Statement of Position ("SOP") 98-5, "Reporting on the Costs of Start-Up Activities." This SOP requires that all nongovernmental entities expense costs of start-up activities (pre-opening, pre-operating and organizational costs) as those costs are incurred and requires the write-off of any unamortized balances upon implementation. SOP 98-5 is effective for financial statements issued for periods beginning after December 15, 1998. The Company will adopt SOP 98-5 in the first quarter of 1999. Adoption of the SOP is not expected to have a material impact on the 1999 results of operations.

Unamortized Loan Costs

Debt discount and issuance costs incurred in connection with the placement of long-term debt are capitalized and amortized to interest expense, principally on the bonds outstanding method.

Self-Insurance

The Company is self-insured for various levels of general liability, workers' compensation and employee medical and life insurance coverage. Insurance reserves include the present values of projected settlements for claims.

Earnings Per Share ("EPS")

Basic EPS is computed by dividing net income available to common stockholders (net income less preferred dividends of $10 million in 1998 and $13 million in 1997) by the weighted average number of common shares outstanding for the period.

The weighted average number of common shares outstanding for 1998, 1997 and 1996 were 250 million, 250 million and 197 million, respectively. Diluted EPS reflects the potential dilution that could occur if securities or other contracts to issue common stock were exercised or converted. The dilutive effect of the assumed exercise of stock options and convertible securities increased the weighted average number of common shares by 28 million, 31 million and 12 million for 1998, 1997 and 1996, respectively. In addition, the increase to net income resulting from interest on convertible securities assumed to have not been paid was $15 million, $15 million and $9 million for 1998, 1997 and 1996, respectively.

Use of Estimates

The preparation of financial statements in conformity with generally accepted accounting principles requires management to make estimates and assumptions that affect the reported amounts of assets and liabilities and disclosure of contingent assets and liabilities at the date of the financial statements and the reported amounts of revenue and expenses during the reporting period. Actual results could differ from those estimates.

Reclassifications

The consolidated financial statements for prior years reflect certain reclassifications to conform with classifications adopted in 1998. These classifications have no effect on net income.

INVENTORIES

Included in inventories at December 31, 1998 and 1997 are unsold intervals at the Company's vacation ownership properties of $42 million and $32 million, respectively. Inventories are valued at the lower of cost or estimated net realizable value.

INVESTMENTS

Investments at December 31, 1998 and 1997 are as follows:

(in millions)	1998	1997
Equity investments		
Hotels (seven in 1998, eight in 1997)	$ 33	52
Other	58	41
Vacation ownership notes receivable	107	86
Other notes receivable	40	19
Marketable securities	24	35
Total	$ 262	233

PROPERTY AND EQUIPMENT

Property and equipment at December 31, 1998 and 1997 are as follows:

(in millions)	1998	1997
Land	$ 379	166
Buildings and leasehold improvements	2,296	1,546
Furniture and equipment	540	384
Property held for sale or development	37	39
Construction in progress	71	18
	3,323	2,153
Less accumulated depreciation	840	780
Total	$2,483	1,373

ACCOUNTS PAYABLE AND ACCRUED EXPENSES

Accounts payable and accrued expenses at December 31, 1998 and 1997 are as follows:

(in millions)	1998	1997
Accounts and notes payable	$ 28	87
Accrued compensation and benefits	63	44
Other accrued expenses	219	137
Total	$ 410	268

LONG-TERM DEBT

Long-term debt at December 31, 1998 and 1997 is as follows:

(in millions)	1998	1997
Industrial development revenue bonds at adjustable rates, due 2015	$ 82	82
Senior notes, with an average rate of 7.6%, due 2001 to 2017	1,117	1,174
Senior notes, with an average rate of 7.2%, due 2002 to 2004	625	623
Mortgage notes, 5.9% to 8.4%, due 1999 to 2016	145	116
5% Convertible subordinated notes due 2006	492	491
Commercial paper	—	280
Revolving loans	635	—
Other	3	8
Debt allocated to discontinued gaming operations	—	(1,306)
	3,099	1,468
Less current maturities	62	31
Net long-term debt	$3,037	1,437

Interest paid, net of amounts capitalized, was $130 million, $74 million and $55 million in 1998, 1997 and 1996, respectively. Capitalized interest amounted to $4 million and $2 million in 1998 and 1997, respectively. No interest was capitalized in 1996.

Debt maturities during the next five years are as follows:

(in millions)	
1999	$ 62
2000	53
2001	170
2002	572
2003	483

In order to equalize the indebtedness between Hilton and Park Place at the time of the spin-off, pro forma for the merger of Park Place and Grand, Hilton and Park Place agreed to an allocation of the December 31, 1998 debt balances and entered into a debt assumption agreement. Pursuant to the debt assumption agreement, Park Place assumed and agreed to pay 100% of the amount of each payment required to be made by Hilton under the terms of the indentures governing Hilton's $300 million 7.375% Senior Notes due 2002 and its $325 million 7% Senior Notes due 2004. These notes remain in Hilton's long-term debt balance and a long-term receivable from Park Place in an equal amount is included in the Company's 1998 consolidated balance sheet. In the event of an increase in the interest rate on these notes as a result of certain actions taken by Hilton or certain other limited circumstances, Hilton will be required to reimburse Park Place for any such increase. Hilton is obligated to make any payment Park Place fails to make, and in such event Park Place shall pay to Hilton the amount of such payment together with interest, at the rate per annum borne by the applicable notes plus two percent, to the date of such reimbursement.

In order to facilitate the transfer of debt balances in connection with the spin-off, in December 1998 Park Place entered into a long-term credit facility and completed a senior subordinated note offering. Park Place used the proceeds from the new facility and note offering to repay $1,066 million of Hilton's commercial paper borrowings, representing an estimate of Park Place's share of the obligation. The distribution agreement entered into between Hilton and Park Place calls for a final reconciliation and allocation of certain debt and cash balances, as defined. The reconciliation resulted in an additional amount due Hilton from Park Place of $73 million. This balance is reflected in current assets in the accompanying consolidated financial statements. A pro rata portion of Hilton's historical outstanding public and corporate bank debt balances and related interest expense has been allocated to Park Place for prior periods.

By virtue of an agreement with Prudential to restructure the joint venture ownership of the Hilton Hawaiian Village, effective June 1, 1998 the Company was deemed to control the joint venture, thus requiring consolidation of this previously unconsolidated entity. The agreement also called for the refinancing of the joint venture's existing debt under a new joint venture revolving credit facility. In accordance with the terms of the agreement, this new facility was used to borrow an additional $294 million which was loaned to a Prudential affiliate and subsequently redeemed to increase the Company's investment in the joint venture from 50% to 98%. The consolidation of the joint venture, which includes the total borrowings under the new facility, resulted in an increase in consolidated debt of $480 million.

During 1996, the Company entered into a long-term revolving credit facility with an aggregate commitment of $1.75 billion, which expires in 2001. At December 31, 1998, $155 million was outstanding, leaving approximately $1.6 billion of the revolving credit facility available to the Company at such date. Borrowings will generally bear interest at the London Interbank Offered Rate ("LIBOR") plus a spread based on the Company's public debt rating or a leverage ratio. The all in cost of borrowings under the facility was approximately LIBOR plus 60 basis points as of December 31, 1998.

In October 1997, the Company filed a shelf registration statement ("Shelf") with the Securities and Exchange Commission registering up to $2.5 billion in debt or equity securities. At December 31, 1998, available financing under the Shelf totaled $2.1 billion. The terms of any additional securities offered pursuant to the Shelf will be determined by market conditions at the time of issuance.

In accordance with the terms of the indenture governing the Company's $500 million 5% Convertible Subordinated Notes due 2006, effective January 4, 1999, the conversion price was adjusted to $22.17, reflecting the gaming spin-off.

Provisions under various loan agreements require the Company to comply with certain financial covenants which include limiting the amount of outstanding indebtedness.

FINANCIAL INSTRUMENTS

Cash Equivalents and Long-Term Marketable Securities

The fair value of cash equivalents and long-term marketable securities is estimated based on the quoted market price of the investments.

Long-Term Debt

The estimated fair value of long-term debt is based on the quoted market prices for the same or similar issues or on the current rates offered to the Company for debt of the same remaining maturities.

The estimated fair values of the Company's financial instruments at December 31, 1998 and 1997 are as follows:

(in millions)	1998		1997	
	Carrying Amount	Fair Value	Carrying Amount	Fair Value
Cash and equivalents and long-term marketable securities	$ 71	71	40	40
Long-term debt (including current maturities)	3,099	3,123	1,468	1,517

INCOME TAXES

The provisions for income taxes for the three years ended December 31 are as follows:

(in millions)	1998	1997	1996
Current			
Federal	$ 98	168	66
State, foreign and local	31	34	18
	129	202	84
Deferred	7	(78)	(5)
Total	$ 136	124	79

During 1998, 1997 and 1996 the Company paid income taxes, including amounts paid on behalf of the discontinued gaming operations, of $165 million, $150 million and $83 million, respectively.

The income tax effects of temporary differences between financial and income tax reporting that gave rise to deferred income tax assets and liabilities at December 31, 1998 and 1997 are as follows:

(in millions)	1998	1997
Deferred tax assets		
Accrued expenses	$ 2	8
Self-insurance and other reserves	26	29
Benefit plans	23	6
Pre-opening costs	11	—
Foreign tax credit carryovers (expire beginning in 2000)	21	3
Disposition of assets	24	30
Other	4	—
	111	76
Valuation allowance	(3)	(3)
	108	73
Deferred tax liabilities		
Fixed assets, primarily depreciation	(30)	(14)
Equity investments	(80)	(59)
Other	(15)	(5)
	(125)	(78)
Net deferred tax liability	$ (17)	(5)

The reconciliation of the Federal income tax rate to the Company's effective tax rate is as follows:

	1998	1997	1996
Federal income tax rate	35.0%	35.0	35.0
Increase (reduction) in taxes			
State and local income taxes, net of Federal tax benefits	4.2	4.0	3.9
Foreign taxes, net	—	.4	.3
Spin-off costs	.8	—	—
Other	.5	.1	(.5)
Effective tax rate	40.5%	39.5	38.7

STOCKHOLDERS' EQUITY

Four hundred million shares of common stock with a par value of $2.50 per share are authorized, of which 265 million and 251 million were issued at December 31, 1998 and 1997, respectively, including treasury shares of four million and two million in 1998 and 1997, respectively. Authorized preferred stock includes 25 million shares of preferred stock with a par value of $1.00 per share. In October 1998, 15 million shares of 8% PRIDES convertible preferred stock were converted into 14 million shares of common stock. Fifteen million shares of 8% PRIDES were issued and outstanding at December 31, 1997; no preferred shares were issued or outstanding at December 31, 1998.

To reflect the spin-off of the gaming business, the $3.3 billion book value of net assets of discontinued gaming operations as of December 31, 1998 was charged against the Company's retained earnings and additional paid-in capital.

The Company's Board of Directors has approved the repurchase by the Company of up to 20 million shares of its common stock pursuant to a stock repurchase program. The timing of the stock purchases are made at the discretion of the Company's management. At December 31, 1998, the Company had repurchased 4.3 million shares or 22 percent of the total authorized to be repurchased. The Company may at any time repurchase up to 15.7 million of the remaining shares authorized for repurchase.

The Company has a Share Purchase Rights Plan under which a right is attached to each share of the Company's common stock. The rights may only become exercisable under certain circumstances involving actual or potential acquisitions of the Company's common stock by a specified person or affiliated group. Depending on the circumstances, if the rights become exercisable, the holder may be entitled to purchase units of the Company's junior participating preferred stock, shares of the Company's common stock or shares of common stock of the acquiror. The rights remain in existence until July 2008 unless they are terminated, exercised or redeemed.

The Company applies APB Opinion 25 and related interpretations in accounting for its stock-based compensation plans. Accordingly, compensation expense recognized was different than what would have otherwise been recognized under the fair value based method defined in SFAS No. 123, "Accounting for Stock-Based

Compensation." Had compensation cost for the Company's stock-based compensation plans been determined based on the fair value at the grant dates for awards under those plans consistent with the method of SFAS No. 123, the Company's net income and net income per share would have been reduced to the pro forma amounts indicated below:

(in millions, except per share amounts)	1998	1997	1996
Income from continuing operations	$ 183	178	116
Discontinued gaming operations	92	61	(41)
Net income	$ 275	239	75
Basic EPS			
Income from continuing operations	$ .69	.66	.59
Discontinued gaming operations	.37	.25	(.21)
Net income	$ 1.06	.91	.38
Diluted EPS			
Income from continuing operations	$ .69	.66	.59
Discontinued gaming operations	.35	.24	(.21)
Net income	$ 1.04	.90	.38

At December 31, 1998, 33 million shares of common stock were reserved for the exercise of options under the Company's Stock Incentive Plans. Options may be granted to salaried officers, directors and other key employees of the Company to purchase common stock at not less than the fair market value at the date of grant. Generally, options may be exercised in installments commencing one year after the date of grant. The Stock Incentive Plans also permit the granting of Stock Appreciation Rights ("SARs"). No SARs have been granted as of December 31, 1998.

On December 31, 1998, the effective date of the spin-off, all outstanding options under the Stock Incentive Plans were adjusted to represent options to purchase an equivalent number of shares of Hilton common stock and shares of Park Place common stock. The exercise price for options to purchase Hilton common stock were adjusted based on relative values of Hilton and Park Place common stock at the date the Company's stock began trading on an exdividend basis.

The fair value of each option grant is estimated on the date of grant using the Black-Scholes option-pricing model with the following weighted-average assumptions used for grants in 1998, 1997 and 1996, respectively: dividend yield of one percent for each of the three years; expected volatility of 34, 32 and 27 percent; risk-free interest rates of 5.51, 6.49 and 6.33 percent and expected lives of six years for each of the three years.

A summary of the status of the Company's stock option plans as of December 31, 1998, 1997 and 1996, and changes during the years ending on those dates is presented below:

	Options Price Range (per share)	Weighted Average Price (per share)	Options Outstanding	Available for Grant
Balance at December 31, 1995	$ 4.68 – 12.16	$ 8.71	6,825,740	346,504
Authorized		—	—	12,000,000
Granted	11.88 – 18.70	13.28	9,777,900	(9,777,900)
Exercised	4.68 – 12.16	7.08	(2,135,426)	—
Cancelled	4.72 – 17.15	11.03	(668,758)	653,158
Balance at December 31, 1996	4.68 – 18.70	12.08	13,799,456	3,221,762
Authorized		—	—	6,200,000
Granted	15.95 – 21.30	16.73	3,046,990	(3,046,990)
Exercised	4.72 – 16.23	9.32	(1,418,185)	—
Cancelled	7.46 – 17.15	13.87	(796,642)	795,892
Balance at December 31, 1997	4.68 – 21.30	13.23	14,631,619	7,170,664
Authorized		—	—	12,000,000
Granted	12.17 – 27.53	18.23	9,113,850	(9,113,850)
Exercised	4.72 – 18.38	10.04	(692,067)	—
Cancelled	10.48 – 21.30	15.71	(2,359,632)	2,359,632
Balance at December 31, 1998	$ 4.68 – 27.53	$ 15.25	20,693,770	12,416,446

The following table summarizes information about stock options outstanding at December 31, 1998:

		Options Outstanding			Options Exercisable	
Range of Exercise Price	Number Outstanding	Weighted Average Remaining Contractual Life	Weighted Average Exercise Price		Number Exercisable	Weighted Average Exercise Price
$ 4.68 – 11.88	7,999,918	2.73	$11.32		4,867,168	$10.99
12.51 – 16.59	7,554,652	8.91	14.57		1,321,687	15.41
16.65 – 27.53	5,139,200	9.22	22.39		357,750	17.51
$ 4.68 – 27.53	20,693,770	6.60	$15.25		6,546,605	$12.24

Effective January 1, 1997, the Company adopted the 1997 Employee Stock Purchase Plan by which the Company is authorized to issue up to two million shares of common stock to its full-time employees. Under the terms of the Plan, employees can elect to have a percentage of their earnings withheld to purchase the Company's common stock.

EMPLOYEE BENEFIT PLANS

The Company has a noncontributory retirement plan ("Basic Plan") covering substantially all regular full-time, nonunion employees. The Company also has plans covering qualifying employees and non-officer directors ("Supplemental Plans"). Benefits for all plans are based upon years of service and compensation, as defined.

The Company's funding policy is to contribute not less than the minimum amount required under Federal law but not more than the maximum deductible for Federal income tax purposes. After December 31, 1996, employees will not accrue additional benefits for future service under either the Basic or Supplemental Plans. Plan assets will be used to pay benefits due employees for service through that date.

The following sets forth the funded status for the Basic Plan as of December 31, 1998 and 1997:

(in millions)	1998	1997
Actuarial present value of benefit obligation		
Projected benefit obligation for service rendered to date	$ (225)	(214)
Plan assets at fair value, primarily listed securities and temporary investments	257	242
Projected benefit obligation less than plan assets	32	28
Unrecognized gain	(45)	(41)
Accrued pension cost	$ (13)	(13)
Pension cost includes the following components		
Interest cost on projected benefit obligation	$ 15	15
Expected return on plan assets	(15)	(17)
Net periodic pension cost	$ —	(2)

Included in plan assets at fair value are equity securities of Hilton and Park Place of $21 million and $32 million at December 31, 1998 and 1997, respectively. The following sets forth the funded status for the Supplemental Plans as of December 31, 1998 and 1997:

(in millions)	1998	1997
Actuarial present value of benefit obligation		
Projected benefit obligation for service rendered to date	$ (8)	(17)
Plan assets at fair value	—	12
Projected benefit obligation in excess of plan assets	(8)	(5)
Unrecognized net loss	4	1
Accrued pension cost	$ (4)	(4)
Pension cost includes the following components		
Interest cost on projected benefit obligation	$ 1	1
Expected return on plan assets	(1)	(3)
Net periodic pension cost	$ —	(2)

The discount rate used in determining the actuarial present values of the projected benefit obligations was 6.75 percent in 1998 and 7 percent in 1997. The expected long-term rate of return on assets is 7.25 percent. The projected benefit obligation and accumulated benefit obligation were $8 million and $8 million, respectively, as of December 31, 1998. The projected benefit obligation, accumulated benefit obligation, and fair value of plan assets for pension plans with accumulated benefit obligations in excess of plan assets were $17 million, $17 million and $12 million, respectively, as of December 31, 1997.

A significant number of the Company's employees are covered by union sponsored, collectively bargained multi-employer pension plans. The Company contributed and charged to expense $11 million, $9 million and $5 million in 1998, 1997 and 1996, respectively, for such plans. Information from the plans' administrators is not sufficient to permit the Company to determine its share, if any, of unfunded vested benefits.

The Company also has other employee investment plans whereby the Company contributes certain percentages of employee contributions. The cost of these plans is not significant.

POSTRETIREMENT BENEFITS OTHER THAN PENSIONS

The Company provides life insurance benefits to certain retired employees. Under terms of the plan covering such life insurance benefits, the Company reserves the right to change, modify or discontinue these benefits. The Company does not provide postretirement health care benefits to its employees. The cost of the benefits provided is not significant.

LEASES

The Company operates seven properties under noncancellable operating leases, all of which are for land only, having remaining terms up to 44 years. Upon expiration of three of the leases, the Company has renewal options of 30, 30 and 40 years. Six leases require the payment of additional rentals based on varying percentages of revenue or income. Minimum lease commitments under noncancelable operating leases approximate $13 million annually through 2003 with an aggregate commitment of $215 million through 2042.

COMMITMENTS AND CONTINGENCIES

At December 31, 1998, the Company had contractual commitments at its wholly owned or leased properties for major expansion and rehabilitation projects of approximately $130 million.

Various lawsuits are pending against the Company. In management's opinion, disposition of these lawsuits is not expected to have a material effect on the Company's financial position or results of operations.

REVIEW QUIZ

When you feel you have covered all of the material in this chapter, answer these questions. Choose the *best* answer.

1. The figure accountants calculate by dividing Current Assets by Current Liabilities is called the:

    a. current ratio.
    b. restricted cash.
    c. additional paid-in capital.
    d. net working capital.

2. The ability of a business to pay its future obligations depends, in part, on:

    a. the ratio of current assets to long-term liabilities.
    b. the relative amounts of long-term financing by owners and creditors.
    c. whether the business's total liabilities and owners' equity equal total assets.
    d. whether the business's current assets are depreciated.

3. All of the following are limitations of the balance sheet *except:*

    a. it is based on the cost principle, and therefore often understates the value of assets.
    b. it fails to reveal the financial flexibility of the operation.
    c. it fails to reflect many elements of value to the operation.
    d. many amounts reported are based on estimates and therefore are not exact.

4. Current assets are listed on the balance sheet in:

    a. alphabetical order.
    b. order of decreasing liquidity.
    c. order of increasing amounts of assets.
    d. order of decreasing amounts of assets.

5. A hotel corporation issued 1,000 shares of common stock with a par value of $1.00 per share for $5,000. An accountant should enter _____ as Common Stock and _____ as Paid-In Capital in Excess of Par.

    a. $5,000; $–0–
    b. $2,500; $2,500
    c. $1,000; $4,000
    d. $4,000; $1,000

6. For a sole proprietorship, the Owner's Equity section of the balance sheet would include:

    a. retained earnings.
    b. a single capital account.
    c. several capital accounts.
    d. treasury stock.

REVIEW QUIZ *(continued)*

7. The full disclosure principle is the main reason for the use of which of the following?

   a. footnotes
   b. Prepaid Expenses line
   c. report format
   d. account format

Answer Key: 1-a-C1, 2-b-C1, 3-b-C2, 4-b-C3, 5-c-C3, 6-b-C3, 7-a-C4

Each question is linked to a competency. Competencies are listed on the first page of the chapter. An answer reading 3-b-C4 translates to:

   3: the question number
   b: the correct answer
   C4: the competency number

Chapter 7 Outline

Control Accounts and Subsidiary Ledgers
Specialized Journals
    Sales Journal
    Cash Receipts Journal
    Purchases Journal
    Cash Disbursements Journal
General Ledger
General Journal
Payroll Journal
Specialized Journals for Lodging
    Operations
Computerized Systems
    Hardware
    Software
    Hotel Computer Systems

Competencies

1. Define *control account* and *subsidiary ledger* and describe the relationship between them.

2. Explain the functions of specialized journals, including sales journals, cash receipts journals, purchases journals, and cash disbursements journals.

3. Describe the general ledger, the general journal, the payroll journal, and specialized journals for the lodging industry.

4. Explain features and functions of computerized accounting systems and property management systems.

7

Specialized Journals and Subsidiary Ledgers

The MANUAL ACCOUNTING SYSTEM discussed in this chapter uses several specialized journals and subsidiary ledgers. The addition of these specialized journals and subsidiary ledgers to a manual system results in greater efficiency. In manual systems, each transaction is recorded in a general journal and posted individually to general ledger accounts. Specialized journals allow for vastly reduced postings, and specialized ledgers allow for a much smaller general ledger.

However, the complete manual accounting system we describe in this chapter is less efficient than an automatic system, so we will briefly discuss the highly computerized accounting systems prevalent in hospitality businesses today. Remember, though, that to thoroughly understand a fully automated accounting system, one must first understand the basics of a manual system.

We will use the Sample Restaurant to illustrate a complete manual accounting system that uses special journals and subsidiary ledgers. This food service facility has 50 seats and is open six days of the week. Some customers choose to pay cash for food, while others pay with credit cards.

Control Accounts and Subsidiary Ledgers

When a hospitality business has only a few guests and suppliers, it can establish separate accounts for each in its general ledger. However, as a business grows and its number of guests and suppliers increases, the business operates more efficiently if it sets up **control accounts** in its general ledger for accounts receivable and accounts payable. That is, all transactions affecting guest accounts are debited or credited to a single control account, Accounts Receivable, in the general ledger. A hospitality business can also establish a **subsidiary ledger** of accounts receivable to account for the activities of each guest. Likewise, the hospitality business can establish a single control account, Accounts Payable, for recording all transactions with suppliers, as well as a subsidiary ledger of accounts payable to account for business activities with each individual supplier.

Thus, the balance of the Accounts Receivable control account in the general ledger *must* equal the sum of the balances of individual guest accounts in the **accounts receivable subsidiary ledger**. Likewise, the balance of the Accounts Payable control account in the general ledger *must* equal the sum of the supplier accounts in the **accounts payable subsidiary ledger**.

245

The subsidiary ledger accounts provide the detail for each account. For example, assume Mary Jones, a previous guest, charged three nights' stay at $40 per night on April 30. The accounts receivable subsidiary ledger would contain an account for Mary Jones reflecting the $120 charge for the three days of her stay (April 27–29). The $120 charge would be included in the total of the Accounts Receivable account in the general ledger along with amounts due from other current and past guests.

Further assume in our example that this motel had four other outstanding accounts receivable. The T-accounts for the guests from the subsidiary ledger and the accounts receivable from the general ledger would look like this:

Control Ledger
General Ledger

Accounts Receivable—Trade

20X1	
Apr. 30 (balance)	600

Accounts Receivable Subsidiary Ledger

Bill Adams

20X1	
Apr. 30 (balance)	160

Fred Dills

20X1	
Apr. 30 (balance)	80

Mary Jones

20X1	
Apr. 30 (balance)	120

Walter Miller

20X1	
Apr. 30 (balance)	160

Barb Smith

20X1		
Apr. 30 (balance)	80	

The sum of the balances of the accounts receivable accounts for guests in the accounts receivable subsidiary ledger equals the $600 balance of the Accounts Receivable—Trade control account, as shown below:

Bill Adams	$160
Fred Dills	80
Mary Jones	120
Walter Miller	160
Barb Smith	80
Total	$600

Any time a transaction affects a control account, it also affects an account in a subsidiary ledger. When the transaction is journalized, the recording must indicate which account in the subsidiary ledger is affected. Posting will be made to both the control account and the account in the subsidiary ledger. For example, assume a hotel purchases food worth $300 on account from General Foods, Inc., and records the transaction as follows:

		Post. Ref.	Debit	Credit
July 1	Food Purchases	401	$300	
	Accounts Payable—			
	General Foods, Inc.	201/✓		$300

The food purchase amount is posted as a debit to Food Purchases (account #401) in the general ledger. Accounts Payable (account #201) in the general ledger is credited for $300, and the General Foods, Inc. account in the accounts payable subsidiary ledger is also credited for $300. The posting to the account in the accounts payable subsidiary ledger is indicated with a check mark (✓), while postings to general ledger accounts are indicated with the account number of the appropriate general ledger accounts as shown above in the Post. Ref. (posting reference) column.

The number of control accounts and subsidiary ledgers maintained by a hospitality business depends on the business's information needs. When detailed information for similar types of accounts should be maintained, a control account and related subsidiary ledger should also be established. The most common control accounts and subsidiary ledgers are for accounts receivable and accounts payable.

In the lodging segment of the hospitality industry, Accounts Receivable— Trade consists of accounts receivable for current guests and nonguests. These accounts are generally kept in two separate ledgers. The related subsidiary ledgers are typically called the *guest ledger* and the *city ledger.*

The **guest ledger** consists of accounts for guests currently staying in the lodging facility, while the **city ledger** consists of accounts for noncurrent guests and local businesses. The guest ledger is maintained in the front office and the accounts are maintained in guestroom order to facilitate posting various charges to the guest accounts. The city ledger is generally maintained in the accounting office for posting cash received on account. These separate ledgers result in greater efficiency in processing accounting transactions than a single accounts receivable subsidiary ledger would afford.

In addition to control accounts and subsidiary ledgers, hospitality firms use specialized journals. Each specialized journal is used for recording transactions of a particular nature.

Specialized Journals

The use of only the general journal to record transactions is adequate for the very smallest businesses. However, accounting systems in larger businesses are more efficient if the firms use a special journal for each type of transaction. For example, a firm might use a different specialized journal to record each type of activity, such as cash disbursements, purchases, and sales.

Several advantages of using specialized journals include increased efficiency and improvements in internal control. Increased efficiencies include:

1. Time saved in recording transactions. Just one line is used in the journal, since debits and credits are recorded in the appropriate columns and no explanation is required.

2. Time saved in posting to the ledger accounts. Transactions recorded in the general journal are posted individually to general ledger accounts. With specialized journals, column *totals*—not individual transactions—are posted to the appropriate general ledger accounts.

Specialized journals provide several safeguards that improve internal control. They reduce the potential for errors in the following ways:

1. The division of duties prevents one employee from handling any single transaction from beginning to end. For example, one employee records a meal charged in the hotel's restaurant and another posts the amount to the guest's account while a third, the cashier, collects the amount due when the guest checks out of the hotel.

2. Since the general ledger accounts have significantly fewer entries, the potential for errors in posting is greatly reduced.

Several journals are designed to systematically record the major recurring types of transactions. The following specialized journals, illustrated in this section of the chapter, pertain to the Sample Restaurant:

1. **Sales journal**, used to record sales of food on account

2. **Cash receipts journal**, used to record all cash received by the business, including cash sales, collection of accounts, and other cash inflows

3. **Purchases journal**, used to record all purchases of food on account

4. **Cash disbursements journal**, used to record all checks written by the Sample Restaurant

In addition, the Sample Restaurant uses a general journal to record transactions and activities that are not recorded in one of the specialized journals. The Sample Restaurant uses the general journal to record adjusting and closing entries.

The various ledger account pages contain a posting reference column. The accounting employee records the sources of the postings in this column. For example, the employee writes an *S* in this column if the transaction was originally recorded in the sales journal. Businesses commonly use the following abbreviations in the posting reference column for the five journals:

Journal	Abbreviation
Sales journal	S
Cash receipts journal	CR
Purchases journal	P
Cash disbursements journal	CD
General journal	GJ

Each entry in these specialized journals must be supported by evidence that proves that the transaction did occur. For example, each charge sale must be supported by a server check that indicates the date, the amount of the sale, the food sold to the customer, and the customer's signature acknowledging the purchase. Required documentation might also include a supplier invoice to support each cash disbursement. The supplier invoice would reveal the date of the purchase, the invoice number, the items purchased, and the amount of the purchase.

Sales Journal

Sales in most hospitality businesses may be either cash or *charge* (also known as *credit*) sales. The sales journal is used to record the charge sales, while cash sales are recorded in the cash receipts journal (discussed in the next section of this chapter). The sales journal of the Sample Restaurant has the following column headings:

Date	Customer	Server Check No.	Accts. Rec. Dr. 105 Sales Cr. 301	
			Amount	✓

The date of the sale is recorded in the Date column. The customer's name is recorded to show which accounts receivable subsidiary ledger account is to be debited by the amount of the sales transaction. The number of the server check that documents the sale is recorded in the Server Check Number column. The Accounts Receivable and Sales column is for recording the amount due the Sample

Restaurant and the amount of the sale. A check mark is placed in the "✔" column when the amount is posted to the customer's account in the subsidiary ledger.

Exhibit 1 shows the Sample Restaurant's sales journal for May. Remember, only charge sales are recorded in this journal, while cash sales are recorded in the cash receipts journal. The sales journal shows that only five charge sales were made during May. The name of each customer making a food purchase was recorded in the sales journal, along with the server check number and the amount. (Other server checks were used in cash sales.) A check was placed in the "✔" column as each amount was posted to the customer's account. To ensure that customers' accounts are updated, amounts are posted daily to them. The posting reference of *S1* (*sales* journal, page 1) is entered by each posting in the customer's account and also by the totals posted to general ledger accounts. The total of $219.57 for the month was posted at the end of May to the general ledger accounts—as a debit to Accounts Receivable (account #105) and as a credit to Sales (account #301). These two account numbers are written in the sales journal under the total amount of $219.57 to reflect the completed posting to the general ledger accounts.

As discussed previously, the total of the accounts receivable subsidiary accounts must equal the balance of the control account, Accounts Receivable. The sum of the accounts in the accounts receivable subsidiary ledger of $33.28 + $43.19 + $29.22 + $67.08 + $46.80 equals $219.57, the balance of the accounts receivable control account in the general ledger.

Cash Receipts Journal

A hospitality business uses a cash receipts journal to record all its cash inflows. The major column headings in the cash receipts journal reflect the most frequent cash transactions. Less frequent sources of cash are usually recorded in the Other Accounts columns of the cash receipts journal. The following are the Sample Restaurant's cash receipts journal column headings:

		Cash Dr. 101	Accounts Rec. Cr. 105		Sales Cr. 301	Other Accounts Cr.			
Date	Description		Amount	✔		Acct. Title	Acct. #	Amount	✔

The Date column is for recording the date of the cash receipt. The Description column allows a brief description of the activity, such as "cash sales" or "sale of capital stock." Each transaction recorded in the cash receipts journal involves cash; therefore, a cash amount will be recorded in the Cash column for each activity. The Accounts Receivable columns are for recording the amount of the cash received on account from customers and also for entering a check in the "✔" column when the amounts are posted to the customers' accounts in the accounts receivable subsidiary ledger. Customers' accounts should be posted daily to maintain current account balances. When a customer pays on account, the bookkeeper should indicate the customer's name in the Description column, such as "payment on account—Fred Weeks." The Sales column is used to record cash sales, while the Other Accounts columns are used to record all cash activities

Exhibit 1 Sales Journal

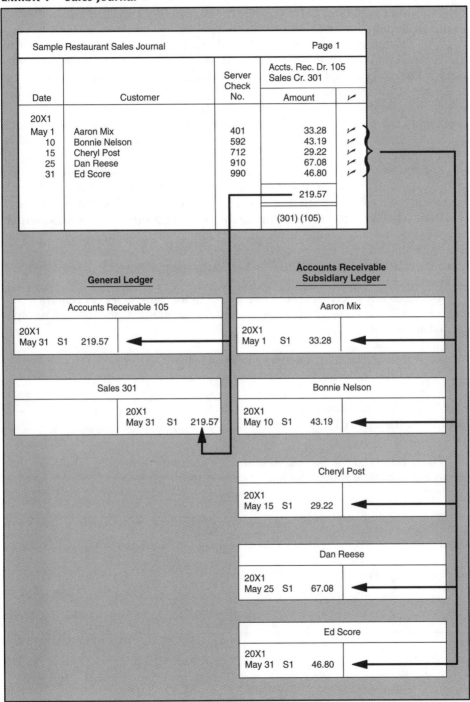

other than those just described. For example, in a sale of capital stock for $1,000, Cash would be debited for $1,000, while the Capital Stock account (account #257) would be credited for $1,000.

Exhibit 2 is the Sample Restaurant's cash receipts journal for May 20X1, which shows detail only for May 1–4 and May 31. All cash receipts are recorded in this journal. The totals of the Cash, Accounts Receivable, and Sales columns are posted to the respective general ledger accounts at the end of the month. Amounts are posted to accounts in the accounts receivable subsidiary ledger on a daily basis. A check is placed in the "✔" column next to the amount in the journal when the posting is completed. Each item in the Other Accounts columns is posted individually to the appropriate general ledger account. During May, the Capital Stock account was affected when the Sample Restaurant sold 100 shares of stock for $10 each for a total of $1,000. The *total* of this column is not posted to any account, since each amount in the column is posted individually, and so indicated with a check mark.

In each ledger account, the source of the posting *CR1* (for *cash receipts* journal, page *1*) is shown alongside the amount and the date. As we noted with the sales journal postings to the accounts receivable subsidiary ledger, the amounts posted to the individual accounts of $20.00 + $43.19 must equal the total of $63.19 posted to the control account in the general ledger.

The Accounts Receivable control account in the general ledger reflects a balance of $156.38 after it receives postings from the sales journal and the cash receipts journal at the end of May:

Accounts Receivable 105

20X1			20X1		
May 31	S1	219.57	May 31	CR1	63.19
May 31	(balance)	156.38			

The accounts in the Sample Restaurant's accounts receivable subsidiary ledger after postings from the sales and cash receipts journals would be as follows:

Aaron Mix

20X1			20X1		
May 1	S1	33.28	May 4	CR1	20.00
May 31	(balance)	13.28			

Bonnie Nelson

20X1			20X1		
May 10	S1	43.19	May 31	CR1	43.19
May 31	(balance)	–0–			

Exhibit 2 Cash Receipts Journal

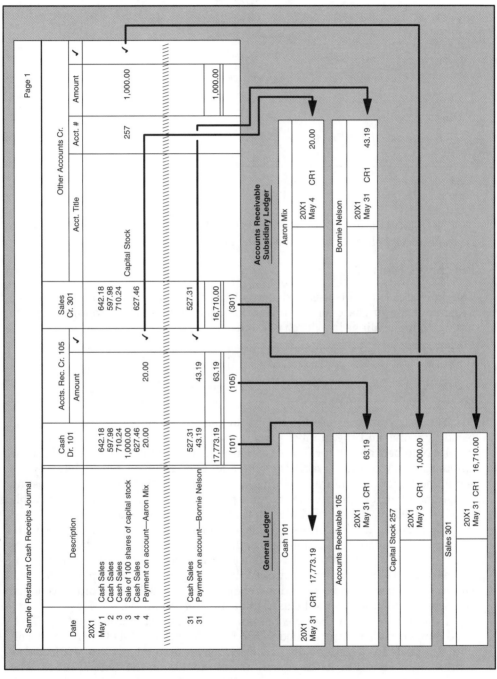

Sample Restaurant Cash Receipts Journal — Page 1

Date	Description	Cash Dr. 101	Accts. Rec. Cr. 105 Amount	✓	Sales Cr. 301	Other Accounts Cr. Acct. Title	Acct. #	Amount	✓
20X1 May 1	Cash Sales	642.18			642.18				
2	Cash Sales	597.98			597.98				
3	Cash Sales	710.24			710.24				
3	Sale of 100 shares of capital stock	1,000.00				Capital Stock	257	1,000.00	✓
4	Cash Sales	627.46			627.46				
4	Payment on account—Aaron Mix	20.00	20.00	✓					
31	Cash Sales	527.31			527.31				
31	Payment on account—Bonnie Nelson	43.19	43.19	✓					
		17,773.19	63.19		16,710.00			1,000.00	
		(101)	(105)		(301)				

General Ledger

Cash 101
20X1 May 31	CR1	17,773.19

Accounts Receivable 105
20X1 May 31	CR1	63.19

Capital Stock 257
20X1 May 3	CR1	1,000.00

Sales 301
20X1 May 31	CR1	16,710.00

Accounts Receivable Subsidiary Ledger

Aaron Mix
20X1 May 4	CR1	20.00

Bonnie Nelson
20X1 May 31	CR1	43.19

Cheryl Post		
20X1		
May 15 S1	29.22	

Dan Reese		
20X1		
May 25 S1	67.08	

Ed Score		
20X1		
May 31 S1	46.80	

The total of these accounts of $156.38 is and must be equal to the balance of the accounts receivable control account in the general ledger.

Purchases Journal

The purchases journal is used to record all purchases on account. For the Sample Restaurant, the purchases on account are food items for resale. The following are the basic column headings in a purchases journal:

Date	Supplier	Invoice No.	Accts. Pay. Cr. 201 Food Purch. Dr. 401	
			Amount	✓

The Date column is used to record the date of the purchase. The supplier is listed by name, and the number from the supporting invoice is recorded in the Invoice Number column for future reference. A single column is provided for the amount since Accounts Payable is credited and Food Purchases is debited by the same amount for each transaction. Checks in the check column indicate the posting of the amount to the appropriate accounts payable account in the accounts payable subsidiary ledger. Just as the individual accounts receivable accounts are posted daily, so the individual accounts payable accounts should be posted daily to maintain up-to-date records of amounts owed. A hospitality business that purchases goods other than food for resale would use additional columns, and the Food Purchases column would be separate from accounts payable. For example, such a firm would record beverage, food, and gift shop items for resale in separate accounts, and separate columns would be used in the purchases journal.

Exhibit 3 shows the Sample Restaurant's purchases journal for May 20X1. Food purchases on account totaled $4,686.34 for May. The total of the Amount column was posted as a credit to the Accounts Payable account (account #201) and as a debit to the Food Purchases account (account #401) in the general ledger. The cross-reference noted in the ledger accounts is *P1* (for *purchases* journal, page *1*). The account numbers for these two accounts, 401 and 201, are noted under the total

Exhibit 3   Purchases Journal

Sample Restaurant Purchases Journal			Page 1	
		Invoice No.	Accts. Pay. Cr. 201 Food Purchases Dr. 401	
Date	Supplier		Amount	✓
20X1				
May 1	Food Corp.	1450	601.27	✓
7	Spartan Co.	629	1,194.00	✓
11	Chips, Inc.	428	246.05	✓
19	Food Corp.	1506	797.00	✓
24	ABC Beverages	112	429.81	✓
31	Spartan Co.	707	1,418.21	✓
			4,686.34	
			(401) (201)	

General Ledger

Accounts Payable 201	
	20X1 May 31 P1 4,686.34

Food Purchases 401	
20X1 May 31 P1 4,686.34	

Accounts Payable Subsidiary Ledger

ABC Beverages	
	20X1 May 24 P1 429.81

Chips, Inc.	
	20X1 May 11 P1 246.05

Food Corp.	
	20X1 May 1 P1 601.27
	May 19 P1 797.00

Spartan Co.	
	20X1 May 7 P1 1,194.00
	May 31 P1 1,418.21

of the Amount column in the purchases journal to indicate posting of the totals. Each transaction amount has been posted to an account in the accounts payable subsidiary journal and so indicated with a check in the "✔" column of the journal. Each posting in the accounts payable subsidiary ledger account reveals the date and the source, which in this example is P1 for each amount.

The total postings to the accounts payable subsidiary ledger must equal the total posted to the Accounts Payable control account in the general ledger.

Cash Disbursements Journal

Accountants use the cash disbursements journal to record all transactions involving the payment of cash. Most hospitality businesses pay their bills by check, since this provides greater control over cash. The columns of a cash disbursement journal will vary by the business, depending on the purposes of the disbursements. A fairly simple cash disbursements journal would have the following column headings:

Date	Payee/ Description	Check No.	Cash Cr. 101	Accounts Pay. Dr. 201		Payroll Exp. Dr. 501	Other Accounts Dr.			
				Amount	✔		Acct. Title	Acct. #	Amount	✔

The Date column is for recording the date of the cash disbursement. The Payee/Description column is used for recording to whom the check is written and an explanation. For example, a payment to XYZ Corporation for its invoice #500 might be shown as "XYZ Corp., invoice #500." The Check No. column is for recording the numbers of the company's checks. (For control purposes checks should be used in numerical order. The employee writing the checks should void any unusable checks by writing *VOID* across the face of the check.) The first amount column is for cash since each transaction will involve cash. The Accounts Payable column is further divided into an amount column and a check (✔) column. The check column is used to indicate posting to the accounts payable subsidiary ledger account. In this particular journal form, a column is provided for payroll expense to record the amounts paid to employees. Finally, the last four columns pertain to accounts that will be debited. Examples of such accounts include Rent Expense, Supplies Expense, and Utilities Expense. For each transaction, the account title, account number, and amount must be recorded. The check column is used to indicate the posting to each account in the general ledger.

Exhibit 4 contains the Sample Restaurant's cash disbursements journal for the month of May. Disbursements for May totaled $11,257.56; this amount was posted as a credit to the Cash account in the general ledger. Three charge bills from suppliers of food, which were recorded earlier in the purchases journal, were paid. The Accounts Payable control account in the general ledger was debited for $2,041.32, and the individual accounts in the accounts payable subsidiary ledger were debited the day of payment so that they were kept current. Payroll Expense in the general ledger was posted for total amounts paid to Sample Restaurant employees. Businesses often maintain a separate payroll journal. Since the Sample Restaurant

Sample Restaurant Cash Disbursements Journal

Date	Payee/Description	Check No.	Cash Cr. 101	Accts. Pay. Dr. 201 Amount	✓	Payroll Exp. Dr. 501	Other Accounts Dr. Acct. Title	Acct. #	Amount	✓
20X1										
May 1	Pleasant Supplies—Inv. 468	501	49.15				Supplies Exp.	510	49.15	
2	Kern Office Supplies—Inv. 915	502	64.28				Office Supplies Exp.	511	64.28	
3	Realty Rentals—Rent for May	503	2,000.00				Rent Expense	515	2,000.00	
8	Food Corp.—Inv. 1450	504	601.27	601.27						
12	Miller Ins. Agency—Ins. for May	505	200.00				Insurance Exp.	514	200.00	
15	Pleasant Supplies—Inv. 530	506	72.81				Supplies Exp.	510	72.81	
19	Spartan Co.—Inv. 629	507	1,194.00	1,194.00						
23	Chips, Inc.—Inv. 428	508	246.05	246.05						
31	Melody Adams—Payroll	509	640.00			640.00				
31	Nelson Boyd—Payroll	510	720.00			720.00				
31	Omar Cousy—Payroll	511	710.00			710.00				
31	Paul Ditmar—Payroll	512	1,020.00			1,020.00				
31	Ron East—Payroll	513	820.00			820.00				
31	Steve Floyd—Payroll	514	920.00			920.00				
31	Wes Hills—Payroll	515	2,000.00			2,000.00				
			11,257.56	2,041.32		6,830.00			2,386.24	
			(101)	(201)		(501)				

General Ledger

Cash 101

20X1
May 31 CD1 11,257.56

Accounts Payable 201

20X1
May 31 CD1 2,041.32

Payroll Expense 501

20X1
May 31 CD1 6,830.00

Supplies Expense 510

20X1
May 1 CD1 49.15
15 CD1 72.81

Office Supplies Expense 511

20X1
May 2 CD1 64.28

Rent Expense 515

20X1
May 3 CD1 2,000.00

Insurance Expense 514

20X1
May 12 CD1 200.00

Accounts Payable Subsidiary Ledger

Food Corp.

20X1
May 8 CD1 601.27

Spartan Co.

20X1
May 19 CD1 1,194.00

Chips, Inc.

20X1
May 23 CD1 246.05

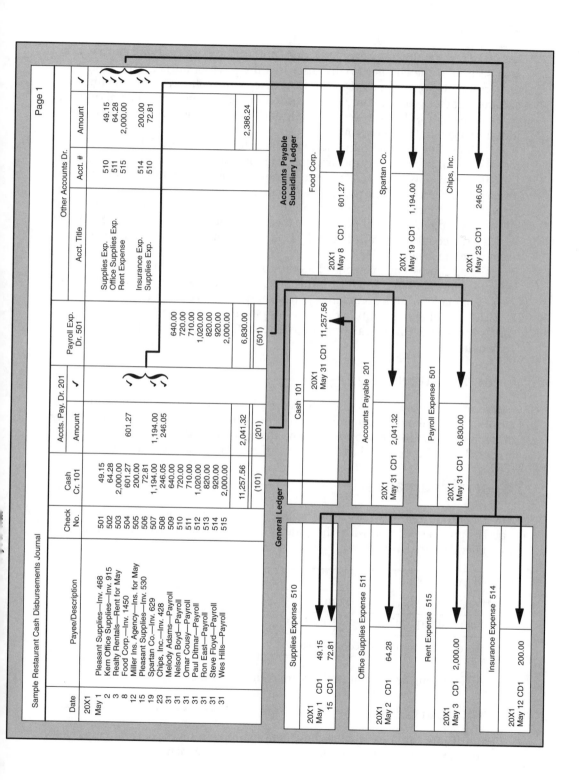

has just a few employees, however, it does not use a separate payroll journal. (The next section of the chapter briefly discusses the payroll journal.) The remaining disbursements were recorded in the Other Accounts columns. The account title, account number, and amount were recorded for each transaction. Furthermore, a check in the journal by each amount indicates that the amounts were posted to the individual general ledger accounts.

Each posting to an account indicates the date; the source, *CD1* (*cash disbursements* journal, page 1); and the amount. The total of each amount column except for Other Accounts is posted, and the account number is written below the total amount to indicate that the posting has occurred. The amounts of the three checks written to suppliers were posted to the supplier accounts in the accounts payable subsidiary ledger. The total postings to these three accounts ($601.27 + $1,194.00 + $246.05) equal the total of $2,041.32 posted to the Accounts Payable control account in the general ledger.

The Accounts Payable control account and the accounts payable subsidiary ledger accounts in T-account form appear in Exhibit 5 as they would look after postings were made from the purchases journal and the cash disbursements journal.

The sum of the accounts in the accounts payable subsidiary ledger of $2,645.02 equals the May 31, 20X1 balance of the Accounts Payable control account in the general ledger.

General Ledger

After amounts from the specialized ledgers have been posted at the end of the month, a trial balance of general ledger accounts is prepared to prove the equality of debits and credits. Exhibit 6 contains the Sample Restaurant's general ledger accounts, and Exhibit 7 is the trial balance of the general ledger accounts.

General Journal

The general journal is used to record transactions that do not fit in a specialized journal. The purchase of land with a hospitality company's stock would be recorded in the general journal as follows:

Land (Acct. #150)	$10,000	
Common Stock (Acct. #250)		$10,000
To record acquisition of land with 1,000		
shares of the company's common stock.		

All adjusting and closing entries are recorded in the general journal.

Payroll Journal

A **payroll journal** is used when hospitality companies have several employees. The column headings of a payroll journal may look like this:

Exhibit 5   Accounts Payable Control and Detailed Accounts

General Ledger	Accounts Payable Subsidiary Ledger

Accounts Payable 201

20X1		20X1		
May 31 CD1 2,041.32	May 31 P1 4,686.34			
	Balance 2,645.02			

ABC Beverages

	20X1		
	May 24 P1	429.81
	Balance	429.81

Chips, Inc.

20X1		20X1		
May 23 CD1 246.05	May 11 P1 246.05
	Balance 0.00

Food Corp.

20X1	20X1		
May 8 CD1 601.27	May 1 P1 601.27
	May 19 P1 797.00
	Balance 797.00

Spartan Co.

20X1	20X1		
May 19 CD1 1,194.00	May 7 P1 1,194.00
	May 31 P1 1,418.21
	Balance 1,418.21

					Deductions			Net Pay
Date	Employee	Check No.	Salary Expense Dr. 501		Fed. Inc. Taxes Payable Cr. 207	FICA Taxes Payable Cr. 208	St. Inc. Taxes Payable Cr. 209	Payroll Cash Cr. 102

The Date column is used to record the date of each check. The employee's name is recorded in the Employee column, and the check number is recorded in the Check No. column. The gross amount of the check is recorded under Salary Expense, while deductions (for taxes due) are recorded in three columns: Federal Income Taxes Payable, FICA Taxes Payable, and State Income Taxes Payable. The

Exhibit 6   Sample Restaurant General Ledger

Account Title ___Cash___   Account No. ___101___

Date		Accounts/Explanation	Post. Ref.	Debit	Credit	Balance
20X1						
May	31	Cash receipts for May	CR 1	1 7 7 7 3 19		1 7 7 7 3 19
	31	Cash disbursements for May	CD 1		1 1 2 5 7 56	6 5 1 5 63

Account Title ___Accounts Receivable___   Account No. ___105___

Date		Accounts/Explanation	Post. Ref.	Debit	Credit	Balance
20X1						
May	31	Sales on account	S 1	2 1 9 57		2 1 9 57
	31	Collections during May	CR 1		6 3 19	1 5 6 38

Account Title ___Accounts Payable___   Account No. ___201___

Date		Accounts/Explanation	Post. Ref.	Debit	Credit	Balance
20X1						
May	31	Purchases on account for May	P 1		4 6 8 6 34	4 6 8 6 34
	31	Payments on account for May	CD 1	2 0 4 1 32		2 6 4 5 02

Account Title ___Capital Stock___   Account No. ___257___

Date		Accounts/Explanation	Post. Ref.	Debit	Credit	Balance
20X1						
May	3	Sale of 100 shares	CR 1		1 0 0 0 00	1 0 0 0 00

Account Title ___Sales___   Account No. ___301___

Date		Accounts/Explanation	Post. Ref.	Debit	Credit	Balance
20X1						
May	31	Sales on account	S 1		2 1 9 57	2 1 9 57
May	31	Cash sales	CR 1		1 6 7 1 0 00	1 6 9 2 9 57

Exhibit 6 *(continued)*

Account Title		Food Purchases		Account No. 401				
Date		Accounts/Explanation	Post. Ref.	Debit		Credit		Balance
20X1								
May	31	Purchases during May	P 1	4 6 8 6 34				4 6 8 6 34

Account Title		Payroll Expense		Account No. 501				
Date		Accounts/Explanation	Post. Ref.	Debit		Credit		Balance
20X1								
May	31	Payroll expense for May	CD 1	6 8 3 0 00				6 8 3 0 00

Account Title		Supplies Expense		Account No. 510				
Date		Accounts/Explanation	Post. Ref.	Debit		Credit		Balance
20X1								
May	1	Purchased supplies	CD 1	4 9 15				4 9 15
	15	Purchased supplies	CD 1	7 2 81				1 2 1 96

Account Title		Office Supplies Expense		Account No. 511				
Date		Accounts/Explanation	Post. Ref.	Debit		Credit		Balance
20X1								
May	2	Purchased office supplies	CD 1	6 4 28				6 4 28

Account Title		Insurance Expense		Account No. 514				
Date		Accounts/Explanation	Post. Ref.	Debit		Credit		Balance
20X1								
May	12	Insurance expense for May	CD 1	2 0 0 00				2 0 0 00

Account Title		Rent Expense		Account No. 515				
Date		Accounts/Explanation	Post. Ref.	Debit		Credit		Balance
20X1								
May	3	Rent expense for May	CD 1	2 0 0 0 00				2 0 0 0 00

Exhibit 7   Trial Balance

	Trial Balance Sample Restaurant		
Account Title	Account Numbers	Debits	Credits
Cash	101	$ 6,515.63	
Accounts Receivable	105	156.38	
Accounts Payable	201		$ 2,645.02
Capital Stock	257		1,000.00
Sales	301		16,929.57
Food Purchases	401	4,686.34	
Payroll Expense	501	6,830.00	
Supplies Expense	510	121.96	
Office Supplies Expense	511	64.28	
Insurance Expense	514	200.00	
Rent Expense	515	2,000.00	
		$ 20,574.59	$20,574.59

difference between salary expense and the deductions is net pay, which is the amount of each check. The net pay amount is recorded in the Payroll Cash column. The only expense account shown in this payroll journal is Salary Expense, while the three liability accounts are used to record payroll tax amounts due to various governmental agencies. Payroll Cash is a checking account used only for payroll purposes. There may be many more deductions, such as those for other taxes and for life insurance, health insurance, and savings bonds. The process remains the same: salary expense less deductions equals net pay.

Specialized Journals for Lodging Operations

In lodging operations, certain specialized journals are maintained in the front office for recording transactions involving guests. The three journals we'll discuss are the front office cash receipts and disbursements journal, the allowance journal, and the transfer journal.

The **front office cash receipts and disbursements journal** is used for recording cash transactions involving lodging guests. The column headings of this journal are as follows:

			Cash Receipts			Cash Disbursements		
Room No.	Guest	✓	Cash Debit	Credits		Cash Credit	Debit	
				Guest	City		Guest	City

The room number pertains to the lodging guest's room number, while the guest's name is recorded to show which guest account in one of the subsidiary ledgers should be debited or credited for the activity. The posting reference column indicates that the amount has been posted to the guest account in the subsidiary ledger. Cash receipts received from current or former guests are recorded in the Cash column. The credit is recorded under either the guest or city columns, depending on where the guest's ledger account is located. Cash disbursements for specific guests, such as payments for packages received COD, are also recorded in this journal. The amount expended is debited to the guest's account and recorded in the appropriate column (Guest or City, depending on the location of the guest's ledger account), and the Cash account is credited.

Amounts recorded in the front office cash receipts and disbursements journal should be posted as soon as possible to guests' ledger accounts to avoid unposted charges when guests check out of the lodging facility.

Allowance vouchers are recorded in the **allowance journal**. The following are the column headings of this journal:

Date	Voucher No.	Guest	Room No.	✓	Guest Cr.	City Cr.	Room Sales Allow. Dr.	Food Sales Allow. Dr.	Telephone Sales Allow. Dr.	Other Accounts Dr.			
										Acct. Title	Acct. #	Amount	✓

The Date column is used to record the date of the voucher. The allowance voucher number is recorded in the Voucher No. column. Guests' names are recorded in the Guest column, while current guests' room numbers are recorded in the Room No. column. The posting reference column indicates that the amount has been posted to the guest's ledger account. Since allowances are issued to reduce charges, a credit results in a reduction to the guest's account. The amount is recorded in the Guest or City column, depending on the location of the guest's account. The amount is also debited to a sales allowance account. This particular allowance journal form allows for debits to Room Sales Allowances, Food Sales Allowances, or Telecommunications Sales Allowances. If other accounts were to be debited, such as Beverage Sales Allowance, the amount and account number would be recorded in the two columns on the right side of this journal. The monthly totals are posted to the proper general ledger accounts.

The **transfer journal** records the transfer of one person's account to another in the same ledger or to another ledger. For example, suppose a guest checks out of the hotel and is to be billed direct. Since the individual is no longer a hotel guest, his or her account would be transferred from the guest ledger to the city ledger.

The column headings of a transfer journal would look like this:

Date	Guest	Room No.	Guest Ledger				City Ledger			
			Debit	✓	Credit	✓	Debit	✓	Credit	✓

The Date column records the date of the transfer. The guest's name and room number are recorded in the Guest and Room No. columns, respectively. The Guest Ledger Debit column is used to record transfers to an account in the guest ledger, while the Guest Ledger Credit column records transfers from an account in the guest ledger. The City Ledger columns relate to similar transfers involving accounts in the city ledger. All posting reference columns are for indicating that the amount has been recorded in the ledger account.

Computerized Systems

The accounting system described in this chapter is a manual system that uses physical journals and ledgers. In practice, however, only the smallest hospitality organizations still use such manual systems.

Instead of manual accounting systems, many hospitality organizations use fully integrated computerized systems. The major advantages of computerized accounting systems are their speed, accuracy, and efficiency. Hospitality businesses have become so large and complex that they can provide the highest possible level of services only by using computers.

Technological advances have made computers affordable for smaller hospitality businesses. Computers, commonly used for reservations and front office accounting, are now used by many accounting operations in small and medium-sized lodging and food service establishments.

Many computer systems perform real-time processing, an operating feature that processes input very quickly, updates files, and makes output immediately available on a current basis. A system of this kind is invaluable to a hotel, which may conduct business 24 hours a day, 365 days a year.

Computer systems possess two major components: hardware and software. *Hardware* is the equipment that makes up a computer system: keyboards, monitors, printers, disk drives, tape drives, and other input/output devices. *Software* refers to the instructions and programs that direct computer operations.

Hardware

The major hardware components of a microcomputer system are a central processing unit (CPU), a display screen, a keyboard, and disk drives.

The CPU is the control center of a computer system. Inside are the circuits and mechanisms that process and store information and send instructions to the other components of the system. The same physical frame that houses the CPU may also include the disk drives.

Information can be entered into or retrieved from the CPU using a keyboard similar to a typewriter keyboard. Data can be entered, updated, and recalled at will using the keyboard, a mouse, a touch-sensitive screen, or other devices.

The information requested through keyboard commands may be printed on paper by means of a printer or displayed on a *screen*, which is also called a *monitor* or *video display terminal.*

Volumes of data can be stored (filed) on storage devices such as magnetic tape units or magnetic disk units. Data stored on tape units must be in a sequential arrangement; the updating or retrieval of information on these units is time-consuming because of this sequential operation. Magnetic disks store data in an arrangement that allows random access. Magnetic disk storage units allow almost immediate posting and quick access to any record.

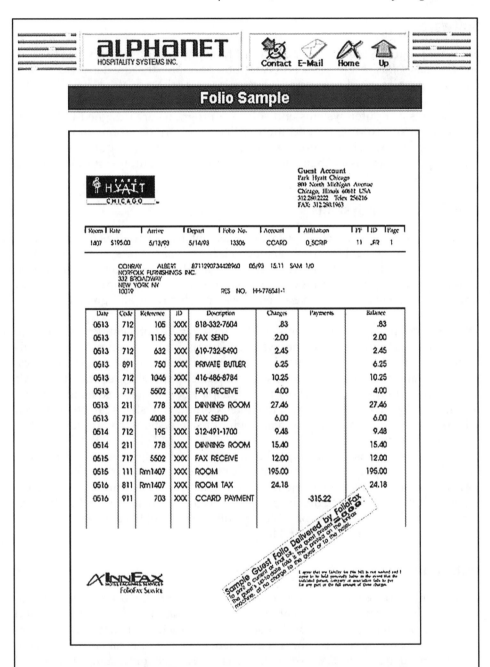

AlphaNet Hospitality Systems manufactures a special, quiet fax machine called an Inn-Fax Machine (promoted on their Internet site at http://www.alphanet.net/com bine.cgi?content=ahs/products/innfax/folio). Guests can receive copies of their folios at the touch of a button from their guestrooms. (Courtesy of AlphaNet Telecom Inc.)

Software

Software programs tell the computer what to do, how to do it, and when to do it. *Applications software* refers to sets of computer programs that are designed for specific uses such as word processing, electronic spreadsheet analysis, and database management.

Today's computer systems and software programs are designed to be user-friendly—easier to operate and more efficient. Many programs have built-in options through which operators can request help from the computer itself. Computer suppliers may assist their customers by providing computer installation and employee training.

Hotel Computer Systems

Computer systems for hotel property management are as varied as the hotels they serve. They are available for both small and large hotels. Some systems are modular and can be expanded to fit the needs of the hotel and its management. A computer-based property management system (PMS) offers opportunities for improved guest services, increased employee productivity, and greater management efficiency.

Property management systems are designed to give hotel employees access to the hotel's electronic information system. Various types of computer terminals allow direct access and communication within the hotel using this information system. Users at remote locations can instantly update the hotel's accounts. Terminals are usually equipped with keyboards and display screens (and sometimes printers) and are located in vital areas of the hotel. Computer systems can be interfaced with telephone call accounting systems, point-of-sale systems, and in-house entertainment systems.

PMS applications can be divided into two broad functional areas: front office and back office applications. PMS front office applications integrate such functions as reservations, rooms management, and guest accounting within a hotel's information network. PMS back office applications typically include such functions as accounts receivable, accounts payable, payroll accounting, fixed asset accounting, financial reporting, and the general ledger.

Summary

All accounting transactions could be recorded in a general journal and posted to general ledger accounts that might include separate accounts for each guest and supplier. However, hospitality businesses are more efficient when they use specialized journals and ledgers. Businesses use a ledger of accounts for customers, generally referred to as a *subsidiary accounts receivable ledger,* for tracking charges and payments from each customer. The total of these accounts equals the total in the control account Accounts Receivable in the general ledger. Likewise, the accounts payable subsidiary ledger consists of an account for each supplier; the total of the accounts in this ledger equals the balance of the control account Accounts Payable.

Specialized journals are established to record sales, cash disbursements, cash receipts, and purchases. These journals greatly reduce the number of postings to general ledger accounts. And, as different personnel are assigned to maintaining the ledgers and journals, more effective internal control is achieved.

A hotel operation has specialized journals maintained in the front office to account for hotel guest activities. Three major specialized journals are the front office cash receipts and disbursements journal, the allowance journal, and the transfer journal.

Most of the chapter focuses on manual accounting systems. However, many of today's hospitality firms use some computerization, which makes a firm's accounting operations more efficient.

Key Terms

accounts payable subsidiary ledger—A subsidiary ledger that holds the accounts of those suppliers from which the hospitality firm purchases items on account.

accounts receivable subsidiary ledger—A subsidiary ledger that holds the accounts of those guests of the hospitality firm who purchase things on account.

allowance journal—A journal used to record allowance vouchers when a sale is discounted.

cash disbursements journal—A journal used to record all transactions involving the payment of cash.

cash receipts journal—A journal used to record all cash inflows into a hospitality firm, including cash sales and cash collections.

city ledger—A subsidiary ledger with an alphabetical listing of accounts receivable from guests who have already checked out of the hotel and any other receivables.

control accounts—Accounts used to summarize all similar transactions that occur in a hospitality firm, such as all accounts receivable transactions.

front office cash receipts and disbursements journal—A journal used to record cash receipts and disbursements involving lodging guests.

guest ledger—A subsidiary ledger that lists the accounts receivable of guests currently staying in the hotel.

payroll journal—A journal containing a record of each payroll check issued, along with the corresponding gross pay and various deductions for federal tax, state tax, city tax, FICA, employee health care contributions, and miscellaneous contributions such as union dues.

purchases journal—A journal used to record all purchases made on account.

sales journal—A journal used for posting all sales transactions on account.

subsidiary ledger—A special ledger that provides more detailed information about an account, is controlled by the general ledger, and is used when there are several accounts with a common characteristic.

transfer journal—A journal used to record the transfer of one person's account to another in the same ledger or to another ledger.

Review Questions

1. What is a *control account?*
2. Why do businesses use specialized journals?
3. How do businesses record purchases on account?
4. What are *subsidiary ledgers?*
5. When should activities of hotel guests be posted to the subsidiary ledger accounts, and why then?
6. When are column totals of specialized journals posted, and why then?
7. How do hospitality firms record payroll accruals at the end of the accounting period?
8. When should control accounts be established?
9. What disbursements are recorded in the front office cash receipts and disbursements journal?
10. What journals are maintained in the front office of a lodging property?

Problems

Problem 1

Identify the journal in which each of the following transactions would be recorded. Assume the business uses the specialized journals discussed in this chapter, as well as a general journal.

1. Cash beverage sales are for $1,500.
2. Beverages purchased on account totaled $800.
3. An adjusting entry to recognize bad debt expenses of $500.
4. Charge food sales total $2,000.
5. Wages of $500 for James Haslett, an employee, for the pay period.
6. A payment to a beverage supplier of $500 on account.
7. A payment from a restaurant patron of $150 on his account.
8. A utility bill payment of $200.

Problem 2

The Dansville Café uses the following journals:

- Sales journal
- Cash receipts journal

- Purchases journal
- Cash disbursements journal
- Payroll journal
- General journal

Several business transactions and activities of the Dansville Café are as follows:

1. Lunch sales for cash totaled $454.48 on May 31.
2. Lunch sales on account totaled $128.14 on May 31.
3. Food purchased on account from Food Corp. costs $647.
4. Fresh fruit purchased with cash (check no. 1897) costs $147.
5. Consumers Electric Co. was paid $647 for electricity used during April.
6. Jack Jones, the cafe manager, was paid a salary of $2,400 for May.
7. The federal income taxes total of $648, withheld from employee checks during May, was deposited with Bank One.
8. The account receivable of James Nopay, for $58, was deemed uncollectible and written off on May 31.
9. Wages of $1,254 were accrued at the end of May.
10. Frost Pak, Inc., a supplier, was paid $300 on account.

Required:

Indicate the journal used to record each transaction of activity.

Problem 3

The Haslett Diner allows selected customers to charge meals. The sales on account and cash payments from Gregory Case were as follows for April 20X1:

April	Sales	Cash Payment
1	$14.72	—
2	12.47	—
7	—	$20.00
10	6.50	—
15	7.28	—
22	14.15	—
29	13.12	—
30	—	30.00

The balance of Case's account at the beginning of April 20X1 was $50.00.

Required:

Determine the balance of the Case's account at the end of April 20X1.

Problem 4

The Leslie Grill purchased food on account from several suppliers during June as follows:

Date	Supplier	Amount
June 4	Bates Meats	$847.15
6	Lash Dairy	148.71
7	Aguiler Supply	749.92
12	Jake's Frozen Foods	652.66
15	Lash Dairy	129.46
18	Spartan Foods	597.77
21	Bates Meats	668.88
22	Minoso's Foods	372.22
25	Lash Dairy	172.71
27	Aguiler Supply	497.73
30	Jake's Frozen Foods	455.54

Required:

1. Post the above amounts to T-accounts in the accounts payable subsidiary ledger. Assume the above transactions were recorded on page 5 of the purchases journal.
2. Assume the accounts payable control account had a $–0– balance on May 31. What is the balance of the accounts payable control account after posting the total from the purchases journal to the accounts payable control account?

Problem 5

The Howell Hotel (HH) purchases its produce from Mellon Farms on account and pays the purveyor twice a month. On April 30, 20X1, HH owed Mellon Farms $215.45. Purchases on account and cash payments to Mellon Farms for May 20X1 were as follows:

May	Purchase	Cash Payment
2	$115.42	—
5	—	$215.45
7	89.15	—
11	136.42	—
15	79.36	—
19	47.15	—
20	—	204.57
24	78.15	—
29	123.41	—

Required:

Determine the amount owed to Mellon Farms at the end of May 20X1.

Problem 6

The Leslie Grill has made the following payments on account during June:

Date	Check No.	Supplier	Amount
June 8	9894	Bates Meats	$300.00
10	9903	Lash Dairy	148.71
14	9943	Bates Meats	300.00
18	9987	Aguiler Supply	749.92

23	10014	Bates Meats	300.00
27	10029	Jake's Frozen Foods	600.66
30	10051	Lash Dairy	129.46

In addition, spoiled food costing $52.00 was returned to Jake's Frozen Foods on June 27 and credit was issued to the Leslie Grill.

Required:

1. Based on the above information and the purchases on account from Problem 4, prepare T-accounts and determine how much the Leslie Grill owes each of its suppliers at the end of June. Assume that all payments were recorded on page 8 of the cash disbursements journal.

2. What is the total amount the Leslie Grill owes to all suppliers at the end of June?

Challenge Problems

Problem 7

The North Woods Motel (NWM), a 20-room lodging facility, generally does not extend credit to its guests beyond check-out. However, a few extremely loyal guests have been extended credit. The balances of their accounts as of January 31, 20X3, are as follows: M. Terrace $194.28; J. K. Weed $275.29; F. M. Fordham $84.21; Martin Block $64.28; Mary Cervantes $124.91. The balance of the city ledger control account (acct. #112) is $742.97.

The following transactions during February 20X3 involve these five customers:

Feb. 3   M. Terrace stayed at the NWM for two nights and $75.26 was charged to his account.

5   A check for $275.29 was received from J. K. Weed for payment on account.

7   F. M. Fordham charged $275.20 for dinner for a small group to her account.

11   Martin Block checked out of the NWM and charged $59.42 to his account.

13   Mary Cervantes paid $100.00 on her account.

14   J. K. Weed checked out of the motel and charged $85.22 to her account.

17   Martin Block paid $50.00 on his account.

19   M. Terrace stayed one night at the NWM and charged $41.40 to his account.

22   F. M. Fordham paid $200.00 on her account.

23   A check for $200.00 was received from M. Terrace on his account.

28   Mary Cervantes charged $94.20 to her account after staying for two nights at the NWM.

Required:

Prepare a sales journal (see Exhibit 1), a cash receipts journal (see Exhibit 2), and T-accounts for each of the five guests who are extended credit. Also, prepare a T-account for the city ledger control account. When preparing the T-accounts, include the balance as of January 31, 20X3.

1. Record each sales transaction in the sales journal (assume all sales were for rooms and are recorded on page 10).

2. Record each cash transaction in the cash receipts journal on page 12.

3. Post all charges to the guest accounts. Then post all amounts received from guests to their accounts. Post totals from the two journals to the city ledger control account.

4. Prepare a schedule of receivables and compare it to the balance of the city ledger control account at the end of February 20X3.

Problem 8

The Okemos Cafe made the following food purchases and cash disbursements during September 20X4:

1. On September 2, $452.00 of meat was purchased from Borden Meats on account (invoice 1349).

2. Food supplies costing $337.42 were purchased from Givens Foods on account on September 4 (invoice 15872).

3. Check 475 for $550.00 was written to Ganakas Beverages on September 6 as payment on account.

4. Beverages costing $185.21 were purchased on account from Ganakas Beverages on September 7 (invoice K-4871).

5. On September 8, food costing $687.09 was purchased on account from Spartan Enterprises (invoice 9876).

6. Borden Meats delivered $398.15 of meat on account on September 10 (invoice 1398).

7. Check 476 for $452.00 was written to Borden Meats on September 12.

8. Additional checks written on September 12 were as follows:

Check #	Payee	Amount	Acct. #	Account Title
477	Givens Foods	$337.42	201	Accounts Payable
478	Richard Smith	480.00	501	Payroll Expense
479	Sandy Rhodes	420.00	501	Payroll Expense
480	Twyla Miller	380.00	501	Payroll Expense
481	Rose Aquaro	400.00	501	Payroll Expense
482	William Jones	390.40	501	Payroll Expense
483	R. J. Realty	800.00	520	Rent Expense
484	Okemos Power	450.29	510	Utilities Expense
485	Motor Repair Inc.	227.94	508	Repair Expense

9. On September 15, meat costing $567.50 was purchased on account from Borden Meats (invoice 1420).

10. Food costing $695.00 was purchased on account from Spartan Enterprises on September 17 (invoice 9902).

11. Beverages costing $345.00 were purchased on account from Ganakas Beverages on September 21 (invoice K-4997).

12. Check 486 was written for $687.09 to Spartan Enterprises on September 24 for payment on account.

13. Checks written on September 26 were as follows:

Check #	Payee	Amount	Acct. #	Account Title
487	Richard Smith	$480.00	501	Payroll Expense
488	Sandy Rhodes	425.00	501	Payroll Expense

489	Twyla Miller	385.00	501	Payroll Expense
490	Rose Aquaro	398.00	501	Payroll Expense
491	William Jones	405.00	501	Payroll Expense
492	*Ingham Newspaper*	85.00	506	Advertising
493	Bank One	290.00	502	Employee Benefits
494	Blue Cross	875.50	502	Employee Benefits

14. On September 29, meat costing $627.91 was purchased on account from Borden Meats (invoice 1435).

Required:

1. Prepare a cash disbursements journal (see Exhibit 4) and a purchases journal (see Exhibit 3). Record all disbursements for payroll in the cash disbursements journal. These transactions are recorded on page 18 of each journal.

2. Record all of the above transactions in the two journals and total the columns of each journal.

Problem 9

Use information provided in Problem 8 to solve this problem.

Required:

1. Make T-accounts for each of the following general ledger accounts:

Account Title	Acct. #	Account Balance September 1, 20X4
Cash	101	$9,521.00
Accounts Payable	201	2,678.20
Food Purchases	401	—
Payroll Expense	501	—
Employee Benefits	502	—
Advertising Expense	506	—
Repair Expense	508	—
Utilities Expense	510	—
Rent Expense	520	—

2. Make T-accounts for the accounts payable subsidiary ledger as follows:

Suppliers	September 1, 20X4 Balance
Borden Meats	$697.45
Givens Foods	846.92
Ganakas Beverages	650.00
Spartan Enterprises	483.83

3. Post the totals from the cash disbursements and purchases journals (solution to Problem 8) to the general ledger and subsidiary ledger accounts.

4. Post the amounts pertaining to suppliers to the proper accounts in the accounts payable subsidiary ledger.

5. Prepare a list of accounts payable accounts and compare the total to the Accounts Payable control account.

Problem 10

The Mason Dairy Cream is preparing to open on June 7, 20X8. It will maintain three special-ized journals: a cash receipts journal, a purchases journal, and a cash disbursements journal. It will also use a general journal. Its general ledger will consist of the following:

Account Title	Acct. #	Account Title	Acct. #
Cash	101	Food Purchases	401
Equipment	150	Payroll Expense	501
Accumulated Depreciation	151	Utilities Expense	503
Accounts Payable	201	Supplies Expense	505
E. Mason, Capital	250	Advertising Expense	507
Sales	301	Rent Expense	509
		Depreciation Expense	511

Transactions for June 20X8 are as follows:

June 1   E. Mason invests $15,000 in the business.

2    $500 rent for June is paid (check 101).

3   Equipment costing $8,000 is purchased with cash (check 102).

4   Food costing $850 is purchased on account from Supplies, Inc. (invoice 1872).

5   *Webberville Times* is paid $200 for advertising (check 103).

6    $180 in supplies are purchased (check 104).

7   Cash sales total $750.50.

10–15   Cash sales total $2,810.

19   Food is purchased on account from Ice Cream, Inc., for $690 (invoice 4897).

20   *Webberville Times* is paid $250 for advertising (check 105).

21   Three employees are paid wages:

Aaron Dakan	$150.00	check 106
Laurie Golden	140.50	check 107
Marla Maps	162.00	check 108

22    $625 in food is purchased on account from Supplies, Inc. (invoice 1926).

22   Ice Cream, Inc., is paid $500 on account (check 109).

19–23   Cash sales total $2,545.

26   Supplies, Inc., is paid $850 on account (check 110).

27   Food costing $590 is purchased from Springtime Co. on account (invoice F-3941).

28   The utility bill for the first 20 days of June of $350.50 is paid (check 111).

26–30   Cash sales total $2,458.

The depreciation on the equipment for June totals $200.

Required:

1. Record transactions for June 20X8 in the proper journals. All journal pages should be numbered page 1.
2. Establish T-accounts for each general ledger account and post entries to them.
3. Establish T-accounts for each food supplier and post all appropriate activity to these accounts.
4. Record the depreciation expense in the general journal and post the amounts to the proper accounts.
5. Prepare a trial balance of general ledger accounts.

REVIEW QUIZ

When you feel you have covered all of the material in this chapter, answer these questions. Choose the *best* answer.

1. Which of the following must have a balance that equals the sum of individual account balances in corresponding subsidiary ledgers?

   a. general ledger
   b. control account
   c. cash disbursements journal
   d. city ledger

2. The credit entry of each transaction recorded in the purchases journal is to the _____ account.

   a. Food Purchases
   b. Accounts Payable
   c. Accounts Receivable
   d. Cash

3. Which of the following journals would be affected if a banquet planner charged the amount due to a restaurant for a banquet?

   a. sales journal
   b. purchases journal
   c. cash receipts journal
   d. cash disbursements journal

4. Mary, a hotel manager, wants to check on the amount of a transaction that involved invoice number 1309 from Peter's Plumbing Services. Her hotel uses a system of specialized journals and subsidiary ledgers. Mary would be most likely to find information about this transaction in:

   a. the cash receipts journal.
   b. the city ledger.
   c. either the cash receipts journal or the general journal.
   d. either the purchases journal or the cash disbursements journal.

5. The Bigbucks Hotel exchanges five thousand shares of common stock for ten acres of land. This transaction would be recorded in the:

   a. sales journal.
   b. ledgers for the Land account and the Cash account.
   c. cash disbursements journal.
   d. general journal.

REVIEW QUIZ *(continued)*

6. Which of the following components of a computer system is considered software?

    a. CPU
    b. spreadsheet applications
    c. keyboard
    d. magnetic disk storage units

7. Telephone call accounting systems, point-of-sale systems, and in-house entertainment systems are all examples of which of the following?

    a. front office applications
    b. back office applications
    c. systems with which a property management system can be interfaced
    d. central processing units that process information and send instructions to other system components

Answer Key: 1-b-C1, 2-b-C2, 3-b-C2, 4-d-C2, 5-d-C3, 6-b-C4, 7-c-C4

Each question is linked to a competency. Competencies are listed on the first page of the chapter. An answer reading 3-b-C4 translates to:

    3: the question number
    b: the correct answer
    C4: the competency number

Chapter 8 Outline

Internal Control of Cash
Voucher System
    Preparation of a Voucher
Petty Cash
Bank Reconciliation
    Preparing a Bank Reconciliation
    Illustration of a Bank Reconciliation
Gross Method of Recording Purchases
Net Method of Recording Purchases
Credit Card Sales
Integrated Cash Management for Multi-
    Unit Operations

Competencies

1. Describe assets that accountants represent as Cash or Cash Equivalents, and describe procedures that help ensure internal control of a firm's cash.

2. Explain the purpose of a voucher system and how it works.

3. Describe the petty cash fund and the accounting procedures related to it.

4. Explain the purpose for performing bank reconciliations, and demonstrate how to prepare a bank reconciliation.

5. Compare and demonstrate the gross and net methods of recording purchases.

6. Distinguish between the two types of credit cards, and demonstrate how to account for sales that involve each type.

7. Describe an integrated cash management system.

8

Cash

ASSETS AND LIABILITIES are listed on the balance sheet in order of liquidity. Liquidity measures an operation's ability to convert assets to cash. This chapter discusses **cash**, the most liquid current asset.

Cash is a very critical asset for hospitality businesses. The amount of cash a firm holds may not be related to the amount of income it generates. Certainly investors and managers are concerned that the firm generates an adequate profit, but cash is more critical on a day-to-day basis. It is cash, not income, that pays employee wages and the firm's sales taxes, vendors' bills, rent, utilities expenses, and so forth. Although adequate income ensures the long-run survival of the firm, cash keeps the operation running smoothly.

Cash refers not only to the currency and coins that a hospitality firm holds, but also to **time deposits**, demand deposits, money orders, certificates of deposit, and credit card slips signed by the firm's customers. Cash that is formally restricted for a long-term purpose such as for equipment replacement should be listed under Noncurrent Assets.

It is not uncommon for a business to list Cash and Equivalents in place of Cash on the balance sheet. **Cash equivalents** would include very liquid short-term investments held by the firm, such as commercial paper or treasury bills.

Internal Control of Cash

Cash is the most vulnerable of all assets. It is therefore essential to have an effective system of internal control over cash in all phases of the operation. The theft of cash is always possible. The following is a list of general procedures that help ensure that cash is adequately controlled:

1. Cash-handling duties should be segregated.

2. Bookkeeping and cash-handling duties should be separated.

3. All expenditures should be paid by check.

4. Mechanical devices should be used to help safeguard cash.

5. Servers and cashiers should use prenumbered sales tickets.

6. Cash should be deposited daily.

7. Employees should be bonded.

8. Internal and external audits should be performed periodically.

9. A voucher system should be implemented.

Each of these procedures is discussed in this section.

Segregation of Duties. The responsibility for handling cash transactions should be divided among two or more individuals. The segregation of cash-handling duties does not guarantee that fraud will not be perpetrated; it simply makes fraud more difficult because it makes collusion necessary for fraud to occur.

The following example involving the deposit of cash illustrates the advantages of segregating duties. Any cash or checks mailed to the firm should be recorded by the employee who opens the mail. This employee should forward the cash and checks to another employee, who will prepare the bank deposit. The employee opening the mail should also prepare a list of the day's receipts and send a copy of it to the controller. The person preparing the bank deposit should forward a duplicate deposit ticket to the controller. The controller can then compare the list of cash receipts with the day's deposit ticket to look for any discrepancies.

Separate Bookkeeping and Cash-Handling Duties. Employees who have access to cash should not have access to accounting records such as the cash receipts or cash disbursements journals. Similarly, employees who have access to the accounting records should not have access to cash. Separating the bookkeeping and cash-handling duties can be a very challenging chore in small operations with limited personnel available.

Pay for All Expenditures by Check. All disbursements should be made by check after proper authorization procedures are completed. Checks written for more than a certain amount should require two signatures. The only exception to paying by check should be the small business transactions that invariably occur, such as postage stamp purchases or small freight charges. Such small expenditures should be paid out of a petty cash fund, which will be discussed in more detail later in this chapter.

Use of Mechanical Devices. Whenever feasible, mechanical devices should be integrated into the hospitality operation to assist in safeguarding cash. Cash registers, time clocks, and check protectors are examples of such devices. The cash register, for example, should record all transactions on a two-ply tape that is locked inside the register and inaccessible to the employee operating the machine. At the end of a shift, the employee operating the cash register should count the cash and transfer it to the cashier's office where the cash receipts will be listed on a deposit slip. A third employee from the accounting department should remove the tape from the machine, compare the total to the cash amount listed by the cashier, and record the cash sales in the appropriate journal.

Use of Prenumbered Sales Tickets. All restaurant servers should be given prenumbered sets of sales slips that they must account for at the end of each shift. To prevent fraudulent use of sales slips by servers, some food service operations charge a fixed amount of dollars for each sales slip that is unaccounted for at the end of a shift. However, managers must ensure that such charges do not put an employee below the minimum wage for the pay period.

Daily Deposits of Cash. All of the operation's cash receipts should be deposited daily and intact in the bank. All checks received from guests should immediately be restrictively endorsed with the words *for deposit only.* Miscellaneous small expenditures should never be paid for out of the day's receipts; instead, they should be paid for through the petty cash fund.

Employee Bonding. Key employees who handle cash should be bonded by an insurance company.

Audit Procedures. Periodic reviews of the internal control system policies and procedures that safeguard cash should be performed internally by the company's auditors and externally by independent Certified Public Accountants.

Voucher System. A voucher system should be implemented to control cash disbursements. The next section of this chapter discusses the workings of a voucher system.

Voucher System

A **voucher** is a business's written authorization to make a cash payment. Firms use the voucher system to provide better control over cash disbursements. Use of the voucher system ensures that, before a firm makes any cash payment, transactions are verified, approved in writing, and recorded by the firm's employees. Whenever an obligation to pay cash is incurred, a numerically sequenced voucher is attached to the invoice supporting the obligation.

A sample of a voucher is shown in Exhibit 1. Notice that space is provided for the payee's name and address, the date the voucher originates, and the date the payment is due. Also provided are blanks for the invoice date and number, the credit terms, and the amount of the invoice.

Accounting employees fill in the second section of the voucher to indicate verification and approval. This section provides spaces for approval dates and for the initials of employees responsible for checking extensions and footings on the invoice, or of the employee who checks to see if the quantities originally ordered match those on the receiving report.

The final section of the voucher lists names of accounts that may be debited or credited with the amount of the transaction. The list of accounts helps the accounting department to journalize the transaction correctly.

Preparation of a Voucher

An accounting department employee initiates the voucher process when the firm receives an invoice from a supplier of goods or services. The employee enters the dates, the invoice number, and the amounts and terms of sale in the appropriate places on the voucher. Then he or she attaches the invoice to the voucher and sends both documents to another employee, who will check extensions and verify prices and quantities.

Exhibit 1   Sample Voucher

Voucher
Leisure Time Hotel
Miami, Florida
Voucher #1563

Date of Voucher	___/___/___	
Due Date of Payment	___/___/___	
Invoice Date	___/___/___	Invoice Number #_____
Invoice Amount	$_____	Terms of Sale _____
Discount Available	$_____	
Net Amount of Invoice	$_____	

Verification and Approval

	Individual	Date
Quantities Compared with Receiving Report	_____	_____
Prices Compared with Purchase Order	_____	_____
Credit Terms Checked with Purchase Order	_____	_____
Footings and Extensions Checked	_____	_____
Ledger Accounts Identified and Approved	_____	_____
Payment Authorized	_____	_____

Voucher #1563 Invoice Amount	$_____	Date of Voucher	___/___
Discount Available	$_____	Payment Due Date	___/___
Net Amount of Invoice	$_____		

Payee Name _____   Date Check Drawn   ___/___
Address   _____   Check Number   #_____
               _____   Amount of Check $_____
                                                 Recorded in Voucher Register—Initial _____

Ledger Account Identification

Account Debited	Account Credited
Wages Expense	Vouchers Payable
Administrative Salaries	
Purchases	
Utilities	
Marketing	
Property Operation & Maintenance	
Rent	
Insurance	
Administrative & General	
Other	

After completing the checking and verification procedures, the second employee initials and dates the voucher and forwards it to a third employee, who indicates which accounts are to be debited and credited. The debit will frequently be to an expense account, but sometimes will be to an asset or liability account. The credit will be to a short-term liability account called Vouchers Payable. The balance sheet will not normally list Vouchers Payable among the liabilities; instead, it includes the amount of the outstanding vouchers in Accounts Payable.

The voucher is then entered in a voucher register and is placed in a tickler file. The tickler file could be housed in an accordion folder that has a pocket for each of the 31 days in a month. If a particular bill is due on the 15th of the month, it is placed in the 15 pocket of the folder. The tickler file is checked every day for bills that are due to ensure that bills are paid when due but not before. The unpaid voucher file in essence becomes the accounts payable subsidiary ledger.

When a bill is due to be paid, an employee in the accounting department removes the voucher from the file and prepares a check for the treasurer (who is in the finance department) to sign. In an ideal system of internal control, no single person or department should prepare a check *and* sign it. At this time, the voucher amount is recorded in the check register. The journal entry for this transaction would be:

Vouchers Payable	$XXX	
Cash		$XXX

Once the check is prepared, it is forwarded along with the supporting documentation to the treasurer for an authorized signature. At this time, the treasurer reviews the voucher, signs the check, and perforates the voucher with a stamp that reads *PAID*, and the voucher is sent back to the accounting department to be filed. Finally, the check is mailed directly to the billing firm by the treasurer.

Petty Cash

Although a hospitality business would prefer to have all purchases paid for by check using the voucher system, that is not always possible. For instance, a small COD package may arrive or a small purchase of postage stamps or office supplies may be necessary. Such miscellaneous expenditures are paid out of a small fund of cash called the **petty cash** fund.

A business starts a petty cash fund by cashing a check for an amount that it considers adequate to cover small, miscellaneous transactions. A person designated as the custodian of the fund keeps the cash under his or her control in an envelope, a cardboard box, or a drawer.

The entry to start a petty cash fund for $100 would be:

Petty Cash	$100	
Cash		$100

Note that the total amount of cash held by the company has not changed as a result of this entry. Rather, the composition of cash has changed. There is now $100 more in actual cash in the firm and $100 less in **demand deposits**. Petty Cash is not listed separately on the balance sheet; instead, it is included in the Cash amount.

Disbursements from the petty cash fund should be supported by receipts such as cash register tapes, invoices, or other documents. At any given time, the total of the cash and receipt amounts should equal the amount of the fund; in this case, the cash and receipt amounts should total $100.

When the cash in the fund is reduced to a level considered inadequate to cover likely expenditures, the fund is said to need reimbursing or replenishing. A check is drawn and cashed for an amount that will replenish the fund (that is, bring it back to its original level).

To illustrate the reimbursement of a petty cash fund, assume that an examination of the fund for the Chippewa Motel reveals $18 in cash and the following receipts: postage, $38; freight charges, $27; and office supplies, $17. Based on this information, the entry to reimburse the fund would be:

Postage Expense	$38	
Freight Expense	27	
Office Supplies	17	
Cash		$82

If the original amount of the petty cash fund proves to be too low and must be increased by $50, the following entry would be made:

Petty Cash	$50	
Cash		$50

Note that the most common entry involving the petty cash fund is the entry to reimburse the fund. This particular journal entry does not involve the Petty Cash account.

Occasionally an employee, when reimbursing the petty cash fund, will find that the receipts and remaining cash do not equal the amount of the fund. For example, a $100 fund may contain $12 and the following receipts: spare parts, $23; shop supplies, $18; freight charges, $32; and postage, $13. If the credit to Cash was entered as simply the total of the debits to the expense accounts, the fund would not be properly reimbursed. Remember, reimbursing means bringing the fund back to its original balance. In this case, there is a $2 shortage unaccounted for in the fund.

To avoid underfunding or overfunding the petty cash fund, businesses follow this three-step procedure to reimburse it:

1. Debit the expense accounts relating to the receipts in the fund.

2. Subtract the amount of the remaining cash from the amount of the fund, and credit Cash for that amount.

3. If the credit entry does not equal the debit entries, use the Cash Short and Over account to balance the entry.

For the example just given, this procedure would result in the following journal entry:

Spare Parts	$23	
Shop Supplies	18	
Freight Expense	32	
Postage Expense	13	
Cash Short and Over	2	
Cash		$88

Cash Short and Over is a miscellaneous expense or revenue account, depending on its balance at the end of the year. A debit balance indicates expense, while a credit balance indicates revenue. At the end of the fiscal period, it is closed into the Income Summary account just as the other nominal accounts are.

Bank Reconciliation

A **bank reconciliation** is a monthly procedure that provides additional control over cash. The bank reconciliation explains any differences between the bank's cash balance and the cash balance in the company's books. A company starts its bank reconciliation when it receives a statement from the bank.

The bank statement provides a list of the deposits made by the company, the company's checks that have cleared the bank during the month, and other miscellaneous debits and credits to the bank balance. Included with the bank statement are the company's canceled checks that have cleared the bank.

Any differences in the bank and book balances of cash may be due to any of the following five possible reasons:

1. Deposits in transit

2. Outstanding checks

3. NSF checks

4. Bank service charges

5. Credits for interest earned or receivables collected

The following section describes each of these in more detail.

Deposits in transit are deposits made by the company at the end of the month but not included on the bank statement. For example, a restaurant may drop a deposit in the bank's night depository on June 30. The bank would probably then record it as a July 1 deposit and include it on the July bank statement.

Outstanding checks are checks written by the hospitality firm to third parties who have not yet presented them to the bank for collection.

NSF checks are checks that the bank returned to the hospitality business because the customer writing the check did not have enough funds to cover it. *NSF* stands for *Not Sufficient Funds*. NSF checks are often called *bounced checks*.

Bank service charges are charges for services provided by the bank, such as fees for new checks or fees charged to the bank customer for collecting notes receivable.

Another common charge would be the monthly bank fee for processing bank credit card slips that the firm has deposited.

Credits for interest earned or receivables collected. If the checking account earned interest on the average balance held in the account, a credit would appear on the bank statement for this amount. Occasionally a hospitality firm will leave a note receivable with the bank for collection, such as when both the maker of the note and the payee do business at the same bank. When the receivable is collected by the bank, the credit appears on the current bank statement.

Preparing a Bank Reconciliation

Although there are several ways to proceed when preparing a bank reconciliation, we recommend the following steps:

1. Compare the deposits listed on the bank statement with the deposits listed in the company's records. Any deposit not listed on the bank statement represents a deposit in transit and should be added to the balance listed on the bank statement.

2. Put the canceled checks in numerical order. Compare the amounts on the bank statement with the amounts on the checks and investigate any discrepancies. Compile a list of checks that have been written but not returned with the bank statement. The sum of check amounts from this list, which is called an *outstanding check list,* should be subtracted from the *balance per bank* (that is, the balance listed on the bank statement). The outstanding check list from the previous month's bank reconciliation should be examined and any canceled checks received with the current statement should be checked off that list. Any checks still not returned should be included on the current month's outstanding check list.

3. Add any credit memoranda listed on the bank statement to the *balance per books* (that is, the balance listed in the company's books). These credit memoranda could include such items as interest earned or notes receivable collected.

4. Deduct from the balance per books any debit memoranda on the bank statement, such as bank service charges, credit card fees, or NSF checks.

5. Make any necessary corrections resulting from errors made by either the bank or the company. For example, perhaps the company entered a $56 amount in the check register when the check was actually written for $65. This would necessitate a reduction in the balance per books of $9.

6. After making all necessary adjustments to both the bank and book balances, verify that the adjusted balances are equal.

7. Make any necessary adjusting entries to the books. Note that items requiring adjusting entries will appear in the portion of the bank reconciliation dealing with the adjusted *book* balance.

Exhibit 2   Bank Statement

Bank Statement
First National City Bank of Mt. Pleasant, MI

Customer: Bayview Hotel
Account #:   408576
Address: 22900 Dock Street, Clinton, MI 49068

Previous statement balance:	$ 324.81
5 credits totaling	7,490.00
12 debits totaling	2,182.41
NSF check	50.00
Bankcard draft fees	8.00
Interest @ 5.25%	4.23
Current statement balance	5,578.63
Average collected balance	932.29

Deposits and Other Credits

Date	Amount	
6/3	$1,500.00	regular deposit
6/8	500.00	regular deposit
6/18	1,090.00	regular deposit
6/20	500.00	credit memo
6/25	3,900.00	regular deposit

Checks

Date	Check #	Amount		Date	Check #	Amount
6/2	1188	$247.72		6/17	1195	$163.09
6/5	1189	264.88		6/19	1196	120.75
6/8	1190	334.98		6/20	1197	45.00
6/10	1191	554.43		6/24	1199	31.50
6/12	1192	50.11		6/25	1201	258.24
6/15	1193	81.87		6/30	1203	29.84

Illustration of a Bank Reconciliation

Assume that the Bayview Hotel received the bank statement shown in Exhibit 2. Furthermore, assume that the balance per books is currently $5,265.10. The following checks were written in June but not returned with the bank statement:

Check #	Amount
1194	$ 75.00
1198	23.82
1200	146.58
1202	12.90

An examination of the deposits on the bank statement reveals that a deposit the hotel made on June 30 for $400.00 is not included on the statement. The credit memo for $500.00 on June 20 represents the collection of a note receivable by the bank. The current cash balance on the bank statement is $5,578.63.

Suppose that check #1197 for $45.00 for office supplies was incorrectly recorded on the books as $54.00. Using this information along with the bank statement, the bank reconciliation at June 30 would appear as follows:

Bayview Hotel
Bank Reconciliation
June 30, 20X4

Balance per bank statement, June 30, 20X4			$5,578.63
Add: Deposit in transit: June 30			400.00
Deduct: Outstanding checks:			
	#1194	$ 75.00	
	#1198	23.82	
	#1200	146.58	
	#1202	12.90	(258.30)
Adjusted bank balance:			$5,720.33
Balance per books, June 30, 20X4			5,265.10
Add: Note receivable collected by bank		$500.00	
Interest earned during June		4.23	
Error in recording check #1197		9.00	513.23
Deduct: NSF check		$ 50.00	
Bankcard draft processing fees		8.00	(58.00)
Adjusted book balance:			$5,720.33

The bank reconciliation for the Bayview Hotel indicates that the correct cash balance at June 30 is $5,720.33. Remember, the books currently have a cash balance of $5,265.10. The important last step in the reconciliation process is to make the necessary journal entries to adjust the cash balance. For this example, the entries would be as follows:

Cash	$513.23	
Notes Receivable		$500.00
Interest Income		4.23
Office Supplies		9.00

Accounts Receivable	$50.00	
Bank Service Charges	8.00	
Cash		58.00

Gross Method of Recording Purchases

An additional control procedure over cash disbursements involves accounting for purchases of inventory on account. To understand the gross method of recording purchases, assume that a hospitality firm receives an invoice for a $1,000 inventory purchase. The invoice is dated March 1 with terms of 2/10, *n*/30. The "2/10" means that the buyer may take a 2 percent discount if the invoice is paid within 10 days of the invoice date. The "*n*/30" means that if the discounted invoice is not paid within 10 days of the invoice date, the entire amount (net) is due within 30 days of the invoice date. The $1,000 purchase of inventory on account would be recorded as follows under the **gross recording method:**

Purchases	$1,000	
Accounts Payable		$1,000

This entry reflects the total invoice price.

The subsequent payment within the discount period (by March 11) would be recorded this way:

Accounts Payable	$1,000	
Cash		$980
Purchase Discounts		20

Note that Purchase Discounts is reduced by the discounted portion (2% × $1,000).

If the 2 percent discount on this invoice is not taken, the entry on the payment date would be as follows:

Accounts Payable	$1,000	
Cash		$1,000

Net Method of Recording Purchases

A major disadvantage of the gross method is that it does not reveal discounts that are lost. In addition, recording invoices at their gross billing inflates accounts payable if a company customarily takes most or all discounts in its normal accounts payable cycle. The net method of recording purchases uses the invoice amount *minus* any potential cash discount. With the **net recording method,** cash discounts are recorded upon receipt of an invoice, enabling an operation to measure purchasing and payment efficiency.

Under the net method of recording purchases, the discount is anticipated and the purchases and accounts payable are recorded at net price (invoice price less the cash discount). Upon payment, any discounts lost are recorded in an expense account called Discounts Lost.

Assume that a firm makes an inventory purchase for $1,000 dated March 1 with terms of 2/10, *n*/30. Under the net method, the entry to record the invoice is:

Purchases	$980
Accounts Payable	$980

In this case, the entry reflects the net invoice price.

If the invoice is paid within the discount period, the entry would be:

Accounts Payable	$980
Cash	$980

However, if the invoice is not paid within the discount period, the discount is lost and the invoice is due in full. The entry upon payment would be:

Accounts Payable	$980
Discounts Lost	20
Cash	$1,000

The Discounts Lost account is listed separately on the income statement as an additional operating expense. Like other expense accounts, it is closed into the Income Summary account at the end of the fiscal period.

The gross method of recording purchases provides a record of the discounts taken in the Purchase Discounts account, while the net method provides a record of the discounts lost in an expense account called Discounts Lost. Since they are mutually exclusive methods and most managers would prefer to have a record of the discounts lost, the net method is generally preferred. Exhibit 3 summarizes the gross and net methods of recording purchases.

Credit Card Sales

Guests use credit cards extensively to pay for goods and services in most areas of the hospitality industry. When a guest pays a bill with a credit card, the hospitality firm keeps a copy of the credit slip, which is essentially a check drawn on the credit card company. The firm should process signed credit card slips into its bank account as promptly as possible.

There are basically two types of credit cards: bankcards and nonbankcards. Visa and MasterCard are examples of bankcards. When hospitality firms deposit signed Visa or MasterCard drafts given to them by guests, the bank accepts them for immediate deposit.

The journal entry for the deposit of $800 worth of bankcard drafts is recorded in the same way a cash sale is. The entry in this instance would be:

Cash	$800
Sales	$800

Exhibit 3   Gross and Net Methods of Recording Purchases of Inventory

GROSS METHOD			NET METHOD		
Purchase of Inventory:			**Purchase of Inventory:**		
Inventory	$1,000		Inventory	$980	
Accounts Payable		$1,000	Accounts Payable		$980
Payment within Discount Period:			**Payment within Discount Period:**		
Accounts Payable	$1,000		Accounts Payable	$980	
Cash		$980	Cash		$980
Purchase Discount		20			
Payment after Discount Period:			**Payment after Discount Period:**		
Accounts Payable	$1,000		Accounts Payable	$980	
Cash		$1,000	Discounts Lost	20	
			Cash		$1,000

Usually once a month the bank will charge the hospitality firm 1.5 to 3.5 percent for processing the bankcard drafts. The charge will appear on the firm's monthly bank statement as a service charge and will be deducted from the firm's cash balance. Most firms consider this monthly charge a very reasonable one since it allows the firm to avoid the costs of credit investigation and collection on those particular accounts.

Examples of nonbankcards are Diners Club and American Express. Hospitality firms cannot deposit the drafts from these credit cards directly into their bank accounts. Instead, they are required to mail the drafts directly to the credit card companies. Consequently, when guests use nonbankcards, hospitality firms must wait for the credit card companies to reimburse them for the guests' purchases. The following entry would be made on the books if guests signed $600 worth of drafts using American Express cards:

Accounts Receivable—American Express	$600	
Sales		$600

Between six and ten days later, after American Express received the signed slips, it would remit to the firm the amount of the slips less a fee of 3 to 5 percent. On the day that the firm received the cash, the firm would make the following entry, assuming a 4 percent American Express fee:

Cash	$576	
Credit Card Expense	24	
Accounts Receivable—American Express		$600

Credit Card Expense would be included among the other selling expenses on the income statement, which include such accounts as Sales Salaries and Advertising.

Integrated Cash Management for Multi-Unit Operations

More and more restaurants and hotels are expanding into multi-unit operations. As a company progresses from a single-unit operation to one with several units, it should adopt an integrated cash management system. Such a system centralizes the collection and disbursement of cash at the corporate level. Cash received at the unit level is quickly transferred to corporate headquarters. Similarly, cash disbursements for the individual units are also made at the corporate level.

The integrated cash management system represents an attempt to provide better internal control over cash. By consolidating cash at the corporate level, a properly installed system will reduce the overall cash balances that the firm holds.

Another important aspect of this type of system involves cash forecasting. Under this system, both the individual units and the corporation prepare integrated cash budgets for the short term and the long term. Cash forecasting indicates when the corporation will need to borrow money and also allows management to consider how to invest excess cash when it accumulates.

Summary

The asset *cash* is critical to the day-to-day operations of hospitality firms. *Cash* refers not only to currency and coins, but also to time deposits, demand deposits, money orders, certificates of deposit, and signed credit card slips. Since cash is both highly desirable and mobile, it is essential that management safeguard it with an effective system of internal control.

This internal control system should include the segregation of duties, the separation of bookkeeping and cash-handling duties, payment of expenditures by check using a voucher system, use of mechanical devices to help safeguard and control cash, use of prenumbered sales tickets, daily deposits of cash, bonding of employees, and periodic internal and external audits. There should be an adequate petty cash procedure in place to take care of small cash expenditures.

Not only is it necessary to carefully monitor cash as it flows through the company, it is also necessary to verify that all transactions involving the bank are compared to the bank statement. This is accomplished through a procedure known as the *bank reconciliation.*

Other control procedures over cash transactions include using the *net method* of recording purchases (rather than the *gross method)*, monitoring credit card sales, and installing an integrated system for multi-unit operations.

⊶ Key Terms

bank reconciliation—A monthly procedure that provides additional control over cash by explaining any differences between the bank's cash balance and the book's cash balance. A firm starts the bank reconciliation procedure when it receives a bank statement from the bank. The statement provides a list of the deposits made by the company, the checks that have cleared the bank during the month, and miscellaneous debits and credits to the bank balance.

cash—A category of current assets consisting of cash in house banks, cash in checking and savings accounts, and certificates of deposit. Cash is shown on the balance sheet at its stated value.

cash equivalents—Short-term, highly liquid investments such as treasury bills and money market accounts.

demand deposit—A checking account with a commercial bank.

gross recording method—A method of recording cash discounts that uses the full invoice amount as the basis of a journal entry. If the discount is realized, it may be treated as a reduction of the account originally debited (nonrevenue treatment) or as other income (revenue treatment).

NSF check—A check for which there are "Not Sufficient Funds" in the bank to cover payment; also known as a *bounced check*.

net recording method—A method of recording cash discounts that uses the invoice amount minus any potential cash discount as the basis of a journal entry. If the anticipated discount is realized, then no later adjustment is required. If the anticipated discount is not realized, it may be recorded to an expense account called Discounts Lost.

petty cash—A small amount of cash set aside to be used when items must be purchased on the spur of the moment or when it isn't feasible to go through the normal voucher and check procedure to buy an item.

time deposit—A savings account with a commercial bank.

voucher—A business's written authorization to make a cash payment; also, a written document used for posting a transaction to a guest account.

Review Questions

1. What items other than coins or currency might be included in the balance sheet account Cash?

2. What major procedures did the chapter recommend for providing internal control over cash?

3. How does the net method of recording purchases differ from the gross method? How would firms that use each method make journal entries for a $1,000 invoice with a 2 percent discount?

4. What are the journal entries for the establishment of a petty cash fund for $100, increasing the fund by $50, and decreasing the fund by $25?

5. What is the account classification (i.e., asset, liability, etc.) of the account Cash Short and Over? How is it disposed of at the end of the fiscal period?

6. What is the three-step procedure for making the journal entry to replenish the petty cash fund?

7. What is the purpose of a bank reconciliation? What is the chapter's recommended procedure for completing a bank reconciliation?

8. What kinds of transactions require additions to book balances? subtractions from book balances? What kinds of transactions require additions to bank balances? subtractions from bank balances?

9. How does the voucher system help establish control over disbursements? Where is the Vouchers Payable account found on the balance sheet?

10. What is the purpose of establishing an integrated cash management system in a multi-unit operation?

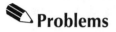 **Problems** —————————————————————————————————

Problem 1

Required:

Using the following information, calculate the amount that would be included in Cash and Cash Equivalents on the Waywest Hotel balance sheet at December 31, 20X4.

Signed credit card slips—Diners Club	$ 250
Time deposits	3,256
Money orders	350
Receivable from Bob Golden	200
Petty cash	100
Signed credit card slips—Visa	480
Shares of stock in Motors International	1,000
Certificates of deposit	2,000

Problem 2

Explain the mechanics of the voucher system and include explanations of the following terms: Voucher, voucher register, check register, vouchers payable, and tickler file.

Problem 3

Journalize the following transactions involving the petty cash fund for the Sunshine Motel:

1. Establish a petty cash fund on February 1, 20X4, for $150.
2. Increase the fund to $200 on March 1, 20X4.
3. Eliminate the petty cash fund on November 15, 20X4.

Problem 4

The custodian of the petty cash fund for the Wade Inn examined the $100 fund and found $10 cash and the following receipts:

Taxi fare, $15; postage, $29; office supplies, $18; parking receipts, $20; and freight charges, $12.

Required:

Make the journal entry for the replenishment of the fund.

Problem 5

Lakeside Restaurant purchased inventory from Valley Packing, receiving an invoice dated February 3, 20X4, for $2,000 with terms 2/10, $n/30$.

Required:

Using the net method of recording purchases, complete the following:

1. Record the purchase of the inventory.
2. Record the payment of the invoice within the discount period.
3. Record the payment of the invoice after the discount period.

Problem 6

The Oyster Restaurant has deposited $1,200 in bankcard drafts in its local bank on June 15, 20X4. On June 17, 20X4, the restaurant is paid $2,000 for a banquet, receiving a credit card draft on American Express (a non bankcard). On June 22, 20X4, American Express remits to Oyster a check for the June 17, 20X4, draft less a 3 percent fee.

Required:

1. Record the journal entries for June 15.
2. Record the journal entries for June 17.
3. Record the journal entries for June 22.

Challenge Problems

Problem 7

The following information relates to the Clearwater Lake Restaurant checking account for the month of April:

Balance of cash per books, 4/30/20X4	$3,735
Balance of cash per bank, 4/30/20X4	3,528
Outstanding checks as of 4/30/20X4	256
Bank service charges for April	12
Deposit in transit at 4/30/20X4	422
NSF check returned with statement	38
Error in recording check #1568—	
(Office Supplies) recorded as	98
should be	89

Required:

Prepare a bank reconciliation for the restaurant for April 30, 20X4.

Problem 8

Chippewa Golf Club purchased merchandise on the following dates:

Date	Vendor	Amount	Terms
April 5	Golf Unlimited	$30,000	2/10, $n/60$
April 12	Pro Line Sports	$20,000	1/10, $n/30$

Required:

Using the *gross* method of recording purchases, complete the following:

1. Record the purchases of April 5 and April 12.

2. Record the payment of the April 5 invoice as if it had been paid on April 15 and the payment of the April 12 invoice as if it had been paid on April 20.

3. Record the payment of the April 5 invoice as if it had been paid on April 17 and the payment of the April 12 invoice as if it had been paid on April 24.

4. Record all of the above transactions under the *net* method.

Problem 9

During July, several events occurred at the Flamingo Resort.

a. On July 1, a Petty Cash Fund was established in the amount of $100.

b. On July 15, the fund was replenished since it had a balance of $4 with the following receipts:

Postage	$30
Office Supplies	$25
Shipping Charges to UPS	$40

c. On July 16, the fund was increased to $200.

d. On July 31, the fund was replenished since it had a balance of $12 with the following receipts:

Spare Parts	$35
Stamps	$28
Shop Supplies	$27
Inventory	$100

Required:

Journalize all of the necessary transactions for July in chronological order.

Problem 10

N 2 Surfing Resort's June bank statement showed the following deposits and checks:

N 2 Surfing Resort
Bank Statement

Deposits			Checks		
Date	**Amount**		**Date**	**Number**	**Amount**
06/01	$2,205.60		06/01	652	$1,261.50
06/05	$3,872.42		06/03	654	$1,000.00
06/17	$5,105.18		06/08	655	$1,250.00
06/22	$2,764.87		06/12	656	$800.00
06/30	$1,835.92		06/16	657	$627.31
			06/18	659	$250.00
			06/25	660	$861.12
			06/30	662	$500.00

The cash records per books for June showed the following:

Cash Receipts Journal		Cash Payments Journal		
Date	**Amount**	**Date**	**Number**	**Amount**
06/04	$3,872.42	06/01	654	$1,000.00
06/16	$5,105.18	06/03	655	$1,250.00
06/21	$2,764.87	06/09	656	$800.00
06/29	$1,853.92	06/10	657	$672.31
06/30	$1,386.45	06/11	658	$300.00
		06/12	659	$250.00
		06/20	660	$861.12
		06/22	661	$387.50
		06/28	662	$500.00
		06/29	663	$500.00

The bank statement for June 30 showed a cash balance of $12,458.27; the cash balance per books on that date was $12,174.62. The outstanding checks list for May included the following:

Number	Amount
648	$328.05
649	$150.00
652	$1,261.50

There was a debit memo of $22.00 for bank service charges that was included with the bank statement. The bank made no errors, while the company made two errors.

Required:

Prepare a bank reconciliation for the company as of June 30.

REVIEW QUIZ

When you feel you have covered all of the material in this chapter, answer these questions. Choose the *best* answer.

1. The Sleeper's Motel is a small operation with limited accounting staff. The general manager wants to maintain internal control over cash. For the sake of internal control of cash, it would be best for a person who handled cash to maintain:

    a. the cash receipts journal.
    b. the cash disbursements journal.
    c. the general journal.
    d. any of the above.

2. In which of the following situations should a hotel employee prepare a voucher?

    a. A guest submits a check in payment for a stay.
    b. A supplier submits an invoice for goods delivered.
    c. A guest rents a cellular phone from the hotel.
    d. The hotel's bank sends the hotel the monthly statement for its account.

3. A petty cash fund of $100 is replenished during a certain month. The journal entry to record this would credit:

    a. Cash.
    b. Petty Cash.
    c. Vouchers Payable.
    d. Accounts Payable.

4. Charles, a hotel accountant, notices that there is a difference between the bank statement's balance and the balance in the hotel records for the hotel's account. All of the following are common causes for this difference *except:*

    a. deposits in transit.
    b. NSF checks.
    c. bank service charges.
    d. a shortage of hotel revenue.

5. The account that is used in the gross method of recording purchases that is not used in the net method of recording purchases is:

    a. Discounts Lost.
    b. Purchase Discounts.
    c. Cash.
    d. Accounts Payable.

REVIEW QUIZ *(continued)*

6. A hotel submits credit card slips that total $2,000 to American Express for payment. Suppose that American Express charges a 4 percent processing fee. The amount the hotel will receive is:

   a. $2,080.
   b. $2,000.
   c. $1,920.
   d. $80.

7. In an integrated cash management system, cash disbursements for individual operating units are made:

   a. by the individual units.
   b. by staff at corporate headquarters.
   c. when corporate headquarters has received the requisite cash from the owner.
   d. at the request of guests only.

Answer Key: 1-c-C1, 2-b-C2, 3-a-C3, 4-d-C4, 5-b-C5, 6-c-C6, 7-b-C7

Each question is linked to a competency. Competencies are listed on the first page of the chapter. An answer reading 3-b-C4 translates to:

   3: the question number
   b: the correct answer
   C4: the competency number

Chapter 9 Outline

Uncollectible Accounts Expense (Bad Debts)
    Direct Write-Off Method
    Allowance Method
Notes Receivable
    Interest-Bearing Notes
Notes Payable
    Non-Interest-Bearing Notes

Competencies

1. Define terms associated with receivables and payables, and outline ways to avoid bad debt losses.

2. Describe and demonstrate the direct write-off method of accounting for bad debt expense, and identify its major flaw.

3. Describe and demonstrate the allowance method of accounting for bad debt expense.

4. Describe and demonstrate the aging of accounts receivable method of estimating bad debt expense.

5. Describe and demonstrate the percentage of sales method of estimating bad debt expense.

6. Describe notes receivable, demonstrate how to account for honored and dishonored notes receivable, and demonstrate how to change an account receivable to a note receivable.

7. Demonstrate how to account for interest-bearing and non-interest-bearing notes payable.

9

Receivables and Payables

This chapter discusses accounts receivable and notes receivable, which are both current assets. It also addresses short-term notes payable and accounts payable. The term **creditor** refers to the company that has either an account receivable or a note receivable on its books, while the term **debtor** refers to the company with an account payable or a note payable on its books.

Accounts receivable are very liquid current assets that a company expects to convert into cash generally within 30 to 60 days. These assets are typically listed after "Cash" or "Cash and Equivalents" on the balance sheet.

Hotels generally keep accounts receivable in two subsidiary ledgers. The accounts receivable pertaining to guests currently staying in the hotel are kept in a *guest ledger*. The second ledger, called a *city ledger*, is an alphabetical file of accounts receivable pertaining to guests who have checked out of the hotel. It also contains accounts of any other receivables.

It is important that the sales personnel of any hospitality firm understand that a credit sales transaction is not completed until the cash from the sale is collected. It is relatively easy to sell goods and services on credit but often more difficult to collect the cash from the sales. To avoid uncollectible account losses, or what are often called *bad debt losses*, companies should establish proper credit-checking procedures before extending credit.

It is fairly easy to avoid bad debt losses when accepting credit cards. Before accepting a signed credit card draft in payment of a sale, the seller should request an authorization code from the appropriate credit card company when the dollar amount of the sale exceeds a certain figure. Once the authorization code is granted, the credit card company cannot return to the seller for payment if the owner of the credit card fails to pay for the purchase.

The firm must also have a formal set of credit-checking procedures in place when dealing with open account credit. The payment histories and current statuses of the accounts of existing guests would normally determine whether additional credit should be extended.

A credit check should always be completed for a new guest. This involves investigating the guest's references, examining the guest's financial statements when available, and checking with local credit bureaus or a national credit-checking firm such as Dun & Bradstreet, Inc.

No matter how efficient a credit investigation may be, some accounts receivable will still not be paid when due. Therefore, hospitality companies should establish policies for dealing with past-due accounts. The following is an example of such a policy:

Exhibit 1   Methods Used to Account for Bad Debts

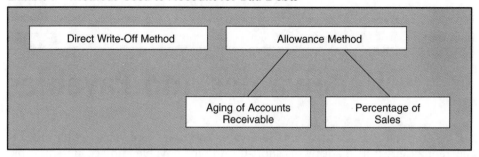

1. Send a courteous reminder letter to the guest when the account becomes past due.

2. If there is no response to the first letter, send a second letter with a sterner tone.

3. If the client doesn't respond to the second letter, follow it up with a phone call from the credit manager.

4. If the first three steps don't succeed, the firm's attorney should write a letter to the guest.

5. If the first four steps fail, the account should be turned over to a collection agency. If the account is small, the client should be taken to small-claims court.

This is just one of several sets of procedures for handling past-due accounts. The key is to establish a well-considered set of procedures before an account becomes past due.

Uncollectible Accounts Expense (Bad Debts)

Any firm that extends credit will eventually experience bad debt losses regardless of the effectiveness of its system of credit investigation. Bad debts can be accounted for in one of two basic ways: the direct write-off method or the allowance method. Exhibit 1 shows these basic methods of handling bad debts expense.

Direct Write-Off Method

Under the **direct write-off method,** an account receivable is written off at the time that it is determined to be uncollectible. Assume that the $150 account receivable of a former guest, I. Leftown, is determined to be uncollectible. Using the direct write-off method, the journal entry in this instance would be:

Provision for Doubtful Accounts	$150	
Accounts Receivable/I. Leftown		$150

This expense account, Provision for Doubtful Accounts, would be closed along with the other expense accounts at the end of the fiscal period and listed under Administrative and General Expenses on the income statement.

If the $150 were eventually collected from I. Leftown, the following journal entries would be made:

Accounts Receivable/I. Leftown	$150	
Provision for Doubtful Accounts		$150

Cash	$150	
Accounts Receivable/I. Leftown		$150

Notice that it is necessary to make two entries when such an account is paid. The first entry reestablishes the account receivable on the books and reduces the expense account. If the second entry were the only entry made, I. Leftown's account would have a credit balance, which in the case of a receivable is actually a liability.

The direct write-off method is only occasionally used in business because it has a major flaw. Assume, in the example discussing I. Leftown, that the account receivable was journalized in December 20X3 and the account was written off in June 20X4. In this example, the revenue from the sale would be reported in the 20X3 income statement, while the expense relating to the revenue (i.e., the bad debt) would be reflected in the 20X4 income statement. The obvious flaw in the direct write-off method is that it violates the matching principle. Businesses could use the direct write-off method, however, when the amount of the mismatch of revenues and expenses is immaterial.

Allowance Method

Most accountants prefer the **allowance method** of accounting for bad debts to the direct write-off method because it better matches expenses with revenues. It makes use of a contra-asset account called Allowance for Doubtful Accounts. Accountants using the allowance method estimate bad debts expense at the end of each accounting period. For example, a hospitality firm with $30,000 in accounts receivable on December 31, 20X3, may be unable, at that time, to identify which receivables will prove uncollectible in the future. From experience, however, they can estimate the dollar amount of the receivables that will be written off. Once the estimate is made, the following journal entry is entered on the books:

Provision for Doubtful Accounts	$XXX	
Allowance for Doubtful Accounts		$XXX

If a hospitality firm had cash of $18,500, accounts receivable of $30,000, and a balance in the Allowance for Doubtful Accounts account of $3,000, the Current Assets section of the balance sheet would be as follows:

Current Assets		
Cash & Equivalents		$18,500
Accounts Receivable	$30,000	
Less: Allowance for Doubtful Accounts	3,000	$27,000

Exhibit 2   Sample Aging of Accounts Receivable Schedule

			December 31, 20X3			
Guest	Amount	Current	1–30	30–60	60–90	Over 90
Darryl Brile	$ 250		$ 250			
Scott Miller	300	$ 300				
June Stephens	700			$ 700		
Mike Toddard	500					$ 500
Sarah Wynn	250				$ 250	
(Others)	28,000	23,000	1,900	1,200	1,400	500
	$30,000	$23,300	$2,150	$1,900	$1,650	$1,000

Once a specific account is determined to be uncollectible as in the following example involving a $300 receivable, the account is written off against the Allowance account as follows:

Allowance for Doubtful Accounts	$300	
Accounts Receivable/XYZ		$300

The following illustration involving the write-off of a $300 receivable shows that the entry has no effect on the carrying value of Accounts Receivable:

Before write-off:		
Accounts Receivable	$30,000	
Less: Allowance for Doubtful Accounts	3,000	27,000
After write-off:		
Accounts Receivable	$29,700	
Less: Allowance for Doubtful Accounts	2,700	27,000

The term *carrying value* refers to the balance in the asset account Accounts Receivable less the balance in the related contra-asset account Allowance for Doubtful Accounts.

Under the allowance method, two different approaches may be used to estimate uncollectibles: the aging of accounts receivable method (the balance sheet approach) and the percentage of sales method (the income statement approach).

Aging of Accounts Receivable Method. Under this allowance method, an **aging of accounts receivable** schedule is compiled, as illustrated in Exhibit 2.

Once the columns of the aging schedule are totaled, historical percentages are applied to the totals to determine the balance in the allowance account. Assume that a firm expects, from experience, to lose the following percentages of bad debts:

Days Past Due	Percentage Considered Uncollectible
0 (Current)	1
1–30	2
30–60	3
60–90	4
over 90	32.55

Using these percentages, the Sleeptite Motel would estimate bad debts as follows:

Days Past Due	Accounts Receivable Amount	Percentage Considered Uncollectible	Estimated Uncollectible Accounts
Current	$23,300	1	$233.00
1–30	2,150	2	43.00
30–60	1,900	3	57.00
60–90	1,650	5	82.50
over 90	1,000	32.55	325.50
	$30,000		$741.00

It is important to note that this analysis indicates that the correct balance in the Allowance for Doubtful Accounts account should be $741. We now need to examine the existing balance in the account before making the journal entry. If the Allowance account shows a credit balance of $34, the entry should be as follows:

Provision for Doubtful Accounts	$707	
Allowance for Doubtful Accounts		$707

This T-account shows the status of the Allowance account before and after the journal entry:

Allowance for Doubtful Accounts	
	34
	707
Balance	741

If the Allowance account had a debit balance of $34 before the adjusting entry, the journal entry would change as illustrated below:

Provision for Doubtful Accounts	$775	
Allowance for Doubtful Accounts		$775

The following T-account shows the status of the Allowance account before and after this journal entry:

Allowance for Doubtful Accounts	
34	775
	Balance 741

Percentage of Sales Method. Whereas the aging of accounts receivable method focuses on the balance sheet, the **percentage of sales method** focuses on the income statement. Under the percentage of sales method, the firm looks at the historical amount of bad debts as a percentage of net credit sales. For example, the Sleeptite Motel may have found that bad debts averaged 2 percent of net credit sales over the last five years.

To estimate this year's bad debts, the firm simply applies 2 percent to the amount of net credit sales for the year. If for Sleeptite the net credit sales amount were $35,000 for 20X3, the bad debts would be computed as $35,000 × .02 = $700. Based on this calculation, the journal entry would be:

Provision for Doubtful Accounts	$700	
Allowance for Doubtful Accounts		$700

It is very important to note that once the amount of bad debts is estimated under this method, the existing balance in the Allowance for Doubtful Accounts account is ignored when constructing the journal entry. This is in direct contrast to the aging technique. Assuming that the balance in the Allowance account was a credit of $34 before the entry, the account would change, as illustrated below:

Allowance for Doubtful Accounts

		34
		700
	Balance	734

Notes Receivable

While accounts receivable represent verbal promises to receive cash, notes receivable are written promises to receive cash in the future. The individual or company promising to pay is called the **maker** of the note, while the individual expecting to be paid is called the **payee**. Exhibit 3 is an example of a promissory note for $2,000.

Interest-Bearing Notes

An interest-bearing note is a note on which interest accrues over the life of the note. In the promissory note shown in Exhibit 3, Charles White, the maker, has signed an interest-bearing note and agreed to pay the payee, Oakbrook Motel, $2,000 plus interest at 12 percent per annum over the life of the note. The principal and interest due at maturity are referred to as the **maturity value**. The basic formula for calculating simple interest on a note is Interest = Principal × Rate × Time. The interest on the note shown in Exhibit 3 would be calculated as follows:

$$\text{Interest} = \text{Principal} \times \text{Rate} \times \text{Time}$$
$$= \$2,000 \times .12 \times \frac{60}{360}$$
$$= \$40$$

For the sake of simplicity, we will assume that there are 360 days in a year.

Exhibit 3   Interest-Bearing Note

$2,000	Topeka, Kansas	June 15, 20X3

Sixty days after date I promise to pay to the order of Oakbrook

Motel - - - - - - Two thousand and no/100 - - - - - - dollars payable at

First City Bank of Topeka with an interest at 12 percent.

<u>Charles White</u>

The maturity value on the note would be:

$$
\begin{aligned}
\text{Maturity Value} \quad &= \quad \text{Principal} + \text{Interest} \\
&= \quad \$2,000 + \$40 \\
&= \quad \$2,040
\end{aligned}
$$

Accounting for Notes Receivable. Now let us examine the journal entries used in accounting for notes receivable. Assuming that the Oakbrook Motel received the note in exchange for renting a large block of rooms, the entry on the date of the sale would be:

Notes Receivable	$2,000	
Rooms Revenue		$2,000

On the maturity date of the note, the entry to record the receipt of the cash would be:

Cash	$2,040	
Notes Receivable		$2,000
Interest Income		40

Calculating Maturity Dates. The actual maturity date of the note would be August 14, calculated as follows:

Days remaining in June (June 16–30)	15
Days in July	31
Days needed in August	14
Total days of note	60

Note: When calculating the maturity date for this type of note, accountants do not count the date that the note is issued. For example, the maturity date for Charles White's note was calculated from June 16, the day *after* he took out the note.

Sometimes, however, the time period of a note is stated in months rather than days. For notes of this type, the maturity date falls on the same date of the month on which the note was written. For example, if a three-month note is written on August 4, its maturity date is November 4.

Exchange of Account Receivable for Note Receivable. Occasionally a company may purchase goods or services from a hospitality firm, fully intending to pay the account receivable according to the regular terms. If, for some reason, payment is not made at the end of the credit period, the seller may allow the purchaser to sign a note receivable. The exchange of the account receivable for the note receivable in the amount of $10,000 would be journalized as follows:

Notes Receivable	$10,000	
Accounts Receivable		$10,000

Dishonored Notes. However, if the maker fails to pay a note receivable when due, the note is said to be dishonored. If the $2,000 note to the Oakbrook Motel were dishonored on the due date, the following entry would be made:

Accounts Receivable	$2,040	
Notes Receivable		$2,000
Interest Income		40

Notice that the note is written off the books, the interest is recorded and the total is debited to Accounts Receivable.

Discounting a Note Receivable. Occasionally the payee of a note receivable is unable to wait until the maturity date of the note to receive payment. If the maker of the note has a good credit rating, the payee could take the note to a bank and discount it before maturity. *Discounting* simply means cashing a note in before it is due and receiving less than the maturity value in the process.

Assume that 30 days after the Oakbrook Motel accepted the note from Charles White, the treasurer takes the note to the local bank, which discounts it at a rate of 14 percent. In this case, the cash that Oakbrook would receive, usually called the *proceeds*, would be calculated using the same formula used to calculate simple interest (Interest = Principal × Rate × Time), but substituting Discount in place of Interest, Maturity Value in place of Principal, Discount Rate in place of Rate, and Discount Period in place of Time.

$$\text{Discount} = \text{Maturity Value} \times \text{Discount Rate} \times \text{Discount Period}$$
$$= \$2,040 \times .14 \times \frac{30}{360}$$
$$= \$24$$

$$\text{Proceeds} = \text{Maturity Value} - \text{Discount}$$
$$= \$2,040 - \$24$$
$$= \$2,016$$

Exhibit 4 Discount Period for a Note

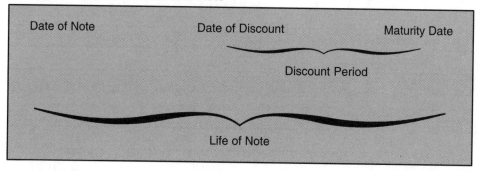

Observe that the bank discount rate can be different from the rate on the note. In this case, the bank discount rate is 14 percent while the note rate is 12 percent. Also notice that the discount period consists of the time that elapses between the discount date and the due date, as illustrated in Exhibit 4. The journal entry to record the proceeds on the discount date for the note would be:

Cash	$2,016	
Notes Receivable		$2,000
Interest Income		16

In this case, the actual proceeds realized when the note is discounted are more than the face amount of the note payable. This will not necessarily always be the case. If the bank discount rate had been 20 percent and the note had been discounted 20 days after issuance, the proceeds would have been $1,995. The journal entry would have been written in this way:

Cash	$1,995	
Interest Expense	5	
Notes Receivable		$2,000

The Oakbrook Motel has a **contingent liability** to the bank for the note once it is discounted and until it is finally paid by the maker. Assume in the case of its $2,000 note that the maker does not pay on the maturity date. Oakbrook would have to pay the bank the maturity value of the note and would make the following journal entry:

Accounts Receivable	$2,040	
Cash		$2,040

Note Receivable Spanning Two Fiscal Periods. Sometimes the receipt and collection of a note span two fiscal periods. Consider a $3,000, two-month, 12 percent note received on December 1, 20X3. The journal entry on December 31, 20X3, to record the accrued interest on the note would be:

Interest Receivable	$30	
Interest Income		$30

On February 1, 20X4, the due date of the note, the following entry would be made:

Cash	$3,060	
Interest Receivable		$ 30
Interest Income		30
Notes Receivable		3,000

Notes Payable

The average hospitality firm has several short-term liabilities or payables on its books, including wages payable, taxes payable, accounts payable, and notes payable. The topic of notes payable so closely parallels the topic of notes receivable that we will briefly discuss notes payable here.

A note payable could simply result when a company borrows money on a short-term basis from a bank. For example, assume that on October 1, 20X3, the Bayshore Country Club borrows $12,000 for 120 days at 10 percent from the Kentfield Bank. The journal entry for this transaction would be:

Cash	$12,000	
Notes Payable		$12,000

On December 31, 20X3, the Bayshore would make the following entry for the interest accrued to date on the note:

Interest Expense	$300	
Interest Payable		$300

The journal entry required on the payment date of the note, February 1, 20X4, would be:

Notes Payable	$12,000	
Interest Payable	300	
Interest Expense	100	
Cash		$12,400

Occasionally a firm has an account payable that it is unable to pay when due, and consequently signs a note payable for the amount of the account payable,

Exhibit 5   Note with Interest Included in Face Value

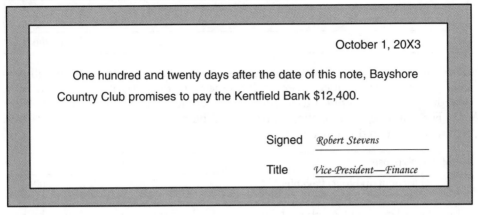

October 1, 20X3

One hundred and twenty days after the date of this note, Bayshore Country Club promises to pay the Kentfield Bank $12,400.

Signed   *Robert Stevens*

Title   *Vice-President—Finance*

agreeing to pay the principal and interest at a later date. If a $5,000 account payable were replaced by a note payable, the journal entry recording it would be:

Accounts Payable	$5,000	
Notes Payable		$5,000

Non-Interest-Bearing Notes

A **non-interest-bearing note** is one that includes the interest in the face value of the note. For example, assume that on October 1, the Bayshore Country Club borrowed $12,000 from the Kentfield bank for 120 days with an interest rate of 10 percent. The bank could simply compute the interest to maturity and include it in the face amount of the note as follows:

$$
\begin{aligned}
\text{Interest} &= \text{Principal} \times \text{Rate} \times \text{Time} \\
&= 12{,}000 \times .1 \times \tfrac{120}{360} \\
&= 400
\end{aligned}
$$

$$
\begin{aligned}
\text{Maturity Value} &= \text{Principal} + \text{Interest} \\
&= 12{,}000 + 400 \\
&= 12{,}400
\end{aligned}
$$

The bank could simply write the note as shown in Exhibit 5. Notice that, despite the fact that this type of note is referred to as a *non-interest-bearing note*, interest is still paid at maturity.

The accounting for non-interest-bearing notes differs from that for interest-bearing notes. In the case of a non-interest-bearing note, at the time the note was borrowed, Bayshore would make the following entry:

Cash	$12,000	
Discount on Notes Payable	400	
Notes Payable		$12,400

The Discount on Notes Payable account is a contra-liability account and will normally carry a debit balance. Over the life of the note, the $400 balance in the account is reduced, and the Interest Expense account is gradually increased by the $400.

For example, an adjusting entry would be made at December 31, 20X3, to accrue interest on the note as shown below:

Interest Expense	$300	
Discount on Notes Payable		$300

The balance sheet at December 31, 20X3, would show the carrying value of the note as $12,300, as illustrated below:

Current Liabilities:
Notes Payable	$12,400	
Less: Discount on Notes Payable	100	12,300

The journal entry on the maturity date of the note would be:

Notes Payable	$12,400	
Interest Expense	100	
Cash		$12,400
Discount on Notes Payable		100

A key point to remember is that the Notes Payable account is always credited for the face value of the note, whether it is interest-bearing or not. Exhibit 6 compares the journal entries for interest-bearing and non-interest-bearing notes.

Summary

The assets Accounts Receivable and Notes Receivable, as well as the liabilities Accounts Payable and Notes Payable, all play a very big role in a company's actual and potential cash flow. (Of course, a company wishes to collect receivables as soon after a sale as possible, and delay the payment of payables as long as possible, provided there are no adverse consequences such as loss of discounts for timely payment.)

To help avoid nonpayment problems, a hospitality business should follow a set of credit-checking procedures before issuing credit to a new guest. Even with a proper credit check, some guests will pay late. Therefore, it is wise to establish procedures for following up on late accounts and for dealing with uncollectible accounts. Two such procedures used when dealing with uncollectible accounts are the direct write-off method and the allowance method. Under the allowance

Exhibit 6   Comparison of Interest-Bearing and Non-Interest-Bearing Notes

Event/Date	Journal Entry for Interest-Bearing Notes		Journal Entry for Non-Interest-Bearing Notes	

Cash Borrowed, October 1	Cash
	   Notes Payable
		$12,000
		     $12,000
			Cash
			Discount on Notes Payable
			   Notes Payable
				$12,000
				400
				   $12,400

Adjusting Entry December 31	Interest Expense
	   Interest Payable
		$ 300
		   $ 300
			Interest Expense
			   Discount on Notes Payable
				$ 300
				   $ 300

Payment Date January 29	Notes Payable
	Interest Expense
	Interest Payable
	   Cash
		$12,000
		100
		300
		   $12,400
			Notes Payable
			Interest Expense
			   Discount on Notes Payable
			   Cash
				$12,400
				100
				   $ 100
				   12,400

method, there are two ways to determine the amount of bad debts to be written off: the aging of accounts receivable method and the percentage of sales method.

The chapter also shows how interest is computed and what entries are used in accounting for it.

Key Terms

aging of accounts receivable method—A method of accounting for bad debts expense in which the aging of accounts receivable schedule (a list of accounts receivable according to length of time outstanding) is used to estimate the total amount of bad debts.

allowance method—A method of accounting for bad debts expense in which accountants set up a contra-asset account called Allowance for Doubtful Accounts at the beginning of a fiscal year, give it a balance equal to the sum of accounts expected to be uncollectible in the coming year, then write off uncollectible accounts against this account; includes *aging of accounts receivable* method and *percentage of sales* method.

contingent liability—A liability that is based on a future event that may or may not take place; it is not yet an actual liability and therefore should not be included in the Liabilities section of the balance sheet. Instead, it should be included in footnotes to the financial statements.

creditor—A company with either an account receivable or a note receivable on its books.

debtor—A company with either an account payable or a note payable on its books.

direct write-off method—A method of accounting for bad debts expense in which an account receivable is written off at the time that it is determined to be uncollectible; does not match expenses with revenues.

dishonored note—A note payable that the maker fails to pay.

maker—The individual or company promising to pay the amount of a note.

maturity value—The principal and interest due at the maturity date of a note.

non-interest-bearing note—A note payable that has the interest included in its face value.

payee—The individual expecting to be paid by the maker of a note.

percentage of sales method—A method of accounting for bad debts expense in which the total amount of bad debts is calculated as a percentage of net credit sales.

Review Questions

1. How does a hotel's guest ledger differ from its city ledger? How do these ledgers relate to a subsidiary ledger?

2. What is the ledger account classification for Allowance for Doubtful Accounts? What is its normal balance?

3. What is a major disadvantage of the direct write-off method of accounting for bad debts?

4. What accounts are debited and credited when a specific account is written off during the year under the allowance method of accounting for bad debts?

5. How does the aging of accounts receivable method differ from the percentage of sales method in accounting for bad debts?

6. If the allowance method of accounting for bad debts indicates a debit balance at the end of the year, were bad debts underestimated or overestimated for the year?

7. How is the maturity value of a note calculated?

8. What is the difference between an interest-bearing note and a non-interest-bearing note?

9. What is the account classification for Discount on Notes Payable? What is its normal balance?

10. Does the year-end adjusted entry for accruing the interest of a non-interest-bearing note increase or decrease the carrying value of the note?

Problems

Problem 1

On June 15, the Pines Restaurant decided to write off the account of Thomas Sunbart in the amount of $350. The restaurant uses the direct write-off method of accounting for bad debts.

Required:

1. Make the necessary journal entry for June 15.
2. On August 10, the restaurant receives a check in the amount of $350 from Sunbart. Make the necessary entry or entries for this date.

Problem 2

The Goal Post Inn has the following notes receivable:

Customer	Date of Note	Terms	Amount
Jarvis Advertising	January 8, 20X3	60 days	$10,000
Methods Inc.	March 12, 20X3	2 months	$8,000
Salvos Engineering	May 22, 20X3	90 days	$4,000
Raphael Corporation	August 15, 20X3	3 months	$6,000
Valspar Technology	October 6, 20X3	180 days	$2,000
Valvomatics	November 1, 20X3	6 months	$12,000

Required:

Determine the maturity dates for the notes. Assume 20X2 was a leap year.

Problem 3

The Downtown Restaurant uses the percentage of sales method of estimating bad debts.

Required:

Using the following information, journalize the necessary entry on December 31, 20X3:

Cash Sales	$200,000
Credit Sales	300,000
Total Sales	$500,000
Expected Bad Debts Percentage	1.5
Current credit balance in the allowance account:	$ 1,500

Problem 4

Following are the terms for a discounted note:

Date of note	June 1
Life of note	90 days
Maturity date of note	?
Discount date of note	July 31
Amount of note	$20,000
Interest rate on note	8%
Discount rate on note	9%

Required:

Calculate the proceeds on the discounted note. Assume 360 days in a year.

Problem 5

The Carolina House Restaurant borrows $30,000 at 14 percent from its bank for three months on December 1, 20X3.

Required:

1. Prepare the journal entry for December 1, 20X3.
2. Prepare the adjusting entry for December 31, 20X3.
3. Prepare the entry for the payment of the principal and interest on the note for March 1, 20X4.

Problem 6

Use all of the information given in Problem 5 to solve this problem. However, assume that the note in Problem 6 is a *non-interest-bearing note.*

Required:

1. Prepare the journal entry for December 1, 20X3.
2. Prepare the adjusting entry for December 31, 20X3.
3. Prepare the entry for the payment of the principal and interest on March 1, 20X4.

Challenge Problems

Problem 7

The Pacific Hotel uses the aging of accounts receivable method of accounting for uncollectible accounts. The current aging of receivables schedule indicates the allowance for bad debts to be $2,500.

Required:

1. Prepare an adjusting entry for December 31, 20X3, assuming a credit balance of $200 in the allowance account.
2. Prepare an adjusting entry for December 31, 20X3, assuming a debit balance of $200 in the allowance account.
3. The $300 balance in Mary Lewis's account is written off the books on January 31, 20X4. Prepare the journal entry.
4. Mary Lewis sends a check for $300 in payment of her account, which was previously written off. Prepare the necessary entry or entries on October 15, 20X4.

Problem 8

The 12/31/X3 accounts receivable of the Cabana Resort Inn are represented by the following:

Guest	Date of Invoice	Terms of Sale	Amount
Lou Shields	Oct. 12	n/30	$ 500

Paul Martin	Sept. 6	n/60	$ 800
John Anthony	Aug. 9	n/30	300
Chris Silas	Dec. 22	n/30	600
Rick Switzer	Nov. 15	n/30	1,500
Bob Sheldon	Sept. 10	n/60	700
Dave Rice	Dec. 19	n/30	300

The firm expects to lose the following percentages of bad debts:

Days Past Due	Percentage Considered Uncollectible
0 (Current)	1
1 – 30	3
31 – 60	4
61 – 90	10
Over 90	20

Required:

1. Prepare an aging of accounts receivable schedule.
2. Prepare the journal entry to allow for bad debts for 12/31/X3, assuming the current balance in the allowance account is $94.

Problem 9

The Southbreeze Hotel uses the aging of accounts receivable method of estimating bad debts. As of December 31, 20X3, the summarized aging schedule and expected loss percentages are as follows:

Aging of Accounts Receivable

	Current	0–30	30–60	60–90	over 90
Amount	$18,000	$2,200	$1,800	$1,000	$750
Loss % expected	1%	2%	4%	10%	30%

Required:

1. Assuming a zero balance in the allowance account, make the necessary journal entry on December 31, 20X3.
2. Assuming a $150 debit balance in the allowance account, make the necessary journal entry on December 31, 20X3.

Problem 10

The Conway Hotel accepts a 120-day, $15,000, 10 percent note from a client on April 1, 20X3, in exchange for conference services.

Required:

1. Prepare the journal entry required on April 1, 20X3.

2. The Conway Hotel decides to discount the note at the local bank on May 1, 20X3, at a rate of 12 percent. Prepare the entry for the discounting of the note.

3. Prepare the necessary journal entry on August 1, 20X3, assuming that the note is dishonored.

REVIEW QUIZ

When you feel you have covered all of the material in this chapter, answer these questions. Choose the *best* answer.

1. A company that has either an account payable or a note payable on its books is called a:

   a. debtor.
   b. creditor.
   c. note maker.
   d. note discounter.

2. The Windmill Café used the direct write-off method of accounting for bad debt expense to recognize Mr. Armstrong's debt as uncollectible. If Mr. Armstrong paid the amount he owes, the journal entry would involve:

   a. crediting Accounts Receivable and debiting Provision for Doubtful Accounts.
   b. debiting Cash and crediting Accounts Receivable.
   c. three journal entries.
   d. two journal entries.

3. Francisco has determined that Mr. Freeloader, a former guest of his hotel, will probably not pay the hotel his debt of $600. Francisco's hotel uses the allowance method of accounting for bad debt expense. Francisco must _____ Allowance for Doubtful Accounts and _____ Accounts Receivable to recognize that the account is uncollectible.

   a. credit; debit
   b. credit; credit
   c. debit; credit
   d. dishonor; discount

4. The aging of accounts receivable schedule for the Rambles Inn showed the following:

	Amount	Percentage Uncollectible
Current	$30,000	.5
1 to 30 days past due	$15,000	1.5
31 to 60 days past due	$5,000	2.5
Over 60 days past due	$5,000	15.0

   Using the amounts and percentages provided, the total amount of estimated uncollectible accounts is:

   a. $950.
   b. $1,250.
   c. $2,600.
   d. impossible to determine.

REVIEW QUIZ *(continued)*

5. The percentage of sales method of estimating bad debt losses focuses on the:

   a. balance sheet.
   b. income statement.
   c. statement of cash flows.
   d. statement of retained earnings.

6. When a meeting planner who owes a hotel money fails to pay an interest-bearing note payable on its due date, what happens to the interest on the note?

   a. It is written off as Provision for Doubtful Accounts.
   b. It is recorded as being part of the face value of the note.
   c. It is recorded as Interest Income.
   d. It is added to Accounts Payable.

7. A non-interest-bearing note with a maturity value of $10,500 has a discount of $500. The cash to be received when the funds are borrowed is _____, while the amount to be paid at maturity is _____.

   a. $10,500; $11,000
   b. $10,000; $11,000
   c. $10,000; $10,500
   d. $10,500; $10,000

Answer Key: 1-a-C1, 2-d-C2, 3-c-C3, 4-b-C4, 5-b-C5, 6-c-C6, 7-c-C7

Each question is linked to a competency. Competencies are listed on the first page of the chapter. An answer reading 3-b-C4 translates to:

   3: the question number
   b: the correct answer
   C4: the competency number

Chapter 10 Outline

Periodic versus Perpetual Inventory
    Systems
        Taking a Physical Inventory
        Transportation Costs
Inventory Valuation Methods
        Comparison and Evaluation of
            Inventory Valuation Methods
Estimating Ending Inventory and Cost of
    Goods Sold
        The Retail Method
        The Gross Profit Method
Lower of Cost or Market (LCM)
Perpetual Inventory System

Competencies

1. Identify broad guidelines for controlling inventory, and explain the role of inventory in the calculation of profit.

2. Explain procedures for taking a physical inventory, and describe the roles of transportation costs and terms of sale in recording inventory.

3. Demonstrate and compare the four basic methods of valuing ending inventory.

4. Demonstrate and distinguish between the retail and gross profit methods of estimating ending inventory.

5. Perform the lower of cost or market (LCM) computation and outline situations in which it is used.

6. Distinguish the perpetual inventory system from the periodic inventory system.

10

Inventory

MERCHANDISE INVENTORY represents the goods that a hospitality firm holds for resale to its guests. In the case of a restaurant, the food and beverages stocked constitute the operation's merchandise inventory. Merchandise inventory is normally expected to be sold within a year. Therefore, it is considered a current asset.

Inventory as a percentage of total assets is relatively low for the average hospitality firm. However, because of its impact on profit, it is important to control and account for inventory carefully. In addition to merchandise inventory, hospitality firms have supplies inventory. A hotel's housekeeping department would keep an inventory of such supplies as brooms, waxes, and mops. Other supplies inventory categories include guestroom amenities and office stocks of stationery. Supplies inventory is considered a current asset on the balance sheet, and is usually listed after cash and receivables.

Inventory is a very portable asset in a hospitality firm and consequently should be maintained under an adequate system of internal control. The following are some of the broad guidelines that should be followed in controlling inventory:

1. There should be a separation between custody of the inventory records and custody of the inventory. The custodian of the inventory should not have access to the inventory records. Conversely, the accountant who maintains the inventory records should not have access to the inventory itself.

2. A physical inventory should be taken periodically using preprinted inventory control forms.

3. Any significant underage or overage of inventory should be reported to the controller when it is discovered.

4. A daily inventory of high-priced items should be taken.

5. The storeroom where the inventory is kept should be secured, and access should be limited to authorized personnel.

Periodic versus Perpetual Inventory Systems

The two basic types of inventory systems are the periodic and the perpetual systems. Except for a brief discussion of the perpetual inventory system at the end of this chapter, the following concepts assume the use of a **periodic inventory system**. Under the periodic inventory system, no continuous record of the inventory items is kept. After the beginning of a fiscal period, one can only estimate the inventory value. When items are purchased, the Purchases account is debited and

Cash or Accounts Payable is credited. When items are sold, the Sales account is credited for the retail value, Cash or Accounts Receivable is debited, and no deduction is made from the Inventory account.

Under the periodic inventory system, the exact dollar amount of the inventory is not known until the next physical inventory is taken. The perpetual inventory system, however, keeps continuous track of inventory as it is purchased as well as when it is sold. At any given time, one can look at the books and know exactly what the value of inventory is.

A firm starts an accounting period with beginning inventory, which is the inventory that remains from the previous period. Purchases made during the current period represent goods bought for resale. Inventory purchases include the purchase cost of goods for sale plus the related shipping cost. *Beginning inventory* and *purchases* added together are referred to as the *cost of goods available for sale*. *Ending inventory* is the inventory left at the end of an accounting period.

Inventory is a unique accounting item. Although Inventory is a balance sheet account, it is also included on the income statement. This is because accountants use Inventory when calculating cost of goods sold for the firm. Cost of goods sold is traditionally computed as follows:

	Beginning inventory
Plus:	Inventory purchases
Equals:	Cost of goods available for sale
Less:	Ending inventory
Equals:	Cost of goods consumed
Less:	Goods used internally (such as Employee Meals—Food & Beverage Department)
Equals:	Cost of goods sold

An important but relatively small category of direct expenses is "Goods used internally." An example of this would be food provided free of charge to employees (Employee Meals—Rooms Department). Many hospitality operations provide free meals to employees as part of their benefits package. Cost of employee meals for the rooms department is subtracted to determine cost of food sold. The cost of employee meals for rooms department employees is shown as an expense in the rooms department.

Cost of goods sold is then subtracted from sales to obtain the gross profit for the operation. An error in either the counting or the valuation of inventory will cause an error in reported income. Exhibit 1 illustrates the effects that an error in ending inventory can have on profit.

When ending inventory is understated, profit is understated. When ending inventory is overstated, profit is overstated. An error in beginning inventory has the opposite effect on profit. An understatement of beginning inventory causes an overstatement of profit. This is shown in Exhibit 2. If, on the other hand, beginning inventory is overstated, profits are understated. The effects of errors in beginning and ending inventory are summarized in Exhibit 3.

Note that, since the ending inventory of one accounting period is the beginning inventory of the next period, the effect of an error in the first period will likewise cause an error in profit in the subsequent period. Although total profits for

Exhibit 1   Effects of Error in Ending Inventory on Profit

Correct Ending Inventory			Incorrect Ending Inventory		
Sales		$100,000	Sales		$100,000
Cost of Goods Sold:			Cost of Goods Sold:		
Beginning Inventory	$ 30,000		Beginning Inventory	$ 30,000	
Purchases	90,000		Purchases	90,000	
Cost of Goods Available	120,000		Cost of Goods Available	120,000	
Ending Inventory	− 40,000		Ending Inventory	− 35,000	
Cost of Goods Sold		80,000	Cost of Goods Sold		85,000
Gross Profit		$ 20,000	Gross Profit		$ 15,000

Exhibit 2   Effects of Error in Beginning Inventory on Profit

Correct Beginning Inventory			Incorrect Beginning Inventory		
Sales		$100,000	Sales		$100,000
Cost of Goods Sold:			Cost of Goods Sold:		
Beginning Inventory	$ 30,000		Beginning Inventory	$ 25,000	
Purchases	90,000		Purchases	90,000	
Cost of Goods Available	120,000		Cost of Goods Available	115,000	
Ending Inventory	− 40,000		Ending Inventory	− 40,000	
Cost of Goods Sold		80,000	Cost of Goods Sold		75,000
Gross Profit		$ 20,000	Gross Profit		$ 25,000

Exhibit 3   Effects of Error in Inventory on Profit

Error in Inventory	Effect on Profit
Beginning Inventory Understated	Overstated
Beginning Inventory Overstated	Understated
Ending Inventory Understated	Understated
Ending Inventory Overstated	Overstated

the two periods will be correct, the individual profit figure for each period will be incorrect. Owners' equity will be incorrect for the first period but will be correct by the end of the second period.

Taking a Physical Inventory

Since an accurate inventory amount is essential to the computation of net income, it is important that the procedures for taking a physical inventory be followed carefully. A physical inventory involves two basic steps. Step one constitutes the actual counting of the inventory items. Care must be taken both in counting the individual items and in recording the cost of each particular item. Employees taking a physical inventory should work in pairs; one employee should count the items while the other writes down the amounts and individual costs of the items. Step two involves the *footing of the inventory*. This means multiplying the items by their costs and adding together the costs of all items of inventory.

It is important to ensure that there is a proper cutoff in taking inventory at the end of the physical inventory period. This means that any items physically in the storeroom but already sold to customers *should not be* included in inventory. In addition, items that are part of an inventory but not physically in the storeroom *should be* included in the ending inventory.

Transportation Costs

Dollar amounts used to record inventory and cost of sales should reflect the total purchase cost involved in obtaining a shipment of goods. The total purchase cost should, therefore, include not only the cost of the merchandise but also the cost of getting the merchandise to the place of business. This cost is variously called *shipping, transportation,* or *freight.*

Some suppliers absorb the expenses involved in transporting goods to the buyer. Other suppliers who deliver will charge the buyer for freight costs. In freight terminology, *FOB* means *free on board.* However, it does not necessarily mean *free freight. FOB* is only one part of the terms of freight. Either the point of origin or the point of destination must be specified to determine whether the buyer or seller pays the additional freight charges required to complete delivery. Two common freight terms are *FOB destination* and *FOB shipping point.*

FOB destination means that the seller will deliver the product free of any freight charges to the destination specified by the buyer. By contrast, *FOB shipping point* indicates point of origin. It basically means that the buyer must pay transportation charges to have the merchandise transported to a specified location.

Items that are in transit at the end of an accounting period must be carefully scrutinized through an examination of the terms of sale. If the seller ships merchandise with terms *FOB destination*, title does not pass to the purchaser until the goods reach the purchaser. Merchandise shipped FOB destination should be included on the seller's books at the end of this particular accounting period. If, on the other hand, the seller ships the goods with the terms *FOB shipping point*, the shipped goods are no longer considered part of the seller's inventory.

Items purchased on terms *FOB destination* should not be included on the books of the purchaser until they arrive, while goods purchased on terms *FOB shipping point* should be included on the purchaser's books at the end of the period even if they have not yet arrived. Items that arrive near year-end in a damaged state and are returned to a supplier before year-end should not be included in the purchaser's year-end inventory.

Inventory Valuation Methods ────────────────────────────

The four basic methods for valuing ending inventory are specific identification; weighted average; first-in, first-out (FIFO); and last-in, first-out (LIFO). It is important to understand that these four inventory valuation techniques are simply methods of valuing the ending inventory on the books. *The method of inventory valuation a business uses does not usually parallel the physical flow of merchandise through the storeroom.*

Using the data listed in the following table, we will illustrate the four inventory valuation methods:

	Number of Units	Cost per Unit	Total Cost
Beginning inventory	25	$10.00	$ 250.00
February 15 purchase	30	11.00	330.00
May 6 purchase	20	13.00	260.00
August 22 purchase	35	14.00	490.00
October 10 purchase	40	15.00	600.00
December 2 purchase	25	16.00	400.00
Available for sale	175		$2,330.00
Units sold	145		
Ending inventory	30		

Notice that there were 175 units available for sale, 145 units sold, and 30 units remaining in ending inventory. In this section, we will use each of the four techniques to value the same 30 units of ending inventory.

The **specific identification method** is used for valuing big-ticket items. Hotel accountants typically use this method to value certain food and beverage items, such as cases of expensive wine. Under this method, the amounts actually paid for individual items determine their value at the end of the period. Food and beverage items are marked at their cost when they are received. These costs are used to value the inventory.

Assuming that the ending inventory of 30 units consisted of 20 units at $16 (December 2 purchase), 2 units at $15 (October 10 purchase), and 8 units at $10 (beginning inventory), the ending inventory under the specific identification method would be valued at $430.

Under the **weighted average method**, the total number of units available for sale is divided into the total cost of the units available for sale. In our example, a unit of ending inventory would be valued at $13.314 per unit, as shown below:

$$\text{Cost of units available for sale} \quad \frac{\$2,330.00}{175} = \$13.314$$
$$\text{Divided by units available}$$

Under this method, the ending inventory would be valued at $399.42, calculated as follows:

$$30 \text{ units @ } \$13.314 = \$399.42 \text{ (or } \$399, \text{ rounded)}$$

The **first-in, first-out (FIFO) method** assumes that the first units into inventory are the first units out of inventory. The ending inventory therefore consists of the latest purchases, while the cost of goods sold consists of the earliest purchases. The 30 units of ending inventory would be valued as follows under FIFO:

25 units from December 2 purchase @ $16.00	= $400.00
5 units from October 10 purchase @ $15.00	= 75.00
Ending inventory value of 30 units, FIFO	$475.00

Exhibit 4   Summary of Inventory Valuation Methods

	Specific ID	Weighted Average	FIFO	LIFO
Sales	$6,000	$6,000	$6,000	$6,000
Cost of Goods Sold:				
Beginning Inventory	250	250	250	250
Purchases	2,080	2,080	2,080	2,080
Cost of Goods Available	2,330	2,330	2,330	2,330
Ending Inventory	380	399	475	305
Cost of Goods Sold	1,950	1,931	1,855	2,025
Gross Profit	$4,050	$4,069	$4,145	$3,975

The 30 units of inventory under FIFO are valued at $475.00, whereas under the weighted average method they were valued at $399.

The **last-in, first-out (LIFO) method** of valuing inventories assumes that the first units in are the last units out of inventory and that the ending inventory consists of the earliest purchases. The value of the ending inventory would be calculated as follows under LIFO:

25 units of beginning inventory @ $10.00	=	$250.00
5 units from February 15 purchase @ $11.00	=	55.00
Ending inventory value of 30 units, LIFO		$305.00

Comparison and Evaluation of Inventory Valuation Methods

The four inventory methods assign different values to the same 30 units of inventory. Exhibit 4 summarizes these four methods and illustrates their effects on income, assuming that sales are $6,000 for the period.

Notice that the information provided in the table indicated a period of rising prices. That is, every time merchandise was ordered, it cost more than it had before. Because of this inflationary climate, FIFO results in the highest value for ending inventory, and LIFO results in the lowest. This occurs because, under FIFO, the latest (higher) costs are assigned to the ending inventory. Under LIFO, the earliest (lowest) costs are assigned to ending inventory. The weighted average method results in a value for the ending inventory somewhere between those for FIFO and LIFO, since it averages all the costs of inventory for the period.

Since FIFO results in the highest value for the ending inventory, it also results in the lowest value for the cost of goods sold for the period and the highest gross profit for the period. On the other hand, since LIFO has the lowest value for the ending inventory, it results in the highest cost of goods sold figure and the lowest gross profit amount. Since LIFO provides the lowest reported income figure, most companies prefer to use it when reporting to the Internal Revenue Service (IRS).

An inventory valuation computation involving a period of falling prices would produce the opposite effect on profits. Under deflationary conditions, FIFO would result in a lower value for the ending inventory and a higher cost of goods sold than LIFO. FIFO would also result in lower reported income than LIFO.

The consistency principle dictates that once a business selects an inventory valuation method, it should use that method in subsequent years. If the business adheres to this generally accepted accounting principle, its reported profit will be more consistent from year to year. However, this does not mean that once an inventory valuation method is selected, a firm may never change methods. If the firm has a valid reason for changing inventory valuation methods, it may do so. Such a change must be disclosed in the notes to the financial statements.

Estimating Ending Inventory and Cost of Goods Sold ———

Hospitality firms always take a physical inventory at the end of each fiscal year, whether they use the periodic or the perpetual inventory method. They do this to accurately compile financial statements and to comply with IRS regulations. On a monthly basis, however, it may be too costly or inconvenient to take a physical inventory. Sometimes it may be impossible to do so, such as when a business is destroyed by a fire or flood. However, companies still need to produce financial statements. In lieu of taking a physical inventory, businesses can use one of two methods to estimate ending inventory. They are the retail method and the gross profit method.

The Retail Method

Although the **retail method of inventory valuation** is used primarily by department stores, hospitality firms can also use it effectively. To implement this method, a firm must maintain records at both cost and retail for beginning inventory and purchases. The retail price is the amount at which the item is priced for sale.

Since an accountant would have a record of both beginning inventory and purchases, he or she should therefore know the cost of goods available for sale at both cost and retail. Recall that at the end of a fiscal period, the items included in cost of goods available must either have been sold or be in ending inventory. With that information and a record of sales for the period, the accountant can subtract cost of goods available at retail from sales at retail and end up with ending inventory at retail.

The books list ending inventory at cost, not retail, so there is one more step in the computation. It involves finding the percentage relationship between cost and retail for the business. This is accomplished by simply dividing *the cost of goods available for sale at cost* by *the cost of goods available for sale at retail*. The resulting percentage is then multiplied by the ending inventory at retail. The result is ending inventory at cost.

The following illustration shows the estimate of ending inventory at July 31, 20X3 for a hypothetical firm. Assume the following:

Beginning inventory at cost	$ 12,376
Beginning inventory at retail:	$ 22,277
Purchases at cost:	$ 76,840
Purchases at retail:	$138,312
Net sales at retail:	$132,068

Using these balances, an estimate of ending inventory would be computed as follows:

	Cost Price	Retail Selling Price
Beginning Inventory	$12,376	$ 22,277
Purchases	+ 76,840	+ 138,312
Cost of Goods Available	89,216	160,589

$$\text{Cost Percentage: } \frac{\$89,216}{\$160,589} = 56\%$$

Subtract Net Sales at Retail		− 132,068
Ending Inventory at Retail		$ 28,521
Ending Inventory at Cost:		
$28,521 × .56	$15,972	

The Gross Profit Method

The basic assumption under the **gross profit method of inventory valuation** is that the gross profit percentage for the firm is fairly constant from period to period. Therefore, if a restaurant's gross profit percentage was 60 percent over the past five years, it can assume that the current period's gross profit percentage is also 60 percent. Recall the relationship between the gross profit percentage and the cost of goods sold percentage: added together, they must equal 100 percent.

Once the accountant obtains the gross profit percentage, he or she goes to the general ledger and adds beginning inventory and purchases to get cost of goods available for sale. Next, the accountant estimates cost of goods sold by multiplying sales by the gross profit percentage. Finally, the accountant determines ending inventory by subtracting cost of goods sold from cost of goods available for sale.

We will use the following example to illustrate the gross profit method:

Beginning inventory, August 1, 20X3	$16,586
Purchases in August	48,522
Sales in August	93,407
Gross profit percentage	53%

Using these account balances and the gross profit ratio of 53 percent, the ending inventory would be $21,207, computed as follows:

Beginning inventory, August 1, 20X3	$16,586
Purchases in August	48,522
Cost of goods available for sale	65,108
Subtract estimated cost of goods sold:	

Exhibit 5   Computation of Lower of Cost or Market

Inventory Item	Number of Units	Cost/ Unit	Current Market Value/Unit	1 Cost	2 Market	3 LCM
A	20	$12	$11	$ 240	$ 220	$ 220
B	15	11	10	165	150	150
C	12	16	17	192	204	192
D	30	14	13	420	390	390
E	18	17	17	306	306	306
				$1,323	$1,270	$1,258

Sales in August	$93,407	
Cost of goods sold % (1 − .53)	× .47	43,901
Estimated ending inventory, August 31, 20X3		$21,207

Lower of Cost or Market (LCM)

Obsolescence, deterioration, or a drop in the current market prices of inventory may cause a firm to lower the value of inventory on its books. The generally accepted accounting principle of conservatism states that inventory should be carried at the lower of cost (on the purchase date) or the market value of the inventory as of the balance sheet date. (This is true for both the periodic and perpetual inventory systems.)

The **lower of cost or market (LCM)** computation can be done either on an item-by-item basis or by comparing total cost with total market value. Exhibit 5 illustrates the lower of cost or market computation. The columns numbered 1 and 2 show the computation on the basis of the lower of total cost or market, while column 3 provides an amount for inventory on an item-by-item basis.

Applying the lower of cost or market value on an item-by-item basis would result in an ending inventory value of $1,258; applying the lower of cost or market to the total of the entire inventory would result in a value of $1,270.

Perpetual Inventory System

Until this point, the chapter discussion has for the most part revolved around periodic inventory systems. The **perpetual inventory system** continuously updates the Merchandise Inventory account. Every time merchandise is purchased for resale, the inventory account is increased. Every time merchandise is sold, the inventory account is decreased.

Under this system, it is not necessary to estimate the ending inventory for interim statement purposes. Rather, one can simply look at the Inventory account to ascertain the inventory's value. A physical inventory is taken at the end of the year to prove that the book inventory matches the actual inventory.

Under the perpetual system, the Purchases account is not used when merchandise is purchased. Instead, the Merchandise Inventory account is debited, as shown below when $2,000 worth of inventory is purchased on account.

Exhibit 6   Periodic versus Perpetual Inventory Systems

Event	Periodic		Perpetual	
Purchased 48 bottles of wine @ $8/bottle	Purchases $384		Merchandise Inventory $384	
	Accounts Payable	$384	Accounts Payable	$384
Sold 10 bottles of wine @ $15/bottle for cash	Cash $150		Cash $150	
	Sales	$150	Sales	$150
			Cost of Goods Sold $ 80	
			Merchandise Inventory	$80

Merchandise Inventory	$2,000	
Accounts Payable		$2,000

Two entries are required under this system when merchandise is sold. The following entries illustrate the cash sale of $4,000 worth of merchandise that has a cost of $1,800.

Cash	$4,000	
Sales		$4,000

Cost of Goods Sold	$1,800	
Merchandise Inventory		$1,800

From these two entries, one can conclude that the gross profit on the sale was $2,200, since Sales minus Cost of Goods Sold equals Gross Profit. Exhibit 6 compares the journal entries that would be made under the periodic and perpetual inventory systems.

Summary

Although inventory as a percentage of total assets is relatively low, its impact on profits can be great. Therefore, inventory must be accounted for and controlled carefully. The two primary types of inventory systems are the periodic and the perpetual systems.

Four basic methods for valuing ending inventory are specific identification; weighted average; first-in, first-out (FIFO); and last-in, first-out (LIFO). Each of these methods provides a slightly different valuation of inventory. Therefore, for the sake of consistency, the firm should use the same method each period, unless it has a valid reason for changing it.

Sometimes it may be necessary to estimate the value of inventory, such as when a fire destroys the inventory and its value must be estimated for insurance purposes, or when a physical inventory would be inconvenient or too costly. Two methods used to estimate the value of inventory are the retail method and the gross profit method.

Occasionally, obsolescence, deterioration, or a drop in the current market prices of inventory may cause a firm to lower the value of inventory on its books to comply with the accounting principle of conservatism.

With the growth of technology, many firms are switching to a perpetual inventory system wherein the value of inventory on hand is updated continuously through the firm's computer systems. Of course, even a perpetual inventory system doesn't entirely eliminate the need to perform physical inventory counts.

Key Terms

first-in, first-out (FIFO) method of inventory valuation—A method of valuing inventory in which the first units into inventory are considered sold first; hence, ending inventory consists of the latest purchases.

gross profit method of inventory valuation—A method of estimating ending inventory based on a historical gross profit percentage for the firm.

last-in, first-out (LIFO) method of inventory valuation—A method of valuing inventory in which the last units into inventory are considered sold first; hence, ending inventory consists of the earliest purchases.

lower of cost or market (LCM)—An accounting procedure for valuing ending inventory based on the generally accepted accounting principle of conservatism.

merchandise inventory—Goods that a hospitality firm holds for resale to guests.

periodic inventory system—A system of accounting for inventory under which cost of goods sold must be computed. There are no continuous inventory records kept, so a physical count of the storeroom is required to determine the inventory on hand.

perpetual inventory system—A system of accounting for inventory that records receipts and issues and provides a continuous record of the quantity and cost of merchandise in inventory.

retail method of inventory valuation—A method of estimating ending inventory based on the relationship between cost and retail price.

specific identification method of inventory valuation—A method of valuing inventory by identifying the actual costs of the purchased and issued units.

weighted average method of inventory valuation—A method of valuing inventory in which the value is determined by averaging the cost of items in the beginning inventory with the cost of items purchased during the period.

Review Questions

1. What major guidelines should a hospitality business follow to control inventory?

2. What are the differences between the periodic and perpetual inventory systems?

3. How is cost of goods sold calculated? How is it related to gross profit?

4. Does an overstatement of ending inventory overstate or understate cost of goods sold for the period? What is the effect of the error on net income for the period?

5. How do the terms under which a supplier ships goods affect inventory valuation and accounting for inventory?

6. How do the LIFO and FIFO methods of inventory valuation differ?

7. How can an area's economic environment affect managers' choices of inventory valuation methods?

8. What special records must be maintained to implement the retail method of estimating inventory?

9. What is the gross profit method of estimating inventory? When would it be necessary to use this method?

10. How is inventory accounted for differently under the perpetual inventory method as opposed to the periodic method?

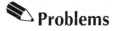

Problems

Problem 1

Based on the following transactions and shipping terms between Coldpac Distributors and Marco's Pizzeria, determine who should include the inventory in question on their 12/31/20X8 balance sheet.

1. Marco's received $4,000 worth of inventory on January 3 that was shipped FOB destination by Coldpac on December 28.

2. Marco's received $5,000 worth of inventory on January 2 that was shipped FOB shipping point on December 24.

3. Marco's received $1,000 worth of inventory on December 29 shipped by Coldpac on December 26 FOB destination. The inventory was defective and was shipped back to Coldpac on December 31.

Problem 2

On July 6, 20X3, the Pro Shop at the Hilton Lagoons Hotel ordered golf clubs and clothing that together cost $8,000, which managers charged to the hotel's account. On July 15, 20X3, the shop sold $2,500 worth of merchandise, which cost $1,400.

Required:

Journalize the entries for July 6 and July 15, assuming:

1. The Pro Shop uses the periodic inventory system.
2. The Pro Shop uses the perpetual inventory system.

Problem 3

The following data is for the month of May 20X8 for the Signature Café:

Purchases	$ 32,400
Ending Inventory	59,000
Cost of Food Sold	29,676

Employee meals are 10 percent of monthly purchases.

Required:

Calculate inventory at May 1, 20X8.

Problem 4

Indicate the effects of the following errors on cost of goods sold and net income:

	Error	Amount
1.	Ending inventory understated	$ 50,000
2.	Beginning inventory overstated	$ 20,000
3.	Ending inventory overstated	$ 30,000
4.	Beginning inventory understated	$ 12,000

Problem 5

The following data is for the month of June 20X3 for the Fairbanks Hotel:

Beginning Inventory	$ 28,300
Purchases	16,200
Ending Inventory	29,500
Employee Meals—Rooms Department	300
Employee Meals—Food & Beverage Department	500

Required:

Calculate the cost of food used and the cost of food sold for the Fairbanks Hotel for the month of June.

Problem 6

The following information relates to the merchandise of the Pro Shop of the Lagoons Resort through May 31, 20X4.

	# of Sets of Golf Clubs	Cost/Set	Total Cost
Beginning Inventory	5	$ 250.00	$ 1,250.00
January 8 purchase	12	265.00	3,180.00
February 12 purchase	20	270.00	5,400.00
March 20 purchase	20	280.00	5,600.00
April 5 purchase	20	290.00	5,800.00
May 18 purchase	10	300.00	3,000.00
Available for sale	87		$ 24,230.00
Sets sold	57		
Ending Inventory	30		

Required:

Journalize the purchase of April 5 and sale of those 20 sets of golf clubs, assuming that each set sells for $495 and that:

1.   The Pro Shop uses the periodic inventory system.
2.   The Pro Shop uses the perpetual inventory system.

Challenge Problems

Problem 7

Using the information provided in Problem 6, complete the following:

Required:

1.   Assume that all sets of golf clubs were sold for $495 each, and that the remaining sets consisted of the following:

>   8   sets from the May 18 purchase
>   18   sets from the April 5 purchase
>   4   sets from Beginning Inventory

Calculate gross profit through May 31 for the Pro Shop.

2.   Assume the same selling price for the golf clubs ($495 each). Using the weighted average method of inventory valuation, calculate gross profit through May 31 for the Pro Shop.

Problem 8

Using the information provided in Problem 6, calculate gross profit through May 31 for the Pro Shop, assuming that:

a. The business uses the FIFO inventory valuation.

b. The business uses the LIFO inventory valuation.

Problem 9

The following data pertaining to the Stellar Cellars Restaurant shows both cost and current market value for five items of inventory.

Required:

Calculate the value of the inventory using lower of cost or market (LCM) on both a unit basis and a total basis.

Inventory Item	# of Units	Cost	Market Value
1	25	$12.60	$12.80
2	20	14.25	13.75
3	15	18.30	18.60
4	18	16.40	15.90
5	32	11.20	11.20

Problem 10

The Pro Shop at the Hilton Lagoons Hotel and Golf Club is compiling its July income statement. It is the middle of the busy season and the manager decides not to take the time to do a physical inventory. Instead, she chooses the retail method of estimating inventory.

Beginning inventory was $18,000 at cost and $35,500 at retail. Purchases for the month amounted to $12,000 at cost and $23,600 at retail. Sales for the month were $26,800.

Required:

Estimate ending inventory using the retail method of inventory valuation.

REVIEW QUIZ

When you feel you have covered all of the material in this chapter, answer these questions. Choose the *best* answer.

1. Inventory:

   a. is used to calculate cost of goods sold, which is necessary for computing gross profits.
   b. is used to calculate the selling price for goods used internally.
   c. is a balance sheet account that has no effect on the income statement.
   d. appears on the income statement instead of the balance sheet.

2. *FOB destination* means freight charges will be paid by the:

   a. hospitality firm that ordered the shipment.
   b. purchasing agent.
   c. freight company.
   d. supplier.

3. A hotel had 5 jars of gourmet fudge topping on hand that cost $10.00 apiece when they were purchased on January 1, 20X1. During the year, three purchases of the topping were made as follows:

March 1	15 units @ $11.00
July 14	12 units @ $12.00
November 4	20 units @ $13.00

   At the end of the year, 18 units were on hand. Calculate the value of the ending inventory using the weighted average method.
   a. $238.50
   b. $214.27
   c. $193.00
   d. $180.00

4. Which of the following inventory valuation methods is generally used for valuing big-ticket items?

   a. weighted average method
   b. FIFO
   c. specific identification method
   d. LIFO

REVIEW QUIZ *(continued)*

5. Given the following information, estimate the value of ending inventory, using the gross profit method:

Beginning Inventory	$400
Purchases	$100
Sales	$300
Gross profit percentage	50%

    a. $150
    b. $200
    c. $300
    d. $350

6. Using the information below, calculate the lower of cost or market (LCM) on an item-by-item basis:

Coasters	10 units purchased at $1.00 each; the market value is now $2.00 each
Special glasses	10 units purchased at $5.00 each; the market value is now $4.00 each
Nozzles	10 units purchased at $3.00 each; the market value is now $3.00 each

    a. $60
    b. $70
    c. $75
    d. $80

7. The Merchandise Inventory account is continuously updated using the _____ inventory system.

    a. periodic
    b. precision
    c. perpetual
    d. weighted average

Answer Key: 1-a-C1, 2-d-C2, 3-b-C3, 4-c-C3, 5-d-C4, 6-d-C5, 7-c-C6

Each question is linked to a competency. Competencies are listed on the first page of the chapter. An answer reading 3-b-C4 translates to:

3: the question number
b: the correct answer
C4: the competency number

Chapter 11 Outline

Property and Equipment
    Lump Sum Purchase
    Depreciation of Property and
        Equipment
Intangible Assets
Other Assets

Competencies

1. Identify and describe assets that are
    classified as Property and Equipment
    on the balance sheet, demonstrate how
    to account for them, and distinguish
    between revenue expenditures and
    capital expenditures.

2. Explain and demonstrate the
    straight-line method of depreciation.

3. Explain and demonstrate the units of
    production method of depreciation.

4. Explain and demonstrate the
    sum-of-the-years' digits method of
    depreciation.

5. Explain and demonstrate the double
    declining balance method of
    depreciation.

6. Explain and demonstrate how to
    account for china, glassware, silver,
    linens, and uniforms.

7. Explain and demonstrate how to
    account for revisions of useful lives of
    assets and the sale, disposal, or
    exchange of property and equipment.

8. Describe assets that typically are listed
    as Intangible Assets or Other Assets on
    the balance sheet, and demonstrate
    and explain how to account for them.

11

Property, Equipment, and Other Assets

THE ASSETS of a hospitality firm are typically organized into two main categories: Current Assets and Noncurrent Assets. Current assets are those that are expected to be converted into cash within a year, such as inventory or receivables. Noncurrent assets are expected to have a life of greater than a year.

The four major categories of noncurrent assets include Property and Equipment, Investments, Noncurrent Receivables, and Other Assets. Noncurrent receivables are simply amounts owed to the firm (by owners and officers) that are not due within 12 months. Only the Property and Equipment and Other Assets categories are discussed in this chapter.

Property and Equipment

The Property and Equipment group includes those assets that are depreciated, such as buildings and equipment, and those that are not depreciated, namely land. The Property and Equipment assets were formerly called Fixed Assets. Today, the term *fixed asset* is rarely found on a company's financial statements. The percentage of total assets that are in the Property and Equipment group for a hospitality firm is substantially greater than that for a manufacturing firm. Property and Equipment assets constitute 55 to 85 percent of the total assets of a hospitality firm; this group of assets generally represents only about 30 percent of the assets of a manufacturing firm.

The *Uniform System of Accounts for the Lodging Industry,* Ninth Revised Edition, uses the following classifications for the Property and Equipment group of assets: Land, Buildings, Furnishings and Equipment, Leaseholds, Leasehold Improvements, Construction in Progress, and China, Glassware, Silver, Linen, and Uniforms. Similar assets held under capital leases, if material, should be separately presented on the balance sheet or in notes to the financial statements.

Expenditures for Property and Equipment assets are capital expenditures, as opposed to revenue expenditures. **Revenue expenditures** are those expenditures a hospitality firm makes for which the benefits are expected to be received within a year. Examples of revenue expenditures include wages expense and utilities expense. **Capital expenditures**, on the other hand, are expenditures for which the benefits are expected to be received over a period greater than one year. For example, when a hotel is built, its owners expect to realize its benefits over many years, not just one. It is important that capital expenditures be recorded as capital expenditures rather than as revenue expenditures because of the impact these entries have on the income statement. If a capital expenditure with a life of ten years is recorded as a revenue expenditure, all of the expense will be recorded in one year instead of spread over ten years, which would distort the income statements for all ten years. In this case, net income for year 1 would be understated, whereas net income for years 2 through 10 would be overstated.

Occasionally a company may purchase an item that is technically a capital expenditure, but treat it as a revenue expenditure because the amount is immaterial. An example of this would be the purchase of a $20 calculator.

Property and equipment should be recorded at cost when purchased. The costs of these assets should include all reasonable and necessary expenditures required to get the asset in operating condition. Examples of expenditures that ought to be included in the cost of Property and Equipment are such items as freight charges, sales tax on the purchase, and installation charges. Charges that would not be considered reasonable and necessary include repairs due to damages in handling or a traffic ticket incurred by the truck driver during delivery.

The following will illustrate the recording of an asset's purchase. Assume that the Oakdale Inn has just purchased some exercise equipment from a supplier. The list price of the equipment is $40,000 with terms of 2/10, *n*/60. Under these terms, the Inn receives a 2 percent discount for paying within 10 days; otherwise, the full amount is due in 60 days. The Inn, in this case, is able to pay within the cash discount period. Also assume that sales tax of $1,568 must be paid. Freight charges of $650 and installation costs of $290 are to be paid by the Inn. The Inn also purchases a two-year maintenance contract on the equipment at a total cost of $1,000. Based on this information, the cost to be recorded for the asset is determined as follows:

List price of equipment	$40,000
Less 2% cash discount	800
Net price	39,200
Sales tax	1,568
Freight charges	650
Installation charges	290
Cost of equipment	$41,708

Notice that the maintenance contract is not added to the cost of the equipment and depreciated over the asset's life. Instead, the $500 for the next 12 months would be recorded as a prepaid expense, while the coverage for the second year would be deferred.

When land is purchased, all of the reasonable and necessary expenditures to buy the land are included in the purchase price. These expenditures include property taxes paid, title opinions, surveying costs, brokerage commissions, and any excavating expenses required to get the land into proper condition.

Occasionally a hospitality firm will lease an asset under an agreement requiring the firm to record the lease as a **capital lease**. When this occurs, the leased asset is recorded as an asset on the lessee's books and is included under Property and Equipment as "Leased Asset under Capital Lease."

When a business leases a building, it often finds it necessary to make extensive improvements before opening. Such improvements made to walls, carpeting, ceiling, and lighting are called **Leasehold Improvements,** an asset that is to be amortized over the remaining life of the lease or the life of the improvement, whichever is shorter. For example, assume that the Surfside Restaurant leased a building for ten years and immediately spent $50,000 on improvements that had a life of five years. The restaurant would amortize $10,000 of the cost of the improvements each year with the following entry:

Amortization of Leasehold Improvements	$10,000	
Leasehold Improvements		$10,000

Construction in Progress is another asset commonly found in the Property and Equipment section of a hospitality firm's balance sheet. Construction in progress represents all labor, materials, advances on contracts, and interest on construction loans that are incurred in the current construction of property and equipment.

China, Glassware, Silver, Linen, and Uniforms is a unique Property and Equipment asset account found on hospitality firm balance sheets. This asset is an important asset for hospitality firms to control. If silverware is carelessly thrown away with the garbage, for example, there will be an increase in expenses and a corresponding decrease in net income. These assets will be discussed in detail later in this chapter.

Lump Sum Purchase

Occasionally the purchase of two or more assets is made for one price. This is referred to as a **lump sum** (or basket) **purchase.** Sometimes this will include a building, which is depreciable, and land, which is nondepreciable. In this case, the procedure for placing individual assets on the books is as follows. Both assets should be appraised at their current market values. The values of the individual assets are then added up, and each asset is expressed as a percentage of the total appraised value. Next, those respective percentages are multiplied by the total purchase price of the combined assets, and the individual assets are then recorded at their respective amounts.

Assume that a restaurant business makes a lump sum purchase of land, building, and equipment for $500,000. The individual asset accounts would be debited for amounts based on the following computations:

ASSET	APPRAISED VALUE	PERCENTAGE OF TOTAL	APPORTIONMENT OF COST
Land	$300,000	50%	$250,000
Building	240,000	40%	200,000
Equipment	60,000	10%	50,000
	$600,000	100%	$500,000

Depreciation of Property and Equipment

The process by which property or equipment is expensed over its life is called **depreciation**. The total amount of depreciation that can be taken over the life of an asset is equal to the cost of the asset less its salvage or scrap value. Through the matching process, every year in the life of an asset, an amount is placed in a contra-asset account called Accumulated Depreciation and the carrying value of the asset is reduced by the same amount. It is important to realize that no one writes a check for depreciation. Depreciation is different from most other expenses in that it is a noncash expense. Depreciation is also not a fund of cash set aside by a company. However, depreciation does save cash in this way: It provides a tax shelter for the firm, since it, like other expenses, reduces taxable income. Property and Equipment assets are typically shown on the books at their book values or at what are sometimes called *carrying values*. *Book value* (also called *net book value*) is determined when the accumulated depreciation on the asset to date is subtracted from the cost of the asset. Accumulated Depreciation is a contra-asset account and carries a credit balance.

Methods of Depreciation. The four basic methods used to depreciate assets are straight-line, sum-of-the-years' digits, double declining balance, and units of production. Sum-of-the-years' digits and double declining balance are called **accelerated methods of depreciation** because they result in the highest charges in the first year, with lower and lower charges in successive years. These accelerated methods allocate the largest portion of an asset's depreciation costs to the early years of the asset's estimated useful life.

An important concept relating to depreciation is the **salvage value** or residual value of the asset. This is the estimated value of the asset at the end of its useful life. Most of the depreciation methods take salvage value into consideration; the double declining balance method does not.

Straight-line depreciation is the simplest of the four methods. Under this technique, the same amount of depreciation is taken on the asset in each year of its life. To compute the annual depreciation under straight-line, one simply takes the cost of the asset less its salvage value and divides that figure by the estimated life of the asset. For example, assume that a delivery truck costs the firm $34,000, and has a salvage value of $4,000 and a life of five years. As shown in the following illustration, the annual depreciation under straight-line would be $6,000 per year:

Cost of truck	$34,000
Less salvage value	4,000
Depreciable cost	$30,000 ÷ 5 Yrs. = $6,000 annual depreciation

Total depreciation over life: $6,000 × 5 = $30,000

Under the **units of production depreciation** method, depreciation taken is based on the usage of the asset. In the preceding example of the $34,000 delivery truck with a $4,000 salvage value, the depreciation would be computed in the following way: First, the number of useful miles of the truck would be estimated.

Assume that this figure is 100,000. We would divide this into the cost less salvage value of $30,000. This would give a depreciation rate of $.30 per mile. If, in the first year of its use, the truck had been driven 12,000 miles, the depreciation taken for the first year would be 12,000 miles times $.30, or $3,600.

Under the **sum-of-the-years' digits depreciation** method, the years of the asset's life are added together; the resulting total becomes the denominator in a fraction used to calculate each year's depreciation. For instance, using the truck example once again, we would sum the years of its life in this way:

$$5 + 4 + 3 + 2 + 1 = 15$$

The following is a quick formula for figuring this:

$$\frac{n(n + 1)}{2}$$

$$\text{where, if } n = 5, \quad \frac{5(6)}{2} = 15$$

The first year we would take $\frac{5}{15}$ of the difference between the cost and the salvage value, a difference of $30,000, and get $10,000 depreciation. Depreciation for the other years is shown in the following table:

Table I

Cost of truck			$34,000
Less salvage value			4,000
Depreciable cost			$30,000

YEAR	RATE	DEPRECIABLE COST	ANNUAL DEPRECIATION
1	5/15	$30,000	$10,000
2	4/15	30,000	8,000
3	3/15	30,000	6,000
4	2/15	30,000	4,000
5	1/15	30,000	2,000
Total Depreciation			$30,000

The **double declining balance depreciation** method ignores salvage value while computing annual depreciation. Under this method, the straight-line rate of depreciation is calculated first with the division of the life of the asset into 100 percent. In the example of the $34,000 truck, we would divide 5 (years) into 100 (%) and get 20 percent per year. Then the straight-line rate of 20 percent would be multiplied by two to get the double declining rate, which would be 40 percent. Thus, in the first year of depreciation for the truck, the depreciation would be $34,000 times 40 percent, or $13,600. In the second year, the $34,000 cost minus the first year's depreciation of $13,600 would yield $20,400, which would be multiplied by 40 percent to get the second year's depreciation of $8,160. The remaining years' depreciation is illustrated in the following table. Notice that although the salvage value is not used in the computation of the annual depreciation under this method, one must be careful not to depreciate the asset below the salvage value in the later years. Also notice that the depreciation in year 5 is limited to $406 rather than 40 percent of $4,406 so that the asset is not depreciated below its $4,000 salvage value.

Table II

Cost of truck			$34,000
YEAR	RATE	DECLINING BALANCE	ANNUAL DEPRECIATION
1	40%	$34,000	$13,600
2	40%	20,400	8,160
3	40%	12,240	4,896
4	40%	7,344	2,938
5	40%	4,406	406
Total Depreciation			$30,000

Depreciation for Fractional Periods. If the $34,000 truck had been purchased on September 1, 20X3, the depreciation taken in 20X3 under the straight-line method would have been $2,000 for the four months it was owned, as follows:

$$\text{Depreciable cost of } \$30,000 \div 5 \text{ Years} = \$6,000$$

$$\text{Depreciation for September–December 20X3} = \$6,000 \times \tfrac{4}{12} = \$2,000$$

Calculation of the depreciation for the truck for September through December of 20X3 and full-year 20X4 under the sum-of-the-years' digits method would be as follows:

Year 20X3

$$\text{Depreciable cost of } \$30,000 \times \tfrac{5}{15} \times \tfrac{4}{12} = \$3,333$$

Year 20X4

$$\text{Depreciable cost of } \$30,000 \times \tfrac{5}{15} \times \tfrac{8}{12} = \$6,667$$

$$+ \ \$30,000 \times \tfrac{4}{15} \times \tfrac{4}{12} = \underline{2,667}$$

Total Depreciation $9,334

If the truck were being depreciated under the double declining balance method, the depreciation for 20X3 and 20X4 would be $4,533 and $11,787, respectively, as illustrated:

Year 20X3

$$\text{Cost} = \$34{,}000 \times 40\% \times \tfrac{4}{12} = \$4{,}533$$

Year 20X4

Declining balance of $\$34{,}000 - 4{,}533 = \$29{,}467 \times 40\% = \$11{,}787$

China, Glassware, Silver, Linen, and Uniforms. Properties use a variety of methods to charge the cost of china, glassware, silver, linen, and uniforms to operations. Listed below are examples of these methods:

1. Consider these items part of inventory and physically count and reflect the aggregate cost of the items on hand.

2. Capitalize the base stock of these items and then expense the cost of the items subsequently bought and placed in service.

3. Initially capitalize the base stock and then depreciate that amount to 50 percent of the cost over a reasonably short period. Properties that use this method take no further depreciation and expense the cost of items subsequently bought and placed in service.

Each of these methods has conceptual merit; however, in order to foster uniformity, the following method is preferable: Capitalize the cost of the initial complement of these items. Then depreciate this capitalized cost over a period not to exceed 36 months and expense replacements when they are placed in service. Reserve stocks of these items should be considered inventory until they are placed in service. The total accumulated depreciation should appear as a separate line item. This amount is then subtracted from the Total Property and Equipment line to determine Net Property and Equipment.[1]

Assume for example that a property purchased an initial stock of China, Glassware, Silver, Linen, and Uniforms for $15,000 cash on November 30, 20X1. The property has chosen to write off the stock over 30 months. On December 15, replacement items were purchased for $1,000, but not placed into service. The journal entries from November 30 until December 31, 20X1, for this asset are recorded below:

China, Glassware, Silver, Linen, and Uniforms	$15,000	
Cash		$15,000
China, Glassware, Silver, Linen, and Uniforms	$1,000	
Cash		$1,000
Depreciation Expense—China, Glassware, Silver, Linen, and Uniforms	$500	
Accumulated Depreciation—China, Glassware, Silver, Linen, and Uniforms		$500

At December 31, 20X1, this property's income statement would include $500 of depreciation expense for china, glassware, silver, linen, and uniforms, and the balance sheet would include the following:

China, Glassware, Silver, Linen, and Uniforms		$16,000
Less: Accumulated Depreciation—China, Glassware, Silver, Linen, and Uniforms	(500)	$15,500

Financial versus Tax Reporting. Any of the depreciation methods discussed here can be used for financial reporting purposes. Tax legislation in 1981 and 1982 liberalized tax depreciation rules with the enactment of an Accelerated Cost Recovery System (ACRS), which provided for faster recovery (depreciation) of capital expenditures. For tax reporting purposes, all assets acquired after 1981 must be depreciated with either straight-line depreciation or ACRS. Under ACRS, assets are arbitrarily placed into one of six property class lives. Predetermined rates are then applied to the asset's cost with salvage value ignored. The Tax Reform Act of 1986 created the Modified Accelerated Cost Recovery System (MACRS), which provided for eight classes of property and lengthened the recovery periods. In financial accounting, a building may be depreciated over 30 years or more. MACRS currently allows, for tax purposes, recovery over 31.5 years. Similarly, furnishings and equipment may be depreciated over seven to ten years (or more) for financial accounting purposes, while the same items are depreciated for tax purposes over five years under MACRS. Thus, the timing of reported net income for financial purposes can be significantly different from that for taxable income.

In the later years of an asset's life, the deduction for depreciation, especially that for furnishings and equipment, will be greater for financial accounting than for tax accounting. At the end of the asset's life, the deduction for depreciation will be the same in total for both financial reporting and tax accounting. The difference is in the timing of the deduction. Firms may now choose to use optional straight-line depreciation with half-year convention instead of MACRS. (*Half-year convention* means that, regardless of the month of the year when an asset is purchased, one-half of a year's depreciation is taken in the year of purchase.)

Revision of Useful Lives of Assets. Occasionally during the life of a depreciable asset, a revision is made regarding the asset's useful life. In this situation, the remaining depreciable cost of the asset is simply spread over its remaining life. Assume in the case of the $34,000 delivery truck that, after three years of its life, managers determined that its total life was eight years instead of five years. The depreciation for year 4 would be computed as follows:

Depreciable cost	$30,000
Depreciation for years 1, 2, & 3	18,000
Remaining depreciable cost	12,000
Remaining life: 5 years	
Depreciation for year 4: $12,000 ÷ 5 = $2,400	

Disposal of Property and Equipment. Occasionally a firm will take a Property and Equipment asset off the books because the asset is being scrapped, sold, or traded in. If an asset is scrapped and has been fully depreciated, it is necessary to remove both the asset and related accumulated depreciation from the books. Assume that a truck with a cost of $34,000 and a salvage value of zero was fully depreciated. In this case, the following entry would be made:

Accumulated Depreciation—Truck	$34,000	
Truck		$34,000

If the same asset is scrapped before it is fully depreciated, a different entry is made. Assume that the same truck costing $34,000 has been depreciated in the amount of $28,000. In this case, the journal entry would be:

Accumulated Depreciation—Truck	$28,000	
Loss on Disposal of Asset	6,000	
Truck		$34,000

The loss on the disposal of this asset would be closed into the Income Summary account at the end of the next fiscal period.

Sometimes Property and Equipment assets are disposed of through a sale that results in a gain or loss. Suppose the same truck had a book value of $6,000, based on a cost of $34,000 and an accumulated depreciation balance of $28,000. If this truck were sold for $8,000, the following journal entry would be made:

Cash	$ 8,000	
Accumulated Depreciation—Truck	28,000	
Truck		$34,000
Gain on Disposal of Asset		2,000

The gain of $2,000 is simply the difference between the selling price of $8,000 and the book value of $6,000.

Assume the same facts concerning the $34,000 truck, except that it is sold for $4,000. Since it had a book value of $6,000 and was sold for $4,000, a loss of $2,000 would result. The journal entry to record this transaction would be as follows:

Cash	$ 4,000	
Accumulated Depreciation—Truck	28,000	
Loss on Disposal of Asset	2,000	
Truck		$34,000

Exchange of Property and Equipment Assets. Property and Equipment assets, such as the truck, are commonly exchanged or traded in for similar assets. Assume that the $34,000 truck is exchanged along with $36,000 cash for a new truck that has a list price of $38,000. At the time of the exchange, the old $34,000 truck has accumulated depreciation of $28,000; hence, it has a book value of $6,000. Notice that, although the book value is $6,000, the firm is getting only $2,000 on the trade-in. Therefore, there is a loss of $4,000. The entry to record the exchange is:

Truck—New	$38,000	
Accumulated Depreciation—Old Truck	28,000	
Loss on Disposal of Asset	4,000	
Cash		$36,000
Truck—Old		34,000

Notice how this entry would change if, instead, the hospitality firm were given $7,000 on the trade-in and consequently had to pay only $31,000 for the new truck. In this case, the journal entry would be:

Truck—New	$37,000	
Accumulated Depreciation—Old Truck	28,000	
Cash		$31,000
Truck—Old		34,000

The Financial Accounting Standards Board (FASB) has stated that no gains are to be recorded on exchanges. Instead, the gain is to be reflected in the value of the asset acquired. Two points should be noted concerning these two entries:

1. The generally accepted accounting principle of conservatism states that losses should be recorded, but not gains.

2. Tax reporting rules differ from financial reporting rules. In reporting for tax purposes, neither gains nor losses are recorded on exchanges of similar assets.

Intangible Assets

Intangible assets are assets that have long lives but no physical substance. Common intangible assets are franchises, trademarks, patents, goodwill, copyrights, leaseholds, and leasehold improvements.

The **franchise** is a very common intangible asset in the hospitality business. It is the right to do a certain business in a given geographical area for a certain period of time. Holiday Hospitality Worldwide and Taco Bell are examples of companies that grant franchises around the world.

A **trademark** is defined as a name, mark, or character given legal protection. McDonald's Golden Arches is an example of a trademark.

A **patent** is an exclusive right given by the federal government for use and sale of a product. Patent protection is granted for a period of 17 years. The recipe for Coca-Cola is an example of a patent.

Goodwill is the excess of purchase price over the appraised value of assets. Goodwill exists when the expected future earnings are greater than the normal rate for the industry. However, goodwill is put on the books only when it is purchased by a company.

A **copyright** is an exclusive right over a literary or artistic work. Copyrights are granted to the creator and extend for the life of the creator plus 50 years. Copyrights should be amortized over their lives or over the years in which revenue from the work is expected, whichever is shorter. Operating manuals are an example of the kind of item that should be copyrighted.

A **leasehold** is a right to lease a given property for a fixed number of years. A leasehold could be put on the books if a lease requires the lessee to pay the last year's rent in advance. The advance payment is debited to Leaseholds; in the last year of the lease, the advance payment is transferred to Rent Expense.

Leasehold improvements (mentioned earlier in the chapter) should be amortized over the life of the improvements or the life of the lease, whichever is shorter.

Intangible assets, when purchased, are placed in an asset account, as illustrated below in the case of a franchise being purchased for $100,000:

Franchise Fee	$100,000	
Cash		$100,000

Intangible assets are amortized under a straight-line technique over a period of up to 40 years. **Amortization** is a process similar to depreciation. For example, assume that a hospitality firm purchases a franchise granting it rights for a period of up to 20 years in exchange for $50,000. Every year the firm would make a journal entry debiting Amortization Expense for $2,500 and crediting Franchise Fee for $2,500. The Amortization Expense account would be closed to the Income Summary account at the end of each fiscal period.

Other Assets

The Other Assets category on the balance sheet typically includes these four areas:

- Security Deposits
- Deferred Charges
- Deferred Income Taxes
- Other

Security deposits include funds deposited to secure occupancy or utility services (such as telecommunications, water, electricity, and gas) and any similar types of deposits.

Deferred charges, also called *deferred assets* or *deferred expenses,* are expenses that are prepaid yet are noncurrent. They are distinguished from Prepaid Expenses that would show up in the Current Assets section of the balance sheet. Since they are noncurrent, they benefit future periods. Examples include advertising and maintenance expenses or financing costs related to long-term debt.

Deferred income taxes result from the tax effects of temporary differences between the bases of noncurrent assets and noncurrent liabilities for financial and income tax reporting purposes.

Other is a miscellaneous category for items that do not fit neatly into the other three categories. Items included here are the cash surrender value of life insurance on the officers of the company, organization costs such as legal fees, and any intangible assets carried on the books.

The *USALI* requires that **preopening expenses** be expensed when incurred. Hospitality firms outside the United States may be allowed to amortize preopening expenses, depending on local conventions and laws.

Summary

Property and Equipment, Intangible Assets, and Other Assets are assets that have a life of greater than one year. Assets in the Property and Equipment group are depreciated over their lives. It is important to include all reasonable and necessary expenditures in the cost of an asset.

The commonly used depreciation methods are straight-line, units of production, sum-of-the-years' digits, and double declining balance. The latter two are called *accelerated methods of depreciation* because they take more depreciation in the early years of the asset's life and less depreciation in the later years. Salvage value or residual value is the value of the depreciable asset at the end of its useful life. An asset cannot be depreciated below salvage value. When a depreciable asset is purchased during a fiscal year, it is necessary to calculate the depreciation for only part of the year. Occasionally a revision is made in the life of a depreciable asset. In this event, the remaining depreciable cost is spread over the remaining useful life of the asset.

When Property and Equipment assets are disposed of, it is necessary to calculate the gain or loss on the sale. In the case of exchanges of property assets, losses are recognized but gains are not. Financial and tax rules differ in the case of gains or losses on exchange of similar assets.

The Other Assets category includes items such as security deposits, deferred charges, deferred income taxes, and intangible assets, such as goodwill and unamortized franchise fees.

Endnotes

1. This section is based on the discussion of China, Glassware, Silver, Linen, and Uniforms on pages 9 and 10 of *Uniform System of Accounts for the Lodging Industry,* Ninth Revised Edition (East Lansing, Mich.: Educational Institute of the American Hotel & Motel Association, 1996; © Hotel Association of New York City).

Key Terms

accelerated methods of depreciation—Methods of depreciation that result in higher depreciation charges in the first year; charges gradually decline in amount over the lives of fixed assets. Sum-of-the-years' digits and double declining balance are accelerated methods of depreciation.

amortization—The systematic transfer of the partial cost of an intangible long-lived asset (such as purchased goodwill, franchise rights, and trademarks) to an expense called Amortization. The asset cost is generally reduced and shown at its remaining cost to be amortized.

capital expenditure—An expenditure for which the benefits are expected to be received over a period of greater than one year. It is recorded to an asset account and not directly to expense.

capital lease—A classification of lease agreements that are of relatively long duration and are generally noncancellable and in which the lessee assumes responsibility for executory costs. For accounting purposes, capital leases are capitalized in a way similar to that for the purchase of a fixed asset (i.e., recorded as an asset with recognition of a liability).

China, Glassware, Silver, Linen, and Uniforms—A unique Property and Equipment asset account found on a hospitality firm's balance sheet.

Construction in Progress—An asset commonly found in the Property and Equipment section of a hospitality firm's balance sheet. It represents all labor, materials, advances on contracts, and interest on construction loans that are incurred in the current construction of property and equipment.

copyright—An exclusive right over a literary or artistic work granted by the federal government to the creator and extended for the life of the creator plus 50 years. Copyrights should be amortized over their lives or over the years in which revenue from the work is expected, whichever is shorter.

deferred charges—Expenses that are prepaid yet are noncurrent. Since they are noncurrent, they benefit future periods. They are distinguished from prepaid expenses that would show up in the Current Assets section of the balance sheet. Examples include advertising and maintenance expenses or financing costs related to long-term debt. Also called *deferred assets* or *deferred expenses.*

deferred income taxes—When the income taxes on the statement of income exceed the amount of liability to government tax agencies for the year, the business records the excess as deferred income taxes. This excess generally represents timing differences with respect to payment dates of taxes.

depreciation—The systematic transfer of part of a tangible long-lived asset's cost to an expense called Depreciation. The asset cost is generally not reduced, but is offset by an entry to the Accumulated Depreciation account, which represents the depreciation recorded on an asset from the point at which it was acquired. Depreciation is usually associated with assets classified as Property and Equipment, but not with land.

double declining balance depreciation—An accelerated method of depreciation that ignores salvage value in the computation of annual depreciation. Although the salvage value is ignored, one must be careful not to depreciate the asset below its salvage value in the later years.

franchise—A common intangible asset found in the hospitality business. It is the right to do a certain business in a given geographical area for a certain period of time.

goodwill—An intangible asset that is the excess of the purchase price over the appraised value of a company's assets. Goodwill exists when the expected future earnings of an operation are greater than the normal rate for the industry. Goodwill is put on the books, however, only when it is purchased by a company.

intangible assets—Noncurrent assets that do not have physical substance; their value is derived from rights or benefits associated with their ownership. Examples include franchises, leaseholds, goodwill, patents, copyrights, and trademarks. When intangible assets are purchased, they are placed in an asset account and amortized under a straight-line technique over a period of up to 40 years.

leasehold—The right to use property or equipment by virtue of a lease for a fixed number of years. It could be put on the books if a lease requires the lessee to pay the last year's rent in advance.

leasehold improvements—Renovations or remodeling performed on leased buildings or space prior to the commencement of operations. For accounting purposes, all leasehold improvements are capitalized (i.e., recorded as an asset with recognition of a liability). This asset is to be amortized over the remaining life of the lease or the life of the improvement, whichever is shorter.

lump sum purchase—The purchase of two or more assets made for one price. Sometimes this will include a building, which is depreciable, and land, which is nondepreciable.

patent—An exclusive right granted by the federal government to use, manufacture, sell, or lease a product or design. The right is granted for 17 years.

preopening expense—Costs associated with certain business activities that occur before a company is operational. They include amounts spent for employee training, salaries, and wages; and advertising and promotional expenses.

revenue expenditure—An expenditure a hospitality firm makes for which the benefits are expected to be received within a year. Examples include wages expense and utilities expense.

salvage value—Estimated market value of an asset at the time it is to be retired from use. Also called *residual value*.

security deposits—Funds deposited to secure occupancy or utility services (such as telecommunications, water, electricity, and gas) and any similar types of deposits.

straight-line depreciation—A method of distributing depreciation expense evenly throughout the estimated life of an asset (that is, the same amount of depreciation is taken on the asset in each year of its life).

sum-of-the-years' digits depreciation—A method that uses a fraction in computing depreciation expense. The numerator of the fraction is the remaining years of the asset's estimated useful life. This figure changes with each year's computation of depreciation. The denominator of the fraction is the sum of the digits of the asset's useful life. This figure remains constant with each year's computation of depreciation. Each year's depreciation expense is determined by multiplying this fraction by the asset's cost less its salvage value. This method is an accelerated method of depreciation and hence assigns more depreciation in the early years and less in the later years.

trademark—A name, mark, or character given legal protection. It is an intangible asset.

units of production depreciation—A method of depreciation in which depreciation is taken based on the usage of the asset.

 **Review Questions**

1. How valid are the following two statements about depreciation?

   a. Depreciation represents a fund of cash set aside for the replacement of an asset.

   b. Depreciation has no effect on the taxes an organization pays.

2. What does *accelerated depreciation* mean? Which depreciation methods are considered accelerated?

3. What are the differences between financial and tax reporting of gains or losses on the exchange of a Property and Equipment asset?

4. What are some common expenditures included in the cost of a Property and Equipment asset?

5. How does a revenue expenditure differ from a capital expenditure? What are some examples of each?

6. What is the preferred procedure used to account for china, glassware, silver, linen, and uniforms?

7. How are the values of individual assets determined in the case of a lump-sum or basket purchase?

8. How is the gain or loss on the sale of a Property and Equipment asset calculated?

9. What is *salvage value* or *residual value*? Which depreciation methods take the salvage value into account when the annual depreciation is calculated?

10. What four specific items could be included in the Other Assets section of the balance sheet?

**Problems** ————————————————————————————

Problem 1

For each of the following purchases, does the purchase represent a capital or a revenue expenditure?

a. Complete remodeling of a restaurant dining room at a cost of $80,000.
b. Repainting the exterior of a delivery truck at a cost of $500.
c. Purchase of a pizza oven at a cost of $18,000.
d. Purchase of a dozen pencil sharpeners with a life of ten years at a total cost of $65.
e. Overhaul of the engine on a tour bus at a cost of $5,000, extending the life of the bus by five years.
f. Purchase of a computer system at a cost of $35,000.

Problem 2

Indicate whether the assets below should be listed on the balance sheet under Current Assets or Property and Equipment:

Inventory
Land
Accounts Receivable
Leaseholds
Construction in Progress
Prepaid Expenses

China, Glassware, Silver, Linen, and
Uniforms
Notes Receivable
Furnishings and Equipment
Building
Short-Term Investments

Problem 3

The Bay View Restaurant has purchased a new dishwasher for its own use.

Required:

Using the following information, determine the proper amount to be capitalized in the asset account Equipment.

Invoice price of equipment	$8,000
Cash discount allowed: 2% of invoice	160
Freight-in paid	300
Speeding ticket given to our truck driver while the driver was delivering equipment	25
Installation costs	150
Sales tax on purchase	308
Repair of damages due to equipment being dropped off truck	200

Problem 4

The Tree Line Inn has purchased a shuttle bus to transport guests to and from a local ski lodge. The cost of the bus is $40,000; its salvage value is $4,000; and its life is five years with expected usable mileage of 100,000.

Required:

Calculate the first year's depreciation under each of the following methods:

1. Straight-line.
2. Units of production, assuming the bus traveled 15,000 miles in year 1.
3. Sum-of-the-years' digits.
4. Double declining balance.

Problem 5

The Shamrock Restaurant purchased $12,000 worth of China, Linen, Glassware, Silver, and Uniforms (CLGS&U) on open account on May 1, 20X1. On August 12, 20X1, the restaurant purchased $400 worth of CLGS&U for cash. The restaurant plans to write off the original purchase over 20 months. Using the preferred approach presented in the text, journalize the necessary entries on May 1, May 31, and August 12, 20X1.

Problem 6

Blue Lake Inn purchased an ice machine with a ten-year life on January 6, 20X3. The $3,500 purchase was recorded as a debit to Equipment Expense and a credit to Cash.

Required:

This capital expenditure was recorded as a revenue expenditure. Determine the effect of this error on the following (assume straight-line depreciation and no salvage value):

1. The amount of understatement or overstatement of Operating Income in 20X3 and 20X4.
2. The amount of understatement or overstatement of Property and Equipment in 20X3 and 20X4.

Problem 7

Empire Hotels recently purchased a parcel of land, a building, and some furnishings for $1,200,000 cash. The land was appraised $400,000, the building at $1,400,000, and the furnishings at $200,000.

Required:

Journalize the entry to record this lump sum purchase.

Challenge Problems

Problem 8

Deli Catering is trading in its old delivery truck for a new model with a list price of $24,000. The old truck cost $18,000 and has accumulated depreciation of $15,000.

Required:

1. Record the exchange, assuming the additional cash paid is $20,000.
2. Record the exchange, assuming the additional cash paid is $22,000.
3. Explain how the recognition of the gains or losses would differ under tax reporting rules.

Problem 9

For the year 20X1, the Landmark Restaurant had sales of $800,000 and expenses of $700,000 excluding depreciation. The building is being leased and the only depreciable asset is equipment in the amount of $100,000. The equipment has a life of 10 years with zero salvage value. Calculate the earnings before tax for 20X1 if:

1. The equipment is depreciated under straight-line depreciation.
2. The equipment is depreciated under double declining balance depreciation.

Problem 10

The Valley Hotel is remodeling its fitness center and disposing of exercise equipment that cost $20,000 and has accumulated depreciation of $18,000.

Required:

Record the disposal under each of the following conditions:

1. The equipment is scrapped.
2. The equipment is sold for $4,000.
3. The equipment is sold for $1,000.

REVIEW QUIZ

When you feel you have covered all of the material in this chapter, answer these questions. Choose the *best* answer.

1. Scotty's Enterprises purchases land, a building, and equipment for a lump sum of $2,500,000. The land has a current market value of $1,500,000; the building, $1,200,000; and the equipment, $300,000. Scotty should record this purchase with a debit to Land of:

   a. $1,250,000.
   b. $1,500,000.
   c. $3,000,000.
   d. $1,200,000.

2. The Mountaintop Resort purchased a shuttle bus to ferry skiers from the resort to a nearby summit. The bus cost $65,000 and has a salvage value of $5,000. Its estimated useful life is 10 years, assuming a usage of 10,000 miles each year. During the first year, the bus traveled 10,000 miles, just as expected. The first year's depreciation for the bus under the straight-line method of depreciation is:

   a. $13,000.
   b. $6,500.
   c. $6,000.
   d. $10,000.

3. The Mountaintop Resort purchased a shuttle bus to ferry skiers from the resort to a nearby summit. The bus cost $65,000 and has a salvage value of $5,000. Its estimated useful life is 10 years, assuming a usage of 10,000 miles each year. During the first year, the bus traveled 10,000 miles, just as expected. The first year's depreciation for the bus under the units of production method of depreciation is:

   a. $3,000.
   b. $6,500.
   c. $6,000.
   d. $6,091.

4. In the sum-of-the-years' digits method of depreciation, the year numbers of an asset's life are added together to yield the:

   a. dollar amount of depreciation.
   b. denominator of a fraction used to calculate each year's depreciation.
   c. asset's salvage value.
   d. percentage used to calculate each year's depreciation.

5. The method of depreciation that ignores salvage value is the _____ method.

   a. straight-line
   b. double declining balance
   c. sum-of-the-years' digits
   d. units of production

REVIEW QUIZ *(continued)*

6.   Marty's Restaurant made a major purchase of china, glassware, silver, and linens as part of a change to the restaurant's decor. The purchase of $12,000 is to be written off over 24 months. Each month, Marty should debit the account Depreciation Expense—China, Glassware, Silver, and Linens for:

    a. $1,200.
    b. $2,000.
    c. $500.
    d. $200.

7.   The generally accepted accounting principle of _____ implies that losses from an exchange of assets should be recorded but not gains.

    a. matching
    b. going concern
    c. conservatism
    d. full disclosure

Answer Key: 1-a-C1, 2-c-C2, 3-c-C3, 4-b-C4, 5-b-C5, 6-c-C6, 7-c-C7

Each question is linked to a competency. Competencies are listed on the first page of the chapter. An answer reading 3-b-C4 translates to:

  3: the question number
  b: the correct answer
  C4: the competency number

Chapter 12 Outline

Notes Payable
Accounting for Payroll-Related Liabilities
    Payroll Records
    Regular Pay and Overtime Pay
    Payroll Journal Entries
    Reporting Tips
Other Current Liabilities
    Property Taxes

Competencies

1. Identify and describe current liabilities that hospitality firms commonly carry.

2. Distinguish between notes payable and accounts payable, and demonstrate how to account for notes payable.

3. Describe payroll systems, internal control policies and procedures that are appropriate for them, and some of the forms, records, and procedures required in payroll systems.

4. Demonstrate how to calculate regular and overtime pay and describe the circumstances under which each is due to staff.

5. Demonstrate how to make payroll journal entries, and describe the payroll taxes imposed on U.S. employers and the related forms and procedures.

6. Describe payroll accounting for tipped employees with respect to employee tip reporting, minimum wage, tip credit, net pay, and overtime pay.

7. Demonstrate how to account for property taxes.

12

Current Liabilities and Payroll

THIS CHAPTER covers the major current liabilities of the hospitality firm, with an emphasis on payroll liabilities. Liabilities are debts of the organization that are typically classified on the basis of their maturity. Long-term liabilities are expected to be paid off over a period of greater than a year; they include bonds payable and mortgages payable. Current liabilities are expected to be paid off within a year. Current liabilities include accounts payable, notes payable, and wages payable.

The amounts of most current liabilities are exact and known to exist for the firm. For example, if the company purchases $15,000 worth of merchandise from a supplier, the liability is recorded at $15,000. A company may know of the existence of certain other liabilities, but may be uncertain of their amounts. These liabilities are referred to as *estimated liabilities*. Examples include liabilities for product warranty and liability for income tax. If a firm expects to have a liability resulting from product warranty, it would estimate that amount and record the liability accordingly. In the case of a $50,000 estimated liability for product warranty, the journal entry would be:

Warranty Expense	$50,000	
Liability for Warranty		$50,000

When a company estimates its income taxes and determines them to be approximately $80,000, it makes the following journal entry:

Income Tax Expense	$80,000	
Income Tax Payable		$80,000

The term **loss contingency** refers to situations in which a liability is reasonably estimable; while it is not certain in nature, it is rather probable. An example of a loss contingency would be a pending lawsuit. In this case, the liability should be put on the books at its estimated amount.

A **contingent liability**, on the other hand, is a liability that is based on some future event. A common contingent liability is a debt guarantee that a company has agreed to. For example, a parent company might agree to guarantee the debt of a subsidiary should the subsidiary fail to pay the debt. It is important to realize that contingent liabilities are not real liabilities and therefore should not be included in the Liabilities section of the balance sheet. Instead, they should be included as footnotes to the financial statements.

Notes Payable

Accounts payable are the most common current liability on the books of hospitality firms. They represent amounts owed to suppliers of goods or services due in one year or less. Typically these liabilities have maturities of 30, 60, or 90 days.

Like accounts payable, notes payable are current liabilities, but they differ in this way: a note payable is a written promise to pay an amount in the future, whereas an account payable is an oral promise to pay. A note payable, because it is in writing, represents a more stringent claim on the debtor. A firm might sign a note payable in the following situation. Suppose the firm owed a supplier an amount on open account represented by an account payable, and was unable to pay at the maturity date. In this case, the supplier could require the debtor to sign a note to promise to pay the principal with interest at some future date.

Assume that a company exchanged an account payable for a note payable in the amount of $10,000 with interest at 12 percent due in 90 days. It would make the following journal entry:

Accounts Payable	$10,000	
Notes Payable		$10,000

In 90 days, at the maturity date of the note, the following journal entry would be made when payment is made on the note:

Notes Payable	$10,000	
Interest Expense	300	
Cash		$10,300

The interest is calculated based on the basic formula Interest = Principal × Rate × Time, or $10,000 × .12 × $\frac{90}{360}$. (To simplify matters, we are assuming that there are 360 days in a year rather than 365.)

Alternatively, a company could sign a note payable simply upon borrowing cash from a bank. Assume that the Alpine Company borrowed $15,000 from the Commercial Bank on November 1, 20X1, agreeing to pay principal and interest at 8 percent in six months. On November 1, 20X1, the journal entry for borrowing the money at the bank would be:

Cash	$15,000	
Notes Payable		$15,000

Assuming that financial statements were not prepared at the end of November, the Alpine Company would make the following adjusting entry on December 31, 20X1, to accrue the interest on the note for November and December:

Interest Expense	$200	
Interest Payable		$200

Country-Specific Sites

In addition to the sites listed below, country-specific information can be found at Ernst & Young's "Doing Business In" and KPMG's "International Tax"

Argentina

- Administracion Federal de Ingresos Publicos

Australia

- Government Sites
    o Australian Government Home Page
    o Australian Taxation Office - ATO Assist
    o Commonwealth Budget, 1998-99
    o Department of Finance
    o Department of the Treasury

- State Taxation Offices
    o New South Wales
    o Queensland
    o South Australia
    o Tasmania
    o Victoria
    o Western Australia

- Other Resources
    o Australian Tax Practice
    o Australia Wide Taxation Training Services
    o Coopers & Lybrand 1998 Budget Executive Brief
    o Deloitte Articles
    o KPMG Tax Online
    o ICAA Tax Reform Site
    o Legal Information Index
    o Online Tax News
    o OZ TAX - Australian Taxation Index
    o SolNet
    o Taxability
    o Taxation Institute of Australia
    o Tax on Australia

Austria

- Österreichisches Steuerrecht

Taxsites.com provides links to many Internet sites that relate to accounting or taxes. This page of their site (http://www.taxsites.com/international.html) may be particularly help-ful to accountants who serve clients outside their home countries. (Courtesy of Schmidt Enterprises, LLC, 2 November 1998) © 1995–1998 Schmidt Enterprises, LLC/Maintained by Dennis Schmidt/E-Mail:webmaster@taxsites.com

The amount of interest ($200) was determined as follows:

$$\text{Interest} = \text{Principal} \times \text{Rate} \times \text{Time}$$
$$= \$15,000 \times .08 \times \frac{60}{360}$$

On the maturity date of the note, it is important that the firm recall the entry it made on December 31, 20X1, because that entry affects the entry made on the payment date. On May 1, 20X2, the payment date of this note, the following journal entry would be made:

Notes Payable	$15,000	
Interest Expense	400	
Interest Payable	200	
Cash		$15,600

The $15,600 represents the total principal of $15,000 plus the interest of $600 on the note.

Our discussion so far has assumed that the note payable was written for the principal only. Sometimes, however, the interest is included in the face amount of the note. For example, in the case of the preceding $15,000 note, the bank could add the $600 interest to the principal and make the note for $15,600. The November 1, 20X1, journal entry in this case would be:

Cash	$15,000	
Discount on Notes Payable	600	
Notes Payable		$15,600

It would be incorrect on November 1 to debit Interest Expense for the difference between the cash received and the amount of the note payable. This is because the $600 difference is not yet interest expense; rather, it will accrue as interest expense over the life of the note. Since it is not yet interest expense, the proper account to use is Discount on Notes Payable, which is a contra-liability account with a debit balance. This note would require the following journal entry on December 31, 20X1, to accrue interest:

Interest Expense	$200	
Discount on Notes Payable		$200

Finally, in this case, the following journal entry would be made on May 1, 20X2, the maturity date of the note:

Notes Payable	$15,600	
Interest Expense	400	
Discount on Notes Payable		$ 400
Cash		15,600

Accounting for Payroll-Related Liabilities

Payroll represents a very large expense for hospitality operations. It usually represents the greatest expense for the club and lodging industries; in the restaurant industry, payroll expense runs closely behind the cost of food and beverage sold. Our discussion of payroll begins with the following list of the most important control features that should be in place for this major liability:

1. Payroll functions should be segregated wherever possible. As in all accounting procedures, there should be an attempt to segregate by function; the area of payroll is certainly no exception. This can be a problem in small operations that don't have many employees. However, the following functions should be performed by separate individuals where possible:

   - Authorization of employment and establishment of wage rates for employees.

   - Reporting of hours worked by employees.

   - Actual preparation of the payroll.

   - Signing of the payroll checks.

   - Distribution of checks to employees. Checks should be distributed to employees by individuals independent of the payroll department. Some larger companies with hundreds or even thousands of employees will use what is called the *payoff test;* that is, they will require a periodic "shaking of hands" of employees receiving the checks to make certain the individuals actually exist.

   - Reconciliation of payroll bank accounts by an independent party.

2. The human resources (personnel) department should be the only department allowed to add individuals to or delete them from the labor force. In addition, this department should be the only one that provides the payroll department with employees' wage rates.

3. Proper procedures should be in place for recording time worked, including the use of time clocks where possible.

4. Employees should be paid by check only, not in cash. In addition, a special **imprest payroll account** should be used. An imprest payroll account is one into which only the exact amount of a given payroll period is deposited. Payroll checks totaling that deposit are then written on that account. Once all of the checks clear the bank, there is nothing left in the account.

5. Payroll sheets and employee paychecks should be independently checked.

6. Any unclaimed payroll checks should be immediately returned to the controller who will hold them until the employees return to work and pick up their checks directly from the controller.

Exhibit 1   Sample Employee Time Card

	MORNING IN	NOON OUT	NOON IN	NIGHT OUT	EXTRA IN	EXTRA OUT	

WEEK ENDING _____ 20 _____

Form No. 1212

No.

NAME

DAY	MORNING IN	NOON OUT	NOON IN	NIGHT OUT	EXTRA IN	EXTRA OUT	TOTAL

TOTAL TIME _____ HRS.

RATE _____

TOTAL WAGES FOR WEEK $ _____

Payroll Records

The Fair Labor Standards Act (FLSA), commonly known as the *federal wage and hour law,* covers such things as equal pay for equal work, recordkeeping require-ments, minimum wage rates, and overtime pay. Hospitality firms, except for cer-tain small operations, are subject to this act.

To comply with the FLSA, employers must keep records of the time worked by hourly employees. Time cards or time sheets are generally used to satisfy this requirement. The time cards or sheets can be administered manually or through an electronic time clock. An example of an employee time card is shown in Exhibit 1.

Companies will typically keep a **master payroll file** of records that include important information on employees. The information in the file would include

Exhibit 2   IRS Form W-4—Employee's Withholding Allowance Certificate

Form **W-4**	**Employee's Withholding Allowance Certificate**	OMB No. 1545-0010
Department of the Treasury Internal Revenue Service	► **For Privacy Act and Paperwork Reduction Act Notice, see page 2.**	**1999**

1 Type or print your first name and middle initial	Last name	2 Your social security number

Home address (number and street or rural route)

3 ☐ Single ☐ Married ☐ Married, but withhold at higher Single rate.
Note: *If married, but legally separated, or spouse is a nonresident alien, check the Single box*

City or town, state, and ZIP code

4 If your last name differs from that on your social security card, check here. **You** must call 1-800-772-1213 for a new card . . . ► ☐

5 Total number of allowances you are claiming (from line H above or from the worksheets on page 2 if they apply) . | **5**
6 Additional amount, if any, you want withheld from each paycheck . . . . | **6** $
7 I claim exemption from withholding for 1999, and I certify that I meet **BOTH** of the following conditions for exemption:
 • Last year I had a right to a refund of **ALL** Federal income tax withheld because I had **NO** tax liability **AND**
 • This year I expect a refund of **ALL** Federal income tax withheld because I expect to have **NO** tax liability.
 If you meet both conditions, write "EXEMPT" here . . . . ► | **7**

Under penalties of perjury, I certify that I am entitled to the number of withholding allowances claimed on this certificate, or I am entitled to claim exempt status.
Employee's signature
(Form is not valid
unless you sign it) ►   Date ►

8 Employer's name and address (Employer: Complete 8 and 10 only if sending to the IRS)	9 Office code (optional)	10 Employer identification number

Cat. No. 10220Q

Exhibit 3   Payroll Journal

Payroll Journal

NAME	PAY PERIOD ENDING	TAXES PAYABLE AND ACCRUED			ACCOUNTS PAYABLE			NET PAY	CHECK NUMBER
		F.I.C.A.	ST. INCOME WH	TOTAL CREDIT	RET. CONT.	HEALTH INS.	TOTAL CREDIT	CASH IN BANK CREDIT	

employee names, addresses, Social Security numbers, and wage rates, as well as deduction information for the employees.

An important form filled out by the employee and given to the employer is Internal Revenue Service (IRS) form W-4, which helps the employer calculate the amount of taxes withheld from the individual employee's payroll check. The front of a W-4 form is shown in Exhibit 2. W-4 forms are also completed for state and city income tax withholdings. Another payroll record is the **payroll journal** shown in Exhibit 3. This lists a record of each payroll check issued by the company along with the corresponding gross pay and various deductions for federal, state, city, and Social Security taxes; employee health care contributions; and miscellaneous contributions such as union dues. IRS form W-2, which employers must provide to employees annually, is shown in Exhibit 4. A file called an **employee's earnings**

Exhibit 4   IRS Form W-2—Wage and Tax Statement

a Control number	22222	Void ☐	For Official Use Only ► OMB No. 1545-0008		
b Employer identification number				1 Wages, tips, other compensation	2 Federal income tax withheld
c Employer's name, address, and ZIP code				3 Social security wages	4 Social security tax withheld
				5 Medicare wages and tips	6 Medicare tax withheld
				7 Social security tips	8 Allocated tips
d Employee's social security number				9 Advance EIC payment	10 Dependent care benefits
e Employee's name (first, middle initial, last)				11 Nonqualified plans	12 Benefits included in box 1
				13 See instrs. for box 13	14 Other
				15 Statutory employee ☐ Deceased ☐ Pension plan ☐ Legal rep. ☐ Deferred compensation ☐	
f Employee's address and ZIP code					

16 State Employer's state I.D. no.	17 State wages, tips, etc.	18 State income tax	19 Locality name	20 Local wages, tips, etc.	21 Local income tax

Form **W-2** Wage and Tax Statement   **1999**

Copy A For Social Security Administration—Send this entire page with Form W-3 to the Social Security Administration; photocopies are **not** acceptable.

Cat. No. 10134D

Department of the Treasury—Internal Revenue Service

For Privacy Act and Paperwork Reduction Act Notice, see separate instructions.

Exhibit 5   Sample Employee's Earnings Record

NAME:
ADDRESS:
SOCIAL SECURITY NUMBER:

Employee's Earnings Record

Pay Period Ending	EARNINGS				Wages for WH	Meals & Lodging	Wages for F.I.C.A.	DEDUCTIONS						NET PAY
	Regular	Overtime	Gross	Tips				F.I.C.A.	Fed. Income WH	St. Income WH	Ret. Cont.	Health Ins.		

record is also kept for each individual employee of the operation. An example of this file is shown in Exhibit 5. This record is used to compile information for government reporting of employees' wages. Some taxes apply to earnings up to a certain dollar amount only; this record is used to make sure that those caps are not exceeded.

Regular Pay and Overtime Pay

According to the FLSA, regular pay for an employee is based on a 40-hour work-week. *Regular hourly rate* refers to the rate per hour that is used to compute regular pay. The FLSA also requires that overtime pay be given for any hours worked in excess of 40 hours in a week. *Overtime hourly rate* refers to the rate per hour used to compute overtime pay. The FLSA requires that overtime be paid at the rate of 1.5 times the employee's regular hourly rate.

To calculate the overtime pay for some employees, it may be necessary to convert a weekly wage into an hourly rate. For example, assume that an employee is hired at a weekly wage of $218 for a 40-hour workweek. The regular hourly rate for this employee would be $5.45, calculated as follows:

$$\text{Regular Hourly Rate} = \frac{\text{Weekly Wage}}{\text{Number of Hours in Regular Workweek}}$$

$$= \frac{\$218}{40}$$

$$= \$5.45$$

Now that the regular hourly rate has been calculated, the overtime rate can easily be determined. Since the FLSA requires the overtime rate to be 1.5 times the regular hourly rate, this employee would have an hourly overtime rate of $8.175, calculated as follows:

$$\text{Overtime Hourly Rate} = \text{Regular Hourly Rate} \times 1.5$$

$$= \$5.45 \times 1.5$$

$$= \$8.175$$

Payroll Journal Entries

There are two major journal entries involving payroll. These two separate and distinct entries are referred to as *the entry to record the payroll* and *the entry to record the payroll taxes*.

The Entry to Record Payroll. It may be useful to think of the payroll entry as a "check stub" entry, because if we had only one employee and that employee's check stub were in front of us, we could use the stub's information to journalize the entry. The following items would be included in the payroll entry:

1. *Gross Pay.* Gross pay is calculated by multiplying the hours the employee worked for the pay period by the hourly rate, including any overtime premium. In the case of salaried employees, gross pay for a month, for example, would be $\frac{1}{12}$ of their annual salaries.

2. *Federal Income Tax (FIT).* Exhibit 6 is an example of withholding tables employers refer to for this deduction. The withholding amounts for federal income tax vary depending on marital status. Exhibit 6 shows an excerpt from the table that

Exhibit 6   Excerpt from Withholding Table for Married Persons—Biweekly Payroll Record

MARRIED Persons—BIWEEKLY Payroll Period
(For Wages Paid in 1998)

At least	But less than	0	1	2	3	4	5	6	7	8	9	10
$0	$250	0	0	0	0	0	0	0	0	0	0	0
250	260	1	0	0	0	0	0	0	0	0	0	0
260	270	3	0	0	0	0	0	0	0	0	0	0
270	280	4	0	0	0	0	0	0	0	0	0	0
280	290	6	0	0	0	0	0	0	0	0	0	0
290	300	7	0	0	0	0	0	0	0	0	0	0
300	310	9	0	0	0	0	0	0	0	0	0	0
310	320	10	0	0	0	0	0	0	0	0	0	0
320	330	12	0	0	0	0	0	0	0	0	0	0
330	340	13	0	0	0	0	0	0	0	0	0	0
340	350	15	0	0	0	0	0	0	0	0	0	0
350	360	16	0	0	0	0	0	0	0	0	0	0
360	370	18	2	0	0	0	0	0	0	0	0	0
370	380	19	3	0	0	0	0	0	0	0	0	0
380	390	21	5	0	0	0	0	0	0	0	0	0
390	400	22	6	0	0	0	0	0	0	0	0	0
400	410	24	8	0	0	0	0	0	0	0	0	0
410	420	25	9	0	0	0	0	0	0	0	0	0
420	430	27	11	0	0	0	0	0	0	0	0	0
430	440	28	12	0	0	0	0	0	0	0	0	0
440	450	30	14	0	0	0	0	0	0	0	0	0
450	460	31	15	0	0	0	0	0	0	0	0	0
460	470	33	17	1	0	0	0	0	0	0	0	0
470	480	34	18	3	0	0	0	0	0	0	0	0
480	490	36	20	4	0	0	0	0	0	0	0	0
490	500	37	21	6	0	0	0	0	0	0	0	0
500	520	39	24	8	0	0	0	0	0	0	0	0
520	540	42	27	11	0	0	0	0	0	0	0	0
540	560	45	30	14	0	0	0	0	0	0	0	0
560	580	48	33	17	2	0	0	0	0	0	0	0
580	600	51	36	20	5	0	0	0	0	0	0	0
600	620	54	39	23	8	0	0	0	0	0	0	0
620	640	57	42	26	11	0	0	0	0	0	0	0
640	660	60	45	29	14	0	0	0	0	0	0	0
660	680	63	48	32	17	1	0	0	0	0	0	0
680	700	66	51	35	20	4	0	0	0	0	0	0
700	720	69	54	38	23	7	0	0	0	0	0	0
720	740	72	57	41	26	10	0	0	0	0	0	0
740	760	75	60	44	29	13	0	0	0	0	0	0
760	780	78	63	47	32	16	0	0	0	0	0	0
780	800	81	66	50	35	19	3	0	0	0	0	0
800	820	84	69	53	38	22	6	0	0	0	0	0
820	840	87	72	56	41	25	9	0	0	0	0	0
840	860	90	75	59	44	28	12	0	0	0	0	0
860	880	93	78	62	47	31	15	0	0	0	0	0
880	900	96	81	65	50	34	18	3	0	0	0	0
900	920	99	84	68	53	37	21	6	0	0	0	0
920	940	102	87	71	56	40	24	9	0	0	0	0
940	960	105	90	74	59	43	27	12	0	0	0	0
960	980	108	93	77	62	46	30	15	0	0	0	0
980	1,000	111	96	80	65	49	33	18	2	0	0	0
1,000	1,020	114	99	83	68	52	36	21	5	0	0	0
1,020	1,040	117	102	86	71	55	39	24	8	0	0	0
1,040	1,060	120	105	89	74	58	42	27	11	0	0	0
1,060	1,080	123	108	92	77	61	45	30	14	0	0	0
1,080	1,100	126	111	95	80	64	48	33	17	2	0	0
1,100	1,120	129	114	98	83	67	51	36	20	5	0	0
1,120	1,140	132	117	101	86	70	54	39	23	8	0	0
1,140	1,160	135	120	104	89	73	57	42	26	11	0	0
1,160	1,180	138	123	107	92	76	60	45	29	14	0	0
1,180	1,200	141	126	110	95	79	63	48	32	17	1	0
1,200	1,220	144	129	113	98	82	66	51	35	20	4	0
1,220	1,240	147	132	116	101	85	69	54	38	23	7	0
1,240	1,260	150	135	119	104	88	72	57	41	26	10	0
1,260	1,280	153	138	122	107	91	75	60	44	29	13	0
1,280	1,300	156	141	125	110	94	78	63	47	32	16	1
1,300	1,320	159	144	128	113	97	81	66	50	35	19	4
1,320	1,340	162	147	131	116	100	84	69	53	38	22	7
1,340	1,360	165	150	134	119	103	87	72	56	41	25	10
1,360	1,380	168	153	137	122	106	90	75	59	44	28	13

applies to a married individual who is paid biweekly and who files jointly with his or her spouse. Recent actual rates for a married person filing jointly are shown in the following table:

INCOME	TAX RATE
$0–$41,200	15%
$41,200–$99,600	$6,180 + 28% of excess
$99,600–$151,750	$22,532 + 31% of excess
$151,750–271,050	$38,698.50 + 36% of excess
$271,050 and up	$81,646.50 + 39.6% of excess

Suppose a married individual files a joint return and has a taxable income of $45,000. Based on the rates in the above table, the federal tax liability for this individual would be $7,244, determined as follows:

$$\text{Tax Liability} = \$6,180 + 28\% \text{ of Excess } (\$45,000 - \$41,200)$$
$$= \$6,180 + 28\% \text{ of } \$3,800$$
$$= \$7,244$$

3. *Social Security Taxes.* Social Security taxes result from the **Federal Insurance Contributions Act (FICA)**. The current rate for FICA taxes is 7.65 percent. This rate is actually a combination of two rates: 6.2 percent on the first $72,600 of income, plus 1.45 percent on all income. (Note: These are the 1999 figures.)

4. *State Income Tax (SIT).* States vary widely in the amount of state income tax assessed, ranging from zero percent in several states to North Dakota's rate of about 12 percent.

5. *Miscellaneous deductions.* Other deductions from an individual's pay might include local income tax, the employee's contribution to health care benefits, union dues taken by the employer and later remitted to the union, or a payroll deduction for items such as charitable contributions.

All of these current liabilities, such as FIT, SIT, FICA, and miscellaneous deductions, are eventually remitted to the respective agencies. From the time period in which they are deducted from employee wages until they are remitted to the agencies, they are considered current liabilities for the hospitality firm.

6. *The amount of the employee's net pay.* Net pay, of course, is simply gross pay minus the various deductions. It is the amount the payroll check is written for.

Let us assume for a given pay period that a hotel had sales salaries and administrative salaries of $30,000 and $19,000, respectively. Let us also assume that the total federal income tax withheld for this pay period was $13,720, the state income tax withheld was $2,254, the FICA deduction was $3,749, and the health insurance deduction $980, making the net pay $28,297. The entry to record this transaction would be as follows:

Sales Salaries	$30,000	
Administrative Salaries	19,000	
FIT Payable		$13,720
SIT Payable		2,254
FICA		3,749
Health Insurance Payable		980
Salaries Payable		28,297

This entry would be made on the date the payroll was computed. On the date the payroll was actually paid to the employees and the amount of net pay transferred into the payroll imprest fund, the journal entry would be:

| Salaries Payable | $28,297 | |
| Cash | | $28,297 |

Note the large difference in this case between the gross payroll of $49,000 and the net pay to the employees of $28,297.

The Entry to Record Payroll Taxes. The second major entry involving payroll is the one recording the employer's payroll taxes. **Payroll taxes** represent additional taxes paid by the employer based on employee wages. The three major elements of payroll taxes are the employer's FICA tax contribution and its contributions under the **Federal Unemployment Tax Act (FUTA)** and the **State Unemployment Tax Act (SUTA)**.

We have already discussed FICA taxes in relation to the first payroll entry. The Federal Insurance Contribution Act also states that the employer must match the amounts withheld from employees' pay for Social Security taxes. As a result, the dollar amount of the credit to FICA Tax Payable in the first journal entry (that is, the entry to record the payroll) will be the same dollar amount in this second journal entry. Employers are required to report the amounts of FICA taxes for employees on Federal Form 941, which is filed quarterly. The first page of Federal Form 941 is shown in Exhibit 7. Employers are now able to report FICA taxes electronically by touch-tone phone with Form 941 Telefile.

The Federal Unemployment Tax Act (FUTA) establishes a tax that pays unemployment wages to people who have lost their jobs. This fund is financed through taxes levied on employer payrolls. The 1997 federal unemployment tax was 6.2 percent on employee's wages up to $7,000. This tax is no longer levied on an employee's wages after the first $7,000.

States must contribute dollars into the federal unemployment fund. To do so, they levy their own state unemployment tax rates. These rates vary by state, but, whatever that rate is, employers are allowed to use the state tax rate as a credit against the federal rate. For example, assume that a state levied a 5.4 percent state

Exhibit 7   IRS Form 941—Employer's Quarterly Federal Tax Return

Form **941**	**Employer's Quarterly Federal Tax Return**	
(Rev. January 1999) Department of the Treasury Internal Revenue Service	► See separate instructions for information on completing this return. Please type or print.	

Enter state code for state in which deposits were made ONLY if different from state in address to the right ► [ ] (see page 2 of instructions).

			OMB No. 1545-0029
Name (as distinguished from trade name)		Date quarter ended	T
Trade name, if any		Employer identification number	FF
			FD
Address (number and street)		City, state, and ZIP code	FP
			I
			T

IRS Use

If address is different from prior return, check here ►

```
1  1  1  1  1  1  1  1  1  1      2      3  3  3  3  3  3  3  3      4  4  4      5  5  5
   6     7      8  8  8  8  8  8  8      9  9  9  9  9      10 10 10  10 10 10 10 10 10
```

If you do not have to file returns in the future, check here ► [ ]   and enter date final wages paid ►

If you are a seasonal employer, see **Seasonal employers** on page 1 of the instructions and check here ► [ ]

1	Number of employees in the pay period that includes March 12th . ►	**1**		
2	Total wages and tips, plus other compensation	**2**		
3	Total income tax withheld from wages, tips, and sick pay	**3**		
4	Adjustment of withheld income tax for preceding quarters of calendar year	**4**		
5	Adjusted total of income tax withheld (line 3 as adjusted by line 4—see instructions) . . .	**5**		
6	Taxable social security wages	**6a**	× 12.4% (.124) =	**6b**
	Taxable social security tips	**6c**	× 12.4% (.124) =	**6d**
7	Taxable Medicare wages and tips . . .	**7a**	× 2.9% (.029) =	**7b**
8	Total social security and Medicare taxes (add lines 6b, 6d, and 7b). Check here if wages are not subject to social security and/or Medicare tax . . . . ► [ ]		**8**	
9	Adjustment of social security and Medicare taxes (see instructions for required explanation) Sick Pay $ _____ ± Fractions of Cents $ _____ ± Other $ _____ =		**9**	
10	Adjusted total of social security and Medicare taxes (line 8 as adjusted by line 9—see instructions)		**10**	
11	**Total taxes** (add lines 5 and 10)		**11**	
12	Advance earned income credit (EIC) payments made to employees		**12**	
13	Net taxes (subtract line 12 from line 11). **If $1,000 or more, this must equal line 17, column (d) below (or line D of Schedule B (Form 941))**		**13**	
14	Total deposits for quarter, including overpayment applied from a prior quarter		**14**	
15	**Balance due** (subtract line 14 from line 13). See instructions		**15**	

16 **Overpayment.** If line 14 is more than line 13, enter excess here ► $ _____
and check if to be: [ ] Applied to next return   **OR**   [ ] Refunded.

* **All filers:** If line 13 is less than $1,000, you need not complete line 17 or Schedule B (Form 941).
* **Semiweekly schedule depositors:** Complete Schedule B (Form 941) and check here . . . . ► [ ]
* **Monthly schedule depositors:** Complete line 17, columns (a) through (d), and check here . . . . ► [ ]

17	Monthly Summary of Federal Tax Liability. Do not complete if you were a semiweekly schedule depositor.			
	(a) First month liability	**(b)** Second month liability	**(c)** Third month liability	**(d)** Total liability for quarter

Sign Here   Under penalties of perjury, I declare that I have examined this return, including accompanying schedules and statements, and to the best of my knowledge and belief, it is true, correct, and complete.

Signature ►   Print Your Name and Title ►   Date ►

For Privacy Act and Paperwork Reduction Act Notice, see back of form.   Cat. No. 17001Z   Form **941** (Rev. 1-99)

unemployment rate while the federal rate was 6.2 percent. This would result in a federal unemployment tax rate of only .8 percent, calculated as follows:

$$6.2\% - 5.4\% = .8\%$$

With the information given in the earlier example for the payroll of the hotel, and using a federal unemployment rate of 6.2 percent and a state rate of 5.4 percent, the hotel would make the following journal entry (assuming no employee had earned $7,000 yet) to record its payroll taxes:

Payroll Tax Expense	$6,787	
FICA Tax Payable		$3,749
Federal Unemployment Tax Payable		
($49,000 × .8%)		392
State Unemployment Tax Payable		
($49,000 × 5.4%)		2,646

The debit to Payroll Tax Expense is simply the total of the three credits to the liability accounts. (The annual unemployment tax return for reporting federal taxes is Form 940; the form is shown in Exhibit 8.)

Once again, let us point out that these are two separate and distinct entries: One records the payroll and the other records the payroll tax expense. The only connection between the two entries is the FICA Tax Payable credit amount, which should be the same in both journal entries. Note the cost of employees to the employer; that is, in this example, it costs the employer the gross wages of $49,000 plus the payroll taxes of $6,787. This represents a total cost to the employer of $55,787.

Employees often do not realize what the costs of their employment actually are to the employer. In this case, there is a 14 percent difference between the gross wages of the employees and the total payroll cost to the employer (and this does not include the cost of any additional benefits the employer provides to its employees). Since fringe benefits and payroll taxes can be costly, hospitality firms may hire independent contractors rather than employees to perform certain services. Suppose that an independent contractor could provide a service such as accounting, data processing, or repair work for the hotel. If the employer hired this independent contractor, the employer would not have to pay payroll taxes. The IRS rules for determination of employee status versus independent contractor status are detailed and very strict, and are beyond our scope.

Reporting Tips

Certain employees in the hospitality industry, such as table servers, commonly receive tips from customers. There are both federal and state regulations on tip reporting, and the calculation of tip reporting can be complex. The form that the government provides for reporting tips, Form 4070 (shown in Exhibit 9), is the employee's report of tips to the employer.

Exhibit 8   IRS Form 940—Employer's FUTA Tax Return

Form **940**	**Employer's Annual Federal**	OMB No. 1545-0028
Department of the Treasury Internal Revenue Service (99)	**Unemployment (FUTA) Tax Return** ▶ **See separate instructions for information on completing this return.**	**1998**

		T	
⌐ Name (as distinguished from trade name)	Calendar year ⌐	FF	
		FD	
Trade name, if any		FP	
		I	
Address and ZIP code	Employer identification number	T	
∟			⌐

A   Are you required to pay unemployment contributions to only one state? (If "No," skip questions B and C) .   ☐ **Yes** ☐ **No**

B   Did you pay all state unemployment contributions by February 1, 1999? ((1) If you deposited your total FUTA
   tax when due, check "Yes" if you paid all state unemployment contributions by February 10. (2) If a 0%
   experience rate is granted, check "Yes." (3) If "No," skip question C.) . . . .   ☐ **Yes** ☐ **No**

C   Were all wages that were taxable for FUTA tax also taxable for your state's unemployment tax? . . . . .   ☐ **Yes** ☐ **No**

   If you answered "No" to any of these questions, you must file Form 940. If you answered "Yes" to all the
   questions, you may file Form 940-EZ, which is a simplified version of Form 940. (Successor employers see
   Special credit for successor employers on page 3 of the instructions.) You can get Form 940-EZ by calling
   1-800-TAX-FORM (1-800-829-3676) or from the IRS's Internet Web Site at **www.irs.ustreas.gov.**

   If you will not have to file returns in the future, check here, and complete and sign the return . . . . ▶ ☐
   If this is an Amended Return, check here . . . . ▶ ☐

Part I	**Computation of Taxable Wages**		

1   Total payments (including payments shown on lines 2 and 3) during the calendar year for
   services of employees . . . . | **1** |

2   Exempt payments. (Explain all exempt payments, attaching additional
   sheets if necessary.) ▶ ------------------------------------
   -- | **2** |

3   Payments for services of more than $7,000. Enter only amounts over the
   first $7,000 paid to each employee. Do not include any exempt payments
   from line 2. The $7,000 amount is the Federal wage base. Your state
   wage base may be different. **Do not use your state wage limitation** . | **3** |

4   Total exempt payments (add lines 2 and 3) **4**

5   **Total taxable wages** (subtract line 4 from line 1) . . . . ▶ **5**

Be sure to complete **both sides** of this return, and sign in the space provided on the back.
For Privacy Act and Paperwork Reduction Act Notice, see separate instructions.   Cat. No. 11234O   Form **940** (1998)

DETACH HERE

Form **940-V**	**Form 940 Payment Voucher**	OMB No. 1545-0028
Department of the Treasury Internal Revenue Service	Use this voucher only when making a payment with your return.	**1998**

Complete boxes 1, 2, 3, and 4. Do not send cash, and do not staple your payment to this voucher. Make your check or money order payable to the
"United States Treasury". Be sure to enter your employer identification number, "Form 940", and "1998" on your payment.

1 Enter the amount of the payment you are making	**2** Enter the first four letters of your last name (business name if partnership or corporation)	**3** Enter your employer identification number
▶ $.		

Instructions for Box 2	**4** Enter your business name (individual name for sole proprietors)
—Individuals (sole proprietors, trusts, and estates)— Enter the first four letters of your last name.	Enter your address
—Corporations and partnerships—Enter the first four characters of your business name (omit "The" if followed by more than one word).	Enter your city, state, and ZIP code

(continued)

Exhibit 8 *(continued)*

Form 940 (1998)   Page **2**

Part II   **Tax Due or Refund**

1   Gross FUTA tax. Multiply the wages in Part I, line 5, by .062 . . . .   **1**
2   Maximum credit. Multiply the wages in Part I, line 5, by .054 . . .   **2**
3   **Computation of tentative credit** (Note: *All taxpayers must complete the applicable columns.*)

(a) Name of state	(b) State reporting number(s) as shown on employer's state contribution returns	(c) Taxable payroll (as defined in state act)	(d) State experience rate period		(e) State experience rate	(f) Contributions if rate had been 5.4% (col. (c) x .054)	(g) Contributions payable at experience rate (col. (c) x col. (e))	(h) Additional credit (col. (f) minus col.(g)). If 0 or less, enter -0-.	(i) Contributions paid to state by 940 due date
			From	To					

3a   Totals . . . ▶
3b   **Total tentative credit** (add line 3a, columns (h) and (i) only—for late payments also see the instructions for
     Part II, line 6 . . . . ▶

4
5
6   **Credit:** Enter the smaller of the amount in Part II, line 2 or line 3b; or amount from the worksheet
     in the line 6 instructions **6**
7   **Total FUTA tax** (subtract line 6 from line 1). If the result is over $100, also complete Part III . .   **7**
8   Total FUTA tax deposited for the year, including any overpayment applied from a prior year . .   **8**
9   **Balance due** (subtract line 8 from line 7). Pay to the "United States Treasury". If you owe more
     than $100, see "Depositing FUTA Tax" on page 3 of the instructions . . . . ▶   **9**
10   **Overpayment** (subtract line 7 from line 8). Check if it is to be: ☐ **Applied to next return**
     or ☐ **Refunded** . . . . ▶   **10**

Part III   **Record of Quarterly Federal Unemployment Tax Liability** *(Do not include state liability.)* Complete only if
     line 7 is over $100. See page 6 of the instructions.

Quarter	First (Jan. 1–Mar. 31)	Second (Apr. 1–June 30)	Third (July 1–Sept. 30)	Fourth (Oct. 1–Dec. 31)	Total for year
Liability for quarter					

Under penalties of perjury, I declare that I have examined this return, including accompanying schedules and statements, and, to the best of my knowledge and belief, it is true, correct, and complete, and that no part of any payment made to a state unemployment fund claimed as a credit was, or is to be, deducted from the payments to employees.

Signature ▶   Title (Owner, etc.) ▶   Date ▶

Exhibit 9   **IRS Form 4070—Employee's Report of Tips to Employer**

Form **4070** (Rev. July 1996) Department of the Treasury Internal Revenue Service	**Employee's Report of Tips to Employer** ▶ For Paperwork Reduction Act Notice, see back of form.	OMB No. 1545-0065

Employee's name and address	**Social security number**
Employer's name and address (include establishment name, if different)	1 Cash tips received
	2 Credit card tips received
	3 Tips paid out
Month or shorter period in which tips were received	4 Net tips (lines **1** + **2** − **3**)
from , 19 , to , 19	
Signature	Date

Certain provisions of state and federal laws allow employers to apply a tip credit against the minimum wage of tipped employees. In this way, the employer can reduce the amount of gross wages paid to those employees. Assume, for example, that the minimum wage is $5.15 per hour and that the state allows a 40 percent maximum tip credit. Under these conditions, the employer could apply a credit of $2.06 (40% of $5.15) toward the hourly wage of tipped employees as long as the actual tips received by the employees were not less than the maximum allowable tip credit. In this case, the employer would comply with the law by paying employees $3.09 per hour ($5.15 − $2.06).

The next illustration shows how the gross wages payable to an employee are calculated when the actual tips received by the employee are greater than the maximum tip credit. Assume that an employee who worked 40 hours reports tips of $90, and is paid a minimum wage of $5.15 per hour. Also assume that the employer applies a maximum tip credit of $2.06. The gross wages payable to this employee would be calculated as follows:

Gross Wages: 40 hours at $5.15/hour		$206.00
Less lower of:		
Maximum FLSA tip credit (40 hours at $2.06)	$82.40	
Actual tips received	90.00	
Allowable tip credit		− 82.40
Gross wages payable by employer		$123.60

If the actual tips received by the employee were less than the maximum allowed tip credit, the *tips received* would be subtracted from the gross wages of $206 to determine the actual gross wages payable by the employer.

It is important to note that the gross taxable earnings of a tipped employee include both the gross wages payable by the employer and the actual tips received by the employee.

The Tax Equity and Fiscal Responsibility Act of 1982 (TEFRA) established regulations that govern tip-reporting requirements for food and beverage operations. The regulations state that the tips reported by hospitality establishments should be at least 8 percent of the qualified gross receipts of the business. Receipts from banquets, for which gratuities and service charges are often charged automatically, do not qualify. If the tips reported do not meet this 8 percent requirement, the deficiency is called a *tip shortfall*. When there is a shortfall, the employer must provide each directly tipped employee with an information sheet showing the tips reported by the employee and the tips that should have been reported.

The 8 percent tip regulation does not apply to all food and beverage operations. Cafeteria and fast-food operations, for example, are exempt from the regulation.

Other Current Liabilities

Accounts payable, notes payable, wages payable, and taxes payable resulting from payroll are the major current liabilities in hospitality operations. A review of the balance sheets of restaurant and lodging operations would also disclose other liabilities, such as unearned revenue, the current portion of long-term debt, income taxes payable, advance deposits, and other accrued items. A current liability that warrants discussion is property taxes.

Property Taxes

Property taxes are taxes on real estate and personal property (such as restaurant equipment and fixtures) levied by local taxing entities such as townships, cities, or counties. These property taxes are *ad valorem* **taxes**; that is, they are based on the assessed value of the asset itself. Once that value is determined by an authorized assessor of the taxing entity, the voted millage rate is applied to the value of the asset. A **mill** is a tax dollar per $1,000 of valuation. Assume, for example, that a restaurant is assessed at a value of $300,000 with a tax rate of 45 mills. The property taxes would amount to $13,500, shown in this calculation:

$$\$300,000 \div \$1,000 = 300 \times 45 \text{ mills} = \$13,500$$

The bill for $13,500 would not normally be received until December. In actual practice, most businesses receive two tax bills, one for summer and one for winter taxes; in this case, an adjustment would be made twice a year.

Normally, the hospitality firm would estimate the annual property taxes and accrue a portion of that amount every month, and adjust to the actual tax rate when it receives the bill. For example, assume that the estimated tax on the restaurant was $12,000 for the year, or $1,000 per month. The monthly journal entry would be as follows:

| Property Tax Expense | $1,000 | |
| Property Tax Payable | | $1,000 |

Next, assume that the bill for $13,500 was received on December 1, 20X1, and was payable on February 14, 20X2. The entry on December 31, 20X1, would adjust the estimated tax to the actual tax:

| Property Tax Expense | $2,500 | |
| Property Tax Payable | | $2,500 |

The entry on February 14, 20X2, the day on which the taxes are due, would be as follows:

| Property Tax Payable | $13,500 | |
| Cash | | $13,500 |

Summary

Current liabilities are those liabilities that are expected to be paid off within one year. Examples include accounts payable, notes payable, and wages payable. Most current liabilities are known and exact in amount; a few are known, but the amount must be estimated; and a very few are not only unknown in amount, but are not even certain to arise (such as a potential lawsuit judgment against the firm). Nevertheless, they must be recorded on the company's books.

Payroll, along with all of its related tax liabilities, represents one of the largest current liabilities for the hospitality firm, if not the largest. As such, payroll requires a good system of controls. One of the primary means of control is the segregation of the various payroll-related duties.

Other current liabilities are property taxes on real estate and personal property (such as restaurant equipment and fixtures) levied by local taxing authorities such as townships, cities, or counties. Tax bills are generally received twice a year, but are reflected in monthly journal entries to more closely match expenses with revenues for the period.

Key Terms

ad valorem **tax**—A tax based on the assessed value of the asset itself, usually a fixed percentage of the value.

contingent liability—A liability that is based on a future event that may or may not take place; it is not yet an actual liability and therefore should not be included in the Liabilities section of the balance sheet. Instead, it should be included in footnotes to the financial statements.

employee's earnings record—A record for each employee of the operation, used to record gross pay, taxes withheld, deductions, and net pay; used to compile information for reporting employee wages to governments.

Federal Insurance Contributions Act (FICA)—The federal law governing the national Social Security system, which imposes a payroll tax on the employee and the employer.

Federal Unemployment Tax Act (FUTA)—A federal law imposing a payroll tax on the employer for the purpose of funding national and state unemployment programs.

imprest payroll account—A control account into which only the exact amount of payroll funds for a given payroll period is deposited. Payroll checks totaling that deposit are then written on that account. Once all of the checks clear the bank, there is nothing left in the account.

loss contingency—A situation in which a liability is reasonably estimable, though uncertain but still rather probable in nature. An example would be a pending lawsuit against the company that the company's counsel expected to lose. Such a liability should be put on the books at its estimated amount.

master payroll file—A file containing information, including employee names, addresses, Social Security numbers, wage rates, and payroll deduction information.

mill—A tax dollar per $1,000 of valuation.

payroll journal—A journal containing a record of each payroll check issued, along with the corresponding gross pay and various deductions for federal tax, state tax, city tax, FICA, employee health care contributions, and miscellaneous contributions such as union dues.

payroll taxes—Additional taxes paid by the employer based on employee wages. The three major elements of payroll taxes are the employer's Federal Insurance Contributions Act (FICA) tax contribution, Federal Unemployment Tax Act (FUTA) tax contribution, and State Unemployment Tax Act (SUTA) tax contribution.

State Unemployment Tax Act (SUTA)—An unemployment tax rate levied by individual states. States must contribute dollars into the federal unemployment fund; to do this, they levy their own state unemployment tax rates. The tax rates vary by state, but whatever the state's rate is, employers are allowed to use the state tax rate as a credit against the federal rate.

Review Questions

1. What is the difference between a current liability and a long-term liability?

2. What are the differences between estimated liabilities, contingent liabilities, and loss contingencies?

3. What type of note payable results in the use of a Discount on Notes Payable account? What type of account is Discount on Notes Payable? What is the account's normal balance?

4. What six major control features can a firm use to safeguard payroll?

5. What basic items should be included in a payroll master file?

6. What information is provided in a payroll journal? What information is provided by an employee earnings record?

7. What are the differences between the entry to record *payroll* and the entry to record *payroll taxes*?

8. What does the acronym *FICA* stand for? Is a FICA tax an employer tax or an employee tax?

9. What do the acronyms *FUTA* and *SUTA* represent? Are FUTA and SUTA taxes paid by the employer, the employee, or both?

10. What do the terms *ad valorem* and *mill* mean?

Problems

Problem 1

Longview Hotels operates ten properties in the Midwest. The company employs the following procedures to control payroll:

a. Tom Johnson, the human resources manager, carefully interviews all prospective employees, authorizes their hiring, prepares the payroll, and distributes the checks.

b. Donna Miller, the front desk manager, deletes individuals from her department's labor force and provides payroll employees with front desk employees' wage rates.

c. At the end of each shift, hotel dining room employees write down their hours on a blank sheet of paper and place it on the desk of the food and beverage manager.

d. All employees are paid by checks drawn on the general bank account of the company.

e. All individual paychecks are kept in the respective departments until they are claimed by employees.

Required:

Draft a memo suggesting changes that the operation ought to make to better control payroll.

Problem 2

Indicate which of the following items should appear in the financial statements of Holen Hotel and where they would appear.

a. A $100,000 lawsuit pending against the hotel that the hotel's attorney believes the hotel will probably lose.

b. FICA taxes payable.

c. Estimated property taxes.

d. A commitment to pay a certain entertainer $30,000 if he performs at the hotel in six months.

e. Estimated income taxes.

f. The guarantee of $250,000 worth of a subsidiary's debt.

Problem 3

Indicate whether each of the following items is a real liability, loss contingency, or contingent liability:

a. Debt guarantee of a subsidiary's loan

b. Note payable due in 90 days

c. Liability for income tax

d. Salaries payable

e. Liability due to a pending lawsuit

f. Liability for product warranty

g. Accounts payable

Problem 4

Lakeside Restaurant, Inc., borrowed $40,000 from Empire Savings on November 1, 20X1. The note was written for $40,000 at 12 percent interest for 90 days and was due on February 1, 20X2.

Required:

Create the journal entries needed for Lakeside for November 1, 20X1; December 31, 20X1; and February 1, 20X2.

Problem 5

One of the key control features for payroll involves the separation of payroll functions.

Required:

1. List three functions that should be performed by separate individuals where possible.
2. List three other control features that should be in place for payroll.

Problem 6

You have been asked to prepare the entry to record the payroll on February 15, 20X1, for Hotel Properties, Inc. The gross wages are $8,000 for administrative salaries and $6,000 for sales salaries. The federal income tax rate is 28 percent, the state income tax rate is 4.6 percent, and the FICA rate is 7.65 percent for all employees. All wages are subject to these taxes. In addition to taxes withheld, the employer has withheld $128 for the employees' contribution to a health insurance plan.

Required:

1. Prepare the necessary journal entry to record the payroll of Hotel Properties, Inc., on February 15, 20X1.
2. Prepare the journal entry that would be made on the date the payroll was actually paid.

Problem 7

Using the information given in Problem 6 and the following additional information, make the journal entry necessary to record Hotel Properties, Inc., *payroll taxes* on February 15, 20X1:

- Federal unemployment tax rate (FUTA) is 6.2 percent.
- State unemployment tax rate (SUTA) is 4.2 percent. (The full 4.2 percent state rate can be used as a credit against the federal rate.)
- All employees' wages are subject to federal and state unemployment taxes.

Challenge Problems

Problem 8

The payroll journal for Northport Enterprises, Inc., is shown. Using the information provided in the following journal, construct the entry to record the payroll for the company. Brown and Pung are administrative personnel, while the other employees are sales personnel.

Payroll Journal								
Name	Pay Period Ending	Gross Wages	FICA	Federal Inc. Tax	State Inc. Tax	Health Ins.	Net Pay	Check #
Brown, J.	2/12/X1	$800	$50.00	$224.00	$38.40	$18.00	$469.60	4265
Smith, T.	"	750	46.87	210.00	36.00	-0-	457.13	4266
Woods, L.	"	725	45.31	203.00	34.80	18.00	423.89	4267
Pung, A.	"	825	51.56	231.00	39.60	20.00	482.84	4268
Jones, B.	"	600	37.50	168.00	28.80	9.00	356.70	4269

Problem 9

Ralph Jenkins is the assistant manager of the Hemlock Hotel. Tom Patterson, the owner of the hotel, has asked you to compute the hotel's total cost of employing Jenkins.

Required:

1. Using the following information, compute the total annual expense that Jenkins represents for the hotel.

Jenkins' gross salary	$32,000
FICA tax rate	7.65% on earnings up to $72,600
SUTA	5.20% on earnings up to $7,000
FUTA	6.20% on earnings up to $7,000
Federal Income Tax Rate	28% on all earnings
State Income Tax Rate	5.4% on all earnings

2. Compare the cost to the hotel of employing Jenkins with the amount Jenkins sees in his check.

Problem 10

The payroll journal for the SeaGate Hotel on the June 30 payday shows the following:

Employee	Gross Wages	Federal Income Tax	FICA	State Income Tax	Health Insurance	Union Dues	Net Pay
M. Cleaves	$400	$112	$25	$19	$ 9	$10	$225
A. Hutson	375	105	23	18	8	10	$211
T. Peterson	360	100	22	17	–	–	$221
J. Klein	410	116	26	20	12	12	$224

Assume that SeaGate's FUTA rate is 5.8 percent, that its SUTA rate is 4.8 percent, and that the full state rate can be used as a credit against the federal rate. Also assume that all wages are subject to federal and state unemployment taxes and that all wages are subject to FICA taxes. Round to the nearest dollar.

<u>Required:</u>

1. Record the entry for SeaGate's payroll on June 30.
2. Record the entry for SeaGate's payroll tax expense on June 30.

REVIEW QUIZ

When you feel you have covered all of the material in this chapter, answer these questions. Choose the *best* answer.

1. A lawsuit pending against a hotel is expected to result in a $50,000 judgment against the hotel. This is an example of a(n):

   a. estimated liability.
   b. actual liability.
   c. contingent liability.
   d. loss contingency.

2. A hotel borrowed $20,000 from the bank on November 1, 20X1, at an annual interest rate of 12 percent. The first quarterly loan payment is due February 1, 20X2. The accrued interest on February 1, 20X2, would equal _____.

   a. $300
   b. $400
   c. $500
   d. $600

3. The balance of an imprest payroll bank account should be:

   a. equal to the sum of the outstanding payroll checks for the pay period.
   b. equal to the gross payroll after employees have cashed their checks.
   c. equal to payroll expense for the period.
   d. $0.

4. A certain employee has an hourly rate of $10. This week, the employee has worked a total of 44 hours, four hours of which are considered overtime hours, for which this employer chooses to pay double-time. The employee's gross pay:

   a. is $400.
   b. is $440.
   c. is $480.
   d. cannot be determined because the tax rates have not been provided.

5. Hospitality firm income and wages are subject to certain taxes in the United States. Federal Unemployment Tax Act taxes are collected from:

   a. employees only.
   b. employers only.
   c. employers and employees alike.
   d. none of the above.

REVIEW QUIZ *(continued)*

6. Alena works in a state with a $6.00 minimum wage and a 30 percent maximum tip credit. If Alena worked 40 hours and received actual tips of $100 one week, her gross wages payable by her employer for that week would be:

    a. $240.
    b. $198.
    c. $168.
    d. $68.

7. Omar's Oasis Motel has a building worth $350,000, according to a recent valuation. If the tax rate for the motel's district is 50 mills, the motel's property taxes will be:

    a. $12,500.
    b. $16,000.
    c. $17,500.
    d. $35,000.

Answer Key: 1-d-C1, 2-d-C2, 3-a-C3, 4-c-C4, 5-b-C5, 6-c-C6, 7-c-C7

Each question is linked to a competency. Competencies are listed on the first page of the chapter. An answer reading 3-b-C4 translates to:

    3:   the question number
    b: the correct answer
    C4: the competency number

Chapter 13 Outline

Advantages of Partnerships
    Ease of Formation
    No Partnership Taxes
    Synergy
Disadvantages of Partnerships
    Limited Life
    Mutual Agency
    Unlimited Liability
General versus Limited Partnerships
Partners' Capital and Drawing Accounts
Formation of a Partnership
    Division of Income
Admission of a New Partner
Withdrawal of a Partner
Liquidation of a Partnership

Competencies

1. Outline characteristics of business partnerships and their advantages and disadvantages.

2. Distinguish between a general partnership and a limited partnership.

3. Describe partners' drawing and capital accounts, how partnerships are formed, and common ways to divide partnership income.

4. Explain and demonstrate how to account for the admission of a new partner, the withdrawal of a partner, and the liquidation of a partnership.

13

Partnerships

THE FOUR FORMS of business organization are the sole proprietorship, the partnership, the limited liability company, and the corporation. This chapter covers basic accounting principles for the second form of business, the partnership. Accounting for assets and liabilities in a partnership is basically the same as it is for a sole proprietorship; however, there are a few changes in the equity section of the balance sheet.

First we will discuss what a business partnership is all about: two or more individuals engaged in some economic activity. The partners co-own all the assets and liabilities of the entity and share, in some manner, in its profits or losses. Although some partnership agreements are oral, most are written, and should include at least the following important details:

1. The names of the partners

2. The amount of the investments of each individual partner

3. The profit-sharing arrangement

4. The buy/sell agreement of the partnership

Advantages of Partnerships

Compared to a corporation, a partnership has three major advantages. These are ease of formation, lack of partnership taxes, and synergy.

Ease of Formation

It is relatively easy to form a partnership. Partners get together, decide on the amounts of their investments and their profit sharing, and start the business. The process is much different from the process of forming a corporation, where articles of incorporation, as well as other important documents, must be drawn up.

No Partnership Taxes

Unlike the corporation, the partnership itself pays no taxes on its profits. However, the partnership must file a partnership tax return. This may seem confusing, but the partnership return is simply an informational return. The partnership is a form of business organization through which profits flow to the individual tax returns of the partners. The individual partners pay taxes on their shares of the profits.

Synergy

In its basic form, **synergy** means that the total effect of something is greater than the sum of its individual effects. For example, suppose an individual owns a restaurant and is extremely good at dealing with customers and promoting the business, but poorly manages the accounting work, the ordering, and various other duties. Let's further suppose that there is a second individual who owns a restaurant on the other side of town. This person is very detail-oriented, and very effectively keeps the books, works behind the scenes, plans the menu, and so forth, but does not work very well with the public. Each of these two individuals may adequately manage his or her own restaurant, but if the two people formed a partnership and each specialized in their respective areas of expertise, the resulting restaurant would make more money than the individual restaurants did on their own.

Disadvantages of Partnerships

The partnership form of business organization also has a few disadvantages, including limited life, mutual agency, and unlimited liability.

Limited Life

A partnership is like a sole proprietorship in that the life of the business is contingent on the owners. If a partner were to leave the partnership, or if a partner died, a whole new partnership would have to be drawn up for the remaining partners or any new partners joining the partnership. In other words, the partnership itself has a life limited to the lives of the individual partners.

Mutual Agency

The term **mutual agency** refers to the fact that partners are responsible for their partners' individual business actions. For example, suppose that a partnership is owned by Partners A, B, and C. If Partner A decided to increase the inventory by 50 percent and to purchase that inventory on open account, Partners B and C would be just as liable for the purchase as Partner A. Mutual agency pertains only to actions that relate to the partnership, not to any partner's personal debts or actions.

Unlimited Liability

Like the owner of a sole proprietorship, partners have **unlimited liability** with regard to the business. This means that if the business should fail, the business's creditors could seize the partners' personal assets. (This is not the case in the corporate form of business organization, where the owners have limited liability, or in limited liability companies.)

General versus Limited Partnerships

The partnerships described so far are called **general partnerships**, in which all of the partners are called *general partners* and have unlimited liability. Partners can avoid unlimited liability if they form a **limited partnership**. This is a partnership in which one or more of the partners have limited liability; that is, their liability is limited to the amount of their investment in the partnership, and their personal assets are not vulnerable to their business's creditors. Every partnership must have at least one general partner; several criteria must be met in the case of a limited partnership. These criteria are covered in advanced textbooks.

Partners' Capital and Drawing Accounts

In some sole proprietorships, the owner has a capital and a drawing account in the equity section of the general ledger accounts. In the case of a partnership, the equity accounts are expanded so that each partner has both a capital account and a drawing account. The following partial balance sheet shows the Owners' Equity section for the Jenkins and Phillips partnership.

Partial Balance Sheet		
Owners' Equity Section		
Ralph Jenkins, Capital	$150,000	
Betty Phillips, Capital	$175,000	
Total Capital		$325,000

   Assume that during the fiscal year 20X1 Jenkins drew $50,000 out of the partnership, while Phillips drew $60,000 out. The journal entries to close those drawing accounts into the partners' capital accounts would be as follows:

Ralph Jenkins, Capital	$50,000	
Ralph Jenkins, Drawing		$50,000

Betty Phillips, Capital	$60,000	
Betty Phillips, Drawing		$60,000

Formation of a Partnership

Now we will examine how a partnership begins and how the accounting entries are journalized in the early stages. Often the partners coming together bring personal assets from a previous business. Sometimes these assets are worth substantially more than the books of the individual sole proprietorships show they are worth. As a result, when assets are brought into a partnership, they are recorded on the books at fair market value rather than at cost at the time the partnership is formed.

   Let's assume that George Clark and John Barry are going to pool their assets and liabilities to form a partnership in the restaurant business. Clark will bring in land that cost him $30,000 but now has a fair market value of $80,000, and a building that cost him $50,000 and now has a fair market value of $150,000. In addition, Clark will bring inventory that is on the books at $10,000 and a note payable in the amount of $25,000. Barry, on the other hand, will bring to the partnership $150,000 in cash and equipment that has a fair market value of $80,000. The assets and liabilities of this partnership will be at their stated amounts, except for the land and building, which will be brought on at $80,000 and $150,000, respectively, their fair market values.

The journal entries for the formation of this partnership would be as follows:

Land	$ 80,000	
Building	150,000	
Inventory	10,000	
Notes Payable		$ 25,000
George Clark, Capital		215,000

Cash	$150,000	
Equipment	80,000	
John Barry, Capital		$230,000

The balance sheet of the partnership after these entries were made would appear as illustrated below:

Balance Sheet Clark & Barry Restaurant January 1, 20X1			
Cash	$150,000	Notes Payable	$ 25,000
Inventory	10,000	George Clark, Capital	215,000
Equipment	80,000	John Barry, Capital	230,000
Building	150,000		
Land	80,000		
		Total Liability and	
Total Assets	$470,000	Equity	$470,000

Division of Income

There are many possible ways to divide income, but we will limit our discussion to three common methods:

- Division of income in a fixed ratio, the simplest method.

- Division of income with salary distributed first, followed by remaining income in a fixed ratio.

• Division of income with salary distributed first, followed by a percentage of the partners' beginning capital balances, concluded by a division of the remaining income in some fixed ratio. This is the most complex profit-sharing arrangement.

Division of Income—Fixed Ratio. The simplest way for two partners to divide income is to use a 50-50 ratio. However, they don't always do so. Partners may decide, for various reasons, to divide income on a 60-40 basis, a 70-30 basis, or even a 90-10 basis. Assume that two partners, Robbins and Byrd, form a partnership with Robbins contributing $80,000 and Byrd, $100,000. Assume also that the two partners agree to share profits in the ratio of 60 percent for Robbins to 40 percent for Byrd. At the end of 20X1, profits of $80,000 would be divided as shown below:

Robbins	Byrd	Income $80,000
$48,000	$32,000	$80,000

This format would result in Robbins receiving $48,000 and Byrd $32,000 of the $80,000 profit for the year. The schedule shows that the full $80,000 is distributed and that the partners' profit-sharing amounts equal the $80,000 balance.

Division of Income with Salary and Fixed Ratio. Next, assume that Robbins and Byrd form a partnership with the same capital contributions as in the previous example, and agree to pay Robbins a $30,000 salary and Byrd a $20,000 salary. After the salary is distributed, the remaining profits will be divided in the same 60-40 ratio. If in 20X1 the partnership earned $80,000, the division of profits under this profit-sharing arrangement would appear as follows:

	Robbins	Byrd	Income $80,000
Salary	$30,000	$20,000	$50,000
Profits	18,000	12,000	30,000
Total	$48,000	$32,000	$80,000

The illustration shows that under these circumstances Robbins would receive $48,000 and Byrd $32,000 for a total of $80,000.

Division of Income with Salary, Interest on Beginning Capital Balances, and the Remainder in a Fixed Ratio. Assume that Robbins and Byrd form the same partnership with the same capital contributions as in the previous examples, but agree to share profits as follows:

1. Salary of $30,000 to Robbins, $20,000 to Byrd,

2. Interest at 10 percent on beginning capital balances for both partners, and

3. The remainder in a 60-40 ratio.

If profits for 20X1 were again $80,000, the division of profits would appear as follows:

	Robbins	Byrd	Income $80,000
Salary	$30,000	$20,000	$50,000
Interest (10% of beginning capital balance)	8,000	10,000	18,000

	Robbins	Byrd	Income $80,000
Profits (remainder)	7,200	4,800	12,000
Total	$45,200	$34,800	$80,000

Under this profit-sharing arrangement, Robbins would end up with $45,200 while Byrd would receive $34,800, once again totaling the $80,000 annual profit.

Occasionally, a partnership does not earn enough profit to meet all of the provisions of the profit-sharing agreement. Suppose that a partnership has the same profit-sharing agreement mentioned in the previous example. Also suppose that the partnership profit amounted to only $60,000. Under these circumstances, the division of profits would appear as shown in this table:

	Robbins	Byrd	Income $60,000
Salary	$30,000	$20,000	$50,000
Interest (10% of beginning capital balance)	8,000	10,000	18,000
Loss	(4,800)	(3,200)	(8,000)
Total	$33,200	$26,800	$60,000

Under this profit-sharing arrangement, Robbins would receive $33,200 and Byrd $26,800 for a total of $60,000. Notice that even though there was a "loss" in the middle of the computations, we still continued the computations as if there were enough profit.

Admission of a New Partner

Admission of a new partner into a partnership can be accomplished in one of two distinct ways: An individual can buy an existing partner's entire interest from that partner or he or she can invest cash or other assets in the partnership for an equity interest. The journal entries for these two situations are very different.

It is very simple to account for the first situation. Assume, for instance, that Wood and Conrad have a partnership with $60,000 in each partnership equity account and that they share profits equally. Next assume that Hale buys Conrad's entire equity interest by paying Conrad $80,000. The journal entry for this transaction on the partnership books would appear as follows:

Conrad, Capital	$60,000	
Hale, Capital		$60,000

The amount that Hale pays for Conrad's interest is irrelevant to this journal entry in the partnership books. Conrad is leaving the partnership; therefore, her total equity is removed from the books and replaced by Hale's interest. In this instance, no cash entered or exited the partnership.

Now we will consider the admission of a new partner into the partnership by way of an investment of cash in the partnership. Assume the same facts exist for the partners mentioned previously; that is, Wood's capital is $60,000 and Conrad's capital is $60,000. Wood and Conrad agree to admit Hale into the partnership for a $\frac{1}{3}$ interest in exchange for an investment of $60,000. The journal entry in this case would be:

Cash	$60,000	
Hale, Capital		$60,000

The partners' equity accounts on the balance sheet after this transaction would appear as follows:

Owners' Equity Section of the Balance Sheet	
Wood, Capital	$ 60,000
Conrad, Capital	60,000
Hale, Capital	60,000
Total Capital	$180,000

Now consider the original partnership of Wood and Conrad, but with these differences: they agree to admit Hale for a $\frac{1}{3}$ interest based on an investment of $90,000 in the partnership. Notice that Hale is paying $90,000 cash for an equity interest of $70,000. This $20,000 difference could be due to undervaluation of assets that have been on the partnership books for many years. The $70,000 equity interest is computed as follows:

Equity in the partnership before new partner	$120,000
+ New equity brought in by the new partner	90,000
Total Equity after admission of new partner	$210,000
$\frac{1}{3}$ of $210,000 = Equity interest of new partner	$ 70,000

The journal entry to record the admission of Hale under these circumstances would be as follows:

Cash	$90,000	
Hale, Capital		$70,000
Wood, Capital		10,000
Conrad, Capital		10,000

Since Hale is paying $90,000 for an equity interest of $70,000, the $20,000 difference represents a bonus to the original partners, who divide it between them on the basis of their 50-50 profit-sharing arrangement. After this journal entry, the partners' capital accounts would have been as follows:

Hale, Capital	$ 70,000
Wood, Capital	70,000
Conrad, Capital	70,000
Total Capital	$210,000

Occasionally, an existing partnership may be so eager to admit a new partner (either because of the incoming partner's assets or expertise) that it does so for less than the value of the equity interest. If, for example, Wood and Conrad had agreed to admit Hale for a $\frac{1}{3}$ interest in the partnership based on an investment of $30,000, the computation of Hale's equity interest would have been as follows:

Equity of the old partnership	$120,000
+ New equity coming into the partnership	30,000
Total Equity after admission of new partner	$150,000
Total Equity divided by 3 = Capital per partner	$ 50,000

The journal entry to record this would be as follows:

Cash	$30,000	
Wood, Capital	10,000	
Conrad, Capital	10,000	
Hale, Capital		$50,000

After this journal entry, the partnership capital accounts would be as follows:

Wood, Capital	$50,000
Conrad, Capital	$50,000
Hale, Capital	$50,000

The $20,000 difference between the cash invested in the partnership and the new partner's equity interest represents a bonus to the new partner that comes out of the capital accounts of the old partners.

Withdrawal of a Partner

The withdrawal of a partner can result either when a partner dies or simply when a partner wishes to leave the partnership. The withdrawal of a partner, like the admission of a partner, could occur in one of two ways. First, if a partner withdraws by receiving a cash settlement from an outside individual, the entry is very simple. The outgoing partner's capital account is debited for the amount that was in the account, and the incoming partner's capital account is credited for the amount of the outgoing partner's capital regardless of the amount paid for the interest. The transaction is handled this way because the cash paid for the partnership interest goes directly to the outgoing partner and not into the partnership. In the second way of leaving a partnership, the outgoing partner receives cash from the partnership equal to the value of his or her interest. The entry for this is also simple: the outgoing partner's Capital account is debited and Cash is credited for the amount of the settlement. On the other hand, if the outgoing partner receives an amount for his or her interest that is more or less than the book value of the interest, a bonus would be paid either to the outgoing partner or to the remaining partners. The entries would be similar to those entries for the admission of a partner, only in reverse.

Liquidation of a Partnership

The last event to occur chronologically in the life of a partnership is its liquidation. At the time of liquidation, the assets are converted to cash, the debts are paid, and the balance is distributed to the partners based on the balances in their capital accounts. Notice the important last step in the liquidation—that is, that the liquidating cash dividend (the final distribution paid to the partners based on their capital accounts) paid to the partners is not distributed according to their profit-sharing agreement; rather, it is based on their final equity balances.

To illustrate a simple liquidation of a partnership, assume that Field, Stream, and Woods, who share profits equally, produce the following balance sheet on June 30, 20X1.

Field, Stream, and Woods Balance Sheet June 30, 20X1			
Assets		**Liabilities & Owners' Equity**	
Cash	$ 50,000	Notes Payable	$ 40,000
Equipment	130,000	Field, Capital	50,000
		Stream, Capital	70,000
		Woods, Capital	20,000
Total Assets	$180,000	Total Liabilities & OE	$180,000

If the equipment were sold for $100,000, the first journal entry would be:

Cash	$100,000	
Loss on Disposal of Equipment	30,000	
Equipment		$130,000

Next, the loss would be distributed to the partners by means of the following journal entry:

Field, Capital	$10,000	
Stream, Capital	10,000	
Woods, Capital	10,000	
Loss on Disposal of Equipment		$30,000

At this point, the capital balances of the partners would be $40,000, $60,000, and $10,000 for Field, Stream, and Woods, respectively. The next entry would occur when the note payable was paid off, and would simply be:

Notes Payable	$40,000	
Cash		$40,000

At this point, the balance sheet of the partnership would appear as follows:

Balance Sheet			
Cash	$110,000	Field, Capital	$ 40,000
		Stream, Capital	60,000
		Woods, Capital	10,000
Total Assets	$110,000	Total Owners' Equity	$110,000

The final entry for the liquidation of this partnership would be:

Field, Capital	$40,000	
Stream, Capital	60,000	
Woods, Capital	10,000	
Cash		$110,000

Once again, notice that when the liquidating dividend is paid, the profit-sharing agreement is disregarded and the cash is distributed based on the final capital balances in the partners' accounts.

In this next illustration, we will assume the same facts that we did before, except that the equipment in this case sells for $55,000 rather than $130,000. In this case, the journal entry for the disposal of the equipment would be:

Cash	$55,000	
Loss on Disposal of Equipment	75,000	
Equipment		$130,000

The loss would then be distributed to the partners by means of the following journal entry:

Field, Capital	$25,000	
Stream, Capital	25,000	
Woods, Capital	25,000	
Loss on Disposal of Equipment		$75,000

At this point, the partners' balances in their capital accounts would be $25,000, $45,000, and ($5,000) respectively for Field, Stream, and Woods. The note payable would be disposed of as it was before, with a debit to Notes Payable and a credit to Cash of $40,000. At this point, the partnership's balance sheet would appear as follows:

Balance Sheet			
Cash	$65,000	Field, Capital	$25,000
		Stream, Capital	45,000
		Woods, Capital	(5,000)
Total Assets	$65,000	Total Owners' Equity	$65,000

At this point, Field and Stream would ask Woods to pay the $5,000 deficit in her partnership account. If Woods was able to pay the $5,000, the entry would be:

Cash	$5,000	
Woods, Capital		$5,000

This would produce a zero balance in Woods's capital account.

The final journal entry for the liquidation of this partnership would be as follows:

Field, Capital	$25,000	
Stream, Capital	45,000	
Cash		$70,000

If, however, Field and Stream asked Woods to pay the $5,000 and she could not, the $5,000 deficit in her account would be distributed to the remaining partners based on their profit-sharing arrangement, which at this point would be 50-50. The journal entry to record this would be:

Field, Capital	$2,500	
Stream, Capital	$2,500	
Woods, Capital		$5,000

The final entry for this partnership liquidation would be:

Field, Capital	$22,500	
Stream, Capital	42,500	
Cash		$65,000

Summary

A business partnership is an entity made up of two or more individuals engaged in some economic activity. The partners co-own all the assets and liabilities of the entity and also share in some manner in the profits or losses of the enterprise. Although some partnership agreements are oral, most are written and should include at least the names of the partners, the amounts of the investments of each individual partner, the profit-sharing arrangement, and the buy/sell agreement of the partnership.

Some of the advantages of a partnership are

- Its ease of formation
- The fact that there are no partnership taxes to be paid
- The potential for synergy

Some disadvantages of the partnership form of business organization are:

- Its limited life
- Mutual agency
- Unlimited liability

The rest of the chapter discussed the differences between general and limited partnerships; the partners' capital and drawing accounts; the formation of a partnership; the division of the income produced by the partnership; the admission of a new partner; the withdrawal of a partner; and, finally, the steps necessary for the liquidation of a partnership.

Key Terms

general partnership—A form of business organization in which all of the partners are called *general partners* and have unlimited liability for the debts of the partnership.

limited partnership—A partnership in which one or more of the partners have limited liability. That is, their liability is limited to the amounts of their investment in the partnership and their personal assets are not vulnerable to their business's creditors. Every partnership must have at least one general partner, and there are several criteria that must be met in the case of a limited partnership.

mutual agency—The responsibility of partners in a partnership for their partners' individual business actions. Mutual agency pertains only to actions that relate to the partnership, not to any partner's personal debts or actions.

synergy—The interaction of two or more separate individuals or agencies to achieve an effect of which each is individually incapable; more commonly, "the whole is greater than the sum of its parts."

unlimited liability—The type of liability experienced by a sole proprietorship or a partnership. The liability of sole proprietors or partners extends beyond their investments in the business to their personal assets.

Review Questions

1. What is the difference between a general partnership and a limited partnership?

2. What are the disadvantages of the partnership form of business organization?

3. How does the balance sheet of a partnership differ from that of a sole proprietorship?

4. What are the major items that ought to be included in a partnership agreement?

5. In what two different ways can a new partner be admitted to a partnership?

6. Dewey, Cheatum, and Howe share partnership profits in a $\frac{1}{4}$, $\frac{1}{2}$, and $\frac{1}{4}$ ratio, respectively. If Howe were paid a $30,000 bonus to leave the partnership, how would the bonus affect the capital accounts of Dewey and Cheatum?

7. Land and See, who share profits in a $\frac{2}{3}$ -$\frac{1}{3}$ ratio respectively, are liquidating their partnership. After the assets have been converted to cash and the liabilities have been paid, the accounts have the following balances: Cash, $30,000; Land, Capital $18,000; and See, Capital $12,000. What would be the final closing entry for the partnership?

8. Duke and Earl form a partnership to start a fine dining restaurant. What is Duke's liability for Earl's actions in each of the following situations?

   a. Earl orders $25,000 worth of food and beverages from American Foods, Inc., for use in the restaurant.

   b. Earl purchases a personal automobile for driving to and from the restaurant, and signs a note for $18,000.

   c. Earl signs a lease on a building for the restaurant, agreeing to pay $3,000 per month.

d. Earl signs a home improvement loan in the amount of $8,000 for an addition to his home.

9. What are the three common profit-sharing agreements discussed in the chapter, and what are their characteristics?

10. Discuss the validity of the following three statements:

a. Partnerships pay no taxes.

b. Partnerships file no tax returns.

c. Partners pay no tax on partnership profits.

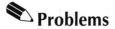# Problems

Problem 1

Cook and Sell are forming a partnership to start a catering business. Cook's contribution will be cash of $20,000, equipment that cost $8,000 and has a fair market value of $10,000, and inventory worth $10,000. Sell's contribution includes land that cost $15,000 and is now worth $40,000, a building with a fair market value of $80,000 and a mortgage of $60,000, and equipment worth $5,000.

Required:

Determine the capital balances for the two partners at the date of the partnership's formation.

Problem 2

Griffin and Hall are partners in the motel business. On January 1, 20X1, their capital balances were $50,000 and $40,000 respectively. During 20X1 Griffin drew $25,000 and Hall drew $30,000 out of the partnership. The profit for 20X1 was $60,000 and is to be divided in the ratio of 40 percent for Griffin to 60 percent for Hall.

Required:

Determine the capital balances of Griffin and Hall for December 31, 20X1.

Problem 3

Reed, Dolan, and Gates are partners in a ski resort and have agreed to share profits in the following way: salaries of $25,000 to Reed, $35,000 to Dolan, and $40,000 to Gates. The remaining profit will be distributed as follows: 30 percent to Reed, 20 percent to Dolan, and 50 percent to Gates.

Required:

Assuming the partnership earned a profit of $150,000 in 20X1, compute the amount that each partner would earn in 20X1.

Problem 4

Haul and Oates start a partnership with the following assets:

Asset	Market Value	Cost	Original Asset Owned by Haul	Oates
Cash	$ 50,000	$ 50,000	X	
Building	100,000	75,000		X
Inventory	30,000	40,000	X	
Equipment	60,000	80,000		X
Supplies	10,000	10,000	X	
Land	200,000	100,000		X

Required:

1. What is the amount of Haul's capital in the partnership?
2. What is the amount of Oates's capital in the partnership?

Problem 5

Street has $80,000 in capital and Barnes has $60,000 in capital in a restaurant partnership. They have agreed that Street will sell her entire interest to Townes for $80,000 in cash.

Required:

1. Write the journal entry for this sale.
2. Write the journal entry if the sale is made for $90,000.

Problem 6

Siggy, Babbs, and Emily are partners in a small contract food service business. The equity in the partnership accounts is $20,000 each.

Required:

Construct the journal entry for the withdrawal of Emily under each of the following two sets of circumstances:

1. The partnership pays Emily $20,000 for her entire interest.
2. Sarah pays Emily $25,000 for her interest and is admitted to the partnership for a $\frac{1}{3}$ interest.

Problem 7

Fox and Wolfe are partners in a destination resort operation with capital balances of $120,000 each. They share profits equally. They are badly in need of cash and have agreed to admit Lyon for $90,000 in exchange for a $\frac{1}{3}$ equity interest in the partnership.

Required:

1. Journalize the entry for the admission of Lyon.
2. Illustrate the Owners' Equity section of the balance sheet after the admission of Lyon.

Challenge Problems

Problem 8

Cleaves, Klein, and Hunter form a partnership with the following assets:

Partner	Asset	Cost Basis of Asset	Market Value of Assets
Cleaves	Cash	$100,000	
Klein	Building	80,000	$160,000
	Equipment	60,000	40,000
Hunter	Cash	50,000	
	Inventory	60,000	50,000

The partnership agreement calls for profit sharing in the following way:
Salaries of $40,000 to Cleaves
                     $50,000 to Klein
                     $30,000 to Hunter
Interest of 10 percent on beginning of year capital balances.
Remaining profits distributed as follows:
        40% to Cleaves
        30% to Klein
        30% to Hunter

Required:

Assume the profit before wages and interest for Year 1 was $200,000.

1. Prepare a balance sheet for the starting date of the partnership.
2. Determine the division of profits for the partners in Year 1.

Problem 9

At 12/31/20X1, Smith's and Wesson's drawing and capital accounts are as follows:

Partner	Balance
Smith, Capital	$50,000
Smith, Drawing	70,000
Wesson, Capital	80,000
Wesson, Drawing	30,000

The profit-sharing agreement is as follows:

a. Salary of $30,000 to Smith and $20,000 to Wesson.

b. Divide the remaining profit or loss in a 60-40 ratio with 60 percent to Smith and 40 percent to Wesson.

Required:

Based on the existing account balances and profit sharing agreement, determine the ending balances in the partners' accounts if the business had a $50,000 loss in this year.

Problem 10

Hill and Dale are partners in a successful resort called the Timberline Inn. The general ledger accounts of the partnership appear as follows:

Cash	$ 20,000
Accounts Receivable	45,000
Inventory	23,000
Equipment	23,000
Land	180,000
Buildings	450,000
Accounts Payable	16,000
Mortgage Payable	325,000
Hill, Capital	220,000
Dale, Capital	180,000

Hill and Dale have agreed to admit Valley on 12/31/20X1 for $200,000 cash to a $\frac{1}{3}$ interest in the partnership.

Required:

1. Journalize the entry to admit Valley.
2. Compile the balance sheet for the partnership at December 31, 20X1, after the admission of Valley.

REVIEW QUIZ

When you feel you have covered all of the material in this chapter, answer these questions. Choose the *best* answer.

1. A major disadvantage of the partnership form of business is:

    a. limited life.
    b. ease of formation.
    c. lack of partnership taxes.
    d. synergy.

2. If the partnership of Appleby and Kent should fail, the business's creditors could lawfully seize the personal assets of both partners. Which of the following terms best describes this situation?

    a. synergy
    b. limited liability
    c. mutual agency
    d. unlimited liability

3. Solomon wants to start a business with his parents, who want a minimum of financial risk. The parents do not want their personal assets to serve as a guarantee for any loans Solomon takes out for the business. Given the following options, the business should take the form of a:

    a. partnership with synergy in effect.
    b. general partnership.
    c. limited partnership.
    d. liquidation partnership.

4. In the partnership "Byrd and Kennedy," Kennedy gets 40 percent of the profits. Also, Byrd receives $30,000 as a salary, and Kennedy's salary is $35,000. How much would Kennedy be entitled to for an accounting period in which the business earned $200,000?

    a. $54,000
    b. $80,000
    c. $89,000
    d. $92,000

5. The Harper & Stilton partnership divides its profit, in part, according to a 10 percent interest rate on each partner's average capital balance. Harper had a beginning capital balance of $100,000 at the start of this fiscal year and, after nine months, contributed another $20,000 of capital. Harper made no more contributions that fiscal year. How much profit accrues to Harper for the year from interest?

    a. $10,000
    b. $10,500
    c. $12,000
    d. $360,000

REVIEW QUIZ *(continued)*

6. Under which of the following conditions are assets converted to cash, debts paid, and any remaining balance distributed to the partners of a partnership?

   a. The partnership is liquidated.
   b. The partnership loses a limited partner.
   c. The partnership admits a new partner.
   d. The partnership sells much of its equipment.

7. Which of the following business transactions can involve a debit to a partner's capital account?

   a. admission of a new partner
   b. liquidation of a partnership
   c. withdrawal of a partner
   d. any of the above

Answer Key: 1-a-C1, 2-d-C1, 3-c-C2, 4-c-C3, 5-b-C3, 6-a-C4, 7-d-C4

Each question is linked to a competency. Competencies are listed on the first page of the chapter. An answer reading 3-b-C4 translates to:

   3: the question number
   b: the correct answer
   C4: the competency number

Chapter 14 Outline

Financial Statements
Advantages and Disadvantages of the
   Corporation
Taxes
Organizational Structure
Forming a Corporation
Common Stock
Dividends
Retained Earnings
Stock Subscription Plan
Preferred Stock
Cash Dividends Compared to Stock
   Dividends
Stock Splits
Treasury Stock
Book Value per Share of Common Stock
     Book Value versus Market Value per
     Share

Competencies

1. Identify unique features of corporate
    financial statements, and outline
    advantages and disadvantages of the
    corporate form of business.

2. Explain how corporations' taxes are
    accounted for and how corporations
    are structured and formed.

3. Describe common stock and cash
    dividends and demonstrate how to
    account for them.

4. Demonstrate how to prepare a
    statement of retained earnings and
    how to account for a stock
    subscription plan.

5. Distinguish between common and
    preferred stock, and describe preferred
    stock.

6. Describe stock dividends and stock
    splits and demonstrate how to account
    for them.

7. Describe treasury stock and
    demonstrate how to account for it.

8. Demonstrate how to calculate book
    value per share of stock, and explain
    why this figure and the market value
    per share interest shareholders.

14

Corporate Accounting

THERE ARE FOUR basic forms of business organization: the sole proprietorship, the partnership, the limited liability company, and the corporation. Corporation accounting is by far the most difficult of the four forms' accounting requirements.

Financial Statements

The financial statements produced for corporations are basically the same as the statements produced for the sole proprietorship, partnership, or LLC—in most areas. There are very few, if any, changes in the Assets and Liabilities sections. However, there are major changes in the equity section of the balance sheet. The Stockholders' Equity section of the balance sheet can be very complex compared to the equity section of a balance sheet produced for the other three business forms.

The Stockholders' Equity section of the balance sheet includes two major sections: Paid-In Capital and Earned Capital. The Paid-In Capital section includes the amounts of capital paid into the corporation over its life. Typical paid-in capital accounts include Common Stock, Preferred Stock, Additional Paid-In Capital, and Common Stock Subscribed.

Earned Capital represents the capital that the corporation has earned through profits over its life and has not been paid out in dividends. These accumulated earnings are recorded in an account called Retained Earnings. All of these capital accounts will be discussed in detail in this chapter.

A corporation is very different from the other forms of organization. A corporation is a legal entity in itself, given a life in the state in which it is incorporated. Since the corporation has a life, it can be taken to court and can enter into long-term contracts, which is not possible to do in the case of partnerships and sole proprietorships.

Advantages and Disadvantages of the Corporation

There are advantages and disadvantages of the corporate form of organization. The advantages of incorporation include limited liability. This is very important because it limits the potential losses of the owners to the amount of their original investments. (This is not true of the sole proprietorship or partnership, where the owners can lose amounts beyond their original investment.) Another advantage of the corporation is that it has unlimited life. The life of a sole proprietorship or partnership is limited to the lives of the owners. However, a corporation continues regardless of any changes in ownership. Another advantage of the corporate form of organization is its ease in acquiring capital. Corporations can acquire large amounts of capital with relatively little difficulty compared to partnerships or sole proprietorships. In addition, shares of ownership in a corporation are easily transferable. It could take many months for a sole proprietor to turn over the business to another individual. However, in the case of a huge corporation, thousands of shares of stock can change hands as the result of a simple phone call. The corporation also benefits from professional management. The corporation is organized differently from the sole proprietorship or partnership in that a professional management team runs it and its owners are usually uninvolved in day-to-day management.

Disadvantages of the corporate form of business include **double taxation**, which can be a severe disadvantage. Since corporations are legal entities, they are required to pay taxes on their profits. Later, when the profits are distributed to the owners as dividends, the owners must pay taxes again. The issue of taxation is a complex one; further discussion of it is beyond our scope.

Regulation is another disadvantage of the corporate form of business. Federal and state government agencies require many more reports of corporations than they require of other business forms.

Taxes

The corporation is the only form of business that pays taxes on profits. In sole proprietorships, partnerships, and LLCs, the owners pay taxes only on their personal tax returns.

In the case of the corporation, income taxes are estimated quarterly. The following accounting entry would be made in the event of a $25,000 tax liability:

| Income Tax Expense | $25,000 | |
| Income Tax Payable | | $25,000 |

The liability will appear in the Current Liabilities section of the balance sheet, while Income Tax Expense will appear at the bottom of the income statement just before Net Income.

Organizational Structure

The organizational structure of the corporation is different from the other forms of business. The owners of a corporation vote for members of the corporation's board of directors, which is responsible for setting broad policy guidelines for the operations of the business and is not involved in its daily management. The board's responsibilities include hiring individuals to manage the company's day-to-day activities.

Forming a Corporation

To form a corporation, individuals must apply to a state for organization within that state. After the necessary paperwork is submitted and approved, the state allows a corporation to begin operating its business. There are many costs involved in forming a corporation. These costs include legal fees, promoter's fees, and fees paid to the state for incorporating. Corporations may account for **organization costs** by placing them in an intangible-asset account called Organization Costs and writing them off over a number of years. Organization costs should not be written off over a period of greater than 40 years. Federal tax law states that organization costs for tax purposes may be written off over a shorter period of time, but no less than five years.

Common Stock

The basic unit of ownership in a corporation is a share of stock. The term **capital stock** refers broadly to ownership in a corporation. When a corporation applies to a state for a charter, it is required to ask for a certain authorized number of shares of stock. The *authorized number of shares of stock* represents the maximum amount of shares that the company can eventually issue to the public. *Issued shares of stock*, on the other hand, refers to the number of shares of stock that the company has sold to the public. *Outstanding shares of stock* equals issued shares of stock less *treasury stock* (to be discussed later in the chapter). For example, a company that has issued 40,000 shares of stock and purchased back 5,000 shares of treasury stock has 35,000 shares of stock outstanding.

Shares of stock must have either a **par value** or a stated value. Par value or stated value represents the legal capital of the corporation. Although technically there are differences between par value and stated value, we will assume they are similar. Understand that the par value of a stock has no relation to the market value of the stock. Companies will usually set the par value of a stock very low. Let's assume that a certain corporation decided to issue 20,000 shares of par value stock that have a par value of $2 a share, for $10 a share. The journal entry would be as follows:

Cash	$200,000	
Common Stock		$ 40,000
Additional Paid-In Capital in Excess of Par		160,000

Amounts are always entered in the Common Stock account at par value. The excess of the selling price over the par value is credited to an account called Additional Paid-In Capital in Excess of Par. This is an equity account that normally carries a credit balance. The $40,000 common stock and $160,000 paid-in capital represent the legal capital of the firm.

The owners of these shares of stock expect two things in return for the money they gave the corporation for the stock. First, they hope that the shares of stock increase in value. Second, they expect to receive a return of the company's profits every year. Profits returned to the stockholders are referred to as **dividends**.

Dividends

Dividends are paid out of the company's accumulated earnings and are available to stockholders only when dividends are declared by the board of directors. There are four important dividend dates relating to cash dividends. They are the date of declaration, the date of record, the ex-dividend date, and the date of payment.

1. *The date of declaration.* This is the date on which the board of directors announces a future dividend. At this time, the board of directors will state when the payment date will be and what the amount of the dividend will be.

2. *The date of record.* This is the date on which a list of the holders of the shares of stock is compiled so that the dividend checks can be mailed to them.

3. *The ex-dividend date.* On this date, the stock sells without the dividend; that is, even though a dividend will be paid soon on the stock, the new purchaser will not receive the dividend. The ex-dividend date normally precedes the date of record by three days. The purpose of setting an ex-dividend date is to allow the paperwork on exchanges of ownership of shares of stock to be cleared up before the date of record.

4. *The date of payment.* This is the date on which the actual dividend is paid.

Assume that a company declares a $.30 dividend on 50,000 shares of outstanding stock. The journal entry to record the declaration of the dividend would be:

Retained Earnings	$15,000	
Dividends Payable		$15,000

Rather than debit Retained Earnings when a dividend is declared, some corporations will debit an account called Dividends or Dividends Declared. This account will then be closed into Retained Earnings at the end of the fiscal period.

Note that once a dividend is declared by the board of directors, the company must pay the dividend. On the dividend payment date, the following entry would be made in the case of the $.30 dividend just mentioned:

Dividends Payable	$15,000	
Cash		$15,000

Once the dividend is declared, it will be paid shortly thereafter; hence, it is classified as a current liability. No accounting entries are made on either the date of record or the ex-dividend date.

Normally a corporation will not handle the payment of a dividend itself. Rather, it will use a transfer agent and registrar to keep track of the corporation's shareholders and to issue the dividend checks. The transfer agent or registrar is typically a large bank or a trust company.

Retained Earnings

Retained Earnings is an equity account that appears only on the books of a corporation. Whereas partnerships and sole proprietorships close their Income Summary accounts into the owners' capital accounts at the end of a fiscal period, corporations close their Income Summary accounts into Retained Earnings.

Retained Earnings represents the amount of a company's earnings to date that have not been paid out in dividends. Retained earnings is *not* the same as cash for a given corporation. A corporation can have a large amount of cash and no retained earnings or a large amount of retained earnings and no cash. There is not necessarily a relationship between the amounts in these two accounts. One prerequisite for paying a dividend is that the company must have retained earnings. A second prerequisite is that the company also must have the cash on hand to pay the dividend. The third prerequisite is that the dividend must be declared by the board of directors.

The following is a statement of retained earnings for United Hotels.

United Hotels Statement of Retained Earnings For Year Ended December 31, 20X1	
Retained Earnings, January 1, 20X1	$150,000
Net Income for 20X1	48,000
Subtotal	$198,000
Dividends Declared during 20X1	24,000
Retained Earnings, December 31, 20X1	$174,000

On rare occasions a firm may discover an error in the income reported in a prior year. Since the net income of that year has already been closed into Retained Earnings, the correction is logically made to the Retained Earnings account. This correction is called a *prior period adjustment*. The correction should be made to the beginning balance of Retained Earnings, as shown in the following statement:

United Hotels Statement of Retained Earnings For Year Ended December 31, 20X1	
Retained Earnings, January 1, 20X1	$150,000

Add: Error of prior period: Recorded purchase of
    Equipment as an expense rather than an asset
    (net of taxes)
	25,000

Adjusted Retained Earnings	175,000
Net Income for 20X1	48,000
Subtotal	223,000
Dividends Declared during 20X1	24,000
Retained Earnings, December 31, 20X1	$199,000

It is not uncommon for a hospitality firm to operate at a loss in the first years of its existence. When those losses are closed into Retained Earnings, a debit balance is created in that account. This debit balance in Retained Earnings is referred to as a *deficit*. The deficit is subtracted from the rest of the owners' equity, as shown in this illustration:

Stockholders' Equity	
Preferred Stock	$150,000
Common Stock	200,000
Additional Paid-In Capital	600,000
Subtotal	$950,000
Less Deficit	50,000
Total Stockholders' Equity	$900,000

Stock Subscription Plan

Occasionally, a company will offer new shares of stock through what is called a **stock subscription plan**. In this case, individuals choosing to buy new shares of stock in the corporation complete a subscription form, agreeing to buy the stock at a certain price. Assume that a certain corporation receives subscriptions to 5,000 shares of $10 par value stock at a price of $30 a share. The entry to record the subscription of these 5,000 shares of stock would be as follows:

Stock Subscriptions Receivable	$150,000	
Common Stock Subscribed		$ 50,000
Additional Paid-In Capital in Excess of Par		100,000

The Stock Subscriptions Receivable account appears in the Current Assets section of the balance sheet.

Assume that later in the month cash is paid for 3,000 shares of the subscribed stock. In this case, the following two entries would be made:

Cash	$90,000	
Stock Subscriptions Receivable		$90,000

Common Stock Subscribed	$30,000	
Common Stock		$30,000

If a balance sheet were drawn up for the company between the subscription date and the date the new stock is actually issued, the Common Stock Subscribed account would appear on the balance sheet in the equity section. The following is an example of a Stockholders' Equity section of the balance sheet, including Common Stock Subscribed:

Stockholders' Equity	
Common Stock	$1,000,000
Common Stock Subscribed	20,000
Paid-In Capital in Excess of Par	100,000
Retained Earnings	250,000
Total Stockholders' Equity	$1,370,000

Preferred Stock

So far we have discussed one type of stock, **common stock,** which is the most popular form of stock issued by corporations. Another type of stock occasionally found on the books of hospitality firms is called **preferred stock.** Preferred stock has many characteristics that common stock does not have. First, as its name implies, it is preferred in terms of dividend payment. Any given corporation will pay dividends to its preferred stockholders before it pays any dividends to common stockholders. Second, preferred dividends are preferred in the event of the liquidation of the company. If the company should decide to liquidate its assets after paying off its liabilities, preferred stockholders would be paid before common stockholders. Third, preferred stock is generally **cumulative** in nature. This means that if a dividend is not paid in one year, before anything can be paid to the common stockholders in a subsequent year, the past preferred dividend and the current year's dividend must be paid. Most preferred stocks are cumulative; however, a few preferred stocks are noncumulative.

Fourth, preferred stock is **callable**. This means that the corporation has the option of paying the preferred stockholders the par value of the stock (or some other predetermined value above par) in return for the stock certificates. Fifth, preferred stock, unlike common stock, normally gives holders no voting rights. Sixth, some preferred stock is convertible into common stock of the corporation. Seventh, some preferred stock is *participating preferred*. This means that in years when excess profits are earned, preferred stockholders participate with the common stockholders in additional dividend payments.

The journal entries recording the issuance of preferred stock are similar to those used to record common stock.

Cash Dividends Compared to Stock Dividends

People often confuse stock dividends and cash dividends. *Cash dividends* are cash payments to owners of shares of stock that come out of the company's income. **Stock dividends**, on the other hand, are additional shares of stock in the company granted to existing shareholders.

What is the benefit of receiving a stock dividend? If, for instance, a stockholder receives additional stock dividends in the amount of 10 percent of the stock he or she owns and every other stockholder also receives 10 percent more stock than he or she currently owns, is any stockholder really in any better position after the stock dividend than before the stock dividend? Stockholders *may* be in a better position after a stock dividend in two instances. First, if the company keeps the same cash dividend per share after distributing the stock dividend, stockholders are better off, because they receive the same dividend per share times the greater number of shares—a greater overall dividend amount. Second, when a stock dividend is declared, the company's stock will usually drop in value, often making it more attractive to potential investors and thus providing some appreciation potential for the stockholders in the future.

Assume that Hercules Properties Corporation has 200,000 shares of $5 par value stock authorized and 150,000 shares issued and outstanding. Hercules declares a 5 percent stock dividend when the market price of the stock is $20 per share. The journal entry to record this declaration of the stock dividend is:

Retained Earnings	$150,000	
Stock Dividend to Be Distributed		$ 37,500
Additional Paid-In Capital: Stock Dividend		112,500

The $150,000 debit to Retained Earnings is equal to 150,000 shares × 5% × $20/share. The $37,500 credit to Stock Dividend to Be Distributed is equal to 7,500 shares × $5/share. Additional Paid-In Capital is credited for $20 − $5 = $15 × 7,500 shares, or $112,500.

Later, when the stock dividend was actually distributed, the journal entry would be:

Stock Dividend to Be Distributed	$37,500	
Common Stock		$37,500

Notice that in the case of this small stock dividend, Retained Earnings is decreased by the number of shares in the dividend times the current market price of the stock (7,500 shares × $20 = $150,000). The Common Stock account, of course, is increased by the par value of the stock in the second journal entry.

We described this entry as a *small stock dividend* because the dividend amounted to less than 20 to 25 percent of the shares of stock outstanding at the date of the dividend. In the case of a *large stock dividend,* which is defined as a dividend that is greater than 20 to 25 percent of the stock outstanding, the same accounts would be used in the journal entry on the date of declaration, except that Retained Earnings would be debited for the par value of the stock and not the market price of the stock.

Stock Splits

Corporations may want to increase the number of shares of their stock outstanding for various reasons or may want to see the stock price reduced in the marketplace. Both scenarios can be accomplished through the use of a **stock split**. In the case of a two-for-one stock split, a corporation would grant two shares for every one share currently held by the owners. For example, assume that Hercules Property Corporation has 50,000 shares of common stock outstanding at a par value of $10 for

$500,000 worth. After a two-for-one stock split, the company would have 100,000 shares of stock at $5 par value, again yielding $500,000. Note that there is no change in the total assets, no change in total liabilities, and no change in total stockholders' equity. Thus, no journal entry is made in the case of a stock split; instead, a memo is made in the general journal.

Treasury Stock

Treasury stock is common stock that was once issued by a corporation and later repurchased by the same corporation. A company that has treasury stock will show a difference between the number of shares of stock issued and the number of shares outstanding, since treasury stock is not currently outstanding even though it has been issued. There are two basic ways to account for treasury stock. These are the *par method* and the *cost method*. Here, we will discuss only the cost method of accounting for treasury stock.

First, it is important to note that treasury stock is not an asset. Also, since treasury stock is stock that is not outstanding, no dividends are paid on it. Treasury stock shows up in the Stockholders' Equity section of the balance sheet as a reduction to Total Stockholders' Equity. Assume that Pristine Hotels reacquires 5,000 shares of its own stock at a market price of $30 per share. Recording this purchase at cost, the journal entry would be as follows:

Treasury Stock	$150,000	
Cash		$150,000

If later on that treasury stock were sold at cost, the company would merely reverse the preceding entry. However, if 3,000 shares of treasury stock that had been purchased at $30 per share were later sold back to the public at $40 per share, the following entry would be made:

Cash	$120,000	
Treasury Stock		$90,000
Additional Paid-In Capital from Treasury Stock		30,000

If, following that resale, 1,000 shares of treasury stock were resold to the public at $20 per share, the following entry would be made:

Cash	$20,000	
Additional Paid-In Capital from Treasury Stock	10,000	
Treasury Stock		$30,000

Notice that no gains or losses are recorded on the sale of treasury stock. In the second case, in which the treasury stock was resold at a price below its cost, the difference between cost and selling price is debited to the Additional Paid-In Capital account. If there had been no additional paid-in capital, rather than giving

Paid-In Capital a debit balance, accountants would have debited Retained Earnings for $10,000.

Book Value per Share of Common Stock

Common stockholders closely watch the market price of their stock as listed on the organized stock exchanges or the over-the-counter markets. Although of lesser interest to stockholders, book value per share is also a concern to owners.

Book value per share of stock refers to the per-share value of the company's net assets (assets minus liabilities). For a corporation offering only common stock, book value per share of stock is computed by dividing Total Stockholders' Equity by the number of common shares outstanding. For example, assume that Greenwood Hotels, Inc., had the following Stockholders' Equity section:

Common Stock, $5 par (10,000 shares outstanding)	$ 50,000
Additional Paid-In Capital	150,000
Retained Earnings	80,000
Total Stockholders' Equity	$280,000

The book value per share would be $28.00, determined as follows:

Total Stockholders' Equity	$280,000
÷ Common Shares Outstanding	10,000
= Book Value per Share	$ 28

The calculation of book value per share is complicated when the corporation has preferred stock outstanding. First, the preferred stock must be deducted at its call price from the value of the net assets. Second, any dividends in arrears on the preferred stock must be deducted also. The remaining value of the net assets is then divided by the number of common shares outstanding.

For example, assume that Greenwood Hotels, Inc., had 500 shares of $100 par, 8 percent preferred, callable at $105, with $20,000 dividends in arrears. Under these circumstances, book value per share of common stock would be calculated as follows:

Preferred Stock, $100 par, 8%, callable at $105,		
500 shares outstanding		$ 50,000
Common Stock, $5 par, 10,000 shares outstanding		50,000
Additional Paid-In Capital		150,000
Retained Earnings		80,000
Total Stockholders' Equity		$330,000
Total Stockholders' Equity		$330,000
Less Call Value of Preferred Stock		(52,500)
Less Preferred Dividends in Arrears		(20,000)
Equity of Common Stockholders		$257,500
Divided by Common Shares Outstanding	÷	10,000
Equals Book Value per Share of Common Stock	=	$ 25.75

Book Value versus Market Value per Share

Book value per share is based on historical cost figures for the items on the balance sheet. For example, land that was purchased for $500,000 ten years ago has a book value of $500,000, even though it may now be worth $10,000,000. Book value is generally lower than market value for a given company. If a stock happened to be selling at a market price below book value, it could be of interest to potential stockholders, since the sale of the assets at book value would yield enough to pay the debts and leave more dollars per share than the stock was currently selling for in the market.

Summary

Accounting for the corporate form of business organization is more complex than accounting for the sole proprietorship, the partnership, or the limited liability company.

Advantages of the corporate form of business organization include limited liability, unlimited life, ease of acquiring capital, easily transferable shares of ownership, and professional management. Some disadvantages of the corporate form are double taxation (that is, taxes are paid on the profits of the corporation and also on the dividends distributed to the shareholders) and regulation by local, state, and federal governments.

The remainder of the chapter discusses the types of stock issued by a corporation and the accounting procedures associated with them for dividend determination and payment. Also noted are stock splits, treasury stock, book value per share of common stock, market value per share, and the differences between cash dividends and stock dividends.

Key Terms

callable—Subject to a demand for presentation for payment.

capital stock—Shares of ownership of a corporation; general term that covers all classes of common and preferred stock.

common stock—Capital stock of a corporation; stockholders who own common stock generally have voting rights.

cumulative—Refers to the fact that if a dividend is not paid in one year, the past preferred dividend and the current year's dividend must be paid before anything can be paid to the common stockholders in a subsequent year.

dividend—A distribution of earnings to owners of a corporation's stock.

double taxation—This occurs when both corporate profits and dividends paid to stockholders are taxed.

organization costs—Costs incurred before a business is incorporated. They include such things as legal fees, promoter's fees, and fees paid to the state for incorporating.

par value—An arbitrarily selected amount associated with authorized shares of stock; it is also referred to as *legal value.*

preferred stock—Corporate stock that entitles the holder to preferential treatment on dividends, but may not give the holder voting rights.

stock dividend—The payment by a corporation of a dividend in the form of shares of its own stock without change in par value.

stock split—A division of corporate stock by the issuance to existing stockholders of a specified number of new shares with a corresponding lowering of par value for each outstanding share. In the case of a two-for-one stock split, the corporation would grant two shares for every one share previously held by the owners.

stock subscription plan—A stock purchase plan in which individuals choosing to buy new shares of stock in the corporation complete a subscription form, agreeing to buy the stock at a certain price.

treasury stock—A corporation's own capital stock that the corporation has repurchased but not retired or reissued.

 # Review Questions

1. What are the major advantages and disadvantages of the corporate form of business?

2. What is the significance of the par value of a common stock? What is the relationship between par value and market value?

3. What are the four dividend dates? What is the significance of each?

4. What are the main characteristics of preferred stock?

5. How does a firm acquire treasury stock? Where does it appear on the balance sheet?

6. What are the differences between a cash dividend and a stock dividend?

7. How does accounting for a stock dividend differ from accounting for a stock split?

8. What do common stockholders expect to receive in return for their investment?

9. How would the journal entry for a small stock dividend differ from the journal entry for a large stock dividend?

10. Where are the accounts Stock Subscriptions Receivable and Common Stock Subscribed located on the balance sheet?

 # Problems

Problem 1

Condor Hotels, Inc., currently has common stock of $200,000, additional paid-in capital of $800,000, and retained earnings of $75,000. On December 15, 20X1, it issues 10,000 shares of $5 par common stock at $20 per share.

Required:

1. Write the journal entry for December 15, 20X1.
2. Prepare, in good form, the Stockholders' Equity section of the balance sheet after the issuance of the additional shares.

Problem 2

Based on the following information, compile the statement of retained earnings for Top Flight Hotels, Inc., for the year ended December 31, 20X1.

Net income for the year	$ 92,000
Retained earnings as of January 1, 20X1	125,000
Dividends declared during 20X1	46,000
Error of prior period: add $50,000 net of taxes	50,000

Problem 3

The accounts for the Lighthouse Hotel Corporation are given below:

Common Stock	Land
Bonds Payable	Equipment
Accounts Receivable	Treasury Stock
Additional Paid-In Capital—Common Stock	Common Stock Subscribed
Buildings	Accounts Payable
Retained Earnings	Stock Dividend to Be Distributed
Wages Payable	Preferred Stock

Required:

Classify the above accounts as assets, liabilities, or equity, and indicate the normal balance (debit or credit) for each.

Problem 4

Journalize the following transactions for Blue Water Resorts, Inc.

1. Purchased 10,000 shares of its own stock at a price of $20 per share on May 6, 20X1.
2. Resold 4,000 shares of Treasury Stock at $30 per share.
3. Resold 4,000 shares of Treasury Stock at $15 per share.

Problem 5

Vacationland Properties declares a $.70 per share dividend on April 1, 20X1. On that date, the corporation has 15,000 shares of stock issued and 12,000 shares outstanding. The date of record is May 1, 20X1, and the ex-dividend date is April 28, 20X1. The dividend is to be paid on May 15, 20X1.

Required:

Write the necessary journal entries for April 1, April 28, May 1, and May 15.

Problem 6

1. Record the journal entries for Allied Hotels, Inc., for the following transactions:

   a. Received subscriptions for 10,000 shares of $5 par value common stock at a price of $15 per share on August 5, 20X1.

   b. Received a check for payment of 6,000 shares of stock and issued the common stock on August 28, 20X1.

2. Before the stock subscription, the company had $300,000 in common stock, $650,000 in additional paid-in capital, and $95,000 in retained earnings. Prepare a Stockholders' Equity section for August 31, 20X1.

Problem 7

The following is the balance sheet of Treadway Inns, Inc.:

Stockholders' Equity:

6% Preferred Stock, $50 par, callable at $55, 60,000 shares authorized, 30,000 shares issued	$ 1,500,000
Common Stock, $5 par value, 1,000,000 shares authorized, 500,000 shares issued	?
Additional Paid-In Capital—Common Stock	10,000,000
Retained Earnings	8,000,000

Required:

Using the information provided in the partial balance sheet, answer the following questions:

1. What is the dollar amount in the Common Stock account?
2. What is the total dollar amount of stockholders' equity?
3. What is the total amount of legal capital?
4. What is the book value per share of the common stock?
5. What is the average issuance price of the common stock?

Challenge Problems

Problem 8

The Royce Karlton Hotel Corporation had the following transactions for April 20X1:

Date   **Transaction**

4/01   Sold 1,000 shares of common stock, $20 par, for $25 per share.
4/05   Sold 500 shares of 8% preferred stock, $100 par, for $105 per share.
4/08   Declared a 10% common stock dividend on 10,000 common shares when the market price of the stock was $40.

4/15 Declared a dividend of $.20 per share on 10,000 shares of common stock.
4/16 Declared a dividend of $2.00 per share on 2,000 shares of preferred stock.
4/25 Paid the preferred and common stock dividends.
4/27 Distributed the common stock dividend.
4/30 Closed the April income of $200,000 into retained earnings.

Required:

Record the journal entries for the above transactions for April.

Problem 9

Evergreen Resorts, Inc., has 400,000 shares of $2 par value common stock authorized and 200,000 shares issued and outstanding.

Required (all of the following are independent cases):

1. Record the journal entries for the declaration of a 10 percent stock dividend on June 1, 20X1, and the subsequent distribution of the dividend on July 1, 20X1. The market price of the stock on June 1 is $40 and on July 1 is $50.

2. Record the journal entries for the declaration of a 30 percent stock dividend on August 1, 20X1, and subsequent distribution of the dividend on September 1, 20X1. The market price of the stock on August 1 is $55, and on September 1 is $60.

3. A two-for-one stock split is declared on October 1, when the stock price is $65. Record the appropriate entries for this event.

Problem 10

Required:

Compile the equity section of the Balance Sheet for the Sea-Witch Restaurant Company at 12/31/XX based on the following incomplete data:

Additional Paid-In Capital—Common Stock	$860,000
8% Preferred Stock, $100 par, callable at $110, cumulative, 10,000 shares authorized, 6,000 shares issued and outstanding	?
Treasury Stock, 10,000 shares purchased at $8 per share	?
Additional Paid-In Capital—Preferred Stock	30,000
Common Stock, no par, $5 stated value, 500,000 shares authorized, 400,000 shares issued, and 390,000 shares outstanding	?
Deficit	40,000
Common Stock Subscription Receivable	50,000
Common Stock Subscribed	50,000

REVIEW QUIZ

When you feel you have covered all of the material in this chapter, answer these questions. Choose the *best* answer.

1. Which of the following is an advantage of the corporate form of business organization?

    a. unlimited liability
    b. limited life
    c. ease of acquiring capital
    d. freedom from government regulation

2. A certain corporation sold 10,000 shares of $2 par value stock for $10 per share. The total cash received and the amount recorded in the Common Stock account are _____ and _____, respectively.

    a. $20,000; $20,000
    b. $100,000; $100,000
    c. $100,000; $20,000
    d. $20,000; $100,000

3. In which of the following kinds of plans do participants complete forms in which they agree to buy stock at a certain price?

    a. retained earnings plans
    b. stock subscription plans
    c. cash dividend plans
    d. treasury stock plans

4. If a corporation decides to liquidate, stockholders who hold _____ stock will be paid first.

    a. preferred
    b. common
    c. treasury
    d. callable

5. The Successful Corporation has 100,000 outstanding shares of stock. Each share has a par value of $2 and a market value of $10. On the date of declaration of a 5 percent stock dividend, corporate accountants would make a journal entry in which they would debit Retained Earnings for:

    a. $200,000.
    b. $50,000.
    c. $5,000.
    d. $10,000.

REVIEW QUIZ *(continued)*

6. A certain corporation is authorized to sell 100,000 shares of stock. Forty thousand shares have been issued and 3,000 shares have been repurchased as treasury stock. The number of outstanding shares equals:

   a. 100,000.
   b. 60,000.
   c. 40,000.
   d. 37,000.

7. A certain corporation issues both preferred stock and common stock. The total call value of the preferred stock is $80,000. There are no preferred dividends in arrears. Total stockholders' equity amounts to $380,000, and there are 10,000 shares of common stock outstanding. The book value per share of common stock is:

   a. $38.
   b. $30.
   c. $8.
   d. not determinable with the given information.

Answer Key: 1-c-C1, 2-c-C3, 3-b-C4, 4-a-C5, 5-b-C6, 8-d-C7, 7-b-C8

Each question is linked to a competency. Competencies are listed on the first page of the chapter. An answer reading 3-b-C4 translates to:

   3: the question number
   b: the correct answer
   C4: the competency number

Chapter 15 Outline

Disadvantages and Advantages of Bond
  Financing
    Disadvantages of Bond Financing
    Advantages of Bond Financing
Classifying Bonds
Other Features of Bonds
Journal Entries for Issuance of Bonds
    Bonds Sold between Interest Payment
    Dates
Market Value versus Face Value
    Bonds Issued at a Discount
    Bonds Issued at a Premium
Year-End Adjusting Entries for Bonds
  Payable
Effective Interest Rate Method of Bond
  Amortization
Bond Sinking Fund
Convertible Bonds
Retirement of Bonds
Leases
Pensions
Mortgages Payable

Competencies

1. Describe bonds, the advantages and disadvantages of bond financing, and the types of bonds.

2. Demonstrate and explain how to account for bond issues and for bond sales between interest payment dates.

3. Demonstrate and explain how to account for bonds sold at a premium or at a discount.

4. Demonstrate and explain how to make year-end adjusting entries for bonds payable.

5. Describe the effective interest rate method of bond amortization, and explain how to account for bond sinking funds, convertible bonds, and the retirement of bonds.

6. Describe leases, pensions, and mortgages payable, and explain how to account for each.

15

Bonds, Leases, and Mortgages Payable

BONDS PAYABLE are long-term liabilities that the issuing company plans to pay off over a period greater than one year. The holders of the bonds are creditors of the corporation, not owners. In exchange for providing funds to the hospitality firm, the bondholders are paid interest on the bonds, usually semiannually. The bonds are generally sold through an **underwriting firm**.

The underwriting firm is a very important institution in U.S. financial markets. The underwriting firm, or a syndicate of several underwriting firms, will buy the entire bond issue from the corporation that is issuing the bonds. The underwriting firm will then resell the bonds to the public. These bonds can be sold at their face value, at a price above face value (at a *premium*), or at a price below face value (at a *discount*). Premiums and discounts on bonds will be discussed in detail later in this chapter.

The holders of the bonds can keep the bonds until maturity or sell them in what are called the *secondary securities markets.* Bonds of large corporations are readily marketable with prices quoted daily in the financial pages of the newspapers. The following Rally's example from the *Wall Street Journal* shows a typical listing of a bond in the financial pages.

Bonds	Cur Yld	Vol	Close	Net Chg
Rally's $9\frac{7}{8}$ 00	12.5	20	79	+3

Bonds normally have a face value of $1,000 and are quoted as a percentage of face value. This listing shows that the Rally's bond quoted at 79 is actually selling for $790.00 (79% of $1,000). The listing also reveals that Rally's Hamburgers' $9\frac{7}{8}$ percent bonds due in 2000 are currently yielding 12.5 percent. On this particular day, 20 bonds were traded at a closing price of $790 per bond, which represented an increase of $30.00 (net change of 3% of $1,000) per bond over the previous closing price.

The company that issues bonds typically must adhere to many contractual provisions. Technically, the bond contract exists between the firm issuing the bonds and an institution called the *trustee.* The trustee in most cases is a commercial bank. For all practical purposes, however, the agreement is between the bondholders and the corporation issuing the bonds. This agreement is called the **bond indenture** and lists in detail the contractual provisions of the bond. The items listed in the indenture include the interest payment dates and the interest rate on the bond. Any specific collateral on the bonds is also listed in the bond indenture. The *maturity date* (the date the bond is to be paid off) is included in the bond indenture along with any call provisions on the bonds or any convertible provisions. All of these contractual provisions will be discussed later in the chapter.

Disadvantages and Advantages of Bond Financing

Hospitality firms issue bonds to raise large amounts of capital. A hospitality firm needing capital may choose among several alternatives, including bonds, preferred stock, or common stock financing. To decide which method of financing to use, the hospitality firm must consider the advantages and disadvantages of bond financing.

Disadvantages of Bond Financing

First, since the bond indenture includes many contractual provisions that the corporation must comply with, the corporation can find the indenture very restricting. For example, if the corporation earns no profit in a given year, it does not have to pay any dividends on preferred or common stock. However, even in loss years, the bond interest still must be paid on outstanding bonds payable.

A second disadvantage of bond financing over preferred or common stock financing involves the maturity date of the bonds. Preferred and common stock have no maturity date; that is, when these stocks are issued to the public, the public never expects to be paid off by the corporation. If a holder of preferred or common stock decides to sell the stock, he or she sells it in the secondary markets. Such a sale has very little effect on the corporation itself. Bonds, on the other hand, always have a maturity date, thus forcing the firm to plan ahead to accumulate the funds necessary to pay the bond issue off at some future date, or sell another bond issue to pay off the maturing bonds.

A third disadvantage of bond financing concerns the fact that the interest represents a fixed charge. That is, when a bond is issued, both the corporation and the bondholder know exactly the rate that must be paid on the bond until maturity. The same fixed rate is paid on the bonds in good and bad economic times, regardless of the company's profitability. If a bond is issued when the rates are high, the company has to pay those high rates or pay the bond off before its maturity date, which is called *retiring* the bond.

Advantages of Bond Financing

The fixed rates just mentioned as a disadvantage could also be considered an advantage of bond financing. If market rates of interest go up after a company has issued bonds at a low interest rate, the company continues to pay the lower contractual rate.

In addition, since bondholders are paid interest before preferred or common stockholders are paid dividends, bondholders take less risk. As a result, due to the risk/return trade-off pervasive in the financial markets, we expect bonds to yield a lower rate than preferred or common stock.

Exhibit 1   Tax Deductibility of Interest

	Bond Financing	Stock Financing
Earnings before Interest and Taxes	$4,000,000	$4,000,000
Interest	200,000	–0–
Earnings before Tax	3,800,000	4,000,000
Tax (30%)	1,140,000	1,200,000
Net Income after Tax	2,660,000	2,800,000
Dividends	–0–	200,000
Net Income after Tax and Dividends	$2,660,000	$2,600,000

A third advantage of bond financing is that bondholders have no control over the activities of the corporation, unlike common stockholders. As long as the interest is paid on the bonds and the provisions of the indenture are complied with, bondholders have no say in the operation of the business. In contrast, common stockholders can attend a company's annual stockholders' meeting and vote on the board of directors as well as other major issues involving the corporation.

The last major advantage of bond financing is the tax advantage. Stockholders receive dividends on their investments, whereas bondholders receive interest on their investments. The corporation cannot deduct dividends, whether on preferred stock or common stock, for tax purposes. Instead, corporations must pay dividends out of after-tax earnings. However, bond interest, like all other legitimate expenses, serves to reduce the corporation's taxable income. This tax advantage of bond financing is shown in Exhibit 1.

Classifying Bonds

Bond issues can be classified according to the procedure used to pay them off. **Term bonds** are bonds that will be paid off in one lump sum at some future date. Companies must accumulate the large sum of money needed for this payoff, and usually do so through an arrangement called a *sinking fund*. (Sinking funds will be discussed later in this chapter.)

A bond issue can also be paid off through equal installments over its life. This type of bond is called a **serial bond**. The bonds that are to be paid off each year are usually determined through a random selection process. For example, if a bond issue had a 10-year life, 10 percent of the bonds would be randomly selected for retirement each year. With a serial bond, the portion of the long-term bond that comes due within one year or less should be reclassified from the Long-Term Liabilities section to the Current Liabilities section of the balance sheet.

Bonds can also be classified according to the collateral behind the bonds. Secured bonds, sometimes called **mortgage bonds**, are bonds that have some *specific* collateral behind them. For example, a company might issue a mortgage bond with the company's building pledged as specific collateral should the company

Who We Are

About The Bond Market Association

THE BOND MARKET ASSOCIATION

Who We Are
What We Do
Membership
Board of
Directors
Committees
Staff

Policy
Issues
& Advocacy
Legislative
Issues
Legal &
Regulatory
Issues
Market
Practices,
Guidelines
and
Procedures

News
Washington
Update

Who We Are The Bond Market Association, represents securities firms and banks that underwrite, trade and sell debt securities, both domestically and internationally. These debt securities include: Municipal bonds; U.S. Treasury securities; Federal Agency securities; Mortgage and other asset-backed securities, Corporate Debt securities; Money Market instruments; and Repos. Membership is open to any bona fide dealer in bonds and other debt securities, as long as the firm (and its parent, where relevant) agrees to support the Association's objectives. These include endorsement of the goal of "open and free access to the public securities markets throughout the world," with participation of multinational financial institutions not restricted by narrow questions of nationality. At least 20% of its member firms are substantially owned by foreign institutions.

Mission The Bond Market Association speaks for the bond industry and advocates its positions. In New York, Washington, D.C., London and Tokyo, and with issuer and investor groups nationwide, the Association represents its members' interests. It keeps members informed of relevant legislative, regulatory and market practice developments and provides a forum through which the industry can review and respond to current issues. The Association also strives to standardize market practices and commonly used documentation, both to promote efficiency and to reduce costs. It helps members solve common problems and develop more efficient management, operations and communications methods, thereby benefiting not only the industry but the investing and taxpaying public as well. The Association educates legislators, regulators, the press and investors on the size and importance of the bond markets. It publishes books, brochures, manuals and other educational materials, and sponsors seminars, conferences and informational meetings on topics of current interest. The Association also compiles and tracks various industry-related statistics on an historical basis and disseminates the information through published research reports. These combined efforts increase the level of professionalism in the industry and raise public awareness of the role of the markets served by the Association.

The Bond Market Association's Internet site (at http://www.bondmarkets.com) can help readers keep up-to-date on bond financing in hospitality and other industries. (Courtesy of The Bond Market Association)

default on the bond. Bonds that have no specific collateral behind them are called **debenture bonds**. It is important to note that debenture bonds, although they do not have any specific collateral pledged as security, are secured by the company's assets in general. If a company were to go out of business, the mortgage bondholders would seize the asset pledged as specific collateral on that bond and collect those funds gained from the sale of the seized asset. Next, the debenture bondholders and other unsecured creditors would be paid off from the sale of the rest of the assets. Only after all of the secured and unsecured creditors were paid would the stockholders receive some type of liquidating dividend.

Bonds may be classified according to the procedure used to pay interest on them. In the case of **registered bonds**, the bondholders' names are recorded with the corporation or its transfer agent. The transfer agent is usually a bank chosen by the corporation to facilitate the actual payment of the interest for the corporation. When interest payment dates arrive, interest checks are mailed to the registered bondholders.

Coupon bonds, sometimes called *bearer bonds,* are not registered with the corporation that issued them or with its trustee. When an interest payment date for a coupon bond arrives, the bondholder merely detaches a coupon from the bond and presents it at a bank for payment. The bank then forwards the coupon to the corporation's bank for reimbursement for the interest. Most bonds today are registered bonds rather than coupon bonds. Currently, all municipal bonds must be registered bonds; they cannot be coupon bonds.

Other Features of Bonds

Sometimes bond issues are convertible. Convertible bonds can be exchanged at the will of the holder for shares of the corporation's common stock. (Convertible bonds and the entries involving them will be discussed later in this chapter.)

Some bonds also have a call feature. **Callable bonds** can be paid off before maturity at the company's option. Companies issuing callable bonds usually provide some call protection to the bondholders. Call protection ensures that the company issuing the bonds contractually agrees not to call the bonds until a certain number of years have passed after the issuance date. When the bonds are called, the bondholder typically receives a premium on the call date. The premium is a dollar amount above the face value of the bond; it compensates the bondholders for having to reinvest their funds.

Journal Entries for Issuance of Bonds

We will begin our discussion of the issuance of bonds with a very simple example of bonds issued at their face value. Assume that on January 2, 200X, the Alpine Hotel issued $500,000 worth of 8 percent, 10-year bonds, with interest payable on July 2 and January 2. The entry to record this sale follows:

Cash	$500,000	
Bonds Payable		$500,000

The next relevant date involving these bonds would be the first semiannual interest date, July 2. At that time, the company would pay one-half of the annual interest on the bonds and make the following journal entry:

Interest Expense	$20,000	
Cash		$20,000

The interest is calculated using the formula Interest = Principal × Rate × Time. In this example, the formula results in interest of $20,000:

$$
\begin{aligned}
\text{Interest} &= \text{Principal} \times \text{Rate} \times \text{Time} \\
&= \$500{,}000 \times .08 \times \tfrac{1}{2} \\
&= \$20{,}000
\end{aligned}
$$

This same entry would be made every six months over the life of the bond. Following the bond over the rest of its life, the last entry would be for the retirement of the bonds at maturity. This entry, which would be written on January 2, 201X, follows:

Bonds Payable	$500,000	
Cash		$500,000

Bonds Sold between Interest Payment Dates

The entry for the issuance of bonds is complicated when the bond issue is sold between interest payment dates. Issuers of bonds traditionally pay the full amount of interest on each semiannual payment date regardless of how long the bond is held. For example, if the bond in the previous example were dated January 2 and not sold until April 1, the company would still pay the full six months' interest on the first payment date. The firm would, however, require the purchaser of the bond on April 1 to pay the first three months' interest—that is, the interest from January 2 to April 1—in addition to the face value of the bond.

Again, assume that the Alpine Hotel issued $500,000 worth of 8 percent, 10-year bonds. Based on this information and the fact that the bonds were sold on April 1, the journal entry on April 1 for the sale of the bonds would be as follows:

Cash	$510,000	
Bond Interest Payable		$ 10,000
Bonds Payable		500,000

The liability Bond Interest Payable credited in this entry would be listed in the Current Liabilities section of the balance sheet.

The next relevant date for this bond issue would be the first semiannual interest payment date, July 2. On this date, the following entry would be made:

Bond Interest Expense	$10,000	
Bond Interest Payable	10,000	
Cash		$20,000

This entry eliminates the liability of $10,000 that was set up on the date the bonds were sold and records the interest expense of $10,000 for the period of April, May, and June.

Market Value versus Face Value

Until this point in the chapter, we have assumed that bonds have sold at their face value, but in reality, this is not usually the case. Bonds usually sell at a price above or below their face value, resulting in an associated premium or discount. When a firm decides to sell a bond issue in the financial markets, the firm must make a decision regarding the rate investors expect to earn on the bond, based on current and future interest rates. Remember, no matter what the $1,000, 8 percent bond sells for, the holder will receive $80 per year (8% of $1,000) in interest. If potential investors think that the 8 percent coupon rate (sometimes called the *stated rate*) is too low, the price of the bond will fall in order to raise the market rate of interest on the bond, resulting in the sale of the bond at a discount from face value. On the other hand, if investors believe the 8 percent bond is a good buy, they will bid its market price up, resulting in the sale of the bond at a premium over stated value. As you can see, bond prices and bond yields are inversely related. The higher the market price of a bond, the lower the yield, and the lower the market price of a bond, the higher the yield.

Bonds Issued at a Discount

Assume that the bond issue in the previous example sold for $450,000 on January 2 instead of the face value of $500,000. The journal entry to record the sale of this bond follows:

Cash	$450,000	
Discount on Bonds Payable	50,000	
Bonds Payable		$500,000

Bonds Payable is always credited for the face value of the bond issue regardless of the selling price. The Discount on Bonds Payable account is a contra-liability account that carries a debit balance and is offset against Bonds Payable on the balance sheet, as shown here:

Bonds Payable	$500,000	
Less: Discount on Bonds Payable	50,000	$450,000

Although the bond was sold for $450,000, the bondholders expect to receive not $450,000 but rather the face value of $500,000 on the maturity date ten years later. The difference between the selling price and the face value represents additional interest expense to the firm. Rather than calling the $50,000 difference additional interest in the year the bond matures, the matching principal dictates that the $50,000 difference be spread over the life of the bond.

    In the case of this discounted bond, on July 2, the first semiannual interest payment date, the following two entries would be made:

Bond Interest Expense	$20,000	
Cash		$20,000

Bond Interest Expense	$2,500	
Discount on Bonds Payable		$2,500

The $2,500 amortization of the discount is $\frac{1}{20}$ of the total of $50,000, determined as follows:

$50,000 ÷ 20 six-month periods over bond's life = $2,500

The first entry records the cash interest paid; the second entry records the semi-annual amortization of the discount. Traditionally, these two entries are combined into one entry:

Bond Interest Expense	$22,500	
Cash		$20,000
Discount on Bonds Payable		2,500

Bonds Issued at a Premium

Assume that the bonds issued by the Alpine Hotel were sold at a price of $540,000 rather than the face value of $500,000 on January 2. In this case, the journal entry to record the sale of the bonds would be as follows:

Cash	$540,000	
Bonds Payable		$500,000
Premium on Bonds Payable		40,000

The Premium on Bonds Payable account will carry a credit balance and will be added to the amount of the Bonds Payable Account on the balance sheet:

Bonds Payable	$500,000	
Premium on Bonds Payable	40,000	$540,000

Since this bond sold at a premium, the bondholders are paying $540,000 for the bond and at maturity will receive only the face value of $500,000. In this case, the difference of $40,000 should be considered a reduction of interest. Again, rather than being recorded as an offset against revenue in one year, the premium should be amortized over the life of the bond. On July 2, the first interest payment date, the following two entries should be made:

Bond Interest Expense	$20,000	
Cash		$20,000

Premium on Bonds Payable	$2,000	
Bond Interest Expense		$2,000

These two entries could be combined into a compound entry:

Bond Interest Expense	$18,000	
Premium on Bonds Payable	2,000	
Cash		$20,000

Year-End Adjusting Entries for Bonds Payable

Now we will examine the adjusting entry necessary at year-end that results from having a bond issue outstanding. Assume, once again, the same facts concerning the bond selling at a discount. Also assume that the firm's fiscal year ends on September 30. The adjusting entry at September 30 in the first year the bond was issued would be as follows:

Bond Interest Expense	$11,250	
Interest Payable		$10,000
Discount on Bonds Payable		1,250

The $1,250 amortization of the bond discount represents three months' interest (July, August, and September), calculated as follows:

$$\$50,000 \text{ total discount to be amortized}$$
$$(\text{over the 120 months of the bond's life}) \times \tfrac{3}{120} = \$1,250$$

This compound entry combines the following two entries:

Bond Interest Expense	$10,000	
Bond Interest Payable		$10,000

Bond Interest Expense	$1,250	
Discount on Bonds Payable		$1,250

In the case of the preceding bond that sold at a premium, the journal entry at year-end (on September 30) would be a little different. The year-end adjusting entry would be:

Bond Interest Expense	$9,000	
Premium on Bonds Payable	1,000	
Bond Interest Payable		$10,000

This compound entry combines the following two entries:

Bond Interest Expense	$10,000	
Bond Interest Payable		$10,000

Premium on Bonds Payable	$1,000	
Bond Interest Expense		$1,000

Effective Interest Rate Method of Bond Amortization

Until this point, we have amortized the premium or discount on the bond issue by using the straight-line method of amortization. The straight-line method can create confusion among investors, since the annual percentage return would appear to vary over the life of the bond. Recall that bonds pay a fixed return, yet the carrying value is obviously changing over its life, increasing when a bond sells at a discount and decreasing when a bond sells at a premium. Bondholders who expect to receive a fixed return when buying a bond can sometimes be confused by this changing annual effective interest rate.

To avoid this theoretical shortcoming of the straight-line method of amortization, another method can be used instead. It is called the *effective interest rate method*. It is more complicated and will not be discussed in detail. We will state, however, that the effective interest rate method results in the amortization of the discount or premium in a manner that makes the annual yield on the bond the same rate every year over its life.

Bond Sinking Fund

If a bond issue is to be paid off in a lump sum, companies issuing those bonds will usually make annual cash payments into a **bond sinking fund** in order to accumulate the amount due at maturity. Any income from a bond sinking fund is recorded as Other Revenue on the income statement. The fund of cash that is accumulating to pay off the bond is included under the Long-Term Investments category on the balance sheet.

Convertible Bonds

Corporations may issue bonds that can be converted into the company's common stock. Since many investors consider **convertible bonds** more attractive than non-convertible bonds, the issuing corporation can usually sell them at lower rates. While convertible bonds are outstanding, they are like regular bonds in that the holders are paid semiannual interest at a fixed rate. However, the bonds may be converted into the company's common stock when the common stock reaches a certain dollar price. The number of shares the bonds are convertible into is determined through use of the **conversion ratio**.

For example, a $1,000 bond may be converted into 20 shares of the company's common stock when the common stock reaches a price of $50 per share. The $50 stock price in this example is referred to as the **conversion parity price** of the bond. The convertible bond is good for the company due to the lower interest rate, but it is also good for the bondholder. The convertible bondholder has the best of both worlds in enjoying the security of a fixed investment and also the upside potential of the company's common stock. The upside potential results from the fact that since the bond is convertible into stock in a fixed ratio, as the stock goes up in price, the bond also increases in value. For example, if the company's stock goes from $50 to $70 per share, the bond, being convertible into 20 shares of stock, should sell for $1,400 (20 shares × $70/share).

Assume that the Merriway Hotel Corporation has an $800,000 convertible bond issue outstanding. Assume also that the conversion ratio is 20 shares per $1,000 bond, and that the conversion parity price of the common stock is $50 per share for the $5 par value stock. The journal entry to record the entire conversion of this bond issue into common stock would be as follows:

Convertible Bonds Payable	$800,000	
Common Stock		$ 80,000
Additional Paid-In Capital		720,000

The $800,000 debited to Convertible Bonds Payable represents 800 $1,000 bonds. 800 × 20 shares = 16,000 shares; 16,000 shares × $5 par value = $80,000 credited to the Common Stock account. Additional Paid-In Capital is credited for the difference between $800,000 and $80,000.

Retirement of Bonds

A corporation with a bond issue outstanding may decide to **retire** it (that is, pay it off before maturity). This is usually accomplished by purchasing the bonds in the open market. The retirement of the bond issue may result in a gain or loss to the corporation depending on the price paid for the bonds. The gain or loss on retirement is the difference between the purchase price of the bond at its current market value and the carrying value of the bond on the retirement date. If the gain or loss on the bond is material, it should be reported on the income statement as an extraordinary item.

Assume that the Deli-Delite Corporation retired a $1,000,000 bond issue with an unamortized discount of $40,000 by purchasing it for $990 per bond. The journal entry to record the retirement would be:

Bonds Payable	$1,000,000	
Loss on Retirement of Bonds	30,000	
Discount on Bonds Payable		$ 40,000
Cash		990,000

The credit to Cash is for the amount paid for the bond. The credit to Discount on Bonds Payable is the amount of the unamortized discount at the retirement date. The debit to Bonds Payable is for the face value of the bonds. The Loss on Retirement of Bonds is determined by computing the difference between the carrying value of the bond and the purchase price of the bond. The loss of $30,000 would be determined by subtracting the book value of the bond issue of $960,000 ($1,000,000 less the unamortized discount of $40,000) from the $990,000 purchase price of the bond issue.

Leases

The topic of leases is presented in this chapter because certain leases result in long-term liabilities. The two basic types of leases are operating leases and capital leases.

You are probably familiar with operating leases, since leases covering the rental of a telephone, an apartment, or a dorm room are operating leases. Under an **operating lease**, the **lessor** (owner) allows the **lessee** to use the asset in exchange for a fixed periodic rental payment; there is no intent on the lessor's part to sell the asset to the lessee. The journal entry for this type of lease is very simple, as this illustration for the rental payment of $1,000 indicates:

Rental Expense $1,000	
Cash	$1,000

Operating leases are sometimes referred to as *off balance sheet financing,* since the company leasing the asset (the lessee) has all of the uses of the asset yet does not have to put the liability of future payments on its books.

The **capital lease** results in a closer relationship between the lessor and the lessee. The Financial Accounting Standards Board (FASB) has set four criteria for determining whether a lease is a capital lease. If any—not all—of these criteria are met, the lease must be treated as a capital lease:

1. The lease provides for the transferability of ownership to the lessee at some point during the life of the lease.

2. There is a bargain purchase option in the lease. This means that the purchase price at the end of the lease period is substantially less than the leased property's expected market value at the date the option is to be exercised. The bargain price is generally considered substantially less than the market value only if the difference, for all practical purposes, ensures that the bargain purchase option will be exercised.

3. The life of the lease is greater than 75 percent of the economic life of the asset. The term *economic life* refers to the useful life of the leased property.

4. The present value of the minimum lease payments equals 90 percent or more of the property's market value.

If a lease were determined to be a capital lease, such as when equipment worth $50,000 was leased, the following journal entry would be made:

Leased Equipment	$50,000	
Obligations under Capital Lease		$50,000

In this case, Leased Equipment would appear as a long-term asset under Property and Equipment on the balance sheet, and Lease Liability would appear under Long-Term Liabilities on the balance sheet.

Pensions

Accounting for pensions can be very complex, usually requiring the services of an **actuary**. Pensions are typically covered in great detail in intermediate accounting texts. Only a limited discussion of pensions will be presented in this chapter since pensions result in large long-term liabilities for corporations. There are basically two types of pensions: defined contribution pensions and defined benefit pensions.

In the case of **defined contribution pensions**, employers or employees contribute fixed amounts per year into the pension fund. The benefits that individuals receive from the pension are based on the pension's accumulated amount at some future date. The entry to record payment into a pension involves a debit to Pension Fund and a credit to Cash.

The **defined benefit pension** is more complex. In this case, the amount of the benefit is based on some future amount. For example, this future amount may be 75 percent of the average of an employee's salary during the last three years of employment. In this type of pension, each year an evaluation must be made of the accumulated benefits versus the accumulated obligations. This analysis results every year in either a long-term asset or a long-term liability on the corporation's books.

Mortgages Payable

A *mortgage* is another long-term liability. Home mortgages are similar to mortgages on commercial buildings. A fixed monthly payment is made, part of which is interest on the outstanding balance of the mortgage. The rest of the payment reduces the principal on the mortgage.

Let's assume that a building was purchased for $100,000 with a 30-year, 9 percent mortgage, and that the company buying the building agrees to make a monthly payment of $900. The principal, the interest, and the ending balance on the mortgage for the first two months are shown in the following table:

Month	Beginning Balance	Total Payment	Interest	Principal	Ending Balance
1st	$100,000	$900	$750	$150	$99,850
2nd	99,850	900	749	151	99,699

The $750 interest for the first month is determined by multiplying $100,000 by 9 percent and dividing by 12 months. The $900 total payment less the $750 interest equals the principal amount of $150, which reduces the mortgage to $99,850. The journal entry to record the first payment on this mortgage is:

Mortgage Payable	$150	
Interest Expense	750	
Cash		$900

This example involves a fixed monthly payment with increasing amounts applied to the principal over the life of the mortgage. There are instances in which a fixed amount of principal is applied to a mortgage every month, thus varying the payment. This, however, is less common. Mortgage interest is included on the income statement and is closed to the Income Summary account at the end of the fiscal period. The **Mortgage Payable** liability is listed in the Long-Term Liabilities section of the balance sheet except for the portion due within a year. That portion is listed as a current liability.

Summary

Bonds payable represent a long-term liability for a hospitality firm. Bondholders are creditors of the firm, not owners. The following are some disadvantages of issuing bonds to raise capital:

- The bond's contractual provisions can be very restrictive to the corporation.

- Bonds eventually mature and must be paid off, whereas stock does not.

- Interest rates on bonds are fixed and must be paid until the bond issue is retired, even if interest rates in the broader market fall.

Some advantages of issuing bonds follow:

- Those same fixed interest rates may be a good deal for the firm in times of increasing interest rates.

- Since bonds usually represent a lesser degree of risk to the bondholder than common stock, bonds can offer a lower rate of return to the investor and hence a lower cost to the firm.

- Bond interest is paid out of pretax earnings and therefore is not taxed.

Bond issues can be classified according to the procedure used to pay them off. They can be term bonds, which require the firm to establish a bond sinking fund to enable it to pay off the bond issue on the designated date, or serial bonds, which are paid off in installments. Bonds can also be classified by the type of collateral behind them. Secured bonds have specific assets pledged as collateral. Debenture bonds have no specific collateral pledged, but rather have the general assets of the firm pledged as collateral. Bonds can also be classified as registered bonds, coupon bonds, convertible bonds, or callable bonds.

This chapter also discusses the accounting procedures required for the issuance of bonds, the sale of bonds between interest payment dates, determining the market value and the face value of bonds, the issuance of bonds at a discount and at a premium, year-end adjusting entries for bonds payable, the effective interest rate method of bond amortization, and, finally, the retirement of bonds.

Also discussed are operating leases, capital leases, pensions, and mortgages.

Key Terms

actuary—Someone who calculates insurance and annuity premiums, reserves, and dividends.

bond indenture—Written agreement that details the contractual provisions of a bond.

bond sinking fund—A fund established by a company in which it will accumulate annual cash payments toward the amount it must pay in a lump sum at the maturity of a bond issue. Any income from a bond sinking fund is recorded as Other Revenue on the income statement. The fund is included under the Long-Term Investments category on the balance sheet.

callable bond—A bond that, at the company's option, can be paid off before maturity. Companies issuing callable bonds will usually provide some call protection to the bondholders. This means that the company contractually agrees not to call the bonds until a certain number of years have passed after the issuance date and agrees to pay the bondholder a premium on the call date.

capital lease—A classification of lease agreements that are of relatively long duration and are generally noncancelable and in which the lessee assumes responsibility for executory costs. For accounting purposes, capital leases are capitalized in a way similar to that for the purchase of a fixed asset (i.e., recorded as an asset with recognition of a liability).

conversion parity price—The per-share common stock price at which a convertible bond can be converted into shares of the company's common stock; calculated by dividing the value of one bond by the number of shares into which the bond may be converted. A $1,000 bond that could be converted into 20 shares of the company's common stock would have a conversion parity price of $50.

conversion ratio—A ratio that determines the number of shares of common stock into which a convertible bond can be converted. For example, a $1,000 bond may be converted into 20 shares of common stock when the common stock reaches a price of $50 per share.

convertible bond—A bond that can be exchanged at the option of the holder for shares of the corporation's common stock once the common stock reaches a certain price.

coupon bond—A bond with a coupon attached that the holder detaches and presents for payment when the interest payment date arrives. Also called a *bearer bond.*

debenture bond—A bond backed by the general credit of the issuer rather than a specific lien on particular assets.

defined benefit pension—A pension plan wherein the amount of the benefit is based on some future amount. For example, the amount could be 75 percent of the average of an employee's salary during the last three years of employment.

defined contribution pension—A pension plan wherein the employers or employees contribute fixed amounts per year to the pension fund. The benefits that individuals receive from the pension are based on the accumulated amount of the pension at some future date.

lessee—The person or company that makes periodic cash payments called *rent* to a lessor in exchange for the right to use the property.

lessor—The person or company that leases property or equipment to the lessee in exchange for a fixed periodic rental payment.

mortgage bonds—Secured bonds that have some specific collateral behind them.

mortgage payable—A liability listed in the Long-Term Liabilities section of the balance sheet except for the portion due within a year, which is listed as a current liability.

operating lease—A lease similar to a rental agreement without any appearance of present or future ownership of the leased property by the lessee.

registered bond—A bond for which the bondholders' names are recorded with the corporation or its transfer agent.

retire—To retire a bond is to pay it off before its maturity date.

serial bond—A bond issue paid off through equal installments over its life.

term bond—A bond that is to be paid off in one lump sum at some future date.

underwriting firm—A firm, or a syndicate of several firms, that buys an entire bond issue from the corporation issuing the bonds; the underwriting firm buys these for resale to the public.

Review Questions

1. How does a capital lease differ from an operating lease? What are the four FASB criteria for a capital lease?

2. What is the *conversion ratio* of a bond? What is the *conversion parity price?*

3. What are the major advantages and disadvantages of bond financing?

4. What is the difference between a registered bond and a coupon bond? How does a term bond differ from a serial bond?

5. What is the difference between the stated rate on a bond and the effective rate?

6. If a bond sells at a discount, is the stated rate greater than or less than the effective rate?

7. How is the gain or loss on the retirement of a bond calculated?

8. What is the nature of a bond sinking fund? Where is it listed on the balance sheet?

9. What is the difference between a defined benefit pension plan and a defined contribution plan?

10. How does a debenture bond differ from a mortgage bond? What is a *bond indenture?* What is the role of the underwriter in bond financing?

Problems

Problem 1

Record the following journal entries involving the bond transactions for Timber Ridge Hotels:

1. On July 1, 2001, sold $800,000, 8 percent, bonds dated June 1, 2001, at face value.
2. Paid semiannual interest on November 30, 2001.
3. Paid off bond issue on May 31, 2011.

Problem 2

Slide Inns owes $187,000 on a 10 percent long-term mortgage dated April 1, 20X1, which requires a total monthly payment of $1,800.

Required:

Journalize the entry necessary for the May 1, 20X1, monthly payment.

Problem 3

Provide an explanation for all the numbers below for the bond of the Showboat Company:

Bond	Current Yield	Vol	Close	Net Change
Showboat $9\frac{1}{4}$ 08	8.7	15	105 $\frac{3}{4}$	$-\frac{1}{4}$

Problem 4

On April 1, 20X1, American Clubs, Inc., sells a 12 percent bond issue of $700,000 dated March 1, 20X1 at face value.

Required:

1. Journalize the entry necessary on the date of the sale.
2. Record the entry for the payment of semiannual interest on September 1, 20X1.

Problem 5

Hightower Hotels is retiring a bond issue that has a face value of $1 million and a carrying value of $1,050,000. The bonds will be retired at a price of $1,060 per bond.

Required:

Journalize the entry necessary for the retirement of the bond.

Problem 6

North Peaks, Inc., is entering into a lease on June 15, 20X1, for snow-making machines that have a market value of $150,000. The lease payment will be $2,000 per month with the first payment due on July 15, 20X1.

Required:

1. Record the journal entry necessary on June 15, 20X1, if the lease contains a bargain purchase option.
2. Record the journal entry necessary on July 15, 20X1, if the lease is an operating lease.

Challenge Problems

Problem 7

Resort Hotels, Inc., is starting operations by raising $30 million. Earnings before Interest and Taxes are expected to be $20 million this year. The company has a 30 percent tax rate.

Required:

Calculate Earnings after Tax and Dividends under each of the following two financing options:

1. Bond financing: $20 million at 7 percent interest
2. Stock financing: $20 million with 8 percent annual dividend

Problem 8

On October 1, 20X1, Mayfair Hotels, Inc., issued 10-year, 10 percent debenture bonds with $50 million in total face value and with interest payable on April 1 and October 1. The company's year-end is December 31.

Required:

1. Construct the necessary entries for December 31, 20X1, and the journal entry to record payment of bond interest on April 1, 20X2, under each of the following assumptions:

    a. The bonds were issued at 97.
    b. The bonds were issued at 103.

2. What is the carrying value of the bonds at December 31, 20X1, under each of the previous two assumptions?

Problem 9

Apex Resorts Corporation has $500,000 of 9.5 percent convertible bonds outstanding that are convertible into 40 shares of the company's common stock. The bonds currently have an unamortized discount of $20,000. The par value of the company's stock is $10 per share.

Required:

Record the entry necessary for the conversion of half of the bond issue.

Problem 10

Garden Restaurant Corporation issued $12 million of 7 percent, 10-year bonds on April 1, 20X8. The bonds were dated March 1, 20X8, and were sold for $960 apiece. The semiannual interest payment dates are March 1 and September 1.

Required:

1. Journalize the following entries:

   a. Sale of bonds on April 1, 20X8.
   b. Payment of interest and amortization of discount on September 1, 20X8.
   c. Accrual of interest and amortization of discount on December 31, 20X8.
   d. Payment of interest and amortization of discount on March 1, 20X9.
2. Show how the bond would appear on the balance sheet on December 31, 20X8.

REVIEW QUIZ

When you feel you have covered all of the material in this chapter, answer these questions. Choose the *best* answer.

1. Which of the following types of bonds has no specific collateral behind it?

    a. coupon bond
    b. debenture bond
    c. registered bond
    d. mortgage bond

2. A *term bond* is best described as:

    a. an agreement that allows someone to use an asset with no understanding that the user will eventually buy the asset.
    b. the collateral a firm uses to back registered bonds.
    c. a bond that is to be paid off in one lump sum at some future date.
    d. a bond that has some specific collateral behind it.

3. The Echo Hotel issued $500,000 in 12 percent bonds on April 1. The interest payment dates are March 1 and October 1. The cash received from the sale of the bonds would most likely be for _____. (Assume that the market interest rate is 12 percent.)

    a. $440,000
    b. $500,000
    c. $505,000
    d. $560,000

4. The Gargantuan Hotel Corporation sells its 3,000 $1,000 bonds for $2,750,000. Recording this transaction would involve a _____ to Bonds Payable of _____.

    a. credit; $3,000,000
    b. debit; $3,000,000
    c. credit; $2,750,000
    d. debit; $2,750,000

5. A certain bond issue sold for $500,000 instead of its face value of $550,000. The 10-year bonds bear annual interest of 10 percent. The adjusting entry at the end of the first year after the sale of these bonds would involve a credit to Discount on Bonds Payable of:

    a. $1,250.
    b. $5,000.
    c. $2,500.
    d. $5,500.

REVIEW QUIZ *(continued)*

6. The $5 par value common stock of Unified Hotels, Inc., has attained a market value of $50, the conversion parity price for the 800 $1,000 convertible bonds it issued. The conversion ratio is 50 shares per $1,000 bond. The journal entry to record the entire conversion of this bond issue into common stock would credit _____ for $600,000.

    a. Convertible Bonds Payable
    b. Bond Interest Payable
    c. Common Stock
    d. Additional Paid-In Capital

7. A mortgage payable for the Illinois Inn is $1,000,000 at the beginning of the year. At the end of the year, a mortgage payment of $150,000 is to be paid. The annual interest rate on this loan is 10 percent. The reduction in the mortgage payable at the end of the year is:

    a. $0.
    b. $50,000.
    c. $100,000.
    d. $150,000.

Answer Key: 1-b-C1, 2-c-C1, 3-c-C2, 4-a-C3, 5-b-C4, 6-d-C5, 7-b-C6

Each question is linked to a competency. Competencies are listed on the first page of the chapter. An answer reading 3-b-C4 translates to:

  3: the question number
  b: the correct answer
C4: the competency number

Chapter 16 Outline

Accounting for Investments
    Investments in Debt Securities
    Short-Term Equity Investments
    Long-Term Equity Investments
Valuation of Investments
    Held-to-Maturity Securities
    Trading Securities
    Available-for-Sale Securities

Competencies

1. Explain and demonstrate how to account for investments in debt securities (bonds).

2. Explain and demonstrate how to account for investments in equity securities (stocks).

3. Explain and demonstrate the cost, equity, and consolidated statement methods of accounting for investments.

4. Explain and demonstrate the approach to valuation of investments that is recommended by Financial Accounting Standards Board Statement 115.

Investments in Corporate Securities

ACCORDING TO the *Uniform System of Accounts for the Lodging Industry (USALI)*, Ninth Revised Edition, there are two types of investments in securities: short-term and long-term. Short-term investments are readily marketable and are intended to be converted into cash within a year. Long-term investments in corporate securities are those held for more than one year and are included in the Investments category on the balance sheet. The Investments category includes three types of investments:

1. Cash advances to affiliated companies

2. Investments in property or equipment that is not currently used in the business or land held for speculation

3. Equity and debt investments (stocks and bonds) purchased by the company that are not short-term in nature

Accounting for the first two items is simple. The assets are recorded at cost and taken off the books or reclassified when necessary. Accounting for the third item—equity and debt securities—is complex. This chapter discusses equity and debt investments.

Accounting for Investments

Hospitality firms invest in the securities of other companies for one of two reasons:

1. To earn a good return on excess cash held for the short term

2. To exercise influence or control

If the securities are purchased for the short term to obtain a favorable return on excess cash, they are *not* listed under Investments. Instead, a current asset account, Short-Term Investments, is debited for the purchase price. The investments must be immediately convertible at the market price of the securities to be included in the Short-Term Investments account. The method of accounting used for the current asset Short-Term Investments depends on whether a debt or equity security is involved.

Investments in Debt Securities

The accounting for short-term and long-term debt securities is basically the same. When a hospitality firm invests in bonds, it expects to receive interest semiannually on its investment. To understand the investment in **marketable debt securities**, assume that Balboa Hotels purchased bonds on August 1, 20X4, for 97 percent of par. The bonds have a total face value of $100,000 and pay installments of the annual 9 percent interest on May 1 and November 1. Balboa Hotels pays a brokerage commission of $500, plus accrued interest, at the time of purchase. Based on this information, the journal entry on August 1, 20X4, would be:

Debt Investments	$97,500	
Bond Interest Receivable	2,250	
Cash		$99,750

The $97,500 debit to Debt Investments is the cost of the bonds plus the commission. The $2,250 debit to Bond Interest Receivable represents the interest accrued on the bonds from May 1 to August 1 ($100,000 × 9% × $\frac{3}{12}$).

The next relevant entry would be on November 1, 20X4, to record the receipt of six months' worth of interest:

Cash	$4,500	
Bond Interest Receivable		$2,250
Bond Interest Income		2,250

Although the company receives a check for a full six months' worth of interest, recall that it paid for three months' interest in advance on August 1. At the end of the calendar year, another entry would be made to accrue the interest on the bonds. The entry on December 31, 20X4, would be as follows:

Bond Interest Receivable	$1,500	
Bond Interest Income		$1,500

Short-Term Equity Investments

Accounting for **short-term equity investments** (stocks) is simpler than accounting for short-term debt investments (bonds). Recall that investments in stocks yield dividends rather than interest. Dividends are typically paid quarterly. Companies that have investments in the stocks of other companies do not accrue the dividends. Instead, dividend income is recorded when received. The following is the entry for the receipt of $3,000 worth of dividends:

Cash	$3,000	
Dividend Income		$3,000

Realized Gains or Losses from the Sale of Short-Term Equity Investments.
When these securities are sold, the cost of the securities should be written off the
books and the gain or loss on the sale recognized. The gain or loss should be closed
into the Income Summary account at the end of the fiscal period. Assume that
Greatway Hotels sold its holdings in other companies' stocks that had cost $99,000
for $97,000, less a $500 commission. Thus, Greatway received $96,500 from the sale.
The journal entry would be recorded as follows:

Cash	$96,500	
Loss on Sale of Short-Term Investments	2,500	
Short-Term Investments		$99,000

The $2,500 loss is the difference between the net selling price of $96,500 and the
cost of $99,000.

Long-Term Equity Investments

The following section focuses on accounting for long-term equity investments.
The cost method, the equity method, and the consolidated statement method are
discussed.

When the investment in the stock of another company is less than 20 percent
of the investee's stock, the **cost method** is used to account for the investment.
Under the cost method, long-term investments are put on the books at cost, gains
or losses are recognized as of the sale date, and income is recorded when received.

Sometimes the purchaser (the **investor**) purchases such a large percentage of
stock that it can have significant influence or even control over the **investee**. When
significant influence or control exists, the methods used to account for these investments include the equity method and the consolidated statement method. The percentage of ownership determines which of the methods is used. If the company
owns 20 to 50 percent of the investee, the equity method is used. However, if the
investor owns more than 50 percent of the investee, the consolidated statement
approach is used.

The Equity Method. Under the **equity method of accounting for investments,**
the investor records the original investment at cost, then adjusts the value of the
investment over time. The investor increases the value of the investment as the
investee generates income and decreases the value of the investment if the investee loses money. When the investee pays the investor dividends, the value of the
investment decreases, and the investor records the decrease as dividends. For
example, assume that Harris buys 25 percent, or $50,000 worth, of Tweed stock on
November 1, 20X4. On December 31, Tweed reports income of $20,000, and
on January 6 pays a dividend of $10,000. The entries under the equity method are
as follows:

Nov. 1	Investment in Tweed	$50,000	
	Cash		$50,000

Dec. 31	Investment in Tweed	$5,000	
	Income from Investment		$5,000

Jan. 6	Cash	$2,500	
	Investment in Tweed		$2,500

Based on these entries, the value of the investment in Tweed on January 6 would be $52,500, as shown:

Original Investment	$50,000
Plus: Share of Investee's Income	+ 5,000
Less: Dividends Paid	− 2,500
Equals: Investment in Tweed	$52,500

Notice that under the equity method, when the dividends are paid to the investor, the value of the investment drops to reflect the fact that part of the investment has been converted into cash. The income from the investee is reported on the investor's income statement.

The Consolidated Statement Method. If one company owns more than 50 percent of a second company, the first company is said to control the second; the purchaser is called the **parent company** and the purchased company is called the **subsidiary company**. When this occurs, **consolidated financial statements** *normally* are prepared for the one entity. The word *normally* is emphasized because the Financial Accounting Standards Board (see http://www.rutgers.edu/Accounting/raw/fasb) has stated that when two dissimilar companies, such as a bank and a hotel, are in a parent-subsidiary relationship, it would not be useful to combine the statements.

Although the parent and the subsidiary keep separate books during the year, at year-end they report as one consolidated entity. When the parent and the subsidiary combine items for the consolidated balance sheet, they cannot simply add all items for the companies together. If they were to do so, some items, such as a parent's loan of money to its subsidiary, would be counted twice. Therefore, when a parent and subsidiary prepare consolidated financial statements, they must also prepare some intercompany **eliminating entries**. Consolidated financial statements can be very complex for some companies. (A detailed discussion of complex consolidated financial statements is presented in more advanced accounting texts.)

This chapter will discuss three simple examples:

1. The purchase of 100 percent of a subsidiary at book value

2. The purchase of 100 percent of a subsidiary at a price above book value

3. The purchase of less than 100 percent of a subsidiary at book value

Purchase of 100 percent of a subsidiary at book value. A worksheet for a consolidated balance sheet of a parent company, Parentis Hotel, and its subsidiary, Subside Motel, is shown in Exhibit 1. Notice the two eliminating entries marked (a) and

Exhibit 1 Worksheet for Consolidated Balance Sheet

Parentis Hotel and Subside Motel
Worksheet for Consolidated Balance Sheet
January 1, 20X4

	Parentis	Subside	Eliminating Entries Debit	Eliminating Entries Credit	Consolidated Balance Sheet
Cash	$ 10,000	$ 55,000			$ 65,000
Accounts Receivable	20,000	15,000			35,000
Notes Receivable	25,000	—		(a) $ 25,000	—
Inventory	50,000	40,000			90,000
Investment in Subsidiary	140,000	—		(b) 140,000	—
Property & Equipment	105,000	80,000			185,000
Totals	**$350,000**	**$190,000**			**$375,000**
Accounts Payable	$ 40,000	$ 25,000			$ 65,000
Notes Payable	—	25,000	(a) $ 25,000		—
Common Stock	245,000	100,000	(b) 100,000		245,000
Retained Earnings	65,000	40,000	(b) 40,000		65,000
Totals	**$350,000**	**$190,000**	**$165,000**	**$165,000**	**$375,000**

(b) on the worksheet. First, the parent company's Notes Receivable and the subsidiary company's Notes Payable are both eliminated with eliminating entry (a). The $25,000 in this case involves the parent's loan to the subsidiary. This transfer of dollars within the consolidated entity is merely that: a transfer of money within the entity itself. In a sense, the company owes the money to itself; consequently, to avoid double counting, both affected accounts are eliminated.

Eliminating entry (b) involves the Investment in Subsidiary account on the parent's books, which is eliminated against the subsidiary's equity. The Investment in Subsidiary account of $140,000 on the parent's books represents the subsidiary's entire equity. Since the subsidiary's equity or its net assets are represented by the asset account Investment in Subsidiary on the parent's books, double counting would occur if eliminating entries were not made. Note that these eliminating entries are made only on the worksheet and not on each individual company's books—a very important point. The last column of the consolidated worksheet (labeled "Consolidated Balance Sheet") shows the items used to compile the entity's formal consolidated balance sheet.

Purchase of 100 percent of a subsidiary at a price above book value. A parent company could buy a subsidiary for above or below book value. (The discussion of a purchase for an amount below book value is deferred to advanced accounting courses.) A purchase above book value is more likely than a purchase below book value. There are two reasons for this; the first reason involves undervaluation of assets. Because of the cost principle, the subsidiary's assets could have been put on the books at cost and, despite appreciation over the years, would remain on the

Exhibit 2   Worksheet for Consolidated Balance Sheet with Goodwill

Parentis Hotel and Subside Motel
Worksheet for Consolidated Balance Sheet

	Parentis	Subside	Eliminating Entries Debit	Eliminating Entries Credit	Consolidated Balance Sheet
Cash	$ 10,000	$ 55,000			$ 65,000
Accounts Receivable	20,000	15,000			35,000
Notes Receivable	25,000	—		(a) $ 25,000	—
Inventory	50,000	40,000			90,000
Investment in Subsidiary	165,000	—		(b) 165,000	—
Property & Equipment	105,000	80,000			185,000
Goodwill	–0–		(b) $ 25,000		25,000
Totals	$375,000	$190,000			$400,000
Accounts Payable	$ 40,000	$ 25,000			$ 65,000
Notes Payable	—	25,000	(a) 25,000		—
Common Stock	270,000	100,000	(b) 100,000		270,000
Retained Earnings	65,000	40,000	(b) 40,000		65,000
Totals	$375,000	$190,000	$190,000	$190,000	$400,000

books at cost. The second reason involves future excess earning power. If the parent company anticipates that the earnings of the subsidiary will be above normal for the industry, it might pay a premium above book value. If the parent company makes the purchase above book value because some of the subsidiary's assets were under-valued on the subsidiary's books, the entity will attempt to raise the value of these particular assets on the books of the consolidated entity.

If the parent purchases the subsidiary above book value because of the subsidiary's excess earning power, a new account called Goodwill should be put on the consolidated entity's books. If this occurred in the case of the Parentis and Subside companies, the consolidated balance sheet would be compiled as shown in Exhibit 2. In this instance, the parent paid $165,000 for the subsidiary's net assets, which have a book value of only $140,000.

Once again, the note receivable on the parent's books and the note payable on the subsidiary's books are eliminated. In addition, the subsidiary's equity is elimi-nated as well as the investment on the parent's books. In this case, $25,000 of Good-will is put on the consolidated entity's balance sheet.

Purchase of less than 100 percent of a subsidiary at book value. Now we con-sider a situation in which the parent purchases less than 100 percent of the subsid-iary's stock at a price equal to book value. This situation gives rise to a new item on the consolidated balance sheet called minority interest. This item represents the equity interest in the subsidiary that is not owned by the parent, or the portion of the subsidiary's net assets owned by outsiders other than the parent. Assuming that Parentis Company purchased 70 percent of Subside's net assets, the consolidated balance sheet would be compiled as shown in Exhibit 3.

Exhibit 3   Worksheet for Consolidated Balance Sheet with Minority Interest

Parentis Hotel and Subside Motel
Worksheet for Consolidated Balance Sheet

	Parentis	Subside	Eliminating Entries Debit	Eliminating Entries Credit	Consolidated Balance Sheet
Cash	$ 10,000	$ 55,000			$ 65,000
Accounts Receivable	20,000	15,000			35,000
Notes Receivable	25,000	—		(a) $ 25,000	—
Inventory	50,000	40,000			90,000
Investment in Subsidiary	98,000	—		(b) 98,000	—
Property & Equipment	105,000	80,000			185,000
Totals	$308,000	$190,000			$375,000
Accounts Payable	$ 40,000	$ 25,000			$ 65,000
Notes Payable	—	25,000	(a) $ 25,000		—
Common Stock	203,000	100,000	(b) 100,000		203,000
Retained Earnings	65,000	40,000	(b) 40,000		65,000
Minority Interest				(b) 42,000	42,000
Totals	$308,000	$190,000	$165,000	$165,000	$375,000

Eliminating entry (a), which eliminates Notes Receivable and Notes Payable in Exhibit 3, is the same as eliminating entry (a) in the consolidated worksheets shown in Exhibits 1 and 2. Eliminating entry (b) eliminates all of the subsidiary's equity and all of the investment that appears on the parent's books. In addition, eliminating entry (b) sets up the account Minority Interest. Note that the minority interest is in the amount of $42,000 and represents 30 percent of the subsidiary's equity, as shown here:

Common Stock of Subsidiary	$100,000
Retained Earnings of Subsidiary	+ 40,000
Total Equity of Subsidiary	140,000
Times 30%	× .30
Equals Minority Interest	$ 42,000

This chapter has focused on the balance sheet in its discussion of consolidated financial statements. Companies would, of course, have to compile consolidated income statements and other financial statements as well. Discussion of these consolidated statements is usually presented in advanced accounting courses.

Valuation of Investments

Both debt and equity investments can vary significantly over the time that they are held by an investor. Generally, the proper accounting treatment for these investments is to place them on the balance sheet at fair market value on a given balance sheet date.

Automating information for FASB Statement no. 115.

Taking Stock On The Internet

By *Terry J. Ward* and *Jon Woodroof*

Terry J. Ward, is an associate professor of accounting at Middle Tennessee State University in Murfreesboro, Tennessee. **Jon Woodroof**, CPA, PhD, is an assistant professor of accounting at the same university.

EXECUTIVE SUMMARY

- COMPANIES THAT MUST apply Financial Accounting Standards Board Statement no. 115, *Accounting for Certain Investments in Debt and Equity Securities,* can use the Internet and spreadsheet software to do the job most efficiently.
- AN INTERNET WEB PAGE offers, at no charge, up-to-the-minute prices of securities in customized portfolios. That information, when imported into a spreadsheet template, can generate the accounting information that complies with Statement no. 115.
- TWO WORKSHEET TEMPLATES are used: One is for the formulas and the other is a parsing sheet, into which you paste market information copied from the Internet.
- TO GET THE LATEST market information, tap into the Internet and go to http://www.imet.com/pages/login.htp. Users are allowed a maximum of 15 stocks and 15 mutual funds for each login name. Companies can track additional stocks and mutual funds simply by registering under different login/password combinations.
- THE INTERNET IS beginning to revolutionize the way organizations conduct business and the way accountants perform their professional work. CPAs should be prepared to take full advantage of the Internet—for both their own work and for both their clients and employers.

If your company or client is required to track the current market value of securities it owns, then you know what an irksome, time-consuming task that can be. But now, with the help of the Internet, the task can be accomplished almost automatically.

Under Financial Accounting Standards Board Statement no. 115, *Accounting for Certain Investments in Debt and Equity Securities,* businesses must account for the securities in their financial statements. Using two computer tools—the Internet and spreadsheet software—you can do the job with little more than a few mouse clicks.

Terry J. Ward and Jon Woodroof tout the use of the Internet for valuing investments in this January 1997 article from the *Journal of Accountancy Online* (vol. 183, no. 1; see http://www.aicpa.org/pubs/jofa/index.htm for more information). The parent site for this publication is that of the American Institute of Certified Public Accountants (http://www.aicpa.org), which has more resources for aspiring accounting professionals.

According to FASB's Statement 115, *Accounting for Certain Investments in Debt and Equity Securities,* these investments should be grouped into the following three categories:

1. Held-to-maturity securities

2. Trading securities

3. Available-for-sale securities

Held-to-Maturity Securities

Since equity securities have no maturity date, only debt securities fall into this category. These securities should be accounted for at amortized cost, not fair value. The valuation for **held-to-maturity securities** is complex and is generally discussed in intermediate accounting courses.

Trading Securities

Trading securities involve frequent purchase and sale. These securities are purchased with the intention of selling them in a short period of time, generally within three months of purchase. These securities are reported on the balance sheet at fair market value, with the difference between cost and fair market value reported as unrealized gain or loss and included in the income statement of the current year.

In order to illustrate these concepts, consider the trading security portfolio of the Fairview Hotel Company as of December 31, 20XX:

Investment	Cost	Fair Value	Unrealized Gain (Loss)
Agresso Stock	$ 12,000	$ 14,000	$ 2,000
Conservo Corp. Bonds	50,000	49,000	(1,000)
Reservo Corp. Stock	80,000	85,000	5,000
	$142,000	$148,000	$ 6,000

Both the unrealized gain and the increase in the value of the investment portfolio are recorded by the following entry:

Investment Securities Adjustment—Trading	$6,000	
Unrealized Gain on Securities—Income		$6,000

If the value of the portfolio had decreased over the accounting period, an unrealized-loss account would have been debited and the Investment Securities account would have been credited. Any unrealized gains or losses are closed to Income Summary and included on the income statement for the current period.

Available-for-Sale Securities

Available-for-sale securities are purchased with the intention of selling them sometime in the future. If the intent is to sell them within a year, they should be recorded as short-term investments. If the intent is to sell them over 12 months from the purchase date, they should be classified as long-term investments.

Assuming that the investments of the Golden Corporation below are long-term investments, they should be reported at fair market value. The procedure for determining the unrealized gain or loss is the same as that for the case of trading securities, but the journal entry differs. Assume that the Golden Corporation has the following available-for-sale securities at 6/30/XX:

Investment	Cost	Fair Value	Unrealized Gain (Loss)
Conservo Bonds	$ 60,000	$ 61,000	$ 1,000
Retracto Stock	40,000	38,000	(2,000)
	$100,000	$ 99,000	$(1,000)

The journal entry on 6/30/XX would be as follows:

Unrealized Loss—Equity	$1,000	
Investment Securities Adjustment—Available-for-Sale		$1,000

Since these securities are not expected to be sold soon, there is a good chance that there could be further unrealized gains or losses before their sale. Therefore, the unrealized gain or loss is not reported on the income statement but rather as a separate item on the Stockholders' Equity section of the balance sheet.

Summary

The asset account Investments includes cash advances to affiliated companies, property and equipment not currently used in the business, long-term debt, and equity investments. Not all debt and equity investments are put in this asset account. Short-term investments appear in their own Current Assets account, Short-Term Investments.

Three ways of accounting for long-term investments in equity securities are the cost method, the equity method, and the consolidated financial statements method. Under the cost method, investments are put on the books at cost, gains or losses are recognized when sold, and income is recorded when received. Under the equity method, investments are recorded at cost, and their value adjusted as earnings are reported by the subsidiary and dividends are paid.

If an investor owns more than 50 percent of a company, the investor is said to control the subsidiary and is called a *parent company*. In this case, the financial statements of the two entities are combined into a consolidated format.

Key Terms

available-for-sale securities—Debt and equity securities purchased with the intention of selling them sometime in the future. Available-for-sale securities are reported at fair value, with unrealized gains and losses excluded from the income statement's earnings and reported in a separate component of Stockholders' Equity on the balance sheet.

consolidated financial statements—The combined financial statements of a parent corporation and its subsidiary corporations. Parent companies must use the consolidated statement method to account for investments in subsidiaries.

cost method—A method of accounting for investments in which long-term investments are put on the books at cost, gains or losses are recognized as of the sale date, and income is recorded when received.

eliminating entries—Entries used in preparing consolidated financial statements for a parent-subsidiary entity to avoid double counting. For example, a parent's loan of money to its subsidiary would be "eliminated" from (not counted in) the consolidated financial statements, since in effect the entity owes money to itself.

equity method—A method of accounting for an investment in which the investor records the original investment at cost, then adjusts the value of the investment over time. A company owning more than 20 percent but less than 50 percent of the investee uses this method.

held-to-maturity securities—Debt securities that the enterprise has the positive intent and ability to hold to maturity. Held-to-maturity securities are reported at amortized cost.

investee—A company whose stock is purchased.

investor—A company or individual who buys stock in a company.

marketable debt securities—Bonds.

minority interest—The equity interest in a subsidiary that is not owned by the parent, or the portion of a subsidiary's net assets owned by outsiders other than the parent.

parent company—A company that owns greater than 50 percent of another company and is said to control that company.

short-term equity investments—Stocks intended to be converted to cash within one year.

subsidiary company—A company that has been purchased by a parent company, which owns greater than 50 percent of the subsidiary and controls it. See *parent company*.

trading securities—Debt and equity securities that are bought and held principally for the purpose of selling them in the near term (usually within three months of purchase). Trading securities are reported on the balance sheet at fair value, with unrealized gains and losses included in earnings on the income statement.

Review Questions

1. What determines whether an investment is classified in the Short-Term Investments account or the Investments account?

2. What percentage of a company's stock must be held before there is significant influence or control? What is the nature of the account Minority Interest on the books of a consolidated entity? Where does Minority Interest appear on a consolidated balance sheet?

3. Cash Advances to Affiliated Companies is an example of an item listed in the Investments category on the balance sheet. What are the other two items found in this category?

4. What are the common eliminating entries on the worksheet of a consolidated entity?

5. What are the differences between the cost method and the equity method of accounting for an investment?

6. When the parent pays more than the book value for a subsidiary, how is the difference between book value and purchase price recorded on the books of the consolidated entity?

7. When a hospitality firm purchases bonds of another firm with the intent of holding them for a long time, what accounts are involved in the purchase's journal entry if the bonds are bought between interest payment dates?

8. Based on the following information, what would be the eliminating entry on the worksheet of the consolidated entity? (Assume that the parent company bought the subsidiary because of the subsidiary's excess earning power.)

Subsidiary's common stock	$100,000
Retained earnings of subsidiary	50,000
Parent's investment	180,000

9. How are marketable equity securities valued at year-end?

10. Where do short-term and long-term investments appear on a company's balance sheet?

 **Problems** ————————————————————————————————

Problem 1

In the left column of the following table is a list of individual balance sheet items.

Required:

In the right column of the table, write the subclassification under which each of the individual balance sheet items would be found.

Balance Sheet Items	Balance Sheet Subclassifications
Minority Interest	
Marketable Securities	
Land Held for Future Use	
Goodwill	
Cash Advances to Affiliated Companies	
Allowance for Marketable Equity Securities	

Problem 2

Based on FASB 115, write a memo explaining the differences among held-to-maturity securities, trading securities, and available-for-sale securities.

Problem 3

The Brownstone Hotel had several marketable debt securities transactions in the month of May.

Required:

Make the relevant journal entries for the following transactions:

1. Brownstone purchased $100,000 worth of 9 percent bonds at 98 percent of par plus a $600 commission and accrued interest on May 1, 20X4. Interest payment dates are April 1 and October 1.
2. The hotel received a check for six months' interest on October 1, 20X4.
3. The hotel accrued interest income on December 31, 20X4.

Problem 4

Pleasuredine Restaurants, Inc., purchased 3,000 of the 10,000 shares of Telecom Company for $15 per share on November 6, 20X4. On December 31, 20X4, Telecom reports income of $40,000 and, on January 15, 20X5, pays a dividend of $.30 per share.

Required:

1. Record the journal entries for Pleasuredine on November 6, 20X4.
2. Record the journal entries for Pleasuredine on December 31, 20X4.
3. Record the journal entries for Pleasuredine on January 15, 20X5.
4. Determine the value of Pleasuredine's investment in Telecom as of January 15, 20X5.

Problem 5

Skyway Corporation is treating the following securities as trading securities. The cost and fair market value as of December 31, 20XX, for their portfolio are listed below. Record the adjusting entry necessary for December 31, 20XX.

Investment	Cost	Fair Value	Unrealized Gain (Loss)
Bluesky Corp. Stock	25,000	$ 26,000	$ 1,000
Good Earth Corp. Bonds	12,000	10,000	(2,000)
	$ 37,000	$ 36,000	$ (1,000)

Problem 6

Keystone Corporation accounts for the following securities as available-for-sale investments:

Investment	Cost	Fair Value as of 9/30/XX
GreenCo Inc. Stock	$15,000	$18,000
Whitefield Co. Bonds	$16,000	$15,000
Maroontide Co. Bonds	$18,000	$17,000
Golden Co. Stock	$12,000	$18,000

Required:

Journalize the appropriate adjusting entry for 9/30/XX.

Problem 7

Pizza Prince Company purchased 2,000 shares of Empire Corporation on August 15, 20X4, at $45 per share plus a brokerage commission of $300. Quarterly dividend dates are September 15, December 15, March 15, and June 15. The current dividend is $2.70 per share.

Required:

Record any necessary journal entries on the dates shown.

1. August 15, 20X4
2. September 15, 20X4
3. December 15, 20X4
4. December 31, 20X4

Challenge Problems

Problem 8

The information provided in the following table pertains to Cajun Carl's Restaurant and its subsidiary, Louisiana Lil's, as of December 31, 20X4:

	Parent Cajun Carl's	Subsidiary Louisiana Lil's
Cash	$ 18,000	$ 6,000
Accounts Receivable	14,000	2,500
Rent Receivable	15,000	–0–
Inventory	6,000	1,500
Investments	32,000	–0–
Property & Equipment	55,000	40,000
Total Assets	$ 140,000	$ 50,000
Accounts Payable	$ 9,000	$ 3,000
Rent Payable	–0–	15,000
Mortgage Payable	26,000	–0–
Common Stock	47,000	20,000
Retained Earnings	58,000	12,000
Total Liabilities and Owners' Equity	$ 140,000	$ 50,000

Additional information:

1. The Rent Receivable of $15,000 on the parent's books is the $15,000 Rent Payable on the subsidiary's books.

2. Cajun Carl's owns 100 percent of the subsidiary.

Required:

Compile the consolidated balance sheet for Cajun Carl's as of December 31, 20X4, based on the information provided.

Problem 9

Buffy's Hotels buys and sells marketable securities when excess cash is available. All of its marketable securities are classified as current assets.

Required:

Write the necessary journal entry for each of the following transactions.

1. On October 6, purchased 100 shares of Allison Labs common stock at $51\frac{1}{4}$ per share plus brokerage commissions of $280.

2. On October 15, purchased $60,000 worth of 9 percent face value bonds from McGuire International at 97 percent of par plus accrued interest of $2,250 and commission of $300.

3. On November 15, received semiannual interest on McGuire International Bonds.

4. On November 28, purchased 200 shares of Farley Industries common stock at $26\frac{1}{2}$ per share plus brokerage commission of $175.

5. On December 1, received quarterly dividend of $.75 per share on Allison Labs stock.

6. At December 31, 20X4, the market price of Allison Labs stock was $49 per share, while the market price of Farley Industries stock was $27. Make any necessary adjusting entries.

7. On January 25, sold 100 shares of Allison Labs for $49\frac{1}{4}$ per share less commission of $280.

Problem 10

Based on the account balances below, compile the consolidated balance sheet of the Webb Corporation for December 31, 20XX. (Hint: Some of the accounts below may not be needed.)

Account	Balance
Land	$60,000
Unrealized Gain on Available-for-Sale Securities—Equity	5,000
Cash	10,000
Unrealized Loss on Trading Securities—Income	3,000
Minority Interest	50,000
Retained Earnings	?
Building	75,000
Short-Term Investments	20,000

Accounts Receivable	20,000
Accounts Payable	12,000
Common Stock	60,000
Long-Term Investments	18,000
Inventory	25,000
Goodwill	40,000
Notes Payable	10,000
Mortgage Payable	60,000

REVIEW QUIZ

When you feel you have covered all of the material in this chapter, answer these questions. Choose the *best* answer.

1. The International Hospitality Company (IHC) purchased bonds that had a total face value of $250,000 for $242,500 on August 1, 20X1. The bonds pay installments of the 8 percent annual interest on May 1 and November 1. The IHC pays for accrued bond interest in advance, at the time of purchase, when it buys bonds. The IHC's journal entry on the date of bond purchase would debit Debt Investments for _____ and Bond Interest Receivable for _____ and credit Cash for _____.

    a. $242,500; $242,500; $0
    b. $242,500; $2,000; $242,500
    c. $250,000; $7,500; $242,500
    d. $242,500; $5,000; $247,500

2. The Eat Inn Company purchased bonds that had a total face value of $250,000 for $242,500 on August 1, 20X1. The bonds pay installments of the 8 percent annual interest on May 1 and November 1. The company pays for accrued bond interest in advance, at the time of purchase, when it buys bonds. The Eat Inn Company's journal entry on November 1 would debit _____ for _____ and credit Bond Interest Income and Bond Interest Receivable for _____ apiece.

    a. Debt Investments; $10,000; $5,000
    b. Cash; $10,000; $5,000
    c. Debt Investments; $7,500; $3,750
    d. Cash; $7,500; $3,750

3. Venda Vacations, Inc., has invested in 8 percent of the stocks of the Hinterlands Hotel Corporation. The Hinterlands Hotel Corporation pays dividends quarterly, which is typical. Venda Vacations should account for dividends from its investment by:

    a. accruing dividends weekly until they are distributed.
    b. accruing dividends monthly until they are distributed.
    c. recording dividends only when they are received, and then as Dividend Income.
    d. recording dividends as increases in operating income.

4. Morton's Motel recently sold the 6 percent stock interest it had purchased as an investment in another company. Gains or losses on the sale of stocks should be closed into the _____ account.

    a. Income Summary
    b. Cash
    c. Owner's Equity
    d. Dividend Income

REVIEW QUIZ *(continued)*

5. Quid, Inc., owns 10 percent of Frost Pak, and Quid accounts for its invest-
    ment, which was $150,000 on January 1, 20X4, on a cost basis. During 20X4,
    Frost Pak reported net income of $200,000 and paid dividends of $100,000.
    Quid's account Investment in Frost Pak has a balance of _____ at the end
    of 20X4.

    a. $150,000
    b. $170,000
    c. $180,000
    d. $300,000

6. The Kewanee Corporation owns 32 percent of the voting stock of the Adiron-
    dack Hotel. The corporation should account for its holding in this hotel on
    a(n) _____ basis.

    a. cost
    b. consolidated
    c. equity
    d. controlling

7. Available-for-sale securities that are purchased with the intention to resell
    them within a year should be listed on the balance sheet as:

    a. Bonds.
    b. Trading Securities.
    c. Short-Term Investments.
    d. Investments.

Answer Key: 1-d-C1, 2-b-C1, 3-c-C2, 4-a-C2, 5-a-C3, 6-c-C3, 7-c-C4

Each question is linked to a competency. Competencies are listed on the first page of
the chapter. An answer reading 3-b-C4 translates to:

  3:   the question number
  b: the correct answer
 C4: the competency number

Chapter 17 Outline

The Purpose of the Statement of Cash Flows
Classification of Cash Flows
Conversion of Accrual Income to Net Cash
   Flows from Operations
      Direct and Indirect Methods
Preparing the SCF
      Step 1: Determining Net Cash Flows
         from Operating Activities
      Step 2: Determining Net Cash Flows
         from Investing Activities
      Step 3: Determining Net Cash Flows
         from Financing Activities
      Step 4: Presenting Cash Flows by
         Activity on the SCF
      Interpreting the Results
Accounting for Other Transactions

Competencies

1. Explain the purpose and use of the
    statement of cash flows.

2. Identify the general format for a
    statement of cash flows, and classify
    transactions as operating, investing, or
    financing activities.

3. Explain the direct and indirect
    methods of reporting cash flows from
    operations.

4. Explain the preparation of the
    Operating Activities section of a
    statement of cash flows.

5. Explain the preparation of the
    Investing Activities section of a
    statement of cash flows.

6. Explain the preparation of the
    Financing Activities section of a
    statement of cash flows.

7. Describe special situations that may
    need to be accounted for in preparing
    a statement of cash flows.

17

Statement of Cash Flows

TRADITIONALLY, the principal financial statements used by hospitality operations have been the income statement and the balance sheet. The balance sheet shows the financial position of the business at the end of the accounting period. The income statement reflects the results of operations for the accounting period. Although these statements provide extensive financial information, they do not provide answers to such questions as:

1. How much cash was provided by operations?

2. What amount of property and equipment was purchased during the year?

3. How much long-term debt was borrowed during the year?

4. What amount of funds was raised through the sale of capital stock?

5. What amount of dividends was paid during the year?

6. How much was invested in long-term investments during the year?

The **statement of cash flows (SCF)** is designed to answer these questions and many more as it shows the sources and uses of cash for the accounting period.

Our discussion will address the definition of *cash*, the relationship of the SCF to other financial statements, the purposes and uses of the SCF, a classification of cash flows, alternative formats that may be used for the SCF, a four-step approach for preparing the SCF, an illustration of the preparation of the SCF using the Sample Inn, and accounting for other transactions.

The Purpose of the Statement of Cash Flows

The statement of cash flows shows the effects on cash of a business's operating, investing, and financing activities for the accounting period. It explains the change in Cash for the accounting period; that is, if Cash decreases by $3,000 from January 1, 20X1 (the beginning of the accounting period), to December 31, 20X1 (the end of the accounting period), the SCF will reflect the decrease in the sum of cash from the firm's various activities.

For purposes of this statement, *cash* is defined to include both cash and cash equivalents. **Cash equivalents** are short-term, highly liquid investments such as U.S. Treasury bills and money market accounts. Firms use cash equivalents for investing funds that are temporarily not needed for operating purposes. Generally, these short-term investments are made for 90 days or less. Since cash and cash equivalents are considered the same, transfers between Cash and Cash Equivalents are not considered cash receipts or cash disbursements for SCF purposes.

The major purpose of the SCF is to provide information regarding the cash receipts and disbursements of a business that will help users (investors, creditors, managers, and others) to:

1. Assess the organization's ability to generate positive future net cash flows. Although users of financial statements are less interested in the past than in the future, many users, especially external users, must rely on historical financial information to assess an operation's future abilities. Thus, the investor interested in future cash dividends will review the SCF to determine past sources and uses of cash to evaluate the firm's ability to pay future dividends.

2. Assess the firm's ability to meet its obligations. Users of financial statements want to determine the firm's ability to pay its bills as they come due. If a firm has little likelihood of being able to pay its bills, then suppliers will most likely not be interested in selling the firm their goods and services.

3. Assess the difference between the enterprise's net income and cash receipts and disbursements. The SCF allows a user to quickly determine the major net sources of cash and how much relates to the enterprise's operations. Investors, creditors, and other users generally prefer enterprises that are able to generate cash from operations (that is, from their primary purpose for being in business), as opposed to those generating cash solely from financing and investing activities (that is, activities which are incidental to the primary purpose).

4. Assess the effect of both cash and noncash investing and financing during the accounting period. Investing activities relate to the acquisition and disposition of noncurrent assets, such as property and equipment. Financing activities relate to the borrowing and payment of long-term debt and sale and purchase of capital stock. Noncash activities (that is, transactions involving no cash) include such transactions as the acquisition of a hotel in exchange for stock or long-term debt.

The three major user groups of the SCF are management (internal) and investors and creditors (external). Management may use the SCF to (1) assess the firm's liquidity, (2) assess its financial flexibility, (3) determine its dividend policy, and (4) plan investing and financing needs. Investors and creditors will most likely use the SCF to assess the firm's (1) ability to pay its bills as they come due, (2) ability to pay dividends, and (3) need for additional financing, including borrowing debt and selling capital stock.

The relationship of the SCF to other financial statements is shown in Exhibit 1. The statement of retained earnings, mentioned in Exhibit 1, reflects results of operations and dividends declared, and reconciles the Retained Earnings accounts of two successive balance sheets. Net Income from the income statement is transferred to the Retained Earnings account when the temporary accounts (revenues and expenses) are closed at the end of the accounting period. In addition, Net Income is shown on the SCF when the SCF is prepared using the indirect approach (discussed later in this chapter). Finally, the SCF indirectly reconciles

Exhibit 1   Relationship of SCF to Other Financial Statements

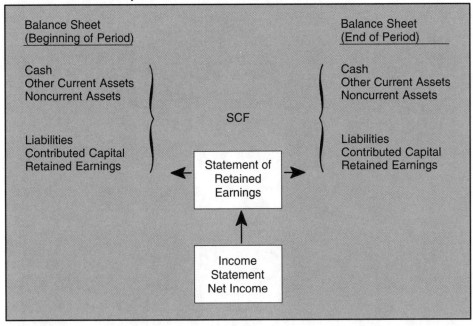

most accounts on the balance sheet other than Cash by showing the sources and uses of cash.

Classification of Cash Flows

The SCF classifies cash receipts and disbursements as operating, investing, and financing activities. Both **cash inflows** and **cash outflows** are included within each category. Exhibit 2 presents classifications of cash flows under the various activities, which are further described below:

- **Operating Activities:** This category includes cash transactions related to revenues and expenses. Revenues (cash inflows) include sales of food, beverages, and other goods and services to lodging guests, as well as interest and dividend income. Expenses (cash outflows) are for operational cash expenditures, including payments for salaries, wages, taxes, supplies, and so forth. Interest expense is also included as an operations cash outflow.

- **Investing Activities:** These activities relate primarily to cash flows from the acquisition and disposal of all noncurrent assets, especially property, equipment, and investments. Also included are cash flows from the purchase and disposal of marketable securities (short-term investments).

- **Financing Activities:** These activities relate to cash flows from the issuance and retirement of debt and the issuance and repurchase of capital stock. Cash

Exhibit 2 Classification of Cash Flows

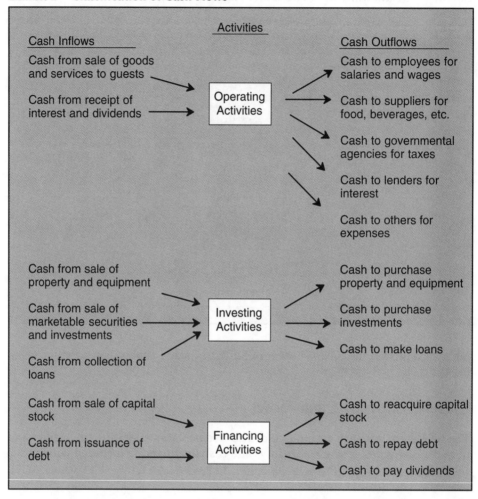

inflows include cash received from issues of stock and both short-term and long-term borrowing. Cash outflows include repayments of loans (although paying the interest expense portion of the debt is an operating activity) and payments to owners for both dividends and any repurchase of stocks. Payments of accounts payable, taxes payable, and the various accrued expenses, such as wages payable, are not payments of loans under financing activities, but they are classified as cash outflows under Operating Activities.

Finally, hospitality enterprises engage in noncash investing and financing activities, such as the exchange of capital stock for a hotel building. Since this represents only an exchange, no cash transaction has occurred. Therefore, these non-cash activities are not shown on the SCF. However, since a major purpose of the

Exhibit 3   Schedule of Noncash Investing and Financing Activities—Gateway Inn

Common stock exchanged for long-term debt	$100,000
Capital lease obligations incurred for use of equipment	50,000
Total	$150,000

Exhibit 4   Basic Format of the SCF

Cash Flows from Operating Activities [direct or indirect approaches may be used]	$XX
Cash Flows from Investing Activities [list cash inflows and outflows]	XX
Cash Flows from Financing Activities [list cash inflows and outflows]	XX
Net Increase (Decrease) in Cash	XX
Cash at the Beginning of the Period	XX
Cash at the End of the Period	$XX
Schedule of Noncash Investing and Financing Transactions	
[list individual transactions]	$XX

SCF is to include financing and investing activities, and since these activities will affect future cash flows, they must be disclosed on a separate schedule of the SCF. Thus, the user of financial information is provided with a complete presentation of investing and financing activities. Exhibit 3 is an example of a supplementary schedule of noncash investing and financing activities of the Gateway Inn.

The basic format of the SCF is shown in Exhibit 4. Generally, cash flows from operating activities are shown first. The indirect or direct approaches (to be discussed later) may be used to show cash flows from operating activities. Cash flows from investing and financing activities follow. Individual cash outflows and inflows are shown in each section. For example, Long-Term Debt may increase by $100,000 due to payment of $50,000 and subsequent borrowing of $150,000. Each cash flow should be shown rather than netting the two flows. Finally, as stated above, a supplementary schedule of noncash investing and financing activities to the SCF must be included.

Conversion of Accrual Income to Net Cash Flows from Operations

A major purpose of the SCF is to show net cash flows from operations. The income statement is prepared on an **accrual basis;** that is, revenues are recorded when they are earned, not when cash is received from guests, and expenses are recorded when incurred, not necessarily when cash is disbursed. Consequently, there may be little correlation between net income and cash flow. Consider the hypothetical Wales Inn, which had $2,000,000 in sales for 20X1. Its accounts receivable (AR) from guests totaled $100,000 at the beginning of the year and $110,000 at the end of the year. The cash received from sales during 20X1 is determined as follows:

$$\text{Cash receipts for sales} = \text{Sales} - \text{increase in AR}$$
$$or + \text{decrease in AR}$$
$$= \$2,000,000 - \$10,000$$
$$= \underline{\underline{\$1,990,000}}$$

Thus, even though the Wales Inn had sales of $2,000,000 as reported on its income statement, it would show cash receipts from sales on its SCF as $1,990,000.

Direct and Indirect Methods

There are two methods of reporting cash flows from operations: the direct and the indirect methods. The **direct method** shows cash receipts from sales and cash disbursements for expenses. This method requires that each item on the income statement be converted from an accrual basis to a cash basis, as were the sales of the Wales Inn above. Another example of this conversion process for the Wales Inn is Payroll Expense. Assume that the Wales Inn reported $700,000 as Payroll Expense for 20X1, and its balance sheet's Accrued Payroll account at the beginning of the year showed $15,000 and at the end of the year showed $20,000. Its cash disbursement for payroll for 20X1 would be determined as follows:

$$\begin{matrix}\text{Cash Disbursement} \\ \text{for Payroll Expense}\end{matrix} = \text{Payroll Expense} - \text{increase in Accrued Payroll}$$
$$or + \text{decrease in Accrued Payroll}$$
$$= \$700,000 - \$5,000$$
$$= \underline{\underline{\$695,000}}$$

So even though payroll expense for the year totaled $700,000 as shown on the income statement, only $695,000 was disbursed during the year.

Some expenses shown on the income statement do not involve any direct cash disbursement and are simply ignored when the direct method is used. For example, depreciation expense is only an adjustment to help match expenses to revenues. Depreciation does not entail any cash, so it is ignored when the direct

Exhibit 5   Basic Formats of the Net Cash Flow from Operating Activities Section

Operating Activities

Direct Method

Cash Flows from Operating Activities:

Cash Receipts from Sales		$ XXX
Interest and Dividends Received		XXX
Total		XXX

Cash Disbursements for:

Payroll	$ XXX	
Purchases of Inventory	XXX	
Other Expenses	XXX	
Interest Expense	XXX	
Income Taxes	XXX	XXX
Net Cash Flows from Operating Activities		$ XXX

Indirect Method

Cash Flows from Operating Activities:

Net Income		$ XXX

Adjustments to Reconcile Net Income to Net Cash
Flows from Operating Activities:

Depreciation Expense	$ XXX	
Gain on Sale of Property	(XXX)	
Loss on Sale of Investments	XXX	
Increase in Accounts Receivable	(XXX)	
Decrease in Inventories	XXX	
•		
•		
•		
Increase in Accrued Payroll	XXX	XXX
Net Cash Flows from Operating Activities		$ XXX

method is used. The same approach is taken for amortization expense and gains and losses on the sale of property and equipment. The basic formats of cash flows from the Operating Activities section of the SCF for both the direct and indirect methods are shown in Exhibit 5.

Most hospitality businesses use the indirect method because the information needed to prepare it is more readily available than that needed for using the direct method. For that reason, the major focus in this chapter will be on the indirect method.

The **indirect method** for determining net cash flows from operations starts with net income. Net income is then adjusted for noncash items included on the income statement. The most common noncash expense deducted to determine net income is depreciation. Therefore, since depreciation is subtracted to compute net income on the income statement, it is added back to net income to compute net cash flows from operating activities. Other items on the income statement that must be added or subtracted include amortization expense and gains and losses on the sale of noncurrent assets and marketable securities.

To illustrate the addback of a loss on the sale of investments, assume that in 20X1 the Wales Inn sold for $200,000 a parcel of underdeveloped land (an investment) that originally cost $250,000. The journal entry to record the sale was as follows:

Cash	$200,000	
Loss on Sale of Investments	50,000	
Investment in Land		$250,000

The $200,000 of cash inflow will be shown as an investing activity on the SCF; however, the loss on sale of investments of $50,000 was included on the income statement in determining net income. Since it was subtracted in determining the Wales Inn's net income and it did not use cash, it must be added back to net income to determine the net cash flows from operating activities for the SCF.

In addition, to determine the net cash flows from operating activities while using the indirect method, the Wales Inn's net income must be adjusted for sales that were recorded but not paid during 20X1. This adjustment is accomplished by subtracting the increase in Accounts Receivable of $10,000 from net income on the SCF. Several similar adjustments must be made using the indirect method. These will be discussed in detail and illustrated in the next section of this chapter.

Regardless of the method used, the result will show the same amount of net cash provided by operating activities. The Financial Accounting Standards Board requires that firms using the indirect method report the amount of interest expense and taxes paid in separate disclosures.

Preparing the SCF

The principal sources of information needed for preparing the SCF are the income statement, the statement of retained earnings, and two successive balance sheets from the beginning and end of the accounting period. In addition, details of transactions affecting any change in noncurrent balance sheet accounts must be reviewed. For example, if a comparison of two successive balance sheets shows the Building account has increased by $5,000,000, the account must be analyzed to determine the reason(s) for the changes. Simply reflecting the net change of $5,000,000 on the SCF is generally not acceptable.

A four-step approach for preparing the SCF is as follows:

1. Determine the net cash flows from operating activities.

2. Determine the net cash flows from investing activities.

3. Determine the net cash flows from financing activities.

4. Present the cash flows by activity on the SCF.

Exhibits 6 and 7 contain balance sheets and a condensed income statement and statement of retained earnings for the Sample Inn. These will be used to illustrate this four-step approach. The preparation of the SCF is illustrated using the indirect method for showing net cash flows from operating activities.

Exhibit 6   Balance Sheets for the Sample Inn

Sample Inn
Balance Sheets
December 31, 20X1 and 20X2

		20X1	20X2
Assets			
Current Assets:			
Cash		$ 5,000	$ 10,000
Accounts Receivable		30,000	26,000
Inventory		10,000	12,000
	Total	45,000	48,000
Investments		50,000	300,000
Property and Equipment:			
Land		200,000	200,000
Building		10,000,000	10,000,000
Equipment		1,000,000	1,100,000
Less: Accumulated Depreciation		(5,000,000)	(5,500,000)
	Total	6,200,000	5,800,000
Total Assets		$ 6,295,000	$ 6,148,000
Liabilities and Owners' Equity			
Current Liabilities:			
Accounts Payable		$ 6,000	$ 6,500
Accrued Payroll		4,000	4,500
Income Taxes Payable		7,000	6,000
Dividends Payable		10,000	15,000
	Total	27,000	32,000
Long-Term Debt		4,500,000	3,750,000
Owners' Equity:			
Capital Stock		1,000,000	1,250,000
Retained Earnings		768,000	1,116,000
	Total	1,768,000	2,366,000
Total Liabilities and Owners' Equity		$ 6,295,000	$ 6,148,000

Step 1: Determining Net Cash Flows from Operating Activities

To determine the net cash flows from operating activities by using the indirect method, we focus first on the income statement by starting with net income of $500,000. Next, we need to adjust net income for items on the income statement that did not provide or use cash. In particular, depreciation expense and the gain on the sale of the investments are considered. Since depreciation was subtracted on the income statement to determine net income, it must be added to net income on the SCF to determine net cash flow from operating activities. Since the gain on the sale of investments is not a cash flow (the proceeds from the sale of investments of $150,000 are an investing activity on the SCF and will be discussed later), the gain of $100,000 must be subtracted from net income on the SCF. Thus, the net cash flows from operating activities are determined at this point as follows:

Exhibit 7   Income Statement and Statement of Retained Earnings for the Sample Inn

Sample Inn
Condensed Income Statement and Statement of Retained Earnings
For the Year Ended December 31, 20X2

Sales	$7,000,000
Cost of Goods Sold	1,000,000
Payroll Expenses	2,450,000
Other Operating Expenses	2,400,000
Income Taxes	250,000
Depreciation Expense	500,000
Gain on the Sale of Investments	100,000
Net Income	500,000
Retained Earnings—12/31/X1	768,000
Dividends Declared	152,000
Retained Earnings—12/31/X2	$1,116,000

Other Information:

1. No property and equipment were disposed of during 20X2.

2. Investment and equipment purchases during 20X2 were made with cash. No funds were borrowed.

3. Investments costing $50,000 were sold for $150,000, resulting in a $100,000 gain on the sale of investments during 20X2.

4. Long-term debt of $250,000 was converted to capital stock in a noncash transaction during 20X2. No other capital stock was issued, and there were no repurchases of capital stock.

5. Interest expense paid during the year totaled $400,000.

Net Cash Flows from Operating Activities:		
Net Income		$500,000
Adjustments to Reconcile Net Income to		
Net Cash Flows from Operating Activities:		
Depreciation Expense	$500,000	
Gain on Sale of Investments	(100,000)	400,000
Partial Net Cash Flows from Operating Activities		$900,000

The second type of adjustment includes changes in current accounts from the balance sheet. The Cash account is not considered, since we are essentially looking at all other balance sheet accounts to determine what caused the change in Cash for purposes of the SCF. In addition, the current liability account Dividends Payable is not considered in determining cash flows from operating activities, as dividends payable relate to financing activities and will be considered later. The changes in the remaining five current accounts and noncash current accounts are fully considered as follows:

Account	Balances—December 31 20X1	20X2	Change in Account Balance
Current Assets:			
Accounts Receivable	$30,000	$26,000	$4,000 (dec.)
Inventory	$10,000	$12,000	$2,000 (inc.)
Current Liabilities:			
Accounts Payable	$ 6,000	$ 6,500	$ 500 (inc.)
Accrued Payroll	$ 4,000	$ 4,500	$ 500 (inc.)
Income Taxes Payable	$ 7,000	$ 6,000	$1,000 (dec.)

A brief explanation follows for each of the above current accounts, including how the change affects net cash flows from operating activities.

Accounts receivable relate directly to sales, which were $7,000,000 for the Sample Inn for 20X2. Sales on account result in cash inflows when the hotel guests pay their bills. However, under accrual accounting, the sale is recorded when services are provided. Most of the sales during 20X2 resulted in cash as the guests paid their accounts, but at year-end, the Accounts Receivable account balance was $26,000. Analysis of the account will reveal how much cash resulted from sales as follows:

Accounts Receivable

12/31/X1 Balance	30,000	Cash Received	7,004,000
Sales to Hotel Guests	7,000,000		
12/31/X2 Balance	26,000		

Alternatively, the cash receipts from hotel guests could be determined as follows:

$$\text{Cash Receipts from Hotel Guests} = \text{AR Beginning Balance} + \text{Sales} - \text{AR Ending Balance}$$

$$= \$30,000 + \$7,000,000 - \$26,000$$

$$= \$7,004,000$$

In preparing the SCF, we need to show a decrease in Accounts Receivable of $4,000, which is added to Net Income as an increase in cash to determine net cash flows from operating activities.

The change in the balances of the Inventory account is an increase of $2,000. Inventory relates to the Purchases and Cost of Goods Sold (food and beverages) accounts. Remember, Cost of Goods Sold is the cost of food and beverage inventory sold, not the cash disbursed for purchases. Therefore, we need to determine the purchases for the year as follows:

	Ending inventory	$ 12,000
+	Cost of goods sold	1,000,000
	Goods available for sale	1,012,000
−	Beginning inventory	10,000
	Purchases	$1,002,000

The $2,000 increase in Inventory causes the accrual basis Cost of Goods Sold to be $2,000 less than Purchases. By assuming that Purchases is the cash amount paid for purchases, we must show a decrease in cash flows from operating activities of $2,000.

However, not all purchases were made for cash. The $500 increase in Accounts Payable represents the difference between purchases on account and cash paid to suppliers during 20X2. An increase in Accounts Payable means the amount of cash paid was less than the amount of purchases. Thus, the $500 increase in Accounts Payable must be added back to the accrual basis net income to determine net cash flows from operating activities. An analysis of the Accounts Payable account shows this as follows:

Accounts Payable

		1/1/X2 Balance	6,000
Payments to Suppliers	1,001,500	Purchases	1,002,000
		12/31/X2 Balance	6,500

The increase in the Accrued Payroll account of $500 represents the difference between the accrual basis payroll costs of $2,450,000 and the cash payments to personnel of $2,449,500. This determination is apparent in the analysis of the Accrued Payroll account as follows:

Accrued Payroll

		12/31/X1 Balance	4,000
Payments for Payroll	2,449,500	Payroll Expense	2,450,000
		12/31/X2 Balance	4,500

Since the payroll payments were $500 less than the payroll expense, the $500 increase in Accrued Payroll is added back to the accrual basis net income to determine net cash flows from operations.

Finally, the decrease of $1,000 in Income Taxes Payable represents the difference between the accrual basis income taxes of $250,000, shown on the condensed income statement of the Sample Inn, and the $251,000 paid, as determined by the analysis of the Income Taxes Payable account as follows:

Income Taxes Payable

		12/31/X1 Balance	7,000
Income Taxes Paid	251,000	Income Tax Expense	250,000
		12/31/X2 Balance	6,000

In reality, the $7,000 of income taxes due at the beginning of 20X1 were paid along with $244,000 of income taxes for 20X2. The remaining $6,000 of taxes for 20X2 will be paid in early 20X3. However, since income taxes paid during 20X2 exceed income tax expenses for 20X2 by $1,000, the $1,000 must be subtracted from the accrual basis net income to determine the net cash flows from operations.

In addition to differences from year to year in the payment of income taxes, a hospitality enterprise may have deferred income taxes over several years. The details of the account for deferred income taxes are beyond our scope.

The Sample Inn's SCF's net cash flows from operating activities based on the above would reflect the following:

Net Cash Flows from Operating Activities:		
Net Income		$500,000
Adjustments to Reconcile Net Income to Net		
Cash Flows from Operating Activities:		
Depreciation Expense	$500,000	
Gain on Sale of Investments	(100,000)	
Decrease in Accounts Receivable	4,000	
Increase in Inventory	(2,000)	
Increase in Accounts Payable	500	
Increase in Accrued Payroll	500	
Decrease in Income Taxes Payable	(1,000)	402,000
Net Cash Flows from Operating Activities		$902,000

In general, the rules for accounting for changes in current accounts in determining net cash flows provided by operating activities are as follows:

- A decrease in a current asset is added to Net Income.

- An increase in a current asset is deducted from Net Income.

- A decrease in a current liability is deducted from Net Income.

- An increase in a current liability is added to Net Income.

Step 2: Determining Net Cash Flows from Investing Activities

Step 2 of the four-step approach to preparing an SCF focuses on investing activities. In general, attention must be directed to noncurrent assets of the Sample Inn.

The investment account increased by $250,000. Further analysis of this account is as follows:

Investments			
12/31/X1 Balance	50,000	Sale of Investments	50,000
Purchase of Investments	300,000		
12/31/X2 Balance	300,000		

The analysis reveals both a sale of investments of $50,000 and a purchase of investments of $300,000. Thus, $300,000 of cash was used to purchase investments, which is a use of cash in the investing activities section of the SCF. However, further analysis of the sale of investments shows the journal entry to record this transaction as follows:

Cash	$150,000	
Investments		$ 50,000
Gain on Sale of Investments		100,000

The entry clearly shows a cash inflow of $150,000. Thus, this source of cash should be shown as an investing activity. Notice that the cost of investments sold ($50,000) and the gain on the sale of investments ($100,000) have no impact on net cash flow from investing activities.

There were no changes in the Land and Building accounts, as no purchases or sales were made during 20X2. Therefore, cash was not affected.

We will look next at the Equipment account. According to note 1 under Other Information, no equipment was disposed of during 20X2. Thus, the $100,000 difference must be due to purchases of equipment. The $100,000 of equipment is shown as a use of cash in determining net cash flows from investing activities.

The Sample Inn's final noncurrent account is Accumulated Depreciation, which increased by $500,000, the exact amount of depreciation expense for the year. Because depreciation does not affect cash, under the indirect method the $500,000 is added back to the accrual basis net income as discussed under Step 1. The change in no way affects investing activities of the Sample Inn.

Now that the noncurrent asset accounts of the Sample Inn have been analyzed, the Investing Activities section of the SCF reflects the following:

Net Cash Flows from Investing Activities:	
Proceeds from Sale of Investments	$ 150,000
Purchase of Investments	(300,000)
Purchase of Equipment	(100,000)
Net Cash Flows from Investing Activities	$(250,000)

Step 3: Determining Net Cash Flows from Financing Activities

To determine the net cash flows from financing activities, we must turn our attention to the noncurrent liabilities and owners' equity accounts. First, the change in the Long-Term Debt account is a decrease of $750,000. The analysis of the Long-Term Debt account is as follows:

Long-Term Debt (LTD)

		12/31/X1 Balance	4,500,000
Conversion to Common			
Stock	250,000		
Payment of LTD	500,000		
		12/31/X2 Balance	3,750,000

The above analysis is based on notes 2 and 4 under Other Information. Note 4 reveals that $250,000 of LTD was converted to capital stock. This is a noncash transaction and will be shown only in a supplementary schedule to the SCF. Note 2 indicates no funds were borrowed; therefore, the remaining $500,000 reduction in LTD had to be due to payment of LTD. The $500,000 payment is a cash outflow from financing activities.

The next account to be analyzed is Capital Stock. The increase for 20X2 is $250,000, which is due to the exchange of capital stock for LTD, as discussed above. According to note 4 under Other Information, there were no other Capital Stock transactions. Since this change in Capital Stock did not involve cash, it is not shown on the SCF. However, since it is a financing activity, it is shown on a supplementary schedule as mentioned previously.

The final account to be analyzed is Retained Earnings. The statement of retained earnings at the bottom of the income statement reflects the detailed changes in this account as follows:

Retained Earnings

		12/31/X1 Balance	768,000
Dividends Declared	152,000	Net Income	500,000
		12/31/X2 Balance	1,116,000

The net income has already been accounted for in the SCF as an operating activity. The declaration of $152,000 of dividends is not a cash activity by itself. For the SCF, the focus is on dividend payments, not dividend declaration. When dividends are declared, they are recorded as a reduction in Retained Earnings and as an increase in Dividends Payable, a current liability account. Therefore, to determine the amount of dividends paid during 20X2, we analyze the Dividends Payable account as follows:

Dividends Payable

		12/31/X1 Balance	10,000
Dividends Paid	147,000	Dividends Declared	152,000
		12/31/X2 Balance	15,000

Effectively, the $5,000 increase in the Dividends Payable account results in Dividends Declared during 20X2 exceeding Dividends Paid by $5,000. The $147,000 of dividends paid is shown in the SCF as a financing activity.

The Sample Inn's SCF Financing Activities section would show the following:

Net Cash Flows from Financing Activities:	
Payment of Long-Term Debt	$(500,000)
Payment of Cash Dividends	(147,000)
Net Cash Flows from Financing Activities	$(647,000)

Exhibit 8   SCF for the Sample Inn

<table>
<tr><td colspan="3" align="center">**Sample Inn**
Statement of Cash Flows
For the Year Ended December 31, 20X2</td></tr>
<tr><td>Net Cash Flows from Operating Activities:</td><td></td><td></td></tr>
<tr><td> Net Income</td><td></td><td>$ 500,000</td></tr>
<tr><td> Adjustments to Reconcile Net Income to Net Cash Flows from</td><td></td><td></td></tr>
<tr><td>   Operating Activities:</td><td></td><td></td></tr>
<tr><td>   Depreciation</td><td>$ 500,000</td><td></td></tr>
<tr><td>   Gain on Sale of Investments</td><td>(100,000)</td><td></td></tr>
<tr><td>   Decrease in Accounts Receivable</td><td>4,000</td><td></td></tr>
<tr><td>   Increase in Inventory</td><td>(2,000)</td><td></td></tr>
<tr><td>   Increase in Accounts Payable</td><td>500</td><td></td></tr>
<tr><td>   Increase in Accrued Payroll</td><td>500</td><td></td></tr>
<tr><td>   Decrease in Income Taxes Payable</td><td>(1,000)</td><td>402,000</td></tr>
<tr><td> Net Cash Flows from Operating Activities</td><td></td><td>902,000</td></tr>
<tr><td>Net Cash Flows from Investing Activities:</td><td></td><td></td></tr>
<tr><td> Sale of Investments</td><td>$ 150,000</td><td></td></tr>
<tr><td> Purchase of Investments</td><td>(300,000)</td><td></td></tr>
<tr><td> Purchase of Equipment</td><td>(100,000)</td><td></td></tr>
<tr><td> Net Cash Flows from Investing Activities</td><td></td><td>(250,000)</td></tr>
<tr><td>Net Cash Flows from Financing Activities:</td><td></td><td></td></tr>
<tr><td> Payment of Long-Term Debt</td><td>$(500,000)</td><td></td></tr>
<tr><td> Dividends Paid</td><td>(147,000)</td><td></td></tr>
<tr><td> Net Cash Flows from Financing Activities</td><td></td><td>(647,000)</td></tr>
<tr><td>Net Increase in Cash during 20X2</td><td></td><td>5,000</td></tr>
<tr><td>Cash at the Beginning of 20X2</td><td></td><td>5,000</td></tr>
<tr><td>Cash at the End of 20X2</td><td></td><td>$ 10,000</td></tr>
<tr><td colspan="3">**Supplementary Schedule of Noncash Financing and Investing Activities**</td></tr>
<tr><td> Exchange of capital stock for long-term debt</td><td></td><td>$ 250,000</td></tr>
<tr><td colspan="3">**Supplementary Disclosure of Cash Flow Information:**</td></tr>
<tr><td> Cash paid during the year for:</td><td></td><td></td></tr>
<tr><td>   Interest</td><td>$ 400,000</td><td></td></tr>
<tr><td>   Income taxes</td><td>$ 251,000</td><td></td></tr>
</table>

Step 4: Presenting Cash Flows by Activity on the SCF

We now are ready to prepare the SCF based on the analysis in Steps 1 through 3. The SCF for the Sample Inn is shown in Exhibit 8. The three activities show cash flows as follows:

Operating activities provided cash	$ 902,000
Investing activities used cash	(250,000)
Financing activities used cash	(647,000)
Total	$ 5,000

The result is a bottom line of $5,000 cash inflow. The Sample Inn's operating activities provided large enough cash inflows to cover the outflows for investing and financing.

In the preparation of the SCF, the net increase in cash of the Sample Inn per the SCF is added to the Sample Inn's Cash account at the beginning of 20X2 to equal the Cash account at the end of 20X2. The $5,000 net increase in the Cash account per the SCF equals the $5,000 increase in cash per the Sample Inn's successive balance sheets (Exhibit 6). This does not *prove* that the SCF is prepared correctly; however, if the $5,000 increase per the SCF had *not* been equal to the change per the successive balance sheets, we would know that we had improperly prepared the SCF. We would then need to locate our mistake and make the correction. Thus, this is at least a partial check on the SCF's accuracy.

Further, notice the supplementary schedule to the SCF, which shows the noncash exchange of capital stock of $250,000 for long-term debt and the supplementary disclosure of the amounts of interest and income taxes paid during 20X2.

Interpreting the Results

The Sample Inn's SCF lends insight to the user as follows:

- While net income increased by $500,000, cash flows from operations increased by $902,000. The major differences are Depreciation Expense of $500,000 and the Gain on Sale of Investments of $100,000.

- Cash flows from operations were sufficient to allow the Sample Inn to (1) pay off LTD of $500,000, (2) pay dividends of $147,000, and (3) use $250,000 for investing purposes.

- Together with the supplementary schedule, the SCF reflects that $750,000 of debt was retired and that no additional funds were borrowed on a long-term basis.

Accounting for Other Transactions

The preparation of the SCF using the Sample Inn was reasonably straightforward. Now we turn our attention to additional situations that may be encountered and that would have to be considered in preparing the SCF.

First, consider the sale of investments for $150,000 that originally cost $200,000. The result is a $50,000 loss on the sale. On the SCF, the $50,000 loss would be added into the Cash Flows from Operating Activities section, as the $50,000 loss on sale of investments would have been subtracted on the income statement to determine net income. Also, the proceeds of $150,000 received from the sale would be reported as sale of investments of $150,000 in the Investing Activities section of the SCF.

Second, consider the current asset account Marketable Securities. This account is used for investments with an expected life of less than one year. Still, the account reflects investments, and accounting for changes in this account would be the same as that for the Investment account. Proceeds from the sale of marketable securities or the cost of the purchase of marketable securities would be reported on the Investing Activities section of the SCF. Any gain or loss on the sale of marketable securities would be included in the Operating Activities section of the SCF.

Third, consider amortization expense. Amortization expense is the write-off of an intangible asset such as franchise costs or goodwill. Like depreciation, amortization is a noncash expense subtracted to determine net income; therefore, it must be added to net income to determine the net cash flows provided by operating activities.

Fourth, consider the sale of property and equipment. Assume a hospitality firm sells a range for $500 and that the range originally cost $1,500 but had been depreciated over the years by $1,300. The gain on the sale would be $300, which is the difference between the proceeds of $500 and the net book value of $200. The gain on the sale would be reported on the income statement as an addition to income, yet the gain is *not* cash, and neither is the sale part of operations. Therefore, the gain on the sale must be subtracted from net income in the Operating Activities section of the SCF. In addition, the proceeds of $500 is an increase in cash that is included in the Investing Activities section of the SCF. If the range had been sold for only $100, a loss on the sale of $100 would have occurred. In this case, the loss on the sale of $100 would be added to net income in the Operating Activities section of the SCF and the proceeds of $100 reported in the Investing Activities section of the SCF.

Fifth, consider a firm's purchase of its own capital stock. Assume a hotel company pays $10,000 to purchase 1,000 shares of its common stock on the market. If the shares are retired, the Capital Stock account is debited. If the stock is held for future reissue, the Treasury Stock account is charged. Either way, the $10,000 expenditure would be included in the Financing Activities section of the SCF.

Sixth, consider the sale of stock. Assume a hotel sells 300 shares of $10 par value common stock for $30 per share. Both the Common Stock and Paid-In Surplus accounts will be credited. The entire proceeds received should be reported in the Financing Activities section of the SCF as "Proceeds from sale of common stock."

Finally, consider the borrowing of funds from a financial institution. Cash is received and a liability is incurred. The entire amount of cash borrowed would be shown as "Proceeds from loan" in the Financing Activities section of the SCF. As the loan was paid off, the amount paid, excluding interest expense, would be reported in the Financing Activities section. Generally, amounts due within one year of the balance sheet date are reported on the balance sheet as "Current maturities of long-term debt." This reclassification of long-term debt does *not* affect cash. Only the payment of the debt affects the cash flows. However, consider a hotel's comparative balance sheet at December 31, 20X2, which reflects the following:

	Dec. 31	
	20X1	20X2
Current Maturities of Long-Term Debt	$ 20,000	$ 20,000
Long-Term Debt (LTD)	$800,000	$900,000

The Current Maturities account is a current liability, while the LTD account is a noncurrent liability account. By definition, the amount of a current liability as of December 31, 20X1, must be paid during 20X2. If you had the above comparative information and nothing more, the analysis would reflect the payment of LTD of $20,000 and funds borrowed of $120,000 as follows:

Current Maturities—LTD

		12/31/X1 Balance	20,000
Payment	20,000		
			–0–
		Reclassification	20,000
			20,000

LTD

		12/31/X1 Balance	800,000
Reclassification	20,000		
			780,000
		Borrowed	120,000
			900,000

The rationale is as follows: The current maturities of LTD of $20,000 as of December 31, 20X1, *was paid* in 20X2. Remember, this was a current liability as of December 31, 20X1. Therefore, the $20,000 balance in current maturities of LTD as of December 31, 20X2, had to be a reclassification of LTD of $20,000 during 20X2. Finally, since the LTD account was reduced by $20,000 during 20X2, and the December 31, 20X2, balance was $900,000, we would assume the difference of $120,000 had to be due to the borrowing of funds on a long-term basis.

Summary

The SCF is an FASB-mandated financial statement that must be issued with other financial statements released to external users. It reflects the inflow and outflow of cash for a period of time.

The SCF must show operating, investing, and financing activities. Operating activities reflect cash flows as they relate to revenues and expenses. Investing activities relate to changes in marketable securities and noncurrent asset accounts. Commonly included in these activities are the purchase and sale of property and equipment. Financing activities relate to payments of dividends payable and long-term debt, borrowing of long-term debt, and sale of capital stock. The net sum of the three activities shown on the SCF must equal the change in the cash amount shown on the two successive balance sheets.

There are two basic approaches to preparing the SCF—the direct and indirect methods. The difference between the two approaches is reflected only in the

Operating Activities section of the SCF. The direct approach shows the direct sources of cash, such as cash receipts from sales, and direct uses of cash, such as disbursements for payroll. The indirect approach starts with net income and adjusts it to account for noncash transactions. Other adjustments for the indirect approach are the changes in current accounts related to operations. Most hospitality firms use the indirect approach because it is easier to prepare.

Key Terms

accrual basis accounting—System of reporting revenues and expenses in the period in which they are considered to have been earned or incurred, regardless of the actual time of collection or payment.

cash equivalents—Short-term, highly liquid investments such as U.S. Treasury Bills and money market accounts.

cash inflows—Cash received by the hospitality organization during the accounting period.

cash outflows—Cash disbursed by the hospitality organization during the accounting period.

direct method—With regard to the statement of cash flows, one of two methods for converting net income to net cash flow from operations. This method shows cash receipts from sales and cash disbursements for expenses and requires that each item on the income statement be converted from an accrual basis to a cash basis.

indirect method—With regard to the statement of cash flows, one of two methods for converting net income to net cash flow from operations. This method starts with net income and then adjusts for noncash items included on the income statement.

statement of cash flows (SCF)—A statement that reflects the cash inflows and outflows of a business for a period of time. It explains the change in Cash by showing the effects on cash of a business's operating, investing, and financing activities for the accounting period.

Review Questions

1. What is the major purpose of the SCF?

2. How do different users of the SCF use this statement?

3. What are the three major classifications of cash flows in the SCF?

4. What are the two alternative approaches to preparing the SCF?

5. How do the two methods of preparing the SCF differ?

6. What supplementary information must be provided when the indirect approach is used in preparing the SCF?

7. How are changes in the various current balance sheet accounts shown on an SCF that was prepared using the indirect approach?

8. Where is a $10,000 loss on the sale of an investment shown on an SCF that is prepared using the indirect approach?

9. How does the sum of the cash flows from the three major classifications on the SCF relate to the change in balance sheet accounts from two successive balance sheets?

10. How is the exchange of common stock for long-term debt shown on the SCF?

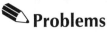 # Problems

Problem 1

The Westside Deli has engaged in several transactions during the year as follows:

1. Purchased a delivery van for $15,000 and paid cash.
2. Sold 100 shares of capital stock with a $5 par value per share for $10 per share.
3. Borrowed $15,000 from the local savings and loan institution on a long-term basis.
4. Paid dividends of $10,000 during the year.
5. Sold investments, with book value of $8,000, for $6,000.
6. Purchased marketable securities (stock in a Fortune 500 company) for $4,500.
7. Repurchased 50 shares of its own capital stock for $300. Stock is to be held for possible resale.
8. Paid $5,600 of long-term debt.
9. Exchanged 100 shares of capital stock for $1,000 of long-term debt owed to First Bank.
10. Purchased vacant land for $10,000 for potential expansion two years hence.

Required:

Identify how each transaction would be classified for the purpose of creating a statement of cash flows.

Problem 2

The Westland Inn had net earnings of $65,000 during 20X5. Included on its income statement for 20X5 were depreciation and amortization expenses of $150,000 and $5,000, respectively. Its current accounts on its comparative balance sheet showed the following.

	December 31	
	20X4	20X5
Cash	$10,000	$12,000
Marketable Securities	25,000	27,000
Accounts Receivable	45,000	40,000
Inventory	15,000	17,000

Prepaid Expense	10,000	8,000
Accounts Payable	25,000	30,000
Accrued Payroll	8,000	10,000
Income Taxes Payable	10,000	8,000
Current Maturities of Long-Term		
Debt	15,000	18,000
Dividends Payable	5,000	8,000

In addition, sales of equipment, marketable securities, and investments during 20X5 were as follows:

1. Equipment that cost $20,000 with accumulated depreciation of $12,000 was sold for $5,000.

2. Investments that cost $20,000 were sold for $25,000.

3. Marketable securities that cost $10,000 were sold for $8,000.

Required:

Prepare a schedule of cash flows from operating activities for 20X4.

Problem 3

Determine the indicated cash flows for the Broad Inn in each of the following situations:

1. During 20X3, the Broad Inn had cash sales of $800,000 and sales on account of $2,540,000. During the same year, Accounts Receivable—Hotel Guests increased by $10,000. Determine the cash received from hotel guests during 20X3.

2. During 20X3, the Broad Inn's board of directors declared cash dividends of $120,000. The Dividends Payable account was $10,000 at the beginning of the year and $15,000 at the end of the year. Determine the dividends paid by the Broad Inn during 20X3.

3. During 20X3, the Broad Inn had cost of food used of $400,000. During the year, Food Inventory increased by $8,000 and the related Suppliers Payable accounts decreased by $5,000. Determine the cash payments for food purchases during 20X3.

4. During the year, the Broad Inn's long-term debt of $1,000,000 as of January 1, 20X3, increased by $500,000 to $1,500,000 as of December 31, 20X3. Also during 20X3, $200,000 of long-term debt was converted to common stock, and $50,000 of long-term debt was reclassified as current debt. Determine the amount of cash that was borrowed and recorded as long-term debt during 20X3.

5. The Broad Inn's Income Tax Expense of 20X3 was $25,000. Its Income Taxes Payable account on the balance sheet was $4,000 at the beginning of the year and $5,000 at the end of the year. Determine the amount of income taxes paid during 20X3.

6. The Broad Inn's balance sheet at the beginning of 20X3 showed Accumulated Depreciation of $500,000 and at the end of the year the Accumulated Depreciation account totaled $600,000. During 20X3 a range that cost $10,000 was sold for $5,000, resulting in a $2,000 gain. The only other journal entry affecting the Accumulated Depreciation account was one for Depreciation Expense. Determine the amount of Depreciation Expense for 20X3.

Problem 4

The Spring Valley Resort had several transactions as shown below. In the columns to the right, describe the type of activity for each transaction and what amount (if any) would be shown on the SCF prepared according to the indirect method. (For example, the payment of utilities is not shown on the SCF because it is subtracted from sales to determine net income, which is shown on the SCF.)

Transaction			Type of Activity	Amount Shown on SCF
1.	Cash	$125,000		
	Common Stock	$100,000		
	Paid-In Capital in			
	Excess of Par	25,000	_____	_____
2.	Cash	$ 25,000		
	Accumulated			
	Depreciation	60,000		
	Equipment	$ 80,000		
	Gain on Sale of			
	Equipment	5,000	_____	_____
3.	Cash	$125,000		
	Treasury Stock	$100,000		
	Paid-In Capital in			
	Excess of Par	25,000	_____	_____
4.	Notes Payable	$ 75,000		
	Common Stock	$ 60,000		
	Paid-In Capital in			
	Excess of Par	15,000	_____	_____
5.	Notes Payable	$100,000		
	Interest Expense	20,000		
	Cash	$120,000	_____	_____
6.	Cash	$ 10,000		
	Accounts Receivable	30,000		
	Sales	$ 40,000	_____	_____
7.	Salaries and Wages	$ 20,000		
	Cash	$ 20,000	_____	_____
8.	Cash	$ 5,000		
	Dividend Income	$ 5,000	_____	_____
9.	Cash	$ 40,000		
	Loss on Sale of			
	Investments	$ 10,000		
	Investments	$ 50,000	_____	_____
10.	Equipment	$ 15,000		
	Notes Payable	$ 15,000	_____	_____

Problem 5

You have been hired by Lisa Idaho, a successful entrepreneur, to prepare a statement of cash flows for her two-year-old hotel, the Minney Motel. The following are copies of the condensed balance sheets and the income statement of the Minney Motel.

Minney Motel
Condensed Balance Sheets
December 31, 20X1 and 20X2

	20X1	20X2
Cash	$ 30,000	$ 40,000
Accounts Receivable	190,000	225,000
Inventory	30,000	35,000
Property and Equipment (net)	1,400,000	1,500,000
Other Assets (Preopening Expenses)	200,000	100,000
Total Assets	$1,850,000	$1,900,000
Accounts Payable	$ 140,000	$ 185,000
Wages Payable	10,000	15,000
Current Maturities—LTD	50,000	50,000
Long-Term Debt	1,000,000	950,000
Total Liabilities	1,200,000	1,200,000
Owners' Equity	650,000	700,000
Total Liabilities and Owners' Equity	$1,850,000	$1,900,000

Minney Motel
Condensed Income Statement
For the Year Ended December 31, 20X2

Sales	$2,000,000
Cost of Goods Sold	300,000
Contribution Margin	1,700,000
Undistributed Operating Expenses	1,050,000
Income before Fixed Charges	650,000
Depreciation Expense	300,000
Amortization of Preopening Expenses	100,000
Income before Tax	250,000
Income Tax	50,000
Net Income	$ 200,000

Additional information:

1. Equipment was purchased for $400,000.
2. Dividends of $150,000 were declared and paid during 20X2.
3. Long-term debt of $50,000 was paid during 20X2 and $50,000 of long-term debt was reclassified as current at the end of 20X2.

Required:

Prepare the SCF for the Minney Motel using the indirect method.

Problem 6

The condensed balance sheets and income statement of the Spartan Inn are as follows:

Spartan Inn
Condensed Balance Sheets
December 31, 20X1 and 20X2

Assets	20X1	20X2
Current Assets:		
Cash	$ 30,000	$ 40,000
Marketable Securities	50,000	50,000
Accounts Receivable	100,000	95,000
Inventory	20,000	25,000
Total Current Assets	200,000	210,000
Investments	100,000	60,000
Property and Equipment:		
Land	500,000	500,000
Building	5,000,000	6,000,000
Equipment	1,000,000	1,000,000
Accumulated Depreciation	(1,600,000)	(2,000,000)
Net Property and Equipment	4,900,000	5,500,000
Total Assets	$ 5,200,000	$ 5,770,000
Liabilities and Owners' Equity		
Current Liabilities:		
Accounts Payable	$ 60,000	$ 70,000
Dividends Payable	30,000	50,000
Current Portion of LTD	100,000	130,000
Total Current Liabilities	190,000	250,000
Long-Term Debt	4,200,000	4,470,000
Capital Stock	500,000	500,000
Retained Earnings	310,000	550,000
Total Liabilities and Owners' Equity	$ 5,200,000	$ 5,770,000

Condensed Income Statement
For the Year Ended December 31, 20X2

Sales	$ 6,000,000
Cost of Sales	1,000,000
Gross Profit	5,000,000
Depreciation	400,000
Other Expenses (Except Depreciation)	4,500,000
Net Operating Income	100,000
Gain on Sales of Investments	300,000
Income Taxes	110,000
Net Income	$ 290,000

Additional information:

1. Dividends declared during 20X2 totaled $50,000.
2. No investments were purchased during 20X2.
3. The current portion of long-term debt at the end of 20X2 was reclassified from noncurrent during 20X2.
4. No equipment or buildings were sold during 20X2.
5. Long-term debt was borrowed to partially finance the building purchase.

Required:

Prepare the Spartan Inn's SCF for 20X2 using the indirect method.

Problem 7

The operations of The McKenzie, a small lodging operation, are becoming more complex. Ms. Jo McKenzie, the owner, has asked for your help in preparing her statement of cash flows. She is able to present you with condensed balance sheets and some additional information.

The McKenzie
Condensed Balance Sheets
December 31, 20X3 and 20X4

	20X3	20X4
Cash	$ 10,000	$ 6,000
Accounts Receivable	26,500	25,500
Investments	10,000	5,000
Equipment	200,000	325,000
Accumulated Depreciation	(20,000)	(40,000)
Total Assets	$ 226,500	$ 321,500
Current Liabilities:		
Accounts Payable	$ 18,000	$ 21,000
Mortgage Payable (Current)	5,000	5,000
Dividends Payable	5,000	5,000
Noncurrent Liabilities:		
Mortgage Payable	75,000	70,000
Notes Payable	-0-	40,000
Common Stock	50,000	100,000
Retained Earnings	73,500	80,500
Total Liabilities and Owners' Equity	$ 226,500	$ 321,500

Additional information for 20X4:

1. Equipment that cost $20,000 depreciated to its salvage value of $2,000 and was sold for $8,000.
2. Common stock, purchased as a long-term investment for $5,000, was sold for $15,000.
3. Dividends declared totaled $15,000.

4. Equipment was purchased for $145,000.

5. Depreciation expense totaled $38,000.

6. Long-term debt of $5,000 was reclassified as current and $5,000 of long-term debt was paid.

7. Common stock of $50,000 was sold and long-term debt of $40,000 (note payable) was borrowed.

8. The McKenzie generated net income of $22,000.

Required:

Prepare the SCF as requested by Ms. McKenzie using the indirect method.

Challenge Problems

Problem 8

The Lakeside Hotel's sales for 20X1 totalled $5,000,000 of which 70 percent are on account. The remainder of the sales were for cash. All sales on account are recorded by debiting Accounts Receivable and crediting the appropriate sales account. Assume that the balance of accounts receivable totaled $100,000 and $120,000 at the beginning and end of the year, respectively.

Required:

1. What was the total amount of cash sales?

2. What was the total amount of cash received from guests who charged their purchases during 20X1?

3. What was the total amount of cash received during 20X1 related to charge sales, regardless of when the sale occurred?

Problem 9

The Oceanview Inn's comparative long-term debt for 20X1 and 20X2 was shown on its balance sheet as follows:
The Oceanview Inn's comparative long-term debt for 20X1 and 20X2 was shown on its balance sheet as follows:

	December 31	
	20X1	20X2
Current Liabilities		
Current Portion—Mortgage Payable	$ 20,000	$ 25,000
Long-Term Liabilities		
Mortgage Payable	$1,000,000	$ 1,200,000
Bonds Payable	–0–	$ 500,000

Assume current liabilities are paid on a timely basis.

Required:

1. What amount of mortgage debt was paid during 20X2?
2. How much was borrowed on a long-term basis during 20X2?

Problem 10

The Valley Café's comparative balance sheet for December 31, 20X1 and 20X2 reflects both Dividends Payable and Retained Earnings. The only entries to the Retained Earnings account are net income and dividends declared. Assume the Valley Café's bills (dividends payable) are paid on a timely basis and that Dividends Payable is a current liability on its balance sheet. The comparative balance sheet shows the following:

	20X1	20X2
Dividends Payable	$10,000	$15,000
Retained Earnings	$50,000	$55,000

Required:

Determine the amount of dividends paid during 20X2 for each of the three independent situations:

1. Net income for 20X2 totaled $20,000.
2. Net income for 20X2 totaled $25,000.
3. Net income for 20X2 totaled $30,000.

REVIEW QUIZ

When you feel you have covered all of the material in this chapter, answer these questions. Choose the *best* answer.

1. The Financier Hotel Company deposits $3,000 in its money market fund because these funds are not immediately needed for operations. This transaction would:

   a. appear on the statement of cash flows as a financing activity.
   b. appear on the statement of retained earnings as a financing activity.
   c. appear on the statement of cash flows as an investing activity.
   d. not appear on the statement of cash flows.

2. Hospitality firms' statements of cash flows often have a separate schedule that details:

   a. noncash investing and financing activities.
   b. operating activities.
   c. cash inflows from investing activities.
   d. procedures for determining whether to use the direct or indirect method of converting accrual income to net cash flows from operations.

3. The difference between the direct and indirect methods of preparing the statement of cash flows is reflected only in the _____ Activities section of the statement of cash flows.

   a. Financing
   b. Operating
   c. Cash Flow
   d. Investing

4. Changes in most kinds of current accounts on the balance sheet are analyzed to compile the:

   a. Operating Activities section of the statement of cash flows.
   b. Investing Activities section of the statement of cash flows.
   c. Financing Activities section of the statement of cash flows.
   d. noncash transaction schedule of the statement of cash flows.

5. The Waterbury Hotel and Water Park had no change in its Buildings account during the past fiscal year. When accountants are preparing a statement of cash flows, any change in the Buildings account would be:

   a. recorded directly on the Investing Activities section of the statement.
   b. ignored, because it would represent a noncash transaction.
   c. analyzed in light of other information to determine whether it should be recorded on the statement of cash flows.
   d. noted in a footnote.

REVIEW QUIZ *(continued)*

6.   The Seven Seas' Retained Earnings account for 20X2 reflects beginning and ending balances of $150,000 and $200,000, respectively, plus dividends declared and the results of operations. During 20X2, dividends of $40,000 were declared. The results of operations for 20X2 were:

   a.   earnings of $50,000.
   b.   earnings of $90,000.
   c.   losses of $10,000.
   d.   losses of $60,000.

7.   Which of the following would be added to net income to help determine net cash flows from operating activities?

   a.   proceeds from the sale of land
   b.   the value of a firm's purchase of its own capital stock
   c.   proceeds from the sale of stock
   d.   amortization expense

Answer Key: 1-d-C1, 2-a-C2, 3-b-C3, 4-a-C4, 5-c-C5, 6-b-C6, 7-d-C7

Each question is linked to a competency. Competencies are listed on the first page of the chapter. An answer reading 3-b-C4 translates to:

   3:   the question number
   b: the correct answer
   C4:   the competency number

Chapter 18 Outline

Analysis of Financial Statements
Horizontal Analysis
Vertical Analysis
Trend Analysis
Ratio Analysis
    Ratio Standards
    Purposes of Ratio Analysis
    Classes of Ratios
Liquidity Ratios
    Current Ratio
    Acid-Test Ratio
    Operating Cash Flows to Current
        Liabilities Ratio
    Accounts Receivable Turnover
    Average Collection Period
Solvency Ratios
    Debt-Equity Ratio
    Long-Term Debt to Total Capitalization
        Ratio
    Number of Times Interest Earned Ratio
    Fixed Charge Coverage Ratio
    Operating Cash Flows to Total
        Liabilities Ratio
Activity Ratios
    Inventory Turnover
    Property and Equipment Turnover
    Asset Turnover
    Paid Occupancy Percentage and Seat
        Turnover
    Complimentary Occupancy
    Average Occupancy per Room
    Multiple Occupancy
Profitability Ratios
    Profit Margin
    Operating Efficiency Ratio
    Return on Assets
    Return on Owners' Equity
    Earnings per Share
    Price Earnings Ratio
    Viewpoints Regarding Profitability
        Ratios
Operating Ratios
    Mix of Sales
    Average Daily Rate
    Revenue per Available Room
    Average Food Service Check
    Food Cost Percentage
    Beverage Cost Percentage
    Labor Cost Percentage
    Limitations of Ratio Analysis

Competencies

1. Describe types of numbers used in financial analysis, and distinguish between the types of financial analysis.

2. Perform horizontal and vertical analyses of comparative balance sheets and comparative income statements.

3. Demonstrate how to calculate trend percentages, and describe the advantages and limitations of trend analysis.

4. Describe standards used in ratio analysis, the purposes of ratio analysis, and common classes of ratios and the general purpose of each class.

5. Calculate common liquidity ratios and describe how creditors, owners, and managers view them.

6. Calculate common solvency ratios and describe how creditors, owners, and managers view them.

7. Calculate common activity ratios and describe how creditors, owners, and managers view them.

8. Calculate common profitability ratios and describe how creditors, owners, and managers view them.

9. Calculate common operating ratios and explain how managers use them to evaluate operational results.

18

Analysis and Interpretation of Financial Statements

THE FINANCIAL STATEMENTS issued by hospitality establishments contain a lot of information. A good understanding of this information requires more than simply reading the reported facts. Users of financial statements must interpret the reported facts to discover aspects of the hospitality firm's financial situation that could otherwise go unnoticed. This is accomplished through various types of analysis that make significant comparisons between related facts reported on financial statements. Analysis makes the figures reported in a financial statement more meaningful, informative, and useful. In particular, analysis generates indicators for evaluating various aspects of a financial situation.

Analysis can provide users of financial statements with answers to such questions as:

1. Is there sufficient cash to meet the establishment's obligations for a given time period?

2. Are the profits of the hospitality operation reasonable?

3. Is the level of debt acceptable in comparison with the stockholders' investment?

4. Is the inventory usage adequate?

5. How do the operation's earnings compare with the market price of its stock?

6. Is the total of accounts receivable reasonable in light of credit sales?

7. Is the hospitality establishment able to service its debt?

In this chapter, we first explain the purposes of financial analysis. Then we will discuss the kinds of analysis, including vertical, horizontal, trend, and ratio analysis. The hypothetical Wonderland Lodge is used to illustrate the concepts discussed. Ratio standards are presented as well as limitations to ratio analysis.

Analysis of Financial Statements

Several types of analysis can be conducted on a company's financial statements. All of these analyses rely on comparisons to enhance the value of the accounting information. For example, suppose a company's net income for 20X3 was $300,000.

By itself, this information is not very useful. However, comparing this amount to Net Income of $250,000 for 20X2, Total Assets of $2,000,000, Total Owners' Equity of $1,000,000, and the Planned Net Income of $275,000 for 20X3 results in much more useful information.

Financial analysis may be expressed as:

1. Absolute changes of an item

2. Relative changes of an item

3. Trend percentages

4. Percentages of single items to a total

5. Ratios

The absolute change in an item may be either an increase or a decrease and simply reflects the dollar change. For example, if a hotel has $10,000 in cash at the end of 20X1 and $15,000 in cash at the end of 20X2, the absolute change is simply $5,000. Absolute changes are reflected on **comparative financial statements** such as that shown in Exhibit 1.

The relative change in an item may also be either an increase or a decrease and simply reflects the percentage change in an item. Expressed another way, the relative change is the absolute change divided by the base of comparison. Using the cash example from above, we determine the relative change as follows:

$$\text{Relative Change} = \frac{\text{Absolute Change}}{\text{Base Amount}}$$

$$= \frac{\$5,000}{\$10,000}$$

$$= \underline{\underline{.5}} \text{ or } \underline{\underline{50}}\%$$

A relative change is always shown as a percentage and is often referred to as a *percentage change.* Relative changes are also reflected on comparative financial statements such as that shown in Exhibit 1. The calculation of absolute or relative changes in comparative financial statements is known as **horizontal analysis.**

Trend percentages are similar to relative changes except that accountants compare several periods to the base period. Using the cash example, assume that Cash at the end of 20X3, 20X4, and 20X5 was $18,000, $20,000, and $25,000, respectively. The trend percentages would be as follows:

20X1	100%
20X2	150%
20X3	180%
20X4	200%
20X5	250%

Trend percentages are useful, as they reflect changes over time. Many hospitality companies provide ten years of summary statistics to allow analysts to compute trends.

Exhibit 1 Comparative Balance Sheets

The Wonderland Lodge
Comparative Balance Sheets
December 31, 20X4 and 20X5

Assets	(1) 20X5	(2) 20X4	(3) Dollars	(4) Percent	(5) 20X5	(6) 20X4
	December 31		Change 20X5 over 20X4		Percent of Total Assets—Dec. 31	
Current Assets:						
Cash	$ 22,500	$ 10,000	$ 12,500	125.00%	1.01%	0.46%
Marketable Securities	25,000	20,000	5,000	25.00%	1.13%	0.91%
Accounts Receivable	110,000	100,000	10,000	10.00%	4.96%	4.56%
Inventories	12,500	9,000	3,500	38.89%	0.56%	0.41%
Prepaid Expenses	8,500	10,000	(1,500)	–15.00%	0.38%	0.46%
Total Current Assets	178,500	149,000	29,500	19.80%	8.05%	6.80%
Property and Equipment:						
Land	200,000	200,000	0	0.00%	9.02%	9.13%
Buildings	1,500,000	1,500,000	0	0.00%	67.61%	68.46%
Furnishings and Equipment	800,000	600,000	200,000	33.33%	36.06%	27.38%
Less: Accumulated Depreciation	500,000	300,000	200,000	66.67%	22.54%	13.69%
Total Property and Equipment	2,000,000	2,000,000	0	0.00%	90.15%	91.28%
Other Assets	40,000	42,000	(2,000)	–4.76%	1.80%	1.92%
Total Assets	$ 2,218,500	$ 2,191,000	$ 27,500	1.26%	100.00%	100.00%
Liabilities and Owners' Equity						
Current Liabilities:						
Accounts Payable	$ 65,000	$ 60,000	$ 5,000	8.33%	2.93%	2.74%
Current Maturities of						
Long-Term Debt	80,000	60,000	20,000	33.33%	3.61%	2.74%
Accrued Expenses	7,000	6,000	1,000	16.67%	0.32%	0.27%
Income Tax Payable	5,000	4,500	500	11.11%	0.23%	0.21%
Total Current Liabilities	157,000	130,500	26,500	20.31%	7.08%	5.96%
Long-Term Liabilities:						
Mortgage Payable	1,300,000	1,380,000	(80,000)	–5.80%	58.60%	62.98%
Total Liabilities	1,457,000	1,510,500	(53,500)	–3.54%	65.68%	68.94%
Owners' Equity:						
Common Stock	500,000	500,000	0	0.00%	22.54%	22.82%
Retained Earnings	261,500	180,500	81,000	44.88%	11.79%	8.24%
Total Owners' Equity	761,500	680,500	81,000	11.90%	34.32%	31.06%
Total Liabilities and						
Owners' Equity	$ 2,218,500	$ 2,191,000	$ 27,500	1.26%	100.00%	100.00%

Financial analysis also includes the comparison of a single item to a total. For example, the comparison of each asset to Total Assets is quite useful. The comparison of each expense to Total Sales provides real insight into a company's operations. Financial statements reduced to percentages are referred to as **common-size statements,** since every element is computed as a percentage of a base. This type of analysis is called **vertical analysis.**

Finally, financial ratios are expressions of logical relationships between certain items in the financial statements. Financial ratios are computed based on items in one or two financial statements. For example, the *current ratio* compares Total Current Assets and Total Current Liabilities from a single financial statement (the balance sheet), while *accounts receivable turnover* compares Average Accounts Receivable (from the balance sheet) to Total Sales (from the income statement).

Exhibits 1 and 2 contain the comparative balance sheets and income statements for 20X4 and 20X5 for the hypothetical Wonderland Lodge, which will be used throughout this chapter to illustrate financial statement analysis. The Wonderland Lodge is a 150-room lodging enterprise with food and beverage facilities. Additional information regarding the property's operations will be provided as we progress through this chapter.

Horizontal Analysis

Horizontal analysis consists of calculating the dollar change and the relative change for two accounting periods. Exhibits 1 and 2 show these calculations in columns 3 and 4.

The dollar change is simply the difference between the 20X5 and 20X4 amounts (columns 1 and 2). When the amount for 20X5 is greater than the amount for 20X4, the dollar difference is positive; when the amount for 20X5 is less than the amount for 20X4, the dollar difference is negative. For example, in Exhibit 1, Cash was $10,000 at the end of 20X4 and $22,500 at the end of 20X5. In other words, there was a positive change of $12,500. On the other hand, Prepaid Expenses decreased by $1,500 from the end of 20X4 to the end of 20X5; the change is therefore a negative number.

In reviewing the balance sheets by focusing on columns 1 through 4, we observe the following:

1. Total Current Assets increased by $29,500 from the end of 20X4 to the end of 20X5. Column 4 reflects the relative increase of 19.8 percent. The largest changes were increases in Cash and Accounts Receivable of $12,500 and $10,000, respectively. Although these amounts are not very different in absolute terms, they constitute a 125 percent relative change in Cash but only a 10 percent relative change in Accounts Receivable. Thus, the relative change provides additional insight to these changes.

2. Total Property and Equipment did not increase, as the total at the end of each year (20X5 and 20X4) was $2,000,000. However, Furnishings and Equipment increased by $200,000 or 33.33 percent, while Accumulated Depreciation increased by $200,000 or 66.67 percent.

3. Total Current Liabilities increased by $26,500 or 20.31 percent from the end of 20X4 to the end of 20X5. The major cause was the increase of $20,000 or 33.33 percent in Current Maturities of Long-Term Debt. Even though the percentage increase in Total Current Liabilities is greater than the percentage increase in Total Current Assets, the dollar change is greater for current assets than for

Exhibit 2   Comparative Income Statements

The Wonderland Lodge
Comparative Income Statements
for the years of 20X5 and 20X4

	December 31		Change 20X5 over 20X4		Percent of Total Revenue—Dec. 31	
	(1) 20X5	(2) 20X4	(3) Dollars	(4) Percent	(5) 20X5	(6) 20X4
Total Revenue	$3,135,000	$2,900,000	$ 235,000	8.10%	100.00%	100.00%
Rooms—Revenue	$2,400,000	$2,200,000	$ 200,000	9.09%	76.56%	75.86%
Payroll & Related Expense	360,000	330,000	30,000	9.09%	11.48%	11.38%
Other Expense	192,000	176,000	16,000	9.09%	6.12%	6.07%
Department Income	1,848,000	1,694,000	154,000	9.09%	58.95%	58.41%
Food & Beverage—Revenue	630,000	600,000	30,000	5.00%	20.10%	20.69%
Cost of Sales	220,500	210,000	10,500	5.00%	7.03%	7.24%
Payroll & Related Expense	189,000	180,000	9,000	5.00%	6.03%	6.21%
Other Expense	126,000	120,000	6,000	5.00%	4.02%	4.14%
Department Income	94,500	90,000	4,500	5.00%	3.01%	3.10%
Telecommunications—Revenue	105,000	100,000	5,000	5.00%	3.35%	3.45%
Cost of Sales	63,000	60,000	3,000	5.00%	2.01%	2.07%
Payroll & Related Expense	25,000	25,000	–0–	0.00%	0.80%	0.86%
Other Expense	10,000	10,000	–0–	0.00%	0.32%	0.34%
Department Income	7,000	5,000	2,000	40.00%	0.22%	0.17%
Total Operated Department Income	1,949,500	1,789,000	160,500	8.97%	62.19%	61.69%
Undistributed Operating Expenses						
Administrative and General	240,000	232,000	8,000	3.45%	7.66%	8.00%
Marketing	130,000	116,000	14,000	12.07%	4.15%	4.00%
Property Operation and Maintenance	312,000	290,000	22,000	7.59%	9.95%	10.00%
Energy Costs	155,000	145,000	10,000	6.90%	4.94%	5.00%
Total Undistributed Operating Expenses	837,000	783,000	54,000	6.90%	26.70%	27.00%
Income after Undistributed Operating Expenses	1,112,500	1,006,000	106,500	10.59%	35.49%	34.69%
Rent, Property Taxes, and Insurance	210,000	180,000	30,000	16.67%	6.70%	6.21%
Interest	190,000	200,000	(10,000)	–5.00%	6.06%	6.90%
Depreciation and Amortization	202,000	202,000	–0–	0.00%	6.44%	6.97%
Income before Income Taxes	510,500	424,000	86,500	20.40%	16.28%	14.62%
Income Taxes	153,150	127,200	25,950	20.40%	4.89%	4.39%
Net Income	$ 357,350	$ 296,800	$ 60,550	20.40%	11.40%	10.23%

Note: Food and Beverage are shown together because a single manager is often responsible for both.

current liabilities. This suggests that the firm probably has the ability to pay its bills as they come due.

4. Long-term debt had decreased by $80,000 by the end of 20X5. Although this may seem like a large sum, it is only a 5.8 percent decrease, since the decrease is compared to a relatively large amount of outstanding long-term debt at the end of 20X4.

5. Finally, Total Owners' Equity increased by $81,000 or 11.9 percent, due solely to the increase in Retained Earnings. Together, both Total Assets and Total Liabilities and Owners' Equity increased by 1.26 percent. We know these increases must be the same, as Assets always must equal Liabilities plus Owners' Equity on a balance sheet.

Horizontal analysis of the Wonderland Lodge's comparative income statements is shown in columns 1 through 4 of Exhibit 2. A few comments are as follows:

1. Total Revenue increased by $235,000 or 8.1 percent from 20X4 to 20X5. Total Revenue consists of revenue from rooms, food and beverage, and telecommunications. The largest increase was $200,000 or 9.09 percent for the rooms department.

2. The operated department income increase of $160,500 is 8.97 percent above the $1,789,000 for 20X4. The largest increase in dollars was from the rooms department with $154,000 or 9.09 percent. However, the $2,000 increase for the telecommunications department was a 40 percent increase over the telecommunications department income of $5,000 for 20X4.

3. Total Undistributed Operating Expenses increased by $54,000 or 6.9 percent. The major increases were in Marketing and Property Operation and Maintenance, which were $14,000 (12.07%) and $22,000 (7.59%), respectively.

4. The major increase in fixed charges was in Rent, Property Taxes, and Insurance of $30,000 or 16.67 percent. Income before Income Taxes increased by $86,500 or 20.4 percent over the 20X4 amount.

5. Finally, Net Income increased by $60,550 or 20.4 percent. Thus, an 8.10 percent increase in Total Revenue resulted in a 20.4 percent increase in Net Income for the Wonderland Lodge during 20X5.

Vertical Analysis

Vertical analysis consists of reducing the balance sheets and income statements to percentages. Exhibits 1 and 2 for the Wonderland Lodge reflect these percentages in columns 5 and 6. For the balance sheet, Total Assets (and, of course, Total Liabilities and Owners' Equity) equals 100 percent, and each asset line item is computed as a percentage of Total Assets. Each line item of liabilities and owners' equity is computed as a percentage of Total Liabilities and Owners' Equity. For the income statement, Total Revenue is 100 percent, and each line item is computed as a percentage thereof.

Vertical analysis allows an analyst to see the change in the composition of assets, liabilities, and owners' equity on the balance sheet from year to year. Looking at Exhibit 1, we can note the following:

1. Total Current Assets increased from 6.80 to 8.05 percent of Total Assets, while Property and Equipment decreased from 91.28 to 90.15 percent. Since Total Assets equals 100 percent for each year, an increase in one or more categories from year to year must be offset by decreases in one or more categories. It is interesting to note that Total Property and Equipment remained constant at $2,000,000 but decreased as a percentage of Total Assets, since Total Assets increased during 20X5.

2. Total Current Liabilities increased as a percentage of Total Liabilities and Owners' Equity from 5.96 percent at the end of 20X4 to 7.08 percent at the end of 20X5. Total Liabilities decreased from 68.94 to 65.68 percent, while Total Owners' Equity increased from 31.06 to 34.32 percent.

Vertical analysis of the Wonderland Lodge's comparative income statements is shown in columns 5 and 6 of Exhibit 2. Total Revenue for each year is set at 100 percent, and each line item is calculated as a percentage thereof. Thus, even though Total Revenue increased in 20X5 by $235,000 (8.1%), the percentages in columns 5 and 6 are both 100 percent. That is, the percentages in columns 5 and 6 for the individual line items reflect changes as they relate to total revenues for their respective years. Note the following:

1. Rooms revenue as a percentage of Total Revenue increased only slightly, from 75.86 percent in 20X4 to 76.56 percent, even though the dollar change was $200,000.

2. Total Operated Department Income increased by $160,500, but this was only a 0.5 percent increase in comparison to Total Revenue.

3. Income before Income Taxes was 16.28 percent and 14.62 percent as a percentage of Total Revenue for 20X5 and 20X4, respectively. Net Income as a percentage of Total Revenue increased from 10.23 percent for 20X4 to 11.4 percent for 20X5.

Trend Analysis

Trend analyses are useful in analyzing financial information over several accounting periods, generally years. Trend percentages, which are used for trend analyses, are calculated as follows:

1. Select several periods of financial information.

2. Assign 100 percent to each amount for the earliest (base) period.

3. Divide the corresponding amounts for later periods for each item by the amount for the base period.

4. Generally, the result in step 3 is multiplied by 100 to yield an index number.

Exhibit 3   Trend Analysis

The Wonderland Lodge
Condensed Income Statements
for the years of 20X1–20X5

	20X1	20X2	20X3	20X4	20X5
Total Revenue	$ 2,000,000	$ 2,350,000	$ 2,650,000	$ 2,900,000	$ 3,135,000
Room Department—Income	$ 1,200,000	$ 1,400,000	$ 1,560,000	$ 1,694,000	$ 1,848,000
Food & Beverage Department— Income	67,000	74,000	80,000	90,000	94,500
Telecommunications Department—Income	3,500	4,000	4,500	5,000	7,000
Total Operated Department Income	1,270,500	1,478,000	1,644,500	1,789,000	1,949,500
Undistributed Operating Expenses	560,000	648,600	725,000	783,000	837,000
Fixed Charges	587,000	597,000	592,000	582,000	602,000
Income before Income Taxes	123,500	232,400	327,500	424,000	510,500
Income Taxes	30,875	65,072	98,250	127,200	153,150
Net Income	$ 92,625	$ 167,328	$ 229,250	$ 296,800	$ 357,350

Trend Percentages
for the years of 20X1–20X5

	20X1	20X2	20X3	20X4	20X5
Total Revenue	100%	118%	133%	145%	157%
Room Department—Income	100%	117%	130%	141%	154%
Food & Beverage Department— Income	100%	110%	119%	134%	141%
Telecommunications Department—Income	100%	114%	129%	143%	200%
Total Operated Department Income	100%	116%	129%	141%	153%
Undistributed Operating Expenses	100%	116%	129%	140%	149%
Fixed Charges	100%	102%	101%	99%	103%
Income before Income Taxes	100%	188%	265%	343%	413%
Income Taxes	100%	211%	318%	412%	496%
Net Income	100%	181%	248%	320%	386%

To illustrate the use of trend percentages in trend analysis, we will use financial information from the Wonderland Lodge's condensed income statements for the years of 20X1 through 20X5 (shown in Exhibit 3). The base year is 20X1; Total Revenue and the other nine line items for 20X1 are set at 100 percent. Total Revenue rises a little every year from 100 percent in 20X1 to 157 percent in 20X5. Since Total Operated Department Income increases a little every year to 153 percent in 20X5 and Undistributed Operating Expenses and Fixed Charges each increase to less than 153 percent, we expect Income before Income Taxes to increase. In fact, it increases significantly each year to 413 percent for 20X5. This *appears* to be due primarily to the relative constancy of fixed charges over the five-year period (reflected in trend percentages varying between 99 and 103 percent for the five-year period). Finally, Net Income increased to 386 percent by 20X5. This is a fairly dramatic increase but appears to be due primarily to the constancy of fixed charges during a time of sizable increases in several other items.

Trends are useful for analyzing financial information over several accounting periods, especially years. However, one must remember the drawbacks in calculating trends. When the base period numbers are zero or negative, the result is not meaningful. An increase in net income to $10,000 in 20X2 from $0 in 20X1 yields a result of infinity, which is not meaningful. In addition, unusually small numbers in the base year will yield large and perhaps somewhat less useful results. For example, assume a firm has net income of $10, $10,000, $12,000, and $15,000 over a four-year period. Since the first year's net income of $10 is the base figure, the percentages for 20X2 through 20X4 would be 100,000 percent, 120,000 percent, and 150,000 percent.

Ratio Analysis

As stated earlier, financial ratios are expressions of logical relationships between certain items in one or two financial statements. **Ratio analysis** is used to evaluate the favorableness or unfavorableness of various financial conditions.

However, a computed ratio is not inherently good or bad, acceptable or unacceptable, reasonable or unreasonable. By itself, a ratio is neutral and simply expresses numerical relationships between related figures. To be useful as indicators or measurements of the success or well-being of a hospitality operation, the computed ratios must be compared with some standard. Only then will the ratios become meaningful and provide users of financial statements with a basis for evaluating the financial conditions.

Ratio Standards

There are basically three different standards that are used to evaluate the ratios computed for a given operation for a given period. Many ratios can be compared to corresponding ratios calculated for the prior period in order to discover any significant changes. For example, the occupancy percentage (discussed later in this chapter) for the current year may be compared to the occupancy percentage of the prior year in order to determine whether the lodging operation is selling more of its available rooms this year. This comparison may be useful in evaluating the effectiveness of the firm's current marketing plans.

Industry averages provide another useful standard against which to evaluate ratios. After calculating the return on investment (discussed later in this chapter) for a given firm, investors may want to compare this with the average return for similar firms in their particular industry segment. This may give investors an indication of the ability of the firm's management to effectively use resources to generate profits for the owners in comparison to other operations in the industry. In addition, managers may want to compare the occupancy percentage or food cost percentage for their own operation to industry averages in order to evaluate their abilities to compete with other operations in their industry segment. Published sources of average industry ratios are readily available.

While ratios can be compared to results of a prior period and also to industry averages, ratios are best compared against planned ratio goals. For example, to control the cost of labor more effectively, management may project a goal for the current year's labor cost percentage (discussed later in this chapter) that is slightly lower than the previous year's levels. The expectation of a lower labor cost percentage may reflect management's efforts to improve scheduling procedures and other factors related to the cost of labor. By comparing the actual labor cost percentage with the planned goal, management is able to assess the success of its efforts to control labor cost.

Different evaluations may result from comparing ratios to these different standards. For example, a food cost of 33 percent for the current period may compare favorably with the prior year's ratio of 34 percent and with an industry average of 36 percent, but may compare unfavorably to the operation's planned goal of 32 percent. Therefore, care must be taken when evaluating the results of operations with ratio analysis.

Purposes of Ratio Analysis

Managers, creditors (including lenders), and investors often have different purposes in using ratio analysis to evaluate the information reported in financial statements.

Ratios help managers monitor the operating performance of their operations and help them evaluate their success in meeting a variety of goals. By tracking a limited number of ratios, hospitality managers are able to maintain a fairly accurate perception of the effectiveness and efficiency of their operations. In a food service operation, most managers compute food cost percentage and labor cost percentage in order to monitor the two largest expenses of their operations. In lodging operations, occupancy percentage is one of the key ratios that managers use on a daily basis. Hospitality establishments often use ratios to express operational goals. For example, management may establish ratio goals as follows:

- Maintain a 1.25 to 1 current ratio.

- Do not exceed a debt-equity ratio of 1 to 1.

- Maintain return on owner's equity of 15 percent.

- Maintain fixed asset turnover of 1.2.

These ratios and many more will be fully explained later in this chapter. The point here is to note that ratios are particularly useful to managers as indicators of how well goals are being achieved. When actual results fall short of goals, ratios help indicate where a problem may be. In the food cost percentage example presented earlier (in which an actual ratio of 33 percent compared unfavorably with the planned 32 percent), additional research would be required to determine the cause(s) of the 1 percent variation. This 1 percent difference may be due to cost differences, sales mix differences, or a combination of the two. Only additional analysis will determine the actual cause(s). Ratio analysis can contribute significant information to such an investigation.

Creditors use ratio analysis to evaluate the solvency of hospitality operations and to assess the riskiness of future loans. For example, the relationship of Current Assets to Current Liabilities, referred to as the *current ratio* (discussed later in this chapter), may indicate an establishment's ability to pay its upcoming bills. In addition, creditors sometimes use ratios to express requirements for hospitality operations as part of the conditions set forth for certain financial arrangements. For example, as a condition of a loan, a creditor may require an operation to maintain a current ratio of 2 to 1.

Investors and potential investors use ratios to evaluate the performance of a hospitality operation as they consider their investment options. For example, the dividend payout ratio (dividends paid divided by earnings) indicates the percentage of earnings paid out by the establishment. Potential investors primarily interested in stock growth may shy away from investing in properties that pay out large dividends.

Ratios are used to communicate financial performance. Different ratios communicate different results. Individually, ratios reveal only part of the overall financial condition of an operation. However, collectively, ratios are able to communicate a great deal of information that may not be immediately apparent from simply reading the figures reported in financial statements.

Classes of Ratios

Ratios are generally classified by the type of information which they provide. Five common ratio groupings are as follows:

1. Liquidity

2. Solvency

3. Activity

4. Profitability

5. Operating

Liquidity ratios reveal the ability of a hospitality establishment to meet its short-term obligations. **Solvency ratios**, on the other hand, measure the extent to which the enterprise has been financed by debt and is able to meet its long-term obligations. **Activity ratios** reflect management's ability to use the firm's assets, while several **profitability ratios** show management's overall effectiveness as measured by returns on sales and investments. Finally, **operating ratios** assist in the analysis of hospitality establishment operations.

Knowing the meaning of a ratio and how it is used is always more important than knowing its classification. We will now turn to an in-depth discussion of individual ratios. For each ratio discussed, we will consider its purpose, the formula by which it is calculated, and the sources of data needed for the ratio's calculation. Exhibits 1 and 2 will be used throughout our discussion of individual ratios.

Liquidity Ratios

The ability of a hospitality establishment to meet its current obligations is important in evaluating its financial position. For example, can the Wonderland Lodge meet its current debt of $157,000 as it becomes due? Several ratios can be computed that suggest answers to this question.

Current Ratio

The most common liquidity ratio is the **current ratio,** which is the ratio of Total Current Assets to Total Current Liabilities and is expressed as a coverage of so many times. Using figures from Exhibit 1, we calculate the 20X5 current ratio for the Wonderland Lodge as follows:

$$\text{Current Ratio} = \frac{\text{Current Assets}}{\text{Current Liabilities}}$$

$$= \frac{\$178,500}{\$157,000}$$

$$= \underline{\underline{1.14 \text{ times}}} \text{ or } \underline{\underline{1.14 \text{ to } 1}}$$

This result shows that for every $1 of current liabilities, the Wonderland Lodge has $1.14 of current assets. Thus, there is a cushion of $.14 for every dollar of current debt. Some shrinkage of inventory and receivables could occur before the Wonderland Lodge would be unable to pay its current obligations with cash from its current assets. The 20X4 current ratio for the Wonderland Lodge was also 1.14 times. Would a current ratio of 1.14 times please all interested parties?

Owners/stockholders normally prefer a low current ratio to a high one, because stockholders view investments in most current assets as less productive than investments in noncurrent assets. Since stockholders are primarily concerned with profits, they prefer a relatively low current ratio.

Creditors normally prefer a relatively high current ratio, as this provides assurance that they will receive timely payments. A subset of creditors, lenders of funds, believe adequate liquidity is so important that they often incorporate a minimum working capital requirement or a minimum current ratio into loan agreements. Violation of this loan provision could result in the lender demanding full payment of the loan.

Management is caught in the middle, trying to satisfy both owners and creditors while maintaining adequate working capital and sufficient liquidity to ensure the smooth operations of the hospitality establishment.

An extremely high current ratio may mean that Accounts Receivable is too high because of liberal credit policies or slow collections, or it may indicate that Inventory is excessive. Since ratios are indicators, management must follow through by analyzing possible contributing factors.

Acid-Test Ratio

A more stringent test of liquidity is the **acid-test ratio.** The acid-test ratio measures liquidity by considering only "quick assets"—cash and near-cash assets. Inventories and prepaid expenses are excluded from Current Assets in determining the total quick assets. In many industries, inventories are significant and their conversion to cash may take several months. The extremes appear evident in the hospitality industry. Some hospitality operations, especially quick-service restaurants, may entirely replenish their food inventory twice a week. On the other hand, some operations may replace the stock of certain alcoholic beverages only once in three months.

The difference between the current ratio and the acid-test ratio is a function of the amounts of inventory and prepaid expenses relative to Current Assets. In some operations, the difference between the current ratio and the acid-test ratio will be minor, while in others, it will be significant. Based on the relevant figures from Exhibit 1, the 20X5 acid-test ratio for the Wonderland Lodge is computed as follows:

$$\text{Acid-Test Ratio} = \frac{\text{Cash, Marketable Securities, and Accounts Receivable}}{\text{Current Liabilities}}$$

$$= \frac{\$157,500}{\$157,000}$$

$$= \underline{\underline{1.00}} \text{ times}$$

The 20X5 acid-test ratio reveals quick assets of $1.00 for every $1.00 of current liabilities. The acid-test ratio is also 1.0 for 20X4. Although the acid-test ratio was 1.0 for 20X4 and 20X5, the Wonderland Lodge was not in extremely difficult financial straits. Many hospitality establishments are able to operate efficiently and effectively with an acid-test ratio of 1.0 or less, for they have minimal amounts of both inventory and accounts receivable.

Operating Cash Flows to Current Liabilities Ratio

A fairly new ratio made possible by the statement of cash flows is the **operating cash flows to current liabilities ratio.** The operating cash flows are taken from the statement of cash flows, while Current Liabilities comes from the balance sheet. This measure of liquidity compares the cash flow from the firm's operating activities to its obligations at the balance sheet date that must be paid within twelve months. Using the relevant figures from Exhibits 1 and 4, we calculate the 20X5 operating cash flows to current liabilities ratio as follows:

$$\text{Operating Cash Flows to Current Liabilities Ratio} = \frac{\text{Operating Cash Flows}}{\text{Average Current Liabilities}}$$

$$= \frac{\$548,850}{.5(\$157,000 + \$130,500)}$$

$$= \underline{\underline{3.818}} \text{ or } \underline{\underline{381.8\%}}$$

The 20X5 ratio of 385.3 percent shows that the Wonderland Lodge provided $3.853 of cash flow from operations during 20X5 for each $1.00 of current debt at the end of 20X5.

Exhibit 4   Statement of Cash Flows

The Wonderland Lodge		
Statement of Cash Flows		
for the year of 20X5		
Net Cash Flows from Operating Activities:		
Net Income		$ 357,350
Adjustments to Reconcile Net Income to Net		
Cash Flows from Operating Activities:		
Depreciation and amortization	$ 202,000	
Increase in accounts receivable	(10,000)	
Increase in inventories	(3,500)	
Decrease in prepaid expenses	1,500	
Increase in accounts payable	5,000	
Increase in accrued expenses	1,000	
Increase in income taxes payable	500	196,500
Net Cash Flows from Operating Activities		553,850
Net Cash Flows from Investing Activities:		
Purchase of Furnishings and Equipment	$ (200,000)	
Purchase of Marketable Securities	(5,000)	
Net Cash Flows from Investing Activities		(205,000)
Net Cash Flows from Financing Activities:		
Payment of Long-Term Debt	(60,000)	
Payment of Dividends	(276,350)	
Net Cash Flows from Financing Activities		(336,350)
Net Increase in Cash during 20X5		12,500
Cash at January 1, 20X5		10,000
Cash at December 31, 20X5		$ 22,500

Accounts Receivable Turnover

In hospitality operations that extend credit to guests, Accounts Receivable is gener-ally the largest current asset. Therefore, in an examination of a firm's liquidity, the "quality" of its accounts receivable must be considered. The **accounts receivable turnover** measures the speed of the conversion of receivables to cash. The faster the accounts receivable are turned over, the more credibility the current and acid-test ratios have in financial analysis.

This ratio is determined by dividing Total Revenue by Average Accounts Receivable. A refinement of this ratio uses only charge sales in the numerator; how-ever, quite often charge sales figures are unavailable to outsiders (stockholders, potential stockholders, and creditors). Regardless of whether Revenue or Charge

Sales is used as the numerator, the calculation should be consistent from period to period. Average Accounts Receivable is the result of dividing the sum of the beginning-of-the-period and end-of-the-period Accounts Receivable by two. Using the relevant figures from Exhibits 1 and 2, we calculate the accounts receivable turnover of the Wonderland Lodge for 20X5 as follows:

$$\text{Accounts Receivable Turnover} = \frac{\text{Total Revenue}}{\text{Average Accounts Receivable*}}$$

$$= \frac{\$3,135,000}{\$105,000}$$

$$= \underline{\underline{29.86}} \text{ times}$$

$$\text{*Average Accounts Receivable} = \frac{\text{Accounts Receivable at Beginning and End of Year}}{2}$$

$$= \frac{\$100,000 + \$110,000}{2}$$

$$= \underline{\underline{\$105,000}}$$

The accounts receivable turnover of 29.86 times indicates that the total revenue for 20X5 is 29.86 times the average receivables. The accounts receivable turnover should be compared with the targeted turnover, and management would generally investigate any difference. An investigation might reveal that changes in the credit policy or collection procedures significantly contributed to the difference.

Although the accounts receivable turnover measures the overall rapidity of collections, it fails to address individual accounts. This matter is resolved by preparing an aging of accounts receivable, which reflects the status of each account. In an aging schedule, each account is broken down to the period when the charges originated. Like credit sales, this information is generally available only to management.

Average Collection Period

A variation of the accounts receivable turnover is the **average collection period,** which is calculated by dividing the accounts receivable turnover into 365 (the number of days in a year). This conversion simply translates the turnover into a more understandable result. For the Wonderland Lodge, the average collection period for 20X5 is as follows:

$$\text{Average Collection Period} = \frac{365}{\text{Accounts Receivable Turnover}}$$

$$= \frac{365}{29.86}$$

$$= \underline{\underline{12}} \text{ days}$$

This means that the Wonderland Lodge was collecting all its accounts receivable on an average of every 12 days throughout 20X5.

Generally, the time allowed for average payments should not exceed the terms of sale by more than 7 to 10 days. Therefore, if the terms of sale are $n/30$ (entire amount is due in 30 days), the maximum allowable average collection period is 37 to 40 days.

The above discussion assumes that all sales are credit sales. However, many hospitality operations have both cash and credit sales. Therefore, the mix of cash and credit sales must be considered when the accounts receivable turnover ratio uses revenue rather than credit sales in the numerator. This is accomplished by allowing for cash sales. For example, if sales are 50 percent cash and 50 percent credit, then the maximum allowable average collection period should be adjusted. An adjusted maximum allowable average collection period is calculated by multiplying the maximum allowable average collection period by credit sales as a percentage of total sales.

In the previous example of a maximum allowable collection period of 37 to 40 days and 50 percent credit sales, the adjusted maximum allowable average collection period is 18.5 to 20 days (37 to 40 days × 5). Generally, only management can make this adjustment because other interested parties do not know the mix of sales.

Solvency Ratios

Solvency ratios measure the degree of debt financing used by a hospitality enterprise and are partial indicators of the establishment's ability to meet its long-term debt obligations. These ratios reveal the equity cushion that is available to absorb any operating losses. Primary users of these ratios are outsiders, especially lenders, who generally prefer less risk to more risk. High solvency ratios show an operation's financial ability to weather financial storms.

Owners like to use debt to increase their **leverage,** which is the use of debt in place of equity dollars to increase the return on the equity dollars already invested. Leverage is used when the return on the investment exceeds the cost of the debt used to finance the investment. When using debt to increase their leverage, owners are, in essence, transferring part of their risk to creditors.

As a further explanation of the concept of leverage, let us consider the following example. Assume that Total Assets of a certain lodging facility is $100, Earnings before Interest and Taxes (EBIT) is $50, and Interest is 15 percent of debt. Further assume that two possible combinations of debt and equity are $80 of debt and $20 of equity, and the reverse ($80 of equity and $20 of debt). Also assume a tax rate of 40 percent. The return on equity for each of the two combinations is calculated in Exhibit 5.

The calculations in Exhibit 5 reveal that each $1 invested by stockholders in the high debt/low equity combination earns $1.14, while every $1 invested by stockholders in the low debt/high equity combination earns only $.35.

This class of ratios includes three groups—those based on balance sheet information, those based on income statement information, and one based on information on the balance sheet and the SCF.

Exhibit 5   Return on Equity

	High Debt/ Low Equity	High Equity/ Low Debt
Debt	$80	$20
Equity	$20	$80
EBIT	$50	$50
Interest—15%	− 12*	− 3**
Income before Taxes	38	47
Income Taxes	− 15.20	− 18.80
Net Income	$22.80	$28.20

Return per $1 of equity:

$$\frac{\text{Net Income}}{\text{Equity}} = \frac{22.80}{20} = \$1.14 \qquad \frac{28.20}{80} = \$.35$$

*Debt × Interest Rate = Interest Expense
  $80 × .15 = $12
**$20 × .15 = $3

Debt-Equity Ratio

The **debt-equity ratio,** one of the most common solvency ratios, compares the hospitality firm's debt to its net worth (owners' equity). The debt-equity ratio indicates the establishment's ability to withstand adversity and meet its long-term debt obligations. Figures from Exhibit 1 can be used to calculate the Wonderland Lodge's debt equity ratio for 20X5:

$$\text{Debt-Equity Ratio} = \frac{\text{Total Liabilities}}{\text{Total Owners' Equity}}$$

$$= \frac{\$1,457,000}{\$761,500}$$

$$= 1.91 \text{ to } 1$$

The Wonderland Lodge's debt-equity ratio of 1.91 to 1 at the end of 20X5 indicates that for each $1 of owners' net worth, the Wonderland Lodge owed creditors $1.91.

Long-Term Debt to Total Capitalization Ratio

Another solvency ratio is the calculation of Long-Term Debt as a percentage of the sum of Long-Term Debt and Owners' Equity, commonly called *total capitalization.* This ratio is similar to the debt-equity ratio except that current liabilities are excluded from the numerator, and long-term debt is added to the denominator of the debt-equity ratio. Current liabilities are excluded because current assets are normally adequate to cover them, which means they are not a long-term concern. Figures from Exhibit 1 can be used to calculate the 20X5 **long-term debt to total capitalization ratio** for the Wonderland Lodge:

$$\text{Long-Term Debt to Total Capitalization Ratio} = \frac{\text{Long-Term Debt}}{\text{Long-Term Debt and Owners' Equity}}$$

$$= \frac{\$1,300,000}{\$2,061,500}$$

$$= 63.06\%$$

Long-Term Debt of the Wonderland Lodge at the end of 20X5 is 63.06 percent of its total capitalization.

Number of Times Interest Earned Ratio

The **number of times interest earned ratio** is based on financial figures from the income statement and expresses the number of times interest expense can be covered. The greater the number of times interest is earned, the greater the safety afforded the creditors. Since interest is subtracted to determine Taxable Income, Income Taxes is added to Net Income and Interest Expense to yield Earnings before Interest and Taxes (EBIT), the numerator of the ratio, while Interest Expense is the denominator. Figures from Exhibit 2 can be used to calculate the 20X5 number of times interest earned ratio for the Wonderland Lodge:

$$\text{Number of Times Interest Earned Ratio} = \frac{\text{EBIT}}{\text{Interest Expense}}$$

$$= \frac{\$700,500}{\$190,000}$$

$$= 3.69 \text{ times}$$

The result of 3.69 times shows that the Wonderland Lodge could cover its interest expense by over three times. In general, a number of times interest earned ratio of greater than four reflects a sufficient amount of earnings for a hospitality enterprise to cover the interest expense of its existing debt. Thus, Wonderland Lodge's management may desire to give some attention to this area.

The number of times interest earned ratio fails to consider fixed obligations other than interest expense. Many hospitality firms have long-term leases that require periodic payments similar to interest. This limitation of the number of times interest earned ratio is overcome by the fixed charge coverage ratio.

Fixed Charge Coverage Ratio

The **fixed charge coverage ratio** is a variation of the number of times interest earned ratio and considers leases as well as interest expense. Hospitality establishments that have obtained the use of property and equipment through leases may find the fixed charge coverage ratio to be more useful than the number of times interest earned ratio. This ratio is calculated the same as the number of times interest earned ratio except that Lease Expense (Rent Expense) is added to both the numerator and the denominator of the equation.

Using figures from Exhibit 2 and assuming that Rent Expense for 20X5 is $50,000, we can calculate the 20X5 fixed charge coverage ratio for the Wonderland Lodge as follows:

$$
\text{Fixed Charge Coverage Ratio} \ = \ \frac{\text{EBIT} + \text{Lease Expense}}{\substack{\text{Interest Expense} \\ \text{and Lease Expense}}}
$$

$$
= \ \frac{\$700{,}500 + \$50{,}000}{\$190{,}000 + \$50{,}000}
$$

$$
= \ \underline{\underline{3.13 \text{ times}}}
$$

The result indicates that earnings prior to lease expense, interest expense, and income taxes cover lease and interest expense 3.13 times.

Operating Cash Flows to Total Liabilities Ratio

The final solvency ratio presented here uses figures from both the statement of cash flows and the balance sheet by comparing operating cash flows to average total liabilities. Both the debt-equity and long-term debt to total capitalization ratios are based on static numbers from the balance sheet. The **operating cash flows to total liabilities ratio** overcomes the deficiency of using debt at a point in time by considering cash flow for a period of time.

Figures from Exhibits 1 and 4 are used to calculate the 20X5 operating cash flows to total liabilities ratio for the Wonderland Lodge as follows:

$$
\substack{\text{Operating Cash Flows to} \\ \text{Total Liabilities Ratio}} \ = \ \frac{\text{Operating Cash Flows}}{\text{Average Total Liabilities}}
$$

$$
= \ \frac{\$553{,}850}{.5(\$1{,}457{,}000 + \$1{,}510{,}500)}
$$

$$
= \ \underline{\underline{.373 \text{ or } 37.3\%}}
$$

This means the Wonderland Lodge's operating cash flows for 20X5 were $.373 for each $1 of debt at the end of 20X5.

Activity Ratios

Activity ratios measure management's effectiveness in using its resources. Management is entrusted with inventory and fixed assets (and other resources) to generate earnings for owners while providing products and services to guests. Since the fixed assets of most lodging facilities constitute a large portion of the operation's total assets, it is essential to use these resources effectively. Although Inventory is generally not a significant portion of Total Assets, management must adequately control it in order to minimize the cost of sales.

Inventory Turnover

The **inventory turnover** shows how quickly the inventory is being used. All things being the same, generally the quicker the inventory turnover the better, because inventory can be expensive to maintain. Maintenance costs include those for storage space, freezers, insurance, personnel expense, recordkeeping, and, of course, the opportunity cost of the funds invested in inventory. Inventories held by hospitality operations are highly susceptible to theft and must be carefully controlled.

Inventory turnovers should generally be calculated separately for food supplies and for beverages. Some food service operations will calculate several beverage turnovers based on the types of beverages available.

Exhibit 6 is a condensed food and beverage department statement of the Wonderland Lodge with food and beverage operations for 20X5 shown separately. Figures from this statement will be used to illustrate the food and beverage turnover ratios.

The 20X5 food inventory turnover ratio for the Wonderland Lodge is calculated as follows:

$$\text{Food Inventory Turnover} = \frac{\text{Cost of Food Used}}{\text{Average Food Inventory*}}$$

$$= \frac{\$177{,}500}{\$7{,}250}$$

$$= 24.5 \text{ times}$$

$$\text{*Average Food Inventory} = \frac{\text{Beginning and Ending Inventories}}{2}$$

$$= \frac{\$6{,}000 + \$8{,}500}{2}$$

$$= \$7{,}250$$

The food inventory turned over 24.5 times during 20X5, or approximately twice per month. The speed of food inventory turnover generally depends on the type of food service operation. A quick-service restaurant generally has a much faster food

Exhibit 6   Condensed Food and Beverage Department Statement

Condensed Food and Beverage Department Statement The Wonderland Lodge for the year of 20X5		
	Food	Beverage
Revenue	$450,000	$180,000
Cost of Sales:		
Beginning Inventory	6,000	3,000
Purchases	180,000	46,000
Less: Ending Inventory	8,500	4,000
Cost of Goods Used	177,500	45,000
Less: Employee Meals	2,000	–0–
Cost of Goods Sold	175,500	45,000
Gross Profit	274,500	135,000
Payroll and Related Expenses	144,000	45,000
Other Expenses	85,000	41,000
Total Expenses	229,000	86,000
Department Income	$ 45,500	$ 49,000

turnover (possibly more than 200 times a year) than does a fine dining establishment. A norm used in the hotel industry for hotels that may have several different types of restaurants and banquets calls for food inventory to turn over four times per month.

Although a high food inventory turnover is desired because it means that the establishment is able to operate with a relatively small investment in inventory, too high a turnover may indicate possible stockout problems. Failure to provide desired food items to guests may result not only in disappointed guests, but also negative goodwill if this problem persists. Too low an inventory turnover suggests that food is overstocked. In addition to the costs to maintain inventory previously mentioned, the cost of spoilage may become a problem.

Using figures from Exhibit 6, we can calculate the 20X5 beverage turnover ratio for the Wonderland Lodge as follows:

$$\text{Beverage Turnover Ratio} = \frac{\text{Cost of Beverages Used}}{\text{Average Beverage Inventory*}}$$

$$= \frac{\$45,000}{\$3,500}$$

$$= \underline{\underline{12.86 \text{ times}}}$$

$$\text{*Average Beverage Inventory} = \frac{\text{Beginning and Ending Inventories}}{2}$$

$$= \frac{\$3,000 + \$4,000}{2}$$

$$= \underline{\underline{\$3,500}}$$

The beverage turnover of 12.86 times means that the average beverage inventory of $3,500 required restocking approximately every 28 days (365 days/year ÷ 12.86). Not all beverage items are sold evenly, so some items would have to be restocked more frequently. A norm used in the hotel industry for hotels that have several different types of lounges and banquets calls for beverage inventory to turn over 1.25 times per month or 15 times per year.

Property and Equipment Turnover

The **property and equipment turnover** is determined by dividing the average total of Property and Equipment into Total Revenue for the period. A more precise measurement would be to use only revenues related to property and equipment usage in the numerator. However, revenue by source is not available to many financial analysts, so Total Revenue is generally used.

This ratio measures management's effectiveness in using property and equipment. A high turnover suggests the hospitality enterprise is using its property and equipment effectively to generate revenue, while a low turnover ratio suggests the establishment is not making effective use of its property and equipment and should consider disposing of part of them.

A limitation of this ratio is that it places a premium on using older (depreciated) property and equipment, since their book value is low. Furthermore, this ratio is affected by the depreciation method employed by the hospitality operation. For example, an operation using an accelerated method of depreciation will show a higher turnover than an operation using the straight-line depreciation method, all other factors being the same.

Using figures from Exhibits 1 and 2, we calculate the 20X5 property and equipment turnover ratio for the Wonderland Lodge as follows:

$$\text{Property and Equipment Turnover} = \frac{\text{Total Revenue}}{\text{Average Property and Equipment*}}$$

$$= \frac{\$3,135,000}{\$2,000,000}$$

$$= \underline{\underline{1.57 \text{ times}}}$$

$$\text{*Average Property and Equipment} = \frac{\text{Total Property and Equipment at Beginning and End of Year}}{2}$$

$$= \frac{\$2,000,000 + \$2,000,000}{2}$$

$$= \$2,000,000$$

The property and equipment turnover of 1.57 times reveals that Total Revenue was 1.57 times the average total property and equipment.

Asset Turnover

Another ratio to measure the efficiency of management's use of assets is the **asset turnover.** It is calculated by dividing Total Revenue by Average Total Assets. The two previous ratios presented, inventory turnover and property and equipment turnover, concerned a large percentage of the total assets. The asset turnover examines the use of total assets in relation to Total Revenues. Limitations of the property and equipment ratio are also inherent in this ratio to the extent that property and equipment make up Total Assets. For most hospitality establishments, especially lodging businesses, property and equipment constitute the majority of the operation's total assets.

Using figures from Exhibits 1 and 2, we can calculate the 20X5 asset turnover for the Wonderland Lodge as follows:

$$\text{Asset Turnover Ratio} = \frac{\text{Total Revenues}}{\text{Average Total Assets*}}$$

$$= \frac{\$3,135,000}{\$2,204,750}$$

$$= 1.42 \text{ times}$$

$$\text{*Average Total Assets} = \frac{\text{Total Assets at Beginning and End of Year}}{2}$$

$$= \frac{\$2,218,500 + \$2,191,000}{2}$$

$$= \$2,204,750$$

The asset turnover of 1.42 times indicates that each $1 of assets generated $1.42 of revenue in 20X5.

Both the property and equipment turnover and the asset turnover ratios are relatively low for most hospitality segments, especially for hotels and motels. The relatively low ratio is due to the hospitality industry's high dependence on property and equipment and its inability to quickly increase output to meet maximum

Exhibit 7   Statement of Retained Earnings and Other Information

Statement of Retained Earnings
The Wonderland Lodge
for the year of 20X5

Retained Earnings—Beginning of Year	$ 180,500
Net Income	357,350
Dividends Declared	(276,500)
Retained Earnings—End of Year	$ 261,350

Other Information

Rooms Sold	43,800
Paid Guests	61,320
Rooms Occupied by Two or More People	15,400
Complimentary Rooms	200*
Average Shares of Common Stock Outstanding	100,000
Food Covers	65,000

*Assume one guest per complimentary room.

demand. It is common for many hotels and motels to turn away customers four nights a week due to excessive demand, and operate at an extremely low level of output (less than 50%) the three remaining nights.

Four additional measures of management's ability to use available assets efficiently are paid occupancy percentage (or seat turnover), complimentary occupancy, average occupancy per room, and multiple occupancy percentage. Although these ratios are not based on financial information, they are viewed as excellent measures of management's effectiveness in selling space, whether it be rooms in a lodging facility or seats in a food service establishment.

Paid Occupancy Percentage and Seat Turnover

Paid occupancy percentage is a major indicator of management's success in selling its "product." It refers to the percentage of rooms sold in relation to the number of rooms available for sale in hotels and motels. In food service operations, it is commonly referred to as **seat turnover** and is calculated by dividing the number of people served by the number of seats available. Seat turnover is commonly calculated by meal period. Most food service facilities experience different seat turnovers for different dining periods. The occupancy percentage for lodging facilities and the seat turnovers for food service facilities are key measures of facility utilization.

Using the "Other Information" listed in Exhibit 7, the annual paid occupancy of the Wonderland Lodge can be determined by dividing total Paid Rooms

Occupied by Available Rooms for sale. If the Wonderland Lodge has 150 rooms available for sale each day, its paid occupancy percentage for 20X5 is calculated as follows:

$$\text{Paid Occupancy Percentage} = \frac{\text{Paid Rooms Occupied}}{\text{Available Rooms*}}$$

$$= \frac{43,800}{54,750}$$

$$= \underline{\underline{80\%}}$$

$$*\text{Available Rooms} = \text{Rooms Available per Day} \times 365 \text{ Days}$$
$$= 150 \times 365$$
$$= \underline{\underline{54,750}}$$

The Wonderland Lodge's 20X5 annual paid occupancy percentage is 80 percent. This percentage does not mean that every day 80 percent of the available rooms were sold, but rather that on the average 80 percent were sold. For example, a hotel experiencing 100 percent paid occupancy Monday through Thursday and 33 percent paid occupancy Friday through Sunday would end up with a combined result of 71.29 percent.

Many factors affect paid occupancy rates in the lodging industry, such as location within an area, geographic location, seasonal factors (both weekly and yearly), rate structure, and type of lodging facility, to mention a few.

Complimentary Occupancy

Complimentary occupancy, as stated in the *USALI*, is determined by dividing the number of complimentary rooms for a period by the number of rooms available. Using figures from the "Other Information" section of Exhibit 7, we can calculate the 20X5 complimentary occupancy for the Wonderland Lodge as follows:

$$\text{Complimentary Occupancy} = \frac{\text{Complimentary Rooms}}{\text{Rooms Available}}$$

$$= \frac{200}{54,750}$$

$$= \underline{\underline{0.37\%}}$$

Average Occupancy per Room

Another ratio to measure management's ability to use lodging facilities is the **average occupancy per room.** This ratio is the result of dividing the number of guests by the number of rooms occupied. Generally, as the average occupancy per room increases, the room rate also increases.

Using figures from the "Other Information" section of Exhibit 7, the 20X5 average occupancy per room for the Wonderland Lodge can be calculated as follows:

$$\text{Average Occupancy per Room} = \frac{\text{Number of Guests}}{\text{Number of Rooms Occupied by Guests}}$$

$$= \frac{61{,}320}{44{,}000}$$

$$= \underline{\underline{1.39}} \text{ guests}$$

The Wonderland Lodge's 20X5 average occupancy per room was 1.39 guests. The average occupancy per room is generally highest for resort properties, where it can reach levels in excess of two guests per room, and lowest for transient lodging facilities.

Multiple Occupancy

Another ratio used to measure multiple occupancy of rooms is **multiple occupancy,** sometimes less accurately called **double occupancy.** This ratio is similar to the average occupancy per room and is determined by dividing the number of rooms occupied by more than one guest by the number of rooms occupied by guests.

Using figures from the "Other Information" section of Exhibit 7, we calculate the multiple occupancy of the Wonderland Lodge for 20X5 as follows:

$$\text{Multiple Occupancy} = \frac{\text{Rooms Occupied by Two or More People}}{\text{Rooms Occupied by Guests}}$$

$$= \frac{15{,}400}{44{,}000}$$

$$= \underline{\underline{35\%}}$$

The multiple occupancy for the Wonderland Lodge during 20X5 indicates that 35 percent of the rooms sold were occupied by more than one guest.

Profitability Ratios ———————————————————————

Profitability ratios reflect the results of all areas of management's responsibilities. All information conveyed by liquidity, solvency, and activity ratios affect the profitability of the hospitality enterprise. The primary purpose of most hospitality operations is the generation of profit. Owners invest for the purpose of increasing their wealth through dividends and through increases in the price of capital stock. Both dividends and stock price are highly dependent upon the profits generated by the operation. Creditors, especially lenders, provide resources for hospitality enterprises to use in the provision of services. Generally, future profits are required

⊕-stock◂home**point**™

about . products . advertising . press . support . contact us

Portfolio
QuoteCenter
FundCenter
Markets
News
Commentary
InvestingTools

[Investing Tools] **stockfinder pro**

Stockfinder Pro (Find up to 100 stocks that meet your criteria) [Go!] [Reset]
Try these sample screens! No Sample Selected ▼ Click here for Help!

Company Name:
Industry: all ▼ **Order By** Symbol ▼ **Descending** ☐

overview
stockfinder
▸ stockfinder pro
fundfinder
fundfinder pro

Price Data	Minimum	Maximum	Revenue & Earnings Data	Minimum	Maximum
Price			Total Revenue (Millions)		
Price 12 month Low			Revenue per Share		
Price 12 month High			Book Value per Share		
Percent Below Price 12 Month High			Revenue Growth Rate %		
Price 4 Week Change %			Earnings per Share		
Price 13 Week Change %			Earnings per Share Growth Rate		
Price 26 Week Change %			Return on Equity		
Price 52 Week Change %			Price to Earnings Ratio		
Size/Capitalization Data	Minimum	Maximum	Price to Book Ratio		
Market Capitalization (Millions)			Annual Yield, Dividend		
Employees, Number of			**Risk Data**	Minimum	Maximum
Shares Outstanding (Millions)			Beta		
Avg Monthly Volume (Millions)			Current Ratio		
			Debt to Equity Ratio		
			Short Interest Ratio		
			Insider Shares Purchased		
			% Insider Ownership		
			% Institutional Ownership		

Data provided by

◆Market Guide

Many of the ratios discussed in this chapter can help hospitality executives choose investment vehicles. Stockfinder Pro (by Stockpoint.com at http://www.stockpoint.com/ neuralsearch.asp) allows Internet users to search for stocks that fit the hospitality firm's ratio criteria for investment. (Courtesy of Stockpoint.com)

to repay these lenders. Managers are also extremely interested in profits because their performance is, to a large degree, measured by the operation's bottom line. Excellent services breed goodwill, repeat customers, and other benefits which ultimately increase the operation's profitability.

The profitability ratios we are about to consider measure management's overall effectiveness as shown by return on sales (profit margin and operating efficiency ratio), return on assets, return on owners' equity, and the relationship between net income and the market price of the hospitality firm's stock (price earnings ratio).

Profit Margin

Hospitality enterprises are often evaluated in terms of their ability to generate profits on sales. **Profit margin,** a key ratio, is determined by dividing Net Income by Total Revenue. It is an overall measurement of management's ability to generate sales and control expenses, thus yielding the bottom line. Net Income is the income remaining after all expenses have been deducted, both those controllable by management and those directly related to decisions made by owner(s) or the board of directors.

Based on figures in Exhibit 2, the 20X5 profit margin of the Wonderland Lodge can be determined as follows:

$$\text{Profit Margin} = \frac{\text{Net Income}}{\text{Total Revenue}}$$

$$= \frac{\$357,350}{\$3,135,000}$$

$$= 11.4\%$$

The Wonderland Lodge's 20X5 profit margin of 11.4 percent is an increase over the profit margin of 10.2 percent of the prior year.

If the profit margin is lower than expected, then expenses and other areas should be reviewed. Poor pricing and low sales volume could be contributing to the low ratio. To identify the problem area, management should analyze both the overall profit margin and the operated departmental margins. If the operated departmental margins are satisfactory, the problem would appear to be with overhead expense.

Operating Efficiency Ratio

The **operating efficiency ratio** is a better measure of management's performance than the profit margin. This ratio is the result of dividing Income after Undistributed Operating Expenses by Total Revenue. Income after Undistributed Operating Expenses is the result of subtracting expenses generally controllable by management from Total Revenue. The remaining fixed charges are expenses relating to the capacity of the hospitality firm, including rent, property taxes, insurance, depreciation, and interest expense. Although these expenses are the results of decisions made by owners or boards of directors and thus are beyond the direct control of active management, management can and should review tax assessments and insurance policies and quotations and make recommendations to the owners or board of directors that can affect the facility's total profitability. In calculating the operating efficiency ratio, income taxes are also excluded, since fixed charges directly affect income taxes.

Using figures from Exhibit 2, we can calculate the 20X5 operating efficiency ratio of the Wonderland Lodge as follows:

$$\text{Operating Efficiency Ratio} = \frac{\text{Income after Undistributed Operating Expenses}}{\text{Total Revenue}}$$

$$= \frac{\$1,112,500}{\$3,135,000}$$

$$= 35.49\%$$

The operating efficiency ratio shows that over $.35 of each $1 of revenue is available for fixed charges, income taxes, and profits.

The next group of profitability ratios compares profits to amounts of either assets or owners' equity. The result in each case is a percentage and is commonly called a *return.*

Return on Assets

The **return on assets (ROA)** ratio is a general indicator of the profitability of an enterprise's assets. Unlike the two preceding profitability ratios drawn only from income statement data, this ratio compares bottom-line profits to the total investment, that is, to Total Assets (listed on the balance sheet). This ratio, or a variation of it, is used by several large conglomerates to measure the performances of their subsidiary corporations operating in the hospitality industry.

Using figures from Exhibits 1 and 2, we can calculate the Wonderland Lodge's 20X5 ROA as follows:

$$\text{Return on Assets} = \frac{\text{Net Income}}{\text{Average Total Assets*}}$$

$$= \frac{\$357,350}{\$2,204,750}$$

$$= 16.21\%$$

$$\text{*Average Total Assets} = \frac{\text{Total Assets at Beginning and End of Year}}{2}$$

$$= \frac{\$2,218,500 + \$2,191,000}{2}$$

$$= \$2,204,750$$

This result means that 16.21 cents of profit were generated for every $1 of Average Total Assets.

A very low ROA may result from inadequate profits or excessive assets. A very high ROA may suggest that older assets will require replacement in the near future, or that additional assets are needed to support growth in revenues. The determination of whether an ROA is low or high is usually based on industry averages and the hospitality establishment's own ROA profile that is developed over time.

ROA may also be evaluated by reviewing profit margin and asset turnovers, because when these ratios are multiplied by each other, they yield ROA:

$$\text{Profit Margin} \quad \times \quad \text{Asset Turnover} \quad = \quad \text{ROA}$$

$$\frac{\text{Net Income}}{\text{Total Revenue}} \quad \times \quad \frac{\text{Total Revenue}}{\text{Average Total Assets}} \quad = \quad \frac{\text{Net Income}}{\text{Average Total Assets}}$$

Return on Owners' Equity

A key profitability ratio is the **return on owners' equity (ROE).** The ROE ratio compares the profits of the hospitality enterprise to the owners' investment. Included in the denominator are all capital stock and retained earnings.

Using relevant figures from Exhibits 1 and 2, we calculate the 20X5 ROE for the Wonderland Lodge as follows:

$$
\begin{aligned}
\text{Return on Owners' Equity} \quad &= \quad \frac{\text{Net Income}}{\text{Average Owners' Equity}^*} \\[2mm]
&= \quad \frac{\$357,350}{\$721,000} \\[2mm]
&= \quad 49.56\%
\end{aligned}
$$

$$
\begin{aligned}
^*\text{Average Owners' Equity} \quad &= \quad \frac{\text{Owners' Equity at Beginning and End of Year}}{2} \\[2mm]
&= \quad \frac{\$761,500 \; + \; \$680,500}{2} \\[2mm]
&= \quad \$721,000
\end{aligned}
$$

In 20X5, for every $1 of owners' equity, 49.56 cents was earned.

To the owner, this ratio represents the end result of all management's efforts. The ROE reflects management's ability to produce for the owners.

Earnings per Share

A common profitability ratio shown on hospitality establishments' income statements issued to external users is **earnings per share (EPS).** The EPS calculation is a function of the firm's capital structure. If only common stock has been issued (that is, there is no preferred stock or convertible debt or similar dilutive securities), then EPS is determined by dividing Net Income by Average Common Shares

Outstanding. When preferred stock has been issued, Preferred Dividends are first subtracted from Net Income; the result is then divided by the average number of common shares outstanding. If any dilutive securities have been issued, the EPS calculation is considerably more difficult and is beyond our scope.[1]

Based on figures from Exhibits 2 and 7, the 20X5 EPS for the Wonderland Lodge can be calculated as follows:

$$\text{Earnings per Share} \;=\; \frac{\text{Net Income}}{\substack{\text{Average Common}\\ \text{Shares Outstanding}}}$$

$$=\; \frac{\$357,350}{\$100,000}$$

$$=\; \underline{\$3.57}$$

Simply stated, in 20X5 the Wonderland Lodge earned $3.57 per common share.

Increases in EPS must be viewed cautiously. For example, all other things being equal, the EPS will rise when an issuing establishment reduces the amount of common stock outstanding by purchasing its own stock (treasury stock). Further, EPS should be expected to increase as a hospitality enterprise reinvests earnings in its operations, because a larger profit can then be generated without a corresponding increase in shares outstanding.

Price Earnings Ratio

Financial analysts often use the **price earnings (PE) ratio** in presenting investment possibilities in hospitality enterprises. It is shown daily in the *Wall Street Journal* for all stocks listed on the New York and American stock exchanges. The PE ratio is computed by dividing the market price per share by the EPS.

Assume that the market price per share of the Wonderland Lodge is $20.00 at the end of 20X5. The PE ratio for the Wonderland Lodge at the end of 20X5 is calculated as follows:

$$\text{Price Earnings Ratio} \;=\; \frac{\text{Market Price per Share}}{\text{Earnings per Share}}$$

$$=\; \frac{\$20}{\$3.57}$$

$$=\; \underline{5.60}$$

The PE ratio of 5.60 indicates that if the 20X5 EPS ratio were maintained, it would take 5.60 years for earnings to equal the market price per share at the end of 20X5.

The PE ratio may vary significantly from one hospitality firm to another. Factors affecting these differences include relative risk, stability of earnings, perceived earnings trend, and perceived growth potential of the stock.

Viewpoints Regarding Profitability Ratios

Owners, creditors, and management obviously prefer high profitability ratios. Owners prefer high profitability ratios because they indicate the return the owners are receiving from their investments. Owners will be most concerned about ROE (return on common stockholders' equity if preferred stock has been issued), because ROE measures the precise return on their investments. Although other profitability measures are important to the owner, the ROE is the "bottom line" to him or her. Other profitability ratios may be relatively low and the ROE may still be excellent. For example, the profit margin could be only 2 percent, but the ROE could be 20 percent, based on the following:

Sales	$100
Net Income	$2
Owners' Equity	$10
Profit Margin	2%
ROE	20%

If the profitability ratios are not as high as other available investments with similar risks, stockholders may become dissatisfied and eventually move their funds to other investments. This move, if not checked, will result in lower stock prices and may make it more difficult for the enterprise to raise funds externally.

Creditors also prefer high, stable, or even growing profitability ratios. Although they desire stockholders to receive an excellent return (as measured by ROE), they will look more to the ROA ratio, because this ratio considers all assets, not simply claims to a portion of the assets, as does ROE. A high and growing ROA represents financial safety and indicates competent management. A high ROA also generally means high profits and cash flow, which suggests safety to the creditor and low risk to the lender.

Managers must keep both creditors and owners happy. Therefore, all profitability ratios are especially important to them. Everything else being the same, the higher the profitability ratios, the better. High ratios indicate that management is performing effectively and efficiently.

Operating Ratios

Operating ratios help management analyze the operations of a hospitality establishment. Detailed information necessary for computing these ratios is normally not available to creditors or even owners who are not actively involved in management. These ratios reflect the actual mix of sales (revenue) and make possible comparisons to sales mix objectives. Further, operating ratios relate expenses to revenues and are useful for control purposes. For example, food cost percentage is calculated and compared to the budgeted food cost percentage to evaluate the overall control of food costs. Any significant deviation is investigated to determine the cause(s) for the variation between actual results and planned goals.

There are literally hundreds of operating ratios that could be calculated. Consider the following examples:

Exhibit 8   Sales Mix

Departments	Sales	Percentage of Total
Rooms	$2,400,000	76.6%
Food	450,000	14.4
Beverage	180,000	5.7
Telecommunications	105,000	3.3
Totals	$3,135,000	100.0%

- Departmental revenues as a percentage of Total Revenue (sales mix)
- Expenses as a percentage of Total Revenue
- Departmental expenses as a percentage of departmental revenues
- Revenues per room occupied, meal sold, and so forth
- Annual expenses per room

This section will consider only some of the most critical ratios, several relating to revenues and several relating to expenses. The revenue ratios include the mix of sales, average daily rate, revenue per available room, and average food service check. The expense ratios include food cost percentage, beverage cost percentage, and labor cost percentage.

Mix of Sales

Hospitality firms, like firms in other industries, try to generate sales as a means of producing profits. In the lodging segment of the hospitality industry, sales by the rooms department contribute more toward overhead costs and profits than the same amount of sales in other departments. In a food service operation, a given sales total can yield different contributions toward overhead and profits, depending on the sales mix. Therefore, it is essential for management to obtain the desired sales mix. To determine the sales mix, departmental revenues are totaled and percentages of the total revenue are calculated for each operated department.

Using figures from Exhibits 2 and 6, Exhibit 8 calculates the 20X5 sales mix for the Wonderland Lodge. The sales mix of a hospitality operation is best compared to the establishment's objectives as revealed in its budget. A second standard of comparison is the previous period's results. A third involves a comparison to industry averages.

An evaluation of revenue by department is accomplished by determining the amount of each department's average sale. For the rooms department, the amount of the average sale is the average room rate; for the food service department, it is the average food service check.

Average Daily Rate

A key rooms department ratio is the average room rate, usually referred to as **average daily rate (ADR).** Most hotel and motel managers calculate the ADR even though rates within a property may vary significantly from single rooms to suites, from individual guests to groups and conventions, from weekdays to weekends, and from busy seasons to slack seasons.

Using figures from Exhibits 2 and 7, we calculate the 20X5 average room rate for the Wonderland Lodge as follows:

$$\text{Average Daily Rate} = \frac{\text{Room Revenue}}{\text{Number of Rooms Sold}}$$

$$= \frac{\$2,400,000}{43,800}$$

$$= \underline{\underline{\$54.79}}$$

The best standard of comparison to use in evaluating an actual average room rate is the rate budgeted as the goal during the period. This average rate should also be calculated individually for each market segment (business groups, tourists, airline crews, and other segments) or by room type.

Revenue per Available Room

Paid occupancy percentage and ADR can be combined into a single ratio called **revenue per available room** or **RevPAR.**

Traditionally, many hoteliers have placed heavy reliance on paid occupancy percentage as a quick indicator of activity and possibly performance. Others have looked at the ADR as an indication of the quality of its operation. However, paid occupancy percentage and average room rate by themselves are somewhat meaningless. One hotel may have a room occupancy of 80 percent and an ADR of $40, while a close competitor has a paid occupancy of 70 percent and an ADR of $60. Which hotel is in the preferable condition? RevPAR provides an answer to this question. It is calculated as follows:

$$\text{RevPAR} = \frac{\text{Room Revenue}}{\text{Available Rooms}}$$

or

$$\text{RevPAR} = \text{Paid Occupancy Percentage} \times \text{ADR}$$

Using the above example, the hotel with the 80 percent paid occupancy and the $40 ADR has a RevPAR of $32, while its competitor has a RevPAR of 70% × $60, or $42. Everything else being the same, hoteliers, creditors, and investors obviously prefer the hotel with the higher RevPAR. In this example, the RevPAR leads us to choose the hotel with the higher ADR, but this will not always be the case. Suppose, for example, that the second hotel in the above example had a paid occupancy of 50 percent instead of 70 percent; its RevPAR would then be $30 ($60 × 50%) and the RevPAR ratio would then favor the hotel with the higher occupancy percentage.

Based on the paid occupancy percentage and the ADR calculated earlier in this chapter, the Wonderland Lodge's RevPAR for 20X2 can be determined as follows:

$$
\begin{aligned}
\text{RevPAR} \quad &= \quad \$54.79 \times 80\% \\
&= \quad \underline{\underline{\$43.83}}
\end{aligned}
$$

Alternatively, using information from Exhibit 2, we can determine RevPAR as follows:

$$
\begin{aligned}
\text{RevPAR} \quad &= \quad \frac{\text{Room Revenue}}{\text{Available Rooms}} \\
&= \quad \frac{\$2,400,000}{150 \times 365} \\
&= \quad \underline{\underline{\$43.83}}
\end{aligned}
$$

Evaluating RevPAR is an improvement over simply looking at occupancy percentage or ADR separately. Many industry executives prefer this combined statistic.

Average Food Service Check

A key food service ratio is the **average food service check.** The ratio is determined by dividing Total Food Revenue by the number of food covers sold during the period.

Using figures from Exhibits 6 and 7, we can calculate the average food service check for 20X5 for the Wonderland Lodge as follows:

$$
\begin{aligned}
\text{Average Food Service Check} \quad &= \quad \frac{\text{Total Food Revenue}}{\text{Number of Food Covers}} \\
&= \quad \frac{\$450,000}{65,000} \\
&= \quad \underline{\underline{\$6.92}}
\end{aligned}
$$

The average food service check is best compared to the budgeted amount for 20X5. It can also be compared to industry averages.

Additional average checks should be calculated separately for beverages. Management may even desire to calculate the average check by dining area or by meal period.

Food Cost Percentage

The **food cost percentage** is a key food service ratio that compares the cost of food sold to Food Sales. Most food service managers rely heavily on this ratio for determining whether food costs are reasonable.

Based on figures from Exhibit 6, the 20X5 food cost percentage for the Wonderland Lodge is determined as follows:

$$\text{Food Cost Percentage} = \frac{\text{Cost of Food Sold}}{\text{Food Sales}}$$

$$= \frac{\$175,500}{\$450,000}$$

$$= \underline{\underline{39\%}}$$

In other words, of every $1 of food sales, $.39 goes toward the cost of food sold. This is best compared to the budgeted percentage for the period. A significant difference in either direction should be investigated by management. Management should be just as concerned about a food cost percentage that is significantly lower than the budgeted goal as it is about a food cost percentage that exceeds budgeted standards. A lower food cost percentage may indicate that the quality of food served is lower than desired, or that smaller portions are being served than are specified by the standard recipes. A food cost percentage in excess of the objective may be due to poor portion control, excessive food costs, theft, waste, spoilage, and so on.

Beverage Cost Percentage

A key ratio for beverage operations is the **beverage cost percentage.** This ratio results from dividing the cost of beverages sold by Beverage Sales.

Based on figures from Exhibit 6, the 20X5 beverage cost percentage for the Wonderland Lodge is calculated as follows:

$$\text{Beverage Cost Percentage} = \frac{\text{Cost of Beverages Sold}}{\text{Beverage Sales}}$$

$$= \frac{\$45,000}{\$180,000}$$

$$= \underline{\underline{25\%}}$$

That is, for each $1 of beverage sales, $.25 is spent on the cost of beverages served. As with the food cost percentage, this ratio is best compared by management to the goal set for that period. Likewise, any significant variances must be investigated to determine the cause(s). Refinements of this ratio include beverage cost percentages by type of beverage sold and by beverage outlet.

Exhibit 9   Operated Department Labor Cost Percentages

$$\text{Labor Cost Percentage} \ = \ \frac{\text{Labor Cost by Departments}}{\text{Department Revenues}}$$

Department	Total Labor Cost	÷ Total Revenue	= Labor Cost Percentage
Rooms	$ 360,000	$2,400,000	15.00%
Food	$ 144,000	$ 450,000	32.00%
Beverage	$ 45,000	$ 180,000	25.00%
Telecommunications	$ 25,000	$ 105,000	23.81%

Labor Cost Percentage

The largest expense in hotels, motels, clubs, and many restaurants is labor. Labor expense includes salaries, wages, bonuses, payroll taxes, and benefits. A general **labor cost percentage** is determined by dividing Total Labor Costs by Total Revenue. This general labor cost percentage is simply a benchmark for making broad comparisons. For control purposes, labor costs must be analyzed by department. The rooms department labor cost percentage is determined by dividing Rooms Department Labor Cost by Rooms Revenue. The food and beverage department labor cost percentage is determined by dividing Food and Beverage Department Labor Cost by Food and Beverage Revenue. Other operated department labor cost percentages are similarly determined.

Exhibit 9 uses figures from Exhibits 2 and 6 to calculate the 20X5 operated department labor cost percentages for the Wonderland Lodge. The food and beverage departments have the highest labor cost percentages at 32 percent and 25 percent, respectively. In most lodging firms, this is usually the case. The standards for these ratios are the budgeted percentages. Since labor costs are generally the largest expense, they must be tightly controlled. Management must carefully investigate any significant differences between actual and budgeted labor cost percentages.

Ratios for other expenses are usually computed as a percentage of revenue. If the expenses are operated department expenses, then the ratio is computed with the operated department revenues in the denominator and the expense in the numerator. An overhead expense ratio will consist of the overhead expense being divided by Total Revenue. For example, marketing expense percentage is determined by dividing the marketing expense by Total Revenue. Using figures for the Wonderland Lodge in 20X5 found in Exhibit 2, the marketing expense percentage can be calculated as 4.15 percent (marketing expense of $130,000 divided by total revenues of $3,135,000).

Limitations of Ratio Analysis

Ratios are extremely useful to owners, creditors, and management in evaluating the financial conditions and operations of hospitality establishments. However, ratios are only indicators. They do not resolve problems or even reveal exactly what the problem is. At best, when they vary significantly from budgeted standards, industry averages, or ratios for past periods, ratios only indicate that there *may be* a problem. Considerably more analysis and investigation are required.

Ratios are meaningful when they result from comparing two related numbers. Food cost percentage is meaningful because of the direct relationship between food costs and food sales. A goodwill/cash ratio is probably meaningless due to the lack of any meaningful relationship between goodwill and cash.

Ratios are most useful when compared to a standard. A food cost percentage of 32 percent has little usefulness until it is compared to a standard such as past performance, industry averages, or the budgeted percentages.

Ratios are often used to compare different hospitality establishments. However, many such comparisons (especially those using operating ratios) will not be meaningful if the two firms are in completely different segments of the industry. For example, comparing ratios for a luxury hotel to ratios for a quick-service restaurant would seldom serve a meaningful purpose.

In addition, if the accounting procedures used by two separate hospitality establishments differ in several areas, then a comparison of their ratios will likely show differences related to accounting procedures rather than to financial positions or operations.

Even though these limitations are present, a careful use of ratios that acknowledges their shortcomings will result in an enhanced understanding of the financial position and operations of various hospitality establishments.

Summary

Financial analysis permits investors, creditors, and operators to receive more valuable information from the financial statements than they could receive from reviewing the absolute numbers reported in the documents. Vital relationships can be monitored to determine solvency and risk, performance in comparison with other periods, and dividend payout ratios.

This chapter looked at four types of financial analysis: horizontal, vertical, trend, and ratio analyses. Horizontal analysis consists of calculating the absolute (dollar) change and the relative (percentage) change in line items for two accounting periods. Vertical analysis consists of reducing financial statement information to percentages of a whole for a given year in order to see the composition of the whole. Trend analysis is similar to horizontal analysis, except that it involves comparing several accounting periods to a single base period. Ratio analysis involves comparing related figures from one or two financial statements and expressing the relationship numerically. Most of this chapter focused on ratio analysis.

There are five major classifications of ratios: liquidity, solvency, activity, profitability, and operating. Although there is some overlap among these categories, each has a special area of concern. Exhibit 10 lists the 30 ratios presented in this chapter and the formulas for each. It is important to be familiar with the types of

Exhibit 10   List of Ratios

Ratio	Formula
Liquidity Ratios:	
1. Current ratio	Current Assets ÷ Current Liabilities
2. Acid-test ratio	(Cash + Marketable Securities + Notes + Accounts Receivable) ÷ Current Liabilities
3. Operating cash flows to current liabilities ratio	Operating Cash Flows ÷ Current Liabilities
4. Accounts receivable turnover	Revenue ÷ Average Accounts Receivable
5. Average collection period	365 ÷ Accounts Receivable Turnover
Solvency Ratios:	
6. Debt-equity ratio	Total Liabilities ÷ Total Owners' Equity
7. Long-term debt to total capitalization ratio	Long-Term Debt ÷ (Long-Term Debt + Owners Equity)
8. Number of times interest earned ratio	EBIT ÷ Interest Expense
9. Fixed charge coverage ratio	(EBIT + Lease Expense) ÷ (Interest Expenses + Lease Expense)
10. Operating cash flows to total liabilities ratio	Operating Cash Flows ÷ Total Liabilities
Activity Ratios:	
11. Inventory Turnover:	
Food inventory turnover	Cost of Food Used ÷ Average Food Inventory
Beverage inventory turnover	Cost of Beverages Used ÷ Average Beverage Inventory
12. Property and equipment turnover	Total Revenue ÷ Average Property and Equipment
13. Asset turnover ratio	Total Revenue ÷ Average Total Assets
14. Paid occupancy percentage	Paid Rooms Occupied ÷ Available Rooms
15. Complimentary occupancy percentage	Complimentary Rooms ÷ Available Rooms
16. Average occupancy per room	Number of Room Guests ÷ Number of Rooms Occupied
17. Multiple occupancy percentage	Rooms Occupied by More than One Person ÷ Number of Rooms Occupied

(continued)

Exhibit 10   *(continued)*

Ratio	Formula
Profitability Ratios:	
18. Profit margin	Net Income ÷ Total Revenue
19. Operating efficiency ratio	Income after Undistributed Operating Expenses ÷ Total Revenue
20. Return on assets	Net Income ÷ Average Total Assets
21. Return on owners' equity	Net Income ÷ Average Owners' Equity
22. Earnings per share	Net Income ÷ Average Common Shares Outstanding
23. Price earnings ratio	Market Price per Share ÷ Earnings per Share
Operating Ratios:	
24. Mix of sales	[Departmental revenues are totaled; percentages of Total Revenue are calculated for each]
25. Average daily rate	Rooms Revenue ÷ Number of Rooms Sold
26. Revenue per available room (RevPAR)	Paid Occupancy Percentage × Average Daily Rate
27. Average food service check	Total Food and Beverage Revenue ÷ Number of Food Covers
28. Food cost percentage	Cost of Food Sold ÷ Food Sales
29. Beverage cost percentage	Cost of Beverages Sold ÷ Beverage Sales
30. Labor cost percentage	Labor Cost by Department ÷ Department Revenue

ratios in each category, to know what each ratio measures, and to be aware of the targets or standards against which they are compared.

For example, a number of liquidity ratios focus on the hospitality establishment's ability to cover its short-term debts. However, each person examining the establishment's financial position will have a desired performance in mind. Creditors desire high liquidity ratios because they indicate that loans will probably be repaid. Investors, on the other hand, like lower liquidity ratios, since current assets are not as profitable as long-term assets. Management reacts to these pressures by trying to please both groups.

The five ratio classifications vary in importance among the three major users of ratios. Creditors focus on solvency, profitability, and liquidity; investors and owners consider these ratios, but highlight the profitability ratios. Managers use all types of ratios, but are especially concerned with operating and activity ratios, which can be used in evaluating the results of operations.

It is important to realize that a percentage by itself is not meaningful. It is only useful when it is compared with a standard: an industry average, a ratio from a past period, or a budgeted ratio. It is the comparison with budgeted ratios that is the most useful for management. Any significant difference should be analyzed to determine its probable cause(s). Once management has fully investigated areas of concern revealed by the ratios, then corrective action can be taken to rectify any problems.

Endnotes

1. The interested student is referred to intermediate accounting texts, most of which contain a full discussion of EPS calculations in various situations.

Key Terms

accounts receivable turnover—A measure of the rapidity of conversion of accounts receivable into cash; revenue divided by average accounts receivable.

acid-test ratio—Ratio of total cash and near-cash current assets to total current liabilities.

activity ratios—A group of ratios that reflect management's ability to use the property's assets and resources.

asset turnover—An activity ratio; total revenues divided by average total assets.

average collection period—The average number of days it takes a hospitality operation to collect all its accounts receivable; calculated by dividing the account receivable turnover into 365 (days in a year).

average daily rate (ADR)—A key rooms department operating ratio; rooms revenue divided by number of rooms sold. Also called *average room rate*.

average food service check—Total food revenue divided by the number of covers for a period.

average occupancy per room—An activity ratio measuring management's ability to use lodging facilities; the number of guests divided by the number of rooms occupied.

beverage cost percentage—A ratio comparing the cost of beverages sold to beverage sales; calculated by dividing the cost of beverages sold by beverage sales.

common-size statements—Financial statements used in vertical analysis whose information has been reduced to percentages to facilitate comparisons.

comparative financial statements—The horizontal analysis of financial statements from the current and previous periods in terms of both absolute and relative variances for each line item.

complimentary occupancy—The number of complimentary rooms for a period divided by the number of rooms available.

current ratio—Ratio of total current assets to total current liabilities expressed as a coverage of so many times; calculated by dividing current assets by current liabilities.

debt-equity ratio—Compares the debt of a hospitality operation to its net worth (owners' equity) and indicates the operation's ability to withstand adversity and meet its long-term obligations; calculated by dividing total liabilities by total owners' equity.

double occupancy—The number of rooms occupied by more than one guest divided by the number of rooms occupied by guests. Sometimes called *multiple occupancy*.

earnings per share (EPS)—A ratio providing a general indicator of the profitability of a hospitality operation by comparing net income to the average number of common shares outstanding. If preferred stock has been issued, preferred dividends are subtracted from net income before calculating EPS.

fixed charge coverage ratio—A variation of the number of times interest earned ratio that considers leases as well as interest expense; the sum of lease expense and earnings before both interest and income taxes divided by the sum of interest expense and lease expense.

food cost percentage—A ratio comparing the cost of food sold to food sales; calculated by dividing the wholesale dollar amount of total sales by the retail dollar amount of total sales.

horizontal analysis—Comparing financial statements for two or more accounting periods in terms of both absolute and relative variances for each line item.

inventory turnover—A ratio showing how quickly a hospitality operation's inventory is moving from storage to productive use; calculated by dividing the cost of products (e.g., food or beverages) used by the average product (e.g., food or beverages) inventory value.

labor cost percentage—A ratio comparing the labor expense for each department to the total revenue generated by the department; total labor cost by department divided by department revenues.

leverage—The use of debt in place of equity dollars to finance operations and increase the return on the equity dollars already invested.

liquidity ratios—A group of ratios that reveal the ability of a hospitality establishment to meet its short-term obligations.

long-term debt to total capitalization ratio—A solvency ratio showing long-term debt as a percentage of the sum of long-term debt and owners' equity; long-term debt divided by the sum of long-term debt and owners' equity.

multiple occupancy—The number of rooms occupied by more than one guest divided by the number of rooms occupied by guests. Sometimes called *double occupancy*.

number of times interest earned ratio—A solvency ratio expressing the number of times interest expense can be covered; earnings before both interest and taxes divided by interest expense.

operating cash flows to current liabilities ratio—A liquidity ratio that compares the cash flow from the firm's operating activities to its obligations at the balance sheet date that must be paid within 12 months; operating cash flows divided by average current liabilities.

operating cash flows to total liabilities ratio—A solvency ratio; operating cash flows divided by average total liabilities.

operating efficiency ratio—A measure of management's ability to generate sales and control expenses; calculated by dividing Income after Undistributed Operating Expenses by total revenue.

operating ratios—A group of ratios that assist in the analysis of hospitality establishment operations.

paid occupancy percentage—A measure of management's ability to efficiently use available assets; the number of rooms sold divided by the number of rooms available for sale.

price earnings (PE) ratio—A profitability ratio used by financial analysts when presenting investment possibilities; the market price per share divided by the earnings per share.

profit margin—An overall measure of management's ability to generate sales and control expenses; calculated by dividing net income by total revenue.

profitability ratios—A group of ratios that reflect the results of all areas of management's responsibility.

property and equipment turnover—A ratio measuring management's effectiveness in using property and equipment to generate revenue; calculated by dividing average total property and equipment into total revenue generated for the period.

ratio analysis—Comparing financial ratios in a business with standards, such as prior performance, industry averages, or planned goals, as a way of evaluating the performance and financial condition of the business.

return on assets (ROA)—A ratio providing a general indicator of the profitability of a hospitality operation by comparing net income to total investment; calculated by dividing net income by average total assets.

return on owners' equity (ROE)—A ratio providing a general indicator of the profitability of a hospitality operation by comparing net income to the owners' investment; calculated by dividing net income by average owners' equity.

revenue per available room (RevPAR)—A combination of paid occupancy percentage and average daily rate; room revenues divided by the number of available rooms or, alternatively, paid occupancy percentage times average daily rate.

seat turnover—An activity ratio measuring the rate at which people are served; the number of people served divided by the number of seats available.

solvency ratios—A group of ratios that measure the extent to which an enterprise has been financed by debt and is able to meet its long-term obligations.

trend analysis—A method of analyzing ratios over more than two time periods. Trend analysis allows management to identify and deal with emerging trends.

trend percentage—Expression of a given period's figure as a percentage of the base period's figure; used for several years' or financial periods' data in *trend analysis*.

vertical analysis—Analyzing individual financial statements by reducing financial information to percentages of a whole; that is, income statement line items are expressed as percentages of total revenue; balance sheet assets are expressed as percentages of total assets.

Review Questions

1. How does ratio analysis benefit creditors?

2. If you were investing in a hotel, which ratios would be most useful? Why?

3. What are the limitations of ratio analysis?

4. How do the three user groups of ratio analysis react to the solvency ratios?

5. What is *leverage*, and why may owners want to increase it?

6. What do activity ratios highlight?

7. How is the profit margin calculated? How is it used?

8. Which standard is the most effective for comparison with ratios?

9. Of what value is the ratio of Food Sales to Total Sales to the manager of a hotel? To a creditor?

10. What is *RevPAR*? What is the reason for its increased use by managers?

Problems

Problem 1

Steve Rannels, the founder of the Houston Hotel, wants to analyze 20X2's operations by comparing them with the 20X1 results. To help him, prepare a comparative income statement using the 20X1 and 20X2 information available.

Houston Hotel
Income Statements
For the years ending December 31, 20X1 and 20X2

	20X1	20X2
Revenues		
Rooms	$ 976,000	$ 1,041,000
Food and Beverage	604,000	626,000
Telephone	50,000	52,000
Total	1,630,000	1,719,000

Direct Expenses		
Rooms	250,000	264,000
Food and Beverage	476,000	507,000
Telephone	68,000	68,000
Total Operational Departmental Income	836,000	880,000
Undistributed Operating Expenses		
Administrative and General	195,000	206,000
Marketing	65,000	68,000
Property Operation and Maintenance	69,000	68,000
Energy Costs	101,000	102,000
Income after Undistributed Operating Expenses	406,000	436,000
Rent, Property Taxes and Insurance	200,000	201,000
Interest	55,000	52,000
Depreciation and Amortization	116,000	116,000
Income before Income Taxes	35,000	67,000
Income Taxes	7,000	17,000
Net Income	$ 28,000	$ 50,000

Note: Rearrange the income statement to conform to the *USALI* format; that is, subtract direct expenses from revenues of operated departments to show departmental incomes.

Problem 2

The following information is the Mobile Inn's balance sheet account balances as of December 31, 20X1 and 20X2. You have been hired by the owner to prepare a financial package for a bank loan, and the package is to include comparative balance sheets.

Assets	20X1	20X2
Cash	$ 16,634	$ 20,768
Accounts Receivable	16,105	11,618
Marketable Securities	10,396	10,496
Inventories	14,554	18,554
Prepaid Expenses	4,158	3,874
Land	116,435	116,435
Building	1,007,090	1,007,090
China, Glass, etc.	269,255	284,934
Accumulated Depreciation	453,263	537,849
Organization Costs	10,000	8,000

Liabilities & Owners' Equity		
Accounts Payable	23,265	20,945
Accrued Expenses	2,047	1,039
Deferred Income Taxes	8,163	7,927
Current Portion of Long-Term Debt	20,407	20,060
Long-Term Debt	553,429	533,369
Retained Earnings	192,853	149,380
Common Stock	261,200	261,200
Treasury Stock	50,000	50,000

Required:

Prepare comparative balance sheets for December 31, 20X1 and 20X2, in accordance with *USALI.* Reflect both percentage and dollar differences between the two years.

Problem 3

Below is selected information from the comparative and common-size asset portion of balance sheets for the LA Grill.

	December 31 20X1	December 31 20X2	Dollar Difference	Common-Size (Dec. 31, 20X2)
Current Assets				
Cash				
House Bank	$_____	$_____	$ (10)	_____%
Demand Deposit	_____	60	_____	.6
Total Cash	_____	_____	(10)	1.0
Accounts Receivable	$ 1,241	_____	_____	14.0
Inventories	_____	_____	_____	_____
Total Current Assets	_____	1,620	201	_____
Investments	_____	_____	25	2.0
Property & Equipment (net)				
Land	957	1,030	_____	_____
Building	4,350	_____	_____	_____
Furniture	_____	_____	(75)	25.0
Other Assets	49	_____	_____	.5
Total Assets	$_____	$_____	$_____	_____%

Required:

Fill in the blanks above. Round all amounts to the nearest dollar.

Challenge Problems

Problem 4

The Louis V Hotel is a 250-room facility with several profit centers. The hotel is open throughout the year, and generally about 2 percent of the rooms are being repaired or renovated at all times; therefore, assume that these rooms are unavailable for sale. During 20X1, the hotel sold 76,400 rooms and experienced an average occupancy per room of 1.42 people. The accounting department has supplied the following information concerning the food department:

Ending Inventory	$ 35,000
Consumption by Employees (free of charge)	5,000
Cost of Food Sales	312,000
Food Cost %	35%
Food Inventory Turnover	12 times

Required:

Determine the following:

1. Paid occupancy rate for 20X1
2. Number of paid guests of 20X1
3. Beginning inventory of food
4. Food sales
5. Multiple occupancy percentage (Assume that no more than two persons occupied a double room.)

Problem 5

The Tahoe Hotel's current assets and current liabilities from the past three years' balance sheets are as follows:

	20X1	20X2	20X3
Current Assets:			
Cash	$ 15,000	$ 20,000	$ 30,000
Marketable Securities	30,000	25,000	20,000
Accounts Receivable (Net)	70,000	85,000	95,000
Inventory—Food	20,000	22,000	25,000
Prepaid Expenses	10,000	12,000	15,000
Total	$ 145,000	$ 164,000	$ 185,000

	20X1	20X2	20X3
Current Liabilities:			
Accounts Payable	$ 60,000	$ 62,000	$ 65,000
Notes Payable	30,000	30,000	30,000
Wages Payable	20,000	22,000	25,000
Taxes Payable	10,000	11,000	12,000
Total	$ 120,000	$ 125,000	$ 132,000

	20X1	20X2	20X3
Selected Operations Data:			
Sales (Total)	$1,000,000	$1,100,000	$1,200,000
Cost of Food Sold	150,000	160,000	168,000
Free Meals—Employees and Others	3,000	3,200	3,400

Required:

1. Compute the following for each year (except as noted):
   a. Current ratio
   b. Acid-test ratio
   c. Accounts receivable turnover (20X2 and 20X3 only)
   d. Inventory turnover (20X2 and 20X3 only)
   e. Working capital
2. Based on the above analysis, comment on the liquidity trend of the Tahoe Hotel.

Problem 6

The financial statements of The 10,000 Lakes Cafe are as follows:

The 10,000 Lakes Cafe
Income Statement
For the year ended December 31, 20X5

Revenue

Food Sales	$1,800,000
Allowances	10,000
Net Revenue	1,790,000
Cost of Food Sold	500,000
Gross Profit	1,290,000

Operating Expenses

Payroll	600,000
Payroll Taxes and Employee Benefits	80,000
Laundry and Dry Cleaning	21,000
Operating Supplies	50,000
Advertising	20,000
Utilities	38,000
Repairs and Maintenance	19,000
Other Operating Expenses	40,000
Total Operating Expenses	868,000
Income after Undistributed Operating Expenses	422,000

Fixed Charges

Rent	20,000
Property Taxes	10,000
Insurance	5,000
Interest	80,000
Depreciation	20,000
Total Fixed Charges	135,000
Income Before Income Taxes	287,000
Income Taxes	101,000
Net Income	$ 186,000

Balance Sheets
December 31, 20X5 and December 31, 20X4

Assets

Current Assets	20X4	20X5
Cash	$ 36,500	$ 34,000
Accounts Receivable	3,400	4,000
Food Inventory	5,000	5,500
Prepaid Expenses	2,600	2,000
Total Current Assets	47,500	45,500

Property and Equipment		
Land	$ 30,000	$ 30,000
Building	960,000	960,000
Furniture and Equipment	248,000	262,000
Less Accumulated Depreciation	35,000	40,000

China, Glassware and Silver	18,000	19,000
Net Property and Equipment	$1,221,000	$1,231,000
Total Assets	$1,268,500	$1,276,500

Liabilities

Current Liabilities		
Accounts Payable	$ 25,000	$ 21,000
Accrued Expenses	7,000	9,000
Current Portion of Long-Term Debt	16,000	16,000
Total Current Liabilities	48,000	46,000
Long-Term Liabilities		
Mortgage Payable, Net of		
Current Portion	940,000	934,000

Owners' Equity

Paid-In Capital:		
Common Stock	150,000	150,000
Additional Paid-In Capital	15,000	15,000
Retained Earnings	115,500	131,500
Total Liabilities and		
Shareholders' Equity	$1,268,500	$1,276,500

Required:

Compute the following ratios for The 10,000 Lakes Cafe for both 20X4 and 20X5 except as noted:

1. Current ratio
2. Acid-test ratio
3. Debt-equity ratio
4. Food inventory turnover for 20X5 only
5. Accounts receivable turnover for 20X5 only
6. Average collection period for 20X5 only
7. Long-term debt to total capitalization ratio
8. Asset turnover ratio for 20X5 only
9. Return on assets for 20X5 only
10. Return on owners' equity for 20X5 only

Problem 7

Using the information provided in Problem 6, compute the following ratios for The 10,000 Lakes Cafe for 20X5.

1. Number of times interest earned ratio
2. Fixed charge coverage ratio
3. Profit margin
4. Earnings per share (Assume 25,000 shares were outstanding.)

5. Average food service check (Assume 164,000 meals were served.)
6. Food cost percentage
7. Labor cost percentage
8. Operating cash flows to current liabilities ratio (Assume operating cash flows were $203,500 for 20X5.)
9. Operating cash flows to total liabilities ratio

Problem 8

The Dallas Budget Inn condensed income statements for the months of July and August 20X1 are as follows:

	July	August
Room Sales	$110,000	$112,000
Labor Expense	50,000	52,000
Laundry Expense	5,000	4,800
Utility Expense	6,500	6,700
Insurance Expense	1,500	1,500
Property Tax Expense	2,100	2,100
Interest Expense	8,000	8,000
Depreciation Expense	15,000	15,000
Income Tax	7,000	7,500
Net Income	$14,900	$14,400

Required:

Convert the two income statements to common-size income statements.

Problem 9

Using the condensed income statements for July and August for the Dallas Budget Inn, prepare comparative income statements. Show both dollar and percentage differences.

Problem 10

Selected information from the Assets sections of the comparative and common-size balance sheets of December 31, 20X1 and 20X2 of the Boloski Lodge is as follows:

	December 31		Dollar	Common Size
	20X1	20X2	Difference	12/31/20X2
Current Assets:				
Cash	$_____	$_____	$1,000	1.0%

Accounts Receivable	150,000	_____	5,000	_____%
Inventory	_____	25,000	_____	_____%
Prepaid Expenses	10,000	_____	_____	_____%
Total	_____	200,000	10,000	10.0%
Investments	_____	_____	(10,000)	10.0%
Property & Equipment:				
Land	_____	_____	-0-	20.0%
Building	_____	_____	50,000	_____%
Equipment	_____	_____	-0-	_____%
Accumulated Depreciation	_____	_____	_____	(10.0)%
Total	_____	_____	_____	_____%
Total Assets	$_____	$_____	$50,000	_____%

Required:

Fill in the blanks in the previous table. Round all percentages to the nearest 0.1 percent.

REVIEW QUIZ

When you feel you have covered all of the material in this chapter, answer these questions. Choose the *best* answer.

1. All of the following types of figures used in financial analysis are typically expressed in percentages *except:*

   a. absolute changes of an item.
   b. relative changes of an item.
   c. trend percentages.
   d. figures used in vertical analysis.

2. Barbara Baggins, owner of the Hobbit Hotel, is new to the hotel business. She thought that her knowledge and experience in real estate development would help her evaluate the success of her investment in the hotel. Three months into the fiscal year, the hotel was earning a profit, but Barbara wasn't sure whether the return on her investment was high or low. Which of the following standards would provide Barbara with a baseline against which to compare the hotel's financial ratios for the quarter?

   a. industry averages
   b. budgeted ratio goals
   c. ratios from a past period
   d. official standards set by government regulations

3. If the Average Accounts Receivable for a certain hotel is $35,000 and its Total Revenue is $750,000, the average collection period is:

   a. 4 percent.
   b. 21 days.
   c. 17 days.
   d. 2.0 days.

4. The Delhi Restaurant's Earnings before Interest and Taxes was $200,000 for 20X4. During 20X4, the Delhi had interest expense of $50,000, income taxes of $60,000, and rent expense of $100,000. The fixed charge coverage ratio for 20X4 is _____ times.

   a. 1.3
   b. 1.5
   c. 2
   d. 2.3

REVIEW QUIZ *(continued)*

5.

Rooms Available for Sale	100,000
Paid Rooms Occupied	60,000
Paid Guests	80,000
Rooms Occupied by 2 or More Guests	10,000

Given the above information, what is the paid occupancy percentage?

a. 10%
b. 60%
c. 80%
d. cannot be determined from the information given

6. Profit margin is determined by dividing:

a. market price per share by earnings per share.
b. income after undistributed operating expenses by total revenue.
c. net income by total revenue.
d. net income by average total assets.

7. The food sales for the XYZ Restaurant were $100,000 for June. The cost of food consumed totaled $38,000. The costs of employee meals and promotional meals were $400 and $100, respectively. The food cost percentage for June was:

a. 38%.
b. 37.5%.
c. 37%.
d. none of the above.

Answer Key: 1-a-C1, 2-a-C4, 3-c-C5, 4-c-C6, 5-b-C7, 6-c-C8, 7-b-C9

Each question is linked to a competency. Competencies are listed on the first page of the chapter. An answer reading 3-b-C4 translates to:

3: the question number
b: the correct answer
C4: the competency number

Index

¡Continuemos!

¡Continuemos!

SEVENTH EDITION

Ana C. Jarvis
Chandler-Gilbert Community College

Raquel Lebredo
California Baptist University

Francisco Mena-Ayllón
University of Redlands

Teleinforme activities prepared by Anny Ewing

INSTRUCTOR'S EDITION

Houghton Mifflin Company   **Boston**   **New York**

Publisher: Rolando Hernández

Sponsoring Editor: Amy Baron

Development Manager: Sharla Zwirek

Development Editor: Rafael Burgos-Mirabal

Editorial Assistant: Erin Kern

Project Editor: Amy Johnson

Production/Design Coordinator: Lisa Jelly Smith

Manufacturing Manager: Florence Cadran

Senior Marketing Manager: Tina Crowley Desprez

Cover Painting © Harold Burch/NYC

Library of Congress Control Number: 2001133271

Student Text ISBN: 0-618-22067-4
Instructor's Edition ISBN: 0-618-22072-0

3456789-DOC-06 05 04

Contents

Introduction to the Instructor's Edition

¡Continuemos!, Seventh Edition, is a complete, fully integrated intermediate Spanish program for two- and four-year colleges and universities. Designed to consolidate the language skills acquired in introductory-level courses and to build communicative skills and cultural competency, *¡Continuemos!*, Seventh Edition, emphasizes the natural use of practical, high-frequency language for communication. This Instructor's Edition describes the program and its objectives, offers suggestions for implementing the various components and the companion texts, and provides an answer key to the cloze exercises in the text.

Program Components

¡Continuemos!, Seventh Edition, features a full range of integrated components, designed with flexibility in mind to accommodate both diverse teaching styles and the varying intermediate Spanish curricula of colleges and universities.

The complete program consists of the following items:

¡Continuemos!, Seventh Edition

- Student's Edition with free Student Audio CD
- Instructor's Edition with Student Audio CD
- Workbook/Laboratory Manual (in print and online versions)
- Audio Program (on CDs or cassettes)
- Student CD-ROM
- Instructor's Resource Manual (Testing Program / Tapescript / Videoscript)
- Video
- Student Website (*http://spanish.college.hmco.com/students*)
- Spanish Web Resources and Instructor Website (*http://spanish.college.hmco.com/instructors*)
- Instructor Class Prep CD-ROM

Companion texts

- *¡Conversemos!*, Third Edition, with free Student Audio CD (*conversation text*)
- *¡Conversemos!* Instructor's Resource Manual
- *Aventuras literarias*, Sixth Edition, with free Student Audio CD (*literary reader*)

New to the Seventh Edition

The *¡Continuemos!* program continues to offer a comprehensive review of basic, first-year grammar structures, while developing students' reading, writing, speaking, and listening skills and increasing their awareness of the cultures from the Spanish-speaking world. In response to suggestions from reviewers and from users of the previous edition, the Seventh Edition provides new opportunities for students to progress from skill-getting to skill-using through a text-specific video, text-specific audio, authentic readings, reading and writing strategy instruction and practice, and an increased emphasis on personalized, open-ended activities. The following lists highlight the major changes in the Student's Edition and in the components.

The Student's Edition

- The scope and sequence has been streamlined to ten lessons to further improve the program's manageability.

- Chosen for their cultural relevance and success in generating student interaction, four new themes—family and personal relations, Spanish-American cuisines, the Latin presence in entertainment worldwide, work and technology—and five new readings strengthen the diverse thematic coverage of the program.

- Throughout each lesson, new listening material, ranging from slow-paced narrations to faster-paced conversation and authentic songs, expose learners to increasingly challenging tasks in order to prepare them for real-life listening situations and interaction.

- Additional, related vocabulary enables learners to converse about target themes early, and contextualized and open-ended practice provides realistic situations and opportunities for the creative use of active vocabulary.

- To support for-recognition and for-production acquisition as well as student understanding, cultural facts and active vocabulary are carefully reentered in grammar examples and explanations, practice, and in *¡Continuemos!*, the cumulative end-of-lesson section.

- Using a geographic focus, each lesson covers products and/or practices. Perspectives are explored through conversations involving cross-cultural comparisons in order to promote discussion and expand students' knowledge of the diverse cultures of the Spanish-speaking world.

- Through the gradual incorporation of reading and writing strategies, the program offers a spiraling approach to strategy instruction. Each lesson focuses on a specific or a combination of strategies for reading and on process-based writing to foster students' independence as critical thinkers.

The Components

○ The *Workbook/Laboratory Manual,* available in print and online versions, reflects the changes in the Student's Edition. The verb conjugation charts have been replaced with a variety of contextualized exercises. New art-based activities and cultural exercises tied to **El mundo hispánico** essays have been added.

○ The Video has been upgraded to reflect the substantially revised thematic scope and sequence.

○ In order to further integrate listening in your classes, the new Student Audio consists of the recorded lesson opening passages, fast-paced conversations followed by one comprehension activity, and folkloric Iberian-American songs.

○ The new *¡Continuemos!* Student CD-ROM is a state-of-the-art multimedia ancillary that provides practice on vocabulary acquisition, on target lesson vocabulary and grammar, as well as on reading, writing, and listening that is primarily based on the target lesson theme. In addition, it offers games and video-based speaking and comprehension activities.

○ The substantially upgraded *¡Continuemos!* website now features an instructor component. This includes additional preconversation support for select discussion activities; a technology integration guide; electronic versions of the Testing Program, the Audioscript, and the Videoscript; and PowerPoint slides that contain grammar charts and explanations. The student component provides online self tests, flashcards, web search activities integrated within writing tasks, and four-skills practice, primarily based on the target lesson country or region (**El mundo hispánico** culture section).

○ The new Instructor Class Prep CD-ROM includes, in electronic format, all the materials in the Instructor's Resource Manual as well as PowerPoint slides of grammar charts and explanations.

Objectives of the Program

The integrated four-skills approach of *¡Continuemos!,* Seventh Edition, prepares intermediate students to use Spanish in real-life situations by emphasizing oral communication and by developing the other basic language skills. To meet these goals, the program has been designed with the following objectives in mind:

○ To reinforce and expand the vocabulary base acquired by students in first-year Spanish. Practical, high-frequency vocabulary presented in culturally authentic contexts takes students beyond the basic survival skills acquired in introductory classes and sets the stage for extended discourse.

○ To review fundamental grammar structures and to foster the mastery of concepts not fully acquired in the first year of study. The presentation of most structures in *¡Continuemos!* expands on the morphological and syntactical elements normally presented in beginning Spanish.

○ To strengthen students' communicative competency by providing ongoing opportunities for oral practice in realistic contexts (cultural discussions, debates, role-plays, and problem-solving situations) that lend themselves to more sophisticated discourse strategies, for example circumlocution and paraphrasing.

○ To broaden students' knowledge of the geography of the Spanish-speaking world, to increase their familiarity with the contemporary cultures from these countries, and to expand their ability to make cross-cultural comparisons.

○ To develop students' ability to read and understand authentic texts from the Spanish-speaking world and to articulate their observations, reactions, and opinions.

○ To develop listening comprehension skills by exposing students to natural language in real-life contexts, as spoken by native speakers from a variety of countries from the Spanish-speaking world.

○ To improve writing skills by providing ongoing practice in contexts that reinforce the vocabulary and structures taught in the text.

Organization of the Textbook

¡Continuemos!, Seventh Edition, consists of ten regular lessons, five self-tests, and a reference section. The reference materials at the end of the text include a summary of syllabification, accentuation, and punctuation rules; a summary of regular and irregular verb conjugations; an answer key to the self-tests; and Spanish–English and English–Spanish vocabularies. To assist instructors in implementing the various features of the text, they are described in detail in this section.

¡Bienvenidos al mundo hispánico!
This introductory section develops cultural competency through new full-color maps, a list of countries, national flags, capitals, nationalities, and questions on the geography of the Spanish-speaking world.

Lessons 1–10
The following features recur in each of the ten text lessons:

Lesson Opener
Each lesson begins with a list of lesson objectives accompanied by a photo that illustrates the lesson theme.

Lesson Opening Passage, *Dígame*, and *Perspectivas socioculturales*
To develop communicative competence, students must be exposed to language samples presented in realistic contexts. The lesson opening passages serve this function as they introduce the new vocabulary and grammatical structures that will be prac-

ticed throughout the lesson within the framework of high-frequency situations that present the lessons' central theme. In the Seventh Edition, the opening passages are recorded in the new Student Audio CD for additional aural reinforcement of the target lesson vocabulary and structures in context. The **Dígame** activity checks comprehension in a question-and-answer activity format. **Perspectivas socioculturales** offers opportunities for cross-cultural discussions on sociocultural concepts or on specific products and/or practices that are covered in the opening passage.

Vocabulario and *Hablemos de todo un poco*

The **Vocabulario** sections list all new words and expressions presented in the dialogues by parts of speech or under the heading **Otras palabras y expresiones**. Entries in this list are to be learned for active use and are reinforced in the lesson's activities. **Ampliación** lists other theme-related, high-frequency words and expressions that expand on the basic ones appearing on the lesson opening passage. Considered active vocabulary, the **Ampliación** entries are also reinforced throughout the lesson's activities and grammar examples. **Hablemos de todo un poco** is the new vocabulary activity section. Always beginning with **Preparación,** a warm-up activity that practices vocabulary items in structured contexts, this section provides discussion topics for using the vocabulary just introduced in open-ended conversation.

Palabras problemáticas

To promote linguistic awareness, this section introduces students to nuances in the usage of specific lexical items that commonly cause difficulties for native speakers of English. These include groups of Spanish words with a single English translation, Spanish synonyms with variations in meaning, and false cognates. **Práctica** activities in a variety of formats reinforce the meanings and usage of the **palabras problemáticas**.

¡Ahora escuche!

This is the first of two in-text listening sections. It consists of a short narration that recycles the vocabulary introduced in the opening passage. The narration is followed by comprehension questions. To carry out this activity, the instructor will find the material in the **Answers to Text Exercises** section of the Instructor's Edition.

El mundo hispánico

Here the lesson's target country or region is explored. First, students read a brief essay that touches upon basic products and/or practices from that country or region. A comprehension check activity follows. Second, through in-class conversation on the **Hablemos de su país** discussion topics, students compare cultural aspects covered in the essay by examining those same aspects in the context of their own country. Finally, **Una tarjeta postal** offers further opportunity for reading or writing practice around cultural aspects of the country or region. In some cases, the text already appears on the postcard (for reading acquisition) and in other cases students are asked to write to peers about some of the products or practices to which they have been exposed, and to explore cultural perspectives by expressing themselves on any cultural aspect they may wish (or the instructor might want them) to focus on.

Estructuras gramaticales

All grammar explanations are presented clearly and succinctly in English, with numerous examples of usage so that students may use these sections for independent study and reference. All grammatical terms are followed by their Spanish equivalents. When appropriate, new structures are compared and contrasted with previously learned Spanish structures or with their English equivalents. The **¡Atención!** heading signals areas of potential interference between Spanish and English or points out important exceptions to the primary grammar rules whenever necessary. Assigning each grammar point as outside reading the day before it will be covered in class allows the instructor to devote more time to illustrating and practicing the grammar in context through the activities provided in the textbook.

Práctica

Each structure introduced in the **Estructuras gramaticales** sections is immediately followed by a subsection entitled **Práctica**, which reinforces the grammar points through exercises that range from controlled drills to contextualized, personalized, and open-ended activities. Among the many exercise formats featured are substitution drills, transformations, fill-ins, personalized questions, sentence completions, and interviews. Many of these exercises are designed to be done either orally or in writing at the instructor's discretion. Cloze exercises may be assigned as written homework to reinforce the new material; the more open-ended activities may be assigned as homework if advance preparation is needed or done orally in class in pairs or groups so that all students have the opportunity to communicate in Spanish.

¡Continuemos!

This end-of-lesson activity section promotes and develops listening and oral proficiency by involving students in realistic communicative and listening situations related to the lesson theme and geographic focus. All of the oral activities are designed for pair or small-group work. The activities engage students in lively, meaningful, and practical tasks such as surveys, listening to near-authentic and authentic material, interviews, debates, and role-plays. The following activities are included in this section:

Una encuesta: Here students conduct a survey of their classmates on topics related to the lesson theme. The results of the survey form the basis for small-group discussion.

¿Comprende Ud.?: This is the second in-text listening section. Students are presented with two different listening tasks. The first one is listening to a fast-paced conversation closely related to the lesson theme and geographic focus, and in which the lesson vocabulary and structures are recycled. The second one is learning a short traditional song that presents at least one of the lesson target structures in an authentic context. The listening material is in the Student Audio CD that accompanies the Student Edition.

Hablemos de...: In this activity, students must read and use information from authentic documents such as newspaper / magazine ads and brochures to answer a series of questions.

¿Qué dirían ustedes?: This sequence of brief role-play situations reinforces the contexts and themes that have been presented throughout the lesson.

¡De ustedes depende!: This activity features a more challenging or elaborate role-play situation; the scenario usually involves several tasks.

Mesa redonda/Debate: To encourage extended oral discourse, this activity asks students to engage in a debate or round-table discussion on a thought-provoking or controversial issue related to the lesson theme.

To prepare students for the **¡Continuemos!** activities, especially in the early lessons, brainstorming sessions that focus on the ways in which the situation might evolve and the vocabulary needed to respond appropriately may prove beneficial, particularly to students experiencing difficulty. Assigning pairs or groups so that weaker students work with more able peers can also be helpful.

Lecturas periodísticas

Chosen for their appeal and accessibility, these authentic readings from newspapers and magazines from Spain, Latin America, and the United States expand students' cultural knowledge while reinforcing the lesson theme. New cultural concepts and noncognate words and phrases are explained in marginal glosses and, occasionally, in footnotes. To develop students' reading skills, **Saber leer** introduces important reading strategies that are recycled and built upon throughout the textbook. **Para leer y comprender** consists of a series of prereading questions. Personalized, open-ended questions (**Desde su mundo**) follow each reading and provide opportunities for students to discuss their own opinions and experiences in relation to the reading topic. Students should be encouraged to employ the reading strategies and to use the prereading questions to help them focus on meaning rather than on translating every word. To check comprehension, students may be asked to paraphrase the selection orally or in writing.

Piense y escriba

As a whole, the end-of-lesson **Piense y escriba** sections constitute a writing skill development program. Writing is a process and it is conceived of as a communicative medium for the development of critical-thinking skills at the intermediate level. Lessons 1 and 2 introduce the concepts of audience and purpose; Lessons 3 and 4 introduce prewriting aspects (generation, selection, and organization of ideas); Lesson 5 focuses on the introduction and the conclusion of written texts; in Lesson 6 students apply all they have hitherto covered about the writing process. Lessons 7 and 9 address peer editing as an activity for revising drafts (for content and organization, as well as for grammatical correctness); Lesson 8 explicitly discusses the fact that good writing requires aural and reading contact with the language. Finally, in Lesson 10, students are asked to approach the given topic as their own writing project.

Teleinforme

In conjunction with the captivating visual images presented on the authentic footage in the **Teleinforme** modules of the revised *¡Continuemos!* Video, the **Teleinforme** activities expand upon and enhance students' cultural knowledge of the Spanish-speaking world. The three activity sections—**Preparación** (previewing), **Comprensión** (postviewing comprehension), and **Ampliación** (postviewing expansion)—are pedagogically designed to fully exploit the video footage and to give students the support they need to comprehend natural speech.

The following strategies are helpful for using **Teleinforme** modules and activities to the best advantage:

○ Model pronunciation of the **Vocabulario** as a previewing activity and instruct students to circle words in the **Vocabulario** as they hear them in the video.

○ Tell students not to worry about understanding every word as they watch the video, but to focus on getting the gist of what is being said. Emphasize that attention to background settings and nonverbal communication will help students to understand what is going on in the video clips.

○ View the video clips as many times as necessary for student comprehension. Using the pause button to freeze an image while you ask a question about it is an excellent way to verify comprehension.

○ Point out locations shown in the video on maps to increase students' familiarity with the geography of the Spanish-speaking world.

¿Están listos para el examen?

These self-tests, which follow Lessons 2, 4, 6, 8, and 10, contain exercises designed to review the vocabulary and structures introduced in the two preceding lessons. Organized by lesson and by grammatical structure, they enable students to determine quickly what material they have mastered and which concepts they ought to review further. The answer key in **Apéndice C** provides immediate verification.

Appendices

The three appendices at the end of the text serve as a useful reference.

Apéndice A: This summary of rules related to Spanish syllabification, use of accent marks, and punctuation will help students to improve their writing skills.

Apéndice B: The conjugations of the highest-frequency regular, stem-changing, and irregular Spanish verbs are organized here in a convenient, readily accessible format for quick reference and review.

Apéndice C: This answer key to five **¿Están listos para el examen?** self tests enables students to check their own progress quickly throughout the course.

End Vocabularies

Spanish–English and English–Spanish vocabularies are provided for students' reference. The Spanish–English vocabulary contains both active and passive vocabulary found in the student text. All active words and expressions are followed by the number of the lesson in which they are activated. No lesson reference is given for passive vocabulary, since students are not expected to internalize these words or expressions. The English–Spanish vocabulary contains only active vocabulary presented in the **Vocabulario** sections of the text.

Supplementary Materials

Workbook / Laboratory Manual

Each lesson of the *Workbook / Laboratory Manual* is correlated to the corresponding lesson in the student's text and is divided into two sections. The **Actividades para escribir** reinforce each grammar point and the lesson vocabulary through a variety of exercise formats, including question-and-answer exercises, dialogue completion, sentence transformation, illustration-based exercises, and crossword puzzles. It also reinforces culture knowledge from the **El mundo hispánico** essay, and ends with a composition assignment. Designed for use with the *¡Continuemos!* Audio Program, the **Actividades para el laboratorio** for each lesson include structured grammar review exercises, listening-and-speaking exercises, pronunciation practice, and a dictation. Answer keys for the workbook exercises and the laboratory dictations are provided to enable students to monitor their progress independently.

Student Audio CD

To further develop listening skills, the Seventh Edition includes a Student Audio CD that comes free of charge with the purchase of a new textbook. The student will find each lesson opening passage recorded for further listening reinforcement of target vocabulary and the target grammatical structures in context. Following each opening passage is the listening material for the in-text listening activities under **¿Comprende Ud.?**. The first activity consists of listening to a relatively fast-paced conversation that integrates the lesson target vocabulary, structures, theme, and country or region. An eight-item-long true/false comprehension activity follows. The second activity is to learn by heart a very brief song from the Iberian-American folklore, which illustrates at least one lesson target structure in an authentic context. The audioscript for each **¿Comprende Ud.?** section appears under its corresponding lesson in the **Answers to Text Exercises,** in the Instructor's Edition.

Audio Program

The Audio Program for *¡Continuemos!*, Seventh Edition, available on CDs or cassettes for student purchase, is fully supported by the *Workbook / Laboratory Manual*. The following recorded material is provided for each lesson:

Estructuras gramaticales
Four to six structured, mechanical exercises that reinforce the grammar concepts.

Diálogos
Realistic simulations of conversations, interviews, newscasts, ads, and editorials, followed by comprehension questions. The last simulation in every lesson provides the students with an opportunity for an authentic comprehension activity.

Lógico o ilógico

A series of statements that checks students' comprehension of lesson vocabulary and structures.

Pronunciación

Ongoing pronunciation practice of words and expressions introduced in each lesson.

Para escuchar y escribir

Tome nota, a listening exercise in which students write information based on what they hear in realistic simulations of radio advertisements, announcements, newscasts, and other types of authentic input, followed by **Dictado**, a dictation covering the target lesson vocabulary and structures.

The *¡Continuemos!* Video

Developed specially for use with *¡Continuemos!*, Seventh Edition, this exciting 60-minute video provides a broad cultural overview of the Spanish-speaking world through authentic television footage from Spain and the Americas. It also improves listening comprehension skills by exposing students to authentic language; that is, the video provides natural contexts for students to see and hear native speakers in real-life situations. To facilitate classroom use, each of the ten **Teleinforme** video modules is approximately five minutes long. The footage presents diverse images of traditional and contemporary life in Spanish-speaking countries through commercials, interviews, travelogues, TV programs, concert broadcasts, and reports on movies, art, and cooking. The video is available on the Student CD-ROM.

The *¡Continuemos!* Student CD-ROM

Free of charge with the purchase of a new textbook, this new multi-media CD-ROM provides preparatory support and additional practice for designated sections of the student text, the student audio, and the video, and targets several dimensions of language acquisition. First, the student will find prelesson preparation activities followed by target lesson vocabulary and grammar practice. Second, the student will be able to do vocabulary build-up activities based on readings and on listening material. In addition, he or she will practice listening, reading, and writing, and will have the opportunity to reinforce writing through listening by working on a writing task based on the listening they will have done. Students will have access to the entire *¡Continuemos!* Video contents. This CD-ROM also provides preparatory, previewing activities for select clips in the *¡Continuemos!* Video. The student will be able to practice viewing comprehension, speaking, as well as target lesson vocabulary and structures in the context of authentic footage. Finally, this ancillary offers games that target vocabulary acquisition.

¡Continuemos! Student Website
(http://spanish.college.hmco.com/students)

The significantly enhanced Student Website provides support and additional practice for sections in the Student Text and Student Audio, as well as for portions of the

Video Program not supported by the *¡Continuemos!* Student CD-ROM. It includes a diagnostic self quiz on the target lesson structures (**¿Cuánto recuerda?**) as well as a self test (**Compruebe cuánto sabe**) designed to be taken once the **Estructuras gramaticales** section on each lesson has been covered. In addition, it also provides further vocabulary build-up instruction and practice; listening, reading, and writing skill development; and, through postconversational writing tasks, it helps to reinforce the speaking-writing pair of skills. It also offers previewing support for clips in the *¡Continuemos!* Video that are not supported by the CD-ROM. This support consists of viewing comprehension, speaking, and target lesson vocabulary and grammar preparatory practice. Web search activities are integrated in the writing tasks. Students will have access to electronic flashcards that will help them practice words, and their definitions, and conjugation paradigms.

¡Continuemos! Instructor Website (*http://spanish.college.hmco.com/instructors*)

In this new component, the instructor will find materials to support his or her class preparation. The instructor will find optional in-class preconversation activities to be used before the **Perspectivas socioculturales** and **Hablemos de su país** cultural conversation activities. To facilitate integration of the rich technology package accompanying the Student's Edition, the instructor will find the **Technology Integration Guide** very useful. Its focus is on the integration of the *¡Continuemos!* Video, the Student Audio, the *¡Continuemos!* Student CD-ROM, and the two (Student and Instructor) *¡Continuemos!* Websites, with the textbook during any given class period and throughout the course. In addition, for the convenience of the instructor, an online version of the contents of the Instructor's Resource Manual is also found on this website.

Instructor Class Prep CD-ROM

For the convenience of the instructor, the materials in the Instructor's Resource Manual (the Testing Program, the Audioscript, and the Videoscript) as well as PowerPoint slides of grammar charts and explanations are made available in electronic format in this new CD-ROM.

Instructor's Resource Manual

This ancillary resource consists of the Testing Program, the Audioscript, and the Videoscript. The completely revised and expanded Testing Program consists of two quizzes for each of the ten textbook lessons and two final examinations, a complete answer key for all test items, and a script for the listening comprehension portion of each quiz and test. The Audioscript contains a written transcript of the contents of the Audio Program while the Videoscript consists of the transcript of the video.

Coordinating *¡Continuemos!* with the Companion Texts

¡Continuemos!, Seventh Edition, and its companion texts may be implemented using a variety of strategies and text combinations to meet individual course objectives

and instructor preferences. The text descriptions and suggestions that follow offer some ideas as to how the three texts may be used in various configurations to suit the requirements of specific courses.

¡Conversemos!, Third Edition

¡Conversemos!, Third Edition, offers an array of lively, communicative pair and small-group activities specifically designed to develop speaking-and-listening skills and to facilitate student interaction. Topically organized, each of its ten lessons contains 10–12 activities based on practical, high-interest topics. Interactive problem-solving tasks, role-plays, realia- and illustration-based activities and conversation starters stimulate meaningful communication as students apply their personal experiences to real-life situations such as defining personal goals, establishing a budget, planning an event, and applying for a job. The engaging, student-centered activities motivate students to use language creatively while reinforcing key language functions such as persuading, obtaining information, responding to requests, expressing preferences, and giving commands. Numerous authentic documents, photographs, illustrations, and readings throughout the text provide points of departure for discussion, debate, and cross-cultural comparison. A free Student Cassette allows students to complete the in-text listening activities independently.

Aventuras literarias, Sixth Edition

Aventuras literarias, Sixth Edition, is a richly diverse collection of fifty manageable, minimally edited selections from the works of classical and contemporary figures in Spanish and Latin American literature. In this edition, grammar points from each *¡Continuemos!* lesson are illustrated in selections in the corresponding chapter of this companion literary reader. Signaled by a cassette icon in the table of contents, key selections are recorded on the 90-minute audiocassette that comes free of charge with each copy of the reader. Brief background information on the author and style of each reading is provided. Numerous glosses and footnotes define new vocabulary and explain cultural points. Prereading activities, vocabulary development, comprehension questions, literary analysis, and discussion and composition activities enhance students' understanding.

Implementation Strategies

Courses Emphasizing Conversation

These courses may combine *¡Continuemos!*, Seventh Edition, with *¡Conversemos!*, Third Edition, by emphasizing independent study of grammar structures and using class time for communicative activities. Many of the activities in *¡Conversemos!* are divided into **Pasos**, allowing instructors to choose the task most suited to their students' interests and abilities.

Courses Emphasizing Literature

¡Continuemos!, Seventh Edition, may be used effectively in conjunction with *Aventuras literarias*, Sixth Edition. Depending on the class schedule and the students'

reading abilities, one, two, or all of the reading selections in a given chapter of the reader may be assigned after or during the presentation of the corresponding lesson in the core text.

Courses Emphasizing Both Conversation and Literature

Instructors who wish to enhance the reading and the conversation component of their intermediate courses may use *¡Conversemos!* and *Aventuras literarias* in conjunction with the core text, alternating discussion of literary selections with activities from *¡Conversemos!* as best fits the course schedule.

Using the Texts Independently

Although *¡Continuemos!*, Seventh Edition, and its companion texts constitute an integrated program, each one may be used as a stand-alone text or in conjunction with other texts.

Lección 1

Dígame, pág. 3 1. Ana María es española; su esposo es norteamericano. 2. Están sentados en la cocina. Están bebiendo café y conversando. 3. Ellos trabajan y estudian. 4. Se va a poner muy contenta. 5. Según Tyler, ella los malcría. 6. Van a tener una reunión familiar. Va a ser en California. 7. Porque se mantienen en contacto de una manera u otra. 8. La tía de Tyler se casa en mayo. La boda va a ser en Nueva Jersey. 9. Van a tener un par de hijos que van a vivir cerca de ellos. 10. No va a haber divorcio porque ellos se llevan muy bien. 11. Se siente un poco nostálgica y piensa que cada vez extraña más a su familia. 12. Un día de éstos va a tomar un avión y va a ir a visitarlos a todos. Ahora se sirve otra taza de café y empieza a escribir.

Perspectivas socioculturales, pág. 3 Answers will vary.

Hablando de todo un poco

Preparación, pág. 5 1. k 2. n 3. s 4. i 5. a 6. d 7. q 8. f 9. p 10. o 11. b 12. r 13. c 14. e 15. h 16. m 17. l 18. j 19. g

A, pág. 6 Answers will vary.

B, pág. 6 Answers will vary.

C, pág. 6 Answers will vary. *Adjectives:* 1. trabajadora 2. optimista 3. tacaño 4. haragana (perezosa) 5. generoso 6. mandona 7. egoísta 8. comprensiva 9. materialista 10. pesimista

D, pág. 6 Answers will vary.

Palabras problemáticas, pág. 8 1. conoces / tomando / Sabes / sé / llevar / preguntar / pedir 2. Sabes / sé / Coge (Toma) (Agarra) / conozco / llevar / sé

¡Ahora escuche!, pág. 8
Querida abuela:

¿Te sientes mejor? Como siempre me dices tú a mí: "Tienes que cuidarte mucho". La verdad es que yo me preocupo por ti, porque estamos tan lejos, y no puedo correr a tu casa y hacerte un poco de sopa o llevarte al médico o sentarme contigo en la cocina y charlar. En fin, mimarte un poco como tú nos mimas a nosotros...

Abuela: tengo buenas noticias para ti. A lo mejor Tyler y yo vamos a Madrid en mayo. Las clases terminan el dieciocho; el veinte vamos a California porque todos los parientes de Tyler tienen una reunión allí, y el veintiocho o el veintinueve podemos salir para España. ¡Por supuesto que espero verte en el aeropuerto con el resto de la familia!

Tyler sigue siendo un marido perfecto. Es amable, comprensivo y generoso y nunca está de mal humor. ¡Por eso le cae bien a todo el mundo!

Bueno, abuela, pronto te escribo otra vez o te llamo por teléfono para decirte cómo van nuestros planes. ¡Te extraño! Un abrazo, Ana María

¿Verdadero o falso? comprehension questions 1. Ana María piensa que su abuela debe cuidarse. (V) 2. Ana María tiene una relación muy especial con su abuela. (V) 3. Tyler y Ana María tienen clases hasta el veinte de mayo. (F) 4. Ana María y Tyler no piensan asistir a la reunión familiar en California. (F) 5. Ana María cree que ella y su esposo pueden salir para España a fines de mes. (V) 6. Ana María espera que su abuela vaya al aeropuerto con sus otros parientes. (V) 7. Ana María no se lleva bien con Tyler. (F) 8. Tyler siempre está frustrado y deprimido. (F) 9. La gente tiene muy buena opinión de Tyler. (V) 10. Ana María echa de menos a su abuela. (V)

Sobre España, pág. 10 1. Los límites de España son: al norte, Francia y el Mar Cantábrico; al sur, el Estrecho de Gibraltar; al este, el Mar Mediterráneo; al oeste, el Océano Atlántico. 2. Las Islas Baleares y las Islas Canarias pertenecen a España. 3. La superficie de España es de unas 195.000 millas cuadradas y su población es de unos cuarenta millones de habitantes. 4. Algunas atracciones de Madrid son sus parques, sus centros culturales, sus museos, plazas, monumentos y sus grandes hoteles y restaurantes. Sí, el turismo tiene mucha importancia en esta ciudad. 5. Hablan el catalán. 6. Las tres ciudades más importantes del sur de España son Granada, Sevilla y Córdoba. Se ve la influencia mora. 7. La Universidad de Salamanca es una de las más antiguas de Europa. 8. La ciudad de Bilbao está situada sobre el Mar Cantábrico. 9. Ocupa el lugar número once. 10. Velázquez, Goya, Dalí y Picasso se distinguen en la pintura; Albéniz, Falla y Casals se distinguen en la música y Cervantes, Machado y García Lorca se distinguen en la literatura. Gaudí se distingue en la arquitectura.

Hablemos de su país, pág. 10 Answers will vary.

Después de leer la tarjeta, pág. 11   1. Sí, se está divirtiendo mucho.   2. Sí, le gusta mucho Granada. Piensa visitar Madrid, Toledo y Barcelona.   3. Están a unas doce millas de África.   4. Porque quiere quedarse allí.   5. No, está conduciendo un Seat.

Estructuras gramaticales, pág. 12   Answers will vary.

A, pág. 13   Answers will vary.

B, pág. 14   Yo soy un chico (una chica) muy popular. Conozco a todos los estudiantes de la Facultad y todos dicen que yo valgo mucho, porque soy muy inteligente. Los viernes y sábados salgo con mis amigos (nunca digo que no a una invitación), pero los domingos no hago nada; desaparezco de la ciudad y no aparezco hasta el lunes por la mañana. Generalmente voy con mi familia a la montaña. Trabajo en una oficina, donde traduzco cartas y documentos. Como no tengo mucho tiempo para estudiar en mi casa, a veces traigo mis libros a la oficina. Yo conduzco un coche muy bonito y tengo bastante dinero; todos los meses pongo dinero en el banco para poder salir de viaje en las vacaciones. Yo reconozco que soy un chico (una chica) de mucha suerte.

C, pág. 14   Answers will vary.

A, pág. 15   1. cuesta / almuerza / servimos / compite   2. enciende / encuentra / mueren / sugiero   3. Recuerdan / cuenta / confiesa / tiene / repite   4. impide / muerde / pierde / despierta

B, pág. 16   Answers will vary.

C, pág. 16   Answers will vary.

A, pág. 18   1. Yo estoy leyendo una carta.   2. Marcelo está durmiendo en su cuarto.   3. Alicia está poniendo los libros en su escritorio.   4. Rosalía está sirviendo el desayuno.   5. Ana y Luis están pidiendo información sobre Salamanca.   6. Ernesto está diciendo que debemos llamar a los abuelos.   7. Silvia está haciendo ejercicio.   8. Ramiro está escribiendo una carta.

B, pág. 18   Answers will vary.

C, pág. 18   Answers will vary.

A, pág. 19   1. A / a / -   2. - / a   3. A / A / a / a   4. a / -   5. -

B, pág. 20   Answers will vary.

A, pág. 21   1. me necesita   2. las necesita   3. te necesita   4. lo necesitan   5. nos necesita   6. la necesitas

B, pág. 22   los / La / -nos / Los / lo / me / te / me

C, pág. 22   1. Sí, puedo invitarlos (los puedo invitar).   2. Sí, yo voy a comprarlas (las voy a comprar).   3. Sí, quiero usarlo (lo quiero usar).   4. Sí, voy a traerlas (las voy a traer).   5. Sí, voy a llamarlo(a) (lo[a] voy a llamar).   6. Sí, te necesito.   7. Sí, puedo llevarlos(as) (Los[as] puedo llevar).   8. Sí, lo tengo aquí.

A, pág. 24   Answers will vary.

B, pág. 24   Answers will vary. *Indirect object structures:*   1. Les pienso mandar mensajes electrónicos a... Sí, (No, no) les voy a dar buenas noticias. Les voy a decir que...   2. Les voy a comprar...   3. Sí (No), mis padres (no) me dan (prestan) dinero...   4. Le cuento mis problemas a...   5. Sí (No), (no) les doy consejos a mis amigos.   6. Sí, le hablo a... (No, no le hablo a nadie)

C, pág. 24   Answers will vary.

A, pág. 27   1. te levantas / Me levanto / me acuesto   2. se queja / se burlan   3. se bañan / nos bañamos / nos lavamos   4. te sientas / te arrodillas   5. te acuerdas / me olvido

B, pág. 27   1. Nos acostamos.   2. Puedo quitármelos (Me los puedo quitar).   3. La probamos.   4. Que me parezco a él.   5. Debo dormir.   6. Se va.   7. Me la pruebo.   8. Me lo pongo.   9. Me duermo.   10. Nos levantamos.

C, pág. 28   Answers will vary. *Possibilities:*   1. ...me levanto.   2. ...se baña y se lava la cabeza.   3. ...se peina.   4. ...te pruebas la ropa.   5. ...nos ponemos el abrigo.   6. ...se van.   7. ...me quito los zapatos.   8. ...se quejan.   9. ...te arrodillas.   10. ...nos acostamos.

Una encuesta, pág. 29   Answers will vary.

¿Comprende Ud.?, pág. 29 and in Student Audio

En Madrid

Ana María y Tyler están en Madrid. Están en la casa de la abuela de Ana María. En este momento están sentados en el balcón, comiendo churros con chocolate.

Ana María —Mañana viene Monserrat, mi amiga de Barcelona. Yo la quiero mucho. Es alegre, amistosa y siempre está de buen humor.

Tyler —¿Ella es la chica que se va a casar con tu primo?

Ana María —Sí, su prometido es mi primo Luis. Él es madrileño, como yo, pero sabe hablar catalán.

Tyler —¿Ella va con nosotros al Museo del Prado el sábado?

Ana María —Sí, pero primero ella y yo vamos a ir de compras a El Corte Inglés. Creo que abuela va con nosotras.

Tyler —Perfecto. Yo me quedo aquí porque tengo un libro de poemas de Antonio Machado que quiero leer.

Ana María —Mi tío Luis viaja a Sevilla la semana próxima y podemos ir con él. También podemos ir a Córdoba y a Granada.

Tyler —Yo quiero ir a Salamanca para ver la universidad. Tu abuela dice que es una de las más antiguas de Europa.

Ana María —¡Tenemos tiempo de hacerlo todo! También tenemos que ir a Bilbao y ver el Mar Cantábrico... !

Tyler —¡Estás muy entusiasmada, cariño! Pero vamos a estar en España dos semanas, no dos meses...

¿Verdadero o falso? comprehension questions 1. Ana María y su esposo están en un hotel de Madrid. (F) 2. La amiga de Ana María generalmente está triste. (F) 3. El primo de Ana María es de Barcelona. (F) 4. Ana María y Monserrat van de compras al Museo del Prado. (F) 5. Tyler prefiere quedarse en la casa de la abuela y leer. (V) 6. El tío de Ana María viaja al sur de España la semana próxima. (V) 7. Una de las universidades más antiguas de Europa está en Salamanca. (V) 8. Ana María y Tyler piensan estar en España menos de un mes. (V)

Song lyrics:

"Aserrín, aserrán"

Aserrín, aserrán, los maderos de San Juan.
Piden pan, no les dan; piden queso, les dan hueso
y les cortan el pescuezo.

Aserrín, aserrán, los maderos de San Juan.
Piden pan, no les dan; piden pata, les dan nata
y les cortan la corbata.

Aserrín, aserrán, los maderos de San Juan.
Piden pan, no les dan; piden rejas, les dan viejas
y les cortan las orejas.

Aserrín, aserrán, los maderos de San Juan.
Piden pan, no les dan; piden patos, les dan gatos
y les cortan los zapatos.

Aserrín, aserrán, los maderos de San Juan.

Hablemos de una invitación de boda, pág. 30 1. El padre de la novia es ingeniero. El padre del novio es arquitecto.

2. El apellido paterno de María Luz es Peña. Su apellido materno es Juncal. 3. La boda va a ser religiosa. Lo sabemos porque se celebrará en la Iglesia de Los Ángeles. 4. La boda se celebrará el diez de junio del 2003 a las seis de la tarde. 5. La recepción va a ser en el Hotel Villa Magna; van a servir una cena. 6. Porque la invitación dice que esperan tener el honor de su presencia.

Lecturas periodísticas

Para leer y comprender, pág. 31 1. Es indispensable la presencia física de los padres. 2. Tienen que trabajar todo el día fuera de casa. 3. Pasan entre 8 y 10 o más horas lejos del hogar. 4. Las tres posibilidades son: un familiar, una guardería o una niñera. 5. Se establece una relación mágica. Los gratificados son el niño y el adulto. 6. Se debe seleccionar a alguien tierna y agradable y tener referencias. 7. Deben ser reducidos. Cada grupo debe tener una maestra fija. 8. Es conveniente visitar el lugar de forma sorpresiva. 9. Debe empezar por comprender y aceptar las razones que lo llevan a dejar a su bebé en manos de otro. La educación de un hijo implica responsabilidad. 10. Los momentos clave son por la mañana, cuando se despierta, y por la noche, cuando se va a dormir. Debe aprovecharlos para dedicárselos al niño. 11. El niño va a tener que seguir el ritmo de los padres. 12. Una hora con mamá y papá es mucho más importante.

Teleinforme

Preparación, pág. 35 Answers will vary.

Comprensión: A, pág. 36 a. B, TT / sí / tú / "Est**á**s guapísima" b. N / sí / tú / "¡Qué elegante v**as**!" c. BB, TT / sí / tú / "¿Cómo est**á**s?" d. B, TT / Answer may vary. / tú / "Tenía muchas ganas de conocer**te**" e. N / no / Ud. / "Encantado de conocer**la**." f. B / no / tú / "No me llam**es** *señora*." g. M / no / N / N h. BB, TT / no / N / N

B, pág. 37 1. D ↔ J 2. D ↔ J 3. A ↔ D 4. J ↔ A 5. J ↔ A 6. A ↔ J

C, pág. 37 1. F (Ángeles y Demetrio hablan.) 2. F (No es sonámbula.) 3. V 4. V 5. F (Ángeles sí quiere ayudar a la abuela.) 6. V 7. V 8. F (No parece que Ángeles y Demetrio estén muy contentos con la idea.)

Ampliación, pág. 37 Answers will vary.

Lección 2

Dígame, pág. 40   1. V   2. F   3. F   4. V   5. F   6. F
7. V   8. V   9. F   10. F

Perspectivas socioculturales, pág. 40   Answers will vary.

Hablando de todo un poco

Preparación, pág. 42   1. especialización / empresas / materias / informática   2. consejero(a) / estudios / requisito
3. horario / matricularse / tardar   4. escuela / promedio /
asistir / universitaria   5. notas / tarde / privada / beca /
del estado   6. cuenta / asistencia   7. odontología / primaria (secundaria) / educación / letras / derecho   8. salón
(aula) / visto / salón (aula) / general   9. comerciales / contadora / sistemas / trabajadora   10. muchísimo / mitad /
física

A, pág. 43   Answers will vary.

B, pág. 43   Answers will vary.

C, pág. 43   Answers will vary.

Palabras problemáticas, pág. 44   Answers will vary.

¡Ahora escuche!, pág. 44   Roberto, un muchacho chileno
que está estudiando en la Universidad de Tejas, tiene un
problema. Durante su primer semestre en la universidad
tomó clases de arte, de música, de educación física y de fotografía. Lo pasó muy bien pero no tomó ningún requisito
general. Esta mañana fue a hablar con el Dr. Leyva, su
consejero, para planear su programa de estudios. El Dr.
Leyva le dijo que necesitaba tomar inglés, física y
matemáticas. Roberto dijo que no quería tomar clases
muy difíciles porque necesitaba mantener un buen promedio pues pensaba solicitar una beca para el próximo año.

Por fin, los dos decidieron que era mejor tomar dos
requisitos y dos cursos electivos. Al medio día, Roberto almorzó con su amiga Marisol y le contó su problema. Ella
le sugirió tomar la clase de psicología de la Dra. Silva, que
ella pensaba tomar, y le dijo que podían estudiar juntos.

¿Verdadero o falso? comprehension questions   1. Roberto
es un estudiante extranjero. (V)   2. Roberto tomó cuatro
requisitos durante su primer semestre. (F)   3. El Dr.
Leyva es el profesor de música de Roberto. (F)   4. El Dr.
Leyva dijo que Roberto necesitaba tomar una clase de
educación física. (F)   5. Roberto va a solicitar una beca
(V)   6. El próximo año, Roberto no va a asistir a clase. (F)
7. Roberto y Marisol almorzaron juntos. (V)   8. Roberto
no le dijo nada a Marisol sobre sus problemas. (F)   9. La

Dra. Silva enseña una clase de psicología. (V)
10. Marisol no quiere estudiar con Roberto. (F)

Sobre México, pág. 46   1. México limita al norte con los
Estados Unidos, al sur con Guatemala y Belice, al este con
el Océano Pacífico y al oeste con el Golfo de México.   2.
Porque hay altas montañas, desiertos, valles fértiles y selvas tropicales.   3. Exporta petróleo, plata, oro, cobre.   4.
El turismo es otra fuente de riqueza.   5. Están en Teotihuacán, cerca de la Ciudad de México.   6. Están las
ruinas de Chichén Itzá y las de Tulum.   7. Conservan
su lengua y sus tradiciones.   8. Tiene unos 24 millones
de habitantes.   9. Los mariachis.   10. Son escritores
famosos.

Hablemos de su país, pág. 46   Answers will vary.

Estructuras gramaticales

A, pág. 50   1. La clase de biología es a las ocho.   2. El
vestido es de rayón.   3. Rodolfo es muy bajo.   4. Elsa
está de mal humor.   5. La mochila está en la residencia
universitaria.   6. Mi hermana es ingeniera.   7. Es mejor
asistir a clase.   8. Elena está de viaje.   9. El profesor está
corrigiendo los exámenes.   10. ¿Quién es esa chica?
11. La estudiante es de Yucatán.   12. Estoy de acuerdo
con mis padres.   13. El concierto es mañana.   14. Mañana
es el ocho de diciembre.   15. El pobre gato está muerto.
16. Mis padres están de vuelta.   17. Marta es inteligente.
18. ¿Dónde es la reunión?   19. Las puertas están abiertas.
20. Teresa es muy joven.

B, pág. 51   Son / están / es / Es / está / es / son / es
/ es / están / está / está / están / estás / es / es / es
/ Estás / es / eres / estás / soy / soy / es / Es / estoy

C, pág. 51   Answers will vary.

D, pág. 51   Answers will vary.

A, pág. 52   1. tus / Mis   2. Nuestra / su / Mi   3. nuestros
/ tu

B, pág. 53   Answers will vary.

A, pág. 54   1. La nuestra   2. la suya   3. el tuyo / El mío
4. Las suyas   5. las mías / las tuyas   6. Los nuestros

B, pág. 54   Answers will vary.

A, pág. 56   1. No se los compra.   2. No me los da.
3. No se lo trae.   4. No nos la trae.   5. No te lo envía.
6. No se las regala.   7. No se las manda.   8. No se los
trae.

B, pág. 56   1. me lo envuelve   2. se lo presto (doy)
3. se los entregamos   4. te la doy (regalo)   5. nos los
trae   6. se la compro (la compro y se la regalo)

C, pág. 57   Answers will vary.

pág. 57   Answers will vary.

pág. 58   - / los / - / la / el / El / la / los / - / el / el / la / El
/ el / - / la / la

A, pág. 59   1. Es abogado.   2. Es un actor muy famoso.
3. Es americano.   4. No, es un demócrata fanático.
5. Es católico.   6. Trabaja de (como) bibliotecaria.
7. Quiero beber media botella de vino.   8. El vino cuesta
cien pesos.   9. Sí, otro plato de sopa.   10. Yo no uso
sombrero.

B, pág. 60   Answers will vary.

A, pág. 61   estudié / regresé (volví) / comí / tomé (bebí) /
miramos / llamó / escribí / preparó / aprendió / visitaron /
conversó (habló) / volví (regresé)

B, pág. 61   Answers will vary.

A, pág. 63   Answers will vary.

B, pág. 63   Answers will vary. *Verb forms:*   1. tuvo   2. estuvieron   3. anduviste   4. quiso   5. dijiste   6. condujimos   7. vinieron   8. trajeron   9. traduje   10. fui

C, pág. 63   Answers will vary.

pág. 64   1. saqué / pagué / Busqué   2. contribuyeron /
leyó   3. huyó / oyó   4. Empecé / toqué   5. almorcé /
llegué

A, pág. 65   1. durmió / Dormí   2. pidieron / pedí / pidió
3. consiguió / conseguí   4. eligió   5. murió   6. sirvieron
/ Servimos   7. repitió / repitió

B, pág. 66   Answers will vary. *Questions:*   1. —¿Cuándo
comenzó a estudiar Ud. en esta universidad?   2. —¿Qué
libros leyó Ud. el semestre pasado?   3. —¿Por qué eligio
Ud. esta clase?   4. —¿A qué hora llegó Ud. a la universidad hoy?   5. ¿Cuándo sacó Ud. un libro de la biblioteca?   6. —¿Cuánto pagó Ud. por su libro de español?
7. —¿Qué pidió Ud. en la cafetería?   8. —¿Qué sirvió
Ud. en la última fiesta que dio?   9. —¿Cuántas horas
durmió Ud. anoche?

C, pág. 66   Answers will vary.

A, pág. 67   Answers will vary.

B, pág. 67   Answers will vary. *Verbs:*   1. vivía   2. éramos
3. comían   4. tenías   5. veías   6. iba   7. hablábamos
8. volvía   9. iban   10. viajaban

C, pág. 68   Answers will vary.

¿Comprende Ud.?, pág. 68 and in Student Audio

En la cafetería de la universidad

*Hace dos semanas que Sergio y Lucía se conocieron cuando se
matriculaban para sus clases en la Universidad de California en
San Diego. Sergio es de Puebla, México, y Lucía es paraguaya.
Ahora están en la cafetería de la universidad hablando de sus
estudios.*

Lucía   —Tuve mucha suerte. Conseguí todas las clases
que quería tomar, y ¿tú?
Sergio   —Yo, solamente dos. Una de informática y otra de
administración de empresas. Las otras dos son
requisitos generales.
Lucía   —Bueno, yo ya los tomé todos el año pasado. Este
semestre voy a tomar todo lo que me gusta.
Sergio   —¿Y cuál es tu especialización?
Lucía   —Quiero ser doctora en filosofía y letras, ¿y tú?
Sergio   —Me voy a dedicar a la programación de informática. Sólo me queda un año para graduarme y
estoy tratando de encontrar un puesto.
Lucía   —Pues yo sé donde lo puedes encontrar. Cuando
te metas en Internet busca la página web de
monster.com, que es uno de los portales de empleo más importantes de los Estados Unidos.
Sergio   —Muchas gracias por la sugerencia. Esta misma
noche lo voy a hacer.

¿Verdadero o falso? comprehension questions   1. Hace
mucho tiempo que Sergio y Lucía son amigos. (F)
2. Sergio va a tomar cuatro clases. (V)   3. A Lucía no le
gusta una de sus clases. (F)   4. Lucía quiere ser profesora
de educación física. (F)   5. Sergio quiere dedicarse a la
computación. (V)   6. Sergio no quiere trabajar este año.
(F)   7. Lucía sabe dónde Sergio puede buscar empleo. (V)
8. El portal de empleo se llama **monster.com.** (V)

Song lyrics:

"¡A la una, a las dos... y a las tres!"

A la una yo nací,
a las dos me bauticé,
a las tres conseguí novio(a),
y a las cuatro me casé.

A las cinco di una fiesta,
a las seis fui a trabajar,

a las siete tomé siesta,
y a las ocho fui a jugar.

A las nueve volví a casa,
a las diez me preparé,
a las once comí pasas,
y a las doce me acosté.

Hablemos de carreras, pág. 68   1. Sus cursos preuniversitarios corrigen las fallas del bachillerato. Nivelan las diferencias entre el liceo y la universidad. Permiten aprobar el primer semestre sin dificultades. Crean y estimulan el hábito de estudios.   2. Más del 70 por ciento de los alumnos resultan aplazados.   3. Ofrecen cursos especiales para los que desean ingresar en la facultad de medicina. 4. Queda en la Plaza Venezuela, Centro Capriles, 1a Mezzanina.   5. Se debe llamar al teléfono 782-82-10 o al 782-48-53.   6. Están abiertas hasta el viernes.

Lecturas periodísticas

Para leer y comprender, pág. 70   1. V   2. V   3. F   4. F   5. F   6. V   7. F   8. V   9. F   10. V

Teleinforme

Preparación, pág. 73   Answers will vary. *Possible answers:*
1. S, U   2. T   3. L   4. L   5. S, U, T, L   6. T   7. S, U, T   8. L   9. S, U   10. T   11. L   12. L   13. S, U, T   14. L   15. L   16. U, T   17. L   18. S   19. U, T   20. S, U   21. S, U   22. S, U   23. L   24. S, U   25. T   26. T, L   27. T   28. S, U, T

Comprensión: A, pág. 73   1. UBAC significa "Upward Bound Alumni Club". UBAC ayuda a los estudiantes que en el colegio pertenecían a Upward Bound. Ayuda a escoger clases; es un club social para que los estudiantes se sientan parte del grupo.   2. Muchos profesores aprenden el español. Los estudiantes latinos son muy tímidos; no se dirigen a la autoridad; no preguntan por qué. Los profesores tienen que extender la mano; hacer algo más que entrar y salir.

B, pág. 74   Nuri: 3, 8, 11, 12, 15, 17, 23   Chuni: 2, 5, 10, 19, 25, 27   Charo: 14, 26

C, pág. 74   Answers will vary.

Ampliación, pág. 74   Answers will vary.

Lección 3

Dígame, pág. 83   1. Pablo estudia en Chile. Rafael Vargas le sirve de guía.   2. Están leyendo la página deportiva.

3. Rafael no fue porque no pudo conseguir entradas. Pablo no fue porque tuvo que estudiar.   4. Piensa que es el mejor boxeador del país.   5. El único deporte que realmente le interesa es el fútbol.   6. Pasaba horas en la calle jugando al fútbol.   7. Fue a acampar. Rubén fue con ellos. 8. A Rubén le gusta pescar, montar a caballo, escalar montañas, bucear...   9. No fue porque le dolía mucho la espalda. Prefirió quedarse en casa.   10. Las conocieron en la fiesta de Olga.   11. Patricia Serna es la nueva campeona de tenis. Le ganó a Marisa Beltrán.   12. Lo ganó el club Fénix. Dos jugadores se lastimaron.

Perspectivas socioculturales, pág. 83   Answers will vary.

Hablando de todo un poco

Preparación, pág. 85   1. bate / guante   2. hipódromo / carreras   3. partido (juego) / reñido / empataron   4. nadadora / esquí 5. campeonato / libre / gimnasta / campeona   6. tienda / caña   7. partido (juego) / pesar / jugadores / tiempo   8. perdí / boxeo / sacar (conseguir) 9. actividades / libre / escalar / vez / poco   10. página / deportes / Olímpicos   11. boxeador / mejorar   12. dieron / marcó   13. montar / esquiar / nadar   14. realidad / servir

A, pág. 85   Answers will vary.

B, pág. 85   Answers will vary.

C, pág. 85   Answers will vary.

Palabras problemáticas, pág. 86   1. echo de menos (extraño)   2. faltaste   3. me los perdí   4. perdieron 5. realiza   6. nos dimos cuenta

¡Ahora escuche!, pág. 87   Carlos y Eduardo son amigos desde hace diez años y a los dos les gustan mucho los deportes y las actividades al aire libre. Carlos juega al tenis y al fútbol y también practica el básquetbol. Eduardo, como casi todos los cubanos, prefiere el béisbol.

Estas vacaciones Eduardo y Carlos van a trabajar como entrenadores en un campamento de verano para niños pobres. Eduardo va a servir de entrenador de béisbol. Como saben que los niños van a necesitar muchas cosas, Carlos y Eduardo les están pidiendo dinero a sus amigos para comprar bates, pelotas, guantes y también uniformes para el equipo. Eduardo piensa que todos se van a divertir mucho.

Silvia, la esposa de Eduardo, cree que éste no va a ser un buen verano para ella, porque Eduardo va a estar muy ocupado; por eso planea irse a la playa los fines de semana con Marta, la novia de Carlos. A ellas les encanta bucear y nadar. Cuando Silvia era niña, quería ser campeona de natación y pasaba mucho tiempo nadando en la piscina de su casa. Es por eso que nada muy bien.

¿Verdadero o falso? comprehension questions   1. Hace muy poco tiempo que Eduardo y Carlos son amigos. (F) 2. A Carlos no le gusta practicar ningún deporte. (F)   3. Eduardo es peruano. (F)   4. Este verano, Eduardo va a servir de entrenador de béisbol. (V)   5. Carlos y Eduardo van a necesitar mucho dinero este verano. (V)   6. Ellos van a comprar muchos artículos deportivos. (V)   7. Este verano, Eduardo piensa divertirse mucho. (V)   8. Silvia piensa viajar con Eduardo en el verano. (F)   9. Marta y Silvia planean muchas actividades para el sábado y para el domingo durante el verano. (V)   10. Cuando era niña, Silvia quería ser campeona de tenis. (F)

Sobre Chile, Perú y Ecuador, pág. 88   1. Los límites de Chile son: al norte, Perú; al sur, el Océano Pacífico; al este, Bolivia y Argentina; al oeste, el Océano Pacífico. El país es largo y estrecho.   2. Exporta minerales, principalmente cobre, y también exporta frutas y vinos. Rafael dice que los vinos chilenos son los mejores del mundo.   3. Se pueden visitar museos interesantísimos como el Museo Precolombino, y parques, como el Parque de Artesanos. 4. Se puede esquiar.   5. Debemos visitar Viña del Mar. 6. La capital de Perú es Lima. Es de gran belleza y valor histórico.   7. Otra ciudad importante es Cuzco. Cerca de allí encontramos las ruinas de Machu Picchu.   8. Quito, la capital de Ecuador, es una de las ciudades más antiguas del hemisferio occidental. Está situada casi directamente en la línea del ecuador.   9. Las islas Galápagos. Deben su nombre a las enormes tortugas que allí viven.

Hablemos de su país, pág. 89   Answers will vary.

Después de leer la tarjeta, pág. 89   1. Son inclinadas y estrechas.   2. Tiene la sensación de estar en el siglo XVI. 3. Está situado en la latitud 0°.   4. Va a visitar Guayaquil.

Estructuras gramaticales

A, pág. 91   1. A ellos les gusta más el baloncesto. 2. David dice que a Ud. le gusta más el fútbol.   3. A la mayoría de la gente le gusta más montar a caballo.   4. A mí me gusta más pescar.   5. ¿A ti te gusta más esquiar? 6. A mí me gusta más la natación.   7. Al entrenador le gusta más practicar los viernes.   8. A nosotros nos gusta más acampar.   9. A Daniel le gusta más la lucha libre. 10. ¿A ti te gustan más esos guantes de pelota?   11. A ellos les gusta más escalar montañas.   12. A Rafael le gusta más bucear.

B, pág. 91   Answers will vary.

C, pág. 91   Answers will vary.

pág. 92   1. me duele   2. me gustan   3. le encanta 4. nos quedan / Nos faltan

A, pág. 93   1. Preterit (completed action): ganó / fuiste / fui / pude / perdí / tuve / ganó / fuiste / se fue / dijo / esquiamos / fui / divertimos / fue / dijo / fuiste / preferí Imperfect: quería (I wanted to) / sabías (you knew) / era (age in the past) / pasaba (habitual action) / quería (indirect discourse) (he wanted) / necesitaba (indirect discourse) / dolía

B, pág. 93   era / llegaste / Eran / fuimos / hiciste / estaba / hacía / fuimos / volvimos / dijo / dolía / vino / Dijo / se llamaba / era / Era / tenía / Hablaba / estaba / jugábamos / ganaba / dijo / iba / viste / fueron / estuvo

C, pág. 94   Answers will vary.

D, pág. 94   Answers will vary.

A, pág. 95   1. pude / sabía / quiso   2. supe / conoció / sabía   3. quería / pudimos   4. conocía / conocí   5. sabía

B, pág. 95   Answers will vary.

A, pág. 97   1. quien / cuyos / que / quién / que / que / quien / que

B, pág. 97   Answers will vary.

A, pág. 98   1. Hace seis meses que tomo clases de natación.   2. Hace tres horas que estamos en el estadio. 3. Hace cuatro días que no veo a mi entrenador.   4. Hace tres meses que no juego al fútbol.   5. Hace veinte minutos que los jugadores están aquí.   6. Hace media hora que ellos están nadando.   7. Hace dos años que practico gimnasia.   8. Hace doce horas que no como.

B, pág. 98   1. Hacía dos horas que ellas hablaban de deportes cuando yo llegué.   2. Hacía 4 días que ella estaba en Quito cuando se enfermó.   3. Hacía veinte minutos que Uds. comentaban el juego cuando yo los llamé. 4. Hacía una hora que el gimnasta practicaba cuando se lastimó.   5. Hacía media hora que ellos jugaban cuando empataron.   6. Hacía quince minutos que jugábamos cuando marcamos un gol.

C, pág. 99   Answers will vary. *Questions:*   1. ¿Cuánto tiempo hace que se casaron tus abuelos?   2. ¿Cuánto tiempo hace que nacieron tus padres?   3. ¿Cuánto tiempo hace que aprendiste a leer?   4. ¿Cuánto tiempo hace que aprendiste a montar en bicicleta?   5. ¿Cuánto tiempo hace que te graduaste de la escuela primaria?   6. ¿Cuánto tiempo hace que empezaste a estudiar en la universidad?   7. ¿Cuánto tiempo hace que te enamoraste por primera vez?

¿Comprende Ud.?, pág. 99 and in Student Audio

En Chile

Paco está en Portillo. Después de esquiar toda la tarde, está hablando con una chica que conoció en el hotel.

Paco —Yo creo que estoy mejorando mi estilo. Me encanta esquiar, pero la última vez que fui a Farellones por poco me mato.

Rocío —¡Vamos! ¡Yo creo que pronto vas a estar listo para los Juegos Olímpicos!

Paco —Cuando tenía quince años me creía un gran atleta. Practicaba tantos deportes que no me quedaba mucho tiempo para estudiar.

Rocío —¿Sí? ¿Jugabas al fútbol? Mi hermano jugaba en un equipo que salió campeón cuatro años seguidos.

Paco —Bueno... mi deporte favorito era el básquetbol. En Santiago tenían equipos muy buenos. Pero un día me lastimé y decidí dedicarme a la natación.

Rocío —¡Yo también nadaba! Mi familia y yo vivíamos en Viña del Mar y yo pasaba todos los fines de semana en la playa.

Paco —Yo fui a Viña del Mar el año pasado para asistir al Festival Internacional de la Canción.

Rocío —¿Piensas ir a Viña del Mar el verano próximo?

Paco —No, pienso ir a Lima a visitar a unos amigos peruanos. Ellos me van a llevar a Cuzco y después a visitar las ruinas de Machu Picchu.

¿Verdadero o falso? comprehension questions: 1. Paco solamente esquía en Portillo. (F)   2. A Paco no le gustaban los deportes cuando era adolescente (F)   3. El hermano de Rocío pertenecía a un equipo muy bueno. (V) 4. Cuando Paco se lastimó, decidió no practicar ningún otro deporte. (F)   5. Rocío nunca iba a la playa cuando era adolescente. (F)   6. El Festival Internacional de la Canción tuvo lugar en Viña del Mar. (V)   7. Todos los amigos de Paco son chilenos. (F)   8. A Paco y a sus amigos no les interesan las ruinas de Machu Picchu. (F)

Song lyrics:

"Las mañanitas"

Éstas son las mañanitas
que cantaba el rey David;
a las muchachas bonitas
se las cantamos aquí.

Despierta, mi bien, despierta,
mira que ya amaneció;
ya los pajarillos cantan,
la luna ya se metió.

Si el sereno de la esquina
me quisiera hacer favor
de apagar su linternita
mientras que pasa mi amor.

Despierta, mi bien, despierta,
mira que ya amaneció;
ya los pajarillos cantan,
la luna ya se metió.

Hablemos de deportes, pág. 100   1. Los cursos se ofrecen en el verano.   2. Lo van a aceptar en Inglaterra. 3. Se ofrecen clases de informática y de artes plásticas. 4. Ofrecen clases de dry ski, esgrima (fencing), karts y motor cross.   5. Sí, puede hacerlo, porque pueden ser externos.

Lecturas periodísticas

Para leer y comprender, pág. 101   1. Es hacer una larga caminata en lugares lejanos, en contacto con la naturaleza y con culturas remotas.   2. Requieren una minuciosa planeación y rigurosa preparación física y mental. 3. Se orientan con brújula y mapas.   4. Es necesario tener en cuenta el terreno, la época del año, los peligros, etc. 5. El guía debe estar preparado en primeros auxilios y conocer perfectamente el terreno.   6. Debe llevar botas cómodas y ligeras, ropa adecuada, una mochila, un botiquín, dos cantimploras, etc.   7. Cuentan con animales como mulas, caballos y yaks y también con porteadores.

Teleinforme

Preparación, pág. 104   Answers will vary. *Possible answers:* 1. F   2. R   3. R   4. FR   5. R   6. F   7. R   8. F   9. FR 10. F   11. FR   12. F   13. F   14. F   15. F   16. F 17. R   18. FR   19. F   20. R   21. R   22. F   23. R 24. FR   25. R   26. R   27. R   28. R   29. F   30. F 31. F   32. F
Follow-up activity: Answers will vary.

Comprensión: A, pág. 104   1, 6, 8, 10, 11, 12, 13, 14, 19, 22, 29, 32

B, pág. 105   1. España probablemente va a ganar el partido.   2. El equipo rumano está en último lugar. 3. Kiko, López, Luis Enrique, Manjarín, Nadal y Pizzi. 4. Se entrenan en Leeds.   5. Si gana, España va a poder clasificar.   6. Los medios de comunicación no se han acordado de la selección rumana en este momento. 7. Answers may vary. (Es posible que les falte motivación.)

C, pág. 105   2, 3, 4, 5, 7, 9, 17, 18, 20, 21, 23, 24, 25, 26, 27, 28

D, pág. 105   1. F   2. V   3. F   4. V   5. V   6. F   7. V 8. V   9. F   10. F   11. F   12. V

Ampliación, pág. 105   Answers will vary.

Lección 4

Dígame, pág. 109   1 Desea que vaya en diciembre. 2. En Paraguay, el 1° de diciembre se celebra el Día de todos los Santos. María Isabel fue a misa.   3. Mañana va a ir al cementerio porque es el Día de los Muertos. Va a llevar flores a la tumba de su abuela.   4. Gustavo es menor que María Isabel. Tiene preparadas varias bromas porque es el Día de los Inocentes.   5. La van a llevar a Caacupé, un pueblo cercano a Asunción. Allí se celebra el Día de la Virgen de Caacupé. Kathy puede tomar parte en una procesión.   6. Se celebra el Día de Nochebuena. Va a disfrutar de una cena típicamente paraguaya.   7. Después de cenar, van a ir a ver los pesebres y a la medianoche van a ir a la Misa del Gallo.   8. Es pleno verano y hace mucho calor.   9. Van a ir todos a un club, al baile de fin de año. 10. Se celebra el Día de los Reyes Magos. Los niños reciben regalos.   11. María Isabel necesita saber el número de vuelo de Kathy para poder ir por ella al aeropuerto.   12. María Isabel va a Bolivia a fines de marzo para asistir a una conferencia.

Perspectivas socioculturales, pág. 109   Answers will vary.

Hablando de todo un poco

Preparación, pág. 110   1. f   2. i   3. h   4. l   5. a   6. o 7. k   8. p   9. e   10. d   11. b   12. j   13. n   14. c 15. g   16. m

A, pág. 111   Answers will vary. *Celebrations in no. 1:*   a. el Año Nuevo   b. el día de los Enamorados   c. el Día de la Madre   d. el Día del Padre   e. el Día de Canadá f. el Día de la Independencia de los Estados Unidos g. el Día del Trabajo   h. el Día de las Brujas   i. el Día de Acción de Gracias   j. el Día de Nochebuena   k. la Víspera de Año Nuevo (Fin de Año)

B, pág. 111   Answers will vary.

Palabras problemáticas, pág. 113   Answers will vary.

¡Ahora escuche!, pág. 113   Carlos y su novia Amanda son de La Paz, la capital de Bolivia. Él es de estatura mediana, inteligente y simpatiquísimo. Ella es baja, bonita, muy eficiente y trabajadora y siempre está de buen humor.

Amanda va a misa todos los domingos y toma parte en todas las procesiones de la iglesia. (Ella quiere que Carlos vaya con ella, pero él generalmente le dice que está ocupado.) No es supersticiosa, pero le gusta leer su horóscopo todos los días.

Carlos dice que él no es supersticioso, pero tiene una pata de conejo y una herradura, y una vez se puso muy contento porque encontró un trébol de cuatro hojas.

Amanda y Carlos siempre les hacen bromas a sus amigos el 28 de noviembre. El año pasado les dijeron a todos que pensaban casarse en diciembre, pero que no podían invitarlos porque planeaban tener la ceremonia en Madrid. Muchos se enojaron, pero después se dieron cuenta de que era una broma.

Carlos espera terminar sus estudios en diciembre y después piensa pedirle a Amanda que se case con él. ¡Ojalá que sean muy felices!

¿Verdadero o falso? comprehension questions: 1. Carlos y Amanda son de la misma nacionalidad. (V)   2. Carlos es más alto que Amanda. (V)   3. A Amanda no le gusta trabajar. (F)   4. Amanda es más religiosa que Carlos. (V) 5. Amanda no sabe cuál es su signo del zodíaco. (F) 6. Carlos tiene tres cosas que él cree que le van a traer buena suerte. (V)   7. Amanda y Carlos hacen bromas el Día de los Inocentes. (V)   8. Amanda y Carlos se casaron en diciembre, en España. (F)   9. Carlos no quiere casarse con Amanda. (F)   10. Todos esperan que Amanda y Carlos se divorcien en seguida. (F)

Sobre Paraguay y Bolivia, pág. 114   1. Los límites de Paraguay son: al norte, Bolivia; al sur, Argentina; al este, Brasil y al oeste, Argentina y Bolivia.   2. Los dos países que no tienen salida al mar son Paraguay y Bolivia.   3. Es la planta hidroeléctrica más grande del mundo.   4. Es tan alta como un edificio de sesenta pisos y tiene una longitud de cinco millas.   5. Podemos visitar las cataratas de Iguazú.   6. Se filmó *La misión.* Escogieron Paraguay debido a su extraordinaria belleza.   7. Se ve la mezcla de las culturas española y guaraní.   8. Es la capital y también el puerto principal del país. Algunos edificios son altos y modernos; otros son casas coloniales.   9. Tiene el lago navegable más alto del mundo: el Titicaca; el aeropuerto más alto del mundo; la capital más alta, una de las ruinas más antiguas, etc.   10. La Paz y Sucre. La Paz es hoy la capital de facto; en Sucre tiene sede el poder judicial.

Hablemos de su país, pág. 115   Answers will vary.

Estructuras gramaticales

A, pág. 119   Answers will vary.

B, pág. 119 *Superlativos absolutos:*   1. simpatiquísimo
2. facilísimo   3. feísimo   4. guapísimo   5. pequeñísimo
6. dificilísimo   7. malísimo   8. grandísimo   9. altísimo
10. buenísimo

C, pág. 119   1. Mario es el mejor estudiante. José no es tan
malo como Juan. Juan es el peor estudiante   2. Oscar es
el mayor de los tres. Daniel es el menor de los tres. Sergio
es mayor que Oscar y menor que Daniel   3. La casa de
Elena es la más pequeña. La casa de Marité es la más
grande. La casa de Marta es más grande que la de Elena y
más pequeña que la de Marité   4. La casa de Eva es más
barata que la casa de Luis. La casa de Luis es más cara que
la casa de Elena.   5. El hotel Miramar no es tan bueno
como el hotel El Azteca. El hotel Santander es el mejor de
los tres.

D, pág. 119   Answers will vary.

A, pág. 121   1. por / para / Para / por   2. por / por / por /
para   3. para / por / para / para / para

B, pág. 121   Answers will vary.

A, pág. 122   1. Por suerte no tuvieron que llevar a nadie al
hospital.   2. ¡No era para tanto!   3. ¡Para eso se puso un
vestido muy elegante!   4. Quiero quedarme aquí para
siempre.   5. Vamos a estar allí por lo menos un mes.
6. Los necesita para tener suerte.   7. Voy a hablar de la
sopa paraguaya y del lechón asado, por ejemplo.   8. Por
aquí nadie cree en la brujería.

B, pág. 122   Por / por / por / por / por / para / para / Por
/ por / por / por / por / por / para / para

pág. 124   1. traiga, divida, conozca, corra, hable, saque
2. mantengas, conserves, decidas, comas, vengas, llegues
3. hable, vea, aprenda, abra, quepa, empiece   4. dedique-
mos, digamos, bebamos, recibamos, volvamos, paguemos
5. hagan, insistan, teman, pongan, viajen, toquen

pág. 125   1. que nosotros pidamos...   2. que Estela
pueda...   3. que tú vayas...   4. que ellos sepan...   5. que
usted empiece...   6. que ustedes mientan...   7. que nosotras durmamos...   8. que tú y yo demos...   9. que Ana y
Eva sirvan...   10. que Roberto esté

A, pág. 127   1. dar / invites   2. ir / vayan   3. hagamos /
visiten   4. vengan / trabaje   5. cambiar / te quedes
6. salir / salgas / salir

B, pág. 127   Answers will vary.

pág. 128   Answers will vary.

A, pág. 129   1. vayas / poder / salgamos   2. sepa / dé
3. estén / puedan   4. estar / estén   5. sepa

B, pág. 130   Answers will vary. *Possibilities:*   1. Ojalá que
no llueva.   2. Es una suerte que mi tío sea presidente
de una compañía. Es de esperar que me dé un empleo.
3. Es una lástima (Siento) que mi amiga esté enferma.
4. Lamento no tener suficiente dinero. (Es lamentable que
yo no tenga suficiente dinero.)   5. Es sorprendente que
mi sobrino sepa nadar.   6. Temo que el profesor dé un
examen hoy. (Ojalá que el profesor no dé un examen
hoy.)

C, pág. 130   Answers will vary.

D, pág. 130   dé / sepan / nos hable / señalar / ayudarlos /
haya / nos aclare / hable / le haga / tener / preguntarle /
nos llamen / se comuniquen / sea

E, pág. 131 *Possibilities:*   1. Siento que tu esposo esté enfermo. Espero que se mejore pronto.   2. Me alegro de
que tus hijos estén bien.   3. Es sorprendente que Teresa y
Jorge se casen.   4. Es una lástima que Olga y Raúl se divorcien.   5. Ojalá (Espero) que José encuentre trabajo
pronto.   6. Me alegro de que Alina tenga un puesto muy
bueno.   7. Es de esperar (Ojalá) que Carlos y Adela
puedan visitarnos este verano.   8. Espero que tú puedas
acompañarlos.

¿Comprende Ud.?, pág. 132 and in Student Audio

Al fin en Paraguay

*María Isabel habla por teléfono con su amiga Carmen sobre el
viaje de Kathy a Paraguay.*

Carmen   —¿Por fin Kathy llegó el 28 de noviembre?
María Isabel   —Sí, y como era el Día de los Inocentes,
                      Gustavo le hizo varias bromas, pero ya ella
                      las esperaba.
Carmen   —¿Adónde fueron?
María Isabel   —Gustavo nos llevó a ver las Cataratas de
                      Iguazú. Nos quedamos dos días allí. Kathy
                      quedó encantada con el viaje.
Carmen   —¿Qué hicieron el día de Nochebuena?
María Isabel   —Tuvimos una cena magnífica en casa, pero
                      a Kathy no le gustó la sopa paraguaya.
                      Dice que eso no es sopa.
Carmen   —¿Fueron al club a esperar el año?
María Isabel   —Sí, y a Kathy le gustó mucho nuestra
                      música. Le regalé algunas cintas de polcas.
Carmen   —¿La llevaste a ver la represa de Itaipú?

María Isabel —No, no pudimos ir.

Carmen —¡Qué lástima!, pero bueno, supongo que pasearon mucho por Asunción.

María Isabel —Sí, y Kathy compró varias cosas hechas de ñandutí para llevárselas a su familia.

Carmen —¿Ella piensa volver a Paraguay?

María Isabel —Sí, dice que le gustó mucho nuestro país, pero yo creo que mi hermano Gustavo le gusto más. Bueno, te dejo porque voy a salir.

[María Isabel abre la puerta y se oye un trueno y el ruido de una fuerte lluvia.)

María Isabel —¡Ay no!, empezó a llover a cántaros. No puedo salir.

¿Verdadero o falso? comprehension questions 1. Kathy no sabía que el 28 de noviembre era el Día de los Inocentes. (F) 2. Kathy y María Isabel fueron solas a las cataratas. (F) 3. A Kathy no le gustó la sopa paraguaya. (V) 4. Kathy piensa que la música paraguaya es muy bonita. (V) 5. Kathy compró varias cintas de polcas paraguayas. (F) 6. Kathy estuvo en la represa de Itaipú. (F) 7. Kathy compró varios regalos para su familia. (V) 8. A Kathy le gustó mucho Paraguay. (V) 9. Kathy no conoció a nadie atractivo en Paraguay. (F) 10. María Isabel no va a salir porque está lloviendo mucho. (V)

Song lyrics:

"La farolera"

La farolera tropezó,
y en la calle se cayó,
y al pasar por un cuartel,
se enamoró de un coronel.

Alcen la barrera
para que pase la farolera
de la puerta al sol;
subió la escalera
y se apagó el farol.

Y a la medianoche se puso a contar,
y todas las cuentas le salieron mal.

Dos y dos son cuatro, cuatro y dos son seis,
seis y dos son ocho, y ocho dieciséis.
y ocho veinticuatro y ocho treinta y dos;
pónganse a cantar si tienen buena voz.

Hablemos del horóscopo, pág. 132 1. No les ha escrito a sus amigos. 2. Su signo es Leo. Sí, porque sus problemas económicos van a desaparecer. 3. Es probable que haya una chica en su futuro porque va a conocer a alguien muy interesante. 4. No, porque va a recibir buenas noticias. 5. Su signo es Virgo. No, porque va a tener buenas posi-

bilidades en el amor. 6. No, no va a resolverlas fácilmente. 7. Su signo es Escorpión. No, porque su horóscopo dice que antes de tomar una decisión, debe pensarlo muy bien. 8. No, porque no debe gastar mucho dinero hoy. 9. No, porque hoy no es un buen día para hacer un viaje. 10. No, no debe darse por vencido. 11. Su signo es Tauro. Sí, yo creo que va a poder ir porque va a recibir mucho dinero. 12. Va a recibir una sorpresa.

Lecturas periodísticas

Para leer y comprender, pág. 134 1. Está situada en el corazón de los Andes, a una altitud de 3.400 metros. 2. Sus antepasados son los incas. 3. Es una fiesta de características propias, donde se mezclan elementos cristianos y andinos. 4. Las sacaban de sus palacios y las llevaban en procesión por las calles de la ciudad. 5. Se trasladan a la catedral las imágenes de las vírgenes y de los santos patronos de las iglesias de Cuzco. El jueves santo son sacadas todas para la impresionante procesión que tiene lugar en la Plaza de Armas. 6. Algunas de estas imágenes son auténticas obras de arte. Se destacan, sobre todo, por la riqueza que las adorna.

Teleinforme

Preparación, pág. 137 Answers will vary.

Comprensión: A, pág. 138 1. tradiciones 2. las familias, las comunidades 3. día de los Difuntos 4. cementerio, las tumbas 5. las casas 6. pan 7. colas, aguardiente 8. bailan, toman 9. el cordón 10. el muerto 11. el cordón 12. maligno, bueno

B, pág. 138 Orden de los elementos de la fiesta: 8, 9, 3, 5, 11, 1, 6, 7, 2, 10, 4

Ampliación, pág. 138 Answers will vary.

Lección 5

Dígame, pág. 146 1. Está preocupada porque Mario tiene el colesterol muy alto. 2. Le dice que baje de peso y que haga ejercicio pero Mario no cree que eso sea necesario. 3. Lucía duda que él cambie de actitud. 4. El único ejercicio que hace es caminar hacia el refrigerador y cambiar los canales en la televisión. 5. El médico quiere que pierda unos quince kilos. 6. Es buena idea hacer ejercicios vigorosos para mantenerse joven. 7. Va a hacerse socio de un club, pero no del que le gusta a Marcelo porque es muy caro. 8. Lucía dice que deben empezar por ponerse a dieta. Mario va a hacer cualquier cosa. 9. Debemos evitar las drogas, el tabaco y el estrés. 10. Los alimentos que contienen fibra. Debemos beber por lo

menos ocho vasos de agua al día.   11. Answers will vary.
12. Answers will vary.

Perspectivas socioculturales, pág. 147   Answers will vary.

Hablando de todo un poco

Preparación, pág. 148   1. canal   2. engordar   3. pulgada
4. sobrar   5. grasa   6. cuerpo   7. libra   8. exagerar
9. cualquier cosa   10. ajo   11. zanahoria   12. pastel
13. cebolla   14. hacerse socio   15. ejercicio ligero
16. mantenerse joven   17. realizar   18. desgraciadamente   19. regla   20. único

A, pág. 149   Answers will vary.

B, pág. 149   Answers will vary.

C, pág. 149   Answers will vary.

Palabras problemáticas, pág. 150   1. me puse   2. Se hizo
3. se convirtió en   4. corto   5. baja

¡Ahora escuche!, pág. 150   Marcela está muy preocupada
porque su hijo Carlitos tiene exceso de peso. El chico
tiene sólo doce años y pesa veinte libras más de lo que
debe pesar. Marcela piensa que su hijo puede tener muchos problemas de salud cuando sea mayor.

Carlitos no hace ningún tipo de ejercicio. Cuando llega
de la escuela, lo único que hace es sentarse a mirar televisión. El niño nunca come frutas ni vegetales y siempre
está comiendo pasteles, papas fritas y hamburguesas.

Marcela está decidida a llevarlo al médico para que lo
ponga a dieta y también va a hacerlo socio de un gimnasio
para que haga ejercicio. Con todo esto, ella espera que
muy pronto Carlitos pueda adelgazar.

El esposo de Marcela también necesita perder peso, de
modo que decide disminuir el consumo de grasas y también ir a caminar todas las mañanas para tratar de mantener un peso adecuado.

¿Verdadero o falso? comprehension questions: 1. El hijo
de Marcela necesita adelgazar. (V)   2. Carlitos tiene diez
años. (F)   3. Es posible que el niño tenga problemas de
salud más tarde. (V)   4. El niño tiene una dieta balanceada. (F)   5. Carlitos come muchas comidas que tienen
muchas calorías. (V)   6. Carlitos tiene que ponerse a
dieta. (V)   7. Marcela se va a hacer socia de un gimnasio.
(F)   8. Es probable que pronto Carlitos sea más delgado.
(V)   9. El esposo de Marcela va a tratar de engordar. (F)
10. El papá de Carlitos planea hacer un ejercicio ligero.
(V)

Sobre Venezuela y Colombia, pág. 152   1. Venezuela limita
al norte con el Mar Caribe y con el Océano Atlántico; al
sur con Brasil; al este con Guyana y al oeste con Colombia. Colombia limita al norte con Panamá y el Mar
Caribe; al sur con Perú y Ecuador; al este con Venezuela y
Brasil y al oeste con el Océano Pacífico.   2. Venezuela
significa "pequeña Venecia." El nombre se lo dio Américo
Vespucio.   3. El Salto Ángel. Más de trescientas islas
pertenecen al país. La más popular es la isla Margarita.
4. El petróleo.   5. En el centro histórico está la casa
donde nació Simón Bolívar. En la parte moderna encontramos autopistas y rascacielos.   6. Fue el Libertador de
América.   7. La capital es Bogotá. Otras ciudades importantes son Medellín y Cartagena.   8. Mario y Lucía
piensan visitar el Museo del Oro y la Catedral de Sal.
9. Porque este autor recibió el Premio Nóbel de Literatura.   10. Sueña con comprar un anillo con una esmeralda porque sabe que las mejores esmeraldas son las de
Colombia.

Hablemos de su país, pág. 152   Answers will vary.

Después de leer la tarjeta, pág. 153   1. Dice que es muy
interesante.   2. En el Museo del Oro hay una colección
de veinte mil piezas.   3. Fueron a una discoteca y
bailaron cumbia.   4. Cartagena es una ciudad colonial.
5. Lucía quiere que Mario le compre una esmeralda.

Estructuras gramaticales

A, pág. 155   1. Evite el estrés y duerma por lo menos seis
horas al día.   2. Disminuya el consumo de sal.   3. No se
preocupe demasiado.   4. Tome la medicina dos veces al
día, pero no la tome con el estómago vacío.   5. Vuelva
en dos semanas.   6. Déle este papel a la recepcionista y
pídale un turno   7. Lláme me si tiene algún problema.
Follow-up: Answers will vary.

B, pág. 155   1. Escriban las cartas.   2. Traduzcan las
cartas (Tradúzcanlas) al español.   3. Vayan al correo.
4. Llévenle los documentos al Sr. Díaz.   5. Preparen todos los informes para esta tarde.   6. Estén aquí mañana
temprano.   7. Busquen otro empleo.

C, pág. 155   Answers will vary.

D, pág. 156   Answers will vary.

A, pág. 157   1. Sentémonos cerca de la ventana.   2. No,
no nos sentemos en la sección de fumar.   3. Pidámosle el
menú.   4. No, no lo pidamos ahora.   5. Sí, digámoselo.
6. Sí, pongámosle aceite y vinagre.   7. Sí, pidámosla.
8. Sí, dejémosle propina.

B, pág. 157   Answers will vary.

C, pág. 157   Answers will vary.

A, pág. 159   Answers will vary.

B, pág. 159   Answers will vary.

A, pág. 160   Answers will vary.

B, pág. 161   Answers will vary.

A, pág. 161   Answers will vary.

B, pág. 161   1. No podemos bajar de peso a menos que hagamos ejercicio.   2. Yo puedo hacerme socio del club con tal de que Uds. me den el dinero.   3. Voy a comprar las verduras para que mamá haga la sopa.   4. Voy a decirles a los socios que estén aquí a las dos en caso de que la dietista quiera hablar con ellos.   5. Voy a limpiar mi casa antes de que mi suegra venga a vernos.   6. No puedo salir de casa sin que los niños me vean.

A, pág. 162   1. Mañana Teresa va a llamar a su novio en cuanto llegue a casa.   2. Siempre esperamos al entrenador hasta que viene.   3. Esta tarde voy a leer la página deportiva tan pronto como llegue el periódico.   4. Ellos van a llevar a María al hospital cuando se den cuenta de que está enferma.   5. Voy a comprar ropa tan pronto como me paguen.

B, pág. 162   Answers will vary.

¿Comprende Ud.?, pág. 163 and in Student Audio

En la consulta del médico

Aunque Silvia se encuentra bien de salud, fue a ver a su médico porque quiere perder un poco de peso. También desea hablarle sobre la dieta que sigue ahora porque duda que sea la dieta adecuada.

Silvia   —Me gustaría saber qué puedo hacer para adelgazar dos o tres kilos.

Médico   —Veamos. Venga aquí. Voy a pesarla. Sí, puede perder dos kilos, pero no más. ¿Qué dieta sigue?

Silvia   —Bueno, por la mañana tomo café con dos tostadas con mantequilla. Para almorzar, pescado o carne, y por la noche, vegetales con jamón.

Médico   —Su dieta es buena, pero hay dos cosas que quiero que haga. Elimine la mantequilla y cocine la carne a la parrilla para que tenga menos grasa. ¡Ah! y coma siempre productos lácteos desgrasados.

Silvia   —Quiero también decirle que últimamente me encuentro algo cansada.

Médico   —¿Hace Ud. algún ejercicio?

Silvia   —Soy socia de un gimnasio, pero llevo varios meses sin poder ir.

Médico   —Bueno, le voy a mandar varios ejercicios para que los haga en su casa y recupere la energía.

Silvia   —Muchas gracias, doctor. ¿Necesito volver a la consulta?

Médico   —Sí, vuelva en un mes.

¿Verdadero o falso? comprehension questions: 1. Silvia va al médico porque está muy mala. (F)   2. Silvia cree que está muy delgada. (F)   3. Silvia come verduras para la cena. (V)   4. El médico piensa que la dieta de Silvia es muy mala. (F)   5. El médico quiere que Silvia elimine las grasas. (V)   6. Silvia va todos los días al gimnasio. (F) 7. El médico quiere que Silvia haga ejercicios en casa. (V) 8. Silvia tiene que volver al médico en dos semanas. (F)

Song lyrics:

"Arroz con leche"

Arroz con leche, me quiero casar
con una señorita de San Nicolás.
Que sepa coser, que sepa bordar;
que sepa abrir la puerta
para ir a jugar.

¡Con ésta, sí; con ésta, no!
¡Con esta señorita me caso yo!

Arroz con leche, me quiero casar
con una señorita de San Nicolás.
Que sea bonita, que sea cortés,
y que me traiga flores cada fin de mes.

¡Con ésta, sí; con ésta, no!
¡Con esta señorita me caso yo!

Hablemos de la salud, pág. 164   1. Se llama Gimnasio Ángel López y está en la calle Amparo Usera, 14.   2. Se debe llamar (Debe llamarse) al número 476-36-82.   3. Lo va a encontrar (Va a encontrarlo) cerrado porque cierran a las dos.   4. No, no está cerrado.   5. Pueden asistir los adultos y los niños.   6. Hay karate y taekwondo.   7. No, los socios no tienen que pagar por usar la sauna.   8. Answers will vary.

Lecturas periodísticas

Para leer y comprender, pág. 166   1. Se deben comer con moderación la grasa, los helados, los quesos, los aderezos para ensaladas y los aceites.   2. Debemos utilizar utensilios de teflón, preparar las carnes al horno o a la parrilla, y las verduras al vapor.   3. Podemos hacer ejercicio regularmente y tratar de hacer actividades divertidas que no incluyan comer.   4. Debemos tener cuidado con las píldoras que prometen derretir la grasa y que quitan el apetito, los suplementos de fibra y los sustitutos de azúcar.   5. Se deben evitar las dietas que enfatizan un tipo de alimento sobre otros, insisten en mezclar únicamente cierto tipo de alimentos y se tienen que seguir con suplementos de minerales y vitaminas.   6. Answers will vary.

Teleinforme

Preparación, pág. 170   Answers will vary. *Possible answers:*
1. (modelo) mente sana-cuerpo sano +   2. cuerpo sano +
3. cuerpo sano -   4. cuerpo sano +   5. cuerpo sano -
6. cuerpo sano -   7. cuerpo sano +   8. mente sana-cuerpo sano -   9. mente sana-cuerpo sano +   10. mente sana-cuerpo sano -   11. cuerpo sano -   12. mente sana-cuerpo sano +   13. mente sana-cuerpo sano +   14. cuerpo sano +
15. cuerpo sano -   16. cuerpo sano +   17. cuerpo sano -
18. cuerpo sano -   19. cuerpo sano -   20. cuerpo sano -
21. cuerpo sano +   22. cuerpo sano -   23. mente sana-cuerpo sano +   24. mente sana-cuerpo sano +   25. cuerpo sano +   26. cuerpo sano +   27. mente sana-cuerpo sano +
Follow-up activity: Answers will vary.

Comprensión: A, pág. 171   1. V   2. F   3. F   4. V   5. V
6. F   7. F   8. F   9. V   10. F

B, pág. 171   1. quemaduras   2. hirviendo, perola   3. ampollas, cicatrices   4. clara   5. batirla   6. cuchara, espátula
7. mucha   8. sencillo

Ampliación, pág. 171   Answers will vary.

Lección 6

Dígame, pág. 174   1. F   2. F   3. F   4. V   5. V   6. F
7. V   8. F   9. F   10. V   11. F   12. V   13. V   14. V

Perspectivas socioculturales, pág. 175   Answers will vary.

Hablando de todo un poco

Preparación, pág. 176   1. o   2. r   3. k   4. t   5. i   6. a
7. c   8. e   9. b   10. g   11. m   12. d   13. f   14. h
15. s   16. l   17. n   18. j   19. q   20. p

A, pág. 177   Answers will vary.

B, pág. 177   Answers will vary.

C, pág. 177   Answers will vary.

Palabras problemáticas, pág. 178   Answers will vary.

¡Ahora escuche!, pág. 178
Querida Cindy:

Como me pides en tu carta, te estoy escribiendo en español. Me preguntas cómo me va en las clases y la verdad es que el programa es magnífico. He aprendido mucho y creo que ya casi hablo como una "tica". Bueno, estoy exagerando, pero realmente mi español ha mejorado mucho.

En las clases que estoy tomando los grupos de estudiantes son pequeños y por eso tenemos la oportunidad de practicar mucho. Los profesores son muy capacitados y tienen mucho interés en que todos aprendamos. Pero no pienses por eso que lo único que hago es estudiar, pues como tengo los fines de semana libres, casi siempre voy de excursión. Unas veces voy con los profesores y otras con Mirta, la hija de los Alvarado, la familia con la que estoy viviendo.

La semana pasada fui con ella al Parque Braulio Carrillo, un parque nacional interesantísimo. Allí vi muchos animales y hasta tuve la suerte de ver un quetzal.

Bueno, Cindy, ¿quieres un buen consejo? Ven a estudiar a Costa Rica. Yo quizás venga a pasar el próximo verano aquí.

Cariños,
Debbie

¿Verdadero o falso? comprehension questions: 1. Cindy no sabe español. (F)   2. Debbie piensa que no ha aprendido mucho en las clases. (F)   3. En las clases hay pocos estudiantes. (V)   4. Los profesores que tiene Debbie no son muy buenos. (F)   5. Debbie sólo tiene tiempo para estudiar. (F)   6. A veces Debbie va de excursión con sus profesores. (V)   7. La familia con la que vive Debbie tiene una hija. (V)   8. Debbie nunca ha visto un quetzal. (F)
9. Debbie cree que Cindy debe venir a estudiar a Costa Rica. (V)   10. Debbie piensa volver a Costa Rica. (V)

Sobre Costa Rica, pág. 179   1. Costa Rica limita al norte con Nicaragua, al sur con Panamá, al este con el Mar Caribe y al oeste con el Océano Pacífico.   2. A los costarricenses los llaman "ticos".   3. Es uno de los mejores de Latinoamérica.   4. Las protege con leyes muy estrictas.
5. Las reservas ecológicas ocupan el 15% de la superficie.
6. Se pueden ver el Océano Pacífico y el Mar Caribe.
7. Los productos principales de exportación son bananas, café y flores.   8. Otra fuente de ingresos del país es el turismo.   9. Puerto Limón está en la costa del Mar Caribe. San José, la capital, no es una ciudad muy grande, pero es muy hospitalaria.

Hablemos de su país, pág. 179   Answers will vary.

Estructuras gramaticales

A, pág. 181   1. No escribas el informe hoy.   2. No pongas la mesa ahora.   3. No hagas la cena.   4. No te laves la cabeza.   5. No traigas las revistas.   6. No te sientes aquí.   7. No te prepares para salir.   8. No le des el dinero a Iván.   9. No le pidas el auto a María.   10. No te acuestes antes de las diez.

B, pág. 182   1. Levántate temprano.   2. Báñate y vístete. 3. No te pongas los pantalones azules; ponte los blancos. 4. Haz la tarea, pero no la hagas mirando televisión. 5. Sal de la casa a las once.   6. Ve al mercado, pero no vayas en bicicleta.   7. Vuelve a casa temprano y dile a Rosa que la fiesta es mañana.   8. Ten cuidado y no le abras la puerta a nadie.   9. Sé bueno y no te acuestes tarde.   10. Cierra las puertas y apaga las luces.   11. Llámame por teléfono si necesitas algo.   12. No mires televisión hasta muy tarde.

C, pág. 182   Answers will vary

D, pág. 182   Answers will vary.

pág. 183   1. Levantaos temprano.   2. Bañaos en seguida. 3. Haced la tarea.   4. No os pongáis los zapatos negros. 5. Poneos el abrigo.   6. Invitad a las chicas.   7. Llevadlas al parque.   8. Llamadnos esta noche.   9. Idos ahora mismo.   10. Venid temprano mañana.

pág. 184   1. apreciado   2. supuesto   3. descubierto 4. envuelto   5. contribuido   6. devuelto   7. comentado 8. parecido   9. celebrado   10. muerto   11. leído 12. roto   13. hecho   14. evitado   15. cubierto 16. puesto   17. huido   18. dicho   19. caído   20. escrito

pág. 185   1. rota   2. preso   3. electo / resueltos   4. encendidas   5. sustituto   6. escrito / confuso   7. despiertos 8. sueltos

A, pág. 186   1. han preguntado / hemos hecho   2. han venido / han vuelto   3. has dicho / he dicho   4. ha escrito / he leído   5. han ido / han alquilado   6. has puesto / he visto

B, pág. 186   has visto / he visto / he estado / has llevado / ha (he) tenido / ha dicho / has sacado / has aprendido

C, pág. 186   Answers will vary.

A, pág. 187   1. Ud. ya había arrancado el coche cuando yo salí de casa.   2. Nosotros ya habíamos cambiado la goma pinchada cuando ellos llegaron.   3. Tú ya habías llamado al club automovilístico cuando él fue al taller de mecánica. 4. El mecánico ya había revisado los frenos cuando tú viniste.   5. Yo ya había pagado la chapa cuando Uds. nos dieron el dinero.   6. Ellos ya habían comprado el acumulador cuando nosotros los llamamos.

B, pág. 187   Answers will vary.

A, pág. 189   1. gran presidente   2. misma clase / Carlos mismo   3. antigua ciudad / ciudad muy interesante 4. lápices rojos   5. mujeres republicanas   6. algunos agentes   7. coche japonés   8. ventana abierta   9. mujer grande   10. ninguna limitación   11. famoso actor 12. única profesora   13. hombre pobre   14. mujer única

B, pág. 190   1. Sí, es un hombre grande.   2. Sí, somos viejos amigos.   3. No, tengo que hablar con el director mismo.   4. Sí, es un hombre pobre.   5. No, es una mujer única.   6. No, quiero usar el mismo libro.   7. Sí, es un hombre viejo.   8. Sí, es un gran actor.   9. No, ¡pobre niña!   10. No, éstas son mis únicas sandalias.

¿Comprende Ud.?, pág. 191 and in Student Audio

¿Adónde vamos hoy?
Esta semana no hay clases en la universidad y Mirta quiere aprovechar para enseñarle a Debbie algunos lugares interesantes de Costa Rica.

Mirta   —Hoy vamos a ir al Parque Nacional de Carara, pero vamos a ir en una excursion y así no tenemos que manejar.
Debbie   —¿A qué hora salimos?
Mirta   —El ómnibus sale a las ocho.

En el parque
Debbie   —Esto es precioso. Me gusta más que el Parque Braulio Carrillo. Aquí he visto más animales, y hay muchísimos pájaros. ¡Y qué bien cantan!

Se oye el canto de los pájaros.
Mirta   —Sí, parece que los pájaros te quieren dar un concierto.
Debbie   —Mira, allí entre los árboles hay dos monos. ¡Qué lindos!
Mirta   —Bueno, vamos ahora a la playa que está cerca de aquí.
Debbie   —Debemos darnos prisa porque pronto nos van a llamar para irnos.

En la playa
Debbie   —Esta playa es muy bonita.

Al rato se oye sonar tres veces la bocina del ómnibus.

Debbie —Ay, nos están llamando para irnos. ¡Qué lástima!

Mirta —No te preocupes. Mañana vamos a ir al Jardín de las Mariposas. Te va a gustar mucho. Hay miles de mariposas.

Debbie —¿Pasado mañana podemos ir al volcán Arenal?

Mirta —Sí, y también quiero llevarte a una plantación de café. Ya sabes que nuestro café es uno de los mejores del mundo.

¿Verdadero o falso? comprehension questions: 1. Debbie y Mirta van a ir en coche al Parque Nacional de Carara. (F)   2. Debbie cree que el Parque Braulio Carrillo es más bonito. (F)   3. En el parque de Carara hay más animales. (V)   4. Las chicas van a ir a una playa. (V)   5. Debbie y Mirta pueden estar mucho tiempo en la playa. (F)   6. Mañana las chicas van a ver muchas mariposas. (V)   7. A Debbie le interesa ir a ver el volcán Arenal. (V)   8. Mirta dice que el café de Costa Rica no es muy bueno. (F)

Song lyrics:

Canción de cuna

Duérmete mi niño, duérmete mi sol;
duérmete, pedazo de mi corazón.

Este niño lindo, que nació de día,
quiere que lo lleven a la dulcería.

Esta niña linda, que nació de noche.
quiere que la lleven a pasear en coche.

Duérmete, mi niño, duérmete, mi sol;
duérmete, pedazo de mi corazón.

Hablemos de programas para estudiantes extranjeros, pág. 191   1. Se llama Novalingua.   2. Está en España, en Barcelona.   3. Avenida Diagonal, 600.   4. Se ofrecen en julio, agosto, septiembre y octubre.   5. El curso dura ochenta horas.   6. El máximo es 8 alumnos por clase.

Lecturas periodísticas

Para leer y comprender, pág. 193   1. Lo que más atrae es su bellísima naturaleza.   2. Sí, para conocer el famoso Parque Nacional de Tortuguero.   3. Recomienda excursiones a la selva, al Valle del Orosí, al Lago Arenal, a los volcanes y al Parque Nacional del Volcán Irazú.   4. Es pequeño, pero elegante y exclusivo; está en lo alto de una montaña; arregla excursiones para los turistas; y es posible disfrutar de la piscina, montar a caballo, ir de excursión al cercano Parque Nacional de Guayabo o simplemente sen-

tarse en el jardín.   5. Podemos visitar la Catedral, el Teatro Nacional y el Museo Nacional.

Teleinforme

Preparación, pág. 196   lugar/pueblo/ciudad: 3, 6, 7, 18; para llegar: 1, 8, 9, 21; alojamiento: 11, 17, 24; comida: 10, 13, 23; actividades: 2, 4, 5, 12, 14, 19, 22; excursiones: 15, 16, 20

Comprensión: A, pág. 197   1. Mar Caribe   2. Talamanca   3. malas   4. banano   5. el turismo   6. Hay hoteles, pensiones y *bed and breakfasts*.   7. Abrió sus puertas en agosto de 1997.   8. baja, baratos   9. Los precios del Hotel Casa Camarona están al alcance del turista costarricense.   10. 17, 8   11. la conservación y mantenimiento del medio ambiente   12. Jamaica, Panamá   13. coco, cacao, ñame, yuca, tubérculos   14. su gente, su paisaje y su tranquilidad y hospitalidad

B, pág. 197   Answers will vary.

Ampliación, pág. 198   Answers will vary.

Lección 7

Dígame, pág. 205   1. Están sentados alrededor de una mesa. Están charlando animadamente.   2. Se habrán graduado para junio.   3. Le gustaría vivir en Managua.   4. Echa de menos a su familia y a sus amigos. Extraña la sopa de pescado que prepara su abuela.   5. Roberto tiene ganas de comer mondongo o arroz con frijoles y tortillas de maíz; Estela quiere comer plátanos fritos con miel de abeja.   6. Porque ya ha comido demasiado.   7. Es una tortilla rellena de carne, frijoles y queso.   8. No habría comido tanto.   9. Dice "buen provecho".   10. Pasaban por lo menos una hora charlando. (Hacían la sobremesa.)   11. Porque se van a poner tristes.   12. Rafael levanta su copa.

Perspectivas socioculturales, pág. 205   Answers will vary.

Hablando de todo un poco

Preparación, pág. 207   1. e   2. h   3. n   4. k   5. o   6. b   7. p   8. a   9. l   10. d   11. r   12. g   13. q   14. j   15. m   16. c   17. i   18. f

A, pág. 207   Answers will vary.

B, pág. 207   Answers will vary.

C, pág. 208   Answers will vary.

Palabras problemáticas, pág. 208   Answers will vary.

¡Ahora escuche!, pág 208   Juana, la cocinera de los Acosta, no vendrá a trabajar mañana, de modo que Elvira y su mamá tendrán que cocinar. Como tienen invitados a cenar piensan preparar una cena especial: ensalada mixta, sopa de pescado, bistec y papas al horno. De postre Elvira decidió preparar un flan.

El señor Acosta irá mañana al supermercado y comprará unas botellas de vino tinto español para la cena; su esposa preparará un ponche de frutas para que los niños puedan brindar con el resto de la familia.

Después de cenar probablemente se quedarán conversando un rato, discutiendo de política y contando chistes, pues, como a casi todos los latinos, les encanta hacer la sobremesa. Más tarde el señor Acosta quiere llevar a su familia y a sus amigos al teatro a ver una comedia musical. Él piensa que todos se van a divertir mucho.

Marcelo, el novio de Elvira, que siempre es bienvenido a las reuniones familiares, irá con ellos al teatro y después llevará a los amigos de la familia al hotel donde se están hospedando.

¿Verdadero o falso? comprehension questions: 1. Juana vendrá mañana a casa de los Acosta. (F)   2. La mamá de Elvira no sabe cocinar. (F)   3. Los Acosta invitaron a unos amigos a cenar. (V)   4. En la cena el plato principal va a ser carne. (V)   5. Elvira va a preparar el postre. (V)   6. El señor Acosta prefiere los vinos chilenos. (F)   7. Los Acosta tienen niños. (V)   8. Los invitados del señor Acosta son norteamericanos. (F)   9. Inmediatamente después de la cena los invitados no van a irse a su casa. (V)   10. La familia Acosta va a ir al teatro a ver un drama. (F)   11. Elvira tiene novio. (V)   12. A la familia Acosta no le gusta la compañía de Marcelo. (F)

Sobre Centroamérica, pág. 210   1. Panamá conecta América Central con Sudamérica. Es famoso por su canal. 2. Es importante porque alrededor del canal gira la economía del país.   3. Nicaragua es el más extenso. 4. Es el mayor lago de agua dulce y en él hay tiburones. 5. La capital es Managua.   6. Es el país más pequeño y más densamente poblado de Centroamérica.   7. Es San Salvador. Es la ciudad más industrializada de América Central.   8. Se diferencia de los demás en que no tiene volcanes.   9. La capital es Tegucigalpa. La mayor atracción turística es Copán.   10. Tikal está en Guatemala y es uno de los sitios arqueológicos más interesantes de toda América.

Hablemos de su país, pág. 210   Answers will vary.

Después de leer la tarjeta, pág. 211   1. Escribe desde Guatemala. Lo está pasando muy bien.   2. Visitó las ruinas de Tikal y también estuvo en Antigua.   3. Dice que es un centro de atracción turística.   4. Dijo que era una de las ciudades más románticas del mundo.   5. No, no piensa estar mucho más tiempo allí.

Estructuras gramaticales

A, pág. 213   Answers will vary.

B, pág. 214   Answers will vary.

C, pág. 214   Answers will vary.

D, pág. 214   me levantaré / me vestiré / saldré / Llegaré / vendrá / me dirá / podré / estará / Haré / invitaré / querrá / estudiaré / iré / preparé / cenaré / tendré

A, pág. 215   Answers will vary.

B, pág. 215   Answers will vary.

A, pág. 217   1. Dijeron que las traerían hoy por la tarde. 2. Dijo que lo cocinaría término medio.   3. Dijo que las freiría.   4. Dijeron que lo pondrían en el horno. 5. Dijo que vendrían mañana.   6. Dijo que no saldría con él.

B, pág. 217   Answers will vary

pág. 218   Answers will vary.

A, pág. 219   Answers will vary.

B, pág. 219   Answers will vary.

A, pág. 220   Answers will vary. *Verbs:*   1. habría invitado 2. habríamos servido   3. habrías empezado   4. habrían servido   5. habrían invitado   6. les habría avisado 7. habríamos tenido   8. había terminado

B, pág. 220   1. Yo me habría levantado mucho más temprano y habría limpiado la casa.   2. Elvira habría comprado comida y gaseosas.   3. Tú habrías traído los discos de música latina.   4. Carlos y Alicia habrían vuelto temprano de la universidad.   5. Víctor y yo habríamos preparado un buen postre.   6. Uds. habrían lavado las copas y las fuentes.

C, pág. 221   Answers will vary.

A, pág. 222   1. al cabeza   2. El cura   3. la capital   4. Los policías   5. la manga / el mango   6. el fondo   7. una fonda   8. la guía   9. el capital   10. una parte / el resto 11. la orden   12. el puerto   13. la punta   14. el frente

B, pág. 222   1. h   2. a   3. i   4. g   5. j   6. b   7. m   8. c
9. e   10. d   11. f   12. n   13. l   14. k   15. q   16. r
17. o   18. p

C, pág. 223   1. La policía / al cabeza / la guardia / el parte
/ el orden / la capital   2. policías / la fonda / el puerto
3. la cura   4. la cabeza   5. modo   6. moda / mangas / la
banda

¿Comprende Ud.?, pág. 224 and in Student Audio

Cruzando fronteras

*Amanda Núñez está en su apartamento, hablando con Sandra
Stevens, su compañera de cuarto.*

Sandra   —Nunca me habría imaginado que tendría una
amiga salvadoreña. Me gustaría visitar El Salvador algún día. Es el país más pequeño de
Centroamérica, ¿verdad?

Amanda   —Sí, pero es el más densamente poblado. Y San
Salvador, la capital, es la ciudad más industrializada de Centroamérica.

Sandra   —El año pasado mi familia y yo fuimos a
Nicaragua. Visitamos Managua, la capital,
pero no vimos el famoso lago Nicaragua. Eso
sí, por primera vez en mi vida vi un volcán...

Amanda   —Yo fui a Honduras y a Guatemala con unas
amigas. Visitamos Tegucigalpa y las ruinas
mayas de Copán. Nos habría gustado visitar
también las ruinas de Tikal, pero no tuvimos
tiempo.

Sandra   —¡Qué lástima! Dicen que es uno de los sitios
arqueológicos más interesantes de toda
América.

Amanda   —Bueno, la próxima vez que vayamos a
Guatemala las visitaremos.

Sandra   —Yo haré un viaje por toda Centroamérica dentro de dos años. Para entonces ya me habré
graduado.

Suena el timbre

Amanda   —¿Quieres abrir la puerta? ¿Quién vendrá a esta
hora?

Sandra   —Será uno de tus muchos admiradores...

Amanda   —[*Se ríe*] Lo dudo, pero sería muy bienvenido...

¿Verdadero o falso? comprehension questions: 1. Sandra
ha estado en El Salvador muchas veces. (F)   2. Casi no
hay industrias en El Salvador. (F)   3. Sandra no tuvo
oportunidad de visitar el lago Nicaragua. (V)   4. Sandra
nunca había visto un volcán antes de ir a Nicaragua. (V)
5. Amanda va a tratar de ver las ruinas de Tikal durante su

próxima visita a Guatemala. (V)   6. Dentro de dos años,
Sandra habrá terminado sus estudios. (V)   7. Amanda
sabe quién es la persona que llama a la puerta. (F)
8. Amanda no tiene ganas de ver a nadie. (F)

Song lyrics:

"La barca"

Se irá, se irá la barca,
se irá, se irá el vapor;
el lunes por la mañana
también se irá mi amor.

La esperaré, paciente,
no dejaré de llorar;
cuando ella vuelva, sonriente,
feliz la iré a esperar.

Se irá, se irá la barca,
se irá, se irá el vapor;
el lunes por la mañana
también se irá mi amor.

Hablemos de comida, pág. 224   1. Debemos ir a La Fonda
de Paco porque el anuncio dice que podemos comer bien
y gastar poco.   2. Debemos ir al restaurante Dandy
porque tiene un "show" de primerísima calidad.
3. Debemos ir al restaurante La Pampa porque tiene
cocina argentina.   4. Debemos ir al Restaurante O'Pazo
porque tiene los mejores pescados y mariscos del mundo.
5. Debemos ir al restaurante Canta Gallo porque tiene un
precio especial para niños.   6. Debemos ir al Casino
Gran Madrid, donde va a actuar el cantante Raphael.
7. Debemos ir al restaurante don Emiliano porque sirve
especialidades regionales mexicanas.

Lecturas periodísticas

Para leer y comprender, pág. 227   1. La podemos considerar un paraíso por su gente, sus bellezas naturales y por
su comida.   2. Son de origen prehispánico.   3. Entre los
postres tenemos buñuelos, torrejas, higos y camotes en
dulce. Entre las bebidas están el atol de elote, la chicha y
el ponche de frutas.   4. El maíz es la base de muchas comidas guatemaltecas, como por ejemplo: las tortillas, los
tamales, los tacos y las enchiladas.   5. Lo consideraban
como una planta sagrada.   6. Nos habla del origen del
teocinte y de la creación del hombre.   7. De los granos
del teocinte los dioses hicieron la carne, los huesos y la
sangre de las primeras criaturas humanas.   8. Se describe
en el libro sagrado de los mayas.   9. Se guiaban por el
calendario lunar.   10. A la diosa Ixcumané.

Teleinforme

Preparación, pág. 231   1. A   2. A   3. V   4. V   5. V
6. V   7. A   8. A   9. A   10. V

Comprensión: A, pág. 231

1. maíz   2. nopal   3. (las tortillas de) maíz   4. nopal
5. maíz   6. nopal   7. maíz   8. (las tortillas de) maíz
9. nopal   10. nopal

B, pág. 232   1. a   2. i   3. d   4. g   5. j   6. h   7. b   8. e
9. f   10. c

C, pág. 232   1. café   2. mucho dinero extranjero
3. montañosas (inaccesibles)   4. la fábrica de la cooperativa   5. bueno   6. segundo / pequeño

D, pág. 233   1/2. el pollo, el caldo (de pollo), la papa (sa-
banera, pastusa, criolla), el maíz (tierno) / las mazorcas, las
alcaparras, la (crema de) leche, el aguacate   3. b

Ampliación, pág. 233   Answers will vary.

Lección 8

Dígame, pág. 236   1. Luis, David y Rebeca son americanos, Nélida es puertorriqueña e Ignacio es salvadoreño.
2. Van a hablar de los problemas sociales y ambientales,
y Rebeca va a dirigir las discusiones.   3. Sugiere que empiecen por los problemas de la contaminación.   4. Según
Luis, las principales causas son los automóviles y las fábricas.
5. La contaminación de las aguas se resolvería si la gente
cooperara.   6. Reciclan periódicos, plásticos, aluminio y
vidrio.   7. Menciona las drogas, los asesinatos, las violaciones y los robos, y éstos no son exclusivos de las grandes
ciudades.   8. No hay ninguna que haya podido resolverlos.   9. Si se hubiera educado mejor al pueblo muchos de
estos problemas se habrían resuelto.   10. Nos hemos
acostumbrado a las comodidades del mundo moderno.

Perspectivas socioculturales, pág. 236   Answers will vary.

Hablando de todo un poco

Preparación, pág. 238   1. c   2. b   3. b   4. a   5. c   6. a
7. b   8. c   9. c   10. a   11. b   12. c   13. a   14. b

A, pág. 239   Answers will vary.

B, pág. 239   Answers will vary.

C, pág. 239   Answers will vary.

D, pág. 239   Answers will vary.

Palabras problemáticas, pág. 240   1. Quedé suspendido(a)
2. gratis   3. fracasó   4. dejar   5. libres

¡Ahora escuche!, pág. 240   Roberto tiene que preparar un
informe para su clase de sociología, y ha decidido hacerlo
sobre los problemas que hay en la ciudad donde él vive.
Uno de los más graves es el de la delincuencia y él cree
que este problema se debe principalmente al uso de las
drogas y a la pobreza. En la ciudad han aumentado los robos, los asesinatos y las violaciones, así como también la
cantidad de pandillas. En su informe, Roberto va a hablar
de las organizaciones que están tratando de ayudar a los
jóvenes para evitar que entren a formar parte de las pandillas, y de los programas creados por el gobierno con ese
fin.

Otro problema que Roberto considera importante
mencionar es el de la contaminación del medio ambiente,
y se propone señalar algunas de las medidas que, según él,
pudieran ayudar a resolver el problema, como por ejemplo, tener un buen programa de reciclaje y aumentar el
uso de productos biodegradables y de combustibles más
limpios. Él cree que, si realmente nos hubiéramos pro-
puesto resolver estos problemas, no habríamos llegado a
esta situación y confía en que podremos solucionarla si todos cooperamos.

¿Verdadero o falso? comprehension questions: 1. Roberto
va a preparar un informe para una de sus clases. (V)
2. Roberto va a hablar de las cosas buenas que hay en su
ciudad. (F)   3. El problema que él considera más grande
es el de la delincuencia. (V)   4. Roberto no cree que las
drogas aumenten el crimen. (F)   5. En la ciudad de
Roberto ha disminuido la violencia. (F)   6. Ahora hay
menos pandillas. (F)   7. Hay organizaciones que tratan de
evitar que existan pandillas. (V)   8. Roberto se preocupa
por la contaminación del medio ambiente. (V)   9. El reciclaje no es importante para evitar la contaminación. (F)
10. Según Roberto, todos debemos cooperar en la solución de los problemas. (V)

Sobre las minorías hispanas, pág. 242   1. Luis nació en
Los Ángeles. Su familia viene de México y él se siente
orgulloso de su origen y su cultura.   2. Se ve en los
nombres de las ciudades y de las calles y en la arquitectura. Es el de los mexicanoamericanos.   3. Han influido
en la música y la comida. Se destacan en la política,
la educación, las artes y la literatura.   4. Unos tres
millones de puertorriqueños han emigrado a Estados
Unidos desde la Segunda Guerra Mundial.   5. Los
puertorriqueños son ciudadanos estadounidenses.

6. Es el grupo más jóven.   7. Sí, se unen y muchos alcanzan altos grados y distinciones.   8. Dejaron Cuba y se unieron a la colonia cubana de Miami. Lograron prosperidad económica.   9. Mantienen las costumbres y tradiciones de Cuba.   10. Se ve en los restaurantes, la radio, la música, etc. Hoy es la ciudad más rica y moderna del mundo hispanohablante.

Hablemos de su país, pág. 243   Answers will vary.

Estructuras gramaticales

A, pág. 246   1. Le dijo a Carlos que escribiera un informe sobre el problema de la contaminación de las aguas. 2. Les dijo a Uds. que trajeran artículos sobre la polución del aire.   3. Les dijo a Mireya y a Saúl que organizaran una mesa redonda.   4. Te dijo a ti que hablaras con otros estudiantes sobre la importancia del reciclaje.   5. A mí me dijo que fuera a la biblioteca y sacara un libro sobre los problemas ambientales.   6. A nosotros nos dijo que estuviéramos aquí mañana a las ocho.

B, pág. 246   1. Dijo que no creía que los problemas fueran fáciles de resolver.   2. Dijo que era una lástima que tantos muchachos se unieran a las pandillas.   3. Dijo que era necesario que identificáramos los problemas más graves. 4. Dijo que era importante que estudiáramos los problemas de las personas sin hogar.   5. Dijo que era urgente que hiciéramos un esfuerzo para solucionar los problemas de la delincuencia.   6. Dijo que no era cierto que la educación fuera nuestra primera prioridad.

C, pág. 246   Answers will vary.

D, pág. 246   Answers will vary.

A, pág. 247   1. tengo   2. fuera / diera   3. puedo / fuera / quieren / tenemos   4. invitaran   5. fuera / tuviera

B, pág. 248   Answers will vary.

A, pág. 249   1. haya escrito / haya hecho / haya terminado   2. haya estado / haya entendido / hayamos podido 3. haya visto / haya ido / hayan invitado / hayan dado

B, pág. 249   *Possible answers:*   1. No creo que el gobierno haya resuelto el asunto de los desperdicios químicos. 2. Me alegro de que ellos se hayan reunido para hablar sobre la contaminación del ambiente.   3. No es verdad que la gente siempre haya llevado los residuos de productos químicos al vertedero.   4. Dudo que nosotros siempre hayamos usado productos biodegradables.   5. Es una lástima que los problemas de la delincuencia se hayan

agravado.   6. Me alegro de que hayamos hablado con las personas que organizan la mesa redonda.   7. Ojalá que todos juntos hayamos identificado los problemas más difíciles de resolver.   8. Siento que el gobernador no se haya reunido con nosotros todavía.   9. Es una lástima que hayas dicho que nuestras iniciativas fracasarán.   10. Espero que nuestros esfuerzos hayan ayudado a educar a la comunidad.

A, pág. 250   1. Mis amigos lamentaron que yo me hubiera mudado tan lejos.   2. El jefe de mi papá sintió que él hubiera dejado la oficina.   3. Raquel no creía que nosotros hubiéramos decidido mudarnos.   4. Mis abuelos se alegraron de que mis padres hubieran vuelto a California. 5. Olga no esperaba que nosotros hubiéramos encontrado una casa grande y barata.

B, pág. 251   *Wording of some answers may vary slightly.* 1. Si me hubieran dado el descuento que yo quería, yo habría comprado el coche.   2. Si me hubieran ofrecido media botella de vino blanco, yo la habría aceptado. 3. Si hubiera habido habitaciones libres en los hoteles, nosotros habríamos pasado un fin de semana en la Costa del Sol.   4. Si hubiera salido temprano de casa, yo habría llegado a tiempo a la cita.   5. Si hubiéramos hecho reservaciones en un hotel, nosotros habríamos ido a Río para la época de carnaval.   6. Si hubiera tenido mis documentos en regla, yo habría ido a Europa.   7. Si hubiera habido un vuelo directo, yo habría tomado el avión.   8. Si me hubieran ofrecido un puesto trabajando con otra persona, yo lo habría aceptado.

C, pág. 251   Answers will vary.

D, pág. 251   Answers will vary

¿Comprende Ud.?, pág. 252 and in Student Audio

En la Universidad Internacional de la Florida
Paco, un chico madrileño, y Adela, una muchacha de la Ciudad de México, están comiendo en la cafetería de la universidad. Mientras comen, comparan los problemas sociales y ambientales de sus respectivas ciudades.

Adela —El peor problema que tenemos en México es el de la contaminación del aire. No creo que tenga solución.

Paco —Pero, ¿no es verdad que el gobierno mexicano ha tomado muchas medidas para eliminar la contaminación?

Adela —Sí, pero aún así la contaminación no se ha eliminado por completo. ¿Y en tu ciudad, Paco?

Paco —Aunque también hay contaminación en Madrid, lo peor para nosotros es el crimen y el consumo de bebidas alcohólicas. Este año ha empeorado bastante.

Adela —Desgraciadamente, ese problema existe en todo el mundo, como también el problema de la droga.

Paco —Es verdad. En Madrid, tanto la droga como el crimen se han convertido en problemas gravísimos entre la juventud.

Adela —Y otro de los grandes problemas que tenemos en México es la contaminación ambiental. Sospecho que es igual en Madrid.

Paco —Sí, pero ya hemos empezado a reciclar periódicos, plásticos, vidrio, aluminio...

¿Verdadero o falso? comprehension questions: 1. Paco y Adela son de España. (F)   2. Adela cree que la contaminación se va a terminar. (F)   3. El gobierno mexicano está tratando de resolver el problema. (V)   4. Según Paco, el crimen en Madrid ha bajado. (F)   5. Según Adela, el crimen se encuentra en todas las ciudades. (V)   6. En España, la droga y el crimen son grandes problemas de la juventud. (V)   7. En México, no hay problemas con el medio ambiente. (F)   8. En España, se reciclan todo tipo de materiales. (V)

Song lyrics:

"La loba"

La loba, la loba
le compró al lobito
zapatos de cuero
y un gorro bonito.

La loba, la loba
se fue de paseo
con su hijito lindo
y su gorro nuevo.

La loba se ha ido
con su buen lobito
su hijito ha crecido,
ya no es chiquitito.

La loba, la loba
está muy enojada
porque ya está vieja
y no tiene nada.

Hablemos de la vida urbana, pág. 252   1. Se llevaron más de medio millón de dólares.   2. No han detenido a nadie.   3. Es el alcalde de la población de Achi, en el Departa-

mento de Bolívar, y fue secuestrado.   4. Detuvo a veintidós carteristas.   5. Se enfrentaron a tiros con un grupo de narcotraficantes.   6. Tres personas resultaron muertas.   7. Answers will vary.

Lecturas periodísticas

Para leer y comprender, pág. 255   1. Los llamados productos "verdes" o "biodegradables".   2. No, porque algunas empresas utilizan el engaño, y otras simplemente presentan alegatos totalmente irrelevantes.   3. No, porque ninguno lo tiene. Desde 1978 los aerosoles con CFC están prohibidos en Estados Unidos.   4. Porque se usa en cientos de productos cuya biodegradabilidad va desde meses hasta miles de millones de años.   5. Es mejor comprar productos reciclados porque estimula a las empresas que los producen. El hecho de que un producto sea reciclable no significa que será reciclado.   6. Debemos comprar frutas y vegetales orgánicos.   7. Debemos llevar bolsas de tela al supermercado.

Teleinforme

Preparación, pág. 258   Answers will vary.

Comprensión: A, pág. 258   1. espacio   2. la luz   3. barro   4. gusanos   5. sueños   6. silencio   7. una sirena   8. socios   9. graffitti   10. maravillas   11. dibujamos, defendemos

B, pág. 259   1. c   2. d   3. a   4. e   5. b   6. f

C, pág. 259   1. Para ella, "latino" tiene un tono menos político que "chicano".   2. Rubén se considera un ciudadano de los Estados Unidos, con descendencia[1] mexicana. Rubén nació en EE.UU. Su madre nació en EE.UU. Sus abuelos eran de México.   3. Hay cuatro hijos en la familia de Javier. Una hermana tiene catorce, la otra tiene dieciséis y su hermano tiene veinte. Todos nacieron en Culiacán.   4. Ruth se sentó con estudiantes anglos. Estas personas se levantaron y cambiaron de asiento. Se sintió insultada, lastimada.   5. Significa "Movimiento Estudiantil Chicano de Aztlán". Aztlán es lo que antes era México, donde vivían los aztecas.

D, pág. 260   Answers will vary. *Possible answers:*   1a. Gwillurmo   1b. Guillermo   2a. parece confuso   2b. sonríe, interesada   3a. OK. That's great!   3b. ¡Muy bien!   4a. Lora   4b. Laura   5a. inatenta, avergonzada   5b. sonríe, orgullosa

Ampliación, pág. 260   Answers will vary.

[1] Utilizó **descendencia** en lugar de **ascendencia**.

Lección 9

Dígame, pág. 267   1. Paola Bianco es una actriz argentina. 2. *La mentira* es una telenovela que se estrenará a mediados de julio en el canal 5.   3. Sí, una de sus películas salió premiada el año pasado.   4. Trabajó con el director y productor uruguayo Rafael Burgos. Sí, piensa volver a trabajar con él.   5. No, va a ser una comedia musical. 6. Paola admira a Andy García y a Antonio Banderas. 7. Está enamorada de Mario Juncal y piensa casarse con él pronto.   8. Sólo se escuchaba esporádicamente en algunas discotecas.   9. Algunos salseros famosos son Celia Cruz, la India y Marc Anthony.   10. Ha llegado hasta Europa y Asia.   11. Se enseñan los pasos básicos de la salsa, el mambo, el merengue o la rumba cubana. Se ha puesto de moda bailar ritmos latinos.   12. Es la nueva reina del *pop* y fue nombrada por los críticos como "la voz del siglo". Sus representantes anunciaron que acababa de lanzar un nuevo disco grabado en español.

Perspectivas socioculturales, pág. 267   Answers will vary.

Hablando de todo un poco

Preparación, pág. 269   1. protagonista / premio   2. entrevista / actriz / encantadora / enamorada   3. sueña /reina 4. bajo /estrenar   5. pistas / pasos / puesto / cámara 6. lanzar / voz / siglo / escuchar   7. mediados / pantallas / desfile / volver   8. telediario / grabo   9. surgir / como 10. cuanto / nombra   11. publicidad

A, pág. 269   Answers will vary.

B, pág. 269   Answers will vary.

C, pág. 269   Answers will vary.

D, pág. 270   Answers will vary.

Palabras problemáticas, pág. 270   1. A mediados 2. mediana   3. bajo   4. abajo   5. medio   6. Debajo

¡Ahora escuche!, pág. 271   A Marisol le encanta la música de Enrique Iglesias, y compra todos los discos del famoso cantante. Ayer le pidió a su hermano Esteban que le comprara el último disco compacto de su cantante favorito y él se lo compró y se lo regaló, porque ayer fue el cumpleaños de Marisol.

Esteban invitó a todos los amigos de su hermana y les dijo que vinieran a la casa de su familia a las siete. Allí la mamá de los chicos tenía una cena lista para todos.

Después de cenar y abrir regalos, todos fueron a una discoteca a bailar.

En la pista de baile, Marisol le enseñó a su hermano los pasos básicos de la salsa y del merengue para que él pudiera bailar con Isabel, la chica de sus sueños. Irene bailó con todos sus amigos. Se divirtieron mucho.

Hoy Marisol volvió de la universidad y, después de cenar y mirar el telediario, fue a su cuarto y se puso a escuchar a Enrique Iglesias.

¿Verdadero o falso? comprehension questions: 1. A Marisol le gusta mucho Enrique Iglesias. (V)   2. Esteban le compró un disco compacto de Enrique Iglesias a Marisol. (V)   3. El disco compacto le costó mucho dinero a Marisol. (F)   4. Marisol celebró su cumpleaños ayer. (V)   5. Marisol y sus amigos cenaron en un restaurante. (F)   6. Marisol recibió solamente un regalo. (F)   7. El hermano de Marisol no sabía bailar la salsa ni el merengue. (V)   8. Marisol no quería que su hermano bailara con Isabel. (F)   9. Irene bailó solamente con su novio. (F)   10. Marisol no fue a la universidad hoy. (F)

Sobre Uruguay y Argentina, pág. 273   1. Acaba de regresar de Uruguay. Fue a una reunión de artistas.   2. Horacio Quiroga es un famoso escritor uruguayo. A Paola le gustaría hacer una película basada en uno de los cuentos de Quiroga.   3. Dice que Montevideo es el centro administrativo, económico y cultural del país y que allí vive casi la mitad de la población de Uruguay. También visitó Punta del Este.   4. Argentina limita al norte con Paraguay y Bolivia; al sur con el Cabo de Hornos; al este con el Océano Atlántico, Uruguay y Brasil y al oeste con Chile.   5. Siempre extraña a su tierra. 6. No conoce todo su país porque es muy grande. Argentina ocupa el octavo lugar en el mundo por su extensión.   7. La Pampa es una inmensa llanura. Se extiende desde el Océano Atlántico hasta los Andes.   8. El Aconcagua es el pico más alto del mundo occidental. 9. Está situada a orillas del Río de la Plata. Los porteños son los que nacieron en Buenos Aires.   10. Se ve en la arquitectura, en sus amplios bulevares y parques, en la moda y en su sistema de educación. Otras influencias europeas son la española, la inglesa y, sobre todo, la italiana.

Hablemos de su país, pág. 273   Answers will vary.

Después de leer la tarjeta, pág. 274   1. Estuvo en Punta del Este.   2. Sí, le gustó mucho.   3. Fue a la playa y tomó el sol.   4. Visitó la avenida 18 de Julio y la Plaza de la Independencia.   5. Es más tranquila que en Buenos Aires.

Estructuras gramaticales

A, pág. 276   verte / pudieras / hubiera tenido / llamara / hayas tenido / te invito / des / hable / habla / llame / llamaras / pueda / vaya / entrevistar / sea / empiece / llame

B, pág. 276   Answers will vary.

A, pág. 278   Answers will vary.

B, pág. 278   Answers will vary.

A, pág. 280   a / de / a / a / de / de / de / a / en / a / de / a / en / a / en / a

B, pág. 280   1. Voy a empezar a estudiar a la(s)... 2. Generalmente llego a la universidad a la(s)...   3. Me gustaría aprender a...   4. Yo te podría enseñar a...   5. Voy a salir. (Me voy a quedar en casa.)   6. Voy a ir a visitar a mi mejor amigo...   7. Me gusta hablar de...   8. Sí, me gustan los chicos (las chicas) de ojos verdes.   9. El mejor actor (La mejor actriz) de este país es...   10. Prefiero viajar en...

A, pág. 281   1. me comprometí con / casarte con / me di cuenta de / enamorada de / soñaba con / me alegro de 2. saliste de / Traté de / Me olvidé de / convinimos en 3. acuérdate de / encontrarse con / insiste en / cuentes conmigo   4. pensando en / Te fijaste en / entré en

B, pág. 281   Answers will vary.

pág. 282   1. No usar el ascensor en caso de incendio. 2. Tengo varios poemas sin publicar.   3. Oímos hablar en inglés.   4. Entrar por la izquierda.   5. Trabajar es necesario.   6. Los vi salir.   7. Me gusta escucharla cantar.   8. Todavía tengo dos regalos sin abrir. 9. Agregar una taza de agua.   10. No fumar aquí. 11. Oímos sonar el teléfono.   12. Estudiar es importante para mí.

A, pág. 284   Answers may vary. *Possibilities:*   1. Acabo de llegar.   2. Porque acabo de comer.   3. Voy a volver a lavarlo.   4. Me dijo que me pusiera a estudiar.   5. Me puse a estudiar.   6. Me voy a poner a estudiar.

B, pág. 284   acaba de llegar / oí entrar / ir / cenar / mirar / bailar / se pone a leer / ir / sin abrir / Vuelve a / ir / hablar

¿Comprende Ud.?, pág. 285 and in Student Audio

En Buenos Aires

Elba y Silvia, dos chicas paraguayas, están de vacaciones en Buenos Aires. Ahora están en el vestíbulo del hotel esperando a unos amigos para ir al teatro.

Silvia   —¡Qué bonita es esta ciudad! Me encanta pasear por sus avenidas y visitar las tiendas.

Elba   —Sí, son magníficas. Ayer estuve de compras en la famosa calle Florida y todas la tiendas allí son muy elegantes. Gasté muchísimo.

Silvia   —Anoche yo fui con Ernesto a un restaurante en la Avenida Nueve de Julio. Comimos una parrillada que me gustó mucho. ¿Qué hiciste tú?

Elba   —Fui al cine con Lisandro. Vimos la película de Paola Bianco, que ganó el premio en el Festival de Cine el año pasado.

Silvia   —Es muy buena. Fue filmada aquí, pero la dirigió el uruguayo Rafael Burgos.

Elba   —¡Ah! Lisandro y Ernesto acaban de llegar. Están en la puerta a la entrada del hotel. Vamos a reunirnos con ellos.

En la calle se oyen las bocinas de varios autos.

Elba   —¡Cuántos automóviles! El tráfico aquí es terrible.

Silvia   —[A los chicos] Llegaron temprano. La función no empieza hasta las nueve. ¿Por qué no vamos un rato a la discoteca del hotel?

Lisandro —Perfecto. Aquí tienen un grupo que toca música latina. Es muy bueno. Oigan, están tocando una cumbia.

Se oye el final de una cumbia y después aplausos.

Elba   —¿Qué lástima! Los músicos van a descansar ahora. Mejor vamos a tomar algo y volvemos cuando empiecen otra vez. Quizás entonces toquen una salsa.

Ernesto   —Buena idea. Vamos.

¿Verdadero o falso? comprehension questions: 1. Elba y Silvia son argentinas. (F)   2. Las chicas están hospedadas en una pensión. (F)   3. A Silvia le gusta mucho Buenos Aires. (V)   4. Elba no compró nada en la calle Florida. (F)   5. Elba vio una película argentina muy buena. (V)   6. Los amigos de Silvia y Elba llegaron tarde a la cita. (F)   7. En el hotel se puede bailar música latina. (V)   8. Los chicos quieren bailar salsa. (V)

Song lyrics:

"Las posadas"

Entren Santos peregrinos, peregrinos...
Reciban este rincón,
que aunque es pobre la morada,
la morada...
se la doy de corazón.

Los peces en el río

Pero mira cómo beben los peces en el río,
pero mira cómo beben por ver al Dios nacido.
Beben y beben, y vuelven a beber
los peces en el río, por ver al Dios nacer.

Hablemos de televisión, pág. 285   1. Hay programas religiosos a las tres y a las tres y media. Se llaman "Club cristiano costarricense" y "Cruzada de Jimmy Swaggart". 2. Puede ver el programa "Aeróbicos". Es a las nueve de la mañana.   3. Le va a interesar el programa "Hola, juventud".   4. La ponen en el canal 2. La protagonista es María Antonieta Pons.   5. Le gustaría ver "Las aventuras de Lassie".   6. Puede mirar las noticias a las doce y cuarto, a las diez de la noche y a las once de la noche. 7. Ponen "Plaza Sésamo", "Scooby Doo" y "Los Pitufos".   8. Va a ver "En ruta al Mundial", en el canal 2. 9. Le recomendaríamos el programa "Cocinando con tía Florita".   10. Comienza a las 8:35 de la mañana y termina a la 1:05 de la mañana del día siguiente. 11. Answers will vary.   12. Answers will vary.

Lecturas periodísticas

Para leer y comprender, pág. 288   1. No, es reconocido a nivel internacional.   2. Nos muestra su crecimiento como persona y como artista.   3. Sí, ha ganado dos Grammys. 4. Los mercados más codiciados son el anglo y el hispano. 5. Secada se inició en el idioma inglés. Después dio el paso al mercado hispano.   6. Jon Secada es cubano. Tenía nueve años cuando llegó a los Estados Unidos.   7. Stevie Wonder, Billy Joel y Elton John, entre otros, tuvieron mucha influencia en su formación como artista.   8. Pudo cultivar sus habilidades y talento como compositor y productor.   9. En el año 1992 lanzó el disco "Jon Secada". Sí, tuvo mucho éxito. Vendió más de seis millones de álbumes.   10. Ganó su segundo Grammy con el disco *Amor*. Sí, ha contribuido al éxito de cantantes como Gloria Estefan, Ricky Martin y Jennifer López.

Teleinforme

Preparación, pág. 291   *Telediario:* noticiero / telediario; *De paseo:* programa informativo; *La botica de la abuela:* pro-grama informativo; *Tradiciones milenarias en la Península de Santa Elena:* documental; *Cartelera TVE:* magazín; *Somos* (Conversaciones con estudiantes de la SDSU); *Futuramente:* anuncio publicitario; *Las chicas de hoy en día:* telecomedia; *Una hija más:* telecomedia; *Aristas:* programa cultural; *América Total:* documental

Comprensión: A, pág. 292   Esmeralda: 1, 2, 11   José Armando: 3, 9, 10   don Rodolfo Peñarreal: 5, 6, 7   Blanca: 4, 8

B, pág. 292   1. volver   2. di   3. mal   4. ver   5. -migo 6. cambiar   7. paga   8. traición   9. sufrir, sufrir 10. olvidé   11. perder   12. sufrir, sufrir   13. veas

C, pág. 293   Juan Pedro López Silva: 2, 4, 11, 14; la presentadora: 1; un niño: 3, 15; una niña: 5, 6, 8, 10, 12, 16; la Chilindrina: 13; Quico: 7; el Chavo: 9

Ampliación, pág. 294   Answers will vary.

Lección 10

Dígame, pág. 297   1. Están leyendo los anuncios clasificados y hay dos que les interesan.   2. Se necesita experiencia en mercadeo y logos para páginas de Internet y conocimientos de Windows® 2000 y Acrobat® 4.0. 3. Ofrece salario, gastos de carro, comisión y beneficios marginales. Se debe mandar a la Oficina de Recursos Humanos.   4. Precisa Director de Producción.   5. A Álvaro siempre se le descompone el carro.   6. Va a mandar su resumé y unas cartas de recomendación.   7. Va a solicitar el puesto de director de producción.   8. Tiene una maestría en mercadeo y relaciones públicas y habla dos idiomas.   9. Álvaro renunció porque pidió un aumento de sueldo y no se lo dieron.   10. Ofrece un seguro de salud y un plan de retiro.   11. Van a celebrar que han conseguido los puestos que querían.   12. Decide comprar un carro nuevo porque está hasta la coronilla de su carro.

Perspectivas socioculturales, pág. 297   Answers will vary.

Hablando de todo un poco

Preparación, pág. 299   1. o   2. t   3. i   4. q   5. a   6. l 7. c   8. e   9. s   10. b   11. g   12. d   13. f   14. j   15. h 16. m   17. k   18. n   19. r   20. p

A, pág. 299   Answers will vary.

B, pág. 299   Answers will vary.

C, pág. 299   Answers will vary.

Palabras problemáticas, pág. 300   1. Usamos el signo "X". 2. Sí, recibí una carta de él (ella). 3. Pongo una señal. 4. Sí, conseguí el trabajo. 5. Un letrero nos lo indica.

¡Ahora escuche!, pág. 300   Juan fue despedido de su trabajo por muchas razones: casi siempre llegaba tarde, muchas veces se dormía en la oficina, se le olvidaba archivar los documentos, y todo lo hacía de mala gana. Juan les dijo a sus compañeros de trabajo que su jefe no quería que siguiera trabajando allí porque, a la larga, él tendría un puesto más importante que el jefe.

Norma, que no tiene pelos en la lengua, le dijo a Juan que el jefe lo había despedido porque estaba hasta la coronilla de él.

Mañana Juan va a ser entrevistado para el puesto de secretario de una compañía que hace letreros. Tiene que usar una computadora, archivar los letreros que recibe como ficheros electrónicos, y mandarles mensajes electrónicos a los vendedores. El sueldo es de veinticinco mil dólares anuales. Juan dice que, si le dan el empleo, va a trabajar para esa empresa por un tiempo, mientras busca un empleo que sea mejor que ése.

¿Verdadero o falso? comprehension questions: 1. Juan recibió un aumento de sueldo. (F)   2. Juan era muy puntual. (F)   3. Juan a veces tenía sueño en la oficina. (V)   4. Juan era muy trabajador. (F)   5. Según Juan, él tendría un puesto muy importante algún día. (V)   6. Norma dice todo lo que piensa. (V)   7. Norma tiene muy buena opinión de Juan. (F)   8. Norma piensa que el jefe de Juan estaba cansado de él. (V)   9. En la compañía que hace letreros necesitan un secretario. (V)   10. El secretario no necesita tener conocimiento de computadoras. (F)   11. El salario que ofrece la compañía es de veinticinco mil dólares mensuales. (F)   12. Juan piensa trabajar para esa compañía hasta jubilarse. (F)

Sobre el Caribe hispánico, pág. 302   1. Tiene la forma de un cocodrilo. Es la mayor de las Antillas.   2. Dijo que era "la tierra más hermosa que ojos humanos vieron". Algunos la llaman "la Perla de las Antillas".   3. Exporta azúcar y tabaco.   4. El danzón, el son, la rumba, el mambo y la salsa.   5. Porque Puerto Rico es un Estado Libre Asociado a los Estados Unidos.   6. El Morro es una antigua fortaleza. El Yunque es un bosque tropical.   7. La comparte con Haití.   8. La primera ciudad fundada en el Nuevo Mundo fue Santo Domingo.   9. Se basa en la agricultura.   10. El deporte más popular es el béisbol.

Hablemos de su país, pág. 302   Answers will vary.

Estructuras gramaticales

A, pág. 304   1. Esta empresa fue fundada en 1998.   2. Todos los aspirantes han sido entrevistados por el jefe.   3. Ese empleado fue despedido la semana pasada.   4. Los gastos de los viajes eran pagados por los ejecutivos.   5. Los contratos serán archivados por los empleados.   6. No creo que ya hayan sido comprados todos los procesadores de textos.

B, pág. 304   Answers will vary.

A, pág. 305   1. Los teléfonos celulares se compraron el mes pasado.   2. Pronto se venderá la maquinaria.   3. El aumento anual no se había incluido en el informe anterior.   4. Ya se han puesto los letreros.   5. Las etiquetas se imprimieron ayer.   6. Se va a anunciar la venta el jueves.   7. Se firmarán los documentos la próxima semana.   8. Se habían eliminado muchos gastos diarios.   9. Las cartas se envían al extranjero los fines de mes.   10. Se entrevistaba a los aspirantes los lunes.

B, pág. 306   1. Se habla español. En Brasil se habla portugués.   2. Se dice "so".   3. Se escribe con una "X".   4. La clase se termina a la(s)...   5. Se sale por la puerta.   6. A mi casa se llega...   7. Se usan abrigos, guantes, etc.   8. Se hace con carne, lechuga, tomate y pan.

A, pág. 307   1. A mí se me perdió el dinero.   2. Al vendedor se le han perdido los contratos.   3. A mí siempre se me olvida hacer reservaciones cuando viajo.   4. A Lorenzo se le olvidó traer las etiquetas.   5. Se echó a reír porque se te quemó la comida.   6. Algunas veces a nosotros se nos olvida firmar los cheques.   7. A ellos se les descompuso el coche.   8. A nosotros se nos perdió nuestro gato.

B, pág. 307   1. No, se le perdió.   2. No, se les rompió.   3. No, se nos olvidó.   4. No, se te manchó.   5. No, se nos descompuso.   6. No, se me murió.

pág. 308   1. por no tener   2. darme ánimo   3. pongo en duda   4. en peligro   5. gato por liebre   6. chispa   7. ridículo   8. pelos en la lengua   9. hagas el tonto (la tonta)   10. hace agua la boca   11. dar marcha atrás   12. pone peros / hace caso   13. da en el clavo

A, pág. 310   Answers will vary

B, pág. 310   1. al pie de la letra   2. no tener pelos en la lengua   3. poner peros   4. dar gato por liebre   5. en el acto   6. a la larga   7. entre la espada y la pared   8. de mala gana   9. al fin y al cabo   10. poner el grito en el cielo

C, pág. 310   1. Hoy estamos a... 2. Sí, al pie de la letra. 3. Hablo en voz baja. 4. Sí, he pescado a... con las manos en la masa. 5. Sí, a veces hacía cosas de mala gana. 6. No sé, pero aquí hay gato encerrado. 7. Sí, iría en el acto. 8. Me sentiría entre la espada y la pared. 9. A la larga, voy a hablarlo muy bien. 10. Sí, estoy hasta la coronilla. 11. Pondría el grito en el cielo. 12. Me caen bien.

¿Comprende Ud.? pág. 311 and in Student Audio

En San Juan

Jorge Torres y su primo, Luis Sandoval, están en un ómnibus en la hermosa ciudad de San Juan. Luis piensa solicitar un puesto en una empresa local y Jorge le está dando consejos.

Jorge —Si quieres llegar a desempeñar un puesto importante, necesitas tener conocimiento de computadoras y hablar muy bien el inglés. Como sabes, es una lengua muy importante en Puerto Rico.

Luis —Bueno, yo tomé varias clases de inglés en Santo Domingo, y practicaba mucho con un chico americano que jugaba en mi equipo de béisbol, pero necesito mejorarlo.

Jorge —Buena idea. ¡Ah! Mañana vas a conocer a Álvaro, mi amigo cubano. Los tres vamos a ir al Viejo San Juan y vamos a visitar el Castillo del Morro, una antigua fortaleza de la época colonial. Es muy interesante.

Luis —¡Perfecto! Otro sitio que quiero conocer es El Yunque. Es un bosque tropical, ¿no?

Jorge —Sí. Hoy en día es una reserva federal. Oye, el sábado es el cumpleaños de la hermana de Álvaro y estamos invitados a su fiesta.

Luis —¿Vamos a bailar? ¡Me encanta la música cubana, sobre todo la rumba y el mambo! [*Canta*] Mambo, qué rico el mambo... Oye, ¿qué tal es la hermana de tu amigo?

Jorge —¡Hermosa! ¡Y tiene mucha chispa! Y un esposo y tres hijos... Levántate, Luis. Nos bajamos en la próxima esquina.

¿Verdadero o falso? comprehension questions: 1. Jorge y Luis están en el coche de Álvaro. (F) 2. Según Jorge, no es necesario hablar inglés para conseguir un buen puesto. (F) 3. Puerto Rico tiene más de una lengua oficial. (V) 4. Luis no practicaba ningún deporte cuando vivía en Santo Domingo. (F) 5. Los tres muchachos van a ir a lugares muy frecuentados por los turistas.

(V) 6. El Yunque es un desierto. (F) 7. A Luis le gustan mucho los ritmos cubanos. (V) 8. Álvaro tiene tres sobrinos. (V)

Song lyrics:

"Adiós, señora"

Naranja dulce, limón partido,
dame un abrazo, que yo te pido;
y si es falso mi juramento
en un momento te olvidaré.

Naranja dulce, limón partido,
dame un abrazo, que yo te pido;
toca la marcha, mi pecho llora,
adiós, señora, que ya me voy.

Hablemos de tecnología, pág. 312   1. Investigan para fabricar robots en serie. 2. Venden kits para montar en casa interesantes prototipos. 3. Se empeña en hacer realidad la ciencia ficción. 4. Significa "presta mucha atención". 5. Ha cambiado la música. 6. Algunos MP3.

¿Qué dirían Uds.?, pág. 312 *Idioms:* 1. dar gato por liebre 2. no tener pelos en la lengua 3. dar ánimo 4. hacérsele agua la boca 5. al pie de la letra 6. de mala gana 7. en el acto 8. dar en el clavo

Lecturas periodísticas

Para leer y comprender, pág. 313   1. El Internet se ha convertido en una necesidad. 2. Las corporaciones y oficinas gubernamentales lo utilizan. 3. Representa el acceso ilimitado a información y un ahorro sustancial. 4. Les provee muchas herramientas necesarias para aumentar su productividad. 5. Se evitan las llamadas de larga distancia, el uso del fax y el gasto excesivo de papel. 6. Tienen la ventaja de personalizar su e-mail y también la de tener su propia página de web.

Teleinforme

Preparación, pág. 316   Answers will vary.

Comprensión: A, pág. 316   1. claro 2. una red de información 3. un ordenador, una línea telefónica, un modem, una compañía que nos conecte a la red 4. El modem 5. Answers will vary. *Possible answers:* fax modem 28800, Netscape versión 2.02, modelos de ordenadores; versión de Windows 6. Answers will vary. *Possible answers:* línea telefónica, datos sobre Amazon, número de usuarios

B, pág. 317   1. F   2. F, S   3. This aspect of the interview isn't mentioned by anyone.   4. C (S)   5. F   6. S   7. S   8. C   9. P   10. P

C, pág. 318   1. Es para grabadores de datos.   2. Hay doscientos (200) puestos.   3. Sí, es necesario.   4. Por turnos.   5. en Madrid   6. Inmediatamente   7. Llamando al 902 30 40 80

Ampliación, pág. 318   Answers will vary.

¡Continuemos!

SEVENTH EDITION

Ana C. Jarvis
Chandler-Gilbert Community College

Raquel Lebredo
California Baptist University

Francisco Mena-Ayllón
University of Redlands

Teleinforme activities prepared by Anny Ewing

Houghton Mifflin Company   **Boston**   **New York**

Publisher: Rolando Hernández

Sponsoring Editor: Amy Baron

Development Manager: Sharla Zwirek

Development Editor: Rafael Burgos-Mirabal

Editorial Assistant: Erin Kern

Project Editor: Amy Johnson

Production/Design Coordinator: Lisa Jelly Smith

Manufacturing Manager: Florence Cadran

Senior Marketing Manager: Tina Crowley Desprez

Cover Painting © Harold Burch/NYC

Library of Congress Control Number: 2001133271

Student Text ISBN: 0-618-22067-4
Instructor's Edition ISBN: 0-618-22072-0

456789-DOC-06 05 04

Contents

Preface

¡Continuemos!, Seventh Edition, is a complete, fully integrated college intermediate Spanish program. It is designed to help you perfect your Spanish by offering a comprehensive review and systematic expansion of the basic structures of Spanish commonly taught at the introductory level, while providing numerous opportunities for developing your listening, speaking, reading, and writing skills and cultural competency. Since it is essential to understand the underlying philosophy and organization of the program to use it to your greatest advantage, below we describe the text and other components in detail.

The Student's Text

The organization of this central component of the *¡Continuemos!*, Seventh Edition, program reflects its emphasis on the active use of Spanish for practical communication in context. Each of the text's ten lessons contains the following features.

- Chapter opener: Each lesson begins with a list of the lesson objectives accompanied by a photo that illustrates the lesson's theme. You will find additional preparatory activities in the Student CD-ROM, under **Ante todo.**

- Lesson opening passage, **Dígame,** and **Perspectivas socioculturales:** New vocabulary and structures are first presented in the context of idiomatic Spanish conversations dealing with the high-frequency situation that is the lesson's central theme. The **Dígame** comprehension activity provides immediate reinforcement of the vocabulary and communicative functions presented in the dialogue. **Perspectivas socioculturales** offers an opportunity to discuss cultural aspects highlighted in the opening passage in the context of your own culture. Your instructor might assign additional preconversational activities.

- **Vocabulario** and **Hablemos de todo un poco:** This section lists the new words and expressions introduced in the dialogues. Entries in the **Vocabulario** (including those under **Ampliación**) are to be learned for active use. **Hablemos de todo un poco** is the vocabulary activity section. **Preparación** is a warm-up activity to the conversation topics that follow it.

- **Palabras problemáticas** and **Práctica:** This section focuses on specific lexical items that cause difficulties for native speakers of English. It includes groups of Spanish words with a single English translation, Spanish synonyms with variations in meaning, and false cognates. **Práctica** activities in a variety of formats reinforce the meanings and usage of the **Palabras problemáticas.**

- **¡Ahora escuche!:** Your instructor might decide to carry out this in-class listening comprehension activity.

- **El mundo hispánico:** This section includes a brief essay on the country or region covered in the lesson. The essay is followed by comprehension questions. The activity **Hablemos de su país** provides further discussion opportunities about aspects featured in the essay, but in the context of your own country. **Una tarjeta postal** offers further reading and writing practice on cultural aspects explored in the section. You will find further vocabulary and writing practice related to this section in the Student Website under **El mundo hispánico.**

- **Estructuras gramaticales** and **Práctica:** Each new grammatical structure featured in the lesson opening passage is explained clearly and concisely in English so that you may use the explanations independently as an out-of-class reference. All explanations are followed by numerous examples of their practical use in natural Spanish. The **¡Atención!** head signals exceptions to the grammar rules presented or instances where knowledge of an English structure may interfere with learning the equivalent Spanish structure. After each explanation, the **Práctica** sections offer immediate reinforcement of new concepts through a variety of structured and communicative activities.

- **¡Continuemos!:** This section stimulates listening comprehension and meaningful communication by involving you in a wide range of interactive tasks related to the lesson theme. **Una encuesta** employs the results of a student-conducted survey as the basis for a small-group discussion. **¿Comprende Ud.?** is a two-activity listening comprehension section that is correlated to recorded passages in the Student Audio CD.[1] **Hablemos de...** requires you to read and use information gained from authentic documents. **¿Qué dirían ustedes?** provides a series of brief role-play situations. **¡De ustedes depende!** presents a more challenging, open-ended role-play scenario. **Mesa redonda/Debate** supplies a conversation starter on a thought-provoking or controversial issue.

- **Lecturas periodísticas:** Chosen for their appeal and accessibility, these authentic readings from newspapers and magazines from Spain, Latin America, and the United States expand your cultural knowledge while reinforcing the lesson's themes. To develop your reading skills, **Saber leer** incorporates proven reading strategies that are recycled and built on throughout the textbook. **Para leer y comprender** consists of a list of prereading questions. You will find further vocabulary build-up and reading activities on this material in the Student CD-ROM under **Lecturas periodísticas.** Personalized, open-ended questions (**Desde su mundo**) follow each reading and provide opportunities for you to discuss your own opinions and experiences in relation to the reading topic.

- **Piense y escriba:** This section introduces one aspect of the writing process per lesson. Toward the last lesson in the program, you will complete your own writing project.

- **Teleinforme:** These activities are designed to be used with the **Teleinforme** modules of the **¡Continuemos!** Video. You will find additional previewing activities on select clips of each video module in the Student CD-ROM and Website under **Video.**

---

[1] You will find more listening and writing activities in the **¿Comprende Ud.?** material on the Student CD-ROM (under **¿Comprende Ud.?**) and Website (under **Canción**).

○ **¿Están listos para el examen?:** These self-tests, which follow Lessons 2, 4, 6, 8, and 10, enable you to review the structures, vocabulary, and culture information of the two preceding lessons. Organized by lesson and by grammatical structure, they allow you to determine quickly what material you have mastered and which concepts you should target for further review. An answer key is provided in Appendix C for immediate verification.

○ Reference Materials: The following sections provide useful reference tools throughout the course:

Maps: Colorful maps and national flags of the Spanish-speaking world appear in the **¡Bienvenidos al mundo hispánico!** section of the textbook for quick reference.

Appendices: **Apéndice A** summarizes the rules of Spanish syllabification, the use of accent marks, and the norms of punctuation. Conjugations of high-frequency regular, stem-changing, and irregular Spanish verbs constitute **Apéndice B**. **Apéndice C** is the answer key to the **¿Están listos para el examen?** self-tests.

Vocabularies: Spanish–English and English–Spanish glossaries list all active vocabulary introduced in the **Vocabulario** lists and in the **Estructuras gramaticales** sections. Active vocabulary is identified by the number of the lesson in which the word or phrase first appears. The Spanish–English vocabulary also lists passive vocabulary, which consists of those words glossed by an English equivalent anywhere in the text.

Supplementary Materials

Workbook / Laboratory Manual (in print and online versions)

Each lesson of the *Workbook / Laboratory Manual* is correlated to the corresponding lesson in your textbook and is divided into two sections. The **Actividades para escribir** offers a variety of writing formats, including question-and-answer exercises, dialogue completion, sentence transformation, illustration-based exercises, and crossword puzzles. It also reinforces culture knowledge from the **El mundo hispánico** essay, and ends with a composition assignment. Designed for use with the *¡Continuemos!* Audio Program, the **Actividades para el laboratorio** for each lesson include grammar review exercises, listening-and-speaking exercises, pronunciation practice, and a dictation. Answer keys for the workbook exercises and the laboratory dictations are provided to enable you to monitor your progress independently.

Student Audio CD

To further develop your listening skills, the Seventh Edition includes a Student Audio CD that comes free of charge with the purchase of a new textbook. You will find each lesson opening passage recorded for further listening reinforcement. Following each opening passage is the listening material for the in-text listening activities under **¿Comprende Ud.?** The first activity consists of listening to a relatively fast-paced conversation that integrates the lesson vocabulary, structures, theme, and country or region. An eight-item long true/false comprehension activity follows. The second activity involves listening to a very brief song from the Iberian-American folklore, which illustrates at least one lesson target structure in an authentic context.

Audio Program

The complete Audio Program (on CD or cassettes) to accompany the *¡Continuemos! Workbook / Laboratory Manual* is available for student purchase. Recorded by native speakers, the ten 60-minute audio lessons develop speaking-and-listening comprehension skills through contextualized exercises that reinforce the themes and content of the textbook lessons. Each lesson contains structured grammar exercises; listening-and-speaking and listening-and-writing activities based on realistic simulations of conversations, interviews, newscasts, ads, and editorials; a comprehension check of key vocabulary and idiomatic expressions; pronunciation practice; and a dictation. Answers to all exercises, except for those that require a written response, are provided in the audio lesson.

The *¡Continuemos!* Video

Thematically linked to the lessons in *¡Continuemos!*, this exciting, 60-minute video provides a unique opportunity to develop listening skills and cultural awareness through authentic television footage from countries throughout the Spanish-speaking world. Each of the ten **Teleinforme** video modules is approximately five minutes long. The footage presents diverse images of traditional and contemporary life in Spanish-speaking countries through commercials, interviews, travelogues, TV programs, and reports on art and cooking. The entire *¡Continuemos!* **Video** is available in the Student CD-ROM.

The *¡Continuemos!* Student CD-ROM

Free of charge with the purchase of a new textbook, this new multi-media CD-ROM provides preparatory support and additional practice for select sections of the student text, the student audio, and the video. First, you will find prelesson preparation activities followed by target lesson vocabulary and grammar practice. Second, you will be able to do vocabulary build-up activities based on readings and on listening material. You will be able to practice listening, reading, and writing, and will have the opportunity to reinforce both your writing and listening skills by working on a writing task based on listening material. This CD-ROM includes the entire *¡Continuemos!* **Video** contents, as well as preparatory, previewing activities for select clips in the video and games. You will be able to practice viewing comprehension, speaking, as well as target lesson vocabulary and structures in the context of authentic footage.

The *¡Continuemos!* Student Website (*http://spanish.college.hmco.com/students*)

The significantly enhanced Student Website provides support and additional practice for sections in the Student Text, Student Audio, and Video Program. It includes a diagnostic self quiz on the target lesson structures (**¿Cuánto recuerda?**) as well as a self test (**Compruebe cuánto sabe**) designed to be taken once the **Estructuras gramaticales** section in each lesson has been covered. In addition, it also provides further vocabulary build-up instruction and practice; listening, reading, and writing skill development, and post-conversational writing tasks that reinforce the speaking-writing pair of skills. It also offers support for clips in the ***¡Continuemos!* Video** that consists of viewing comprehension, speaking, and target lesson vocabulary and grammar preparatory practice. You will find web search activities integrated in the writing tasks and electronic flashcards for further practice of vocabulary and verb conjugation.

We would like to hear your comments on *¡Continuemos!*, Seventh Edition, and reactions to it. Reports on your experiences using this program would be of great interest and value to us. Please write to us, care of Houghton Mifflin Company, College Division, 222 Berkeley Street, Boston MA 02116-3764 or e-mail us at college_mod_lang@hmco.com.

Acknowledgments

We wish to express our sincere appreciation to the following colleagues for the many valuable suggestions they offered in their reviews of the Sixth Edition:

Kurt Barnada, *Elizabethtown College*

Kathy Cantrell, *Whitworth College*

Sara Colburn-Alsop, *Butler University*

Antonio J. Jiménez, *University of San Diego*

Lauren Lukkarila, *Clark Atlanta University*

Anne Roswell Porter, *Ohio University*

Lea Ramsdell, *Towson University*

Lynn C. Vogel-Zuiderweg, *Santa Monica College*

Rodney Wiliamson, *University of Ottawa*

We also extend our appreciation to the World Languages Staff of Houghton Mifflin Company, College Division: Roland Hernández, Publisher; Amy Baron, Sponsoring Editor; Tina Crowley Desprez, Senior Marketing Manager; and Rafael Burgos-Mirabal, Development Editor.

Ana C. Jarvis
Raquel Lebredo
Francisco Mena-Ayllón

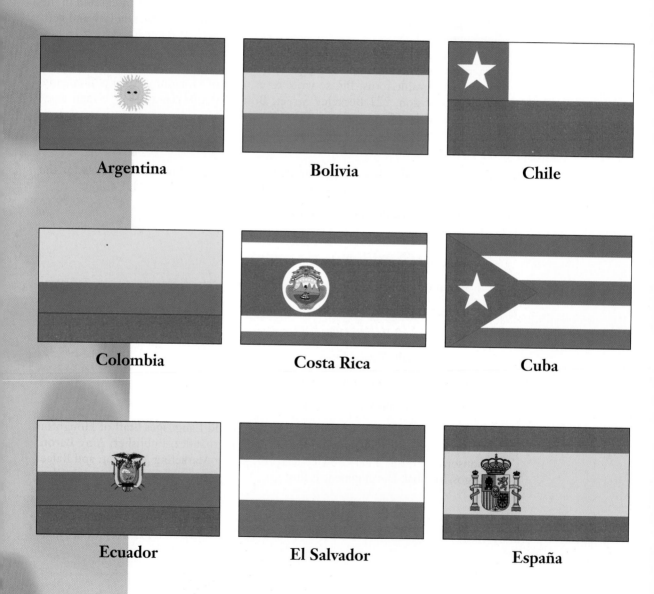

Argentina	Bolivia	Chile
Colombia	Costa Rica	Cuba
Ecuador	El Salvador	España

Estados Unidos

Guatemala

Honduras

México

Nicaragua

Panamá

Paraguay

Perú

Puerto Rico

República Dominicana

Uruguay

Venezuela

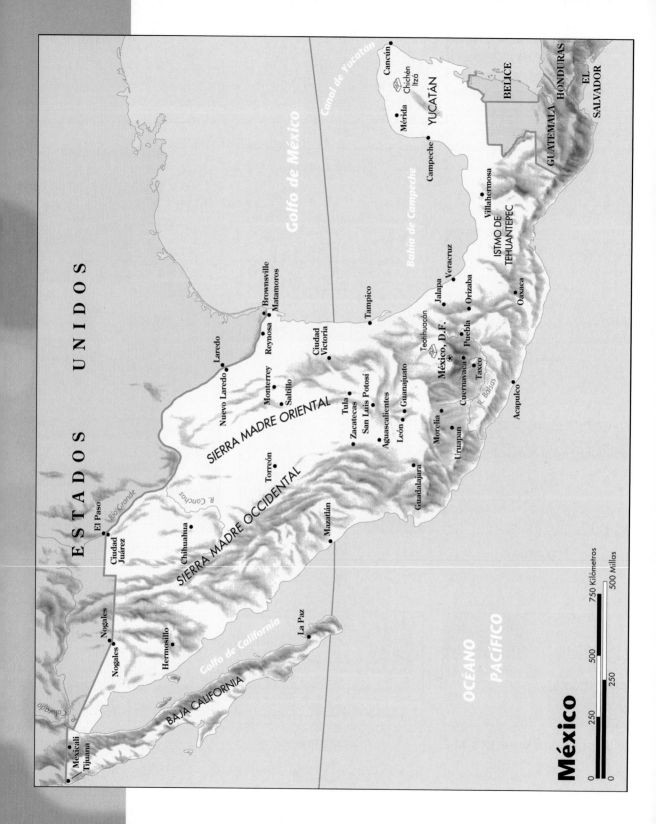

México

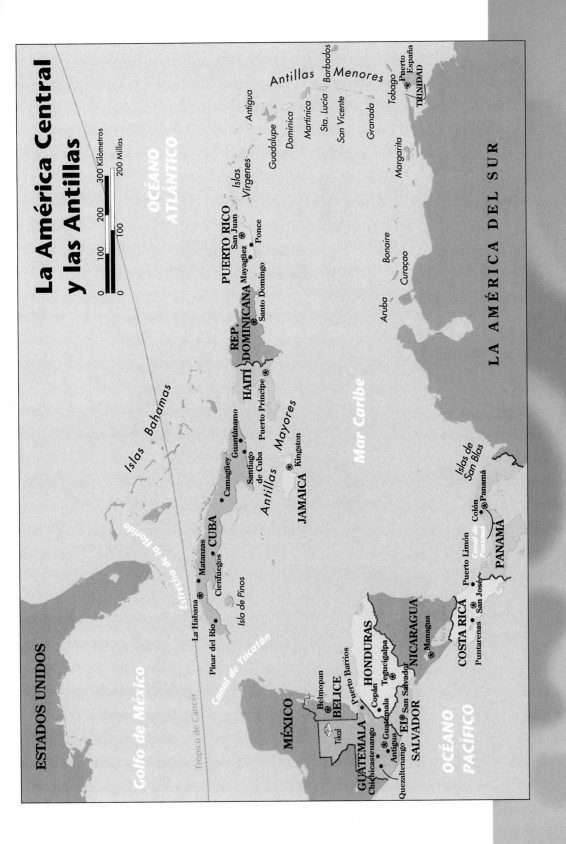

La América Central y las Antillas

ESTADOS UNIDOS

Golfo de México

300 Kilómetros
200 Millas

OCÉANO ATLÁNTICO

Trópico de Cáncer

Islas Bahamas

Estrecho de la Florida

La Habana
Pinar del Río
Matanzas
Cienfuegos
Isla de Pinos
CUBA
Camagüey
Santiago de Cuba
Guantánamo

Canal de Yucatán

Antillas Mayores

JAMAICA
Kingston

PUERTO RICO
San Juan
Mayagüez
Ponce
Islas Vírgenes

HAITÍ
Puerto Príncipe
REP. DOMINICANA
Santo Domingo

Antillas Menores

Antigua
Guadalupe
Dominica
Martinica
Sta. Lucía
San Vicente
Barbados
Granada
Tobago
Puerto España
TRINIDAD

Mar Caribe

MÉXICO

Belmopan
Tikal
BELICE
Puerto Barrios
GUATEMALA
Chichicastenango
Quezaltenango
Antigua
Guatemala
EL SALVADOR
San Salvador
Copán
HONDURAS
Tegucigalpa
NICARAGUA
Managua

OCÉANO PACÍFICO

COSTA RICA
Puntarenas
San José
Puerto Limón

Islas de San Blas
Panamá
Colón
Canal de Panamá
PANAMÁ

Margarita
Aruba
Curaçao
Bonaire

LA AMÉRICA DEL SUR

La América del Sur

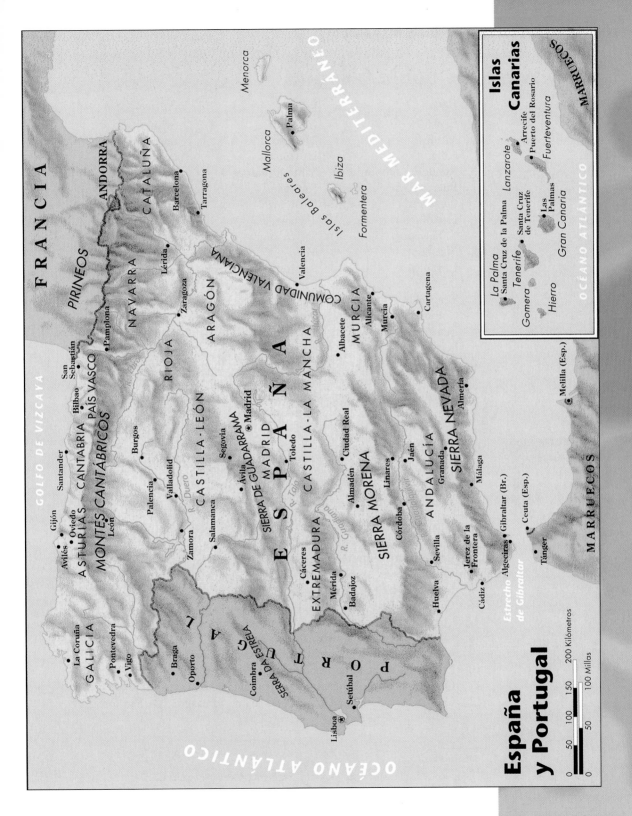

España y Portugal

FRANCIA

PIRINEOS

ANDORRA

GOLFO DE VIZCAYA

PAÍS VASCO

San Sebastián
Pamplona

NAVARRA

CATALUÑA

Lérida
Zaragoza
Barcelona
Tarragona

Santander
Bilbao

CANTABRIA

MONTES CANTÁBRICOS

Gijón
Oviedo
Avilés
León

ASTURIAS

La Coruña
Pontevedra
Vigo

GALICIA

Braga
Oporto
Coimbra

SERRA DA ESTRELA

P O R T U G A L

Lisboa
Setúbal

OCÉANO ATLÁNTICO

Zamora
Salamanca
Valladolid
Palencia
Burgos

CASTILLA-LEÓN

Segovia
Ávila

SIERRA DE GUADARRAMA

MADRID

Madrid
Toledo

E S P A Ñ A

RIOJA

ARAGÓN

COMUNIDAD VALENCIANA

Valencia

R. Ebro

R. Duero

R. Tajo

R. Guadiana

R. Guadalquivir

CASTILLA-LA MANCHA

Ciudad Real
Albacete

MURCIA

Alicante
Murcia
Cartagena

EXTREMADURA

Cáceres
Mérida
Badajoz

SIERRA MORENA

Almadén
Linares
Córdoba
Jaén

ANDALUCÍA

Sevilla
Huelva
Jerez de la Frontera
Cádiz
Algeciras

Gibraltar (Br.)
Ceuta (Esp.)
Tánger

Estrecho de Gibraltar

SIERRA NEVADA

Granada
Almería
Málaga

MAR MEDITERRÁNEO

Menorca
Mallorca
Palma
Ibiza
Formentera

Islas Baleares

MARRUECOS

Melilla (Esp.)

Islas Canarias

La Palma
Santa Cruz de la Palma
Gomera
Tenerife
Santa Cruz de Tenerife
Hierro
Gran Canaria
Las Palmas
Gran Canaria
Lanzarote
Arrecife
Puerto del Rosario
Fuerteventura

MARRUECOS

OCÉANO ATLÁNTICO

0   50   100   150   200 Kilómetros
0   50   100 Millas

xxi

Países de habla hispana

País	*Capital*	*Nacionalidad*
España	Madrid	español(a)
México	México, D.F.[1]	mexicano(a)
Cuba	La Habana	cubano(a)
República Dominicana	Santo Domingo	dominicano(a)
Puerto Rico	San Juan	puertorriqueño(a)
Guatemala	Guatemala	guatemalteco(a)
Honduras	Tegucigalpa	hondureño(a)
El Salvador	San Salvador	salvadoreño(a)
Nicaragua	Managua	nicaragüense
Costa Rica	San José	costarricense
Panamá	Panamá	panameño(a)
Venezuela	Caracas	venezolano(a)
Colombia	Bogotá	colombiano(a)
Ecuador	Quito	ecuatoriano(a)
Perú	Lima	peruano(a)
Bolivia	La Paz	boliviano(a)
Chile	Santiago	chileno(a)
Paraguay	Asunción	paraguayo(a)
Argentina	Buenos Aires	argentino(a)
Uruguay	Montevideo	uruguayo(a)

 En Brasil se habla portugués.[2]
La capital es Brasilia y la nacionalidad es brasileño(a).

¿Cuánto sabe usted sobre el mundo hispánico?

1. ¿Cuál es la capital de España?
2. ¿Qué ciudades importantes hay en el sur de España?
3. ¿Cuáles son los límites de España?
4. ¿Qué separa a España de Francia? ¿y a España de Marruecos?
5. ¿Dónde están las Islas Baleares?
6. ¿Qué ciudades están cerca del Golfo de Vizcaya?
7. ¿Qué ciudades están sobre el Mar Mediterráneo?
8. ¿Qué países de habla hispana son islas?
9. ¿Cuál de estas islas es la más grande y cuál es la más pequeña?
10. ¿En qué países sudamericanos no se habla español?
11. ¿Qué países de Sudamérica no tienen salida al mar?
12. ¿Cuál es la nacionalidad de una persona de Santiago? ¿De San José?

---

[1] Distrito Federal

[2] Tampoco se habla español en Guayana, Surinam y Guayana Francesa.

13. ¿Cuál es la capital de Uruguay? ¿De Paraguay?
14. ¿Con qué países limita Colombia?
15. ¿Con qué países sudamericanos no limita Brasil?
16. ¿Cuáles son los países de Centroamérica?
17. ¿Qué islas están al sureste de Argentina?
18. ¿Qué cordillera (*mountain range*) separa a Argentina de Chile?
19. ¿Con qué países limita México?
20. ¿Qué famoso canal une el Océano Atlántico con el Océano Pacífico?

Sobre las relaciones familiares

Un matrimonio, conversando y desayunando.

OBJETIVOS

Temas para la comunicación

Las relaciones humanas

Estructuras

1. El presente de indicativo
2. El presente progresivo
3. La **a** personal
4. Formas pronominales en función de complemento directo
5. Formas pronominales en función de complemento indirecto
6. Construcciones reflexivas

Regiones y países

España

Lectura

¿Eres un papá de medio tiempo?

Estrategias de lectura

Un autor debe conocer a su público

Estrategias de redacción

¿Para quién escribimos?

Sobre las relaciones familiares

CD-ROM   STUDENT AUDIO
For preparation, do the **Ante
todo** activities found on the
CD-ROM.

*Ana María Hernández es española, pero ahora vive en Nueva York con su esposo Tyler
Robinson, que es norteamericano. Los dos son estudiantes y trabajan medio día.*

*Ahora están sentados en la cocina de su pequeño apartamento, conversando y bebiendo
café.*

ANA MARÍA —Le voy a escribir a mi abuela. Tengo que decirle que a lo mejor
vamos a Madrid en mayo. Ella está un poco enferma y se va a poner
contenta si recibe buenas noticias de su nieta favorita.

TYLER —*(Se ríe)* ¡Qué vanidosa eres! ¿Cómo sabes que tú eres su nieta
favorita?

ANA MARÍA —*(Se ríe también)* ¡Es lo que ella me dice siempre! Pero les dice lo
mismo a mis hermanos y a mis primos. La verdad es que ella nos
mima a todos.

TYLER —Yo creo que los malcría. Pero ése es el papel de las abuelas españolas,
¿no? Oye, en mayo tenemos la reunión familiar con todos mis parientes. Va a ser en California este año.

ANA MARÍA —Ésa es una costumbre típicamente americana, ¿no? Nosotros no
hacemos eso en España, y creo que los latinoamericanos tampoco lo
hacen...

TYLER —Bueno, eso es porque ustedes se mantienen en contacto de una manera u otra. Yo tengo primos a quienes apenas conozco... ¡Ah! También tenemos una boda en Nueva Jersey. Mi tía Mary se casa el dos
de mayo.

ANA MARÍA —¿Tu tía Mary? Ella es viuda, ¿no? Y tiene unos sesenta años...

TYLER —Sí, pero aquí la gente mayor se casa... Muchos prefieren no vivir
solos...

ANA MARÍA —Pero tienen a toda su familia.

TYLER —No necesariamente. Muchas veces sus hijos viven muy lejos y no los
ven a menudo. Entonces el círculo de amigos es muy importante en
su vida.

ANA MARÍA —Pues yo no estoy de acuerdo con ese estilo de vida. Tú y yo vamos a
tener un par de hijos que van a vivir aquí, cerca de nosotros.

TYLER —*(Bromeando)* ¿Y si nos divorciamos? ¿Quién se queda con los niños?

ANA MARÍA —Ellos van a preferir a su mamá, por supuesto... Además, tú y yo nos
llevamos muy bien, de manera que no va a haber divorcio.

*Ana María y Tyler siguen hablando un rato y después él se levanta para irse a trabajar y
ella se prepara para escribir varias cartas. Hoy se siente un poco nostálgica y piensa que cada
vez extraña más a su familia. Piensa que un día de éstos va a tomar un avión a Madrid y
va a ir a visitar a sus padres y a sus hermanos... , a su abuela, a sus tíos y a sus primos... ,
a sus padrinos... Se sirve otra taza de café y empieza a escribir.*

Dígame

En parejas, contesten las siguientes preguntas basadas en el diálogo.

1. ¿Cuál es la nacionalidad de Ana María? ¿Y la de su esposo?
2. ¿Dónde están sentados? ¿Qué están haciendo?
3. ¿Ana María y Tyler trabajan o estudian?
4. Según Ana María, ¿cómo se va a poner su abuela si recibe noticias de ella?
5. Según Ana María, su abuela los mima a todos. ¿Y según Tyler?
6. ¿Qué van a tener Tyler y sus parientes en mayo? ¿Dónde va a ser?
7. Según Tyler, ¿por qué no tienen los hispanos reuniones familiares?
8. ¿Quién se casa en mayo? ¿Dónde va a ser la boda?
9. Según Ana María, ¿cúantos hijos van a tener ellos y dónde van a vivir?
10. Según Ana María, ¿por qué no va a haber divorcio?
11. ¿Cómo se siente Ana María y qué piensa?
12. ¿Qué va a hacer ella un día de éstos? ¿Qué hace ahora?

Perspectivas socioculturales

INSTRUCTOR WEBSITE

Your instructor may assign the preconversational support activities found in **Perspectivas socio-culturales.**

Muchos aspectos sobre la familia varían entre las diferentes culturas. Haga lo siguiente:

a. Lea los temas de conversación que aparecen a continuación y escoja uno de ellos.
b. Durante unos cinco minutos, converse con dos compañeros sobre el tema seleccionado.
c. Participe con el resto de la clase en la discusión del tema cuando su profesor(a) se lo indique.

Temas de conversación

1. **Reuniones familiares.** ¿Celebra su familia reuniones familiares? ¿Y las familias de sus amigos? ¿Cómo las celebran?
2. **Padres e hijos.** ¿Viven sus padres cerca o lejos de donde vive Ud.? ¿Qué ventajas y qué desventajas tiene su situación?
3. **Los ancianos.** ¿Hay ancianos en su familia o conoce usted a algunos de su comunidad? ¿Viven con parientes, cerca de amigos o en alguna comunidad para ancianos?

Vocabulario

Nombres

la boda wedding
el círculo circle
la costumbre custom, habit
la gente mayor older people
la manera, el modo way
la noticia piece of news, news item
el padrino[1] godfather
el papel role
el (la) pariente relative
la reunión reunion, meeting
la vida life

Verbos

bromear to kid, to joke
casarse (con) to get married
divorciarse to get a divorce
extrañar, echar de menos to miss, to be homesick for
malcriar to spoil
mimar to pamper
reírse[2] to laugh
sentirse (e → ie) to feel
tomar to take

Adjetivos

nostálgico(a) homesick
vanidoso(a) vain, conceited
varios(as) several

Otras palabras y expresiones

a lo mejor, quizá(s), tal vez perhaps, maybe
a menudo, frecuentemente often, frequently
además besides
apenas barely, hardly
de manera (modo) que so
estar de acuerdo to agree
llevarse bien to get along
lo mismo the same thing
lo que what, that which
mantenerse en contacto to keep in touch
no va a haber there's not going to be
ponerse contento(a) to be (become) happy
por supuesto, claro, naturalmente of course, naturally
quedarse con to keep
sobre about
trabajar medio día to work part time
un día de éstos one of these days
un par de a couple of
un poco a little
un rato a while
unos(as) about (*before a number*)

Ampliación

Para hablar de estados de ánimo

aburrido(a) bored
alegre, contento(a) happy, glad
de buen (mal) humor in a good (bad) mood
deprimido(a) depressed
enojado(a), enfadado(a) angry
entusiasmado(a) enthused, excited
frustrado(a) frustrated
nervioso(a) nervous

---

[1] **la madrina** godmother

[2] Present indicative: **me río, te ríes, se ríe, nos reímos, os reís, se ríen**

preocupado(a)   worried
tranquilo(a)   calm, tranquil
triste   sad

Para hablar de la personalidad

amable   kind, polite
amistoso(a)   friendly
comprensivo(a)   understanding
egoísta   selfish
generoso(a)   generous
haragán(-ana), perezoso(a)   lazy
mandón(-ona)   bossy
materialista   materialistic
optimista   optimistic
pesimista   pessimistic
realista   realistic
tacaño(a)   cheap, stingy
trabajador(a)   hard-working

Para hablar de las relaciones interpersonales

abrazar, dar un abrazo   to hug, to give a hug
amar, querer (e → ie)   to love
besar, dar un beso   to kiss, to give a kiss
caerle bien a uno   to like
caerle mal a uno   to dislike
el cariño, el amor   love
comprometido(a)   engaged
cuidar   to take care of
dar consejos   to give advice
meterse   to meddle
obedecer (yo obedezco)   to obey
el (la) prometido(a)   fiancé(e)
respetar   to respect

CD-ROM
Go to **Vocabulario** for additional vocabulary practice.

Hablando de todo un poco

Preparación   Encuentre en la columna B las respuestas a las preguntas de la columna A (las listas continúan en la página siguiente).

A

1. ¿Eva está comprometida con Luis?
2. ¿Por qué te cae mal Toto?
3. ¿El papel de la abuela es malcriar a los niños?
4. ¿Pepe está bromeando?
5. ¿Echas de menos a tu padrino?
6. ¿Tú te mantienes en contacto con Ada?
7. ¿Cómo se siente Alina?
8. ¿Fernando es haragán?
9. ¿Olga está contenta?
10. ¿Por qué estás enojada con Elsa?
11. ¿Beatriz es mandona?
12. ¿Tu esposo quiere quedarse con el dinero?
13. ¿Tú visitas a tu abuelo a menudo?
14. ¿Pablo es vanidoso?
15. ¿Tú siempre le cuentas tus problemas a tu hermana?

B

a. Sí, lo extraño mucho.
b. Porque ella dice que tengo malas costumbres.
c. Sí, pero yo no estoy de acuerdo. Yo quiero devolverlo.
d. No, porque ella y yo no nos llevamos bien.
e. No, pero a lo mejor vamos a verlo un día de éstos.
f. Sí, y además me cuida mucho.
g. Sí, lo que pasa es que se cree muy guapo.
h. Sí, por eso nos estamos riendo.
i. Sí. ¡Es que él es muy amistoso!
j. Sí, la boda es en abril.
k. Sí, porque no tienen nada que hacer.
l. Sí, porque ella es muy comprensiva.
m. Porque se mete en todo.
n. Sí, ella siempre está de buen humor.
o. ¡No! ¡Es muy trabajador!

16. ¿Los niños están aburridos?
17. ¿Beto tiene muchos amigos?
18. ¿Tu tía te da consejos?

p. Frustrada y un poco deprimida
q. Sí, siempre está dando órdenes.
r. No, mimarlos.

En grupos de tres o cuatro, hagan lo siguiente.

A. **¿Qué tal están?**

1. Digan si están aburridos(as) o entusiasmados(as), contentos(as) o tristes y por qué.
2. Digan si están deprimidos(as), frustrados(as), preocupados(as) o nerviosos(as) y por qué.
3. Digan si están de buen humor o de mal humor y por qué.
4. Digan si están enojados(as) con alguien (¿con quién? ¿por qué?)
5. Si alguna persona del grupo tiene un problema, los demás (*the others*) tienen que decirle qué puede hacer.

B. **Normas culturales.**   ¿En qué circunstancias hacen ustedes lo siguiente?

1. darle un abrazo a un(a) amigo(a)
2. darle un beso a su mamá (a su papá)
3. dar consejos
4. meterse en la vida de alguien
5. cuidar a alguien (¿a quién?)
6. respetar a alguien (¿a quién?)
7. obedecer a alguien (¿a quién?)

C. **¿Qué le dicen?**   Túrnense usted y un(a) compañero(a) para hacer comentarios apropiados que describan la personalidad de cada persona, de acuerdo a las descripciones dadas.

MODELO: a un primo que siempre dice que él es muy guapo
           ¡Qué vanidoso eres! o *¡Eres muy vanidoso!*

1. a una amiga que trabaja mucho
2. a una hermana que siempre piensa que todo le va a salir bien
3. a un amigo que tiene mucho dinero, pero siempre lleva a su novia a restaurantes baratos
4. a una prima que nunca quiere trabajar
5. a un tío que siempre ayuda a la gente con dinero y tiempo
6. a una prima que siempre le dice a todo el mundo lo que debe hacer
7. a un primo que sólo piensa en sí mismo (*himself*)
8. a una hermana que siempre trata de comprender a sus amigos
9. a una amiga que sólo sale con hombres que tienen mucho dinero
10. a un primo que siempre piensa que todo le va a salir mal

D. **Parientes y amigos.**   Describan a sus parientes y amigos, indicando sus virtudes y sus defectos. Digan cómo son ustedes. Digan qué tipos de personas les caen bien y qué tipos de personas les caen mal.

Palabras problemáticas

A. **Tomar, coger, agarrar** y **llevar** como equivalentes de *to take*

- **Tomar, coger** y **agarrar** son sinónimos cuando se usan para expressar *to take hold of* o *to seize*. En algunos países (Chile, Paraguay, México y Argentina) **coger** se considera una palabra ofensiva y sólo se usan **tomar** y **agarrar.**

  Ana María **toma (coge, agarra)** la pluma y escribe.

- **Llevar** se usa para expresar la idea de *to take* (*someone or something to another location*).

  Yo quiero **llevar** a mi padrino a la reunión.

- **Tomar** también se usa como equivalente de *to take* con respecto a las asignaturas, los medios de transporte y las medicinas.

  Mi prometido está **tomando** una clase de italiano.

  Mi abuela va a **tomar** el avión.

  ¿Por qué no **tomas** la medicina si no te sientes bien?

B. **Saber** y **conocer** como equivalentes de *to know*

- **Saber** quiere decir *to know* (*a fact*) o *to know by heart*. Seguido de un infinitivo significa *to know how* (*to do something*).

  Yo **sé** que mis parientes van a asistir a la boda.

  Mi nieto **sabe** el poema de memoria.

  Mi sobrina no **sabe** nadar.

- **Conocer** significa *to be familiar* o *to be acquainted with* (*a person, a thing, a place, or a work of art*). El verbo **conocer** nunca va seguido de un infinitivo.

  Yo tengo primos a quienes apenas **conozco.**

  ¿Tú **conoces** Nueva York?

  Nosotros **conocemos** los poemas del poeta español Antonio Machado.

C. **Pedir** y **preguntar** como equivalentes de *to ask*

- **Pedir** significa *to ask for* o *to request* (*something*).

  Yo nunca le **pido** dinero a mi madrina.

- **Preguntar** quiere decir *to ask* (*a question*) o *to inquire*. Cuando se usa con la preposición **por** quiere decir *to ask about* (*someone*).

  Le voy a **preguntar** a mi padrino si piensa divorciarse de su esposa.

  Marisol siempre me **pregunta por** ti. ¡Te extraña mucho!

Práctica

Complete los siguientes diálogos y luego represéntelos (*enact them*) con un(a) compañero(a).

1. —¿Tú _____ a Teresa?
   —Sí, ella y yo estamos _____ varias clases juntos.
   —¿_____ su número de teléfono?
   —No, no lo _____.
   —La quiero _____ al cine esta noche. Le voy a _____ si quiere ir conmigo.
   —¿Tienes dinero?
   —No, se lo voy a _____ a mi tío.

2. —¿_____ la dirección de Ana?
   —Sí, la _____ de memoria. (_____ una pluma y escribe la dirección.)
   —¿Dónde queda esta calle? Yo no _____ bien la ciudad.
   —Yo te puedo _____ en mi coche.
   —¡Muchas gracias! Yo no tengo coche y no _____ conducir.

Your instructor may carry out the **¡Ahora escuche!** listening activity found in the **Answers to Text Exercises.**

¡Ahora escuche!

Se leerá dos veces una carta de Ana María a su abuela. Se harán aseveraciones sobre la carta. En una hoja (*sheet*) escriba los números de uno a diez e indique si cada aseveración es verdadera (V) o falsa (F).

FESTIVAL DEL PRADO

SEFARAD III

El mundo hispánico

España en el corazón

STUDENT WEBSITE
Go to **El mundo hispánico** for prereading and vocabulary activities.

Ana María

Se dice que España es un continente en miniatura por su gran diversidad geográfica y cultural, y eso es verdad. Con una superficie de 506.000 kilómetros cuadrados[1] y una población de unos cuarenta millones de habitantes, tiene una increíble variedad de culturas, y no podemos decir que, conociendo una o dos regiones, tenemos una buena idea de lo que es España.

Yo soy de Madrid, la capital de España y, como todo madrileño, estoy enamorada de mi ciudad que, con sus parques, centros culturales, museos, plazas, monumentos y grandes hoteles y restaurantes, es visitada por miles de turistas todos los años. Pero conozco muchas otras ciudades que también tienen mucho que ofrecer. Una de mis favoritas es Barcelona, que está al noreste°, en la costa del Mediterráneo. Allí tengo muchos amigos que siempre

northeast

---

[1] Unas 195.000 millas cuadradas

tratan de enseñarme a hablar catalán, el otro idioma que se habla en Cataluña. Barcelona, la segunda ciudad en importancia, es un centro industrial, vibrante y moderno, y algunos de sus edificios están considerados maravillas arquitectónicas. Los más admirados son los diseñados por el arquitecto Gaudí.

En el sur, Granada, Sevilla y Córdoba, con su influencia mora° en la arquitec-   Moorish
tura y en la música, son verdaderas joyas. Al oeste está Salamanca, que tiene una de las universidades más antiguas de Europa. Al norte, la hermosa ciudad de Bilbao, la capital del País Vasco, situada junto al Mar Cantábrico.

¿Se nota que estoy muy orgullosa de mi país? ¡Ah! Debo decirles que España ocupa, por su desarrollo, el número once entre los 175 países del mundo, según el Informe mundial del desarrollo humano, publicado por la Organización de las Naciones Unidas.

Los millones de turistas que visitan España todos los años no sólo van en busca de playas, de sol, de paisajes naturales y de la excepcional calidad y variedad de su comida y de sus vinos. Van también a admirar sus museos, a conocer de cerca su historia, a visitar la cuna de pintores como Velázquez, Goya, Dalí y Picasso; de músicos como Albéniz, Falla y Casals, y de escritores como Cervantes, Machado y García Lorca.

En la página anterior tienen un mapa de España que les permite ver exactamente dónde está ubicado este hermoso país, así como sus regiones y las islas que son parte del territorio español.

Sobre España

En parejas, túrnense para contestar las siguientes preguntas.

1. ¿Cuáles son los límites de España al norte, al sur, al este y al oeste?
2. ¿Qué islas pertenecen a España?
3. ¿Cuál es la superficie de España? ¿Y la población?
4. ¿Cuáles son algunas de las atracciones de Madrid? ¿Tiene importancia el turismo en esta ciudad?
5. ¿Qué idioma hablan en Barcelona (Cataluña), además del castellano?
6. ¿Cuáles son las tres ciudades más importantes del sur de España? ¿Qué influencia se ve allí?
7. ¿Qué sabemos de la Universidad de Salamanca?
8. ¿Sobre qué mar está situada la ciudad de Bilbao?
9. Entre los países del mundo, ¿qué lugar ocupa España en cuanto a su desarrollo?
10. ¿Qué nombres sobresalen (*stand out*) en el mundo del arte?

Hablemos de su país

INSTRUCTOR WEBSITE
STUDENT WEBSITE
Your instructor may assign the preconversational activities in Hablemos...
(under Hablemos de su país). Go to Hablemos de su país (under ...y escribamos) for postconversational web search and writing activities.

En el mapa aparecen las diversas regiones de España. Reúnase con otro(a) compañero(a) y conteste lo siguiente: ¿Qué regiones hay en su país? ¿Qué elementos (geográficos, sociales, culturales o históricos) las distinguen?

Luego cada pareja compartirá las respuestas con toda la clase. ¿Hay diferencias de opinión sobre cuáles son las regiones y sobre los elementos que las distinguen?

Una tarjeta postal

Esta es una tarjeta postal de Cindy, una amiga norteamericana de Ana María, que está viajando por España.

Querida Ana María:

Lo estoy pasando muy bien aquí, en este país maravilloso. Ahora estoy en Granada, que es una ciudad increíble. De aquí voy a ir a Madrid, a Toledo y a Barcelona. Después quiero visitar las Islas Baleares y también las Islas Canarias, que están a unas doce millas de África, pero pertenecen a España, cosa que yo no sabía. En abril pienso volver a Sevilla para ver la feria. ¡Quiero quedarme en España!

Un abrazo,

Cindy

P.D. ¡Estoy conduciendo un Seat!

Después de leer la tarjeta

1. ¿Cindy se está divirtiendo en España?
2. ¿Le gusta Granada? ¿Qué otras ciudades piensa visitar?
3. ¿A qué distancia de África están las Islas Canarias?
4. ¿Cómo sabemos que a Cindy le encanta España?
5. ¿Cindy está conduciendo un coche americano?

ESPAÑA

Estructuras gramaticales

STUDENT WEBSITE
Do the **¿Cuánto recuerda?** pretest to check what you already know on the topics covered in this **Estructuras gramaticales** section.

1 El presente de indicativo[1]

A Verbos de conjugación irregular

○ The following verbs are irregular in the present indicative tense.

Infinitive	Present Indicative
ser	soy, eres, es, somos, sois, son
estar	estoy, estás, está, estamos, estáis, están
dar	doy, das, da, damos, dais, dan
ir	voy, vas, va, vamos, vais, van
tener	tengo, tienes, tiene, tenemos, tenéis, tienen
venir	vengo, vienes, viene, venimos, venís, vienen
oír (*to hear*)	oigo, oyes, oye, oímos, oís, oyen

Verbs ending in **-tener** are conjugated exactly like the verb **tener**. All verbs ending in **-venir** are conjugated exactly like the verb **venir**.

mantener   *to maintain, to support*   **convenir**   *to be convenient, to suit*
detener   *to stop, to detain*   **intervenir**   *to intervene*
entretener   *to entertain*

—¿Alberto gana un buen sueldo?   *"Does Alberto earn a good salary?"*
—Sí, y **mantiene** a todos sus hermanos.   *"Yes, and he supports all his brothers."*

—¿Tú **intervienes** en los problemas de tu hijo?   *"Do you intervene in your son's problems?"*
—No, yo nunca **intervengo** en sus problemas.   *"No, I never intervene in his problems."*

Práctica

CD-ROM
Go to **Estructuras gramaticales** for additional practice.

Entreviste a un(a) compañero(a), usando las siguientes preguntas.

1. ¿Quién eres?
2. ¿Quiénes son tus padres?
3. ¿De dónde son ustedes?
4. ¿Tienen tú y tu familia reuniones familiares?
5. ¿Vienen a visitarte tus parientes? ¿Vienen a menudo?
6. ¿Tú intervienes en los problemas de tu familia?
7. ¿Tú siempre estás de acuerdo con tus padres?
8. ¿Te mantienes en contacto con todos tus parientes?

---

[1] Please review the conjugations of regular **-ar**, **-er**, and **-ir** verbs in **Apéndice B**.

9. ¿Tú le das un abrazo a tu mejor amigo(a) cuando lo (la) ves?
10. ¿Adónde van tú y tu familia de vacaciones? ¿Tienen vacaciones todos los años?

B Verbos irregulares en la primera persona

○ Many Spanish verbs are irregular in the present tense only in the first person singular. Most verbs ending in a vowel plus **-cer** or **-cir** add a **z** before the **c**.

Common irregular verbs		*Verbs ending in a vowel + -cer or -cir*	
hacer	yo **hago**	conocer	yo **conozco**
poner	yo **pongo**	reconocer (*to recognize;*	yo **reconozco**
salir	yo **salgo**	*to admit*)	
valer (*to be worth*)	yo **valgo**	ofrecer	yo **ofrezco**
traer	yo **traigo**	agradecer (*to thank*)	yo **agradezco**
caer	yo **caigo**	obedecer (*to obey*)	yo **obedezco**
ver	yo **veo**	parecer (*to seem*)	yo **parezco**
saber	yo **sé**	conducir	yo **conduzco**
caber	yo **quepo**	traducir	yo **traduzco**

—¿Tú trabajas los domingos?   "*Do you work on Sundays?*"
—No, yo no **hago** nada los domingos.   "*No, I don't do anything on Sundays.*
    Generalmente **salgo** con mis amigos.   *I generally go out with my friends.*"
—¿Quién conduce cuando sales con   "*Who drives when you go out with your*
    tus amigos?   *friends?*"
—Siempre **conduzco** yo.   "*I always drive.*"

atención

Verbs ending in **-hacer**, **-poner**, and **-parecer** are conjugated exactly like those verbs.

rehacer	*to remake, redo*	**proponer**	*to propose*	**desaparecer**	*to disappear*
suponer	*to suppose*	**aparecer**	*to appear*	**imponer**	*to impose*

—¿Dónde está tu primo?   "*Where's your cousin?*"
—No sé, pero **supongo** que está en casa   "*I don't know, but I suppose he's at his*
    de su madrina.   *godmother's house.*"

—¿Qué haces tú cuando viene tu suegra?   "*What do you do when your mother-in-*
    law comes?"

—¡**Desaparezco**!   "*I disappear!*"

Práctica

CD-ROM
Go to **Estructuras gramaticales** for additional practice.

A. Termine las siguientes oraciones según su propia experiencia. Compare sus respuestas con las de un(a) compañero(a).

1. Yo siempre desaparezco cuando...
2. Yo reconozco que...
3. Yo siempre (nunca) obedezco...
4. Yo les agradezco a mis padres...
5. Yo conozco...
6. Yo sé...
7. Yo nunca veo...
8. Yo supongo que...

B. Lea el siguiente párrafo y vuelva a escribirlo en la primera persona de singular, cambiando las palabras en cursiva (*italic*) según sus propias circunstancias.

Olga es una chica muy popular. Conoce a todos los estudiantes de la Facultad y todos dicen que ella vale mucho, porque es muy inteligente.

Los viernes y sábados sale con *sus amigos* (nunca dice que no a una invitación), pero los domingos *no hace nada*; desaparece de la ciudad y no aparece hasta el lunes por la mañana. Generalmente va *con su familia a la montaña.*

Trabaja en una oficina, donde traduce cartas y documentos. Como no tiene mucho tiempo para estudiar en su casa, a veces trae sus libros a la oficina.

Olga *conduce un coche muy bonito* y tiene *bastante* dinero; *todos los meses* pone dinero en el banco para poder *salir de viaje en las vacaciones.* Ella reconoce que es *una chica de mucha suerte.*

C. Hable con un(a) compañero(a) sobre lo siguiente.

1. la hora en que ustedes salen de su casa por la mañana
2. las cosas que ustedes traen cuando viajan
3. las personas a quienes ustedes ven todos los días
4. algunos parientes a quienes ustedes apenas conocen
5. si hacen ejercicio todos los días y por cuánto tiempo
6. si conducen o no; si conducen rápido; qué tipo de coche conducen

C El presente de indicativo de verbos con cambios en la raíz

○ Certain verbs undergo a stem change in the present indicative, as follows:

preferir (e → ie)		*poder (o → ue)*		*pedir (e → i)*	
prefiero	preferimos	puedo	podemos	pido	pedimos
prefieres	preferís	puedes	podéis	pides	pedís
prefiere	prefieren	puede	pueden	pide	piden

○ Notice that the stem change does not occur in **nosotros** and **vosotros**.

Other stem-changing verbs		
-ar	*-er*	*-ir*
e → ie cerrar	querer	mentir (*to lie*)
comenzar	encender (*to light*)[1]	sugerir
empezar	perder	sentir
pensar	entender	advertir (*to warn*)
confesar		
despertar		
negar (*to deny*)		

---

[1] **Encender** tambien significa *to turn on* cuando se habla de la luz, el radio y el televisor.

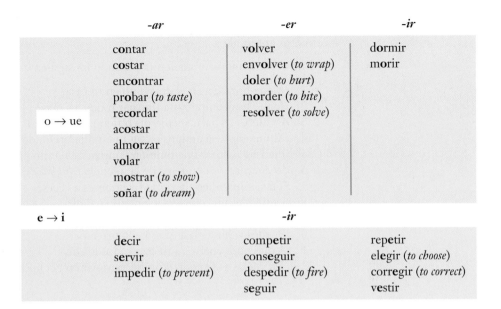

	-ar	*-er*	*-ir*
o → ue	contar costar encontrar probar (*to taste*) recordar acostar almorzar volar mostrar (*to show*) soñar (*to dream*)	volver envolver (*to wrap*) doler (*to hurt*) morder (*to bite*) resolver (*to solve*)	dormir morir

		-ir	
e → i	decir servir impedir (*to prevent*)	competir conseguir despedir (*to fire*) seguir	repetir elegir (*to choose*) corregir (*to correct*) vestir

Práctica

CD-ROM
Go to **Estructuras gramaticales** for additional practice.

A. **Mirando la tele.** A estos anuncios y noticias de un programa de televisión les faltan los verbos. Póngaselos usted, usando el presente de indicativo de los verbos que aparecen en cada lista. Usted y sus compañeros serán los locutores (*announcers*) y cada uno leerá un anuncio.

competir   costar   servir   almorzar

1. Todo _____ menos en el restaurante El Sombrero. Usted _____ por sólo cinco dólares. Nosotros _____ el mejor pollo frito de la ciudad. Ningún otro restaurante _____ con el nuestro en precios ni en servicios.

morir   encender   encontrar   sugerir

2. Si usted _____ la luz y _____ cucarachas (*roaches*) en la cocina, debe usar nuestro producto Anticucarachas. En dos minutos, todas las cucarachas _____. Yo le _____ no esperar un día más.

tener   confesar   recordar   contar   repetir

3. ¿_____ ustedes a la famosa Lolita Vargas? Rosa Barreto nos _____ lo que está pasando en la vida de la famosa actriz. Lolita _____ que _____ un nuevo amor y _____ que éste es el verdadero (otra vez).

morder   perder   impedir   despertar

4. ¡Importante! Un agente de policía _____ un robo en la tienda Libertad. Un perro rabioso _____ a dos personas en un parque. El gobernador Francisco Acosta _____ las elecciones. Un hombre _____ después de estar en coma por seis meses. Film a las once.

B. Ahora, en parejas, escriban dos noticias y dos anuncios originales, usando los verbos aprendidos.

C. Entreviste a un(a) compañero(a), usando las siguientes preguntas.

1. ¿A qué hora sirven el desayuno en tu casa?
2. ¿A qué hora empiezas a trabajar todos los días?
3. ¿Prefieres trabajar medio día o tiempo completo?
4. ¿Almuerzas con amigos o con tu familia? ¿Dónde almuerzas? ¿A qué hora?
5. ¿Piensas asistir a una reunión familiar el verano próximo?
6. ¿Recuerdas a tus amigos de la infancia (*childhood*)?
7. ¿Tú siempre dices la verdad o mientes a veces?
8. ¿Entiendes una conversación en español?
9. ¿Tú consigues periódicos en español?
10. ¿Puedes venir a clase la semana próxima?
11. ¿A qué hora vuelves a tu casa todos los días?
12. ¿Tú vuelas a menudo o prefieres viajar en coche?

2 El presente progresivo

A Formas del gerundio[1]

- To form the present participle (the *-ing* form in English) of regular verbs, the following endings are used:

-ar *verbs:* -ando		-er *and* -ir *verbs:* -iendo	
		correr	corriendo
mimar	mimando		
		escribir	escribiendo

- The following verbs have irregular forms.

1. **-er** and **-ir** verbs whose stems end in a vowel use the ending **-yendo** instead of **-iendo.**

| leer: | le**yendo** | oír: | o**yendo** |
| caer: | ca**yendo** | huir (*to flee*): | hu**yendo** |

2. **-ir** stem-changing verbs change the **e** to **i** and the **o** to **u:**

| mentir: | mintiendo | dormir: | durmiendo |
| servir: | sirviendo | morir: | muriendo |

---

[1] The **gerundio** (**-ando** and **-iendo** forms) is the Spanish equivalent of the English present participle (*-ing* form).

3. Other irregular forms are:

| decir: | **diciendo** | ir: | **yendo**[1] |
| poder: | **pudiendo** | venir: | **viniendo**[1] |

B   Formas y uso del presente progresivo

○ The most commonly used present progressive construction in Spanish is formed with the present tense of the verb **estar** and the **gerundio** of the main verb.

—¿Qué **está haciendo** el Sr. Paz?   *"What is Mr. Paz doing?"*
—**Está hablando** con su sobrino.   *"He's talking with his nephew."*

○ In Spanish, the present progressive indicates an action that is in progress.

—¿Qué **estás leyendo**?   *"What are you reading?"*
—**Estoy leyendo** una carta de mi   *"I'm reading a letter from my great-*
  bisabuelo.   *grandfather."*

atención

The present progressive is never used in Spanish to indicate a future action, as it is in English; the present tense is used instead.

Mañana **salgo** para Bilbao.   *I'm leaving for Bilbao tomorrow.*

The present progressive tense describes temporary actions. Extended or repeated actions are usually described in the present tense.

Mis abuelos **viven** en Sevilla.   *My grandparents live in Sevilla.*

C   El gerundio con los verbos *seguir* y *continuar*

○ **Continuar** or **seguir** + *the present participle* (**gerundio**) may be used in Spanish to indicate an action that started in the past and is still taking place at a given time.

—¿Todavía estás estudiando francés?   *"Are you still studying French?"*
—Sí, yo **continúo estudiando,** pero   *"Yes, I continue (keep on) studying, but*
  no aprendo mucho.   *I'm not learning much."*
—¿**Sigues estudiando** en la   *"Are you still studying at the university?"*
  universidad?
—No, porque tengo problemas   *"No, because I have financial problems."*
  económicos.

-----

[1] These are hardly ever used in the present progressive. The present indicative is used instead:
¿Adónde vas? = Where are you going?

atención

Continuar and **seguir** are *never* followed by the infinitive, as they are in English.

Ellos	**siguen estudiando**	informática.
They	***continue to study***	*computer science.*

Notice that **seguir** and **continuar** are synonymous in this context.

Ellos **siguen (continúan) estudiando.**

Práctica

CD-ROM
Go to **Estructuras gramaticales** for additional practice.

A. Usted y sus amigos están en casa de sus padres. Usando el presente progresivo y los elementos dados, diga lo que está haciendo cada persona. Añada (*Add*) las palabras que sean necesarias.

1. yo / leer / una carta
2. Marcelo / dormir / su cuarto
3. Alicia / poner / libros / escritorio
4. Rosalía / servir / el desayuno
5. Ana y Luis / pedir / información / Salamanca
6. Ernesto / decir / debemos / llamar / abuelos
7. Silvia / hacer / ejercicio
8. Ramiro / escribir / carta

B. Entreviste a un(a) compañero(a), usando las siguientes preguntas. Use **seguir** o **continuar** + gerundio en sus respuestas.

1. ¿Todavía vives en la misma ciudad?
2. ¿Todavía trabajas en el mismo lugar?
3. ¿Todavía estudias en la biblioteca?
4. ¿Todavía planeas ir de vacaciones?
5. ¿Todavía tienes problemas económicos?

C. En parejas, hagan una lista de lo que está ocurriendo en la clase en este momento, usando los verbos **leer, estudiar, hablar, mirar, hacer, charlar** (*to chat*) y **escribir.**

3 La *a* personal[1]

◉ The personal **a** has no equivalent in English. It is used in Spanish before a direct object noun that refers to a specific person or persons.

—Yo no veo **a** todos mis amigos los sábados.	"I don't see all my friends on Saturdays."
—¿**A** quiénes ves?	"Whom do you see?"
—**A** Julio y **a** Teresa.[2]	"Julio and Teresa."

---

[1] Review the concept of the direct object on page 20.

[2] If there are two or more direct objects, the personal **a** is used before each: Llaman **a** Julio y **a** Teresa.

—¿**A** cuál de las chicas conoces?　　　"*Which one of the girls do you know?*"
—**A** ésa que está allí.　　　"*That one over there.*"
—¿Qué hace Carlos en la universidad　"*What's Carlos doing at the university so*
tan temprano?　　　*early?*"
—Espera **a**[1] la Sra. Reyes.　　　"*He's waiting for Mrs. Reyes.*"

○ The personal **a** is also used when the direct object is **quien(es)** or is an indefinite expression such as **alguien** or **nadie**.

—¿Necesitas ver **a** alguien?　　　"*Do you need to see anybody?*"
—No, no necesito ver **a** nadie.　　　"*No, I don't need to see anyone.*"

○ The personal **a** is used when an animal or an inanimate object is personified.

—¿Adónde vas?　　　"*Where are you going?*"
—Voy a llevar **a** mi perrito al
veterinario porque el pobre　　　"*I'm going to take my puppy to the vet*
está enfermo.　　　*because the poor thing is sick.*"
—En España tenemos las montañas　"*In Spain we have the most beautiful*
más hermosas.　　　*mountains.*"
—Para ti, España es el mejor lugar　"*For you, Spain is the best place in the*
del mundo.　　　*world.*"
—Es que yo amo mucho **a** mi país.　"*Well, I love my country very much.*"

○ The personal **a** is not used when the direct object refers to a thing, to an unspecified person, or after the verb **tener**.

—¡Hola! ¿Qué haces aquí?　　　"*Hi! What are you doing here?*"
—Espero un taxi.　　　"*I'm waiting for a taxi.*"

—¿Qué necesitas?　　　"*What do you need?*"
—Necesito un secretario.　　　"*I need a secretary.*"

—¿Tiene Ud. hijos?　　　"*Do you have children?*"
—Sí, tengo cuatro hijos.　　　"*Yes, I have four sons.*"

Práctica

CD-ROM
Go to **Estructuras gramaticales** for additional practice.

A. En parejas, lean los siguientes diálogos usando la **a** en los casos en que se necesita.

1. —¿_____ quién esperas?
   —No espero _____ nadie. Estoy esperando _____ el ómnibus.
2. —¿Cuántos hijos tienes?
   —Tengo _____ dos hijos: Luis y Mario; pero no veo _____ Luis muy
   frecuentemente.
3. —¿_____ cuál de los chicos prefieres? ¿_____ ése o _____ aquél?
   —Prefiero _____ aquél.

---

[1] If the personal **a** is followed by the article **el**, the contraction **al** is formed: Espera **al** Sr. Reyes.

4. —¿Vas a visitar _____ tus padres en Madrid?
   —Sí, y vamos a ir todos a visitar _____ el Museo del Prado.
5. —¿Qué necesitan Uds.?
   —Necesitamos _____ una recepcionista.

B. Entreviste a un(a) compañero(a), usando las siguientes preguntas.

1. ¿A qué parientes ves frecuentemente?
2. ¿Tienes hermanos? ¿Cuántos?
3. ¿Conoces a los padres de tu mejor amigo(a)?
4. ¿A quién quieres mucho? ¿A quién mimas? ¿Malcrías a alguien?
5. ¿Visitas a alguien los domingos?
6. ¿Visitas los museos de arte a veces?
7. ¿Extrañas a alguien?
8. Tú estás muy ocupado(a). ¿Necesitas una secretaria?
9. Si te invitan a una fiesta, ¿a quién llevas, generalmente?
10. ¿Llamas a tus amigos todos los días?

4 Formas pronominales en función de complemento directo

A El complemento directo de la oración

○ The direct object is the object that directly receives the action of the verb.

S   V   D.O.
Él compra **el libro.**

○ In the sentence above, the subject **Él** performs the action expressed by the verb, while **el libro,** the direct object, is directly affected by the action of the verb. The direct object of a sentence may be either a person or a thing. It can be easily identified by saying the subject and verb and then asking the question *what?* or *whom?*

Él compra **el libro.**   *He is buying* **what?**
Alicia mira **a Luis.**   *Alicia is looking at* **whom?**

B Formas de los pronombres de complemento directo

○ The direct object pronouns replace nouns used as direct objects.

	Singular		*Plural*
me	*me*	**nos**	*us*
te	*you* (familiar)	**os**	*you* (**vosotros** form)
lo	*you* (m.), *him, it* (m.)	**los**	*you* (m.), *them* (m.)
la	*you* (f.), *her, it* (f.)	**las**	*you* (f.), *them* (f.)

C Posición de los pronombres personales usados como complemento directo

○ In Spanish, direct object pronouns are placed *before* a conjugated verb. They are attached to the end of an infinitive or a present participle **(gerundio)**.

—¿**Me** llamas este fin de semana?	*"Will you call me this weekend?"*
—No, no[1] **te** llamo.	*"No, I won't call you."*
—No tenemos tiempo de terminar**lo**.	*"We don't have time to finish it."*
—Sí, haciéndo**lo**[2] entre los dos, **lo** terminamos sin problema.	*"Yes, (by) doing it between the two (of us), we'll finish it without (any) problem."*

○ If a conjugated verb and an infinitive or a present participle are used in the same sentence or clause, the direct object pronouns may either be placed before the conjugated verb or attached to the infinitive or present participle.

—¿Cuándo **los** quieres ver?	*"When do you want to see them?"*
—Quiero ver**los** mañana.	*"I want to see them tomorrow."*
—¿Dónde está el periódico? ¿Estás leyéndo**lo**[2]?	*"Where is the paper? Are you reading it?"*
—No, no **lo** estoy leyendo.	*"No, I'm not reading it."*

○ The verbs **saber, decir, pedir,** and **preguntar** generally take a direct object. If the sentence does not have one, the pronoun **lo** must be added to complete the idea. **Lo** is also added to **ser** and **estar**.

—Ana extraña a sus amigos y a sus parientes.	*"Ana misses her friends and her relatives."*
—Sí, **lo** sé.	*"Yes, I know."*
—No sé el número de teléfono de Olga.	*"I don't know Olga's phone number."*
—Puedes preguntar**lo**...	*"You can ask . . ."*
—Él es muy perezoso, ¿verdad?	*"He's very lazy, isn't he?"*
—Sí, **lo** es.	*"Yes, he is."*
—¿Carlos está muy enfadado?	*"Is Carlos very angry?"*
—Sí, **lo** está.	*"Yes, he is."*

Práctica

CD-ROM
Go to **Estructuras gramaticales** for additional practice.

A. Usando el verbo **necesitar**, termine las siguientes oraciones apropiadamente.

MODELO: Yo voy a llevar los libros a casa de Ana porque ella _____.
*Yo voy a llevar los libros a casa de Ana porque ella **los** necesita.*

---

[1] In a negative sentence, the word **no** is placed before the pronoun.

[2] Note that an accent is required on present participles that have attached direct object pronouns. The accent is placed on the **a** or **e** of the participle ending to maintain the original stress: *Estoy mirándola* or *Sigue diciéndolo*.

1. Yo voy a ir a casa de tía Amanda porque ella _____.
2. Las enfermeras van a ir al consultorio del Dr. Torres porque él _____.
3. Tú tienes que ir a la escuela porque el maestro _____.
4. Roberto piensa ir a la casa de sus abuelos porque ellos _____.
5. Nosotros vamos a ir a la oficina de la Srta. Rojas porque ella _____.
6. Yo voy a traer la maleta porque sé que tú _____.

B. Pepe y su hermana Ada están conversando en un restaurante de Madrid. Agregue Ud. (*Add*) los pronombres de complemento directo que faltan.

PEPE —¿Tienes los cheques de viajero?

ADA —Sí, aquí _____ tengo. Oye, ¿a qué hora vas a llamar a mamá por teléfono?

PEPE —_____ voy a llamar a las dos. Papá dice que quiere llevar _____ a todos al parque del Retiro esta tarde.

ADA —Yo quiero invitar a Marcelo y a su hermana.

PEPE —_____ puedes invitar, si quieres, pero ellos ya _____ conocen.

ADA —Pero Marcelo va a venir porque _____ quiere ver a mí...

PEPE —Bueno... Marcelo _____ quiere ver a ti y su hermana _____ quiere ver a mí...

C. Imagínese que Ud. y un(a) compañero(a) están planeando una fiesta en su casa. Túrnense (*Take turns*) para contestar las siguientes preguntas usando siempre pronombres de complemento directo.

1. ¿Tú puedes invitar a todos nuestros amigos?
2. ¿Tú vas a comprar las bebidas?
3. ¿Quieres usar mi radiocasetera?
4. ¿Vas a traer las cintas?
5. ¿Vas a llamar al profesor (a la profesora) de español?
6. ¿Me necesitas para limpiar la casa antes de la fiesta?
7. ¿Puedes llevarnos a casa después de la fiesta?
8. ¿Tienes tu auto aquí?

5 Formas pronominales en función de complemento indirecto

○ In addition to the direct object, the verb of a sentence may take an indirect object.

	D.O.	I.O.			D.O.	I.O.

Él **le** da **el libro a María.**   *He gives **the book to María.***

An indirect object describes *to whom* or *for whom* an action is done. In Spanish, an indirect object pronoun can be used in place of an indirect object. The indirect object pronoun includes the meaning *to* or *for*: **Yo les mando los libros (a los estudiantes).**

A Formas y posición

○ The forms of the indirect object pronouns are as follows:

	Singular		*Plural*
me	*(to, for) me*	**nos**	*(to, for) us*
te	*(to, for) you* (familiar)	**os**	*(to, for) you* (**vosotros** form)
le	*(to, for) you, him, her, it*	**les**	*(to, for) you, them*

○ Like direct object pronouns, indirect object pronouns are usually placed before a conjugated verb.

—¿Qué **te** dice tu hermana en la carta? *"What does your sister say (to you) in the letter?"*

—**Me** dice que no va a haber boda. *"She tells me there isn't going to be a wedding."*

○ When a conjugated verb is followed by an infinitive or a present participle the indirect object pronoun may either be placed in front of the conjugated verb or be attached to the infinitive or present participle.

Le voy a traer una maleta.
Voy a traer**le** una maleta. *I'm going to bring him a suitcase.*

Les está leyendo la noticia.
Está leyéndo**les**[1] la noticia. *She is reading the news item to them.*

○ The third person singular and plural pronouns **le** and **les** are used for both masculine and feminine forms.

—¿Qué **le** vas a traer a él? *"What are you going to bring (for) him?"*
—Voy a traer**le** un libro. *"I'm going to bring him a book."*
—¿Y a Rosa? *"And to Rosa?"*
—**Le** voy a traer una revista. *"I'm going to bring her a magazine."*

○ If the meaning of the pronouns **le** or **les** is ambiguous, the preposition **a** + *personal pronoun or noun* may be used for clarification.

Le doy la carta. (¿**a quién?**) *I'm giving the letter . . . (**to whom?**)*

Le doy la carta { a **Ud.** / a **él.** / a **ella.** / a **María.** }

---

[1] Note that an accent is required on present participles that have attached direct object pronouns. The accent is placed on the **a** or **e** of the participle ending to maintain the original stress: *Estoy mirándola* or *Sigue diciéndolo.*

○ The prepositional phrase **a** + *personal pronoun* may be used for emphasis even when it is not needed for clarification.

Ella quiere dar**me** el dinero **a mí**.   *She wants to give the money to me (and to no one else).*

atención   Prepositional phrases with **a** are not substitutes for the indirect object pronouns. The prepositional phrase is optional, but the indirect object pronouns must always be used.

B Otros usos de las formas pronominales de complemento indirecto

○ Remember that in Spanish the definite article, not the possessive adjective, is used when referring to parts of the body or articles of clothing (including shoes and jewelry). The indirect object pronoun is used in such sentences to indicate the possessor.

—¿Quién **te** corta el pelo?   *"Who cuts your hair?"*
—Alberto.   *"Alberto."*

—¿Qué vestido quieres poner**le** a la niña?   *"Which dress do you want to put on the girl?"*
—Quiero poner**le** el vestido rosado.   *"I want to put her pink dress on her."*

Práctica

CD-ROM
Go to **Estructuras gramaticales** for additional practice.

A. En parejas, hablen de las cosas que cada uno va a traerles a los siguientes parientes en la próxima reunión familiar, y por qué. Sigan el modelo.

MODELO: A mi papá...
          A mi papá le voy a traer una maleta porque la que él tiene es muy vieja.

1. A mi padrino...
2. A mis dos tías...
3. A ti...
4. A mis hermanos...

B. Entreviste a un(a) compañero(a), usando las siguientes preguntas.

1. ¿A quiénes piensas mandarles mensajes electrónicos hoy o mañana? ¿Qué les vas a decir? ¿Les vas a dar buenas noticias?
2. ¿Qué les vas a comprar a tus padres para su aniversario?
3. ¿Tus padres te dan o te prestan dinero a veces?
4. ¿A quién le cuentas tus problemas?
5. ¿Tú les das consejos a tus amigos?
6. ¿Tú le hablas a alguien sobre tu vida? ¿A quién?

C. Imagínese que Ud. está en una fiesta y oye fragmentos de conversaciones. Siempre oye las preguntas, pero nunca oye las respuestas. ¿Qué cree Ud. que contesta cada persona? Complete los diálogos y represéntelos con un(a) compañero(a) usando los pronombres de complemento indirecto en sus respuestas.

1. ANA — Jorge, ¿qué te dice tía Susana de mí?
   JORGE —
2. TERESA —¿Qué me vas a regalar para mi cumpleaños?
   RAFAEL —
3. MARÍA —Elena, ¿qué vestido le vas a poner a tu hija mañana, el rojo o el azul?
   ELENA —
4. LUIS —¿Cuánto dinero vas a darles a los nietos?
   ROSA —
   LUIS —Pero eso es mucho dinero...
5. ROBERTO —¿En qué idioma les hablan a Uds. sus abuelos?
   MONIQUE —
6. MARCOS —Olga, ¿qué le vas a comprar a tu madrina?
   OLGA —

Ahora piensen en otras conversaciones breves que se oyen en la fiesta. Escriban dos más y represéntenlas.

6 Construcciones reflexivas

Usos y formas

- A verb is reflexive when the subject performs and receives the action of the verb. In Spanish, most transitive verbs[1] may be used as reflexive verbs. The use of the reflexive construction is much more common in Spanish than in English.

- When a Spanish verb is used reflexively, the following reflexive pronouns must be used.

	Singular		*Plural*
me	*myself*	**nos**	*ourselves*
te	*yourself* (**tú** form)	**os**	*yourselves* (**vosotros** form)
se	*yourself* (**Ud.** form) / *himself* / *herself*	**se**	*yourselves* (**Uds.** form) / *themselves*

- Note that, except for the third person **se,** the reflexive pronouns have the same forms as the direct and indirect object pronouns.

- The following chart outlines the reflexive forms of **vestirse:** *to dress* (*oneself*), *to get dressed.*

---
[1] Remember that transitive verbs require a direct object to complete the action of the verb: *Luis compró **una casa.*** Without **una casa,** the sentence would have no meaning.

vestirse (e → i)

Yo **me visto.**	*I dress (myself). I get dressed.*
Tú **te vistes.**	*You (fam. sing.) dress (yourself). You get dressed.*
Ud. **se viste.**	*You (form. sing.) dress (yourself). You get dressed.*
Él **se viste.**	*He dresses (himself). He gets dressed.*
Ella **se viste.**	*She dresses (herself). She gets dressed.*
Nosotros **nos vestimos.**	*We dress (ourselves). We get dressed.*
Vosotros **os vestís.**	*You (fam. pl.) dress (yourselves). You get dressed.*
Uds. **se visten.**	*You (form. pl.) dress (yourselves). You get dressed.*
Ellos **se visten.**	*They (m.) dress (themselves). They get dressed.*
Ellas **se visten.**	*They (f.) dress (themselves). They get dressed.*

Yo no **me levanto** muy temprano porque los niños no **se despiertan** hasta las ocho.	*I don't get up very early because the children don't wake up until eight.*

○ Reflexive pronouns function as either direct or indirect objects; they occupy the same position in a sentence that object pronouns do.

    D.O.
Yo **me** lavo.

    I.O.   D.O.
Yo **me** lavo **las manos.**

    I.O. D.O.
Yo **me las** lavo.
     (R.P.)

○ When a reflexive pronoun is used with a direct object pronoun, the reflexive pronoun always precedes the direct object pronoun.

—Tienes que lavarte las manos.	*"You have to wash your hands."*
—Yo siempre **me las** lavo.	*"I always wash them."*

atención   Note that the reflexive pronouns always agree with the subject.

○ Some verbs change meaning when they are used reflexively.

acostar	*to put to bed*	**acostarse**[1]	*to go to bed*
dormir	*to sleep*	**dormirse**	*to fall asleep*
levantar	*to raise, to lift*	**levantarse**	*to get up*
llamar	*to call*	**llamarse**	*to be named*
llevar	*to take*	**llevarse**	*to carry off*
probar (o → ue)	*to taste, to try*	**probarse (o → ue)**	*to try on*
poner	*to put, to place*	**ponerse**	*to put on*
quitar	*to take away*	**quitarse**	*to take off*

---

[1] When a verb is reflexive, the infinitive always ends in **-se.**

ir *to go*	irse *to leave, to go away*
parecer *to seem, to appear*	parecerse *to look like*
sentar *to seat*	sentarse *to sit down*

—¿Quieres **acostarte** ahora?
—Sí, pero primero quiero
   acostar a los niños.

"Do you want to go to bed now?"
"Yes, but first I want to put the children
   to bed."

○ Some verbs are always used with a reflexive construction.

acordarse (o → ue) (de) *to remember*	**burlarse (de)** *to make fun of*
arrepentirse (e → ie) (de) *to regret, to repent*	**quejarse (de)** *to complain*
arrodillarse *to kneel down*	**suicidarse** *to commit suicide*
atreverse (a) *to dare*	

atención   The use of reflexive pronouns does not necessarily mean that the action is reflexive:

Los estudiantes **se quejan** del profesor.
The students complain about the professor (not about themselves).

Práctica

CD-ROM
Go to **Estructuras gramaticales** for additional practice.

A. En parejas, lean los siguientes diálogos usando el presente de indicativo de los verbos de la lista.

acordarse	bañarse	arrodillarse	sentarse	acostarse
olvidarse	burlarse	levantarse	quejarse	lavarse

1. —¿A qué hora _____ tú generalmente?
   —_____ a las seis de la mañana y _____ a las once de la noche.
2. —La Sra. Ruiz _____ de los niños todos los días.
   —Es que ellos siempre _____ de su hijito porque él no sabe nadar.
3. —¿Uds. _____ por la mañana?
   —Sí, _____ y _____ la cabeza.
4. —Para rezar (*to pray*), ¿tú generalmente _____ o _____?
   —Me arrodillo.
5. —¡Qué cabeza tienes! Nunca _____ de traer el libro.
   —Es verdad. Todos los días _____ de traerlo.

B. Conteste las siguientes preguntas, seleccionando el verbo reflexivo o el no reflexivo, según corresponda.

1. ¿Qué hacen Uds. cuando tienen mucho sueño? (acostar, acostarse)
2. Si le duelen los pies, ¿qué puede hacer Ud. con los zapatos? (quitar, quitarse)
3. Para saber si la comida está picante (*spicy*) o no, ¿qué hacen Uds.? (probar, probarse)
4. Si Ud. es muy similar a su padre, ¿qué le dice la gente? (parecer, parecerse)
5. ¿Qué debe hacer Ud. por la noche para no estar cansado(a) al día siguiente? (dormir, dormirse)

6. ¿Qué hace el profesor cuando termina la clase? (ir, irse)
7. Antes de comprar una chaqueta, ¿qué hace Ud.? (probar, probarse)
8. Si hace mucho frío, ¿qué hace Ud. con el abrigo? (poner, ponerse)
9. ¿Qué hace Ud. si la clase es muy aburrida? (dormir, dormirse)
10. ¿Qué hacen Uds. después de despertarse? (levantar, levantarse)

C. Use su imaginación y construcciones reflexivas para decir lo que hacen las siguientes personas, según la información dada.

1. Son las seis de la mañana. Yo...
2. En el baño, mi padre...
3. Frente al espejo, mi hermana...
4. En el probador (*fitting room*), tú...
5. Cuando tenemos frío, nosotros...
6. En el restaurante, después de pagar la cuenta, ellos...
7. Cuando vuelvo a mi casa y me duelen los pies, yo...
8. Cuando el servicio en el restaurante es malo, Uds...
9. Cuando tú rezas...
10. A las once de la noche, nosotros...

STUDENT WEBSITE
Do the **Compruebe cuánto sabe** self test after finishing this **Estructuras gramaticales** section.

	Summary of Personal Pronouns			
Subject	*Direct object*	*Indirect object*	*Reflexive*	*Object of preposition*
yo	me	me	me	mí
tú	te	te	te	ti
usted (*f.*)	la			usted (*f.*)
usted (*m.*)	lo	le	se	usted (*m.*)
él	lo			él
ella	la			ella
nosotros(as)	nos	nos	nos	nosotros(as)
vosotros(as)	os	os	os	vosotros(as)
ustedes (*f.*)	las			ustedes (*f.*)
ustedes (*m.*)	los	les	se	ustedes (*m.*)
ellos	los			ellos
ellas	las			ellas

 **atención**   With the preposition **con, conmigo** and **contigo** are used.

¡CONTINUEMOS!

Una encuesta

Entreviste a sus compañeros de clase para tratar de identificar a aquellas personas que...

1. ...se ponen contentos cuando ven a sus parientes.
2. ...son un poco vanidosos.
3. ...no se llevan bien con algunos de sus parientes.
4. ...se mantienen en contacto con sus parientes.
5. ...asisten a reuniones familiares.
6. ...se sirven una taza de café antes de ir a trabajar.
7. ...son un poco haraganes.
8. ...se sienten nostálgicos o echan de menos a alguien.
9. ...generalmente están de acuerdo con sus padres.
10. ...son amistosos.
11. ...se sienten un poco frustrados a veces.
12. ...piensan viajar a España un día de éstos.

Ahora divídanse en grupos de tres o cuatro y discutan el resultado de la encuesta.

  ## ¿Comprende Ud.?

CD-ROM STUDENT WEBSITE
Go to **De escuchar...a escribir** (in **¿Comprende Ud.?**) on the CD-ROM for activities related to the conversation, and go to **Canción** on the website for activities related to the song.

1. Escuche la siguiente conversación entre Ana María y Tyler durante su viaje por España. El objetivo de la actividad es el de escuchar una conversación a velocidad natural. No se preocupe de entenderlo todo, pues esto no se espera de Ud. Después de escuchar la conversación dos veces, Ud. oirá varias aseveraciones. En una hoja, escriba los números de uno a ocho e indique si cada aseveración es verdadera o falsa.
2. Luego escuche la canción y trate de aprenderla.

Hablemos de una invitación de boda

En parejas, fíjense en esta invitación de boda y contesten las preguntas.

El ingeniero Juan Carlos Peña Sandoval y su esposa
doña María Isabel Juncal Ordóñez
tienen el placer de anunciar el matrimonio de su hija

María Luz Peña Juncal
con
Luis Fernando Arias Calderón,

hijo del arquitecto Gustavo Antonio Arias Acosta
y doña Carmen Anabel Calderón Reyes.

La boda se celebrará en la
Iglesia de Los Ángeles
el día 10 de junio de 2003, a las seis de la tarde.

Inmediatamente después de la ceremonia, habrá
una recepción con cena en el

Hotel Villa Magna

Esperamos tener el honor de su presencia en este dichoso día.

1. ¿Cuál es la profesión del padre de la novia? ¿Y la del padre del novio?
2. ¿Cuál es el apellido paterno de María Luz? ¿Y el materno?
3. ¿La boda va a ser civil o religiosa? ¿Cómo lo sabemos?
4. ¿En qué fecha y a qué hora se celebrará la boda?
5. ¿Dónde va a ser la recepción? ¿Qué van a servir en la recepción?
6. ¿Cómo sabe la persona que recibe esta invitación que está invitada a la recepción?

¿Qué dirían ustedes?

Imagínense que Ud. y un(a) compañero(a) se encuentran en las siguientes situaciones. ¿Qué va a decir cada uno?

1. Uds. están encargados(as) de planear una reunión familiar. Digan dónde y cuándo va a ser, quiénes van a estar allí, qué actividades van a tener y cuánto tiempo va a durar (*last*).
2. Uds. hablan de las diferencias que existen entre mimar y malcriar a los niños, y de cuál debe ser el papel de los abuelos en la crianza (*upbringing*) de los niños.
3. Uds. hablan de la mejor edad para casarse, dando las razones, y también de las ventajas y desventajas de casarse cuando uno es una persona mayor.

¡De ustedes depende!

Una chica española va a venir al estado donde Uds. viven. En grupos de dos o tres, hablen de las cosas que ella debe saber (incluyendo algunas costumbres) para que su estadía sea agradable. Hagan una lista de las cosas que Uds. quieren preguntarle a ella sobre las costumbres de los españoles en cuanto a sus parientes y amigos.

Mesa redonda

Formen grupos de cuatro o cinco estudiantes y hablen de las ventajas y de las desventajas de vivir con sus padres mientras asisten a la universidad. Hablen también sobre la idea de vivir muy cerca de los parientes políticos (*in-laws*).

Lecturas periodísticas

Saber leer   Un autor debe conocer a su público

CD-ROM

Go to **Lecturas periodísticas** for additional prereading and vocabulary activities.

Cuando leemos, debemos tener presente (*keep in mind*) que el escritor o la escritora de un texto siempre desea comunicarse con algún lector (*reader*). Este "lector" es su público. Échele una mirada rápida (*Scan*) al siguiente artículo y conteste la pregunta: ¿A quiénes se dirige la autora? Es decir, ¿cuál es su público?

Para leer y comprender

Al leer el artículo detalladamente, busque las respuestas a las siguientes preguntas.

1. Según la autora, ¿qué es indispensable durante las dos primeras etapas de la infancia?
2. En la actualidad, ¿qué tienen que hacer muchos padres?
3. ¿Cuánto tiempo pasan muchos padres lejos del hogar?
4. En cuanto a las personas que pueden cuidar de los niños mientras los padres trabajan, ¿cuáles son las tres posibilidades?
5. Generalmente, ¿qué se establece entre un niño y un abuelo que quiere cuidarlo? ¿A quiénes gratifica esta situación?
6. Al seleccionar una niñera, ¿qué se debe tener en cuenta?

7. ¿Cómo deben ser los grupos de niños en una guardería? ¿Qué debe tener cada grupo?
8. ¿Qué es conveniente hacer de vez en cuando?
9. Si un papá se siente culpable de tener que dejar a su bebé en una guardería, ¿qué debe hacer? ¿Qué implica la educación de un hijo?
10. ¿Cuáles son los momentos clave en los que el papá o la mamá debe estar presente? ¿Qué pueden hacer los padres los fines de semana?
11. ¿Qué pasa si los padres tienen un horario que no pueden modificar?
12. Según la autora, ¿qué es mucho más importante para el niño que una hora de sueño?

¿Eres un papá de medio tiempo?

Pautas° para educar a los chicos cuando mamá y papá trabajan fuera de casa. Las obligaciones. Los horarios. La culpa°. Los límites.

Guidelines
guilt

Especialmente en las dos primeras etapas de la infancia... la presencia física de los padres es indispensable para la crianza de los hijos...

Después de pasar unas horas en la guardería, esta niñita vuelve a casa con sus padres.

Especialmente en las dos primeras etapas° de la infancia (es decir, desde recién nacidos hasta los cinco años), la presencia física de los padres es indispensable para la crianza° de los hijos, pero los tiempos que corren° te obligan a trabajar todo el día fuera de casa. Sea por el desarrollo de una vocación o por el equilibrio de la economía familiar, hoy tanto papá como mamá pasan entre 8 y 10 o más horas lejos del hogar°.

¿Con quién dejo a mi hijo?

Hay que ser realista. Sólo caben tres posibilidades: un familiar, una guardería° o una niñera°.

Los abuelos

No hay nada mejor que un abuelo con ganas de° cuidar a su nieto. En la mayoría de los casos se establece una relación mágica que no sólo gratifica al niño sino° también al adulto.

La niñera

Con respecto a una niñera, tienes que seleccionar a alguien tierna y agradable. Además, es fundamental tener referencias.

La guardería

En una guardería, los grupos de niños deben ser reducidos y deben estar divididos por edad. Cada grupo debe tener una maestra fija.

De vez en cuando°, es conveniente visitar el lugar de forma sorpresiva para poder observar cómo funciona.

¿Qué hago para no sentirme culpable?

Puedes empezar por comprender y aceptar las razones que te llevan a dejar a tu bebé en manos de otro. La educación de un hijo implica responsabilidad, no culpas.

Pero está todo el día con otra persona...

Hay momentos clave° en los que mamá o papá deben estar presentes. Por la mañana, cuando se despierta, y por la noche, cuando se va a dormir. Es importante darle cariño y prestarle atención y también aprovechar° los fines de semana para dedicárselos al niño.

¿Tengo que adaptarme a sus horarios o mi hijo tiene que adaptarse a los míos?

Si estás sujeto a un horario que no puedes modificar, de alguna manera el niño va a tener que seguir tu ritmo. Un nene° está acostumbrado a dormirse a las nueve de la noche; comparte° con su mamá el baño, la cena y los juegos°. Pero quizás su papá no llega a casa hasta después de las diez. Entonces el padre no ve nunca al hijo y el hijo no ve nunca al padre. Debes ser flexible y comprender que una hora con mamá y papá es mucho más importante que una hora de sueño°.

Adaptado de la revista digital *Papá y mamá* (Argentina)

---

stages
raising
los... the way things are nowadays
home
nursery / nanny
con... willing
but

De... Once in a while
key

take advantage of
little child
he shares
games
sleep

Desde su mundo

1. ¿Tiene Ud. o alguien que Ud. conoce algunos de los problemas que se discuten en este artículo? ¿Cuáles?
2. ¿Está Ud. de acuerdo con las soluciones que ofrece la autora? ¿Por qué?
3. Algunas madres prefieren quedarse en casa con sus hijos pequeños y no trabajar. ¿Qué piensa Ud. de esta idea?

Piense y escriba   ¿Para quién escribimos?

Antes de escribir, es muy importante tener claro para quiénes vamos a escribir. Por ejemplo, es muy distinto escribir una composición para un examen final que escribirle una carta a su novio(a).

Aquí le asignamos a Ud. un público que Ud. ya conoce: desea escribir un artículo breve (*brief*) sobre el tema general de las relaciones humanas. Lo va a publicar en alguna revista estudiantil de su universidad. ¡Sea imaginativo(a)! Haga lo siguiente:

1. Escoja (*Choose*) un tema que quiere presentarle a ese público. Por ejemplo, "mis amigos", "mis tres parientes favoritos", "una reunión de Acción de Gracias (*Thanksgiving*)", "mi vida sentimental", etc.
2. Genere (*Generate*) una lista de subtemas teniendo en cuenta (*keeping in mind*) lo que desea comunicarle a su público sobre el tema. De la lista generada, escoja tres. Por ejemplo, tres posibles subtemas para discutir el tema de "mis amigos" pueden ser:
   a. mi mejor amigo(a)
   b. otros amigos y amigas
   c. lo que nos gusta hacer juntos(as)

   Escriba aquí su tema: _____.

   Ahora, en *a* a *e* abajo, genere cinco subtemas en los que puede discutir el tema escogido:
   a. _____.
   b. _____.
   c. _____.
   d. _____.
   e. _____.

3. Escoja tres. Desarrolle (*Develop*) cada uno de los tres subtemas escogidos en un párrafo distinto (*separate*).
4. Escriba una introducción a los tres párrafos.
5. Resuma o concluya.

MUSEO THYSSEN-BORNEMISZA
PASEO DEL PRADO, 8. 28014 MADRID. TEL.(91) 420 39 44

Pepe Vega y su mundo

Teleinforme

Las tres escenas que siguen son fragmentos de una serie popular de la televisión española de los 1990, Una hija más, *en la que vemos las interacciones de la familia Sánchez: Demetrio y Ángeles, los padres; los hijos Júnior y Dani, y la empleada Nati.*

Preparación

Relaciones interpersonales.   Piense en las relaciones que Ud. tiene con algunos parientes y con otras personas. Conteste las siguientes preguntas para cada una de las relaciones interpersonales que aparecen en el esquema (*table*) presentado abajo:

Persona	1. ¿Cómo lo/la llama?	2. ¿Con qué gesto la saluda o se despide de ésta?
a. su madre o su padre		
b. su hermano(a)		
c. su abuelo(a)		
d. su mejor amigo(a)		
e. su profesor(a) de español		
f. el (la) director(a) del banco		

1. ¿Cómo llama Ud. a esta persona? ¿Por su nombre (como *Sandy*)? ¿Por un nombre familiar (como *Nana*)? ¿Por su título y apellido (como *Mrs. Kelly*)? ¿Por un título (como *Sir*)? etc.

2. Cuando Ud. saluda o se despide de esta persona, ¿qué hace Ud.? ¿La abraza (*hug*)? ¿Le da la mano (*shake hands*)? ¿Le da un beso (*kiss*)? ¿Le toca el brazo o el hombro? etc.

Comprensión

Saludos   0:00–1:41

Demetrio ha invitado a una vieja amiga de su pueblo, Blanca Peláez, a cenar en su casa. Ángeles ha invitado a Paco, el párroco (*parrish priest*) de su iglesia, a participar también en la cena de la familia. En esta parte vamos a ver cómo interaccionan los varios participantes de la escena.

A. Observaciones culturales

1. Vea el video *sin el sonido*. En la columna 1 del esquema, señale cómo se saludan las personas indicadas: ponga **B** si se dan un beso, **BB** si se dan dos besos, **M** si se dan la mano, **T** si se tocan el brazo, **TT** si se tocan los dos brazos o **N** si no hay un saludo de tipo físico.

2. Basándose en la manera en que se saludan, diga si Ud. cree que se conocen o no las personas indicadas. Ponga **sí** o **no** en la columna 2 del esquema.

Las personas	¿Cómo se saludan?	¿Se conocen?	¿Tú o Ud.?	¿Qué dicen?
MODELO:	M	no	tú	"Y **tú** el párroco"
Demetrio ↔ Paco				
a. Paco ↔ Ángeles				
b. Paco ↔ Dani				
c. Demetrio ↔ Blanca				
d. Ángeles ↔ Blanca				
e. Dani ↔ Blanca				
f. Blanca ↔ Dani				
g. Blanca ↔ Paco				
h. Paco ↔ Blanca				

3. Ahora vea el video *con el sonido* y observe quiénes se tratan de **tú** y quiénes de **Ud.** Indique sus observaciones en la columna 3 del esquema. En la columna 4, anote la frase en que oye la forma **tú** o **Ud.**

4. ¿Notó Ud. alguna interacción inesperada (*unexpected*)? Explique cuál y por qué.

CD-ROM
Go to **Video** for further pre-viewing, vocabulary, and structure practice on this clip.

Madres e hijos   1:43–3:15

En esta escena vamos a conocer a Júnior, el hijo mayor de Demetrio y de Ángeles, y a Dani, su hermano menor. Están en el garaje de la casa, donde Ángeles los encuentra y les recuerda que es hora de irse a la escuela. Note la interacción entre hermanos y también la de cada uno de los hijos con su madre.

B. ¿Quién dice qué?   Mire la escena e indique cuáles de los participantes se dicen lo siguiente: Júnior (**J**), Dani (**D**) o Ángeles (**A**).

MODELO: <u>D ↔ J</u> ¡Ayúdame a levantarme! / Pesas demasiado.

1. _____ Tengo paros cardíacos. / Tú estás loco, enano.
2. _____ ¡Eres un cerdo y un egoísta! / ¡Déjame en paz de una vez!
3. _____ Llegarás tarde al autobús del cole. Tendrás que ir a patitas.
4. _____ Necesito la casa para la reunión del viaje de fin de curso. / Ay, lo siento... es imposible.
5. _____ ¡Ya he citado a todos mis compañeros! / Bueno, pues anula la cita.
6. _____ Supongo que habrá más gente con casa entre tus compañeros... Vamos, digo yo. / Vale, un beso.

La abuela: madre y suegra   3:17–5:01

CD-ROM
You will also find this clip under **Video**.

Ha llegado la abuela a casa de los Sánchez. Aquí vemos a la abuela, que viene a confesarles un problema a Demetrio y a Ángeles.

C. ¿Verdadera o falsa?   Indique si las siguientes aseveraciones son verdaderas (**V**) o falsas (**F**). Si son falsas, corríjalas.

1. _____ Ángeles y Demetrio duermen cuando alguien llama a la puerta.
2. _____ La abuela es sonámbula, es decir, camina y habla mientras está dormida.
3. _____ La abuela tiene remordimientos porque recibe ilegalmente la pensión de su esposo.
4. _____ Demetrio sugiere que la abuela alegue (*alleges*) que está senil.
5. _____ Ángeles no quiere ayudar a la abuela.
6. _____ La abuela no quiere ser una carga (*burden*) para nadie.
7. _____ La abuela piensa venir a vivir con Ángeles y Demetrio.
8. _____ Ángeles y Demetrio piensan que es una idea estupenda.

Ampliación

Análisis de la familia.   Haga una de las siguientes comparaciones:

1. Escoja a dos parejas de la familia Sánchez, por ejemplo la de Júnior y Dani, o la de Demetrio y Dani. Describa la relación de cada pareja: ¿Cómo se tratan? ¿Qué diferencias hay en su manera de relacionarse? ¿Cómo explica Ud. las diferencias?
2. Escoja a dos personas de la familia Sánchez y compare su relación con la de alguna pareja parecida en su propia familia. Por ejemplo, la relación de Ángeles y Júnior con la de Ud. y su madre. ¿Hay diferencias en la manera de relacionarse? ¿Hay semejanzas? ¿Puede Ud. hacer alguna generalización comparando a la familia Sánchez con su familia?

LECCIÓN 2

Sistemas educativos

Dos estudiantes conversan frente a la biblioteca de la UNAM, en la ciudad de México.

Sistemas educativos

CD-ROM   STUDENT AUDIO

For preparation, do the **Ante todo** activities found on the CD-ROM.

Ayer fue el primer día para matricularse y Noemí, una chica de Guadalajara, México, fue a hablar con un consejero sobre su programa de estudios en la Universidad de California y le preguntó qué clases debía tomar.

CONSEJERO —Veo que su especialización es administración de empresas.

NOEMÍ —Bueno, no estoy segura, pero creo que sí. ¿Qué asignaturas tengo que tomar este semestre?

CONSEJERO —Lo mejor es tomar todos los requisitos generales primero.

NOEMÍ —Yo tomé matemáticas, biología, psicología y una clase de informática el semestre pasado.

CONSEJERO —Este semestre puede tomar algún curso electivo: arte o educación física, por ejemplo.

NOEMÍ —No sé. Necesito una clase de química y una de física, y no quiero tomar demasiadas unidades porque tengo una beca y necesito mantener un buen promedio.

Después de hablar con su consejero, Noemí almorzó con su amigo Steve en la cafetería de la universidad. Steve leyó el horario de clases de Noemí y lo encontró muy difícil.

STEVE —¿Vas a tomar física y química juntas? Por lo visto eres muy lista. Oye, ¿existen muchas diferencias entre el sistema universitario de México y el de aquí?

NOEMÍ —¡Ya lo creo! Por ejemplo, en mi país no tenemos cursos electivos. Tampoco existen los requisitos generales, porque los estudiantes los toman en la escuela secundaria.

STEVE —Entonces, ¿en la universidad, toman solamente las materias propias de sus respectivas carreras?

NOEMÍ —Sí, por eso cuando yo estaba en la escuela secundaria, tenía que estudiar muchísimo para sacar buenas notas.

STEVE —Pues las mías eran malísimas porque nunca estudiaba. Oye, ¿cuántos años deben estudiar Uds. en la universidad para obtener un título de ingeniero, por ejemplo?

NOEMÍ —Por lo regular, unos cinco años en la facultad de ingeniería. ¿Tú quieres ser ingeniero?

STEVE —A lo mejor... Un amigo mío, que es de Paraguay, dice que la asistencia no es obligatoria allí.

NOEMÍ —Bueno, en Paraguay, como en muchos otros países, hay estudiantes que no asisten a clases. Algunos viven lejos de la universidad o trabajan durante las horas de clases; otros simplemente prefieren estudiar por su cuenta. Solamente van a la universidad a tomar el examen de mitad de curso y el examen final.

STEVE —¡Qué buena idea! Ese sistema me gusta más que el nuestro.

NOEMÍ —Bueno... tiene sus ventajas, pero necesitas ser disciplinado. Oye, ¿vas a la conferencia de la Dra. Reyes?

STEVE   —Yo no sabía que había una conferencia. Nadie me lo dijo. ¿Dónde es?

NOEMÍ   —Es en el aula número cien, donde tenemos las reuniones del club de francés. Empieza a las ocho. ¿Por qué no vamos juntos?

STEVE   —Bueno, paso por ti a las siete y media, a más tardar. ¿Sigues viviendo en la residencia universitaria?

NOEMÍ   —Sí, pero esta vez tienes que ser puntual porque no podemos llegar tarde. La puntualidad es muy importante para mí. ¡Ah!, necesito tu libro de francés, ¿me lo puedes prestar?

STEVE   —Sí, te lo doy esta noche.

NOEMÍ   —Bueno, quedamos en que vienes a las siete y media.

Dígame

En parejas, lean estas aseveraciones basadas en los diálogos, y decidan si son verdaderas o no y por qué.

1. Noemí tuvo que hablar con un consejero antes de matricularse.
2. Noemí no sabe nada de computadoras.
3. Noemí no necesita ninguna clase.
4. Las notas son importantes para Noemí.
5. El sistema educativo de México es muy similar al de los Estados Unidos.
6. Los estudiantes paraguayos deben asistir a clase todos los días.
7. Steve prefiere el sistema educativo de los países hispanos.
8. Noemí quiere ir a la conferencia con Steve.
9. Noemí vive en un apartamento.
10. Noemí necesita el libro de Steve, pero él no se lo puede prestar.

Perspectivas socioculturales

INSTRUCTOR WEBSITE

Your instructor may assign the preconversational support activities found in **Perspectivas socioculturales.**

Noemí le comenta a Steve que hay diferencias entre el sistema de educación mexicano y el norteamericano. Haga lo siguiente:

a. Lea los temas de conversación que aparecen a continuación y escoja uno de ellos.
b. Durante unos cinco minutos, cambie opiniones (o converse) con dos compañeros sobre el tema seleccionado.
c. Participe con el resto de la clase en la discusión del tema cuando su profesor(a) se lo indique.

Temas de conversación

1. **La secundaria.** Durante la secundaria, ¿tomó Ud. requisitos generales que ya no tiene que tomar en la universidad?
2. **La universidad.** En un semestre, ¿puede matricularse solamente en cursos de su especialización? ¿Qué ventajas y qué desventajas presenta su situación?
3. **La carrera.** ¿Va a necesitar realizar estudios de postgrado (*graduate studies*) para ejercer (*practice*) la carrera que desea seguir hoy?

Vocabulario

Nombres

la administración de empresas
business administration

la asignatura, la materia subject (*in a school*)

la asistencia attendance

el aula, el salón de clase classroom

la beca scholarship

la carrera career, course of study

la conferencia lecture

el (la) consejero(a) advisor, counselor

el curso class, course of study

la educación física physical education

la escuela secundaria secondary school (*junior high school and high school*)

la especialización major

el examen de mitad (mediados) de curso, el examen parcial mid-term examination

la facultad school, college (*division within a university*)

el horario de clases class schedule

la informática, la computación computer science

el (la) ingeniero(a) engineer

la nota grade

el país country (*nation*)

el programa de estudios study program

el promedio grade point average

la química chemistry

el requisito requirement

la residencia universitaria dormitory

la reunión, la junta (*Mex.*) meeting

el título degree

la ventaja advantage

Verbos

asistir a to attend

existir to exist

mantener (*conj. like* **tener**) to maintain, to keep

matricularse to register

sacar to get (*a grade*)

tratar de to try to

Adjetivos

demasiados(as) too many

educativo(a) educational, related to education

juntos(as) together

listo(a) smart

malísimo(a) extremely bad

obligatorio(a) mandatory

propio(a) related, own

universitario(a) university, college

Otras palabras y expresiones

a más tardar at the latest

creo que sí (no) I (don't) think so

entre between

esta vez this time

llegar tarde (temprano) to be late (early)

lo mejor the best thing

muchísimo a lot, a great deal

pasar por (alguien) to pick (someone) up

por ejemplo for example

por lo regular as a rule

por lo visto apparently

por su cuenta on their own

ser puntual to be punctual

¡Ya lo creo! I'll say!

Ampliación

Algunas facultades

facultad de arquitectura   school of architecture

facultad de ciencias económicas (comerciales)   school of business administration

facultad de derecho   law school

facultad de educación   school of education

facultad de filosofía y letras   school of humanities

facultad de ingeniería   school of engineering

facultad de medicina   medical school

facultad de odontología   dental school

Algunas profesiones

el (la) abogado(a)   lawyer

el (la) analista de sistemas   systems analyst

el (la) bibliotecario(a)   librarian

el (la) contador(a) público(a)   certified public accountant

el (la) dentista   dentist

el (la) enfermero(a)   nurse

el (la) farmacéutico(a)   pharmacist

el (la) maestro(a)   teacher

el (la) médico(a)   medical doctor

el (la) programador(a)   programmer

el (la) psicólogo(a)   psychologist

el (la) trabajador(a) social   social worker

el (la) veterinario(a)   veterinarian

Otras palabras y expresiones relacionadas con el tema

la escuela primaria (elemental)   grade school, elementary school

la escuela tecnológica   technical school

ingresar en   to enter (*e.g., a university*)

la matrícula   tuition

el profesorado   faculty

el (la) rector(a)   president (*of a university*)

la solicitud   application

la universidad estatal   state university

la universidad privada   private university

el (la) universitario(a)   college student

CD-ROM
Go to **Vocabulario** for additional vocabulary practice.

Hablando de todo un poco

Preparación   **Complete lo siguiente, usando el vocabulario de la Lección 2.**

1. La _____ de Marcos es administración de _____, pero una de sus _____ favoritas es la _____, porque le gusta trabajar con computadoras.

2. Tatiana habló con su _____ sobre su programa de _____. Tiene que tomar química, porque es un _____.

3. Fernando tiene el _____ de clases porque tiene que _____ para el semestre próximo mañana a más _____.

4. Celia terminó la _____ secundaria el año pasado con un _____ de 3,5. Ahora va a _____ a la universidad y va a vivir en la residencia _____.

5. Sergio no sacó muy buenas _____ el semestre pasado porque no estudió mucho. Este semestre piensa ser puntual y no llegar _____ a clase. No va a asistir a una universidad _____ porque no tiene mucho dinero y perdió la _____. Piensa ingresar en una universidad _____.

6. Marina quiere estudiar por su _____, pero la _____ a clase es obligatoria.

7. Los cuatro hermanos tienen ideas muy diferentes. Armando quiere ser dentista, de modo que va a asistir a la facultad de _____. Carlos quiere ser maestro en una escuela _____, de modo que va a asistir a la facultad de _____. Daniel piensa asistir a la facultad de filosofía y _____ y Esteban piensa ingresar en la facultad de _____ porque quiere ser abogado.

8. El profesor Vega está en el _____ de clase, escribiendo en la pizarra. Por lo _____ es muy temprano, porque no hay ningún estudiante en el _____. Por lo _____ los estudiantes empiezan a llegar a las ocho.

9. Eva va a ingresar en la facultad de ciencias _____ porque quiere ser _____ pública. Su papá es analista de _____ y su mamá es _____ social.

10. Tengo que estudiar _____ porque mañana tengo un examen de _____ de curso, pero primero tengo que ir a mi clase de educación _____.

En grupos de tres o cuatro hagan lo siguiente.

A. **Su programa de estudio.**   Digan las materias que están tomando, los requisitos que ya tomaron, los que necesitan y los cursos electivos que piensan tomar.

B. **La carrera.**   Describan la carrera que piensan seguir: la facultad o el departamento en que deben seguirla, si van a trabajar en el campo (*field*) mientras estudian, si asisten a conferencias o reuniones sobre la misma, etc.

C. **Las profesiones.**   Hablen sobre las profesiones de algunos de sus parientes, amigos y de otras personas que Uds. conocen.

Palabras problemáticas

A. **Tiempo, vez** y **hora** como equivalentes de *time*

- **Tiempo** equivale a *time* cuando nos referimos al período o duración de algo.

  Por lo visto ella no quiere estar aquí mucho **tiempo.**

- **Vez** equivale a *time* cuando se habla de series.

  Por lo regular voy a clase dos **veces** por semana.

- **Hora** equivale a *time* cuando se habla de un momento del día o de una actividad específica.

  Es **hora** de cenar.
  El rector no puede ir a las ocho porque a esa **hora** está ocupado.

B. **Estar de acuerdo, ponerse de acuerdo** y **quedar en**

- **Estar de acuerdo** significa **ser de la misma opinión.**

    El profesorado no **está de acuerdo** con lo que dice la Dra. Reyes.

- **Ponerse de acuerdo** equivale a *to come to an understanding.*

    Los dos hablaban a la vez, y no podían **ponerse de acuerdo.**

- **Quedar en** significa *to agree to do something.*

    Quedamos en que esta vez vienes a las siete.

Práctica

Entreviste a un(a) compañero(a) usando las siguientes preguntas.

1. ¿A qué hora empiezas a estudiar?
2. ¿Tienes tiempo para ir a una conferencia hoy?
3. ¿Cuántas veces por semana vas a la biblioteca?
4. A la hora del almuerzo, ¿estás en la universidad o en tu casa?
5. ¿Tú siempre estás de acuerdo con tus profesores?
6. ¿Tú quedaste en verte con algún compañero de clase este fin de semana?

Your instructor may carry out the **¡Ahora escuche!** listening activity found in the **Answers to Text Exercises.** **¡Ahora escuche!** Se leerá dos veces una breve narración sobre el problema de Roberto, un muchacho chileno que estudia en la Universidad de Tejas. Se harán aseveraciones sobre la narración. En una hoja (*sheet*) escriba los números de uno a diez e indique si cada aseveración es verdadera (V) o falsa (F).

ARTE MEXICANO

ARTESANIA FINA
Visítanos en Cuauhtémoc No. 37
Zihuatanejo, Gro. México

El mundo hispánico

México lindo y querido

Noemí

Así comienza una canción popular en la que se muestra el cariño que sentimos los mexicanos por nuestra tierra°. México, uno de los países más grandes del mundo hispano, es una tierra de contrastes naturales. Hay regiones de altas montañas, de desiertos, de valles fértiles y de selvas tropicales.

land

Hoy en día°, la economía de México es una de las más pujantes° del mundo hispano. Entre sus fuentes de riqueza están la exportación de petróleo°, de plata, de oro y de cobre. Otra fuente de ingreso es el turismo: sus hermosas playas —Cancún, Puerto Vallarta y Acapulco, entre otras— son visitadas por millones de turistas, principalmente norteamericanos.

Hoy... Nowadays
vigorous
oil

México es famoso también por su diversidad social, por su artesanía y por sus ruinas arqueológicas. Son muy conocidas las ruinas de Teotihuacán, cerca de la Ciudad de México, donde encontramos las pirámides del Sol y de la Luna. En la península de Yucatán están las ruinas mayas de Chichén Itzá y las de Tulum. Sociedades indígenas como la maya conservan hoy su lengua y sus tradiciones.

STUDENT WEBSITE
Go to **El mundo hispánico** for prereading and vocabulary activities.

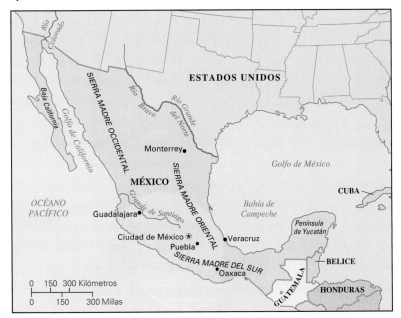

La capital del país, la Ciudad de México, es posiblemente la más poblada del mundo. Allí viven unos 24 millones de personas. En el centro, cerca del Zócalo o plaza principal, coexisten testimonios arquitectónicos de la capital prehispánica azteca con edificios coloniales monumentales como la Catedral Metropolitana y el Palacio Nacional de México. Los mariachis son conocidos en todo el mundo hispano y, para muchos, ellos son la representación de México. En la pintura se destacan° **se**... stand out Diego Rivera, Clemente Orozco y Alfaro Siqueiros. En la literatura tenemos escritores como Carlos Fuentes, Octavio Paz y Mariano Azuela que dan a conocer nuestra historia, y nuestras costumbres y tradiciones. En la página anterior tienen un mapa de mi México. Espero que pronto lo visiten.

Sobre México

En parejas túrnense para contestar las siguientes preguntas.

1. ¿Cuáles son los límites de México al norte, al sur, al este y al oeste?
2. ¿Por qué es México una tierra de contrastes naturales?
3. ¿Qué exporta México?
4. ¿Qué sabe Ud. del turismo en México?
5. ¿Dónde están las pirámides del Sol y de la Luna?
6. ¿Qué ruinas famosas hay en Yucatán?
7. ¿Qué conservan los grupos indígenas de México?
8. ¿Cuál es la población de la Ciudad de México?
9. ¿Qué grupos musicales son representativos de México?
10. ¿Quiénes son Carlos Fuentes, Octavio Paz y Mariano Azuela?

Hablemos de su país

INSTRUCTOR WEBSITE
STUDENT WEBSITE
Your instructor may assign the preconversational activities in Hablemos... (under **Hablemos de su país**). Go to **Hablemos de su país** (under ...**y escribamos**) for postconversational web search and writing activities.

Noemí nos dice que México es muy conocido por sus mariachis. Reúnase con otro(a) compañero(a) y conteste lo siguiente: ¿Qué géneros (*genres*) de música y qué cantantes de los Estados Unidos son famosos en el mundo?

Luego cada pareja compartirá las respuestas con toda la clase. ¿Hay diferencias de opinión?

Una tarjeta postal

Imagínese que Ud. y un(a) compañero(a) están viajando por México. Envíenles una tarjeta postal a sus compañeros de clase, describiendo sus impresiones.

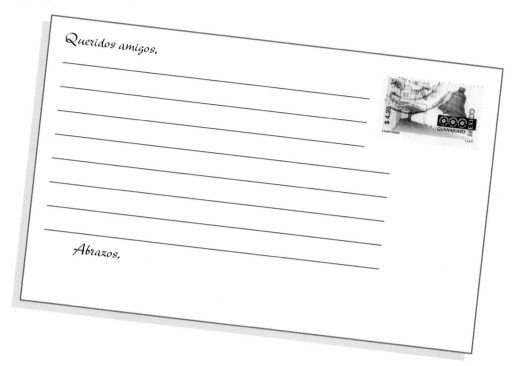

Queridos amigos,

Abrazos,

Estructuras gramaticales

1 Usos de los verbos **ser** y **estar**

○ Both **ser** and **estar** correspond to the English verb *to be*, but they are *not* interchangeable.

A Usos del verbo *ser*[1]

○ **Ser** identifies people, places, or things.

—¿Quién **es** ese muchacho?   "Who is that young man?"
—**Es** José Luis Vargas Peña.   "It's José Luis Vargas Peña."

—¿Cuáles **son** tus ciudades favoritas?   "What are your favorite cities?"
—Guadalajara y Cancún.   "Guadalajara and Cancún."

---

[1] The use of **ser** in the passive voice will be studied in **Lección 10**.

—¿Qué **es** esto?   *"What is this?"*
—**Es** mi programa de estudios.   *"It's my study program."*

- With adjectives, it describes essential qualities such as color, size, shape, nationality, religion, and profession or trade.

—¿Cómo **es** tu casa nueva?   *"What is your new house like?"*
—**Es** grande y muy cómoda.   *"It's big and very comfortable."*

—Juan y Eva **son** farmacéuticos, ¿no?   *"Juan and Eva are pharmacists, aren't they?"*
—No, él **es** arquitecto y ella **es** ingeniera.   *"No, he's an architect and she's an engineer."*

—¿**Son** colombianos?   *"Are they Colombian?"*
—Creo que sí.   *"I think so."*

- With the preposition **de**, it indicates origin, possession, relationship, and the material that things are made of.

—¿De dónde **es** Juan?   *"Where is Juan from?"*
—**Es** de Quito.   *"He is from Quito."*

—¿Roberto **es** el hermano de Daniel?   *"Is Roberto Daniel's brother?"*
—No, **es** su primo.   *"No, he is his cousin."*

—¿De quién **es** el reloj?   *"Whose watch is this?"*
—**Es** de la mamá de Antonio.   *"It's Antonio's mother's."*
—¿**Es** de oro?   *"Is it (made) of gold?"*
—No, **es** de plata.   *"No, it's (made) of silver."*

- It is used to express the time and the date.

—¿Qué hora **es**?   *"What time is it?"*
—**Son** las diez y media.   *"It's ten-thirty."*

—¿Qué fecha **es** hoy?   *"What's the date today?"*
—Hoy **es** el cuatro de abril.   *"Today is April fourth."*

- It is used in impersonal expressions.

—¿Tenemos la reunión hoy?   *"Shall we have the meeting today?"*
—No, **es mejor** tenerla mañana.   *"No, it's better to have it tomorrow."*

—¿**Es necesario** asistir a clase?   *"Is it necessary to attend class?"*
—¡Ya lo creo!   *"I'll say!"*

- With the preposition **para**, it indicates for whom or what something is destined.

—¿Para quién **son** estos regalos?   *"Whom are these gifts for?"*
—**Son** para ti.   *"They're for you."*

—¿Para qué **es** este libro?   *"What is this book for?"*
—**Es** para aprender inglés.   *"It's for learning English."*

○ It is used to indicate where an event is taking place, when *to be* is the equivalent of *to take place*.

—¿Dónde **es** la conferencia?　　*"Where does the lecture take place?"*
—**Es** en el aula 222.　　　　　*"It's in (class)room 222."*

—¿Dónde **es** la fiesta?　　　　*"Where's the party?"*
—**Es** en mi casa.　　　　　　　*"It's at my house."*

B Usos del verbo *estar*

○ **Estar** is used to indicate location of a person, place, or thing.

—¿Dónde **está** tu hermano?　　*"Where is your brother?"*
—**Está** en el banco.　　　　　　*"He's at the bank."*

○ With adjectives, it indicates a current condition or state.

—¿Cómo **está** Antonia hoy?　　　*"How's Antonia today?"*
—**Está** mucho mejor, pero **está**　*"She's much better, but she's very tired."*
muy cansada.

○ With personal reactions, it describes what is perceived through the senses—that is, how a person or thing seems, looks, tastes, or feels.

—¿Te gusta la sopa?　　　　　　*"Do you like the soup?"*
—¡Sí, **está** muy rica!　　　　　*"Yes, it's very tasty!"*

○ With the past participle, it indicates the state or condition resulting from a previous action. In this case, the past participle is used as an adjective and agrees with the subject in gender and number.

—¿No puedes leer las cartas?　　　*"Can't you read the letters?"*
—No, **están** escritas en italiano.　*"No, they're written in Italian."*

○ *To be alive* or *to be dead* are considered states or conditions that are expressed using **estar**.

—¿**Está** vivo?　　　　　　　　*"Is he alive?"*
—No, **está** muerto.　　　　　　*"No, he is dead."*

○ It is used with the present participle forms **-ando** and **-iendo** in the progressive tenses.

—¿Qué **estás haciendo**?　　　　*"What are you doing?"*
—**Estoy haciendo** la tarea.　　　*"I'm doing the homework."*

○ It is also used in many idiomatic expressions:

1. **estar de acuerdo**　*to agree*

Ella dice que necesito un título, pero yo no **estoy de acuerdo**.

2. **estar de buen (mal) humor**　*to be in a good (bad) mood*

Hoy **estoy de buen humor** porque no hay clases.

3. **estar de vacaciones**   *to be on vacation*

Mis padres **están de vacaciones** en Acapulco.

4. **estar en cama**   *to be sick in bed*

Mi hermano **está en cama**. Tiene fiebre.

5. **estar de viaje**   *to be (away) on a trip*

Mis suegros **están de viaje** por Sudamérica.

6. **estar de vuelta**   *to be back*

Los chicos van a tratar de **estar de vuelta** esta noche.

C Adjetivos que cambian de significado

○ Some adjectives change meaning depending on whether they are used with **ser** or **estar**. Here are some of them:

	With ser	*With* estar
aburrido(a)	*boring*	*bored*
verde	*green (color)*	*green (not ripe)*
malo(a)	*bad*	*sick*
listo(a)	*smart, clever*	*ready*

Los estudiantes **están aburridos**. Eso es porque el profesor **es** muy **aburrido**.

Estas manzanas no **están verdes**. **Son** manzanas **verdes**.

Rosa no puede ir a la reunión porque todavía **está mala**. Tiene mucha fiebre.

No quiero ir a ver a ese médico porque dicen que **es** muy **malo**.

¿Estás lista? Ya son las cuatro.

Mi hijo **es** muy **listo**. Es el más inteligente de la clase.

○ Notice that, used with **ser**, these adjectives express an essential quality or a permanent condition. Used with **estar** they express a state or a current, transitory condition.

Práctica

CD-ROM
Go to **Estructuras gramaticales** for additional practice.

A. Forme oraciones con las siguientes palabras o frases usando **ser** o **estar** según corresponda. Añada (*Add*) todos los elementos necesarios, siguiendo el modelo.

MODELO: mesa / metal
          La mesa es de metal.

1. la clase de biología / a las ocho
2. vestido / rayón
3. Rodolfo / muy bajo
4. Elsa / de mal humor
5. mochila / en la residencia universitaria
6. mi hermana / ingeniera
7. mejor / asistir a clase
8. Elena / de viaje

9. profesor / corrigiendo los exámenes
10. quién / esa chica
11. la estudiante / de Yucatán
12. de acuerdo / con mis padres
13. concierto / mañana
14. mañana / ocho de diciembre
15. pobre gato / muerto
16. mis padres / de vuelta
17. Marta / inteligente
18. dónde / la reunión
19. puertas / abiertas
20. Teresa / muy joven

B. Complete el siguiente párrafo usando las formas correctas del presente de **ser** o **estar**, según corresponda.

_____ las cinco de la tarde y Alicia y Fernando _____ conversando en un café de la Alameda. Alicia _____ una muchacha inteligente y simpática. _____ ingeniera y ahora _____ trabajando para una compañía norteamericana. Fernando _____ moreno, alto y muy guapo. Los chicos _____ muy buenos amigos. Alicia _____ argentina y Fernando _____ de Venezuela, pero ahora los dos _____ viviendo en México.

Hoy Alicia _____ de muy buen humor porque su familia _____ de vuelta de un viaje a España, y dentro de unos días comienzan sus vacaciones. Escuchemos lo que _____ diciendo.

FERNANDO —Oye, hoy _____ más bonita que nunca. Esta noche sales con Nicolás, ¿verdad?

ALICIA —¡Ay, no! El pobre _____ muy aburrido y además no _____ muy listo.

FERNANDO —Pero, ¿no _____ tu novio?

ALICIA —¿_____ loco? Para mí lo más importante en un hombre _____ la inteligencia, y él no tiene ninguna.

FERNANDO —¡Qué mala _____ (tú)! Siempre te _____ riendo del pobre chico.

ALICIA —Yo no _____ mala; _____ sincera. Oye, ¿dónde _____ la fiesta de Nora?

FERNANDO —_____ en el hotel Veracruz. ¿Vamos juntos? Paso por ti a las ocho.

ALICIA —¡Buena idea! A las ocho en punto _____ lista.

C. Entreviste a un(a) compañero(a) usando las siguientes preguntas.

1. ¿Cómo estás? ¿Estás de mal humor a veces?
2. ¿Cuándo es tu cumpleaños?
3. ¿A qué horas son tus clases?
4. ¿Adónde vas cuando estás de vacaciones?
5. ¿Cómo son tus padres? ¿De dónde son?
6. ¿Qué crees que está haciendo tu padre (madre) en este momento?
7. ¿A qué hora tienes que estar de vuelta en tu casa hoy?
8. ¿La ventana de tu cuarto está abierta o cerrada?

D. En parejas, y teniendo en cuenta los usos de **ser** y **estar**, preparen cinco preguntas para hacérselas a su profesor(a).

2 Adjetivos y pronombres posesivos

A Adjetivos posesivos

○ The forms of the possessive adjectives are as follows:

Singular	Plural	
mi	mis	*my*
tu	tus	*your* (familiar)
su	sus	*your* (formal), *his, her, its*
nuestro(a)	nuestros(as)	*our*
vuestro(a)	vuestros(as)	*your* (familiar)
su	sus	*your* (formal), *their*

○ Possessive adjectives always precede the nouns they introduce. They agree in number and gender with the nouns they modify, not with the possessor(s).

Yo tengo dos hermanas.   **Mis** hermanas viven en Veracruz con mis padres.

Ellas tienen un amigo.   **Su** amigo es de Guadalajara.

○ **Nuestro** and **vuestro** are the only possessive adjectives that have feminine endings. The others have the same endings for both genders.

nuestro profesor   **mi** profesor
nuestra profesora   **mi** profesora
Nosotros tenemos una casa.   **Nuestra** casa está en la calle Quinta.

○ In Spanish, unlike in English, a possessive adjective must be repeated before each noun it modifies.

Mi madre y **mi** padre son de Yucatán.   *My mother and father are from Yucatán.*

○ Since **su** and **sus** have several meanings, the forms **de él, de ella, de Ud., de Uds., de ellas,** and **de ellos** may be substituted for **su** or **sus** for clarification.

his father   { **su padre**
                          { **el padre de él**

Práctica

CD-ROM
Go to **Estructuras gramaticales** for additional practice.

A. En parejas, lean los siguientes diálogos usando los adjetivos posesivos correspondientes.

1. —¿De dónde son _____ profesores, Paco?
   —_____ profesores son de San Miguel de Allende.

2. —¿Dónde viven Uds.?
   —_____ casa queda en la calle Olmos. ¿En qué calle queda _____ casa, señora?
   —_____ casa queda en la avenida Magnolia.

3. —Nosotros no tenemos _____ libros. ¿Tú sabes dónde están?
    —Sí, están en _____ escritorio, Pedro.

B. Entreviste a un(a) compañero(a) usando las siguientes preguntas.

1. ¿Sabes mi nombre? (Si la respuesta es negativa, dé su nombre.)
2. ¿Cuál es tu materia favorita?
3. ¿Cuál es tu promedio?
4. ¿Dónde vive tu mejor amigo(a)?
5. ¿Conoces a la familia de él (de ella)?
6. ¿Cuáles son las actividades preferidas de Uds.?

B Pronombres posesivos

○ The forms of the possessive pronouns are as follows:

Masculine		Feminine		
Singular	*Plural*	*Singular*	*Plural*	
mío	míos	mía	mías	*mine*
tuyo	tuyos	tuya	tuyas	*yours* (familiar)
suyo	suyos	suya	suyas	*his, hers, yours* (formal)
nuestro	nuestros	nuestra	nuestras	*ours*
vuestro	vuestros	vuestra	vuestras	*yours* (**vosotros** form)
suyo	suyos	suya	suyas	*theirs, yours* (formal)

(el) ... (los) ... (la) ... (las)

○ Possessive pronouns agree in gender and number with the nouns they replace, that is, with the thing possessed, and they are generally preceded by a definite article.

—No encuentro mis libros. "*I can't find my books.*"
—Si quieres, puedes usar **los míos.** "*If you want to, you may use mine.*"

—Éstas son mis plumas. "*These are my pens. Where are yours?*"
  ¿Dónde están **las suyas**?
—**Las nuestras** están en la mesa. "*Ours are on the table.*"

—Mis padres son de México. "*My parents are from Mexico.*"
—**Los míos** también. "*Mine are too.*"

○ Since the third-person forms of the possessive (**el suyo, la suya, los suyos, las suyas**) may be ambiguous, they are often replaced by the following:

el de		Ud.
la de		él
los de		ella
las de		Uds.
		ellos
		ellas

—¿De quién es este diccionario?
—Es el suyo.
—¡Ah! Es el diccionario **de ellas.** (*clarified*)
—Sí, es **el de ellas.**

○ After the verb **ser**, the article is usually omitted if one merely wants to express possession.

—¿De quién son estos libros? *"Whose books are these?"*
—Son **míos.**   *"They are mine."*

○ The definite article is used with the possessive pronoun after **ser** to express *the one that belongs to* (*me, you, him, etc.*).

—Estos libros son **los míos.** *"These books are mine (the ones that belong*
 ¿Cuáles son **los tuyos?**   *to me). Which ones are yours (the ones*
           that belong to you)?"

—Los libros que están sobre *"The books that are on the table are mine*
 la mesa son **los míos.**   *(the ones that belong to me)."*

CD-ROM
Go to **Estructuras gramaticales** for additional practice.

Práctica

A. En parejas, lean los siguientes diálogos. Escojan el pronombre posesivo que corresponda para completar cada uno.

el mío	el tuyo	la suya	la nuestra
las mías	las tuyas	las suyas	los nuestros

1. —La casa de los García está en la calle Paz. ¿Dónde está la de Uds.?
 —_____ está en la calle 25 de Mayo.

2. —Marta está muy contenta con su profesora.
 —¿Sí? Alberto no está muy contento con _____.

3. —Mi horario de clases está aquí. ¿Dónde está _____, Eva?
 —_____ está en mi casa.

4. —Mis hijas están en casa. ¿Dónde están las de Marisol?
 —_____ están en casa también.

5. —¿Cuántas cartas hay?
 —Hay cuatro cartas, dos para ti y dos para mí. Yo tengo _____ y _____ están en tu cuarto.

6. —Estos vestidos son de Oaxaca. ¿De dónde son los vestidos de Uds.?
 —_____ son de Puebla.

B. Entreviste a un(a) compañero(a), usando las siguientes preguntas.

1. Mi casa queda en la calle... ¿Dónde queda la tuya?
2. Mi padre es de... ¿De dónde es el tuyo?
3. Mis profesores son muy buenos. ¿Cómo son los tuyos?

4. Nuestros amigos son de México. ¿De dónde son los amigos de Uds.?

5. Mi amiga tiene todos los libros que necesita. ¿Tu amiga tiene los de ella?

3 Pronombres de complementos directo e indirecto usados juntos

A Usos y posición

- When a direct and an indirect object pronoun are used together, the indirect object pronoun always precedes the direct object pronoun.

  I.O. D.O.

  Ella **me los** compra.

- The indirect object pronouns **le** and **les** change to **se** when used with the direct object pronouns **lo, los, la,** and **las.**

  D.O.   I.O.

  Le digo la verdad [a mi padre].   ~~Le~~   **la** digo.

                                                Se   **la** digo.

  D.O.   I.O.

  Les leo el poema [a los niños].   ~~Les~~   **lo** leo.

                                                Se   **lo** leo.

atención   In the preceding examples, the meaning of **se** may be ambiguous, since it may refer to **Ud., él, ella, Uds., ellos,** or **ellas.** The following prepositional phrases may be added for clarification.

Ella **se** los compra
$\begin{cases} \text{a Ud.} \\ \text{a él.} \\ \text{a ella.} \\ \text{a Uds.} \\ \text{a ellos.} \\ \text{a ellas.} \\ \text{a Roberto.} \\ \text{a los niños.} \end{cases}$

- When two object pronouns are used together, the following combinations are possible.

| me $\begin{cases} \text{lo, la,} \\ \text{los, las} \end{cases}$ | te $\begin{cases} \text{lo, la,} \\ \text{los, las} \end{cases}$ | se $\begin{cases} \text{lo, la,} \\ \text{los, las} \end{cases}$ | nos $\begin{cases} \text{lo, la,} \\ \text{los, las} \end{cases}$ |

- Both object pronouns must always appear together, either *before* the conjugated verb or *after* the infinitive or the present participle. In the latter case, they are always attached to the infinitive or the present participle and a written accent mark must be added on the stressed syllable.

—¿Quién te trajo los exámenes?   *"Who brought you the tests?"*
—**Me los** trajo Alfredo.   *"Alfredo brought them to me."*

—¿A quién quieres regalarle ese libro?   *"To whom do you want to give that book?"*
—Quiero regalár**selo** a Diego.   *"I want to give it to Diego."*
—¿Por qué **se lo** quieres regalar a él?   *"Why do you want to give it to him?"*
—Porque es su cumpleaños.   *"Because it is his birthday."*

—¿No le vas a escribir la carta   *"Aren't you going to write the letter to*
  a Sergio?   *Sergio?"*
—Estoy escribiéndo**sela.**   *"I'm writing it to him."*

CD-ROM
Go to **Estructuras gramati-cales** for additional practice.

Práctica

A. Felipe siempre le hace muchas promesas a todo el mundo, pero no cumple (*doesn't keep*) ninguna. Complete Ud. lo siguiente diciendo todo lo que probablemente no va a hacer.

MODELO: A Juan le promete mandarle un diccionario.
          No se lo va a mandar.

1. A Eva le promete comprarle unos zapatos.
2. A mí me promete darme unos cuadernos.
3. A Uds. les promete traerles un reloj de pared.
4. A nosotros nos promete traernos una cámara fotográfica.
5. A ti te promete enviarte un libro de poemas.
6. A mis primas les promete regalarles unas plumas.
7. A Roberto le promete mandarle unas revistas.
8. A Teresa y a Carmen les promete traerles unos libros.

B. ¿Qué dicen Ud. y las siguientes personas en cada una de las siguientes circunstancias? Complete lo siguiente usando pronombres de complementos directo e indirecto.

MODELO: Mi mamá y yo estamos en una librería y yo veo un libro que me gusta. Mi mamá _____.
          Mi mamá me lo compra.

1. Yo compro un vestido para regalárselo a mi mamá y no me gusta envolver regalos. La empleada _____.
2. Mi mejor amiga quiere comprar algo y no tiene el dinero que necesita. Yo _____.
3. No tenemos tiempo para terminar los exámenes, pero la profesora dice que tenemos que entregarlos. Nosotros _____.
4. Yo tengo una mochila que no uso. Tú la necesitas. Yo _____.
5. Mi compañero(a) de cuarto y yo necesitamos unos libros que están en la casa de mi amiga. La llamamos por teléfono a su casa. Mi amiga _____.

6. Yo estoy en una tienda con mi mejor amiga y a ella le gusta una blusa que hay allí. Es su cumpleaños. Yo _____.

C. Imagínese que Ud. y un(a) compañero(a) de cuarto van a irse de vacaciones y necesitan la ayuda de varias personas durante su ausencia. Indique quién va a hacer qué. Use los pronombres de complementos directo e indirecto.

MODELO: ¿Quién va a darle la comida al gato?
Se la va a dar mi mamá.
(o: *Mi mamá va a dársela.*)

1. ¿Quién va a limpiarles el apartamento?
2. ¿Quién va a cuidarle las plantas a Ud.?
3. ¿Quién va a recogerles el correo?
4. ¿Quién va a darle la comida al perro?
5. ¿Quién me va a abrir la puerta a mí si yo quiero dormir en el cuarto de Uds.?

B Usos especiales

○ With the verbs **decir, pedir, saber, preguntar,** and **prometer,** the direct object pronoun **lo** is used with the indirect object pronoun to complete the idea of the sentence when a direct object noun is not present. Note how this is implied rather than stated in the English examples that follow.

—Oye, el libro es malísimo.	*"Listen, the book is very bad."*
—**¿Se lo** digo a Roberto?	*"Shall I tell (it to) Roberto?"*
—No, ya **lo** sabe.	*"No, he already knows (it)."*
—Yo no tengo dinero para ir al cine.	*"I don't have (any) money to go to the movies."*
—¿Por qué no **se lo** pides **a tu papá**?	*"Why don't you ask your dad (for it)?"*
—Buena idea. ¿Sabes si Julio viene con nosotros?	*"Good idea. Do you know if Julio is coming with us?"*
—No, pero puedo preguntár**selo a él.**	*"No, but I can ask him (that)."*

Práctica

CD-ROM
Go to **Estructuras gramaticales** for additional practice.

Entreviste a un(a) compañero(a), usando las siguientes preguntas.

1. Si no entiendes algo de gramática, ¿a quién se lo preguntas?
2. Si necesitas dinero para comprar libros, ¿a quién se lo pides?
3. ¿Prometes ayudarme con la tarea de español?
4. Si vas a tener una fiesta en tu casa, ¿se lo dices a todos tus amigos?
5. Yo necesito dinero para matricularme; ¿a quién puedo pedírselo?

4 Usos y omisiones de los artículos definidos e indefinidos

A Usos y omisiones del artículo definido

○ The definite article is used more frequently in Spanish than it is in English.

3. ¿De qué nacionalidad es?   (americano)
4. ¿Es republicano?   (no / demócrata / fanático)
5. ¿De qué religión es?   (católico)
6. ¿Qué profesión tiene tu hermana?   (trabajar / bibliotecaria)
7. ¿Qué quieres beber?   (media / botella / vino)
8. ¿Cuánto cuesta el vino aquí?   (cien / pesos)
9. ¿Quieres pedir alguna otra cosa?   (Sí / otro / plato de sopa)
10. Oye, ¿dónde está tu sombrero?   (no usar / sombrero)

B. En parejas, preparen ocho preguntas para hacérselas a su profesor(a). Recuerden los usos y omisiones de los artículos definidos e indefinidos.

Pregúntenle sobre lo siguiente:

1. sus ideas sobre la educación
2. lo que piensa hacer el verano próximo
3. los días que trabaja
4. la hora en que viene a trabajar
5. el color de sus ojos
6. si es americano(a) o no
7. su afiliación política
8. su religión

5   El pretérito

A   El pasado en español

○ There are two simple past tenses in Spanish: the preterit and the imperfect. Each tense expresses a distinct way of viewing a past action. The preterit narrates in the past and refers to a completed action in the past. The imperfect describes in the past; it also refers to a customary, repeated, or continued action in the past, without indicating the beginning or the end of the action.

B   Formas de los pretéritos regulares

○ The preterit of regular verbs is formed as follows.

-ar *verbs*	-er *and* -ir *verbs*	
hablar	*comer*	*vivir*
hablé	comí	viví
hablaste	comiste	viviste
habló	comió	vivió
hablamos	comimos	vivimos
hablasteis	comisteis	vivisteis
hablaron	comieron	vivieron

○ Note that the endings for **-er** and **-ir** verbs are the same.

○ Verbs of the **-ar** and **-er** groups that are stem-changing in the present indicative are regular in the preterit.

C Usos del pretérito

○ The preterit is used to refer to actions or states that the speaker views as completed in the past.

—¿**Compraste** algo ayer?   *"Did you buy anything yesterday?"*
—Sí, **compré** unas blusas.   *"Yes, I bought some blouses."*

—¿A qué hora **volviste** a casa?   *"At what time did you return home?"*
—**Volví** a las dos.   *"I returned at two."*

○ It is also used to sum up a past action or a physical or mental condition or state in the past that is viewed as completed.

—¿Por qué no **asististe** a las clases ayer?   *"Why didn't you attend classes yesterday?"*
—Porque me **dolió** la cabeza todo el día.   *"Because my head ached all day long."*

—¿Es verdad que Daniel viene la   *"Is it true that Daniel is coming next*
   semana próxima?   *week?"*
—Sí. Nos **alegramos** mucho   *"Yes. We were very happy when we got the*
   cuando **recibimos** la noticia.   *news."*

Práctica

CD-ROM
Go to **Estructuras gramaticales** for additional practice.

A. Diga Ud. lo que pasó ayer.

Ayer yo _____ en la biblioteca hasta las tres. Después _____ a casa y _____ una ensalada y _____ un vaso de leche. Mi compañera de cuarto y yo _____ televisión y después ella _____ por teléfono a sus padres y yo _____ unas cartas. Por lo general yo preparo la cena, pero anoche la _____ Gloria porque por fin _____ a cocinar. Después de cenar nos _____ unos amigos. Gloria _____ con ellos hasta muy tarde, porque a ellos les encanta conversar. Yo _____ a la biblioteca para seguir estudiando.

B. Converse con un(a) compañero(a). Háganse preguntas sobre lo que hicieron (*what you did*) ayer, anteayer y la semana pasada usando los verbos de la lista.

trabajar	aprender	salir	escribir
estudiar	volver	ver	comer
visitar	lavar	recibir	asistir

D Verbos irregulares en el pretérito

○ The verbs **ser**, **ir**, and **dar** are irregular in the preterit.

ser	*ir*	*dar*
fui	fui	di
fuiste	fuiste	diste
fue	fue	dio
fuimos	fuimos	dimos
fuisteis	fuisteis	disteis
fueron	fueron	dieron

○ **Ser** and **ir** have the same forms in the preterit. The meaning is made clear by the context of each sentence.

Anoche Rosa **fue** al cine con Miguel. (**ir**)

Last night Rosa went to the movies with Miguel.

George Washington **fue** el primer presidente. (**ser**)

George Washington was the first president.

○ The following verbs have irregular stems and endings in the preterit.

tener[1]	tuv–		
estar	estuv–		
andar	anduv–		
poder	pud–		
poner[1]	pus–	-e	-imos
saber	sup–	-iste	-isteis
caber	cup–	-o	-ieron
hacer[1]	hic–		
venir[1]	vin–		
querer	quis–		
decir[1]	dij–		
traer[1]	traj–	-e	-imos
conducir	conduj–	-iste	-isteis
traducir	traduj–	-o	-eron
producir	produj–		

—¿Qué **hiciste** ayer?
—Fui al cine. ¿Y tú?
—Yo **estuve** en la universidad.

"What did you do yesterday?"
"I went to the movies. And you?"
"I was at the university."

atención The stress in the first person singular and the third person singular forms of the preterit of these verbs is different from that in the respective forms of the preterit of regular verbs. In regular verbs the stress is on the verb ending, while in irregular verbs the stress is on the verb stem. Compare:

	Irregular verbs	*Regular verbs*
1st person singular	pude	hablé, comí
3rd person singular	tuvo	compró, vivió

○ The **c** changes to **z** in the third person singular of the verb **hacer** to maintain the soft sound of the **c**: **él hizo.**

○ All the verbs in the fourth group in the chart above (**decir, traer,** etc.) omit the **i** in the third person plural ending.

—¿Quién **trajo** el coche?
—Lo **trajeron** mis padres.

"Who brought the car?"
"My parents brought it."

---

[1] Verbs of the **tener, poner, hacer, venir, decir,** and **traer** families conjugate exactly as their respective root verbs. Examples of these are **mantener** and **contener; componer** and **reponer; rehacer** and **deshacer; convenir** and **prevenir; predecir** and **bendecir; distraer** and **atraer.**

 The preterit of **hay** (impersonal form of **haber**) is **hubo** (*there was, there were*).

Anoche **hubo** una fiesta.   *Last night there was a party.*

Práctica

CD-ROM
Go to **Estructuras gramaticales** for additional practice.

A. Entreviste a un(a) compañero(a) usando las siguientes preguntas.

  1. ¿A qué hora viniste a la universidad hoy?
  2. ¿Condujiste tu coche a la universidad?
  3. ¿Trajiste el libro de español a la clase?
  4. ¿Pudieron tú y tus compañeros terminar la tarea anoche?
  5. ¿Le diste la tarea al profesor (a la profesora) al comenzar la clase?
  6. ¿Fueron tú y un(a) amigo(a) a la biblioteca ayer?
  7. ¿Tuviste que trabajar ayer?
  8. ¿Dónde estuvieron tú y tus amigos anoche?
  9. ¿Qué hiciste por la noche?
10. ¿Hubo una fiesta en la universidad el fin de semana pasado?

B. Termine las siguientes oraciones en forma original. Use los verbos que están en cursiva (*italic*).

  1. Hoy el veterinario no *tiene* que trabajar, pero anoche...
  2. Ahora los chicos *están* en clase, pero ayer no...
  3. Hoy *andas* por el centro, pero ayer...
  4. Hoy Ud. *quiere* ir a la fiesta, pero anoche no...
  5. Hoy *dices* que no, pero ayer...
  6. Hoy *conducimos* a la universidad, pero ayer...
  7. Hoy *vienen* en ómnibus, pero ayer...
  8. Hoy *traen* los discos y ayer...
  9. Hoy *traduzco* del español al inglés y ayer...
10. Este año *soy* estudiante del profesor Soto, pero el año pasado...

C. En parejas, preparen seis preguntas para su profesor(a) sobre las cosas que él (ella) hizo ayer, la semana pasada, etc.

E Verbos de cambios ortográficos

○ **c → qu** (before **é**). Verbs ending in **-car** change the **c** to **qu** before the final **-é** of the first person singular of the preterit[1]: **buscar—busqué**.

○ **g → gu** (before **é**). Verbs ending in **-gar** change the **g** to **gu** before the final **-é** of the first person singular of the preterit[1]: **pagar—pagué**.

○ **z → c** (before **é**). Verbs ending in **-zar** change the **z** to **c** before the final **é** of the first person singular of the preterit[1]: **empezar—empecé**.

-car *verbs*		-gar *verbs*		-zar *verbs*	
sa**car**	yo sa**qué**	lle**gar**	yo lle**gué**	empe**zar**	yo empe**cé**
to**car**	yo to**qué**	ju**gar**	yo ju**gué**	comen**zar**	yo comen**cé**
bus**car**	yo bus**qué**	pa**gar**	yo pa**gué**	almor**zar**	yo almor**cé**

[1] This change is made to maintain the same sound through the conjugation.

—¿Tocaste en el concierto anoche?   *"Did you play in the concert last night?"*
—Sí, **toqué.** ¿No me oíste?   *"Yes, I played. Didn't you hear me?"*
—No, porque **llegué** tarde.   *"No, because I arrived late."*

—¿Cuándo empezaste a estudiar en   *"When did you start studying at the school of*
la escuela tecnológica?   *technology?"*
—**Empecé** cuando tenía quince años.   *"I started when I was fifteen years old."*

- **gu → gü** (before **é**). Verbs ending in **-guar** change the **gu** to **gü** before the final **-é** of the first person singular of the preterit. Examples of this kind of verb are **averiguar** (*to find out, to guess*): **averigüé,** and **atestiguar** (*to attest, to testify*): **atestigüé.**[1]
- Verbs whose stem ends in a vowel (**a, e, o, u**) change the unaccented **i** of the preterit ending to **y** in the third persons singular and plural.

Infinitive	Third person singular	Third person plural
le**er**	le**yó**	le**yeron**
cre**er**	cre**yó**	cre**yeron**
ca**er**	ca**yó**	ca**yeron**
o**ír**	o**yó**	o**yeron**
constru**ir**	constru**yó**	constru**yeron**
sustitu**ir**	sustitu**yó**	sustitu**yeron**
contribu**ir**	contribu**yó**	contribu**yeron**
hu**ir**	hu**yó**	hu**yeron**

—Dice Aníbal que anoche **huyeron**   *"Aníbal says that ten criminals escaped last*
diez criminales.   *night."*
—¿Lo **oyó** en la radio?   *"Did he hear it on the radio?"*
—No, lo **leyó** en el periódico.   *"No, he read it in the paper."*

CD-ROM
Go to **Estructuras gramaticales** for additional practice.

Práctica

En parejas lean los siguientes diálogos y complétenlos usando el pretérito de los verbos que aparecen entre paréntesis.

1. —Ayer (yo) _____ (sacar) las entradas para el teatro; _____ (pagar) diez euros por cada entrada. ¿Qué hiciste tú?
   —_____ (Buscar) un regalo para Marité, pero no encontré nada.

2. —¿Con cuánto _____ (contribuir) ellos para la Cruz Roja?
   —Con 500 euros. ¿No lo _____ (leer) Ud. en el periódico?

3. —¿Arrestaron al ladrón (*thief*)?
   —No, _____ (huir) cuando _____ (oír) a los policías.

---

[1] This change is made to maintain the same sound through the conjugation. It is discussed further in **Apéndice B,** under **Verbos de cambios ortográficos,** number 3.

4. —¿A qué hora empezaste a tocar el piano?
   —_____ (Empezar) a las nueve y _____ (tocar) hasta las doce.
5. —¿Almorzaste con Adela?
   —No, _____ (almorzar) solo porque _____ (llegar) tarde.

F Verbos que cambian en la raíz

○ All **-ir** verbs that are stem-changing in the present tense change the **e** to **i** and
the **o** to **u** in the third persons singular and plural of the preterit.

e → i		o → u	
pedir	pidió, pidieron	dormir	durmió, durmieron
servir	sirvió, sirvieron	morir	murió, murieron
conseguir	consiguió, consiguieron		
elegir	eligió, eligieron		
repetir	repitió, repitieron		

○ Other verbs that use the **e → i** conjugation are **advertir, competir,** and **mentir.**

—¿Qué **pidieron** los chicos en el   *"What did the children order at the*
 restaurante?   *restaurant?"*
—Tomás **pidió** sopa y pescado y   *"Tomás ordered soup and fish and Teresa*
 Teresa **pidió** bistec.   *ordered steak."*
—¿Cómo **durmieron** Uds. anoche?   *"How did you sleep last night?"*
—Yo dormí bien, pero Carlos no   *"I slept well, but Carlos didn't sleep at all."*
 durmió nada.

Práctica

CD-ROM
Go to **Estructuras gramaticales** for additional practice.

A. Complete los siguientes diálogos usando el pretérito de los verbos de la lista que
 aparece arriba.

1. —¿Cómo _____ Ud. anoche, señora?
   —_____ muy bien, gracias.
2. —¿Qué _____ Uds. en el restaurante?
   —Yo _____ enchiladas y mi esposo _____ tamales.
3. —¿Dónde _____ Ud. esa revista?
   —La _____ en una librería.
4. —¿Cuál de los anillos _____ su hija?
   —El de oro.
5. —¿Hubo un accidente?
   —Sí, pero no _____ nadie.
6. —¿Qué _____ Uds. en la fiesta?
   —_____ sándwiches y cerveza.
7. —¿Cuántas veces _____ la profesora la pregunta?
   —La _____ tres veces.

B. Entreviste a un(a) compañero(a) de clase utilizando la información dada. Use los verbos en el pretérito y la forma **Ud.** Siga el modelo.

MODELO: empezar a estudiar español   (cuándo)
—*¿Cuándo empezó Ud. a estudiar español?*
—*Empecé a estudiar español el año pasado.*

1. comenzar a estudiar en esta universidad   (cuándo)
2. leer libros el semestre pasado   (qué)
3. elegir esta clase   (por qué)
4. llegar a la universidad hoy   (a qué hora)
5. sacar un libro de la biblioteca   (cuándo)
6. pagar por su libro de español   (cuánto)
7. pedir en la cafetería   (qué)
8. servir en la última fiesta que dio   (qué)
9. dormir anoche   (cuántas horas)

C. En parejas, hablen de lo que Uds. hicieron la semana pasada...

... con su familia   ... en la universidad
... con sus amigos   ... en el trabajo
... en la clase de español

6 El imperfecto

A Formas del imperfecto

⊙ The imperfect of regular verbs is formed as follows.

-ar *verbs*	-er *and* -ir *verbs*	
jugar	*tener*	*vivir*
jug**aba**	ten**ía**	viv**ía**
jug**abas**	ten**ías**	viv**ías**
jug**aba**	ten**ía**	viv**ía**
jug**ábamos**	ten**íamos**	viv**íamos**
jug**abais**	ten**íais**	viv**íais**
jug**aban**	ten**ían**	viv**ían**

⊙ Note that the endings for **-er** and **-ir** verbs are the same, and that there is a written accent mark on the **i.**

⊙ There are only three irregular verbs in the imperfect.

ser	*ir*	*ver*
era	iba	veía
eras	ibas	veías
era	iba	veía
éramos	íbamos	veíamos
erais	ibais	veíais
eran	iban	veían

B Usos del imperfecto

○ The imperfect tense in Spanish is equivalent to these three forms in English depending on the context.

Yo **jugaba** al tenis. $\begin{cases} \textit{I used to (would) play tennis.} \\ \textit{I was playing tennis.} \\ \textit{I played tennis (several times).} \end{cases}$

The imperfect tense is used:

○ To refer to habitual or repeated actions in the past, with no reference to when they began or ended.

Cuando **vivía** en México, **iba** al cine todos los sábados.	*When I lived in Mexico, I would go to the movies every Saturday.*
Veíamos a nuestros amigos dos veces por semana.	*We used to see our friends twice a week.*

Práctica

CD-ROM
Go to **Estructuras gramaticales** for additional practice.

A. Entreviste a un(a) compañero(a) de clase usando las siguientes preguntas y dos preguntas originales.

1. ¿Dónde vivías cuando eras niño(a)?
2. ¿A qué escuela ibas? ¿Estudiabas mucho?
3. ¿Qué hacías en la escuela?
4. ¿Tomabas clases de educación física?
5. ¿Qué hacías los fines de semana?
6. ¿Adónde ibas de vacaciones? ¿Con quién?
7. ¿Quién era tu mejor amigo(a)? ¿Cómo era?
8. ¿Veías a tus abuelos a menudo?
9. ¿Cuál era tu programa de televisión favorito?
10. ¿Qué querías ser?

B. Esto es lo que estas personas **hacen ahora,** pero, ¿qué **hacían cuando** eran jóvenes? Use su imaginación y dígalo.

MODELO: Ahora María trabaja mucho...
Ahora María trabaja mucho, pero cuando era joven trabajaba poco.

1. Ahora José vive en Boston...
2. Ahora nosotros somos demócratas...
3. Ahora ellos no comen mucho...
4. Ahora tú tienes mucho dinero...
5. Ahora no ves a tus amigos frecuentemente...
6. Ahora yo no voy mucho al cine...
7. Ahora nosotros hablamos español...
8. Ahora Ud. vuelve a su casa muy temprano...
9. Ahora ellos van a clase todos los días...
10. Ahora Uds. viajan mucho...

STUDENT WEBSITE
Do the **Compruebe cuánto sabe** self test after finishing this **Estructuras gramaticales** section.

C. En grupos de tres hablen de lo que Uds. hacían cuando eran niños...

... en la escuela   ... con sus amigos
... durante las vacaciones   ... con sus padres

¡CONTINUEMOS!

Una encuesta

Entreviste a sus compañeros de clase para tratar de identificar a aquellas personas que...

1. ... están tomando por lo menos tres requisitos generales.
2. ... tienen una beca.
3. ... están tomando por lo menos dos cursos electivos. ¿Cuáles?
4. ... ya saben exactamente qué carrera van a estudiar. ¿Cuál es?
5. ... prefieren no asistir a clase y estudiar por su cuenta.
6. ... prefieren no tener exámenes ni notas.
7. ... mantienen un promedio de "A" en todas sus clases.
8. ... toman más de doce unidades.
9. ... piensan estudiar esta noche.
10. ... siempre son puntuales.

Ahora divídanse en grupos de tres o cuatro y discutan el resultado de la encuesta.

     ## ¿Comprende Ud.?

CD-ROM   STUDENT WEBSITE
Go to **De escuchar...a escribir** (in **¿Comprende Ud.?**) on the CD-ROM for activities related to the conversation, and go to **Canción** on the website for activities related to the song.

1. Escuche la siguiente conversación entre Sergio y Lucía, dos estudiantes latinoamericanos que estudian en la Universidad de California. El objetivo de la actividad es el de escuchar una conversación a velocidad natural. No se preocupe de entenderlo todo, pues esto no se espera de Ud. Después de escuchar la conversación dos veces, Ud. oirá varias aseveraciones. En una hoja, escriba los números de uno a ocho e indique si cada aseveración es verdadera o falsa.

2. Luego escuche la canción y trate de aprenderla.

Hablemos de carreras

En parejas, fíjense en (*notice*) este anuncio y contesten las siguientes preguntas.

1. ¿Cuáles son las ventajas de asistir al Centro de Orientación Pre-Universitaria Andrés Bello?
2. Según el anuncio, ¿qué porcentaje de los alumnos resultan aplazados (*fail*) en el primer semestre?
3. ¿Ofrece el centro cursos especiales para los estudiantes que desean ingresar en la facultad de medicina o en la facultad de filosofía y letras?

4. ¿Dónde queda el centro?
5. ¿A qué número se debe llamar para obtener información acerca de los cursos?
6. ¿Hasta qué día están abiertas las inscripciones?

¿Qué dirían ustedes... ?

Imagínense que Ud. y un(a) compañero(a) se encuentran en las siguientes situaciones. ¿Qué va a decir cada uno?

1. Alguien los (las) invita para ir al cine esta noche y Uds. tienen un examen mañana.
2. Un latinoamericano necesita información sobre el sistema educativo de Estados Unidos.
3. Uds. quieren explicarles a unos amigos algunas cosas sobre el sistema educativo de México.
4. Uds. quieren invitar a un(a) amigo(a) a ir a una conferencia con Uds. Esa persona dice que está ocupada, y Uds. tratan de convencerla de que es mejor ir a la conferencia.

¡De ustedes depende!

Una estudiante latinoamericana va a asistir a la universidad donde Uds. estudian. Ud. y un(a) compañero(a), denle la información que ella necesita con respecto a lo siguiente.

1. días de matrícula
2. cuánto debe pagar por la matrícula
3. cuándo empiezan y terminan las clases
4. requisitos que debe tomar
5. posibilidades de obtener ayuda financiera (*financial aid*)
6. programas especiales
7. clubes y organizaciones
8. lugares donde puede vivir

Mesa redonda

Formen grupos de cuatro o cinco estudiantes y hablen de los problemas de la educación en Estados Unidos, sugiriendo posibles soluciones. Hagan una lista de los problemas y otra de las soluciones. Seleccionen un líder de cada grupo que informe al resto de la clase sobre las ideas discutidas en los grupos.

Lecturas periodísticas

Saber leer El propósito del escritor

CD-ROM

Go to **Lecturas periodísticas** for additional prereading and vocabulary activities.

Relacionada con la pregunta de para quién escribe el escritor, está la pregunta de cuál es el propósito del escritor. El propósito de una noticia o de un artículo de prensa (*press*) es, por lo general, el de informar al público acerca de algún suceso (*event*) o de algún tema. El breve reportaje que presentamos a continuación se publicó en uno de los periódicos españoles de mayor circulación, *El País*, en su versión digital (*online*).

Lea el primer párrafo (la introducción) y conteste lo siguiente: ¿Sobre qué tema nos desea informar el (la) reportero(a)? Es decir, ¿de qué relación entre los campos (*fields*) de la tecnología y de la educación nos va a informar?

Para leer y comprender

Al leer el artículo, decida si las siguientes aseveraciones son verdaderas (V) o falsas (F).

1. La mayoría de los profesores están de acuerdo en que se deben introducir las nuevas tecnologías en los centros escolares.
2. Los estudiantes tienen acceso a mucha información a través de la Red.
3. Según los expertos no es necesario introducir el Internet[1] dentro de las clases.
4. Solamente algunas escuelas y universidades necesitan tener acceso al Internet.

---

[1] *Internet* can be used with or without an article, often depending on the country.

5. Muy pocos profesores participaron en el I Congreso Internacional de Educared.
6. Según Jesús Beltrán toda la tecnología no es suficiente si los profesores y los estudiantes no saben qué hacer con ella.
7. Los profesores no tienen ningún problema en utilizar la nueva tecnología dentro de las clases.
8. El tipo de clase que se puede diseñar va a variar mucho con el uso de Internet.
9. No es necesario que Internet se introduzca en todas las clases.
10. Cada clase debe tener un computador conectado al Internet.

La Red° entra en la educación

Los profesionales piden programas para introducir Internet en el aula y para formar al profesorado. La preocupación por introducir las nuevas tecnologías con fines pedagógicos en los centros escolares es prácticamente unánime entre el profesorado. La urgencia por encontrar una respuesta sobre cómo se puede llevar a cabo° obedece a que la Red se ha metido en la educación, sin darle a ésta tiempo a

reaccionar, a través° de la multitud de información a la que tienen acceso los alumnos a través de ella.

Los expertos aseguran que es necesario introducir Internet en las clases para poder desarollar° una nueva pedagogía adaptada a esta herramienta°. Un gran programa de formación al que tengan fácil acceso todas las escuelas y universidades españolas es otro de los requisitos que mencionaron la semana pasada los

profesores en el I Congreso Internacional de Educared, organizado por la Fundación Encuentro y la Fundación Telefónica y en el que participaron más de 1.600 profesores de toda España.

El catedrático de Psicología, Jesús Beltrán, advirtió que "toda la tecnología, y especialmente Internet, tiene un gran poder, pero no es más que un instrumento, y lo importante es qué sabe hacer el profesorado o el alumno con él". Domingo Gallego, de la Universidad Nacional de Educación a Distancia, habló del panorama actual y de los problemas con los que se enfrentan°. Éstas son dos de sus principales conclusiones:

—**Práctica educativa.** El diseño de la nueva pedagogía se debe hacer desde la práctica educativa. La información de Internet, la conexión entre aulas de diferentes escuelas en tiempo real y el uso de videoconferencias en las propias pantallas° del ordenador° son algunas de las herramientas que cambiarán el papel del profesor y del alumno, su relación y el tipo de clase que se puede enseñar.

---
net

llevar... carry out

---
a... through
develop
tool

---
se... face
screen
computer

Los expertos aseguran que es necesario introducir Internet en las clases para poder desarrollar una nueva pedagogía adaptada a esta herramienta.

Tres estudiantes universitarios en una clase de cibernética.

—**Internet en el aula**. Internet se debe introducir en cada clase. No es suficiente que la Red se use sólo para que los alumnos naveguen por ella un par de veces a la semana.

Sólo si se introduce en las clases se utilizará con fines pedagógicos. Esto requiere un esfuerzo° por parte de las administraciones de hacer un análisis de cada centro y

proporcionar° un ordenador conectado a Internet en cada clase.

Adaptado de *El País Digital* (España)

———
effort

———
furnish

Desde su mundo

1. En la universidad donde Ud. estudia, ¿ofrecen clases a distancia?
2. En su universidad, ¿hay ordenadores conectados a Internet en cada clase?

piense y escriba   ¿Cuál es su propósito como escritor?

STUDENT WEBSITE

CD-ROM

Go to **...y escriba- mos** (in **Hablemos de su país**) on the student website and **De escuchar... a escribir** (in **¿Com- prende Ud.?**) on the CD-ROM for ad- ditional writing practice.

Antes de escribir, debe tener claro el propósito de su comunicación.

Hoy se lo asignamos: Ud. es el (la) director(a) de admisiones de su universidad y va a entrevistar a un(a) joven que termina la escuela secundaria este año y espera matricularse en la universidad en septiembre. Les va a presentar un breve informe sobre el (la) joven a los miembros (*members*) del comité de admisiones.

1. Haga una lista de cinco o seis preguntas que Ud. va a hacerle al (a la) candidato(a).
2. Entreviste a un(a) compañero(a).
3. Considerando la información de la entrevista: ¿cuál es la idea principal que desea co- municar en su informe?
4. Analice u organice la información de la entrevista bajo dos o tres subtemas. Desarrolle cada subtema en un párrafo distinto, siempre teniendo en cuenta la idea principal.
5. Concluya o resuma.

Pepe Vega y su mundo

Teleinforme

Desde la primaria y la secundaria hasta la universidad, la educación formal ocupa gran parte de nuestras vidas. En el video para esta lección, veremos primero aspectos de la transición de la secundaria a la universidad y luego, aspectos de la transición al mundo del trabajo.

Preparación

¿Secundaria, universidad, trabajo o tiempo libre?   Clasifique las siguientes actividades y expresiones según pertenezcan al mundo de la secundaria (**S**), de la universidad (**U**), del trabajo (**T**) o del tiempo libre (**L**).

_____ 1. aprender idiomas
_____ 2. archivos (*filing*)
_____ 3. el ballet clásico
_____ 4. el club social
_____ 5. las computadoras
_____ 6. la contabilidad (*accounting*)
_____ 7. enseñar
_____ 8. la equitación
_____ 9. escoger clases
_____ 10. escribir a máquina (*to type*)
_____ 11. el esquí acuático
_____ 12. el golf
_____ 13. hablar francés
_____ 14. hacer ejercicios aeróbicos
_____ 15. hacer *windsurf*

_____ 16. la informática
_____ 17. la meditación trascendental
_____ 18. la preparatoria
_____ 19. la publicidad (*advertising*)
_____ 20. la química
_____ 21. las matemáticas
_____ 22. los estudiantes
_____ 23. practicar ala delta (*hang-gliding*)
_____ 24. los profesores
_____ 25. el (la) secretario(a)
_____ 26. ser actriz
_____ 27. la taquigrafía (*shorthand*)
_____ 28. el tratamiento de textos (*word processing*)

Comprensión

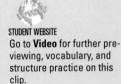

STUDENT WEBSITE
Go to **Video** for further pre-viewing, vocabulary, and structure practice on this clip.

Conversaciones con estudiantes de San Diego State University, parte 1   5:03–6:49

Estas dos entrevistas son fragmentos del programa *Somos*, una serie de conversaciones con estudiantes latinos de San Diego State University. Aquí las dos jóvenes hablan de sus experiencias como estudiantes mexicoamericanas en California y de la transición académica y cultural entre el colegio y la universidad.

A. **¿Qué aprendió Ud.?**   Después de oír cada conversación, conteste las preguntas correspondientes que aparecen a continuación.

1. **Teresa habla de UBAC.** ¿Que significa UBAC? ¿A quiénes ayuda UBAC en San Diego State University? ¿Qué tipo de ayuda da?
2. **Guillermina les da algunos consejos a los profesores de la universidad para que puedan ofrecer un mejor servicio a los estudiantes**

chicanos o mexicoamericanos. Según Guillermina, ¿qué hacen muchos profesores? Según ella, ¿cómo son los estudiantes latinos? Según ella, ¿qué más deberían hacer los profesores?

CD-ROM
Go to **Video** for further previewing, vocabulary, and structure practice on this clip.

En la Agencia Supersonic   6:51–9:09

Las chicas de hoy en día es un programa de comedia producido por la estación nacional de España, la TVE o Televisión Española. Charo y Nuri son dos jóvenes que quieren conseguir trabajo como actrices en Madrid. En este episodio, Nuri busca trabajo para ganarse la vida mientras consigue otro trabajo como actriz. Aquí la vemos en la agencia de colocación Supersonic.

B. ¿Quién menciona qué?   Vea el video y preste atención a las actividades o habilidades que menciona Chuni, la representante de la Agencia Supersonic; las que menciona Nuri, la solicitante rubia (*blond applicant*), y las que menciona Charo, la amiga de Nuri. De la lista en la sección de **Preparación,** ¿cuáles menciona Nuri, cuáles menciona Chuni y cuáles menciona Charo? Escríbalas en tres columnas:

Nuri	*Chuni*	*Charo*

C. En su opinión...

1. ¿Qué tipo de preparación tiene Nuri?
2. ¿Qué tipo de preparación busca Chuni?
3. ¿Qué tipo de trabajo sería apropiado para Nuri?

Ampliación

Consejos.   Un(a) estudiante universitario(a) desea reunirse con su consejero(a) para hablar sobre una de las siguientes situaciones.

a. Va a asistir a un programa en una universidad mexicana.
b. Pronto termina la carrera universitaria y busca su primer trabajo.

En parejas, preparen la representación de un diálogo. ¿Qué problemas o cuestiones se plantea el (la) estudiante? ¿Qué orientación y soluciones propone el (la) consejero(a)?

Lecciones 1 y 2

Tome este examen para ver cuánto ha aprendido. Las respuestas correctas aparecen en el **Apéndice C.**

Lección 1

A El presente de indicativo

Complete las siguientes oraciones usando el presente de indicativo de los verbos que aparecen entre paréntesis.

1. Yo _____ (desaparecer) el sábado y no _____ (aparecer) hasta el domingo. Los martes no _____ (salir) de mi casa.
2. ¿Tú nunca _____ (recordar) lo que _____ (soñar)?
3. Yo _____ (saber) que ellos _____ (almorzar) en la cafetería y _____ (volver) a su casa a las dos. Yo los _____ (ver) todos los días.
4. Cuando el profesor _____ (corregir) los exámenes, siempre _____ (sugerir) algo.
5. Yo _____ (reconocer) que yo lo _____ (traducir) todo al español.
6. Ella les _____ (advertir) que ese perro _____ (morder).
7. Nosotros nunca _____ (entender) lo que el profesor _____ (decir).
8. Yo les _____ (decir) que yo no _____ (caber) aquí.
9. Yo _____ (hacer) la tarea, _____ (poner) los libros en el coche y _____ (ir) a la universidad. Siempre _____ (conducir) el coche de mi papá.
10. Las clases _____ (empezar) en agosto y _____ (terminar) en enero.
11. Él no _____ (negar) que no le gusta bromear. _____ (Confesar) que es muy serio.
12. Ellos _____ (decir) que el señor Leyva _____ (despedir) a los empleados sin motivo. Yo _____ (pensar) que eso está muy mal.

B El presente progresivo

Complete las siguientes oraciones con el equivalente español de las palabras que aparecen entre paréntesis.

1. Roberto _____ español. (*continues to study*)
2. Carlos _____ a sus parientes. (*is visiting*)
3. Ellos _____ en la escuela secundaria. (*continue to teach*)
4. Ella le _____ dinero a su padrino. (*is asking for*)
5. ¿Qué _____ tú ahora? (*are doing*)
6. Yo _____ la comida. (*am serving*)
7. Nosotros _____ sobre la reunión familiar. (*continue to talk*)
8. Arturo _____ la carta de su abuela. (*is reading*)

C La **a** personal

Complete las siguientes oraciones, usando el equivalente español de las palabras que aparecen entre paréntesis.

1. Yo echo de menos _____. (*my parents*)
2. Voy a llevar _____ al veterinario. (*my dog*)
3. No necesitamos ver _____. (*anybody*)
4. Busco _____. (*a secretary*)
5. Voy a llamar _____ y _____. (*my sister-in-law / my mother-in-law*)

D Formas pronominales en función de complemento directo

Conteste las siguientes preguntas en forma afirmativa, reemplazando las palabras en cursiva por los pronombres de complemento directo correspondientes.

1. ¿Conoces *a esas personas que están en la sala?*
2. ¿Hay *agencias de viaje* aquí?
3. ¿*Me* llamas mañana? (Use la forma *tú*)
4. ¿Tus padres *te* visitan todos los días?
5. ¿Tú tienes *los libros* de Marcela?
6. ¿Sabes *que él tiene tu tarjeta de crédito?*
7. ¿Mi abuela *los* conoce *a ustedes?*
8. ¿Pueden ustedes hacer *ese trabajo* hoy?

E Formas pronominales en función de complemento indirecto

Complete las siguientes oraciones, usando el equivalente español de las palabras que aparecen entre paréntesis.

1. Tengo que _____ las noticias. (*give them*)
2. Yo siempre _____ los libros que él necesita. (*buy him*)
3. Ella _____ todas las semanas. (*writes to me*)
4. ¿Tú puedes _____ las revistas? (*send us*)
5. ¿Tus amigos _____ en español? (*speak to you*)
6. Yo siempre _____ la verdad. (*tell her*)
7. ¿Ellos pueden _____ los documentos que usted necesita? (*bring you*)
8. Yo tengo que _____ cien dólares. (*lend her*)

F Construcciones reflexivas

Conteste las siguientes preguntas, usando la información dada entre paréntesis.

1. ¿Qué haces tú por la mañana? (bañarse y vestirse)
2. ¿Qué piensan hacer ustedes? (acostarse temprano)

3. ¿Qué hacen tus tíos en el verano?   (irse de vacaciones)
4. ¿Qué hacen tus compañeros cuando tienen exámenes?   (quejarse)
5. ¿Qué dicen de mí?   (parecerse a tu padre)
6. ¿Qué hacen tú y Luis todos los viernes?   (encontrarse en el café)
7. ¿Qué haces antes de comprar un par de zapatos?   (probárselos)
8. ¿Qué va a hacer ahora?   (lavarse la cabeza)

G ¿Recuerda el vocabulario?

Circule la palabra o frase que no pertenence al grupo.

1. manera   modo   papel
2. bromear   malcriar   mimar
3. casarse   sentirse   divorciarse
4. a lo mejor   apenas   tal vez
5. por supuesto   naturalmente   además
6. enojado   enfadado   triste
7. mandón   amistoso   amable
8. amistoso   egoísta   comprensivo
9. deprimido   alegre   contento
10. afecto   cariño   círculo
11. amar   querer   extrañar
12. abrazar   cuidar   besar
13. frustrado   nervioso   de buen humor
14. obedecer   tomar   respetar

H Cultura

Circule la información correcta.

1. España tiene una población de unos (15, 40, 5) millones de habitantes.
2. Barcelona está en la costa del (Pacífico, Mediterráneo, Atlántico).
3. Córdoba, Sevilla y Granada están en el (sur, norte, oeste) de España.
4. Una de las universidades más antiguas de Europa está en (Bilbao, Madrid, Salamanca).

Lección 2

A Usos de los verbos **ser** y **estar**

Complete las siguientes oraciones, usando **ser** o **estar,** según corresponda.

1. ¿De quién _____ este libro? ¡_____ muy interesante!
2. Estos relojes _____ de plata.
3. Los profesores _____ de vacaciones, pero los consejeros _____ en la universidad.

4. La biblioteca _____ abierta, pero los bancos _____ cerrados.
5. Elsa sabe mucho; _____ muy lista.
6. ¿Quién _____ ese hombre que _____ hablando con Teresa? ¡_____ una persona muy aburrida!
7. Ricardo _____ enfermo. _____ muy aburrido porque no tiene nada que hacer.
8. ¿Dónde _____ la conferencia? ¿Qué hora _____? Yo ya _____ lista para salir.
9. Mi abuelo _____ en cama porque _____ malo. Creo que tiene pulmonía.
10. ¿Para quién _____ el horario de clases?
11. David _____ mexicano, pero no _____ de la Ciudad de México.
12. _____ mejor tomar todos los requisitos primero.
13. No debes comer esas manzanas; _____ verdes.
14. ¡Mmm! Yo _____ comiendo tamales verdes. ¡_____ deliciosos!

B Adjetivos posesivos

Conteste las siguientes preguntas usando en sus respuestas los adjetivos posesivos correspondientes y las palabras que aparecen entre paréntesis.

1. ¿Dónde están los horarios de clases de ustedes?   (en el bolso de mano)
2. ¿De dónde son tus padres?   (de Oaxaca)
3. ¿De dónde es el título del profesor?   (de la Universidad de Guadalajara)
4. ¿Dónde está mi examen?   (en el escritorio)
5. ¿Quién es una buena amiga tuya?   (Amalia)

C Pronombres posesivos

Conteste las siguientes preguntas usando en sus respuestas los pronombres posesivos correspondientes y las palabras que aparecen entre paréntesis.

1. Mis clases son difíciles. ¿Y las tuyas?   (fáciles)
2. Mi abuelo es de Guadalajara. ¿De dónde es el tuyo?   (de Chihuahua)
3. Yo tengo tus libros. ¿Tú tienes los míos?   (no)
4. Nuestro profesor es muy simpático. ¿Y el de ustedes?   (muy simpático también)
5. Mis clases son por la mañana. ¿Cuándo son las de tus amigos?   (por la tarde)

D Pronombres de complementos directo e indirecto usados juntos

Conteste las siguientes preguntas en forma afirmativa, sustituyendo las palabras en cursiva por los pronombres correspondientes.

1. ¿Puedes comprarme *ese diccionario?* (Use la forma *tú*)
2. ¿Les pides *los horarios* a las chicas?
3. ¿Tu papá te da *el dinero que necesitas?*
4. ¿Piensas comprarle *esas plumas* a tu hermano?
5. ¿El profesor les va a dar a ustedes *las notas* hoy?

E Usos y omisiones de los artículos definidos e indefinidos

Complete las siguientes oraciones usando el equivalente español de las palabras que aparecen entre paréntesis.

1. _____ dice que _____ es muy importante (*Dr. Vega / education*)
2. Mi composición tiene _____ palabras, y la composición de Eva tiene solamente _____. (*a thousand / a hundred*)
3. Mi hijo es _____. Es _____. (*a doctor / an excellent doctor*)
4. _____ tiene clases _____ lunes _____ siete. (*Miss Peña / on / at*)
5. Necesito _____ trabajo porque tengo problemas económicos. (*another*)
6. _____ nunca usa _____. (*Mrs. Soto / a hat*)

F El pretérito

Cambie las siguientes oraciones al pretérito.

1. Ellos compran los libros y los traen a la universidad.
2. Piden enchiladas y no las comen. Se las dan a su papá.
3. Ella lo sabe, pero no dice nada.
4. Nosotros vamos al cine porque no tenemos que trabajar.
5. Yo llego a las ocho, pero no comienzo a trabajar hasta las nueve.
6. Yo toco las canciones que ellos eligen.
7. Yo le hablo, pero ella no me oye.
8. Yo no quepo en el coche y por eso no voy.
9. Yo vengo y les doy el dinero, pero ellos no compran nada.
10. Ellos leen el artículo, pero yo no puedo leerlo.
11. Teresa vuelve a su casa a las diez y se acuesta en seguida.
12. Carlos va al teatro. Ellas prefieren quedarse en su casa.

G El imperfecto

Complete las siguientes oraciones, usando el imperfecto de los verbos de la lista.

comprar   ir   ser   hacer   hablar   prestar   ver   salir   asistir

1. Elsa siempre me _____ sus discos compactos.
2. En esa época yo _____ a la universidad.
3. Yo siempre _____ a la casa de ellos, pero nunca _____ a sus abuelos.
4. Ella _____ las cintas para mí.
5. ¿No me dijiste que _____ frío? ¿Dónde está tu abrigo?
6. _____ las seis cuando él llegó al club.
7. Andrés _____ muy bien el inglés.
8. Ellos _____ de su casa cuando sonó el teléfono.

H ¿Recuerda el vocabulario?

Complete las siguientes oraciones usando palabras y expresiones de la **Lección 2.**

1. Elena no asiste a clases. Ella estudia por su _____.
2. La asistencia a clases es _____ en esta universidad.
3. Juan está estudiando la _____ de médico.
4. Yo no pago matrícula porque tengo una _____.
5. Por lo _____ Elvira es muy lista. En todas sus clases _____ un _____ de "A".
6. El examen de _____ de _____ es el doce de marzo.
7. La conferencia empieza a las ocho a más _____.
8. ¿Puedes prestarme tu programa de _____?
9. Voy a preguntarle a mi _____ qué materias debo tomar.
10. Raúl siempre llega tarde. No es nada _____.
11. Eva quiere ser abogada. Estudia en la _____ de _____.
12. Ana vive en la _____ universitaria.
13. Voy a _____ de terminar el trabajo.
14. Luis es _____ público, Carlos es _____ de sistemas y Elvira es _____ social.
15. La avenida Olmos está _____ las calles Quinta y Magnolia.

I Cultura

Circule la información correcta.

1. México exporta oro, plata y (cobre, automóviles, azúcar).
2. Las ruinas de Teotihuacán están cerca de (Guadalajara, la Ciudad de México, Ensenada.)
3. Diego Rivera es famoso en (la música, el cine, la pintura) de México.
4. Octavio Paz es un gran (actor, escritor, ex presidente) mexicano.

Los deportes y las actividades al aire libre

Cuatro amigos, gozando de una caminata.

Los deportes y las actividades al aire libre

CD-ROM   STUDENT AUDIO

For preparation, do the **Ante todo** activities found on the CD-ROM.

Pablo Villalobos es un muchacho peruano, pero hace un año que está estudiando en Santiago, la capital de Chile. Tiene muchos amigos en la universidad y uno de ellos, Rafael Vargas, le sirve de guía muchas veces.

Esta semana no hay clases y Pablo y Rafael están sentados en un café al aire libre leyendo el periódico y comentando la página deportiva mientras toman café.

RAFAEL —Ganó nuestro equipo favorito. ¿Fuiste al estadio a ver el partido? Yo no fui porque no pude conseguir entradas.

PABLO —No, yo también me lo perdí. Quería ir con Sergio, pero tuve que estudiar.

RAFAEL —¿Sabías que Pedro Benítez ganó la pelea anoche? ¡Es el mejor boxeador del país!

PABLO —No me gusta el boxeo. En realidad el único deporte que realmente me interesa es el fútbol.

RAFAEL —A mí también. Cuando yo era chico pasaba horas en la calle jugando al fútbol. Oye, ¿fuiste a patinar con Paco ayer?

PABLO —No, él se fue a Portillo a esquiar. Me dijo que quería mejorar su estilo.

RAFAEL —¿Qué estilo? La última vez que esquiamos juntos por poco se mata.

PABLO —*(Se ríe)* Pero tienes que darte cuenta de que Paco se cree un gran atleta y de que le encanta esquiar.

RAFAEL —Pues para mí, lo mejor es ir a acampar. Hace dos semanas fui con unos amigos y nos divertimos mucho. Rubén fue con nosotros.

PABLO —Sí, a él le encantan las actividades al aire libre: pescar, montar a caballo, escalar montañas, bucear . . .

Página Deportiva

Tenis

Patricia Serna nueva campeona
Ayer la tenista Patricia Serna obtuvo una gran victoria sobre Marisa Beltrán. Con este triunfo quedó clasificada como una de las tres mejores tenistas del mundo.

Fútbol

Fénix ganó 5–3
El domingo pasado el Club Fénix ganó el partido contra los Leones 5 a 3. A pesar de que en el primer tiempo dos de sus jugadores se lastimaron, en el segundo tiempo pudo marcar dos goles más, ganando el partido.

Básquetbol

México le ganó a España
El partido de baloncesto celebrado ayer en el Estadio Metropolitano fue muy reñido. El equipo de la Ciudad de México venció al equipo español por 82 a 80. El entrenador del equipo español estaba furioso y comentó que la próxima vez, su equipo iba a ser el campeón.

RAFAEL —Sí, ayer me dijo que necesitaba mi tienda de campaña y mi caña de pescar para este fin de semana.

PABLO —Ah, ¿fuiste a ver el partido de tenis anteayer?

RAFAEL —No, porque me dolía mucho la espalda y preferí quedarme en casa.

PABLO —(*Bromeando*) Es que tú eres un enclenque.

RAFAEL —Eso no es verdad. Oye, aquí vienen las chicas que conocimos en la fiesta de Olga. Vamos a hablar con ellas . . .

Dígame

En parejas, contesten las siguientes preguntas basadas en el diálogo.

1. ¿Dónde estudia Pablo? ¿Quién le sirve de guía muchas veces?
2. ¿Qué sección del periódico están leyendo Pablo y Rafael?
3. ¿Por qué no fue Rafael a ver el partido? ¿Y Pablo?
4. ¿Qué opinión tiene Rafael de Pedro Benítez?
5. En realidad, ¿cuál es el único deporte que le interesa a Pablo?
6. ¿Qué hacía Rafael cuando era chico?
7. ¿Adónde fue Rafael con sus amigos hace dos semanas? ¿Quién fue con ellos?
8. ¿Qué actividades al aire libre le gustan a Rubén?
9. ¿Por qué no fue Rafael al partido de tenis anteayer? ¿Qué prefirió hacer?
10. ¿Dónde conocieron Rafael y Pablo a las chicas?
11. ¿Quién es la nueva campeona de tenis? ¿A quién le ganó?
12. ¿Quién ganó el partido de fútbol el domingo pasado? ¿Qué pasó en el primer tiempo?

Perspectivas socioculturales

INSTRUCTOR WEBSITE
Your instructor may assign the preconversational support activities found in **Perspectivas socioculturales**.

Hay deportes que son característicos de ciertas culturas. Algunos de éstos se crearon en una cultura particular y luego fueron adoptados por otras. El *jaialai*, por ejemplo, es un deporte que se originó en el País Vasco y que hoy en día se practica en muchas partes del mundo.

Haga lo siguiente:

a. Lea los temas de conversación que aparecen a continuación y escoja uno de ellos.
b. Durante unos cinco minutos, cambie opiniones (o converse) con dos compañeros sobre el tema seleccionado.
c. Participe con el resto de la clase en la discusión del tema cuando su profesor(a) se lo indique.

Temas de conversación

1. **Deportes autóctonos del mundo.** ¿Qué deportes se originaron en su cultura? ¿Qué deportes de su cultura se practican en otras partes del mundo?
2. **Fútbol (balompié o *soccer*) y fútbol americano.** ¿Cuáles son las diferencias que distinguen al balompié del fútbol americano?
3. **La importancia del deporte.** Hable sobre la importancia que tiene el deporte en su sociedad.

Vocabulario

Nombres

el (la) atleta athlete
el baloncesto, el básquetbol
  basketball
el (la) boxeador(a) boxer
el boxeo boxing
el (la) campeón(-ona) champion
la caña de pescar fishing rod
el deporte sport
el (la) enclenque sickly person
el (la) entrenador(a) trainer, coach
el equipo team
el estadio stadium
el fútbol, el balompié soccer
el (la) jugador(a) player
la montaña mountain
la página page
el partido game, match
la pelea fight
la tienda de campaña tent
la vez time (*in a series*)

Verbos

acampar to camp
bucear to go scuba diving
comentar to comment
escalar to climb
esquiar to ski
ganar to win
lastimar(se) to hurt (oneself)

marcar to score (*in sports*)
mejorar to improve
patinar to skate
perderse (e→ie) (algo) to miss out
  on (something)
pescar to fish, to catch a fish
quedarse to stay, to remain
servir (e→i) (de) to serve (as)
vencer to defeat

Adjetivos

deportivo(a) related to sports
reñido(a) close (*in a game*)
sentado(a) seated

Otras palabras y expresiones

a pesar de que in spite of
al aire libre outdoor(s)
darse cuenta de to realize
en realidad in fact
la última vez the last time
montar a caballo to ride on
  horseback
por poco se mata he almost killed
  him(her)self
primer (segundo) tiempo first
  (second) half (*in a game*)
sacar (conseguir) entradas to buy
  (get) tickets

Ampliación

Otras palabras relacionadas con los deportes

el (la) aficionado(a) fan
el árbitro umpire
el bate bat
el béisbol baseball
el campeonato championship
la carrera race

la carrera de autos auto race
la carrera de caballos horse race
empatar to tie (*a score*)
el esquí acuático water skiing
el fútbol americano football
la gimnasia gymnastics
el (la) gimnasta gymnast
el guante de pelota baseball glove

el hipódromo   race track
los Juegos Olímpicos, las Olimpiadas   Olympic Games
la lucha libre   wrestling
el (la) nadador(a)   swimmer

nadar   to swim
la natación   swimming
la pelota   ball
la raqueta   racket

CD-ROM
Go to **Vocabulario** for additional vocabulary practice.

Hablando de todo un poco

Preparación   **Complete lo siguiente, usando el vocabulario de la Lección 3.**

1. Voy al estadio a jugar béisbol. Necesito un _____ y un _____ de pelota.
2. Ellos van al _____ para ver las _____ de caballos.
3. El _____ de fútbol fue muy _____. Los equipos _____ tres a tres.
4. No me gusta la natación porque no soy buena _____. Prefiero practicar el _____ acuático y bucear.
5. Raúl Valdés ganó el _____ de lucha _____. Él es el nuevo campeón y la _____ Marisa Rivas es la _____ de gimnasia.
6. Voy a acampar cerca de un lago. Necesito una _____ de campaña y una _____ de pescar.
7. Mi equipo ganó el _____ de baloncesto; a _____ de que dos de los _____ se lastimaron en el segundo _____.
8. Anoche me _____ la pelea de _____ porque no pude _____ entradas.
9. A Marta le encantan las _____ al aire _____. Sobre todo le gusta _____ montañas, pero la última _____ que lo hizo por _____ se mata.
10. Siempre leo la _____ deportiva porque me interesan mucho los _____. Algún día espero poder ir a ver los Juegos _____.
11. El entrenador de José Díaz, el _____ que perdió la pelea anoche, comentó que José necesita _____ su estilo para poder vencer.
12. Los aficionados no se _____ cuenta del problema que el árbitro tuvo con el atleta que _____ el gol.
13. Me gusta _____ a caballo, _____ en la nieve, patinar y _____ en la piscina.
14. En _____ Elsa va a quedarse aquí porque nos quiere _____ de guía.

En grupos de tres o cuatro, hagan lo siguiente.

A. **Deportes.**   Conversen sobre los deportes que Uds. consideran violentos, los que encuentran interesantes o entretenidos y los que les parecen aburridos. Expliquen por qué.

B. **Campamento de verano.**   Uds. están encargados de organizar las actividades que se van a realizar en un campamento de verano. Digan qué actividades van a incluir y qué van a necesitar para cada una de ellas.

C. **Preguntas.**   Preparen por lo menos ocho preguntas sobre deportes para hacérselas a su profesor(a). Utilicen el vocabulario que acaban de aprender.

Palabras problemáticas

A. **Perderse, perder, faltar a** y **echar de menos** como equivalentes de *to miss*

- **Perderse (algo)** significa **no tener el placer (de hacer algo).**

    ¿No viste el partido? ¡No sabes lo que **te perdiste**!

- **Perder,** cuando se refiere a un medio de transporte, significa **no llegar a tiempo para tomarlo.**

    Perdí el tren de las diez, y ahora debo esperar otro.

- **Faltar a** significa **no asistir.**

    Ayer **falté a** clase porque estaba enferma.

- **Echar de menos (extrañar)** significa **sentir la ausencia de.**

    Cuando estoy de viaje, **echo de menos** a mi familia.

B. **Darse cuenta de** y **realizar**

- **Darse cuenta de** significa **notar, comprender;** equivale al inglés *to realize.*

    Yo no **me di cuenta de** que era tan tarde.

- **Realizar** significa **efectuar** o **ejecutar** una acción y equivale al inglés *to do, to accomplish.*

    La Cruz Roja **realiza** una gran labor.

atención   Notice that **realizar** and *to realize* are not cognates.

Práctica

Complete los siguientes diálogos y luego represéntelos con un(a) compañero(a).

1. —¿Vas a volver a tu país?
   —Sí, porque _____ a mi familia.

2. —¿Tú _____ a las prácticas de balompié la semana pasada?
   —Sí, porque estuve enfermo.

3. —¿Viste los Juegos Olímpicos en la tele anoche?
   —No, _____.

4. —¿Uds. _____ el avión ayer?
   —Sí, llegamos tarde al aeropuerto a pesar de que salimos de casa temprano.

5. —¿David está en Chile trabajando con el Cuerpo de Paz?
   —Sí, y esa organización _____ una gran labor.

6. —¿Por qué no vinieron Uds. antes?
   —No _____ de que era tan tarde.

Your instructor may carry out the **¡Ahora escuche!** listening activity found in the **Answers to Text Exercises.**

¡Ahora escuche!

Se leerá dos veces una breve narración sobre Carlos y Eduardo, dos jóvenes aficionados a los deportes. Se harán aseveraciones sobre la narración. En una hoja escriba los números de uno a diez e indique si cada aseveración es verdadera (V) o falsa (F).

El mundo hispánico

¡Vivan Chile, Perú y Ecuador!

Rafael Vargas

A ver... ¿qué puedo decirles de Chile? Como saben es un país largo y estrecho° situado entre los Andes y el océano Pacífico. Aunque es el más largo de los países sudamericanos, con una extensión de más de 4.300 kms de norte a sur, solamente tiene unos 200 kms de ancho°. El clima es muy variado y es muy posible pasar, en un mismo día, del calor de la costa al frío de la montaña.

narrow

width

Mi país es una de las naciones latinoamericanas de mayor desarrollo° industrial. Exporta minerales, especialmente cobre, pero también es uno de los exportadores más importantes de frutas y, ¿quiénes tienen los mejores vinos del mundo? ¡Los chilenos!

development

Yo nací en Santiago, la capital, una ciudad moderna de más de cinco millones de habitantes. Si vienen a mi ciudad pueden visitar museos interesantísimos como el Museo Precolombino, que tiene artefactos de las culturas indígenas. También pueden pasear por el Parque de Artesanos y comprar objetos de artesanía y escuchar música. Si les gusta esquiar, Portillo y Farellones los esperan a pocos kilómetros de Santiago.

Uno de los centros turísticos más importantes del mundo es Viña del Mar, donde se celebra el famoso Festival Internacional de la Canción.

Siguiendo viaje hacia el norte no deben dejar de visitar Perú, empezando con Lima, su capital, una ciudad de gran belleza y valor histórico. Cuzco, la antigua capital de los incas, es fascinante, y desde allí un viaje en tren los va a llevar a las famosas ruinas de Machu Picchu.

STUDENT WEBSITE
Go to **El mundo hispánico** for prereading and vocabulary activities.

Otro país andino digno de verse° es Ecuador. Quito, su capital, es una de las ciudades más antiguas del hemisferio occidental y está situada casi directamente en la línea del ecuador. Si les interesa la ecología pueden visitar las islas Galápagos, que deben° su nombre a las enormes tortugas° que allí viven.

digno... worth seeing

owe
tortoises

Aquí tienen dos mapas que incluyen estos países.

Sobre Chile, Perú y Ecuador

En parejas, túrnense para contestar las siguientes preguntas.

1. ¿Cuáles son los límites de Chile al norte, al sur, al este y al oeste? ¿Qué aspecto tiene el país en un mapa?
2. ¿Qué exporta Chile? ¿Qué dice Rafael de los vinos chilenos?
3. ¿Qué lugares interesantes se pueden visitar en Santiago?
4. ¿Qué se puede hacer en Portillo y Farellones?
5. ¿Qué ciudad debemos visitar si queremos asistir al Festival de la Canción?
6. ¿Cuál es la capital de Perú? ¿Cómo es?
7. ¿Qué otra ciudad importante podemos visitar? ¿Qué encontramos cerca de allí?
8. ¿Qué sabe Ud. de la capital de Ecuador? ¿Dónde está situada?
9. ¿Qué islas están cerca de Ecuador? ¿A qué deben su nombre estas islas?

Hablemos de su país

INSTRUCTOR WEBSITE
STUDENT WEBSITE
Your instructor may assign the preconversational activities in **Hablemos...** (under **Hablemos de su país**). Go to **Hablemos de su país** (under **...y escribamos**) for postconversational web search and writing activities.

Reúnase con otro(a) compañero(a) y conteste lo siguiente: ¿Qué actividades al aire libre son propias del lugar de donde es Ud.?

Luego cada pareja compartirá las respuestas con toda la clase. Establezcan si las actividades al aire libre varían según los lugares de origen de los miembros de la clase.

Una tarjeta postal

Ésta es una tarjeta postal que Pablo le envía a Rafael desde Ecuador.

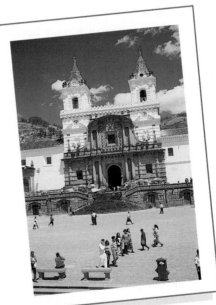

Estimado amigo:

Estoy en Quito, con sus calles inclinadas y estrechas, donde uno tiene la sensación de estar en el siglo XVI. Ayer visité el monumento en la mitad del mundo, situado en la latitud 0°. ¡Tenía un pie en el hemisferio norte y el otro en el hemisferio sur! Mañana salgo para Guayaquil.

Saludos,

Pablo

Después de leer la tarjeta

1. ¿Cómo son algunas de las calles de Quito?
2. ¿Qué sensación tiene Pablo?
3. ¿En qué latitud está situado el monumento en la mitad del mundo?
4. ¿Qué ciudad va a visitar Pablo mañana?

Estructuras gramaticales

1 Verbos que requieren una construcción especial

A *Gustar*

○ The verb **gustar** means *to like* (literally, *to be pleasing* or *to appeal to*). As shown in the following examples, **gustar** is used with indirect object pronouns.

I.O.	Verb	Subject	Subject	Verb	D.O.
Me	gusta	**esa pelota.**	*I*	*like*	*that ball.*
			Subject	Verb	I.O.
			That ball	*appeals*	*to me.*

○ In Spanish, the person who does the liking is the indirect object, and the thing or person liked is the subject.

○ Two forms of **gustar** are used most often: the third person singular **gusta** (**gustó, gustaba,** etc.) if the subject is singular, or the third person plural **gustan** (**gustaron, gustaban,** etc.) if the subject is plural.

Indirect object
  pronouns

Me
Te } **gusta** ← patinar.
Le   ← bucear y nadar.
Nos   ← ese **equipo.**
Os } **gustan** ← los **deportes.**
Les   ← esos **guantes de pelota.**

—¿**Te gustó** el partido?   *"Did you like the game?"*
—Sí, **me gustó** mucho.   *"Yes, I liked it a lot."*

○ The preposition **a** is used with a noun or a pronoun to clarify the meaning or to emphasize the indirect object pronoun.

—**A Juan** no **le** gusta ese atleta.   *"Juan doesn't like that athlete."*
—Pues yo no estoy de acuerdo.   *"Well, I don't agree. I like him very much."*
   A mí me gusta mucho.

—**Me** gustan mucho estos bates.   *"I like these bats very much."*
—**A nosotros nos** gustan más   *"We like the other ones better."*
   los otros.

atención The word **mucho** is placed immediately after **gustar.** The equivalent in Spanish of *to like . . . better* is **gustar más... .**

CD-ROM
Go to **Estructuras gramaticales** for additional practice.

Práctica

A. Vuelva a escribir las siguientes oraciones, sustituyendo **preferir** por **gustar más.** Haga todos los cambios necesarios. Siga el modelo.

MODELO: Yo prefiero ir a un partido de tenis.
A mí me gusta más ir a un partido de tenis.

1. Ellos prefieren el baloncesto.
2. David dice que Ud. prefiere el fútbol.
3. La mayoría de la gente prefiere montar a caballo.
4. Yo prefiero pescar.
5. ¿Tú prefieres esquiar?
6. Yo prefiero la natación.
7. El entrenador prefiere practicar los viernes.
8. Nosotros preferimos acampar.
9. Daniel prefiere la lucha libre.
10. ¿Tú prefieres esos guantes de pelota?
11. Ellos prefieren escalar montañas.
12. Rafael prefiere bucear.

B. Esta actividad tiene dos partes: en la primera, diga lo que les gusta hacer a estas personas; en la segunda, diga qué cosas les gusta(n).

1. Los fines de semana
a mi papá	a mis amigos
a mí	a nosotros
a ti	a Ud.

2. Éstas son las comidas, las bebidas, la ropa, los lugares, etc., que nos/les gusta(n):
a mí	a mis parientes
a mi mamá	a Ud.
a ti	a Uds.
a nosotros	a mi novio(a)

C. En parejas, imagínense que van a pasar el fin de semana juntos(as). Planeen varias actividades, haciéndose preguntas sobre lo que les gusta y lo que no les gusta. Expliquen el porqué de sus preferencias, usando expresiones como **me gusta(n) mucho...** y **me gusta(n) más...**

B Verbos con construcciones similares a *gustar*

O The following frequently used verbs have the same construction as **gustar.** Note the use of the indirect object pronouns.

1. **doler**   *to hurt*

—¡**Me duele** mucho la espalda!   *"My back hurts a lot!"*
—¿Por qué no tomas una aspirina?   *"Why don't you take an aspirin?"*

2. **faltar**   *to be lacking, to need*

—¿Cuánto **te falta** para poder
comprar las entradas?
—**Me faltan** veinte dólares.

*"How much do you need to be able to
buy the tickets?"*
"I need twenty dollars."

3. **quedar**   *to have (something) left*

—Quiero comprar la pelota.
¿Cuánto dinero **nos queda**?
—Solamente **nos quedan** diez
dólares.

*"I want to buy the ball. How much
money do we have left?"*
"We only have ten dollars left."

4. **encantar**   *to love (literally, to delight)*

—Hoy hay un partido de béisbol.
¿Vamos?
—Sí, **me encanta** el béisbol.

*"There's a baseball game today.
Shall we go?"*
"Yes, I love baseball."

Práctica

CD-ROM
Go to **Estructuras gramaticales** for additional practice.

Complete los siguientes diálogos usando los verbos de la lista en la forma correcta.
Luego represéntenlos en parejas.

encantar   faltar   doler   quedar   gustar

1. —¿Quieres jugar al tenis?
   —No, _____ mucho la espalda.

2. —¿Por qué no vas a las carreras de autos?
   —Porque no _____.

3. —¿A Marcelo le gusta el esquí acuático?
   —Sí, ¡_____!

4. —Necesitamos una tienda de campaña, pero sólo _____ treinta dólares y la
   tienda de campaña que queremos cuesta cien dólares. _____ setenta dólares.
   —Bueno, puedes usar tu tarjeta de crédito.

2 El pretérito contrastado con el imperfecto

Principios generales

○ The difference between the preterit and the imperfect may be visualized in the
following way:

The wavy line representing the imperfect shows an action or event taking place
over a period of time in the past. There is no reference as to when the action began or ended. The vertical line representing the preterit shows an action or
event completed in the past.

○ In many instances, the choice between the imperfect and the preterit depends on how the speaker views the action or the event. The following table summarizes some of the most important uses of both tenses.

Imperfect	*Preterit*
1. Describes past actions in the process of happening, with no reference to their beginning or end. ¿Viste a Ana cuando **ibas** para el estadio?	1. Reports past actions or events that the speaker views as finished and completed, regardless of how long they lasted. Anoche él **jugó** al béisbol.
2. Describes a physical, mental, or emotional condition or characteristic in the past. No fui porque **estaba** enferma. **Era** delgada y **tenía** el pelo largo.	2. Sums up a condition or a physical or mental state, viewed as completed. **Estuve** enfermo toda la noche.
3. Refers to repeated or habitual actions in the past. Siempre **íbamos** con Ana.	
4. Describes or sets the stage in the past. **Hacía** frío y **llovía** cuando salí.	
5. Expresses time in the past. **Eran** las once cuando llegué.	
6. Is used in indirect discourse. Ella dijo que no **sabía** nadar.	
7. Describes age in the past. Ella **tenía** seis años.	

CD-ROM
Go to **Estructuras gramaticales** for additional practice.

Práctica

A. En parejas, lean cuidadosamente el diálogo de esta lección y busquen ejemplos del uso del pretérito y del uso del imperfecto. Den las razones por las cuales se usa uno u otro tiempo.

B. Complete el siguiente diálogo usando el pretérito o el imperfecto de los verbos que aparecen entre paréntesis. Después de completarlo, represéntelo en voz alta con un(a) compañero(a).

VÍCTOR —¡Oye! ¿Qué hora _____ (ser) cuando tú _____ (llegar) anoche?

ANDRÉS —_____ (Ser) las doce y media. Gloria y yo _____ (ir) a un partido de fútbol. ¿Qué _____ (hacer) tú ayer?

VÍCTOR —Como el día _____ (estar) muy hermoso y _____ (hacer) calor, Rita y yo _____ (ir) a la playa, pero _____ (volver) temprano porque ella _____ (decir) que le _____ (doler) mucho la cabeza.

ANDRÉS —Ayer a eso de las cuatro _____ (venir) a buscarte un muchacho. _____ (Decir) que _____ (llamarse) John Taylor.

VÍCTOR —¿John Taylor...? No sé quién es... ¿Cómo _____ (ser)?

ANDRÉS —_____ (Ser) rubio, de estatura mediana y _____ (tener) unos veinticinco años... _____ (Hablar) muy bien el español.

VÍCTOR —¡Ah, ya recuerdo! Cuando yo _____ (estar) en la escuela secundaria, él y yo muchas veces _____ (jugar) al baloncesto y él siempre _____ (ganar).

ANDRÉS —Él _____ (decir) que _____ (ir) a volver el sábado por la tarde.

VÍCTOR —Oye, ¿tú _____ (ver) a Marta en el partido de fútbol?

ANDRÉS —Sólo por un momento. ¿Tú y Rita no _____ (ir) al estadio anoche?

VÍCTOR —No, porque la pobre Rita _____ (estar) enferma toda la noche.

C. En parejas, completen cada oración de acuerdo con sus propias experiencias.

1. Cuando mis padres eran jóvenes...
2. Cuando era niño(a)...
3. Yo tenía ocho años cuando...
4. Mi mejor amigo(a) y yo...
5. En 1999, yo...
6. Mi primer(a) novio(a) era...
7. Cuando yo estaba en la escuela secundaria...
8. El verano pasado, mis amigos y yo...
9. Decidí estudiar en esta universidad porque...
10. Un día no pude asistir a clase porque...
11. La semana pasada, mi profesor(a)...
12. Yo le dije a mi profesor(a) que...
13. Ayer, cuando yo venía a la universidad...
14. Anoche mis amigos y yo...

D. En parejas, escojan a algún personaje famoso (jugador, atleta, etc.) y preparen de diez a quince preguntas para hacerle una entrevista sobre su niñez y su juventud (*youth*).

3 Verbos que cambian de significado en el pretérito

◯ Certain Spanish verbs have special English equivalents when used in the preterit tense. Contrast the English equivalents of **conocer, poder, querer,** and **saber** when these verbs are used in the imperfect and preterit tenses.

Imperfect		*Preterit*	
yo **conocía**	*I knew*	yo **conocí**	*I met*
yo **podía**	*I was able (capable)*	yo **pude**	*I managed, succeeded*
yo no **quería**	*I didn't want to*	yo no **quise**	*I refused*
yo **sabía**	*I knew*	yo **supe**	*I found out, learned*

—¿Tú no **conocías** al árbitro?   "*Didn't you know the umpire?*"
—No, lo **conocí** anoche.   "*No, I met him last night.*"

—Por fin **pude** aprender a escalar montañas.

"I finally managed to learn to climb mountains."

—Al principio yo tampoco **podía** hacerlo, pero no es tan difícil.

"At first I couldn't do it either, but it is not so difficult."

—Elena **no quiso** ir al hipódromo. Se quedó en casa.

"Elena refused to go to the race track. She stayed home."

—Yo tampoco **quería** ir, pero al fin fui.

"I didn't want to go either, but in the end I went."

—¿**Sabías** que teníamos un partido de fútbol hoy?

"Did you know we were having a soccer match today?"

—No, lo **supe** esta mañana.

"No, I found out this morning."

Práctica

CD-ROM
Go to **Estructuras gramaticales** for additional practice.

A. Complete lo siguiente con el pretérito o el imperfecto de los verbos estudiados, según corresponda.

1. —¿Por qué no fuiste a la pelea de boxeo?
   —No _____ ir porque tuve que trabajar.
   —Yo no _____ que tú trabajabas por la noche.
   —Y Julio, ¿fue?
   —No, él no _____ ir. Prefirió quedarse en casa.
2. —Ayer _____ que Daniel se casó.
   —Sí, se casó con Nora. Él la _____ la última vez que estuvo en Madrid.
   —Ah, yo no _____ que ella era de Madrid.
3. —¿Llamaste a Sofía?
   —Sí, _____ invitarla a las carreras de caballos, pero (nosotros) no _____ ir porque ella no se sentía bien.
4. —¿Ud. _____ a Carmen?
   —Sí, la _____ en el hipódromo la semana pasada.
5. —¡Tú nadas muy bien!
   —Pues cuando empecé la clase no _____ nada...

B. En parejas, háganse las siguientes preguntas.

1. ¿Conocías al profesor (a la profesora) antes de tomar esta clase?
2. ¿Cuándo lo (la) conociste?
3. ¿Sabías español antes de tomar esta clase?
4. ¿Podías hablar español cuando eras niño(a)?
5. ¿Cuándo supiste quién iba a ser tu profesor(a) de español?
6. ¿Pudiste terminar la tarea antes de venir?
7. Yo no quería venir hoy a clase. ¿Tú querías venir a clase hoy?
8. La última vez que no viniste a clase, ¿no pudiste o no quisiste venir?

4 Los pronombres relativos

◉ Relative pronouns are used to combine and *relate* two sentences that have a common element, usually a noun or pronoun.

A El pronombre relativo *que*

common element

¿Dónde están **los bates?**   ¿Trajiste **los bates?**

R.P.

¿Dónde están los bates **que** trajiste?

○ Notice that the relative pronoun **que** not only helps combine the two sentences, but also replaces the common element (**los bates**)[1] in the second sentence.

common element

¿Cómo se llama **el boxeador?**   **El boxeador** ganó la pelea.

R.P.

¿Cómo se llama el boxeador **que** ganó la pelea?

○ The relative pronoun **que** is invariable, and it is used for both persons and things. It is the Spanish equivalent of *that, which,* or *who*. Unlike its English equivalent, the Spanish **que** is never omitted.

B El pronombre relativo *quien* (*quienes*)

—¿El nadador **con quien**   "*Is the swimmer with whom you were*
hablabas es americano?   *speaking an American?*"
—No, es extranjero.   "*No, he's a foreigner.*"

—¿Quiénes son esos jugadores?   "*Who are those players?*"
—Son los jugadores **de quienes**   "*They're the players about whom José spoke*
te habló José.   *to you.*"

○ The relative pronoun **quien** is only used with persons.

○ The plural of **quien** is **quienes. Quien** does not change for gender, only for number.

○ **Quien** is generally used after prepositions: for example, **con quien, de quienes.**

○ **Quien** is the Spanish equivalent of *whom, that,* or *who.*

○ In written Spanish, **quien** may be used instead of **que** for *who* if the relative pronoun introduces a statement between commas. Compare:

Ésa es la señora **que** compró la casa.   *That is the woman who bought the house.*
Esa señora, **quien** compró la casa,   *That woman, who bought the house, is a*
es una mujer riquísima.   *very rich woman.*

C El pronombre relativo *cuyo*

○ The relative possessive **cuyo(-a, -os, -as)** means *whose*. It agrees in gender and number with the noun that follows it, *not* with the possessor.

Anita, **cuyos padres** por poco se matan en el accidente, fue a verlos.

---

[1] The common element appears in the main clause. This element is called the *antecedent* of the relative pronoun that introduces the subordinate clause, because it is the noun or the pronoun to which the relative pronoun refers.

In a question, the interrogative *whose?* is expressed by **¿de quién(es)...?**

> **¿De quién** es esa caña de pescar?

CD-ROM
Go to **Estructuras gramaticales** for additional practice.

Práctica

A. Jorge y Esteban son compañeros de cuarto en la universidad, pero casi nunca se ven. Cuando no pueden hablarse, se escriben notas. Ésta es una nota que Jorge le dejó a Esteban esta mañana. Complétela, usando los pronombres relativos correspondientes.

Esteban:

El señor a _____ llamamos ayer va a venir a las tres para arreglar el refrigerador. ¿Vas a estar en casa? La chica _____ discos usamos en la fiesta llamó esta mañana. Los necesita para la fiesta _____ ella va a dar esta noche. ¿De _____ son las dos cintas de Gloria Estefan _____ están en la mesa? Alberto y yo comimos los sándwiches _____ preparaste para tu almuerzo. ¡Lo siento!

¡Ah! La chica con _____ fuiste a esquiar quiere que la llames y la muchacha _____ fue con nosotros al hipódromo quiere verte hoy.

Jorge

B. Use su imaginación para escribir la nota que Esteban le escribiría (*would write*) a Jorge, en respuesta a la suya. Cuéntele lo que pasó mientras (*while*) él no estaba.

5 Expresiones de tiempo con *hacer*

○ The expression **hace** + *period of time* + **que** + *verb in the present indicative* is used in Spanish to refer to an action that started in the past and is still going on. It is equivalent to the use of the present perfect or the present perfect progressive + *period of time* in English.

> **Hace + dos horas + que +** los aficionados **están** aquí.
> *The fans have been here for two hours.*

—¿Cuánto tiempo **hace que juegas** en ese equipo?　　"How long have you been playing on that team?"
—**Hace tres años que juego** allí.　　"I've been playing there for three years."

—¿Cuánto tiempo **hace que esperan** al entrenador?　　"How long have you been waiting for the coach?"
—**Hace media hora que lo esperamos**. No sé si va a venir.　　"We've been waiting for him for a half hour. I don't know if he's going to come."

○ The expression **hacía** + *period of time* + **que** + *verb in the imperfect* is used to refer to an action that started in the past and was still going on when another action took place.

> **Hacía + dos meses + que + vivía** aquí cuando **murió**.
> *He had been living here for two months when he died.*

—¿Cuánto tiempo **hacía que el**   *"How long had the champion been here*
  campeón estaba aquí cuando   *when I arrived?"*
  yo llegué?
—**Hacía solamente diez minutos**   *"He had only been here for ten minutes."*
  que estaba aquí.

○ The expression **hace** + *period of time* + **que** + *verb in the preterit* is used to refer to the time elapsed since a given action took place. In this construction, **hace** is equivalent to *ago* in English.

> **Hace + dos horas + que + llegué** al estadio.
> *I arrived at the stadium two hours ago.*

—¿Ese gimnasta todavía está   *"That gymnast is still practicing?"*
  practicando?
—¡Sí! ¡Y **hace tres horas que**   *"Yes! And he started three hours ago!"*
  empezó!
—¿Cuándo terminaron la carrera?   *"When did they finish the race?"*
—**Terminaron hace cinco minutos.**   *"They finished five minutes ago."*

atención

In all of these constructions, if **hace** is placed after the verb, the word **que** is omitted.

Llegó a los Estados Unidos **hace** un año.   *He arrived in the United States a year ago.*

Práctica

CD-ROM
Go to **Estructuras gramati-cales** for additional practice.

A. Vuelva a escribir lo siguiente, indicando el tiempo transcurrido (*elapsed*) entre los diferentes sucesos (*events*). Siga el modelo.

MODELO: Estamos en el año 2004. / Vivo en California desde (*since*) 1989.
           Hace quince años que vivo en California.

1. Estamos en agosto. / Tomo clases de natación desde febrero.
2. Son las cinco de la tarde. / Estamos en el estadio desde las dos de la tarde.
3. Hoy es viernes. / Yo no veo a mi entrenador desde el lunes.
4. Estamos en abril. / No juego al fútbol desde enero.
5. Son las tres y veinte. / Los jugadores están aquí desde las tres.
6. Son las nueve. / Ellos están nadando desde las ocho y media.
7. Estamos en el año 2004. / Practico gimnasia desde el año 2002.
8. Son las nueve de la noche. / No como desde las nueve de la mañana.

B. Escriba oraciones usando la información dada y la construcción **hacía... que**. Siga el modelo.

MODELO: tres años / ellos / trabajar allí / conocerse
           Hacía tres años que ellos trabajaban allí cuando se conocieron.

1. dos horas / ellas / hablar / deportes / yo / llegar
2. cuatro días / ella / estar / Quito / enfermarse
3. veinte minutos / Uds. / comentar / juego / yo / llamarlos
4. una hora / el gimnasta / practicar / él / lastimarse

5. media hora / ellos / jugar / empatar
6. quince minutos / nosotros / jugar / marcar / un gol

C. Entreviste a un(a) compañero(a) de clase sobre lo siguiente. Usen construcciones con **hace** y dé alguna información personal. Siga el modelo.

MODELO: graduarse de la escuela secundaria
E1: —*¿Cuánto tiempo hace que te graduaste de la escuela secundaria?*
E2: —*Hace dos años que me gradué de la escuela secundaria. Mi familia vivía en Omaha en esa época.*

STUDENT WEBSITE
Do the **Compruebe cuánto sabe** self test after finishing this **Estructuras gramaticales** section.

1. casarse sus abuelos
2. nacer sus padres
3. aprender a leer
4. aprender a montar en bicicleta
5. graduarse de la escuela primaria
6. empezar a estudiar en la universidad
7. enamorarse (*to fall in love*) por primera vez

¡CONTINUEMOS!

Una encuesta

Entreviste a sus compañeros de clase para tratar de identificar a aquellas personas que...

1. ...leen la página deportiva todos los días.
2. ...vieron un partido de fútbol (básquetbol, béisbol) la semana pasada.
3. ...prefieren ir al estadio en vez de ver los partidos en televisión.
4. ...van a ver las peleas de boxeo.
5. ...fueron a patinar la semana pasada.
6. ...saben esquiar.
7. ...tienen tiendas de campaña.
8. ...fueron a pescar el verano pasado.
9. ...saben montar a caballo.
10. ...son aficionados a la lucha libre.
11. ...no pueden estar sentadas mucho rato.
12. ...conocen a una persona enclenque.

Y ahora discutan el resultado de la encuesta con el resto de la clase.

¿Comprende Ud.?

CD-ROM STUDENT WEBSITE
Go to **De escuchar...a escribir** (in **¿Comprende Ud.?**) on the CD-ROM for activities related to the conversation, and go to **Canción** on the website for activities related to the song.

1. Paco, el amigo de los chicos que dialogan al inicio de esta lección, está en Portillo, Chile. Escuche la siguiente conversación entre Paco y Rocío, una chica que conoció en el hotel. El objetivo de la actividad es el de escuchar una conversación a velocidad natural. No se preocupe de entenderlo todo, pues esto no se espera de Ud. Después de escuchar la conversación dos veces, Ud. oirá varias aseveraciones. En una hoja, escriba los números de uno a ocho e indique si cada aseveración es verdadera o falsa.
2. Luego escuche la canción y trate de aprenderla.

Hablemos de deportes

En parejas, fíjense en este anuncio y contesten las siguientes preguntas.

Julio–Agosto

Inglés en Verano
Viviendo el Inglés en plena actividad

En España

● Deportes náuticos ● Equitación ● Informática
● Artes plásticas ● Piscinas ● Tenis ● Golf
● Actividades culturales. Todo ello en magníficas
instalaciones en plena naturaleza

Izarra
International College
Residencial o externos. De 8 a 16 años.

Estepona
(Málaga) Residencial o externos. De 8 a 16 años.

En Inglaterra
Residencial Desde 8 años.
Jóvenes y adultos.

Cursos intensivos en
convivencia con chicos
y chicas ingleses
de la misma edad.

● Deportes náuticos
● Dry ski ● Equitación
● Esgrima ● Tenis
● Karts ● Moto cross
● Excursiones ● Cursos para familias

1. ¿En qué estación del año se ofrecen estos cursos?
2. Si una persona de cuarenta años quiere tomar parte en este programa, ¿dónde lo van a aceptar?
3. Además de los deportes, ¿qué otras clases se ofrecen en España?
4. ¿Qué clases ofrecen en Inglaterra que no ofrecen en España?
5. Si una persona quiere tomar los cursos en España, pero no quiere vivir en la escuela, ¿puede hacerlo? ¿Cómo lo saben?

¿Qué dirían ustedes?

Imagínese que Ud. y un(a) compañero(a) se encuentran en las siguientes situaciones. ¿Qué va a decir cada uno?

1. Un amigo de Uds. no pudo ver un partido de fútbol. Cuéntenle lo que pasó.
2. Uds. quieren ir a ver un partido de básquetbol y un(a) amigo(a) no quiere ir. Traten de convencerlo(a) para que vaya con Uds.
3. Uds. están hablando con unos amigos de los eventos deportivos más importantes de la semana.

¡De ustedes depende!

El club de español va a publicar su propio periódico y Ud. y un(a) compañero(a) están a cargo de la sección deportiva. Discutan cuáles son las noticias que van a publicar este mes y lo que van a escribir sobre ellas.

¡Debate!

La clase se va a dividir en dos grupos de acuerdo con la opinión de cada estudiante sobre lo que son unas "vacaciones perfectas". Cada grupo va a hablar de las ventajas de sus vacaciones "ideales" y va a tratar de convencer a los miembros del otro grupo.

1. Unas vacaciones en las que acampamos en la playa, en el bosque o en la montaña, y participamos en toda clase de actividades al aire libre.
2. Unas vacaciones en las que visitamos una ciudad muy interesante, nos hospedamos en buenos hoteles y participamos en todas las actividades típicas de una gran ciudad.

Lecturas periodísticas

Saber leer La lectura *no* es pasiva

CD-ROM
Go to **Lecturas periodísticas** for additional prereading and vocabulary activities.

La lectura requiere la participación **activa** del lector. Para leer activamente, un lector debe asegurarse de tener sus objetivos muy claros antes de leer. Establecidos (*Having established*) los objetivos, hay que definir **estrategias** para alcanzarlos (*attain them*).

Antes de leer la siguiente lectura periodística, considere dos objetivos importantes: conocer en qué consiste la actividad de *trekking*, y practicar y desarrollar sus destrezas (*skills*) de lectura en español. Ahora piense en una o dos estrategias que le van a ayudar a alcanzar estos objetivos. Dos estrategias posibles son: (1) leer primero las preguntas para anticipar la información que debe buscar y (2) echarle una mirada rápida (*skim and scan*) al artículo para tener en mente un contexto general al leer. Antes de leer, ¡ponga en práctica las estrategias que Ud. escogió!

Para leer y comprender

Al leer el artículo detalladamente, busque las respuestas a las siguientes preguntas.

1. ¿Cómo se puede definir la palabra *trekking*?
2. ¿Qué requieren los *trekkings* y por qué?
3. ¿Cómo se orientan los *trekkers*?
4. Señale algunos aspectos que es necesario tener en cuenta al planear un *trekking*.
5. ¿Qué conocimientos debe tener el guía?
6. Nombre algunas de las cosas que debe llevar un(a) *trekker*.
7. ¿Con qué ayuda cuentan los *trekkers* para cargar el equipo?

Caminando hasta el fin del mundo

¿Qué es el trekking*?*

El uso de este anglicismo es mundialmente conocido entre° los aventureros. Es hacer una larga caminata° en lugares lejanos, en contacto con la naturaleza y con culturas remotas. Durante días los *trekkers* se internan en los lugares más fascinantes del mundo: selvas°, desiertos, sierras, altas montañas, los helados reinos° del Ártico y de la Antártida.

Estas expediciones requieren una minuciosa planeación y rigurosa preparación física y mental, ya que° durante días los aventureros se encuentran aislados del resto del mundo, a muchas horas y kilómetros de estaciones de radio, hospitales, carreteras, aeropuertos, en fin, de los servicios y las comodidades° de las grandes civilizaciones. Caminan durante días orientándose con brújula° y mapas, soportando las inclemencias del tiempo y afrontando° los peligros de la naturaleza.

El *trekking* no es extremadamente peligroso, ni está reservado para verdaderos locos de la aventura, pero éste tiene que estar planeado perfectamente tomando en cuenta° el terreno, la época° del año, las condiciones climáticas, los peligros y posibles accidentes, el sistema de carga°, la comida y los puntos de interés de la zona.

Generalmente va un guía especializado en aventura que es el encargado de darle confianza y seguridad al grupo. Está preparado en primeros auxilios° y conoce perfectamente el terreno de acción, así como las plantas, los animales, los poblados° y los paisajes más bellos y espectaculares de la ruta.

La planeación de cada *trekking* debe hacerse cuidadosamente. Cada integrante tiene que cargar° todo su equipo, por lo que es muy importante no cargar cosas innecesarias. Hay que llevar botas cómodas y ligeras°, ropa adecuada, una buena mochila°, un botiquín°, dos cantimploras°, comida energética, cuchillo de campo°, un impermeable, una bolsa de dormir y, si se lleva equipo fotográfico, cargar sólo lo indispensable. Cada *trekking* exige° distinto equipo y herramientas°.

Por lo general, se alquilan animales como mulas, caballos o yaks para cargar el equipo, según el lugar donde se elige ir, o se contratan porteadores° que ayudan con el equipo.

Si Ud. decide ir en un *trekking* va a tener la oportunidad de descubrir y proteger los rincones° más bellos y lejanos de nuestro planeta y de vivir una aventura inolvidable.

Adaptado de la revista *Escala* (México)

> *El trekking no es extremadamente peligroso, ni está reservado para verdaderos locos de la aventura...*

Perú: Un grupo de turistas disfruta de la vista de los majestuosos Andes.

---

among
hike
forests
kingdoms
ya... since
comforts
compass

facing
tomando... keeping in mind
time

loading
primeros... first aid
villages
carry
light
backpack
first aid kit / canteens

cuchillo... pocketknife
demands
tools
bearers

corners

Desde su mundo

1. ¿Qué lugares de su país recomienda Ud. para un *trekking*?
2. ¿A Ud. y a sus amigos les gusta la idea de hacer *trekking*? ¿Por qué o por qué no?

STUDENT WEBSITE

CD-ROM

Go to **...y escribamos** (in **Hablemos de su país**) on the student website and **De escuchar... a escribir** (in **¿Comprende Ud.?**) on the CD-ROM for additional writing practice.

Piense y escriba   Generar ideas

Recuerde las estrategias que Ud. aprendió a utilizar en las **Lecciones 1** y **2** para generar ideas sobre lo que Ud. quiere comunicar.

Hoy le asignamos el siguiente tipo de escrito: un diálogo entre una persona a quien le encantan las actividades al aire libre y una que las odia. Antes de empezar a escribir el diálogo, haga una lista de todas las actividades al aire libre que Ud. conoce, para generar posibles ideas. Puede utilizar como modelo el diálogo entre Pablo Villalobos y Rafael Vargas, que está al inicio de la lección.

Pepe Vega y su mundo

bolsa... sleeping bag

Teleinforme

Los deportes se pueden practicar en grupo o individualmente, para competir o sólo por el placer (pleasure) de llevar a cabo la actividad. Aquí vamos a ver dos actividades muy distintas, pero que tienen algunos aspectos en común: el fútbol, el deporte más popular de todo el mundo hispánico, y el rafting, *una actividad al aire libre muy emocionante.*

Preparación

Clasifique las siguientes expresiones según pertenezcan al mundo del fútbol (**F**), del *rafting* (**R**) o ¡de los dos (**FR**)! Explique brevemente la clasificación de diez de las expresiones.

_____ 1. la alineación (*line-up*)
_____ 2. la balsa inflable (*inflatable raft*)
_____ 3. el cañón (*canyon*)
_____ 4. el capitán (la capitana)
_____ 5. el casco (*helmet*)
_____ 6. el (la) centrocampista (*halfback*)
_____ 7. el chaleco salvavidas (*life jacket*)
_____ 8. clasificarse
_____ 9. correr
_____ 10. la defensa
_____ 11. el entrenamiento (*training*)
_____ 12. el equipo (*team; equipment*)
_____ 13. el estadio
_____ 14. la estrategia
_____ 15. expulsado(a)
_____ 16. el gol

_____ 17. el guía
_____ 18. el hule (*rubber*)
_____ 19. el (la) jugador(a)
_____ 20. maniobrar
_____ 21. los obstáculos
_____ 22. el partido
_____ 23. los pedazos de árboles
_____ 24. los pies
_____ 25. los rápidos [de] clase 3
_____ 26. remar (*to row*)
_____ 27. el río
_____ 28. río abajo (*downstream*)
_____ 29. la selección
_____ 30. la tarjeta amarilla (*yellow card*)
_____ 31. la tarjeta roja
_____ 32. la victoria

Comprensión

STUDENT WEBSITE
Go to **Video** for further previewing, vocabulary, and structure practice on this clip.

Partido de fútbol España-Rumanía   9:11–11:56

En este reportaje de la Televisión Española (RTVE) vamos a oír las opiniones de varias personas sobre un importante partido de fútbol entre España y Rumanía. España espera quedar en la clasificación final para la Eurocopa de Naciones y Rumanía espera conservar su orgullo (*pride*) nacional y deportivo.

A. ¿Qué oye Ud.? Mientras ve el video por primera vez, marque las expresiones de la lista en la sección de **Preparación** que Ud. oye o ve en el reportaje sobre el partido de fútbol España-Rumanía.

B. ¿Cuánto entiende Ud.?   Vea el video por segunda vez y conteste las siguientes preguntas según lo que Ud. entienda.

1. Según este reportaje, ¿quién va a ganar el partido probablemente?
2. ¿En qué lugar está el equipo rumano: en primero o en último lugar?
3. ¿Cuáles de estos nombres corresponden a jugadores del equipo español: Filipescu, Kikó, López, Luis Enrique, Manjarín, Nadal, Pizzi, Popesku?
4. ¿En qué ciudad se entrenan los jugadores: en Madrid, en Londres o en Leeds?
5. ¿Qué va a ocurrir si España gana este partido?
6. ¿Por qué están enfadados los jugadores rumanos?
7. ¿Les falta motivación a los jugadores rumanos?

Rafting en el Río Pacuare   11:58–15:11

CD-ROM
Go to **Video** for further previewing, vocabulary, and structure practice on this clip.

En este episodio del programa *De paseo* de Costa Rica, conocemos al Sr. Rafael Gallo, presidente de la Compañía Ríos Tropicales. Rafael nos habla de la popularidad, la técnica y lo divertido del *rafting* en los ríos de Costa Rica.

C. ¿Qué oye Ud.?   Mientras ve el video por primera vez, marque las expresiones de la lista en la sección de **Preparación** que Ud. oye en el programa sobre el *rafting* en el Río Pacuare.

D. ¿Cuánto entiende Ud.?   Indique si las siguientes oraciones son verdaderas (**V**) o falsas (**F**). Si son falsas, corríjalas.

1. _____ El *rafting* es el deporte de correr.
2. _____ Se usan balsas de hule inflables para hacer el *rafting*.
3. _____ Cualquier persona puede manejar y maniobrar la balsa sin la ayuda de un guía.
4. _____ El Río Corobicí es un río muy tranquilo.
5. _____ Se puede llevar niños o personas de edad avanzada en un río de clase 1 ó 2.
6. _____ Hacer *rafting* en el Río Reventazón es poco emocionante.
7. _____ En un río de clase 3, es el guía el que lleva el control de la balsa y el que debe maniobrarla.
8. _____ Para practicar *rafting* en los ríos de clase 4 o de clase 5 se necesita bastante experiencia.
9. _____ El Pacuare tiene rápidos de clase 1 y de clase 2.
10. _____ Lo más importante del deporte de *rafting* es prestarles atención a las corrientes y al agua.
11. _____ Sólo los niños deben llevar el chaleco salvavidas.
12. _____ Los participantes tienen que sentarse con los pies hacia río abajo.

Ampliación

¡Debate!   Con un(a) compañero(a) prepare un debate o una presentación sobre uno de los siguientes temas.

1. actividad de competencia vs. actividad que no es de competencia
2. actividad de equipo vs. actividad individual
3. actividad organizada vs. actividad poco estructurada

Dé ejemplos de cada tipo de actividad. ¿Qué tienen en común? ¿Cuáles son las diferencias importantes? ¿Quiénes son los participantes? ¿Cuál es la estructura de la actividad? ¿Qué equipo es necesario para llevarla a cabo? ¿Cuáles son las ventajas y desventajas de cada tipo de actividad?

Costumbres y tradiciones

Una celebración, al estilo sevillano.

Costumbres y tradiciones

CD-ROM   STUDENT AUDIO

For preparation, do the **Ante todo** activities found on the CD-ROM.

María Isabel, una chica paraguaya, le escribe una carta a su amiga Kathy, que es de Colorado, para contarle de sus planes para la visita de Kathy a Asunción.

1° de noviembre del 2003

Querida Kathy:

Ojalá que ya estés mejor y no tengamos que cambiar nuestros planes para tu viaje. Ahora tengo mucho trabajo, pero espero poder terminar todos mis proyectos y estar libre durante el mes de diciembre.

Hoy se celebra aquí el Día de todos los Santos, de modo que esta mañana fui a misa. Mañana es el Día de los Muertos y vamos a ir al cementerio a llevar flores a la tumba de mi abuela. ¿Recuerdas que cuando estuvimos en México vimos que allá llevan flores, velas y comida y que pasan la noche en el cementerio? ¡Eso es más interesante que lo que hacemos aquí!

Tú piensas llegar a Asunción el 28 de noviembre, ¿verdad? Ése es el Día de los Inocentes[1]. Te advierto que Gustavo, mi hermano menor, tiene preparadas varias bromas para ti, que es lo que la gente hace aquí ese día.

El 8 de diciembre queremos llevarte a un pueblo cercano a Asunción, que se llama Caacupé, donde se celebra el Día de la Virgen de Caacupé, que es la santa patrona de Paraguay. ¡Vas a poder tomar parte en una procesión!

Tenemos muchos planes para celebrar la Navidad. El 24, el Día de Nochebuena, vas a disfrutar de una cena típicamente paraguaya: lechón asado, pollo y la famosa sopa paraguaya, que no es sopa, sino una especie de pan de maíz. Después vamos a ir a ver los pesebres y a la medianoche, a la Misa del Gallo. No vas a tener una Navidad blanca, porque aquí estamos en pleno verano y hace mucho calor.

El día 31, después de la cena aquí, en casa, vamos a ir todos a un club, al baile de fin de año. A las doce de la noche vamos a brindar con sidra y vamos a ver muchos fuegos artificiales.

Es una lástima que no puedas quedarte hasta el 6 de enero –el Día de los Reyes Magos– que es cuando los niños de por aquí reciben regalos.

Necesito saber el número de tu vuelo para poder ir por ti al aeropuerto. También dime por cuánto tiempo piensas quedarte.

Espero que me escribas pronto. ¡No veo la hora de verte!

Cariños,

María Isabel

P.D. A fines de marzo voy a Bolivia para asistir a una conferencia. ¿Quieres ir conmigo? ¡Tu horóscopo dice que debes viajar más!

---

[1] A day on which people play practical jokes on each other, as we do on April Fool's Day.

Dígame

En parejas, contesten las siguientes preguntas basadas en la carta.

1. ¿En qué mes desea María Isabel que vaya Kathy a Asunción?
2. ¿Qué se celebra en Paraguay el 1° de noviembre? ¿Qué hizo María Isabel por la mañana?
3. ¿Adónde va a ir María Isabel mañana? ¿Por qué? ¿Qué va a llevar al cementerio?
4. ¿Gustavo es mayor o menor que María Isabel? ¿Qué tiene preparado Gustavo y por qué?
5. ¿Adónde van a llevar a Kathy el 8 de diciembre? ¿Qué se celebra allí? ¿Qué va a poder hacer Kathy?
6. ¿Qué se celebra el 24 de diciembre? ¿De qué va a disfrutar Kathy?
7. ¿Qué van a hacer después de cenar? ¿Adónde van a ir a la medianoche?
8. ¿Qué tiempo hace en Paraguay en diciembre?
9. ¿Qué van a hacer el 31 de diciembre?
10. ¿Qué se celebra el 6 de enero? ¿Qué reciben los niños?
11. ¿Qué necesita saber María Isabel y para qué?
12. ¿Qué país va a visitar María Isabel? ¿Cuándo? ¿Qué va a hacer allí?

Perspectivas socioculturales

• •

INSTRUCTOR WEBSITE
Your instructor may assign the preconversational support activities found in **Perspectivas socioculturales.**

Las celebraciones varían entre las diferentes culturas. Haga lo siguiente:

1. Durante unos cinco minutos, converse con dos compañeros sobre el siguiente tema: **¿Cuáles son las principales celebraciones de su cultura?**
2. Participe con el resto de la clase en la discusión del tema cuando su profesor(a) se lo indique.

Vocabulario

Nombres
la broma   practical joke
el cementerio   cemetery
el fin de año   New Year's Eve
la flor   flower
los fuegos artificiales   fireworks
la gente   people
el maíz   corn
la misa   mass
la Misa del Gallo   Midnight Mass
la Nochebuena   Christmas Eve

el pesebre, el nacimiento   manger, nativity scene
los Reyes Magos   the Three Wise Men
el (la) santo(a)   saint
el (la) santo(a) patrón(-ona)   patron saint
la sidra[1]   cider
la tumba   grave
la vela   candle

_____
[1] An alcoholic cider often served in Spanish-speaking countries instead of champagne

Verbos

brindar   to toast
cambiar   to change
disfrutar (de)   to enjoy
pasar   to spend (*time*)

Adjetivos

cercano(a)   nearby
libre   free
querido(a)   dear

Otras palabras y expresiones

a fines de   at the end of

dime   tell me
en pleno verano   in the middle of the summer
es una lástima   it's a pity
no ver la hora de...   not to be able to wait to . . .
por aquí   around here
pronto   soon
sino   but (in the sense of *on the contrary*)
tomar parte en   to take part in
una especie de   a kind of

Ampliación

Algunas celebraciones

Año Nuevo   New Year's Day
los Carnavales   Mardi Gras
Día de Acción de Gracias   Thanksgiving
Día de las Brujas   Halloween
Día de los Enamorados   Valentine's Day
Día de Canadá   Canada Day
Día de la Independencia   Independence Day
Día de la Madre   Mother's Day
Día de Pascua Florida   Easter
Día del Padre   Father's Day
Día del Trabajo   Labor Day
La Semana Santa   Holy Week
Víspera de Año Nuevo (Fin de Año)   New Year's Eve

Palabras relacionadas con las supersticiones

el amuleto   amulet
la bruja   witch
la brujería   witchcraft
el diablo, el demonio   devil, demon
la herradura   horseshoe
la magia negra   black magic
el (la) mago(a)   magician
el mal de ojo   evil eye
la pata de conejo   rabbit's foot
los signos del zodíaco   zodiac signs
el trébol de cuatro hojas   four-leaf clover

CD-ROM
Go to **Vocabulario** for additional vocabulary practice.

Hablando de todo un poco

Preparación   **Encuentre en la columna B las respuestas a las preguntas de la columna A (las listas continúan en la página siguiente).**

A

1. ¿Vas al cementerio a llevar flores y velas?

B

a. El 6 de enero.
b. Sí, y tomé parte en la procesión.

2. ¿Con qué vas a brindar la Víspera de Año Nuevo?

3. ¿Vio él los fuegos artificiales?

4. ¿Qué hiciste tú el día de Nochebuena?

5. ¿Cuándo se celebra el Día de Reyes?

6. ¿Van a viajar Uds. a fines de julio?

7. ¿Qué es la sopa paraguaya?

8. ¿Vas a ir a visitar a tus padres?

9. ¿Ester es supersticiosa?

10. ¿La gente de por aquí cree en las brujas?

11. ¿Fuiste a la fiesta del santo patrón?

12. ¿Dónde pasaron Uds. el Día de los Enamorados?

13. ¿Tienes un amuleto?

14. ¿Piensas cambiar tus planes de viaje?

15. ¿Cuál es otro nombre para el diablo?

16. ¿Te dijo que era un mago famoso?

c. Sí, y es una lástima, pero no estoy libre.

d. Sí, y también en la magia negra.

e. Sí, siempre tiene una pata de conejo, una herradura y un trébol de cuatro hojas.

f. Sí, para la tumba de mi abuela.

g. Demonio.

h. Sí, el Día de la Independencia.

i. Con sidra.

j. Fuimos a un restaurante cercano y disfrutamos de una cena excelente.

k. Es un pan de maíz.

l. Fui a ver los pesebres y después a la Misa del Gallo.

m. Sí, pero era una broma.

n. Sí, para evitar el mal de ojo y la brujería.

o. Sí, queremos ir en pleno verano.

p. Sí, muy pronto. No veo la hora de estar con ellos.

En grupos de tres o cuatro, hagan lo siguiente.

A. El calendario de fiestas.

1. Digan qué se celebra en las siguientes fechas.
   a. el 1 de enero
   b. el 14 de febrero
   c. el segundo domingo de mayo
   d. el tercer domingo de junio
   e. el 1 de julio
   f. el 4 de julio
   g. el primer lunes de septiembre
   h. el 31 de octubre
   i. el cuarto jueves de noviembre
   j. el 24 de diciembre
   k. el 31 de diciembre

2. Ahora hablen sobre las distintas celebraciones que hay durante el año. ¿Qué hacen ustedes y su familia en esos días? ¿Quiénes toman parte en esas actividades? ¿Tienen ustedes algunas costumbres y tradiciones especiales?

B. Supersticiones.   Hablen sobre las supersticiones que mucha gente tiene. ¿Creen ustedes en ellas o no?

Palabras problemáticas

A. **Pensar, pensar (de), pensar (en)** como equivalentes de *to think (of)*

- **Pensar** se usa en los siguientes casos:

  1. Cuando se quiere expresar un proceso mental.

     ¡El problema que tienes tú es que no **piensas**!

  2. Cuando se habla de planear algo.

     El sábado **piensan** ir a una fiesta de Fin de Año.

- **Pensar (de)** es el equivalente en español de *to think (about)* cuando se pide opinión.

  ¿Qué **piensas** tú **de** las supersticiones?

- **Pensar (en)** se usa sólo para indicar un proceso mental, y no para expresar opinión.

  Estoy **pensando en** mi viaje a Bolivia.

B. **Obra** y **trabajo** como equivalentes de *work*

- **Obra** se utiliza principalmente para referirse a un trabajo de tipo artístico o intelectual.

  El profesor de arte nos habló de la **obra** de Picasso.

- **Trabajo** equivale a *work* como sinónimo de *task*.

  No puedo ir al cementerio contigo porque tengo mucho **trabajo**.

C. **Personas, gente** y **pueblo** como equivalentes de *people*

- **Personas** es el equivalente en español de la palabra *people* cuando se refiere a los individuos de un grupo. Puede referirse a un número determinado o indeterminado de individuos.

  Cinco **personas** solicitaron el trabajo.
  Algunas **personas** llegaron muy temprano a la fiesta.

- **Gente**[1] equivale a *people* cuando se usa como nombre colectivo de un grupo. No se usa con números o con las palabras **algunas** y **varias.**

  La **gente** se preocupa demasiado por el dinero.

- **Pueblo** equivale a *people* cuando se refiere a las personas de una misma nacionalidad.

  El **pueblo** paraguayo va a elegir un nuevo presidente.

---

[1] **Gente** is usually used in the singular: La gente **está** asustada. *People are frightened.*

Práctica

Entreviste a un(a) compañero(a), usando las siguientes preguntas.

1. ¿Tienes mucho trabajo esta semana?
2. ¿Qué piensas hacer este fin de semana?
3. ¿En qué estás pensando en este momento?
4. Cuando tienes que decidir algo importante, ¿lo piensas mucho?
5. ¿Tú sabes cuántas personas hay en esta clase?
6. ¿Tú conoces la obra de algún escritor hispanoamericano?
7. ¿Qué piensa la gente del presidente?
8. ¿Qué crees tú que es lo más importante para el pueblo americano?

Your instructor may carry out the ¡Ahora escuche! listening activity found in the Answers to Text Exercises.

¡Ahora escuche!

Se leerá dos veces una breve narración sobre Carlos y Amanda, una pareja de novios que vive en La Paz, Bolivia. Se harán aseveraciones sobre la narración. En una hoja escriba los números de uno a diez e indique si cada aseveración es verdadera (V) o falsa (F).

El mundo hispánico

En el corazón de Sudamérica: Paraguay y Bolivia

María Isabel

Paraguay es pequeño, pero hospitalario y acogedor°.   welcoming
Como Bolivia, no tiene salida al mar, de modo que los ríos son las principales vías de comunicación del país. Sobre el río Paraná se construyó la represa° de   dam
Itaipú, la planta hidroeléctrica más grande del mundo. La presa que retiene las aguas del Paraná es tan alta como un edificio de sesenta pisos y tiene una longitud de cinco millas.

Si vienen a visitar mi país, no deben dejar de ver las famosas cataratas° de Iguazú que en   falls
guaraní, el segundo idioma de los paraguayos, significa "agua grande". Debido a° su espléndida   **Debido**... Due to
belleza°, Paraguay fue escogido como escenario de   beauty
la película *La misión*, filmada en las ruinas jesuíticas, que datan del siglo XVII.

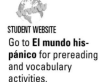

STUDENT WEBSITE
Go to **El mundo hispánico** for prereading and vocabulary activities.

La música paraguaya, así como su artesanía, es una mezcla° de las culturas española y guaraní. Los turistas quedan fascinados con las polcas y las guaranias, y llevan de recuerdo los exquisitos manteles de ñandutí, un tipo de encaje° que sólo se encuentra en Paraguay.   **mixture**   **lace**

La capital, Asunción, es también el puerto principal del país. Aquí, los edificios altos y modernos se mezclan armoniosamente con las casas coloniales, con sus patios donde florecen jazmines y madreselvas°.   **honeysuckle**

Al noroeste de Paraguay está Bolivia, un país de superlativos. Tiene, entre otras cosas, el lago navegable más alto del mundo —el Titicaca— de belleza espectacular, el aeropuerto más alto, la capital más alta y una de las ruinas más antiguas. Bolivia se conoce también por tener dos capitales: La Paz, que hoy día es la capital de facto, y Sucre, donde tiene sede el poder judicial.

Espero que algún día puedan visitar Paraguay y Bolivia, nuestro país vecino°. Mientras tanto, fíjense en el mapa, que les deja ver dónde están situados.   **neighboring**

Sobre Paraguay y Bolivia

En parejas, túrnense para contestar las siguientes preguntas.

1. ¿Cuáles son los límites de Paraguay al norte, al sur, al este y al oeste?
2. ¿Cuáles son los dos países sudamericanos que no tienen salida al mar?
3. ¿Qué sabe usted de la represa de Itaipú?
4. ¿Cómo es la presa que retiene las aguas del río Paraná?

5. ¿Qué cataratas podemos visitar si vamos a Paraguay?
6. ¿Qué famosa película se filmó en Paraguay? ¿Por qué escogieron Paraguay para filmarla?
7. ¿Qué influencias se ven en la música y en la artesanía paraguayas?
8. ¿Qué sabe usted de Asunción? ¿Cómo son los edificios?
9. ¿Cuáles son los "superlativos" que caracterizan a Bolivia?
10. ¿Cuáles son las dos capitales de Bolivia? ¿En qué se distingue cada una?

Hablemos de su país

INSTRUCTOR WEBSITE
STUDENT WEBSITE
Your instructor may assign the preconversational activities in **Hablemos...** (under **Hablemos de su país**). Go to **Hablemos de su país** (under **...y escribamos)** for postconversational web search and writing activities.

El ensayo hace referencia a la riqueza cultural de Paraguay, específicamente en cuanto a idiomas, música y artesanía. Reúnase con otro(a) compañero(a) para contestar una de las siguientes preguntas: ¿Qué idiomas se hablan en su país o región? ¿Se puede decir que la música de su país mezcla elementos de diferentes culturas? ¿Con qué tipos de artesanía se quedan fascinados los turistas que visitan su país?

Luego cada pareja compartirá las respuestas con toda la clase. ¿Hay algún consenso acerca de las respuestas?

Una tarjeta postal

Imagínese que Ud. y un(a) compañero(a) están viajando por Paraguay. Envíenles una tarjeta postal a sus compañeros de clase, describiendo sus impresiones.

Queridos amigos,

_____

_____

_____

_____

_____

_____

_____

Saludos,

Estructuras gramaticales

STUDENT WEBSITE
Do the **¿Cuánto recuerda?** pretest to check what you already know on the topics covered in this **Estructuras gramaticales** section.

1 Comparativos de igualdad y de desigualdad

A Comparativos de igualdad

○ Comparisons of equality of nouns, adjectives, adverbs, and verbs in Spanish use the adjectives **tanto(-a, -os, -as)** or the adverbs **tan, tanto + como,** as follows:

When comparing nouns		*When comparing adjectives or adverbs*		*When comparing verbs*	
tanto (dinero) (*as much*) **tanta** (plata) **tantos** (libros) (*as many*) **tantas** (plumas)	+ **como**	bonita **tan** (*as*) tarde	+ **como**	bebo **tanto** (*as much*)	+ **como**

—¡Tengo mucho trabajo!
—Yo tengo **tanto trabajo como** tú y no me quejo.

"*I have a lot of work!*"
"*I have as much work as you (do) and I don't complain.*"

—Tú compras muchas flores.
—Sí, pero no compro **tantas flores como** tú.

"*You buy a lot of flowers.*"
"*Yes, but I don't buy as many flowers as you (do).*"

—Jaime no es puntual. Siempre llega tarde.
—Es verdad. No es **tan puntual como** nosotros.

"*Jaime is not punctual. He's always late.*"
"*It's true. He's not as punctual as we are.*"

—Ahora no camino **tan rápido como** antes.
—Es verdad...

"*These days I don't walk as fast as I used to (before).*"
"*That's true . . .*"

—Cada vez que haces algo, te quejas.
—Tú te quejas **tanto como** yo, y nunca haces nada.

"*Every time you do something, you complain.*"
"*You complain as much as I (do) and you never do anything.*"

B Comparativos de desigualdad

○ In Spanish, comparisons of inequality of most adjectives, adverbs, and nouns are formed by placing **más** or **menos** before the adjective, adverb, or noun. *Than* is expressed by **que.** Use the following formula.

más (*more*) o **menos** (*less*)	+	adjetivo adverbio nombre	+	**que** (*than*)

—El pesebre de Marta es muy grande.

"*Marta's nativity scene is very big.*"

—Sí, es mucho **más grande que** el nuestro.

"*Yes, it's much bigger than ours.*"

○ When a comparison of inequality includes a numerical expression, the preposition **de** is used as the equivalent of *than*.

—¿Por qué no compras esas velas?

"*Why don't you buy those candles?*"

—Porque cuestan **más de quince** dólares y a mí me quedan **menos de doce.**

"*Because they cost more than fifteen dollars and I have less than twelve left.*"

atención

Más que (*only*) is used in negative sentences when referring to an exact or maximum amount.

—¿Por qué no me das una foto de tu hijo?

"*Why don't you give me a picture of your son?*"

—No puedo, porque no tengo **más que una.**

"*I can't, because I have only one.*"

C El superlativo

○ The superlative of adjectives is formed by placing the definite article before the person or thing being compared.

el		**más** (*most*)	
la	+ **nombre** +	o	+ adjetivo (**de**)
los		**menos** (*least*)	
las			

El Aconcagua es **la** montaña **más alta de** las Américas.

Mt. Aconcagua is the highest mountain in the Americas.

atención

In the example above, note that the Spanish equivalent of *in* is **de.**

—Estas flores cuestan demasiado.

"*These flowers cost too much.*"

—¡Pues son **las menos caras**[1] que tienen aquí!

"*Well, they're the least expensive ones they have here!*"

—Elena no es muy inteligente, ¿verdad?

"*Elena isn't very intelligent, right?*"

—Al contrario, es **la más inteligente**[1] de la clase.

"*On the contrary, she's the most intelligent in the class.*"

○ The Spanish absolute superlative is equivalent to *extremely* or *very* before an adjective in English. This superlative may be expressed by modifying the adjective with an adverb (**muy, sumamente, extremadamente**) or by adding the suffix **-ísimo(-a, -os, -as)** to the adjective.

---

[1] The noun may be omitted because it is understood.

muy mala	mal**ísima**
sumamente difícil	dificil**ísimo**
extremadamente rico	ri**quísimo**[1]
extremadamente largo	lar**guísimo**[2]

atención

If the word ends in a vowel, the vowel is dropped before adding the suffix **-ísimo(a)**.

—¿No te parece que estos   *"Don't you think that these paintings are*
cuadros son muy caros?   *very expensive?"*
—Sí, son **carísimos**, pero me   *"Yes, they are extremely expensive, but I like*
gustan.   *them."*

D Adjetivos y adverbios con comparativos y superlativos irregulares

○ The following adjectives and adverbs have irregular comparative and superlative forms in Spanish.

Adjectives	*Adverbs*	*Comparative*	*Superlative*
bueno	bien	**mejor**	**el (la) mejor**[3]
malo	mal	**peor**	**el (la) peor**[3]
grande		**mayor**	**el (la) mayor**
pequeño		**menor**	**el (la) menor**

○ When the adjectives **grande** and **pequeño** refer to size, the regular forms are generally used.

—¿Tu casa es **más pequeña que**   *"Is your house smaller than mine?"*
la mía?
—No... yo creo que es **más grande**.   *"No . . . I think it's bigger."*

○ When these adjectives refer to age, the irregular forms are used.

—Felipe es **mayor** que tú, ¿no?   *"Felipe is older than you, isn't he?"*
—No, es **menor**. Yo tengo dos   *"No, he's younger. I am two years older than*
años más que él.   *he is."*

○ When **bueno** and **malo** refer to a person's character the regular forms are used.

—Diana no es muy buena...   *"Diana is not very kind . . ."*
—Al contrario, es **la más buena**   *"On the contrary, she is the nicest in the*
de la familia.   *family."*

---

[1] Words ending in **-ca** or **-co** change the **c** to **qu** before adding the suffix **-ísimo(a)** to maintain the hard **c** sound.

[2] Words ending in **-ga** or **-go** change the **g** to **gu** before adding the suffix **-ísimo(a)** to maintain the hard **g** sound.

[3] The adjectives **mejor** and **peor** are placed before the noun: *Ella es mi **mejor amiga**.*

CD-ROM
Go to **Estructuras gramaticales** for additional practice.

Práctica

A. Aquí van a encontrar ustedes información sobre Andrés. Establezcan comparaciones de igualdad o desigualdad entre él y ustedes, según corresponda.

Andrés:

1. ...es sumamente simpático.
2. ...tiene muchísimos planes para el sábado próximo.
3. ...gana tres mil dólares al mes.
4. ...tiene cuatro hermanas.
5. ...trabaja ocho horas al día.
6. ...habla español perfectamente.
7. ...tiene muchísima paciencia.
8. ...bebe mucho café.
9. ...tiene treinta años.
10. ...mide seis pies, cuatro pulgadas.
11. ...escribe muy bien.
12. ...vive en una casa que tiene seis dormitorios y es muy grande.

B. Escriba el superlativo absoluto de los siguientes adjetivos y adverbios y después úselos para describir a personas que ustedes conocen, a lugares, cosas o clases que están tomando.

MODELOS: *Mi novia es inteligentísima.*
San Diego es una ciudad hermosísima.

1. simpático
2. fácil
3. feo
4. guapo
5. pequeño
6. difícil
7. malo
8. grande
9. alto
10. bueno

C. En parejas, lean cuidadosamente la siguiente información, y establezcan comparaciones entre los siguientes elementos.

1. Mario tiene una "A" en español, José tiene una "C" y Juan una "F".
2. Sergio tiene veinte años, Oscar tiene veintiséis y Daniel tiene quince.
3. La casa de Elena tiene tres cuartos, la casa de Marta tiene cinco cuartos y la casa de Marité tiene siete cuartos.
4. La casa de Eva costó $200.000 y la casa de Luis costó $350.000.
5. El hotel Miramar es bueno, el hotel El Azteca es muy bueno y el hotel Santander es excelente.

D. En parejas, hablen de su familia, estableciendo comparaciones entre ustedes y los varios miembros de su familia.

2   Usos de las preposiciones **por** y **para**

A   La preposición *por*

The preposition **por** is used to express the following concepts:

- Period of time during which an action takes place (*during, in, for*)

  Estuvimos en Asunción **por** cuatro semanas.
  Vamos a ir a misa mañana **por** la mañana.

- Means, manner, and unit of measure (*by, for; per*)

  Le hablé **por** teléfono.
  Vinieron **por**[1] avión.
  Me pagan veinte dólares **por** hora.

- Cause or motive of an action (*because of, on account of, on behalf of*)

  No pudieron venir **por** la lluvia.
  Lo hice **por** ellos.

- *in search of, for,* or *to get*

  Fueron **por** el médico.
  Paso **por** ti a las ocho.

- *in exchange for*

  Pagué cien dólares **por** las velas.

- Motion or approximate location (*through, around, along, by*)

  Él huyó **por** la ventana.
  Caminamos **por** la avenida Magnolia.

- With an infinitive, to refer to an unfinished state (*yet*)

  El trabajo está **por** hacer.

- The passive voice (*by*)

  Este libro fue escrito **por** Mark Twain.

- *for;* in the expression *to (mis)take for*

  Habla tan bien el inglés que la **toman por** norteamericana.

B   La preposición *para*

The preposition **para** is used to express the following concepts:

- Destination

  A las ocho salí **para** el cementerio.

- Direction in time, often meaning *by* or *for* a certain time or date

  Necesito los amuletos **para** el sábado.

---

[1] The preposition **en** is also used to refer to means of transportation.

- Whom or what something is for

  Estos amuletos son **para** los muchachos.

- *in order to*

  Necesitamos dinero **para** comprar la sidra.

- Comparison (*by the standard of, considering*)

  Elenita es muy alta **para** su edad.

- Objective or goal

  Carlos estudia **para** ingeniero.

Práctica

CD-ROM
Go to **Estructuras gramaticales** for additional practice.

A. Complete los siguiente mini diálogos, usando **por** o **para**, según corresponda. Después, represéntelos con un(a) compañero(a).

1. —¿Vas a estar en México _____ dos meses? ¿Cuándo vuelves?
   —Tengo que estar de vuelta _____ el quince de agosto.
   —¿_____ matricularte en la universidad?
   —Sí. Oye, ¿tú puedes ir _____ mí al aeropuerto?
   —Sí. ¡No hay problema!
2. —¿Vas a viajar _____ avión?
   —No, yo prefiero viajar _____ tren.
   —¿Cuánto pagaste _____ el pasaje?
   —Quinientos dólares; pero... _____ un viaje a Texas no es caro.
3. —¿Cuándo salen _____ California?
   —Mañana _____ la mañana.
   —¿Compraste muchas cosas?
   —Sí, tengo regalos _____ todos mis sobrinos y _____ mi primo Jorge.
   —¿Él sigue estudiando en la universidad?
   —Sí, estudia _____ médico.

B. En parejas, planeen un viaje. Decidan qué van a hacer con respecto a lo siguiente. Usen **por** o **para** según sea necesario.

1. lugar que van a visitar
2. medio de transporte
3. razones del viaje
4. tiempo que van a estar allí
5. lo que Uds. van a pagar
6. fecha en que Uds. tienen que estar de vuelta

C *Por* y *para* en expresiones idiomáticas

- The following idiomatic expressions use **por.**

por aquí	*around here, this way*	**por eso**	*for that reason, that's why*
por completo	*completely*	**por fin**	*at last, finally*
por desgracia	*unfortunately*	**por lo menos**	*at least*
por ejemplo	*for example*	**por suerte**	*luckily, fortunately*

—¿Terminaste tu trabajo **por completo?**

"Did you finish your work completely?"

—**Por desgracia** no, pero, **por suerte,** es para el viernes.

"Unfortunately, no, but fortunately, it's due Friday."

○ The following idiomatic expressions use **para.**

para siempre *forever*
¿para qué? *what for?*
para eso *for that* (used sarcastically or contemptuously)
no ser para tanto *not to be that important, not to be such a big deal*
sin qué ni para qué *without rhyme or reason*

—Papá estaba furioso conmigo **sin qué ni para qué...**

"Dad was furious with me, without rhyme or reason . . ."

—Es que no compraste el maíz.

"Well, you didn't buy the corn."

—¡No era **para tanto!**

"It wasn't that important!"

—Me llevó a ver los fuegos artificiales.

"He took me to see the fireworks."

—¿Y **para eso** te pusiste un vestido tan elegante?

"And for that you wore such an elegant dress?"

Práctica

CD-ROM
Go to **Estructuras gramaticales** for additional practice.

A. En parejas, reaccionen a lo siguiente, usando las expresiones con **por** o **para** según corresponda.

1. Hubo un accidente. No tuvieron que llevar a nadie al hospital.
2. Estaba furioso porque le hicimos una broma.
3. Ana se puso un vestido muy elegante y su novio la llevó al parque.
4. Me encanta Asunción. Quiero quedarme a vivir aquí.
5. No vamos a estar allí por menos de un mes.
6. Él va a comprar unos amuletos. No sé para qué los necesita.
7. Voy a hablar de comidas típicas de Paraguay: sopa paraguaya, lechón asado...
8. En esta región, nadie cree en la brujería.

B. En parejas, túrnense para leer la siguiente historia, llenando los espacios en blanco con las preposiciones **por** o **para,** según corresponda.

Helen y John planean irse de vacaciones. _____ fin, después de mucho pensarlo, deciden viajar _____ Sudamérica. Piensan estar allí _____ tres meses y van a viajar _____ avión y _____ tren. Van a salir _____ Paraguay el día 10 de junio y piensan estar de vuelta _____ mediados de agosto. _____ suerte este año John va a tener dos meses de vacaciones.

El viaje va a costarles mucho dinero. Van a pagar _____ él casi tres mil dólares, y _____ desgracia eso no incluye más que los pasajes y el hotel. John piensa que en esos países van a tomar a Helen _____ sudamericana porque ella habla muy bien el español, pero ella no lo cree. John no habla español y _____ eso Helen se preocupa un poco _____ él.

Helen se olvidó _____ completo de que _____ estar en Sudamérica tanto tiempo, va a necesitar dejar a alguien en su tienda. Cuando van a comprar los billetes, se da cuenta del problema y dice que va a tener que cancelar el viaje. John no está de acuerdo con ella y le dice que no es _____ tanto porque su hermana puede trabajar en la tienda.

3   El modo subjuntivo

A   Introducción

○ In Spanish, the indicative mood is used to describe events that are factual and definite. The subjunctive mood is used to refer to events or conditions that are subjective in relation to the speaker's reality or experience. Because expressions of volition, emotion, doubt, denial, and unreality all represent reactions to the speaker's perception of reality, they are followed in Spanish by the subjunctive.

○ The Spanish subjunctive is most often used in subordinate or dependent clauses, which are introduced by **que.** The subjunctive is also used in English, although not as often as in Spanish. Consider the following sentence:

*I suggest that he **arrive** tomorrow.*

○ The expression that requires the use of the subjunctive is the main clause, *I suggest.* The subjunctive appears in the subordinate clause, *that he arrive tomorrow.* The subjunctive mood is used because the expressed action is not real; it is only what is *suggested* that he do.

B   Formas del presente de subjuntivo

Verbos regulares

○ To form the present subjunctive of regular verbs, the following endings are added to the stem of the first person singular of the present indicative.

-ar *verbs*	-er *verbs*	-ir *verbs*
hable	aprenda	reciba
hables	aprendas	recibas
hable	aprenda	reciba
hablemos	aprendamos	recibamos
habléis	aprendáis	recibáis
hablen	aprendan	reciban

○ If the verb is irregular in the first person singular of the present indicative, this irregularity is maintained in all other persons of the present subjunctive.

Verb	First person singular (present indicative)	Stem	First person singular (present subjunctive)
conocer	conozco	**conozc-**	**conozca**
traer	traigo	**traig-**	**traiga**
caber	quepo	**quep-**	**quepa**
decir	digo	**dig-**	**diga**
hacer	hago	**hag-**	**haga**
venir	vengo	**veng-**	**venga**
poner	pongo	**pong-**	**ponga**
ver	veo	**ve-**	**vea**

 Verbs ending in **-car, -gar,** and **-zar** change the **c** to **qu,** the **g** to **gu,** and the **z** to **c** before **e** in the present subjunctive:

tocar → **toque**   llegar → **llegue**   rezar → **rece**

CD-ROM
Go to **Estructuras gramaticales** for additional practice.

Práctica

Dé las formas del presente de subjuntivo de los siguientes verbos, según los sujetos indicados.

1. (que) yo: traer, dividir, conocer, correr, hablar, sacar
2. (que) tú: mantener, conservar, decidir, comer, venir, llegar
3. (que) Ana: hablar, ver, aprender, abrir, caber, empezar
4. (que) tú y yo: dedicar, decir, beber, recibir, volver, pagar
5. (que) ellos: hacer, insistir, temer, poner, viajar, tocar

El subjuntivo de los verbos de cambios radicales

○ The **-ar** and **-er** verbs maintain the basic pattern of the present indicative; they change the **e** to **ie** and the **o** to **ue.**

	e → ie		o → ue	
	cerrar *to close*		renovar *to renew*	
-ar *verbs*	cierre	cerremos	renueve	renovemos
	cierres	cerréis	renueves	renovéis
	cierre	cierren	renueve	renueven
	perder *to lose*		volver *to return*	
-er *verbs*	pierda	perdamos	vuelva	volvamos
	pierdas	perdáis	vuelvas	volváis
	pierda	pierdan	vuelva	vuelvan

○ The **-ir** verbs that change the **e** to **ie** and the **o** to **ue** in the present indicative change the **e** to **i** and the **o** to **u** in the first and second person plural of the present subjunctive.

$e \rightarrow ie$		$o \rightarrow ue$	
sentir *to feel*		**morir** *to die*	
sienta	sintamos	muera	muramos
sientas	sintáis	mueras	muráis
sienta	sientan	muera	mueran

○ The **-ir** verbs that change the **e** to **i** in the present indicative maintain this change in all persons of the present subjunctive.

$e \rightarrow i$	
pedir *to request*	
pida	pidamos
pidas	pidáis
pida	pidan

Verbos irregulares

○ The following verbs are irregular in the present subjunctive.

dar	dé, des, dé, demos, deis, den
estar	esté, estés, esté, estemos, estéis, estén
saber	sepa, sepas, sepa, sepamos, sepáis, sepan
ser	sea, seas, sea, seamos, seáis, sean
ir	vaya, vayas, vaya, vayamos, vayáis, vayan

The present subjunctive of **hay** (impersonal form of **haber**) is **haya.**

Práctica

Dé la forma correspondiente del presente de subjuntivo, siguiendo el modelo; añada además una palabra o expresión que complete la idea.

MODELO: yo   abrir   (*que*) *yo abra la puerta*

Sujeto	*Infinitivo*	*Sujeto*	*Infinitivo*
1. nosotros	pedir	6. Uds.	mentir
2. Estela	poder	7. nosotras	dormir
3. tú	ir	8. tú y yo	dar
4. ellos	saber	9. Ana y Eva	servir
5. Ud.	empezar	10. Roberto	estar

4 El subjuntivo con verbos o expresiones de voluntad o deseo

A Con verbos que expresan voluntad o deseo

○ All impositions of will, as well as indirect or implied commands, require the subjunctive in subordinate clauses. The subject in the main clause must be different from the subject in the subordinate clause.

	Main Clause			Subordinate Clause	
Mi	madre	quiere	**que**	yo	**cambie** mis planes.
My	*mother*	*wants*		*me*	*to change my plans.*

○ If there is no change in subject, the infinitive is used.

Mi madre quiere **cambiar sus planes.**   *My mother wants to change her plans.*

○ Some verbs of volition are:

querer	**pedir** (e → i)
desear	**sugerir** (e → ie)
mandar	**aconsejar** (*to advise*)
exigir (*to demand*)[1]	**necesitar**
insistir (**en**)	**rogar** (o → ue) (*to beg, to plead*)
decir	**recomendar** (e → ie)

—Ella **quiere que tú pases** la Semana Santa aquí.   *"She wants you to spend Holy Week here."*

—Yo no puedo venir hasta mayo.   *"I can't come until May."*

—Yo **les**[2] **sugiero a Uds. que tomen** parte en la procesión.   *"I suggest that you take part in the procession."*

—¡Buena idea!   *"Good idea!"*

○ Either the subjunctive or the infinitive may be used with the verbs **prohibir** (*to forbid*), **mandar, ordenar** (*to order*), and **permitir** (*to allow*).

Les **prohíbo hablar** de eso.
Les **prohíbo que hablen** de eso. ⎫   *I forbid you to speak about that.*

No les **permiten aterrizar** aquí.
No les **permiten que aterricen** aquí. ⎫   *They don't allow them to land here.*

Le **ordeno salir.**
Le **ordeno que salga.** ⎫   *I order you to get out.*

Me **van a mandar traerlo.**
Me **van a mandar que lo traiga.** ⎫   *They are going to order me to bring it.*

---

[1] The spelling change for this verb is discussed under **"Verbos de cambios ortográficos,"** number 2, in **Apéndice B.**

[2] The indirect object pronoun is used with the verbs **sugerir, pedir, permitir,** and **decir** when they are followed by a subordinate clause.

CD-ROM
Go to **Estructuras gramaticales** for additional practice.

Práctica

A. En parejas, lean los siguientes diálogos, usando el presente de subjuntivo o el infinitivo de los verbos dados.

1. —Quiero _____ (dar) una fiesta de carnaval.
   —¡Buena idea! Te sugiero que _____ (invitar) a todos tus compañeros de clase.
2. —Los chicos quieren _____ (ir) a ver los fuegos artificiales.
   —Yo creo que los padres les van a prohibir que _____ (ir) solos.
3. —¿Qué nos aconsejas que _____ (hacer) mañana?
   —Les sugiero que _____ (visitar) las cataratas.
4. —Tienes que decirles a tus amigos que _____ (venir) a fines de mes.
   —No puedo, porque mi supervisor insiste en que yo _____ (trabajar) todos los fines de semana.
5. —Yo necesito _____ (cambiar) mis planes. Tengo que regresar a La Paz el domingo.
   —Te ruego que _____ (quedarse) unos días más.
6. —Mis padres me prohíben _____ (salir) con Gustavo.
   —¡Pero te permiten que _____ (salir) con Juan Carlos!
   —¡Me ordenan _____ (salir) con él! ¡Juan Carlos es el hijo de sus mejores amigos!

B. Ud. y su compañero(a) son personas que siempre encuentran soluciones para todo y por eso sus amigos los consultan. ¿Qué sugieren, recomiendan o aconsejan Uds. en cuanto a los siguientes problemas?

1. Los niños están libres mañana y no sé adónde llevarlos.
2. Necesito un coche y no tengo dinero.
3. Mis amigos quieren ir al cine el sábado pero tienen que trabajar.
4. Me duele mucho la cabeza.
5. Me ofrecen un puesto en París y yo no hablo francés.
6. Mi novio(a) y yo queremos ir a la playa el sábado, pero tenemos un examen muy difícil el lunes.
7. Me estoy muriendo de hambre y no tengo tiempo de cocinar.
8. Yo tengo planes para el sábado, pero mis parientes van a venir a visitarme.
9. Mi mamá quiere que vaya a misa con ella, pero yo tengo que terminar un proyecto.
10. El papá de Amalia le prohíbe que salga con Sergio, y ella quiere salir con él.
11. Tenemos que ir por nuestros amigos al aeropuerto y no tenemos coche.
12. Mi mamá va a preparar lechón asado y sopa paraguaya y yo estoy a dieta.

B Con expresiones impersonales que indican voluntad o deseo

○ The subjunctive is used after certain impersonal expressions that indicate will or volition when the verb in the subordinate clause has a stated subject. The most common expressions follow:

es conveniente (conviene)	*it is advisable*	**es necesario**	*it is necessary*
es importante (importa)	*it is important*	**es preferible**	*it is preferable*
es mejor	*it is better*	**es urgente (urge)**	*it is urgent*

—**Es importante** que **celebremos** el Día de Acción de Gracias con nuestra familia.

"It is important that we celebrate Thanksgiving with our family."

—Sí, **es necesario** que **estemos** juntos.

"Yes, it's necessary that we be together."

○ When the subject of a sentence is neither expressed nor implied, the above expressions are followed by an infinitive.

—¿Qué **es necesario hacer** para tener buena suerte?

"What is necessary to do to have good luck?"

—**Es necesario encontrar** un trébol de cuatro hojas.

"It's necessary to find a four-leaf clover."

CD-ROM
Go to **Estructuras gramaticales** for additional practice.

Práctica

Entreviste a un(a) compañero(a), usando las siguientes preguntas.

1. ¿Qué es importante que hagamos cuando tengamos un día libre? ¿Descansar o invitar a un(a) amigo(a) a pasar el día con nosotros? ¿Por qué?
2. ¿Es mejor ir a cenar con un par de amigos o dar una fiesta e invitar a todo el mundo? ¿Por qué?
3. ¿Tú crees que es preferible que viajemos a un país extranjero o que vayamos a una ciudad de los Estados Unidos? ¿Por qué?
4. ¿Es preferible tomarse unas vacaciones cortas cada tres meses o tomarse vacaciones largas una vez al año? ¿Por qué?
5. ¿Es conveniente viajar durante la temporada de verano o conviene viajar cuando hay pocos turistas? ¿Por qué?
6. ¿Urge que vayamos por nuestros amigos al aeropuerto o es mejor que ellos tomen un taxi?

5 El subjuntivo con verbos o expresiones impersonales de emoción

A Con verbos de emoción

○ In Spanish, the subjunctive is always used in the subordinate clause when the verb in the main clause expresses any kind of emotion, such as happiness, pity, hope, surprise, fear, and so forth.

○ Some common verbs that express emotion are:

alegrarse (de)	**sentir**
esperar	**sorprenderse (de)**
lamentar	**temer**

Main Clause	Subordinate Clause
(Yo) espero	que **(Elena) pueda** ir al cine.

Main Clause	Subordinate Clause
(Él) teme	que **(nosotros) no podamos** ir al cine.

○ The subject of the subordinate clause must be different from that of the main clause for the subjunctive to be used. If there is no change of subject, the infinitive is used.

(Yo) espero poder ir al cine.	*I hope to be able to go to the movies.*
(Ella) teme no **poder ir** al cine.	*She is afraid she won't be able to go to the movies.*

—¿Cuánto nos van a dar ellos para la fiesta de Navidad?

"How much are they going to give us for the Christmas party?"

—**Espero** que nos **den** unos cincuenta dólares.

"I hope they give us about fifty dollars."

—**Temo** que no **puedan** darnos tanto.

"I'm afraid they can't give us that much."

B Expresiones impersonales que denotan emoción

○ When an expression denotes emotion in the main clause of a sentence, the subjunctive is required in the subordinate clause if it contains a subject that is either expressed or implicit. The most common expressions are:

es de esperar	*it's to be hoped*	**es (una) lástima**	*it's a pity*
es lamentable	*it's regrettable*	**ojalá**	*it's to be hoped, if only . . .*
es sorprendente	*it's surprising*	**es una suerte**	*it's lucky*

—**Es una lástima** que Jorge no **pueda** ir con nosotros a la Misa del Gallo.

"It's a pity that Jorge can't go with us to Midnight Mass."

—**Ojalá** que Alberto **esté** libre y **pueda** ir.

"It's to be hoped that Alberto is free and can go."

Práctica

CD-ROM
Go to **Estructuras gramaticales** for additional practice.

A. En parejas, lean los siguientes diálogos usando el subjuntivo o el infinitivo de los verbos dados.

1. —Espero que tú _____ (ir) al gimnasio con nosotros.
   —Siento no _____ (poder) ir hoy, pero espero que nosotros _____ (salir) juntos mañana.
2. —Es una lástima que mi hija no _____ (saber) tocar el piano.
   —Es verdad. Ojalá que Emilia le _____ (dar) clases este verano.
3. —Es de esperar que mis amigos _____ (estar) listos a las ocho.
   —Temo que no _____ (poder) estar listos a esa hora.
4. —Me alegro de _____ (estar) aquí con ustedes.
   —Siento que mis padres no _____ (estar) aquí también.
5. —Víctor nos va a llevar a la casa de Hugo.
   —Es una suerte que él _____ (saber) su dirección.

B. Usando cada una de las expresiones impersonales de la página 129, ¿qué diría Ud. en estas situaciones?

1. Dicen que mañana va a llover. Ud. quiere ir a la playa.
2. Ud. necesita un empleo. Su tío es presidente de una compañía.
3. Ud. quiere llevar a su amiga al cine, pero ella está muy enferma.
4. Le ofrecen un coche muy barato, pero Ud. no tiene suficiente dinero.
5. Su sobrino tiene menos de un año y ya sabe nadar perfectamente.
6. Hoy es lunes. Ud. no estudió la lección y el profesor muchas veces da exámenes los lunes.

C. Use su imaginación y complete las siguientes frases de forma original. Compare sus respuestas con las de un(a) compañero(a).

1. Es sorprendente que...
2. Es lamentable que...
3. Me alegro de que...
4. Ojalá que...
5. Temo que...

6. Es de esperar que...
7. Lamento que...
8. Es una suerte que...
9. Es una lástima que...
10. Espero que...

D. **Nuestra gente.**   Complete el siguiente diálogo, usando los verbos entre paréntesis en el subjuntivo o el infinitivo, según corresponda.

En el programa de radio Nuestra gente *entrevistan al Sr. Manuel Peña, director de un programa de ayuda a las minorías de origen hispano.*

PERIODISTA   —Yo quiero que Ud. nos _____ (dar) los datos necesarios para informar al público sobre la labor que realiza su organización.

SR. PEÑA   —Sí, es importante que los miembros de los grupos minoritarios _____ (saber) cuáles son las ventajas que ofrece nuestro programa.

PERIODISTA   —Primero quiero que _____ (hablarnos) de las clases de inglés para adultos.

SR. PEÑA   —Ofrecemos clases nocturnas de inglés, y conviene _____ (señalar—*to point out*) que son gratis. Estoy seguro de que muchas personas van a asistir a ellas. Queremos _____ (ayudarlos) también a conseguir empleo.

PERIODISTA   —Es necesario que _____ (haber) programas similares en otras ciudades. Y ahora, Sr. Peña, quiero que _____ (aclararnos) algunos puntos sobre la ayuda legal que ofrece el programa.

SR. PEÑA   —Yo no puedo darle mucha información sobre esto. Le sugiero que _____ (hablar) con nuestro abogado y que _____ (hacerle) la misma pregunta.

PERIODISTA   —Yo sé que nuestros oyentes (*listeners*) van a _____ (tener) muchas preguntas para Ud. Señoras y señores, si desean _____ (preguntarle) algo al Sr. Peña, les aconsejo que _____ (llamarnos) ahora. El número es 813–4392.

SR. PEÑA   —Ojalá que las personas interesadas _____ (comunicarse) con nosotros.

PERIODISTA   —Es de esperar que así _____ (ser).

Ahora represente el diálogo con un(a) compañero(a). Escriban dos preguntas que los oyentes pueden hacerle al Sr. Peña.

E. **La carta de Maité.**   Ayer llegó a su casa la siguiente carta de su amiga Maité. Responda a su carta por escrito, expresando alegría, temor, sorpresa u otras emociones en respuesta a sus noticias, y añada algunas recomendaciones.

Queridos amigos:

Espero que todos estén bien. ¡Cuántas noticias tengo para Uds.!

Mario, mi esposo, está muy enfermo y está en el hospital. Estoy muy preocupada por él. Mis hijos están más o menos bien. Teresa y nuestro vecino Jorge, que se odiaban, se van a casar. Por desgracia, Olga y Raúl se van a divorciar. José está tratando de encontrar trabajo, pero no tiene suerte; Alina, en cambio, acaba de conseguir un puesto muy bueno.

Ayer hablé con Carlos y Adela y me dijeron que piensan visitarlos a Uds. este verano. ¡Ojalá que yo pueda acompañarlos!

Un beso de

Maité

STUDENT WEBSITE
Do the **Compruebe cuánto sabe** self test after finishing this **Estructuras gramaticales** section.

¡CONTINUEMOS!

Una encuesta

Entreviste a sus compañeros de clase para tratar de identificar a aquellas personas que...

1. ...creen que romper un espejo trae mala suerte.
2. ...creen que un trébol de cuatro hojas o una pata de conejo traen buena suerte.
3. ...nunca pasan por debajo de una escalera (*ladder*).
4. ...leen su horóscopo todos los días.
5. ...evitan viajar el viernes 13.
6. ...vieron alguna vez una procesión.
7. ...fueron alguna vez a la Misa del Gallo.
8. ...son del mismo signo que el profesor (la profesora). ¿Cuál es?
9. ...van a veces al cementerio a llevar flores.
10. ...hacen bromas el primero de abril.
11. ...brindan con champán el 31 de diciembre.
12. ...van a ver los fuegos artificiales el 4 de julio.

Y ahora, discuta el resultado de la encuesta con el resto de la clase.

¿Comprende Ud.?

1. Escuche la siguiente conversación telefónica que tiene María Isabel con su amiga Carmen sobre el viaje de Kathy a Paraguay. El objetivo de la actividad es el de escuchar una conversación a velocidad natural. No se preocupe de entenderlo todo, pues esto no se espera de Ud. Después de escuchar la conversación dos veces, Ud. oirá varias aseveraciones. En una hoja, escriba los números de uno a diez e indique si cada aseveración es verdadera o falsa.

2. Luego escuche la canción y trate de aprenderla.

Hablemos del horóscopo

Después de leer el horóscopo que aparece a continuación, hable con un(a) compañero(a) acerca de los horóscopos de las siguientes personas, según las fechas de nacimiento indicadas.

ARIES

21 de marzo a 19 de abril
No va a encontrar soluciones fáciles para sus problemas.

TAURO

20 de abril a 20 de mayo
Va a recibir mucho dinero.

GÉMINIS

21 de mayo a 21 de junio
Va a conocer a alguien muy interesante.

CÁNCER

22 de junio a 22 de julio
No debe gastar mucho dinero hoy.

LEO

23 de julio a 22 de agosto
Sus problemas económicos van a desaparecer.

VIRGO

23 de agosto a 21 de septiembre
Buenas posibilidades en el amor.

LIBRA

22 de septiembre a 22 de octubre
No debe darse por vencido.

ESCORPIÓN

23 de octubre a 21 de noviembre
Antes de tomar una decisión debe pensarlo muy bien.

SAGITARIO

22 de noviembre a 21 de diciembre
Va a recibir buenas noticias.

CAPRICORNIO

22 de diciembre a 19 de enero
Hoy no es buen día para hacer un viaje.

ACUARIO

20 de enero a 19 de febrero
A fines de esta semana va a recibir una sorpresa.

PISCIS

20 de febrero a 20 de marzo
Debe escribirles a sus amigos.

1. Esteban nació el 22 de febrero. ¿Qué no ha hecho últimamente?
2. Raquel nació el 13 de agosto. ¿Cuál es su signo? ¿Cree Ud. que pronto va a tener dinero? ¿Por qué?
3. Francisco nació el 10 de junio. ¿Cree Ud. que hay una chica en su futuro?
4. Dolores nació el 18 de diciembre. ¿Debe estar preocupada por el futuro? ¿Por qué?
5. Ana nació el 3 de septiembre. ¿Cuál es su signo? ¿Cree Ud. que va a tener problemas con su novio?
6. Roberto nació el 4 de abril. Si tiene dificultades, ¿va a resolverlas fácilmente?
7. Luis nació el 4 de noviembre. ¿Cuál es su signo? ¿Debe actuar impulsivamente? ¿Por qué?
8. Marisa nació el 13 de julio. ¿Cree Ud. que hoy es un buen día para ir de compras? ¿Por qué?
9. Diego nació el 8 de enero. Él planea salir para México hoy. Según su horóscopo, ¿es una buena idea?
10. Raúl nació el 19 de octubre. Quiere casarse con Teresa y ella no acepta. ¿Debe darse por vencido (*give up*)?
11. María nació el 26 de abril. ¿Cuál es su signo? María quiere ir de vacaciones a Sudamérica. ¿Cree Ud. que va a poder ir? ¿Por qué lo cree?
12. Diana nació el 14 de febrero. ¿Qué va a pasar el sábado o el domingo?

Y a Ud., ¿qué le dice su horóscopo para hoy?

¿Qué dirían ustedes?

Imagínese que Ud. y un(a) compañero(a) se encuentran en las siguientes situaciones. ¿Qué va a decir cada uno?

1. En una reunión con sus amigos, todos hablan de supersticiones. Comenten las que Uds. tienen o conocen.
2. Un(a) estudiante latinoamericano(a) va a pasar la Navidad en la ciudad de Uds. Háblenle de lo que se hace en Estados Unidos para celebrar esta fiesta.
3. Uds. van a dar una charla para un grupo de estudiantes mexicanos. Háblenles de las fiestas que se celebran en Estados Unidos.

¡De ustedes depende!

El Club de Español va a organizar una fiesta de Navidad típicamente hispana. Ud. y un(a) compañero(a) están a cargo de preparar las actividades y de seleccionar el menú (comidas y bebidas). Tengan en cuenta lo siguiente.

1. ¿Cómo celebran la Navidad en México?
2. ¿Saben Uds. algunos villancicos (*Christmas carols*) en español?
3. ¿Qué comidas van a servir?
4. ¿Qué bebidas van a servir?
5. ¿Qué tipo de música van a escuchar?

Mesa redonda

Formen grupos de cuatro o cinco estudiantes y hablen sobre la importancia de tener tradiciones familiares. Comenten las que tienen Uds. en su familia, especialmente las que se relacionan con el Día de Acción de Gracias, la Navidad u otra celebración religiosa y el Año Nuevo.

Lecturas periodísticas

Saber leer Creación de contextos: sus conocimientos

CD-ROM

Go to **Lecturas periodísticas** for additional prereading and vocabulary activities.

Lea el título de la siguiente lectura periodística. ¿Sabe de qué va a tratar? Posiblemente no del todo. En el ensayo (*essay*) *El mundo hispánico* de la **Lección 3,** Ud. encontró algunos datos sobre Cuzco, una ciudad peruana. Repáselos.

¿Hay alguna palabra desconocida en el título? Posiblemente Ud. no conozca la palabra **corpus.** ¿Ha oído esa misma palabra en otros contextos? Si no, antes de leer, ayúdese usando la propia lectura para crear algunos conocimientos y contextos sobre la palabra: rápidamente, busque las oraciones de la lectura en las que aparece **corpus** y léalas.

Para leer y comprender

Al leer detalladamente el artículo, busque las respuestas a las siguientes preguntas.

1. ¿Dónde y a qué altitud está situada la ciudad de Cuzco?
2. ¿Quiénes son los antepasados (*ancestors*) de los peruanos?
3. ¿Cómo es la fiesta del Corpus Christi de Cuzco?
4. ¿Qué hacían los indios de la antigüedad con las momias de sus reyes?
5. ¿Qué hacen en Cuzco la víspera de la fecha del Corpus? ¿Qué pasa el jueves santo?
6. ¿Qué son algunas de estas imágenes? ¿Por qué se destacan?

El Corpus de Cuzco

En la transparente atmósfera cuzqueña todavía° vive el espíritu de los incas. Aquí, en el corazón de los Andes, a una altitud de 3.400 metros, los peruanos de hoy sacan° las imágenes en procesión para celebrar una de las fiestas más importantes de la ciudad, el Corpus Christi.

La antigua capital del fabuloso Imperio inca, Cuzco, conserva todavía su antiguo esplendor. La mayoría de los habitantes de Cuzco son descendientes directos de aquéllos que levantaron el imperio incaico. Por eso no es extraño encontrar todavía ceremonias religiosas y fiestas folklóricas que reproducen fielmente° las que se celebraban hace más de quinientos años. Una de las más importantes es la conmemoración del día del Corpus Christi, que atrae° a gran número de visitantes de todos los puntos de Perú. El Corpus de Cuzco es una fiesta de características propias, donde se mezclan elementos cristianos y andinos.

La celebración del Corpus sustituye a otra fiesta mucho más antigua en Cuzco. En los tiempos del Imperio inca, en cierta fecha, las momias de los reyes —los que habían poseído el título de *Inca*, nombre que luego se extendió a toda la población— eran sacadas de sus palacios y llevadas en procesión por las calles de la ciudad.

Después de la conquista, hasta el día de hoy, en la víspera de la fecha del Corpus se trasladan° a la catedral las imágenes de las vírgenes y de los santos patronos de las iglesias de

Cuzco, y el jueves santo son sacadas todas para la impresionante procesión que tiene lugar en la Plaza de Armas. Algunas de estas imágenes son auténticas obras de arte, pero, sobre todo, se destacan° por la riqueza que

las adorna, en ocasiones varios cientos de kilos de plata maciza°.

Adaptado de la revista *Ronda* (España)

---

se... stand out

solid

---

still

take out

faithfully

attracts

se... are moved

La antigua capital del fabuloso imperio inca, Cuzco, conserva todavía su antiguo esplendor.

Procesión del Corpus Christi en Cuzco, Perú.

Desde su mundo

¿Cuáles son algunas tribus indias de los Estados Unidos? ¿Qué sabe Ud. de ellas?

piense y escriba   La selección y organización de las ideas

Ud. va a escribir sobre las fiestas que su familia celebra. ¿Cuál es la más importante para Ud.? ¿Por qué? ¿Cómo la celebran Ud. y su familia? Haga lo siguiente:

1. Haga una lista de las fiestas que celebra su familia.
2. Seleccione la fiesta más importante para Ud.
3. Haga una lista de lo que hacen Ud. y su familia para celebrar la fiesta más importante.

Ahora Ud. necesita definir un **criterio de organización** para discutir lo que hacen en la fiesta: ¿en orden de importancia, en orden cronológico o de otra manera (*other way*)?

Ahora, escriba la composición. No se olvide de resumir o concluir.

Pepe Vega y su mundo

Teleinforme

En esta lección vamos a ver costumbres y tradiciones de Ecuador y de Argentina. El Día de los muertos (o de los difuntos) se celebra en todo el mundo católico. En la península de Santa Elena, en Ecuador, esta celebración presenta costumbres y tradiciones únicas. La fiesta del gaucho en Argentina es una fiesta tradicional que gira en torno (revolves around) al caballo, un animal muy importante en la crianza de ganado (cattle-raising), y a otros aspectos de la cultura y de la sociedad ganaderas.

Preparación

¿Probable o improbable?   Clasifique cada una de las siguientes expresiones. ¿Será probable (**P**) o improbable (**I**) que se refiera a una de estas fiestas o a ambas?

	Día de los difuntos (**D**)	Fiesta del gaucho (**G**)
MODELO: los abuelos	*P*	*I*
las actividades folklóricas	*P*	*P*

	D	G		D	G
el aguardiente (*brandy*)	___	___	las espuelas (*spurs*)	___	___
el algodón hilado (*twisted cotton*)	___	___	la familia	___	___
los animales	___	___	la identidad étnica	___	___
bailar	___	___	el jinete (*rider*)	___	___
los bisabuelos (*great-grandparents*)	___	___	la lucha	___	___
el caballo	___	___	el maligno (*the devil*)	___	___
la carne	___	___	la mesa	___	___
la casa	___	___	la montura (*mount of horse*)	___	___
la celebración	___	___	la morcilla (*blood sausage*)	___	___
el cementerio	___	___	el muerto	___	___
los chinchulines (*kind of sausage*)	___	___	el paisano (*peasant*)	___	___
el chorizo (*spicy sausage*)	___	___	el pan	___	___
la cola (*tail*)	___	___	los pantalones anchos (*wide*)	___	___
la comunidad	___	___	rezar (*to pray*)	___	___
el cordón (*rope belt*)	___	___	la sábana (*sheet*)	___	___
los costillares asados (*grilled ribs*)	___	___	el sombrero	___	___
la danza	___	___	la tradición	___	___
el desfile (*parade*)	___	___	la tropilla (*drove of horses*)	___	___
domar (*to break [a horse]*)	___	___	la tumba (*grave*)	___	___

Comprensión

Día de los difuntos   15:13–18:20

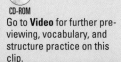
CD-ROM
Go to **Video** for further previewing, vocabulary, and structure practice on this clip.

El Día de los muertos, o de los difuntos, se celebra en muchos países católicos el 2 de noviembre. En este video, producido por la Fundación Pro-Pueblo del Ecuador, vemos algunos aspectos de cómo se celebra este día en Santa Elena, una región de Ecuador que queda en la costa del Pacífico.

A. ¿Cuánto entiende Ud.?   Mientras Ud. ve el video, complete las siguientes oraciones.

1. La gente de la costa del Guayas tiene distintas _____ que no se encuentran en otras partes de Ecuador.
2. Estas tradiciones unifican a _____ y _____.
3. La celebración del _____ es diferente en la zona de Santa Elena.
4. Todo el mundo va al _____ para arreglar _____ de sus queridos muertos.
5. La parte principal de la celebración se realiza en _____.
6. Todo el mundo hace _____ en formas especiales para darles a comer[1] a los muertos.
7. Las amas de casa también les compran a los muertos _____ o _____.
8. De noche, todos _____ y _____ para despedirse de los muertos por otro año.
9. En la zona de Santa Elena se acostumbra ponerle _____ al muerto.
10. Durante el velado (*wake, vigil*), las mujeres se quedan en casa con _____.
11. Los hombres están abajo haciendo _____.
12. Decían los abuelos que el cordón sirve para defenderse del _____, para que el muerto salga al camino del _____.

Fiesta del gaucho   18:22–21:07

STUDENT WEBSITE
Go to **Video** for pre-viewing, vocabulary, and structure practice on this clip.

El gaucho es uno de los símbolos de la República Argentina. Este reportaje nos da un resumen de las actividades que se realizan durante la fiesta del gaucho. El caballo y la carne asada son el centro de la fiesta.

B. ¿Qué pasa cuándo?   Ponga en orden cronológico los elementos de la fiesta.

1. _____ Después de comer y de beber, los gauchos demuestran la destreza.
2. _____ El caballo no quiere, corcovea, brinca, se retuerce.
3. _____ Toma lugar el desfile de los paisanos con mostachos, espuelas, sombreros y pantalones anchos.
4. _____ El sol se encamina hacia el ocaso y el día empieza a morir.
5. _____ Es el turno de las tropillas.
6. _____ Esta vez hay competencia: cada gaucho muestra su tropilla para ganar el premio.
7. _____ La paz se rompe entre el hombre y el animal: es la prueba de la doma.
8. _____ Se presentan las actividades folklóricas.
9. _____ Se presentan las danzas de los niños.
10. _____ Luego, es el turno de otro gaucho, y de otro, y de otro...
11. _____ Se come una buena dosis de carne: morcillas, chorizos, chinchulines y el asado.

Ampliación

¡De fiesta!   Prepare una lista de los elementos de un día de fiesta especial de su país o de su familia. ¿Cuáles son los elementos más importantes de la celebración? ¿Qué se come? ¿Cuáles son las actividades? ¿Cómo son los vestidos? ¿Se decora el lugar de manera especial? ¿Hay elementos únicos en su manera de celebrar? ¿Hay elementos que contribuyen a la identidad étnica, familiar o nacional? Descríbalos.

---

[1] Por lo general se dice "dar **de** comer".

Lecciones 3 y 4

Tome este examen para ver cuánto ha aprendido. Las respuestas correctas aparecen en el **Apéndice C**.

Lección 3

A Verbos que requieren una construcción especial

Complete las siguientes oraciones con el equivalente español de las palabras que aparecen entre paréntesis.

1. _____ el baloncesto que el tenis. (*Carlos likes better*)
2. _____ las carreras de caballos. (*We love*)
3. Me voy a quitar los zapatos porque _____. (*my feet hurt a lot*)
4. ¿Cuánto dinero _____, Anita? (*do you need?* [*do you lack*])
5. Sólo _____ diez dólares a los chicos. (*have left*)

B El pretérito contrastado con el imperfecto

Complete las siguientes oraciones usando los verbos que aparecen entre paréntesis. Tenga en cuenta los usos del pretérito y del imperfecto.

1. Cuando yo _____ (ser) niña, _____ (vivir) con una familia sudamericana, y ellos siempre me _____ (hablar) en español.
2. El sábado pasado ellos _____ (ir) al estadio.
3. _____ (Hacer) frío y _____ (llover) mucho cuando Luis _____ (llegar).
4. Anoche ellos me _____ (decir) que (yo) _____ (deber) estudiar más.
5. En esa época a él le _____ (encantar) ir a restaurantes y _____ (comer) muchísimo.
6. _____ (Ser) las ocho cuando Mario _____ (empezar) a hablar de deportes y _____ (terminar) a las diez.
7. Ayer yo _____ (estar) enfermo todo el día y por eso no _____ (terminar) el trabajo.
8. Teresa no _____ (venir) ayer porque le _____ (doler) la cabeza.

C Verbos que cambian de significado en el pretérito

Complete el siguiente diálogo usando el pretérito o el imperfecto de los verbos **querer**, **saber**, **conocer** y **poder**, según corresponda.

En una fiesta

INÉS   —¿Por qué no vino Gustavo?
NORA   —No _____ venir porque no se sentía bien.
INÉS   —Yo tampoco _____ venir, pero cuando _____ que ese equipo iba a jugar, decidí venir.
NORA   —Yo no _____ que ese equipo jugaba hoy.
INÉS   —Yo _____ hoy al entrenador. ¡Es simpatiquísimo!
NORA   —¿Carlos Torres? Yo ya lo _____.
INÉS   —Estoy muy contenta porque _____ conseguir su autógrafo para mi hermanita.

D Los pronombres relativos

Combine cada par de oraciones, sustituyendo el elemento que tienen en común por el pronombre relativo correspondiente. Siga el modelo.

> MODELO: Ésa es la señora. La señora vino ayer.
> *Ésa es la señora* **que** *vino ayer.*

1. Ésa es la chica española. Yo te hablé de la chica española.
2. La señora está triste. El hijo de la señora tuvo un accidente.
3. El libro es muy interesante. Compré el libro ayer.
4. Vamos a visitar a los niños. Compramos los bates para los niños.
5. El anillo es de oro. Compré el anillo en México.

E Expresiones de tiempo con **hacer**

Conteste las siguientes preguntas usando la información dada entre paréntesis.

1. ¿Cuánto tiempo hace que Ud. no come? (seis horas)
2. ¿Cuánto tiempo hacía que Uds. esperaban cuando yo llegué? (media hora)
3. ¿Cuánto tiempo hace que los jugadores vinieron a esta ciudad? (un año)

F ¿Recuerda el vocabulario?

Complete las siguientes oraciones con palabras y expresiones de la **Lección 3**.

1. No me gustan mucho las actividades al _____ libre.
2. ¿Tú tienes una tienda de _____?
3. Mi _____ favorito es el tenis.
4. Nos encanta _____ montañas.
5. Hubo un _____ de fútbol americano ayer.
6. Uno de los jugadores se _____. Lo llevaron al hospital.
7. Luis está leyendo la página _____.
8. Quiero ver ese partido. No me lo quiero _____.
9. A _____ de que jugaron muy bien, perdieron 110 a 108. El partido fue muy _____.
10. El atleta por _____ se mata en el segundo _____.
11. A mi hermano no le gusta _____ a caballo.
12. Fuimos al _____ para ver la carrera de _____.
13. Me gusta mucho el _____ acuático.
14. Ella ganó una medalla de oro en los últimos _____ Olímpicos.
15. Alberto es campeón de _____ libre.

G Cultura

Circule la información correcta.

1. Chile está situado entre los Andes y el Océano (Atlántico, Pacífico).
2. Chile tiene unos (200, 1.000) kilómetros de ancho.
3. La capital de Chile es (Valparaíso, Santiago).

4. Las ruinas de Machu Picchu están cerca de (Cuzco, Lima).
5. La capital de Ecuador es (Quito, Lima).

Lección 4

A Comparativos de igualdad y de desigualdad

Complete las siguientes oraciones con el equivalente español de las palabras que aparecen entre paréntesis.

1. Yo no pasé _____ en Lima _____ en Quito. (*as much time / as*)
2. Esta semana, yo tengo _____ como tú. (*as many meetings*)
3. Esta sidra es _____ la que tú compraste. (*better than*)
4. Yo tengo _____ cien dólares. (*less than*)
5. Estela es _____ yo. (*much older than*)
6. Ese chico es _____ la clase. (*the tallest in*)
7. Mi casa es _____ la tuya. (*smaller than*)
8. ¿Tú eres _____ yo? (*younger than*)
9. Paco come _____ nosotros. (*as much as*)
10. Laura es una mujer _____. (*extremely intelligent*)

B Usos de las preposiciones **por** y **para**

Complete las siguientes oraciones, usando **por** o **para,** según corresponda.

1. Mañana salgo _____ México. Voy _____ avión y pienso estar allí _____ un mes. Tengo que estar de regreso _____ el diez de junio _____ empezar mis clases.
2. _____ suerte tengo un poco de comida _____ Jaime.
3. Después de la clase te voy a llamar _____ teléfono _____ decirte lo que tienes que estudiar.
4. Papá se puso furioso cuando le dije que el dinero era _____ Jorge. ¡No era _____ tanto!
5. Queríamos hacer el viaje _____ avión pero, _____ desgracia, suspendieron los vuelos _____ la niebla, así que tuvimos que pagar cien dólares _____ el alquiler de un coche _____ poder llegar a tiempo.
6. Mi hijo estudia _____ médico y _____ eso yo nunca tengo dinero.
7. ¿A qué hora pasas _____ mí? Quiero ir a pasear _____ el centro.
8. Necesito información. _____ ejemplo, ¿ _____ quién fue escrita esa novela?
9. Rubén es muy alto _____ su edad.
10. _____ esa fecha, debemos tener el trabajo terminado _____ completo.

C El subjuntivo con verbos de voluntad o deseo

Complete las siguientes oraciones usando el infinitivo o el subjuntivo de los verbos que aparecen entre paréntesis, según corresponda.

1. Él nos sugiere que _____ (ir) a la Misa del Gallo.
2. Ellos no quieren que sus hijos _____ (ser) supersticiosos.
3. Quiero que Uds. _____ (disfrutar) de la fiesta de Año Nuevo.

4. Te ruego que no _____ (dejar) solos a los niños. No quiero que _____ (estar) mucho tiempo solos.

5. Mi padre me aconseja que me _____ (dedicar) a estudiar, pero yo prefiero _____ (trabajar).

6. Te prohíbo que _____ (usar) amuletos.

7. Mi mamá nos exige que siempre _____ (decir) la verdad. No quiere que le _____ (mentir).

8. Los niños insisten en que el Día de Reyes nosotros _____ (acostar) temprano y que _____ (levantar) temprano.

9. Él siempre me pide que (yo) _____ (poner) el nacimiento, pero no me quiere _____ (ayudar) cuando lo hago.

10. A Teresa no le permiten _____ (brindar) con sidra.

D El subjuntivo con expresiones impersonales de voluntad o deseo

Forme oraciones con las siguientes frases, comenzando con las expresiones que aparecen entre paréntesis. Use el subjuntivo o el infinitivo, según corresponda.

1. estudiar todos los días (Es importante)
2. ir al hospital (Es urgente)
3. ella saber conducir (Es conveniente)
4. viajar en pleno verano (Es mejor)
5. ustedes venir a fines de enero (Es necesario)
6. nosotros comprar flores (Es preferible)

E El subjuntivo con verbos de emoción

Forme oraciones con las siguientes frases. Use el subjuntivo o el infinitivo, según corresponda.

1. Siento / tú no puedes ir a misa hoy
2. Lamento / ella no ve los fuegos artificiales
3. Me alegro de / Uds. están libres hoy
4. Ellos temen / ellos no tienen tiempo
5. Sergio siente / nosotros no vamos con él
6. Ellos se alegran de / ellos viven por aquí
7. Espero / Elsa viene pronto
8. Temo / él no sabe dónde es la fiesta
9. Espero / mi hijo pasa más tiempo conmigo

F El subjuntivo con verbos o expresiones impersonales de emoción

Complete las siguientes oraciones usando los verbos que aparecen entre paréntesis.

1. Es de esperar que ellos _____ (poner) el pesebre hoy.
2. Es sorprendente que tú no _____ (llevar) flores al cementerio.
3. Ojalá que ellos no nos _____ (preparar) muchas bromas.
4. Es una lástima que mi esposo no _____ (estar) aquí.

5. Es una suerte que ellos _____ (poder) venir hoy.

6. Es lamentable que nosotros _____ (tener) que cambiar nuestros planes.

G ¿Recuerda el vocabulario?

Complete las siguientes oraciones con palabras y expresiones de la **Lección 4**.

1. Los niños de por _____ creen en los tres _____ Magos.
2. El 24 de diciembre celebramos la _____ y el 25 la _____ .
3. En los Estados Unidos se celebra el Día de _____ de Gracias.
4. Fuimos al cementerio a visitar la _____ de mi bisabuela. Llevamos _____ y flores.
5. El 4 de julio fuimos a ver los _____ artificiales.
6. En la fiesta de _____ de Año nosotros _____ con sidra.
7. La Virgen de Caacupé es la _____ patrona Paraguay.
8. Eva está enferma y por eso no puede ir a la fiesta. ¡Es una _____!
9. Marcelo tomó _____ en el desfile del _____ de la Independencia.
10. Ella cree que una _____ de conejo y un _____ de cuatro hojas traen buena suerte.
11. El 31 de diciembre es la _____ de Año Nuevo.
12. Leo es un _____ del zodíaco.

H Cultura

Circule la información correcta.

1. Paraguay y (Perú, Bolivia) no tienen salida al mar.
2. La represa de Itaipú se construyó sobre el río (Paraná, Paraguay).
3. La música paraguaya es una mezcla de las culturas española y (guaraní, inca).
4. La capital de Paraguay es (Montevideo, Asunción).
5. Paraguay fue escogido como escenario de la película (*Evita*, *La misión*).

LECCIÓN 5

Mente sana en cuerpo sano

OBJETIVOS

Temas para la comunicación

La salud personal

Estructuras

1. El imperativo: **Ud.** y **Uds.**
2. El imperativo de la primera persona del plural
3. El subjuntivo para expresar duda, incredulidad y negación
4. El subjuntivo para expresar lo indefinido y lo inexistente
5. Expresiones que requieren el subjuntivo o el indicativo

Regiones y países

Venezuela y Colombia

Lectura

Tácticas y estrategias de la pérdida de peso

Estrategias de lectura

Creación de contextos: la formulación de preguntas

Estrategias de redacción

La introducción y la conclusión

En un gimnasio, este grupo participa en una clase de boxeo para hacer ejercicio.

Mente sana en cuerpo sano

CD-ROM   STUDENT AUDIO

For preparation, do the **Ante todo** activities found on the CD-ROM.

Lucía y su esposo Mario viven en Caracas, Venezuela. Lucía está muy preocupada porque Mario tiene el colesterol muy alto. El médico le dice que baje de peso y que haga ejercicio, pero Mario no cree que eso sea necesario. Lucía duda que él cambie de actitud.

LUCÍA   —Oye, Mario. El otro día me dijiste que querías adelgazar y que siempre estabas cansado. Aquí hay un artículo que quiero que leas cuando tengas tiempo.

MARIO   —Puedo leerlo ahora mismo. (*Lee.*) Diez reglas infalibles para conservar la salud... Ya me estás dando lata. Yo siempre como bien y hago ejercicio...

LUCÍA   —El único ejercicio que tú haces es caminar hacia el refrigerador y cambiar los canales en la televisión. Y ahora que lo pienso, ¿quién se comió las albóndigas, las chuletas y el pastel de manzana que sobró?

MARIO   —Yo creo que fue el perro.

LUCÍA   —En serio, ¿por qué no te haces socio de un gimnasio? Marcelo conoce uno que es muy bueno.

MARIO   —Tú quieres que yo vaya al gimnasio, que levante pesas, que tome clases de karate... En fin, esperas que me convierta en un superhombre.

LUCÍA   —¡Cómo exageras, Mario! Pero el médico quiere que pierdas unos quince kilos[1].

MARIO   —¡Bah! Ese doctor quiere que yo viva contando calorías y muriéndome de hambre. Además, yo no soy gordo; lo que pasa es que soy bajo para mi peso.

LUCÍA   —(*Se ríe.*) Sí, para ese peso tienes que medir un metro noventa... Pero, según un estudio realizado últimamente, es necesario hacer ejercicios vigorosos frecuentemente para mantenerse joven.

MARIO   —¡Ajá! ¡Lo que tú quieres es un esposo joven! Bueno, te voy a hacer caso. Hagámonos socios de un club, pero no vayamos al que le gusta a Marcelo, porque es carísimo. Necesitamos encontrar uno que sea más económico.

LUCÍA   —Está bien, pero empecemos por ponernos a dieta.

MARIO   —Bueno, con tal de que me dejes en paz, hago cualquier cosa.

Mario lee las reglas para conservar la salud.

---

[1] En los países de habla hispana se usa el sistema métrico decimal. Un kilo equivale a 2,2 libras; un centímetro equivale a 0,39 pulgadas y un metro equivale a 3,2 pies.

Diez reglas infalibles para conservar la salud

Si quiere mantenerse sano y sentirse siempre lleno de energía, es importante que haga lo siguiente:

1. Tenga una dieta balanceada.
2. Haga ejercicio todos los días.
3. Evite las drogas y el tabaco.
4. Evite el estrés y duerma de seis a ocho horas todas las noches.
5. Beba moderadamente o no beba.
6. Disminuya el consumo de grasas.
7. Aumente el consumo de alimentos que contienen fibra.
8. Limite el consumo de sal.
9. Beba por lo menos ocho vasos de agua al día.
10. Mantenga un peso adecuado.

Dígame

En parejas, contesten las siguientes preguntas basadas en el diálogo.

1. ¿Por qué está preocupada Lucía?
2. ¿Qué le dice el médico a Mario? ¿Cree él que eso es necesario?
3. ¿Qué duda Lucía?
4. Según Lucía, ¿cuál es el único ejercicio que hace Mario?
5. ¿Cuántos kilos quiere el médico que pierda Mario?
6. ¿Por qué es una buena idea hacer ejercicios vigorosos?
7. ¿Qué dice Mario que va a hacer? ¿Por qué no quiere ir al gimnasio que le gusta a Marcelo?
8. ¿Qué dice Lucía que deben hacer los dos? ¿Qué va a hacer Mario con tal de que Lucía lo deje en paz?
9. Según el artículo, ¿qué debemos evitar si queremos tener buena salud?
10. ¿Qué alimentos son buenos para la salud? ¿Cuántos vasos de agua debemos beber al día?
11. ¿Ud. cree que Mario va a empezar a cuidarse más? ¿Por qué o por qué no?
12. De las reglas mencionadas en el artículo, ¿cuáles son las dos más importantes para Ud.?

Perspectivas socioculturales

INSTRUCTOR WEBSITE
Your instructor may
assign the precon-
versational support
activities found in
**Perspectivas socio-
culturales.**

En todo el mundo, la gente va creando conciencia (*are becoming aware*) de la importancia de la salud preventiva. Haga lo siguiente:

1. Durante unos cinco minutos, converse con dos compañeros sobre el siguiente tema: En su sociedad, ¿se le da suficiente importancia a prevenir los problemas de la salud?
2. Participe con el resto de la clase en la discusión del tema cuando su profesor(a) se lo indique.

Vocabulario

Nombres

la albóndiga meatball
el alimento food, nourishment, nutrient
el canal channel
la chuleta chop
el consumo consumption
el cuerpo body
el estrés, la tensión nerviosa stress
la grasa fat
la libra pound
la mente mind
el pastel pie
el peso weight
el pie foot
la pulgada inch
la regla rule
la salud health
el (la) socio(a) member

Verbos

adelgazar, perder (e → ie) (bajar de) peso to lose weight
aumentar to increase
caminar to walk

convertirse (e → ie) (en) to become
disminuir (yo disminuyo)[1] to decrease, to lessen
evitar to avoid
exagerar to exaggerate
hacerse to become
mantenerse (*conj. like* **tener**) to keep oneself, to stay (*e.g., young or healthy*)
medir (e → i) to be . . . tall,[2] to measure
realizar to do, to make
sobrar to be left over

Adjetivos

joven young
lleno(a) full
sano(a) healthy
único(a) only

Otras palabras y expresiones

ahora mismo right now
al (por) día a (per) day
cambiar de actitud to change one's attitude

---

[1] This change is discussed in **Apéndice B**, under **"Verbos de cambios ortográficos,"** number 10.

[2] **¿Cuánto mide Ud.?** = How tall are you?

cualquier cosa   anything
darle lata (a alguien)   to annoy or pester (somebody)
dejar en paz   to leave alone
hacer caso   to pay attention, to obey
hacer ejercicio   to exercise
hacerse socio(a)   to become a member (*of a club*)
levantar pesas   to lift weights

lo que pasa es que   the truth of the matter is that
lo siguiente   the following
mantenerse joven   to keep young
morirse (o → ue) de hambre   to die of hunger, to starve to death
ponerse a dieta   to go on a diet
últimamente   lately
una dieta balanceada   a balanced diet

Ampliación

Otras palabras relacionadas con la salud y la nutrición

el calcio   calcium
los carbohidratos, los hidratos de carbono   carbohydrates
descansar   to rest
el ejercicio ligero   light exercise
engordar, ganar peso   to gain weight
la fuente de energía   energy source
el hierro   iron
la proteína   protein
el reposo   rest
la vitamina   vitamin

Algunos vegetales

el ají, el pimiento verde   green pepper
el ajo   garlic
el apio   celery
el brécol, el bróculi   broccoli
la cebolla   onion
la espinaca   spinach
el hongo, la seta   mushroom
la lechuga   lettuce
el pepino   cucumber
el rábano   radish
la remolacha   beet
el repollo, la col   cabbage
la zanahoria   carrot

Hablando de todo un poco

CD-ROM
Go to **Vocabulario** for additional vocabulary practice.

Preparación   Circule la palabra o frase que no pertenece en cada grupo.

1. albóndiga	chuleta	canal
2. bajar de peso	adelgazar	engordar
3. bróculi	pulgada	espinaca
4. sobrar	hacer ejercicio	levantar pesas
5. hierro	calcio	grasa
6. remolacha	cuerpo	rábano
7. pie	libra	pulgada
8. exagerar	disminuir	aumentar

9. en seguida	cualquier cosa	ahora mismo
10. ajo	ají	pimiento verde
11. repollo	col	zanahoria
12. pastel	apio	pepino
13. hongo	cebolla	seta
14. ponerse a dieta	morirse de hambre	hacerse socio
15. fuente de energía	ejercicio ligero	carbohidrato
16. no dejar en paz	mantenerse joven	dar lata
17. realizar	obedecer	hacer caso
18. últimamente	recientemente	desgraciadamente
19. regla	brécol	alimento
20. una dieta balanceada	sano	único

En grupos de tres o cuatro, hagan lo siguiente:

A. **Platos vegetarianos.**   Hablen de las verduras que necesitan usar para preparar los siguientes platos:

1. una ensalada mixta
2. una sopa de verduras
3. un guiso (*stew*) de vegetales
4. sándwiches de verduras

B. **Comidas saludables**

1. Hablen de los alimentos que tienen carbohidratos, de los que tienen proteína, de los que tienen calcio, de los que tienen hierro y de los que tienen diversas vitaminas importantes.
2. Ahora preparen el menú de la cena más balanceada y saludable que puedan ofrecerles a sus compañeros de clase.

C. **Normas diarias de prevención**

1. ¿Qué cosas deben hacer y qué deben evitar para tener buena salud?
2. ¿Qué comidas se deben comer y qué comidas se deben evitar si hacemos dieta?
3. ¿Qué ejercicios se pueden hacer para mantenerse en forma?

Palabras problemáticas

A. **Bajo** y **corto** como equivalentes de *short*

- **Bajo** es el opuesto de **alto;** equivale a *short* cuando se refiere a estatura (*height*).

  Mi hermana sólo mide cinco pies; es muy **baja.**

- **Corto** es el opuesto de **largo;** equivale a *short* cuando se refiere a longitud (*length*).

  Ese vestido no te queda muy bien. Te queda muy **corto.**

  La distancia entre tu casa y la de mis padres es muy **corta.**

B. **Convertirse, ponerse** y **hacerse** como equivalentes de *to become*

- **Convertirse en** es equivalente a *to turn into*.

  Hizo mucho frío y el agua **se convirtió en** hielo.

  Ganó la lotería y, de la noche a la mañana (*overnight*), **se convirtió en** un hombre rico.

- **Ponerse** (+ adjetivo) equivale a *to become* cuando se refiere a adoptar o asumir cierta condición o estado.

  Él **se puso** pálido (*pale*) cuando nos vio.

  Yo **me pongo** nerviosa cuando tengo exámenes.

- **Hacerse** equivale a *to become* cuando se refiere a una profesión u oficio.

  Marta **se hizo** médica y Luis **se hizo** electricista.

Práctica

Complete los siguientes diálogos y represéntelos con un(a) compañero(a).

1. —¿Por qué sacaste una "F" en el examen de ayer?
   —Porque _____ muy nervioso.

2. —¿Qué sabes de Luis?
   —_____ abogado y ahora vive en Chile.

3. —¿Gonzalo perdió todo su dinero?
   —Sí, _____ un hombre pobre de la noche a la mañana.

4. —¿El viaje de Buenos Aires a Asunción es largo?
   —No, es _____ si vas en avión.

5. —¿Elena es alta o _____?
   —Es de estatura mediana.

Your instructor may carry out the **¡Ahora escuche!** listening activity found in the **Answers to Text Exercises**.

¡Ahora escuche!

Se leerá dos veces una breve narración sobre ciertos problemas que tiene Carlitos. Se harán aseveraciones sobre la narración. En una hoja escriba los números de uno a diez e indique si cada aseveración es verdadera (V) o falsa (F).

El mundo hispánico

Dos países sudamericanos

Lucia y Mario

Cuando Américo Vespucio llegó a estas tierras y vio las casas sobre pilotes° donde vivían los indígenas en las orillas° del lago Maracaibo, recordó las de Venecia y nombró el lugar Venezuela, que significa "pequeña Venecia". Situado al norte de Sudamérica, Venezuela es un país tropical que tiene lugares de extraordinaria belleza. Aquí está el famoso Salto° Ángel, que es el más alto del mundo y que constituye una de las mayores atracciones del país. Hay más de trescientas islas que pertenecen a Venezuela. El año pasado nosotros fuimos de vacaciones a Margarita, que, por sus hermosas playas, es la más popular entre los turistas.

stakes
shores

waterfall

El petróleo es una de las mayores fuentes de riqueza° de nuestro país y éste es su principal producto de exportación. Nosotros vivimos en Caracas, la capital, una ciudad llena de contrastes. En el centro histórico está la casa donde nació Simón Bolívar,

fuentes ... sources of wealth

STUDENT WEBSITE
Go to **El mundo hispánico** for prereading and vocabulary activities.

el Libertador de América. Esta casa es hoy un museo nacional. En la parte moderna encontramos autopistas y rascacielos° que se extienden por toda la ciudad. ¡Ah!, y estamos muy orgullosos del sistema de carreteras de Venezuela porque es el más extenso de Latinoamérica.   skyscrapers

El mes próximo vamos a ir a Colombia, nuestro país vecino. Colombia es el cuarto país en extensión en América Latina. Nosotros pensamos pasar varios días en Bogotá, la capital, porque allí tenemos muy buenos amigos. También queremos visitar Medellín, la segunda ciudad en tamaño del país, y la antigua ciudad de Cartagena, famosa por sus edificios coloniales.

En Bogotá no queremos dejar de visitar el Museo del Oro ni la famosa Catedral de Sal que se construyó en las minas de sal en 1954. Las minas están a sólo 35 millas de la capital. Mario quiere comprar algunos de los libros de Gabriel García Márquez, el escritor colombiano que en 1982 recibió el Premio Nobel de Literatura. Yo sueño con comprar un anillo° con una esmeralda porque las esmeraldas   ring
de este país están consideradas como las mejores del mundo. Miren el mapa de Venezuela y de Colombia en la página anterior para que tengan una buena idea de estos países.

Sobre Venezuela y Colombia

En parejas, túrnense para contestar las siguientes preguntas.

1. ¿Cuáles son los límites de Venezuela al norte, al sur, al este y al oeste? ¿Cuáles son los límites de Colombia?
2. ¿Qué significa el nombre Venezuela y quién le dio este nombre al país?
3. ¿Qué famoso salto se encuentra en Venezuela? ¿Cuántas islas pertenecen al país? ¿Cuál es la más popular?
4. ¿Cuál es el principal producto de exportación de Venezuela?
5. ¿Qué encontramos en el centro histórico de Caracas? ¿Qué se ve en la parte moderna?
6. ¿Quién fue Simón Bolívar?
7. ¿Cuál es la capital de Colombia? ¿Qué otras ciudades importantes hay?
8. En Bogotá, ¿qué lugares piensan visitar Mario y Lucía?
9. ¿Por qué le interesa a Mario comprar libros de Gabriel García Márquez?
10. ¿Con qué sueña Lucía? ¿Por qué?

Hablemos de su país

Américo Vespucio le dio a Venezuela este nombre, que significa "pequeña Venecia", porque el lugar le recordó a Venecia. Reúnase con otro(a) compañero(a) y conteste lo siguiente: ¿Cómo se llama la región donde vive o de donde es originalmente? ¿Sabe por qué se la nombró así?

Luego cada pareja compartirá las respuestas con toda la clase.

Una tarjeta postal

Ésta es una tarjeta postal que Lucía, quien visita Colombia con su esposo Mario, le manda a una de sus amigas.

Querida Inés:

¡Qué interesante es Bogotá! Ayer estuvimos en el Museo del Oro, que tiene una colección de veinte mil piezas, la mayoría de ellas de arte prehispánico. Por la noche fuimos a una discoteca a bailar cumbia.

La semana pasada estuvimos en Cartagena, una ciudad colonial. Todavía estoy tratando de convencer a Mario para que me compre una esmeralda.

Un abrazo,

Lucía

Después de leer la tarjeta

1. ¿Qué dice Lucía de Bogotá?
2. ¿Qué hay en el Museo del Oro?
3. ¿Adónde fueron Lucía y Mario anoche? ¿Qué tipo de música bailaron?
4. ¿Qué sabemos de Cartagena?
5. ¿Qué quiere Lucía que Mario le compre?

Estructuras gramaticales

1 El imperativo: **Ud. y Uds.**

○ The command forms for **Ud.** and **Uds.**[1] are identical to the corresponding present subjunctive forms.

A Formas regulares

		Ud.		Uds.	
-ar verbs	cantar	cant	**-e**	cant	**-en**
-er verbs	beber	beb	**-a**	beb	**-an**
-ir verbs	vivir	viv	**-a**	viv	**-an**

—¿A qué hora salimos mañana?　　*"What time shall we leave tomorrow?"*
—**Salgan** a las siete.　　*"Leave at seven."*

—¿Qué hago ahora?　　*"What shall I do now?"*
—**Lea** este artículo.　　*"Read this article."*

 Negative **Ud./Uds.** commands are formed by placing **no** in front of the verb.

No salgan mañana.

B Formas irregulares

	dar	*estar*	*ser*	*ir*
Ud.	dé	esté	sea	vaya
Uds.	den	estén	sean	vayan

—¿Cuándo quiere que vaya al club?　　*"When do you want me to go to the club?"*
—**Vaya** hoy mismo.　　*"Go today." (this very day)*

C Posición de las formas pronominales con el imperativo

○ With *affirmative commands*, the direct and indirect object pronouns and the reflexive pronouns are *attached to the end of the verb*, thus forming only one word.

—¿Le traigo las cartas?　　*"Shall I bring you the letters?"*
—Sí, **tráigamelas**[2].　　*"Yes, bring them to me."*

---

[1] The commands for **tú** will be studied in **Lección 6**.

[2] Accents in affirmative commands are discussed in **Apéndice A,** under "**El acento ortográfico**," number 7.

○ With *negative commands*, the pronouns are *placed before the verb*.

—¿Tengo que hacerlo ahora?　　　　　　　*"Do I have to do it now?"*

—No, no **lo haga** todavía; descanse un rato.　*"No, don't do it yet; rest a while."*

CD-ROM
Go to Estructuras **gramaticales** for additional practice.

Práctica

A. Ud. es médico(a) y está hablando con uno de sus pacientes. Usando el imperativo, dígale lo que tiene que hacer y lo que no debe hacer.

1. evitar el estrés y dormir por lo menos seis horas al día
2. disminuir el consumo de sal
3. no preocuparse demasiado
4. tomar la medicina dos veces al día, pero no tomarla con el estómago vacío
5. volver en dos semanas
6. darle este papel a la recepcionista y pedirle un turno
7. llamarlo(a) si tiene algún problema

Ahora dígale a su paciente tres cosas más que debe o no debe hacer.

B. Ud. tiene dos empleados que encuentran toda clase de excusas para no hacer lo que Ud. les dice. Escriba las órdenes que Ud. les da, usando el imperativo.

1. —_____
   —Ahora no podemos escribir las cartas porque no tenemos tiempo.
2. —_____
   —Tampoco podemos traducirlas al español porque no tenemos suficiente vocabulario.
3. —_____
   —Ahora no podemos ir al correo porque nos duelen los pies.
4. —_____
   —No podemos llevarle los documentos al Sr. Díaz porque él está de vacaciones en España.
5. —_____
   —No podemos preparar todos los informes para esta tarde porque tenemos que ir a almorzar.
6. —_____
   —No podemos estar aquí mañana temprano porque los dos vivimos muy lejos.
7. —_____
   —Bueno... podemos encontrar otro empleo fácilmente.

C. En parejas, hagan una lista de sugerencias para los que quieren lograr los siguientes objetivos. Usen el imperativo.

1. mantener un promedio alto en la universidad
2. pasar un fin de semana divertido en la ciudad donde está la universidad
3. mantener buenas relaciones con sus padres y hermanos
4. tener "mente sana en cuerpo sano"

D. Ahora el (la) profesor(a) va a dividir la clase en varios grupos de hombres y mujeres. Cada grupo discutirá las estrategias y las prácticas necesarias para ser "superhombres" o "supermujeres" y hará una lista de sugerencias, usando el imperativo. Al terminar la discusión, cada grupo le presentará sus recomendaciones a la clase.

2 El imperativo de la primera persona del plural

A. Usos y formas

- The first person plural of an affirmative command (*let's* + *verb*) may be expressed in two different ways in Spanish.

  1. By using the first person plural of the present subjunctive.

     —**Hablemos** con los socios del club.   *"Let's talk with the members of the club."*

     —Sí, **hagámoslo** hoy mismo.   *"Yes, let's do it today."*

  2. By using **vamos a** + *infinitive.*

     Vamos a hacer lo siguiente.   *Let's do the following.*

- To express a negative first person plural command, only the subjunctive is used.

  No caminemos hoy.   *Let's not walk today.*

- With the verb **ir,** the present indicative is used for the affirmative command. The subjunctive is used only for the negative.

  Vamos.   *Let's go.*
  No vayamos.   *Let's not go.*

B. Posición de las formas pronominales

- As with the **Ud.** and **Uds.** command forms, direct and indirect object pronouns and reflexive pronouns are attached to an affirmative command, but precede a negative command.

  —¿Qué le decimos a Oscar?   *"What do we say to Oscar?"*
  —**Digámosle**[1] que tiene que perder peso.   *"Let's tell him that he has to lose weight."*

  —No, no **le digamos** eso.   *"No, let's not tell him that."*

- When the first person plural command is used with a reflexive verb, the final **s** of the verb is dropped before adding the reflexive pronoun **nos.**

  Vistamoś + nos → **Vistámonos.**[1]
  Levantemoś + nos → **Levantémonos.**[1]

---

[1] Like the other affirmative commands, the **nosotros** affirmative command takes an accent on the vowel of the verb's stressed syllable when object pronouns are attached: **comprémosle, comprémoselas...**

◉ The final **s** is also dropped before adding the indirect object pronoun **se.**

Digamos + selo → **Digámoselo.**
Pidamos + selo → **Pidámoselo.**

CD-ROM
Go to **Estructuras gramaticales** for additional practice.

Práctica

A. Ud. y un(a) compañero(a) están en un restaurante. Usen la información dada para decir lo que van a hacer.

MODELO: —¿Para qué hora reservamos la mesa?   (las nueve)
            —*Reservémosla para las nueve.*

1. ¿Dónde nos sentamos?   (cerca de la ventana)
2. ¿Nos sentamos en la sección de fumar?   (no)
3. ¿Qué le pedimos al mozo?   (el menú)
4. ¿Pedimos el vino ahora?   (no)
5. ¿Le decimos al mozo que el bistec está crudo?   (sí)
6. ¿Le ponemos aceite y vinagre a la ensalada?   (sí)
7. ¿Pedimos la cuenta ahora?   (sí)
8. ¿Le dejamos propina al mozo?   (sí)

B. Ud. y un(a) compañero(a) van a ir de viaje. Digan todo lo que deben hacer con respecto a lo siguiente.

MODELO: pasajes
            E1:   —*Compremos los pasajes.*
            E2:   —*Sí, vamos a comprar los pasajes.*

1. los documentos
2. las reservaciones
3. los cheques de viajero
4. el perro
5. el coche
6. las maletas
7. la casa
8. todas las puertas y ventanas

C. Ud. y un(a) compañero(a) van a ponerse a dieta y están tratando de planear actividades para adelgazar. Cuando uno(a) de Uds. propone una actividad, el otro (la otra) la rechaza y propone otra. Propongan unas seis actividades, siguiendo el modelo.

MODELO: E1:   —*Caminemos dos horas todos los días.*
            E2:   —*No, no caminemos dos horas; caminemos una.*

3 El subjuntivo para expresar duda, incredulidad y negación

A El subjuntivo para expresar duda o incredulidad

○ When the verb of the main clause expresses doubt or uncertainty, the verb in the subordinate clause is in the subjunctive.

—Luis cree que Rosa necesita disminuir el consumo de sal.	*"Luis thinks Rosa needs to decrease her salt intake."*
—**Dudo** que ella lo **haga**.	*"I doubt that she will do it."*
—¿Tú vas a ir con él?	*"Are you going with him?"*
—**Dudo** que **pueda** ir.	*"I doubt that I can go."*

atención

When doubt is expressed, the subjunctive always follows the verb **dudar** even if there is no change of subject. When no doubt is expressed, and the speaker is certain of what is said in the subordinate clause, the indicative is used.

Dudo que **pueda** hacerse socio.	*I doubt that he can become a member.*
No dudo que **puede** hacerse socio.	*I don't doubt that he can become a member.*

○ The subjunctive follows certain impersonal expressions that indicate doubt. The most common expressions are:

es difícil[1] *it is unlikely*	**es (im)probable** *it's (im)probable,*
es dudoso *it is doubtful*	*it's (un)likely*
es (im)posible[2] *it is (im)possible*	**puede ser** *it may be*

—¿Quieres ir al gimnasio este fin de semana?	*"Do you want to go to the gym this weekend?"*
—**Es difícil** que yo **tenga** el fin de semana libre, pero **puede ser** que Daniel **pueda** ir contigo.	*"It's unlikely that I'll have the weekend off, but maybe Daniel can go with you."*

○ The verb **creer** is followed by the subjunctive when it is used in negative sentences to express disbelief. It is followed by the indicative in affirmative sentences when it expresses belief or conviction.

—Yo **creo** que **podemos** hacer ejercicio.	*"I think we can exercise."*
—No, **no creo** que **tengamos** tiempo.	*"No, I don't think we'll have time."*

atención

When the verb **creer** is used in a question, the indicative is used if no doubt or opinion is expressed. The subjunctive is used to express doubt about what is being said in the subordinate clause.

¿**Crees** que **podemos** hacer ejercicio?	(Yo creo que sí, o no expreso mi opinión.)
¿**Crees** que **podamos** hacer ejercicio?	(Yo lo dudo.)

---

[1] If there is no subject, the infinitive is used with **difícil**.
    Es difícil **poder** estudiar aquí.

[2] If there is no subject, the infinitive is used with **(im)posible**.
    Es imposible **salir** por esa puerta.

B El subjuntivo para expresar negación

○ When the verb in the main clause denies what is said in the subordinate clause, the subjunctive is used.

—Dicen que ese médico es millonario.
—Pues él **niega** que su capital **pase** de los quinientos mil dólares.

—Ellos deben de tener mucho dinero porque gastan mucho.
—Es verdad que gastan mucho, pero **no es cierto** que **tengan** mucho dinero.

"They say that doctor is a millionaire."
"Well, he denies that his capital exceeds five hundred thousand dollars."

"They must have a lot of money because they spend a lot."
"It's true that they spend a lot, but it isn't true that they have a lot of money."

When the verb in the main clause does not deny, but rather confirms, what is said in the subordinate clause, the indicative is used.

Él **no niega** que su capital **pasa** de los quinientos mil dólares.
Es cierto que **tienen** mucho dinero.

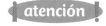
CD-ROM
Go to **Estructuras gramaticales** for additional practice.

Práctica

A. En parejas, den su opinión sobre las siguientes aseveraciones, expresando duda, incredulidad o negación.

1. Olga pesa (*weighs*) cien libras. Necesita perder peso.
2. Luis duerme once horas por noche.
3. Nosotros siempre estamos sentados, mirando la tele. Hacemos mucho ejercicio.
4. El apio tiene mucha grasa.
5. Susana come solamente carne y pasta. Tiene una dieta balanceada.
6. Pedro come muy poco y hace ejercicio. Quiere engordar.
7. Marcelo fuma mucho, pero dice que puede dejar de fumar fácilmente.
8. Paco come mucha carne y mucho queso para que le baje el colesterol.
9. Fernando mide un metro noventa. Es bajo.
10. Levantar pesas es un ejercicio ligero.

B. Complete las siguientes frases de un modo original. Luego compare sus respuestas con las de un(a) compañero(a).

1. No es verdad que yo...
2. Yo no niego que mis padres...
3. Es difícil que un estudiante...
4. No es posible que un niño...
5. Es cierto que mis clases...
6. Es dudoso que nosotros...
7. Estoy seguro(a) de que Uds...
8. Creo que mi amiga...
9. Yo no creo que el profesor...
10. Yo niego que mi familia...

4 El subjuntivo para expresar lo indefinido y lo inexistente

○ The subjunctive is always used when the subordinate clause refers to an indefinite, hypothetical, or nonexistent object or person.

—Busco una persona que **hable** francés. — *"I'm looking for someone who speaks French."*

—Aquí no hay nadie que **sepa** hablar francés. — *"There's no one here who knows how to speak French."*

—Queremos una casa que **tenga** piscina. — *"We want a house that has a swimming pool."*

—En este barrio no hay ninguna casa que **tenga** piscina. — *"In this neighborhood there is no house that has a swimming pool."*

—¿Hay algún restaurante aquí que **sirva** comida mexicana? — *"Is there any restaurant here that serves Mexican food?"*

—No, no hay ningún restaurante aquí que **sirva** comida mexicana. — *"No, there is no restaurant here that serves Mexican food."*

atención

Note that the personal **a** is not used when the noun does not refer to a specific person. If the subordinate clause refers to existent, definite, or specified objects, persons, or things, the indicative is used.

Aquí hay una chica que **sabe** hablar francés. — *There is a girl here who knows how to speak French.*

Vivo en una casa que **tiene** piscina. — *I live in a house that has a swimming pool.*

Aquí hay muchos restaurantes que **sirven** comida mexicana. — *There are many restaurants here that serve Mexican food.*

CD-ROM
Go to **Estructuras gramaticales** for additional practice.

Práctica

A. ¿Qué es lo que estas personas tienen y qué buscan o quieren? ¿Qué hay y qué no hay? Dígalo Ud. usando su imaginación. Luego compare sus respuestas con las de un(a) compañero(a).

1. Yo quiero una casa que...
2. Nosotros buscamos un gimnasio que...
3. En la ciudad donde yo vivo hay muchos restaurantes que...
4. En la clase de español no hay nadie que...
5. Yo prefiero vivir en una ciudad que...
6. Mi amiga busca un esposo que...
7. En esta universidad hay muchos profesores que...
8. En nuestra familia no hay nadie que...
9. Yo tengo un amigo que...
10. Mis padres necesitan a alguien que...
11. En mi barrio hay muchas chicas que...
12. No hay ningún estudiante que...
13. En el gimnasio, no hay miembros que...
14. En el club hay personas que...
15. Necesitamos seguir una dieta que...

B. Ud. y un(a) compañero(a) de clase van a representar el papel de una persona que es nueva en una ciudad y el de otra que es residente. La persona nueva pide información acerca de las cosas que se pueden encontrar en la ciudad y el (la) residente contesta sus preguntas. Siga el modelo.

MODELO: —¿Hay algunas casas que sean baratas?
              —No, no hay ninguna que sea barata.

              (Sí, hay algunas que son baratas.)

5 Expresiones que requieren el subjuntivo o el indicativo

A Expresiones que siempre requieren el subjuntivo

⊙ Some expressions are always followed by the subjunctive. Here are some of them.

a fin de que *in order that*	**en caso de que** *in case*
a menos que *unless*	**para que** *so that*
antes (de) que *before*	**sin que** *without*
con tal (de) que *provided that*	

—¿No va al gimnasio?   *"Aren't you going to the gym?"*
—No puedo ir **a menos que** Ana   *"I won't be able to go unless Ana takes me."*
  me **lleve.**
—La voy a llamar **para que venga**   *"I'll call her so that she'll come for you."*
  por Ud.
—Está bien, pero llámela **antes de**   *"Okay, but call her before she leaves home."*
  que salga de su casa.

Práctica

CD-ROM
Go to **Estructuras gramaticales** for additional practice.

A. Termine las siguientes oraciones según su propia experiencia. Compare sus respuestas con las de sus compañeros(as).

1. Siempre vengo a mis clases, a menos que...
2. Voy a estudiar mucho en caso de que el profesor (la profesora)...
3. Voy a llamar a un(a) compañero(a) de clase para que...
4. No voy a poder terminar el trabajo sin que tú...
5. El sábado voy a ir a la biblioteca con tal de que...
6. No voy a comprar los libros para el semestre próximo antes de que...

B. Combine cada par de oraciones en una sola, utilizando las expresiones estudiadas. Haga los cambios necesarios.

1. No podemos bajar de peso.
   Hacemos ejercicio.
2. Yo puedo hacerme socio del club.
   Uds. me dan el dinero.
3. Voy a comprar las verduras.
   Mamá hace la sopa.

4. Voy a decirles a los socios que estén aquí a las dos.
   La dietista quiere hablar con ellos.
5. Voy a limpiar mi casa.
   Mi suegra viene a vernos.
6. No puedo salir de casa.
   Los niños me ven.

B Expresiones que requieren el subjuntivo o el indicativo

● The subjunctive is used after certain conjunctions of time when the main clause expresses a future action or is a command. Notice that the actions in the subordinate clauses of the following examples have not yet occurred.

—¿Vamos a la estación ahora?   *"Are we going to the station now?"*
—No, vamos a esperar **hasta que venga**   *"No, we are going to wait until Eva*
   Eva.   *comes."*
—Bueno, llámeme **en cuanto** ella **llegue.** *"Well, call me as soon as she arrives."*

Some conjunctions of time are:

así que	*as soon as*	**en cuanto**	*as soon as*
cuando	*when*	**hasta que**	*until*
después (de) que	*after*	**tan pronto (como)**	*as soon as*

If there is no indication of a future action, the indicative is used.

Hablé con ella **en cuanto** la **vi.**   *I spoke with her as soon as I saw her.*
Siempre **hablo** con ella **en cuanto** la **veo.** *I always speak with her as soon as I see her.*

CD-ROM
Go to **Estructuras gramaticales** for additional practice.

Práctica

A. Cambie las siguientes oraciones apropiadamente.

1. Todos los días Teresa llama a su novio en cuanto llega a casa.
   Mañana...
2. Vamos a esperar al entrenador hasta que venga.
   Siempre esperamos al entrenador...
3. Ayer leí la página deportiva tan pronto como llegó el periódico.
   Esta tarde...
4. Ellos llevaron a María al hospital cuando se dieron cuenta de que estaba enferma.
   Ellos van a llevar a María al hospital...
5. Yo siempre compro ropa tan pronto como me pagan.
   Voy a comprar ropa...

B. Complete los siguientes diálogos de una manera original y represéntelos con un(a) compañero(a).

1. —¿A qué hora vamos a salir para el club?
   —En cuanto...

2. —¿Hasta cuándo vas a esperar a Ernesto?
   —Hasta que...
3. —¿Cuándo te vas a poner a dieta?
   —Tan pronto como...
4. —¿Vas a ir a caminar con Sergio?
   —Sí, así que...
5. —¿Cuándo me vas a dejar en paz?
   —Cuando...
6. —¿Cuándo crees tú que Nora va a dejar de fumar?
   —En cuanto...
7. —¿Van a ir Uds. al gimnasio hoy?
   —Sí, después de que Raúl...
8. —¿Hasta cuándo van a estar Uds. aquí?
   —Hasta que...

STUDENT WEBSITE
Do the **Compruebe cuánto sabe** self test after finishing this **Estructuras gramaticales** section.

¡CONTINUEMOS!

Una encuesta

Entreviste a sus compañeros de clase para tratar de identificar a aquellas personas que...

1. ...hacen ejercicio por lo menos tres veces por semana.
2. ...tienen una dieta balanceada.
3. ...no fuman.
4. ...no toman bebidas alcohólicas.
5. ...beben por lo menos ocho vasos de agua al día.
6. ...levantan pesas.
7. ...toman clases de karate.
8. ...practican algún deporte.
9. ...son socios de un gimnasio.
10. ...viven contando calorías.
11. ...siguen todas las reglas que aparecen en el artículo.
12. ...duermen más de seis horas al día.

Ahora, divídanse en grupos de tres o cuatro y discutan el resultado de la encuesta.

  ## ¿Comprende Ud.?

CD-ROM   STUDENT WEBSITE
Go to **De escuchar...a escribir** (in **¿Comprende Ud.?**) on the CD-ROM for activities related to the conversation, and go to **Canción** on the website for activities related to the song.

1. Escuche la siguiente conversación entre Silvia y su médico, que hablan sobre cómo mantener la salud. El objetivo de la actividad es el de escuchar una conversación a velocidad natural. No se preocupe de entenderlo todo, pues esto no se espera de Ud. Después de escuchar la conversación dos veces, Ud. oirá varias aseveraciones. En una hoja, escriba los números de uno a ocho e indique si cada aseveración es verdadera o falsa.

2. Luego escuche la canción y trate de aprenderla.

Hablemos de la salud

En parejas, fíjense en este folleto y contesten las siguientes preguntas.

Tenemos para ti el más avanzado *programa de trabajo cardiovascular* **en Fitness Professional.**

¡anímate y ven!

GIMNASIO ANGEL LOPEZ

Clases de prueba de todas las actividades, sin compromiso

Y muchos otros servicios.

En más de 2000 m².

Actividades

- Aerobic
- Karate infantil y adulto
- Taekwondo
- Gimnasia de mantenimiento
- Gimnasia Rítmica
- Ballet
- Gimnasia con aparatos
- Musculación
- Peso libre olímpico
- Squash
- Sauna (gratuita para socios)

y además

- Gabinete médico y dietético
- Rehabilitación
- Centro de belleza
- Bronceador U.V.A.
- Preparación para cuerpos especiales: Policía, Bomberos, Academias Militares, etc…

Estamos a tu disposición de:
9,00 h. a 22,30 h. lunes a viernes
9,00 h. a 14,00 h. sábados y domingos

Amparo Usera, 14

28026 Madrid

Telf. 476 36 82

¡No cerramos a mediodía!

1. ¿Cómo se llama el centro deportivo y en qué calle está?
2. ¿A qué número de teléfono se debe llamar para pedir información?
3. Si alguien va al gimnasio un sábado a las tres de la tarde, ¿lo va a encontrar abierto? ¿Por qué?
4. ¿Está cerrado el gimnasio de doce a una de la tarde?
5. ¿Qué miembros de la familia pueden asistir al gimnasio?
6. ¿Qué actividades de origen oriental hay en el gimnasio?
7. ¿Los socios del gimnasio tienen que pagar por usar la sauna?
8. De las actividades que ofrece el gimnasio, ¿cuáles les interesan a Uds.?

¿Qué dirían ustedes?

Imagínese que Ud. y un(a) compañero(a) se encuentran en las siguientes situaciones. ¿Qué va a decir cada uno?

1. Un amigo quiere que Uds. le den algunos consejos para perder peso.
2. Un amigo que tiene una vida muy sedentaria les pregunta qué cambios puede hacer para tener una vida más activa.
3. Uds. tienen que dar una pequeña charla sobre la importancia de tener buenos hábitos para conservar la salud.

¡De ustedes depende!

Ud. y su compañero(a) están encargados(as) de aconsejar a estudiantes de habla hispana con problemas de salud. Díganles a estas personas lo que deben hacer y qué alimentos y bebidas deben o no deben consumir.

1. José tiene el colesterol muy alto.
2. Ana sufre de insomnio.
3. Raquel es demasiado delgada.
4. Mario siempre está cansado.
5. Alina es anémica.
6. Marcos sufre de estrés.

Mesa redonda

Según varias encuestas, muchos niños en los Estados Unidos no tienen una buena alimentación. En grupos de cuatro o cinco estudiantes hablen de los problemas que existen, sus causas y las posibles soluciones. Para cada grupo seleccionen un líder que informe al resto de la clase sobre sus ideas.

Lecturas periodísticas

Saber leer   Creación de contextos: la formulación de preguntas

CD-ROM
Go to **Lecturas periodísticas** for additional prereading and vocabulary activities.

Recuerde que la lectura requiere la participación **activa** del lector *antes y durante* la actividad. Otra estrategia para asegurarse de que su lectura sea activa es la de (*that of*) crear contextos formulando preguntas sobre lo que va a leer o sobre lo que está leyendo.

Varios encabezados (*headings*) dividen la siguiente lectura periodística en secciones. Haga lo siguiente.

1. Lea el título y los encabezados.
2. En esta ocasión, le sugerimos las preguntas, una por encabezado.
   a. **Es mejor que...**   ¿Qué hábitos debemos modificar para perder peso?
   b. **Cuidado con...**   ¿Con qué cosas debemos tener cuidado si (*if*) queremos perder peso?
   c. **Evite las dietas que...**   ¿Qué dietas se deben evitar?
   d. **Prefiera los programas que...** ¿Qué programas nos pueden ayudar a perder peso?
3. En parejas, den una respuesta a cada una de las preguntas (antes de leer el artículo).
4. Lea el artículo y compare sus respuestas con las respuestas que se dan en la lectura a cada una de las preguntas.

Para leer y comprender

Al leer detalladamente el artículo, busque las respuestas a las siguientes preguntas.

1. ¿Qué alimentos se deben comer con moderación?
2. ¿Cómo debemos preparar los alimentos?
3. Además de comer adecuadamente, ¿qué otras cosas podemos hacer para perder peso?
4. ¿Con qué debemos tener cuidado?
5. ¿Qué tipos de dietas se deben evitar?
6. ¿Cuál de los programas señalados en el artículo es el más eficaz para no volver a ganar el peso perdido?

Tácticas y estrategias de la pérdida de peso

Es mejor que...

- coma despacio°.
- evite tentaciones. Saque los alimentos de alto contenido calórico del refrigerador y de la despensa°. Tenga en casa únicamente lo que va a comer.
- coma menos grasa. Use azúcares naturales de granos, frutas y verduras.
- coma menos helado, quesos, aderezos° para ensaladas y aceites.
- evite los bocadillos de paquete°, las galletas° y los postres con alto contenido de grasas.
- use utensilios de teflón.

- prepare las carnes al horno o a la parrilla°, y las verduras al vapor°, en lugar de freírlas° en grasa.
- coma productos lácteos° desgrasados°.
- haga ejercicio regularmente.
- trate de hacer actividades divertidas que no incluyan el comer.
- acuda a terapia individual o de grupo si tiene dificultad para mantener su peso.

Cuidado con...

- las píldoras° o productos que prometen "derretir"° la grasa.
- las píldoras que quitan el apetito (tienen efectos indeseables° y,

cuanto más° se usan, menos eficaces son).
- los suplementos de fibra.
- cualquier plan que prometa "quemar"° la grasa.
- los tratamientos en que cubren el cuerpo con cera° y otros materiales.
- los sustitutos de azúcar (y el azúcar).

Evite las dietas que...

- enfatizan un tipo de alimento sobre otros, como toronjas° u otras frutas.
- insisten en mezclar° únicamente cierto tipo de alimentos.

Una frutería en la ciudad de Buenos Aires, Argentina

slowly	
pantry	
dressings	
bocadillos... packaged snacks / cookies	

a la... grilled / **al...** steamed	
en... instead of frying them	
milk	
skimmed	
pills	
melt	
undesirable	

cuanto... the more	
burn	
wax	
grapefruits	
mix	

- se tienen que seguir con suplementos de minerales y vitaminas, especialmente si esas "fórmulas especiales" se venden con la dieta.

Prefiera los programas que...

- sugieren alimentos de bajo contenido calórico, especialmente bajos en grasa y azúcar.

- ofrecen variedad, para que sean más estimulantes.
- se ajustan a su tipo de vida.
- enfatizan cambios en sus hábitos alimenticios° y estilo de vida para que el peso pueda mantenerse constante.

- han sido desarrollados° por expertos y no por alguien sin conocimientos de nutrición.

—————
hábitos... eating habits

—————
developed

Desde su mundo

1. De los consejos que aparecen en el artículo, ¿cuáles ya había oído Ud.?
2. ¿Qué problemas puede Ud. señalar (*point out*) en la alimentación de muchos norteamericanos?
3. ¿Cree Ud. que estos consejos les son útiles a muchas personas? ¿Por qué o por qué no?

piense y escriba   La introducción y la conclusión

STUDENT WEBSITE

CD-ROM

Go to **...y escribamos** (in **Hablemos de su país**) on the student website and **De escuchar... a escribir** (in **¿Comprende Ud.?**) on the CD-ROM for additional writing practice.

La introducción a una composición presenta el tema. En ésta, Ud. también trata de interesar a sus lectores en el tema. En la conclusión, Ud. resume para ayudar a sus lectores a recordar las ideas principales que Ud. les quiso comunicar.

Sin embargo, la introducción y la conclusión de los textos varían según los objetivos que Ud. tenga al escribir. Por ejemplo, en una carta a un amigo suyo, la introducción es un saludo y la conclusión es una despedida, y ambos (*both*) son informales.

Su propósito al escribir en esta ocasión es el siguiente: Ud. tiene una amiga cuya meta (*goal*) para el nuevo año es perder peso. Le va a escribir una carta personal en la que le da consejos sobre lo que debe y lo que no debe comer, y sobre el tipo de ejercicio que debe hacer.

Al escribir la introducción y la conclusión de su carta, hágase las siguientes preguntas, respectivamente:

- **En la introducción:** ¿De qué manera desea presentarle sus opiniones a su amiga e interesarla en los consejos que le quiere dar?
- **En la conclusión:** ¿Cómo quiere despedirse de su amiga y darle fin (*close*) a esta comunicación personal? ¡Sea imaginativo(a)!

Pepe Vega y su mundo

 # Teleinforme

Como vimos en esta lección, hay muchas reglas que una persona puede seguir para mantener una mente sana y un cuerpo sano. Pero a veces ocurren accidentes inesperados que afectan la salud mental o la física. ¿Qué hacemos entonces? Vamos a ver dos segmentos de video que nos muestran que sí se puede mantener una mente sana o un cuerpo sano a pesar de (in spite of) accidentes pequeños (como una quemadura) o catastróficos (como la paraplejia).

Preparación

¿Mente sana, cuerpo sano o las dos cosas?   Clasifique las siguientes expresiones según representen aspectos positivos (+) o negativos (–) de una mente sana o de un cuerpo sano. Si cree que la expresión no tiene relación con la categoría, no escriba nada.

	MENTE SANA	CUERPO SANO
1. **MODELO:** la vida activa	+	+
2. la ampolla (*blister*)		
3. la apendicitis		
4. el calcio		
5. el catarro		
6. la cicatriz (*scar*)		
7. la clara de huevo (*egg white*)		
8. la depresión		
9. descansar		
10. la esquizofrenia		
11. fumar		
12. hacer *jogging*		
13. hacer meditación		
14. hacer yoga		
15. la lesión medular		
16. levantar pesas (*to lift weights*)		
17. las malas posturas		
18. la parálisis		
19. la paraplejia		
20. la pierna rota (*broken leg*)		
21. las proteínas		
22. la quemadura (*burn*)		
23. reestructurar el cuerpo		
24. relajarse		
25. el remedio		
26. la silla de ruedas (*wheelchair*)		
27. tocar la guitarra		

Dé un ejemplo más de cada una de las siguientes categorías: cuerpo sano (–), cuerpo sano (+), mente sana-cuerpo sano (+), y mente sana-cuerpo sano (–).

Comprensión

CD-ROM
Go to **Video** for further pre-viewing, vocabulary, and structure practice on this clip.

Fuera de campo: Lluís Remolí[1]   21:09–24:26

Cartelera TVE es un programa semanal de la Televisión Española que ofrece un re-sumen (*summary*) de los programas que se presentan durante la semana que empieza. A veces también presenta reportajes sobre figuras conocidas de TVE. En este repor-taje vamos a conocer a Lluís Remolí, periodista que sufrió un accidente que lo dejó parapléjico.

---

[1] Luis se escribe *Lluís* en catalán y en valenciano, dos idiomas regionales de España.

A. ¿Verdadera o falsa? Indique si las siguientes oraciones son verdaderas (**V**) o falsas (**F**). Si son falsas, corríjalas.

_____ 1. Lluís Remolí usa una silla de ruedas.
_____ 2. A Lluís no le gusta vivir con la silla.
_____ 3. Lluís da clases de *jogging* todos los jueves por la tarde.
_____ 4. Ha pasado más de diez años usando la silla.
_____ 5. En sus clases, Lluís les enseña a reestructurar el cuerpo y a relajarse.
_____ 6. Para Lluís, el primer elemento de libertad es el coche.
_____ 7. Lluís no puede conducir; por eso siempre toma taxi.
_____ 8. Lluís vive con una compañera de trabajo.
_____ 9. La pasión absoluta de Lluís es la guitarra.
_____ 10. Lluís es una persona muy deprimida.

Remedio para quemaduras   24:28–25:46

STUDENT WEBSITE   CD-ROM
Go to **Video** for further pre-viewing, vocabulary, and structure practice on this clip.

La botica de la abuela es un programa de la Televisión Española para aprender a preparar remedios en nuestra propia casa, como antiguamente lo hacían nuestras abuelas.

B. **Complete las instrucciones.** Escoja o escriba las palabras correctas para completar las instrucciones de Txumari Alfaro, el presentador.

1. Vamos a utilizar la clara de un huevo para las _____.
2. Se puede uno(a) quemar con agua (invierno / hirviendo / ardiendo) o con una (perinola / perla / perola).
3. La clara de huevo se usa para que no salgan _____ y luego no deje _____.
4. Primero hay que tomar la (clara / yema / cáscara) del huevo.
5. Luego hay que _____ un poco.
6. Cuando se queme, rápidamente tome la clara batida y aplíquela con una _____ o con una _____ en la zona quemada.
7. Se debe aplicar (muy poca / mucha / bastante) clara de huevo.
8. Es un remedio (en silla / complicado / sencillo).

Ampliación

¡**Cuidémonos!** Haga una de las siguientes actividades.

1. La botica de Ud.: Prepare una presentación sobre otro remedio sencillo que Ud. (¡o su abuela!) conoce. Por ejemplo: vinagre para una picadura de abeja (*bee sting*), hielo para un tobillo torcido (*sprained ankle*), etc.
2. Mente sana en cuerpo sano: ¿Cuáles son los elementos más importantes de una vida sana para Lluís Remolí? Comente las semejanzas y las diferencias entre la vida de Lluís y la de Ud.

Una estudiante americana en Costa Rica

OBJETIVOS

Temas para la comunicación

Estudios en el extranjero • Los automóviles

Estructuras

1. El imperativo: **tú** y **vosotros**
2. El participio
3. El pretérito perfecto y el pluscuamperfecto
4. Posición de los adjetivos

Regiones y países

Costa Rica

Lectura

Costa Rica, la Suiza de América

Estrategias de lectura

El estudio de palabras clave de acuerdo con el propósito de la lectura

Estrategias de redacción

¡Pongámoslo todo en práctica!

Un grupo de estudiantes universitarios, listos para ir de excursión.

Una estudiante americana en Costa Rica

CD-ROM   STUDENT AUDIO
For preparation, do the **Ante todo** activities found on the CD-ROM.

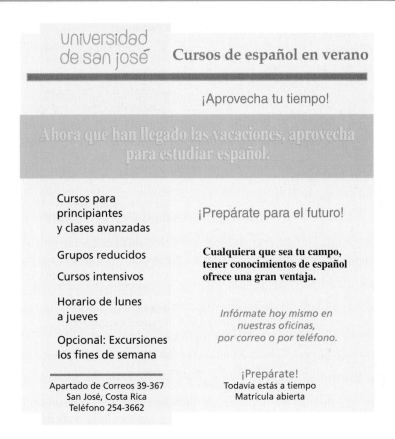

Éste es el anuncio que Debbie había leído cuando estaba estudiando español en la universidad. Ella nunca había estado fuera de su país, de modo que había pasado mucho tiempo tratando de decidir qué debía hacer. Al fin había decidido matricularse en una clase avanzada.

Ahora está en San José, adonde llegó el mes pasado. Debbie está viviendo con los Alvarado, una familia costarricense, y se ha hecho muy buena amiga de Mirta Alvarado que, como es hija única, considera a Debbie como una hermana.

Hoy es viernes y como las chicas están libres, han decidido ir al Parque Nacional Braulio Carrillo a pasar el día. En este momento están en una agencia de automóviles porque quieren alquilar un coche.

MIRTA   —Fíjate en ese descapotable rojo de dos puertas. Es un coche hermoso.

DEBBIE   —No mires los coches caros. Acuérdate de que no tenemos mucho dinero. Pregúntale al empleado cuánto cobran por kilómetro.

Mirta habla con el empleado y vuelve con la información.

MIRTA —Nos dan un buen precio por un coche de cambios mecánicos. Ésos no gastan mucha gasolina.

DEBBIE —Yo prefiero un coche automático. Oye, mi licencia para manejar es de los Estados Unidos; ¿es válida aquí?

MIRTA —Sí... ¿No recuerdas que tú ya has manejado aquí?

DEBBIE —Claro, ¡qué tonta soy! Ah, ¿necesitamos sacar seguro?

MIRTA —Sí, sácalo cuando alquilemos el coche. Es mejor estar aseguradas. (*Bromeando*) ¡Especialmente si tú conduces!

DEBBIE —No seas mala. Oye, ¿cuánto tiempo crees que vamos a demorar en llegar al parque?

MIRTA —Unas tres horas. A eso de las doce estamos allí.

Dígame

En parejas, lean las siguientes aseveraciones basadas en el anuncio y en el diálogo. Decidan si cada aseveración es verdadera (V) o falsa (F).

1. Las clases que anuncia la universidad empiezan en enero.
2. Según el anuncio, ser bilingüe no ofrece ninguna ventaja.
3. Si una persona no sabe español no puede participar en este programa.
4. En estas clases los grupos de estudiantes son pequeños.
5. Debbie había estudiado español antes.
6. Debbie ha viajado a muchos países extranjeros.
7. Hace un mes que Debbie está en San José.
8. Los Alvarado son de Guatemala.
9. Los Alvarado tienen varios hijos.
10. A Mirta le encanta el descapotable rojo.
11. Debbie no puede conducir en Costa Rica con su licencia de los Estados Unidos.
12. Las chicas pueden sacar un seguro en la agencia de alquiler de automóviles.
13. Ir de San José al Parque Braulio Carrillo lleva más de dos horas.
14. Las chicas van a llegar al parque al mediodía.

Perspectivas socioculturales

INSTRUCTOR WEBSITE
Your instructor may assign the preconversational support activities found in **Perspectivas socioculturales**.

El español es una lengua que muchos universitarios estudian hoy en Norteamérica. Haga lo siguiente:

a. Lea los temas de conversación que aparecen a continuación y escoja uno de ellos.
b. Durante unos cinco minutos, converse con dos compañeros sobre el tema seleccionado.
c. Participe con el resto de la clase en la discusión del tema cuando su profesor(a) se lo indique.

Temas de conversación

1. **En su universidad.** ¿Se matriculan en su universidad muchos estudiantes en cursos para aprender español? ¿Cuáles cree Ud. que son las razones principales para el estudio del español en la región donde vive?
2. **En el extranjero.** ¿Piensa Ud. continuar sus estudios de español en algún país del mundo hispánico?

Vocabulario

Nombres

la agencia de alquiler de automóviles car rental agency
el anuncio   ad
el campo   field
el conocimiento   knowledge
la licencia para manejar (de conducir)   driver's license
la matrícula   registration
el precio   price
el (la) principiante   beginner
el seguro   insurance

Verbos

aprovechar   to take advantage of
demorar   to take (*time*)
fijarse   to notice
gastar   to spend
prepararse   to get ready

Adjetivos

asegurado(a)   insured
costarricense   Costa Rican

descapotable, convertible convertible
malo(a)   mean
tonto(a)   silly, dumb
válido(a)   accepted

Otras palabras y expresiones

a eso de   at about
a tiempo   on time
al fin   finally
cualquiera que sea   whatever it may be
de cambios mecánicos   standard shift
de dos puertas   two-door
fuera   out
sacar seguro   to take out insurance
todavía   yet, still

Ampliación

Otras palabras relacionadas con el automóvil

el acumulador, la batería   battery
arrancar   to start (*a motor*)
la camioneta, la furgoneta   van
la chapa, la placa   license plate
chocar   to collide
el club automovilístico   auto club
el freno   brake

funcionar   to work, to function
el gato, la gata (*Costa Rica*)   jack
la goma pinchada (ponchada)   flat tire
la grúa, el remolcador   tow truck
la llanta, el neumático   tire
remolcar   to tow
el semáforo   traffic light
el taller de mecánica   repair shop

CD-ROM
Go to **Vocabulario** for additional vocabulary practice.

Hablando de todo un poco

Preparación   Encuentre en la columna B las respuestas a las preguntas de la columna A (las listas continúan en la página siguiente).

A

1. ¿Tu coche no arranca?
2. ¿Tu auto está asegurado?
3. ¿Es un coche automático?
4. ¿Emilia tuvo un accidente?
5. ¿Para qué necesitas el gato?
6. ¿No pudiste parar?
7. ¿Qué es la "Triple A"?
8. ¿Por qué paraste?
9. ¿Llevaste el coche al taller de mecánica?
10. ¿El coche necesita un acumulador nuevo?
11. ¿Cuál es el número de la chapa?
12. ¿Tú vas a cambiar la llanta?
13. ¿Pablo llegó a tiempo?
14. ¿Conoces Nicaragua?
15. ¿Es una ventaja tener conocimiento de español?
16. ¿Fernando es costarricense?
17. ¿Para qué fueron a la agencia de alquiler de automóviles?

B

a. No, porque los frenos no funcionaban.
b. Todavía no, porque lo tienen que remolcar.
c. Un club automovilístico.
d. No, es mejor que lo haga el mecánico.
e. Porque el semáforo está en rojo.
f. No, vino a eso de las dos y todos se habían ido.
g. Sí, porque no arranca.
h. No, yo nunca he estado fuera de mi país.
i. Para cambiar una goma pinchada.
j. No sé... El anuncio no menciona los precios.
k. No, es de cambios mecánicos.
l. Sí, es de San José.
m. No me fijé.
n. Para alquilar un coche.
o. No, necesito un remolcador.
p. ¡Tres horas! Yo fui la única que la esperó.

18. ¿Cuánto cuestan los coches nuevos?
19. ¿Gastaste todo tu dinero?
20. ¿Cuánto tiempo demoró Ada para prepararse?

q. Sí, porque tuve que pagar la matrícula.
r. No, tengo que sacar seguro.
s. Sí, cualquiera que sea tu campo.
t. Sí, chocó con una camioneta.

En grupos de tres o cuatro, hagan lo siguiente.

A. **¿Qué sabes?**   Conversen sobre su campo de especialización, sobre los conocimientos que tienen y los que esperan obtener, y sobre lo que pagan de matrícula.

B. **Problemas y soluciones.**   Digan qué deben tener en cuenta (*keep in mind*) cuando van a alquilar un coche, cuáles son algunos de los problemas que la gente tiene con su coche y posibles soluciones.

C. **Un anuncio.**   Preparen un anuncio de su programa ideal de estudios de verano. En éste, Ud. invita a personas interesadas a que soliciten información. El anuncio se publicará en el periódico de su comunidad.

Palabras problemáticas

A. **Pasado(a)** y **último(a)** como equivalentes de *last*

- **Pasado(a)** equivale a *last* cuando se usa con una unidad de tiempo.

   ¿Pagaste la matrícula la semana **pasada**?
   Ana tomó el curso para principiantes el año **pasado**.

- **Último(a)** significa *last* (*in a series*).

   Éste es el **último** informe que debo escribir.
   Diciembre es el **último** mes del año.

B. **Sobre, de, acerca de, a eso de** y **unos** como equivalentes de *about*

- **Sobre, de** y **acerca de** son equivalentes de *about* cuando se habla de un tema específico.

   Debo escribir un informe **sobre** los cursos de verano.
   Las chicas hablan **de** Costa Rica.
   Están hablando **acerca de** su viaje.

- **A eso de** es equivalente de *about* o *at about* cuando se refiere a una hora del día.

   Ellos llegaron a la agencia **a eso de** las tres.

- **Unos** es el equivalente de *about* o *approximately* cuando se usa con números. No se usa para hablar de la hora.

   La camioneta costó **unos** 30.000 dólares.

Práctica

En parejas, contesten las siguientes preguntas usando en sus respuestas las palabras problemáticas.

1. ¿Cuántos años creen Uds. que tiene el profesor (la profesora)?
2. ¿De qué creen Uds. que va a hablar el profesor en la próxima clase?
3. ¿A qué hora va a empezar la clase?
4. En el calendario hispánico, ¿qué es el domingo?
5. ¿Qué lección estudiaron en clase hace una semana?

Your instructor may carry out the **¡Ahora escuche!** listening activity found in the Answers to Text Exercises.

¡Ahora escuche!

Se leerá dos veces una carta que Debbie le escribe a su amiga Cindy desde San José, Costa Rica. Se harán aseveraciones sobre la carta. En una hoja escriba los números de uno a diez e indique si cada aseveración es verdadera (V) o falsa (F).

El mundo hispánico

La Suiza de América

Mirta Alvarado

Una de las cosas que nos enorgullecen° a los "ticos", como llaman a los costarricenses, es que tenemos uno de los mejores sistemas educativos de Latinoamérica. Eso es porque el Gobierno gasta un alto porcentaje del presupuesto° en la educación.

También estamos orgullosos de nuestras selvas pluviales vírgenes, que están protegidas por estrictas leyes°. Costa Rica tiene 24 parques nacionales y reservas ecológicas que ocupan el 15% de su superficie°. Como estos parques y reservas están abiertos al público, el país cuenta con un creciente ecoturismo.

Una gran atracción turística es el volcán Irazú, una de las montañas más altas de Costa Rica. Desde su cumbre° es posible ver a veces el Mar Caribe y el Océano Pacífico.

El país no tiene minerales y sus ingresos° provienen principalmente de la agricultura. Actualmente Costa Rica es el mayor exportador mundial de bananas. También exporta café y flores. Otra fuente de ingresos es el turismo, que aumenta cada año.

nos... *makes us proud*

budget

laws

area

top

income

Aunque mi familia es de Puerto Limón, en la costa del Mar Caribe, ahora vivimos en la capital, San José. San José no es una ciudad muy grande, pero los turistas quedan encantados con nuestra hospitalidad.

En este mapa pueden ver dónde está situado mi país.

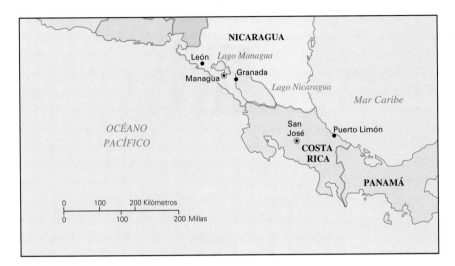

STUDENT WEBSITE
Go to **El mundo hispánico** for prereading and vocabulary activities.

Sobre Costa Rica

En parejas, túrnense para contestar las siguientes preguntas.

1. ¿Con qué limita Costa Rica al norte, al sur, al este y al oeste?
2. ¿Qué sobrenombre (*nickname*) tienen los costarricenses?
3. ¿Cómo es el sistema educativo de Costa Rica?
4. ¿Cómo protege el gobierno de Costa Rica las selvas pluviales?
5. ¿Qué ocupa el 15% de la superficie del país?
6. ¿Qué se puede ver a veces desde la cumbre del volcán Irazú?
7. ¿Cuáles son los productos principales de exportación del país?
8. ¿Cuál es otra fuente de ingresos del país?
9. ¿Qué sabe Ud. de Puerto Limón?

Hablemos de su país

INSTRUCTOR WEBSITE
STUDENT WEBSITE
Your instructor may assign the preconversational activities in **Hablemos...**

Reúnase con otro(a) compañero(a) para discutir las ventajas y desventajas del sistema educativo de su país.

Luego cada pareja compartirá las respuestas con toda la clase. ¿Están todos de acuerdo en cuáles son las ventajas y las desventajas?

(under **Hablemos de su país**). Go to **Hablemos de su país** (under **...y escribamos**) for postconversational web search and writing activities.

Una tarjeta postal

Imagínese que Ud. y un(a) compañero(a) están viajando por Costa Rica. Envíenles una tarjeta postal a sus compañeros de clase, describiendo sus impresiones.

Queridos amigos:

_____

_____

_____

_____

_____

Saludos,

Estructuras gramaticales

STUDENT WEBSITE
Do the **¿Cuánto recuerda?** pretest to check what you already know on the topics covered in this **Estructuras gramaticales** section.

1 El imperativo: **tú** y **vosotros**

A La forma *tú*

○ The affirmative command form for **tú** has the same form as the third person singular of the present indicative.

Verb	Present indicative	Familiar command (tú)
trabajar	él trabaja	**trabaja**
beber	él bebe	**bebe**
escribir	él escribe	**escribe**
cerrar	él cierra	**cierra**
volver	él vuelve	**vuelve**
pedir	él pide	**pide**

—Ya compré el acumulador. ¿Qué
quieres que haga ahora?
—**Cambia** la llanta y **revisa** los frenos.

"I already bought the battery. What do
you want me to do now?"
"Change the tire and check the brakes."

○ Eight verbs have irregular affirmative **tú** command forms.

decir	**di**	salir	**sal**
hacer	**haz**	ser	**sé**
ir	**ve**	tener	**ten**
poner	**pon**	venir	**ven**

—Robertito, **ven** acá. **Hazme** un favor.
Ve a casa de Carlos y **dile** que mi
coche no funciona.
—Bien. Ahora vuelvo.

"Robertito, come here. Do me a favor.
Go to Carlos's house and tell him my
car is not working."
"Okay. I'll be right back."

○ The negative **tú** command uses the corresponding forms of the present
subjunctive.

trabajar	no **trabajes**
volver	no **vuelvas**
tener	no **tengas**

—Ana, **no gastes** tanto dinero.
—¡No me **digas** que no puedo comprar
el coche!

"Ana, don't spend so much money."
"Don't tell me I can't buy the car!"

Object and reflexive pronouns used with **tú** commands are positioned just as they
are with formal commands.

Cómpra**selo**. (*affirmative*)
No **se lo** compres. (*negative*)

Buy it for him.
Don't buy it for him.

Práctica

CD-ROM
Go to **Estructuras gramaticales** for additional practice.

A. Claudia, Rebeca y Mireya son compañeras de cuarto. Cada vez que Claudia le
dice a Rebeca que haga algo, Mireya le dice que no lo haga. Haga Ud. el papel
de Mireya.

1. Escribe el informe hoy.
2. Pon la mesa ahora.
3. Haz la cena.
4. Lávate la cabeza.
5. Trae las revistas.
6. Siéntate aquí.
7. Prepárate para salir.
8. Dale el dinero a Iván.
9. Pídele el auto a María.
10. Acuéstate antes de las diez.

B. Su hermano se va a quedar solo en la casa. Dígale lo que debe (o no debe) hacer.

1. levantarse temprano
2. bañarse y vestirse
3. no ponerse los pantalones azules; ponerse los blancos
4. hacer la tarea, pero no hacerla mirando televisión
5. salir de la casa a las once
6. ir al mercado, pero no ir en bicicleta
7. volver a casa temprano y decirle a Rosa que la fiesta es mañana
8. tener cuidado y no abrirle la puerta a nadie
9. ser bueno y no acostarse tarde
10. cerrar las puertas y apagar las luces
11. llamarlo(la) a Ud. por teléfono si necesita algo
12. no mirar televisión hasta muy tarde

C. Ud. va a ir a Costa Rica a tomar un curso por un mes, y un(a) amigo(a) se queda en su casa. Dígale qué debe hacer respecto a lo siguiente.

1. su ropa sucia
2. el correo (*mail*)
3. los vecinos
4. los libros de la biblioteca
5. el gato
6. la comida
7. los mensajes
8. el jardín
9. la cuenta del teléfono
10. la ventana del baño

D. En parejas, hagan el papel de los siguientes personajes. Cada uno de Uds. debe dar dos órdenes afirmativas y dos negativas. ¡Sean originales!

1. una madre (un padre) a su hijo(a)
2. un(a) maestro(a) a un(a) estudiante que siempre saca malas notas
3. una mujer a su esposo (un hombre a su esposa)
4. un(a) médico(a), hablándole a un(a) niño(a) que está enfermo(a)
5. un(a) estudiante a otro(a)
6. un(a) muchacho(a) a su compañero(a) de cuarto que nunca hace nada

B La forma *vosotros*[1]

○ The affirmative **vosotros** command is formed by changing the final **r** of the infinitive to **d**.

hablar → hablad   comer → comed   venir → venid

○ If the affirmative **vosotros** command is used with the reflexive pronoun **os**, the final **d** is omitted (except with the verb **ir** → **idos**).

bañar   **bañad**
bañarse   **bañaos**

---

[1] This form is used only in Spain. The **Uds.** command form is used in the rest of the Spanish-speaking world.

○ The present subjunctive is used for the negative **vosotros** command.

bañar   **no bañéis**
bañarse   **no os bañéis**

CD-ROM
Go to **Estructuras gramaticales** for additional practice.

Práctica

Cambie los siguientes mandatos de la forma **tú** a la forma **vosotros.**

1. Levántate temprano.
2. Báñate en seguida.
3. Haz la tarea.
4. No te pongas los zapatos negros.
5. Ponte el abrigo.

6. Invita a las chicas.
7. Llévalas al parque.
8. Llámanos esta noche.
9. Vete ahora mismo.
10. Ven temprano mañana.

2 El participio

A Formas

○ The past participle is formed by adding the following endings to the stem of the verb.

-ar *verbs*	-er *verbs*	-ir *verbs*
prepar **-ado**	vend **-ido**	recib **-ido**

○ Verbs ending in **-er** have a written accent mark over the **i** of the **-ido** ending when the stem ends in **-a, -e,** or **-o.**

caer   **ca-ído**   creer   **cre-ído**
traer   **tra-ído**   leer   **le-ído**

○ The past participle of verbs ending in **-uir** does not have a written accent mark.

constr**uir**   constru**-ido**
contrib**uir**   contribu**-ido**

○ The past participle of the verb **ir** is **ido.**

○ The following verbs have irregular past participles.

abrir   **abierto**   hacer   **hecho**
cubrir   **cubierto**   morir   **muerto**
decir   **dicho**   poner   **puesto**
describir **descrito**   resolver   **resuelto**
descubrir **descubierto**   romper   **roto**
devolver   **devuelto**   ver   **visto**
envolver   **envuelto**   volver   **vuelto**
escribir   **escrito**

Práctica

Dé el participio de los siguientes verbos.

1. apreciar	6. devolver	11. leer	16. poner
2. suponer	7. comentar	12. romper	17. huir
3. descubrir	8. parecer	13. hacer	18. decir
4. envolver	9. celebrar	14. evitar	19. caer
5. contribuir	10. morir	15. cubrir	20. escribir

B El participio usado como adjetivo

○ In Spanish, most past participles may be used as adjectives. As such, they must agree in gender and number with the nouns they modify.

—¿Qué compraste cuando fuiste a Costa Rica?

"What did you buy when you went to Costa Rica?"

—Compré unas joyas **hechas** en San José.

"I bought some jewelry made in San José."

—¿Está **cerrada** la agencia?

"Is the agency closed?"

—No, está **abierta** hasta las diez.

"No, it's open until ten."

○ A few verbs have two forms for the past participle. The regular form is used in forming compound tenses[1], and the irregular form is used as an adjective. The most common ones are:

Infinitive	*Regular form*	*Irregular form*
confundir	**confundido**	**confuso**
despertar	**despertado**	**despierto**
elegir	**elegido**	**electo**
imprimir	**imprimido**	**impreso**
prender (*to arrest*)	**prendido**	**preso**
soltar	**soltado**	**suelto**
sustituir	**sustituido**	**sustituto**

—¿Has **despertado** a los niños?

"Have you awakened the children?"

—Sí, están **despiertos.**

"Yes, they are awake."

---

[1] See **"El pretérito perfecto y el pluscuamperfecto"** in this lesson.

CD-ROM
Go to **Estructuras gramaticales** for additional practice.

Práctica

Complete las siguientes oraciones, usando los participios de los verbos que aparecen en la lista.

sustituir	elegir	romper	despertar	encender
confundir	escribir	prender	resolver	soltar

1. La ventana de la sala está _____.
2. Prendieron al ladrón (*thief*). Hace una semana que está _____.
3. El presidente _____ dijo que iba a resolver los problemas económicos, pero hasta ahora los problemas no están _____.
4. Las luces del coche están _____.
5. Nuestro profesor está enfermo y hoy tuvimos un profesor _____.
6. Su informe ya está _____, pero yo no lo entiendo porque está muy _____.
7. Ellos durmieron muy poco. Están _____ desde las tres de la mañana.
8. Los toros estaban _____ y corrían por las calles.

3   El pretérito perfecto y el pluscuamperfecto

A   El pretérito perfecto

○ The Spanish present perfect tense is formed by combining the present indicative of the auxiliary verb **haber** with the past participle of the main verb in the singular masculine form. This tense is equivalent to the English present perfect (*have + past participle*, as in *I have spoken*.)

haber *(present indicative)*	Past participle	
he	**hablado**	*I have spoken*
has	**comido**	*you have eaten*
ha	**vuelto**	*he, she has, you have returned*
hemos	**dicho**	*we have said*
habéis	**roto**	*you have broken*
han	**hecho**	*they, you have done, made*

—**Hemos leído** el anuncio de la universidad.   *"We have read the university ad."*

—¿Y qué **han decidido**?   *"And what have you decided?"*

atención   In Spanish, the auxiliary verb **haber** cannot be separated from the past participle in compound tenses as it can in English.

Yo nunca **he visto** eso.   *I **have** never **seen** that.*

○ Direct object pronouns, indirect object pronouns, and reflexive pronouns are placed before the auxiliary verb.

—¿Has visto a Marta hoy?   *"Have you seen Marta today?"*
—No, no **la he visto** todavía.   *"No, I haven't seen her yet."*

—¿Qué **le han comprado** a Bárbara   *"What have you bought Barbara for*
para su cumpleaños?   *her birthday?"*
—**Le hemos comprado** una furgoneta.   *"We have bought her a van."*

CD-ROM
Go to **Estructuras gramati-**
cales for additional practice.

Práctica

A. En parejas, lean los siguientes diálogos, usando el pretérito perfecto de los verbos indicados.

1. (preguntar) —¿Ya _____ Uds. el precio?
   (hacer)   —No, todavía no lo _____.
2. (venir)   —¿Ya _____ los chicos del taller de mecánica?
   (volver)   —Sí, ya _____.
3. (decir)   —¿Qué le _____ tú?
   (decir)   —Le _____ que llame una grúa.
4. (escribir)   —Jorge te _____ una carta.
   (leer)   —Sí, pero yo todavía no la _____.
5. (ir)   —¿Ya _____ ellos a la agencia de automóviles?
   (alquilar)   —Sí, y ya _____ la camioneta.
6. (poner)   —¿Dónde _____ (tú) la placa del coche?
   (ver)   —¡Yo no la _____!

B. Complete el siguiente diálogo con verbos en el pretérito perfecto. Luego represéntelo con un(a) compañero(a).

—Hola, Ramiro, ¿qué tal?
—Bien, gracias. Oye, ¿_____ a Jorge? ¡No lo encuentro por ninguna parte!
—No, hoy no lo _____. Yo _____ muy ocupada preparando mi coche para el viaje a Arizona. Creo que al fin está listo.
—¿Lo _____ al taller de mecánica?
—Sí, porque últimamente _____ problemas con los frenos y también tenía una goma pinchada.
—¿Te fijaste si el motor funcionaba bien?
—Sí, el mecánico me _____ que ya todo está en orden.
—¿Ya _____ seguro? Recuerda que todavía no _____ a manejar muy bien.
—¡No seas malo! Yo ya estoy conduciendo perfectamente.
—Bueno, si tienes algún problema, cualquiera que sea, llámame.
—Muchas gracias, pero espero no necesitar ayuda.

C. Converse con un(a) compañero(a) sobre las cosas que Uds. nunca han hecho y las que siempre han querido hacer. Hablen de los lugares donde nunca han estado y de los que han visitado.

B El pluscuamperfecto

○ The past perfect, or pluperfect, tense is formed by using the imperfect tense of the auxiliary verb **haber** with the past participle of the main verb. This tense is equivalent to the English past perfect (*had + past participle*, as in *I had spoken.*). Generally, the past perfect tense expresses an action that has taken place before another action in the past.

haber (imperfect)	Past participle	
había	hablado	*I had spoken*
habías	comido	*you had eaten*
había	vuelto	*he, she, you had returned*
habíamos	dicho	*we had said*
habíais	roto	*you had broken*
habían	hecho	*they, you had done, made*

—¿Alquilaste el coche?   *"Did you rent the car?"*
—No, porque Berta ya lo **había alquilado.**   *"No, because Berta had already rented it."*

—No sabía que **habían elegido** presidenta de la clase a María Ruiz.   *"I didn't know they had chosen María Ruiz as president of the class."*
—Sí, ella es la presidenta electa.   *"Yes, she is the president-elect."*

Práctica

CD-ROM
Go to **Estructuras gramaticales** for additional practice.

A. Combine los siguientes pares de oraciones usando el pluscuamperfecto para indicar que la acción de la primera oración es anterior a la de la segunda. Siga el modelo.

MODELO: Roberto puso la mesa. / Yo llegué a casa.
             Roberto ya había puesto la mesa cuando yo llegué a casa.

1. Ud. arrancó el coche. / Yo salí de casa.
2. Nosotros cambiamos la goma pinchada. / Ellos llegaron.
3. Tú llamaste al club automovilístico. / Él fue al taller de mecánica.
4. El mecánico revisó los frenos. / Tú viniste.
5. Yo pagué la chapa. / Uds. nos dieron el dinero.
6. Ellos compraron el acumulador. / Nosotros los llamamos.

B. Converse con un(a) compañero(a). Háganse las siguientes preguntas.

1. Antes de venir a esta universidad, ¿habías asistido tú a otra?
2. ¿Habías estudiado otro idioma antes de estudiar español?
3. ¿Habías tomado otra clase de español antes de tomar ésta?
4. Para el 15 de septiembre, ¿ya habías vuelto de tus vacaciones?
5. Cuando empezaron las clases, ¿ya habías comprado todos los libros que necesitabas?

6. Cuando tú llegaste a casa anoche, ¿ya habías terminado la tarea para hoy?
7. Hoy a las cinco de la mañana, ¿ya te habías levantado?
8. Cuando tú llegaste a clase, ¿ya había llegado el (la) profesor(a)?
9. El año pasado para esta fecha, ¿ya habías terminado tus exámenes?

4   Posición de los adjetivos

A   Adjetivos que van detrás y adjetivos que van delante del sustantivo

○ While most adjectives may be placed either before or after the noun in Spanish, certain adjectives have a specific position.

○ Descriptive adjectives—those that distinguish the noun from others of its kind—generally follow the noun. Adjectives of color, shape, nationality, religion, and ideology are included in this group, as are past participles used as adjectives.

—¿Tienes un **coche japonés**?	*"Do you have a Japanese car?"*
—No, prefiero los **coches americanos**.	*"No, I prefer American cars."*
—¿Cuáles son los libros sobre ecología?	*"Which ones are the books on ecology?"*
—Esos dos **libros rojos** y este **libro azul**. Son tres **libros muy interesantes**.	*"These two red books and this blue book. They are three very interesting books."*
—¿Cuál es tu cuarto?	*"Which one is your room?"*
—El que tiene la **puerta cerrada**.	*"The one with the closed door."*

atención   Adjectives modified by adverbs are also placed after the noun:

Son unas clases **muy interesantes**.

○ Adjectives that express a quality or fact that is generally known about the modified noun are usually placed before the noun.

—¿Qué ciudad van a visitar?	*"What city are you going to visit?"*
—La **antigua ciudad** de Cuzco.	*"The old city of Cuzco."*

○ Possessive, demonstrative, and indefinite adjectives and ordinal[1] and cardinal numbers are also placed before the noun.

—¿Quiénes van a la fiesta?	*"Who is going to the party?"*
—**Mis dos hermanos** y **algunos amigos**.	*"My two brothers and some friends."*

○ The adjectives **mejor** and **peor** are placed in front of the noun.

—¿Cuál es el **mejor hotel**?	*"Which is the best hotel?"*
—El Hotel San José.	*"The San José Hotel."*

---

[1] Except with personal titles (**Enrique Octavo**) and with chapter titles (**Lección primera**).

○ Adjectives that are normally placed after the noun may precede it for emphasis or as a poetic device.

—Leí un **hermoso poema** sobre Costa Rica.
"I read a beautiful poem about Costa Rica."

—¿Por qué no me lo prestas para leerlo?
"Why don't you lend it to me so I can read it?"

○ When two or more adjectives modify the same nouns in a sentence, they are placed after the noun. The last two are joined by the conjunction **y.**

Es una **mujer hermosa y elegante.**
She is a beautiful and elegant woman.

Era una **casa blanca, grande y bonita.**
It was a pretty, large, white house.

B Adjetivos que cambian de significado según la posición

○ The meaning of certain adjectives changes according to whether they are placed before or after the noun. Some common ones are:

grande	un hombre **grande**	*(big)*
	un **gran**[1] hombre	*(great)*
pobre	el señor **pobre**	*(poor, not rich)*
	el **pobre** señor	*(poor, unfortunate)*
único	una mujer **única**	*(unique)*
	la **única** mujer	*(only)*
viejo	un amigo **viejo**	*(old, elderly)*
	un **viejo** amigo	*(long-time)*
mismo	la mujer **misma**	*(herself)*
	la **misma** mujer	*(same)*

Práctica

CD-ROM
Go to **Estructuras gramaticales** for additional practice.

A. Complete las oraciones usando los adjetivos de la siguiente lista en el género y el número correspondientes (algunos pueden usarse dos veces). Coloque los adjetivos **antes o después** del sustantivo, según el sentido de la frase.

republicano
pobre
único *(dos veces)*
rojo
grande *(dos veces)*

algunos
japonés
antiguo
ningún

abierto
muy interesante
mismo *(dos veces)*
famoso

1. George Washington fue un _____ presidente _____.
2. Carlos y María van a tomar la _____ clase _____. _____ Carlos _____ me lo dijo.
3. Atenas, la _____ ciudad _____ griega, es una _____ ciudad _____.
4. Necesito los _____ lápices _____.
5. La organización de _____ mujeres _____ no está de acuerdo con el presidente.

---

[1] **Grande** becomes **gran** before a masculine or feminine singular noun.

6. Hablé con _____ agentes _____ de policía sobre el accidente.
7. Ella va a comprar un _____ coche _____.
8. La _____ ventana _____ es la de mi cuarto.
9. Es una _____ mujer _____; es gorda y muy alta.
10. No tiene _____ limitación _____ en su trabajo.
11. El _____ actor _____ norteamericano Richard Gere va a estar presente en la fiesta.
12. Solamente Marta enseña español. Es la _____ profesora _____ de español.
13. No tiene dinero; es un _____ hombre _____.
14. No hay nadie como ella. ¡Es una _____ mujer _____!

B. En parejas, túrnense para contestar las preguntas, usando uno de los adjetivos de la lista. Recuerden que estos adjetivos tienen diferentes significados según la posición. Usen cada adjetivo de la lista dos veces.

MODELO: ¿Tienes otros profesores además del Dr. Ávila?   (no)
                   No, él es mi único profesor.

mismo   grande   único   viejo   pobre

1. Él es un hombre muy alto y gordo, ¿verdad?   (sí)
2. ¿Uds. ya eran amigos cuando eran niños?   (sí)
3. ¿No puedes hablar con la secretaria en vez de hablar con el director?   (no)
4. ¿Dices que ese hombre gana solamente mil pesos al mes y tiene diez hijos?   (sí)
5. No hay otra mujer como Sofía, ¿verdad?   (no)
6. ¿No quieres usar otro libro?   (no)
7. ¿Dices que ese hombre tiene noventa y ocho años?   (sí)
8. Es un actor magnífico, ¿verdad?   (sí)
9. ¿La niña no tiene padres?   (no)
10. ¿No tienes otras sandalias?   (no)

STUDENT WEBSITE
Do the **Compruebe cuánto sabe** self test after finishing this **Estructuras gramaticales** section.

¡CONTINUEMOS!

Una encuesta

Entreviste a sus compañeros de clase para tratar de identificar a aquellas personas que...

1. ...planean ir a estudiar a un país extranjero. ¿Adónde?
2. ...han vivido fuera de su país.
3. ...siempre llegan a tiempo a sus clases.
4. ...ya han decidido cuál es su campo de especialización.
5. ...tienen un amigo costarricense.
6. ...son hijos únicos.
7. ...habían estudiado español antes de venir a esta universidad.

8. ...han tomado un curso de español intensivo.
9. ...siempre aprovechan bien su tiempo.
10. ...tienen un coche de dos puertas.
11. ...conducen un coche de cambios mecánicos.
12. ...creen que es mejor tener asegurado el coche.
13. ...no tienen un gato en el maletero de su coche.
14. ...han chocado alguna vez.
15. ...siempre paran cuando el semáforo tiene la luz amarilla.

Ahora divídanse en grupos de tres o cuatro y discutan el resultado de la encuesta.

¿Comprende Ud.?

1. Mirta y Debbie, las amigas que dialogan al inicio de la lección, están de paseo por Costa Rica. Escuche la siguiente conversación entre ellas. El objetivo de la actividad es el de escuchar una conversación a velocidad natural. No se preocupe de entenderlo todo, pues esto no se espera de Ud. Después de escuchar la conversación dos veces, Ud. oirá varias aseveraciones. En una hoja, escriba los números de uno a ocho e indique si cada aseveración es verdadera o falsa.
2. Luego escuche la canción y trate de aprenderla.

Hablemos de programas para estudiantes extranjeros

En parejas, lean el anuncio y luego contesten las siguientes preguntas.

IDIOMAS INTENSIVOS

– Duración 80 horas. Diario, de 9 a 13 o de 17 a 21 horas.
– Grupos reducidos, máximo 8 alumnos clase.
– Profesorado titulado y experto en métodos activos.
– Sistemas de vídeo y prácticas en laboratorio de idiomas.
– Especial inglés empresarial de dos semanas de duración.
– También cursos personalizados con horario flexible.
– CURSOS DE INGLÉS EN INGLATERRA, en residencias o familias.

INICIOS: Del 4 al 31 de julio. Del 4 al 31 de agosto. Del 4 de septiembre al 3 de octubre.

NOVALINGUA   Avenida Diagonal, 600 (junto plaza Francesç Marcià). Teléfono 200 11 12. Barcelona.

1. ¿Cómo se llama el instituto de idiomas?
2. ¿En qué país está?
3. ¿Cuál es la dirección del instituto?
4. ¿En qué meses se ofrecen las clases?
5. ¿Cuánto tiempo dura el curso?
6. ¿Cuántos alumnos hay por clase?

¿Qué dirían ustedes?

Imagínense que Ud. y un(a) compañero(a) se encuentran en las siguientes situaciones. ¿Qué va a decir cada uno?

1. Escojan un país del mundo hispánico adonde quieren ir a estudiar español. Hablen de los tipos de clases que quieren tomar, de los lugares que quieren visitar y del tiempo que van a pasar allí.
2. Uds. van a alquilar un coche. Describan el tipo de coche que quieren y digan por cuánto tiempo lo necesitan.

¡De ustedes depende!

Un grupo de estudiantes costarricenses va a visitar la ciudad donde Ud. vive. Ud. y un(a) compañero(a) de clase denles la información que ellos necesitan con respecto a lo siguiente.

1. la mejor época del año para visitar la ciudad
2. ropa adecuada
3. lugares donde pueden hospedarse, incluyendo precios
4. lugares de interés que ellos pueden visitar
5. actividades recreativas en las que pueden participar
6. actividades culturales
7. recuerdos que pueden comprar para sus familiares y amigos

Mesa redonda

Formen grupos de cuatro o cinco estudiantes y hablen sobre las ventajas de ir a un país de habla hispana a estudiar español. Hablen también de las cosas que pueden hacer para practicar más el español, aumentar su vocabulario y conocer mejor la cultura hispana, de modo que algún día lleguen a dominar (*master*) el español.

VILLAS RINCONADA DEL VALLE

Lecturas periodísticas

Saber leer   El estudio de palabras clave de acuerdo con el propósito de la lectura

CD-ROM
Go to **Lecturas pe-riodísticas** for additional prereading and vocabulary activities.

Por lo general, el lector puede ayudarse a comprender la idea general de lo que significa una expresión desconocida y, a veces, saber su significado más o menos exacto, haciendo lo siguiente:

1. Estudiar brevemente la palabra o expresión desconocida en cuanto...
   a. ...a la forma o función gramatical (por ejemplo, ¿es verbo, nombre o adjetivo?) y
   b. ...al significado (por ejemplo, ¿qué palabras que conozco se parecen a ésta? ¿qué significan?)
2. Usar el contexto (la oración o el párrafo) en que aparece la expresión, para ayudarse a descifrar su significado.

Sin embargo, recuerde, como siempre, que debe leer teniendo muy claro el propósito de su lectura.

Haga lo siguiente: Estudie las palabras o expresiones que aparecen a continuación, pues son importantes para los propósitos didácticos de esta actividad de lectura. Intente descifrar lo que significan utilizando sus conocimientos de la forma y significado de las mismas en su contexto.

> **lo que más atrae**
> **se crían**
> **campestres**
> **consejo**
> **estancia**

Para leer y comprender

Al leer el artículo detalladamente, busque las respuestas a las siguientes preguntas.

1. En Costa Rica, ¿qué es lo que más atrae al visitante?
2. ¿Es una buena idea hacer un viaje a Limón? ¿Por qué?
3. ¿Qué excursiones recomienda el artículo?
4. ¿Qué le ofrece al turista el hotel Casa Turire?
5. ¿Qué lugares de interés podemos visitar en San José?

Costa Rica, la Suiza de América

Esta república centroamericana está siendo descubierta cada día más por el turismo internacional, y **lo que más atrae** es su bellísima° naturaleza. Sus parques nacionales, sus ríos, sus montañas y su increíble fauna (¡pájaros° y mariposas° como en ningún otro lugar!) son una atracción muy poderosa°.

El itinerario ideal de este viaje es por lo menos de una semana, distribuido entre San José y quizás° un viaje a Limón, para conocer el famoso Parque Nacional de Tortuguero, en la costa del Caribe, donde **se crían** unas misteriosas e impresionantes tortugas marinas. Estableciendo el "centro de operaciones" en San José, tenemos a nuestra disposición una cantidad variada de excursiones de un día y de medio día, y vale la pena° tomar varias de ellas.

El paseo en el Tren Histórico por la selva° es fascinante. También se puede escoger entre un día en el Valle del Orosí, la excursión de todo el día al Lago Arenal y a los volcanes o la de medio día al Parque Nacional del Volcán Irazú.

Una idea excelente es pasar unos días en hoteles **campestres**, como el hotel Casa Turire, a sólo una hora y media de San José. Muy pequeño, pero elegante y exclusivo, el hotel está en lo alto° de una montaña, bajo la cual pasa el río Reventazón (por donde podemos ir en balsa° y hacer excursiones que el propio hotel arregla). Allí podemos disfrutar de la piscina, montar a caballo, irnos de excursión al cercano Parque Nacional de Guayabo o simplemente sentarnos en el jardín y dejarnos entretener por el sonido de las aguas del río y de los exóticos pájaros.

En San José podemos pasar dos o tres días agradables, tomando excursiones y conociendo algunos sitios de interés como la Catedral, el Teatro Nacional y el Museo Nacional.

Como ven, las opciones son muchas, por lo que nuestro **consejo** es contactar una buena agencia y planear un viaje que incluya San José y la **estancia** en algún hotel campestre. Así podrán hacer un viaje realmente inolvidable° a uno de los países más bellos y amistosos de nuestra América Latina.

Adaptado de la revista *Vanidades* (Hispanoamérica)

> *Estableciendo el "centro de operaciones" en San José, tenemos a nuestra disposición una cantidad variada de excursiones de un día y de medio día...*

Bosque tropical en Costa Rica.

---

very beautiful

---

birds / butterflies
powerful
perhaps
vale... it's worth it
rain forest

---

en... on top of
raft
unforgettable

Desde su mundo

1. Después de leer el artículo, ¿quiere Ud. visitar Costa Rica? ¿Por qué sí o por qué no?
2. ¿Ud. prefiere pasar sus vacaciones en ciudades grandes o en lugares de gran belleza natural? ¿Por qué?

Piense y escriba   ¡Pongámoslo todo en práctica!

STUDENT WEBSITE

CD-ROM

Go to **...y escriba-mos** (in **Hablemos de su país)** on the student website and **De escuchar... a escribir** (in **¿Comprende Ud.?)** on the CD-ROM for additional writing practice.

Ahora, ponga en práctica todo lo que ya sabe (**Lecciones 1** a **5**) al enfrentar (*face*) la siguiente situación.

Ud. es redactor(a) de una revista de viajes. Debe escribir un breve artículo (la introducción, tres párrafos de desarrollo y la conclusión) sobre algún lugar que Ud. conozca. Recuerde los siguientes puntos:

- Determinar el público para el cual escribirá.
- Tener claro su propósito.
- Definir el tema y generar ideas sobre éste.
- Seleccionar las ideas que desea discutir y organizarlas según el tema y los subtemas sobre los que ha decidido escribir.
- Escribir una introducción interesante.
- Resumir o concluir.

Pepe Vega y su mundo

Teleinforme

La costa del Caribe de Costa Rica ofrece muchas atracciones para los viajeros aventureros. El video nos presenta un destino popular de esta parte de Costa Rica: Puerto Viejo de Limón. La zona al norte de la ciudad de Limón es accesible sólo por barco o por avión; no hay carreteras porque la región es refugio ecológico. El viejo puerto de Limón queda al sur de la ciudad de Limón y sí es accesible por tierra. Aquí hay playas bonitas y comodidades para los turistas que buscan relajarse frente al mar.

Preparación

Consejos turísticos.   Una amiga costarricense le da algunos consejos para sus vacaciones en la costa del Caribe de Costa Rica. Ud. apunta sus recomendaciones en el orden en que ésta se las dice a Ud. Ahora, como Ud. quiere pasar unas vacaciones muy buenas, ¡trate de organizar mejor sus apuntes! Clasifique las recomendaciones bajo las categorías apropiadas.

1. Tomar autobús desde Limón Centro.
2. Montar en bicicleta.
3. Bribri y Sixaola: cerca de la frontera con Panamá
4. Bucear.
5. Pasear a caballo.
6. Cahuita: playa, surf
7. Cieneguita
8. Alquilar coche.
9. Cruzar el puente sobre el Río La Estrella.
10. El Continente: comida internacional
11. Hotel Casa Camarona: barato en temporada baja
12. Hacer *kayaking*
13. La Tortuga: con comida tradicional caribeña
14. Nadar.
15. Parque Nacional Cahuita (arrecifes de coral)
16. Parque Nacional Tortuguero (tortuga verde)
17. Pensión del Tío José: muy barata
18. Puerto Viejo de Limón: playas
19. Hacer *surfing*.
20. Refugio de Gandoca-Manzanillo (banco natural de ostión de mangle [*giant oysters*])
21. Tomar la Carretera 36.
22. Hacer *rafting*.
23. Tico Tico: comida rápida
24. Hay varios *bed and breakfasts*.

lugar/pueblo/ciudad:

para llegar:

alojamiento (*lodging*):

comida:

actividades:

excursiones:

Comprensión

STUDENT WEBSITE   CD-ROM
Go to **Video** for further previewing, vocabulary, and
structure practice on this
clip.

Puerto Viejo de Limón   25:48–31:38

De paseo es una serie de programas educativos producidos por SINART/Canal 13 en Costa Rica. Cada programa presenta bellas imágenes de un lugar determinado de Costa Rica. El programa ofrece información importante sobre cada lugar: cómo llegar, su historia, su gente y por qué se debe visitar. En este programa, vamos a visitar Puerto Viejo de Limón.

A. **Información.**   Mientras Ud. ve el video, escoja o escriba, según corresponda, la(s) respuesta(s) correcta(s).

1. Puerto Viejo de Limón está en la costa del (Mar Caribe / Océano Pacífico / Golfo de México).
2. Para llegar a Puerto Viejo hay que dirigirse hasta el Cantón de (Bribri / Sixaola / Talamanca).
3. La carretera hacia Puerto Viejo está en _____ condiciones.
4. Llegando a Puerto Viejo se pasa por plantaciones de (yuca / banano / café).
5. La economía de Puerto Viejo está basada en gran parte en _____.
6. ¿Qué tipos de alojamiento hay en Puerto Viejo?
7. ¿Cuándo abrió sus puertas el Hotel Casa Camarona?
8. Estamos en la temporada (baja / alta). En esta temporada los hoteles son más (caros / baratos).
9. ¿Cómo son los precios del Hotel Casa Camarona para el turista costarricense?
10. El hotel tiene (7 / 16 / 17) habitaciones y (80 / 18 / 8) empleados.
11. Este hotel debe respetar muchas obligaciones con respecto a _____.
12. Puerto Viejo de Limón fue fundado por negros que vinieron de (Cuba / Jamaica / Panamá / Nicaragua).
13. Cultivaron (papas / café / coco / cacao / ñame / yuca / plátanos / tubérculos).
14. Según Edwin Patterson, las tres características principales de Puerto Viejo son _____.

B. **¿Quién hace qué?**   Mire de nuevo los primeros 30 segundos del video y escriba oraciones para describir a las personas que hacen las siguientes actividades. Use su imaginación y al menos un adjetivo para describir a estas personas. ¡Preste atención a la posición de los adjetivos!

Algunos adjetivos posibles: joven   dos   un   único
grande   pequeño   varios   atlético   solo   concentrado

MODELO: caminar por la playa
         Dos mujeres **jóvenes** caminan por la playa.

1. hacer *kayaking*
2. jugar con pelota y paletas (*paddleball*)
3. descansar en la playa

4. tomar el sol
5. usar bronceador (*tanning lotion*)
6. secarse con una toalla

Ampliación

Comente Ud.   Usando la información que aprendió sobre Costa Rica y Puerto Viejo de Limón, haga una de las siguientes actividades.

1. Ud. es el nuevo presentador o la nueva presentadora del programa *De paseo*. Escoja dos minutos del video sobre Puerto Viejo de Limón y prepare una narración original.
2. Ud. es reportero(a) para la sección *Viajes* del periódico de su pueblo de origen o de la universidad donde estudia. Prepare un reportaje turístico sobre Puerto Viejo de Limón.

Lecciones 5 y 6

Tome este examen para ver cuánto ha aprendido. Las respuestas correctas aparecen en el **Apéndice C**.

Lección 5

A El imperativo: **Ud. y Uds.**

Conteste las siguientes preguntas, usando el imperativo (**Ud.** o **Uds.**). Utilice la información que aparece entre paréntesis y reemplace las palabras en cursiva con los complementos correspondientes.

1. ¿Cuándo hacemos *ejercicio*?   (ahora)
2. ¿A quién le leo *el artículo*?   (a Mario)
3. ¿Compro *los alimentos*?   (no)
4. ¿Llamamos *al médico* ahora?   (no)
5. ¿Qué *me* pongo?   (el abrigo)
6. ¿Adónde voy?   (al gimnasio)
7. ¿A quién se lo decimos?   (a nadie)
8. ¿Evito *el tabaco*?   (sí)
9. ¿Bebemos *ocho vasos de agua*?   (sí)
10. ¿A qué hora *me* levanto?   (a las siete)

B El imperativo de la primera persona del plural

Conteste las siguientes preguntas, siguiendo el modelo.

MODELO: ¿Dónde ponemos los libros? (en la mesa)
         Pongámoslos en la mesa.

1. ¿A qué hora nos levantamos mañana? (a las seis)
2. ¿A qué hora nos acostamos esta noche? (a las once)
3. ¿Nos bañamos por la mañana o por la tarde? (por la mañana)
4. ¿Qué le decimos a Mario? (que necesita hacer ejercicio)
5. ¿Se lo decimos al médico? (no)
6. ¿A quién le damos el dinero? (a Ernesto)

C El subjuntivo para expresar duda, incredulidad y negación

Cambie las siguientes oraciones de acuerdo con los nuevos comienzos.

1. Yo creo que ellos evitan las grasas. Yo no creo...
2. Es verdad que ella siempre camina mucho. No es verdad...
3. Yo no dudo que Uds. pueden mejorar su salud. Yo dudo...
4. Ellos no creen que nosotros seamos socios del club. Ellos creen...

5. Yo estoy seguro de que ellos van con Marta. Yo no estoy seguro...
6. Es cierto que ellos tienen mucho estrés en el trabajo. No es cierto...

D El subjuntivo para expresar lo indefinido y lo inexistente

Complete las oraciones con el indicativo o el subjuntivo según sea necesario.

1. Buscamos una casa que _____ (tener) cinco dormitorios; ahora tenemos una casa que _____ (tener) tres dormitorios.
2. ¿Hay alguien aquí que _____ (poder) levantar pesas?
3. Yo no conozco a nadie que lo _____ (saber).
4. Hay muchas personas que no _____ (seguir) las reglas de la salud.
5. Buscamos a alguien que _____ (conocer) al dueño del club.
6. No hay nadie que _____ (querer) hacerse socio de ese club.

E Expresiones que requieren el subjuntivo o el indicativo

Complete las oraciones con el indicativo o el subjuntivo según sea necesario.

1. No podemos ir al gimnasio a menos que ellos _____ (llevarnos).
2. Vamos a empezar a hacer ejercicio en cuanto ellos _____ (llegar).
3. Siempre vamos al club cuando _____ (tener) tiempo.
4. Voy a llamarlo tan pronto como yo _____ (terminar).
5. Quizás tú y yo _____ (poder) hacernos ricos, pero lo dudo.
6. Vamos a ir con tal de que Ud. _____ (ir) también.
7. Dora no va a dejarme en paz hasta que le _____ (hacer) caso.

F ¿Recuerda el vocabulario?

Diga las siguientes frases de otra manera, usando el vocabulario de la **Lección 5**.

1. lo que comemos
2. mantequilla, margarina, aceite, etc.
3. tiene doce pulgadas
4. perder peso
5. opuesto de aumentar
6. opuesto de viejo
7. opuesto de enfermo
8. mineral que encontramos en la leche
9. vegetal que tiene muy pocas calorías
10. pimiento verde
11. sinónimo de col
12. tensión nerviosa

G Cultura

Complete cada una de las siguientes oraciones con la palabra adecuada.

1. El Salto _____ es el más alto del mundo.
2. El _____ es una de las fuentes de riqueza de Venezuela.
3. _____ es la capital de Venezuela.
4. Simón Bolívar es conocido (*known*) como el _____ de América.
5. Las _____ de Colombia son las más famosas del mundo.

Lección 6

A El imperativo: **tú**

Complete las siguientes oraciones, usando la forma **tú** del imperativo.

1. _____ (Ir) a la agencia de automóviles, _____ (alquilar) un automóvil y _____ (sacar) seguro.
2. _____ (Venir) aquí, Anita, _____ (hacerme) un favor: _____ (cerrar) la puerta y _____ (abrir) las ventanas.
3. _____ (Hablar) con Jorge y _____ (decirle) que venga mañana.
4. _____ (Ser) bueno, Luis, y _____ (prestarme) el gato.
5. _____ (Comprar) un coche automático; no _____ (comprar) uno de cambios mecánicos.
6. _____ (Sentarse) al lado de la ventana; no _____ (sentarse) aquí.
7. _____ (Tener) paciencia.
8. _____ (Salir) con Marta; no _____ (salir) con Roberto.

B El participio

Complete las siguientes oraciones, usando los participios de los verbos entre paréntesis en función de adjetivo.

1. No pude entrar porque la puerta estaba _____ (cerrar).
2. Yolanda no durmió anoche; estuvo toda la noche _____ (despertar).
3. Ya no tiene problemas. Todos sus problemas están _____ (resolver).
4. Las cartas estaban _____ (escribir) en francés.
5. Compré unas joyas _____ (hacer) en Costa Rica.

C El pretérito perfecto y el pluscuamperfecto

Complete las oraciones, usando el pretérito perfecto o el pluscuamperfecto de los verbos entre paréntesis.

1. Nosotros no _____ (ver) a nuestros compañeros hoy.
2. Cuando yo llegué a la agencia ya Marta _____ (alquilar) el coche.
3. Cuando empezó el curso ya nosotros _____ (matricularse).
4. Ellos no _____ (llevar) el coche al taller de mecánica hoy.

D Posición de los adjetivos

Complete las siguientes oraciones, usando el equivalente español de las palabras que aparecen entre paréntesis.

1. Pasé la tarde hablando con _____. (*an old friend*)
2. Ella era la _____ que tenía hijos. (*the only woman*)
3. Les serví _____. (*a good Spanish wine*)
4. _____ me dijo que no era necesario estudiar esa lección. (*The teacher herself*)
5. Había _____ en el museo. (*some very interesting paintings*)

E ¿Recuerda el vocabulario?

Complete las siguientes oraciones usando el vocabulario aprendido en la **Lección 6**.

1. Leí un _____ sobre coches en Internet.
2. Es un curso para _____. No es una clase avanzada.
3. Ellos llegaron a _____ de las diez de la noche.
4. No es un coche _____. Es de _____ mecánicos.
5. El coche no arranca; necesito una _____ nueva.
6. Debemos parar porque el _____ está en rojo.
7. ¿Cuál es el número de la _____ de tu automóvil?
8. Llamemos una _____ para remolcar el coche.

F Cultura

Complete cada una de las siguientes oraciones con la palabra adecuada.

1. Costa Rica tiene uno de los mejores sistemas _____ de Latinoamérica.
2. Las reservas ecológicas de Costa Rica ocupan el _____ de la superficie del país.
3. Una de las montañas más altas de Costa Rica es el volcán _____.
4. Costa Rica exporta principalmente _____, _____ y _____.
5. La capital de Costa Rica es _____.

¡Buen provecho!

En el Centro Mercado en Honduras, dos mujeres mayas venden pasteles.

¡Buen provecho!

CD-ROM   STUDENT AUDIO

For preparation, do the **Ante todo** activities found on the CD-ROM.

En una fiesta del Club Internacional de la Universidad de California, cinco estudiantes centroamericanos, sentados alrededor de una mesa, charlan animadamente. Los cinco amigos son: Estela Vidal, de Guatemala; Rafael Mena, de Nicaragua; Roberto Ortiz, de Honduras; Amanda Núñez, de El Salvador; y Oscar Varela, de Panamá.

ESTELA —¿Vamos a la fiesta de Marité mañana? ¡Tenemos que aprovechar estos últimos meses para estar juntos!

AMANDA —Tienes razón. Para junio nos habremos graduado y... ¡quién sabe adónde iremos a parar todos!

RAFAEL —Supongo que yo volveré a mi país. Me gustaría vivir en Managua. La verdad es que me sería difícil quedarme a vivir aquí...

OSCAR —A mí también. Echo de menos a mi familia, a mis amigos... Extraño la comida, sobre todo la sopa de pescado que prepara mi abuela... ¡Y no veo la hora de tomar una chicha[1] con mis amigos en nuestra fonda favorita!

ROBERTO —Yo tengo ganas de comer mondongo con papas, como lo prepara mi mamá... o arroz con frijoles y tortillas de maíz...

ESTELA —Plátanos fritos con miel de abeja... ¡Yo comería un plato de eso ahora mismo!

AMANDA —¡Ay, no me hables de comer! ¡Yo no podría tragar un bocado más...! Bueno... quizá una pupusa...

OSCAR —¿Qué es eso?

AMANDA —Tortilla rellena de carne, frijoles y queso. ¡Son riquísimas! Especialmente cuando las hace mi tía Marta. Oye, Roberto, ¿quieres un poco más de ensalada?

ROBERTO —No, yo estoy satisfecho, pero, ¿qué veo? ¡Hay flan con crema! ¡De haberlo sabido, no habría comido tanto!

AMANDA —Pues... ¡buen provecho!, como decimos siempre en mi país. Hasta mi hermanito más pequeño lo dice.

OSCAR —Eso es muy español... ¡y la sobremesa[2]! En mi casa, después de comer, pasábamos por lo menos una hora charlando o contando chistes... ¡o discutiendo sobre política! ¡Cómo me gustaría estar en mi casa ahora mismo, oyendo la risa de mis hermanos...!

ESTELA —Y a mí me parece ver a mi mamá... trayendo fuentes de comida a la mesa, charlando con amigos que muchas veces llegaban al mediodía... ¡sin avisar, por supuesto! (*Se ríe*) Pero todos eran siempre bienvenidos.

RAFAEL —Bueno, basta de recuerdos... ¡O nos pondremos tristes! (*Levanta la copa.*) ¡Un brindis!

TODOS —(*Levantan las copas también.*) ¡Salud!

---

[1] **chicha:** Bebida hecha con frutas, agua y azúcar.

[2] **sobremesa:** Generalmente los hispanos se quedan sentados alrededor de la mesa y conversan después de comer.

Dígame

En parejas, contesten las siguientes preguntas basadas en el diálogo.

1. ¿Dónde están sentados los chicos? ¿Qué están haciendo?
2. ¿Para cuándo se habrán graduado los chicos?
3. ¿Dónde le gustaría vivir a Rafael?
4. ¿A quiénes echa de menos Oscar? Sobre todo, ¿qué comida extraña?
5. ¿Qué tiene ganas de comer Roberto? ¿Y Estela?
6. ¿Por qué cree Ud. que Amanda dice que no podría tragar un bocado más?
7. ¿Qué es una pupusa?
8. ¿Qué no habría hecho Roberto de haber sabido que había flan?
9. ¿Qué frase dice el hermanito de Amanda cuando van a comer?
10. ¿Qué hacían Oscar y su familia después de comer?
11. ¿Por qué dice Rafael "basta de recuerdos"?
12. ¿Quién levanta su copa para hacer un brindis?

Perspectivas socioculturales

INSTRUCTOR WEBSITE
Your instructor may assign the preconversational support activities found in **Perspectivas socioculturales**.

La comida de un país varía de región en región. Haga lo siguiente:

a. Lea los temas de conversación que aparecen a continuación y escoja uno de ellos.
b. Durante unos cinco minutos, converse con dos compañeros sobre el tema seleccionado.
c. Participe con el resto de la clase en la discusión del tema cuando su profesor(a) se lo indique.

Temas de conversación

1. **La cocina de su región.** ¿Cuáles son los platos más populares de la región donde Ud. vive: de primer plato, de plato principal (*main course*) y de postre?
2. **Sus preferencias gastronómicas.** ¿Tiene Ud. algunos platos favoritos? ¿Cuáles son?

Vocabulario

Nombres
el bocado   bite, morsel
el brindis   toast
el chiste   joke
la copa   glass, goblet
la fonda   inn
la fuente   serving dish
la miel de abeja   honey
el mondongo   tripe and beef knuckles
el plátano   plantain, banana
el recuerdo   memory

Verbos
avisar   to inform, to give notice
discutir   to discuss, to argue
tragar   to swallow

Adjetivos
bienvenido(a)   welcome
relleno(a)   stuffed

rico(a), sabroso(a)   tasty, delicious
satisfecho(a)   full, satisfied

Otras palabras y expresiones
alrededor   around
animadamente   lively
basta   enough
buen provecho   enjoy your meal, bon appetit
de haberlo sabido   had I known
ir a parar   to end up
ponerse triste   to become sad
¡Salud!   Cheers!, To your health!
sobre todo   above all
tener ganas de   to feel like

Ampliación

Para hablar de comidas
el bistec
{
bien cocido   well cooked, well done
medio crudo   rare
término medio   medium-rare
}

las chuletas
{
de cerdo   pork
de cordero   lamb
de ternera   veal
}

pescados
{
el atún   tuna
el bacalao   cod
el salmón   salmon
la sardina   sardine
la trucha   trout
}

Formas de cocinar
asar   to roast, to barbecue
cocinar al horno, hornear   to bake
cocinar al vapor   to steam
freír   to fry
hervir (e → ie)   to boil

Para hablar de bebidas
la cerveza   beer
la gaseosa   soft drink
la ginebra   gin
el ponche   punch
el ron   rum

el vino
{
blanco   white
rosado   rosé
tinto   red
}   wine

CD-ROM
Go to **Vocabulario** for additional vocabulary practice.

Hablando de todo un poco

Preparación   Encuentre en la columna B las respuestas a las preguntas de la columna A.

A

1. ¿Qué necesitas para hacer el brindis?
2. ¿Serviste una fuente de carne asada?
3. Elsa es muy simpática, ¿verdad?
4. ¿Qué están haciendo tus amigos?
5. ¿Estás satisfecho?
6. ¿Uds. quieren postre? Tenemos flan.
7. ¿Adónde vamos a ir a parar esta noche?
8. ¿Uds. comen el bistec bien cocido?
9. ¿Quieres comer más mondongo?
10. ¿Vinieron sin avisar?
11. ¿Extrañas la comida de tu país?
12. ¿Raúl va a traer ron y ginebra?
13. ¿Crees que van a ponerse tristes?
14. ¿Qué tienes ganas de comer?
15. ¿Qué dijo Mario cuando levantó su copa?
16. ¿Vas a cocinar las papas al horno?
17. ¿Qué les vas a decir cuando empiecen a comer?
18. ¿El cordero está muy picante?

B

a. No, medio crudo o término medio.
b. No, pero de haberlo sabido, no habríamos comido tanto.
c. No, las voy a hervir o a freír.
d. Sí, pero siempre son bienvenidos.
e. Vino rosado o vino tinto.
f. Sí, tiene mucha pimienta.
g. No, cerveza, gaseosa y ponche.
h. No, un pavo relleno muy rico.
i. ¡Buen provecho!
j. Plátanos fritos con miel de abeja.
k. Están discutiendo animadamente alrededor de la mesa.
l. No, basta, no podría tragar un bocado más.
m. ¡Salud!
n. Sí, siempre está contando chistes.
o. Sí, he comido muy bien.
p. A una fonda.
q. Sí, porque están hablando de sus recuerdos.
r. Sí, sobre todo las pupusas.

En grupos de tres o cuatro, hagan lo siguiente.

A. **¿Qué vas a traer?**   Uds. están planeando un "potluck". Decidan qué comida va a traer cada estudiante de la clase. Asegúrense de que haya variedad.

B. **Una comida elegante.**   Uds. están encargados(as) de preparar comida para tres estudiantes extranjeros. Decidan qué van a servir teniendo en cuenta lo que cada uno prefiere.

1. A Marité le encanta el pescado.
2. Carlos come mucha carne.
3. Olga prefiere comer chuletas, pero no come carne de cerdo.

Ahora decidan qué bebidas van a servirle a cada uno de acuerdo con el tipo de comida. Olga no toma bebidas alcohólicas. Para terminar, uno de Uds. propone un brindis.

C. **Las maneras de cocinar.**   Hablen de las formas en que Uds. cocinan distintos tipos de comida. ¿Qué fríen, qué cocinan al horno, qué hierven, qué cocinan al vapor, qué asan?

Palabras problemáticas

A. **Picante, caliente** y **cálido** como equivalentes de *hot*

- **Picante** es el equivalente de *hot* (*spicy*) cuando hablamos de comida.

  La carne está muy **picante.** Tiene mucha pimienta.

- **Caliente** se usa cuando nos referimos a la temperatura de las cosas.

  El café está muy **caliente.**

- **Cálido** equivale a *hot* o *warm* cuando hablamos del clima.

  El clima de Hawai es muy **cálido.**

B. **Pequeño, poco** y **un poco de**

- **Pequeño** significa **chico,** y se refiere al tamaño de un objeto o de una persona.

  Mi hermana es muy **pequeña.**

- **Poco** significa **no mucho.**

  Tengo **poco** dinero. Necesito conseguir más.

- **Un poco de** significa **una pequeña cantidad de.**

  ¿Quieres **un poco de** pescado?

Práctica

En parejas, contesten las siguientes preguntas, usando en sus respuestas las palabras problemáticas aprendidas.

1. ¿Le gusta la comida con mucha pimienta? ¿Por qué o por qué no?
2. Generalmente, ¿come Ud. mucho?
3. ¿Toma Ud. té helado?
4. En un buffet, ¿se sirve Ud. mucho de cada comida?
5. Si le ofrecen un trozo de torta, ¿toma Ud. un trozo grande?
6. Cuando Ud. va de vacaciones, ¿escoge un lugar de clima frío?

Your instructor may carry out the **¡Ahora escuche!** listening activity found in the **Answers to Text Exercises.**

¡Ahora escuche!

Se leerá dos veces una narración sobre los Acosta, un matrimonio que tiene invitados mañana para la cena. Se harán aseveraciones sobre la narración. En una hoja escriba los números de uno a doce e indique si cada aseveración es verdadera (V) o falsa (F).

El mundo hispánico

Centroamérica

Oscar Varela

Tengo que dar una charla sobre Centroamérica en la Casa Hispánica y, como es natural, empezaré por hablar de mi país. Panamá conecta América Central con Sudamérica y es la nación hispanoamericana de más reciente creación. Es un país montañoso, un poco más pequeño que Carolina del Sur, y es conocido mundialmente por su famoso canal, alrededor del cual gira° la actividad económica del país. El canal perteneció° a los Estados Unidos hasta el año 1999, pero ahora es propiedad de Panamá. Las dos ciudades más grandes y más importantes de mi país son la ciudad de Panamá, la capital, y Colón.

La mitad del país está cubierta de bosques° y esto ha empezado a atraer a turistas interesados en la ecología. Nosotros esperamos que muy pronto el turismo sea otra fuente importante de ingresos.

Al norte de Panamá está Costa Rica. Yo no hablaré de este país porque la próxima semana lo

STUDENT WEBSITE
Go to **El mundo hispánico** for prereading and vocabulary activities.

revolves
belonged

forest

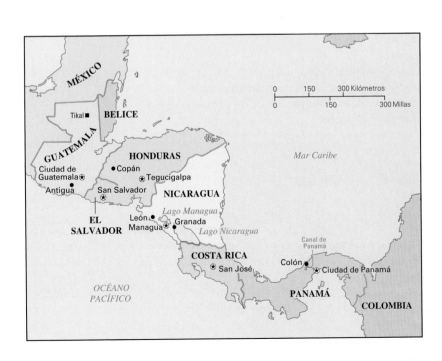

hará un profesor costarricense. Pasemos entonces a Nicaragua, que es el país más extenso de la América Central y que es conocido como la "Tierra° de los lagos°". Una cosa interesante es que en el lago Nicaragua, que es el mayor lago de agua dulce° del mundo, hay tiburones°. Managua, la capital, está situada al oeste del país, que es la región más poblada.

land/lakes

fresh/sharks

El país más pequeño y el más densamente poblado de Centroamérica es El Salvador. Como tiene más de doscientos volcanes se le ha llamado la "Tierra de los volcanes". La capital del país, San Salvador, es la más industrializada de las ciudades de América Central.

Al este de El Salvador está Honduras, que es el único país de Centroamérica donde no hay volcanes. Este país cuenta hoy con el mayor bosque de pinos del mundo. La capital de Honduras es Tegucigalpa y la mayor atracción turística del país es Copán, unas ruinas mayas de singular encanto°.

charm

Otro de los países centroamericanos cuyo territorio fue parte del imperio maya es Guatemala. Aquí, aunque el idioma oficial es el español, la mayor parte de los indígenas hablan sus propias lenguas. En este país encontramos las ruinas de Tikal, uno de los sitios arqueológicos más interesantes de toda América. Guatemala es un país de volcanes, montañas y bellos paisajes°. Su clima es muy agradable y por eso se conoce como "el país de la eterna primavera".

landscapes

Sobre Centroamérica

En parejas, túrnense para contestar las siguientes preguntas.

1. ¿Qué conecta Panamá? ¿Por qué es famoso mundialmente?
2. ¿Qué importancia tiene el canal para la economía del país?
3. ¿Cuál es el país más extenso de la América Central?
4. ¿Qué saben Uds. del lago Nicaragua?
5. ¿Cuál es la capital de Nicaragua?
6. ¿Qué saben Uds. de El Salvador?
7. ¿Cuál es la capital de El Salvador? ¿Qué la distingue?
8. ¿En qué se diferencia Honduras de los demás países centroamericanos?
9. ¿Cuál es la capital de Honduras? ¿Cuál es la mayor atracción turística del país?
10. ¿Dónde está Tikal? ¿Qué importancia tiene?

Hablemos de su país

INSTRUCTOR WEBSITE
STUDENT WEBSITE
Your instructor may assign the pre-conversational activities in
Hablemos... (under **Hablemos de su país**). Go to
Hablemos de su país (under...**y escribamos**) for post-conversational web search and writing activities.

El ensayo hace referencia a aspectos de interés de los países centroamericanos. Reúnase con un(a) compañero(a) para pensar en aspectos de interés natural, urbano o histórico de su región. Prepárense para ensayar (*rehearse*) la representación (*skit*) de una conversación entre el director o la directora de turismo de su región y un(a) visitante. Representen la conversación ante la clase.

Una tarjeta postal

Estela fue de vacaciones a su país y les mandó esta tarjeta a sus amigos.

Queridos amigos:

Lo estoy pasando muy bien en Guatemala. Ayer visité Tikal, las famosas ruinas mayas. También estuve en Antigua, que es un centro de atracción turística. Es un lugar encantador. Con razón Aldous Huxley[1] la calificó como una de las ciudades más románticas del mundo. Espero verlos pronto.

Cariños,

Estela

Después de leer la tarjeta

1. ¿Desde dónde escribe Estela? ¿Cómo lo está pasando?
2. ¿Qué ruinas visitó? ¿En qué otros lugares estuvo?
3. ¿Qué dice Estela de Antigua?
4. ¿Qué dijo Aldous Huxley de Antigua?
5. ¿Estela piensa estar mucho tiempo más en Guatemala?

---

[1] En 1933, este escritor inglés viajó por México, Honduras, Guatemala y el Caribe. Sus impresiones se publicaron en el libro *Beyond the Mexique Bay* (1934).

Estructuras gramaticales

STUDENT WEBSITE
Do the **¿Cuánto recuerda?** pretest to check what you already know on the topics covered in this **Estructuras gramaticales** section.

1 El futuro

A Usos y formas

○ The Spanish future tense is the equivalent of the English *will* or *shall* + *a verb*.

Ellos **serán** bienvenidos.   *They will be welcome.*

The Spanish future form is not used to express willingness, as is the English future. In Spanish this is expressed with the verb **querer.**

¿**Quiere** Ud. esperar?   *Will you (please) wait?*

○ Most verbs are regular in the future tense. It is formed by adding the following endings to the infinitive.

Infinitive		*Stem*	*Endings*	
trabajar	yo	trabajar-	**é**	trabajar**é**
aprender	tú	aprender-	**ás**	aprender**ás**
escribir	Ud.	escribir-	**á**	escribir**á**
hablar	él	hablar-	**á**	hablar**á**
decidir	ella	decidir-	**á**	decidir**á**
dar	nosotros(-as)	dar-	**emos**	dar**emos**
ir	vosotros(-as)	ir-	**éis**	ir**éis**
caminar	Uds.	caminar-	**án**	caminar**án**
perder	ellos	perder-	**án**	perder**án**
recibir	ellas	recibir-	**án**	recibir**án**

○ All endings, except the **nosotros** form, have written accent marks.

—¿Adónde **irán** Uds. el próximo verano?   *"Where will you go next summer?"*

—**Iremos** a Panamá.   *"We will go to Panama."*

—¿Ya **estarán** de vuelta para fines de agosto?   *"Will you (already) be back by the end of August?"*

—Sí, estoy seguro de que para esa fecha **estaremos** de vuelta.   *"Yes, I'm sure that by that date we will be back."*

—¿De qué **hablarás** en la reunión?   *"What will you speak about in the meeting?"*

—**Hablaré** de Centroamérica.   *"I will speak about Central America."*

◯ The following verbs are irregular in the future tense. The future endings are added to a modified form of the infinitive.

Infinitive	Modified stem	Endings	Future (yo-form)
haber[1]	habr-		habré
caber (to fit)	cabr-		cabré
querer	querr-		querré
saber	sabr-	-é	sabré
poder	podr-	-ás	podré
poner	pondr-	-á	pondré
venir	vendr-	-emos	vendré
tener	tendr-	-éis	tendré
salir	saldr-	-án	saldré
valer	valdr-		valdré
decir	dir-		diré
hacer	har-		haré

◯ In the first group, the final vowel of the infinitive is dropped.

◯ In the second group, the final vowel of the infinitive is dropped and the letter **d** is inserted.

◯ In the third group, contracted stems are used.

—¿Qué **harán** los estudiantes?
—**Tendrán** que volver a la universidad.

"What will the students do?"
"They will have to return to the university."

—¿A qué hora **saldrán** Uds. para Managua?

"What time will you leave for Managua?"

—**Saldremos** muy temprano.

"We will leave very early."

Práctica

CD-ROM
Go to **Estructuras gramaticales** for additional practice.

A. En parejas, túrnense para decir lo que estas personas harán en las siguientes situaciones.

1. Queremos comer algo sabroso.
   Uds. _____.
2. Tengo ganas de comer pescado.
   Tú _____.

---

[1] Remember that as a main verb, **haber** is used only in the third person singular. **Habrá** = *there will be.*

3. Pedro tiene mucha sed.
   Él _____.
4. Tú quieres celebrar tu cumpleaños.
   Yo _____.
5. Uds. quieren hacer un brindis.
   Nosotros _____.
6. Las chicas necesitan comprar plátanos.
   Ellas _____.
7. Elsa necesita dinero.
   Ella _____.
8. Yo quiero ir al mercado y no tengo coche.
   Tú _____.

B. Esto es lo que pasa generalmente. Use la imaginación para decir algo diferente que pasará en el futuro.

1. Ella sale con sus amigos.
   La semana que viene _____.
2. Yo pido gaseosa en el restaurante.
   Esta noche _____.
3. Nosotros vamos a la reunión por la tarde.
   El sábado _____.
4. Tú vienes a comer a las ocho.
   Mañana _____.
5. Mamá hace chuletas de cerdo.
   El domingo _____.
6. Los chicos comen sándwiches de atún.
   El lunes _____.
7. Uds. pueden ir al mercado por la mañana.
   Este fin de semana _____.
8. Yo tengo que preparar el almuerzo.
   El martes _____.
9. Ud. vuelve a su casa a las cuatro.
   Mañana _____.
10. Ellos sirven el desayuno a las siete.
    El jueves _____.

C. Una amiga de Uds. va a dar una fiesta y necesita ayuda. En parejas, hagan una lista de diez cosas que Uds. y otros amigos harán para ayudarla.

D. Esto es lo que pasó ayer. Vuelva a escribir el siguiente párrafo para decir lo que pasará mañana, usando el futuro de los verbos en cursiva.

Ayer, como todos los días, *me levanté* temprano, *me vestí* y *salí* para la universidad. *Llegué* tarde por el tráfico. Al llegar, el profesor *vino* y *me dijo*: "Necesita entregar el informe sobre los países centroamericanos". Yo no *pude* dárselo porque no *estaba* terminado. *Hice* la tarea y después *invité* a Nora, una compañera de clase, a almorzar pero, como siempre, no *quiso* ir conmigo. Por la tarde *estudié* en la biblioteca y después *fui* al mercado para comprar varias cosas para la comida, *preparé* la comida y *cené*. En fin, *tuve* un día muy ocupado.

B El futuro para expresar probabilidad o conjetura

○ The future tense is frequently used in Spanish to express probability or conjecture in relation to the present. Phrases such as *I wonder, probably, must be,* and *do you suppose* express the same idea in English.

—¿A qué hora **será** la reunión?	*"What time do you suppose the meeting is?"*
—No sé... **será** a las diez y media.	*"I don't know . . . it must be at about ten-thirty."*
—¿Dónde **estará** Manuel?	*"I wonder where Manuel is?"*
—**Estará** en la fonda.	*"He must be at the inn."*
—¿Cuánto **valdrán** esas copas?	*"I wonder how much those goblets are worth (cost)?"*
—**Valdrán** unos veinte dólares.	*"They probably cost about twenty dollars."*

Deber + *infinitive* is also used to express probability.

Debe costar mucho dinero.   *It must cost (probably costs) a lot of money.*

Práctica

A. Ud. y un(a) compañero(a) están en la fiesta de Mario. Háganse las siguientes preguntas y traten de adivinar las respuestas. Usen el futuro para expresar probabilidad.

1. Oye, ¿tú sabes lo que está celebrando Mario?
2. ¿Quién es la chica que está hablando con él?
3. Es muy joven... ¿Cuántos años crees que tiene?
4. ¿Qué está haciendo la mamá de Mario en la cocina?
5. Estela no está aquí todavía. ¿A qué hora va a venir?
6. Estas chuletas están muy ricas. ¿De qué son?
7. Mario me dijo que íbamos a bailar. ¿Cuándo empieza el baile?
8. Mario no tiene discos compactos. ¿Quién los va a traer?
9. Mario no toma bebidas alcohólicas. ¿Qué crees que van a servir para tomar?
10. No tengo reloj. ¿Qué hora es?

B. En parejas hablen sobre lo siguiente, usando el futuro para expresar probabilidad.

MODELO: un chico que Uds. han visto en la Casa Hispánica
    E1: —*¿Quién será aquel chico?*
    E2: —*Será el nuevo estudiante.*

1. adónde van sus amigos a las ocho de la noche
2. dónde va a ser la cena
3. cómo van a preparar los bistecs
4. qué hay en el refrigerador
5. dónde están las fuentes
6. quién va a servir la comida
7. cuándo van a hacer el brindis
8. quiénes van a contar los chistes

2 El condicional

A Usos y formas

O The conditional tense corresponds to the English *would*[1] + *a verb*.

1. The conditional states *what would happen* if a certain condition were true.

   Yo no lo **haría.**   *I wouldn't do it (if I were you, etc.).*[2]

2. The conditional is also used as the future of a past action. The future states what will happen; the conditional states what would happen.

   Él dice que **llegará** tarde.   *He says that he will be late.*
   Él dijo que **llegaría** tarde.   *He said that he would be late.*

3. The Spanish conditional, like the English conditional, is also used to express a request politely.

   ¿Me **haría** Ud. un favor?   *Would you do me a favor?*

O Like the future tense, the conditional tense uses the infinitive as the stem and has only one set of endings for all verbs, regular and irregular.

Infinitive		*Stem*		*Endings*
trabajar	yo	trabajar-	ía	trabajaría
aprender	tú	aprender-	ías	aprenderías
escribir	Ud.	escribir-	ía	escribiría
ir	él	ir-	ía	iría
ser	ella	ser-	ía	sería
dar	nosotros(-as)	dar-	íamos	daríamos
hablar	vosotros(-as)	hablar-	íais	hablaríais
servir	Uds.	servir-	ían	servirían
estar	ellos	estar-	ían	estarían
preferir	ellas	preferir-	ían	preferirían

O All of the conditional endings have written accents.

—¿Cuánto te dijo que **costaría** el vino tinto?   *"How much did he say the red wine would cost?"*
—Dijo que **costaría** unos cien dólares.   *"He said it would cost about a hundred dollars."*

—¿Qué **preferirían** comer Uds.?   *"What would you rather eat?"*
—**Preferiríamos** comer ternera.   *"We would rather eat veal."*

---

[1] When *would* is used to refer to a repeated action in the past, the imperfect is used in Spanish.

[2] For the use of the conditional in *if*-clauses, see **Lección 8.**

⊙ The same verbs that are irregular in the future are also irregular in the conditional. The conditional endings are added to the modified form of the infinitive.

Infinitive	Modified stem	Endings	Conditional (yo-form)
haber[1]	habr-		habría
caber	cabr-		cabría
querer	querr-		querría
saber	sabr-		sabría
poder	podr-	-ía	podría
		-ías	
poner	pondr-	-ía	pondría
venir	vendr-	-íamos	vendría
tener	tendr-	-íais	tendría
salir	saldr-	-ían	saldría
valer	valdr-		valdría
decir	dir-		diría
hacer	har-		haría

Los niños **tendrían** que comer porque ya es tarde.
Ellos dijeron que **vendrían** a las seis.
David dijo que **saldría** temprano.
Podríamos servir cordero asado.

The children would have to eat because it's late.
They said they would come at six.
David said he would leave early.
We could serve roasted lamb.

Práctica

CD-ROM
Go to **Estructuras gramaticales** for additional practice.

A. Conteste las siguientes preguntas usando el condicional y la información dada entre paréntesis.

MODELO: ¿Qué dijeron de las botellas de ron? (no caber aquí)
Dijeron que no cabrían aquí.

1. ¿Cuándo dijeron que iban a traer las truchas? (hoy por la tarde)
2. ¿Cómo dijo Juan que iba a cocinar el bistec? (término medio)
3. ¿Qué dijo Paco que iba a hacer con las sardinas? (freírlas)
4. ¿Dónde dijeron ellos que iban a poner el salmón? (ponerlo en el horno)
5. ¿Qué dijo Arturo de las chicas? (venir mañana)
6. ¿Qué dijo Sara de Roberto? (no salir con él)

B. ¿Qué cree Ud. que harían Ud. o las siguientes personas en cada una de estas situaciones? Conteste usando el condicional.

1. A su mejor amigo(a) le regalan cien dólares.
2. Ud. tiene un examen y unos amigos lo (la) invitan a una fiesta la noche antes.
3. Su familia tiene hambre y no hay comida en la casa.

---

[1] **habría** = *there would be*

4. Sus padres desean comprar ginebra y no tienen suficiente dinero.
5. Un amigo suyo le pide veinte dólares y Ud. sabe que él nunca paga.
6. Hay un(a) chico(a) muy antipático(a) que la (lo) invita a salir.
7. Necesitamos cerveza.
8. Uds. desean tomar algo caliente.
9. Tú y yo necesitamos diez dólares para comprar el ponche.
10. Mis padres tienen invitados este fin de semana.

B El condicional para expresar probabilidad o conjetura

○ The conditional tense is frequently used to express probability or conjecture in relation to the past.

—Anoche fui a visitar a Enrique y no estaba en su casa. ¿Dónde **estaría**?	*"Last night I went to see Enrique and he wasn't home. Where do you suppose he was?"*
—**Iría** a la casa de Juan.	*"He probably went to Juan's house."*
—No encuentro el vino rosado. ¿Dónde lo **guardaría** Elsa?	*"I can't find the rosé wine. Where do you suppose Elsa keeps it?"*
—Lo **pondría** en la cocina.	*"She probably put it in the kitchen."*

CD-ROM
Go to **Estructuras gramaticales** for additional practice.

Práctica

Su compañero(a) de cuarto siempre quiere saber lo que están haciendo los vecinos. Use Ud. su imaginación para tratar de adivinar las respuestas. Use el condicional para expresar conjetura.

1. ¿Qué hora era cuando llegaron anoche?
2. ¿Por qué llegaron tan tarde?
3. ¿Quién era el muchacho que estaba con ellos?
4. ¿De dónde vinieron?
5. Uno de ellos tenía un paquete en la mano. ¿Qué era?
6. Estuvieron conversando hasta muy tarde. ¿De qué hablaban?
7. ¿A qué hora se acostaron?
8. ¿A qué hora se levantaron esta mañana?
9. ¿Qué desayunaron?
10. ¿A qué hora salieron de su casa?

3 El futuro perfecto y el condicional perfecto

A El futuro perfecto

○ The future perfect is used to refer to an action that will have taken place by a certain point in the future. It is formed with the future tense of the auxiliary verb **haber** + *the past participle of the main verb.* The future perfect in English is expressed by *shall* or *will have* + *past participle.*

haber (future)	Past participle	
habré	hablado	*I will have spoken*
habrás	comido	*you will have eaten*
habrá	vuelto	*he, she, you will have returned*
habremos	dicho	*we will have said*
habréis	roto	*you will have broken*
habrán	hecho	*they, you will have done, made*

—¿Estará Tito en casa para las ocho?
—Sí, estoy segura de que ya **habrá vuelto** para esa hora.

—¿Ya **habrán terminado** Uds. de cenar para las ocho?
—Sí, para entonces ya **habremos terminado**.

"Will Tito be home by eight?"
"Yes, I'm sure that he'll have returned by that time."

"Will you have finished having dinner by eight?"
"Yes, by then we will have finished."

Práctica

CD-ROM
Go to **Estructuras gramaticales** for additional practice.

A. Diga lo que habrán hecho Ud. y las siguientes personas para las fechas u horas indicadas.

1. Para junio, nosotros...
2. Para el 20 de diciembre, yo...
3. Para fines de este verano, mis padres...
4. Para mañana por la tarde, mi amigo...
5. Para la semana próxima, tú...
6. Para mañana a las siete, Uds...
7. Para las diez de la noche, yo...
8. Para las cuatro, mis compañeros de clase...

B. Converse con un(a) compañero(a) sobre lo que habrá pasado en sus vidas y en las de sus familiares y amigos para el año 2010.

B El condicional perfecto

○ The conditional perfect (expressed in English by *would have* + *past participle of the main verb*) is used for the following purposes.

1. It indicates an action that would have taken place (but didn't), if a certain condition had been true.[1]

De haberlo sabido, no **habría comido** tanto.

Had I known, I wouldn't have eaten so much.

---

[1] For the use of the conditional perfect in *if*-clauses, see **Lección 9**.

2. It refers to a future action in relation to the past.

Él **dijo** que para mayo **se habrían graduado.**

He said that by May they would have graduated.

○ The conditional perfect is formed with the conditional of the verb **haber** + *the past participle of the main verb.*

haber (conditional)	Past participle	
habría	hablado	*I would have spoken*
habrías	comido	*you would have eaten*
habría	vuelto	*he, she, you would have returned*
habríamos	dicho	*we would have said*
habríais	roto	*you would have broken*
habrían	hecho	*they, you would have done, made*

—El clima de ese lugar era cálido y húmedo. De haberlo sabido, no **habría ido** allí.

"The climate in that place was warm and humid. Had I known, I wouldn't have gone there."

—En otras palabras, tus vacaciones no fueron muy buenas...

"In other words, your vacation wasn't very good . . ."

—¿Cuántos años más deben estudiar Ana y Paco para graduarse?

"How many more years must Ana and Paco study to graduate?"

—Ellos dijeron que dentro de dos años **habrían terminado.**

"They said that in two years they would have finished."

CD-ROM
Go to **Estructuras gramaticales** for additional practice.

Práctica

A. ¡Planee mejor que Manuel! Aquí tiene una lista de las cosas que Manuel hizo y de las que no hizo cuando tuvo una fiesta en su casa. Diga lo que Ud. y otras personas habrían hecho. Use la información dada.

1. No invitó a todos sus amigos. (yo)
2. Sirvió solamente vino blanco. (nosotros)
3. Empezó la fiesta después de las nueve. (tú)
4. Sirvió únicamente una clase de pescado. (Uds.)
5. No invitó a sus padres a la fiesta. (sus hermanas)
6. No les avisó a sus vecinos que tenía una fiesta. (Ud.)
7. Tuvo la fiesta el jueves. (Nora y yo)
8. Terminó la fiesta a las once. (Carlos)

B. Mi familia y yo planeábamos tener una reunión en mi casa. Cambie los infinitivos al condicional perfecto para indicar lo que cada uno de nosotros habría hecho.

1. Yo: levantarme más temprano y limpiar la casa
2. Elvira: comprar comida y gaseosa
3. Tú: traer los discos de música latina

4. Carlos y Alicia: volver temprano de la universidad
5. Víctor y yo: preparar un buen postre
6. Uds.: lavar las copas y las fuentes

C. Converse con un(a) compañero(a) sobre lo que habrían hecho, y lo que no habrían hecho en la escuela secundaria, de haber sabido lo que saben ahora.

4 Género de los nombres: casos especiales

Sustantivos que cambian de significado según el género

○ A few nouns in Spanish vary in meaning according to differences in gender indicated by masculine or feminine articles. The following nouns have a single invariable form.

Masculino		*Femenino*	
el cabeza	*leader*	**la** cabeza	*head*
el capital	*money, capital*	**la** capital	*capital city*
el corte	*cut, style*	**la** corte	*court*
el cura	*priest*	**la** cura	*healing*
el frente	*front, battlefront*	**la** frente	*forehead*
el guardia	*guard*	**la** guardia	*security force*
el guía	*guide*	**la** guía	*guidebook, directory*
el orden	*order, method*	**la** orden	*order, command*
el parte	*official communication*	**la** parte	*part, portion*
el policía	*policeman*	**la** policía	*police (organization)*[1]

Ellos quieren ir a **la capital,** pero no tienen **el capital** que necesitan.

○ Other nouns that change meaning according to gender change both the article and the ending.

Masculino		*Femenino*	
el bando	*faction, party*	**la** banda	*band, musical group*
el derecho	*right, law*	**la** derecha	*right (direction)*
el fondo	*bottom, fund*	**la** fonda	*inn*
el lomo	*back of an animal*	**la** loma	*hill*
el mango	*handle of a utensil, fruit*	**la** manga	*sleeve*
el modo	*way, manner*	**la** moda	*fashion*
el palo	*stick*	**la** pala	*shovel*
el puerto	*port*	**la** puerta	*door*
el punto	*dot, period*	**la** punta	*point, tip*
el resto	*rest, leftover*	**la** resta	*subtraction*
el suelo	*ground*	**la** suela	*sole*

Me ensucié **la manga** de la camisa con **el mango** de la sartén.

---

[1] **la agente de policía** = *policewoman*

CD-ROM
Go to **Estructuras gramaticales** for additional practice.

Práctica

A. Complete las siguientes oraciones, usando las palabras de las listas anteriores junto con sus correspondientes artículos definidos o indefinidos.

1. Llevaron _____ de los terroristas a la estación de policía.
2. _____ estaba en la iglesia.
3. Mamá nos llevó a conocer _____ de Brasil.
4. _____ prendieron a los ladrones.
5. Me rompí _____ del vestido con _____ de la sartén.
6. El azúcar siempre se queda en _____ de la taza.
7. No paramos en un hotel sino en _____.
8. Encontré tu dirección en _____ de teléfonos.
9. Pusimos todo _____ en el banco.
10. Sr. Roca, coma Ud. _____ del flan y deje _____ para los niños.
11. Los soldados no obedecieron _____ del general.
12. Los barcos ya están en _____.
13. Se me rompió _____ del lápiz y ahora no puedo escribir.
14. Los soldados murieron en _____ de batalla (*battle*).

B. Encuentre en la columna B la definición que corresponde a cada una de las palabras de la columna A.

A	B
1. la corte	a. espalda de un animal
2. el lomo	b. grupo musical
3. la suela	c. opuesto de *izquierda*
4. el palo	d. parte del cuerpo humano
5. el orden	e. la manera
6. la banda	f. facción o partido
7. el guía	g. pedazo de madera
8. la derecha	h. lugar donde trabaja el juez
9. el modo	i. parte del zapato
10. la cabeza	j. método
11. el bando	k. operación aritmética
12. la loma	l. herramienta (*tool*)
13. la pala	m. persona que acompaña a un grupo
14. la resta	n. elevación del terreno
15. el suelo	o. signo de puntuación
16. la puerta	p. parte de la cabeza
17. el punto	q. piso
18. la frente	r. lugar por donde entramos o salimos

C. A continuación le ofrecemos parte de la transcripción de un telediario (*T.V. news broadcast*) centroamericano. En parejas, completen los anuncios comerciales y las noticias con el equivalente español de las palabras de la lista. Luego, represéntenlo.

security force	*sleeves*	*the police*
your head	*the capital* (*city*)	*way*
fashion	*the leader*	*policemen*
official communication	*the inn*	*the cure*
the order	*the band*	*the port*

1. Y ahora tenemos para Uds. las últimas noticias. Nicaragua: _____ detuvo esta mañana _____ de una organización terrorista que había atacado a _____ del palacio presidencial. Según _____ oficial, ya se ha restablecido _____ en _____.

2. En la ciudad de Esmeralda, debido a la tormenta, dos _____ resultaron heridos al tratar de ayudar a varias personas que estaban cenando en _____ La Madrileña cuando el techo (*roof*) cayó sobre ellas. Varios barcos que estaban en _____ también sufrieron daños por la tormenta.

3. Otra noticia muy importante: Un científico francés afirma que acaba de descubrir _____ para el cáncer.

4. Si le duele _____, tome Mejoral. Recuerde: *Mejor mejora Mejoral.*

5. ¿Se va de vacaciones? El mejor _____ de viajar es, como siempre, con la Aerolínea Nacional.

6. La tienda La Elegancia presentó hoy una exhibición con la nueva _____ de invierno. Llamaron la atención las enormes _____ y el nuevo estilo de pantalones, que sólo llegan hasta la rodilla. Mientras las modelos desfilaban, _____ musical tocaba música moderna.

STUDENT WEBSITE
Do the **Compruebe cuánto sabe** self test after finishing this **Estructuras gramaticales** section.

Venga este fin de semana:

Lagunas de
TORREMOLINOS

Km.79, nueva Autopista a Puerto Quetzal

¡CONTINUEMOS!

Una encuesta

Entreviste a sus compañeros de clase para tratar de identificar a aquellas personas que...

1. ...comen chuletas de cordero o de ternera.
2. ...prefieren la carne bien cocida.
3. ...comen comida my picante.
4. ...comen bacalao.
5. ...han comido mondongo alguna vez.
6. ...comen pavo relleno en Navidad.
7. ...tienen una buena receta para hacer ponche.
8. ...dicen "salud" cuando brindan.
9. ...no ven la hora de irse de vacaciones.
10. ...tienen buenos recuerdos de su infancia.
11. ...a veces hacen la sobremesa.
12. ...van a visitar a sus amigos sin avisar.
13. ...usan miel de abeja en vez de azúcar.
14. ...saben muchos chistes.
15. ...discuten sobre política con sus amigos.

Ahora divídanse en grupos de tres o cuatro y discutan el resultado de la encuesta.

¿Comprende Ud.?

CD-ROM   STUDENT WEBSITE
Go to **De escuchar...
a escribir** (in **¿Comprende Ud.?**) on the CD-ROM for activities related to the conversation, and go to **Canción** on the website for activities related to the song.

1. Escuche la siguiente conversación entre Amanda Núñez, la chica salvadoreña que conocimos al inicio de la lección, y Sandra Stevens, su compañera de cuarto. El objetivo de la actividad es el de escuchar una conversación a velocidad natural. No se preocupe de entenderlo todo, pues esto no se espera de Ud. Después de escuchar la conversación dos veces, Ud. oirá varias aseveraciones. En una hoja, esscriba los números de uno a ocho e indique si cada aseveración es verdadera o falsa.
2. Luego escuche la canción y trate de aprenderla.

Hablemos de comida

En parejas, estudien los siguientes anuncios. Decidan a qué lugar irían en cada una de las situaciones en la página 226. Expliquen por qué.

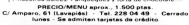

1. Uds. quieren comer bien, pero no tienen mucho dinero.
2. Quieren llevar a unos amigos a un restaurante donde puedan divertirse además de comer.
3. Tienen un amigo de Buenos Aires que vive en España hace mucho tiempo y que se siente nostálgico.
4. A una amiga de Uds. le gusta comer langosta.
5. Invitan a almorzar a dos amigos que tienen hijos pequeños.
6. El sábado quieren llevar a un grupo de cubanos a escuchar a un cantante.
7. Van a comer con una amiga mexicana que hace mucho tiempo no come la comida de su país.

¿Qué dirían Uds.?

Imagínese que Ud. y un(a) compañero(a) se encuentran en las siguientes situaciones. ¿Qué va a decir cada uno?

1. Uds. son los (las) cocineros(as) este fin de semana y tienen que preparar el desayuno, el almuerzo y la cena para seis personas. Discutan lo que van a hacer.
2. Cada uno(a) de Uds. quiere que el otro (la otra) salga con una amiga (un amigo) este fin de semana. Traten de convencerse mutuamente de que la "cita a ciegas" (*blind date*) es una buena idea.
3. Uds. van a encontrarse en un restaurante para cenar. Hagan planes.

¡De ustedes depende!

Uds. les están diciendo a unos amigos latinoamericanos cómo preparar estos platos típicos de los Estados Unidos:

1. una hamburguesa
2. un perro caliente
3. un pavo relleno
4. un pastel de manzanas

Hablen de los ingredientes que necesitan para cada plato. [palabras útiles: carne molida (*ground meat*), mayonesa, mostaza (*mustard*)]

Mesa redonda

Formen grupos de cuatro o cinco estudiantes y hablen de la importancia de estar en familia a la hora de cenar y de aprovechar este tiempo para conversar y estar juntos. Hablen también de las causas que impiden que muchas familias puedan hacerlo. Sugieran algunas soluciones.

Lecturas periodísticas

Saber leer   El uso de varias estrategias

CD-ROM
Go to **Lecturas periodísticas** for additional prereading and vocabulary activities.

Ud. ya ha aplicado el uso de varias estrategias simultáneamente. Por ejemplo, en la **Lección 6**, Ud. estudió ciertas palabras clave de acuerdo con el propósito específico que tenía Ud. al leer. En la **Lección 5**, Ud. se fijó en la estructura de la lectura (los cuatro encabezados) y respondió a preguntas derivadas de los encabezados. Éstas se formularon para crear un contexto antes de leer. Así creó contextos.

Antes de leer la siguiente lectura periodística, escoja dos o tres estrategias de las que ya se han presentado:

- Hágase la pregunta: ¿A qué tipo de público se dirige el (la) autor(a) de la lectura? (de la **Lección 1**)
- Hágase la pregunta: ¿Qué propósito(s) tiene el (la) autor(a) al escribir el artículo? (de la **Lección 2**)
- Para leer activamente, siempre tenga muy presente los objetivos de la lectura. (de la **Lección 3**)
- Cree contextos recordando todo lo que sabe sobre el tema (de la comida centroamericana). (de la **Lección 4**)
- Cree contextos formulando preguntas y contestándoselas antes de leer. (de la **Lección 5**)
- Estudie algunas palabras clave según sus objetivos. (de la **Lección 6**)

Para leer y comprender

Al leer detalladamente el artículo busque las respuestas a las siguientes preguntas.

1. ¿Por qué cosas podemos considerar a Guatemala un paraíso?
2. ¿Qué origen tienen los frijoles, los moles y los chiles?
3. Cite algunos postres guatemaltecos. Cite algunas bebidas.
4. ¿Qué alimento ocupa el primer lugar en la cocina guatemalteca? Cite algunas de las comidas hechas de éste.
5. ¿Cómo consideraban los indígenas de México y de Centroamérica el teocinte?
6. ¿De qué nos habla el Popol-Vuh?
7. ¿Qué hicieron los dioses de los granos del teocinte?
8. ¿Dónde se describe el proceso evolutivo del maíz?
9. ¿Qué usaban los hombres y las mujeres para guiarse en el cultivo del maíz?
10. ¿A qué diosa llaman "la abuela del maíz"?

La cocina guatemalteca

Guatemala no sólo es un paraíso por su gente y sus bellezas naturales sino también por su comida.

En la cocina guatemalteca hay una gran variedad de frijoles, moles, chiles y muchos otros alimentos de origen prehispánico. También tienen postres muy sabrosos, por ejemplo: buñuelos, torrejas, platanitos en mole, quesadillas, higos° y camotes° en dulce, y deliciosas bebidas como el atol de elote° o de plátano, chicha, rosa de jamaica y caldo de frutas°.

Sin embargo, en el comer cotidiano° del guatemalteco, el maíz ocupa el primer lugar. Hay muchas comidas a base de maíz: tortillas, tamales, tacos, enchiladas y otras.

El maíz, según una de las hipótesis más antiguas, surgió° del teocinte[1] mexicano, considerado por los indígenas de México y Centroamérica como planta sagrada°. Principal fuente de

_____
[1] Palabra de origen nahuatl, que significa "alimento de dioses".

alimentación de nuestros pueblos, está ligado° a aspectos mágicos y mitológicos. El Popol-Vuh[2] nos habla de su origen y de la creación del hombre: de los granos blancos y amarillos del teocinte, los dioses harían la carne, los huesos y la sangre° de las primeras criaturas humanas.

El libro sagrado de los mayas describe el proceso evolutivo del maíz en la edad matriarcal hasta que llega a adquirir formas más o menos semejantes a las que tiene ahora, con mazorcas° y granos perfectamente desarrollados. En aquel tiempo los hombres talaban° los árboles y las mujeres sembraban y cosechaban en pequeña escala, guiándose por el calendario lunar. La tradición atribuye a la diosa Ixcumané el nacimiento del maíz, por lo que se la llama "la abuela del maíz". Éste se convierte así en el típico exponente de la cultura maya.

Adaptado de *Publicaciones Serie Latinoamericana*

_____
[2] Libro que conserva la tradición oral de los mayas. Se le ha llamado la "Biblia maya".

> El maíz, según una de las hipótesis más antiguas, surgió del teocinte mexicano, considerado por los indígenas de México y Centroamérica como planta sagrada.

Comprando frutas y vegetales en un mercado al aire libre.

figs / yams	daily	tied
tender corn	appeared	blood
caldo... punch	sacred	ears of corn
		cut down

Desde su mundo

1. ¿Qué alimentos de origen indio se comen en este país?
2. ¿Hay en su ciudad algunos restaurantes que sirvan comida latinoamericana? ¿De qué países?
3. ¿Ha comido Ud. algunos de los platos que se mencionan en el artículo? ¿Cuáles?

piense y escriba Taller de redacción I

STUDENT WEBSITE

CD-ROM

Go to **...y escribamos** (in **Hablemos de su país**) on the student website and **De escuchar... a escribir** (in **¿Comprende Ud.?**) on the CD-ROM for additional writing practice.

El proceso de escribir debe incluir una fase de colaboración con lectores que editen y corrijan el escrito. Teniendo esto en cuenta, haga lo siguiente:

1. Va a escribir un artículo sobre algunos de sus platos favoritos. Incorpore las fases que ya conoce.
2. Intercambie el artículo con otro(a) compañero(a) de clase. Edítense los artículos. Como editor(a), tenga en cuenta las siguientes pautas de organización y de unidad del contenido, identifique lo que no esté claro o lo que podría aclararse y proponga soluciones.
   a. ¿Cuál es el tema?
   b. ¿Cuál es la idea principal que el (la) autor(a) desea comunicar sobre el tema?
   c. ¿Cómo ha decidido abordar (*approach*) la comunicación de tal idea? Por ejemplo, ¿en qué subtemas analizó la idea principal?
   d. ¿Puede describir el (los) criterio(s) de organización que utilizó? ¿Utiliza el mismo criterio a lo largo de todo el artículo?
   e. ¿Se desarrolla cada subtema claramente?
   f. En fin, ¿tiene el artículo unidad de contenido?
3. Vea lo que le ha indicado su editor(a) y prepare la versión final.

Pepe Vega y su mundo

 Teleinforme

La cocina hispanoamericana incorpora ingredientes de todas partes del mundo. Sin embargo, se calcula que casi el 80% de los alimentos que se comen en el mundo entero son de origen americano. Vamos a ver tres aspectos de la cocina de Centro y Sudamérica: ejemplos de productos americanos autóctonos, ejemplos de productos que trajeron los europeos a las Américas y un plato típico que combina alimentos de ambos tipos.

Preparación

Clasificación. ¿Cuánto sabe Ud. de los orígenes de los alimentos? Intente clasificar los siguientes alimentos y productos según su origen, sea americano (**A**) o del "Viejo Mundo" (**V**).

_____	1. el aguacate/la palta (*avocado*)
_____	2. el ají/pimiento/chile
_____	3. el ajo
_____	4. el café
_____	5. el plátano
_____	6. la caña de azúcar
_____	7. el maíz
_____	8. el nopal (*prickly pear cactus*)
_____	9. la papa
_____	10. el trigo (*wheat*)

Comprensión

CD-ROM
You will also find this clip under **Video**.

Alimentos americanos   31:40–34:06

El nopal y el maíz son alimentos muy comunes en México y en Centroamérica. El nopal, un tipo de cacto, es casi desconocido como alimento en los EE.UU. El maíz es uno de los alimentos básicos de la gastronomía indígena americana. Estos dos fragmentos de video, producidos por la emisora nacional de España, ofrecen una perspectiva europea al conocimiento de estos productos típicamente americanos.

A. ¿Qué se come? Mientras que Ud. ve y escucha el video, indique con una **X** la información que se relaciona con cada tipo de alimento.

	el nopal	el maíz
1. Es la base de la alimentación hispanoamericana.		
2. Es la comida más barata que existe.		
3. Se asan a la plancha o a la brasa.		
4. Lo consumían los aztecas.		
5. Lo consumían los mayas.		
6. Los campesinos aspiran a exportarlo.		
7. Primero se cuece y luego se muele.		
8. Se comen en vez del pan de trigo.		
9. Se consume en ensalada o en escabeche.		
10. Se hacen zumos (jugos).		

CD-ROM
Go to **Video** for further previewing, vocabulary, and
structure practice for the clip
on sugar.

Del Viejo Mundo a América   34:08–36:50

Hay muchos alimentos que hoy se cultivan en Centroamérica que no son originarios de esas tierras. Dos ejemplos son la caña de azúcar, de origen asiático, y el café, de origen africano. Estos productos fueron introducidos en las Américas durante la colonización. En el video veremos la importancia actual de la caña de azúcar y del café en la economía de El Salvador.

B. Vocabulario técnico.   En la primera parte del video vemos cómo se cultiva la caña de azúcar, cómo se transporta y cómo se prepara para el consumo. Van a oír algunas palabras conocidas y otras desconocidas. Basándose en lo que ya saben, y en lo que escuchan y ven en el video, emparejen (*match*) las definiciones de la columna B con los términos de la columna A. (Las palabras se presentan en el orden en que se oyen en el video.)

A	B
_____ 1. la siembra	a. acción de arrojar (*throw*) las semillas (*seeds*) en la tierra
_____ 2. consagrado	b. comida esencial
_____ 3. la cosecha	c. comida ligera que se hace por la tarde
_____ 4. la carreta	d. acción de recoger los productos maduros (*ripe*)
_____ 5. la molienda	e. azúcar negra compacta en bloques
_____ 6. mezclado	f. botella para darles de beber a los bebés
_____ 7. la base alimenticia	g. carro de madera, generalmente con dos ruedas
_____ 8. la panela o el papelón	h. combinado
_____ 9. el biberón	i. dedicado
_____ 10. la merienda	j. acción de moler (*to grind*) granos o frutos

C. ¿Qué entiende Ud.?   Lea las siguientes oraciones. Luego, mientras ve la segunda parte del video sobre la producción del café en El Salvador, escriba o escoja la respuesta correcta, según corresponda.

1. En las colinas de algunos de los volcanes de El Salvador se siembra _____.
2. El Sr. Chaves dice que el cultivo del café produce muchas *divisas*, es decir que genera (mucho dinero extranjero/mucho conflicto/muchos trabajos).
3. El café se cosecha en áreas muy _____.
4. El proceso agroindustrial se completa en (las montañas/el campo/la fábrica de la cooperativa).
5. El café de El Salvador y de todo Centroamérica tiene fama de _____.
6. El Salvador es el (primer/segundo/tercer) productor de café a pesar de (*in spite of*) ser el país más (grande/trópico/pequeño) de Centroamérica.

CD-ROM
Go to **Video** for further pre-viewing, vocabulary, and structure practice on this clip.

El ajiaco

36:52–37:57

Colombia recibe muchas influencias y comparte muchos alimentos con los demás países de América Latina. En el último segmento de video de esta lección, veremos un plato típico de Colombia, que combina ingredientes diversos.

D. ¿Cuáles son los ingredientes?

1. Viendo el video *sin el sonido*, trate de identificar los elementos del plato que prepara el cocinero. Ponga una **X** al lado de los alimentos que ve en el video.

_____ a. el aguacate	_____ e. el arroz	_____ i. la leche
_____ b. el ají	_____ f. el caldo	_____ j. el maíz
_____ c. el ajo	_____ g. el plátano	_____ k. la papa
_____ d. las alcaparras	_____ h. la carne	_____ l. el pollo

2. Mire de nuevo el video, esta vez *con sonido*, y averigüe cuáles de los ingredientes menciona el cocinero.

3. Este plato se llama *ajiaco*. Probablemente su nombre viene de un ingrediente que el cocinero ni siquiera (*doesn't even*) menciona por ser tan común en la cocina latinoamericana. ¿Cuál es?

a. el ajo   b. el ají   c. el arroz   d. el frijol

Ampliación

¿Correcciones?   ¿Cuánto sabe Ud. ahora del origen de los alimentos? Fíjese si sus respuestas en la primera parte (**Preparación**) son correctas y cambie las que no lo son, de acuerdo con lo que Ud. vio en el video.

Comerciantes.   Imagine que Ud. quiere comercializar un producto centroamericano para el mercado extranjero. Puede ser un producto poco conocido como el nopal de México, u otro muy común, como el café de El Salvador. ¿Cómo lo haría? En equipos de tres, preparen una campaña para venderles su producto a los otros miembros de la clase.

Nuestras grandes ciudades: problemas y soluciones

Vista del Centro Mundial Financiero en la ciudad de Nueva York.

OBJETIVOS

Temas para la comunicación

Problemas urbanos

Estructuras

1. El imperfecto de subjuntivo
2. El imperfecto de subjuntivo en oraciones condicionales
3. El pretérito perfecto de subjuntivo
4. El pluscuamperfecto de subjuntivo

Regiones y países

Estados Unidos

Lectura

En el supermercado

Estrategias de lectura

Su auto-adiestramiento como lector

Estrategias de redacción

Los buenos escritores

Nuestras grandes ciudades: problemas y soluciones

CD-ROM   STUDENT AUDIO
For preparation, do the **Ante todo** activities found on the CD-ROM.

El club de español de la Universidad Internacional de la Florida, en Miami, ha organizado una mesa redonda para hablar de los problemas sociales y ambientales de las grandes ciudades. Cuatro estudiantes de diferentes países toman parte en la discusión. Luis Muñoz, de ascendencia mexicana; Ignacio Arango, de El Salvador; Nélida Hidalgo de Puerto Rico, y David Robinson de Nueva York. Rebeca Bernal, nacida en Miami de padres cubanos, es la presidenta del club y va a dirigir la mesa redonda.

REBECA —Bueno, creo que primero debemos identificar los problemas y después hablar de las posibles soluciones. ¿Por dónde empezamos: por los problemas del medio ambiente, de la vivienda, de la delincuencia... ? ¿Ignacio?

IGNACIO —Yo sugiero que empecemos por los problemas de la contaminación del medio ambiente, que no sólo siguen siendo graves, sino que están empeorando más y más, al menos en mi país, en la Ciudad de México, en Los Ángeles...

REBECA —Estoy segura de que todas las ciudades grandes tienen el problema, aunque poco a poco se están dando pasos para resolverlo. ¿Cuál es la situación en México, Luis?

LUIS —Bueno, la contaminación del aire es un problema muy serio y no se resolverá si la gente sigue dependiendo tanto del automóvil, y las fábricas no usan combustibles más limpios.

NÉLIDA —Y si seguimos usando pulverizadores de productos químicos y produciendo tanta basura.

REBECA —Exactamente. ¿Y qué me dicen de la contaminación de las aguas? ¿Luis?

LUIS —Ése es otro problema que se podría solucionar si la gente cooperara y llevara los residuos de productos químicos a los vertederos públicos, en lugar de ponerlos en la basura o echarlos por los desagües de las casas.

REBECA —Afortunadamente, podemos utilizar productos biodegradables y reciclar todo tipo de materiales. Aquí en Miami reciclamos periódicos, plásticos, aluminio y vidrio. ¿Tienen buenos programas de reciclaje en El Salvador, Ignacio?

IGNACIO —Hay algunos, pero dudo que la cooperación haya sido total. Sin embargo, yo opino que los problemas del medio ambiente son más fáciles de resolver que los problemas sociales.

DAVID —Estoy de acuerdo. En todas las ciudades existen los problemas de las pandillas, de las personas sin hogar y de los que viven en la miseria. Estos problemas son muy complejos y cada día parecen agravarse.

REBECA —Tienes razón. Según las últimas estadísticas, ni aun los pueblos pequeños están libres de las drogas y de otros problemas sociales como los asesinatos, las violaciones y los robos. ¿Cuál es la situación en Puerto

Rico, Nélida?

NÉLIDA —El gobierno y muchas organizaciones están tratando de resolver estos problemas, pero no hay ninguna que haya podido resolverlos todos.

IGNACIO —Eso es cierto. Muchos de estos problemas se habrían solucionado ya si se hubiera educado mejor al pueblo.

LUIS —Las cosas no habrían llegado a este punto si no nos hubiéramos acostumbrado a las comodidades del mundo moderno, sobre todo el coche.

DAVID —(*Riéndose*) Luis, no trates de convencer a los americanos a no usar el coche, porque tus esfuerzos fracasarán.

Dígame

En parejas, contesten las siguientes preguntas basadas en el diálogo.

1. ¿Cuál es la nacionalidad de cada uno de los participantes de la mesa redonda?
2. ¿De qué van a hablar y quién va a dirigir las discusiones?
3. ¿Qué sugiere Ignacio?
4. Según Luis, ¿cuáles son las principales causas de la contaminación del aire?
5. ¿Cómo dice Luis que podría solucionarse el problema de la contaminación de las aguas?
6. ¿Qué cosas reciclan en Miami?
7. ¿Qué problemas sociales menciona Rebeca? ¿Son estos problemas exclusivos de las grandes ciudades?
8. Según Nélida, ¿hay alguna organización que haya podido resolver estos problemas?
9. Según Ignacio, ¿qué habría pasado si se hubiera educado mejor al pueblo?
10. Según Luis, ¿a qué nos hemos acostumbrado todos?

Perspectivas socioculturales

INSTRUCTOR WEBSITE
Your instructor may assign the preconversational support activities found in **Perspectivas socioculturales.**

En todas las comunidades hay problemas de algún tipo. Haga lo siguiente:

1. Durante unos cinco minutos, converse con dos compañeros sobre los problemas de la región donde Ud. vive:
   • con respecto al medio ambiente
   • con respecto a la vivienda
   • con respecto a la educación
2. Participe con el resto de la clase en la discusión de los problemas cuando su profesor(a) se lo indique. La clase propondrá soluciones que su comunidad, el gobierno y la industria deberían considerar.

Vocabulario

Nombres

el asesinato   murder
la basura   garbage, trash
el combustible   fuel
la contaminación, la polución
   pollution
la delincuencia   delinquency, crime
el desagüe   sewer, drain
el desecho, el desperdicio   waste
la droga   drug[1]
la estadística   statistic
la fábrica, la factoría   factory
el gobierno   government
la ley   law
el medio ambiente   environment
la miseria, la pobreza   poverty
la pandilla   gang
el pueblo   town
el pulverizador   spray, spray can
el residuo   by-product
el robo   robbery, burglary
el vertedero   disposal site, dump
la violación   rape
la vivienda   housing

Verbos

agravarse, empeorarse   to become
   worse
cooperar   to cooperate
depender   to depend
dirigir   to direct, to moderate

echar   to throw
educar   to educate
fracasar   to fail
identificar   to identify
nacer   to be born
organizar   to organize
reciclar   to recycle
resolver (o → ue), solucionar   to
   solve

Adjetivos

ambiental   environmental
cada   each
complejo(a)   complex
grave, serio(a)   serious
limpio(a)   clean
químico(a)   chemical
redondo(a)   round

Otras palabras y expresiones

al menos   at least
aunque   although
dar pasos   to take steps
de ascendencia...   of . . . descent
de habla hispana   Spanish-speaking
en lugar de, en vez de   instead of
hay que (+ *inf.*)   one must, it is necessary to
las personas sin hogar   the homeless
ni aun   not even
poco a poco   little by little
todo tipo de   all kinds of

Ampliación

Otras palabras relacionadas con los problemas de las grandes ciudades

el arma   weapon
el asalto   assault, hold-up, attack

asesinar   to murder
el (la) asesino(a)   murderer, assassin
la huelga   strike
el ladrón, la ladrona   thief, burglar

---

[1]Generalmente la palabra **droga** no se usa para referirse a medicinas.

la pena capital, la pena de muerte
  death penalty
la prisión, la cárcel   prison, jail
rescatar   to rescue
el rescate   rescue; ransom
secuestrar   to kidnap

Palabras relacionadas con el gobierno
el (la) alcalde(-sa)   mayor
la campaña electoral   electoral campaign
las elecciones   elections
el (la) gobernador(a)   governor
postularse (para)   to run for

CD-ROM
Go to **Vocabulario** for additional vocabulary practice.

Hablando de todo un poco

Preparación   **Circule la respuesta apropiada a cada pregunta.**

1. ¿Dónde debemos echar los residuos de productos químicos?
   a. En la basura.
   b. En el desagüe.
   c. En el vertedero municipal.
2. ¿Cuáles son algunas causas de la delincuencia?
   a. Las estadísticas y la ley.
   b. Las drogas y la pobreza.
   c. Las elecciones y los alcaldes.
3. ¿Roberto está en la cárcel porque mató a su esposa?
   a. Sí, cometió una violación.
   b. Sí, cometió un asesinato.
   c. Sí, cometió un robo.
4. ¿Cuáles son algunos problemas relacionados con el medio ambiente?
   a. La polución y la contaminación de las aguas.
   b. Las huelgas y las pandillas.
   c. Los asaltos y la miseria.
5. ¿Para qué va a postularse ella en este pueblo?
   a. Para ladrona.
   b. Para asesina.
   c. Para alcaldesa.
6. ¿Cómo podemos ayudar a evitar la contaminación ambiental?
   a. Reciclando vidrios y periódicos.
   b. Solucionando problemas complejos.
   c. Usando combustibles menos limpios.
7. ¿Los problemas que tiene el gobierno son graves?
   a. Sí, cada día cooperan más.
   b. Sí, cada día empeoran más.
   c. Sí, cada día nacen más.
8. ¿Aquí hay muchas personas sin hogar?
   a. Sí, al menos hay que eliminar los pulverizadores.
   b. Sí, hay que disminuir el número de fábricas.
   c. Sí, poco a poco hay que aumentar el número de viviendas.

9. ¿Uds. van a participar en la mesa redonda?
   a. No, porque no tenemos armas.
   b. No, porque no nos van a rescatar.
   c. No, aunque nos gustaría hacerlo.
10. ¿Fracasó la reunión para organizar la campaña electoral?
   a. No, fue un éxito.
   b. No, no pudieron identificarla.
   c. No, fue gratis.
11. ¿Tus amigos son de habla hispana?
   a. Sí, dependen de sus padres.
   b. Sí, son de ascendencia española.
   c. Sí, son libres.
12. ¿El gobernador está de acuerdo con la pena capital?
   a. No, quiere asesinarla.
   b. No, no quiere dirigirla.
   c. No, quiere dar pasos para eliminarla.
13. ¿Secuestraron a esa señora?
   a. Sí, y pidieron un rescate.
   b. Sí, y la educaron.
   c. Sí, y eliminaron los desechos.
14. ¿Raúl aprobó el examen?
   a. No, dejó de trabajar.
   b. No, quedó suspendido.
   c. No, recibió todo tipo de ayuda.

En grupos de tres o cuatro, hagan lo siguiente.

A. **La contaminación.**   Hablen sobre las causas de la contaminación del aire y del agua, las dificultades y las posibles soluciones.

B. **Actividades criminales.**   Conversen sobre distintos tipos de actividades criminales, sus causas y las posibles soluciones.

C. **La pobreza.**   Hablen sobre la pobreza, las personas sin hogar, las causas de estos problemas y las posibles soluciones.

D. **Promesas.**   Hablen de las promesas que Uds. harían si se postularan para alcalde (alcaldesa), gobernador(a) o presidente(a).

Palabras problemáticas

A. **Fracasar, quedar suspendido** y **dejar de** como equivalentes de *to fail*

- **Fracasar** es lo opuesto de **tener éxito.**

  La organización **fracasó** totalmente.

- **Quedar suspendido** se usa para indicar una nota no satisfactoria en un examen o curso.

  El muchacho puertorriqueño **quedó suspendido** en el examen de inglés.

- **Dejar de** es el equivalente de *to fail (to do something)*.

  No **dejen de** reciclar el vidrio y los periódicos.

B. **Libre** y **gratis** como equivalentes de *free*

- **Libre** significa **independiente, accesible, disponible.**

  Tenemos libertad. Somos **libres.**

  ¿Está **libre** este taxi?

- **Gratis** significa que se obtiene **sin pagar.**

  Los conciertos son **gratis** durante el verano.

Práctica

Complete los siguientes diálogos y léalos con un(a) compañero(a).

1. —¿Cómo te fue en el examen?
   —¡Muy mal! _____ _____. Saqué una "F".

2. —¿Tenemos que pagar por los libros?
   —No, son _____.

3. —¿Tuvo éxito el programa?
   —No, _____ totalmente.

4. —Mañana tenemos un examen.
   —Sí, no podemos _____ de ir a clase.

5. —Ahora es difícil conseguir casa en las ciudades grandes.
   —Sí, y hay pocos apartamentos _____.

Your instructor may carry out the ¡Ahora escuche! listening activity found in the Answers to Text Exercises.

¡Ahora escuche!

Se leerá dos veces una breve narración sobre Roberto, un chico que debe preparar un informe sobre los problemas de la ciudad donde vive. Se harán aseveraciones sobre la narración. En una hoja escriba los números de uno a diez e indique si cada aseveración es verdadera (V) o falsa (F).

El mundo hispánico

Los Estados Unidos hispánicos

En este país viven más de treinta millones de hispanos. De éstos, algunos ya estaban aquí cuando llegaron los primeros angloparlantes; otros, la gran mayoría, vinieron por diferentes motivos: unos en busca de° libertad, otros por razones económicas, otros buscando un cambio para sus vidas o las de sus hijos. Aunque hay personas de todos los países hispanos, los grandes grupos minoritarios son los de origen mexicano, puertorriqueño y cubano. Luis, Nélida y Rebeca van a hablarles un poco de los grupos que cada uno de ellos representa.

en... in search of

Luis

Yo nací en Los Ángeles, pero soy de ascendencia mexicana. Estoy muy orgulloso de mi origen y de mi cultura. En California, como en Texas, Arizona y otros estados, se ve la influencia hispana en los nombres de las ciudades, de las calles y en la arquitectura. El grupo minoritario más numeroso es el de los mexicoamericanos. Nosotros hemos enriquecido la cultura americana con nuestra música y las delicias de la exquisita comida mexicana. Hoy en día, muchos mexicoamericanos se destacan en la política, en la educación, en las artes y en la literatura.

STUDENT WEBSITE
Go to **El mundo hispánico** for prereading and vocabulary activities.

Nélida

Yo soy de Puerto Rico, pero vivo con mis padres en Nueva York. Desde la Segunda Guerra° Mundial, unos tres millones de puertorriqueños han emigrado de la isla a Estados Unidos. En la ciudad de Nueva York residen más puertorriqueños que en San Juan, la capital de Puerto Rico. A diferencia de otros grupos hispanos, nosotros somos ciudadanos estadounidenses, y podemos entrar y salir del país libremente°. Nosotros formamos una de las poblaciones más jovenes de todos los grupos étnicos. Gran número de puertorriqueños ingresan todos los años en las fuerzas armadas americanas, y muchos de ellos alcanzan altos grados y distinciones.

war

freely

Rebeca

En 1970, mis padres dejaron la isla de Cuba para escaparse del régimen comunista de Fidel Castro y se unieron a la colonia cubana de Miami. Como la mayoría de los cubanos, nuestra familia logró prosperidad económica después de muchos esfuerzos. Aunque yo me considero ciudadana americana, en mi casa mantenemos las costumbres y tradiciones de Cuba. Como Uds. ven, aquí en Miami se ve nuestra influencia en todas partes: en los restaurantes, en la radio, en la televisión, en la música, etc. En gran parte, gracias al impulso cubano, se puede decir que Miami es hoy la ciudad más rica y moderna del mundo hispanohablante.

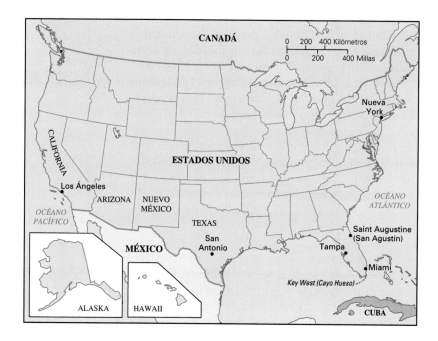

Sobre las minorías hispanas

En parejas, túrnense para contestar las siguientes preguntas.

1. ¿En qué ciudad nació Luis Muñoz y de dónde viene su familia? ¿De qué se siente orgulloso?
2. ¿En qué se ve la influencia hispana en muchos estados? ¿Cuál es el grupo minoritario más numeroso?
3. ¿En qué aspectos de la cultura han influido principalmente los mexicoamericanos? ¿En qué se destacan actualmente?
4. ¿Qué pasó después de la Segunda Guerra Mundial?

5. ¿Cuál es la diferencia entre los puertorriqueños y las personas que vienen de otros países?
6. ¿Qué característica especial tienen los puertorriqueños como grupo?
7. ¿Se unen los puertorriqueños a las fuerzas americanas? ¿Qué alcanzan muchos de ellos?
8. ¿Qué hicieron los padres de Rebeca en 1970? ¿Cómo les fue económicamente?
9. ¿Qué mantienen Rebeca y su familia?
10. ¿Dónde se ve la influencia cubana en Miami? ¿Qué se puede decir de Miami hoy en día?

Hablemos de su país

INSTRUCTOR WEBSITE
STUDENT WEBSITE
Your instructor may assign the pre-conversational activities in **Hablemos...** (under **Hablemos de su país**). Go to **Hablemos de su país** (under...**y escribamos**) for postconversational web search and writing activities.

Reúnase con otro(a) compañero(a) para hablar de los orígenes de los diversos grupos que componen la sociedad de su país. ¿Qué aportaciones (*contributions*) ha brindado (*has shared*) cada grupo a la sociedad?

Luego cada pareja compartirá las respuestas para discutir las aportaciones de cada grupo social.

Una tarjeta postal

Imagínense que Ud. y un(a) compañero(a) están de vacaciones en Miami, en Los Ángeles o en Nueva York. Envíenles una tarjeta postal a sus compañeros de clase dándoles sus impresiones sobre la influencia hispana en la ciudad que Uds. están visitando.

Queridos amigos:

_____

_____

_____

_____

_____

_____

Saludos,

Estructuras gramaticales

STUDENT WEBSITE
Do the **¿Cuánto recuerda?** pretest to check what you already know on the topics covered in this **Estructuras gramaticales** section.

1 El imperfecto de subjuntivo

○ The imperfect subjunctive has two sets of endings: the **-ra** endings (which are more commonly used) and the **-se** endings. The imperfect subjunctive of all verbs is formed by dropping the **-ron** ending of the third person plural of the preterit and adding the corresponding endings.

-ra *endings*		-se *endings*	
-ra	-´ramos[1]	-se	-´semos[1]
-ras	-rais	-ses	-seis
-ra	-ran	-se	-sen

---

[1] Notice the written accent mark on the first person plural form: **comiéramos, comiésemos.**

Verb	Third person plural Preterit	Stem	First person singular imperfect subjunctive -ra *form*	-se *form*
llegar	llegaron	**llega-**	llegara	llegase
beber	bebieron	**bebie-**	bebiera	bebiese
recibir	recibieron	**recibie-**	recibiera	recibiese
ser	fueron	**fue-**	fuera	fuese
saber	supieron	**supie-**	supiera	supiese
decir	dijeron	**dije-**	dijera	dijese
poner	pusieron	**pusie-**	pusiera	pusiese
servir	sirvieron	**sirvie-**	sirviera	sirviese
andar	anduvieron	**anduvie-**	anduviera	anduviese
traer	trajeron	**traje-**	trajera	trajese

○ The imperfect subjunctive is used:

1. When the verb in the main clause is in a past tense (preterit, imperfect, or past perfect) or in the conditional (or conditional perfect) and requires the subjunctive in the subordinate clause.

   —¿Qué les pidió que hicieran?   *"What did he ask you to do?"*
   —**Nos pidió** que **recicláramos**   *"He asked us to recycle the newspapers."*
   los periódicos.

   —**Me gustaría** que **limpiaras**   *"I would like you to clean the garage."*
   el garaje.
   —No tengo tiempo hoy.   *"I don't have time today."*

2. When the verb in the main clause is in the present, but the subordinate clause refers to the past.

   —Es una lástima que Carlos no   *"It's a pity that Carlos didn't come*
   viniera ayer.   *yesterday."*
   —Estuvo muy ocupado.   *"He was very busy."*

3. To express an impossible or improbable wish.

   —Oscar se va a Miami otra vez.   *"Oscar is going to Miami again."*
   —¡Ojalá **tuviera** tanto dinero   *"I wish I had as much money as he does!"*
   como él!

CD-ROM
Go to **Estructuras gramati-cales** for additional practice.

Práctica

A. El Dr. Montoya, que está dando un curso sobre los problemas ambientales, les ha dado a Ud. y a otros miembros de la clase varias instrucciones. Usando el imperfecto de subjuntivo, exprese lo que el profesor ha dicho. Siga el modelo.

MODELO: A Marisa: Busque las estadísticas sobre el uso de pulverizadores.
Le dijo a Marisa que buscara las estadísticas sobre el uso de pulverizadores.

1. A Carlos: Escriba un informe sobre el problema de la contaminación de las aguas.
2. A Uds.: Traigan artículos sobre la polución del aire.
3. A Mireya y a Saúl: Organicen una mesa redonda.
4. A ti: Hable con otros estudiantes sobre la importancia del reciclaje.
5. A mí: Vaya a la biblioteca y saque un libro sobre los problemas ambientales.
6. A todos nosotros: Estén aquí mañana a las ocho.

B. Un amigo suyo no asistió a la conferencia del profesor Carreras sobre los problemas sociales. Háblele Ud. acerca de algunas de las ideas que el profesor expresó. Siga el modelo.

MODELO: Quiero que Uds. comprendan el problema.
Dijo que quería que comprendiéramos el problema.

1. No creo que los problemas sean fáciles de resolver.
2. Es una lástima que tantos muchachos se unan a las pandillas.
3. Es necesario que identifiquemos los problemas más graves.
4. Es importante que estudiemos los problemas de las personas sin hogar.
5. Es urgente que hagamos un esfuerzo para solucionar los problemas de la delincuencia.
6. No es cierto que la educación sea nuestra primera prioridad.

C. En parejas, hablen de lo que sus padres les dijeron que hicieran o que no hicieran en cada una de las siguientes situaciones.

MODELO: la primera vez que fue a una fiesta
Me dijeron que volviera a las doce.

1. su primera cita
2. la primera vez que condujo
3. cuando empezó a tomar clases en la universidad
4. cuando viajó solo(a) por primera vez
5. cuando se mudó a su apartamento
6. cuando buscó trabajo por primera vez

D. Compare su infancia o adolescencia con las de un(a) compañero(a) usando las siguientes frases.

1. Era una lástima que...
2. Dudaba que...
3. No creía que...
4. Era necesario que...
5. Era difícil que...
6. Yo sentía que...
7. Era importante que...
8. Me alegraba mucho de que...

2 El imperfecto de subjuntivo en oraciones condicionales

Conditional sentences that contain a subordinate clause starting with **si** (*if*) require the use of the imperfect subjunctive when the verb of the main clause is in the conditional tense. In this construction, the *if*-clause may express

1. a contrary-to-fact situation (one that is not true)
2. a hypothetical situation
3. a supposition

Cond.   Imp. Sub.   Imp. Subj.   Cond.
Iría si **tuviera** dinero.   Si **tuviera** dinero, iría.

> Subordinate clause   Main clause
> **si** + imperfect subjunctive ↔ conditional

—¿Vas a irte de vacaciones este verano?

—Bueno, si **tuviera** dinero iría a Hawai, pero como no lo tengo, me quedaré en casa.

"Are you going to go on vacation this summer?"

"Well, if I had money I would go to Hawaii, but since I don't have it, I'll stay at home."

atención

When the *if*-clause expresses something that is real or likely to happen, the indicative is used after **si** in the subordinate clause, and the present or the future is used in the main clause.

Ind.   Fut.   Ind.   Pres.
Si **tengo** dinero **iré** a Hawai.   Si **tengo** dinero **voy** a Hawai.

○ The imperfect subjunctive is used after the expression **como si...** (*as if . . .*) because this expression implies a contrary-to-fact condition.

—Nora habla **como si supiera** mucho de política internacional.

—Sí, pero realmente sabe poco.

"Nora speaks as if she knew a lot about international politics."

"Yes, but in reality she knows little."

Práctica

CD-ROM
Go to **Estructuras gramaticales** for additional practice.

A. En parejas, completen los siguientes diálogos usando el imperfecto de subjuntivo o el presente de indicativo.

1. —¿Vas a ir a la conferencia esta noche?
   —Voy a ir si no ____ (tener) que trabajar.

2. —Adela se compró un abrigo que costó cinco mil dólares.
   —¡Está loca! Gasta dinero como si ____ (ser) millonaria.
   —Sí, si su padre no le ____ (dar) tanto dinero no sería tan irresponsable.

3. —¿Adónde vas a ir de vacaciones?
   —Si ____ (poder), voy a ir al sur de California.
   —Si yo ____ (ser) tú, no dejaría de visitar San Diego.
   —Si los chicos ____ (querer) ir y nosotros ____ (tener) tiempo, iremos.

4. —¿Vas a participar en la mesa redonda?
   —No creo que me inviten, pero si me _____ (invitar) aceptaría con mucho gusto.

5. —¿Vas a aceptar el trabajo en esa fábrica?
   —Lo aceptaría si el salario _____ (ser) mejor y no _____ (tener) que vivir en ese pueblo.

B. Imagínese que Ud. y un(a) compañero(a) están haciendo planes para el verano y están hablando de lo que les gustaría hacer y no pueden. Terminen las siguientes oraciones de una manera original. Comparen sus oraciones con las de otro grupo.

1. Yo iría a Cuba si...
2. Mi amigo(a) y yo vamos a tomar una clase si...
3. Tú tendrás que trabajar si...
4. Elba visitaría a sus tíos si...
5. Mi familia y yo nos mudaríamos (*would move*) si...
6. Ignacio y Miguel no tomarían clases si...
7. Yo pasaré unos días en la playa si...
8. Darío nos invitará a su cabaña si...
9. Tú podrías pasar más tiempo con tu familia si...
10. Uds. saldrán de viaje en agosto si...

3   El pretérito perfecto de subjuntivo

The present perfect subjunctive is formed with the present subjunctive of the auxiliary verb **haber** + *the past participle of the main verb*. It is used in the same way as the present perfect in English, but only in sentences that require the subjunctive in the subordinate clause.

Yo dudo que ellos **hayan fracasado.**   *I doubt that they have failed.*

		Present subjunctive of **haber**	Past participle of main verb
que	yo	**haya**	trabajado
	tú	**hayas**	aprendido
	Ud., él, ella	**haya**	recibido
	nosotros(as)	**hayamos**	abierto
	vosotros(as)	**hayáis**	escrito
	Uds., ellos, ellas	**hayan**	hecho

—Espero que **hayas sacado** la basura.   *"I hope you have taken out the garbage."*
—Sí, y la cocina ya está limpia.   *"Yes, and the kitchen is already clean."*

—¿Crees que Juan ha resuelto sus problemas?   *"Do you think Juan has solved his problems?"*
—No, no creo que los **haya resuelto** todavía.   *"No, I don't think he has solved them yet."*

CD-ROM
Go to **Estructuras gramaticales** for additional practice.

Práctica

A. En parejas, completen las siguientes conversaciones usando el pretérito perfecto de subjuntivo. Luego léanlas en voz alta.

1. —Hoy tenemos que entregar el informe, ¿verdad?
   —Sí, y espero que Alicia ya lo _____ (escribir).
   —Dudo que _____ (hacer) nada porque tiene un examen hoy.
   —David fue a buscarla a la universidad. Ojalá que ella ya _____ (terminar) el examen porque él tiene que volver a la fábrica.

2. —¿Conoces a alguien que _____ (estar) ayer en la conferencia de la Dra. Covarrubias?
   —Bueno, Pedro estuvo allí, pero no creo que _____ (entender) nada de lo que ella dijo.
   —Es una lástima que nosotros no _____ (poder) ir.

3. —Espero que Carmela _____ (ver) a la chica que organiza la mesa redonda.
   —No, no creo que _____ (ir) a verla todavía.
   —Me alegro de que nos _____ (invitar) a participar, pero temo que para el fin de semana todavía no nos _____ (dar) la información que necesitamos.

B. Ud. y un(a) compañero(a) tienen un amigo que trabaja organizando su comunidad. Reaccionen a las cosas que él cuenta, usando el pretérito perfecto de subjuntivo. Empiecen con expresiones como **me alegro de que, ojalá que, siento que, espero que, no es verdad que, es una lástima que, dudo que o no creo que.** Utilicen cada expresión por lo menos una vez. Sigan el modelo.

MODELO: Este año han organizado un buen programa de reciclaje.
          Dudo que este año hayan organizado un buen programa de reciclaje.

1. El gobierno ha resuelto el asunto de los desperdicios químicos.
2. Ellos se han reunido para hablar sobre la contaminación del ambiente.
3. La gente siempre ha llevado los residuos de productos químicos al vertedero.
4. Nosotros siempre hemos usado productos biodegradables.
5. Los problemas de la delincuencia se han agravado.
6. Hemos hablado con las persons que organizan la mesa redonda.
7. Todos juntos hemos identificado los problemas más difíciles de resolver.
8. El gobernador no se ha reunido con nosotros todavía.
9. Yo he dicho que nuestras iniciativas fracasarán.
10. Nuestros esfuerzos han ayudado a educar a la comunidad.

4 El pluscuamperfecto de subjuntivo

The pluperfect subjunctive is formed with the imperfect subjunctive of the auxiliary verb **haber** + *the past participle of the main verb*. It is used in the same way as the past perfect tense in English, but only in sentences that require the subjunctive in the subordinate clause.

Yo dudaba que él **hubiera salido.**   *I doubted that he had gone out.*

		Imperfect subjunctive of haber	Past participle of main verb
que	yo	**hubiera**	**trabajado**
	tú	**hubieras**	**aprendido**
	Ud., él, ella	**hubiera**	**recibido**
	nosotros(as)	**hubiéramos**	**abierto**
	vosotros(as)	**hubierais**	**escrito**
	Uds., ellos, ellas	**hubieran**	**hecho**

—¿Conseguiste el empleo?

—No, no me lo dieron porque necesitaban a alguien que ya **hubiera terminado** sus estudios.

—¿Había alguien allá que **hubiera estado** en San Antonio?

—No, no había nadie que **hubiera estado** allí.

"Did you get the job?"

"No, they didn't give it to me because they needed someone who had already finished his studies."

"Was there anyone there who had been in San Antonio?"

"No, there was no one there who had been there."

⊙ The pluperfect subjunctive is used instead of the imperfect subjunctive in an *if*-clause when the verb in the main clause is in the conditional perfect.

Yo habría ido	si **hubiera tenido** tiempo.
I would have gone	*if I had had time.*

⊙ The pluperfect subjunctive is used after the expression **como si...** to refer to a contrary-to-fact action in the past. This is expressed in English by the past perfect indicative (*had + past participle*).

Se quejó	**como si hubiera trabajado** todo el día.
He complained	*as if he had worked all day long.*

—¿Te fijaste qué hambre tenía Juancito?

—Sí, comió **como si** no **hubiera comido** por una semana.

—Si yo **hubiera comido** todo eso, me **habría enfermado.**

"Did you notice how hungry Juancito was?"

"Yes, he ate as if he hadn't eaten for a week."

"If I had eaten all that, I would have gotten sick."

CD-ROM
Go to **Estructuras gramaticales** for additional practice.

Práctica

A. Andrés y su familia se han mudado a California. Haga Ud. el papel de Andrés y diga cuál fue la reacción de las siguientes personas. Utilice el pluscuamperfecto de subjuntivo.

MODELO: Ana sintió / mi hermana / no quedarse en Tejas
           Ana sintió que mi hermana no se hubiera quedado en Tejas.

1. Mis amigos lamentaron / yo / mudarme tan lejos
2. El jefe de mi papá sintió / él / dejar la oficina
3. Raquel no creía / nosotros / decidir mudarnos
4. Mis abuelos se alegraron de / mis padres / volver a California
5. Olga no esperaba / nosotros / encontrar una casa grande y barata

B. Diga lo que Ud. habría hecho si las circunstancias hubieran sido diferentes. Siga el modelo.

MODELO: En la tienda había un vestido azul, pero Ud. quería uno rojo.
           Si el vestido hubiera sido rojo, yo lo habría comprado.

1. Ud. necesitaba comprar un coche, pero no le dieron el descuento que Ud. quería.
2. Le ofrecieron media botella de vino tinto, pero Ud. prefiere vino blanco.
3. Uds. querían pasar un fin de semana en la Costa del Sol, pero en los hoteles no había habitaciones libres.
4. Ud. tenía una cita a las cinco y media, pero no llegó a tiempo porque salió de su casa muy tarde.
5. Uds. querían ir a Río para la época de carnaval, pero no habían hecho reservaciones en ningún hotel.
6. Ud. quería ir a Europa, pero no tenía sus documentos en regla (*in order*).
7. El avión hacía escala en Puebla, y Ud. quería ir en un vuelo directo.
8. Le ofrecieron un puesto en el que Ud. debía trabajar bajo las órdenes de su padre, pero Ud. prefiere trabajar con otra persona.

C. Amplíe cada oración, usando la expresión **como si.** Siga el modelo.

MODELO: Eva habló de él.
           Eva habló de él como si lo hubiera conocido antes.

1. Los chicos se rieron.
2. Estábamos cansados.
3. Pasó la luz roja.
4. Me dieron las gracias.
5. Se perdieron.
6. Escribió sobre el asesinato.

D. Juan se está quejando de sus problemas. Ud. y un(a) compañero(a) le dicen que todo esto no habría pasado si él hubiera hecho ciertas cosas.

MODELO: Quedé suspendido en el examen.
           Esto no habría pasado si hubieras estudiado más.

1. Me duele el estómago y estoy muy lleno.
2. No tengo dinero.
3. Estoy muy cansado.
4. Mi casa no está limpia.
5. No tengo comida en el refrigerador.
6. Estaba enfermo y ahora me siento peor.
7. Mi coche no tiene gasolina.
8. Engordé mucho.
9. Mi novia me dejó por otro.

STUDENT WEBSITE
Do the **Compruebe cuánto sabe** self test after finishing this **Estructuras gramaticales** section.

¡CONTINUEMOS!

Una encuesta

Entreviste a sus compañeros de clase para tratar de identificar a aquellas personas que...

1. ...se preocupan por el medio ambiente.
2. ...reciclan los periódicos.
3. ...usan productos biodegradables.
4. ...pertenecen a una asociación de vecinos.
5. ...han trabajado en una fábrica.
6. ...creen que la educación debe ser la primera prioridad del gobierno.
7. ...nunca usan pulverizadores de productos químicos.
8. ...han participado en una mesa redonda.
9. ...nunca echan productos químicos por el desagüe.
10. ...siempre llevan los residuos de productos químicos a un vertedero público.
11. ...creen que debemos proteger la naturaleza.
12. ...creen que necesitamos un nuevo alcalde.

Ahora divídanse en grupos de tres o cuatro y discutan el resultado de la encuesta.

¿Comprende Ud.?

CD-ROM STUDENT WEBSITE
Go to **De escuchar...a escribir** (in **¿Comprende Ud.?**) on the CD-ROM for activities related to the conversation, and go to **Canción** on the website for activities related to the song.

1. Escuche la siguiente conversación entre Paco y Adela, que conversan sobre los problemas sociales y ambientales de sus ciudades. El objetivo de la actividad es el de escuchar una conversación a velocidad natural. No se preocupe de entenderlo todo, pues esto no se espera de Ud. Después de escuchar la conversación dos veces, Ud. oirá varias aseveraciones. En una hoja, escriba los números de uno a ocho e indique si cada aseveración es verdadera o falsa.
2. Luego escuche la canción y trate de aprenderla.

Hablemos de la vida urbana

En parejas, fíjense en las siguientes noticias y después contesten las preguntas que siguen.

Roban enmascarados medio millón de dólares a banco neoyorquino

NUEVA YORK. Enero 24 (EFE)—Tres enmascarados penetraron en una sucursal del "Chase Manhattan Bank" de Brooklyn, a través del sótano, esposaron a cinco empleados y se llevaron más de medio millón de dólares, en lo que constituye uno de los más importantes robos de banco en la historia de Nueva York.

Las autoridades investigan el atraco, perpetrado a última hora de la tarde del lunes, pero no han detenido todavía a nadie, dijo a EFE Joseph Valiquette, portavoz de la Oficina Federal de Investigación (FBI).

Guerrilleros secuestran a un alcalde

BOGOTA, Enero 8 (UPI) — El alcalde de la población de Achí, en el Departamento de Bolívar, Ricardo Alfonso Castellanos, fue secuestrado por miembros del Ejército de Liberación Nacional (ELN), informaron las autoridades.

La policía detuvo en los últimos días a 22 carteristas

JESUS DUVA, Madrid

Veintidós delincuentes, dedicados a la sustracción de carteras y bolsos de mano, fueron detenidos en los últimos tres días por funcionarios de la Brigada de Seguridad Ciudadana de la Policía Nacional. Los sospechosos fueron capturados in fraganti cuando actuaban en la zona centro de la capital.

Tres muertos en enfrentamiento entre policías y narcotraficantes

MEXICO, Enero 26 (UPI) — Policías federales se enfrentaron a tiros con un grupo de narcotraficantes en la aldea de Turicato, en el agitado estado mexicano de Michoacán, resultando tres personas muertas, según informaron las autoridades.

1. ¿Cuánto dinero se llevaron los enmascarados que asaltaron el banco de Brooklyn?
2. ¿A cuántas personas han detenido las autoridades por este asalto?
3. ¿Quién es Ricardo Alfonso Castellanos y qué le sucedió?
4. ¿A quiénes detuvo la Policía Nacional de la ciudad de Madrid?
5. ¿Con quiénes se enfrentaron los policías federales en Turicato?
6. ¿Cuál fue el resultado del encuentro?
7. ¿Qué nos demuestra la lectura de estas noticias?

¿Qué dirían ustedes?

Imagínese que Ud. y un(a) compañero(a) se encuentran en las siguientes situaciones. ¿Qué va a decir cada uno?

1. Uds. dirigen la asociación de vecinos (*neighbors*) de su barrio. Decidan cuáles van a ser sus prioridades para este año.
2. Uds. quieren darle dinero a una organización que trata de resolver los problemas sociales que afectan las grandes ciudades. Hablen de la labor que realizan varias organizaciones.
3. Uds. están en un país de habla hispana y fueron testigos (*witnesses*) de un robo a un banco. Cuéntenle a la policía lo que vieron.

¡De ustedes depende!

Uds. le están dando una clase de defensa personal a un grupo de estudiantes latinoamericanos. Háblenles sobre lo siguiente y díganles lo que deben o no deben hacer en cada caso.

1. el peligro (*danger*) de caminar solos (solas) por la noche
2. qué hacer si alguien trata de robarles la cartera
3. las ventajas de tomar una clase de karate o yudo
4. las cosas que tienen que tener en cuenta cuando tienen una cita con alguien que no conocen muy bien
5. las precauciones que deben tomar cuando están en el coche

¡Debate!

La clase se dividirá en dos grupos para discutir la pena de muerte. El primer grupo tratará de demostrar que es una medida necesaria y justa para combatir el crimen y la violencia. El segundo grupo dará una serie de razones para no tenerla, señalando que el gobierno no tiene derecho a quitarle la vida a nadie.

Lecturas periodísticas

Saber leer: Su auto-adiestramiento° como lector

self-training

CD-ROM
Go to **Lecturas periodísticas** for additional prereading and vocabulary activities.

En las **Lecciones 1** a **6**, presentamos individualmente algunas estrategias, pero recuerde que lo mejor es poner en práctica tantas como sus conocimientos sobre el tema o sus propósitos al leer lo requieran. La lectura nunca debe ser pasiva, de modo que debe incorporar las diversas estrategias que aprenda o que ya conozca.

La siguiente lectura periodística se titula "En el supermercado". ¿Qué estrategias le conviene utilizar en esta ocasión? Aquí tiene algunas sugerencias:

1. Siempre es esencial empezar teniendo claros sus propósitos al leer.
2. Leer las preguntas de comprensión lo(la) ayuda (a) a saber el tipo de información que deberá buscar al leer y (b) a crear contextos que lo(la) ayuden a leer con atención y de manera activa.
3. Tener presente el tema de la **Lección 8** y los demás conocimientos que Ud. tenga sobre el tema lo(la) podría ayudar a hacerse preguntas (*hypothesize*) sobre lo que va a tratar un artículo que se titula "En el supermercado".
4. En este punto, echarle una mirada rápida al primer párrafo (en cursiva) y leer la primera oración de los demás párrafos, lo(la) ayuda a crear contextos y a comprobar (¡o mejorar!) las hipótesis que Ud. se haya hecho sobre lo que se discute en la lectura periodística.

Para leer y comprender

Al leer detalladamente el artículo, busque las respuestas a las siguientes preguntas.

1. ¿Qué tipo de productos ha proliferado en los supermercados?
2. ¿Podemos confiar en los alegatos que presentan algunas empresas?
3. ¿Debemos preferir los aerosoles que anuncian que no tienen CFC? ¿Por qué?
4. ¿Por qué dice el artículo que la palabra "biodegradable" se presta a confusión?
5. ¿Es mejor comprar productos reciclables o productos reciclados? ¿Por qué?
6. ¿Qué tipos de frutas y vegetales debemos comprar?
7. ¿Cómo podemos disminuir el consumo de las bolsas de plástico?

En el supermercado

Una verdadera revolución se ha iniciado en un sitio que tú conoces muy bien: el supermercado, donde desde hace algún tiempo comienzan a proliferar los llamados productos "verdes" o "biodegradables".

Empresas de prestigio y otras menos conocidas se preocupan por el ambientalismo°, y ésa es una actitud encomiable° pero con la que hay que estar alertas porque el alegato° se presta para ser malinterpretado. Algunas empresas utilizan el engaño°, y otras simplemente presentan alegatos totalmente irrelevantes.

Por ejemplo, nótese el caso de los aerosoles. Desde 1978, en pro de la protección de la capa de ozono que protege contra los rayos ultravioletas, el gobierno de Estados Unidos prohibió su contenido de clorofluorocarbono o CFC. A esta fecha, son muchísimos los productos que anuncian en su etiqueta° que están libres de CFC, como si existieran en el mercado otros con el peligroso químico.

La famosa palabra "biodegradable" también se presta a confusión. La vemos en el supermercado en cientos de productos cuya biodegradabilidad va desde meses hasta miles de millones de años.

"Biodegradable" se convierte así en una palabra mágica, pero que en muchas instancias realmente no tiene sentido práctico si se desea preservar el planeta. ¡Hasta el plutonio es biodegradable si se tiene en cuenta que podría desaparecer en unos pocos millones de años!

"Reciclable" es otro concepto que a los aficionados al ambientalismo les fascina, pero el hecho° de que un producto sea reciclable no significa que será reciclado ni que exista la tecnología para que efectivamente pueda volver a utilizarse.

Averigua° si realmente hay mercado para el reciclaje de determinados productos en tu área de residencia. Comprar un producto reciclable por el hecho de que lo dice su etiqueta no ayuda en nada pero adquirir un artículo confeccionado° con material reciclado es una contribución porque estimula a la empresa que lo produjo.

A veces, incluso° es mejor comprar productos sin empaque o fórmulas concentradas, como en el caso de los detergentes. Compra frutas y vegetales orgánicos y, siempre que sea posible, lleva tu propia bolsa de tela° al supermercado para evitar el consumo de las de plástico o papel.

Comprar en favor del ambiente es una actividad que requiere usar la lógica y estar realmente bien informado.

Adaptado de la revista *Imagen* (Puerto Rico)

> *Algunas empresas utilizan el engaño°, y otras simplemente presentan alegatos totalmente irrelevantes.*

Estantes de un supermercado en Caracas, Venezuela.

---

environmentalism / praiseworthy / claim
deceit

label

fact
Find out
made
even
cloth

Desde su mundo

1. ¿Qué productos biodegradables o reciclables compra Ud. en el supermercado?
2. Mencione tres medidas (*measures*) que Ud. considera importantes para proteger el medio ambiente.

Piense y escriba   Los buenos escritores

STUDENT WEBSITE

CD-ROM

Go to **...y escribamos** (in **Hablemos de su país**) on the student website and **De escuchar... a escribir** (in **¿Comprende Ud.?**) on the CD-ROM for additional writing practice.

Los buenos escritores tratan de mantener el mayor contacto posible con la lengua escrita y hablada. Es importante cultivar dos destrezas indispensables para mejorar la redacción en español: leer y escuchar activamente. Mediante estas destrezas:

1. se refuerza el vocabulario y las maneras de expresarse que Ud. ya conoce.
2. se adquiere nuevo vocabulario y se aprenden nuevas maneras de expresarse en español.

Piense en algunas medidas concretas que lo (la) van a ayudar a mejorar su redacción en español.

Pepe Vega y su mundo

No tengo coche porque no quiero contribuir a la contaminación del aire.

Teleinforme

La limpieza, la inmigración y la educación son tres desafíos (challenges) *importantes de la vida urbana. A menudo se pueden encontrar soluciones en la solidaridad y en los esfuerzos de la gente afectada; a veces, la solución es simplemente cuestión de un cambio de perspectiva.*

Preparación

Términos.   A continuación aparecen algunos términos que designan diversas identidades americanas. ¿Los reconoce Ud.? Defina los términos que Ud. conoce. Algunos términos tienen significados parecidos. Trate de explicar las diferencias.

1. centroamericano(a)
2. chicano(a)
3. costarricense
4. cubano(a)
5. estadounidense
6. gringo(a)
7. guatemalteco(a)
8. hispano(a)
9. hispanoamericano(a)
10. hondureño(a)
11. latino(a)
12. latinoamericano(a)
13. mexicano(a)
14. mexicoamericano(a)
15. puertorriqueño(a)
16. sudamericano(a)
17. tico(a)
18. cubanoamericano(a)

Comprensión

CD-ROM
You will also find
this clip under
Video.

Grafitis en San José   37:59–41:19

En esta lección vamos a ver los grafitis de San José en un reportaje producido por SINART/Canal 13 de Costa Rica. Mientras exploran estos escritos murales, pregúntense: ¿Son los grafitis una forma de contaminación o una muestra (*example*) artística de la cultura urbana?

A. Unos grafitis incompletos.   Complete los siguientes grafitis según aparecen en el video.

1. San José perdió el _____ de la vida.
2. ...y sean tus espinas defensa contra _____ artificial...
3. Mi alma cara de _____.
4. ...rellenarles de _____ que verticalicen el horizonte de las mariposas.
5. En el clavo de la pared cuelgan mis _____.
6. San José termina en la tragedia del _____.
7. En la espuma de los trastos _____ cantó mi destino de Navegante.
8. Santa Claus y Batman son _____.
9. Lea _____ 96.
10. Hay _____ perdidas en las copas de los dedos.
11. En las sombras los _____; en la luz los _____.

B. ¿Quién dice qué?   Encuentre en la columna B la opinión expresada por la persona de la columna A.

A

1. la mujer de las gafas
2. el hombre joven de la camisa azul/verde
3. el hombre del bigote y las gafas de sol
4. la mujer de las gafas de sol
5. el hombre del coche
6. el hombre joven de la camisa blanca

B

a. Dicen cosas muy raras... la verdad.
b. Hay gente que lo pinta por pintarlo nada más.
c. Me parece que no está bien hecho...
d. Que está bien o está mal. Mal cuando se expresa algo que es indebido, tal vez mal educado; bien cuando expresa algo bien y en sí también son culturales, entonces es parte también de nosotros.
e. Que les pinten las casas a los otros pero a mí me gustan mucho.
f. [Es algo] como de transmitir esos mensajes en los periódicos, me entiendes, [todo] en la prensa que la gente lo vea pero como no pueden entonces lo hacen en las paredes.

CD-ROM
Go to **Video** for further previewing, vocabulary, and structure practice on this clip.

Conversaciones con estudiantes de la San Diego State University, parte 2   41:21–44:19

Estas conversaciones fueron tomadas del programa *Somos*. Nos presentan las perspectivas de algunos estudiantes latinos y chicanos de la San Diego State University. Aquí conoceremos a cinco jóvenes que hablan de sus vidas entre dos culturas.

C. ¿Qué aprendió Ud.?   Después de oír cada conversación, conteste las preguntas correspondientes que aparecen a continuación.

1. **Guadalupe habla de los términos "latino" y "chicano".** Para ella, ¿cuál es la diferencia entre los dos términos?
2. **Rubén habla de su identidad.** ¿Cómo se considera él? ¿Dónde nació Rubén? ¿Y su madre? ¿Y sus abuelos?
3. **Javier habla de su familia.** ¿Cuántos hijos hay en la familia de Javier? ¿Qué edades tienen? ¿Dónde nacieron todos?
4. **Ruth habla de los problemas raciales que ha tenido en la universidad.** ¿Con quiénes se sentó un día en el auditorio? ¿Qué hicieron estas personas cuando Ruth se sentó? ¿Cómo se sintió Ruth?
5. **Carmen habla de MEChA y Aztlán.** ¿Qué significa MEChA? ¿Qué es Aztlán?

Hazte maestro   44:21–44:54

Este *spot* publicitario fue creado por la Asociación de Agencias Publicitarias Hispanas para Futuramente, una campaña contra la crisis educativa de los hispanos en EE.UU. El anuncio propone una solución para cambiar las vidas de los alumnos hispanos en las escuelas primarias de este país.

D. Observaciones.   Escuche y mire bien el anuncio. Luego, escriba lo que oye o ve, según habla la maestra anglófona (*English-speaking*) o el maestro hispano.

	a. Maestra anglófona	b. Maestro hispano
1. pronunciación del nombre del niño hispano		
2. reacción del alumno		
3. expresión de aprobación		
4. pronunciación del nombre de la niña hispana		
5. reacción de la alumna		

Ampliación

¡Debate!   Formen equipos para discutir los siguientes temas. Discutan los argumentos a favor y los argumentos en contra. Usen ejemplos tomados de su propia experiencia o de la vida de alguien que Uds. conocen.

1. la inmigración en los EE.UU.
2. la educación bilingüe
3. los grafitis

¿Están listos para el examen?

Lecciones 7–8

Tome este examen para ver cuánto ha aprendido. Las respuestas correctas aparecen en el **Apéndice C**.

Lección 7

A El futuro

Complete las siguientes oraciones con el futuro de los verbos que aparecen entre paréntesis.

1. Yo sé que ella me _____ (decir) que nosotros _____ (tener) que trabajar más.
2. Andrea _____ (salir) para Panamá la semana próxima.
3. Mañana _____ (haber) una fiesta en mi casa, pero yo no _____ (poder) invitar a Juan.
4. Los muchachos _____ (poner) todo su dinero en el banco.
5. Tú y yo no _____ (caber) en el coche de Ana, de modo que _____ (ir) en autobús.
6. Como Uds. no _____ (querer) venir mañana, yo _____ (hacer) todo el trabajo solo.

B El futuro para expresar probabilidad o conjetura

Conteste las siguientes preguntas usando el futuro de probabilidad y las palabras entre paréntesis.

1. ¿Dónde está Ramiro? (la fonda)
2. ¿A qué hora se van a levantar los chicos? (a las nueve)
3. ¿Qué hora es? (las once)
4. ¿Cuánto cuesta ese coche? (15,000 dólares)
5. ¿Cuándo viene Teresa? (el domingo)

C El condicional

Complete el párrafo con el condicional de los verbos que aparecen entre paréntesis.

¿Qué _____ (hacer) nosotros sin nuestros padres, Rosa? Tú no _____ (tener) dinero para estudiar y yo no _____ (poder) comprar ropa. Los chicos _____ (pasar) hambre y Paco _____ (vivir) en la calle. ¡ _____ (ser) un desastre!

D El condicional para expresar probabilidad o conjetura

Conteste las siguientes preguntas usando el condicional y las palabras entre paréntesis.

1. ¿Qué hora era cuando Carlos llegó? (las diez)
2. ¿Dónde estaba él? (en el cine)
3. ¿Con quién estaba? (con Marisa)
4. ¿Adónde fueron antes de venir? (a la cafetería)

E El futuro perfecto y el condicional perfecto

Complete las siguientes oraciones con el equivalente español de las palabras entre paréntesis.

1. Para el verano, Juan y yo _____ las clases. (*will have finished*)
2. Tere, tú _____ para el año 2006, ¿no? (*will have graduated*)
3. Para el verano, Andrés ya _____ empleo. (*will have found*)
4. Yo _____ tanto dinero por ese coche. (*wouldn't have paid*)
5. Ellas _____ la verdad, señora. (*wouldn't have told you*)

F Género de los nombres: casos especiales

Dé las palabras que corresponden a las siguientes definiciones.

1. parte de la cabeza
2. espalda de un animal
3. grupo musical
4. manera
5. operación aritmética
6. opuesto de la izquierda
7. persona que acompaña a un grupo
8. elevación del terreno
9. método
10. signo de puntuación

G ¿Recuerda el vocabulario?

Complete las siguientes oraciones con palabras y expresiones de la **Lección 7**.

1. Julio es muy simpático. Siempre está contando _____.
2. Hagamos un _____. ¡Salud!
3. Necesito una _____ para tomar vino.
4. No me gusta la miel de _____.
5. Nunca están de acuerdo. Siempre están _____.
6. No tengo _____ de ir contigo al cine hoy.
7. Me gusta el bistec bien _____, y no _____ medio.
8. Budweiser es una _____ muy famosa.
9. Siempre servimos _____ blanco con el pescado.
10. De haberlo _____, no habría venido.

H Cultura

Circule la palabra que mejor complete cada oración.

1. Panamá es un poco más (grande, pequeño) que Carolina del Sur.
2. Al norte de Panamá está (Nicaragua, Costa Rica).
3. A Nicaragua se la conoce como la "Tierra de los (ríos, lagos)".
4. La mayor atracción turística de Honduras es (Copán, Tikal).
5. Por su clima, Guatemala se conoce como "El país de (los volcanes, la eterna primavera)".

Lección 8

A El imperfecto de subjuntivo

Cambie del discurso directo al discurso indirecto. Siga el modelo.

MODELO: El profesor me dijo: "Identifica los problemas".
El profesor me dijo que identificara los problemas.

1. Él les advirtió: "Usen productos biodegradables".
2. Luis nos dijo: "Lean las noticias sobre la contaminación".
3. Ellos nos rogaron: "No se unan a las pandillas".
4. Él te aconsejó: "Coopera con los demás".
5. Ellos me pidieron: "Saca la basura".
6. La profesora le aconsejó: "Haga un esfuerzo por mejorar".

B El imperfecto de subjuntivo en oraciones condicionales

Complete las siguientes oraciones, usando los verbos que aparecen entre paréntesis.

1. Si _____ (tratar) de resolver todos esos problemas, fracasarían.
2. Habla como si nuestra ciudad no _____ (tener) problemas sociales.
3. Si ellos nos lo _____ (pedir), los ayudaríamos.
4. Esas organizaciones trabajan como si _____ (estar) seguras del éxito.
5. Uds. ayudarían mucho si _____ (reciclar) los periódicos.
6. ¡Ojalá ese presidente _____ (poder) resolver todos los problemas ambientales!

C Los tiempos compuestos del subjuntivo

Complete las siguientes oraciones con el presente perfecto o el pluscuamperfecto de subjuntivo.

1. Dudo que ellos _____ (hacer) un esfuerzo.
2. Yo habría aceptado el trabajo si Uds. me lo _____ (dar).
3. Espero que tú ya le _____ (ofrecer) el puesto.
4. Habla de la ley como si él la _____ (hacer).
5. Me alegro de que el programa no _____ (empezar) todavía.
6. Dudaban que el gobierno _____ (dar) la noticia.
7. Si ellos me lo _____ (permitir) yo lo habría hecho.
8. No creo que Uds. _____ (resolverlo) todo.
9. Siento que nosotros no _____ (ir) a la fábrica.
10. No es verdad que los alcaldes _____ (ponerse) de acuerdo.

D ¿Recuerda el vocabulario?

Encuentre en la columna B las respuestas a las preguntas de la columna A.

A

1. ¿Adónde debemos llevar los residuos de productos químicos?
2. ¿Con qué debemos sustituir los productos químicos?
3. ¿Dónde echa mucha gente los productos químicos?
4. ¿Qué debemos reciclar?
5. ¿Qué problemas parecen agravarse cada día?
6. ¿Qué debemos hacer para resolver estos problemas?
7. ¿Cuáles son algunos de los problemas sociales?
8. ¿Cómo llamamos a los que no tienen dónde vivir?
9. ¿Qué deben usar las fábricas?
10. ¿A quién debemos educar para poder resolver los problemas de las ciudades?

B

a. Los periódicos y el vidrio.
b. Los robos y los asesinatos.
c. Cooperar todos.
d. Al pueblo.
e. Con productos biodegradables.
f. Las personas sin hogar.
g. En los desagües.
h. Combustibles más limpios.
i. Al vertedero (municipal).
j. Los problemas sociales.

E Cultura

Circule la palabra que mejor complete cada oración.

1. En los Estados Unidos viven más de (quince, treinta) millones de hispanos.
2. El grupo minoritario más numeroso en California es el de los (cubanoamericanos, mexicoamericanos).
3. La capital de Puerto Rico es (San Juan, San José).
4. Los puertorriqueños (son, no son) ciudadanos estadounidenses.
5. Gracias a los (mexicanos, cubanos), Miami es hoy la ciudad más rica del mundo hispanohablante.

El mundo del espectáculo

El famoso cantante puertorriqueño Ricky Martin.

El mundo del espectáculo

CD-ROM   STUDENT AUDIO

For preparation, do the **Ante todo** activities found on the CD-ROM.

Desfile de estrellas

En una entrevista con Jorge Salgado, la actriz argentina Paola Bianco habló de su papel en la telenovela *La mentira*, que se estrenará a mediados de julio en el canal 5. Habló también del premio que ganó en el Festival de Cine el año pasado. Agregó que pensaba volver a trabajar bajo la dirección del famoso director y productor uruguayo Rafael Burgos en su próxima película, que va a ser una comedia musical. La encantadora actriz confesó que sueña con actuar algún día con actores latinos como Andy García y Antonio Banderas. En su vida personal, Paola no pudo negar que estaba muy enamorada de Mario Juncal y que pronto se casaría con él.

¡El boom de la salsa!

Hasta hace unos doce años, la música latina o la música de salsa sólo se escuchaba esporádicamente en algunas discotecas. Hoy los salseros como Celia Cruz, la India, Marc Anthony y muchos otros, tienen innumerables aficionados.

La salsa ha invadido Europa y Asia, pero Los Ángeles y Nueva York siguen siendo las grandes fábricas de la música y el baile latinos.

Últimamente han surgido en muchas ciudades del mundo varias escuelas de baile, donde se aprenden los pasos básicos de la salsa, el mambo, el merengue o la rumba cubana. La gente pasa horas en las pistas de baile para mejorar su estilo. ¡Bailar ritmos latinos se ha puesto de moda!

En cuanto al pop, Christina Aguilera es la nueva reina, nombrada por los críticos como "La voz del siglo". Sus representantes anunciaron que acababa de lanzar un nuevo disco grabado en español.

Dígame

En parejas, contesten las siguientes preguntas basadas en los artículos.

1. ¿Quién es Paola Bianco y cuál es su nacionalidad?
2. ¿Qué es *La mentira* y cuándo se va a estrenar? ¿En qué canal?
3. ¿Salió premiada alguna de las películas de Paola Bianco?
4. ¿Con qué director y productor trabajó Paola antes? ¿Piensa volver a trabajar con él?
5. La película que ella piensa filmar, ¿va a ser un drama?
6. ¿A qué actores latinos admira Paola?
7. ¿De quién está enamorada y cuándo piensa casarse con él?
8. ¿Qué pasaba hace unos doce años con la música latina?
9. ¿Quiénes son algunos salseros famosos? ¿Han tenido mucho éxito?
10. ¿Hasta qué continentes ha llegado la salsa?
11. ¿Qué se enseña hoy en día en algunas escuelas de baile? ¿Qué se ha puesto de moda en la actualidad?
12. ¿Quién es Christina Aguilera? ¿Qué anunciaron sus representantes?

Perspectivas socioculturales

INSTRUCTOR WEBSITE
Your instructor may assign the preconversational support activities found in **Perspectivas socioculturales.**

En todo el mundo, los Estados Unidos ejercen una gran influencia en los campos del espectáculo y del entretenimiento. Al mismo tiempo, la música latina también va dejando notar su influencia en la América del Norte, Europa y Asia. Haga lo siguiente:

a. Lea los temas de conversación que aparecen a continuación y escoja uno de ellos.
b. Durante unos cinco minutos, cambie opiniones (o converse) con dos compañeros sobre el tema seleccionado.
c. Participe con el resto de la clase en la discusión del tema cuando su profesor(a) se lo indique.

Temas de conversación

1. **Los Estados Unidos y el mundo.** ¿Cómo se nota la influencia estadounidense en otras regiones del mundo en los campos del espectáculo y del entretenimiento?
2. **El mundo del entretenimiento latino.** ¿Cómo se nota la influencia de la música y del entretenimiento latinos en su país?

Vocabulario

Nombres

la actriz (el actor)   actress (actor)
el desfile   parade
la entrevista   interview
el espectáculo, el show   show
la estrella   star
la mentira   lie
el paso   step
la pista de baile   dance floor
el premio   award
el (la) productor(a)   producer
la reina   queen
el siglo   century
el (la) televidente   TV viewer
la telenovela   soap opera
la voz   voice

Verbos

actuar   to act, to perform
agregar, añadir   to add
escuchar   to listen (to)

estrenar   to show for the first time
grabar   to record, to tape
lanzar   to release
nombrar   to name
soñar (o → ue)   to dream
surgir   to appear

Adjetivos

enamorado(a)   in love
encantador(a)   charming

Otras palabras y expresiones

a mediados de   around the middle of
acabar de (+ *inf.*)   to have just (done something)
bajo   under
como   like
en cuanto a   as for
ponerse de moda   to become fashionable
volver a (+ *inf.*)   to do something again (over)

Ampliación

Palabras relacionadas con los medios de comunicación

cámara lenta   slow motion
el documental   documentary
el (la) editor(a)   editor
la editorial   publishing company
el (la) locutor(a)   announcer, speaker, commentator

las noticias   news
la pantalla   screen
el (la) protagonista   protagonist
la publicidad   publicity
el reportaje   report, interview
el telediario, las telenoticias   TV news

CD-ROM
Go to **Vocabulario** for additional vocabulary practice.

Hablando de todo un poco

Preparación   **Complete lo siguiente, usando el vocabulario de la Lección 9.**

1. Mireya León tiene el papel principal en la telenovela *La promesa*. Ella es la _____ de la obra y espera recibir un _____ por su actuación.
2. En la _____ de anoche con el locutor Jorge Rivas, la _____ Estela Vargas habló del productor de su última película. Ella dijo que era una persona _____ y añadió que estaba muy _____ de él y que pensaban casarse muy pronto.
3. La famosa cantante Christina Aguilera _____ con llegar a ser la nueva _____ de los espectáculos de música latina.
4. El actor Fernando Soler dice que actuar _____ la dirección de Bruno Vázquez es un gran honor. Él piensa que su última película se va a _____ en septiembre en numerosos cines.
5. El domingo pasado vi, en un documental, cómo se enseñan en las _____ de baile los _____ básicos de algunos de los ritmos latinos que hoy se han _____ de moda en nuestro país. Muchos de los bailes se mostraron a _____ lenta.
6. El cantante español Enrique Iglesias acaba de _____ un nuevo disco. Muchos críticos consideran la _____ de Iglesias como una de las mejores del _____ XXI y opinan que _____ cantar a Iglesias es siempre un placer.
7. A _____ de esta semana vimos en las _____ de nuestros televisores un _____ de estrellas con muchos artistas famosos. El programa se va a _____ a presentar próximamente.
8. Siempre veo el _____ de las ocho de la noche porque me interesan mucho las noticias. Cuando no puedo ver el programa lo _____ para verlo después.
9. Acaba de _____ un grupo de cantantes de salsa que son considerados por los críticos _____ los mejores en su género.
10. El reportaje de Mario Lizaso en _____ al último festival de cine es muy interesante. En él, Lizaso _____ a los artistas que considera los peores del año.
11. Anoche leí un editorial sobre la importancia de la _____ en el aumento de la venta de discos de música latina.

En grupos de dos o tres, hagan lo siguiente.

A. **Gustos y preferencias.**   Conversen sobre los tipos de programa de televisión que les gustan y los que no les gustan y digan por qué.

B. **La música.**   Hablen sobre los tipos de música que se han puesto de moda últimamente y si a ustedes les gusta o no escucharla.

C. **Los reyes.**   Digan a quiénes consideran ustedes el rey y la reina del *pop* y los últimos discos que estas personas han lanzado.

D. **Entrevista.** En grupos de tres, prepárense para hacer el papel de dos entrevistadores que desean preguntarle a un actor o a una actriz de cine o de televisión sobre sus próximos proyectos, incluyendo el papel que va a tener, quién va a dirigirlo(a), el tipo de película o telenovela, la fecha del estreno, etc. Ensayen y representen la entrevista ante la clase.

Palabras problemáticas

A. **A mediados de, mediano** y **medio**

- **A mediados de** se usa como equivalente de *around the middle of* (*a month, a year, etc.*).

  La encantadora actriz se casará **a mediados de** año.

- **Mediano(a)** equivale a *average, middle*.

  El protagonista es un hombre rubio, no muy guapo, de estatura **mediana**.

- **Medio** equivale a (*the*) *middle* o *half*.

  Las chicas estaban en el **medio** de la pista de baile.

  El niño acaba de comerse **medio** pastel.

B. **Debajo de, bajo** y **abajo** como equivalentes de *below*

- **Debajo de** equivale a *below* como sinónimo de *underneath*.

  Ponen los bolsos **debajo del** asiento.

- **Bajo** es el equivalente de *under* o *below* y se usa tanto en sentido literal como figurado.

  La temperatura está a veinte grados **bajo** cero.

  Elena está en la guía telefónica **bajo** "Fernández".

  Trabajan **bajo** la supervisión de la Dra. Ortega.

- **Abajo** es el opuesto de **arriba** (*above*). Equivale a *downstairs* cuando nos referimos a un edificio o a una casa.

  Mi hermano me está esperando **abajo**.

Práctica

Complete los siguientes diálogos, y luego léalos con un(a) compañero(a).

1. —¿Cuándo llega el editor?
   —_____ de septiembre.

2. —¿La actriz es muy alta?
   —No, es de estatura _____.

3. —¿Has trabajado alguna vez _____ la dirección de Rafael Burgos?
   —No, nunca.

4. —¿El director nos espera _____?
   —No, arriba.

5. —¿Dónde están jugando los chicos?
   —En el _____ de la calle.

6. —¿Dónde pusiste el bolso de mamá?
   —_____ del asiento.

Your instructor may carry out the **¡Ahora escuche!** listening activity found in the **Answers to Text Exercises.**

¡Ahora escuche!

Se leerá dos veces una breve narración sobre el cumpleaños de Marisol. Se harán asseveraciones sobre la narración. En una hoja escriba los números de uno a doce e indique si cada aseveración es verdadera (V) o falsa (F).

El mundo hispánico

De Uruguay a la tierra del tango

Paola Bianco

STUDENT WEBSITE
Go to **El mundo hispánico** for prereading and vocabulary activities.

Acabo de regresar de Uruguay, donde asistí a una reunión de artistas. En este país se le da una gran importancia a todas las manifestaciones del arte y de la cultura. Yo admiro mucho a los escritores uruguayos, y algún día me gustaría hacer una película basada en uno de los cuentos del famoso escritor Horacio Quiroga.

No es la primera vez que visito este pequeño país, pero siempre encuentro allí algo interesante. Montevideo, la capital, es el centro administrativo, económico y cultural del país. Allí vive casi la mitad de su población, que es de unos tres millones de habitantes.

Además de estar en Montevideo pasé una semana en el Balneario de Punta del Este, uno de los más famosos centros turísticos de América Latina.

Me gusta mucho viajar y he visto ciudades grandes y hermosas, pero donde-quiera que esté°, extraño a mi tierra. Eso sí, Argentina es tan grande que ni los pro-pios argentinos la hemos recorrido totalmente. El país ocupa el octavo lugar en el mundo por su extensión territorial. Aquí encontrarán grandes ríos, extensas llanuras, lagos y glaciares, así como enormes ciudades y pueblos pequeños. Es, en su mayor parte, una llanura (la Pampa) que se extiende desde el Océano Atlántico hasta Los Andes, donde está el Aconcagua, el pico más alto del mundo occidental.

A orillas° del Río de la Plata está situada la hermosa ciudad de Buenos Aires. Como buena porteña —como nos llaman a los que nacimos en Buenos Aires— yo pienso que mi ciudad es realmente "el París de Sudamérica". La influencia francesa se ve en la arquitectura, en sus amplios bulevares y parques, en la moda y en el sis-tema de educación.

Otras influencias europeas que se notan son la española, la inglesa, y principal-mente la italiana, tanto en la comida como en el idioma hablado.

Como dice un tango muy famoso, Buenos Aires es "la reina del Plata".

dondequiera...
wherever I may be

shores

Sobre Uruguay y Argentina

En parejas, túrnense para contestar las siguientes preguntas.

1. ¿De dónde acaba de regresar Paola? ¿Por qué fue allí?
2. ¿Quién es Horacio Quiroga? ¿Qué le gustaría hacer a Paola algún día?
3. ¿Qué dice Paola de Montevideo? ¿Qué otros lugares visitó en Uruguay?
4. ¿Con qué limita Argentina al norte, al sur, al este y al oeste?
5. ¿Qué pasa cuando Paola viaja por otros países?
6. ¿Por qué no conoce Paola todo su país? ¿Qué lugar ocupa Argentina por su extensión?
7. ¿Qué es la Pampa? ¿De dónde a dónde se extiende?
8. ¿Qué es el Aconcagua?
9. ¿Dónde está situada la ciudad de Buenos Aires? ¿Quiénes son los porteños?
10. ¿En qué se ve la influencia francesa? ¿Qué otras influencias europeas se notan allí?

Hablemos de su país

INSTRUCTOR WEBSITE
STUDENT WEBSITE
Your instructor may assign the pre-conversational activities in **Hablemos...** (under **Hablemos de su país**). Go to **Hablemos de su país** (under **...y escribamos**) for post-conversational web search and writing activities.

Reúnase con otro(a) compañero(a) y conteste lo siguiente: ¿Qué manifestaciones culturales tienen una gran importancia en la región donde vive?

Luego cada pareja compartirá las respuestas con toda la clase. Discutan todas las manifestaciones culturales que las diversas parejas encontraron.

Taller de Teatro Físico POLIMNIA Presenta :
1er Festival Internacional de Mimo y Teatro Físico en el Caribe
22 al 27 de mayo 2001
Teatro Raúl Juliá
Museo de Arte de Puerto Rico

Una tarjeta postal

Ésta es una tarjeta postal que Rafael Burgos le mandó a Paola desde Montevideo.

Querida Paola:

Ayer volví de Punta del Este. El Festival de Cine estuvo magnífico. Aproveché el tiempo para ir a la playa a tomar el sol.

Ahora estoy de vuelta en Montevideo. Estuve caminando por la avenida 18 de Julio y después fui a la Plaza de la Independencia, que es una plaza enorme en el corazón de la ciudad. Aquí la vida es mucho más tranquila que en Buenos Aires, de modo que estoy descansando.

Un abrazo,

Rafael

Después de leer la tarjeta

1. ¿Dónde estuvo Rafael hasta ayer?
2. ¿Le gustó el Festival de Cine?
3. ¿Qué más hizo en Punta del Este?
4. ¿Cuáles son dos de los lugares que visitó en Montevideo?
5. ¿Cómo es la vida en Montevideo?

Estructuras gramaticales

STUDENT WEBSITE
Do the **¿Cuánto recuerda?** pretest to check what you already know on the topics covered in this **Estructuras gramaticales** section.

1 El subjuntivo: resumen general

A Resumen de los usos del subjuntivo en las cláusulas subordinadas

Use the SUBJUNCTIVE . . .
- After verbs of volition, when there is change of subject:

  Yo quiero que él lo **grabe.**

- After verbs of emotion, when there is a change of subject:

  Me alegro de que tú **estés** aquí.

- After impersonal expressions, when there is a subject:

  Es necesario que él **estudie.**

Use the SUBJUNCTIVE . . .
- To express doubt and denial:
  Dudo que **pueda** actuar.

  Niego que él **esté** aquí.

- To refer to something indefinite or nonexistent:

  Busco una casa que **sea** cómoda.
  No hay nadie que lo **sepa.**

- With certain conjunctions when referring to a future action:

  Cenarán cuando él **llegue.**

- In an *if*-clause, to refer to something contrary-to-fact, impossible, or very improbable:

  Si **pudiera,** iría.
  Si el presidente me **invitara** a la Casa Blanca, yo aceptaría.

Use the INFINITIVE . . .
- After verbs of volition, when there is no change of subject:

  Yo quiero **grabar**lo.

- After verbs of emotion, when there is no change of subject:

  Me alegro de **estar** aquí.

- After impersonal expressions, when speaking in general:

  Es necesario **estudiar.**

Use the INDICATIVE . . .
- When there is no doubt or denial:
  No dudo que **puede** actuar.

  No niego que él **está** aquí.

- To refer to something specific:

  Tengo una casa que **es** cómoda.
  Hay alguien que lo **sabe.**

- With certain conjunctions when the action has been completed or is habitual:

  Cenaron cuando él **llegó.**
  Siempre cenan cuando él **llega.**

- In an *if*-clause, when not referring to anything that is contrary-to-fact, impossible, or very improbable:

  Si **puedo,** iré.
  Si Juan me **invita** a su casa, aceptaré.

CD-ROM
Go to **Estructuras gramaticales** for additional practice.

Práctica

A. Complete el siguiente diálogo, usando los verbos entre paréntesis en el infinitivo, el indicativo o el subjuntivo, según corresponda. Después, represéntelo con un(a) compañero(a).

EVA —Hola, Mario. Me alegro de _____ (verte). Siento que tú no _____ (poder) venir a la fiesta anoche.

MARIO —Si _____ (tener) tiempo, habría venido, pero tuve que trabajar. Le dije a Paco que te _____ (llamar).

EVA —No creo que _____ (tener) que trabajar hasta las nueve. Lo que pasa es que cuando yo _____ (invitarte) a mis fiestas nunca vienes.

MARIO —Cuando _____ (dar) otra fiesta, vendré. Oye, ¿conoces a alguien que _____ (hablar) francés? Mi hermano necesita una traductora.

EVA —Sí, conozco a una chica que lo _____ (hablar) muy bien. ¿Quieres que la _____ (llamar)?

MARIO —Sí, por favor. Me gustaría que la _____ (llamar).

EVA —Pues la llamaré en cuanto _____ (poder), y le diré que _____ (ir) a ver a tu hermano.

MARIO —Sí, porque él quiere _____ (entrevistar) a la persona tan pronto como _____ (ser) posible, de manera que _____ (empezar) a trabajar a principios de mes.

EVA —Entonces es importante que la _____ (llamar) hoy mismo.

B. Complete las siguientes oraciones para expresar sus deseos, esperanzas (*hopes*), planes y lo que hace generalmente. Compare sus respuestas con las de un(a) compañero(a).

1. Yo espero que mi profesor(a)...
2. Quiero que mis padres...
3. Dudo que el próximo año...
4. Me alegro de que mis amigos...
5. Ojalá que...
6. Necesito un coche que...
7. No hay nadie en mi familia que...
8. Siempre voy al cine cuando...
9. Yo viajaré este verano si...
10. Yo compraría una casa si...

B Concordancia de los tiempos con el subjuntivo

⊙ In sentences that require the subjunctive, the verb in the main clause determines which subjunctive tense must be used in the subordinate clause. The models that follow show the possible combinations.

Main clause (indicative)	Subordinate clause (subjunctive)
Present Future Present perfect Command[1]	Present subjunctive *or* Present perfect subjunctive

Es necesario que **terminemos** la entrevista hoy.

It's necessary that we finish the interview today.

Saldremos cuando él **llegue.**

We'll leave when he arrives.

Le **he pedido** a Dios que me **ayude.**

I have asked God to help me.

Me alegro de que te **hayan escuchado.**

I'm glad that they have listened to you.

Sentirá mucho que no **hayamos recibido** el premio.

She'll be very sorry that we haven't received the award.

Dile que **vaya** al desfile.

Tell him to go to the parade.

Main clause (indicative)	Subordinate clause (subjunctive)
Preterit Imperfect Conditional	Imperfect subjunctive *or* Pluperfect subjunctive

Le **dije** que lo **leyera** por lo menos una vez.

I told him to read it at least once.

Yo no **creía** que ella **tuviera** ganas de ver la película.

I didn't believe that she wanted to see the movie.

Me **gustaría** que **grabaras** la entrevista.

I would like you to tape the interview.

Si él **hubiera estado** aquí no **habría permitido** esto.

If he had been here, he wouldn't have allowed this.

Me **alegré** de que ellos **hubieran ganado** el premio.

I was glad that they had won the award.

○ When the verb in the main clause is in the present but the action in the subordinate clause refers to the past, the imperfect subjunctive is used.

Main clause (indicative)	Subordinate clause (subjunctive)
Present	Imperfect subjunctive

Siento que no **vinieras** a mediados de mes.

I'm sorry you didn't come around the middle of the month.

---

[1] Only the present subjunctive may be used after the command.

CD-ROM
Go to **Estructuras gramaticales** for additional practice.

Práctica

A. Complete las siguientes oraciones, usando el presente, presente perfecto, imperfecto o pluscuamperfecto de subjuntivo. Use todas las combinaciones posibles.

1. Siento mucho que en ese canal...
2. Yo no habría tenido necesidad de trabajar si...
3. Nosotros preferiríamos que la programación...
4. El director nos ordenó que...
5. Pídele a tu amigo que...
6. El público estará muy contento cuando...
7. Nosotros esperábamos que los críticos...
8. Te he pedido muchas veces que...
9. Yo habría ido al estreno si...
10. Dudo que ese actor siempre...
11. Me alegro de que ayer nosotros(as)...
12. Yo temía que la película...

B. Imagínense que Ud. y un(a) compañero(a) son, respectivamente, el director (la directora) y el productor (la productora) de una película. Hablen de lo siguiente:

1. lo que ustedes quieren que hagan los actores
2. lo que ustedes esperaban que hicieran los periodistas
3. lo que ustedes temen que digan los críticos
4. lo que les gustaría que hiciera el público
5. lo que habrían podido hacer si hubieran tenido más dinero
6. el tipo de actor y actriz que buscan para los papeles principales
7. lo que ustedes dudan que puedan lograr (*achieve*)
8. lo que ustedes van a hacer cuando terminen de filmar la película

2   Usos de algunas preposiciones

◉ The preposition **a** (*to*, *at*, *in*) expresses direction towards a point in space or a moment in time. It is used in the following instances.

1. To refer to a time of day.

   A las cinco pasan el documental.

2. After a verb of motion when it is followed by an infinitive, a noun, or a pronoun.

   Siempre venimos **a** grabar aquí.

3. After the verbs **enseñar, aprender, comenzar,** and **empezar,** when they are followed by an infinitive.

   Van a **empezar a** entrevistar a los actores.

   Te voy a **enseñar a** bailar rumba.

   Yo quiero **aprender a** dirigir películas.

4. After the verb **llegar.**

Cuando **llegó al** festival, vio al director.

5. Before a direct object noun that refers to a specific person.[1] It may also be used to personify an animal or a thing.

Yo no aguanto **a** ese crítico.

Soltaron **al** perro.

Amo **a** mi país.

○ The preposition **de** (*of, from, about, with, in*) indicates possession, material, and origin. It is also used in the following instances:

1. With time of day, to refer to a specific period of the day or night.

Escuchamos las noticias a las ocho **de** la noche.

2. After the superlative, to express *in* or *of.*

Orlando es el más encantador **de** la familia.

Ella es la más alta **de** las tres.

3. To describe personal characteristics.

Es morena **de** ojos negros. Con razón la toman por uruguaya.

4. As a synonym for **sobre** or **acerca de** (*about*).

Hablan **de** todo menos **de** la película premiada.

○ The preposition **en** (*at, in, on, inside, over*) generally refers to something within an area of time or space. It is used in the following instances:

1. To refer to a definite place.

De haberlo sabido, me habría quedado **en** la pista de baile.

2. As a synonym for **sobre** (*on*).

Robertito está sentado **en** la cama.

3. To indicate means of transportation.

Nunca volveré a viajar **en** tren.

4. To refer to the way something is said.

Dijo que estaba enamorado, pero no lo dijo **en** serio; lo dijo **en** broma.

---

[1] Remember that, if the direct object is not a specific person, the personal **a** is not used, except with **alguien** and **nadie.**

Busco un buen maestro.   No busco **a nadie.**

CD-ROM
Go to **Estructuras gramaticales** for additional practice.

Práctica

A. En parejas, completen el siguiente párrafo usando las preposiciones **a, de** o **en,** según corresponda.

Ayer _____ las cinco _____ la tarde vinimos _____ entrevistar _____ la famosa actriz Eva Vargas. Eva es una _____ las más famosas estrellas _____ la televisión mexicana. La actriz nos habló _____ su última telenovela y nos dijo que comenzó _____ trabajar _____ la televisión cuando era muy joven. También nos dijo que iba _____ casarse con el actor chileno Pedro Allende. Según Eva, él es muy guapo; es rubio, _____ ojos verdes y muy simpático. Cuando se casen van _____ vivir _____ Chile. La próxima semana, Eva va _____ viajar _____ avión _____ Chile para reunirse con Pedro.

B. Entreviste a un(a) compañero(a) usando las siguientes preguntas. Preste especial atención al uso de las preposiciones.

1. ¿A qué hora vas a empezar a estudiar mañana?
2. ¿A qué hora llegas a la universidad generalmente?
3. ¿Qué te gustaría aprender a hacer?
4. ¿Qué me podrías enseñar a hacer tú?
5. El próximo sábado, ¿vas a salir o te vas a quedar en casa?
6. ¿Cuándo vas a ir a visitar a tu mejor amigo?
7. ¿De qué te gusta hablar con tus amigos?
8. ¿Te gustan los chicos (las chicas) de ojos verdes?
9. Para ti, ¿quién es el mejor actor (la mejor actriz) de este país?
10. ¿Prefieres viajar en tren o en avión?

3 Verbos con preposiciones

The prepositions **con, de,** and **en** are used with certain verbs to connect the verbs to *someone* or *something*.

○ Expressions with **con**

casarse con *to marry*	La actriz **se casó con** un médico.
comprometerse con *to get engaged to*	Dora **se comprometió con** Luis.
contar con *to count on*	Sé que puedo **contar con** los editores.
encontrarse con *to meet (encounter)*	**Me encontré con** mis amigos ayer.
soñar con *to dream about (of)*	**Sueño con** trabajar con una editorial.

○ Expressions with **de**

acordarse de *to remember*	¿**Te acordaste de** grabar la telenovela?
alegrarse de *to be glad about*	**Me alegro de** verte.
darse cuenta de *to realize*	Ella **se dio cuenta de** que todo era mentira.
enamorarse de *to fall in love with*	El locutor **se enamoró de** una de las actrices.

olvidarse de   *to forget*
salir de   *to leave (a place)*
tratar de   *to try to*

¿**Te olvidaste de** llamar al editor?
Salí de la oficina del productor a las dos.
Traté de terminar de escribir el reportaje.

● Expressions with **en**

confiar en   *to trust*
convenir en   *to agree on*

No **confío en** ese director.
Convinimos en filmar la escena a
cámara lenta.

entrar en   *to enter (a place)*
fijarse en   *to notice*
insistir en   *to insist on*
pensar en   *to think about*

Entró en la oficina del director.
¿**Te fijaste en** el vestido de la reina?
Ella **insistió en** ir al desfile.
Estoy **pensando en** una película que vi.

Práctica

A. Complete los siguientes diálogos con el equivalente español de las palabras que
aparecen entre paréntesis. Luego represéntelos con un(a) compañero(a).

1. —¡Felicítame: Ayer _____ Roberto!   (*I got engaged to*)
   —¡Pero yo creía que tú ibas a _____ Luis!   (*marry*)
   —Sí, pero _____ que no estaba _____ él.   (*I realized / in love with*)
   —¡Pobre Luis! Él _____ ser tu esposo. Pero _____ que seas tan feliz.
   (*was dreaming of / I'm glad*)

2. —¿A qué hora _____ casa, Anita?   (*did you leave*)
   —A las siete. _____ salir más temprano, pero no pude. Además _____ los
   libros y tuve que volver.   (*I tried / I forgot*)
   —Bueno, me voy. Rafael y yo _____ encontrarnos a las nueve.   (*agreed to*)

3. —Paquito, _____ que Olga viene hoy para _____ nosotros.   (*remember /
   to meet*)
   —Ella siempre _____ ir con nosotros y yo no la soporto. ¡No _____ !
   (*insists on / count on me*)

4. —Estoy _____ Gustavo. ¿ _____ lo contento que estaba? ¡Ganó el premio
   del mejor empleado!   (*thinking about / Did you notice*)
   —Sí, lo felicité tan pronto como _____ la oficina.   (*I entered*)

B. En grupos de tres o cuatro, digan lo que ha ocurrido últimamente en la vida sentimental de algunas de las personas que ustedes conocen. Usen las expresiones
aprendidas.

MODELO: Mi hermano se dio cuenta de que su novia no lo quería.

4 El infinitivo

A Algunos usos del infinitivo

In Spanish, the infinitive is used in the following ways:

○ As a noun.

1. Subject of the sentence

—Fue un viaje horrible. Volví cansadísima.
"It was a horrible trip. I came back exhausted."

—¡Y dicen que **viajar** calma los nervios!
"And they say traveling calms the nerves!"

2. Object of a verb, when the infinitive is dependent on that verb

—¿Adónde **quieren ir?**
"Where do you want to go?"

—**Queremos ir** al cine.
"We want to go to the movies."

3. Object of a preposition (In Spanish, the infinitive, not the present participle is used after a preposition.)

—¿Qué hiciste **antes de salir** de casa?
"What did you do before leaving home?"

—Grabé la película.
"I taped the movie."

○ As the object of the verbs **oír, ver,** and **escuchar.**

—¿A qué hora llegaste anoche? No te **oí llegar.**
"What time did you arrive last night? I didn't hear you come in."

—A eso de las doce.
"Around twelve."

○ As a substitute for the imperative, to give instructions or directions.

NO FUMAR
NO SMOKING

SALIR POR LA DERECHA
EXIT ON THE RIGHT

○ After the preposition **sin,** to indicate that an action has not been completed or has not yet occurred.[1] This usage is equivalent to the use of the past participle and the prefix *un-* in English.

—¿Vas a servir vino con la cena?
"Are you going to serve wine with dinner?"

—Sí, tengo una botella **sin abrir.**
"Yes, I have an unopened bottle."

---

[1] One exception is the verb **parar. Sin parar** means *without stopping.*

Ana habla **sin parar.**   *Ana talks without stopping.*

CD-ROM
Go to **Estructuras gramaticales** for additional practice.

Práctica

Vuelva a escribir las siguientes frases, cambiando las palabras en cursiva por una construcción en la que se utilice el infinitivo.

1. No *use* el ascensor en caso de incendio.
2. Tengo varios poemas *que no he publicado*.
3. Oímos *que hablaban* en inglés.
4. *Entren* por la izquierda.
5. *El trabajo* es necesario.
6. Los vi *cuando salían*.
7. Me gusta escucharla *cuando ella canta*.
8. Todavía tengo dos regalos *que no he abierto*.
9. *Agregue* una taza de agua.
10. No *fumen* aquí.
11. Oímos *que sonaba* el teléfono.
12. *El estudio* es importante para mí.

B Frases verbales con el infinitivo

○ **Acabar + de** + *infinitive*

Acabar (in the present tense) + **de** + *infinitive* is used in Spanish to express that something *has just happened* at the moment of speaking.

Yo	**acabo de**	**ver**	el espectáculo.
I	*have just*	*seen*	*the show.*

—Luis Vélez **acaba de lanzar** su nuevo álbum.   *"Luis Velez has just released his new album."*
—Yo pienso comprarlo.   *"I plan to buy it."*

When **acabar** is conjugated in the imperfect tense, the expression means that something *had just happened*.

Yo **acababa de escuchar** las noticias cuando ella llegó.

○ **Volver + a** + *infinitive*

Volver + a + *infinitive* is used in Spanish to indicate the repetition of an action. In English, it means *to do something over* or *to repeat it*.

—¿Te gustó la película?   *"Did you like the movie?"*
—Sí, me gustó tanto que pienso **volver a verla.**   *"Yes, I liked it so much that I plan to see it again."*

○ **Ponerse + a** + *infinitive*

In Spanish, **ponerse + a** + *infinitive* indicates that an action is beginning to take place. In English, it means *to start* or *to begin to do something*.

—Tengo que terminar este reportaje para mañana.

"I have to finish this report for tomorrow."

—Entonces tienes que **ponerte a escribir** ahora mismo.

"In that case, you have to start writing right away."

—¿Qué hiciste anoche después que yo me fui?

"What did you do last night after I left?"

—**Me puse a** ver el telediario.

"I started watching the TV news broadcast."

CD-ROM
Go to **Estructuras gramaticales** for additional practice.

Práctica

A. Conteste las siguientes preguntas, usando frases verbales con el infinitivo.

1. ¿Cuánto tiempo hace que Ud. llegó?
2. ¿Por qué no quiere Ud. comer nada?
3. Ud. lavó su coche ayer y anoche llovió. ¿Qué va a hacer? ¡Su coche está sucio!
4. Ud. sacó una "D" en su informe. ¿Qué le dijo el profesor que hiciera?
5. ¿Qué hizo Ud. anoche cuando llegó a su casa?
6. Mañana Ud. tiene un examen. ¿Qué va a hacer en cuanto llegue a su casa hoy?

B. **Teatro minúsculo.** En parejas, completen el siguiente diálogo, usando los infinitivos o frases con infinitivos correspondientes. Después, hagan el papel de Roberto y Amalia.

ROBERTO   —(*Que _____ a casa y está muy cansado*) Hola... ¿Dónde está el periódico? ¿Qué hay para comer? (*Se sienta.*)

AMALIA   —(*Sorprendida*) ¿Eres tú, Roberto? ¡Ah! No te _____. ¡Entraste muy silenciosamente! Oye, hoy es la fiesta de Rosaura. ¿Quieres _____? ¡Es un baile en el Club Náutico!

ROBERTO   —¡No! Después de _____ quiero _____ televisión y luego acostarme. ¡Estoy muy cansado!

AMALIA   —¡Pero es un baile! ¡Y _____ es un buen ejercicio! ¡Y te pone de buen humor!

ROBERTO   —(*Toma el periódico y _____.*) No, gracias. Prefiero estar de mal humor...

AMALIA   —Bueno, si no quieres _____ a la fiesta, ¿por qué no tomamos un poco de vermut antes de la cena? Tenemos una botella _____.

ROBERTO   —No... prefiero comer algo. Tengo hambre.

AMALIA   —(*_____ insistir*) ¿Estás seguro de que no quieres _____ al baile? ¡Roberto! ¿Por qué no me contestas?

ROBERTO   —Porque _____ contigo es una pérdida de tiempo (*a waste of time*). ¡Tú nunca me escuchas!

AMALIA   —¡Aguafiestas (*Spoilsport*)!

STUDENT WEBSITE
Do the **Compruebe cuánto sabe** self test after finishing this **Estructuras gramaticales** section.

¡CONTINUEMOS!

Una encuesta

Entreviste a sus compañeros de clase para tratar de identificar a aquellas personas que...

1. ...conocen personalmente a alguna persona famosa.
2. ...han visto la película que ganó el Óscar el año pasado.
3. ...tuvieron el papel principal en alguna obra de teatro estudiantil.
4. ...han ganado algún premio.
5. ...han asistido al estreno de una película últimamente.
6. ...prefieren las películas musicales.
7. ...tienen una videograbadora.
8. ...creen que hay demasiada violencia en los programas de televisión.
9. ...siempre miran el telediario por la noche.
10. ...se encuentran con sus amigos para ir al cine.
11. ...miran documentales a veces.
12. ...miran telenovelas.
13. ...creen que pueden dirigir una película.
14. ...se casarían con una estrella de cine.

Ahora divídanse en grupos de tres o de cuatro y discutan el resultado de la encuesta.

¿Comprende Ud.?

CD-ROM STUDENT WEBSITE
Go to **De escuchar...a escribir** (in **¿Comprende Ud.?**) on the CD-ROM for activities related to the conversation, and go to **Canción** on the website for activities related to the song.

1. Escuche la siguiente conversación entre Elba y Silvia, dos chicas paraguayas que están de vacaciones en Buenos Aires, Argentina. El objetivo de la actividad es el de escuchar una conversación a velocidad natural. No se preocupe de entenderlo todo, pues esto no se espera de Ud. Después de escuchar la conversación dos veces, Ud. oirá varias aseveraciones. En una hoja, escriba los números de uno a ocho e indique si cada aseveración es verdadera o falsa.
2. Luego escuche la canción y trate de aprenderla.

Hablemos de televisión

En parejas, fíjense en la guía de televisión que aparece a continuación y luego contesten las preguntas que siguen.

Vea hoy

• La hija del penal,
a la 1 p.m.; canal 2. Con María Antonieta Pons.

• Melodía fatal,
a las 9 p.m.; canal 2. Con Roy Thines e Yvette Mimieux.

• Hola, Juventud,
a las 4:30 p.m.; canal 4. El popularímetro de la música nacional, con Nelson Hoffmann.

Programación

8:35 (2) Buenos días con música.
8:55 (2) Ayer y hoy en la historia.
9:00 (2) Aeróbicos.
9:30 (2) En ruta al mundial.
10:00 (6) Música.
11:00 (6) Capitán Raimar.
11:30 (2) Acción en vivo. (6) El sargento Preston.
11:45 (7) Las aventuras de Lassie.
12:00 (6) Mundo de juguete.

12:15 (7) Telenoticias.
12:30 (2) En contacto directo.
1:00 (2) Tanda del Dos: "La hija del penal". (6) Comentarios con el Dr. Abel Pacheco. (7) La monja voladora.
1:05 (6) Notiséis.
1:30 (7) Mi mujer es hechicera.
1:40 (6) Los tres chiflados.
2:00 (7) Cocinando con tía Florita: Pastel de Cuaresma.
2:05 (6) Tarzán.
2:15 (13) Carta de ajuste.
2:30 (7) Plaza Sésamo.
2:40 (4) Patrón y música.
3:00 (2) Mi marciano favorito. (4) Club cristiano costarricense. (6) Superamigos. (7) El fantasma del espacio y los herculoides. (13) Introducción a la U.
3:30 (2) De to2 para to2. (4) Cruzada de Jimmy Swaggart. (6) Seiscito. (7) Capitán Peligro. (13) El mar y sus secretos.
4:00 (2) Video éxitos del Dos. (4) Club 700. (6) Los Pitufos. (7) El inspector Gadget. (13) Las aventuras de Heidi.
4:30 (4) Hola, juventud. (6) He Man y los amos del Universo. (7) Super héroes. (11) Jesucristo T.V. (13) UNED.
5:00 (2) Teleclub. (6) M.T.V. (7) El justiciero. (11) El pequeño vagabundo. (13) Don Quijote de La Mancha.
5:30 (7) Scooby Doo. (11)

Marvel super heroes. (13) Villa alegre.
5:50 (4) Cenicienta.
6:00 (2) Angélica. (6) Notiséis. (7) Telenoticias. (11) Amar al salvaje. (13) Testigos del ayer.
6:10 (4) Atrévete.
6:30 (6) El Chavo. (13) Aurelia, canción y pueblo.
7:00 (4) Cristal. (6) Lotería. (7) Aunque Ud. no lo crea. (11) Las Amazonas. (13) Pensativa.
7:30 (2) Tú o nadie.
8:00 (4) Rebeca. (6) Comentarios con el Dr. Abel Pacheco. (7) Los magníficos. (11) Mae West. (13) Noches de ópera.
8:05 (6) Miniseries del Seis: "El guerrero misterioso".
8:30 (2) En contacto directo.
9:00 (2) Cine del martes: "Melodía fatal". (4) Voleibol en vivo. (7) Vecinos y amigos.
9:55 (11) De compras.
10:00 (4) Revista mundial. (6) Rituales. (7) Best sellers. (11) Noticiero C.N.N. (13) Cuentos de misterio.
10:30 (4) Despedida. (6) Para gente grande. (13) Despedida y cierre.
11:00 (7) Telenoticias.
11:30 (2) Los profesionales. (6) Notiséis.
12:30 (2) En contacto directo.
1:00 (2) Ayer y hoy en la historia.
1:05 (2) Buenas noches.

Información suministrada por las televisoras.

1. ¿A qué horas hay programas religiosos y cómo se llaman?
2. Necesito hacer ejercicio. ¿Qué programa puedo ver? ¿A qué hora es?
3. ¿Qué programa(s) le va(n) a interesar a la gente joven?
4. ¿En qué canal ponen la película "La hija del penal" y quién es la protagonista?
5. A Paquito le gustan los perros. ¿Qué programa creen Uds. que le gustaría ver?
6. ¿A qué hora puedo mirar la televisión para ver las noticias?
7. ¿Qué programas infantiles ponen hoy en la televisión?
8. A Juan le gustan los deportes. ¿Qué programa creen Uds. que va a ver hoy? ¿En qué canal?
9. A mi mamá le gusta cocinar. ¿Qué programa le recomendarían?
10. ¿A qué hora comienza y termina la programación de hoy?
11. ¿Qué programas les interesa ver y por qué?
12. ¿Qué programas les parecen los menos interesantes?

¿Qué dirían ustedes?

Imagínese que Ud. y un(a) compañero(a) se encuentran en las siguientes situaciones. ¿Qué va a decir cada uno?

1. Uds. quieren conocerse mejor. Entrevístense.
2. Uds. han visto una película muy popular. Una amiga quiere saber de qué trata la película y qué opinión tienen Uds. sobre la misma.
3. Uds. están hablando de sus programas favoritos.

¡De ustedes depende!

El famoso actor español Antonio Banderas viene a visitar la universidad a la que Uds. asisten. Ud. y un(a) compañero(a) están a cargo de entrevistarlo. Preparen las preguntas que le van a hacer, incluyendo lo siguiente.

1. fecha y lugar de nacimiento
2. algo sobre su niñez
3. sus experiencias de la escuela
4. dónde pasó su juventud
5. las mujeres en su vida
6. su vida actual
7. planes para el futuro

¡Debate!

La clase se dividirá en dos grupos: los que están a favor de la censura en los medios de comunicación y los que se oponen a ella. El primer grupo tratará de demostrar que algún tipo de censura es necesaria para proteger al público, sobre todo a los niños. El segundo grupo dará una serie de razones para demostrar que toda censura va contra la libertad de expresión.

Salón de belleza La Época

- Expertos peluqueros y barberos
- Especialidad en permanentes
- Tenemos los mejores equipos y los precios más bajos para hombres y mujeres.

Abierto de lunes a sábado de 9 a 5
Calle Bolívar No. 439

Para pedir su turno llame al teléfono 287–2308

Martes precios especiales para mayores de 50 años.

Lecturas periodísticas

Saber leer   Volver a leer con propósito

CD-ROM
Go to **Lecturas periodísticas** for additional prereading and vocabulary activities.

La "relectura" de un escrito depende, en parte, de los propósitos que Ud. tenga al leer.

1. Antes de leer por primera vez este artículo sobre un joven cantante hispano, piense en sus propósitos como lector(a) y utilice estrategias que lo (la) ayuden a alcanzarlos (*reach*). Considere algunos de los siguientes propósitos generales:

   - Para enterarse de algún aspecto de la música latina de los Estados Unidos.
   - Para conocer mejor a este famoso cantante.
   - Para conocer aspectos del mundo del espectáculo y del entretenimiento.
   - _____.

   Haga la primera lectura.

2. Luego pregúntese: ¿qué propósitos tiene al volver a leer el artículo? Considere los siguientes:

   - Para enterarse mejor de los detalles que le interesaron sobre la música latina de los Estados Unidos, sobre Jon Secada, sobre el mundo del espectáculo, etc.
   - Para responder mejor a algunas de las preguntas de comprensión.
   - Para relacionar mejor los datos de información que le interesaron.
   - _____.

   Ahora, vuelva a leer el artículo.

Para leer y comprender

Al leer el artículo detalladamente, busque las respuestas a las siguientes preguntas.

1. ¿Jon Secada es reconocido solamente a nivel local?
2. ¿Qué nos muestra Jon Secada al lanzar su álbum propio?
3. ¿Ha ganado algún premio? ¿Cuál?
4. ¿Cuáles son los mercados más codiciados?
5. ¿En qué idioma se inició Secada? ¿Qué pasó después?
6. ¿Cuál es la nacionalidad de Jon Secada? ¿Cuántos años tenía cuando llegó a los Estados Unidos?
7. ¿Quiénes han tenido mucha influencia en su formación como artista?
8. ¿Qué pudo hacer Jon Secada gracias a la relación con Gloria y Emilio Estefan?
9. ¿Qué disco lanzó en el año 1992? ¿Tuvo éxito? ¿Cuántos álbumes vendió?
10. ¿Con qué disco ganó su segundo Grammy? ¿Ha colaborado Jon Secada con otros cantantes? ¿Con cuáles, por ejemplo?

Jon Secada

Reconocido internacionalmente por su talento como intérprete, productor y compositor, Jon Secada volvió a los estudios de grabación°, pero esta vez para lanzar un álbum propio, producción en donde nos muestra su crecimiento° como persona y como artista.

El disco *La mejor parte de mí (Best Part of Me)* es en inglés y en él Secada incluye ritmos modernos y contemporáneos, acompañados de un estilo innovador y original. Ganador de dos Grammys y con ventas° de más de 20 millones de dólares alrededor del mundo, Secada es considerado uno de los artistas con mayor prestigio dentro de los mercados más codiciados: el anglo y el hispano.

A diferencia de la mayoría de los artistas, dentro de su carrera como intérprete, Secada se inició en el idioma inglés y después dio el paso al mercado hispano, donde desde su debut ha conservado un gran prestigio. Nacido en La Habana, Cuba, Jon Secada emigró a los Estados Unidos a la edad de nueve años, y en la ciudad de Miami creció° escuchando la música de Stevie Wonder, Billy Joel y Elton John, entre otros; estos talentos han tenido mucha influencia en su formación como artista.

Su relación profesional y personal con Gloria y Emilio Estefan le permitió a Jon cultivar sus habilidades y talento como compositor y productor y en 1992, apoyado° por Estefan, hizo su lanzamiento al mercado hispano con el disco *Jon Secada,* álbum que logró un éxito increíble y llegó a vender más de seis millones de álbumes alrededor del mundo. Secada se mantuvo en los primeros lugares de las listas de popularidad de *Billboard* con el tema "Otro día más sin verte", el cual lo llevó a ganar su primer Grammy. En 1995 y luego de un álbum intermedio titulado *Heart, Soul and a Voice,* Jon Secada lanza *Amor,* que le dio a ganar su segundo Grammy en la categoría de Mejor Presentación Pop Latina. Intérprete de gran talento, Jon Secada ha colaborado con otros cantantes como Gloria Estefan —con quien coescribió *Coming Out of the Dark,* Ricky Martin y Jennifer López, por mencionar a algunos.

Su relación profesional y personal con Gloria y Emilio Estefan le permitió a Jon cultivar sus habilidades y talento como compositor y productor

Jon Secada, famoso cubano intérprete, productor y compositor.

---

recording
development
sales
grew up

---

supported

Desde su mundo

1. ¿Le gustaría a Ud. formar parte de algún programa de entretenimiento?
2. ¿Cree Ud. que es fácil la vida de las estrellas? ¿Por qué sí o por qué no?

Piense y escriba   Taller de redacción II

STUDENT WEBSITE

CD-ROM

Go to **...y escriba-
mos** (in **Hablemos
de su país**) on the
student website
and **De escuchar...
a escribir** (in **¿Com-
prende Ud.?**) on
the CD-ROM for ad-
ditional writing
practice.

Ud. va a escribir un artículo muy breve (de tres a cuatro párrafos) sobre el mundo del espectáculo.

Hoy un(a) compañero(a) editará algunos aspectos gramaticales de su composición. Ud., a su vez (*in turn*), le servirá de editor(a) a uno de sus compañeros de clase. Al revisar el trabajo de su compañero(a), tenga en cuenta las siguientes pautas (*guidelines*):

1. **Nombres y adjetivos:** que haya concordancia (*agreement*) de género y de número.
2. **Verbos:** que guarden concordancia en persona y número con el sujeto.
3. **Tiempos verbales:** que sea el tiempo verbal adecuado y que esté formado correctamente.
4. **Modos verbales:** que sea el modo adecuado (subjuntivo o indicativo) y que esté formado correctamente.

Vea las indicaciones que le ha hecho su editor(a) y prepare la versión final.

Pepe Vega y su mundo

Teleinforme

Como hemos podido ver a lo largo de (throughout) *los teleinformes anteriores, en los países hispánicos existe una programación muy variada. Los programas de los Estados Unidos tienen también una presencia considerable en la televisión de todos los países hispánicos (y del resto del mundo), pero a veces sucede lo contrario. Por ejemplo, ¡el programa mexicano* El chavo del ocho *se menciona en varios episodios del programa de dibujos animados* Los Simpson!

Preparación

Trate de definir por categorías los programas que Ud. ha visto en las lecciones anteriores. A continuación aparecen en una columna las categorías y en la otra los nombres de los programas y los segmentos de video.

CATEGORÍA	PROGRAMA
programa especial	*Telediario* (Partido de fútbol España-Rumanía; La fiesta del gaucho)
programa de concursos (*game show*)	
documental	*De paseo:* (Puerto Viejo de Limón, *Rafting* en el Río Pacuare)
programa informativo	
magazín (programa en que se combinan entrevistas, reportajes y variedades)	*La botica de la abuela* (Remedio para quemaduras)
noticiero / telediario	*Tradiciones milenarias en la Península de Santa Elena* (Día de los difuntos)
programa de dibujos animados	*Cartelera TVE:* (Fuera de campo: Lluís Remolí)
programa de cocina	
programa cultural	*Somos* (Conversaciones con estudiantes de la SDSU)
anuncio publicitario o *spot*	*Futuramente* (Hazte maestro)
telecomedia	*Las chicas de hoy en día* (En la Agencia Supersonic)
telenovela (*soap opera*)	*Una hija más* (Saludos, Madre e hijos, La abuela: madre y suegra)
	Aristas (Grafitis en San José)
	América Total (Alimentos americanos, Del Viejo Mundo a América, El ajiaco)

Comprensión

CD-ROM
Go to **Video** for further previewing, vocabulary, and structure practice on this clip.

Esmeralda   44:56–47:17

Esmeralda es una telenovela mexicana, de la cadena (*network*) Televisa, que cuenta la historia de una niña que nace ciega (*blind*), su padre rico que sólo quiere tener un hijo y la partera (*midwife*) que cambia a la niña por el hijo de una mujer pobre que murió.

A. ¿Quién es quién?   Después de ver el video, escriba el nombre del personaje al que corresponde cada una de las siguientes descripciones. Los personajes son Esmeralda, José Armando, don Rodolfo Peñarreal y Blanca. Hay más de una descripción para cada personaje.

	DESCRIPCIÓN	PERSONAJE
1.	una chica que nace ciega	_____
2.	Su belleza y sensualidad hace que todos los hombres la deseen.	_____
3.	el único hombre que gana el amor de Esmeralda	_____
4.	la verdadera madre de Esmeralda	_____
5.	el verdadero padre de Esmeralda	_____
6.	Su hijo será hombre porque él lo quiere así.	_____
7.	señor rico y poderoso	_____
8.	Ella dio a luz a una niña, una niña que nació muerta.	_____
9.	un huerfanito	_____
10.	Sus ojitos tienen luz.	_____
11.	la ladrona de las fresas	_____

Manny Manuel: "Y sé que vas a llorar"   47:19–49:29

STUDENT WEBSITE
Go to **Video** for further previewing, vocabulary, and structure practice on this clip.

Manny Manuel es un joven cantante puertorriqueño. Su música vibra con los ritmos del Caribe. Vamos a ver parte de un concierto especial producido por la Televisión Española. La canción que canta aquí Manny Manuel combina el ritmo del *merengue* con una letra (*lyrics*) que muestra un tema muy popular: el amor y la traición (*betrayal*).

B. Una canción incompleta.   Escuche la primera parte de la canción y escoja las palabras correctas para completar los versos siguientes.

Y ahora tú quieres (1. volver / regresar / hablar)
Después que todo te (2. vi / di / oí)
Y me aventaste al olvido (*you forgot me*).

Ahora que todo va (3. mal / bien / allá)
Ahora sí me quieres (4. hablar / ver / oír)
Y quieres hablar con (5. -migo / una amiga / un amigo).

Recuerda que te advertí
Que todo puede (6. cambiar / quedar)
Y hoy cambiada has venido.

Y ya verás que al final
El que la hace la (7. haga / para / paga).
Y el dolor de tu (8. canción / traición / amor)
Ya no lo curas con nada.

Y sé que vas a llorar, llorar.
Y sé que vas a (9. sofreír, sofreír / sufrir, sufrir / subir, subir)
Cuando comprendas que te (10. recordé / olvidé / oí bien),
Que hoy te toca (11. verdad / verde / perder).

Y sé que vas a llorar, llorar.
Y sé que vas a (12. sofreír, sofreír / sufrir, sufrir / subir, subir)
Cuando me (13. veas / olvides / vayas) del brazo de ella,
Cuando te acuerdes de mí.

El chavo del ocho   49:31–52:12

El chavo del ocho es un programa de comedia creado por la Estación Televisa de México. Cuenta la historia de la Chilindrina, Quico y el Chavo, quienes conviven en un humilde patio de vecinos (*neighborhood*). Aunque ya no hay nuevos episodios, los viejos se siguen transmitiendo y siguen encantando a los niños de todo el mundo hispánico. Aquí veremos una muestra del programa con varias entrevistas a algunos aficionados (*fans*) de un colegio de España.

C. ¿Quién dice qué?   En este segmento hablan varias personas y, a menudo, ¡todas a la vez! Para separar las oraciones, identifique a cada uno de los hablantes que dicen las siguientes cosas. En el caso de los niños, sólo indique si es niño o niña.

Juan Pedro López Silva   la Chilindrina
la presentadora   Quico
un niño   el Chavo
una niña

LO QUE DICE	HABLANTE
1. "Nuestro compañero Juan Pedro López Silva busca en el colegio la opinión de los chavales sobre esta serie."	_____
2. "¡Ay, muy bien, hijo, y ¿qué vas a contar, hijo?"	_____
3. "Pues... ¡que es muy bonito!"	_____
4. "Altea, ¿tú crees que si los inversores en bolsa vieran *El chavo del ocho* estarían como más eufóricos y más alegres?"	_____
5. "Eh, pues, sí, más... más graciosos, más..."	_____
6. "¡Chusma, chusma! ¡Pff!"	_____
7. "Sí, mami. Chusma, chusma. ¡Pff!"	_____

CD-ROM
You will also find this clip under **Video.**

8. "Chespirito interpreta al Chavo."   _____

9. "Bueno, pero no se enoje."   _____

10. "Juan Carlos Villagrán interpreta a Quico."   _____

11. "¿Qué me dices de la Chilindrina?"   _____

12. "Pues que se llama María Antonieta, y que es la hija de don Ramón."   _____

13. "Yo soy una niña muy obediente."   _____

14. "Mira qué coleta más bonita tiene Carmen."   _____

15. "Yo nunca me lo pierdo. Y es un payaso el Chavo del ocho."   _____

16. "...en el canal 2 de la Televisión Española y a las seis menos cuarto."   _____

Ampliación

Ahora le toca a Ud.   Ud. trabaja para una estación de televisión como productor o productora. Necesita decidir los programas y películas que su estación transmitirá durante la mañana, la tarde o la noche de cierto día. ¿Qué tipos de programa escogería Ud.? ¿Por qué?

El mundo del trabajo y la tecnología

Una ejecutiva en su oficina.

El mundo del trabajo y la tecnología

Student Audio

Álvaro Montero, un joven cubano, y Jorge Torres, dominicano, viven en Puerto Rico y los dos están buscando trabajo. En este momento, leen los anuncios clasificados y éstos son los que les interesan:

Vendedores por Internet

- Experiencia en mercadeo y logos para páginas de Internet
- Conocimiento de Windows® 2000 y Acrobat® 4.0
- Poseer auto en buenas condiciones
- Preferiblemente con título académico, curso en venta/mercadeo, comunicaciones o computadoras
- Amplio conocimiento en Internet
- Responsable, dinámico(a), entusiasta

Ofrecemos:
Salario, gastos de auto, comisión, beneficios marginales

Favor de enviar su resumé a:

Oficina de Recursos Humanos
Apartado 12345
San Juan, PR 00936-2345
Fax (787) 745-5568

ARTES GRÁFICAS

Importante empresa con maquinaria moderna y especializada para la impresión de etiquetas, letreros, libros y revistas precisa:

Director de Producción

- *Disponible para viajar al extranjero*
- *Edad de 30 a 50 años*
- *Con capacidad de organización*
- *Con un mínimo de 3 años de experiencia*
- *Conocimientos de informática*
- *Se ofrecen excelentes condiciones*

Enviar solicitud a:
calle Ponce, 498
San Juan, Puerto Rico
00936-2345

CD-ROM

For preparation, do the **Ante todo** activities found on the CD-ROM.

ÁLVARO —Mira, Jorge, el puesto de vendedor por Internet es perfecto para mí, porque yo tengo experiencia y los conocimientos que piden.

JORGE —Sí, pero se necesita a alguien que tenga un carro en buenas condiciones y el tuyo siempre se te descompone...

ÁLVARO —(*Se ríe.*) Es verdad... pero voy a mandar mi resumé y también unas cartas de recomendación de mi jefe anterior.

JORGE —Pues a mí me interesa el puesto de director de producción. Lo voy a solicitar.

Una semana después, Álvaro tiene una entrevista con la Sra. Paz.

SRA. PAZ —Así que Ud. tiene una maestría en mercadeo y relaciones públicas.

ÁLVARO —Sí, señora. Además, soy bilingüe.

SRA. PAZ	—¿Sabe utilizar los programas de Excel y Access para la introducción de datos?
ÁLVARO	—Sí, he usado varios, incluidos los que Ud. menciona.
SRA. PAZ	—Ud. no fue despedido de su empleo, ¿verdad?
ÁLVARO	—No, renuncié porque pedí un aumento y no me lo dieron.
SRA. PAZ	—Bueno, sus calificaciones son excelentes. Ud. ya sabe cuál es el sueldo. Además ofrecemos beneficios adicionales: un seguro de salud y un plan de retiro para los empleados.

Varios días después, Jorge habla con Álvaro por teléfono.

JORGE	—Hola, Álvaro. ¿Conseguiste el puesto que querías?
ÁLVARO	—Sí, lo conseguí. ¿Y tú, Jorge?
JORGE	—¡También lo conseguí! ¿Qué tal si lo celebramos esta noche?
ÁLVARO	—¡Muy buena idea! Oye, Jorge, como estoy hasta la coronilla de mi carro, pensaba salir ahora para comprar un auto nuevo. ¿Me acompañas?

Dígame

En parejas, contesten las siguientes preguntas basadas en los diálogos.

1. ¿Qué están leyendo Álvaro y Jorge en este momento? ¿Hay algunos anuncios que les interesen?
2. ¿Qué experiencia y qué conocimiento se necesitan para el puesto de vendedor por Internet?
3. ¿Qué ofrece la compañía? ¿A qué oficina se debe mandar el resumé?
4. ¿Qué precisa la compañía de artes gráficas?
5. ¿Qué problema tiene Álvaro con su auto?
6. ¿Qué le va a mandar Álvaro a la compañía?
7. ¿Qué puesto va a solicitar Jorge?
8. ¿Qué título tiene Álvaro y cuántos idiomas habla?
9. ¿Álvaro fue despedido de su empleo anterior o renunció? ¿Por qué?
10. ¿Qué beneficios adicionales ofrece la compañía?
11. ¿Qué van a celebrar Álvaro y Jorge esta noche?
12. ¿Qué decide hacer Álvaro y por qué?

Perspectivas socioculturales

INSTRUCTOR WEBSITE
Your instructor may assign the preconversational support activities found in **Perspectivas socioculturales.**

En muchos países, cada día es más importante poseer experiencia en el uso y manejo de medios tecnológicos. Haga lo siguiente:

1. Durante unos cinco minutos, converse con dos compañeros sobre el siguiente tema: **¿Qué experiencias relacionadas con la tecnología necesitan tener Uds. al salir a buscar su primer trabajo?**
2. Participe con el resto de la clase en la discusión del tema cuando su profesor(a) se lo indique.

Vocabulario

Nombres

el apartado postal, el apartado de correos   post office box
el aumento   increase
el beneficio adicional (marginal)   fringe benefit
el (la) empleado(a)   employee
la empresa   business
la etiqueta   label
el extranjero   abroad
el gasto   expense
el (la) jefe(a)   boss
el letrero   sign
la maquinaria   machinery
el mercadeo   marketing
el puesto, el empleo   job
el retiro, la jubilación   retirement
el sueldo, el salario   salary
el (la) vendedor(a)   salesperson

la venta   sale

Verbos

descomponerse   to break down
despedir (e → i)   to fire (*i.e., from a job*)
incluir   to include
precisar   to need
renunciar   to resign
solicitar   to apply

Adjetivos

anterior   previous
bilingüe   bilingual
disponible   available

Otras palabras y expresiones

así que...   so...
estar hasta la coronilla de   to be fed up with

Ampliación

La tecnología moderna

archivar (almacenar) información   to store information
el archivo, el fichero   file (electronic)
la composición de textos   word processing
el correo electrónico   e-mail
el disco duro   hard drive
diseñar programas   to design programs
el escáner   scanner
la memoria   memory
navegar la red   to surf the net
el ordenador (la computadora) portatil, la microcomputadora   laptop, notebook
el teléfono móvil (celular)   cellular phone

Para hablar del trabajo

anual   yearly
archivar   to file
el (la) aspirante, el (la) postulante   applicant
contratar, emplear   to hire
el contrato   contract
desempeñar un puesto   to hold a position
diario   daily
el (la) ejecutivo(a)   executive
mensual   monthly
semanal   weekly
tiempo extra   overtime

Hablando de todo un poco

Preparación   **Encuentre en la columna B las respuestas a las preguntas de la columna A.**

A	B
1. ¿Eva no está en los Estados Unidos?	a. Según ese letrero, cerca de la capital.
2. ¿Quién es Alberto Salas?	b. Al segundo aspirante.
3. ¿Tito ya no trabaja allí?	c. Sí, precisa dinero.
4. ¿Adela ya no quiere trabajar aquí?	d. No, semanal.
5. ¿Dónde estamos?	e. Sí, cien mil dólares anuales.
6. ¿Vas a hablar con el director?	f. Sí, un ordenador portátil.
7. ¿Va a solicitar un empleo que pague más?	g. El de contadora.
8. ¿Gana un buen sueldo?	h. No, porque no tengo computadora.
9. ¿Cómo se comunican ustedes?	i. No, lo despidieron.
10. ¿A quién contrataron?	j. La archivé.
11. ¿Qué puesto desempeñaba?	k. Apartado postal 234.
12. ¿Ése es el salario mensual?	l. No, no está disponible.
13. ¿Usas una computadora?	m. Un aumento de salario.
14. ¿Qué hiciste con la información?	n. Sí, nunca hace lo que le digo.
15. ¿Navegas la red?	o. No, ella vive en el extranjero.
16. ¿Qué pidieron los empleados?	p. Un seguro de salud y un plan de retiro.
17. ¿Cuál es la dirección?	q. No, piensa renunciar.
18. ¿Dices que estás hasta la coronilla de él?	r. Sí, en mercadeo.
19. ¿Usted tiene una maestría?	s. Por correo electrónico.
20. ¿Qué beneficios incluyen?	t. Mi jefe anterior.

En grupos de tres o cuatro hagan lo siguiente:

A. Su trabajo ideal.   Hablen de los tipos de puestos a los que Uds. aspiran, el horario que desean tener, el sueldo y los beneficios y cuál de estos aspectos es el más importante para Uds. Den razones.

B. La tecnología.   Hablen de la tecnología moderna que utilizan, de los equipos que necesitan y de los que no necesitan, de las cosas que les interesa hacer en computadora y en línea (*online*), y de cómo la tecnología les facilita su vida diaria.

C. Es hora de quejarse.   Aquí tienen Uds. una oportunidad de quejarse. En grupos, comenten sobre las cosas, las personas y las situaciones de las cuales Uds. están hasta la coronilla.

Palabras problemáticas

A. **Letrero, signo** y **señal** como equivalentes de *sign*

- **Letrero** equivale a *printed sign*.

  Hay un **letrero** que dice: "Aquí se habla inglés".

- **Signo** es una indicación que se usa en las escrituras o en las matemáticas.

  El **signo** "×" indica multiplicación.

- **Señal** significa **marca** o **nota** que se pone en las cosas para distinguirlas de otras.

  Pon una **señal** en el libro para saber dónde está la sección gramatical.

B. **Conseguir** y **recibir** como equivalentes de *to get*

- **Conseguir** es el equivalente de *to get* cuando es sinónimo de *to obtain*.

  Mi hermano **consiguió** un buen empleo.

  Carlos no **consiguió** habitación en el hotel.

- **Recibir** significa **tomar lo que le envían a uno.** Es el equivalente de *to get* cuando éste es sinónimo de *to receive*.

  Ayer **recibí** una carta de mi padre.

Práctica

Conteste las siguientes preguntas, usando en sus respuestas las palabras problemáticas aprendidas.

1. ¿Qué usamos para indicar multiplicación?
2. ¿Le escribió su mejor amigo(a)?
3. ¿Qué pone Ud. en un libro para marcar la página que está leyendo?
4. ¿Le dieron el trabajo que solicitó?
5. En la carretera, ¿qué nos indica cuál es el límite de velocidad?

Your instructor may carry out the **¡Ahora escuche!** listening activity found in the **Answers to Text Exercises.**

¡Ahora escuche!

Se leerá dos veces una breve narración sobre Juan, que fue despedido de su trabajo. Se harán aseveraciones sobre la narración. En una hoja escriba los números de uno a doce e indique si cada aseveración es verdadera (V) o falsa (F).

El mundo hispánico

El Caribe hispánico [las Antillas]

STUDENT WEBSITE
Go to **El mundo hispánico** for prereading and vocabulary activities.

Álvaro Montero

Yo era muy joven cuando salí de La Habana, pero todavía recuerdo mi país. La figura de la isla es parecida a la de un cocodrilo y, como es larga y estrecha, tiene extensas costas en las que se encuentran playas de gran belleza. Según dijo Colón cuando llegó a la isla, Cuba es "la tierra más hermosa que ojos humanos vieron". Hoy algunos la llaman "la Perla de las Antillas".

Cuba es la mayor de las Antillas. Tiene como principales exportaciones el azúcar y el tabaco. Nuestros *habanos* o *puros* son los preferidos de los buenos fumadores. También es muy popular en todo el mundo la música cubana: el danzón, el son, la rumba, el mambo y los ritmos afrocubanos que hoy se conocen con el nombre de *salsa*.

Como, por razones políticas, no puedo vivir en mi país, me siento muy feliz de estar aquí en Puerto Rico, país que se parece tanto a mi Cuba de antes. Puerto Rico es un Estado Libre Asociado a los Estados Unidos. El país tiene unas cien millas de largo, es bastante montañoso y tiene numerosos ríos.

Puerto Rico tiene hermosas playas y muchos lugares de interés. Uno de los más visitados por los turistas es el Viejo San Juan, la sección Antigua de su capital. Allí se encuentra el Castillo del Morro, una antigua fortaleza de la época colonial. Otro sitio de interés es la región del Yunque, un bosque tropical que es hoy una reserva federal.

Cuando salí de Cuba, viví durante un año en la República Dominicana. Este país ocupa las dos terceras partes de la isla que Colón llamó La Española. El resto de la isla corresponde a Haití.

La República Dominicana tiene una extensión que equivale, más o menos, a la mitad de la superficie de Kentucky. Su capital, Santo Domingo, fue la primera ciudad europea fundada en el Nuevo Mundo.

La economía del país se basa principalmente en la agricultura, a pesar de que su territorio es muy montañoso. El turismo comienza ahora a ser considerado una fuente de riqueza.

En la República Dominicana, como en los demás países del Caribe, la música y el baile son muy populares. En cuanto a los deportes, el béisbol es el que tiene más fanáticos. Sammy Sosa, el famoso jugador dominicano del equipo de los Chicago Cubs, es uno de los muchos caribeños (antillanos) que juegan en las Grandes Ligas del béisbol norteamericano.

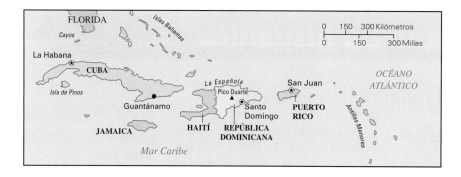

Aquí tienen un mapa del Caribe para que conozcan el área.

Sobre el Caribe hispánico [las Antillas]

En parejas, túrnense para contestar las siguientes preguntas.

1. ¿Qué forma tiene Cuba? ¿Es la menor o la mayor de las Antillas?
2. ¿Qué dijo Colón al ver a Cuba? ¿Cómo la llaman algunos hoy?
3. ¿Qué exporta Cuba principalmente?
4. ¿Cuáles son algunos géneros de música cubana?
5. ¿Por qué es el inglés uno de los idiomas de Puerto Rico?
6. ¿Qué es el Castillo del Morro? ¿Qué es El Yunque?
7. ¿Con qué país comparte la isla la República Dominicana?
8. ¿Cuál fue la primera ciudad europea fundada en el Nuevo Mundo?
9. ¿En qué se basa la economía de la República Dominicana?
10. ¿Cuál es el deporte más popular de los países del Caribe hispánico?

Hablemos de su país

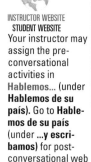

El Viejo Quebec, en Canadá, y la parte antigua de Nueva Orleans, en los Estados Unidos, son centros históricos con una fuerte influencia francesa. Reúnase con otro(a) compañero(a) para contestar la siguiente pregunta: ¿En qué otros lugares que Ud. conoce se pueden apreciar influencias de otros países?

Luego cada pareja compartirá las respuestas con toda la clase. ¿Cuántos lugares fueron discutidos?

Una tarjeta postal

Imagínense que Ud. y un(a) compañero(a) están de vacaciones en una de las islas del Caribe hispánico. Envíenles una tarjeta postal a sus compañeros de clase dándoles sus impresiones sobre la isla.

Queridos amigos:

_____

_____

_____

_____

_____

_____

_____

Saludos,

Cuba 65

Orquídeas Cubanas

Estructuras gramaticales

1 La voz pasiva

○ The passive voice is formed in Spanish in the same way as it is in English.[1] The subject of the sentence does not perform the action of the verb, but receives it.

América **fue descubierta** por los españoles.[2]

America was discovered by the Spaniards.

○ The passive voice is formed in the following way:

subject + **ser** + *past participle* + **por** + *agent*

---

[1] This construction is used less frequently in Spanish than in English.

[2] Active voice: Los españoles **descubrieron** América.

Only the verb **ser** can be used as the auxiliary verb. The past participle must agree with the subject in gender and number.

$$\text{América fue} \quad \text{descubierta} \quad \text{por} \quad \text{los españoles.}$$
subject + **ser** + *past participle* + **por** + *agent*

○ The passive voice may be used whether the agent is identified specifically or not.

Esa empresa **fue fundada** por el Sr. Rivas. (agent identified)
Esa empresa **fue fundada** en 1997. (agent implied)

—¿Quién construyó ese hospital?	*"Who built that hospital?"*
—Ese hospital **fue construido** por la Compañía Torres.	*"That hospital was built by the Torres Company."*
—¿Quién archivará esa información?	*"Who will file that information?"*
—La información **será archivada** por el secretario.	*"The information will be filed by the secretary."*

○ When the action expresses a mental or emotional condition, **de** may be substituted for **por**.

Era amado de todos.　　*He was loved by all.*

atención　The tense of the verb **ser** in the passive voice matches the tense of the verb in the active voice.

Esa asociación **fue fundada** por ellos el año pasado.	**Fundaron** esa asociación el año pasado.

CD-ROM
Go to **Estructuras gramaticales** for additional practice.

Práctica

A. Cambie las siguientes oraciones a la voz pasiva.

MODELO:　La compañía Argos diseñó los programas.
　　　　Los programas fueron diseñados por la compañía Argos.

1. Fundaron esta empresa en 1998.
2. El jefe ha entrevistado a todos los aspirantes.
3. Despidieron a ese empleado la semana pasada.
4. Los ejecutivos pagaban los gastos de los viajes.
5. Los empleados archivarán los contratos.
6. No creo que ya hayan comprado todos los procesadores de textos.

B. Use las siguientes preguntas para entrevistar a un(a) compañero(a).

1. ¿En qué año fue fundada la universidad?
2. ¿Por quiénes fue escrito este libro de español?
3. ¿En qué año fue descubierta América?
4. ¿Sabes por quiénes fueron fundadas las misiones de California?
5. ¿Dónde crees que será construida la primera ciudad espacial?

6. ¿Ha sido descubierta ya una cura para el cáncer?
7. ¿Qué noticia importante fue publicada la semana pasada en todos los periódicos?
8. ¿Qué películas crees que serán nominadas como las mejores del año?

2 Construcciones con **se**

A El *se* pasivo

◉ A reflexive construction with **se** is often used in Spanish instead of the passive voice when the subject is inanimate and the agent is not specified. The verb is used in the third person singular or plural, depending on the subject.

El banco **se abre** a las diez.   *The bank opens at ten.*
Los bancos **se abren** a las diez.   *The banks open at ten.*

B El *se* impersonal

◉ **Se** is also used as an indefinite subject in Spanish. As such it is equivalent to the impersonal *one* or the colloquial *you* in English.

—¿Cómo **se sale** de aquí?   *"How does one (do you) get out of here?"*
—Por aquella puerta.   *"Through that door."*

◉ **Se** is frequently used in impersonal sentences implying orders, regulations, or ads.

Se prohíbe fumar.   *Smoking is forbidden.*
Se compran autos usados.   *Used cars bought.*

Práctica

CD-ROM
Go to **Estructuras gramaticales** for additional practice.

A. Vuelva a escribir las siguientes oraciones, usando el **se** pasivo. Siga el modelo.

MODELO: La carta fue entregada ayer.
          La carta se entregó ayer.

1. Los teléfonos celulares fueron comprados el mes pasado.
2. Pronto será vendida la maquinaria.
3. El aumento anual no había sido incluido en el informe anterior.
4. Los letreros ya han sido puestos.
5. Las etiquetas fueron impresas ayer.
6. La venta va a ser anunciada el jueves.
7. Los documentos serán firmados la próxima semana.
8. Muchos gastos diarios habían sido eliminados.
9. Las cartas son enviadas al extranjero los fines de mes.
10. Los aspirantes eran entrevistados los lunes.

B. Use las siguientes preguntas para entrevistar a un(a) compañero(a).

1. ¿Qué lengua se habla en Chile? ¿Y en Brasil?
2. ¿Cómo se dice "así que" en inglés?
3. ¿Cómo se escribe el signo de multiplicar?
4. ¿A qué hora se termina la clase?
5. ¿Cómo se sale de aquí?
6. ¿Cómo se llega a tu casa?
7. ¿Qué ropa se usa en el invierno?
8. ¿Cómo se hace una hamburguesa?

3 Usos especiales de **se**

El uso de *se* para referirse a acciones imprevistas

○ The reflexive **se** is used with the corresponding indirect object pronoun and the verb in the third person singular or plural to describe an accidental or unexpected action.

Se	me		perdió	el dinero.
	I		*lost*	*the money.*
Se	le		rompieron	los vasos.
	He / She / You (Ud.)		*broke*	*the glasses.*

atención Note that the verb is used in the singular or plural, according to the subject that appears immediately after it. Only the following combinations of pronouns are possible.

se $\begin{cases} \textbf{me} \\ \textbf{te} \\ \textbf{le} \\ \textbf{nos} \\ \textbf{os} \\ \textbf{les} \end{cases}$ Siempre se $\begin{cases} \textbf{me} \text{ pierden las llaves.} \\ \textbf{te} \text{ manchan los pantalones.} \\ \textbf{le} \text{ descompone el coche.} \\ \textbf{nos} \text{ rompen los vasos.} \\ \textbf{os} \text{ olvida firmar los contratos.} \\ \textbf{les} \text{ descompone el ordenador portátil.} \end{cases}$

—A mí siempre **se me pierde** o **se me olvida** algo. ¡Es terrible!

"*I always lose or forget something. It's terrible!*"

—A Elena también **se le olvida** todo. Dicen que ese tipo de persona es muy inteligente.

"*Elena also forgets everything. They say that that type of person is very intelligent.*"

—En ese caso yo debo ser genio.

"*In that case I must be a genius.*"

atención The indirect object pronoun indicates the person involved, but **a** + *noun* or *pronoun* may be added for emphasis or clarification.

A Elena se le olvida todo.

CD-ROM
Go to **Estructuras gramaticales** for additional practice.

Práctica

A. Aquí se describen los problemas de diferentes personas. Vuelva a escribirlos para expresar que la acción es accidental o inesperada. Siga el modelo.

MODELO: Elsa perdió las llaves del coche.
A Elsa se le perdieron las llaves del coche.

1. Yo perdí el dinero.
2. El vendedor ha perdido los contratos.
3. Cuando viajo, siempre olvido hacer reservaciones.
4. Lorenzo olvidó traer las etiquetas.
5. Se echó a reír porque tú quemaste la comida.
6. Algunas veces olvidamos firmar los cheques.
7. Ellos descompusieron el coche.
8. Se perdió nuestro gato.

B. Conteste las siguientes preguntas usando el verbo entre paréntesis. Siga el modelo.

MODELO: —¿Firmaste el contrato? (olvidar)
—*No, se me olvidó.*

1. ¿Leyó Carlos el anuncio? (perder)
2. ¿Trajeron ellos el escáner? (romper)
3. ¿Archivaron Uds. las cartas? (olvidar)
4. ¿Hice yo el letrero? (manchar)
5. ¿Usaron Uds. el ordenador portátil? (descomponer)
6. ¿Llevaste tu perrito al veterinario? (morir)

4 Algunas expresiones idiomáticas comunes

A Expresiones idiomáticas con *dar, tener, poner* y *hacer*

○ Idioms with **dar**

1. **dar ánimo**   *to cheer up*

   David está triste. Voy a tratar de **darle ánimo.**

2. **dar gato por liebre**   *to deceive, to defraud*

   Este anillo no es de oro. Te **dieron gato por liebre.**

3. **dar marcha atrás**   *to back up*

   Dio marcha atrás y rompió la puerta del garaje.

4. **dar en el clavo**   *to hit the nail on the head*

   Cuando ella dijo que él iba a renunciar, **dio en el clavo.**

○ Idioms with **tener**

1. **tener chispa**   *to be witty*

   Todo lo que dice es muy cómico. **Tiene** mucha **chispa.**

2. **no tener pelos en la lengua**   *to be outspoken, to be frank*

   Mi jefa dice exactamente lo que piensa. **No tiene pelos en la lengua.**

3. **por no tener (algo)**   *for the lack of (something)*

   El postulante no pudo conseguir el puesto **por no tener** experiencia como contador.

○ Idioms with **poner**

1. **poner en duda**   *to doubt*

   Al principio **puso en duda** lo que le decíamos, pero después quedó convencido.

2. **poner en peligro**   *to endanger*

   Para salvar a su hijo, **puso en peligro** su vida.

3. **poner peros**   *to find fault*

   ¡Nunca te gustan mis ideas! ¡A todo le **pones peros**!

4. **ponerse en ridículo**   *to make a fool of oneself*

   Siempre estás diciendo tonterías y **poniéndote en ridículo.**

○ Idioms with **hacer**

1. **hacer caso**   *to obey; to pay attention*

   Ellos nunca me **hacen caso.**

2. **hacer(se) (de) la vista gorda**   *to overlook*

   Su secretaria siempre llega tarde, pero él **se hace de la vista gorda.**

3. **hacerse el tonto (la tonta)**   *to play dumb*

   Tú entiendes muy bien lo que te digo, pero **te haces el tonto.**

4. **hacérsele a uno agua la boca**   *to make one's mouth water*

   ¡Mmm! Cuando pienso en el postre de hoy, **se me hace agua la boca.**

Práctica

CD-ROM
Go to **Estructuras gramaticales** for additional practice.

Complete las siguientes oraciones, usando las expresiones idiomáticas estudiadas, según corresponda.

1. No pudo comprar el coche _____ suficiente dinero.
2. ¡Estoy tan triste! ¿Por qué no vienes a _____?
3. Yo sé que lo van a despedir. ¡No lo _____!

4. El doctor dice que si no me opero, estoy poniendo mi vida ____.
5. Me dijeron que la pulsera era de oro y no es verdad; es de cobre (*copper*). Me dieron _____.
6. Es inteligente y tiene un gran sentido del humor. ¡La verdad es que tiene _____!
7. Ese hombre dice muchas tonterías; siempre se pone en _____.
8. Ella siempre dice exactamente lo que piensa; no tiene _____.
9. Tú sabes muy bien de lo que te estoy hablando. ¡No te _____!
10. ¡Qué comida tan estupenda! Sólo de verla se me _____.
11. Para sacar el coche del garaje, tienes que _____.
12. Nada le gusta; a todo le _____. Y nunca hace lo que le digo. No me _____.
13. Puedes creer lo que dice, porque siempre _____.

B Otras expresiones idiomáticas comunes

1. **¿A cuánto estamos hoy?**[1]   *What date is today?*

   A ver... **¿a cuánto estamos hoy?** A 13 de marzo, ¿no?

2. **a la larga**   *in the long run*

   Si los empleados siguen trabajando así, **a la larga** se van a cansar.

3. **al fin y al cabo**   *after all*

   Le van a dar el puesto. **Al fin y al cabo,** tiene un título en mercadeo.

4. **al pie de la letra**   *exactly, to the letter*

   El jefe quiere que sigamos sus instrucciones **al pie de la letra.**

5. **algo por el estilo**   *something like that*

   Se llama Adela... Delia... o **algo por el estilo.**

6. **aquí hay gato encerrado**   *there's something fishy here*

   Lo que está pasando es muy extraño... **Aquí hay gato encerrado...**

7. **con las manos en la masa**   *red-handed*

   Pescaron (*They caught*) al ladrón **con las manos en la masa.**

8. **de mala gana**   *reluctantly*

   Si lo vas a hacer **de mala gana,** prefiero que no lo hagas.

9. **en el acto**   *immediately, at once, right away, instantly*

   Entrevistó al hombre y lo contrato **en el actó.**

10. **en voz alta (baja)**   *aloud, in a loud voice (in a low voice)*

    No hablen **en voz alta** porque el niño está durmiendo. ¡Hablen **en voz baja!**

---

[1] También se dice **¿A cómo estamos hoy?**

11. **entre la espada y la pared**   *between a rock and a hard place*

No sé qué hacer en esta situación. Estoy **entre la espada y la pared.**

12. **poner el grito en el cielo**   *to hit the roof*

Cuando le dijeron que tenía que trabajar tiempo extra, **puso el grito en el cielo.**

CD-ROM
Go to **Estructuras gramaticales** for additional practice.

Práctica

A. Complete las siguientes oraciones y compare sus experiencias y opiniones con las de un(a) compañero(a).

1. Se me hace agua la boca cuando...
2. Yo nunca pongo en duda...
3. A mí siempre se me pierden...
4. Yo me hago el tonto (la tonta) cuando...
5. Sudo la gota gorda cuando...
6. Yo siempre hablo en voz baja cuando...
7. Yo pongo el grito en el cielo cuando...
8. A mí siempre se me olvida(n)...

B. De las expresiones idiomáticas que Ud. aprendió en esta lección, ¿cuáles seleccionaría Ud. como equivalentes de lo siguiente?

1. exactamente
2. decir todo lo que se piensa
3. encontrarlo todo mal
4. engañar (*to deceive*)
5. inmediatamente
6. con el paso del tiempo
7. decidir entre dos problemas igualmente difíciles
8. sin deseos
9. después de todo
10. gritar furiosamente

C. Conteste las siguientes preguntas, usando en sus respuestas las expresiones idiomáticas estudiadas, según corresponda.

1. ¿Qué fecha es hoy?
2. ¿Hace exactamente todo lo que le dicen sus padres?
3. Si alguien está durmiendo, ¿cómo habla Ud.?
4. ¿Ha pescado Ud. a alguien haciendo algo que no debía?
5. Cuando Ud. era pequeño(a), ¿hacía a veces cosas que no quería hacer porque sus padres se lo ordenaban?
6. Alberto y Elsa escribieron exactamente la misma composición. ¿Cómo cree Ud. que sucedió eso?
7. Si su mejor amigo(a) le dijera que lo (la) necesitaba urgentemente, ¿iría Ud. a verlo(la) inmediatamente?

STUDENT WEBSITE
Do the **Compruebe cuánto sabe** self test after finishing this **Estructuras gramaticales** section.

8. Si Ud. tuviera que trabajar tiempo completo y no graduarse a tiempo o estudiar y no tener dinero, ¿cómo se sentiría?
9. ¿Qué va a pasar si Ud. aprende un poco de español cada día?
10. ¿Está Ud. cansado(a) de tener que trabajar todos los días? ¿De su supervisor(a)?
11. ¿Qué haría Ud. si alguien le robara su coche?
12. ¿Qué piensa Ud. de sus compañeros de clase?

¡CONTINUEMOS!

Una encuesta

Entreviste a sus compañeros de clase para tratar de identificar a aquellas personas que...

1. ...tienen un apartado postal.
2. ...trabajan para una empresa muy grande.
3. ...están planeando su jubilación.
4. ...están hasta la coronilla de alguien.
5. ...han usado un escáner recientemente.
6. ...usan mucho su teléfono celular.
7. ...tienen que trabajar tiempo extra a veces.
8. ...han solicitado trabajo recientemente.
9. ...utilizan el correo electrónico con frecuencia.
10. ...esperan desempeñar un puesto importante algún día.
11. ...ponen el grito en el cielo cuando se enojan.
12. ...creen que es importante ser bilingües.
13. ...precisan tener más memoria en su computadora.
14. ...han recibido un aumento de sueldo recientemente.

Ahora, en grupos de tres o cuatro, discutan el resultado de la encuesta.

¿Comprende Ud.?

CD-ROM   STUDENT WEBSITE
Go to **De escuchar...a escribir** (in **¿Comprende Ud.?**) on the CD-ROM for activities related to the conversation, and go to **Canción** on the website for activities related to the song.

1. Escuche la siguiente conversación entre Jorge Torres y su primo Luis Sandoval en un autobús de San Juan, Puerto Rico. El objetivo de la actividad es el de escuchar una conversación a velocidad natural. No se preocupe de entenderlo todo, pues esto no se espera de Ud. Después de escuchar la conversación dos veces, Ud. oirá varias aseveraciones. En una hoja, escriba los números de uno a ocho e indique si cada aseveración es verdadera o falsa.
2. Luego escuche la canción y trate de aprenderla.

Hablemos de tecnología

En parejas, fíjense en los anuncios y contesten las siguientes preguntas.

Robots: el futuro ya está aquí

C3PO y R2D2 están a punto de salir de la pantalla. Muchas empresas de todo el mundo investigan para fabricar pronto robots en serie y algunas venden ya por Internet kits para montar en casa interesantes prototipos. La tecnología punta se empeña en hacer realidad la ciencia ficción.

Ábrete de orejas

La música no es lo mismo desde que ha aparecido el formato MP3. Las discográficas se han rendido ya a sus poderes. Hemos recorrido las tiendas en busca de los más novedosos y revolucionarios reproductores. Algunos te van a sorprender.

1. ¿Qué hacen muchas empresas de todo el mundo?
2. ¿Qué venden ya algunas por Internet?
3. ¿Qué es lo que la tecnología punta (*state-of-the-art*) se empeña en hacer realidad?
4. ¿Qué crees que significa la expresión idiomática "ábrete de orejas"?
5. ¿Qué ha cambiado el formato MP3?
6. ¿Qué te va a sorprender?

¿Qué dirían Uds.?

Imagínese que Ud. y una amiga están comentando lo que les ha pasado a otros amigos de Uds. Reaccionen a la información dada, usando las expresiones idiomáticas adecuadas a cada situación.

1. Pedro compró un reloj que él creyó que era de oro y no lo era.
2. Marta le dijo a su jefe exactamente lo que pensaba de él.
3. Fernando está muy desanimado.
4. Julio piensa en el flan que va a comer esta noche.
5. Raquel sigue exactamente las instrucciones.
6. Olga no quería limpiar su casa, pero tuvo que hacerlo.
7. Le dije a Paco que lo necesitaba y a los cinco minutos estaba en mi casa.
8. Elsa dijo que el candidato iba a perder y perdió.

¡De ustedes depende!

Imagínense que Ud. y un(a) compañero(a) están encargados(as) de preparar un folleto de propaganda turística sobre la ciudad donde viven o estudian. Discutan los siguientes puntos, necesarios para escribir el folleto.

1. ¿Cuándo fue fundada la ciudad y por quién(es)?
2. ¿Qué lugares interesantes se pueden visitar?
3. ¿En qué restaurantes se come bien?
4. ¿A qué hora se abren y se cierran las tiendas, los bancos, etc.?
5. ¿Qué tipo de ropa se debe llevar?
6. ¿Qué fiestas populares se celebran y en qué fechas?
7. ¿Cómo se llega a esa ciudad?
8. ¿Qué otros idiomas, además del inglés, se hablan allí?
9. ¿Qué actividades culturales hay?
10. Otras cosas que Uds. consideren interesantes.

¡Debate!

La clase se dividirá en dos grupos: los que creen que la tecnología es muy útil y resuelve la mayoría de los problemas y los que piensan que en muchos casos deshumaniza al individuo. Cada grupo dará una serie de razones para defender su punto de vista.

Lecturas periodísticas

Saber leer   ¡Ahora le toca a Ud.![1]

CD-ROM
Go to **Lecturas periodísticas** for additional prereading and vocabulary activities.

Hoy le asignamos la tarea de leer el siguiente artículo publicado en la revista *Puerto Rico digital*, versión "en línea". Trata del Internet en casa y en el trabajo. En esta ocasión, el cómo leerlo... ¡será su pequeño proyecto de lectura!

Para leer y comprender

Al leer detalladamente el artículo, busque las respuestas a las siguientes preguntas.

1. ¿En qué se ha convertido el Internet?
2. ¿Qué entidades utilizan el Internet como herramienta?
3. ¿Qué representa el Internet para el consumidor residencial?
4. ¿Qué les provee a las empresas el acceso al Internet?
5. ¿Qué gastos pueden evitar las empresas al conectarse con el Internet?
6. ¿Qué otras ventajas tienen los negocios al conectarse al Internet?

---

[1] *Now it's your turn!*

El acceso al Internet

Acceso residencial. El Internet se ha convertido en una necesidad, no sólo en el trabajo, sino también en el hogar. Cada día son más las corporaciones, oficinas gubernamentales y otras entidades°, que lo valoran como una herramienta°, como al fax, al beeper y al teléfono móvil o celular. Pero el acceso al Internet es mucho más.

Para el consumidor residencial representa, además del acceso ilimitado a diversas fuentes de información, un ahorro° sustancial para su bolsillo. Si necesita obtener una imagen, informarse sobre algún negocio, comprar mercancía° de todo tipo, hacer alguna reservación para ir de vacaciones, o simplemente entretenerse, puede hacerlo desde la comodidad° de su hogar con sólo escribir una frase y apretar° un botón. El tener acceso a la más grande y actualizada fuente de información tiene muchas ventajas.

Acceso corporativo. El acceso al Internet les provee a las empresas muchas de las herramientas necesarias para aumentar su productividad y nuevas formas para servir mejor a sus clientes. Conectando la red° de su empresa al Internet obtiene acceso a la base de datos más grande del mundo, puede beneficiarse con el medio° de comunicación mundial más rápido, eficiente y económico, y mantiene su empresa un paso adelante en el mundo de los negocios°. Esto representará ahorros en gastos operacionales, al poder utilizar el e-mail o correo electrónico y así evitar las llamadas de larga distancia, el uso del fax y el gasto excesivo de papel. Además, el poder comunicarse con los colegas y con otros negocios, sin la necesidad de reunirse en un mismo lugar, representará un mejor uso del tiempo, tan escaso° sobre todo hoy en día°. Entre las ventajas de conectar su negocio al Internet se encuentran la de personalizar el sistema de e-mail (al registrar su *nombre de dominio*, por ejemplo *compañía.com*) y tener su propia página de Web. ¡Conozca las ventajas de conectar su empresa con la red cibernética!

Adaptado de *Puerto Rico digital*

> *Además, el poder comunicarse con los colegas y con otros negocios, sin la necesidad de reunirse en un mismo lugar, representará un mejor uso del tiempo, tan escaso sobre todo hoy en día.*

Agente de viajes haciendo uso del Internet en su trabajo.

---

institutions
tool

saving
merchandise
comfort
press

network
means
business
scarce / **hoy**... nowadays

Desde su mundo

1. ¿El Internet es una herramienta para Ud.? ¿Por qué sí o por qué no?
2. ¿Qué cree Ud. que se pierden aquellas personas que no están conectadas al Internet?

STUDENT WEBSITE

CD-ROM

Piense y escriba   ¡Ahora le toca a Ud.!

Le asignamos la tarea de redacción: Escribirá un breve artículo sobre los cambios que la tecnología ha traído a su vida. Este artículo se publicará en la revista de su clase de español, *Nuestros escritos*. Como para la lectura periodística de esta lección, el cómo escribir el artículo... ¡será su pequeño proyecto de redacción!

Go to ...**y escribamos** (in **Hablemos de su país**) on the student website and **De escuchar... a escribir** (in ¿**Comprende Ud.?**) on the CD-ROM for additional writing practice.

Pepe Vega y su mundo

Teleinforme

En estos tres fragmentos de video veremos algunos aspectos del trabajo y la tecnología: las empresas virtuales en Internet, la importancia de la entrevista de trabajo y una oferta de trabajo televisada.

Preparación

¿Cómo presentarse para un trabajo?   Para conseguir un trabajo, Ud. debe demostrar sus cualidades y su capacidad para desempeñar el trabajo. Hay varios modos de presentarse: la carta de trabajo, el curriculum vitae o resumé, y la entrevista de trabajo. Clasifique la siguiente información según se presente mejor: en una carta (C), en un curriculum vitae (CV) o en una entrevista (E), o si no se debe presentar (N).

_____ 1. si es discapacitado(a) (*disabled*)
_____ 2. si sabe hablar otros idiomas
_____ 3. si tiene coche propio y permiso de conducir
_____ 4. si tiene experiencia en un puesto similar
_____ 5. si vive en la zona del trabajo
_____ 6. su aspecto físico
_____ 7. su conocimiento en informática
_____ 8. su disponibilidad para trabajar por turnos (*in shifts*)
_____ 9. su edad
_____ 10. el salario deseado
_____ 11. su formación profesional
_____ 12. su sentido del humor

Comprensión

CD-ROM
Go to **Video** for further previewing, vocabulary, and structure practice on this clip.

El comercio virtual   52:14–54:02

¿Recuerda Ud. cuando la Internet no era algo común para la mayoría de nosotros? En el reportaje que sigue, realizado para la serie española *Empléate a fondo* veremos la Internet y sus posibilidades ilimitadas en los inicios de la explosión virtual.

A. **Fijarse en los detalles.**   Lea las siguientes oraciones. Luego, mientras ve el informe sobre la Internet y el comercio virtual, escriba o escoja la respuesta correcta, según corresponda.

1. Mayté Cabezas, la presentadora, nos dice que el informe sobre Internet va a ser muy (técnico/difícil de entender/claro).

2. Internet es, simplemente, _____.

3. Según el locutor (*speaker*), ¿cuáles de los siguientes elementos son necesarios para tener acceso a la Internet?

_____ un ordenador   _____ un modem
_____ un teléfono   _____ una empresa virtual
_____ una línea telefónica   _____ una calculadora
_____ una compañía que nos
       conecte a la red

4. _____ es el aparato que convierte la señal telefónica en datos que pueden ser vistos en nuestro ordenador.

5. Fíjese (*Notice*) en el aspecto visual del reportaje. Dé tres ejemplos de imágenes que indican que este reportaje se hizo en la década de 1990 y no hoy. Explique.

6. Escuche la última parte del informe sobre las empresas virtuales. ¿Hay información que le parece anticuada (*outdated*) u obsoleta? Explique por qué.

La entrevista de trabajo   54:04–57:46

CD-ROM
You will also find this clip under **Video**.

Ahora escucharemos varias perspectivas sobre lo que debe ser una entrevista de trabajo. Primero, veremos otro informe de la serie *Empléate a fondo*; luego, Mayte nos presenta a un orientador sociolaboral. Finalmente, escucharemos a cuatro jóvenes entrevistados en el metro de Madrid.

B. ¿Qué es lo más importante?   Indique con una **X** cuáles de los siguientes aspectos de una entrevista son importantes para cada persona que habla.

Aspecto	Felipe de la Cruz	Carlos (chico 1)	Silvia (chica 1)	Paco (chico 2)	Ana (chica 2)
1. buscar información sobre la empresa					
2. cuidar su imagen personal					
3. hablar bien					
4. no preparar la entrevista					
5. preparar preguntas sobre el puesto					
6. seguir la dirección de la entrevistadora					
7. ser simpática y agradable					
8. ser sincero y decir la verdad					
9. vestirse de manera apropiada					
10. vestirse según sus gustos personales					

Oferta de empleo   57:48–58:39

STUDENT WEBSITE
Go to **Video** for further previewing, vocabulary, and structure practice on this clip.

El programa español *Empléate a fondo* no sólo ofrece consejos sobre cómo conseguir un trabajo, sino que también les presenta ofertas de varias clases de trabajo a los televidentes. Aquí vemos a un locutor presentándonos unos puestos para grabadores de datos (*data entry clerks*).

C. ¡Apúntelo bien!   Imagine que Ud. busca empleo y le interesa la oferta que nos describe Antolín Romero. Antes de ver el video, lea la siguiente lista de preguntas. Luego, mientras ve el video, apunte (*jot down*) la información que le falta.

1. ¿Para quiénes es esta oferta de trabajo? _____
2. ¿Cuántos puestos hay? _____
3. ¿Es necesario tener experiencia en un puesto similar? _____
4. ¿Se debe estar disponible para trabajar de día, de noche o por turnos? _____
5. ¿Dónde se debe residir? _____
6. ¿Cuándo empieza el trabajo? _____
7. ¿Cómo se puede saber más? _____

Ampliación

Ud. entrevista.   En grupos de cinco, imagine que una persona es entrevistador(a) y que los otros son los cuatro jóvenes que vimos en el último segmento. Los jóvenes son candidatos para uno de los siguientes empleos (escoja uno):

repartidor(a) de pizza
grabador(a) de datos
ingeniero(a) técnico(a)
profesor(a) de francés
(u otro puesto que Uds. escojan)

Prepare una serie de preguntas para entrevistar a los aspirantes. ¿Quién conseguirá el puesto?

La Internet.   Imagine que Ud. se va a presentar para un puesto en una empresa de comercio virtual. ¿Cómo podría Ud. prepararse para la entrevista *usando la Internet*?

Lecciones 9 y 10

Tome este examen para ver cuánto ha aprendido. Las respuestas correctas aparecen en el **Apéndice C**.

Lección 9

A El subjuntivo: resumen general

Complete las siguientes oraciones con los verbos que aparecen entre paréntesis. Use el indicativo, el infinitivo o el subjuntivo.

1. Ellos querían que yo les _____ (traer) los discos.
2. Es mejor que (tú) _____ (ver) al productor.
3. Dile que te _____ (dar) la guía de espectáculos.
4. No habrían suprimido el programa si _____ (ser) bueno.
5. No habrá nadie que _____ (poder) grabarlo.
6. Siento que ayer nosotros no _____ (conseguir) los papeles principales.
7. Hay muchas personas que _____ (ir) al desfile.
8. Me alegro de _____ (estar) aquí.
9. Irán a ver el espectáculo si _____ (tener) tiempo.
10. No creo que _____ (haber empezar) la telenovela todavía.
11. Si nosotros _____ (salir) ahora, llegaríamos mañana.
12. Por suerte podremos salir en cuanto _____ (llegar) la actriz.
13. Es verdad que ellos _____ (ganar) el premio ayer.
14. El periodista no quería _____ (hacer) la entrevista hoy.
15. Nosotros no queremos que ellos _____ (escuchar) ese programa.

B Usos de algunas preposiciones

Complete las siguientes oraciones usando las preposiciones **a, de** y **en**, según corresponda.

1. Ayer, _____ las nueve _____ la mañana, fuimos _____ visitar _____ Isabel.
2. Le dije _____ Gustavo que yo quería que él empezara _____ enseñarme _____ bailar tan pronto como llegáramos _____ Acapulco.
3. Me olvidé _____ decirte que íbamos _____ volver _____ coche.
4. Yo salí sin darme cuenta _____ que había dejado _____ la gata _____ la calle.
5. Mis hermanos y yo convinimos _____ que hablaríamos _____ todo, menos _____ política.
6. No te acordaste _____ decirle que la ropa estaba _____ la cama.
7. Adela es morena, _____ ojos verdes, y es la chica más simpática _____ la familia.
8. Cuando te dije que él se había enamorado _____ mí, lo dije _____ broma.
9. Insistió _____ entrar _____ ese restaurante.
10. Oscar nunca confía _____ nadie.

C Verbos con preposiciones

Complete las siguientes oraciones usando el equivalente español de las frases dadas.

1. Carlos ya no quiere _____ Aurora porque está _____ Marta. (*marry / in love with*)
2. Yo no _____ su número de teléfono. (*remember*)
3. Armando y yo _____ _____ casa a las diez. (*agree on / leave*)
4. Ellos siempre _____ _____ nosotros los domingos. (*insist on / meet*)
5. _____ que Uds. no _____ él. (*I am glad / trust*)

D El infinitivo

Complete las siguientes oraciones con el equivalente de las palabras entre paréntesis.

1. Ellos dicen que _____ es bueno. (*eating fruit*)
2. Ellas _____ al desfile. (*wanted to go*)
3. _____ a la entrevista, ellos nos llamaron. (*Before going to*)
4. Mi abuela _____ la telenovela. (*wanted to see*)
5. Los periodistas dijeron que tenían tres reportajes _____. (*unfinished*)
6. Él volvió a las doce; _____. (*I heard him come in*)
7. El letrero dice: _____. (*No smoking*)
8. Los chicos _____ de la editorial. (*have just returned*)
9. _____ para el examen. (*I'm going to start studying*)

E ¿Recuerda el vocabulario?

Complete las siguientes oraciones usando el vocabulario de la **Lección 9**.

1. Hoy _____ una película de la _____ Julia Roberts.
2. No es verdad; es _____.
3. Ellos vuelven de su viaje a _____ de junio.
4. Ricardo es encantador; estoy muy _____ de él.
5. La música latina se ha puesto de _____ ahora.
6. Ana está aprendiendo los _____ básicos de la salsa.
7. No puedo ver la telenovela. La voy a _____.
8. Celia Cruz es la _____ de la salsa.
9. La _____ por televisión es muy importante para aumentar las ventas.
10. Hay cien años en un _____.

F Cultura

Conteste las siguientes preguntas.

1. ¿Qué país se conoce como "la tierra del tango"?
2. ¿Cuál es el pico más alto del mundo occidental?
3. ¿A orillas de que río está situada la ciudad de Buenos Aires?
4. ¿Cómo llaman a las personas que nacen en Buenos Aires?
5. ¿Qué influencia europea se nota en Argentina?

Lección 10

A La voz pasiva

Conteste las siguientes preguntas usando la voz pasiva y la información dada entre paréntesis.

1. ¿Quién escribió esa novela?   (Cortázar)
2. ¿Cuándo construirán ese hospital?   (en el 2006)
3. ¿Quién ha publicado ese libro?   (la Editorial Losada)
4. ¿Quién firma los documentos?   (el director)
5. ¿Quién traducía las cartas?   (el Sr. Ruiz)

B Construcciones con se

Complete las siguientes preguntas, usando el **se** pasivo o el **se** impersonal y los verbos dados entre paréntesis.

1. ¿Qué lengua _____ (hablar) en Brasil?
2. ¿Cómo _____ (decir) "jubilación" en inglés?
3. ¿Dónde _____ (vender) escáners?
4. ¿Por dónde _____ (entrar) en este edificio?
5. ¿A qué hora _____ (cerrar) los bancos?
6. ¿Cómo _____ (poder) obtener el puesto de vendedor?

C El uso de se para referirse a acciones imprevistas

Complete las siguientes oraciones, usando construcciones con **se** para indicar que la acción es accidental.

1. Ayer a mí _____ (romper) los platos.
2. A nosotros siempre _____ (perder) las llaves.
3. Anoche _____ (descomponer) el televisor a Juan.
4. A ti siempre _____ (olvidar) los libros.
5. A esos pobres chicos _____ (morir) el gato ayer.

D Algunas expresiones idiomáticas comunes

Complete las siguientes oraciones con el equivalente español de las expresiones idiomáticas que aparecen entre paréntesis.

1. Julio _____ y chocó con un árbol.   (*backed up*)
2. Yo nunca _____ lo que tú me dices.   (*doubt*)
3. Voy a visitar a Rosa para _____.   (*cheer her up*)
4. ¡Eso es de plástico! Ellos _____.   (*deceived you*)
5. No sé qué decidir; estoy _____.   (*between a rock and a hard place*)

E ¿Recuerda el vocabulario?

Complete las siguientes oraciones usando el vocabulario de la **Lección 10**.

1. El número de mi _____ postal es 524.
2. A Rosa le _____ del trabajo ayer.
3. Habla demasiado. Estoy hasta la _____ de él.
4. Un sinónimo de sueldo es _____.
5. Voy a solicitar el _____ de vendedor.
6. _____ a su trabajo porque no quería viajar al _____.
7. Ella es diseñadora de _____.
8. Yo no tengo un teléfono _____ en mi coche.
9. Tengo que pagar todas las semanas porque los pagos son _____.
10. ¡No me gusta _____ la red!

F Cultura

Conteste las siguientes preguntas.

1. ¿Cómo llaman a Cuba?
2. ¿Cuáles son las principales exportaciones de Cuba?
3. ¿Qué es el viejo San Juan?
4. ¿Qué es el Castillo del Morro?
5. ¿Qué dos países comparten la isla que Colón llamó "La Española"?
6. ¿Cuál es el deporte más popular en la República Dominicana?

Apéndice A: Algunas reglas generales

Separación de palabras

A. Vocales

1. A vowel or a vowel combination can constitute a syllable.

   e-ne-ro   a-cuer-do   Eu-ro-pa   ai-re   u-no

2. Diphthongs and triphthongs are considered single vowels and cannot be divided.

   vie-ne   Dia-na   cue-ro   es-tu-diáis   bui-tre

3. Two strong vowels (**a**, **e**, or **o**) do not form a diphthong and are separated into two syllables.

   em-ple-o   le-an   ro-e-dor   tra-e-mos   lo-a

4. A written accent mark on a weak vowel (**i** or **u**) breaks the diphthong; thus the vowels are separated into two syllables.

   rí-o   dú-o   Ma-rí-a   Ra-úl   ca-í-mos

B. Consonantes

1. A single consonant forms a syllable with the vowel that follows it.

   mi-nu-to   ca-sa-do   la-ti-na   Re-na-to

atención **ch**, **ll** and **rr** are considered single consonants.

   co-che   a-ma-ri-llo   ci-ga-rro

2. Consonant clusters composed of **b**, **c**, **d**, **f**, **g**, **p**, or **t** with **l** or **r** are considered single consonants and cannot be separated.

   su-bli-me   cre-ma   dra-ma   flo-res   gra-mo   te-a-tro

3. When two consonants appear between two vowels, they are separated into two syllables.

   al-fa-be-to   mo-les-tia   me-ter-se

atención When a consonant cluster composed of **b**, **c**, **d**, **f**, **g**, **p**, or **t** with **l** or **r** appears between two vowels, the cluster joins the following vowel.

   so-bre   o-tra   ca-ble   te-lé-gra-fo

4. When three consonants appear between two vowels, only the last one goes with the following vowel.

   ins-pec-tor   trans-por-te   trans-for-mar

323

 When there is a cluster of three consonants in the combinations described in rule 2, the first consonant joins the preceding vowel and the cluster joins the following vowel.

es-cri-bir   im-plo-rar   ex-tran-je-ro

El acento ortográfico

In Spanish, all words are stressed according to specific rules. Words that do not follow the rules must have a written accent mark to indicate the change of stress. The basic rules for accentuation are as follows:

1. Words ending in a vowel, **n**, or **s** are stressed on the next to the last syllable.

   ver-de   re-**ten**-go   ro-**sa**-da   es-**tu**-dian   co-**no**-ces

2. Words ending in a consonant, except **n** or **s**, are stressed on the last syllable.

   es-pa-**ñol**   pro-fe-**sor**   pa-**red**   tro-pi-**cal**   na-**riz**

3. All words that do not follow these rules, and also those that are stressed on the second from the last syllable, must have a written accent mark.

   ca-**fé**   co-**mió**   ma-**má**   sa-**lón**   fran-**cés**
   án-gel   **lá**-piz   **mú**-si-ca   de-**mó**-cra-ta

4. The interrogative and exclamatory pronouns and adverbs have a written accent mark to distinguish them from the relative forms.

   ¿Qué comes?
   ¡Qué calor hace!

5. Words that have the same spelling but different meanings have a written accent mark to differentiate one from another.

el	*the*	él	*he, him*
mi	*my*	mí	*me*
tu	*your*	tú	*you*
te	*you, yourself*	té	*tea*
si	*if*	sí	*yes*
mas	*but*	más	*more*
solo	*alone*	sólo	*only*

6. The demonstrative pronouns have a written accent mark to distinguish them from the demonstrative adjectives.

éste	ésta	ése	ésa	aquél	aquélla
éstos	éstas	ésos	ésas	aquéllos	aquéllas

7. Affirmative commands with object pronouns have written accent marks if the word has two or more syllables after the stress.

   Tráigamela.   Cómpralo.   Pídasela.

Uso de las mayúsculas

In Spanish, only proper nouns are capitalized. Nationalities, languages, days of the week, and months of the year are not considered proper nouns.

Jamie Ballesteros es de Buenos Aires, pero sus padres no son argentinos, son de España. El sábado, tres de junio, Jaime y sus padres, el doctor[1] Juan Ballesteros y su esposa, la señora[1] Consuelo Ballesteros, salen para Madrid.

Puntuación

1. Inverted question marks and exclamation marks must be placed at the beginning of questions and exclamations.

   —¿Tú quieres ir con nosotros?
   —¡Por supuesto!

2. A comma is not used before **y** or **o** at the end of a series.

   Estudio francés, historia, geografía y matemáticas.

3. In a dialogue, a dash is frequently used instead of quotation marks.

   —¿Cómo estás, Pablo?
   —Muy bien, ¿y tú?

Estudio de cognados

A. Cognates

Cognates are words that are the same or similar in two languages. It is extremely valuable to be able to recognize them when learning a foreign language. Following are some principles of cognate recognition in Spanish.

1. Some words are exact cognates; only the pronunciation is different.

general	terrible	musical	central	humor	banana
idea	mineral	horrible	cultural	natural	terror

2. Some cognates are almost the same, except for a written accent mark, a final vowel, or a single consonant in the Spanish word.

región	comercial	arte	México	posible	potente
personal	península	oficial	importante	conversión	imposible

3. Most nouns ending in *-tion* in English end in **-ción** in Spanish.

conversación	solución	operación	cooperación

4. English words ending in *-ce* and *-ty* end in **-cia**, **cio**, **-tad**, and **-dad** in Spanish.

importancia	precipicio	libertad	ciudad

---

[1]These words are capitalized only when they are abbreviated: **Dr., Sra.**

5. The English ending -*ous* is often equivalent to the Spanish ending **-oso(a)**.

famoso   amoroso   numeroso   malicioso

6. The English consonant *s*- is often equivalent to the Spanish **es-**.

escuela   estado   estudio   especial

7. English words ending in -*cle* end in **-culo** in Spanish.

artículo   círculo   vehículo

8. English words ending in -*y* often end in **-io** in Spanish.

laboratorio   conservatorio

9. English words beginning with *ph*- begin with **f-** in Spanish.

farmacia   frase   filosofía

10. There are many other easily recognizable cognates for which no rule can be given.

millón   deliberadamente   estudiar   millonario   mayoría
ingeniero   norte   enemigo   monte

B. False cognates

False cognates are words that look similar in Spanish and English, but have very different meanings. Some common ones are as follows:

English word	*Spanish equivalent*	*False cognate*
actually	realmente	actualmente (*nowadays*)
application	solicitud	aplicación (*diligence*)
card	tarjeta	carta (*letter*)
character (*in lit.*)	personaje	carácter (*personality, nature*)
embarrassed	avergonzado(a)	embarazada (*pregnant*)
exit	salida	éxito (*success*)
library	biblioteca	librería (*bookstore*)
major (*studies*)	especialidad	mayor (*older, major in armed services*)
minor (*studies*)	segunda especialidad	menor (*younger*)
move (*from one home to another*)	mudarse	mover (*move something*)
question	pregunta	cuestión (*matter*)
subject	asunto, tema	sujeto (*subject of a sentence*)

Apéndice B: Verbos

Verbos regulares: Modelos de los verbos que terminan en *-ar, -er, -ir*

Infinitive

amar (*to love*)	**comer** (*to eat*)	**vivir** (*to live*)

Present Participle

amando (*loving*)	**comiendo** (*eating*)	**viviendo** (*living*)

Past Participle

amado (*loved*)	**comido** (*eaten*)	**vivido** (*lived*)

A. Simple Tenses

Indicative Mood
Present

(*I love*)	(*I eat*)	(*I live*)
amo	como	vivo
amas	comes	vives
ama	come	vive
amamos	comemos	vivimos
amáis	coméis	vivís
aman	comen	viven

Imperfect

(*I used to love*)	(*I used to eat*)	(*I used to live*)
amaba	comía	vivía
amabas	comías	vivías
amaba	comía	vivía
amábamos	comíamos	vivíamos
amabais	comíais	vivíais
amaban	comían	vivían

Preterit

(*I loved*)	(*I ate*)	(*I lived*)
amé	comí	viví
amaste	comiste	viviste
amó	comió	vivió
amamos	comimos	vivimos
amasteis	comisteis	vivisteis
amaron	comieron	vivieron

Future

(*I will love*)	(*I will eat*)	(*I will live*)
amaré	comeré	viviré
amarás	comerás	vivirás
amará	comerá	vivirá
amaremos	comeremos	viviremos
amaréis	comeréis	viviréis
amarán	comerán	vivirán

Conditional

(*I would love*)	(*I would eat*)	(*I would live*)
amaría	comería	viviría
amarías	comerías	vivirías
amaría	comería	viviría
amaríamos	comeríamos	viviríamos
amaríais	comeríais	viviríais
amarían	comerían	vivirían

Subjunctive Mood
Present

([*that*]) *I* [*may*] *love*)	([*that*] *I* [*may*] *eat*)	([*that*] *I* [*may*] *live*)
ame	coma	viva
ames	comas	vivas
ame	coma	viva
amemos	comamos	vivamos
améis	comáis	viváis
amen	coman	vivan

Imperfect

(two forms: -ra, -se)

([*that*] *I* [*might*] *love*)	([*that*] *I* [*might*] *eat*)	([*that*] *I* [*might*] *live*)
amara -ase	comiera -iese	viviera -iese
amaras -ases	comieras -ieses	vivieras -ieses
amara -ase	comiera -iese	viviera -iese
amáramos -ásemos	comiéramos -iésemos	viviéramos -iésemos
amarais -aseis	comierais -ieseis	vivierais -ieseis
amaran -asen	comieran -iesen	vivieran -iesen

Imperative Mood

(*love*)	(*eat*)	(*live*)
ama (tú)	come (tú)	vive (tú)
ame (Ud.)	coma (Ud.)	viva (Ud.)
amemos (nosotros)	comamos (nosotros)	vivamos (nosotros)
amad (vosotros)	comed (vosotros)	vivid (vosotros)
amen (Uds.)	coman (Uds.)	vivan (Uds.)

B. Compound Tenses

Perfect Infinitive

haber amado	haber comido	haber vivido

Perfect Participle

habiendo amado	habiendo comido	habiendo vivido

Indicative Mood
Present Perfect

(*I have loved*)	(*I have eaten*)	(*I have lived*)
he amado	he comido	he vivido
has amado	has comido	has vivido
ha amado	ha comido	ha vivido
hemos amado	hemos comido	hemos vivido
habéis amado	habéis comido	habéis vivido
han amado	han comido	han vivido

Pluperfect

(*I had loved*)	(*I had eaten*)	(*I had lived*)
había amado	había comido	había vivido
habías amado	habías comido	habías vivido
había amado	había comido	había vivido
habíamos amado	habíamos comido	habíamos vivido
habíais amado	habíais comido	habíais vivido
habían amado	habían comido	habían vivido

Future Perfect

(*I will have loved*)	(*I will have eaten*)	(*I will have lived*)
habré amado	habré comido	habré vivido
habrás amado	habrás comido	habrás vivido
habrá amado	habrá comido	habrá vivido
habremos amado	habremos comido	habremos vivido
habréis amado	habréis comido	habréis vivido
habrán amado	habrán comido	habrán vivido

Conditional Perfect

(*I would have loved*)	(*I would have eaten*)	(*I would have lived*)
habría amado	habría comido	habría vivido
habrías amado	habrías comido	habrías vivido
habría amado	habría comido	habría vivido
habríamos amado	habríamos comido	habríamos vivido
habríais amado	habríais comido	habríais vivido
habrían amado	habrían comido	habrían vivido

Subjunctive Mood
Present Perfect

(*[that] I [may] have loved*)	(*[that] I [may] have eaten*)	(*[that] I [may] have lived*)
haya amado	haya comido	haya vivido
hayas amado	hayas comido	hayas vivido
haya amado	haya comido	haya vivido
hayamos amado	hayamos comido	hayamos vivido
hayáis amado	hayáis comido	hayáis vivido
hayan amado	hayan comido	hayan vivido

Pluperfect

(*[that] I [might] have loved*)	**(two forms: -ra, -se)** (*[that] I [might] have eaten*)	(*[that] I [might] have lived*)
hubiera -iese amado	hubiera -iese comido	hubiera -iese vivido
hubieras -ieses amado	hubieras -ieses comido	hubieras -ieses vivido
hubiera -iese amado	hubiera -iese comido	hubiera -iese vivido
hubiéramos -iésemos amado	hubiéramos -iésemos comido	hubiéramos -iésemos vivido
hubierais -ieseis amado	hubierais -ieseis comido	hubierais -ieseis vivido
hubieran -iesen amado	hubieran -iesen comido	hubieran -iesen vivido

Verbos de cambios radicales

A. Verbos que terminan en *-ar* y *-er*

Stem-changing verbs are those that have a change in the root of the verb. Verbs that end in **-ar** and **-er** change the stressed vowel **e** to **ie,** and the stressed **o** to **ue.** These changes occur in all persons, except the first and second persons plural of the present indicative, present subjunctive, and imperative.

The -*ar* and -*er* Stem-changing Verbs

Infinitive	*Present Indicative*	*Imperative*	*Present Subjunctive*
cerrar	cierro	——	cierre
(*to close*)	cierras	cierra	cierres
	cierra	cierre	cierre
	cerramos	cerremos	cerremos
	cerráis	cerrad	cerréis
	cierran	cierren	cierren
perder	pierdo	——	pierda
(*to lose*)	pierdes	pierde	pierdas
	pierde	pierda	pierda
	perdemos	perdamos	perdamos
	perdéis	perded	perdáis
	pierden	pierdan	pierdan
contar	cuento	——	cuente
(*to count, to tell*)	cuentas	cuenta	cuentes
	cuenta	cuente	cuente
	contamos	contemos	contemos
	contáis	contad	contéis
	cuentan	cuenten	cuenten
volver	vuelvo	——	vuelva
(*to return*)	vuelves	vuelve	vuelvas
	vuelve	vuelva	vuelva
	volvemos	volvamos	volvamos
	volvéis	volved	volváis
	vuelven	vuelvan	vuelvan

Verbs that follow the same pattern are:

acordarse	*to remember*	llover	*to rain*
acostar(se)	*to go to bed*	mostrar	*to show*
almorzar	*to have lunch*	mover	*to move*
atravesar	*to go through*	negar	*to deny*
cocer	*to cook*	nevar	*to snow*
colgar	*to hang*	pensar	*to think, to plan*
comenzar	*to begin*	probar	*to prove, to taste*
confesar	*to confess*	recordar	*to remember*
costar	*to cost*	rogar	*to beg*
demostrar	*to demonstrate, to show*	sentar(se)	*to sit down*
despertar(se)	*to wake up*	soler	*to be in the habit of*
empezar	*to begin*	soñar	*to dream*
encender	*to light, to turn on*	tender	*to stretch, to unfold*
encontrar	*to find*	torcer	*to twist*
entender	*to understand*		

B. Verbos que terminan en -ir

There are two types of stem-changing verbs that end in **-ir**:

Type I: The -ir Stem-changing Verbs

The verbs of this type change stressed **e** to **ie** in some tenses and to **i** in others, and stressed **o** to **ue** or **u**. These changes occur as follows.

Present Indicative: all persons except the first and second persons plural change **e** to **ie** and **o** to **ue**.

Preterit: third person, singular and plural, changes **e** to **i** and **o** to **u**.

Present Subjunctive: all persons change **e** to **ie** and **o** to **ue**, except the first and second persons plural, which change **e** to **i** and **o** to **u**.

Imperfect Subjunctive: all persons change **e** to **i** and **o** to **u**.

Imperative: all persons except the second person plural change **e** to **ie** and **o** to **ue**, and first person plural changes **e** to **i** and **o** to **u**.

Present Participle: changes **e** to **i** and **o** to **u**.

Infinitive	Indicative		Imperative	Subjunctive	
	Present	*Preterit*		*Present*	*Imperfect*
sentir	siento	sentí	——	sienta	sintiera (-iese)
(*to feel*)	sientes	sentiste	siente	sientas	sintieras
	siente	sintió	sienta	sienta	sintiera
Present	sentimos	sentimos	sintamos	sintamos	sintiéramos
Participle	sentís	sentisteis	sentid	sintáis	sintierais
sintiendo	sienten	sintieron	sientan	sientan	sintieran
dormir	duermo	dormí	——	duerma	durmiera (-iese)
(*to sleep*)	duermes	dormiste	duerme	duermas	durmieras
	duerme	durmió	duerma	duerma	durmiera
Present	dormimos	dormimos	durmamos	durmamos	durmiéramos
Participle	dormís	dormisteis	dormid	durmáis	durmierais
durmiendo	duermen	durmieron	duerman	duerman	durmieran

Other verbs that follow the same pattern are:

advertir	*to warn*	mentir	*to lie*
arrepentir(se)	*to repent*	morir	*to die*
consentir	*to consent, to pamper*	preferir	*to prefer*
convertir(se)	*to turn into*	referir	*to refer*
divertir(se)	*to amuse oneself*	sugerir	*to suggest*
herir	*to wound, to hurt*		

Type II: The *-ir* Stem-changing Verbs

The verbs in the second category are irregular in the same tenses as those of the first type. The only difference is that they only have one change: **e** to **i** in all irregular persons.

| Infinitive | Indicative | | Imperative | Subjunctive | |
	Present	Preterit		Present	Imperfect
pedir	pido	pedí	——	pida	pidiera (-iese)
(*to ask for,*	pides	pediste	pide	pidas	pidieras
to request)	pide	pidió	pida	pida	pidiera
Present	pedimos	pedimos	pidamos	pidamos	pidiéramos
Participle	pedís	pedisteis	pedid	pidáis	pidierais
pidiendo	piden	pidieron	pidan	pidan	pidieran

Verbs that follow this pattern are:

competir	*to compete*	reír(se)	*to laugh*
concebir	*to conceive*	reñir	*to fight*
despedir(se)	*to say good-bye*	repetir	*to repeat*
elegir	*to choose*	seguir	*to follow*
impedir	*to prevent*	servir	*to serve*
perseguir	*to pursue*	vestir(se)	*to dress*

Verbos de cambios ortográficos

Some verbs undergo a change in the spelling of the stem in some tenses, in order to keep the sound of the final consonant. The most common ones are those with the consonants **g** and **c**. Remember that **g** and **c** in front of **e** or **i** have a soft sound, and in front of **a**, **o**, or **u** have a hard sound. In order to keep the soft sound in front of **a**, **o**, or **u**, we change **g** and **c** to **j** and **z**, respectively. And in order to keep the hard sound of **g** or **c** in front of **e** and **i**, we add a **u** to the **g** (**gu**) and change the **c** to **qu**. The most important verbs of this type that are regular in all the tenses but change in spelling are the following.

1. Verbs ending in **-gar** change **g** to **gu** before **e** in the first person of the preterit and in all persons of the present subjunctive.

pagar   *to pay*
Preterit: pa**gu**é, pagaste, pagó, etc.
Imperative: paga, pa**gu**e, pa**gu**emos pagad, pa**gu**en
Pres. Subj.:   pa**gu**e, pa**gu**es, pa**gu**e, pa**gu**emos, pa**gu**éis, pa**gu**en

Verbs with the same change: **colgar, jugar, llegar, navegar, negar, regar, rogar.**

2. Verbs ending in **-ger** or **-gir** change **g** to **j** before **o** in the first person of the present indicative and before **a** in all the persons of the present subjunctive.

proteger   *to protect*
Pres. Ind.:   protejo, proteges, protege, etc.
Imperative: protege, proteja, protejamos, proteged, protejan
Pres. Subj.:   proteja, protejas, proteja, protejamos, protejáis, protejan

Verbs with the same pattern: **coger, corregir, dirigir, escoger, exigir, recoger.**

3. Verbs ending in **-guar** change **gu** to **gü** before **e** in the first person of the preterit and in all persons of the present subjunctive.

averiguar   *to find out*
Preterit: averigüé, averiguaste, averiguó, etc.
Imperative: averigua, averigüe, averigüemos, averiguad, averigüen
Pres. Subj.:   averigüe, averigües, averigüe, averigüemos, averigüéis, averigüen

The verb **apaciguar** has the same changes as above.

4. Verbs ending in **-guir** change **gu** to **g** before **o** in the first person of the present indicative and before **a** in all persons of the present subjunctive.

conseguir   *to get*
Pres. Ind.:   consigo, consigues, consigue, etc.
Imperative: consigue, consiga, consigamos, conseguid, consigan
Pres. Subj.:   consiga, consigas, consiga, consigamos, consigáis, consigan

Verbs with the same change: **distinguir, perseguir, proseguir, seguir.**

5. Verbs ending in **-car** change **c** to **qu** before **e** in the first person of the preterit and in all persons of the present subjunctive.

tocar   *to touch, to play (a musical instrument)*
Preterit: toqué, tocaste, tocó, etc.
Imperative: toca, toque, toquemos, tocad, toquen
Pres. Subj.:   toque, toques, toque, toquemos, toquéis, toquen

Verbs that have the same pattern: **atacar, buscar, comunicar, explicar, indicar, pescar, sacar.**

6. Verbs ending in **-cer** or **-cir** preceded by a consonant change **c** to **z** before **o** in the first person of the present indicative and before **a** in all persons of the present subjunctive.

torcer   *to twist*
Pres. Ind.:   tuerzo, tuerces, tuerce, etc.
Imperative: tuerce, tuerza, torzamos, torced, tuerzan
Pres. Subj.:   tuerza, tuerzas, tuerza, torzamos, torzáis, tuerzan

Verbs that have the same change: **convencer, esparcir, vencer.**

7. Verbs ending in **-cer** or **-cir** preceded by a vowel change **c** to **zc** before **o** in the first person of the present indicative and before **a** in all persons of the present subjunctive.

conocer *to know, to be acquainted with*
Pres. Ind.: conozco conoces, conoce, etc.
Imperative: conoce, conozca, conozcamos, conoced, conozcan
Pres. Subj.: conozca, conozcas, conozca, conozcamos, conozcáis, conozcan

Verbs that follow the same pattern: **agradecer, aparecer, carecer, entristecer** (*to sadden*), **establecer, lucir, nacer, obedecer, ofrecer, padecer, parecer, pertenecer, reconocer, relucir.**

8. Verbs ending in **-zar** change **z** to **c** before **e** in the first person of the preterit and in all persons of the present subjunctive.

rezar *to pray*
Preterit: recé, rezaste, rezó, etc.
Imperative: reza, rece, recemos, rezad, recen
Pres. Subj.: rece, reces, rece, recemos, recéis, recen

Verbs that have the same pattern: **abrazar, alcanzar, almorzar, comenzar, cruzar, empezar, forzar, gozar.**

9. Verbs ending in **-eer** change the unstressed **i** to **y** between vowels in the third persons singular and plural of the preterit, in all persons of the imperfect subjunctive, and in the present participle.

creer *to believe*
Preterit: creí, creíste, creyó, creímos, creísteis, creyeron
Imp. Subj.: creyera(ese), creyeras, creyera, creyéramos, creyerais, creyeran
Pres. Part.: creyendo
Past Part.: creído

Leer and **poseer** follow the same pattern.

10. Verbs ending in **-uir** change the unstressed **i** to **y** between vowels (except **-quir**, which has the silent **u**) in the following tenses and persons.

huir *to escape, to flee*
Pres. Ind.: huyo, huyes, huye, huimos, huís, huyen
Preterit: huí, huiste, huyó, huimos, huisteis, huyeron
Imperative: huye, huya, huyamos, huid, huyan
Pres. Subj.: huya, huyas, huya, huyamos, huyáis, huyan
Imp. Subj.: huyera(ese), huyeras, huyera, huyéramos, huyerais, huyeran
Pres. Part: huyendo

Verbs with the same change: **atribuir, concluir, constituir, construir, contribuir, destituir, destruir, disminuir, distribuir, excluir, incluir, influir, instruir, restituir, sustituir.**

11. Verbs ending in **-eír** lose one **e** in the third persons singular and plural of the preterit, in all persons of the imperfect subjunctive, and in the present participle.

reír   *to laugh*
Preterit: reí, reíste, rio, reímos, reísteis, rieron
Imp. Subj.:   riera(ese), rieras, riera, riéramos, rierais, rieran
Pres. Part.:   riendo

Sonreír and **freír** have the same pattern.

12. Verbs ending in **-iar** add a written accent to the **i,** except in the first and second persons plural of the present indicative and subjunctive.

fiar(se)   *to trust*
Pres. Ind.:   (me) fío, (te) fías, (se) fía, (nos) fiamos, (os), fiáis, (se) fían
Pres. Subj.:   (me) fíe, (te) fíes, (se) fíe, (nos) fiemos, (os) fiéis, (se) fíen

Other verbs that follow the same pattern: **ampliar, criar, desviar, enfriar, enviar, guiar, telegrafiar, vaciar, variar.**

13. Verbs ending in **-uar** (except **-guar**) add a written accent to the **u,** except in the first and second persons plural of the present indicative and subjunctive.

actuar   *to act*
Pres. Ind.:   actúo, actúas, actúa, actuamos, actuáis, actúan
Pres. Subj.:   actúe, actúes, actúe, actuemos, actuéis, actúen

Verbs with the same pattern: **acentuar, continuar, efectuar, exceptuar, graduar, habituar, insinuar, situar.**

14. Verbs ending in **-ñir** lose the **i** of the diphthongs **ie** and **ió** in the third persons singular and plural of the preterit and all persons of the imperfect subjunctive. They also change the **e** of the stem to **i** in the same persons.

teñir   *to dye*
Preterit: teñí, teñiste, **tiñó,** teñimos, teñisteis, **tiñeron**
Imp. Subj.:   tiñera(ese), tiñeras, tiñera, tiñéramos, tiñerais, tiñeran

Verbs that follow the same pattern: **ceñir, constreñir, desteñir, estreñir, reñir.**

Verbos irregulares de uso frecuente

adquirir   *to acquire*
Pres. Ind.:   adquiero, adquieres, adquiere, adquirimos, adquirís, adquieren
Pres. Subj.:   adquiera, adquieras, adquiera, adquiramos, adquiráis, adquieran
Imperative: adquiere, adquiera, adquiramos, adquirid, adquieran

andar   *to walk*
Preterit: anduve, anduviste, anduvo, anduvimos, anduvisteis, anduvieron
Imp. Subj.:   anduviera (anduviese), anduvieras, anduviera, anduviéramos, anduvierais, anduvieran

caber   *to fit, to have enough room*
Pres. Ind.:   quepo, cabes, cabe, cabemos, cabéis, caben
Preterit: cupe, cupiste, cupo, cupimos, cupisteis, cupieron
Future: cabré, cabrás, cabrá, cabremos, cabréis, cabrán
Conditional: cabría, cabrías, cabría, cabríamos, cabríais, cabrían
Imperative: cabe, quepa, quepamos, cabed, quepan
Pres. Subj.:   quepa, quepas, quepa, quepamos, quepáis, quepan
Imp. Subj.:   cupiera (cupiese), cupieras, cupiera, cupiéramos, cupierais, cupieran

caer   *to fall*
Pres. Ind.:   caigo, caes, cae, caemos, caéis, caen
Preterit: caí, caíste, cayó, caímos, caísteis, cayeron
Imperative: cae, caiga, caigamos, caed, caigan
Pres. Subj.:   caiga, caigas, caiga, caigamos, caigáis, caigan
Imp. Subj.:   cayera (cayese), cayeras, cayera, cayéramos, cayerais, cayeran
Past Part.:   caído

conducir   *to guide, to drive*
Pres. Ind.:   conduzco, conduces, conduce, conducimos, conducís, conducen
Preterit: conduje, condujiste, condujo, condujimos, condujisteis, condujeron
Imperative: conduce, conduzca, conduzcamos, conducid, conduzcan
Pres. Subj.:   conduzca, conduzcas, conduzca, conduzcamos, conduzcáis, conduzcan
Imp. Subj.:   condujera (condujese), condujeras, condujera, condujéramos,
                 condujerais, condujeran
                 (*All verbs ending in* **-ducir** *follow this pattern.*)

convenir   *to agree* (See **venir**)

dar   *to give*
Pres. Ind.:   doy, das, da, damos, dais, dan
Preterit: di, diste, dio, dimos, disteis, dieron
Imperative: da, dé, demos, dad, den
Pres. Subj.:   dé, des, dé, demos, deis, den
Imp. Subj.:   diera (diese), dieras, diera, diéramos, dierais, dieran

decir   *to say, to tell*
Pres. Ind.:   digo, dices, dice, decimos, decís, dicen
Preterit: dije, dijiste, dijo, dijimos, dijisteis, dijeron
Future: diré, dirás, dirá, diremos, diréis, dirán
Conditional: diría, dirías, diría, diríamos, diríais, dirían
Imperative: di, diga, digamos, decid, digan
Pres. Subj.:   diga, digas, diga, digamos, digáis, digan
Imp. Subj.:   dijera (dijese), dijeras, dijera, dijéramos, dijerais, dijeran
Pres. Part.:   diciendo
Past Part.:   dicho

detener   *to stop, to hold, to arrest* (See **tener**)

elegir   *to choose*
Pres. Ind.   elijo, eliges, elige, elegimos, elegís, eligen
Preterit: elegí, elegiste, eligió, elegimos, elegisteis, eligieron
Imperative: elige, elija, elijamos, elegid, elijan
Pres. Subj.:   elija, elijas, elija, elijamos, elijáis, elijan
Imp. Subj.:   eligiera (eligiese), eligieras, eligiera, eligiéramos, eligierais, eligieran

entender   *to understand*
Pres. Ind.:   entiendo, entiendes, entiende, entendemos, entendéis, entienden
Imperative: entiende, entienda, entendamos, entended, entiendan
Pres. Subj.:   entienda, entiendas, entienda, entendamos, entendáis, entiendan

entretener   *to entertain, to amuse* (See **tener**)

estar   *to be*
Pres. Ind.:   estoy, estás, está, estamos, estáis, están
Preterit: estuve, estuviste, estuvo, estuvimos, estuvisteis, estuvieron
Imperative: está, esté, estemos, estad, estén
Pres. Subj.:   esté, estés, esté, estemos, estéis, estén
Imp. Subj.:   estuviera (estuviese), estuvieras, estuviera, estuviéramos, estuvierais, estuvieran

extender   *to extend, to stretch out* (See **entender**)

haber   *to have*
Pres. Ind.:   he, has, ha, hemos, habéis, han
Preterit: hube, hubiste, hubo, hubimos, hubisteis, hubieron
Future: habré, habrás, habrá, habremos, habréis, habrán
Conditional: habría, habrías, habría, habríamos, habríais, habrían
Pres. Subj.:   haya, hayas, haya, hayamos, hayáis, hayan
Imp. Subj.:   hubiera (hubiese), hubieras, hubiera, hubiéramos, hubierais, hubieran

hacer   *to do, to make*
Pres. Ind.:   hago, haces, hace, hacemos, hacéis, hacen
Preterit: hice, hiciste, hizo, hicimos, hicisteis, hicieron
Future: haré, harás, hará, haremos, haréis, harán
Conditional: haría, harías, haría, haríamos, haríais, harían
Imperative: haz, haga, hagamos, haced, hagan
Pres. Subj.:   haga, hagas, haga, hagamos, hagáis, hagan
Imp. Subj.:   hiciera (hiciese), hicieras, hiciera, hiciéramos, hicierais, hicieran
Past Part.:   hecho

imponer   *to impose, to deposit* (See **poner**)

introducir   *to introduce, to insert, to gain access* (See **conducir**)

ir   *to go*
Pres. Ind.:   voy, vas, va, vamos, vais, van
Imp. Ind.:   iba, ibas, iba, íbamos, ibais, iban
Preterit: fui, fuiste, fue, fuimos, fuisteis, fueron

Imperative:	ve, vaya, vayamos, id, vayan
Pres. Subj.:	vaya, vayas, vaya, vayamos, vayáis, vayan
Imp. Subj.:	fuera (fuese), fueras, fuera, fuéramos, fuerais, fueran

jugar   *to play*

Pres. Ind.:	juego, juegas, juega, jugamos, jugáis, juegan
Imperative:	juega, juegue, juguemos, jugad, jueguen
Pres. Subj.:	juegue, juegues, juegue, juguemos, juguéis, jueguen

obtener   *to obtain* (See **tener**)

oir   *to hear*

Pres. Ind.:	oigo, oyes, oye, oímos, oís, oyen
Preterit:	oí, oíste, oyó, oímos, oísteis, oyeron
Imperative:	oye, oiga, oigamos, oíd, oigan
Pres. Subj.:	oiga, oigas, oiga, oigamos, oigáis, oigan
Imp. Subj.:	oyera (oyese), oyeras, oyera, oyéramos, oyerais, oyeran
Pres. Part.:	oyendo
Past Part.:	oído

oler   *to smell*

Pres. Ind.:	huelo, hueles, huele, olemos, oléis, huelen
Imperative:	huele, huela, olamos, oled, huelan
Pres. Subj.:	huela, huelas, huela, olamos, oláis, huelan

poder   *to be able*

Pres. Ind.:	puedo, puedes, puede, podemos, podéis, pueden
Preterit:	pude, pudiste, pudo, pudimos, pudisteis, pudieron
Future:	podré, podrás, podrá, podremos, podréis, podrán
Conditional:	podría, podrías, podría, podríamos, podríais, podrían
Pres. Subj.:	pueda, puedas, pueda, podamos, podáis, puedan
Imp. Subj.:	pudiera (pudiese), pudieras, pudiera, pudiéramos, pudierais, pudieran
Pres. Part.:	pudiendo

poner   *to place, to put*

Pres. Ind.:	pongo, pones, pone, ponemos, ponéis, ponen
Preterit:	puse, pusiste, puso, pusimos, pusisteis, pusieron
Future:	pondré, pondrás, pondrá, pondremos, pondréis, pondrán
Conditional:	pondría, pondrías, pondría, pondríamos, pondríais, pondrían
Imperative:	pon, ponga, pongamos, poned, pongan
Pres. Subj.:	ponga, pongas, ponga, pongamos, pongáis, pongan
Imp. Subj.:	pusiera (pusiese), pusieras, pusiera, pusiéramos, pusierais, pusieran
Past Part.:	puesto

querer   *to want, to wish, to love*

Pres. Ind.:	quiero, quieres, quiere, queremos, queréis, quieren
Preterit:	quise, quisiste, quiso, quisimos, quisisteis, quisieron
Future:	querré, querrás, querrá, querremos, querréis, querrán

Conditional: querría, querrías, querría, querríamos, querríais, querrían
Imperative: quiere, quiera, queramos, quered, quieran
Pres. Subj.: quiera, quieras, quiera, queramos, queráis, quieran
Imp. Subj.: quisiera (quisiese), quisieras, quisiera, quisiéramos, quisierais, quisieran

resolver *to decide on, to solve*
Pres. Ind.: resuelvo, resuelves, resuelve, resolvemos, resolvéis, resuelven
Imperative: resuelve, resuelva, resolvamos, resolved, resuelvan
Pres. Subj.: resuelva, resuelvas, resuelva, resolvamos, resolváis, resuelvan
Past Part.: resuelto

saber *to know*
Pres. Ind.: sé, sabes, sabe, sabemos, sabéis, saben
Preterit: supe, supiste, supo, supimos, supisteis, supieron
Future: sabré, sabrás, sabrá, sabremos, sabréis, sabrán
Conditional: sabría, sabrías, sabría, sabríamos, sabríais, sabrían
Imperative: sabe, sepa, sepamos, sabed, sepan
Pres. Subj.: sepa, sepas, sepa, sepamos, sepáis, sepan
Imp. Subj.: supiera (supiese), supieras, supiera, supiéramos, supierais, supieran

salir *to leave, to go out*
Pres. Ind.: salgo, sales, sale, salimos, salís, salen
Future: saldré, saldrás, saldrá, saldremos, saldréis, saldrán
Conditional: saldría, saldrías, saldría, saldríamos, saldríais, saldrían
Imperative: sal, salga, salgamos, salid, salgan
Pres. Subj.: salga, salgas, salga, salgamos, salgáis, salgan

ser *to be*
Pres. Ind.: soy, eres, es, somos, sois, son
Imp. Ind.: era, eras, era, éramos, erais, eran
Preterit: fui, fuiste, fue, fuimos, fuisteis, fueron
Imperative: sé, sea, seamos, sed, sean
Pres. Subj.: sea, seas, sea, seamos, seáis, sean
Imp. Subj.: fuera (fuese), fueras, fuera, fuéramos, fuerais, fueran

suponer *to assume* (See **poner**)

tener *to have*
Pres. Ind.: tengo, tienes, tiene, tenemos, tenéis, tienen
Preterit: tuve, tuviste, tuvo, tuvimos, tuvisteis, tuvieron
Future: tendré, tendrás, tendrá, tendremos, tendréis, tendrán
Conditional: tendría, tendrías, tendría, tendríamos, tendríais, tendrían
Imperative: ten, tenga, tengamos, tened, tengan
Pres. Subj.: tenga, tengas, tenga, tengamos, tengáis, tengan
Imp. Subj.: tuviera (tuviese), tuvieras, tuviera, tuviéramos, tuvierais, tuvieran

traer *to bring*
Pres. Ind.: traigo, traes, trae, traemos, traéis, traen
Preterit: traje, trajiste, trajo, trajimos, trajisteis, trajeron
Imperative: trae, traiga, traigamos, traed, traigan
Pres. Subj.: traiga, traigas, traiga, traigamos, traigáis, traigan
Imp. Subj.: trajera (trajese), trajeras, trajera, trajéramos, trajerais, trajeran
Pres. Part.: trayendo
Past Part.: traído

valer *to be worth*
Pres. Ind.: valgo, vales, vale, valemos, valéis, valen
Future: valdré, valdrás, valdrá, valdremos, valdréis, valdrán
Conditional: valdría, valdrías, valdría, valdríamos, valdríais, valdrían
Imperative: vale, valga, valgamos, valed, valgan
Pres. Subj.: valga, valgas, valga, valgamos, valgáis, valgan

venir *to come*
Pres. Ind.: vengo, vienes, viene, venimos, venís, vienen
Preterit: vine, viniste, vino, vinimos, vinisteis, vinieron
Future: vendré, vendrás, vendrá, vendremos, vendréis, vendrán
Conditional: vendría, vendrías, vendría, vendríamos, vendríais, vendrían
Imperative: ven, venga, vengamos, venid, vengan
Pres. Subj.: venga, vengas, venga, vengamos, vengáis, vengan
Imp. Subj.: viniera (viniese), vinieras, viniera, viniéramos, vinierais, vinieran
Pres. Part.: viniendo

ver *to see*
Pres. Ind.: veo, ves, ve, vemos, veis, ven
Imp. Ind.: veía, veías, veía, veíamos, veíais, veían
Preterit: vi, viste, vio, vimos, visteis, vieron
Imperative: ve, vea, veamos, ved, vean
Pres. Subj.: vea, veas, vea, veamos, veáis, vean
Imp. Subj.: viera (viese), vieras, viera, viéramos, vierais, vieran
Past Part.: visto

Apéndice C: Respuestas a las secciones ¿Están listos para el examen?

Lección 1

A. 1. desaparezco / aparezco / salgo 2. recuerdas / sueñas 3. sé / almuerzan / vuelven / veo 4. corrige / sugiere 5. reconozco / traduzco 6. advierte / muerde 7. entendemos / dice 8. digo / quepo 9. hago / pongo / voy / conduzco 10. empiezan / terminan 11. niega / Confiesa 12. dicen / despide / pienso

B. 1. sigue (continúa) estudiando 2. está visitando 3. siguen (continúan) enseñando 4. está pidiendo 5. estás haciendo 6. estoy sirviendo 7. seguimos (continuamos) hablando 8. está leyendo

C. 1. a mis padres 2. a mi perro 3. a nadie 4. un(a) secretario(a) 5. a mi cuñada / a mi suegra

D. 1. Sí, las conozco. 2. Sí, las hay. 3. Sí, te llamo mañana. 4. Sí, mis padres me visitan todos los días. 5. Sí, yo los tengo. 6. Sí, lo sé. 7. Sí, tu abuela nos conoce. 8. Sí, podemos hacerlo (lo podemos hacer) hoy.

E. 1. darles 2. le compro 3. me escribe 4. mandarnos 5. te hablan 6. le digo 7. traerle 8. prestarle

F. 1. Me baño y me visto. 2. Pensamos acostarnos temprano. 3. Se van de vacaciones. 4. Se quejan. 5. Dicen que te pareces a tu padre. 6. Nos encontramos en el café. 7. Me los pruebo. 8. Me voy a lavar (Voy a lavarme) la cabeza.

G. 1. papel 2. bromear 3. sentirse 4. apenas 5. además 6. triste 7. mandón 8. egoísta 9. deprimido 10. círculo 11. extrañar 12. cuidar 13. de buen humor 14. tomar

H. 1. 40 2. Mediterráneo 3. sur 4. Salamanca

Lección 2

A. 1. es / Es 2. son 3. están / están 4. está / están 5. es 6. es / está / Es 7. está / Está 8. es / es / estoy 9. está / está 10. es 11. es / es 12. Es 13. están 14. estoy / Están

B. 1. Nuestros horarios de clase están en el bolso de mano. 2. Mis padres son de Oaxaca. 3. Su título es de la Universidad de Guadalajara. 4. Tu (Su) examen está en el escritorio. 5. Una buena amiga mía es Amalia.

C. 1. Las mías son fáciles. 2. El mío es de Chihuahua. 3. No, yo no tengo los tuyos. 4. El nuestro es muy simpático también. 5. Las de ellos son por la tarde.

D. 1. Sí, puedo comprártelo (te lo puedo comprar). 2. Sí, se los pido. 3. Sí, me lo da. 4. Sí, pienso comprárselas (se las pienso comprar). 5. Sí, nos las va a dar (va a dárnoslas) hoy.

E. 1. El doctor Vega / la educación 2. mil / cien 3. médico / un médico excelente 4. La señorita Peña / los / a las 5. otro 6. La señora Soto / sombrero

F. 1. Ellos compraron los libros y los trajeron a la universidad. 2. Pidieron enchiladas y no las comieron. Se las dieron a su papá. 3. Ella lo supo, pero no dijo nada. 4. Nosotros fuimos al cine porque no tuvimos que trabajar. 5. Yo llegué a las ocho, pero no comencé a trabajar hasta las nueve. 6. Yo toqué las canciones que ellos eligieron. 7. Yo le hablé, pero ella no me oyó. 8. Yo no cupe en el coche y por eso no fui. 9. Yo vine y les di el dinero, pero ellos no compraron nada. 10. Ellos leyeron el artículo, pero yo no pude leerlo. 11. Teresa volvió a su casa a las diez y se acostó en seguida. 12. Carlos fue al teatro. Ellas prefirieron quedarse en su casa.

G. 1. prestaba 2. asistía 3. iba / veía 4. compraba 5. hacía 6. Eran 7. hablaba 8. salían

H. 1. cuenta 2. obligatoria 3. carrera 4. beca 5. visto / mantiene / promedio 6. mitad / curso 7. tardar 8. estudios 9. consejero(a) 10. puntual 11. facultad / derecho 12. residencia 13. tratar 14. contador / analista / trabajadora 15. entre

I. 1. cobre 2. la Ciudad de México 3. la pintura 4. escritor

Lección 3

A. 1. A Carlos le gusta más 2. Nos encantan 3. me duelen mucho los pies 4. te falta 5. les quedan

B. 1. era / vivía / hablaban 2. fueron 3. Hacía / llovía / llegó 4. dijeron / debía 5. encantaba / comía 6. Eran / empezó / terminó 7. estuve / terminé 8. vino / dolía

C. 1. quiso (pudo) / quería / supe / sabía / conocí / conocía / pude

D. 1. Ésa es la chica española de quien yo te hablé.
2. La señora cuyo hijo tuvo un accidente está triste. 3. El libro que compré ayer es muy interesante. 4. Vamos a visitar a los niños para quienes compramos los bates.
5. El anillo que compré en México es de oro.

E. 1. Hace seis horas que no como. 2. Hacía media hora que esperábamos cuando Ud. llegó (tú llegaste). 3. Hace un año que los jugadores vinieron a esta ciudad.

F. 1. aire 2. campaña 3. deporte 4. escalar 5. partido (juego) 6. lastimó 7. deportiva 8. perder 9. pesar / reñido 10. poco / tiempo 11. montar 12. hipódromo / caballos 13. esquí 14. Juegos 15. lucha

G. 1. Pacífico 2. 200 3. Santiago 4. Cuzco 5. Quito

Lección 4

A. 1. tanto tiempo / como 2. tantas reuniones 3. mejor que 4. menos de 5. mucho mayor que 6. el más alto de 7. más pequeña que 8. menor que 9. tanto como 10. inteligentísima

B. 1. para / por / por / para / para 2. Por / para 3. por / para 4. para / para 5. por / por / por / por / para 6. para / por 7. por / por 8. Por / por 9. para 10. Para / por

C. 1. vayamos 2. sean 3. disfruten 4. dejes / estén 5. dedique / trabajar 6. uses 7. digamos / mintamos 8. acostemos / levantemos 9. ponga / ayudar 10. brindar

D. 1. Es importante estudiar todos los días. 2. Es urgente ir al hospital. 3. Es conveniente que ella sepa conducir. 4. Es mejor viajar en pleno verano. 5. Es necesario que Uds. vengan a fines de enero. 6. Es preferible que nosotros compremos flores.

E. 1. Siento que tú no puedas ir a misa hoy. 2. Lamento que ella no vea los fuegos artificiales. 3. Me alegro de que Uds. estén libres hoy. 4. Ellos temen no tener tiempo. 5. Sergio siente que nosotros no vayamos con él. 6. Ellos se alegran de vivir por aquí. 7. Espero que Elsa venga pronto. 8. Temo que él no sepa dónde es la fiesta. 9. Espero que mi hijo pase más tiempo conmigo.

F. 1. pongan 2. lleves 3. preparen 4. esté 5. puedan 6. tengamos

G. 1. aquí / Reyes 2. Nochebuena / Navidad 3. Acción 4. tumba / velas 5. fuegos 6. Fin / brindamos 7. santa 8. lástima 9. parte / Día 10. pata / trébol 11. víspera 12. signo

H. 1. Bolivia 2. Paraná 3. guaraní 4. Asunción 5. *La misión*

Lección 5

A. 1. Háganlo ahora. 2. Léaselo a Mario. 3. No, no los compre. 4. No, no lo llamen ahora. 5. Póngase el abrigo. 6. Vaya al gimnasio. 7. No se lo digan a nadie. 8. Sí, evítelo. 9. Sí, bébanlos. 10. Levántese a las siete.

B. 1. Levantémonos a las seis. 2. Acostémonos a las once. 3. Bañémonos por la mañana. 4. Digámosle que necesita hacer ejercicio. 5. No, no se lo digamos. 6. Démoselo a Ernesto.

C. 1. Yo no creo que ellos eviten las grasas. 2. No es verdad que ella siempre camine mucho. 3. Yo dudo que Uds. puedan mejorar su salud. 4. Ellos creen que nosotros somos socios del club. 5. Yo no estoy seguro de que ellos vayan con Marta. 6. No es cierto que ellos tengan mucho estrés en el trabajo.

D. 1. tenga / tiene 2. pueda 3. sepa 4. siguen 5. conozca 6. quiera

E. 1. nos lleven 2. lleguen 3. tenemos 4. termine 5. podamos 6. vaya 7. haga

F. 1. alimentos 2. grasas 3. un pie 4. adelgazar 5. disminuir 6. joven 7. sano 8. calcio 9. apio (lechuga, rábano, pepino) 10. ají 11. repollo 12. estrés

G. 1. Ángel 2. petróleo 3. Caracas 4. Libertador 5. esmeraldas

Lección 6

A. 1. Ve / alquila / saca 2. Ven / hazme / cierra / abre 3. Habla / dile 4. Sé / préstame 5. Compra / compres 6. Siéntate / te sientes 7. Ten 8. Sal / salgas

B. 1. cerrada 2. despierta 3. resueltos 4. escritas 5. hechas

C. 1. hemos visto 2. había alquilado 3. nos habíamos matriculado 4. han llevado

D. 1. un viejo amigo 2. única mujer 3. un buen vino español 4. La profesora (maestra) misma 5. algunas pinturas muy interesantes

E. 1. anuncio 2. principiantes 3. eso 4. automático / cambios 5. batería 6. semáforo 7. chapa (placa) 8. grúa

F. 1. educativos   2. quince por ciento   3. Irazú
4. bananas / café / flores   5. San José

Leccíon 7

A. 1. dirá / tendremos   2. saldrá   3. habrá / podré
4. pondrán   5. cabremos / iremos   6. querrán / haré

B. 1. Estará en la fonda.   2. Se levantarán a las nueve.
3. Serán las once.   4. Costará quince mil dólares.
5. Vendrá el domingo.

C.   haríamos / tendrías / podría / pasarían / viviría /
Sería

D. 1. Serían las diez.   2. Estaría en el cine.   3. Estaría
con Marisa.   4. Irían a la cafetería.

E. 1. habremos terminado   2. te habrás graduado
3. habrá encontrado   4. no habría pagado   5. no le
habrían dicho

F. 1. la frente   2. el lomo   3. la banda   4. el modo
5. la resta   6. la derecha   7. el guía   8. la loma   9. el
orden   10. el punto

G. 1. chistes   2. brindis   3. copa   4. abeja   5. discutiendo   6. ganas   7. cocido / término   8. cerveza
9. vino   10. sabido

H. 1. pequeño   2. Costa Rica   3. *lagos*   4. Copán
5. *la eterna primavera*

Leccíon 8

A. 1. Él les advirtió que usaran productos biodegradables.
2. Luis nos dijo que leyéramos las noticias sobre la
contaminación.   3. Ellos nos rogaron que no nos
uniéramos a las pandillas.   4. Él te aconsejó que
cooperaras con los demás.   5. Ellos me pidieron que
sacara la basura.   6. La profesora le aconsejó que hiciera
un esfuerzo por mejorar.

B. 1. trataran   2. tuviera   3. pidieran   4. estuvieran
5. reciclaran   6. pudiera

C. 1. hayan hecho   2. hubieran dado   3. hayas ofrecido
4. hubiera hecho   5. haya empezado   6. hubiera dado
7. hubieran permitido   8. lo hayan resuelto   9. hayamos
ido   10. se hayan puesto

D. 1. i   2. e   3. g   4. a   5. j   6. c   7. b   8. f   9. h
10. d

E. 1. treinta   2. mexicoamericanos   3. San Juan   4. son
5. cubanos

Leccíon 9

A. 1. trajera   2. veas   3. dé   4. hubiera sido   5. pueda
6. consiguiéramos   7. van   8. estar   9. tienen   10. haya
empezado   11. saliéramos   12. llegue   13. ganaron
14. hacer   15. escuchen

B. 1. a / de / a / a   2. a / a / a / a   3. de / a / en   4. de /
a / en   5. en / de / de   6. de / en   7. de / de   8. de / en
9. en / en   10. en

C. 1. casarse con / enamorado de   2. me acuerdo de
3. convenimos en / salir de   4. insisten en / encontrarse
con   5. Me alegro de / confíen en

D. 1. comer fruta   2. querían ir   3. Antes de ir
4. quería ver   5. sin terminar   6. yo lo oí entrar
7. No fumar   8. acaban de volver   9. Voy a empezar
(comenzar) a estudiar

E. 1. estrenan / actriz   2. mentira   3. mediados
4. enamorada   5. moda   6. pasos   7. grabar   8. reina
9. propaganda (publicidad)   10. siglo

F. 1. Argentina se conoce como "la tierra del tango".   2. Es
el Aconcagua.   3. Buenos Aires está situada a orillas del Río
de la Plata.   4. Las llaman porteñas.   5. En Argentina se
nota la influencia francesa, española, inglesa e italiana.

Leccíon 10

A. 1. Esa novela fue escrita por Cortázar.   2. Ese hospital
será construido en el 2005.   3. Ese libro ha sido
publicado por la Editorial Losada.   4. Los documentos
son firmados por el director.   5. Las cartas eran
traducidas por el Sr. Ruiz.

B. 1. se habla   2. se dice   3. se venden   4. se entra
5. se cierran   6. se puede

C. 1. se me rompieron   2. se nos pierden   3. se le
descompuso   4. se te olvidan   5. se les murió

D. 1. dio marcha atrás   2. pongo en duda   3. darle ánimo
4. te (le) dieron gato por liebre   5. entre la espada y la pared

E. 1. apartado   2. despidieron   3. coronilla   4. salario
5. puesto   6. Renunció / extranjero   7. programas
8. celular (móvil)   9. semanales   10. navegar

F. 1. La llaman "La Perla de las Antillas".   2. Las principales exportaciones son el azúcar y el tabaco.   3. Es la
sección antigua de San Juan, la capital de P.R.   4. Es una
antigua fortaleza de la época colonial.   5. La República
Dominicana y Haití son los dos países que comparten la
isla.   6. El deporte más popular en ese país es el béisbol.

Vocabulario

The Spanish-English Vocabulary contains all active and passive vocabulary that appears in the student text. Active vocabulary is identified by lesson number and includes words and expressions that appear in the vocabulary lists that follow the lesson-opening passages and in charts and word lists that are part of the grammar explanations. Passive vocabulary consists of words and expressions that are given an English gloss in **El mundo hispánico** and **Una tarjeta postal** sections, in **Lecturas periodísticas** readings, photo captions, exercises, activities, and authentic documents.

The English-Spanish Vocabulary contains only those words and expressions that are considered active.

Español—Inglés

A

a to, at, in, 9
  ¿—cuánto estamos hoy? what's the date today?, 10
  —eso de at about, 6
  —fin de que in order that, 5
  —fines de at the end of, 4
  —la larga in the long run, 10
  —la parrilla grilled
  —lo mejor perhaps, maybe, 1
  —más tardar at the latest, 2
  —mediados de around the middle of (*a month, a year*), 9
  —menos que unless, 5
  —menudo often, frequently, 1
  —pesar de que in spite of, 3
  —su vez in turn
  —tiempo on time, 6
  —través de through, via
abajo below, downstairs, 9
abogado(a) (*m., f.*) lawyer, 2
abordar to board, to approach, 2
abrazar to hug, to give a hug, 1
aburrido(a) bored, 1; boring, 2
acabar de (+ *inf.*) to have just (*done something*), 9
acampar to camp, 3
Acción de Gracias (*f.*) Thanksgiving
acerca de about, 6
acogedor(a) welcoming
aconsejar to advise, 4
acordarse (o → ue) (de) to remember, 1

acostar (o → ue) to put to bed, 1
acostarse (o → ue) to go to bed, 1
actor (*m.*) actor, 9
actriz (*f.*) actress, 9
actuar to act, to perform, 9
acumulador (*m.*) battery, 6
adelgazar to lose weight, 5
además besides, 1
aderezo (*m.*) dressing
administración de empresas (*f.*) business administration, 2
advertir (e → ie) to warn, 1
aficionado(a) (*m., f.*) fan, 3
afrontar to face
agarrar to take, 1
agencia de alquiler de automóviles (*f.*) car rental agency, 6
agente de policía (*m., f.*) policeman, policewoman, 7
agradecer to thank, 1
agravarse to become worse, 8
agregar to add, 9
aguafiestas (*m., f.*) spoilsport
ahora mismo right now, 5
ahorro (*m.*) saving
ají (*m.*) green pepper, 5
ajo (*m.*) garlic, 5
al a + el
  —aire libre outdoor(s), 3
  —día a day, 5
  —fin finally, 6
  —fin y al cabo after all, 10
  —menos at least, 8

  —pie de la letra exactly, to the letter, 10
  —vapor steamed
albóndiga (*f.*) meatball, 5
alcalde (*m.*) mayor, 8
alcaldesa (*f.*) mayor, 8
alcanzar to attain, to reach
alegato (*m.*) claim
alegre happy, glad, 1
alegrarse de to be glad, 4
algo por el estilo something like that, 10
alimenticio(a) related to food
alimento (*m.*) food, nourishment, nutrient, 5
alrededor around, 7
amable kind, polite, 1
amar to love, 1
ambiental environmental, 8
ambientalismo (*m.*) environmentalism
ambos(as) both
amistoso(a) friendly, 1
amor (*m.*) love, 1
amuleto (*m.*) amulet, 4
analista de sistemas (*m., f.*) systems analyst, 2
ancho (*m.*) width
anillo (*m.*) ring
animadamente lively, 7
anterior previous, 10
antes (de) que before, 5
anual yearly, 10

345

anuncio (*m.*)   ad, 6
añadir   to add, 9
Año Nuevo (*m.*)   New Year's Day, 4
aparecer (*conj. like* **parecer**)   to appear, 1
apartado de correos (*m.*)   post office box, 10
apartado postal (*m.*)   post office box, 10
apenas   barely, hardly, 1
apio (*m.*)   celery, 5
aportación (*f.*)   contribution
apoyado(a)   supported
apretar (e → ie)   to press
aprovechar   to take advantage of, 6
aquí hay gato encerrado   there's something fishy here, 10
árbitro (*m.*)   umpire, 3
archivar   to file, 10
   —(almacenar) información   to store information, 10
archivo (*m.*)   file (electronic), 10
arma (*f.*)   weapon, 8
arrancar   to start (*a motor*), 6
arrepentirse (e → ie) (de)   to regret, to repent, 1
arriba   above, 9
arrodillarse   to kneel, 1
asalto (*m.*)   assault, hold-up, attack, 8
asar   to roast, to barbecue, 7
asegurado(a)   insured, 6
asesinar   to murder, 8
asesinato (*m.*)   murder, 8
asesino(a) (*m., f.*)   murderer, assassin, 10
así que   as soon as, 5; so, 10
asignatura (*f.*)   subject (*in school*), 2
asistencia (*f.*)   attendance, 2
asistir a   to attend, 2
aspirante (*m., f.*)   applicant, 10
atleta (*m., f.*)   athlete, 3
atraer (*cong. like* **traer**)   to attract
atreverse (a)   to dare, 1
atún (*m.*)   tuna, 7
aula (*f.*)   classroom, 2
aumentar   to increase, 5
aumento (*m.*)   raise, 10
aunque   although, 8
auto-adiestramiento (*m.*)   self-training
averiguar   to find out
avisar   to inform, to give notice, 7
ayuda financiera (*f.*)   financial aid

B

bacalao (*m.*)   cod, 7
bajar de peso   to lose weight, 5

bajo   under, 9
bajo(a)   short, 5
balompié (*m.*)   soccer, 3
baloncesto (*m.*)   basketball, 3
balsa (*f.*)   raft
banda (*f.*)   band, musical group, 7
bando (*m.*)   faction, party, 7
básquetbol (*m.*)   basketball, 3
basta   enough, 7
basura (*f.*)   garbage, trash, 8
bate (*m.*)   bat, 3
batería (*f.*)   battery, 6
beca (*f.*)   scholarship, 2
béisbol (*m.*)   baseball, 3
belleza (*f.*)   beauty
bellísimo(a)   beautiful
beneficio adicional (marginal) (*m.*)   fringe benefit, 10
besar   to kiss, to give a kiss, 1
bibliotecario(a) (*m., f.*)   librarian, 2
bien cocido(a)   well cooked (done), 7
bienvenido(a)   welcome, 7
bilingüe   bilingual, 10
blanco(a)   white, 7
bocadillo de paquete (*m.*)   packaged snack
bocado (*m.*)   bite, morsel, 7
boda (*f.*)   wedding, 1
bosque (*m.*)   forest
botiquín (*m.*)   first aid kit
boxeador(a) (*m., f.*)   boxer, 3
boxeo (*m.*)   boxing, 3
brécol (*m.*)   broccoli, 5
breve   brief
brillar   to glitter
brindar   to toast, 4; to share
brindis (*m.*)   toast, 7
bróculi (*m.*)   broccoli, 5
broma (*f.*)   practical joke, 4
bromear   to kid, to joke, 1
bruja (*f.*)   witch, 4
brujería (*f.*)   witchcraft, 4
brújula (*f.*)   compass
bucear   to scuba dive, 3
buen provecho   enjoy your meal, bon appétit, 7
burlarse (de)   to make fun of, 1

C

caber   to fit
cabeza (*m.*)   leader; (*f.*) head, 7
cada   each, 8
caerle bien a uno   to like, 1
caerle mal a uno   to dislike, 1
calcio (*m.*)   calcium, 5

caldo de frutas (*m.*)   punch
cálido(a)   hot (*climate*), 7
caliente   hot, 7
cámara lenta (*f.*)   slow motion, 9
cambiar   to change, 4
cambiar de actitud   to change one's attitude, 5
caminar   to walk, 5
caminata (*f.*)   hike
camioneta (*f.*)   van, 6
camote (*m.*)   yam
campaña electoral (*f.*)   electoral campaign, 8
campeón(-ona) (*m., f.*)   champion, 3
campeonato (*m.*)   championship, 3
campo (*m.*)   field, 6
canal (*m.*)   channel, 5
cantimplora (*f.*)   canteen
caña de pescar (*f.*)   fishing rod, 3
capital (*m.*)   money, capital; (*f.*) capital city, 7
carbohidratos (*m. pl.*)   carbohydrates, 5
cárcel (*f.*)   prison, jail, 8
carga (*f.*)   loading
cargar   to carry
cariño (*m.*)   love, 1
carnavales (*m. pl.*)   Mardi Gras, 4
carne molida (*f.*)   ground meat
carrera (*f.*)   career, course of study, 2; race, 3
   —de autos (*f.*)   auto race, 3
   —de caballos (*f.*)   horse race, 3
casarse (con)   to get married, 1; to marry, 9
cataratas (*f. pl.*)   falls
cebolla (*f.*)   onion, 5
cementerio (*m.*)   cemetery, 4
cera (*f.*)   wax
cercano(a)   nearby, 4
cerdo (*m.*)   pork, 7
cerveza (*f.*)   beer, 7
chapa (*f.*)   license plate, 6
charlar   to chat
chiste (*m.*)   joke, 7
chocar   to collide, 6
chuleta (*f.*)   chop, 5
círculo (*m.*)   circle, 1
cita a ciegas (*f.*)   blind date
claro   of course, naturally, 1
clave   key
club automovilístico (*m.*)   auto club, 6
cocinar al horno   to bake, 7
cocinar al vapor   to steam, 7
coger   to take, 1
col (*f.*)   cabbage, 5

combustible (*m.*) fuel, 8
comentar to comment, 3
como since, 2; like, 9
comodidad (*f.*) comfort
compartir to share, 8
complejo(a) complex, 8
composición de textos (*f.*) word processing, 10
comprensivo(a) understanding, 1
comprometerse (con) to get engaged (to), 9
comprometido(a) engaged, 1
computación (*f.*) computer science, 2
computadora portátil (*f.*) lap top, notebook, 10
con ganas de willing
con las manos en la masa redhanded, 10
con tal de que provided that, 5
concordancia (*f.*) agreement
confeccionado(a) made
conferencia (*f.*) lecture, 2
confiar en to trust, 9
conocer to know, to be familiar with, 1
conocimiento (*m.*) knowledge, 6
conseguir (e → i) to get, to obtain, 10
consejero(a) (*m., f.*) adviser, counselor, 2
consumo (*m.*) consumption, 5
contador(a) público(a) (*m., f.*) certified public accountant, 2
contaminación (*f.*) pollution, 8
contar con (o → ue) to count on, 9
contento(a) happy, glad, 1
contratar to hire, 10
contrato (*m.*) contract, 10
convenir (*conj. like* **venir**) to be convenient, to suit, 1
—en to agree on, 9
convertible convertible, 6
convertirse (e → ie) (en) to become, 5
cooperar to cooperate, 10
copa (*f.*) glass, goblet, 7
cordero (*m.*) lamb, 7
corregir (e → i) to correct, 1
correo (*m.*) mail
—electrónico (*m.*) e-mail, 10
corte (*m.*) cut, style; (*f.*) court, 7
corto(a) short, 5
costarricense Costa Rican, 6
costumbre (*f.*) custom, habit, 1
cotidiano(a) daily
crecer to grow

crecimiento (*m.*) development
creer que sí (no) (not) to think so, 2
crianza (*f.*) upbringing, raising
cualquier cosa anything, 5
cualquiera que sea whatever it may be, 6
cuando when, 5
cuanto más the more
cucaracha (*f.*) roach
cuchillo de campo (*m.*) pocket knife
cuerpo (*m.*) body, 5
cuidar to take care of, 1
culpa (*f.*) guilt
cumbre (*f.*) top
cumplir to keep (*a promise*)
cura (*m.*) priest; (*f.*) healing, 7
cursiva (*f.*) italic
curso (*m.*) class, course of study, 2
cuyo(a) whose, 3

D

dar to give
  —ánimo to cheer up, 10
  —consejos to give advice, 1
  —en el clavo to hit the nail on the head, 10
  —fin to close
  —gato por liebre to deceive, to defraud, 10
  —lata to annoy, to pester, 5
  —marcha atrás to back up, 10
  —pasos to take steps, 8
  —un abrazo to hug, to give a hug, 1
  —un beso to kiss, to give a kiss, 1
darse cuenta de to realize, 3
de about, 6; of, from, with, in, 9
  —ascendencia... of . . . descent, 8
  —buen (mal) humor in a good (bad) mood, 1
  —cambios mecánicos standard shift, 6
  —dos puertas two doors, 6
  —haberlo sabido had I known (it), 7
  —habla hispana Spanish speaking, 8
  —mala gana reluctantly, 10
  —manera (modo) que so, 1
  —quién whose, 3
  —vez en cuando once in a while, 5
debajo de below, underneath, 9
deber to owe
debido a due to
dejar de to fail (*to do something*), 8
dejar en paz to leave alone, 5
delincuencia (*f.*) delinquency, crime, 8

demasiados(as) too many, 2
demonio (*m.*) devil, demon, 4
demorar to take (*time*), 6
dentista (*m., f.*) dentist, 2
depender to depend, 8
deporte (*m.*) sport, 3
deportivo(a) related to sports, 3
deprimido(a) depressed, 1
derecha (*f.*) right (*direction*), 7
derecho (*m.*) right fielder; right, law, 7
derretir (e → i) to melt
desagüe (*m.*) sewer, drain, 8
desaparecer (*conj. like* **parecer**) to disappear, 1
desarrollado(a) developed
desarrollar to develop
desarrollo (*m.*) development
descansar to rest, 5
descapotable convertible, 6
descomponerse (*conj. like* **poner**) to break down, 10
desde since
desecho (*m.*) waste, 8
desempeñar un puesto to hold a position, 10
desfile (*m.*) parade, 9
desgrasado(a) skimmed
despacio slowly
despedir (e → i) to fire (*i.e., from a job*), 10
despensa (*f.*) pantry
desperdicio (*m.*) waste, 8
después de que after, 5
destacar to stand out
destreza (*f.*) skill
día (*m.*) day
  —de Acción de Gracias (*m.*) Thanksgiving, 4
  —de Canadá (*m.*) Canada Day, 4
  —de la Independencia (*m.*) Independence Day, 4
  —de la Madre (*m.*) Mother's Day, 4
  —de la Pascua Florida (*m.*) Easter, 4
  —de las Brujas (*m.*) Halloween, 4
  —de los Enamorados (*m.*) Valentine's Day, 4
  —del Padre (*m.*) Father's Day, 4
  —del Trabajo (*m.*) Labor Day, 4
diablo (*m.*) devil, demon, 4
diario(a) daily, 10
dieta balanceada (*f.*) balanced diet, 5
digital online
digno(a) de verse worth seeing
dime tell me, 4

dirigir to direct, to moderate, 8
disco duro (*m.*) hard drive, 10
discutir to discuss, to argue, 7
diseñar programas to design programs, 10
disfrutar (de) to enjoy, 4
disminuir to decrease, to lessen, 5
disponible available, 10
distinto(a) different, 8; separate
divorciarse to get a divorce, 1
documental (*m.*) documentary, 9
doler (o → ue) to hurt, 1
dominar to master
dondequiera que esté wherever I may be
dormir (o → ue) to sleep, 1
dormirse (o → ue) to fall asleep, 1
droga (*f.*) drug(s), 8
dulce fresh (*water*)
durar to last

E

echar to throw, 8
  —de menos to miss, to be homesick for, 1
  —una mirada rápida to scan, to skim
editor(a) (*m., f.*) editor, 9
editorial (*f.*) publishing company, (*m.*) editorial, 9
educación física (*f.*) physical education, 2
educar to educate, 8
educativo(a) educational, related to education, 2
egoísta selfish, 1
ejecutivo(a) (*m., f.*) executive, 10
ejercer to practice
ejercicio ligero (*m.*) light exercise, 5
elecciones (*f. pl.*) elections, 8
elegir (e → i) to choose, 1
elote (*m.*) tender corn
empatar to tie (*a score*), 3
empeorarse to become worse, 8
empleado(a) (*m., f.*) employee, 10
emplear to hire, 10
empleo (*m.*) job, 10
empresa (*f.*) business, 10
en at, in, on, inside, over, 9
  —busca de in search of
  —caso de que in case, 5
  —cuanto as soon as, 5
  —cuanto a as for, 9
  —el acto immediately, at once, right away, instantly, 10
  —línea online, 10

—lo alto de on top of
—lugar de instead of, 8
—pleno verano in the middle of summer, 4
—realidad in fact, 3
—regla in order
—vez de instead of, 8
—voz alta aloud, 10
—voz baja in a low voice, 10
enamorado(a) in love, 9
enamorarse de to fall in love with, 9
encabezado (*m.*) heading
encaje (*m.*) lace
encantador(a) charming, 9
encantar to love (*literally*, to delight), 3
encanto (*m.*) charm
encargar to order, 3
encender (e → ie) to light, to turn on, 1
enclenque (*m., f.*) sickly person, 3
encomiable praiseworthy
encontrarse (o → ue) con to meet (encounter), 9
enfadado(a) angry, 1
enfermero(a) (*m., f.*) nurse, 2
enfrentar(se) (con) to face
engañar to deceive
engaño (*m.*) deceit
engordar to gain weight, 5
enojado(a) angry, 1
enorgullecer to make proud
ensayar to rehearse
ensayo (*m.*) essay
entidad (*f.*) institution
entrar en to enter (*a place*), 9
entre between, 2; among
  —la espada y la pared between a rock and a hard place, 10
entrenador(a) (*m., f.*) trainer, coach, 3
entretener (*conj. like* **tener**) to entertain, 1
entrevista (*f.*) interview, 9
entusiasmado(a) enthused, excited, 1
envolver (o → ue) to wrap, 1
época (*f.*) time
equipo (*m.*) team, 3
es it is
  —conveniente (conviene) it is advisable, 4
  —difícil it is unlikely, 5
  —dudoso it is doubtful, 5
  —de esperar it's to be hoped, 6
  —importante (importa) it is important, 4
  —(im)posible it is (im)possible, 5

—(im)probable it is (im)probable, 5
—lamentable it's regrettable, 4
—una lástima it's a pity, 4
—mejor it is better, 4
—necesario it is necessary, 4
—preferible it is preferable, 4
—sorprendente it's surprising, 4
—una suerte it's lucky, 4
—urgente it is urgent, 4
escalar to climb, 3
escáner (*m.*) scanner, 10
escaso(a) scarce
escoger to choose
escuchar to listen (to), 9
escuela primaria (elemental) (*f.*) grade school, elementary school, 2
escuela secundaria (*f.*) secondary school (*junior high school and high school*), 2
escuela tecnológica (*f.*) technical school, 2
esfuerzo (*m.*) effort, 10
especialización (*f.*) major, 2
espectáculo (*m.*) show, 9
esperanza (*f.*) hope
esperar to hope, 4
espinaca (*f.*) spinach, 5
esquí acuático (*m.*) waterskiing, 3
esquiar to ski, 3
esta vez this time, 2
establecer to establish
estadio (*m.*) stadium, 3
estadística (*f.*) statistic, 8
estar to be, 2
  —de acuerdo to agree, 2
  —de buen (mal) humor to be in a good (bad) mood, 2
  —de vacaciones to be on vacation, 2
  —de viaje to be (away) on a trip, 2
  —de vuelta to be back, 2
  —en cama to be sick in bed, 2
  —en liquidación (venta) to be on sale, 3
  —hasta la coronilla de to be fed up with, 10
estatura (*f.*) height
estrella (*f.*) star, 9
estrenar to show for the first time, 9
estrés (*m.*) stress, 5
estudios de posgrado (*m. pl.*) graduate studies
etapa (*f.*) stage
etiqueta (*f.*) label, 10
evitar to avoid, 5
exagerar to exaggerate, 5

examen (*m.*) **de mitad (mediados) de curso** midterm examination, 2

examen parcial (*m.*) midterm examination, 2

exigir to demand, 4

existir to exist, 2

extranjero (*m.*) abroad, 10

extrañar to miss, to be homesick for, 1

F

fábrica (*f.*) factory, 8

factoría (*f.*) factory, 8

facultad (*f.*) school, college (*division within a university*), 2

—**de arquitectura** school of architecture, 2

—**de ciencias económicas (comerciales)** school of business administration, 2

—**de derecho** law school, 2

—**de educación** school of education, 2

—**de filosofía y letras** school of humanities, 2

—**de ingeniería** school of engineering, 2

—**de medicina** medical school, 2

—**de odontología** dental school, 2

faltar to be lacking, to need, 3

—**a** to miss, 3

farmacéutico(a) (*m., f.*) pharmacist, 2

fichero (*m.*) file (electronic), 10

fielmente faithfully

fijarse to notice, 1

fin de año (*m.*) New Year's Eve, 4

flor (*f.*) flower, 4

fonda (*f.*) inn, 7

fondo (*m.*) bottom, fund, 7

fracasar to fail, 8

freír (*cong. like* **reír**) to fry, 7

freno (*m.*) brake, 6

frente (*m.*) front, battlefront; (*f.*) forehead, 7

frecuentemente often, frequently, 1

frustrado(a) frustrated, 1

fuegos artificiales (*m. pl.*) fireworks, 4

fuente (*f.*) serving dish, 7

fuente de energía (*f.*) energy source, 5

fuera out, 6

funcionar to work, to function, 6

furgoneta van, 6

fútbol (*m.*) soccer, 3

fútbol americano (*m.*) football, 3

G

galleta (*f.*) cookie

ganar to win, 3

—**peso** to gain weight, 5

gaseosa (*f.*) soft drink, 7

gastar to spend (*money*), 6

gasto (*m.*) expense, 10

gata (*f.*) jack (*Costa Rica*), 6

gato jack (*of a car*), 6

generar to generate

género (*m.*) genre

generoso(a) generous, 1

gente (*f.*) people, 4

—**mayor** (*f.*) older people, 1

gimnasia (*f.*) gymnastics, 3

gimnasta (*m., f.*) gymnast, 3

ginebra (*f.*) gin, 7

girar to revolve

gobernador(a) (*m., f.*) governor, 8

gobierno (*m.*) government, 8

goma (*f.*) **pinchada (ponchada)** flat tire, 6

grabación (*f.*) recording

grabar to record, to tape, 9

grande big, great, 6

grasa (*f.*) fat, 5

gratis free, 8

grave serious, 8

grúa (*f.*) tow truck, 6

guante de pelota (*m.*) baseball mitt, 3

guardería (*f.*) nursery

guardia (*m.*) guard; (*f.*) security force, 7

guerra (*f.*) war

guía (*m.*) guide; (*f.*) guidebook, 7

guiso (*m.*) stew

gustar to like (*literally*, to be pleasing to *or* to appeal to), 3

H

hábito (*m.*) habit

habría there would be, 7

hace un tiempo some time ago, 4

hacer to do, to make

—**caso** to pay attention, to obey, 5

—**ejercicio** to exercise, 5

hacerse to become, 5

—**(de) la vista gorda** to overlook, 10

—**el (la) tonto(a)** to play dumb, 10

—**preguntas** to hypothesize

—**socio(a)** to become a member, 5

hacérsele a uno agua la boca to make one's mouth water, 10

haragán(-ana) lazy, 1

hasta que until, 5

hay que (+ *inf.*) one must, it is necessary to, 8

hecho (*m.*) fact

herradura (*f.*) horseshoe, 4

herramienta (*f.*) tool

hervir (e → ie) to boil, 7

hierro (*m.*) iron, 5

higo (*m.*) fig

hipódromo (*m.*) race track, 3

hogar (*m.*) home

hoja (*f.*) leaf, 8; sheet

hongo (*m.*) mushroom, 5

hora (*f.*) time, 2

horario de clases (*m.*) class schedule, 2

hornear to bake, 7

hoy en día nowadays

huelga (*f.*) strike, 8

I

identificar to identify, 8

impedir (e → i) to prevent, 1

imponer (*conj. like* **poner**) to impose, 1

incluir to include, 10

incluso even

indeseable undesirable

infancia (*f.*) childhood

informática (*f.*) computer science, 2

ingeniero(a) (*m., f.*) engineer, 2

ingresos (*m. pl.*) income

inolvidable unforgettable

insistir en to insist on, 9

intervenir (*conj. like* **venir**) to intervene, 1

ir to go, 1

—**a parar** to end up, 7

irse to leave, to go away, 1

J

jefe(a) (*m., f.*) boss, 10

joven (*m., f.*) young man (woman), 4; young, 5

jubilación (*f.*) retirement, 10

juego (*m.*) game

Juegos Olímpicos (*m. pl.*) Olympic Games, 3

jugador(a) (*m., f.*) player, 3

junta (*f.*) meeting, (*Mex.*), 2

juntos(as) together, 2

L

la última vez the last time, 3

lácteo(a) dairy, containing milk

ladrón(ona) (*m., f.*) thief, burglar, 8

lago (*m.*) lake

lamentar to regret, 4

lanzar to release, 9

lastimar(se) to hurt (oneself), 3

lechuga (*f.*) lettuce, 5

lector(a) (*m., f.*) reader

letrero (*m.*) sign, 4

levantar to raise, to lift, 1

　—pesas to lift weights, 5

levantarse to get up, 1

ley (*f.*) law, 8

libra (*f.*) pound, 5

libre free, 4

libremente freely

licencia (de conducir) (*f.*) driver's license, 6

ligado(a) tied

ligero(a) light

limpio(a) clean, 8

listo(a) smart, clever, ready, 2

llamar to call, 1

llamarse to be named, 1

llanta (*f.*) tire, 6

llegar tarde (temprano) to be late (early), 2

lleno(a) full, 5

llevar to take, 1

llevar a cabo to carry out, to take place

llevarse to carry off, 1

llevarse bien to get along, 1

lo mejor the best thing, 2

lo mismo the same thing, 1

lo que what, that which, 1

lo que pasa es que the truth of the matter is that, 5

lo siguiente the following, 5

locutor(a) (*m., f.*) announcer, speaker, commentator, 9

lograr to achieve, 12

loma (*f.*) hill, 7

lomo (*m.*) back of an animal, 7

longitud (*f.*) length

los (las) demás (*m., f.*) the others

lucha libre (*f.*) wrestling, 3

M

macizo(a) solid

madreselva (*f.*) honeysuckle

madrina (*f.*) godmother

maestro(a) (*m., f.*) teacher, 2

magia negra (*f.*) black magic, 4

mago(a) (*m., f.*) magician, 4

maíz (*m.*) corn, 4

mal de ojo (*m.*) evil eye, 4

malcriar to spoil, 1

malísimo(a) extremely bad, 2

malo(a) bad, sick, 2; mean, 6

mandar to order, 4

mandón(-ona) bossy, 1

manera (*f.*) way, 1

manga (*f.*) sleeve, 7

mango (*m.*) handle of a utensil; fruit, 7

mantener (*conj. like* **tener**) to maintain, to support, 1; to keep, 2

mantenerse (*conj. like* **tener**) to keep oneself, to stay, 5

　—en contacto to keep in touch, 1

　—joven to keep young, 5

maquinaria (*f.*) machinery, 10

marcar to score (*sports*), 3

mariposa (*f.*) butterfly

materia (*f.*) subject (*in school*), 2

materialista materialistic, 1

matrícula (*f.*) tuition, 2; registration, 6

matricularse to register, 2

mazorca (*f.*) ear of corn

mediano(a) average, middle, 9

médico(a) (*m., f.*) medical doctor, 2

medida (*f.*) measure

medio (*m.*) middle, half, 9; means

medio ambiente (*m.*) environment, 8

medio crudo(a) rare, 7

medir (e → i) to be . . . tall, to measure, 5

mejorar to improve, 3

memoria (*f.*) memory, 10

mensual monthly, 10

mente (*f.*) mind, 5

mentir (e → ie) to lie, 1

mentira (*f.*) lie, 9

mercadeo (*m.*) marketing, 10

mercancía (*f.*) merchandise

meta (*f.*) goal, 12

meterse to meddle, 1

mezcla (*f.*) mixture

mezclar to mix

microcomputadora (*f.*) lap top, notebook, 10

miel de abeja (*f.*) honey, 7

miembro (*m.*) member

mientras while

mimar to pamper, 1

misa (*f.*) mass (*Catholic*), 4

Misa del Gallo (*f.*) Midnight Mass, 4

miseria (*f.*) poverty, 8

mismo(a) oneself, same, 6

mochila (*f.*) backpack

moda (*f.*) fashion, 7

modo (*m.*) way, 1; manner, 7

mondongo (*m.*) tripe and beef knuckles, 7

montaña (*f.*) mountain, 3

montar a caballo to ride on horseback, 3

moro(a) Moorish

morder (o → ue) to bite, 1

morirse (o → ue) de hambre to die of hunger, to starve to death, 5

mostaza (*f.*) mustard

mostrar (o → ue) to show, 1

muchísimo a lot, a great deal, 2

N

nacer to be born, 8

nacimiento (*m.*) manager, nativity scene, 4

nadador(a) (*m., f.*) swimmer, 3

nadar to swim, 3

natación (*f.*) swimming, 3

naturalmente of course, naturally, 1

navegar la red to surf the net, 10

negar (e → ie) to deny, 1

negocio (*m.*) business

nene (*m.*) little child

nervioso(a) nervous, 1

neumático (*m.*) tire, 6

ni aun not even, 8

niñera (*f.*) nanny

no no

　—más que only, 4

　—ser para tanto not to be that important, 4

　—tener pelos en la lengua to be outspoken, to be frank, 10

　—va a haber there's not going to be, 1

　—ver la hora de not to be able to wait to, 4

Nochebuena (*f.*) Christmas Eve, 4

nombrar to name, 9

noreste northeast

nostálgico(a) homesick, 1

nota (*f.*) grade, 2

noticia (*f.*) piece of news, news item, 1

noticias (*f. pl.*) news, 9

O

obedecer to obey, 1

obligatorio(a) mandatory, 2

obra (*f.*) work (*of art*), 4

ojalá if only, it's to be hoped, 4

Olimpiadas (*f. pl.*) Olympic Games, 3

olvidarse de to forget, 9

optimista   optimistic, 1
orden (*m.*)   order, method; (*f.*) order, command, 7
ordenador (*m.*)   computer
  —**portátil** (*m.*)   lap top, notebook, 10
ordenar   to order, 4
organizar   to organize, 8
orilla (*f.*)   shore
otra manera   other way
oyente (*m., f.*)   listener

P

padrino (*m.*)   godfather, 1
página (*f.*)   page, 3
país (*m.*)   country (nation), 2
paisaje (*m.*)   landscape
pájaro (*m.*)   bird
pala (*f.*)   shovel, 7
pálido(a)   pale
palo (*m.*)   stick, 7
pandilla (*f.*)   gang, 8
pantalla (*f.*)   screen, 9
papel (*m.*)   role, 1
para   by, for, in order to, by the standard of, considering, 4
  —**eso**   for that, 4
  —**que**   so that, 5
  ¿—**qué?**   what for?, 4
  —**siempre**   forever, 4
parecer   to seem, to appear, 1
parecerse   to look like, 1
pariente (*m., f.*)   relative, 1
parientes políticos (*m., f.*)   in-laws
parte (*m.*)   official communication; (*f.*) part, portion, 7
partido (*m.*)   game, match, 3
pasado(a)   last, 6
pasar   to spend (*time*), 4
  —**por (alguien)**   to pick (someone) up, 2
paso (*m.*)   step, 9
pastel (*m.*)   pie, 5
pata de conejo (*f.*)   rabbit's foot, 4
patinar   to skate, 3
pauta (*f.*)   guideline
pedir (e → i)   to ask for, to request (*something*), 1
pelea (*f.*)   fight, 3
peligro (*m.*)   danger
pelota (*f.*)   ball, 3
pena capital (*f.*)   death penalty, 8
pena de muerte (*f.*)   death penalty, 8
pensar (e → ie) (en)   to think (about), 9
pepino (*m.*)   cucumber, 5

pequeño(a)   little, 7
perder (e → ie)   to miss, 3
  —**peso**   to lose weight, 5
perderse (*algo*) **(e → ie)**   to miss out on (*something*), 3
pérdida de tiempo (*f.*)   waste of time
perezoso(a)   lazy, 1
permitir   to allow, 4
personas (*f. pl.*)   people, 4
personas sin hogar (*f. pl.*)   the homeless, 8
pertenecer   to belong
pesar   to weigh
pescar   to fish, to catch a fish, 3
pesebre (*m.*)   manger, nativity scene, 4
pesimista   pessimistic, 1
petróleo (*m.*)   oil, petroleum, 9
picante   spicy, hot, 7
pie (*m.*)   foot, 5
píldora (*f.*)   pill, 6
pilote (*m.*)   stake
pimiento verde (*m.*)   green pepper, 5
pista de baile (*f.*)   dance floor, 9
placa (*f.*)   license plate, 6
plátano (*m.*)   plantain, banana, 7
plato principal (*m.*)   main course, 7
poblado (*m.*)   village
pobre   poor, unfortunate, 6
pobreza (*f.*)   poverty, 8
poco(a)   little (*quantity*), 7
poco a poco   little by little, 8
poderoso(a)   powerful
policía (*m.*)   policeman; (*f.*) police organization, 7
polución (*f.*)   pollution, 8
ponche (*m.*)   punch, 7
poner   to put, to place, 1
  —**el grito en el cielo**   to hit the roof, 10
  —**en duda**   to doubt, 10
  —**en peligro**   to endanger, 10
  —**peros**   to find fault, 10
ponerse   to put on, 1; to become, 5
  —**a** (+ *inf.*)   to start, to begin (+ *inf.*), 9
  —**a dieta**   to go on a diet, 5
  —**contento(a)**   to be (become) happy, 1
  —**de acuerdo**   to come to an understanding, 2
  —**de moda**   to become fashionable, 9
  —**en ridículo**   to make a fool of oneself, 10
  —**triste**   to become sad, 7

por   during, in, for, by, per, because of, on account of, on behalf of, in search of, in exchange for, through, around, along, by, 4
  —**aquí**   around here, 4
  —**completo**   completely, 4
  —**desgracia**   unfortunately, 4
  —**ejemplo**   for example, 2
  —**eso**   for that reason, that's why, 4
  —**fin**   at last, finally, 4
  —**lo menos**   at least, 4
  —**lo regular**   as a rule, 2
  —**lo visto**   apparently, 2
  —**no tener (algo)**   for the lack of (*something*), 10
  —**poco se mata**   he almost killed himself, 3
  —**su cuenta**   on their own, 2
  —**suerte**   luckily, fortunately, 4
  —**supuesto**   of course, naturally, 1
porteador (*m.*)   bearer
postulante (*m., f.*)   applicant, 10
postularse   to run for, 8
precio (*m.*)   price, 6
precisar   to need, 10
preguntar   to ask (*a question*), to inquire, to ask about (*someone*), 1
premio (*m.*)   award, 9
prender   to arrest
prensa (*f.*)   press
preocupado(a)   worried, 1
prepararse   to get ready, 6
presupuesto (*m.*)   budget
primer (segundo) tiempo (*m.*)   first (second) half (*in game*), 3
primeros auxilios (*m. pl.*)   first aid
principiante (*m., f.*)   beginner, 6
prisión (*f.*)   prison, jail, 8
probador (*m.*)   fitting room, 5
probar (o → ue)   to taste, to try, 1
probarse (o → ue)   to try on, 1
productor(a) (*m., f.*)   producer, 9
profesorado (*m.*)   faculty, 2
programa de estudios (*m.*)   study program, 2
programador(a) (*m., f.*)   programmer, 2
prohibir   to forbid, 4
promedio (*m.*)   grade point average, 2
prometido(a) (*m., f.*)   fiancé(e), 1
pronto   soon, 4
propaganda (*f.*)   advertising, promotional material, 2
propio(a)   related, own, 2

proponer (*conj. like* **poner**)   to propose, 1
proporcionar   to furnish
protagonista (*m., f.*)   protagonist, 9
proteína (*f.*)   protein, 5
psicólogo(a) (*m., f.*)   psychologist, 2
publicidad (*f.*)   publicity, 9
pueblo (*m.*)   people, 4; town, 8
puede ser   it may be, 5
puerta (*f.*)   door, 7
puerto (*m.*)   port, 7
puesto (*m.*)   job, 10
pujante   vigorous
pulgada (*f.*)   inch, 5
pulverizador (*m.*)   spray, spray can, 8
punta (*f.*)   point, tip, 7
punto (*m.*)   dot, period, 7

Q

que   that, which, who, 3; que, 4
quedar   to have (*something*) left, 3
   —en   to agree to do something, 2
   —suspendido(a)   to fail (*a course*), 8
quedarse   to stay, to remain, 3
   —con   to keep, 1
quejarse (de)   to complain, 1
quemar   to burn
querer (e → ie)   to love, 1
querido(a)   dear, 4
quien   whom, that, who, 3
química (*f.*)   chemistry, 2
químico(a)   chemical, 8
quitar   to take away, 1
quitarse   to take off, 1
quizá(s)   perhaps, maybe, 1

R

rábano (*m.*)   radish, 5
raqueta (*f.*)   racket, 3
rascacielos (*m.*)   skyscraper
realista   realistic, 1
realizar   to do, to accomplish, 3; to make, 5
recibir   to get, to receive, 10
reciclar   to recycle, 8
rector(a) (*m., f.*)   president (*of a university*), 2
recuerdo (*m.*)   memory, 7; souvenir, 2
red (*f.*)   network
redondo(a)   round, 8
regla (*f.*)   rule, 5
rehacer (*conj. like* **hacer**)   to remake, to redo, 1
reina (*f.*)   queen, 9

reino (*m.*)   kingdom
reírse (e → i)   to laugh, 1
relleno(a)   stuffed, 7
remolacha (*f.*)   beet, 5
remolcador (*m.*)   tow truck, 6
remolcar   to tow, 6
renunciar   to resign, 10
reñido(a)   close (*game*), 3
repollo (*m.*)   cabbage, 5
reportaje (*m.*)   report, interview, 9
reposo (*m.*)   rest, 5
represa (*f.*)   dam
representación (*f.*)   skit
representar   to enact
requisito (*m.*)   requirement, 2
rescatar   to rescue, 8
rescate (*m.*)   rescue, ransom, 8
residencia universitaria (*f.*)   dormitory, 2
residuo (*m.*)   by-product, 8
resolver (o → ue)   to solve, 1
respetar   to respect, 1
resta (*f.*)   subtraction, 7
resto (*m.*)   rest, leftover, 7
resultar aplazado(a)   to fail
retiro (*m.*)   retirement, 10
reunión (*f.*)   meeting, 2
Reyes Magos (*m. pl.*)   Three Wise Men, 4
rezar   to pray, 5
rico(a)   tasty, delicious, 7
rincón (*m.*)   corner
riqueza (*f.*)   wealth
robo (*m.*)   robbery, burglary, 8
rogar (o → ue)   to beg, to plead, 4
ron (*m.*)   rum, 7
rosado(a)   rosé, 7

S

saber   to know (*a fact*) or (*by heart*), 1
sabroso(a)   tasty, delicious, 7
sacar   to get (*a grade*), 2; to take out
   —(conseguir) entradas   to buy (get) the tickets, 3
   —seguro   to take out insurance, 6
sagrado(a)   sacred
salario (*m.*)   salary, 10
salir (de)   to leave (*a place*), 9
salmón (*m.*)   salmon, 7
salón de clases (*m.*)   classroom, 2
salto (*m.*)   waterfall
salud (*f.*)   health, 5
¡Salud!   Cheers!, To your health!, 7
sangre (*f.*)   blood

sano(a)   healthy, 5
santo(a) (*m., f.*)   saint, 4
   —patrón(ona) (*m., f.*)   patron saint, 4
sardina (*f.*)   sardine, 7
satisfecho(a)   full, satisfied, 7
secuestrar   to kidnap, 8
seguro (*m.*)   insurance, 6
selva (*f.*)   forest, rain forest
semáforo (*m.*)   traffic light, 6
Semana Santa (*f.*)   Holy Week, 4
semanal   weekly, 10
sentado(a)   seated, 3
sentar (e → ie)   to seat, 1
sentarse (e → ie)   to sit down, 1
sentirse (e → ie)   to feel, 1; to regret, 4
señal (*f.*)   sign, 10
señalar   to point out
ser   to be, 2
   —puntual   to be punctual, 2
serio(a)   serious, 8
servir (e → i) (de)   to serve (as), 3
seta (*f.*)   mushroom, 5
show (*m.*)   show, 9
si   if
sí mismo(a) (*m., f.*)   himself, herself
sidra (*f.*)   cider, 4
siglo (*m.*)   century, 9
signo (*m.*)   sign, 10
   —del zodíaco (*m.*)   zodiac sign, 4
sin que   without, 5
sin qué ni para qué   without rhyme or reason, 4
sino   but (on the contrary), 4
sobrar   to be left over, 5
sobre   about, 1; on, 9
   —todo   above all, 7
sobrenombre (*m.*)   nickname
sobresalir   to stand out
socio(a) (*m., f.*)   member, 5; partner
solicitar   to apply, 10
solicitud (*f.*)   application, 2
solucionar   to solve, 8
soñar (o → ue)   to dream, 9
   —con   to dream about, 9
sorprenderse de   to be surprised
subrayar   to underline
suceso (*m.*)   event
suela (*f.*)   sole, 7
sueldo (*m.*)   salary, 10
suelo (*m.*)   ground, 7
sueño (*m.*)   sleep
suicidarse   to commit suicide, 1
superficie (*f.*)   area

suponer (*conj. like* **poner**)   to suppose, 1
surgir   to appear, 9

T

tacaño(a)   cheap, stingy, 1
tal vez   perhaps, maybe, 1
talar   to cut down
taller de mecánica (*m.*)   repair shop, 6
tan pronto (como)   as soon as, 5
tanto(a)   as much, 4
tantos(as)   as many, 4
techo (*m.*)   roof
tecnología punta (*f.*)   state-of-the-art
tela (*f.*)   cloth
telediario (*m.*)   TV news, 9
teléfono móvil (celular) (*m.*)   cellular phone, 10
telenoticias (*f.*)   TV news, 9
telenovela (*f.*)   soap opera, 9
televidente (*m., f.*)   TV viewer, 9
temer   to fear, 4
tener chispa   to be witty, 10
tener en cuenta   to keep in mind
tener ganas de   to feel like, 7
tener presente   to keep in mind
tensión nerviosa (*f.*)   stress, 5
término medio   medium-rare, 7
ternera (*f.*)   veal, 7
tiburón (*m.*)   shark
tiempo (*m.*)   time, 2
   —extra (*m.*)   overtime, 10
tienda de campaña (*f.*)   tent, 3
tierra (*f.*)   land
tinto(a)   red, 7
título (*m.*)   degree, 2
todavía   yet, still, 6
todo tipo de   all kinds of, 8
tomar   to take, 1
   —en cuenta   to keep in mind
   —parte en   to take part in, 4

tonto(a)   silly, dumb, 6
toronja (*f.*)   grapefruit
tortuga (*f.*)   tortoise
trabajador(a)   hard-working
trabajador(a) social (*m., f.*)   social worker, 2
trabajar medio día   to work part time, 1
trabajo (*m.*)   work, 4
tragar   to swallow, 7
tranquilo(a)   calm, tranquil, 1
transcurrido(a)   elapsed
trasladar   to move
tratar de   to try to, 2
trébol de cuatro hojas (*m.*)   four-leaf clover, 4
triste   sad, 1
trucha (*f.*)   trout, 7
tumba (*f.*)   grave, 4
turnarse   to take turns

U

últimamente   lately, 5
último(a)   last (*in a series*), 6
un   a, an
   —día de estos   one of these days, 1
   —par de   a couple of, 1
   —poco   a little, 1
   —rato   a while, 1
una especie de   a kind of, 4
único(a)   only, 5; unique, 6
universidad estatal (*f.*)   state university, 2
universidad privada (*f.*)   private university, 2
universitario(a) (*m., f.*)   college student, 2; (*adj.*) university, college, 2
unos(as)   about (*with numbers*), 1

V

valer   to be worth, 1
—la pena   to be worth it
válido(a)   accepted, 6
vanidoso(a)   vain, conceited, 1
varios(as)   several, 1
vecino(a) (*m., f.*)   neighbor
vela (*f.*)   candle, 4
vencer   to defeat, 3
vendedor(a) (*m., f.*)   salesperson, 10
venta (*f.*)   sale, 10
ventaja (*f.*)   advantage, 2
verde   green, not ripe, 2
vertedero (*m.*)   disposal site, dump, 8
vestirse (e → i)   to dress (oneself), to get dressed, 1
veterinario(a) (*m., f.*)   veterinarian, 2
vez (*f.*)   time (*in a series*), 2
vida (*f.*)   life, 1
viejo(a)   old, elderly, long-time, 6
vino tinto (*m.*)   red wine, 7
violación (*f.*)   rape, 8
Víspera de Año Nuevo (Fin de Año)   New Year's Eve, 4
vitamina (*f.*)   vitamin, 5
vivienda (*f.*)   housing, 8
volver (o → ue) a (+ *inf.*)   to do something again (over), 9
voz (*f.*)   voice, 9

Y

¡Ya lo creo!   I'll say!, 2
ya que   since

Z

zanahoria (*f.*)   carrot, 5

English—Spanish

A

a un, una
—**couple of** un par de, 1
—**day** al día, 5
—**great deal** muchísimo, 2
—**kind of** una especie de, 4
—**little** un poco, 1
—**lot** muchísimo, 2
—**while** un rato, 1
about sobre, 1; (*before a number*) unos(as), 1; (*with time*) a eso de, acerca de, de, sobre, 6
above arriba, 9
—**all** sobre todo, 7
abroad extranjero (*m.*), 10
accepted válido(a), 6
accomplish realizar, 3
act actuar, 9
actor actor (*m.*), 9
actress actriz (*f.*), 9
ad anuncio (*m.*), 6
add añadir, agregar, 9
advantage ventaja (*f.*), 2
advise aconsejar, 4
adviser consejero(a) (*m., f.*), 2
after después de, 2; después (de) que, 5
—**all** al fin y al cabo, 10
ago hace + *time* + que, 3
agree estar de acuerdo, 2
—**on** convenir (*conj. like* **venir**) en, 9
—**to do something** quedar en, 2
all kinds of toda clase de, 8
allow permitir, 4
along por, 4
aloud en voz alta, 10
although aunque, 8
amulet amuleto (*m.*), 4
angry enojado(a), enfadado(a), 1
announcer locutor(a) (*m., f.*), 9
annoy dar lata, 5
anything cualquier cosa, 5
apparently por lo visto, 2
appeal to gustar, 3
appear aparecer, 1; parecer, 1; surgir, 9
applicant aspirante (*m., f.*), postulante (*m., f.*), 10
application solicitud (*f.*), 2
apply solicitar, 10
argue discutir, 7

around por, 4; alrededor, 7
—**here** por aquí, 4
—**the middle of** (*a month, a year*) a mediados de, 9
as tan, 4
—**a rule** por lo regular, 2
—**for** en cuanto a, 9
—**many** tantos(as), 4
—**much** tanto(a), 4
—**soon as** tan pronto (como), en cuanto, así que, 5
assassin asesino(a) (*m., f.*), 8
assault asalto (*m.*), 8
at a, en, 9
—**about** a eso de, 6
—**last** por fin, 4
—**least** por lo menos, 4; al menos, 8
—**once** en el acto, 10
—**the end of** a fines de, 4
—**the latest** a más tardar, 2
athlete atleta (*m., f.*), 3
attack asalto (*m.*), 8
attend asistir a, 2
attendance asistencia (*f.*), 2
auto club club automovilístico (*m.*), 6
auto race carrera de autos (*f.*), 3
available disponible, 10
average mediano(a), 9
avoid evitar, 5
award premio (*m.*), 9

B

back (*of an animal*) lomo (*m.*), 7
back up dar marcha atrás, 10
bad malo(a), 2
bake cocinar al horno, hornear, 7
balanced diet dieta balanceada (*f.*), 5
ball pelota (*f.*), 3
banana plátano (*m.*), 7
band banda (*f.*), 7
barbecue asar, 7
barely apenas, 1
baseball béisbol (*m.*), 3
—**glove** guante de pelota (*m.*), 3
basketball baloncesto (*m.*), básquetbol (*m.*), 3
bat bate (*m.*), 3
battery acumulador (*m.*), batería (*f.*), 6
be ser, estar, 2
—**acquainted with** conocer, 1
—**away (on a trip)** estar de viaje, 2

—**back** estar de vuelta, 2
—**born** nacer, 8
—**convenient** convenir (*conj. like* **venir**), 1
—**familiar with** conocer, 1
—**fed up with** estar hasta la coronilla de, 10
—**frank** no tener pelos en la lengua, 10
—**glad about** alegrarse de, 4
—**happy** ponerse contento(a), 1
—**homesick for** extrañar, echar de menos, 1
—**in a good (bad) mood** estar de buen (mal) humor, 2
—**lacking** faltar, 3
—**late (early)** llegar tarde (temprano), 2
—**left over** sobrar, 5
—**named** llamarse, 1
—**on vacation** estar de vacaciones, 2
—**outspoken** no tener pelos en la lengua, 10
—**pleasing to** gustar, 3
—**punctual** ser puntual, 2
—**sick in bed** estar en cama, 2
—**surprised** sorprenderse, 4
—**witty** tener chispa, 10
—**worth** valer, 1
because of por, 4
become convertirse (e → ie) (en), hacerse, ponerse, 5
—**a member** hacerse socio(a), 5
—**fashionable** ponerse de moda, 9
—**happy** ponerse contento(a), 1
—**sad** ponerse triste, 7
—**worse** agravarse, empeorarse, 8
beer cerveza (*f.*), 7
beet remolacha (*f.*), 5
before antes (de) que, 5
beg rogar (o → ue), 4
beginner principiante (*m., f.*), 6
below abajo, bajo, debajo de, 9
besides además, 1
best thing lo mejor, 2
between entre, 2
—**a rock and a hard place** entre la espada y la pared, 10
big grande, 6
bilingual bilingüe, 10
bite morder (o → ue), 1; bocado (*m.*), 7

black magic   magia negra (*f.*), 4
body   cuerpo (*m.*)
boil   hervir (e → ie), 7
bon appétit   buen provecho, 7
bored   aburrido(a), 1
boring   aburrido(a), 2
boss   jefe(a) (*m., f.*), 10
bossy   mandón(ona), 1
bottom   fondo (*m.*), 7
boxer   boxeador(a) (*m., f.*), 3
boxing   boxeo (*m.*), 3
brake   freno (*m.*), 6
break down   descomponerse (*conj. like* **poner**), 10
broccoli   bróculi (*m.*), brécol (*m.*), 5
burglar   ladrón(ona) (*m., f.*), 8
burglary   robo (*m.*), 8
business   empresa (*f.*), 10
business administration   administración de empresas (*f.*), 2
but   sino, 4
buy (get) tickets   sacar (conseguir) entradas, 3
by   por, para, 4
   —the standard of   para, 4
by-product   residuo (*m.*), 8

C

cabbage   repollo (*m.*), col (*f.*), 5
calcium   calcio (*m.*), 5
call   llamar, 1
calm   tranquilo(a), 1
camp   acampar, 3
Canada Day   Día de Canadá (*m.*), 4
candle   vela (*f.*), 4
capital   capital (*m.*), 7
capital city   capital (*f.*), 7
car rental agency   agencia de alquiler de automóviles (*f.*), 6
carbohydrates   carbohidratos (*m. pl.*), 5
career   carrera (*f.*), 2
carrot   zanahoria (*f.*), 5
carry off   llevarse, 1
catch a fish   pescar, 3
celery   apio (*m.*), 5
cellular phone   teléfono móvil (celular) (*m.*), 10
cemetery   cementerio (*m.*), 4
century   siglo (*m.*), 9
certified public accountant   contador(a) público(a) (*m., f.*), 2
champion   campeón(ona) (*m., f.*), 3
championship   campeonato (*m.*), 3
change   cambiar, 4
   —one's attitude   cambiar de actitud, 5

channel   canal (*m.*), 5
charming   encantador(a), 9
cheap   tacaño(a), 1
cheer up   dar ánimo, 10
Cheers!   ¡Salud!, 7
chemical   químico(a), 8
chemistry   química (*f.*), 2
choose   elegir (e → i), 1
chop   chuleta (*f.*), 5
Christmas Eve   Nochebuena (*f.*), 4
cider   sidra (*f.*), 4
circle   círculo (*m.*), 1
class   curso (*m.*), 2
class schedule   horario de clases (*m.*), 2
classroom   aula (*f.*), salón de clases (*m.*), 2
clean   limpio(a), 8
clever   listo(a), 2
climb   escalar, 3
close   (*ref. to games*)   reñido(a), 3
coach   entrenador(a) (*m., f.*), 3
cod   bacalao (*m.*), 7
college   (*division within a university*) facultad (*f.*), 2; (*adj.*) universitario(a), 2
   —student   universitario(a) (*m., f.*), 2
collide   chocar, 6
come to an understanding   ponerse de acuerdo, 2
command   orden (*f.*), 7; (*verb*) ordenar, mandar, 3
comment   comentar, 3
commentator   locutor(a) (*m., f.*), 9
commit suicide   suicidarse, 1
complain   quejarse (de), 1
completely   por completo, 4
complex   complejo(a), 8
computer science   informática (*f.*), computación (*f.*), 2
conceited   vanidoso(a), 1
considering   para, 4
consumption   consumo (*m.*), 5
contract   contrato (*m.*), 10
convertible   descapotable, convertible, 6
cooperate   cooperar, 8
corn   maíz (*m.*), 4
correct   corregir (e → i), 1
Costa Rican   costarricense (*m., f.*), 6
count on   contar (o → ue) con, 9
country   (*nation*)   país (*m.*), 2
counselor   consejero(a) (*m., f.*), 2
course of study   carrera (*f.*), curso (*m.*), 2
court   corte (*f.*), 7
crime   delincuencia (*f.*), 8

cucumber   pepino (*m.*), 5
custom   costumbre (*f.*), 1
cut   corte (*m.*), 7

D

daily   diario(a), 10
dance floor   pista de baile (*f.*), 9
dare   atreverse (a), 1
dear   querido(a), 4
death penalty   pena capital (*f.*), pena de muerte (*f.*), 8
deceive   dar gato por liebre, 10
decrease   disminuir, 5
defeat   vencer, 3
defraud   dar gato por liebre, 10
degree   título (*m.*), 2
delicious   rico(a), sabroso(a), 7
delight   encantar, 3
delinquency   delincuencia (*f.*), 8
demand   exigir, 4
demon   demonio (*m.*), diablo (*m.*), 4
dental school   facultad de odontología (*f.*), 2
dentist   dentista (*m., f.*), 2
deny   negar (e → ie), 1
depend   depender, 8
depressed   deprimido(a), 1
design programs   diseñar programas, 10
detain   detener (*conj. like* **tener**), 1
devil   demonio (*m.*), diablo (*m.*), 4
die of hunger   morirse (o → ue) de hambre, 5
direct   dirigir, 8
directory   guía (*f.*), 7
disappear   desaparecer (*conj. like* **parecer**), 1
discuss   discutir, 7
dislike   caerle mal a uno, 1
disposal site   vertedero (*m.*), 8
do   realizar, 3
   —something again (over)   volver (o → ue) a (+ *inf.*), 9
documentary   documental (*m.*), 9
door   puerta (*f.*), 7
dormitory   residencia universitaria (*f.*), 2
dot   punto (*m.*), 7
doubt   poner en duda, 10
drain   desagüe (*m.*), 8
dream   soñar (o → ue), 9
dream about (of)   soñar (o → ue) con, 9
dress (oneself)   vestirse (e → i), 1
driver's license   licencia (de conducir) (*f.*), 6

drug(s)   droga (*f.*), 8
dumb   tonto(a), 6
dump   vertedero (*m.*), 8
during   por, 4

E

e-mail   correo electrónico (*m.*), 10
each   cada, 8
Easter   Día de Pascua Florida (*m.*), 4
editor   editor(a) (*m., f.*), 9
editorial   editorial (*f.*), 9
educate   educar, 8
educational   educativo(a), 2
elections   elecciones (*f. pl.*), 8
electoral campaign   campaña electoral (*f.*), 8
elementary school   escuela primaria (elemental) (*f.*), 2
employee   empleado(a) (*m., f.*), 10
end up   ir a parar, 7
endanger   poner en peligro, 10
energy source   fuente de energía (*f.*), 5
engaged   comprometido(a), 1
engineer   ingeniero(a) (*m., f.*), 2
enjoy   disfrutar (de), 4
   —your meal   buen provecho, 7
enough   hasta, 7
enter   ingresar (*e.g., a university*) 2; (*a place*) entrar en, 9
entertain   entretener (*conj. like* **tener**), 1
enthused   entusiasmado(a), 1
environment   medio ambiente (*m.*), 8
environmental   ambiental, 8
evil eye   mal de ojo (*m.*), 4
exactly   al pie de la letra, 10
exaggerate   exagerar, 5
excited   entusiasmado(a), 1
executive   ejecutivo(a) (*m., f.*), 10
exercise   hacer ejercicio, 5
exist   existir, 2
expense   gasto (*m.*), 10
extremely bad   malísimo(a), 2

F

faction   bando (*m.*), 7
factory   fábrica (*f.*), factoría (*f.*), 8
faculty   profesorado (*m.*), 2
fail   fracasar, 8; (*a course*) quedar suspendido(a), 8; (*to do something*) dejar de, 8
fall asleep   dormirse (o → ue), 1
fall in love with   enamorarse de, 9
fan   aficionado(a) (*m., f.*), 3
fashion   moda (*f.*), 7
fat   grasa (*f.*), 5

Father's Day   Día del Padre (*m.*), 4
fear   temer, 4
feel   sentirse (e → ie), 6
   —like   tener ganas de, 7
fiancé(e)   prometido(a) (*m., f.*), 1
field   campo (*m.*), 6
fight   (*noun*) pelea (*f.*), 3; (*verb*) pelear(se), 7
file   archivar, 10; archivo (*m.*), fichero (*m.*), 10
finally   por fin, 4; al fin, 6
find fault   poner peros, 10
fire   (from a job) despedir (e → i), 10
fireworks   fuegos artificiales (*m. pl.*), 4
first (second) half (*in a game*) primer (segundo) tiempo (*m.*), 3
fish   pescar, 3
fishing rod   caña de pescar (*f.*), 3
flat tire   goma pinchada (ponchada) (*f.*), 6
flower   flor (*f.*), 4
following   lo siguiente, 5
food   alimento (*m.*), 5
foot   pata (*f.*), 8; pie (*m.*), 5
football   fútbol americano (*m.*), 3
for   por, para, 4
   —example   por ejemplo, 2
   —that   para eso, 4
   —that reason   por eso, 4
   —the lack of (something)   por no tener (*algo*), 10
forbid   prohibir, 4
forehead   frente (*f.*), 7
forever   para siempre, 4
forget   olvidarse de, 9
fortunately   por suerte, 4
four-leaf clover   trébol de cuatro hojas (*m.*), 4
free   libre, 4; gratis, 8
frequently   a menudo, frecuentemente, 1
friendly   amistoso(a), 1
fringe benefit   beneficio adicional (marginal) (*m.*), 10
from   de, 9
front   frente (*m.*), 7
frustrated   frustrado(a), 1
fry   freír (e → i), 7
fuel   combustible (*m.*), 8
full   lleno(a), 5; satisfecho(a), 7
function   funcionar, 6
fund   fondo (*m.*), 7

G

gain weight   engordar, ganar peso, 5
game   partido (*m.*), 3

gang   pandilla (*f.*), 8
garbage   basura (*f.*), 8
garlic   ajo (*m.*), 5
generous   generoso(a), 1
get   conseguir (e → i), recibir, 10
   —a divorce   divorciarse, 1
   —a grade   sacar, 2
   —along   llevarse bién, 1
   —dressed   vestirse (e → i), 1
   —engaged to   comprometerse con, 9
   —married   casarse (con), 1
   —ready   prepararse, 6
   —up   levantarse, 1
gin   ginebra (*f.*), 7
give   dar
   —a hug   abrazar, dar un abrazo, 1
   —a kiss   besar, dar un beso, 1
   —advice   dar consejos, 1
   —notice   avisar, 7
glass   vidrio (*m.*), 3; copa (*f.*), 7
go   ir, 1
   —away   irse, 1
   —on a diet   ponerse a dieta, 5
   —scuba diving   bucear, 3
   —to bed   acostarse (o → ue), 1
goblet   copa (*f.*), 7
godfather   padrino (*m.*), 1
godmother   madrina (*f.*), 1
governor   gobernador(a) (*m., f.*), 8
grade   nota (*f.*), 2
grade point average   promedio (*m.*), 2
grade school   escuela primaria (elemental) (*f.*), 2
grave   tumba (*f.*), 4
great   gran, 6
green   verde, 2
green pepper   ají (*m.*), pimiento verde (*m.*), 5
ground   suelo (*m.*), 7
guard   guardia (*m.*), 7
guide   guía (*m.*), 7
guidebook   guía (*f.*), 7
gymnast   gimnasta (*m., f.*), 3
gymnastics   gimnasia (*f.*), 3

H

habit   costumbre (*f.*), 1
had I known   de haberlo sabido, 7
half   medio(a), 9
Halloween   Día de las Brujas (*m.*), 4
handle of a utensil   mango (*m.*), 7
happy   alegre, contento(a), 1
hard drive   disco duro (*m.*), 10
hardly   apenas, 1

hard-working trabajador(a), 1
have just (done something) acabar de (+ *inf*.), 9
have (something) left quedar, 3
he almost killed himself por poco se mata, 3
head cabeza (*f*.), 7
healing cura (*f*.), 7
health salud (*f*.), 5
healthy sano(a), 5
hill loma (*f*.), 7
hire contratar, emplear, 10
hit the nail on the head dar en el clavo, 12
hit the roof poner el grito en el cielo, 10
hold a position desempeñar un puesto, 10
hold-up asalto (*m*.), 8
Holy Week Semana Santa (*f*.), 4
homeless personas sin hogar (*f*.), 8
homesick nostálgico(a), 1
honey miel de abeja (*f*.), 7
hope esperar, 4
horse race carrera de caballos (*f*.), 3
horseshoe herradura (*f*.), 4
hot caliente, cálido(a), picante, 7
housing vivienda (*f*.), 8
hug abrazar, dar un abrazo, 1
hurt doler (o → ue), 1
hurt (oneself) lastimar(se), 3

I

identify identificar, 8
if only ojalá, 4
I'll say! ¡ya lo creo!, 2
immediately en el acto, 10
impose imponer (*conj. like* **poner**), 1
improve mejorar, 3
in por, 4; a, de, en, 9
  —a good (bad) mood de buen (mal) humor, 1
  —a loud voice en voz alta, 10
  —a low voice en voz baja, 10
  —case en caso de que, 5
  —exchange for por, 4
  —fact en realidad, 3
  —love enamorado(a), 9
  —order that a fin de que, 5
  —order to para, 4
  —search of por, 4
  —spite of a pesar de, 3
  —the long run a la larga, 10
  —the middle of summer en pleno verano, 4
inch pulgada (*f*.), 5

include incluir, 10
increase aumentar, 5; (*noun*) aumento (*m*.), 10
Independence Day Día de la Independencia (*m*.), 4
inform avisar, 7
inn fonda (*f*.), 7
inside en, 19
insist on insistir en, 19
instantly en el acto, 10
instead of en lugar de, en vez de, 8
insurance seguro (*m*.), 6
insured asegurado(a), 6
intervene intervenir (*conj. like* **venir**), 1
interview (*noun*) entrevista (*f*.), reportaje (*m*.), 9; (*verb*) entrevistar, 11
iron hierro (*m*.), 5
it is es
  —a pity es (una) lástima, 4
  —advisable es conveniente (conviene), 4
  —better es mejor, 4
  —doubtful es dudoso, 5
  —important es importante (importa), 4
  —(im)possible es (im)posible, 5
  —(im)probable es (im)probable, 5
  —necessary es necesario, 4
  —necessary to hay que (+ *inf*.), 8
  —preferable es preferible, 4
  —urgent es urgente, 4
  —regrettable es lamentable, 4
  —surprising es sorprendente, 4
  —to be hoped es de esperar, ojalá, 4
  —unlikely es difícil, 5
it may be puede ser, 5

J

jack gato (*m*.), gata (*f*.) (*Costa Rica*), 6
jail cárcel (*f*.), prisión (*f*.), 8
joke bromear, 1; chiste (*m*.), 7

K

keep quedarse con, 1; guardar, 9; mantener (*conj. like* **tener**), 2
  —in touch mantenerse en contacto, 1
  —young mantenerse joven (*conj. like* **tener**), 5
kid bromear, 1
kidnap secuestrar, 8
kind amable, 1
kiss besar, dar un beso, 1
kneel down arrodillarse, 1
knowledge conocimiento (*m*.), 6

L

label etiqueta (*f*.), 10
Labor Day Día del Trabajo (*m*.), 4
lamb cordero (*m*.), 7
lap top ordenador (*m*.) (computadora (*f*.)) portátil, microcomputadora (*f*.), 10
last pasado(a), 6; (*in a series*) último(a), 6
last time la última vez, 3
lately últimamente, 5
laugh reírse (e → i), 3
law derecho (*m*.), 9; ley (*f*.), 8
law school facultad de derecho (*f*.), 2
lawyer abogado(a) (*m*., *f*.), 2
lazy haragán(ana), perezosa(a), 1
leader cabeza (*m*.), 7
leave irse, 1; (*a place*) salir de, 9
  —alone dejar en paz, 5
lecture conferencia (*f*.), 2
leftover resto (*m*.), 7
lessen disminuir, 5
lettuce lechuga (*f*.), 5
librarian bibliotecario(a), (*m*., *f*.), 2
license plate chapa (*f*.), placa (*f*.), 6
lie mentir (e → ie), 1; mentira (*f*.), 9
life vida (*f*.), 1
lift levantar, 1
  —weights levantar pesas, 5
light encender (e → ie), 1
light exercise ejercicio ligero (*m*.), 5
like caerle bien a uno, 1; (*verb*) gustar, 3; como, 9
listen (to) escuchar, 9
little (*quantity*) poco(a), pequeño(a), 7
  —by little poco a poco, 8
lively animadamente, 7
long-time viejo(a), 6
look like parecerse, 1
lose weight adelgazar, perder (bajar de) peso, 5
love amar, querer (e → ie), 1; encantar, 3; cariño (*m*.), amor (*m*.), 1
luckily por suerte, 4

M

magician mago(a) (*m*., *f*.), 4
maintain mantener (*conj. like* **tener**), 1
major especialización (*f*.), 2
make realizar, 5
  —a fool of oneself ponerse en ridículo, 10
  —fun of burlarse (de), 1
  —one's mouth water hacérsele a uno agua la boca, 10

mandatory   obligatorio(a), 2
manger   nacimiento (*m.*), pesebre (*m.*), 4
manner   modo (*m.*), 7
Mardi Gras   Carnavales (*m. pl.*), 4
marry   casarse con, 9
mass   misa (*f.*), 4
match   partido (*m.*), 3
materialistic   materialista, 1
maybe   a lo mejor, quizá(s), tal vez, 1
mayor   alcalde (*m.*), alcaldesa (*f.*), 10
mean   malo(a), 6
meatball   albóndiga (*f.*), 5
meddle   meterse, 1
medical doctor   médico(a) (*m., f.*), 2
medical school   facultad de medicina (*f.*), 2
medium-rare   término medio, 7
meet   encontrarse (o → ue) con, 9
meeting   reunión (*f.*), junta (*Mex.*) (*f.*), 2
member   socio(a) (*m., f.*), 5
memory   recuerdo (*m.*), 7; memoria (*f.*), 10
method   orden (*m.*), 7
middle   medio (*m.*), 9; mediano(a), 9
Midnight Mass   Misa del Gallo (*f.*), 4
mid-term examination   examen de mitad (mediados) de curso, examen parcial (*m.*), 2
mind   mente (*f.*), 5
miss   echar de menos, 1; faltar (a), perder (e → ie), 3
—out on (*something*)   perderse (e → ie) (algo), 3
moderate   dirigir, 8
money   capital (*m.*), 7
monthly   mensual, 10
morsel   bocado (*m.*), 7
Mother's Day   Día de la Madre (*m.*), 4
mountain   montaña (*f.*), 3
murder   (*noun*) asesinato (*m.*), 8; (*verb*) asesinar, 8
murderer   asesino(a) (*m., f.*), 8
mushroom   hongo (*m.*), seta (*f.*), 5
musical group   banda (*f.*), 7

N

name   nombrar, 9
nativity scene   nacimiento (*m.*), pesebre (*m.*), 4
naturally   por supuesto, claro, naturalmente, 1
nearby   cercano(a), 4
need   faltar, 3; precisar, 10
nervous   nervioso(a), 1

New Year's Day   Año Nuevo (*m.*), 4
New Year's Eve   Fin de Año (*m.*), Víspera de Año Nuevo (*f.*), 4
news   noticias (*f.*), 9
—item   noticia (*f.*), 1
not even   ni aun, 8
not to be able to wait to   no ver la hora de, 4
not to be that important   no ser para tanto, 4
notebook computer   ordenador (*m.*) (computadora (*f.*)) portátil, microcomputadora (*f.*), 10
notice   fijarse, 6
nourishment   alimento (*m.*), 5
nurse   enfermero(a) (*m., f.*), 2
nutrient   alimento (*m.*), 5

O

obey   obedecer, 1; hacer caso, 5
of   de, 9
—course   por supuesto, claro, naturalmente, 1
—. . . descent   de ascendencia..., 8
official communication   parte (*m.*), 7
often   a menudo, frecuentemente, 1
old   viejo(a), 6
older people   gente mayor (*f.*), 1
Olympic Games   Juegos Olímpicos (*m. pl.*), Olimpiadas (*f. pl.*), 3
on   sobre, en, 9
—account of   por, 4
—behalf of   por, 4
—their own   por su cuenta, 2
—time   a tiempo, 6
one must   hay que (+ *inf.*), 8
one of these days   un día de estos, 1
onion   cebolla (*f.*), 5
only   no más que, 4; único(a), 5
optimistic   optimista, 1
order   (*verb*) mandar, ordenar, 4; (*noun*) order (*m., f.*), 7
organize   organizar, 8
out   fuera, 9
outdoor(s)   al aire libre, 3
over   en, 9
overlook   hacer(se) (de) la vista gorda, 10
overtime   tiempo extra (*m.*), 10
own   propio(a), 2

P

page   página (*f.*), 3
pamper   mimar, 1
parade   desfile (*m.*), 9
part   parte (*f.*), 7

party   bando (*m.*), 7
patron saint   santo(a) patrón(ona) (*m., f.*), 4
pay attention   hacer caso, 5
people   gente (*f.*), personas (*f. pl.*), pueblo (*m.*), 4
per   por, 4
perform   actuar, 9
perhaps   a lo mejor; quizá(s), tal vez, 1
period   época (*f.*), 8; punto (*m.*), 7
pessimistic   pesimista, 1
pester   dar lata, 5
pharmacist   farmacéutico(a) (*m., f.*), 2
physical education   educación física (*f.*), 2
pick (someone) up   pasar por (alguien), 2
pie   pastel (*m.*), 5
piece of news   noticia (*f.*), 1
place   (*verb*) poner, 1; lugar (*m.*), 2
plantain   plátano (*m.*), 7
play dumb   hacerse el (la) tonto(a), 10
player   jugador(a) (*m., f.*), 3
plead   rogar (o → ue), 4
point   punta (*f.*), 7
police (organization)   policía (*f.*), 7
policeman   policía (*m.*), 7
policewoman   agente de policía (*f.*), 7
polite   amable, 1
pollution   contaminación (*f.*), polución (*f.*), 8
poor   pobre, 6
pork   cerdo (*m.*), 7
port   puerto (*m.*), 7
portion   parte (*f.*), 7
post office box   apartado postal (de correos) (*m.*), 10
pound   libra (*f.*), 5
poverty   miseria (*f.*), pobreza (*f.*), 8
practical joke   broma (*f.*), 4
president   (*of a university*) rector(a) (*m., f.*), 2
prevent   impedir (e → i), 1
previous   anterior, 10
price   precio (*m.*), 6
priest   cura (*m.*), 7
prison   cárcel (*f.*), prisión (*f.*), 8
private university   universidad privada (*f.*), 2
producer   productor(a) (*m., f.*), 9
programmer   programador(a) (*m., f.*), 2
propose   proponer (*conj. like* **poner**), 1
protagonist   protagonista (*m., f.*), 9
protein   proteína (*f.*), 5
provided that   con tal de que, 5
psychologist   psicólogo(a) (*m., f.*), 2

publicity publicidad (*f.*), 9
publishing company editorial (*f.*), 9
punch ponche (*m.*), 7
put poner, 1
—**on** ponerse, 1
—**to bed** acostar (o → ue), 1

Q

queen reina (*f.*), 9

R

rabbit's foot pata de conejo (*m.*), 4
race carrera (*f.*), 3
race track hipódromo (*m.*), 3
racket raqueta (*f.*), 3
radish rábano (*m.*), 5
raise levantar, 1
ransom rescate (*m.*), 8
rape violación (*f.*), 8
rare medio crudo, 7
ready listo(a), 2
realistic realista, 1
realize darse cuenta (de), 3
record (*noun*) disco (*m.*), 4; (*verb*)
  grabar, 9
recycle reciclar, 8
red-handed con las manos en la
  masa, 10
red wine vino tinto (*m.*), 7
redo rehacer (*conj. like* **hacer**), 1
register matricularse, 2
registration matrícula (*f.*), 6
regret arrepentirse (e → ie) (de), 1;
  lamentar, sentir (e → ie), 4
related propio(a), 2
related to sports deportivo(a), 3
relative pariente (*m., f.*), 1
release lanzar, 9
reluctantly de mala gana, 10
remain quedarse, 3
remake rehacer (*conj. like* **hacer**), 1
remember acordarse (o → ue) (de), 1
repair shop taller de mecánica (*m.*), 6
repent arrepentirse (e → ie) (de), 1
report informe (*m.*), 8; reportaje (*m.*),
  9
request (*something*) pedir (e → i), 1
requirement requisito (*m.*), 2
rescue (*noun*) rescate (*m.*), 8; (*verb*)
  rescatar, 8
resign renunciar, 10
respect respetar, 1
rest (*noun*) reposo (*m.*), 5; resto (*m.*),
  7; (*verb*) descansar, 5
retirement jubilación (*f.*), retiro (*m.*),
  10

reunion reunión (*f.*), 1
ride on horseback montar a caballo, 3
right derecho (*m.*), 7; (*direction*)
  derecha (*f.*), 7
right away en el acto, 10
right now ahora mismo, 5
roast asar, 7
robbery robo (*m.*), 8
role papel (*m.*), 1
rosé rosado(a), 7
round redondo(a), 8
rule regla (*f.*), 5
rum ron (*m.*), 7
run for postularse (para), 8

S

sad triste, 1
saint santo(a) (*m., f.*), 4
salary salario (*m.*), sueldo (*m.*), 10
sale venta (*f.*), 10
salesperson vendedor(a) (*m., f.*), 10
salmon salmón (*m.*), 7
same mismo(a), 6
—**thing** lo mismo, 1
sardine sardina (*f.*), 7
satisfied satisfecho(a), 7
scanner escáner (*m.*), 10
scholarship beca (*f.*), 2
school (*division within a university*)
  facultad (*f.*), 2
—**of architecture** facultad de
  arquitectura (*f.*), 2
—**of business administration**
  facultad de ciencias económicas
  (comerciales) (*f.*), 2
—**of education** facultad de
  educación (*f.*), 2
—**of engineering** facultad de
  ingeniería (*f.*), 2
—**of humanities** facultad de
  filosofía y letras (*f.*), 2
score marcar (*in sports*), 3
screen pantalla (*f.*), 9
seat sentar (e → ie), 1
seated sentado(a), 3
secondary school escuela secundaria
  (*f.*), 2
security force guardia (*f.*), 7
seem parecer, 1
selfish egoísta, 1
serious grave, serio(a), 8
serve (as) servir (e → i) (de), 3
serving dish fuente (*f.*), 7
several varios(as), 1
sewer desagüe (*m.*), 8
short bajo(a); corto(a), 5

shovel pala (*f.*), 7
show mostrar (o → ue), 1; enseñar, 3;
  (*on TV*) dar, 11; espectáculo (*m.*), 9
—**for the first time** estrenar, 9
sick malo(a), 2
sickly person enclenque (*m., f.*), 3
sign letrero (*m.*), señal (*f.*), signo
  (*m.*), 10
silly tonto(a), 6
sit down sentarse (e → ie), 1
skate patinar, 3
ski esquiar, 3
sleep dormir (o → ue), 1
sleeve manga (*f.*), 7
slow motion cámara lenta (*f.*), 9
smart listo(a), 2
so de manera (modo) que, 1; así que,
  10
—**that** para que, 5
soap opera telenovela (*f.*), 9
soccer fútbol (*m.*), balompié (*m.*), 3
social worker trabajador(a) social
  (*m., f.*), 2
soft drink gaseosa (*f.*), 7
sole suela (*f.*), 7
solve resolver (o → ue), 1; solucionar,
  8
something like that algo por el estilo, 10
soon pronto, 4
Spanish speaking de habla hispana, 8
speaker locutor(a) (*m., f.*), 9
spend (*time*) pasar, 4; (*money*) gastar, 6
spinach espinaca (*f.*), 5
spoil malcriar, 1
sport deporte (*m.*), 3
spray pulverizador (*m.*), 8
spray can pulverizador (*m.*), 8
stadium estadio (*m.*), 3
standard shift de cambios mecánicos,
  6
star estrella (*f.*), 9
start (*a motor*) arrancar, 6
starve to death morirse (o → ue) de
  hambre, 5
state university universidad estatal
  (*f.*), 2
statistic estadística (*f.*), 8
stay quedarse, 3; mantenerse (*conj. like*
  tener), 5
steam cocinar al vapor, 7
step paso (*m.*), 9
stick palo (*m.*), 7
still todavía, 6
stingy tacaño(a), 1
stop detener (*conj. like* **tener**), 1

store information   archivar (almacenar) información, 10

stress   estrés (*m.*), tensión nerviosa (*f.*), 5

strike   huelga (*f.*), 8

study program   programa de estudios (*m.*), 2

stuffed   relleno(a), 7

style   corte (*m.*), 7

subject   (*in school*) materia (*f.*), asignatura (*f.*), 2

subtraction   resta (*f.*), 7

suit   convenir (*conj. like* **venir**), 1

support   mantener (*conj. like* **tener**), 1

suppose   suponer (*conj. like* **poner**), 1

surf the net   navegar la red, 10

swallow   tragar, 7

swim   nadar, 3

swimmer   nadador(a) (*m., f.*), 3

swimming   natación (*f.*), 3

systems analyst   analista de sistemas (*m., f.*), 2

T

take   agarrar, coger, llevar, tomar, 1
  —**advantage of**   aprovechar, 6
  —**away**   quitar, 1
  —**care of**   cuidar, 1
  —**off**   quitarse, 1
  —**out insurance**   sacar seguro, 6
  —**part in**   tomar parte en, 4
  —**steps**   dar pasos, 8
  —**time**   demorar, 6
  —**turns**   turnarse

tape   grabar, 9

taste   probar (o → ue), 1

tasty   rico(a), sabroso(a), 7

teacher   maestro(a) (*m., f.*), 2

team   equipo (*m.*), 3

technical school   escuela tecnológica (*f.*), 2

tell me   dime, 4

tent   tienda de campaña (*f.*), 3

than   que, 4

Thanksgiving   Día de Acción de Gracias (*m.*), 4

that   que, 3
  —**which**   lo que, 1; quien, 3

that's why   por eso, 4

the truth of the matter is that. . .   lo que pasa es que..., 5

there would be   habría, 7

there's not going to be   no va a haber, 1

there's something fishy here   aquí hay gato encerrado, 10

thief   ladrón(-ona) (*m., f.*), 8

think about   pensar (e → ie) en, 9

think so (not)   creer que sí (no), 2

this time   esta vez, 2

this way   por aquí, 4

Three Wise Men   Reyes Magos (*m. pl.*), 4

through   por, 4

throw   tirar, 8; echar, 8

tie   (*a score*) empatar, 3

time   hora (*f.*), tiempo (*m.*), (*in a series*) vez (*f.*), 2

tip   punta (*f.*), 7

tire   llanta (*f.*), neumático (*m.*), 6

to   a, 9
  —**the letter**   al pie de la letra, 10
  —**toast**   brindar, 4; brindis (*m.*), 7
  —**your health!**   ¡Salud!, 7

together   juntos(as), 2

too many   demasiados(as), 2

tow   remolcar, 6
  —**truck**   grúa (*f.*), remolcador (*m.*), 6

town   pueblo (*m.*), 8

traffic light   semáforo (*m.*), 6

trainer   entrenador(a) (*m., f.*), 3

tranquil   tranquilo(a), 1

trash   basura (*f.*), 8

tripe and beef knuckles   mondongo (*m.*), 7

trout   trucha (*f.*), 7

trust   confiar en, 9

try   probar (o → ue), 1; tratar de, 2
  —**on**   probarse (o → ue), 1

tuition   matrícula (*f.*), 2

tuna   atún (*m.*), 7

turn on   (*lights*) encender (e → ie), 1

TV news   telediario (*m.*), telenoticias (*f.*), 9

TV viewer   televidente (*m., f.*), 9

two door   de dos puertas, 6

U

umpire   árbitro (*m.*), 3

under   bajo, 9

understanding   comprensivo(a), 1

unfortunate   pobre, 6

unfortunately   por desgracia, 4

unique   único(a), 6

university   (*adj.*) universitario(a), 2

unless   a menos que, 5

until   hasta que, 5

V

vain   vanidoso(a), 1

Valentine's Day   Día de los Enamorados (*m.*), 4

van   camioneta (*f.*), furgoneta (*f.*), 6

veal   ternera (*f.*), 7

veterinarian   veterinario(a) (*m., f.*), 2

vitamin   vitamina (*f.*), 5

voice   voz (*f.*), 9

W

walk   caminar, 5

warn   advertir (e → ie), 1

waste   desecho (*m.*), desperdicio (*m.*), 8

water skiing   esquí acuático (*m.*), 3

way   manera (*f.*), modo (*m.*), 1

weapon   arma (*f.*), 8

wedding   boda (*f.*), 1

weekly   semanal, 10

weight   peso (*m.*), 5

welcome   bienvenido(a), 7

well cooked (done)   bien cocido(a), 7

what   lo que, 1

what for?   ¿para qué?, 4

What date is today?   ¿A cuánto estamos hoy?, 10

whatever it may be   cualquiera que sea, 6

when   cuando, 5

which   que, 3

white wine   vino blanco (*m.*), 7

who   que, 3

whom   quien, 3

whose   cuyo(a), de quién, 3

win   ganar, 3

witch   bruja (*f.*), 4

witchcraft   brujería (*f.*), 4

with   de, 9

without   sin que, 5
  —**rhyme or reason**   sin qué ni para qué, 4

word processing   composición de textos (*f.*), 10

work   funcionar, 6
  —**part time**   trabajar medio día, 1

worried   preocupado(a), 1

wrap   envolver (o → ue), 1

wrestling   lucha libre (*f.*), 3

Y

yearly   anual, 10

yet   todavía, 6

young   joven, 5

Z

zodiac sign   signo del zodíaco (*m.*), 4

Índice

Credits

Text Credits

p. 32: Adapted from *Papá y Mamá*; p. 71: Reprinted by permission of El País Internacional, S.A.; p. 102: "Caminando hasta el fin del mundo," by Alfredo Martínez, as appeared in *Escala*, September 1995. Reprinted by permission of *Escala*; p. 135: Adapted from "El corpus de Cuzco," by Ángel Martínez Bermejo from *Ronda*, June 1987; p. 167: Adapted from "Tácticas y estrategias de la pérdida de peso," from *Más*, Summer 1990; p. 194: Adapted from "Costa Rica: La Suiza de América," by Mari Rodriguez Ichaso. From *Vanidades* 33, No. 16, August 4, 1993. Reprinted by permission from Editorial América, S.A., D/B/A Editorial Televisa; p. 228: Adapted from Publicaciones Serie Latinoamericana; p. 256: "Buscando en el supermercado," from *Imagen*, May 1992. Reprinted by permission of *Revista Imagen*, Casiano Communications, Inc., San Juan, Puerto Rico; p. 314: Reprinted by permission from *Puerto Rico Digital*.

Photo and Art Credits

p. 1: © Henry Sims/Getty Images; p. 9: © Robert Frerck/Odyssey/Chicago; p. 11: © Mark Antman/The Image Works; p. 30: Simulated realia by Uli Gersiek; p. 32: © Bob Daemmrich/The Image Works; p. 35: Cartoon by Mark Heng; p. 38: © Robert Frerck/Odyssey/Chicago; p. 45: © David R. Frazier/Stock Boston; p. 71: © Mark Harmel/Getty Images; p. 81: © David Simson/Stock Boston; p. 87: © Flash! Light/Stock Boston; p. 89: © Robert Fried/Robert Fried Photography; p. 102: © Ulrike Welsch; p. 107: © Robert Frerck/Odyssey/Chicago; p. 113: © Bill Jarvis; p. 135: © Mary Altier/Index Stock Imagery; p. 144: © Marc Romanelli/Getty Images; p. 151: © Mark Scott/Getty Images; p. 153: © Robert Frerck/Odyssey/Chicago; p. 167: © Franken/Stock Boston; p. 172: © Bill Bachmann/PhotoEdit; p. 173: Simulated realia by Uli Gersiek; p. 178: © Robert Fried/Stock Boston; p. 194: © Art Gingert/Comstock; p. 203: © Jeff Greenberg/PhotoEdit; p. 209: © Esbin-Anderson/The Image Works; p. 211: © Robert Frerck/Odyssey/Chicago; p. 228: © Frerck/Odyssey/Chicago; p. 234: © Tom Wurl/Stock Boston; p. 241 (top): © Bill Jarvis; p. 241 (bottom) © David Young-Wolff/PhotoEdit; p. 242: © Bob Daemmrich/The Image Works; p. 256: © Peter Menzel/Stock Boston; p. 265: © AFP/Corbis; p. 271: © Alain Daussin/Getty Images; p. 274: © Owen Franken/Stock Boston; p. 289: © Mark Wilson/Getty Images; p. 290: Cartoon by Mark Heng; p. 295: © Bonnie Kamin/PhotoEdit; p. 296: Simulated realia by Uli Gersiek; p. 301: © Robert Frerck/Odyssey/Chicago; p. 314: © Michael Newman/PhotoEdit; p. 315: Cartoon by Mark Heng

Video Credits

The *Video to Accompany ¡Continuemos!, Seventh Edition* is a coproduction of PICS, Houghton Mifflin Company and AltamirA Educational Solutions. © 2003 PICS/The University of Iowa.

Producer: Anny A. Ewing, AltamirA Educational Solutions
PICS Director: Sue K. Otto, The University of Iowa

1a. *Saludos*, excerpted from *Una hija más 4: Familia cristiana*, © Televisión Española, S.A. 1990.

1b. *Madre e hijos*, excerpted from *Una hija más 15: La llegada de la abuela*, © Televisión Española, S.A. 1991.

1c. *La abuela: madre y suegra*, excerpted from *Una hija más 15: La llegada de la abuela*, © Televisión Española, S.A. 1991.

2a. *Conversaciones con estudiantes de la San Diego State University, Parte 1*, excerpted from *Somos* (We are) © San Diego State University, 1995.

2b. *En la Agencia "Supersonic"*, excerpted from *Las chicas de hoy en día 2: Se buscan la vida*, © Televisión Española, S.A. 1991.

3a. *Partido de fútbol España-Rumanía*, excerpted from *Telediario*, © Televisión Española, S.A. 1996.

3b. *Rafting en el Río Pacuare*, excerpted from *De paseo*, © SINART/Canal 13, 1997.

4a. *Día de los difuntos*, excerpted from *Tradiciones milenarias en la península de Santa Elena*, © Fundación Pro-Pueblo, 1996.

4b. *Fiesta del gaucho*, excerpted from *Telediario*, © Televisión Española, S.A. 1989.

5a. *Fuera de campo: Lluís Remolí*, excerpted from *Cartelera TVE*, © Televisión Española, S.A. 1997.

5b. *Remedio para quemaduras*, excerpted from *La botica de la abuela*, © Televisión Española, S.A. 1997.

6. *Puerto Viejo de Limón*, excerpted from *De paseo*, © SINART/Canal 13, 1997.

7a. *Alimentos americanos*, excerpted from *Mujeres de América Latina: México-La rebelión de las lloronas*, © Televisión Española, S.A. 1992; and *América Total: Hijos del volcán*, © Televisión Española, S.A. 1996.

7b. *Del Viejo Mundo a América*, excerpted from *América Total: Hijos del volcán*, © Televisión Española, S.A. 1996.

7c. *El ajiaco*, excerpted from *América Total: Bacatá*, © Televisión Española, S.A. 1995.

8a. *Grafitis en San José*, excerpted from *Aristas*, © SINART/Canal 13, 1997.

8b. *Conversaciones con estudiantes de la San Diego State University, Parte 2*, excerpted from *Somos* (We are) © San Diego State University, 1995.

8c. *Hazte maestro*, courtesy of the Association of Hispanic Advertising Agencies, *Futuramente* © 2002.

9a. *Esmeralda*, excerpted from *Cartelera TVE*, © TVE Televisión Española, 1996; courtesy of Protele, a Division of Televisa International, L.L.C.

9b. *Manny Manuel: Y sé que vas a llorar*, excerpted from *Especial Manny Manuel*, © TVE Televisión Española, 1996.

9c. *El chavo del ocho*, excerpted from *Cartelera TVE*, © TVE Televisión Española, 1996; courtesy of Protele, a Division of Televisa International, L.L.C.

10a. *El comercio virtual*, excerpted from *Empléate a fondo*, © Televisión Española, S.A. 1998.

10b. *La entrevista de trabajo*, excerpted from *Empléate a fondo*, © Televisión Española, S.A. 1997.

10c. *Oferta de empleo*, excerpted from *Empléate a fondo*, © Televisión Española, S.A. 1997.